NEW PHOTOS UPDATED VIEWS

standard catalog of®

FARM TRACTORS

1890-1980

2nd Edition

C.H. Wendel

Published by

700 East State Street • Iola, WI 54990-0001
715-445-2214 • 888-457-2873

Our toll-free number to place an order or obtain a free catalog is (800) 258-0929.

Library of Congress Catalog Number: 2005906856

ISBN: 0-87349-726-0

Designed by Kay Sanders
Edited by Tom Collins

Printed in the United States of America

Pricing advisory panelists:

Craig Anderson

Kurt Aumann

Tom Bitters

Keith Crawford

John Davis

Tom Detwiler

Ed Dina

Dan Ehlerding

Tom Graverson

Ken Guile

Jack Heald

Jeff Huff

Kenneth Johnson

John Kasmiski

Wilbert Kercher

Dennis Lefebers

Byron Lukes

Rick Mannen

Dave Preuhs

Elwyn Suehring

Larry Swenson

Ken Updike

Wayne Witse

Contents

Introduction

For more than 40 years, I've collected literature about old engines, tractors, and farm equipment. I admit that what I thought were high prices for a stack of old tractor catalogs 30 years ago is a bargain today. Yet I had no interest then or now in the capital appreciation of what I was buying. Instead I was interested in preserving some of these materials and using them as resource materials for the books I wanted to write.

My approach over the years has been to write books that people wanted to read. I have always held that the whole idea of a good book is one that the reader picks up and can't put down until finished (or sleep intervenes). For me, page after page of corporate history is probably the best method of inducing sleep known to man, but I've always felt that the pages should come alive to the reader—they should be vibrant and carry the message through printed word and pictorial content.

Another important aspect of historical research is accuracy. In perusing various books written in the past quarter century I have noted glaring errors. Sometimes these occur because of typographical errors, while others were based on erroneous information gathered over the decades. Where possible, I have tried to find the primary source data (if it exists). Barring that, I have cross-referenced the data to maintain accuracy. Even with all of the precautions, safeguards, file cards, databases, and other working tools, this book is certain to contain errors. Companies will have been omitted that should have been included and so on. I apologize in advance for these shortcomings.

Readers familiar with the first edition of this book will be pleased to find a significant addition to the content with the inclusion of data from the Nebraska Tractor Test Laboratory. A brief discussion of the lab and its testing can be found on the following page. This information greatly expands the amount of technical data presented in this book, plus moves coverage forward to include models built up through the early 1980s.

Tractor Grading Guide

Condition is one of the most important factors in determining the price of a tractor. The following is a general grading guide for vintage tractors:

Condition 1

A tractor that is new or restored to new condition, both mechanically and cosmetically. Steel wheels may have rubber lugs or flattened rubber tread so it can travel in parades or at shows. A tractor in this condition need not be restored to better-than-new precision.

Condition 2

A tractor that is well restored or an extremely well maintained tractor that can be featured in a parade or used for belt power. It is complete with all correct parts. Iron wheels may have had lugs removed and replaced with rubber cleats or flat tread.

Condition 3

A tractor that is functional or restorable. It runs, but it needs restoration or replacement of parts and cosmetics to a fine operating and eye-appealing condition.

Condition 4

A tractor that may or may not be functional. It is weathered, wrecked, incomplete or greatly deteriorated, rusty, or stripped to the point of being useful for parts only.

Abenaque Machine Works

WESTMINSTER STATION, VERMONT

Abenaque gas engines first appeared about 1893, being the inventive work of John A. Ostenburg. Ostenburg secured numerous patents for his engines, with the cooling system being a unique feature of many models. In 1908, the company announced this 15 hp "gasoline traction engine." Weighing some 5-1/2 tons, it used the company's own stationary engine mounted on a heavy steel chassis. This single-cylinder tractor used an 8-5/8 x 12-1/2-inch bore and stroke; operating speed was 270 rpm.

In 1915, Abenaque Machine Works filed for bankruptcy. The family of Frederick M. Gilbert, one of the company founders, ultimately ended up with the company. After several difficult years, the company again took bankruptcy in 1921, with the assets finally being sold in 1923. Shown here is the 1911 version of the Abenaque tractor. It was a highly refined version of the 1908 model, although it retained the single-cylinder engine. Like the earlier 1908 model, two sizes were offered—15- and 25-hp. A unique feature was a choice of three forward speeds along with a reverse gear.

COLLECTOR VALUES	1	2	3	4
1908 ABENAQUE	–	–	$30,000-$50,000	–

Acason Farm Tractor Company

DETROIT, MICHIGAN

Acason Motor Truck Company was organized in 1915, continuing in the truck business for a decade. Presumably, the Acason Farm Tractor Company was a division of the parent company. The latter first appears in 1918 as a manufacturer of a tractor attachment for automobiles. Little is known of this device, aside from a very few advertisements. This tractor conversion was designed specifically for use with the Model T Ford automobile. Acason closed its doors forever in 1925.

Acason attachment for automobiles

COLLECTOR VALUES	1	2	3	4
CONVERSION KIT	–	–	$1,000	–

1908 Abenaque tractor

Acme Cultivator Company

LEETONIA, OHIO

Acme garden cultivator

This firm built the Acme and Acme Jr. garden cultivators for some years, beginning in the 1920s. The company appears to have been active as late as 1946. Originally the company was located at Leetonia, Ohio. Until at least 1948 they were at Columbiana, Ohio, and offered repair parts for these machines.

COLLECTOR VALUES	1	2	3	4
GARDEN CULTIVATOR	$950	$650	$400	$250

Acme Harvesting Machine Company

PEORIA, ILLINOIS

Acme had beginnings at least back into the 1890s, if not earlier. Ostensibly, the company was organized to build grain binders and other harvesting machinery, but by 1918 the firm was offering a unique convertible farm tractor.

The tracklayer model shown here was a conversion from the company's wheel-type tractor; a change described as relatively easy to make. Due to strong competition, and the inability to launch an intensive advertising campaign, Acme tractor virtually disappeared by 1920. An Acme tracklayer in condition grade 3 recently sold for $25,000.

Acme 12-25 conventional tractor

Acme's 12-25 conventional tractor, like the twin tracklayer, was listed in various machinery directories for 1918 and 1919. The model shown here was simple and straightforward in design. It used a four-cylinder engine. Aside from a few advertisements and trade announcements, little is known of the Acme conventional tractor. They are a relatively rare find. An Acme 12-25 in condition grade 3 recently sold for $20,000.

Acme tracklayer

Adams-Farnham tractor

Adams-Farnham Company

MINNEAPOLIS, MINNESOTA

In 1909 this company was incorporated in Minne-apolis. The principals were P. W. and G. L. Farnham, along with H. W. Adams. The firm manufactured numerous items, including steam engine governors, gasoline engines, and gasoline tractors. The latter, built only in 1909 and 1910, weighed about 5-1/2 tons. Beyond this basic information, no specifications for the Adams-Farnham have been located. The company quit business in 1911, and in 1915 Harry W. Adams reappeared as the general manager of the Common Sense Tractor Company, also of Minneapolis.

Adams Husker Company

MARYSVILLE, OHIO

About 1910 Adams began offering its "Little Traction Gear" to the farmer. It was a complete running gear to which the farmer could mount an engine. The Adams gear was offered in three sizes, with the No. 0 being for engines up to 9 hp. The No. 1 gear could handle engines up to 13 hp, and the big No. 2 was capable of handling a 20-hp engine. Patent No. 1,118,835 covering this device was issued in 1915. By the time the patent was issued, the market for convertible outfits was fast diminishing as farmers were looking for a small, lightweight tractor suitable for any farm task. A condition grade 3 No. 0 (kit only) is currently valued at $3,500.

Adams "Little Traction Gear" condition grade 3, No. 0—$3,000, kit only

Adams Sidehill Tractor Company

THE DALLES, OREGON

Sometime in the 1920s, a special tractor design was developed for use on steep sidehills. It was the brainchild of E. G. Adams from The Dalles, Oregon. In 1927 a company was organized to manufacture this unique design, but aside from this illustration in a 1927 issue of American Thresherman magazine, little is known of the company or this uncommon tractor design.

Adams Sidehill tractor

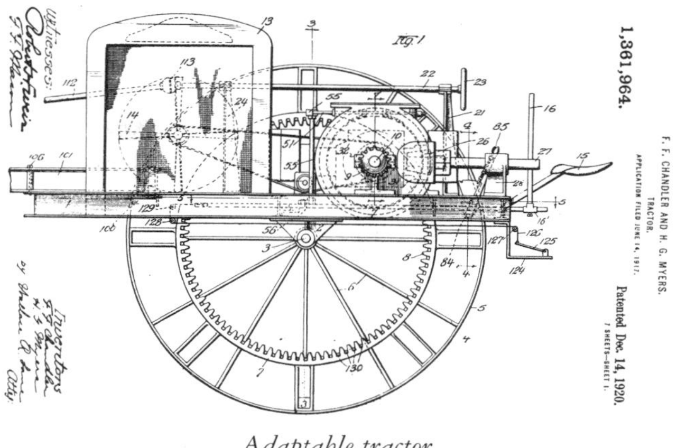

Adaptable tractor

Adaptable Tractor Company

INDIANAPOLIS, INDIANA

The 1920 patent drawing illustrated here is the only remaining evidence of the Adaptable tractor. That same year Adaptable Tractor Company was incorporated to manufacture its new design, intended to be adaptable to virtually every farm power use. As with the vast majority of these universal designs, sales were nothing sensational. This fact, and the post-war depression of the time, effectively put an end to the Adaptable Tractor Company—almost before it got started.

Advance Thresher Company

BATTLE CREEK, MICHIGAN

Jack Junkin was a well-known tractor and machinery designer. Junkin designed the big Advance 35-70 tractor, illustrated here, about 1910. He was also a major player in the design of Minneapolis Steel & Machinery Company's Twin City tractor. A comparison of the Advance 35-70 with the Twin City 40 illustrates the similarities. When M. Rumely Co. bought out Advance in 1911, Junkin went along with the merger and was responsible for polishing the design of the Rumely Oil Pull tractors. Unfortunately, the Advance 35-70 never got off the ground, and likely no more than a few prototypes were ever manufactured. None of these tractors are known to exist.

Advance 35-70 tractor

Advance-Rumely Thresher Company

LA PORTE, INDIANA

Much has been written about Advance-Rumely Thresher Company, despite the fact that production of the Rumely OilPull ceased in 1931. It remains popular among vintage tractor enthusiasts.

The company had roots going back to 1852, when Meinrad Rumely opened a blacksmith and machine shop at Portland, Indiana. By 1856 the company had entered the threshing machine business and, with great demand for the Rumely machine, the business grew rapidly. Until 1882 the company operated as a partnership between Meinrad and his brother John as M. & J. Rumely Company. At this point, Meinrad bought out his brother's interest, forming the M. Rumely Company at La Porte.

Edward A. Rumely, grandson of the founder, joined the firm in the early 1900s, and by 1908 was convinced of the need for a "successful" tractor. Edward set out to acquire the best minds in the business including John A. Secor, the man chiefly responsible for developing the volume-governed engine. Secor also was an early proponent of higher compression that had been used previously.

Edward Rumely was also acquainted with Rudolph Diesel, and was greatly influenced by Diesel's ideas regarding high-compression engines. Also added to the team was William H. Higgins, the Rumely factory superintendent.

Rumely, Secor, Higgins and others took the lead in developing the first prototypes in 1908, with testing carried out in 1909. The experiments were so successful the company moved quickly to build a tractor factory, shipping its first tractor on February 21, 1910.

The overwhelming success of the Rumely OilPull led the firm to acquire Gaar, Scott & Company of Richmond, Indiana, in October 1911, followed by the purchase of Advance Thresher Company of Battle Creek, Michigan. A year later, Rumely bought out the Northwest Thresher Company of Stillwater, Minnesota. The latter had developed a tractor by this time, and it was marketed for a few years as the Rumely GasPull.

In 1912 Rumely acquired the designs for a unique orchard tractor from Joshua Hendy Iron Works, Sunnyvale, California. It was marketed as the Rumely ToeHold tractor, but this model was only in production for a short time, if it ever went into full production.

During 1913 the company experienced financial difficulties, and in 1915 went into receivership. A new firm—Advance-Rumely Thresher Company—emerged, without the Rumely family.

In 1915, probably about the time the firm was reorganized, a new lightweight 8-16 plowing tractor was offered, followed in 1916 by a larger 12-24 model. Both were out of the market by 1917. In 1921 the company announced its new "line-drive" tractor, essentially a mechanical horse...the tractor was operated entirely with a pair of leather lines, just like driving a team of horses! Only a few of these tractors were built and the idea was abandoned.

Rumely 1908 prototype

In 1924 Advance-Rumely made the last of its major acquisitions, the Aultman & Taylor Machinery Company at Mansfield, Ohio. The purchase was intended to put Rumely in a better marketing position because it eliminated a strong competitor. Unfortunately, the market for big heavyweight tractors quickly disappeared, so the purchase did little for Rumely's sagging sales.

The Toro Motor Cultivator was acquired in 1927, the basis for the Rumely DoAll tractor, a convertible machine that could be used either as a conventional tractor or as a motor cul-tivator. Sales were disappointing for the DoAll, and sales for the time-honored Rumely OilPull tractors were also weak by this time.

With the onset of the Great Depression in 1929, Advance-Rumely was no longer able to continue on its own. A 1931 merger made Rumely a part of Allis-Chalmers Manufacturing Company.

For more information on Advance-Rumely, refer to one of the the Author's previous titles, including The Allis-Chalmers Story (Krause: 2004); Unusual Vintage Tractors (Krause: 1996); Encyclopedia of American Farm Tractors (Crestline/ Motorbooks: 1979); and Allis-Chalmers Tractors (Motorbooks: 1992).

In 1908 Rumely began experiments on a new tractor design. Shown is what would soon become the famous Rumely OilPull. This prototype was not equipped with fenders and other niceties, but it embodied many of the features that would be characteristic of all OilPull tractors. Especially obvious is the radiator design that would be greatly modified on the production models, but used the engine exhaust to create an induced draft over the radiator tubes.

Type B 25-45 OilPull

The Type B 25-45 OilPull emerged in 1910, remaining in production during 1911 and 1912. During 1910, the first year of production, 100 units were built, almost 700 in 1911, plus another 150 in 1912. The 25-45 rating meant the tractor was capable of 25 drawbar and 45 belt hp, a rating system widely used up to about 1930.

The photograph below, at an unknown location, illustrates the 25-45 OilPull coupled to a large plow. In those days, fuel was often delivered in large wooden or steel barrels. Reportedly, some ingenious engineers chained a full drum to a rear wheel, and drove forward slightly to raise it off the ground. As shown here, fuel is being pumped into the tractor's main fuel tank.

COLLECTOR VALUES	1	2	3	4
B 25-45 OILPULL	$120,000	$100,000	$75,000	$40,000

25-45 Oil Pull

Type E 30-60 OilPull

Production of the big 30-60 Rumely tractor began in 1910, and continued until 1923. Nearly 2,500 of these tractors were built during that time. Shown in this photograph with a 14-bottom plow, tractors like the 30-60 OilPull were responsible for converting thousands of acres of prairie into tillable and productive farmland. On the belt, the 30-60 was capable of pulling the largest thresher or a large sawmill with relative ease.

Rumley Oil Pull Type E 30-60 engine

Nebraska Test Data

Model: Type E 30-60 OilPull

Test No. 8

Date Tested: April 23 to May 11, 1920

Despite some maintenance problems, the 13-ton 30-60 OilPull gave test engineers a problem in finding enough ballast to come up with an accurate maximum drawbar test. Only 27.91 hp appeared in the rated load test, due to the dynamometer car operator not applying enough load. Test engineers noted the 30-60 would have carried a 30-hp load for 10 hours without difficulty. On the maximum drawbar test, a pull of 10,025 lbs. was achieved at a speed of 1.87 mph. This corresponded to 49.91 drawbar hp—far above the nominal rating of 30. An impressive performance on the belt manifested test figures of 75.6 hp at maximum load, and achieving 7.05 hp-hours per gallon of kerosene fuel. At this load, the 30-60 burned about 10-3/4 gallons of fuel per hour. Two 10 x 12-inch cylinders were used, along with Bosch low tension ignition, and a Rumely carburetor design. Early in the test it was necessary to regrind the valves, and in following days various minor repairs and adjustments were made. Because of its weight and other design features, slippage on the maximum load tests was held to slightly more than 10 percent.

COLLECTOR VALUES	1	2	3	4
E 30-60 OILPULL	$100,000	$90,000	$70,000	$40,000

Type F 15-30 OilPull

Type G 20-40 OilPull

Type E 30-60 frame

For the early series of OilPull tractors, also known as the "heavyweight" style, the chassis design was essentially the same, varying mostly in physical size and dimensions. The foundation was quite simple, but was built to withstand the heaviest loads that might be encountered with a comfortable margin of safety. Note the massive gearing that transmitted power to the drive wheels.

In the 1911-1914 period, Rumely built nearly 2,500 of its 15-30 OilPull tractors. This was essentially the same tractor as the larger 30-60, but the 15-30 was a single-cylinder model. None were built in 1915, but the follow-ing year the 15-30 re-emerged as the Model F, 18-35 tractor. The slight increase in the hp rating came from a small increase in crankshaft speed, as well as capitalizing on the power reserves already built into the tractor. Production ended in 1918.

COLLECTOR VALUES	1	2	3	4
F 15-30 OILPULL	$65,000	$45,000	$30,000	$15,000
F 18-35 OILPULL	$65,000	$45,000	$30,000	$15,000

With the end of the Model F 18-35 OilPull in 1918 came the introduction of the new Type G 20-40 model. This tractor was a two-cylinder design with an 8 x 10 inch bore and stroke, compared to the 10 x 12 cylinder dimensions for the big 30-60. Cold weather operation was always a problem because there were few suitable anti-freeze solutions available. This was not a problem for the OilPull because it used oil as a coolant, and was never subject to freezing. Production of the 20-40 tractor ended in 1924.

Rumely ToeHold tractor

Nebraska Test Data

Model: Type G 20-40 OilPull

Test No. 11

Date Tested: May 6 to May 22, 1920

From the carefully detailed Nebraska Tractor Test charts, a great many conclusions can be drawn in addition to the obvious matters of hp and drawbar pull. An analysis of coolant temperature at various loads revealed that for most OilPull models, coolant temperatures rose substantially when operating at reduced loads. Part of Rumely's success in burning low-grade fuels depended on maintaining a coolant temperature somewhat higher than the so-called industry standard. In the case of the 20-40 OilPull, a coolant temperature of 217° F was recorded while operating at half load. This figure dropped to 193° F on the rated load test. To accommodate the higher temperatures, OilPull tractors used an oil coolant. Brief specifications included a two-cylinder 8 x 10 inch engine rated at 450 rpm. Slightly more than 46 brake hp was developed on the maximum load test, with fuel consumption totaling 5.7 gallons per hour. A maximum drawbar pull of 6,365 lbs. was recorded. This test was made at a ground speed at 1.77 mph and calculated to slightly more than 30 drawbar hp, half again as much as the manufacturer's rating.

COLLECTOR VALUES	1	2	3	4
G 20-40 OILPULL	$32,000	$25,000	$16,000	$8,000

A 14-28 OilPull tractor first appeared in 1917. Production of this model continued into 1918 when it was slightly modified, and then offered as the Type H 16-30 OilPull. The 16-30 was a very popular tractor, because it was well suited to the needs of the average grain and livestock farm. (In comparison, the 30-60 was too large for the average farm, and the 20-40 was well suited to large farms or for pulling a grain separator.) Type H 16-30 tractors used a 7 x 8-1/2 inch bore and stroke, and were rated at 530 rpm.

14-28 OilPull and Type H 16-30 OilPull

GasPull 20-40 tractor

16-30 Oil Pull tractor

Nebraska Test Data

Model: Type H 16-30 OilPull

Test No. 9

Date Tested: April 24 to May 21, 1920

Although the big 30-60 OilPull had only a single forward speed, the 16-30 traveled 2.1 mph in low gear and 3 mph in high. A two-cylinder 7 x 8-1/2 inch engine powered this model—it had a rated speed of 530 rpm, compared to 375 rpm for the 30-60. High-tension ignition was featured, using a Bosch DU2 magneto. Weighing 9,500 lbs., the 16-30 came up with 30-1/2 brake hp and set a new record for fuel efficiency, developing 9.94 hp-hours per gallon, or 3.07 gph. During the rated drawbar test of nearly 10 hours, 2.668 gallons of fuel were burned per hour, and a drawbar hp of 16.68 was attained. On the maximum load test, 22.9 hp was achieved, with a maximum pull of 4,674 lbs. at 1.84 mph. The OilPull design required an exceptionally large amount of water. Test No. 9 indicated 2-3/4 gallons of water per hour were used. With the high compression engines used in the OilPull tractors, and a comparatively high jacket temperature available with the oil coolant, large quantities of water were necessary to minimize or prevent preignition, especially with low-grade fuels. Ordinarily, about a third of the total fuel-water mixture entering the engine consisted of water. In winter, when freezing was a problem, expensive high-test gasoline was often substituted for the warm weather kero-sene-water mixture.

COLLECTOR VALUES	1	2	3	4
H 16-30 OILPULL	$28,000	$23,000	$15,000	$8,000

Type K 12-20 OilPull

During the 1918-1925 period, Advance-Rumely offered its Type K 12-20 OilPull tractor. Of the same general design as its larger brothers, the 12-20 used a two-cylinder, 6 x 8 inch engine rated at 560 rpm. The tractor was generally underrated for its capacity. Although rated at 20 belt hp, it was capable of 26 or more horses on the belt. One of the Author's uncles bought a new 12-20 in the early 1920s, using it to operate a corn sheller for some years, finally trading it off for a truck-mounted corn sheller in the late 1930s.

Nebraska Test Data

Model: Type K 12-20 OilPull
Test No. 10
Date Tested: May 1 to May 21, 1920

As with several other OilPull models, the little 12-20 featured a Bosch DU2 magneto as standard equipment. With this exception, virtually everything about the 12-20, and the entire OilPull series, was designed and built in the Rumely factories. A separate needle valve on the carburetor was provided to adjust the water feed to the fuel mixture. During Test No. 10, it was noted that frequent adjustments of the water needle were necessary to accommodate varying loads. Brief specifications included a two-cylinder, 6 x 8 inch engine rated at 560 rpm. Two forward speeds were provided of 2.1 and 3.26 mph. Nearly 26 belt hp was delivered on the maximum load test, but on the rated load test, Rumely came through with an efficiency of 10.82 hp-hours per gallon of kerosene fuel, or 1.8555 gallons per hour. Slightly more than 15 hp was developed on the maximum drawbar test, with the 6,600 lb. 12-20 pulling 2,780 lbs. at 2.02 mph. No major repairs were made during the 44 hours of test running time.

COLLECTOR VALUES	1	2	3	4
K 12-20 OILPULL	$30,000	$25,000	$15,000	$10,000

In 1912 Rumely announced its new ToeHold tractor, a design purchased from Joshua Hendy Iron Works in California. This venture was short-lived and, aside from the initial announcements, very little is known of the ToeHold tractor. Rated at 14 drawbar and 28 belt hp, the Toe-Hold was equipped with a two-cycle engine, com-pletely unlike the heavy and substantial engines on which Rumely had built its reputation.

Advance-Rumely "8-16" tractor

Advance-Rumely announced its new "8-16" tractor in 1916 for $750 cash, f.o.b. La Porte, Indi-ana. It was an approach to the need for light-weight tractors and, like others of its design, met with generally poor farmer acceptance. Rumely also introduced its "12-24" tractor in 1917, with production of both models ending in 1918. The plows could be easily removed so that the tractor could be used for other purposes.

COLLECTOR VALUES	1	2	3	4
8-16	$25,000	$19,000	$14,000	$8,000

GasPull tractors made their first appearance in 1912, subsequent to Rumely's purchase of Northwest Thresher Company of Stillwater, Minnesota. Initially the GasPull was rated as a 20-40 tractor, and had been sold under a variety of names prior to the Rumely takeover. During 1912 or 1913 the tractor was re-rated downward as a 15-30 model. It remained on the market until 1915, probably about the time M. Rumely Company was reorganized as Advance-Rumely Thresher Company. A GasPull 20-40 in condition grade 2 is currently valued at $40,000.

COLLECTOR VALUES	1	2	3	4
GASPULL 20-40	$60,000	$40,000	$28,000	$15,000

Advance-Rumely "Line-Drive" tractor

An aberration from Advance-Rumely was this little "line-drive" tractor that the company announced in 1921. The design never appears to have gone beyond a couple of units in the prototype stage—likely both still existing in the hands of private collectors. The current collector value, condition grade 2, is $20,000. So-called line-drive tractors were intended to entice farmers unwilling to give up their horses for tractor power, and instead substituting a "mechanical horse."

Type S 30-60 OilPull

In 1924 Advance-Rumely announced the "new Lightweight OilPull." It was much more compact and featured a pressed steel frame, replacing the structural steel chassis of earlier models. Rated speed was 470 rpm. Production of the Type S 30-60 continued into 1928, with only about 500 being built.

Nebraska Test Data

Model: Type S 30-60 OilPull

Test No. 103

Date Tested:

September 6 to September 13, 1924

As with previous Rumely models, the Type S 30-60 OilPull featured a Secor-Higgins carburetor designed and built in the Rumely factory, and used exclusively by that firm. Other features included a Bosch DU4 magneto and Rumely's unique cooling system, with its special oil as the coolant. Weighing 17,500 lbs., the 30-60 carried a two-cylinder horizontal, valve-in-head engine with a 9 x 11-inch bore and stroke, that was rated at 470 rpm. Three forward speeds were provided of 2, 2-1/2, and 3 mph. Slightly more than 40 drawbar hp was exhibited in all three maximum load tests, but in low gear the 30-60 pulled 8,350 lbs. at 1.82 mph. Kerosene was used throughout the 38 hours of testing. At its rated 60 brake hp, the Type S gave a recorded fuel economy of 10.85 hp-hours per gallon, also consuming 7.305 gallons of water per hour during this test. Under maximum brake load, 70.16 hp was recorded, with a total consumption of 8.593 gallons per hour and an economy rating of 9.16 hp-hours per gallon. Water consumption through the Secor-Higgins carburetor totaled 12.21 gallons per hour (gph) during this test.

COLLECTOR VALUES	1	2	3	4
S 30-60 OILPULL	$45,000	$35,000	$22,000	$12,000

Type R 25-45 OilPull tractor engine

Type R 25-45 OilPull tractors were part of the 1924-1927 line. All of the Lightweight Series used a completely redesigned engine. The cutaway photo shown here illustrates the method of providing forced-feed lubrication to all essential engine parts. This was combined with a splash system in the bottom of the crankcase so that every moving part was always bathed in oil.

Nebraska Test Data

Model: Type R 25-45 OilPull

Test No. 116

Date Tested: July 7 to July 14, 1925

In the rated brake hp test a fuel economy of 10.67 hp-hours per gallon of kerosene was recorded for the 25-45. Fuel consumption totaled 4.27 gallons per hour, with 5.62 gallons of water added to the fuel mixture during the same period. In the maximum load test, 50.57 brake hp was developed, with economy slipping to 9.42 hp-hours per gallon. Maximum drawbar load tests were made in all three forward gears, with the rated test in second gear showing a pull of 3,824 lbs. at 2.69 mph for 27.42 hp. The low gear maximum test gave 6,321 lbs. of pull at 1.935 mph for 32.64 drawbar hp. Other than minor adjustments, no repairs or adjustments were necessary. Weighing 11,900 lbs., the 25-45 carried Rumely's own two-cylinder horizontal, valve-in-head engine. Using a 7-13/16 x 9-1/2-inch bore and stroke, it was rated at 540 rpm. Standard equipment included a Bosch DU4/2 Ed.22 magneto, Manzel lubricator, Donaldson air cleaner, and a Secor-Higgins carburetor designed and built in the Rumely factories.

COLLECTOR VALUES	1	2	3	4
R 25-45 OILPULL	$20,000	$17,000	$15,000	$6,500

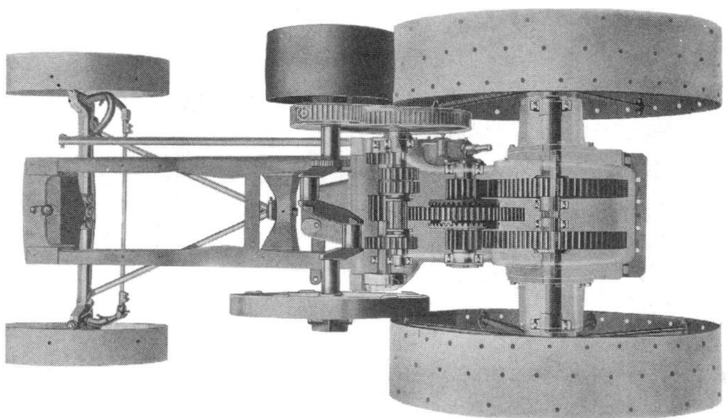

Type M 20-35 OilPull

The new Lightweight OilPull had all gears enclosed and running in oil. This was a great advantage over the earlier models with their exposed gearing. Another of the first Light-weight series was the Type M 20-35 OilPull. It was very popular, with nearly 3,700 units manufactured during the 1924 through 1927 production run. The 20-35 was a popular threshing trac-tor and was capable of handling all but the very largest separators. It was also quite capable of handling a silo filler and many other farm power needs.

Nebraska Test Data

Model: Type M 20-35 OilPull

Test No. 111

Date Tested: March 29 to April 15, 1925

To begin the 1925 testing season, Rumely sent a 20-35 OilPull under Serial No. 79 to the Tractor Test Laboratory. Although maximum drawbar load tests were taken in all three forward gears, the rated load test was taken in second gear and revealed an average pull of 3,017 lbs. at 2.63 mph over the 10-hour test. A maximum pull of 4,850 lbs. was made in low gear, at a speed of 2.13 mph and 16.48 percent slippage. This corresponded to 27.54 maximum drawbar hp. All OilPull models used kerosene fuel. At rated brake hp, the 20-35 gave a fuel economy of 11.22 hp-hours per gallon, burning 3.154 gph while developing 35.39 hp. Economy slipped to 8.43 hp-hours per gallon at a maximum brake load of 43.07 hp. The 20-35 featured Rumely's own two-cylinder horizontal, valve-in-head engine with a 6-13/16 x 8-1/4-inch bore and stroke. Rated speed was 640 rpm. Standard equipment included a Manzel lubricator, Donaldson air cleaner, American Bosch DU4/2 Ed.22 magneto, and Rumely's own Secor-Higgins carburetor. Total weight was 8,750 lbs.

COLLECTOR VALUES	1	2	3	4
M 20-35 OILPULL	$15,000	$12,000	$10,000	$5,000

Smallest of the Lightweight OilPull series was the Type L 15-25 tractor. More than 4,800 of these tractors were built in the 1924-1927 period. It could handle a 24- or 28-inch separator, especially if the large size was equipped with ball-and-roller bearings. A spring-mounted front axle cushioned the tractor for easier steering and operation. The Model L was also available as a special Orchard & Vineyard Tractor.

Nebraska Test Data

Model: Type L 15-25 OilPull
Test No. 112
Date Tested: March 29 to April 16, 1925

Except for physical size, the 15-25 OilPull of this test differed little from the 20-35 noted in Test No. 111. Engine design and standard accessories were identical except that the 15-25 carried a 5-13/16 x 7-inch bore and stroke with a rated speed of 755 rpm. Total weight was 6,050 lbs. Only minor repairs were necessary during the 40-hour test. At its rated brake hp the 15-25 came through with an economy of 10.88 hp-hours per gallon while developing a load of 25.19 hp. Water consumption in the fuel mixture totaled 3.765 gph, compared to 2.314 gallons of kerosene during the same period. At maximum load, 30.52 brake hp was developed—an economy rating of 8.42 hp-hours per gallon. Slightly more than 2,300 lbs. of drawbar pull was recorded in the 10-hour rated drawbar test using second gear, giving 16.01 drawbar hp. Although maximum load tests were made in all three forward gears, the best pull in terms of total lbs. came in low gear with 3,327 on the dynamometer, and a recorded 18.48 drawbar hp.

COLLECTOR VALUES	1	2	3	4
L 15-25 OILPULL	$25,000	$18,000	$13,000	$7,000

For 1928 the Lightweight OilPull Series was slightly modified and re-rated upward on hp output. The earlier 15-25 Type L became the Type W 20-30 tractor. Initially, the Lightweight OilPull tractors used a solid disc flywheel, but its "sounding board" effect was objectionable because it took normal engine noises and amplified them to unacceptable levels. Many of these tractors were retrofitted with a spoked flywheel.

Type W 20-30 OilPull

Nebraska Test Data

Model: Type W 20-30 OilPull
Test No. 141
Date Tested: September 15 to September 24, 1927

Previously tested under No. 112, the 20-30 had an engine speed of 850 rpm, compared to 755 rpm for the 15-25 previously noted. Most other differences between the two tractors were cosmetic. At rated brake hp, the 20-30 burned 3.143 gallons of kerosene per hour and yielded an economy of 9.62 hp-hours per gallon. Along with the fuel, 2.47 gallons of water

Type L 15-25 OilPull

were added into the fuel mixture through the special Rumely carburetor. The maximum load test revealed 35.36 brake hp with an economy of 7.89 hp-hours per gallon. Three forward speeds of 2.2, 2.9, and 3.5 mph were built into the 20-30. The rated drawbar test taken in second gear indicated a fuel economy of 6.06 hp-hours per gallon, while a maximum drawbar load test in low gear gave a recorded pull of 3,995 lbs. at 2.34 mph for 24.89 drawbar hp. Total weight of this tractor was 6,776 lbs.

COLLECTOR VALUES	1	2	3	4
W 20-30 OILPULL	$12,000	$10,000	$8,000	$5,000

Type X 25-40 Oil Pull

Rated to handle four plows or a 32-inch grain separator, the Type X 25-40 OilPull tractor replaced the earlier Type M 20-35. This model was rated at 700-725 rpm. Both the 20-30 "W" and the 25-40 "X" could be delivered as a winch tractor for industrial applications. The tractor was specially equipped with a heavy front-mounted winch. An obvious change between the original Lightweight Series and the second series of 1928 was the relocation of the coolant expansion tank to just above the radiator. Production of the 25-40 began in 1928 and ended in 1930.

Nebraska Test Data

Model: Type X 25-40 OilPull

Test No. 143

Date Tested: October 6 to October 13, 1927

Test No. 111 covered basically the same tractor as noted here, except the crankshaft speed was increased from 640 rpm for the Test No. 111 model to 725 rpm for the tractor used in this test. No major mechanical changes were made. Rated drawbar hp tests indicate a fuel economy of 7.91 hp-hours per gallon of kerosene over the 10-hour test. The best drawbar pull in terms of total lbs. came in low gear with 5,385 lbs. appearing at the dynamometer with a speed of 2.22 mph. Final figures indicate 37.79 total drawbar hp for this test. Maximum brake hp tests yielded 50.26 hp, along with an economy of 9.78 hp-hours per gallon. Fuel consumption totaled 5.768 gph, with an additional 5.43 gallons of water being added to the fuel mixture. Rated brake hp trials show 11.15 hp-hours per gallon of fuel, with total consumption of 3.632 gph. Total weight of this tractor was 9,440 lbs. Engine specifications for the 25-40, excepting crankshaft speed, are noted in Test No. 111.

COLLECTOR VALUES	1	2	3	4
X 25-40 OILPULL EARLY STYLE, LARGE FLYWHEEL	$18,000	$13,000	$8,000	$5,000
X 25-40 OILPULL LATE STYLE, SMALLER FLYWHEEL	$16,000	$13,000	$7,000	$4,000

Rumely crawler tractor

Sometime during the 1928 to 1930 period, Advance-Rumely developed a crawler tractor built over a 20-30 or a 25-40 chassis. Little is known of this tractor—except an original factory photograph in the author's hands, proving that a prototype was actually built. Despite the qualities of the design, the Great Depression certainly eliminated the possibility for a sequel.

During 1929, Advance-Rumely converted 100 of its earlier Type R 25-45 tractors into the new Type Y 30-50 model. Another 145 tractors were built and numbered as Model Ys. Design changes were relatively minor, and the increased power output was achieved by raising the high idle speed to 635 rpm. Despite the quality of the 30-50 and other OilPull models, farmers were now beginning to find numerous row-crop tractors on the market. For larger jobs, many compa-nies were offering small and compact unit-frame designs and sales of the OilPull continued to decline.

Nebraska Test Data

Model: Type Y 30-50 OilPull

Test No. 145

Date Tested: October 13 to October 24, 1927

The Model "Y" of this test was virtually identical to the Model "R" 25-45 tested in 1925, except engine speed was increased from 540 to 635 rpm. Engine specifications for this tractor are otherwise the same as noted under Test No. 116. Weighing 13,025 lbs., the 30-50 made its best maximum pull in low gear where it delivered 6,965 lbs. at the drawbar, traveling at a speed of 2.54 mph. Rated drawbar tests in second gear indicated a fuel economy of 6.75 hp-hours per gallon of kerosene. Brake hp test results show a maximum of 63.32 hp for the 30-50, well over the manufacturer's nominal rating. Under this load the 30-50 squeezed 8.85 hp hours out of each gallon of fuel—this figure rose to 10.79 on the rated brake hp test. In the

Rumely Type Y 30-50

latter case, fuel consumption totaled 4.667 gph, with an additional 3.29 gallons of water being added to the fuel mixture. Except for two broken intake valve springs, no repairs or adjustments were required during the 33-hour test run.

COLLECTOR VALUES	1	2	3	4
Y 30-50 OILPULL	$22,000	$17,000	$12,000	$8,000

Type Z 40-60 OilPull

The last of the OilPull tractors was the Type Z 40-60. Built only in 1929, some of these tractors were converted to Type Z from the earlier Type S 30-60 model. Sales were so poor some of these tractors were later retrofitted to their original 30-60 configuration. After Allis-Chalmers bought out Rumely in 1931, the stocks of remaining OilPull tractors were marketed until depleted, the end of the venerable Rumely OilPull tractor.

COLLECTOR VALUES	1	2	3	4
Z 40-60 OILPULL	$58,000	$40,000	$30,000	$15,000

Advance-Rumely bought out the Toro tractor line in 1927 and began converting it into the Rumely DoAll. This convertible tractor came onto the market in 1928 and remained there until the 1931 buyout by Allis-Chalmers. Unfortunately, the notion of a convertible tractor had already outlived its usefulness. Farmers had already developed a taste for the universal farm tractor in the Farmall and others that quickly came onto the market. The hard work of converting a tractor and then back again was not popular with most farmers.

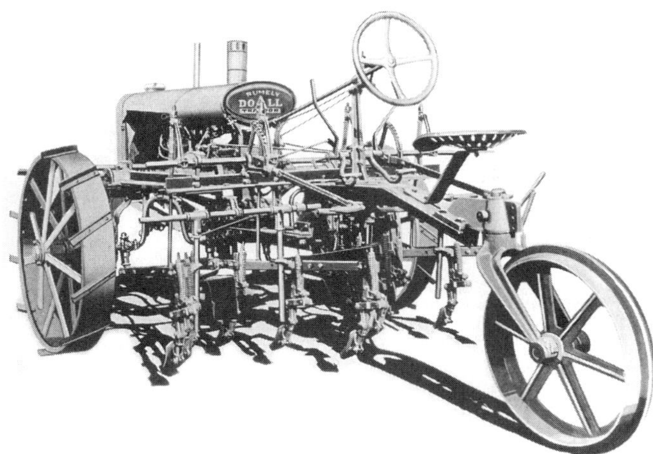

Rumely DoAll cultivator

Rumely DoAll tractor

Rumely DoAll tractors looked just like any small conventional model in their normal mode, but it took lots of work to change over to cultivating work when necessary. The DoAll had limited sales in the 1928 to 1931 period when only about 3,000 units were built. Meanwhile, International Harvester was building its Farmall tractor by the tens of thousands, and this left very little market share for the Advance-Rumely DoAll design.

Nebraska Test Data

Model: DoAll Tractor

Test No. 154

Date Tested: October 29 to November 24, 1928

Closing out the 1928 test season was Rumely's DoAll tractor. Only one problem occurred during the 40-hour test run—to keep the transmission in gear during the rated load and maximum drawbar tests, a method of locking the gear shift lever in place was improvised. Advertised speeds of 2.625 and 3.75 mph were provided. Total tractor weight was 3,702 lbs. At rated drawbar load the DoAll pulled 1,466 lbs. at 2.98 mph, yielding an economy of 4.98 hp-hours per gallon. A maximum drawbar load test in low gear manifested 16.32 drawbar hp with a pull of 2,012 lbs. at 3.04 mph. Maximum brake hp testing resulted in a fuel economy of 9.1 hp-hours per gallon, with the DoAll producing 21.61 brake hp in the maximum operating load test. Rumely powered the DoAll with a four-cylinder Waukesha vertical, L-head engine. With a 3-1/2 x 4-1/2 inch bore and stroke, it was rated at 1,400 rpm. Also included was an Eisemann GV4 magneto, Stromberg MI carburetor, Waukesha governor, and Donaldson-Simplex air cleaner.

COLLECTOR VALUES	1	2	3	4
DOALL TRACTOR	$8,000	$5,000	$3,500	$2,000

Rumely 6A tractor

In 1930 Advance-Rumely finally moved into conventional tractor designs with its Rumely 6A model. This rather attractive design sold very poorly, because when Allis-Chalmers took over in 1931, there still were 700 of the 6A tractors on hand. The new ownership continued selling the 6A until stocks were depleted, so the 6A appeared in some tractor directories until 1934. Allis-Chalmers had little interest in promoting the 6A because it had already developed its own successful tractor line. Thus came the end of Advance-Rumely.

Nebraska Test Data

Model: Rumely 6A

Test No. 185

Date Tested: October 28 to November 19, 1930 and April 7 to April 14, 1931

Cold weather prevented completion of Test No. 185 in 1930, so it was continued the following season. Previously submitted under test No. 181, then withdrawn for unknown reasons, the 6A was able to successfully complete its test the second time around. Test notes indicated that it was necessary to regrind the valves, and in a minor disaster, the fan hub broke, requiring a new fan and radiator before testing could continue. The 6A used a special six-cylinder Waukesha engine. It was rated at 1,365 rpm and carried a 4-1/4 x 4-3/4 inch bore and stroke. Featured also was an American Bosch U6 magneto and a Zenith 156 carburetor. Burning gasoline fuel, the 6A delivered a fuel efficiency of 8.63 hp-hours per gallon at its rated load of 43.23 brake hp. Efficiency rose slightly to 8.79 at maximum load of 48.37 hp. Advertised speeds of 2.82, 3.66, and 4.72 mph were built into the 6A—the rated drawbar test demonstrated 27.1 hp while pulling a 3,263 lb. load at 3.11 mph. Fuel economy was recorded at 5.71 hp-hours per gallon. Maximum drawbar pull came in the low gear test, with a recorded 33.57 hp. This consisted of a 4,273 lb. pull at 2.95 mph and slippage of 9.96 percent. Total weight of the 6A was 6,370 lbs.

COLLECTOR VALUES	1	2	3	4
RUMELY 6A	$8,000	$6,500	$5,500	$3,500

Aerco Corporation

HOLLYDALE, CALIFORNIA

See: Earthmaster Farm Equipment

Agrimotor Tractor Company

WICHITA, KANSAS

The Mid-West 9-18 appears in the trade directories only for 1921, although it may have been built for a localized market during a longer period. This 3,300 lb. tractor was equipped with a Gile two-cylinder horizontal engine with a 5 x 6-1/2-inch bore and stroke. It offered only a single forward speed, plus reverse. Very little is known of the company aside from its 1921 listing in the trade directories.

Ajax Auto Traction Company

PORTLAND, OREGON

In 1912 Ajax announced its No. 1 tractor. It used a four-cylinder opposed engine with the crankshaft mounted parallel to the chassis. The cylinders were 6 x 8-inch bore and stroke. The company also offered a No. 2 model, with a four-cylinder opposed engine built with a 7 x 10-inch bore and stroke. The No. 2 weighed in at 13 tons! Little is known of this venture...it ended shortly after it began.

Ajax No. 1 tractor

Ajax-Picrom Company

SAN FRANCISCO, CALIFORNIA

Ajax-Picrom Co. appears to have built a tractor about 1915, but no additional information has ever been located on its history or products.

Alamo Engine & Mfg. Company

HILLSDALE, MICHIGAN

By 1900 Alamo had already emerged as a major manufacturer of gasoline engines. This Alamo file photo illustrates one of the company's earliest attempts at converting an Alamo stationary engine into a usable tractor. The engine is about 6 hp. A simple clutch pulley was used to control the forward movement of the tractor.

Agrimotor Mid-West 9-18

A 1905 Alamo catalog illustrated the company's approach to a gasoline traction engine. A large Alamo engine, probably of 15 or 20 hp, was mounted on a traction chassis, but the cooling system is not shown. After a short time in the tractor business, Alamo opted to specialize in the engine business, doing so with great success for many years.

Alamo gasoline traction engine

Albaugh-Dover Company

CHICAGO, ILLINOIS

See: Square Turn Tractor Company

Albert Lea Tractor & Mfg. Company

ALBERT LEA, MINNESOTA

Sexton tractor

In the August 1917 issue of Agrimotor Magazine, George L. Sexton detailed his reasons why small tractors were needed for "every farm of 60 acres or more." Seeing a huge need, Sexton organized the Albert Lea company to manufacture the small Sexton tractor. It was equipped with a four-cylinder vertical engine with a 4-3/4 x 6-inch bore and stroke, giving it about 25 to 30 belt hp. The company appears to have begun about 1913, and was perpetually short of money, as indicated by numerous reorganizations and mergers. Finally, in 1917 Albert Lea Grader & Mfg. Company was organized to take over the assets of the tractor company. Little more was found about the Sexton.

Early Alamo tractor

Alberta Foundry & Machine Company

MEDICINE HAT, ALBERTA

14-28 "Canadian" tractor

In 1919, Alberta Foundry & Machine Company Ltd. first offered its 14-28 "Canadian" tractor, the only one to be built in the western provinces. The design came from R. B. Hartsough, an original partner in the Transit Thresher Company of Minneapolis. A unique feature was a wooden frame that could be shortened or lengthened. Another feature was the use of replace-able wooden spokes in the drivewheels. After the initial announcement, little more was heard of the "Canadian" tractor.

Thorobred 18-30 tractor

Allen-Burbank Motor Company

LOS ANGELES, CALIFORNIA

The Thorobred 18-30 tractor was marketed by Allen-Burbank Motor Co. in the 1920-1923 period. It was essentially a built-up tractor that used a Beaver four-cylinder motor and a Nuttall selective shift transmission. In 1923 the company was merged into Community Mfg. Company, also of Los Angeles, and for further information the reader is directed to that heading.

Algona Manfacturing Company

ALGONA, IOWA

Over the past 40 years the Author has collected names of engine and tractor manufacturers. For many years, we kept these on index cards and one such card appears for this company. However, we have no record of where we obtained this information, nor have we subsequently found further information on the company.

Allegheny Gear Works

PITTSBURGH, PENNSYLVANIA

About 1920 an advertisement appeared for the Allegheny 12-20 3-plow tractor. Priced at $450, it included a "Buda motor, worm drive, cut steel gears, roller and ball bearings, all moving parts enclosed, complete with governor and fenders." No illustration of the tractor has been found.

S. L. Allen & Company

PHILADELPHIA, PENNSYLVANIA

S. L. Allen & Co. was actively engaged in manu-facturing cultivators by the 1890s and its Planet Jr. line was known around the world. In 1920 the company made a brief entry into the tractor busi-ness with its Planet Jr. tractor of "universal" design. It was configured to handle cultivators, plows, and numerous other implements, and could also be equipped with the sulky shown in the photo for various drawbar work. Production of the Planet Jr. apparently ended in 1921. The company remained active in the cultivator business, eventually building various styles of walk-behind garden tractors. As with many manufacturers, production was suspended on most mod-els during World War II. Production resumed after the war, but ended again in the early 1950s

Planet Jr. Garden Tractor

Nebraska Test Data

Model: Planet Jr. Garden Tractor

Test No. 234

Date Tested: June 5 to June 19, 1935

Only one gear was built into the Planet Jr. garden tractor, with ground speed being controlled by a hand throttle. At 2.08 mph in the 10-hour rated load test, this tractor pulled 227 lbs. and delivered 1.26 hp with an economy of 3.49 hp-hours per gallon. A maximum pull of 292 lbs.

was achieved with an output of 1.36 hp. Brake tests at 2.07 rated hp indicated 5.88 as the fuel economy, with 6.19 hp-hours per gallon appearing at maximum load of 2.31 hp. The Planet Jr. was equipped with a single-cylinder Toro L-head engine. Rated at 1,800 rpm, it featured a 2-3/4 x 3-1/4-inch bore and stroke. Also featured was an Eisemann Model 71-F flywheel magneto, a Tillotson M-20-A carburetor, and an Air Maze air cleaner. Total unit weight was 500 lbs. Only minor repairs and adjustments were required during the 42-hour test.

Allen Tractor Company

CHICAGO, ILLINOIS

Allen Tractor Co. was incorporated at Chicago in 1916. Aside from the corporate announcement, nothing further has been located concerning the company or its products.

Allen Water Ballast Tractor Company

LOCATION UNKNOWN

This company was once referenced in a magazine article, but no address was provided and no additional information has been located.

Allied Motors Corporation

MINNEAPOLIS, MINNESOTA

Allied was building and marketing Viking and Standard Twin garden tractors in 1936, but further information regarding the activities of Allied Motors remains elusive. Allied acquired the Standard Twin garden tractor in 1930 or 1931, but the acquisition date of the Viking line is unknown.

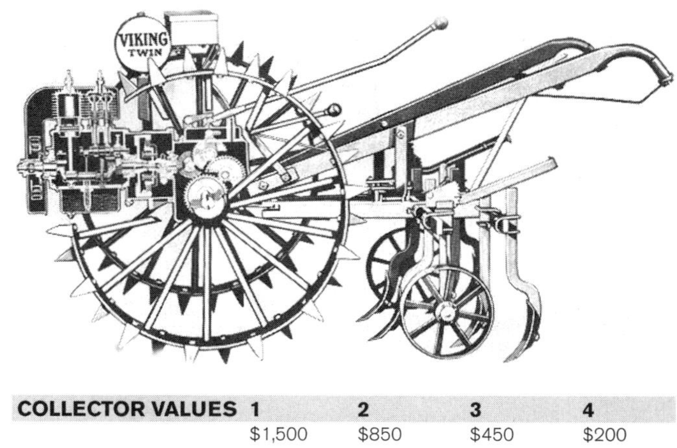

COLLECTOR VALUES	1	2	3	4
	$1,500	$850	$450	$200

Allied Truck & Tractor Corporation

MINNEAPOLIS, MINNESOTA

Allied was incorporated in April 1920 and the Allied 10-20 tractor appeared in the 1921-1924 directories. Weighing about 4,900 lbs., the 10-20 was a convertible tractor, and is shown in the photograph with the sulky truck attached. By 1920 the popularity of this design was waning, and just around the corner was the announcement of the Farmall all-purpose row-crop tractor.

Allied 10-20 tractor

Alligator Tractor Company

ST. LOUIS, MISSOURI

In 1964 Alligator announced its small Model 66 crawler tractor. The 66-G was equipped with a Wisconsin two-cylinder engine, while the diesel model used a Deutz single-cylinder engine. Both were about 53-cid, and both mod-els weighed slightly over 2,000 lbs. The Alligator continued to appear during the next two years, but the company's activities after that time are unknown.

Alligator Model 66 crawler tractor

COLLECTOR VALUES	1	2	3	4
MODEL 66	$2,500	$2,000	$1,500	$500

Allis-Chalmers Mfg. Company

MILWAUKEE, WISCONSIN

Allis-Chalmers had its beginnings in 1901 with the merger of Edward P. Allis Company, Fraser & Chalmers, Gates Iron Works, and Dickson Mfg. Company. Until 1914 the company confined its manufacturing efforts to large industrial machinery, everything from gigantic Corliss steam engines to sawmills, flour milling machinery, and a host of other items. In 1914, the company took an interest in the tractor business, eventually releasing its 10-18 tractor that year.

Sales of the 10-18 tractor were not at all exciting, but the company moved forward, introducing its 15-30, a conventional wheel tractor in 1918. From this point forward Allis-Chalmers tractors made their presence known throughout the industry. Even though the A-C tractor line never was among the top-selling brands, it earned a position of respect wherever it was used.

In 1929 Allis-Chalmers released its Model U tractor, which was destined to make history in the tractor business. The model was unique, but more importantly, the 1932 Model U became the first American farm tractor sold with pneumatic tires. Farmers and manufacturers scorned the idea at first, but in a short time, farmers were clamoring for rubber tires on their tractors, so the industry followed along, although grudgingly at first.

History was again made in 1933 when Allis-Chalmers introduced its WC row-crop tractor. This lightweight, powerful tractor was the first to use a "square engine" that had a 4-inch bore and stroke. WC tractors quickly proved themselves as sturdy, gutsy, and very reliable. By the time production of the WC ended in 1948, the company had built more than 178,000 units.

Other unique features were introduced to the tractor industry during the company's long career that ended in 1985 by merging with Deutz interests to form the Deutz-Allis line. Speculation provides many suggestions for the merger. Viewed in the larger sense, the farm tractor industry of 1985 was no longer able to support the production capacity and facilities of an earlier time.

The author has compiled several titles relating to Allis-Chalmers including: The Allis-Chalmers Story (Krause 2004); Encyclopedia of American Farm Tractors (Crestline/Motorbooks: 1979); and Allis-Chalmers Tractors (Motorbooks: 1992).

Allis-Chalmers 10-18

Allis-Chalmers introduced its 10-18 tractor in 1914. The tractor's unique design probably did not enhance its sales potential, and it took until the early 1920s for the company to sell all of the 10-18 tractors it had built. Yet, Allis-Chalmers persevered, constantly looking for better designs. Very few 10-18 tractors remain, making them highly valued among vintage tractor enthusiasts.

COLLECTOR VALUES	1	2	3	4
10-18	$30,000	$23,000	$17,000	$7,000

Allis-Chalmers 6-12

Between 1919 and 1923, Allis-Chalmers offered the 6-12 tractor, which was similar to several of its contemporaries, most notably the Moline Universal. The photograph shows a two-row cultivator mounted to the 6-12, but many other implements could be used as well. The cultivator could be easily detached, and a simple sulk attachment connected to the tractor frame for pulling a wagon or other towed implement.

Nebraska Test Data

Model: Allis-Chalmers 6-12

Test No. 54

Date Tested: August 17 to August 26, 1920

Representing an entirely different approach to farm power than most of the tractors previously tested (except the Moline Universal), the Allis-Chalmers 6-12 was billed as an "All-Purpose" machine. Using the well known LeRoi engine, it came just within the limits set by the manufacturer's nominal rating. A single forward speed of 2-1/2 mph was provided, with the rated drawbar test revealing 6.29 hp and a 1,046 lb. pull. Gasoline fueled the 6-12 throughout the test. At rated brake hp, 12.08 was the final figure after a two-hour run. Fuel consumption totaled 1.7 gph, with an economy rating of 7.11 hp-hours per gallon. The cooling system was more adequate than in many earlier test models, with coolant temperatures varying from 199 to 205 degrees F throughout the procedures. Standard equipment included a Dixie magneto and Kingston Model L carburetor. Bore and stroke dimensions of the LeRoi engine were 3-1/8 x 4-1/2 inches. The same engine was adapted to many different motor cultivators, combines and other equipment requiring about 12 brake hp. Rated speed was 1,200 rpm. Total weight of the 6-12 was only 2,500 lbs.

COLLECTOR VALUES	1	2	3	4
6-12 (WITH 1-BOTTOM PLOW)	$15,000	$11,000	$6,000	$4,000

Allis-Chalmers 6-12 and Galion Light Premier road graders

Rural roads of the 1920s were usually maintained by the farmers within a township. Small road graders were a blessing that permitted driving into town or around the neighborhood over a relatively smooth road. Shown here is a 6-12 Allis-Chalmers coupled to a Galion Light Pre-mier road grader. With this integrated outfit, one man could control the grader and the tractor with relative ease.

In 1918 Allis-Chalmers launched its new 18-30 tractor. Its unit-frame design was extremely modern for the time and the 18-30 tractor continued in various forms for several seasons. Allis-Chalmers guaranteed the 18-30 to have 3,000 lbs. of drawbar pull in low gear that came from a big four-cylinder engine with a 4-3/4 x 6-1/2-inch bore and stroke. To counter competitors' claims, the company noted: "The Allis-Chalmers 18-30 is not an "assembled" tractor. With the exception of the magneto, carburetor and such special accessories, every part of the tractor is factory-built by the Allis-Chalmers Mfg. Co." This 18-30 is from a 1921 A-C catalog.

Nebraska Test Data

Model: Allis-Chalmers 18-30

Test No. 55

Date Tested: August 23 to September 6, 1920

Under Serial No. 5729, the 18-30 was equipped with the company's own four-cylinder vertical, valve-in-head engine rated at 830 rpm and carrying a 4-3/4 x 6-1/2-inch bore and stroke. Low gear gave a ground travel of 2.31 mph, with 2.82 mph being the speed in high gear. Total weight was 6,000 lbs. Except for minor adjustments, no mechanical problems occurred during the test run of 33 hours. Using low gear, a maximum drawbar pull of 3,500 lbs. was achieved, or to state the matter another way, drawbar pull was slightly over 58 percent of total weight. On this test, 20.19 maximum drawbar hp was calculated. As with the entire procedure, kerosene was used as fuel, and at rated load, 30.58 hp was recorded over the two-hour run. Fuel economy came to an impressive 9.30 hp-hours per gallon, with total consumption being 3.29 gph. The Dixie Model 46 magneto and Kingston Dual carburetor were standard equipment.

Nebraska Test Data

Model: Allis-Chalmers 18-30

Test No. 83

Date Tested: September 15 to September 24, 1921

The 18-30 was retested in 1921 after a minor modification. One problem affecting the model was excessive water consumption due to the design of the "air washer," a popular air cleaner used during the 1920s. By adding a spacer, the volume of air space was substantially increased, and with the addition of another baffle the problem was solved. This unit also had Allis-Chalmer's own four-cylinder vertical engine, with valve-in-head design and a 4-3/4 x 6 _-inch bore and stroke. Rated speed was 930 rpm. A Kingston Model L carburetor and an Eisemann Model G-4 magneto came as regular equipment. The sliding gear transmission permitted two forward speeds of 2.58 and 3.16 mph. In the rated brake hp test, a fuel economy of 9.81 hp-hours per gallon resulted in a total consumption of 3.937 gph and an output of 38.62 hp. Fuel economy dropped minimally during the maximum load test, which revealed 43.73 hp. At the drawbar, a maximum pull of 3,510 lbs. was achieved in low gear. With a speed of 2.52 mph a maximum of 23.62 drawbar hp was recorded. The 18-30 weighed 6,640 lbs.

COLLECTOR VALUES	1	2	3	4
18-30	$12,000	$8,000	$5,500	$1,850

Allis-Chalmers 12-20

Allis-Chalmers developed its 12-20 tractor during 1920, introducing it early the following year. Following its outstanding performance in the Nebraska test, it was re-rated upward to a 15-25 tractor for 1922.

Nebraska Test Data

Model: Allis-Chalmers 12-20

Test No. 82

Date Tested: September 13 to September 24, 1921

In the rated brake hp tests, an impressive fuel economy of 9.71 hp-hours per gallon appeared for this 3-plow unit. This corresponded with 2.811 gallons of fuel consumed per hour at a load of 27.28 hp. Under maximum brake hp conditions, the 12-20 cranked out 33.18 hp with an economy rating of 8.6 hp-hours per gallon. Drawbar tests revealed a maximum pull of 3,000 lbs. in low gear, pulling this load at a speed of 2.55 mph for a maximum of 20.40 drawbar hp. Weighing only 4,550 lbs., the 12-20 carried a Midwest four-cylinder vertical, valve-in-head engine with a 4-1/8 x 5-1/4-inch bore and stroke, and had a rated speed of 1,100 rpm. Two forward speeds were available of 2.3 and 3.1 mph. Standard equipment included a Kingston Model L carburetor and a Dixie Model 46-C magneto. The governor was designed and built by Midwest. Only minor repairs were necessary, including a refitting of the top piston rings in two cylinders that were sticking because of being fitted too tightly.

COLLECTOR VALUES	1	2	3	4
12-20	$12,000	$8,000	$5,500	$1,850
15-30	$8,500	$6,500	$4,500	$1,850

By the beginning of the 1922 season, Allis-Chalmers had re-rated its 12-20 tractor as the Model L 15-25. Weighing 4,400 lbs., the 15-25 had a guaranteed drawbar pull in low gear of 2,750 lbs. Rated speed for the four-cylinder engine was 1,100 rpm, and it featured positive force-feed lubrication. Production of the Model L, 15-25 tractor ended in 1927.

Allis-Chalmers 18-30

Allis-Chalmers Model L 15-25

COLLECTOR VALUES	1	2	3	4
MODEL L 15-25	$8,500	$6,500	$4,500	$1,500

Production of the Allis-Chalmers 15-25 Special Road Maintenance Tractor ran concurrently with the normal production run for the 15-25. However, this modified version used heavier rear wheels, while the front wheels were equipped with high ribs for better steering control. The extra weight of the wheels and other special accessories boosted the operating weight of this style to 5,600 lbs.

In 1921 or 1922 Allis-Chalmers rerated the 18-30 tractor upward to a 20-35 rating, probably because of the results of Nebraska Test No. 83 in September 1921. The big four-cylinder engine used a 4-3/4 x 6-1/2-inch bore and stroke, and was rated at 930 rpm. Removable cylinder sleeves were a standard feature. Production of the 20-35 continued until 1930 when it was replaced with the Model E 25-40 tractor.

Allis-Chalmers 15-25 Special Road Maintenance Tractor

Allis-Chalmers 20-35

Nebraska Test Data

Model: Allis-Chalmers 20-35

Test No. 151

Date Tested: June 18 to June 26, 1928

No repairs or adjustments were required on the 20-35 during some 39 hours of test time. Weighing 7,095 lbs., this tractor was a successor to the 18-30 model tested earlier under Test No. 83. As in the earlier test, a four-cylinder vertical engine was used, with a 4-3/4 x 6-1/2-inch bore and stroke. Rated at 930 rpm, it featured an I-head design. Other features included two forward speeds of 2-1/2 and 3-1/4 mph, along with an Eisemann GS4 magneto and Kingston Model L carburetor. The 20-35 made a maximum drawbar pull of 4,400 lbs. in low gear for a recorded total of 33.2 drawbar hp. At rated drawbar load, fuel consumption came to 4.014 gph for an economy of 5.29 hp-hours per gallon. Maximum brake hp of 44.29 was accompanied with 8.83 hp-hours per gallon, compared to 8.35 at rated hp. The 20-35 recorded its highest coolant temperature of 179 degrees F during the rated brake hp test. Many early tractors operated at or near the boiling point through the test procedures.

COLLECTOR VALUES	1	2	3	4
20-35 SHORT FENDER	$6,800	$5,500	$2,500	$750
20-35 LONG FENDER	$10,500	$7,500	$3,200	$1,850

With the end of the 20-35 in 1930 came its replacement, the Model E 25-40 tractor. This new model boasted a big four-cylinder engine with a 5 x 6-1/2-inch bore and stroke. Production of the Model E 25-40 continued until 1936.

Allis-Chalmers Model E 25-40

Nebraska Test Data

Model: Allis-Chalmers Model E 25-40

Test No. 193

Date Tested: June 18 to June 26, 1931

Using distillate fuel, the Allis-Chalmers Model E had a maximum permissible rating of 27 drawbar and 42 belt hp under the tractor rating codes. This model was somewhat larger than the 20-35 tested under Test No. 151 of 1928. Brief specifications included the company's own four-cylinder, I-head engine with a 5 x 6-1/2-inch bore and stroke with a rated speed of 1,000

Model UC 19-30 row crop

rpm. Two forward speeds of 2-1/2 and 3-1/4 mph were provided, along with such accessories as an Eisemann G4 magneto, Zenith C6EV carburetor, and a Donaldson air cleaner. Weighing 7,200 lbs., the E produced 27.69 hp in the rated drawbar test, pulling 2,703 lbs. at 3.84 mph and yielding an economy of 6.18 hp-hours per gallon. Using low gear it developed 33.82 maximum drawbar hp with a pull of 4,133 lbs. at 3.07 mph. Under its maximum of 47 brake hp the E received a rating of 8.6 hp-hours per gallon, with a substantially higher economy of 9.73 at rated load of 42.24 brake hp.

COLLECTOR VALUES	1	2	3	4
MODEL E 25-40	$8,500	$6,000	$3,000	$1,500

Allis-Chalmers Model U 19-30

In 1929 Allis-Chalmers introduced its Model U 19-30 tractor. This new design was much lighter and more compact than its predecessors and production of this highly successful model continued until 1952. Initially the Model U was equipped with a Continental four-cylinder engine, but in 1932 it was replaced with the company's own engine, with a 4-3/4 x 5-inch bore and stroke. In 1936 the engine was modified slightly by giving it a 4-1/2-inch bore and more power. The Model U was the first tractor to be equipped with pneu-matic tires. This is the same tractor as the "United" from United Tractor & Equipment Company, Chicago, Illinois.

Nebraska Test Data

Model: Allis-Chalmers/"United"

Test No. 170

Date Tested: October 21 to November 7, 1929

Gasoline was used throughout Test No. 170. The featured engine was a Continental four-cylinder vertical style using an L-head design. Rated at 1,200 rpm, it carried a 4-1/4 x 5-inch bore and stroke. A Continental governor, Donaldson air cleaner, Eisemann G4 magneto and Schebler HD carburetor were also included as standard equipment. No repairs or adjustments were required during the 35-hour test. Weighing 4,821 lbs., this tractor had three advertised speeds of 2-1/3, 3-1/3, and 5 mph. Intermediate gear was used for the rated drawbar test. At 19.28 hp the "United" pulled a load of 1,934 lbs. at 3.74 mph and yielded 6.19 hp-hours per gallon. Maximum pull occurred in low gear with 3,679 lbs. at 2.61 mph and slippage of 8.5 percent. At maximum load, 36.04 brake hp was registered, along with fuel consumption of 4.181 gph and 8.38 hp-hours per gallon. This dropped to 8.25 at rated load of 30.27 hp, with fuel consumption coming in at 3.671 gph in the rated load test.

Cultivating style with dished rear wheels

Nebraska Test Data

Model: Allis-Chalmers Model U

Test No. 237

Date Tested: July 15 to August 5, 1935

This Model U was equipped with the company's own four-cylinder I-head engine with a 4-3/8 x 5 inch bore and stroke rated at 1,200 rpm. Because this tractor was available with either steel wheels or rubber tires, dual tests were made. The fuel economy test run in third gear using steel wheels indicated 16.86 hp, along with a pull of 1,087 lbs. at 5.83 mph. Economy was recorded at 6.14 hp-hours per gallon of distillate. The same four-hour test on rubber tires gave an appreciably higher figure of 8.57 on fuel economy, along with an output of 22.72 hp and a pull of 1,680 lbs. at 5.07 mph. The rated drawbar test in second gear was performed on the steel-wheel version. It indicated 19.35 hp, an economy of 6.85, and a pull of 1,891 lbs. at 3.84 mph. Brake testing at the 31.07 rated hp manifested an economy of 9.56 hp-hours per gallon, with the U attaining an economy figure of 9.94 at operating maximum load of 33.18 hp. A Zenith K-5 carburetor and Bendix-Scintilla C-4 magneto rounded out the accessory items. The U weighed 5,030 lbs. on steel wheels and 5,140 lbs. on rubber tires. Advertised speeds of 2.33, 3.33, 5, and 10 mph were provided, although fourth gear was recommended only for the rubber-tired model.

COLLECTOR VALUES	1	2	3	4
MODEL U 19-30	$5,000	$3,500	$1,500	$500

Late in 1930 Allis-Chalmers introduced its Model UC row-crop tractor. It was essentially the same as the Model U standard-tread model, except for the row-crop design. A major feature of the Model UC was the company's development of a "5-minute hitch" system. It was possible to simply drive the tractor into the cultivator, using only a pair of pli-ers to make the connections. Production of the UC continued until 1951.

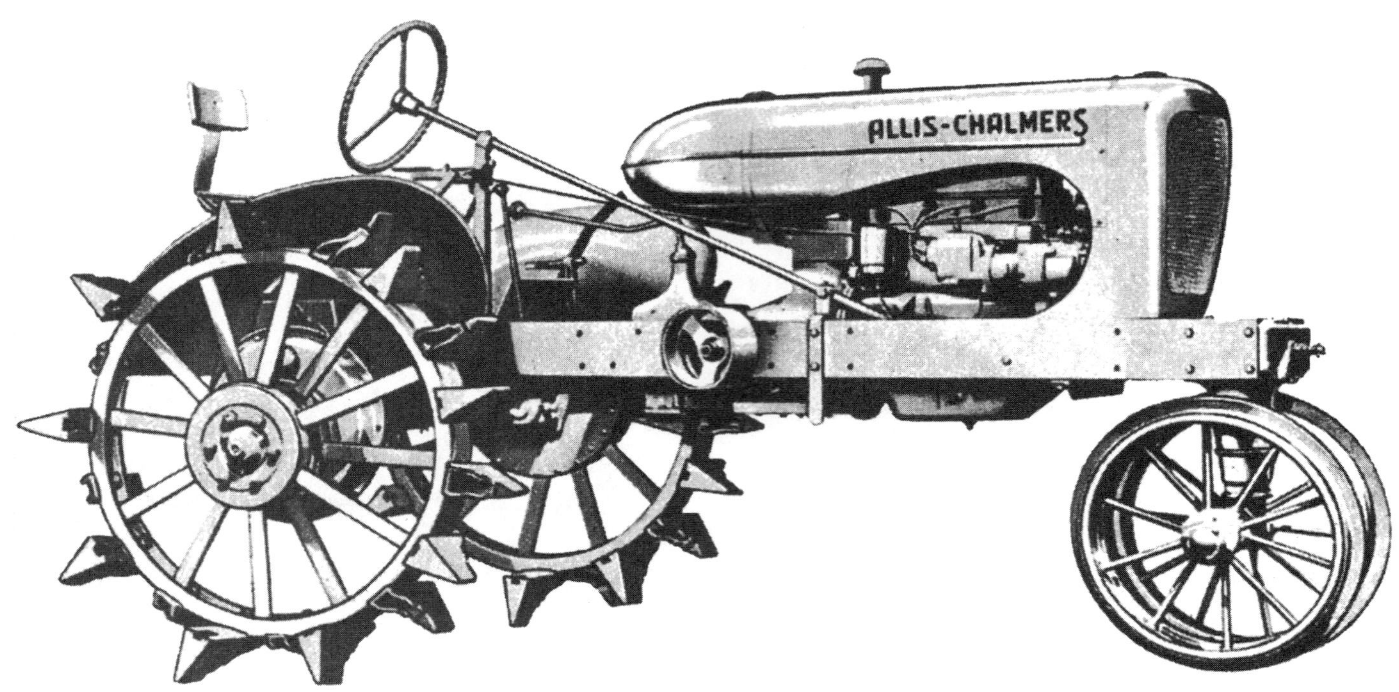

Cultivating style on skeleton steel wheels

Nebraska Test Data

Model: Allis-Chalmers "All-Crop"
Test No. 189
Date Tested: April 17 to May 13, 1931

Featuring a four-cylinder Continental engine, this new Allis-Chalmers row-crop tractor was not given a hp rating by the manufacturer, although under prevailing rating codes it was limited to 18 drawbar and 31 belt hp. A Zenith C5E carburetor was used for the test tractor, with this style and a Kingston carburetor being used at various times during the production run. Also included was an Eisemann GL4 magneto. Of L-head design, the Continental engine was rated at 1,200 rpm and carried a 4-1/4 x 5-inch bore and stroke. Using gasoline, the rated drawbar test at 17.77 hp indicated 5.33 hp-hours per gallon while pulling an 1,812-lb. load at 3.68 mph. A maximum load test in low gear gave 24.98 drawbar hp, along with a 3,763-lb. pull at 2.49 mph. Advertised speeds were 2-1/3, 3-1/3, and 5 mph. Rated brake hp tests at 31.11 hp gave a fuel economy of 9.56 hp-hours per gallon. This figure dropped to 8.82 when under the maximum load of 36.09 hp. Except for tightening the fan belt once, no repairs or adjustments were required during the 46-hour test. Total weight of the "All-Crop " tractor was 5,965 lbs.

Nebraska Test Data

Model: Allis-Chalmers Model UC
Test No. 238
Date Tested: July 16 to August 8, 1935

As with the Model U tractor noted in Test No. 237, this version of the Model UC featured an Allis-Chalmers four-cylinder I-head engine with a 4-3/8 x 5-inch bore and stroke, and rated at 1,200 rpm. It was also tested both with rubber tires and on steel wheels. The four-hour fuel economy test on steel indicated an efficiency of 5.35 hp-hours per gallon, compared to 8.96 on rubber tires. Rated drawbar tests were made on steel wheels, and in second gear the UC delivered 18.9 hp, along with a pull of 1,808 lbs. at 3.92 mph and a fuel economy of 6.18 hp-hours per gallon. The second gear maximum load test on rubber tires gave a pull of 2,593 lbs. at 3.06 mph. At its rated 30.93 brake hp the UC delivered a fuel economy of 10.2 hp-hours per gallon with a slightly diminished economy of 9.83 at operating maximum load of 33.52 hp. Advertised speeds of 2-1/3, 3-1/3, 5, and 10 mph were provided, although fourth gear was recommended only for the rubber-tired version. A Zenith K-5 carburetor and Bendix-Scintilla C-4 magneto rounded out the accessory items. Except for grease leakage from the final drive, no repairs or adjustments were noted during the test run of 71 hours.

COLLECTOR VALUES	1	2	3	4
MODEL UC 19-30				
CONTINENTAL MOTOR	$8,500	$3,800	$2,000	$1,400
UM ENGINE	$7,000	$3,000	$1,000	$600

Introduced in 1933, the Model WC was the first tractor in the industry to use a "square engine" meaning that the engine had the same bore and stroke—in this instance, 4 inches. From the beginning the WC was a very popular tractor, and by the time production ended in 1948, some 178,000 had been built. Shown here is a "flat-top" design of 1936, referring to models produced through early 1938 in which the open radiator tank had a "flat" top. During 1938 the Allis-Chalmers tractor line was streamlined and modernized, resulting in the "styled" Model WC. Many different configurations were available to suit various crop requirements and farming practices. The standard cultivating style on rubber tires was the most popular, although the others were required in certain areas. Production of the WC tractor ended in 1948.

Allis-Chalmers Model WC

WC row crop on rubber tires

WC row crop on steel wheels

WC tractor with wide front axle

Model WC with single front wheel

Nebraska Test Data

Model: Allis-Chalmers WC

Test No. 223

Date Tested: May 2 to May 16, 1934

With this test a new era in tractor testing began—the first tractor to be tested using pneumatic tires. A comparative test was conducted. The rated drawbar load test in second gear, and using steel wheels gave 12.15 hp, along with a pull of 1,201 lbs. at 3.79 mph and slippage of 7.8 percent. Fuel economy came in at 6.5 hp-hours per gallon. The same test using rubber tires indicated 12.08 hp, along with a pull of 1,402 lbs. at 3.23 mph and slippage of 12.2 percent. Fuel economy was recorded at 7.28 hp-hours per gallon. A separate fuel economy test of four hours on each wheel type gave a total of 5.62 hp-hours per gallon on steel and 8.18 on rubber tires. At its rated 20.91 brake hp, economy figures totaled 10.17 hp-hours per gallon, and were within hundredths of the same figure when operating at maximum load of 21.48 hp. Allis-Chalmers equipped this tractor with its own four-cylinder I-head engine rated at 1,300 rpm and using a 4-inch bore and stroke. Also included was a Bendix-Scintilla C-4 magneto, along with a Kingston carburetor and United air cleaner. Both styles had forward speeds of 2-1/2, 3-1/2, and 4-3/4 mph, while a fourth gear of 9-1/4 mph was recommended only for the rubber-tired version. On steel the WC weighed 3,190 lbs., while on rubber the weight jumped to 3,792 lbs.

Nebraska Test Data

Model: Allis-Chalmers WC (Distillate)

Test No. 303

Date Tested: May 31 to June 14, 1938

Over a period of 58 hours, Nebraska Tractor Test engineers evaluated the distillate-powered WC on rubber tires and steel wheels. Testing for rated drawbar hp was made on steel—it indicated a pull of 1,447 lbs. using second gear and traveling 3.84 mph. With an output of 14.81 hp, economy came in at 7.62 hp-hours per gallon. A four-hour fuel economy test on factory rubber and using second gear indicated an output of 17.68 hp, along with a pull of 1,925 lbs. at 3.44 mph and an economy of 9.36 hp-hours per gallon. When equipped with steel wheels the WC weighed in at 3,175 lbs., compared to 4,545 lbs. on rubber tires. Testing for rated brake load gave an economy figure of 10.96 while developing 23.04 hp. By comparison, the operating maximum load test recorded 24.21 hp with an economy of 10.99 hp-hours per gallon. Rated at 1,300 rpm, this WC used a four-cylinder I-head engine of the company's own design. It featured a 4-inch bore and stroke. Accessories on this tricycle tractor design were a Fairbanks-Morse FM4B magneto and a Zenith 124-1/2 carburetor. Also featured were 11.25 x 24 inch rear tires.

Nebraska Test Data

Model: Allis-Chalmers WC (Gasoline)

Test No. 304

Date Tested: June 2 to June 16, 1938

This was not the same tractor used in Test No. 303. It was equipped with the proper manifold for burning gasoline instead of distillate. This tractor was tested first on steel wheels, and then on rubber tires. It offered four forward speeds of 2-1/2, 3-1/2, 4-3/4, and 9 mph. Testing for rated brake load indicated an economy of 11.55 hp-hours per gallon with an output of 26.8 hp. By comparison, at operating maximum load of 28.44 hp, economy rose slightly to 11.58. Testing for rated drawbar load was made on steel wheels, and with an output of 17.67 hp, economy dropped into place at 8.13 hp-hours per gallon with a load of 1,727 lbs. at 3.84 mph. A four-hour fuel economy test in second gear using rubber tires manifested an economy figure of 9.46 with an output of 19.05 hp, along with a pull of 2,118 lbs. at 3.37 mph. Except for a minor oil leak around the governor lever, no repairs or adjustments were noted during 63 hours of engine running time.

COLLECTOR VALUES	1	2	3	4
WC WAUKESHA	$28,500	$18,000	$10,000	$5,000
WC FLAT-TOP, 1934-38	$4,000	$2,800	$1,000	$450
WC TRACTOR "STYLED"	$3,000	$2,000	$1,200	$450

Allis-Chalmers Model RC

From 1939 through 1941, Allis-Chalmers built a few Model RC tractors. The RC was essentially built over the WC chassis but used a smaller engine. Production was suspended during World War II and never resumed.

Nebraska Test Data

Model: Allis-Chalmers RC (Distillate)

Test No. 316

Date Tested: April 19 to April 24, 1939

Testing for rated brake hp indicated a fuel economy of 11.82 hp-hours per gallon with a 16.24-hp load. When working at operating maximum load, the RC cranked out 18.14 hp with a slightly improved fuel economy of 12.26 hp-hours per gallon. Testing for rated drawbar load indicated 12.11 hp with a pull of 1,221 lbs. at 3.72 mph (third gear) and a fuel economy of 9.45 hp-hours per gallon of distillate. Operating maximum load shows a maximum first-gear pull of 2,840 lbs. at 1.66 mph and an output of 12.60 mph. The RC tested carried Serial No. RC sign chassis was used with 10 x 28-inch rear rubber tires, along with 4.75 x 15-inch front tires. Engine 3004. Weighing in at 4,005 lbs., it featured four forward speeds of 2, 2.8, 3.75, and 7.5 mph. The tricycle-de equipment included a Fairbanks-Morse FM4B magneto and a Zenith 61AJ7 carburetor. Allis-Chalmers featured its own four-cylinder I-head engine, rated at 1,500 rpm and carrying a 3-3/8 x 3-1/2-inch bore and stroke. No repairs or adjustments were noted during 51 hours of engine running time.

Allis-Chalmers introduced its Model WF trac-tor in 1937, keeping it in production until 1951. This 23 hp tractor was a standard-tread (fixed width) version of the Model WC row-crop tractor. One of the major features was a four-speed transmission with a high gear that permitted road speeds up to 10 mph. Equipped with rubber tires, the WF weighed 3,600 lbs. Pneumatic tires were standard equipment, although steel wheels could also be furnished. When equipped with steel wheels, fourth gear—or road gear—was blocked out and could not be used.

Allis-Chalmers Model WF

COLLECTOR VALUES	1	2	3	4
MODEL WF (UNSTYLED)	$7,000	$5,000	$3,200	$1,200
MODEL WF (STYLED)	$7,000	$5,000	$3,200	$1,200

Allis-Chalmers Model WD

In 1948 the WC tractor was retired and replaced with a new model known as the WD. A major feature of the WD was its "two-clutch power control system" that was essentially a live power take off (PTO) system. The foot-operated clutch controlled all power operations, while a separate hand clutch could be used to start and stop the tractor, leaving the PTO shaft in operation. The WD also offered a full hydraulic system, plus the advantage of pow-er shifting to change the wheel tread width. Eventu-ally, these improvements were added to virtually every other tractor on the market. Production of the WD continued into 1954.

Nebraska Test Data

Model: Allis-Chalmers WD

Test No. 399

Date Tested: July 16 to July 30, 1948

"Tractor fuel" was introduced in the mid-1940s as an alternative to using distillate or gasoline. Typically, it carried an octane rating of about 42, compared to a typical gasoline octane rating of about 74. The Allis-Chalmers WD presented for this test was equipped to burn "tractor fuel." Testing at an operating maximum load of 25.08 belt hp yielded a fuel economy of 10.52 hp-hours per gallon, compared to an economy of 10.37 when under the rated load of 23.54 belt hp. Standard equipment included 11 x 28-inch rear and 5.50 x 16-inch front tires. Bare tractor weight was 3,388 lbs. No repairs or adjustments were noted during 46-1/2 hours of engine operating time, although testing was done without the hydraulic pump listed as special equipment. Featured was a four cylinder I-head engine with a 4-inch bore and stroke. Rated at 1,499 rpm, it carried a Fairbanks-Morse magneto and Marvel-Schebler TSX-159 carburetor. Advertised speeds of 2-1/2, 3-3/4, 5, and 9-3/4 mph were used and second gear was selected for the rated load drawbar test. At a rated load of 19.34 drawbar hp, the WD pulled 1,989 lbs. at 3.65 mph and yielded a fuel economy of 9.44 hp-hours per gallon. A maximum low-gear pull of 3,425 lbs. at 2.3 mph was determined.

Nebraska Test Data

Model: Allis-Chalmers WD

Test No. 440

Date Tested: May 17 to June 1, 1950

Weighing 3,721 lbs., this WD was loaded with another 1,168 lbs. of weight on each rear wheel during drawbar tests. Advertised speeds of 2.5, 3.75, 5, and 9.75 mph were provided. Third gear was used for the rated-load test, which produced a rated 23.56 drawbar hp, with a load of 1,818 lbs. at 4.86 mph and slippage of 4.73 percent. Fuel economy was registered at 9.97 hp-hours per gallon. Standard equipment included 5.50 x 16-inch front and 11 x 28-inch rear tires. A low-gear maximum pull of 4,304 lbs. was achieved at 2.18 mph against a slippage of 17.35 percent. Allis-Chalmers supplied its own four-cylinder I-head engine for the WD. Rated at 1,400 rpm, it used a 4-inch bore and stroke with a 201-cid engine. No repairs or adjustments were noted during 40-1/2 hours of engine running time. An operating maximum load of 32.57 belt hp yielded a fuel economy of 11.76 hp-hours per gallon. This figure dropped slightly to stand at 11.66 under a rated load of 30.55 belt hp.

COLLECTOR VALUES	1	2	3	4
MODEL WD	$3,500	$2,000	$1,000	$500

Introduced in 1953, the WD-45 boasted substan-tially more hp than its predecessor, the WD. This model had a four-cylinder 226-cid engine with a 4 x 4-1/2-inch bore and stroke. Production of the WD-45 ended in 1957. It was available in various chassis configurations, and was also available in diesel or LP-gas models.

Nebraska Test Data

Model: Allis-Chalmers WD-45

Test No. 499

Date Tested: July 29 to August 10, 1953

The 226-cid WD-45 was rated at 1,400 rpm and achieved a maximum engine torque of 287.9 lbs.-ft. at 867 rpm. This tractor was equipped with a four-cylinder I-head engine with a 4 x 4-_-inch bore and stroke. Over 42-1/2 hours of operating time, no repairs or adjustments were noted. Standard tire equipment included 13 x 28-inch rear and 5.50 x 16-inch front rubber.

Allis-Chalmers Model WD-45

Advertised speeds of 2-1/2, 3-3/4, 5, and 11-1/4 mph were provided with third gear was used for Test H. The bare tractor weighed 3,955 lbs., with 1,900 lbs. added to each rear wheel during Tests F, G, and H. Test H produced a fuel economy of 10.64 hp-hours per gallon. This 10-hour run was made with an output of 30.18 drawbar hp, a pull of 2,250 lbs. at 5.03 mph, and slippage of 4.86 percent. Test G yielded a low-gear maximum pull of 5,441 lbs. at 2.11 mph. With a Test D rated belt load of 38.61 hp, the WD-45 achieved 11.94 hp-hours per gallon. That climbed to 12.34 under a Test C operating maximum load of 40.47 hp.

Nebraska Test Data

Model: Allis-Chalmers WD-45 (Distillate)

Test No. 511

Date Tested: October 26 to October 31, 1953

Tractor fuel was used in this model during 41 hours of operating time. Test C indicated a fuel economy of 11.01 hp-hours per gallon under a load of 32.24 belt hp. At a Test D rated belt load of 28.89 hp, fuel economy dipped slightly to 10.69 hp-hours per gallon. This model carried a four-cylinder I-head engine with a 4 x 4-1/2-inch bore and stroke. Rated at 1,400 rpm, it attained a maximum torque of 231.7 lbs.-ft. at 789 rpm. Standard equipment included 13 x 28-inch rear and 5.50 x 16-inch front tires, with forward speeds of 2-1/2, 3-3/4, 5, and 11-1/4 mph. Bare weight was 3,955 lbs., with an additional 1,482 lbs. of weight added to each rear wheel during Tests F, G, and H. The latter test was run in third gear. On conclusion of this 10-hour run, fuel economy was pegged at 9.23 hp-hours per gallon. During Test H an output of 23.22 hp was recorded, with a pull of 1,715 lbs. at 5.08 mph against a 3.61 percent slippage. Test G elicited a low-gear maximum pull of 4,634 lbs. at 2.21 mph with 11.94 percent slippage.

Nebraska Test Data

Model: Allis-Chalmers WD-45 (LPG)

Test No. 512

Date Tested: October 26 to November 4, 1953

This interesting variation of a well-known tractor series carried the same basic specifications as the distillate model noted in Test No. 511, except for the special LP-gas equipment. Like the WD-45 previously noted, a 226-cid engine was featured, but the LP-gas model used a compression ratio of 7.2:1, compared to 4.75:1 on the distillate model and 6.45:1 for the gasoline model noted in Test No. 499. This engine reached a peak torque of 275.6 lbs.-ft. with an engine speed of 1,250 rpm. The tractor was built with a rated speed of 1,400 rpm. Test H, run in third gear, indicated a rated drawbar output of 30.32 hp, along with a pull of 2,261 lbs. at 5.03 mph, slippage of 4.27 percent, and a fuel economy of 8.34 hp-hours per gallon of propane. Test G secured a low-gear maximum pull of 5,421 lbs. at 2.07 mph. Belt testing indicated a fuel economy of 9.54 hp-hours per gallon of propane under a Test C operating maximum load of 42.12 belt hp. This figure declined to 9.25 at a Test D rated load of 38.45 belt hp. No repairs or adjustments were noted during 42 hours of operating time.

Nebraska Test Data

Model: Allis-Chalmers WD-45 (Diesel)

Test No. 563

Date Tested: October 4 to October 11, 1955

Using a 3-7/16 x 4-1/8-inch, four-cylinder diesel engine, this tractor achieved a maximum engine torque of 259 lbs.-ft. with an engine speed of 1,169 rpm with engine speed rated by the company at 1,625 rpm. Displacement was 230 cid. Standard equipment for this 4,285-lb. tractor included 13 x 28-inch rear and 5.50 x 16-inch front tires, along with forward speeds of 2-1/2, 4, 5-2/5, and 12 mph. No repairs or adjustments were noted during 41 hours of running time. Test H, run in third gear, indicated a rated drawbar output of 30.48 hp, along with a pull of 2,311 lbs. at 4.95 mph and a slippage of 4.47 percent. Drawbar fuel economy was scored at 12.52 hp-hours per gallon of diesel fuel. Test G produced a low-gear maximum pull of 5,908 lbs. at 2.06 mph against a slippage of 16.34 percent. During Tests F, G, and H an additional 1,890 lbs. was added to each rear wheel. Belt hp tests indicated a fuel economy of 14.04 hp-hours per gallon of fuel under a Test B 100 percent maximum load of 43.29 hp. Economy rose to stand at 14.13 when under a Test D rated load of 38.86 hp.

COLLECTOR VALUES	1	2	3	4
MODEL WD-45	$6,000	$3,500	$1,200	$500
MODEL WD-45 DIESEL	$7,000	$4,000	$1,200	$800

Allis-Chalmers Model A standard-tread

Model A standard-tread tractors were offered 1936 to 1942. This style sold rather poorly compared with the WC, but its $1,500 price tag was probably a deterrent. Most farmers saw little need for a standard-tread tractor when its WC row-crop model would do almost everything around the farm. With the onset of World War I, production ended for the Model A, and did not resume after the war.

COLLECTOR VALUES	1	2	3	4
MODEL A	$14,000	$8,500	$5,500	$2,000

Allis-Chalmers Model B

Production of the Model B Allis-Chalmers tractor began in 1937, and continued for 20 years. Initially, this

small tractor was priced at only $495. Many different attachments were available, including the one-row cultivator shown in the photo. Model B tractors were equipped with a four-cylinder engine with a 3-1/4 x 3-1/2-inch bore and stroke. Rated speed was 1,400 rpm. This model used a rear-mounted belt pulley, available as an extra-cost option. Also available was an industrial version Model IB tractor.

Nebraska Test Data

Model: Allis-Chalmers Model B
Test No. 302
Date Tested: May 31 to June 8, 1938

Three forward speeds of 2-1/2, 4 and 7-3/4 mph were built into the Allis-Chalmers B tractor. Weighing but 2,620 lbs., it was presented for testing equipped with 7.00 x 24 rear tires and 5.00 x 15 inch front rubber tires. Distillate fuel was used throughout some 42 hours of testing. Test D for rated brake hp indicated an economy of 11.14 hp-hours per gallon with an output of 14 hp. Under Test C for operating maximum load, economy remained almost identical at 11.13, but hp increased slightly to 15.14. Test H for rated drawbar load indicated 10.31 hp with a pull of 1,074 lbs. at 3.6 mph over the 10-hour test run. Economy figures compiled from this test indicated 9.47 hp-hours per gallon. The B was equipped with the company's own four-cylinder engine rated at 1,400 rpm and carried a 3-1/4 x 3-1/2-inch bore and stroke. Accessories included a Rockford clutch, upholstered seat, Fairbanks-Morse FR4B magneto, Handy governor, and a Zenith 61A7 carburetor. A broken fuel line was replaced with a new one and no other repairs or adjustments were noted.

Nebraska Test Data

Model: Allis-Chalmers Model B
Test No. 439
Date Tested: May 17 to May 24, 1950

This Allis-Chalmers Model B was tested using gasoline. The company's own four-cylinder engine was featured. Of I-head design with a 125.3-cubic inch displacement, it was rated at 1,500 rpm and used a 3-7/8 x 3 _-inch bore and stroke. No repairs or adjustments were required during 43-1/2 hours of engine operating time. Standard equipment included 4.00 x 15-inch front and 10 x 24-inch rear tires. The bare tractor weighed 2,251 lbs., but for Tests F, G, and H an additional 875 lbs. of weight was added to each rear wheel. Advertised speeds of 2-1/2, 4, and 7-1/2 mph were provided, with second gear being used for Test H. At a rated drawbar load of 15.66 hp the B pulled 1,373 lbs. at 4.28 mph with a slippage of 4.65 percent. Test G manifested a low-gear maximum pull of 2,667 lbs. at 2.42 mph. Belt testing revealed a fuel economy of 11.45 hp-hours per gallon under a Test C operating maximum load of 21.17 belt hp. At a Test D rated hp of 19.46, fuel economy came in at 11.22 hp-hours per gallon.

COLLECTOR VALUES	1	2	3	4
MODEL B TRACTOR	$2,700	$1,500	$750	$300

Between 1940 and 1950 Allis-Chalmers built some 90,000 copies of its Model C tractor. The four-cylinder engine carried a 3-3/8 x 4-1/2 inch bore and stroke. This yielded nearly 22 belt-hp with an operating speed of 1500 rpm. A host of implements were available for the Model C, making it an ideal choice for the small farm.

COLLECTOR VALUES	1	2	3	4
MODEL C TRACTOR	$2,600	$1,500	$750	$500

Allis-Chalmers Model C

Nebraska Test Data

Model: Allis-Chalmers Model C (Distillate)
Test No. 363
Date Tested: October 28 to November 6, 1940

Allis-Chalmers used its own four-cylinder I-head engine in this tractor. Rated at 1,500 rpm, it carried a 3-3/8 x 3-1/2 inch bore and stroke. Also included was a Fairbanks-Morse FMJ4B magneto and a Zenith 61AJ7 carburetor. Three forward speeds of 2-1/2, 3-1/4, and 7-1/2 mph were standard equipment, along with 9 x 24-inch rear and 4.00 x 15-inch front tires. Test weight was 3,205 lbs. This tractor was tested using distillate fuel. Test H was run in second gear, and at a speed of 3.38 mph and slippage of 8 percent, the Model C pulled a load of 1,407 lbs. Under a rated output of 12.68 drawbar hp, fuel economy stood at 9.4 hp-hours per gallon at the end of this 10-hour run. The low-gear maximum pull as recorded in Test G was 2,368 lbs. at a speed of 1.87 mph and slippage of 19.24 percent for an output of 11.83 drawbar hp. Test C, under a maximum operating load of 18.82 brake-hp yielded an economy of 12.08 hp-hours per gallon, while at a rated belt load of 17.24 hp, economy dropped to 11.64 hp-hours per gallon. During the limbering-up test, a leaky fuel tank was replaced. No other repairs or adjustments were noted during 53 hours of engine operating time.

Nebraska Test Data

Model: Allis-Chalmers Model C (Gasoline)
Test No. 364
Date Tested: October 28 to November 7, 1940

A comparison of this test with No. 363 indicates that two entirely different tractors were used. Serial No. CE-93G was presented for this test, while in Test No. 363, Serial No. CE-79K was used. With the exception of special equipment required for distillate fuel, both tractors were virtually identical. Test C, with an operating maximum load of 21.83 brake-hp, yielded a fuel economy of 11.86 hp-hours per gallon. Test D, using gasoline, delivered an economy of 11.77 hp-hours per gallon with a rated load of 20.27 brake hp. Second gear was used for Test H, and under a rated load of 14.15 drawbar-hp, the Model C pulled 1,557 lbs. at 3.41 mph with a slippage of 8.21 percent and a fuel economy of 9.69 hp-hours per gallon. A maximum low-gear pull of 2,352 lbs. was noted in Test G with a slippage of 17.9 percent, a ground speed of 1.93 mph, and an output of 12.1 drawbar hp. No repairs or adjustments were noted during 45 hours of engine operating time.

COLLECTOR VALUES	1	2	3	4
MODEL C	$2,600	$1,500	$750	$300

Allis-Chalmers Model CA

The Model CA tractor replaced the Model C in 1950. Production of this model continued until 1957. In addition to all the features found on the Model C, the Model CA was equipped with the company's Traction Booster system and Power Shift rear wheels. The 125-cid engine was also used as a stationary power unit.

Nebraska Test Data

Model: Allis-Chalmers Model CA

Test No. 453

Date Tested: October 31 to November 9, 1950

Allis-Chalmers featured its own four-cylinder I-head engine in the CA tractor. Rated at 1,650 rpm, it used a 3-3/8 x 3-1/2 inch bore and stroke for a 125 cubic inch displacement. Standard equipment included forward gears of 2, 3-1/2, 4-1/2, and 11-1/4 mph, along with 10 x 24-inch rear and 4.00 x 15-inch front tires. Weighing 2,763 lbs., the CA gained an additional 1,048 lbs. of ballast on each rear wheel during Tests F, G, and H. A low-gear maximum pull of 3,557 lbs. was noted in Test G. Second gear was chosen for Test H, and it revealed a rated output of 17.83 drawbar-hp, and a pull of 2,073 lbs. at 3.23 mph under a slippage of 6.66 percent. Under this load, drawbar fuel economy was recorded at 10.29 hp-hours per gallon. No repairs or adjustments were noted during 47 hours of engine running time. Under a Test D rated belt load of 22.69 hp, the CA delivered 11.66 hp-hours per gallon. A Test C operating maximum load was 24.79 belt hp and fuel economy came in at 11.79 hp-hours per gallon.

COLLECTOR VALUES	1	2	3	4
MODEL CA	$2,700	$1,500	$750	$300

In a radical departure from conventional design, Allis-Chalmers introduced its Model G tractor in 1948, continuing production until 1955. This small tractor was immensely popular with truck gardeners, in particular, although it also saw limited use on grain and livestock farms. Many different attachments were available, including a wide variety of cultivators.

Nebraska Test Data

Model: Allis-Chalmers Model G

Test No. 398

Date Tested: July 16 to July 30, 1948

A Continental AN-62 four-cylinder, L-head engine powered the Allis-Chalmers G tractor. Rated at 1,800 rpm, it featured a 2-3/8 x 3-1/2-inch bore and stroke. Also featured was a Delco-Remy electrical system and a Marvel-Schebler TSV-13 carburetor. Forward speeds of 2.25, 3.5, and 7 mph were included, along with a "special low" of 1.6 mph. No repairs or adjustments were noted during 45 hours of engine operating time. Without additional weights, the Model G weighed in at 1,549 lbs. Test H was run in second gear at a speed of 3.2 mph. A pull of 851 lbs. with a slippage of 7.8 percent was recorded, along with an output of 7.26 drawbar hp and a fuel economy of 7.64 hp-hours per gallon. A maximum low-gear pull of 1,143 lbs. was noted in Test G. At a Test C operating maximum load of 10.07 belt hp, fuel economy was recorded at 9.06 hp-hours per gallon. Fuel economy slipped slightly to 8.74 under a Test D rated load of 9.37 belt hp. Tire equipment included 6 x 30-inch rear and 4.00 x 12-inch front rubber.

Allis-Chalmers Model G

COLLECTOR VALUES	1	2	3	4
MODEL G	$3,850	$2,500	$1,500	$700
(ADD $500 FOR HYDRAULICS)				

Although Allis-Chalmers introduced its D-Series tractors in 1957, the small D-10 did not go into production until 1959 and it remained in the line until 1967. Like other D-Series tractors, the D-10 was modified during the production run. Initially it used a 138.7-cid engine with a 3-3/8 x 3-7/8-inch bore and stroke. In late 1961 or early 1962 the engine bore was increased to 3-1/2 inches for a displacement of 149 cubic inches.

Allis-Chalmers D-10

Nebraska Test Data

Model: Allis-Chalmers D-10
Test No. 724
Date Tested: October 13 to October 20, 1959

The D-10 used a 138.7-cid engine and 10 x 24-inch rear and 5.00 x 15-inch front tires. Weighing in at 2,860 lbs., the D-10 was burdened with 795 lbs. of ballast on each rear wheel and 176 lbs. on each front tire, giving an aggregate weight of 4,801 lbs. during most of the drawbar test runs. Using third gear, fuel economy was recorded at 11.19 hp-hours per gallon at a maximum of 25.73 available hp. This two-hour run also yielded a pull of 2,409 lbs. at 4.01 mph and slippage of 8.55 percent. A 10-hour run made at 75 percent pull produced a fuel economy figure of 10.77 with a drawbar output of 21.66 hp. Statistics from this run also included a pull of 1,817 lbs. at 4.47 mph and slippage of 5.34 percent. A maximum of 28.51 PTO hp was delivered at rated engine speed. This two-hour run also recorded a fuel economy of 12.74 hp-hours per gallon. No repairs or adjustments were noted during 37-1/2 hours of operating time.

Nebraska Test Data

Model: Allis-Chalmers D-10
Test No. 812
Date Tested: April 3 to April 18, 1962

A four-cylinder, 149-cid engine was featured in this D-10 tractor. Rated at 1,650 rpm, it used a 3-1/2 x 3-7/8-inch bore and stroke. Standard equipment included 11 x 24-inch rear and 5.00 x 15-inch front tires. Also featured was a selective gear, fixed-ratio transmission with forward speeds of 2.0, 3.5, 4.5, and 11.4 mph. No repairs or adjustments were recorded during 39-1/2 hours of running time. The D-10 carried a test weight of 5,560 lbs. through the addition of front and rear ballast, although bare tractor weight was 3,001 lbs. Using third gear, a two-hour drawbar economy run made at 28.78 maximum available hp indicated a pull of 2,523 lbs. at 4.28 mph with 6.41 percent slippage. Fuel economy was observed at 11.38 hp-hours per gallon. The economy figure changed slightly to 11.12 in a 10-hour economy run made at 75 percent pull. This test noted an output of 25.19 hp, a pull of 1,993 lbs. at 4.74 mph and 4.82 percent slippage. A two-hour PTO run made at rated engine speed indicated an output of 33.46 PTO hp, with an observed fuel economy of 13.05 hp-hours per gallon.

COLLECTOR VALUES	1	2	3	4
D-10	$7,500	$5,500	$4,000	$1,500

Allis Chalmers D-12 tractor

From 1959 to 1967 Allis-Chalmers offered its D-12 tractor. Initially, the D-10 and the D-12 used the same 138.7-cid engine, but in late 1961 or 1962 this was changed to a larger 149-cid motor. Each had a different operating width: the D-10 stood 58 inches wide, while the D-12 had a width of 69 inches.

Nebraska Test Data

Model: Allis-Chalmers D-12
Test No. 723
Date Tested: October 13 to October 20, 1959

Rated at 1,650 rpm, the D-12 used an Allis-Chalmers four-cylinder engine with a 3-3/8 x 3-7/8-inch bore and stroke for a 138.7 cubic inch displacement. At rated engine speed the D-12 delivered a maximum of 28.56 PTO hp and a resultant fuel economy of 12.21 hp-hours per gallon. Weighing 2,945 lbs., the D-12 was loaded to 5,449 lbs. during most of the drawbar testing. Standard equipment included 11 x 24-inch rear and 5.00 x 15-inch front tires. Also included were four forward speeds of 2, 3.5, 4.5, and 11.4 mph. A two-hour run using third gear at maximum available power produced an output of 23.56 drawbar hp with a pull of 2,057 lbs. at 4.29 mph and slippage of 6.18 percent. Fuel economy totaled 10.73 hp-hours per gallon. The figure dipped slightly to 10.28 in a 10-hour run made at 75 percent pull. Statistics for this run included an output of 20.37 hp, a pull of 1,640 lbs. at 4.66 mph and slippage of 4.19 percent. No repairs or adjustments were noted during 39 hours of operation.

Allis-Chalmers D-14 tractor

Nebraska Test Data

Model: Allis-Chalmers D-12
Test No. 813
Date Tested: April 4 to April 1962

Weighing in at 3,051 lbs., the D-12 assumed a test weight of 5,630 lbs. through the addition of front and rear ballast. This tractor featured a selective gear, fixed-ratio transmission with the same forward speeds as previously noted for the D-10 of Test No. 812. Using third gear, a two-hour drawbar economy run indicated an output of 29.43 maximum available hp, along with a pull of 2,595 lbs. at 4.25 mph and 6.56 percent slippage. A fuel economy of 10.56 hp-hours per gallon was recorded, rising to 10.87 in a 10-hour run made at 75 percent pull. The 10-hour run also recorded an output of 25.97 hp, a pull of 1,990 lbs. at 4.89 mph and 4.18 percent slippage. Standard equipment included a 149-cid four-cylinder engine. Rated at 1,650 rpm, it carried a 3-1/2 x 3-7/8-inch bore and stroke. At rated engine speed an observed maximum of 33.32 PTO hp was recorded, with a fuel economy of 12.21 hp-hours per gallon. No repairs or adjustments were recorded during 36-1/2 hours of operating time.

COLLECTOR VALUES	1	2	3	4
MODEL D-12	$7,500	$5,500	$4,000	$1,500

Built only from 1957 to 1960, the D-14 tractor was available fueled by LP gas in addition to the standard gasoline. Using the four-cylinder, 149 cubic inch A-C engine, both models were capable of about 35 PTO hp. This popular A-C engine featured a 3-1/2 x 3-7/8-inch bore and stroke. Rated speed was 1650 rpm. In 1960 this tractor carried a list price of $2,875.

Nebraska Test Data

Model: Allis-Chalmers D-14
Test No. 623
Date Tested: June 1 to June 7, 1957

During 44 hours of operation, no repairs or adjustments were noted for the D-14 tractor. Weighing 3,623 lbs., it featured 12 x 26-inch rear and 5.50 x 16-inch front tires. During Tests F, G, and H an additional 1,563 lbs. was added to each rear wheel. Using direct engine drive, four forward speeds of 2-1/5, 3-3/4, 4-3/4, and 12 mph were available. In the Power Director range, another four speeds about 30 percent slower than direct-drive were added. Test H, run in the high range of third gear, gave a rated output of 24.5 drawbar hp. This test also indicated a pull of 1,866 lbs. at 4.92 mph and slippage of 4.84 percent. Fuel economy was scored at 10.35 hp-hours per gallon. Using the low range of first gear gave a Test G maximum drawbar pull of 4,841 lbs. at 1.36 mph against a slippage of 15.77 percent. The D-14 featured a four-cylinder engine rated at 1,650 rpm and using a 3-1/2 x 3-7/8-inch bore and stroke for a 149-cubic inch displacement. Test L indicated that 105 percent of rated-speed torque was available from 84 percent down to 75 percent of rated rpm. Under a Test C operating maximum load of 32.62 belt hp, fuel economy was posted at 12.01 hp-hours per gallon, slipping to 11.88 at a Test D rated belt load of 30.75 hp.

Allis-Chalmers D-14 LPG version

Nebraska Test Data

Model: Allis-Chalmers D-14 (LPG)
Test No. 645
Date Tested: April 1 to April 12, 1958

The necessary propane equipment was the only visual difference between this tractor and the D-14 gasoline model of Test No. 623. Both tractors carried the same tires and engine, but

Allis-Chalmers D-15

the LPG version had a 8.5:1 compression ratio. Rated at 1,650 rpm, this tractor had a 149 cubic inches of displacement and weighed 3,711 lbs. Portions of the drawbar testing used an additional 1,627 lbs. of ballast on each rear wheel. Test G, when run in the low range of first gear, yielded a maximum pull of 5,017 lbs. at 1.38 mph with a slippage of 13.16 percent. The 10-hour run of Test H was made in the high range of third gear. With a rated output of 23.02 drawbar hp, this tractor pulled 1,648 lbs. at 5.24 mph with a slippage of 3.47 percent. Fuel economy was recorded at 7.28 hp-hours per gallon of propane fuel. During 39 hours of running time, no repairs or adjustments were recorded. At a Test D rated belt load of 28.25 hp, fuel economy came in at 8.69 hp-hours per gallon of propane, climbing to 9.04 under a Test C operating maximum load of 30.98 belt hp.

COLLECTOR VALUES	1	2	3	4
D-14	$4,000	$3,000	$2,500	$1,800

From 1960 to 1967, Allis-Chalmers offered its D-15 tractor in gasoline, diesel, and LP-gas versions. The original series used the same 149-cid engine as in the D-14 tractor, but in 1963, the new Series II D-15 was equipped with a larger 160-cid engine. This four-cylinder model had a 3-5/8 x 3-7/8-inch bore and stroke. Rated speed was 2000 rpm. In 1967 this model sold for $4,430. These tractors were also available in a special High-Clearance version.

Nebraska Test Data

Model: Allis-Chalmers D-15 (Gasoline)

Test No. 795

Date Tested: May 12 to May 23, 1961

Standard equipment for this tractor included 14.9 x 26-inch rear and 6.00 x 16-inch front tires. Also featured was a selective gear, fixed-ratio transmission that included operator-controlled partial range power shifting. Thus, a total of eight forward speeds were available, ranging from 1.9 to 15.3 mph. Without ballast, the D-15 weighed 3,985 lbs., but additional front and rear wheel ballast increased this figure to 7,481 lbs. Using the low range of third gear, 35.33 maximum available hp was evidenced during a two-hour drawbar economy run. With an accrued total of 10.41 hp-hours per gallon of gasoline, the D-15 pulled 3,132 lbs. at 4.23 mph with 5.84 percent slippage. A 10-hour economy run, made at 75 percent pull, noted an economy figure of 9.81. This test saw an output of 28.33 drawbar hp, a pull of 2,380 lbs. at 4.46 mph and 4.27 percent slippage. The D-15 gasoline model was equipped with a four-cylinder engine rated at 2,000 rpm. Using a 3-1/2 x 3-7/8-inch bore and stroke, it had a 149 cubic inch displacement. At rated engine speed a maximum output of 40.00 PTO hp was evidenced, together with a fuel economy of 11.86 hp-hours per gallon. The economy figure rested at 12.08 in a one-hour run made at 540 PTO rpm and a corresponding engine speed of 1,623 rpm. This test saw an output of 33.85 PTO hp.

Nebraska Test Data

Model: Allis-Chalmers D-15 (Diesel)

Test No. 796

Date Tested: May 12 to May 26, 1961

The four-cylinder 3-9/16 x 4-3/8-inch diesel engine provided a displacement of 175 cubic inches. With this exception, the D-15 Diesel presented for Test No. 796 was virtually the same tractor as the D-15 gasoline style. At its rated speed of 2,000 rpm, a maximum output of 36.51 PTO hp was observed, with a fuel economy of 12.72 hp-hours per gallon. A slightly higher economy figure of 13.78 resulted from another PTO run made at 540 rpm and a corresponding crankshaft speed of 1,623 rpm. This test indicated an output of 34.36 PTO hp. Using the low range of third gear, 33.32 maximum available hp was evidenced during a two-hour fuel economy run. Economy came in at 10.94 hp-hours per gallon. The 10-hour drawbar run, made at 75 percent pull, noted an output of 26.53 hp, a pull of 2,196 lbs. at 4.53 mph and 4 percent slippage, with fuel economy of 9.86 hp-hours per gallon. No repairs or adjustments were required during 39-1/2 hours of operating time.

Nebraska Test Data

Model: Allis-Chalmers D-15 (LPG)

Test No. 797

Date Tested: May 12 to May 26, 1961

This third variation of the D-15 tractor differed primarily in the necessary engine modifications and a slightly altered exterior appearance. While the gasoline engine of Test No. 795 used a 7.75:1 compression ratio, this tractor featured an 8.9:1 compression ratio. Rated speed was 2,000 rpm. At this speed a maximum of 37.44 PTO hp was observed. This load produced a fuel economy of 9.38 hp-hours per gallon of propane fuel. The same test, when run at 540 PTO rpm and a corresponding crankshaft speed of 1,623 rpm, indicated an output of 30.83 hp and an economy figure of 9.41. Transmission and tire equipment remained the same as it had for D-15 models in the two previous tests. Weighing in at 4,036 lbs., this LP-gas model took on a test weight of 7,535 lbs. through the addition of front and rear wheel ballast. The low range of third gear yielded a maximum of 33.22 available drawbar hp during the two-hour economy run. With an economy of 8.25 hp-hours per gallon of propane, the D-15 LPG pulled 2,942 lbs. at 4.23 mph with 5.77 percent slippage. A 10-hour run, made at 75 percent pull, noted an output of 26.77 drawbar hp, a pull of 2,242 lbs. at 4.48 mph and 4.18 percent slippage. A fuel economy of 7.81 hp-hours per gallon of propane was accrued during the test. No repairs or adjustments were recorded during 42 hours of operating time.

Nebraska Test Data

Model: Allis-Chalmers D-15 Series II

Test No. 837

Date Tested: April 30 to May 13, 1963

At its rated engine speed of 2,000 rpm, the D-15 Series II tractor yielded a maximum output of 46.18 PTO hp and delivered a fuel economy of 12.21 hp-hours per gallon. A second PTO run made at 540 rpm with a corresponding engine speed of 1,760 rpm noted an economy figure of 12.12 along with an output of 42.35 hp. This tractor was equipped with a four-cylinder, 160-cid engine with a 3-5/8 x 3-7/8-inch bore and stroke. Also featured was a selective gear, fixed-ratio transmission that included partial range power shifting. In all, eight forward speeds were available ranging from 1.8 to 15.3 mph. No repairs or adjustments were required during 46-1/2 hours of operating time. Tire equipment included 14.9 x 26- inch rear and 6.00 x 16-inch front rubber. Weighing 4,025 lbs., a test weight of 7,950 lbs. emerged through the addition of front and rear ballast. Using fourth gear, and at 38.33 maximum available drawbar hp, a pull of 3,761 lbs. was recorded at 3.82 mph with 7.24 percent slippage. Fuel economy was posted at 10.07 hp-hours per gallon. A 10-hour drawbar run at 75 percent pull noted an economy figure of 10.16. This test indicated an output of 31.67 hp, a pull of 2,892 lbs. at 4.11 mph and 4.71 percent slippage.

Nebraska Test Data

Model: Allis-Chalmers D-15 Series II LPG

Test No. 838

Date Tested: April 30 to May 14, 1963

Except for the difference in engine design necessitated by the use of propane fuel, this tractor was identical to that previously noted in Test No. 837. Weighing 4,090 lbs., the D-15 LPG model assumed a test weight of 8,105 lbs. by the addition of front and rear ballast. No repairs or adjustments were noted during 44-1/2 hours of operating time. Using fourth gear, and at 36.02 maximum available drawbar hp, a two-hour test run indicated a pull of 3,530 lbs. at 3.83 mph with 7.34 percent slippage. The 10-hour run at 75 percent pull noted an economy figure of 7.91, an output of 30.12 hp, a pull of 2,811 lbs. at 4.02 mph and 5.16 percent slippage. The D-15 LPG delivered a maximum of 43.55 PTO hp at the rated engine speed of 2,000 rpm. Also indicated was an economy of 9.37 hp-hours per gallon of propane. The economy figure rose to 9.51 in a test made at 540 rpm on the PTO shaft and a corresponding engine speed of 1,760 rpm. This test noted an output of 39.66 PTO hp.

Allis-Chalmers D-17 series

Allis-Chalmers D-17 tractors were built from 1958 to 1967. During this time the D-17 underwent various modifications, finally clos-ing out production with the Series IV. Shown here is the 1958 version, and this one with the single-front wheel, a style that was popular in certain areas.

Nebraska Test Data

Model: Allis-Chalmers D-17

Test No. 635

Date Tested: November 14 to November 25, 1957

At a Test D rated belt load of 46.48 hp, the D-17 delivered a fuel economy of 11-59 hp-hours per gallon. By comparison, this figure rose to 12.18 under a Test C operating maximum load of 50.34 hp. Test L indicated that 115 percent of rated-speed torque was available at 60 percent of the rated engine speed, which in this case was 1,650 rpm. The D-17 featured a four-cylinder, 226-cid engine with a 4 x 4-1/2-inch bore and stroke. Standard features also included 14 x 28-inch rear and 6.00 x 16-inch front tires, along with advertised speeds ranging from 2-3/5, to 12 mph in direct-drive along with another four choices from 1-4/5 to 8-1/2 mph when using the Power-Director. Weighing 4,659 lbs., the D-17 was burdened with an additional 2,223 lbs. of weight on each rear wheel during Tests F, G, and H. Test G, using low gear in direct drive, produced a maximum pull of 7,059 lbs. at 2.3 mph with a slippage of 13.84 percent. The 10-hour run of Test H, run in the high range of third gear, achieved a drawbar fuel economy of 9.88 hp-hours per gallon. This test, run at a rated load of 36.77 drawbar hp, indicated a pull of 2,587 lbs. at 5.33 mph with a slippage of 4.6 percent. No repairs or adjustments were noted during 48-1/2 hours of running time.

Nebraska Test Data

Model: Allis-Chalmers D-17 Diesel
Test No. 636
Date Tested: November 14 to November 26, 1957

Weighing 4,867 lbs., the D-17 Diesel was equipped with 14 x 28-inch rear and 6.00 x 16-inch front tires. During Tests F, G, and H an additional 2,250 lbs. was added to each rear wheel. Eight forward speeds were available, as previously noted in Test No. 635, with a total range of 1-4/5 to 12 mph. At a 100 percent maximum drawbar load, using the high range of first gear, this tractor achieved a pull of 7,126 lbs. at 2.25 mph with a slippage of 15.32 percent, per Test G. At a Test H rated drawbar load of 35.87 hp, a pull of 2,529 lbs. was recorded at 5.32 mph with a slippage of 4.25 percent. Fuel economy in this test totaled 12.02 hp-hours per gallon of diesel fuel. Allis-Chalmers equipped this tractor with a six-cylinder I-head engine rated at 1,650 rpm, and carrying a 3-9/16 x 4-3/8-inch bore and stroke for a 262 cubic inch displacement. Test L indicated that 107 percent of rated-speed torque was available all the way from 85 percent down through 75 percent of rated engine rpm. Test D, run at a rated belt load of 45.52 hp, yielded a fuel economy of 13.98 hp-hours per gallon of fuel. At a 100 percent maximum belt load of 51.14 hp, fuel economy came in at 13.73 hp-hours per gallon. No repairs or adjustments were reported during 39-1/2 hours of engine operating time.

Nebraska Test Data

Model: Allis-Chalmers D-17 Propane
Test No. 644
Date Tested: April 1 to April 12, 1958

Using the same four-cylinder, 4 x 4-1/2-inch engine as found on the gasoline model noted in Test No. 635, this propane-powered model featured an 8.25:1 compression ratio. Rated speed was 1,650 rpm, along with a 226 cubic inch displacement. Other features included 14 x 28-inch rear and 6.00 x 16-inch front tires, plus eight forward speeds ranging from 1-4/5 to 12 mph. The 4,751-lb. basic tractor weight was augmented with 2,192 lbs. of ballast on each rear wheel during a majority of the drawbar testing. Test H, run in the high range of third gear, and at an output of 36.16 drawbar hp, indicated a pull of 2,367 lbs. at 5.73 mph and slippage of 4.04 percent. Fuel economy was recorded at 7.73 hp-hours per gallon of propane. Test G, run in the low range of first gear indicated a pull of 6,956 lbs. at 1.58 mph with a slippage of 14.97 percent. No repairs or adjustment were recorded during 45-1/2 hours of operating time. Test D, run at a rated belt load of 45.09 hp, produced a fuel economy of 9.16 hp-hours per gallon of propane, rising to 9.64 under a Test C operating maximum load of 49.37 hp.

Allis-Chalmers D-19 Tractor

A short production run, lasting only from 1961 to 1963 is noted for the Allis-Chalmers D-19 tractors. Capable of about 70 PTO hp, the D-19 used a six-cylinder, 262-cid engine and the D-19 diesel used the same engine as the D-17 diesel. However, the D-17 operated at 1650 rpm, while the D-19 diesel had a governed speed of 2000 rpm.

Nebraska Test Data

Model: Allis-Chalmers D-19
Test No. 810
Date Tested: April 3 to April 19, 1962

At its rated 2,000 rpm crankshaft speed the D-19 delivered a maximum output of 71.54 PTO hp, together with an economy of 11.48 hp-hours per gallon. Another PTO run, made at 540 rpm on the PTO shaft and a corresponding engine speed of 1,759 rpm, noted an output of 65.19 hp, together with an economy figure of 11.73. This tractor was equipped with the company's own six-cylinder engine carrying a 3-9/16 x 4-3/8-inch bore and stroke for a 262 cubic inch displacement. Also featured was a selective gear fixed-ratio transmission that included partial range power shifting. Eight forward speeds were provided, ranging from 1.9 to 13.9 mph. This 6,645 lb. tractor used 18.4 x 34-inch rear and 7.50 x 16-inch front tires. During testing, the weight was increased to 11,045 lbs. by the addition of rear wheel ballast. A two-hour drawbar economy run, made in fifth gear, and delivering a maximum output of 63.91 hp, noted a pull of 5,371 lbs. at 4.46 mph and 6.45 percent slippage. Also recorded was a fuel economy of 9.43 hp-hours per gallon. The economy figure stood at 9.02 in a 10-hour drawbar run made at 75 percent pull. This test recorded an output of 51.47 hp, a pull of 4,028 lbs. at 4.79 mph, and 4.48 percent slippage. No repairs or adjustments were required during 40-1/2 hours of operating time.

Allis-Chalmers D-19 series

Nebraska Test Data

Model: Allis-Chalmers D-19 LPG
Test No. 814
Date Tested: April 9 to April 19, 1962

While the D-19 gasoline model of Test No. 810 used a compression ratio of 8 to 1, this specially equipped propane version carried a 9.65:1 compression ratio. Both models used virtually the same 262 CID engine, and both models featured a nearly identical chassis and drive train. Weighing 6,785 lbs., this tractor assumed a test weight of 11,160 lbs. through the addition of rear wheel ballast. Using fifth gear, a two-hour run at 58.29 maximum available hp saw a fuel economy of 7.8 hp-hours per gallon of propane fuel. Also indicated was a pull of 4,826 lbs. at 4.53 mph with 5.65 percent slippage. The economy figure stood at 7.69 in a 10-hour run made at 75 percent pull. Other statistics from this test include an output of 48.9 hp, a pull of 3,758 lbs. at 4.88 mph and 3.84 percent slippage. No repairs or adjustments were required during 39-1/2 hours of operating time. At its rated engine speed of 2,000 rpm, an observed maximum of 66.19 PTO hp was recorded, together with a fuel economy of 8.97 hp-hours per gallon of propane. A slight improvement in economy with a figure of 9.15 was evidenced in a second PTO run made at a 540 rpm output speed and a corresponding crankshaft speed of 1,759 rpm. This test indicated an output of 59.88 PTO hp.

Allis Chalmers D-19 High clearance Diesel

Nebraska Test Data

Model: Allis-Chalmers D-19 High-Clearance Diesel
Test No. 811
Date Tested: April 3 to April 18, 1962

A virtually identical chassis and power train was featured in this model and the D-19 gasoline version of Test No. 811. However, this model featured the company's own six-cylinder turbocharged diesel rated at 2,000 rpm. Using a 3-9/16 x 4-3/8-inch bore and stroke, it had 262 cubic inches of displacement and featured a 14:1 compression ratio. The bare tractor weight of 6,835 lbs. was raised to a test weight of 11,210 lbs. through the addition of rear wheel ballast. Using fifth gear, and at 62.05 maximum available hp, a two-hour economy run saw a pull of 5,162 lbs. at 4.51 mph with 5.57 percent slippage—fuel economy in this test was observed at 11.54 hp-hours per gallon. The economy figure sagged slightly to 10.76 in a ten-hour economy run made at 75 percent pull. The latter test indicated an output of 50.31 hp, a pull of 3,852 lbs. at 4.9 mph and 4.08 percent slippage. No repairs or adjustments were recorded during 41-1/2 hours of operating time. At rated engine speed, 66.92 maximum PTO hp was observed, together with a fuel economy of 12.84 hp-hours per gallon. The economy figure rose somewhat to stand at 13.35 in another PTO run made at the standard 540 rpm output speed and a corresponding engine speed of 1,760 rpm. This test noted an output of 64.83 PTO hp.

Allis-Chalmers D-21 tractors were built between 1963 and 1969. This big tractor was available with a gasoline or a diesel engine. The latter was a 426 cid, six-cylinder style with a 4-1/4 x 5-inch bore and stroke. Rated speed was 2200 rpm. Initially the D-21 used a naturally aspirated engine and was capable of about 103 PTO hp. In 1965, a turbocharger was added and this raised the power level to 128 PTO hp.

Allis-Chalmers D-21 series

Nebraska Test Data

Model: Allis-Chalmers D-21 Diesel
Test No. 855
Date Tested: October 15 to October 21, 1963

At its rated engine speed of 2,200 rpm the D-21 delivered a maximum output of 103.06 PTO hp while yielding an economy of 14.44 hp-hours per gallon. This tractor was equipped with the company's own six-cylinder engine. Also featured was a selective gear fixed-ratio transmission with eight forward speeds from 1.6 to 16.2 mph. The 10,745 lb. tractor weight was supported on 24.5 x 32-inch rear and 11.00 x 16-inch front tires. During testing, the addition of front and rear ballast raised this figure to 18,515 lbs. Fourth gear was used for the drawbar economy runs. At 93.09 maximum available hp, economy was posted at 13.09 hp-hours per gallon in a two-hour run. Also recorded was a pull of 7,738 lbs. at 4.51 mph with 4.91 percent slippage. The 10-hour run at 75 percent pull saw an economy figure of 13.26 while delivering 74.94 hp at the drawbar. Manifested, too, was a pull of 5,848 lbs. at 4.81 mph with 3.37 percent slippage. No repairs or adjustments were noted during 37 hours of operating time.

Nebraska Test Data

Model: Allis-Chalmers D-21 Series II Diesel
Test No. 904
Date Tested: June 22 to June 28, 1965

Weighing 10,675 lbs., the D-21 Series II model was burdened with front and rear ballast for a total test weight of 18,965 lbs. Standard equipment included 24.5 x 32-inch rear and 11.00 x 16-inch front tires. Also featured was an eight-speed selective gear fixed-ratio transmission with a range from 1.6 to 16.2 mph. Using fourth gear, this tractor delivered 116.41 maximum available drawbar hp in the two-hour economy run. Against this load, fuel economy was pegged at 14.69 hp-hours per gallon. Other statistics included a pull of 9,740 lbs. at 4.48 mph and 5.99 percent slippage. The 10-hour economy run at 75 percent pull saw an economy of 13.63 hp-hours per gallon against a load of 95.6 hp. Also recorded was a pull of 7,373 lbs. at 4.86 mph and 4.56 percent slippage. No repairs or adjustments were reported during 37-1/2 hours of operating time. Allis-Chalmers equipped this tractor with its own six-cylinder, turbocharged engine. Rated at 2,200 rpm, it carried a 4-1/4 x 5-inch bore and stroke for a 426 cubic inch displacement. Operating at rated engine speed, 127.75 maximum PTO hp was observed, together with an economy of 16.66 hp-hours per gallon of diesel fuel.

Allis-Chalmers 160

Nebraska Test Data

Model: Allis-Chalmers 160 Diesel

Test No. 1028

Date Tested: October 27 to November 4, 1969

A Perkins three-cylinder, 152.7-cid engine was featured in this tractor. Rated at 2,250 rpm, it used a 3.6 x 5.0-inch bore and stroke. At rated engine speed, a two-hour PTO run saw an economy of 15.02 hp-hours per gallon against a maximum load of 40.36 hp. At 540 PTO rpm and a corresponding crankshaft speed of 2,156 rpm, the economy figure rested at 15.17 with an output of 39.77 hp. No repairs or adjustments were required during 45 hours of operation. Features included a selective gear fixed-ratio transmission with synchronized 9th and 10th speeds. A total range of 0.6 to 15.5 mph was offered. Weighing 4,680 lbs., this tractor was furnished with 13.6 x 28-inch rear and 6.00 x 16-inch front tires. Additional front and rear ballast raised the total test weight to 6,070 lbs. Operating in seventh gear, the two-hour economy run manifested an economy of 13.05 hp-hours per gallon with a maximum available output of 36.71 drawbar hp. Further test data includes a pull of 2,833 lbs. at 4.86 mph and 6.47 percent total slippage. The 10-hour run at 75 percent pull noted an economy of 12.96 hp-hours per gallon under an output of 29.32 hp. Other statistics included a pull of 2,133 lbs. at 5.15 mph and slippage of 5.13 percent.

Allis-Chalmers 170 series

Nebraska Test Data

Model: Allis-Chalmers 170 Diesel

Test No. 965

Date Tested: October 13 to October 27, 1967

Allis-Chalmers equipped this model with a four-cylinder, 235.9-cid Perkins engine. Rated at 1,800 rpm, it used 3-7/8 x 5-inch bore and stroke. At rated engine speed, a maximum output of 54.04 PTO hp was achieved, as was an economy of 16.38 hp-hours per gallon. The economy figure rose slightly higher to stand at 16.41 in a PTO run made at 1,624 crankshaft rpm, a PTO speed of 540 rpm, and a total output of 50.59 hp. No repairs or adjustments were reported during 43-1/2 hours of operating time. Weighing in at 5,950 lbs., this unit was equipped with 18.4-28-inch rear and 7.5-16-inch front tires. During drawbar testing, additional ballast raised this figure to 9,160 lbs. The chassis design included a selective gear fixed-ratio transmission with partial range power shifting. The eight forward speeds ranged from 2.0 to 13.3 mph. Drawbar economy was recorded at 14.13 hp-hours per gallon in the two-hour economy run—it was operated at 47.39 maximum available hp. Also recorded in this test was a pull of 4,008 lbs. at 4.43 mph and slippage of 6.98 percent. The 10-hour run at 75 percent pull saw an output of 39.43 hp and a corresponding economy figure of 13.94 hp-hours per gallon. This test noted a pull of 3,083 lbs. at 4.8 mph with 5.1 percent slippage.

Nebraska Test Data

Model: Allis-Chalmers 170

Test No. 970

Date Tested: October 16 to October 27, 1967

Except for a gasoline engine, this tractor was nearly a carbon copy of the 170 model previously noted in Test No. 965. Replacing the Perkins Diesel engine was the company's own four-cylinder, 226-cid gasoline engine. Rated at 1,800 rpm, it used a 4 x 4-1/2-inch bore and stroke. No repairs or adjustments were recorded during 45-1/2 hours of operating time. At rated engine speed, 54.12 maximum PTO hp delivered an economy of 12.45 hp-hours per gallon. When operating at 540 PTO rpm and a corresponding engine speed of 1,624 rpm, an output of 51.46 hp yielded an economy of 12.91 hp-hours per gallon. Fifth gear was used for the drawbar economy runs. The two-hour test at 46.93 maximum available hp saw a pull of 3,973 lbs. at 4.43 mph with slippage totaling 6.75 percent. Fuel economy was posted at 10.73 hp-hours per gallon. The fuel economy figure came in at 9.97 during the 10-hour economy run. Operating at 75 percent pull, this test indicated an output of 38.81 hp, a pull of 3,083 lbs. at 4.72 mph and 4.93 percent slippage. This tractor's bare weight of 5,720 lbs. was augmented by additional front and rear ballast for a total test weight of 9,010 lbs.

Allis-Chalmers 180

Nebraska Test Data

Model: Allis-Chalmers 180 Diesel

Test No. 964

Date Tested: October 13 to October 27, 1967

Weighing 6,510 lbs., this model featured 18.4-28-inch rear and 7.50-16 inch front tires as standard equipment. Additional ballast totaling 1,880 lbs. on each rear wheel brought the total test weight to 10,300 lbs. No repairs or adjustments were recorded during 48-1/2 hours of operating time. Partial range power shifting was featured in the selective gear fixed-ratio transmission. Eight forward speeds from 2.3 to 14.5 mph were provided. In fourth gear, 55.28 maximum available drawbar hp was demonstrated in the two-hour economy run, and an economy of 13.05 hp-hours per gallon was achieved. The test recorded a pull of 4,956 lbs. at 4.18 mph and slippage of 7.44 percent. The 10-hour run at 75 percent pull indicated an economy of 12.17 hp-hours per gallon against a load of 46.19 hp. Reported too was a pull of 3,759 lbs. at 4.61 mph with slippage of 5.2 percent. Allis-Chalmers equipped this tractor with its own six-cylinder, 301-cid diesel engine. Rated at 2,000 rpm, it used a 3-7/8 x 4-1/4-inch bore and stroke. At rated engine speed, 64.01 PTO hp was observed with an economy of 15.24 hp-hours per gallon. A second PTO run made with an output speed of 540 rpm and a corresponding crankshaft speed of 1,964 rpm, saw an output of 63.9 hp and a fuel economy of 15.31 hp-hours per gallon. No repairs or adjustments were noted during 48 hours of operating time.

Allis-Chalmers 175 series

Nebraska Test Data

Model: Allis-Chalmers 175

Test No. 1156

Date Tested: April 1 to April 11, 1974

Operating at its rated speed of 1,800 rpm, the 175 delivered 60.88 maximum PTO hp while achieving 11.97 hp-hours per gallon. Operating at 540 PTO rpm and a corresponding engine speed of 1,622 rpm, 56.02 PTO hp was observed, as was an economy of 11.78 hp-hours per gallon. This tractor was equipped with a four-cylinder, 226-cid engine with a 4 x 4-1/2-inch bore and stroke. The selective gear fixed-ratio transmission featured partial range power shifting. Its eight forward speeds ranged from 2.0 to 13.1 mph. No repairs or adjustments were required during 47 total hours of operating time. Using fifth gear, the two-hour economy run at 51.8 maximum available drawbar hp saw a pull of 4,450 lbs. at 4.37 mph with slippage totaling 8.24 percent. Fuel economy was posted at 10.22 hp-hours per gallon. The 10-hour run at 75 percent pull indicated an economy of 9.64 hp-hours per gallon under a load of 42.52 drawbar hp. Also recorded was a pull of 3,412 lbs. at 4.67 mph with slippage totaling 5.83 percent. The Model 175 weighed in at 6,390 lbs. Additional rear wheel ballast raised the total test weight to 8,400 lbs. Standard equipment included 18.4-26-inch rear and 7.50-16-inch front tires.

Nebraska Test Data

Model: Allis-Chalmers Crop-Hustler 175 Diesel

Test No. 1043

Date Tested: May 26 to June 3, 1970

Weighing 5,925 lbs., this model used 16.9-28 rear and 6.50-16 inch front tires. Additional rear wheel ballast gave a total test weight of 8,400 lbs. Features included a selective gear fixed-ratio transmission with partial range power shifting. The eight forward speeds ranged from 2.1 to 13.7 mph. An economy of 12.73 hp-hours per gallon was established under a maximum available output of 54.06 drawbar hp. The two-hour drawbar economy run also recorded a pull of 4,272 lbs. at 4.75 mph and slippage of 7.81 percent. For the 10-hour run at 75 percent pull, an economy of 13.33 hp-hours per gallon was achieved under a load of 43.24 hp. Other statistics include a pull of 3,216 lbs. at 5.04 mph and 6.12 percent slippage. This tractor was equipped with a Perkins four-cylinder, 235.9-cid engine. Rated at 2,000 rpm, it used a 3.875 x 5.000-inch bore and stroke. At rated engine speed, 62.47 maximum PTO hp was observed, as was an economy of 14.89 hp-hours per gallon. Operating at 540 PTO rpm and a corresponding crankshaft speed of 1,624 rpm, the economy stood at 15.07 under a load of 54.62 hp. No repairs or adjustments were required during 52-1/2 hours of operating time.

Allis-Chalmers 185

Nebraska Test Data

Model: Allis-Chalmers Crop Hustler 185 Diesel

Test No. 1044

Date Tested: May 26 to June 3, 1970

Using the company's own six-cylinder, 301 cid engine, this tractor developed 74.87 maximum PTO hp at a rated engine speed of 2,200 rpm and achieved 14.13 hp-hours per gallon. The design included a 3.87 x 4.250-inch bore and stroke. Operating at 540 PTO rpm and a corresponding engine speed of 1,962 rpm, an economy of 14.57 hp-hours per gallon was realized under a load of 70.72 hp. Features of this 6,710 lb. tractor included a selective gear fixed-ratio transmission with partial range power shifting. Its eight forward speeds ranged from 1.99 to 16.06 mph. No repairs or adjustments were reported during 44 hours of running time. The drawbar performance runs included a two-hour test at 63.82 maximum available drawbar hp and this test yielded 12.00 hp-hours per gallon. Operating in fourth gear, this test also recorded a pull of 5,235 lbs. at 4.57 mph and slippage of 8.41 percent. The 10-hour run at 75 percent pull saw an economy of 11.89 hp-hours per gallon under a load of 52.91 hp. Further data included a pull of 3,984 lbs. at 4.98 mph and 6.01 percent slippage. Standard equipment included 18.4-28-inch rear and 9.5L-15 inch front tires. Additional front and rear ballast raised the total test weight to 9,400 lbs.

Allis-Chalmers 190 series

Nebraska Test Data

Model: Allis-Chalmers 190 Diesel
Test No. 886
Date Tested: April 10 to April 16, 1965

This 7,845 lb. tractor featured 18.4-34-inch rear and 7.50-16 inch front tires. The addition of rear wheel ballast raised this figure to a total test weight of 11,255 lbs. Also featured was a selective gear fixed-ratio transmission with partial range power shifting. Eight forward speeds were available ranging from 2.1 to 13.6 mph. Drawbar fuel economy was observed at 12.23 hp-hours per gallon in a two-hour run made at 65.33 maximum available hp. Also recorded was a pull of 5,714 lbs. at 4.29 mph with 7.72 percent slippage. Economy was registered at 11.73 hp-hours per gallon in the 10-hour drawbar run made at 75 percent pull. This test, made at 52.52 drawbar hp, noted a pull of 4,278 lbs. at 4.6 mph with 5.57 percent slippage. The One-Ninety Diesel used the company's own six-cylinder, 301-cid engine. Rated at 2,200 rpm, it carried a 3-7/8 x 4-1/4-inch bore and stroke. At rated engine speed, fuel economy was posted at 14.33 hp-hours per gallon against an output of 77.2 PTO hp. The same test, when run at 540 PTO rpm and a corresponding engine speed of 1,937 rpm, saw an output of 72.33 PTO hp, together with an economy of 14.58 hp-hours per gallon. No repairs or adjustments were required during 43-1/2 hours of operating time.

Nebraska Test Data

Model: Allis-Chalmers 190 XT Diesel
Test No. 887
Date Tested: April 10 to April 16, 1965

The addition of a turbo-charger constituted the major difference between this tractor and the tractor of Test No. 886. Both tractors carried the same six-cylinder, 301-cid engine, and both were designed with a 16.25:1 compression ratio. The inconsequential additional weight of the turbo-charger equipment was the only difference in weight between the two tractors. Using fourth gear, an economy of 13.87 hp-hours per gallon was realized in a two-hour drawbar run at 79.12 maximum available hp. This test saw a pull of 7,128 lbs. at 4.16 mph with 9.89 percent slippage. Fuel economy came in at 13.07 hp-hours per gallon in a 10-hour drawbar run made at 75 percent pull. This test, made at 66.51 drawbar hp, saw a pull of 5,430 lbs. at 4.59 mph and slippage of 6.83 percent. Shown here during the actual PTO runs, the 190 XT Diesel delivered a maximum of 93.64 hp while achieving an economy of 16.42 hp-hours per gallon. Another PTO run made at 540 rpm on the output shaft, and with a corresponding engine speed of 1,937 rpm saw an economy of 16.78 against an output of 89.71 hp. No repairs or adjustments were reported during 41 hours of running time.

Nebraska Test Data

Model: Allis-Chalmers 190 XT (LPG)
Test No. 927
Date Tested: November 9 to November 17, 1965

This tractor was equipped to burn propane fuel and carried the same engine as the 190 Diesel, though a 9:1 compression ratio was used to accommodate the LPG. At rated engine speed, 85.25 maximum PTO hp was observed, together with an economy of 8.58 hp-hours per gallon of propane. A second run at 540 PTO rpm and a corresponding engine speed of 1,937 rpm saw an output of 76.36 PTO hp and an economy figure of 8.78. This 7,715 lb. tractor featured the same tires and transmission as the standard 190. No repairs or adjustments were required during 41 hours of running time. During drawbar testing, the addition of rear wheel ballast gave a total test weight of 11,295 lbs. Operating in fourth gear, a two-hour economy run at 71.95 maximum available drawbar hp saw an economy figure of 7.17. Also recorded was a pull of 6,422 lbs. at 4.2 mph and slippage of 8.91 percent. The 10-hour run at 75 percent pull indicated an economy of 7.3 hp-hours per gallon of propane against an output of 61.30 drawbar hp. Other statistics from this test included a pull of 5,036 lbs. at 4.56 mph and slippage of 6.13 percent.

Nebraska Test Data

Model: Allis-Chalmers 190
Test No. 928
Date Tested: November 9 to November 16, 1965

Rated at 2,200 rpm, this gasoline-fueled tractor featured the company's own six-cylinder, 265-cid engine. It used a 3-3/4 x 4-inch bore and stroke. At rated engine speed, 75.37 maximum PTO hp was observed, along with an economy of 10.86 hp-hours per gallon. Operating at 540 PTO rpm and a corresponding engine speed of 1,938 rpm, the economy figure was recorded at 11.36 under an output of 70.18 hp. No repairs or adjustments were reported during 40 hours of operating time. The tires and transmission were the same as other 190 models. Bare tractor weight was 7,665 lbs. and the addition of rear wheel ballast raised this figure to a test weight of 11,295 lbs. Operating in fourth gear, the two-hour economy run at 63.10 maximum available hp saw an economy of 8.77 hp-hours per gallon. Also recorded was a pull of 5,477 lbs. at 4.32 mph and slippage of 7.0 percent. The 10-hour run at 75 percent saw an economy of 8.2 hp-hours per gallon against a load of 50.84 drawbar hp. This test was made at a pull of 4,190 lbs. with a speed of 4.55 mph and slippage of 5.53 percent.

Nebraska Test Data

Model: Allis-Chalmers 190 XT
Test No. 929
Date Tested: November 9 to November 16, 1965

This tractor shared many features with the 190 of Test No. 928, but carried a larger engine—a six-cylinder, 301-cid version. Rated at 2,200 rpm, it featured a 3-7/8 x 4-1/4-inch bore and stroke. Operating at rated speed, 89.53 maximum PTO hp was observed, together with an economy of 11.15 hp-hours per gallon. At a PTO speed of 540 rpm and a corresponding engine speed of 1,937 rpm, 82.3 PTO hp was recorded, as was an economy figure of 11.46. This tractor offered the same transmission and tires as other 190s. Weighing in at 7,675 lbs., it was burdened with additional rear wheel ballast for a total test weight of 11,355 lbs. Fourth gear was used for the drawbar economy runs. Operating at 76.65 maximum available hp, the two-hour run saw an economy of 9.06 hp-hours per gallon. Also recorded was a pull of 6,827 lbs. at 4.21 mph and slippage of 9.82 percent. During the 10-hour run at 75 percent pull, 60.78 drawbar hpwas observed, as was an economy of 8.73 hp-hours per gallon. The 10-hour run was made under a pull of 5,031 lbs. at 4.53 mph and under slippage of 6.6 percent. No repairs or adjustments were recorded during 40 hours of running time.

Allis-Chalmers 220

Nebraska Test Data

Model: Allis-Chalmers 220 Diesel

Test No. 1017

Date Tested: June 17 to June 24, 1969

No repairs or adjustments were reported for this tractor during 40-1/2 hours of operating time. Weighing 12,160 lbs., it was equipped with 24.5-32-inch rear and 10.00-16-inch front tires. Additional front and rear ballast raised the total test weight to 20,050 lbs. Features included a selective gear fixed-ratio transmission with eight forward speeds and a range of 1.7 to 17.4 mph. Fourth gear was selected for the drawbar economy runs. The two-hour test at 117.21 maximum available drawbar hp saw an economy of 13.54 hp-hours per gallon while pulling a load of 10.086 lbs. at 4.36 mph. Slippage totaled 7.18 percent. By comparison, the 10-hour run at 75 percent pull achieved an economy of 12.21 hp-hours per gallon against an output of 98.12 hp. Other statistics of this test include a pull of 7,797 lbs. at 4.72 mph with 5.56 percent slippage. Allis-Chalmers equipped this model with its own six-cylinder, 426-cid turbocharged diesel engine. Rated at 2,200 rpm, it carried a 4.25 x 5.00-inch bore and stroke. At rated engine speed it developed 135.95 maximum PTO hp and achieved 15.66 hp-hours per gallon.

Allis-Chalmers 210

Nebraska Test Data

Model: Allis-Chalmers
Landhandler 210 Diesel

Test No. 1065

Date Tested: May 3 to May 13, 1971

The six-cylinder turbocharged diesel engine featured in this model had a rated speed of 2,200 rpm. Using a 4.25 x 5.00-inch bore and stroke gave a 426 cubic inch displacement. At rated engine speed, 122.4 maximum PTO hp was observed, as was an economy of 15.21 hp-hours per gallon of fuel. No repairs or adjustments were reported during 46 hours of operating time. The 210 Diesel featured a selective gear fixed-ratio transmission with eight forward speeds in a range from 1.48 to 16.25 mph. Also featured were 20.8-38-inch rear and 10.00-16-inch front tires. Bare weight was 12,425 lbs.—additional front and rear ballast raised this figure to a test weight of 18,045 lbs. Operating in fourth gear, the two-hour economy run at 104.95 maximum available drawbar hp saw a pull of 8,854 lbs. at 4.44 mph with slippage totaling 7.66 percent. Also recorded was an economy of 13.14 hp-hours per gallon. The 10 -hour run at 75 percent pull witnessed an economy figure of 11.85 against an output of 83.35 hp. Also recorded was a pull of 6,560 lbs. at 4.76 mph and slippage of 5.62 percent.

Nebraska Test Data

Model: Allis-Chalmers 5020 Diesel

Manufactured by Toyosha
Co. Ltd. Osaka, Japan

Test No. 1270

Date Tested: April 6 to April 15, 1978

Weighing 2,060 lbs., the 5020 was equipped with 11.2-10-24-inch rear and 4.00-12-inch front wheels. Additional front and rear ballast gave a total test weight of 3,358 lbs. This tractor carried an eight speed selective gear fixed-ratio transmission with selections ranging from 0.9 to 8.6 mph. Using seventh gear, the two-hour drawbar run at 17.37 maximum available hp indicated an economy of 11.07 hp-hours per gallon. Also recorded was a pull of 1,135 lbs. at 5.74 mph and slippage totaling 6.69 percent. The 10-hour run at 75 percent pull indicated an economy of 10.51 hp-hours per gallon under a load of 14.41 drawbar hp. Also indicated was a pull of 893 lbs. at 6.05 mph and slippage totaling 5.27 percent. No repairs or adjustments were required during 36-_ hours of operation. The 5020 was equipped with a Toyosha two-cylinder diesel engine. Rated at 2,500 rpm, it used a 3.62 x 3.74-inch bore and stroke for a 77 cubic inch displacement. At rated engine speed, 21.79 maximum PTO hp was developed and with an economy of 13.7 hp-hours per gallon. Operating at 540 PTO rpm and a corresponding engine speed of 2,326 rpm, an economy of 13.99 hp-hours per gallon was manifested under a load of 20.78 PTO hp.

Nebraska Test Data

Model: Allis-Chalmers 5030 Diesel

Manufactured by Toyosha
Co. Ltd. Osaka, Japan

Test No. 1271

Date Tested: April 6 to April 21, 1978

Weighing in at 2,530 lbs., the 5030 used 12.4-24-inch rear and 5.00-15-inch front tires. Additional front and rear ballast gave a total test weight of 3,876 lbs. A selective gear fixed-ratio transmission was used—its eight forward speeds ranged from 1.0 to 13.0 mph. Operating in fifth gear, the two-hour drawbar run at 22.47 maximum available hp indicated a pull of 1,976 lbs. at 4.26 mph and slippage totaling 7.58 percent. Fuel economy was posted at 11.64 hp-hours per gallon. The 10-hour run at 75 percent pull established an economy of 11.48 hp-hours per gallon of fuel under a load of 18.90 drawbar hp. Other data from this test includes a pull of 1,594 lbs. at 4.45 mph and slippage totaling 6.27 percent. No repairs or adjustments were required during 34-1/2 hours of engine operating time. The 5030 was equipped with a Toyosha two-cylinder diesel engine. Rated at 2,500 rpm, it carried a 3.82 x 3.94-inch bore and stroke for a 90.1 cubic inch displacement. At rated engine speed, 26.42 maximum PTO hp was observed, as was an economy of 13.49 hp-hours per gallon. Operating at 540 PTO rpm and a corresponding engine speed of 2,326 rpm, an economy of 13.82 hp-hours per gallon was noted under a load of 25.61 PTO hp.

Nebraska Test Data

Model: Allis-Chalmers 5040 Diesel
Manufactured by Uzina Tractorul
(UTB), Brasov, Romania
Test No. 1230
Date Tested: October 27 to November 5, 1976

This Romanian-built model featured a Uzina three-cylinder diesel engine. Rated at 2,400 rpm, it carried a 3.74 x 4.33-inch bore and stroke for a 143 cubic inch displacement. At rated engine speed, 40.05 maximum PTO hp appeared, as did an economy of 14.01 hp-hours per gallon. Operating at 540 PTO rpm and a corresponding engine speed of 1,966 rpm, an economy of 15.47 hp-hours per gallon was manifested under a load of 36.69 PTO hp. This tractor offered a selective gear fixed-ratio transmission with nine forward speeds ranging from 0.5 to 15.2 mph. Using seventh gear, the two-hour economy run at 35.23 maximum available drawbar hp saw a pull of 2,642 lbs. at 5.00 mph with slippage of 5.97 percent. Fuel economy was posted at 12.58 hp-hours per gallon. The 10-hour run at 75 percent pull indicated an economy of 12.74 hp-hours per gallon under a load of 28.73 hp. Other statistics from this test include a pull of 2,015 lbs. at 5.35 mph and slippage of 4.31 percent. No repairs or adjustments were reported during 44 hours of engine operating time. Weighing in at 4,060 lbs., the 5040 was equipped with 13.6-28-inch rear and 6.00-16-inch front tires. Additional front and rear ballast gave a total test weight of 6,240 lbs.

Nebraska Test Data

Model: Allis-Chalmers 5050 Diesel
Manufactured by Fiat Trattori
S.P.A., Modena, Italy
Test No. 1240
Date Tested: April 26 to May 4, 1977

The 5050 Diesel featured a Fiat three-cylinder engine. Rated at 2,700 rpm, it used a 4.055 x 4.330-inch bore and stroke for a 168 cubic inch displacement. At rated engine speed, 51.46 maximum PTO hp appeared and 14.68 hp-hours per gallon was observed. Operating at 540 PTO rpm and a corresponding engine speed of 2,159 rpm, an economy of 16.10 hp-hours per gallon appeared under a load of 47.16 PTO hp. No repairs or adjustments were reported during 43 hours of operation. Features included a selective gear fixed-ration transmission offering 12 forward speeds with a range of 0.5 to 16.4 mph. Also featured were 16.9-9-28 rear and 7.50-16 inch front tires. The bare weight of 4,410 lbs. was raised to a total test weight of 7,690 lbs. using front and rear ballast. Using ninth gear, the two-hour drawbar economy run at 43.29 maximum available hp saw a pull of 2,855 lbs. at 5.69 mph and slippage of 5.06 percent. Fuel economy was posted at 12.58 hp-hours per gallon. By comparison, the 10-hour run at 75 percent pull noted 13.01 hp-hours per gallon under a load of 35.27 drawbar hp. Other statistics from this test included a pull of 2,236 lbs. at 5.92 mph and slippage of 3.71 percent.

Allis-Chalmers 5020 and 5030

Nebraska Test Data

Model: Allis-Chalmers 6060 Diesel, 8-Speed

Test No. 1397

Date Tested: June 9 to June 22, 1981

The 6060 used a four-cylinder turbocharged engine rated at 2,300 rpm. Its 3.876 x 4.250 inch bore and stroke yielded a 200 cubic inch displacement. At rated engine speed, 63.83 maximum PTO hp was observed, as was 15.82 hp-hours per gallon. Operating at 540 PTO rpm and a corresponding engine speed of 2,226 rpm, an economy figure of 16.26 was set with a load of 64.90 PTO hp. No repairs or adjustments were required during 37-1/2 hours of operating time. Weighing in at 6,465 lbs., the 6060 was equipped with 15.5-38-inch rear and 7.50-16-inch front tires. Additional front and rear ballast gave a total test weight of 8,945 lbs. Eight forward speeds ranging from 1.5 to 14.9 mph were provided in the selective gear fixed-ratio transmission. Using fifth gear, the two-hour test at 50.87 maximum available drawbar hp witnessed a pull of 3,949 lbs. at 4.83 mph. Slippage totaled 6.28 percent, and fuel economy was posted at 13.27 hp-hours per gallon. The 10-hour run at 75 percent pull indicated an economy of 11.99 hp-hours per gallon of fuel with a load of 42.67 drawbar hp. Also recorded was a pull of 3,041 lbs. at 5.26 mph and slippage totaling 4.32 percent.

A-C 6070 Diesel

Nebraska Test Data

Model: Allis-Chalmers 6070 Diesel

Test No. 1545

Date Tested: October 19 to October 26, 1984

Weighing 7,460 lbs., the 6070 featured 16.9-34-inch rear and 7.50-16-inch front tires. Additional front and rear ballast gave a total test weight of 10,515 lbs. No repairs or adjustments were required during 32 hours of operating time. A selective gear fixed-ratio transmission offered 12 speeds ranging from 1.0 to 17.2 mph. Operating in seventh gear, the two-hour drawbar test at 58.35 maximum available hp indicated a pull of 5,081 lbs. at 4.31 mph. Slippage totaled 8.0 percent, and fuel economy was posted at 13.38 hp-hours per gallon. The 10-hour run at 75 percent pull indicated 12.30 hp-hours per gallon against a load of 47.68 drawbar hp. Other test data included a pull of 3,836 lbs. at 4.66 mph and slippage of 5.91 percent. The 6070 was equipped with an Allis-Chalmers four-cylinder turbocharged engine. Rated at 2,300 rpm, it carried a 3.875 x 4.250-inch bore and stroke for a 200-cubic-inch displacement. At rated engine speed, 70.78 maximum PTO hp appeared and 16.18 hp-hours per gallon was achieved. Operating at 540 PTO rpm and a corresponding engine speed of 2,228 rpm, the economy figure was 16.45 against a load of 71.01 PTO horsepower.

Allis-Chalmers 5050

A-C 6080 Diesel

Nebraska Test Data

Model: Allis-Chalmers 6080 Diesel, 12-Speed
Test No. 1398
Date Tested: June 8 to June 20, 1981

The four-cylinder, 200-cid diesel engine featured in the 6080 tractor was turbocharged and inter-cooled. Rated at 2,300 rpm, it carried a 3.876 x 4.250-inch bore and stroke for a 200-cubic-inch displacement. At rated engine speed, 83.66 maximum PTO hp was delivered, together with an economy of 16.68 hp-hours per gallon. Operating at 1,000 PTO rpm and a corresponding engine speed of 2,408 rpm, an economy of 15.70 hp-hours per gallon was established under a load of 74.49 PTO hp. No repairs or adjustments were necessary during 40 hours of operation. Weighing 7,590 lbs., this tractor was equipped with 18.4-34-inch rear and 7.50-16-inch front tires. Additional front and rear ballast gave a total test weight of 11,790 lbs. Twelve forward speeds, ranging from 1.0 to 18.0 mph, were provided in the selective gear fixed-ratio transmission. Using eighth gear, the two-hour economy run at 70.50 maximum available drawbar hp indicated 14.27 hp-hours per gallon. Also revealed was a pull of 4,609 lbs. at 5.74 mph and 5.3 percent slippage. The 10-hour run at 75 percent pull established 12.81 hp-hours per gallon against a load of 57 drawbar hp. Other test data included a pull of 3,469 lbs. at 6.16 mph and 3.7 percent slippage.

Allis-Chalmers 6140

Nebraska Test Data

Model: Allis-Chalmers 6140 Diesel
Manufactured by Toyosha Co., Osaka, Japan
Test No. 1445
Date Tested: August 30 to September 8, 1982

At the rated engine speed of 2,500 rpm, the 6140 delivered 41.08 maximum PTO hp together with an economy of 13.08 hp-hours per gallon. With a PTO speed of 540 rpm and a corresponding engine speed of 2,277 rpm, 13.47 hp-hours per gallon was observed under a load of 38.04 PTO hp. This tractor was equipped with a Toyosha three-cylinder engine. Its 3.858 x 4.055-inch bore and stroke gave a 142-cubic-inch displacement. No repairs or adjustments were necessary during 41 hours of operation. Standard equipment included 14.9-28-inch rear and 7.50-16-inch front tires. Also featured was a selective gear fixed-ratio transmission with a speed range of 0.8 to 17.7 mph. Weighing 4,460 lbs., the 6140 assumed a total test weight of 6,195 lbs. after the addition of front and rear ballast. Operating in seventh gear, the two-hour drawbar run at 33.31 maximum available horsepower saw a pull of 2,402 lbs. at 5.2 mph. Slippage totaled 6.61 percent, and fuel economy was registered at 10.87 hp-hours per gallon. In contrast, the fuel economy stood at 10.25 hp-hours per gallon in the 10-hour run at 75 percent pull. This test, run at 27.17 drawbar hp, also indicated a pull of 1,838 lbs. at 5.54 mph and slippage of 5.54 percent.

Allis-Chalmers 6040

Allis-Chalmers 7000

Nebraska Test Data

Model: Allis-Chalmers 7000 Power Shift Diesel
Test No. 1195
Date Tested: November 8 to November 20, 1975

This tractor used a selective gear fixed-ratio transmission with "on-the-go" power shifting. Its twelve forward speeds ranged from 1.9 to 19.3 mph. Using eighth gear, the two-hour economy run at 89.46 maximum available drawbar hp saw a pull of 5,521 lbs. at 6.08 mph with slippage of 5.99 percent. Fuel economy was posted at 13.21 hp-hours per gallon. The 10-hour run at 75 percent pull noted an economy of 12.27 hp-hours per gallon under a load of 74.29 drawbar hp. This load resulted from a pull of 4,278 lbs. at 6.51 mph with slippage totaling 4.46 percent. Weighing 9,550 lbs., this model featured 18.4-38 rear and 10.00-16 inch front tires. Additional front and rear ballast boosted the total test weight to 12,580 lbs. No repairs or adjustments were required during 46 hours of operation. At its rated speed of 2,200 rpm, a maximum output of 106.44 PTO hp was observed with a posted economy of 15.64 hp-hours per gallon. The economy figure rested at 15.70 under a load of 105.85 PTO hp. These results were derived from a test run at 1,000 PTO rpm and a corresponding engine speed of 2,159 rpm. The six-cylinder turbocharged engine featured in this model carried a 3.875 x 4.250 inch bore and stroke for 301 cubic inches of displacement.

Nebraska Test Data

Model: Allis-Chalmers 7010
Power Director Diesel, 20-Speed
Test No. 1345
Date Tested: May 1 to May 13, 1980

Weighing 11,260 lbs., the 7010 featured 18.4-38 rear and 10.00-16 inch front tires. Additional front and rear ballast gave a total test weight of 12,790 lbs. Partial range power shifting was featured in the selective gear fixed-ratio transmission. Its 20 forward speeds varied from 1.6 to 18.8 mph. Using eleventh gear, the two-hour drawbar test at 87.83 maximum available hp indicated a pull 5,448 lbs. at 6.05 mph with slippage totaling 7.6 percent. Fuel economy for this test came to 12.59 hp-hours per gallon. The 10-hour run at 75 percent pull indicated an economy of 11.48 hp-hours per gallon under a load of 75.38 drawbar hp. Also revealed was a pull of 4,254 lbs. at 6.64 mph with slippage totaling 5.38 percent. An Allis-Chalmers six-cylinder turbocharged engine was featured; its 3.875 x 4.250 inch bore and stroke gave a displacement of 301 cubic inches. At its rated speed of 2,300 rpm, a maximum PTO output of 106.53 hp was observed, as was an economy of 15.24 hp-hours per gallon of fuel. Operating at 1,000 PTO rpm and a corresponding engine speed of 2,253 rpm, an economy of 15.48 hp-hours per gallon was achieved under a load of 107.52 PTO hp. No repairs or adjustments were required during 41 hours of operating time.

Allis-Chalmers 7010 and 7020

Nebraska Test Data

Model: Allis-Chalmers
7010 Power Shift Diesel, 12-Speed
Test No. 1346
Date Tested: May 2 to May 14, 1980

At its rated speed of 2,300 rpm, this tractor achieved an economy of 15.21 hp-hours per gallon under a maximum load of 106.72 PTO hp. Operating at 1,000 PTO rpm and a corresponding engine speed of 2,253 rpm, an economy of 15.43 hp-hours per gallon was recorded under, a load of 106.33 PTO hp. This tractor used the company's own six-cylinder turbocharged engine. A displacement of 301 cubic inches resulted from the 3.875 x 4.250 inch bore and stroke. No repairs or adjustments were necessary during 33 hours of engine operating time. Weighing 11,375 lbs., the 7010 was equipped with 18.4-38 rear and 10.00-16 inch front tires. Additional front and rear ballast gave a total test weight of 12,740 lbs. Partial range power shifting was featured in the selective gear fixed-ratio transmission. Its 12 forward speeds ranged from 1.8 to 18.4 mph. Using seventh gear, the two-hour economy test at 89.10 maximum available drawbar hp saw a pull of 5,480 lbs. at 6.10 mph with slippage totaling 6.93 percent. Fuel economy in this test totaled 12.43 hp-hours per gallon. In contrast, the 10-hour run at 75 percent pull saw an economy figure of 11.35 under a load of 75.43 drawbar hp. Also indicated was a pull of 4,217 lbs. at 6.71 mph and slippage of 4.83 percent.

Nebraska Test Data

Model: Allis-Chalmers
7020 Power Director Diesel
Test No. 1260
Date Tested: October 10 to October 21, 1977

This 7020 Power-Director was equipped with a two-range system that made 20 speeds available, ranging from 1.7 to 19.4 mph. It featured a 301-cid, six-cylinder turbocharged and intercooled engine. Under a maximum output of 123.85 PTO hp, an economy of 15.83 hp-hours per gallon of fuel was recorded. Operating at 1,000 PTO rpm and a corresponding engine speed of 2,253 rpm, an economy figure of 16.08 was established under a load of 125.51 PTO hp. No repairs or adjustments were reported for this tractor during 41-1/2 hours of operating time. Using eighth gear, the two-hour economy run at 102.09 maximum available drawbar hp established an economy of 13.09 hp-hours per gallon under a load of 102.09 drawbar hp. Also indicated was a pull of 7,983 lbs. at 4.8 mph and slippage of 7.51 percent. The 10-hour run at 75 percent pull achieved an economy of 12.08 hp-hours per gallon against a load of 84.67 drawbar hp. Other statistics include a pull of 6,132 lbs. at 5.18 mph and slippage totaling 5.31 percent.

Allis-Chalmers 7030

Nebraska Test Data

Model: Allis-Chalmers 7030 Diesel
Test No. 1119
Date Tested: March 13 to March 30, 1973

Rated at 2,300 rpm, the 7030 developed 130.98 maximum PTO hp and yielded an economy of 15.37 hp-hours per gallon. At 1,000 PTO rpm and a corresponding engine speed of 2,253 rpm, an economy of 15.45 hp-hours per gallon resulted from an output of 131.14 PTO hp. This tractor was equipped with a six-cylinder turbocharged engine with a 4.25 x 5.00 inch bore and stroke for a 426 cubic inch displacement. No repairs or adjustments were required during 65 hours of operation. Standard equipment for this 12,430 lb. model included 20.8-38 rear and 11.00-16 inch front tires. Additional rear wheel ballast raised the total test weight to 16,560 lbs. The selective gear fixed-ratio transmission offered partial range power shifting. Its 20 forward speeds ranged from 1.5 to 19.0 mph. Using ninth gear, the two-hour drawbar run at 110.29 maximum available hp saw an economy of 12.92 hp-hours per gallon. Also recorded was a pull of 8,076 lbs. at 5.12 mph with 7.24 percent slippage. The 10-hour run at 75 percent pull noted an economy of 11.9 hp-hours per gallon with a load of 91.66 drawbar hp. Other statistics include a pull of 6,229 lbs. at 5.52 mph and 5.62 percent slippage.

Allis-Chalmers 7040 and 7045

Nebraska Test Data

Model: Allis-Chalmers 7040 Diesel
Test No. 1166
Date Tested: October 29 to November 7, 1974

At its rated engine speed of 2,300 rpm, the 7040 developed 136.49 maximum PTO hp with an observed fuel economy of 15.19 hp-hours per gallon. Operating at 1,000 PTO rpm and a corresponding engine speed of 2,252 rpm, an economy of 15.35 hp-hours per gallon appeared with a load of 136.26 PTO hp. The six-cylinder, 426-cid, turbocharged engine used a 4.25 x 5.00 inch bore and stroke. Also featured were 20 forward speeds ranging from 1.6 to 18.8 mph. These were available through the selective gear fixed-ratio transmission that included partial range power shifting. No repairs or adjustments were required during 58 hours of operating time. Using eighth gear, the two-hour economy run at 114.23 maximum available drawbar hp saw a pull of 8,981 lbs. at 4.77 mph with slippage totaling 6.75 percent. Fuel economy was established at 12.94 hp-hours per gallon. The 10-hour run at 75 percent pull noted an economy figure of 11.86 against a load of 92.48 hp. Also recorded was a pull of 6,772 lbs. at 5.12 mph with 5.12 percent slippage. Standard equipment for this 11,795 lb. tractor included 20.8-38 rear and 11.00-16 inch front tires. Additional front and rear ballast raised the total test weight to 17,380 lbs.

Nebraska Test Data

Model: Allis-Chalmers 7040 Power Shift Diesel
Test No. 1196
Date Tested: November 3 to November 20, 1975

Weighing 12,378 lbs., this tractor was equipped with 20.8-38 rear and 11.00-16 inch front tires. Additional front and rear ballast gave a total test weight of 17,355 lbs. The selective gear fixed-ratio transmission included partial range power shifting. Its 12 forward speeds ranged from 1.8 to 18.4 mph. Using fifth gear, the two-hour economy run at 114.34 maximum available drawbar hp saw a pull of 9,298 lbs. at 4.61 mph and slippage of 7.57 percent. Fuel economy was established at 13.05 hp-hours per gallon. The 10-hour run at 75 percent pull saw an economy of 12.29 hp-hours per gallon under a load of 95.58 drawbar hp. Also manifested in this test was a pull of 7,201 lbs. at 4.98 mph and slippage totaling 5.23 percent. No repairs or adjustments were required during 51-1/2 hours of operating time. At its rated speed of 2,300 rpm, this model delivered 136.30 maximum PTO hp and achieved an economy of 15.31 hp-hours per gallon of fuel. Operating at 1,000 PTO rpm and a corresponding engine speed of 2,253 rpm, an economy of 15.51 hp-hours per gallon appeared under a load of 136.15 PTO hp. Features included an Allis-Chalmers six-cylinder turbocharged engine. Its 426 cubic inch displacement resulted from a 4.25 x 5.00 inch bore and stroke.

Nebraska Test Data

Model: Allis-Chalmers
7045 Power Director Diesel
Test No. 1261
Date Tested: October 12 to October 25, 1977

At its rated engine speed of 2,300 rpm, the 7045 delivered 146.18 maximum PTO hp and achieved an economy of 14.43 hp-hours per gallon. Operating at 1,000 PTO rpm and a corresponding engine speed of 2,253 rpm, an economy of 14.62 hp-hours per gallon resulted from a load of 146.46 PTO hp. This model was equipped with a Allis-Chalmers six-cylinder turbocharged engine. Its 426 cubic inch displacement resulted from a 4.25 x 5.00 inch bore and stroke. Repairs and adjustments noted during 46-1/2 hours of operating time were of relatively minor importance. The selective gear fixed-ratio transmission offered twenty forward speeds ranging from 1.8 to 20.1 mph. Operating in eighth gear, the two-hour run at 122.90 maximum available drawbar hp saw an economy of 12.16 hp-hours per gallon. Also recorded was a pull of 8,974 lbs. at 5.14 mph and slippage totaling 5.13 percent. The 10-hour run at 75 percent pull indicated an economy of 11.4 hp-hours per gallon against a load of 101.45 drawbar hp. Other statistics include a pull of 6,902 lbs. at 5.51 mph and slippage totaling 3.75 percent. Weighing in at 14,235 lbs., this unit was equipped with dual 20.8-38 rear and 11.00-16 inch front tires. Additional front and rear ballast gave a total test weight of 18,980 lbs.

Nebraska Test Data

Model: Allis-Chalmers
7045 Power Shift Diesel, 12-Speed
Test No. 1308
Date Tested: May 3 to May 8, 1979

Dual 20.8-38 rear and 11.00-16 inch front tires were standard equipment for this 14,600-pound tractor. Additional front and rear ballast gave a total test weight of 18,990 lbs.. The selective gear fixed-ratio transmission offered partial range power shifting. Its 12 forward speeds ranged from 2.0 to 19.7 mph. Fifth gear was selected for the two-hour drawbar economy run. Operating at 123.35 maximum available hp, this test saw a pull of 9,380 lbs. at 4.93 mph, slippage of 5.29 percent and an economy of 12.58 hp-hours per gallon. The 10-hour test at 75 percent pull noted an economy of 11.71 hp-hours per gallon of fuel under a load of 102.69 drawbar hp. Also indicated was a pull of 7,277 lbs. at 5.29 mph and slippage of 3.82 percent. An Allis-Chalmers six-cylinder turbocharged engine was featured. Rated at 2,300 rpm, it carried a 4.25 x 5.00 inch bore and stroke for a 426 cubic inch displacement. At rated engine speed, 146.88 maximum PTO hp appeared and an economy of 14.76 hp-hours per gallon was achieved. Operating at 1,000 PTO rpm and a corresponding engine speed of 2,253 rpm, an economy of 14.92 hp-hours per gallon resulted from a load of 146.67 PTO hp. No repairs or adjustments were required during 36-1/2 hours of operating time.

Nebraska Test Data

Model: Allis-Chalmers 7050 Diesel
Test No. 1120
Date Tested: March 14 to March 30, 1973

The 7050 Diesel used the same 426-cid engine as previously noted for the 7030 Diesel of Test No. 1119. In this case, the engine was turbocharged and intercooled. At its rated speed of 2,300 rpm, 156.49 maximum PTO hp was observed and an economy of 15.93 hp-hours per gallon was achieved. Operating at 1,000 PTO rpm and a corresponding engine speed of

Allis-Chalmers 7050

2,253 rpm, an economy of 16.04 hp-hours per gallon was achieved under a load of 156.63 PTO hp. No repairs or adjustments were reported during 55-1/2 hours of operating time. The gear train was virtually identical to that already noted in Test No. 1119, as were the tire sizes. In this case, dual rear wheels were used to improve traction. Weighing 14,525 lbs., this tractor gained additional front and rear ballast for a total test weight of 19,530 lbs. Operating in ninth gear, the two-hour economy run at 131.54 maximum available drawbar hp saw an economy of 13.47 hp-hours per gallon. Also recorded was a pull of 9.028 lbs. at 5.46 mph and slippage of 4.96 percent. The 10-hour run at 75 percent pull saw an economy of 12.67 hp-hours per gallon against a load of 107.64 drawbar hp. Other statistics include a pull of 6,935 lbs. at 5.82 mph and slippage of 3.5 percent.

Allis-Chalmers 7060

Nebraska Test Data

Model: Allis-Chalmers 7060 Diesel

Test No. 1167

Date Tested: October 30 to November 11, 1974

Weighing 13,990 lbs., the 7060 was equipped with dual rear wheels of 20.8-38 inch size, along with 14L-16 inch front tires. Additional front and rear ballast raised the total test weight to 20,490 lbs.. The selective gear fixed-ratio transmission offered partial range power shifting. Its 20 forward speeds ranged from 1.7 to 19.4 mph. Using eighth gear, the two-hour economy run at 136.12 maximum available drawbar hpsaw a pull of 10,073 lbs. at 5.07 mph with slippage totaling 5.33 percent. Fuel economy came in at 13.63 hp-hours per gallon. The 10-hour run at 75 percent pull gave an economy of 12.75 hp-hours per gallon under a load of 111.93 drawbar hp. Also recorded was a pull of 7,784 lbs. at 5.39 mph with slippage totaling 4.43 percent. No repairs or adjustments were required during 49-1/2 hours of operating time. At its rated speed of 2,300 rpm, the 7060 developed 161.51 maximum PTO hp and achieved an economy of 15.87 hp-hours per gallon. At a 1,000 rpm speed on the PTO shaft and a corresponding crankshaft speed of 2,252 rpm, fuel economy came in at 15.99 hp-hours per gallon under a load of 160.44 PTO hp. This tractor was equipped with a six-cylinder turbocharged and intercooled diesel engine. Its 426 cubic inch displacement was derived from a 4.25 x 5.00 inch bore and stroke.

Nebraska Test Data

Model: Allis-Chalmers 7060 Power Shift Diesel

Test No. 1197

Date Tested: November 5 to November 19, 1975

At its rated speed of 2,300 rpm, this model developed 161.42 maximum PTO hp while achieving an economy of 15.87 hp-hours per gallon. Operating at 1,000 PTO rpm and a corresponding engine speed of 2,252 rpm, an economy of 16.08 hp-hours per gallon was observed under a load of 161.65 PTO hp. This tractor featured a six-cylinder, 426-cid turbocharged, intercooled diesel engine with a 4.25 x 5.00 inch bore and stroke. No repairs or adjustments were necessary during 51 hours of operating time. Weighing in at 14,645 lbs., the standard equipment package included dual 20.8-38 rear tires plus 14L-16 inch front tires. Additional front and rear ballast raised the test weight to 20,560 lbs.. Operating in fifth gear, the two-hour economy run at 141.67 maximum available drawbar hp saw a pull of 10,755 lbs. at 4.94 mph and slippage totaling 4.77 percent. Fuel economy was registered at 13.80 hp-hours per gallon. The 10-hour run at 75 percent pull saw an economy of 12.98 hp-hours per gallon against a load of 116.25 drawbar hp. Also recorded was a pull of 8,198 lbs. at 5.32 mph and slippage totaling 3.35 percent.

Nebraska Test Data

Model: Allis-Chalmers 7080 Diesel

Test No. 1168

Date Tested: October 30 to November 13, 1974

At its rated speed of 2,550 rpm, the 7080 developed 181.51 maximum PTO hp and achieved an economy of 15.71 hp-hours per gallon. This tractor was equipped with a six-cylinder turbocharged and intercooled engine with a 4.25 x 5.00 inch bore and stroke for a 426 cubic inch displacement. Also featured was a 20-speed transmission ranging from 1.6 to 18.3 mph. It was of the selective gear fixed-ratio type and included partial range power shifting. At 148.89 maximum drawbar hp, the two-hour economy run indicated a pull of 12,192 lbs. at 4.58 mph with slippage totaling 6.42 percent. Fuel economy was posted at 13.23 hp-hours per gallon. The 10-hour run at 75 percent pull saw an economy figure of 12.11 against a load of 124.54 drawbar hp. Other statistics of this test include a pull of 9,470 lbs. at 4.93 mph with slippage of 4.82 percent. Dual

Allis-Chalmers 7080

Allis-Chalmers 7580

20.8-38 inch rear tires and 18.4-16 inch front tires were featured. Weighing 14,605 lbs., the 7080 gained additional front and rear ballast for a total test weight of 21,720 lbs..

Nebraska Test Data

Model: Allis-Chalmers 7580 4WD Diesel

Test No. 1229

Date Tested: October 26 to November 8, 1976

The 7580 weighed 23,520 lbs. and featured dual 23.1-30 tires on all four corners. Additional front and rear ballast gave a total test weight of 25,000 lbs.. The selective gear fixed-ration transmission offered partial range power shifting. Its 20 forward speeds ranged from 1.5 to 17.6 mph. Using eighth gear, the two-hour drawbar run at 153.7 maximum available hp noted a pull of 12,393 lbs. at 4.65 mph and slippage totaling 3.69 percent. Fuel economy was recorded at 12.22 hp-hours per gallon. The 10-hour run at 75 percent pull noted an economy of 11.39 hp-hours per gallon against a load of 127.26 drawbar hp. Also recorded was a pull of 9,713 lbs. at 4.91 mph and slippage totaling 2.83 percent. The 7580 was equipped with an Allis-Chalmers six-cylinder turbocharged and intercooled engine. Rated at 2,550 rpm, it used a 4.25 x 5.00 inch bore and stroke for a 426 cubic inch displacement. At rated engine speed, 186.35 maximum PTO hp was observed, as was an economy of 14.81 hp-hours per gallon. No repairs or adjustment were required during 53-1/2 hours of operating time.

Nebraska Test Data

Model: Allis-Chalmers 8010 Powershift Diesel

Test No. 1446

Date Tested: August 30 to September 10, 1982

Weighing 12,630 lbs., the 8010 assumed a total test weight of 13,185 lbs. after the addition of front and rear ballast. Standard equipment included 18.4-38 inch rear tires and 10.00-16 inch front tires. Also featured was a selective gear fixed-ratio transmission with 6-range power shifting. Forward speeds varied from 1.8 to 18.4 mph. Running in seventh gear, the two-hour drawbar test at 91.46 maximum available hp indicated an economy of 12.57 hp-hours per gallon. Also observed in this test was a pull of 5,559 lbs. at 6.17 mph and slippage of 6.96 percent. The 10-hour run at 75 percent pull noted an economy of 11.48 hp-hours per gallon of fuel under a load of 73.95 drawbar hp. Likewise noted was a pull of 4,163 lbs. at 6.66 mph and 4.8 percent slippage. No repairs or adjustments were necessary during 40 hours of operating time. At its rated speed of 2,300 rpm the 8010 delivered 107.38 maximum PTO hp with a consequent economy of 14.79 hp-hours per gallon. Operating at 1,000 PTO rpm and a corresponding crankshaft speed of 2,252 rpm, an economy figure of 15.01 was established under a load of 109.55 PTO hp. This tractor was equipped with the company's own six-cylinder turbocharged engine. The 3.875 x 4.250 inch bore and stroke gave a 301 cubic inch displacement.

Allis-Chalmers 8030

Nebraska Test Data

Model: Allis-Chalmers 8030 Powershift Diesel

Test No. 1447

Date Tested: August 31 to September 13, 1982

The 8030 featured an Allis-Chalmers six-cylinder turbocharged engine. Rated at 2,500 rpm, it carried a 4.25 x 5.00 inch bore and stroke for a 426 cubic inch displacement. At rated engine speed, 133.75 maximum PTO hpwas observed, as was an economy of 15.06 hp-hours per gallon of fuel. Operating at 1,000 PTO rpm and a corresponding engine speed of 2,252 rpm, an economy figure of 15.25 was established under a load of 134.42 PTO hp. No repairs or adjustments were required during 36 hours of operating time. A 6-range power shift was featured in the selective gear fixed-ratio transmission. Its 12 forward speeds ranged from 1.8 to 18.4 mph. Using seventh gear, the two-hour drawbar run at 115.22 maximum available hp saw a pull of 6,816 lbs. at 6.34 mph. Slippage totaled 4.67 percent and fuel economy came in at 12.93 hp-hours per gallon. The 10-hour run at 75 percent pull indicated an economy of 11.87 hp-hours per gallon under a load of 93.86 drawbar hp. Other statistics include a pull of 5,165 lbs. at 6.81 mph and slippage totaling 3.52 percent. The 8030 weighed in at 15,015 lbs., but additional

Allis-Chalmers 8010

front and rear ballast gave a total test weight of 17,100 lbs. Standard equipment included dual 18.4-38 inch rear tires and 11.00-16 inch front tires.

Allis-Chalmers 8050

Nebraska Test Data

Model: Allis-Chalmers 8050 Powershift Diesel
Test No. 1448
Date Tested: September 1 to September 17, 1982

The 8050 used an Allis-Chalmers six-cylinder turbocharged and inter-cooled engine. Rated at 2,300 rpm, it carried a 4.25 x 5.00 inch bore and stroke for a 426 cubic inch displacement. At rated engine speed, 152.40 maximum PTO hp was observed, as was an economy of 15.66 hp-hours per gallon. Operating at 1,000 PTO rpm and a corresponding engine speed of 2,252 rpm, an economy figure of 15.88 was established under a load of 155.15 PTO hp. No repairs or adjustments were required for this tractor during 41 hours of operation. The selective gear fixed-ratio transmission featured 6-range power shifting. Its 12 forward speeds varied from 2.0 to 19.7 mph. Operating in fifth gear, the two-hour drawbar test at 131.44 maximum available hp set an economy of 13.71 hp-hours per gallon. This test also established a pull of 10,072 lbs. at 4.89 mph and slippage totaling 6.02 percent. By comparison, the 10-hour run at 75 percent pull set an economy figure of 12.73 under a load of 105.06 drawbar hp. Other statistics include a pull of 7,575 lbs. at 5.2 mph and slippage of 4.2 percent. Standard equipment included dual 20.8-38 inch rear tires and 14L-16 inch front tires. Weighing 15,305 lbs., this model assumed a total test weight of 19,380 lbs. by the addition of front and rear ballast.

Allis-Chalmers 8070

Nebraska Test Data

Model: Allis-Chalmers 8070 Powershift Diesel
Test No. 1449
Date Tested: September 1 to September 16, 1982

At its rated engine speed of 2,400 rpm the 8070 delivered 170.72 maximum PTO hp, meanwhile achieving an economy of 15.97 hp-hours per gallon. Operating at 1,000 PTO rpm and a corresponding engine speed of 2,253 rpm, an economy figure of 16.48 was established under a load of 171.44 PTO hp. This tractor carried an Allis-Chalmers six-cylinder turbocharged and inter-cooled engine. Its 4.25 x 5.00 inch bore and stroke gave a 426 cubic inch displacement. Weighing 16,850 lbs., the 8070 assumed a total test weight of 22,370 lbs. by the addition of front and rear ballast. Standard equipment included dual 20.8-38 inch rear tires and 18.4-16 inch front tires. Also featured was a selective gear fixed-ratio transmission with a 6-range power shift. Its 12 forward speeds varied from 2.0 to 16.8 mph. Operating in seventh gear, the two-hour drawbar test at 145.36 maximum available hp indicated an economy of 13.67 hp-hours per gallon. Also indicated was a pull of 9,260 lbs. at 5.89 mph with slippage totaling 4.54 percent. The 10-hour run at 75 percent pull recorded an economy of 12.59 hp-hours per gallon under a load of 117.58 drawbar hp. Other data includes a pull of 7,061 lbs. at 6.24 mph and slippage totaling 3.51 percent.

A-C Monarch "50"

Nebraska Test Data

Model: Allis-Chalmers Monarch 50
Test No. 179
Date Tested: June 27 to July 3, 1930

Weighing 15,100 lbs., the Monarch 50 featured a huge four-cylinder, vertical, I-head engine with a 5-1/4x 6-1/2 inch bore and stroke. Rated at 1,000 rpm, it included an Eisemann GV4 magneto and Zenith C-6 carburetor as standard equipment. Advertised speeds of 1.82, 2.76, and 3.99 mph were built into the "50." Using intermediate gear and burning gasoline, this tractor developed 44.09 drawbar hp on the rated load test, pulling 6,000 lbs. at 2.76 mph. Fuel consumption totaled 5.673 gallons per hour with economy coming in at 7.77 hp-hours per gallon. Slippage on this test was only 0.65 percent. The low gear maximum test gave 50.14 drawbar hp, with a pull of 10,573 lbs. at 1.78 mph and slippage of 3.03 percent. Rated brake hp testing manifested a fuel efficiency of 9.54 hp-hours per gallon. This figure dropped slightly to 9.29 when developing its maximum of 62.18 brake hp. Except for tightening the water pump packing gland once during the test, no repairs or adjustments were required. Note that A-C listed its Monarch tractor production as being at Springfield, Illinois, rather than Milwaukee (where it had been immediately after the purchase), or Watertown, Wisconsin, where the Monarch company originated.

Allis-Chalmers Model L Crawler

Nebraska Test Data

Model: Allis-Chalmers Model L

Test No. 200

Date Tested: March 17 to April 11, 1932

Tractor rating codes permitted the "L" to carry 60 drawbar and 80 belt hp. This tractor featured a huge six-cylinder I-head engine withg a 5-1/4 x 6-1/2 inch bore and stroke and a rated speed of 1,050 rpm. Also included were two Zenith C6EV carburetors, along with an Eisemann GV6 magneto and a Pomona air cleaner. With an operating weight of 22,027 lbs., this tractor also featured six forward speeds of 1.94, 2.45, 3.05, 4.1, 5.2, and 6.47 mph. In low gear it developed 75.66 drawbar hp, pulling a load of 15,086 lbs. at 1.88 mph, and having a slippage of only 3.42 percent, pulling over 68 percent of its own weight in the maximum drawbar load test. At rated drawbar of 61.69 hp, the L pulled 9,562 lbs. at 2.42 mph, delivering an economy of 7.48 hp-hours per gallon. Rated brake hp tests at 80.46 hp indicated fuel consumption of 9.576 gallons power hour (gph) and an economy of 8.4 hp-hours per gallon. This figure improved slightly to 8.46 under maximum brake load of 91.93 hp. Test notes indicated a flake of solder obstructed the fuel tank outlet and was removed. Then no further adjustments were required.

Nebraska Test Data

Model: Allis-Chalmers Model L

Test No. 338

Date Tested: November 23 to November 28, 1939

Weighing 26,105 lbs., this later Model L featured forward speeds of 1.48, 1.94, 2.68, 3.5, 4.9, and 6.41 mph. Also included was a belt pulley 20 inches in diameter with a 15-inch face. Test C reveals a fuel economy of 10.33 hp-hours per gallon and an output of 108.84 maximum brake hp. It also indicates fuel consumption of 10.538 gallons per hour under this load. Test D at a rated load of 93.65 brake hp noted a fuel economy of 10.21 hp-hours per gallon. This tractor was equipped with two Zenith 62AX-J10 carburetors and a Fairbanks-Morse RV6B magneto. Rated at 1,050 rpm, the Allis-Chalmers six-cylinder I-head engine had a 5-1/4 x 6-1/2 inch bore and stroke. Test H for rated drawbar hp gave a fuel economy of 8.35 hp-hours per gallon. Under a load of 13,727 lbs. the Model L moved at 1.89 mph with a slippage of 2.4 percent and a rated output of 69.34 drawbar hp. This figure was pegged at 90.42 in Test G, using first gear. At 100 percent maximum load, the Model L pulled 23,851 lbs. at 1.42 mph with slippage of 4.32 percent. Hp-hours per gallon in the 100 percent maximum load drawbar tests was not recorded.

Allis-Chalmers Model L-O Crawler

Nebraska Test Data

Model: Allis-Chalmers Model L-O

Test No. 287

Date Tested: September 9 to September 22, 1937

Allis-Chalmers featured its own six-cylinder engine in the L-O tractor, which used fuel injection with spark ignition. Rated at 1,050 rpm, the L-O carried a 5-1/4 x 6-1/2 inch bore and stroke. Integral equipment included a Deco fuel system, Mallory ignition, and a United air cleaner. Six forward speeds of 1.48, 1.94, 2.68, 3.5, 4.9, and 6.41 mph, and two reverse speeds of 1.72 and 2.25 mph were available. Test weight, including operator, was 24,925 lbs. Test H for rated drawbar load included an output of 61.08 hp with a pull of 12,077 lbs. at 1.9 mph and slippage of 2.17 percent. Fuel economy was recorded at 9.77 hp-hours per gallon. The low gear maximum pull was recorded at 20,273 lbs., or about 81 percent of total tractor weight. This test also revealed an output of 76.42 drawbar hp. Test D for rated brake load manifested a fuel economy figure of 12.02 hp-hours per gallon of diesel fuel with an output of 79.92 hp. Economy rose slightly to 12.46 at a maximum load of 91.56 hp. The fuel transfer pump pressure gauge failed during the maximum drawbar tests and was replaced. No other repairs or adjustments were noted.

Allis-Chalmers Crawler Tractors

After buying out the Monarch crawler line in 1928, Allis-Chalmers continued manufacturing Monarch tractors with little change until about 1931 when the Model L crawler appeared. A year later came the Model M, which remained in produc-tion for a decade—a long time in the rapidly changing tractor business. The standard gauge for the Model M was 40 inches, and the company also offered the Model WM built on a 50-inch track gauge.

Nebraska Test Data

Model: Allis-Chalmers Model M

Test No. 216

Date Tested: September 23 to October 9, 1933

Advertised speeds of 2.23, 3.2, 4.15, and 5.82 mph were built into the Allis-Chalmers M tractor. Using second gear, the rated drawbar test at 22.98 hp revealed a pull of 2,714 lbs. at 3.18 mph and a fuel economy of 7.5 hp-hours per gallon. The maximum drawbar pull in low gear indicated 29.65 hp, along with a pull of 5,166 lbs. at 2.15 mph. Rated brake hp tests at 32.01 hp gave total fuel consumption figures at 3.219 gallons per hour with an efficiency of 9.94 hp-hours per gallon. This dropped almost imperceptibly to 9.91 at the maximum load of 35.43 hp. Allis-Chalmers equipped this tractor with its own four-cylinder I-head engine with a 4-3/8 x 5 inch bore and stroke, and a rated speed of 960 rpm. Also included was an Eisemann GL4 magneto, a Zenith K5 carburetor, a Vortox air cleaner and a Rockford clutch. Total tractor weight was 6,620 lbs.. No repairs or adjustments were necessary during the 46-1/2 hours of running time. This unit was built at the Springfield (Illinois) Works.

Nebraska Test Data

Model: Allis-Chalmers Model M

Test No. 239

Date Tested: August 1 to August 9, 1935

While not rated by the manufacturer, this tractor had a maximum permissible rating of 22.79 drawbar and 31.64 belt hp as recommended by the tractor rating codes of S.A.E. and A.S.A.E. The "M" embodied the same four-cylinder engine used in the Model U, making this tractor a crawler model of the same Allis-Chalmers tractor series. Weighing in at 6,855 lbs. the M featured four speeds of 1.83, 2.23, 3.2, and 4.15 mph. In low gear it pulled 5,009 lbs., or 73 percent of its own weight, doing so at a speed of 2.05 mph and developing 27.43 hp. Rated drawbar tests in second gear, and at an output of 22.61 hp indicated a pull of 2,709 lbs. at 3.13 mph, with a fuel economy of 7.32 hp-hours per gallon of distillate. At its rated 31.78 brake hp, a figure of 9.79 hp-hours per gallon was attained, with a nearly identical figure at the maximum load of 31.78 hp. No repairs or adjustments were required during the 50-hour test. This later Model M was noted as a product of Milwaukee.

Allis-Chalmers Model K Crawler

Nebraska Test Data

Model: Allis-Chalmers "Special K"

Test No. 215

Date Tested: September 21 to October 4, 1933

Although not rated by the manufacturer, this tractor assumed maximum ratings of 35.51 drawbar and 49.29 belt hp under existing tractor rating codes. Using gasoline, it developed 35.7 hp in the rated drawbar test, achieving a fuel economy of 7.14 hp-hours per gallon. This test also indicated a pull of 4,304 lbs. at 3.11 mph. The low gear maximum load test gave 47.87 hp with an 8,865 lb. pull at 2.03 mph, for nearly 76 percent of its 11,670 lb. operating weight. Standard equipment included th1e company's own four-cylinder I-head engine with a 5 x 6-1/2 inch bore and stroke and a rated speed of 1,050 rpm. Three forward speeds of 2.08, 3.1, and 4.5 mph were also provided, along with accessory items such as an Eisemann GL4 magneto and a Zenith C-6 carburetor. At its rated 49.59 belt hp the "Special K" delivered a fuel economy of 10.04 hp-hours per gallon. This total dropped slightly to 9.38 at maximum load of 55.24 hp. No repairs or adjustments were required during this test.

Nebraska Test Data

Model: Allis-Chalmers Model S-O

Test No. 286

Date Tested: September 16 to September 25, 1937

Except for a single minor adjustment, no other repairs were recorded for the Allis-Chalmers S-O tractor during some 44 hours of operating time. Five forward speeds of 1.51, 2.32, 3.25, 4.55, and 6.37 mph were featured. Test H for rated drawbar load was made in second gear. It recorded a pull of 7.786 lbs. at 2.3 mph and slippage of 0.97 percent with a total output of 47.78 hp. Fuel economy was 9.34 hp-hours per gallon. A maximum pull of 16,732 lbs. was recorded in low gear. Traveling at a speed of 1.41 mph the S-O delivered 62.97 drawbar hp in this test with slippage of 6.33 percent. Test D for rated belt load indicated 66.64 hp, along with an economy of 11.67 hp-hours per gallon of diesel fuel. An improved economy figure of 12.37 was noted under maximum load of 74.82 brake hp. Weighing in at 20,100 lbs., the S-O featured a four-cylinder A-C I-head engine with a 5-3/4 x 6-1/2 inch bore and stroke. Rated at 1,050 rpm, it used fuel injection with spark ignition. Also included was a Deco fuel system, Mallory ignition, Pierce governor, United air cleaner, and Rockford clutch.

Allis-Chalmers Model M Crawler

Allis-Chalmers Model WK-O Crawler

Nebraska Test Data

Model: Allis-Chalmers Model WK-O

Test No. 285

Date Tested: August 26 to September 2, 1937

Weighing an even 6-1/2 tons, the WK-O diesel tractor featured speeds of 1.72, 2.59, 3.26, and 5.92 mph. Drawbar Test G records a maximum low gear pull of 11,685 lbs. at a speed of 1.62 mph and slippage of 6.24 percent for an output of 50.45 drawbar hp. Test H for rated load was made in second gear. With an output of 39.8 hp the WK-O pulled 5,814 lbs. at 2.57 mph under a slippage of 1.59 percent. Fuel economy was recorded at 9.49 hp-hours per gallon of commercial diesel fuel. At its rated 53.41 brake hp the WK-O yielded an economy of 11.86 hp-hours per gallon with an improved total of 12.79 under maximum load of 59.06 brake hp. This tractor was equipped with an A-C four-cylinder engine featuring fuel injection and spark ignition. Rated at 1,050 rpm, it carried a 5-1/4 x 6-1/2 inch bore and stroke. Equipment included a Deco fuel system, Mallory ignition, and a United air cleaner. The fuel injectors were cleaned during the belt tests but no other repairs or adjustments were noted during 54 hours of operation.

Allis-Chalmer Model WK Crawler

Nebraska Test Data

Model: Allis-Chalmers Model WK

Test No. 336

Date Tested: November 21 to November 27, 1939

Weighing in at 13,340 lbs., the WK tractor offered forward speeds of 1.72, 2.59, 3.26, and 5.92 mph. Second gear was used for the rated drawbar test. Upon completion of this 10-hour trial, Test H indicated a fuel economy of 8.96 hp-hours per gallon, along with a pull of 6,063 lbs. at 2.57 mph and slippage of 1.52 percent for an output of 41.5 rated drawbar hp. Test G for operating maximum load indicates a first-gear pull of 11,785 lbs. at 1.65 mph and slippage of 4.32 percent for a total of 51.85 hp. This tractor was equipped with the company's own four-cylinder I-head engine rated at 1,050 rpm and carrying a 5 x 6-1/2 inch bore and stroke. This was complemented with a Fairbanks-Morse FMO4-B magneto and a Zenith 62AJ12 carburetor. Brake hp tests indicate a fuel economy of 10.31 hp-hours per gallon under Test C, along with an output of 62.15 hp. Test D for rated load pegged this figure at 54.54, along with an economy of 10.39 hp-hours per gallon. No repairs or adjustments were recorded during 36 hours of engine operating time.

Allis-Chalmers Model WS Crawler

Nebraska Test Data

Model: Allis-Chalmers Model WS

Test No. 337

Date Tested: November 18 to November 24, 1939

Test C notes a fuel economy of 10.27 hp-hours per gallon nder an operating maximum load of 84.34 brake hp. By comparison, Test D notes an economy figure of 10.38 with an output of 72.92 rated belt hp. Using first gear, the WS made a maximum pull of 17,843 lbs. in Test G. At a speed of 1.44 mph, the WS delivered 68.72 maximum drawbar hp, experiencing a slippage of 5 percent. The 10-hour run of Test H indicates 53.8 rated drawbar hp and an economy of 8.06 hp-hours per gallon. In this test the WS had a ground speed of 2.29 mph and slippage of 2.1 percent. Advertised speeds of 1.52, 2.32, 3.25, 4.55, and 6.37 mph were offered, along with a Rockford clutch and Zenith 62A12 carburetor. A Delco-Remy 12-volt ignition was used, but the generator and starter were by Auto-Lite. Allis-Chalmers used its own four-cylinder I-head engine in the WS tractor. Rated at 1,050 rpm, it carried a 5-3/4 x 6-1/2 inch bore and stroke. During 36 hours of engine operating time, no repairs or adjustments were recorded.

The HD-Series crawlers were launched with the HD-14 in 1939, and full production commenced the following year. With 132 drawbar hp, the HD-14 weighed in at 29,000 lbs. It was equipped with a GM 6-71 diesel engine, a standard for the A-C crawler line for some years to come. Numerous models and styles of HD-Series crawlers were built subsequent to 1939 and the line stayed in production until 1965.

Allis-Chalmers Model HD-14 Crawler

Nebraska Test Data

Model: Allis-Chalmers HD-14

Test No. 362

Date Tested: October 15 to November 5, 1940

A General Motors six-cylinder, two-cycle diesel engine was featured in the HD-14 tractor. Rated at 1,500 rpm, it carried a 4-1/4 x 5 inch bore and stroke just like the smaller models of this series. Standard equipment included six forward speeds of 1.72, 2.18, 2.76, 3.5, 4.36, and 7 mph. Second gear was chosen for Test H. At 99.39 rated drawbar-hp, the HD-14 pulled a 17,568 pound load at 2.12 mph with a slippage of 3.29 percent and a fuel economy of 12.58 hp-hours per gallon. A maximum drawbar pull of 28,019 lbs. occurred in low gear. The HD-14 weighed in at 28,750 lbs., thus it pulled more than 97 percent of its own weight in this test. Test G also indicates a ground speed of 1.63 mph and 5.64 percent slippage for this pull, along with an output of 122.09 drawbar hp. Test C and Test B observed a 100 percent maximum load of 145.39 brake hp and an economy of 15.18 hp-hours per gallon of diesel fuel. Test D at a rated load of 128.17 brake hp resulted in an identical fuel economy rating. No repairs or adjustments were noted during 62 hours of engine operating time.

Allis-Chalmers Model HD-10W Crawler

Nebraska Test Data

Model: Allis-Chalmers HD-10W

Test No. 361

Date Tested: October 15 to October 25, 1940

At a rated drawbar load of 65.55 hp, the HD-10W delivered a fuel economy of 11.62 hp-hours per gallon of diesel fuel as noted in Test H. Other data extracted from this test includes a pull of 12,159 lbs. at 2.02 mph with slippage of 2.13 percent. Second gear was used for this test. A 100 percent maximum pull of 19,002 lbs. was recorded in Test G. Using first gear, the HD-10W pulled this load at a speed of 1.6 mph with slippage of 4.83 percent and an output of 81.25 drawbar hp. Advertised speeds of 1.69, 2.06, 2.68, 3.78, 4.62, and 6.03 mph were attained with standard equipment. Test weight was 21,630 lbs. During 63 hours of engine operating time no repairs or adjustments were noted. Tests C and B indicated a fuel economy of 14.41 hp-hours per gallon of fuel under a 100 percent maximum load of 98.47 brake hp. A nearly identical economy of 14.14 mpg appeared in Test D under a rated brake load of 86.45 hp. This tractor was equipped with a General Motors four-cylinder, two-cycle diesel engine. Rated at 1,600 rpm, it carried a 4-1/4 x 5 inch bore and stroke. Standard equipment included a GM fuel injection system.

Allis-Chalmers Model HD-7W Crawler

Nebraska Test Data

Model: Allis-Chalmers HD-7W

Test No. 360

Date Tested: October 15 to October 21, 1940

Weighing in at 14,175 lbs., the HD-7W tractor featured a General Motors three-cylinder vertical, two-cycle diesel engine. Rated at 1,500 rpm, it carried a 4-1/4 x 5 inch bore and stroke. This engine also featured a GM fuel injection system. No repairs or adjustments were recorded during 49 hours of engine operating time. The HD-7W was equipped with transmission speeds of 1.84, 2.55, 3.45, and 5.82 mph. In Test G a low gear maximum pull of 12,171 lbs. was recorded at a speed of 1.77 mph and with slippage of 4.43 percent for an output of 57.31 maximum drawbar hp. A rated 45.45 drawbar hp was noted in Test H. At a speed of 2.52 mph and with slippage of 1.24 percent, the HD-7W pulled 6,753 lbs. and yielded a fuel economy of 11.32 hp-hours per gallon of diesel fuel. Test C and Test B were combined for the 100 percent maximum belt hp test, and under a load of 68.68 hp this tractor produced a fuel economy of 14.2 hp-hours per gallon. A slightly lower economy of 13.98 was registered in Test D with a rated load of 60.52 brake horsepower.

Allis-Chalmers Model HD-5B Crawler

Nebraska Test Data

Model: Allis-Chalmers HD5B

Test No. 396

Date Tested: July 2 to July 14, 1948

Weighing in at 11,815 lbs., the HD-5B featured forward speeds of 1.46, 2.44, 3.30 3.96, and 5.47 mph. This tractor was equipped with a General Motors two-cylinder, two-cycle, I-head diesel engine. Rated at 1,800 rpm, it used a 4-1/4 x 5 inch bore and stroke. Also included was a Delco-Remy 12-volt electrical system and GM fuel injection equipment. No repairs or adjustments were noted during 38 hours of engine operating time. Test H was run in second gear, and at a load of 30.22 drawbar hp the HD-5B pulled 4,682 lbs. at 2.42 mph with a slippage of 1.15 percent. Fuel economy came in at 9.63 hp-hours per gallon of diesel fuel. A low-gear maximum pull of 10.059 lbs. at 1.41 mph was recorded in Test G. Slippage rose to 4.33 percent in this test. Test B and C were combined for the 100 percent maximum belt load. At 47.85 belt hp, fuel economy was noted at 12.69 hp-hours per gallon. A very slight drop in economy to 12.45 hp-hours per gallon was noted at a Test D rated load of 42.71 belt hp.

Allis-Chalmers Model HD-19 Crawler

Nebraska Test Data

Model: Allis-Chalmers HD-19

Test No. 397

Date Tested: July 2 to July 16, 1948

Weighing in at an immense 40,395 lbs., the HD-19 featured a torque converter drive with speeds ranging up to 7 mph. Because of the hydraulic torque converter, rated load and maximum load were the same, both on belt and on drawbar testing. Using the low gear range, the HD-19 made a maximum pull of 37,536 lbs. at 1.08 mph under a slippage of 4.9 1 percent. The high gear range yielded a maximum pull of 16,132 lbs. at 2.36 mph with an output of 101.53 drawbar hp. Fuel economy was not recorded in these tests. Test C and Test B, run at 100 percent maximum belt load indicated an output of 129.08 hp, along with an economy of 11.02 hp-hours per gallon. Instead of the usual one hour test time, the test was limited to 30 minutes as a safety measure for the dynamometer installation. No repairs or adjustments were noted during 38 hours of engine operating time. The HD-19 was equipped with a General Motors six-cylinder I-head diesel engine. Rated at 1,750 rpm, it carried a 4-1/4 x 5 inch bore and stroke. Also included was a Delco-Remy electrical system and GM fuel injection equipment. Using low gear range, Test H was run at a rated drawbar load of 110.64 hp. At a speed of 1.65 mph it pulled 25,111 lbs. with a slippage of 2.44 percent, yielding a fuel economy on the drawbar of 9.5 hp-hours per gallon.

Allis-Chalmers Model HD-9 Crawler

Nebraska Test Data

Model: Allis-Chalmers HD-9

Test No. 463

Date Tested: July 17 to July 28, 1951

A General Motors 4-71 two-cycle diesel engine was featured in the HD-9 tractor. Of four-cylinder design, this engine was rated at 1,600 rpm, carried a 4–1/4 x 5 inch bore and stroke, and had a 284 cubic inch displacement. A 12-volt electrical system was standard equipment. During 39-1/2 hours of operating time, no repairs or adjustments were noted. With a weight of 19,945 lbs., the HD-9 delivered a low-gear maximum pull of 19,035 lbs. at 1.3 mph under a slippage of 6.2 percent. Test G was run in all forward gears. Test H, for rated drawbar load, was run in second gear. At 54.46 hp, the HD-9 pulled 9,858 lbs. at 2.07 mph with a slippage of 1.46 percent. Fuel economy totaled 11.14 hp-hours per gallon. Advertised speeds of 1.39, 2.1, 2.93, 3.77, 4.41, and 5.68 mph were a standard feature. Fuel economy was recorded at 133.33 hp-hours per gallon under a Test D rated belt load of 71.93 hp. This figure was slightly increased to 13.51 at a Test B maximum belt load of 79.1 hp.

Allis-Chalmers Model HD-15 Crawler

Nebraska Test Data

Model: Allis-Chalmers HD-15

Test No. 464

Date Tested: July 17 to August 2, 1951

In 50-1/2 hours of operating time, no repairs or adjustments were recorded for the HD-15 tractor. Advertised speeds of 1.39, 2.09, 2.97, 3.87, 4.46, and 5.8 mph were featured, with second gear being used for Test H. At a rated load of 81.95 drawbar hp, the HD-15 pulled 14,949 lbs. at 2.06 mph with a slippage of 1.96 percent. By the conclusion of this 10-hour run, fuel economy was pegged at 11.23 hp-hours per gallon of diesel fuel. Test G delivered a low-gear maximum pull of 29,400 lbs. at 1.34 mph against a slippage of 2.49 percent, or a maximum drawbar output of 105.04 hp. Total weight of the HD-15 was 30,985 lbs. Belt hp testing indicated a fuel economy of 13.44 hp-hours per gallon under a Test D rated load of 105.73 hp. A slightly improved fuel economy figure of 13.75 was manifested in the Test B maximum load run made at 117.68 hp. Standard equipment included a General Motors 6-71 two-cycle diesel engine rated at 1,600 rpm. Its 4-1/4 x 5-inch bore and stroke gave a 426 cubic inch displacement.

Allis-Chalmers Model HD-20 Crawler

Nebraska Test Data

Model: Allis-Chalmers HD-20

Test No. 465

Date Tested: July 20 to August 3, 1951

Due to the limited capacity of the dynamometer, no belt tests were made on this tractor. Weighing 42,625 lbs., the HD-20 featured a General Motors 6-110 two-cycle diesel engine. Rated at 1,700 rpm, it used a 5 x 5.6-inch bore and stroke for a 660 cubic inch displacement. This engine carried an 18:1 compression ratio and used a 24-volt electrical system. An important feature of the HD-20 tractor was a torque converter that automatically loaded the engine by controlling the forward travel speed according to the load applied. Because of this system, rated load and maximum load were approximately the same. Low and high gear ranges were provided with this system. Using low range, a maximum pull of 41,321 lbs. at 0.96 mph was achieved with a slippage of 5.77 percent. Test H, run at a rated drawbar load of 114.87 hp over 10 hours, revealed a pull of 28,544 lbs. at 1.51 mph with a 2.82 percent slippage. Fuel economy in this test totaled 12.91 hp-hours per gallon of diesel fuel. Prior to beginning Test H the high idle adjustment was changed, otherwise no repairs or adjustments were noted over 42 hours of engine operating time.

Allis-Chalmers Model HD-21 Crawler

Nebraska Test Data

Model: Allis-Chalmers HD-21

Test No. 550

Date Tested: July 6 to July 18, 1955

Weighing 44,725 lbs., the HD-21 was equipped with an Allis-Chalmers six-cylinder, supercharged engine. Rated at 1,800 rpm, this engine carried a 5-1/4 x 6-1/2-inch bore and stroke for an 844 cubic inch displacement. This tractor was equipped with a three-stage hydraulic torque converter that automatically loaded the engine by controlling the forward travel according to the load applied so rated load and maximum load were approximately the same. Using the low gear range, speeds of 0 to 3 mph were available, while in high range the speed could be varied from 0 to 7.5 mph. Using low-gear range, a maximum drawbar pull of 40,563 lbs. was recorded at 1.22 mph with a slippage of 8.84 percent, for an output of 132.26 hp. The 10-hour Test H run was also made in the low gear range and indicated a rated drawbar output of 129.67 hp, a pull of 29,070 lbs. at 1.67 mph, and slippage of 2.76 percent, Fuel economy in this test totaled 13.974 hp-hours per gallon of diesel fuel. Due to the limited capacity of the dynamometer, no belt tests were run on this tractor.

Allis-Chalmers Model HD-16 Crawler

Nebraska Test Data

Model: Allis-Chalmers HD-16

Test No. 551

Date Tested: July 6 to July 18, 1955

Weighing 32,135 lbs., the HD-16 featured a 3-stage torque converter that automatically loaded the engine by controlling the forward travel speed according to the load applied so rated load and maximum load were approximately the same. Using the low-gear range, a maximum drawbar pull of 29,130 lbs. was achieved at a speed of 1.35 mph against a slippage of 4.27 percent. This equated to 104.96 drawbar hp. Test H, run for 10 hours in the medium gear range, delivered a rated drawbar output of 103-14 hp. During this test the HD-16 pulled 15,060 lbs. at 2.57 mph with a slippage of 1.71 percent. Fuel consumption totaled 10.177 gallons per hour for a fuel economy of 10.13 hp-hours per gallon of diesel fuel. Due to the limited capacity of the dynamometer, no belt tests were made on this tractor. Standard equipment included an Allis-Chalmers six-cylinder four-cycle engine rated at 1800 rpm. Using a 5-1/4x 6-1/2-inch bore and stroke it had an 844 cubic inch displacement. No repairs or adjustments were recorded during 29 hours of operating time.

Allis-Chalmers Model HD-16A Crawler

Nebraska Test Data

Model: Allis-Chalmers HD-16A

Test No. 552

Date Tested: July 6 to July 18, 1955

Although this tractor had the same basic designation as the model noted in Test No. 551, some fundamental changes were evident. Instead of the torque converter drive, this tractor featured a standard transmission with speeds of 1.4, 2.1, 3, 3.9, 4.5, and 5.8 mph. Also featured in this 32,375 pound tractor was an Allis-Chalmers six-cylinder, four-cycle diesel engine with a 5-1/4 x 6-1/2-inch bore and stroke for an 844 cubic inch displacement. Rated at 1,600 rpm, it achieved a maximum torque of 774.4 lbs.-ft. with an engine speed of 1,300 rpm. Test G yielded a low-gear maximum pull of 28,743 lbs. at 1.32 mph with a slippage of 6.15 percent. The ten-hour run of Test H was made in second gear. With a rated drawbar output of 93.56 hp, the HD-16 A pulled 17,162 lbs. at 2.04 mph with a slippage of 2.68 percent and delivered a fuel economy of 12.12 hp-hours per gallon of fuel. Test B, run at a 100 percent maximum belt load of 133.83 hp scored a fuel economy of 14.72 hp-hours per gallon of fuel, with this figure slipping to 14.54 at a Test D rated belt load of 120.35 hp. During 39-1/2 hours of operating time, no repairs or adjustments were noted.

Allis-Chalmers Model HD-6B Crawler

Nebraska Test Data

Model: Allis-Chalmers HD-6B

Test No. 580

Date Tested: July 7 to July 14, 1956

Weighing 13,580 lbs., this tractor featured forward speeds of 1.46, 2.44, 3.3, 3.96, and 5.47 mph. No repairs or adjustments were reported during 37-1/2 hours of operating time. Test G, run in low gear, achieved a maximum drawbar pull of 12,636 lbs. at 1.37 mph with a slippage of 7.51 percent. The 10-hour rated drawbar run of Test H was made in second gear. At a rated output of 39.46 hp, the HD-6B pulled 6,242 lbs. at 2.37 mph with a slippage of 2.89 percent. Fuel economy was scored at 9.45 hp-hours per gallon. An Allis-Chalmers four-cylinder diesel engine was featured. It carried a 4-7/16 x 5-9/16-inch bore and stroke for a 344 cubic inch displacement. Rated at 1,800 rpm, it achieved 124 percent of rated engine torque at 65 percent of rated speed. The combined run of Test B & C, made at a 100 percent maximum belt load of 60.51 hp produced a fuel economy of 11.48 hp-hours per gallon. This figure rose to 12.05 under a Test D rated load of 54.83 hp.

Allis-Chalmers Model HD-11B Crawler

Nebraska Test Data

Model: Allis-Chalmers HD-11B

Test No. 581

Date Tested: July 9 to July 13, 1956

At a Test D rated belt load of 80.82 hp, this tractor scored a fuel economy of 12.78 hp-hours per gallon of diesel. Fuel economy rose slightly to stand at 12.96 at a Test B 100 percent maximum belt load of 89.75 hp. Rated at 1,800 rpm, the HD-11B delivered a peak torque of 122 percent over rated torque at 60 percent of rated speed. Weighing 22,375 lbs., the HD-11B featured an Allis-Chalmers six-cylinder diesel engine with a 4-7/16 x 5-9/16-inch bore and stroke for a 516 cubic inch displacement. No repairs or adjustments were reported during 38 hours of running time. Advertised speeds of 1.39, 2.1, 2.93, 3.77, 4.41, and 5.68 mph were available and the rated drawbar run of Test H was made in second gear. At a load of 59.33 hp, this tractor pulled 10,646 lbs. at 2.09 mph with a slippage of 0.97 percent. Fuel economy was pegged at 10.34 hp-hours per gallon. Test G indicated a low-gear maximum pull of 20,468 lbs. at 1.33 mph under a slippage of 4.57 percent.

Allis-Chalmers Model HD-21A Crawler

Nebraska Test Data

Model: Allis-Chalmers HD-21A

Test No. 664

Date Tested: August 26 to September 3, 1958

Weighing 47,455 lbs., the HD-21A featured a three-stage hydraulic torque converter system that automatically loaded the engine by controlling the forward travel speed according to the load applied. Due to the limited capacity of the dynamometer, no belt tests were conducted. The low-speed range gave infinitely variable speeds from 0 to 3.1 mph, while the high-speed range permitted speeds ranging from 0 to 8 mph. Test H, run in low gear for 10 hours at a 100 percent maximum of 144.01 hp yielded a pull of 36,224 lbs. at 1.49 mph with 4.45 percent slippage. Fuel economy came in at 11.44 hp-hours per gallon. This tractor featured an Allis-Chalmers AC-21000 six-cylinder, turbocharged engine. Rated at 1,825 rpm, it carried a 5-1/4 x 6-1/2-inch bore and stroke for an 844.3 cubic inch displacement. Also featured was a 24-volt electric starting system. The tracks were adjusted during the test, but no other repairs or adjustments were noted during 40 hours of running time.

Allis-Chalmers Model H-3 Crawler

Nebraska Test Data

Model: Allis-Chalmers H-3

Test No. 793

Date Tested: May 12 to May 25, 1961

Including both the low and high ranges, this tractor had eight forward speeds from 1.2 to 4.8 mph. Weighing in at 7,395 lbs. it made a low-gear maximum pull of 7,893 lbs. at 1.17 mph with 6.39 percent slippage. Using the high range of second gear, the two-hour drawbar economy run at 25.48 maximum available hp saw a pull of 5,099 lbs. at 1.87 mph with 3.41 percent slippage. During this test a fuel economy of 8.8 hp-hours per gallon was accrued. The economy figure slipped slightly to stand at 8.42 on the 10-hour drawbar run, made at 75 percent pull. This test yielded an output of 21.56 hp, and saw a pull of 4,026 lbs. at 2.01 mph with 3.13 percent slippage. No repairs or adjustments were required during 44 hours of operation. Allis-Chalmers equipped the H-3 with its own four-cylinder engine rated at 1,650 rpm. It carried a 3-1/2 x 3-7/8-inch bore and stroke for a 149 cubic inch displacement. At rated engine speed, a maximum of 32.11 PTO hp was developed, with a fuel economy of 11.26 hp-hours per gallon.

Allis-Chalmers Model HD-3 Crawler

Nebraska Test Data

Model: Allis-Chalmers HD-3

Test No. 794

Date Tested: May 12 to May 26, 1961

Although this was basically the same tractor as the H-3 gasoline model of Test No. 793, the use of a diesel engine plus other minor changes brought it in with a test weight of 7,645 lbs. Standard features included an Allis-Chalmers four-cylinder diesel engine rated at 1,650 rpm, and using a 3-9/16 x 4-3/8- inch bore and stroke. This design included a 15.5:1 compression ratio. At rated engine speed a maximum of 32.53 PTO hp was developed with the test realizing a fuel economy of 12.68 hp-hours per gallon. No repairs or adjustments were noted during 39-1/2 hours of running time. Transmission equipment for this tractor was virtually the same as previously noted in Test No. 793. Using the high range of second gear, the two-hour drawbar economy run, made at 26.17 maximum available hp, indicated a pull of 5,262 lbs. at 1.86 mph with 3.67 percent slippage. Fuel economy totaled 10.22 hp-hours per gallon. The economy figure rose slightly to stand at 10.48 in a 10-hour drawbar economy run made at 75 percent pull. This test recorded an output of 22.17 hp, a pull of 4,169 lbs. at 1.99 mph and 3.22 percent slippage.

COLLECTOR VALUES	1	2	3	4
F 75 CRAWLER	$15,000	$12,000	$6,000	$3,000
H 6-TON CRAWLER	$18,000	$10,000	$5,000	$3,000
H 50 CRAWLER	$14,000	$10,000	$6,000	$3,000
H-3 & HD-3 CRAWLER	$6,000	$4,500	$3,000	$2,000
HD-4 CRAWLER	$6,000	$4,500	$3,000	$2,000
HD-5 CRAWLER	$8,000	$6,000	$4,000	$2,000
HD-6 CRAWLER	$8,000	$6,000	$4,000	$2,000
HD-7 CRAWLER	$9,000	$7,000	$3,500	$1,000
HD-9 CRAWLER	$9,000	$7,000	$3,500	$1,000
HD-10 CRAWLER	$9,000	$7,000	$3,500	$1,000
HD-10W CRAWLER	$9,000	$7,000	$3,500	$1,500
HD-11 CRAWLER	$8,000	$6,000	$4,500	$3,000
HD-15 CRAWLER	$8,000	$6,000	$4,500	$2,000
HD-16 CRAWLER	$8,000	$6,000	$4,500	$2,000
HD-19 CRAWLER	$8,000	$6,000	$4,500	$2,000
HD-20 CRAWLER	$8,000	$6,000	$4,500	$2,000
HD-21 CRAWLER	$10,000	$8,000	$4,000	$2,000
K 35 CRAWLER	$8,000	$6,000	$4,000	$1,500
L & LO CRAWLER	$9,000	$7,000	$4,000	$1,000
LD CRAWLER	$9,000	$7,000	$4,000	$1,500
M CRAWLER	$6,000	$4,000	$2,000	$500
S & SO CRAWLER	$9,000	$7,000	$4,000	$1,000

Alma Mfg. Company

ALMA, MICHIGAN

See: McVicker Engineering Company

A trade note of 1909 indicates that Alma was building the McVicker four-cylinder chain drive tractor. This may have been the same tractor referred to under the heading of McVicker Engineering Company, also in this volume.

Altgelt Tractor Company

ADDRESS UNKNOWN

A magazine article published sometime between 1915 and 1920 made a passing reference to this firm, but no additional information has ever been located.

American-Abell Engine & Thresher Company

TORONTO, ONTARIO

American-Abell Universal Farm Tractor

American-Abell had roots in the threshing machine business going back to 1847. By 1886 the firm was building Cock O' The North steam traction engines. In 1902 the firm was sold jointly to Advance Thresher Co. and Minneapolis Threshing Machine Co. When M. Rumely Co. bought out Advance in 1912, Minneapolis sold its share for cash to Rumely. In 1911 American-Abell offered its Universal Farm Motor. It was the same tractor built by Universal Tractor Co. at Stillwater, Minnesota.

American Engine & Tractor Company

CHARLES CITY, IOWA

American announced its 15-30 tractor in 1918. This model was equipped with a Beaver four-cylinder engine that had a 4-3/4 x 6 inch bore and stroke. It was rather pricey for its day, with a retail tag of $1,895. Production ended shortly after it began, and in 1919 the firm became known as American Tractor & Foundry Company.

American Farm Machinery Company

MINNEAPOLIS, MINNESOTA

Kinkade garden tractor

Among other products, American built the Kinkade garden tractors. The company was incorporated December

Weber tractor, American Gas Engine Company

24, 1921, and remained in business until 1955. Shown here is one example of the Kinkade tractor; this one is from the early 1920s. American traced its ancestry to the Andrews Tractor Company, and then the Andrews-Kinkade Tractor Company.
See: Andrews-Kinkade

COLLECTOR VALUES	1	2	3	4
GARDEN TRACTOR	$850	$400	$250	$150

American Fork & Hoe Company

MONTROSE, IOWA

During 1953 this company was listed as the manufacturer for the Gro-Mor garden tractors, as well as for the Held garden tractor. The latter had formerly been built by the Frank Held Tractor Company. Aside from this listing, nothing further has been located.

COLLECTOR VALUES	1	2	3	4
GRO-MOR, HELD GARDEN TRACTORS	$800	$600	$400	$250

American Gas Engine Company

KANSAS CITY, MISSOURI

The Weber tractor first made its appearance in 1914. American Gas Engine Co. was the resulting reorganization of the Weber Gas Engine Co., also in Kansas City. It is likely the tractor was at least in development prior to the reorganization of the company. This tractor is identical to that offered concurrently by Phoenix Mfg. Company at Winona, Minnesota. Aside from a few advertisements, little is known of the Weber tractor.

American Gas Tractor Company

MINNEAPOLIS, MINNESOTA

The October 1910 issue of Gas Review magazine discussed the new tractor being developed by American Gas Tractor Company, noting that the company was not yet ready to put it on the market. A table of tractor specifications in the March 1911 issue of Gas Review notes the American tractor used a four-cylinder engine with a 7-1/4 x 8-inch bore and stroke for a rating of 60 belt hp. Weighing nearly nine tons, the American tractor sold for $3,500.

American Implement Company

CLEVELAND, OHIO

In 1919 American Implement Co. offered three tractor models. All were equipped with four-cylinder engines. Included was the American Junior, a 10-20 tractor. It used a 3 x 5-1/2-inch bore and stroke. The American was a 15-30 tractor, and its engine carried a 3-3/4 x 5-1/8-inch bore and stroke. Topping the line was the American Combined, a big tractor with a 30-58 hp rating. Its four-cylinder engine used a 5-1/2 x 7-inch bore and stroke.

American Implement Corporation

LOS ANGELES, CALIFORNIA

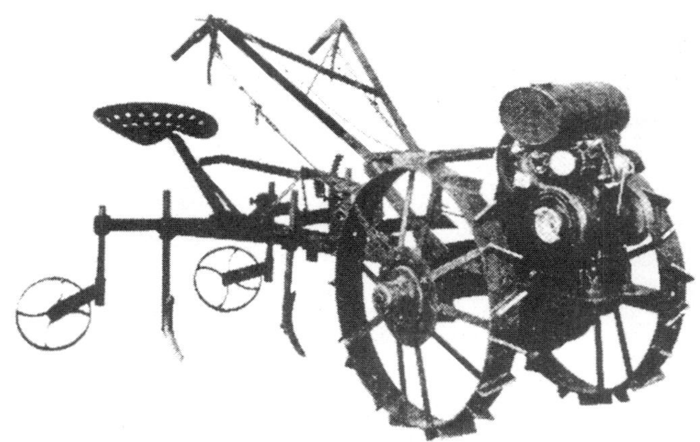

American "General" Model 600 garden tractor

The American garden tractor is listed in the 1948 issue of Farm Implement News Buyer's Guide. Its American "General" Model 600 garden tractor weighed 950 lbs. and used a Gladden single cylinder, Model 75 engine with a 2-3/4 x 3-inch bore and stroke. Further information has not been found.

COLLECTOR VALUES	1	2	3	4
MODEL 600 GARDEN TRACTOR	$500	$300	$200	$100

American Mfg. Company

INDIANAPOLIS, INDIANA

A trade note of 1913 indicates this company was organized "to build tractors" but no further information has been located concerning this firm.

American Merchandise Mart

PHILADELPHIA, PENNSYLVANIA

This company offered its Farmwell Jr. garden tractor in the late 1940s. The 1948 Buyer's Guide from Farm Implement News notes the Farmwell only for this year and no further details have been located.

American Standard Tractor Company

MINNEAPOLIS, MINNESOTA

This firm appears in the 1920 tractor directories, although a suitable illustration of the tractor has not been located. The company remained in business until 1922. Rated at 17 drawbar and 23 belt hp, this tractor was equipped with the "American Standard" transmission, which was claimed to be very simple and durable. Gilbert Amonsen of Minneapolis secured Patent No. 1,318,471 covering the engine used for the tractor. It was two-cycle with a very unusual port design.

American Steel Tractor Company

CANTON, OHIO

American Steel Tractor

This is a 1947 model built by American Steel Tractor Corporation of Canton, Ohio. It was tested in Nebraska in June 1947. It failed nearly all the tests. The engine overheated under heavy load and the rear end got so hot water had to be poured on it to cool it during the tests. Only five units were ever built and the tractor never made it to production. The results of the Nebraska testing left hard feelings between the engineers and the company, which resulted in dissolution of the venture. Three of the five tractors still exist. The tractor in the photo sold at the Ed Spiess Auction for $17,000.

American 15-30

American Swiss Magneto Company

TOLEDO, OHIO

Macultivator Company at Sandusky, Ohio, went out of business in the late 1920s, probably about 1929 or 1930. American Swiss Magneto took over the Macultivator line and continued to offer parts for them through the 1950s, though how long it manufactured the garden tractors is unclear.

See: Macultivator Company

COLLECTOR VALUES	1	2	3	4
MACULTIVATOR GARDEN TRACTOR	$750	$500	$200	$100

American 3-Way Prism Company

LAPORTE, INDIANA

The September 1914 issue of Gas Power magazine notes this company was about to begin building a small tractor offering 15 drawbar hp and 24 belt hp. It was to be equipped with a four-cylinder vertical engine with a total weight of the tractor about 5,000 lbs. Because 3-Way Prism was best known as a manufacturer of architectural lighting systems (including skylights and sidewalk lights), this was an unusual venture. Aside from this mention, no further information has ever been located on the company's proposed tractor.

American Tractor & Foundry Company

CHARLES CITY, IOWA

This firm was the immediate successor of American Engine & Tractor Company. It appears the company was reorganized or renamed in late 1919 or early 1920. No traces of its tractors have been found. A 1920 issue of the Patent Office Gazette illustrated the company trademark for the "Americo" tractors and engines, noting the company first used this tradename in February 1920, but after this time the firm disappeared from view.

See: American Engine & Tractor Company

Trademark for "Americo" tractors

American Tractor Company

DES MOINES, IOWA

This firm is listed in 1916 as the manufacturer of the American Oil Tractor. Rated at 18 drawbar and 35 belt hp, the American Oil Tractor used a four-cylinder engine with a 5 x 7-inch bore and stroke. The tractor was of conventional four-wheel design with the engine placed paral-lel to the tractor frame and between the rear wheels. It weighed 6,300 lbs. and sold for $1,600.

American Tractor Corporation

PEORIA, ILLINOIS

The American tractor, the work of John W. Kinross, emerged in 1918. American, like many other companies, withered under fierce competition and the postwar depression of the early 1920s.

The American 15-30 shown here weighed 4,600 lbs., and was priced at $1,765. Power was provided by an Erd four-cylinder motor with a 4 x 6-inch bore and stroke. This model was replaced by the Yankee 15-25 in 1920. Production of the American and Yankee models ended about 1922.

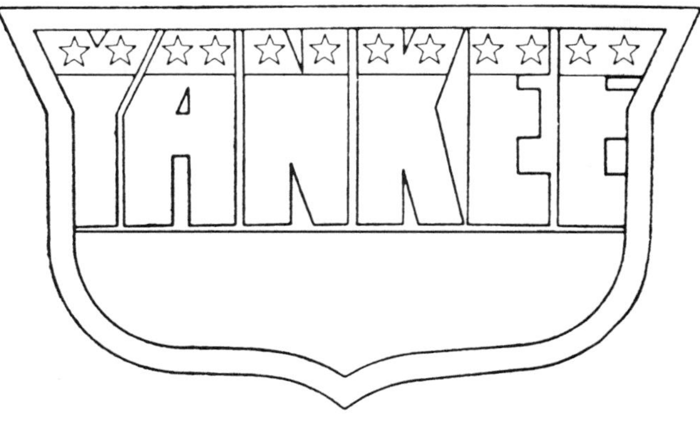

"Yankee" trademark

In a trademark application of 1920, American Tractor Corporation claimed that the "Yankee" trademark shown here had first been used April 1, 1918.

American Tractor Company

DETROIT, MICHIGAN

No information available.

American Tractor Company

PITTSBURGH, PENNSYLVANIA

No information available.

American Tractor Corporation

CHURUBUSCO, INDIANA

American began building its crawler tractors in late 1949, with full-fledged production coming the following year.

Terratrac GT-25

From 1950 to 1953 Ameri-can offered the Terratrac GT-25. Weighing less than two tons, the GT-25 had a turning radius of only six feet. Options included a PTO shaft, belt pulley, and a hydraulic lift system.

The Terratrac GT-30 was built from 1951 to 1954. This model was capable of about 25 drawbar hp and, like other Terratrac models of the period, was available with an optional three-point hitch system. It was equipped with a Continental F-140 engine. During this same period, American also built the similar GT-34 crawler, and from 1952 to 1954 it offered the DT-34, the company's first diesel-powered crawler tractor.

Terratrac GT-30

Nebraska Test Data

Model: Terratrac GT-30

Test No. 471

Date Tested: May 19 to May 27, 1952

Weighing 4,471 lbs., the Terratrac GT-30 featured a four-cylinder Continental Red Seal engine. Rated at 1,850 rpm, this engine carried a 3-3/16 x 4-3/8-inch bore and stroke for a 140 cubic inch displacement. Advertised speeds of 1.78, 2.81, and 4.61 mph were featured, with the 10-hour rated drawbar load run of Test H being made in second gear. At a rated load of 19.85 drawbar hp the GT-30 pulled 2,727 lbs. at 2.73 mph with a slippage of 3.12 percent. Fuel economy was recorded at 8.55 hp-hours per gallon. Test G achieved a low-gear maximum pull of 4,518 lbs. at 1.64 mph. Effective with the 1952 testing season, torque in lbs.-ft. was listed in each test. The GT-30 achieved a maximum torque of 241.5 lbs.-ft. at 1,152 rpm engine speed. Test D, at a rated belt load of 26.81 hp yielded a fuel economy of 10.71 hp-hours per gallon, and climbed slightly to 11.02 under a Test C operating maximum load of 28.92 belt hp. No repairs or adjustments were noted during 41 hours of operating time.

COLLECTOR VALUES	1	2	3	4
GT-30 TERRATRAC	$6,000	$4,000	$2,500	$1,000

During 1954 American introduced a new tractor series with its Terratrac 200 crawler, which was similar to the Terratrac GT-30 it replaced. American also introduced the Terratrac 300 crawler in 1954, and it remained in production until 1958. The Terratrac 400 and Terratrac 500 tractors also made their debut in 1954. The latter was equipped with a torque converter and was also known as the Terramatic.

Terratrac 200 crawler

In 1956, J.I. Case Company bought out American Tractor Company, making it the basis for the con-tinuing line of Case crawler tractors. In 1957 American introduced its Terratrac 600 crawler, the largest the company had built, and production continued until 1962. American Tractor's concept of using a torque converter drive on smaller tractors had never been tried before, although Allis-Chalmers HD-21was equipped with one. Case applied the torque converter concept to its wheel tractors in the form of the Case-O-Matic drive.

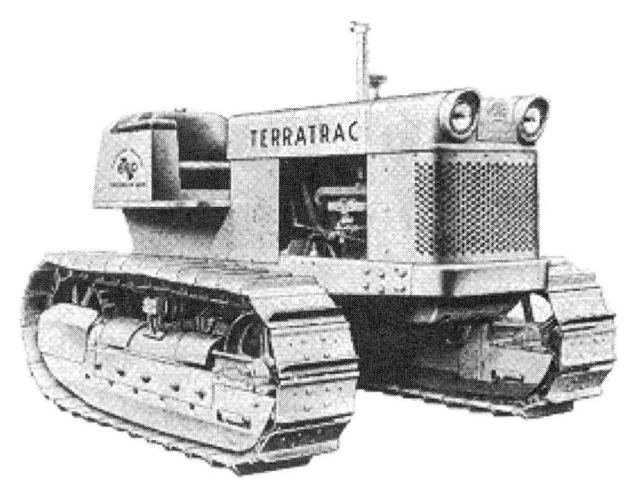

Terratrac 600 crawler

American Tractor and Harvester Company

STUTTGART, ARKANSAS

No information available.

American Tractor & Implement Company

CINCINNATI, OHIO

In 1920 the American Ground Hog tractor appeared. Weighing 6200 lbs., it had a

17-1/2 -31 hp rating. It featured an Erd four-cylinder engine with a 4 x 6-inch bore and stroke. This tractor listed at $2,800.

American Well Works

AURORA, ILLINOIS

Aurora traction engine

American Well Works was established in 1866 and the company developed a line of internal combustion engines in the 1890s. Sometime around 1898 American designed and manufactured its Aurora traction engine. Production likely contin-ued for only a short time, and few details have been found con-cerning the Aurora tractor.

Anderson Company

MINNESOTA TRANSFER, MINNESOTA

Anderson tractor

A single-page circular describing the Anderson tractor is about the only information that has been uncovered regarding this company. Rated at 25 belt hp, the Anderson used a four-cylinder engine. With a single drive wheel, the complicated differential gearing was eliminated. The specific date of manufacture is unknown, but it was probably sometime around 1915.

Anderson Foundry & Machine Company

ANDERSON, INDIANA

A trade note from around 1915 indicates that Anderson Foundry was entering the tractor business, but no further information has been located. Anderson did make a substantial mark in the oil and diesel engine business at least into the 1920s.

Andrews Tractor Company

MINNEAPOLIS, MINNESOTA

Andrews tractor

George C. Andrews organized this company in 1914, ostensibly to build the tractor he had designed. Andrews applied for a patent on the drive mechanism of his tractor and Patent No. 1,311,943 was issued in 1919. A friction-drive transmission provided infinitely variable ground speeds from 1 to 4 mph. Initially, the Andrews was equipped with a four-cylinder, two-cycle engine that delivered 10 drawbar and 20 belt hp. The company was reorganized as Andrews-Kinkade Tractor Company in 1921.

Andrews-Kinkade Tractor Company

MINNEAPOLIS, MINNESOTA

In 1921 Andrews Tractor Co. was reorganized as Andrews-Kinkade Tractor Co. Within a very short time, perhaps only a few weeks, the company was again reorganized as American Farm Machinery Company. The new company went on to build the Kinkade garden tractors for several years. Despite all the corporate changes, the company introduced its Andrews 18-36 tractor. This machine used a Climax four-cylinder engine with a 5 x 6-1/2-inch bore and stroke. The tractor was marketed for only a short time.

See: American Farm Machinery Company; Andrews Tractor Company

Angola Engine & Foundry Company

ANGOLA, INDIANA

This firm was in the gasoline engine business by 1904, and was listed as a builder of "gasoline traction engines" between 1904 and 1909. The company built very few engines during its existence, which ended in 1911. No images or specifications have been located.

Ann Arbor Hay Press Company

ANN ARBOR, MICHIGAN

Ann Arbor had a long career in the hay press business, eventually selling out to Oliver Farm Equipment Company in the 1940s. In 1910 the company offered this self-propelled hay press, one of the earliest self-propelled balers on the market. Although the traction gearing was not heavy enough for heavy drawbar loads, it was able to move the machine from place to place.

Ann Arbor self-propelled hay press

Andrews 18-36 tractor

Antigo Tractor Corporation

ANTIGO, WISCONSIN

Antigo Quadpull tractor

The Antigo Quadpull tractor was listed in vari-ous directories between 1921 and 1923. The unique four-wheel-drive design was of interest to some farmers, and with a 15-25 hp rating the Quadpull was sufficiently large for the average farm. Weighing 4,500 lbs., the Quadpull had all gears enclosed and running in oil.

Appleton Mfg. Company

BATAVIA, ILLINOIS

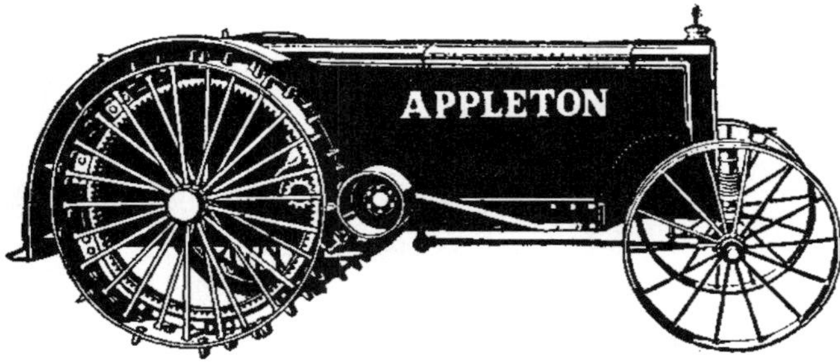

14-28 tractor

This company was established in 1872 to build various farm machines, including corn shellers, wood saws and feed grinders. By the early 1900s the company had gained considerable status, and in 1917 its 14-28 tractor was announced. By 1919 the tractor was rated downward to a 12-20 model, although it continued to use the same Buda four-cylinder engine. Rated at 1,050 rpm, the engine featured a 4-1/4 x 5-1/2-inch bore and stroke. Production of the 12-20 tractor ended about 1924. The company remained in business until about 1950.

COLLECTOR VALUES	1	2	3	4
12-20 (1917-1924)	$7,000	$5,000	$2,000	$1,000

Ariens Company

BRILLION, WISCONSIN

Ariens C tiller

Ariens Company first appears in the trade directories in the 1930s. However, by 1948 the company was the largest of its kind in the country, specializing in garden tillers. Shown here is the Ariens C tiller of 1941. It used a 5-1/2 hp engine. At the time, Ariens was building similar machines in sizes up to 14 hp. Ariens builds and markets a full line of tillers and snowblowers today.

COLLECTOR VALUES	1	2	3	4
C TILLER	$850	$700	$400	$250

A.P. Armington

EUCLID, OHIO

Armington 10-20

During 1921 and 1922 the Armington 10-20 was offered at a list price of $1,100. The Arm-ington featured a friction-drive transmission, providing infinitely variable speeds, both forward and reverse. Weighing 3,800 lbs., it used a Waukesha four-cylinder engine with a 3-3/4 x 5-1/4-inch bore and stroke.

Arnold-Sandberg Machine Company

TERRE HAUTE, INDIANA

The April 1911 issue of Gas Review magazine illustrated the Arnold-Sandberg tractor, which was developed by D.B. Arnold and others. Weighing 4,300 lbs., it was equipped with a two-cylinder 15 hp engine. This tractor had features that would later be embodied in successful row-crop tractors. Unfortunately, designers probably never thought of their machine as a row-crop tractor. Aside from its 1911 announcement, it doesn't appear the Arnold-Sandberg gained great fame or saw any extensive production.

Arnold-Sandberg tractor

Aro Tractor Company

MINNEAPOLIS, MINNESOTA

Aro Trademark

Aro Tractor Company first appeared in the 1921 trade directories. Its small garden tractor was called a 3-6, meaning it had 3 drawbar and 6 belt hp. Weighing 1,000 lbs., it was priced at $465. The company apparently remained in business until the late 1920s. A trademark application indicated Aro first used the illustrated mark on or about February 1, 1921. Numerous companies attempted to market power cultivators and garden tractors in the 1920s. A few succeeded...but most did not.

Aro small garden tractor

Arrow Mfg. Company

DENVER, COLORADO

The Arrow All-Purpose tractor was listed in trade directories for 1948 only. This small tractor was equipped with an Onan two-cylinder engine with a 3 x 2-3/4-inch bore and stroke. A small, simple little tractor, it used a twin V-belt drive with a tightener as the clutch.

Arthurdale Farm Equipment Corporation

ARTHURDALE, WEST VIRGINIA

Co-op No. 3

Duplex Machinery Company at Battle Creek, Michigan sent a Co-op tractor to Nebraska's Tractor Test Laboratory in 1936. (See Test No. 275 in the Duplex listing.) A year or so later the name changed to Co-Operative Mfg. Co., and the 1940 trade directories listed this firm as the manufacturer of the Co-op No. 2 and Co-op No. 3 tractors. After World War II began that all ended for Co-op tractor line.

See: Co-Operative Mfg. Co.; Duplex Machinery Company

Athey Tractor Company

CHICAGO, ILLINOIS

No information available

Atlantic Machine & Mfg. Company

CLEVELAND, OHIO

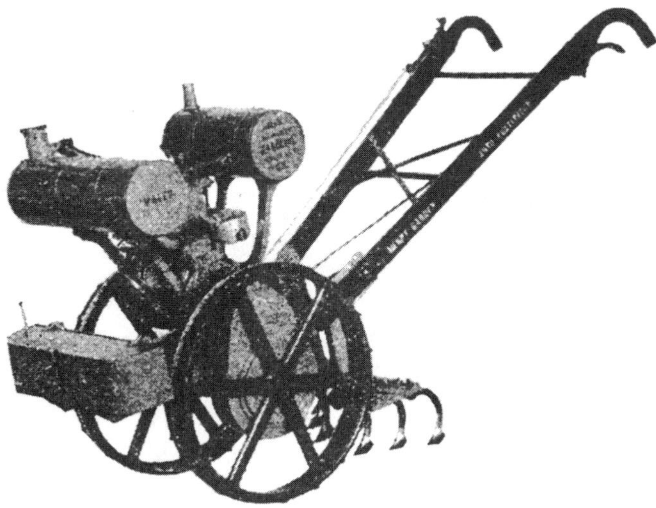

Merry Garden Tractor

In 1920 the Merry Garden Tractor appeared. This walk-behind unit weighed 360 lbs., and was powered by a 2-hp engine. By 1924 the Merry was being built by Federal Foundry Supply Co., also of Cleveland. Federal appears only as a parts supplier for the Merry by the early 1930s.

COLLECTOR VALUES	1	2	3	4
MERRY GARDEN TRACTOR	$1,500	$850	$450	$250

Atlas Engineering Company

CLINTONVILLE, WISCONSIN

Atlas tractor

About 1927 Atlas Engineering Co. was formed as a successor to the Topp-Stewart Tractor Company, also of Clintonville. The latter had its beginnings in 1917, and was organized a year earlier as the Four Wheel Tractor Company. The design was by D. S. Stewart, who was also involved with the Antigo Tractor Company, Antigo, Wisconsin. Stewart's partner was Dr. Charles Topp. The model shown here was rated at 30 drawbar and 45 belt hp.

COLLECTOR VALUES	1	2	3	4
ATLAS	$45,000	–	–	$4,500

Aulson Tractor Company

WAUKEGAN, ILLINOIS

Aulson 12-25 tractor

In 1918 Aulson announced its new 12-25 tractor. Weighing 5,800 lbs., it used a four-cylinder engine with a 5 x 6-1/2-inch bore and stroke. For 1919 the belt hp rating was raised to 34, using the same engine as before, but taking advantage of the vastly underrated designation used the previous year. After 1919 the Aul-son disappeared from the trade directories.

COLLECTOR VALUES	1	2	3	4
AULSON 12-25	–	–	$10,000	–

Aultman & Taylor Machinery Company

MANSFIELD, OHIO

Aultman-Taylor 30-60

In late 1910 or early 1911 Aultman & Taylor introduced its 30-60 tractor. The early model, illustrated below, used an induced draft radiator. Weighing almost 25,000 lbs., the 30-60 remained on the market until the company was bought out by Advance-Rumely Thresher Company in January 1924.

The square radiator of the earlier models was replaced with a round tubular style in late 1913 or early 1914. Dual fans pulled air through 196 two-inch tubes in the 120-gallon radiator. The four-cylinder engine carried a 7 x 9-inch bore and stroke and was rated at 500 rpm. The 30-60 was capable of pulling more than 9,000 lbs. Two clutches were used—one in the flywheel-controlled forward ground travel, and one on the belt pulley or bandwheel used for belt work, or for reverse.

Nebraska Test Data

Model: Aultman-Taylor 30-60

Test No. 30

Date Tested: June 30 to July 20, 1920

Although the 30-60 OilPull of Test No. 8 made Rumely's claims of great power and fuel economy quite evident, the Aultman-Taylor 30-60 proved to be even more powerful, and slightly more fuel efficient. In the maximum brake hp tests, 75.49 maximum hp was developed using kerosene. Even under this load, 7.46 hp hours were developed for each gallon of fuel, for a total consumption of 10.12 gph. The same test conducted with gasoline produced an economy rating of 8.8 hp-hours per gallon, with total consumption coming to 9.1 gph. By changing from kerosene to gasoline, hp rose to the maximum 80.1. A similar situation occurred at the drawbar. Slightly over 58 hp was developed when operating on either gasoline or kerosene, but drawbar pull came to 9,160 lbs. at a speed of 2.38 mph. Drivewheel slippage was slightly over 4 percent. During the 44 hours of testing, only minor adjustments and repairs were necessary. Rated at 550 rpm, the 30-60 carried a four-cylinder, horizontal, valve-in-head engine with a 7-inch bore and stroke. Shipping weight was 24,450 lbs.

COLLECTOR VALUES	1	2	3	4
30-60				
ROUND RADIATOR	$70,000	$50,000	$30,000	$8,500
SQUARE RADIATOR	–	$51,000	–	–

Aultman-Taylor 25-50

Early in 1915 the Aultman-Taylor 25-50 came on the market. It was virtually a clone of the 30-60, varying primarily in its physical size. The four-cylinder engine used a 6 x 9-inch bore and stroke. The 25-50 remained on the market until 1918.

COLLECTOR VALUES	1	2	3	4
25-50	$60,000	$45,000	$28,000	$12,000

Aultman-Taylor 18-36

Aultman & Taylor introduced its 18-36 tractor in late 1915. Its four-cylinder engine operated at 600 rpm and carried a 5 x 8-inch bore and stroke. This model was of the same basic design as the ever-popular 30-60 tractor. The smaller-sized machines found competition very difficult in a market that was being inundated by a host of lightweight tractors. It appears the 18-36 was revamped and rerated as the 22-45 tractor in 1918.

COLLECTOR VALUES	1	2	3	4
18-36	$50,000	$45,000	$35,000	$12,000

Aultman-Taylor 22-45

With the 1918 introduction of the 22-45 Aultman-Taylor tractor, the company phased out the 18-36 and 25-50 models. Following the same general design as the 30-60, the 22-45 used a four-cylinder engine with a 5-1/2 x 8-inch bore and stroke. Weighing almost 13,000 lbs., the 22-45 was the only heavyweight Aultman-Taylor design to use a two-speed transmission. This tractor remained in the Aultman-Taylor line until the 1924 buyout by Advance-Rumely.

Nebraska Test Data

Model: Aultman-Taylor 22-45
Test No. 32
Date Tested: July 1 to July 19, 1920

The Aultman-Taylor 22-45 model had its share of problems during the test. On several occasions it was necessary to clean or repair the carburetor, a Model E Kingston. Because of a poor cylinder casting, the head gasket for cylinders 3 and 4 burned out and had to be replaced. Due probably to the fault of the operator, the left countershaft bearing burned out and had to be re-babbitted and the countershaft drive gear was noticeably worn by the end of testing. Brief specifications for the 22-45 included a four-cylinder horizontal, valve-in-head engine with a 5-1/2 x 8-inch bore and stroke. Rated speed was 600 rpm. Two forward speeds were available of 2.13 and 2.93 mph. Shipping weight was 12,880 lbs. A total of 46-2/3 maximum brake hp was recorded. On the rated load test, 5.36 gallons of fuel were burned per hour, and an economy of 8.38 hp-hours per gallon was recorded. Running in low gear, the 22-45 pulled 4,986 lbs. at a speed of 2.46 mph for a maximum of 28.1 drawbar hp. Kerosene was used throughout the tests.

COLLECTOR VALUES	1	2	3	4
22-45 (1916-24)	$50,000	$45,000	$35,000	$12,000

Aultman-Taylor 15-30

During 1918 Aultman-Taylor announced its new 15-30 tractor. This was the company's first (and only) entry into lightweight tractor market—lightweight compared with the 30-60 and its cousins. The four-cylinder Climax engine used a 5-1/2 x 6-inch bore and stroke. Production continued until the Advance-Rumely buyout of 1924.

Nebraska Test Data

Model: Aultman-Taylor 15-30
Test No. 31
Date Tested: July 1 to July 8, 1920

Featuring a 5 x 6-1/2-inch bore and stroke, 15-30 was rated at 900 rpm and weighed 8,240 lbs. The four-cylinder vertical engine was of L-head design. A single forward speed of 2.49 mph was provided in the test model. Standard equipment included a Kingston Model L carburetor and an Eisemann Model G4 magneto. Kerosene fuel was used throughout the test. During the two-hour rated load test, 30.4 brake hp was developed with a fuel consumption of 4.08 gph, resulting in an economy of 7.44 hp-hours per gallon. On maximum load, 34.37 brake hp was recorded, with fuel consumption of 5.79 gph. Slightly more than 2,800 lbs. of pull was recorded at the drawbar, at a speed of 2.8 mph and a crankshaft speed of 944 rpm. Slightly more than 21 drawbar hp resulted from this test. Minor problems occurred but none were significant. Coolant temperatures ranged from 163 to 191 degrees throughout the test procedures.

COLLECTOR VALUES	1	2	3	4
15-30	$25,000	$20,000	$10,000	$5,000

F. C. Austin Company

CHICAGO, ILLINOIS

F.C. Austin had a long career in building construction machinery, but built agricultural-oriented machinery for a few years starting around 1914. In 1920 the F. C. Austin Machinery Company was incorporated. It took over the assets of the parent firm, along with a couple of other construction machinery manufacturers, and quietly left the tractor business.

The company offered this gasoline road roller about 1914. It consisted of a huge single-cylinder engine that was built by Austin, along with the heavy framework and ballast that made it an effective road roller.

Austin 18-35 Multipedal crawler tractor

About 1916 or 1917 Austin introduced its 18-35 Multipedal crawler tractor. Weighing more than five tons, it was equipped with an Automatic four-cylinder engine featuring a 5-1/2 x 6-inch bore and stroke. Exceptionally long tracks were used; they were carried on six rollers. The final drive was through heavy chain to the bull gears.

Austin 12-20 crawler tractor

About 1917 Austin developed its 12-20 crawler tractor. It carried a Buffalo four-cylinder engine with a 4 x 5- inch bore and stroke. The compact design of the 12-20 should have gained it some popularity in the agricultural trade, but the company made only a small effort to enter this market. Instead, it appears that Austin focused its attention on the construction industry.

Little is known of the Austin 12-20, which debuted in 1919. Apparently a four-wheel-drive design, it is shown in the photo equipped with special road planing equipment. The company was primarily interested in building construction machinery, particularly for road building. Austin line made little impact on the agricultural market.

Austin 12-20 tractor

Austin 20-40 crawler tractor

Austin gasoline road roller

In 1919 and 1920 Austin offered its 20-40 crawler tractor. This one was a remodeled and enlarged version of the earlier 18-35 Multipedal design. At this time Austin also announced a big 125 hp crawler, rated to pull 12,500 lbs. at the drawbar. The 75-125 model was equipped with a six-cylinder Buffalo engine with a 7-1/2 x 9-inch bore and stroke.

Austin 15-30 tractor

In 1920 the Austin 15-30 appeared, the only conventional four-wheel design to come from the Austin factories. Production of the Austin 15-30, along with the rest of the tractor line, ended at the time of the merger, and the new company apparently ended all efforts in the tractor business.

Auto Tractor Company

CHICAGO, ILLINOIS

This firm was one of the first to make an attachment that converted an automobile into a tractor. With this particular attachment the family car could be changed to a tractor with relative ease, and still be ready for church on Sunday, or for a family outing. Most farmers, and perhaps their wives as well, held this idea in disdain, so most of the tractor conversion kits never met with great success. This one was available in 1913, and perhaps earlier.

Auto Tractor Company

SAN FRANCISCO, CALIFORNIA

No information available.

Auto-Track-Tractor Syndicate

SAN FRANCISCO, CALIFORNIA

Beginning about 1920 the Auto-Track 30-50 crawler tractor was on the market, remaining there until about 1924. Aside from trade references to this model, little else is known about the company. The 30-50 was equipped with a Buda four-cylinder engine with a 5 x 6-1/2 -inch bore and stroke. The spring-mounted track rollers are unusual and feature extensive use of ball and roller bearings. This was an asset to the design as well. The 30-50 weighed nearly five tons.

Automotive Corporation

TOLEDO, OHIO

The Automotive tractor was built at Fort Wayne, Indiana, starting around 1918. The company built a new plant and moved to Toledo, Ohio, in 1920. Probably due in part to intense competition at the time, the Automotive tractor left the scene about 1922.

Early Automotive 12-24 tractor

Auto Tractor attachment in use

The Automotive 12-24 first appeared sometime around 1918. It was a line-drive tractor, using three leather lines to control all operations of the tractor from a towed implement or wagon. Initially the Automotive used a Buda four-cylinder engine with a 3-3/4 x 5-1/2-inch bore and stroke.

Beginning with the 1920 model, Automotive 12-24 tractors were equipped with a larger Hercules four-cylinder engine; the latter used a 4 x 5-1/8-inch bore and stroke. This engine was vastly improved, using a five-bearing crankshaft, along with full force-feed lubrication.

Late Automotive 12-24 tractor

Automotive Motor Plow Company

CARTHAGE, MISSOURI

No information available

Autopower Company

DETROIT, MICHIGAN

"HELPING HENRY"

AUTOPOW

In 1916 Autopower Co. began offering special devices that enabled the family car to be used for farm power needs. In some cases this simply consisted of jacking up one hind wheel, attaching a suitable pulley, and connecting a belt to the feed grinder or the wood saw. Among these devices was the "AUTOPLOW" and the "HELPING HENRY." The latter was presumably for attachment to the inimitable Ford Model T.

Avery Company

PEORIA, ILLINOIS

Avery Power Machinery Company

PEORIA, ILLINOIS

Avery Company had its beginnings in 1874, and by 1891 was building steam traction engines. The company entered the tractor business in 1909, and manufactured a number of models until financial problems emerged in the early 1920s. The firm declared bankruptcy in 1924 and was reorganized as Avery Farm Machinery Company and at this time it left the tractor market. Avery reentered the tractor business in 1938 with the Ro-Trak, but production of that model was stopped in 1941 with the outbreak of World War II. It marked the end of the Avery tractors.

In 1909 the company announced its "Farm and City Tractor." Round wooden plugs in the wheels provided necessary traction, and the final drives were with heavy roller chains. This model was furnished with a four-cylinder engine with a 4-3/4 x 5-inch bore and stroke. It was capable of 36 hp. Production ended in 1914.

Avery 25 H.P. tractor

Farm and City Tractor

COLLECTOR VALUES	1	2	3	4
FARM AND CITY TRACTOR	$50,000	$40,000	$20,000	$10,000

During 1909 Avery Company built this big single-cylinder tractor. Equipped with a 12 x 18-inch bore and stroke, it should have had about 60 hp with a rated speed of 350 rpm. Avery took it to the 1910 Winnipeg Tractor Demonstration, and it performed so poorly that it was withdrawn.

New Avery tractor

With Avery's original 1910 tractor design a failure, the company came out with a completely new model in 1911. Rated at 20 drawbar and 35 belt hp, this model used a two-cylinder engine with a 7-3/4 x 8-inch bore and stroke. Although it would undergo further changes and refinements, the design would typify Avery tractors for some years to come. The New Avery Gas Traction Engine first appeared in 1912, only a few months after the initial 1911 prototypes. The addition of a half-cab and a completely redesigned cooling system were the most obvious changes. Weighing almost six tons, the 20-35 was priced at about $1,800. Production of this model ended in 1915.

COLLECTOR VALUES	1	2	3	4
20-35	$68,000	$50,000	$30,000	$18,000

Avery 40-80 and 45-65

During 1912 Avery Company developed its 40-80 model, announcing it publicly in January 1913. This big $2,650 tractor weighed 22,000 lbs. The four-cylinder engine used a 7-3/4 x 8-inch bore and stroke and had a rated speed of 600 rpm. The 40-80 designation remained until 1920 when it was tested at Nebraska. Its performance there dictated that the tractor be rerated as a 45-65, and this occurred in October 1920.

Nebraska Test Data

Model: Avery 45-65

Test No. 44

Date Tested: July 26 to August 3, 1920

Although this Avery model walked into the test procedures with a 40-80 manufacturer's rating, it left with a somewhat different rating of 45-65 hp. With an engine speed of 634 rpm, the Avery was able to pull 7,812 lbs. at 2-1/4 mph on the rated drawbar test, for a calculated total of 46.93 hp. At maximum load, 49.97 drawbar hp was obtained, with a maximum pull of 8,475 lbs.. These results were somewhat higher than the nominal rating, prompting the company to raise it to 45 drawbar hp. On the brake hp tests the story was different. Instead of the 80 nominal hp ascribed by the company, only 69.23 was actually available on the maximum load test. During the two-hour rated load test, 65.73 brake hp was developed at a crankshaft speed of 612 rpm. The resultant fuel economy was 7.26 hp-hours per gallon on rated load, rising to a figure of 8.41 on maximum load. Rated load fuel consumption totaled 9.06 gph. Weighing 22,000 lbs., the 45-65 carried the familiar Avery four-cylinder, horizontal opposed engine, but with a 7-3/4 x 8-inch bore and stroke. Forward speeds of 2 and 3 mph were provided. This giant could easily pull eight to 10 moldboard plows or 18 disc plows, according to contemporary Avery advertising.

COLLECTOR VALUES	1	2	3	4
40-80	$85,000	$60,000	$35,000	$15,000

Production of the 12-25 Avery tractor began late in 1912. Weighing 7,500 lbs., the 12-25 was equipped with a two-cylinder engine with a 6-1/2 x 7-inch bore and stroke.

Avery 12-25

Nebraska Test Data

Model: Avery 12-25

Test No. 71

Date Tested: March 25 to June 13, 1921

A summary of Test No. 71 failed to note why testing was spread out over nearly three months to perform about 35 hours of running time. Perhaps the engineer's notes might give a clue: "Before any official data was taken, the rear exhaust valve was ground and both spark plugs were replaced by long-skirted plugs. The pistons were taken out and turned down about .005 inch. At the end of the maximum drawbar test, the compression of rear cylinder was weak." Despite these problems, the Test Report states: "there were no indications of undue wear in any part, nor any weakness that might require early repair." Brief specifications noted a two-cylinder engine of Avery's own design, carrying a 6-1/2 x 7 inch stroke. Rated speed was 700 rpm. Standard equipment items were a K-W Model TK magneto and a Kingston Model E carburetor. Total weight was 7,500 lbs. At rated drawbar load, 13.77 hp was developed using low gear. This resulted in a pull of 2,441 lbs. at 2.12 mph. At rated brake load, 25.2 hp was developed with a fuel economy of 8.08 hp-hours per gallon. Fuel consumption on this test totaled 3.12 gallons per hour.

COLLECTOR VALUES	1	2	3	4
12-25	$35,000	$25,000	$18,000	$10,000

Avery 12-25 Nursery Tractor

About 1916 Avery announced its specially equipped 12-25 Nursery Tractor. This special design featured a high-clearance front axle, along with a protective tunnel for tender nursery stock. The half-cab had been removed, and the platform had been modified. Production of this design was probably quite limited.

Avery 8-16

During 1914 the Avery line grew to include its small 8-16 model. Essentially the same design as its larger cousins, the 8-16 used a two-cylinder engine with a 5-1/2 x 6-inch bore and stroke. Rated speed was 750 rpm. Although the 8-16 began life with a list price of $900, this dropped to $700 by 1917. Production of this model continued until about 1922.

Nebraska Test Data

Model: Avery 8-16

Test No. 72

Date Tested: March 28 to May 31, 1921

As with earlier Avery models, the 8-16 featured a horizontal, valve-in-head opposed engine—in this case with a 5-1/2 x 6-inch bore and stroke. Rated speed was 750 rpm. Regular accessory equipment included a Kingston Model E carburetor and a K-W magneto. The 8-16 was equipped with two forward speeds, 2-1/4 and 3-1/2 mph. Total weight was 4,900 lbs. As with the 12-25 Avery tested under No. 71, the pistons were removed and relieved. All valves were ground after the limbering-up run, and the kerosene gasifiers were exchanged for gasoline equipment to develop rated belt hp. Using this fuel, 16.66 brake hp was indicated in the rated load test. Total fuel consumption came to 2.15 gallons per hour for an economy of 7.76 hp-hours per gallon. On the drawbar, 9.99 maximum hp was achieved, corresponding to a 1,690 pound pull at 2.22 mph. Some 42 hours were required to complete the tests. Avery ads rated this tractor ideal for pulling two moldboard plows, or two or three disc plows.

COLLECTOR VALUES	1	2	3	4
8-16	$35,000	$25,000	$18,000	$10,500

Avery 25-50

Avery's 25-50 tractor saw first light in 1914. This model started with a retail price of $2,300, but eventually this price fell due to competition. Weighing 12,500 lbs., the 25-50 carried a four-cylinder engine with a 6-1/2 x 7-inch bore and stroke. Production continued into 1922 when it was replaced with an improved model. In 1915 Avery announced electric starting and electric lights as an available option for its tractors. It does not appear this option gained much favor because no mention of it has been found in subsequent years.

Nebraska Test Data

Model: Avery 25-50

Test No.43

Date Tested: July 26 to July 30, 1920

The 25-50 featured a valve-in-head, four-cylinder, horizontal, opposed engine. It had a 6-1/2 x 8-inch bore and stroke, with a rated speed of 700 rpm. In low gear a ground speed of 2 mph was realized, and in high gear, things moved right along at 3 mph. The ever-popular Kingston carburetor and K-W magneto were no less a feature in the 25-50. Kerosene fuel was used throughout the test and, in contrast to some of the smaller Avery models, fuel economy actually increased under maximum load as compared to rated load. In this, 7.91 hp-hours per gallon were calculated at rated load, while on the maximum load of 56.68 hp, 8.05 hp hours resulted. Throughout the drawbar and brake tests, coolant temperatures ranged from 208 to 212 degrees F. Nearly 31.5 maximum drawbar hp was recorded in the maximum drawbar pull test using low gear, for a maximum pull of 4,415 lbs. Except for adjusting the clutch and installing a new governor spring, mechanical repairs were of no consequence. Test engineers did note the tractor cab required additional bracing "to hold it rigidly to the engine frame." Avery claimed a capacity of five or six moldboard plows or 12 disc plows for the 25-50.

COLLECTOR VALUES	1	2	3	4
25-50	$40,000	$30,000	$20,000	$10,000

Avery 18-36 tractor

Early in 1916 Avery announced its 18-36 tractor. It came along about the time that the old 20-35 was taken from production. Avery made tractor history in 1916 by being the first tractor manufacturer to use replaceable cylinder sleeves in its tractor engines. This tractor carried a four-cylinder engine using the same 5-1/2 x 6-inch bore and stroke as the little 8-16 tractor, although the latter had but a two-cylinder engine. Production of the 18-36 ended about 1921.

Nebraska Test Data

Model: Avery 18-36

Test No. 58

Date Tested: August 25 to September 9, 1920

From a design viewpoint, the 18-36 was virtually identical to the Avery models tested earlier in 1920. To its credit, no repairs or adjustments were noted throughout the test. At this point in the history of farm tractor development, few tractors could make this boast. Ground speeds could be chosen from two possibilities: low gear of 2.8 mph or high gear of 4 mph. Weighing 9,250 lbs., the 18-36 pulled a maximum of 4,590 lbs., or nearly 50 percent of its own weight. The resultant 27.5 maximum drawbar hp gave an ample reserve over Avery's nominal rating of 18 drawbar hp. Kerosene was used throughout the test. At rated brake hp, 6.31 hp-hours per gallon were recorded, along with a total consumption of 5.81 gph. Under maximum load, 44.5 hp was noted. The 18-36 carried Avery's usual four-cylinder, horizontal, opposed engine. A 5-1/2 x 6-inch bore and stroke was featured, with an operating speed of 800 rpm. Avery claimed this model could easily pull four or five moldboard or eight disc plows.

COLLECTOR VALUES	1	2	3	4
18-36	$25,000	$20,000	$15,000	$7,500

Avery 14-28 tractor

During 1919 Avery introduced its 14-28 tractor. This broadened the Avery line to eight distinct models, plus several styles of motor cul-tivators. Because of the unrelenting competition at the time, sales of the 14-28 were likely unrewarding, and production ceased by 1922.

Nebraska Test Data

Model: Avery 14-28

Test No. 42

Date Tested: July 21 to August 2, 1920

Weighing 7,540 lbs., the Avery 14-28 featured two forward speeds of 2-1/2 and 3-1/2 mph. At the drawbar, it made a maximum pull of 3,049 lbs. in low gear, or about 41 percent of its own weight. Fuel economy on the rated drawbar load was a rather disappointing 4.94 hp-hours per gallon of kerosene at a load of 17.68 hp. Rated brake hp revealed a far better fuel economy of 8.24 hp-hours per gallon, with a consumption of 3.42 gph and a load of 28.16 hp. Under maximum load conditions, 31.83 hp was recorded, with an economy of 7.63 hp-hours per gallon of kerosene. A K-W magneto and Kingston carburetor were standard features. A valve-in-head design was featured on the four-cylinder, horizontal, opposed engine. Specifications included a 4-5/8-inch bore and 7-inch stroke with a rated speed ranging from 700 to 900 rpm. Only minor adjustment problems were noted, although the valves were reground near the end of the test. Avery claimed that the 14-28 could easily pull three or four moldboard plows or five or six disc plows.

COLLECTOR VALUES	1	2	3	4
14-28	$18,000	$14,000	$10,000	$5,000

Avery 5-10 tractor

Originally priced at $295 the Avery 5-10 tractor made its debut in January 1916. Of special note, the operator's seat was located ahead of the rear wheels, with a large platform to the rear. This model used a four-cylinder engine rated at 1200 rpm, and carried a 3 x 4-inch bore and stroke. Production continued at least into 1919.

COLLECTOR VALUES	1	2	3	4
5-10	$7,000	$5,000	$3,000	$1,500

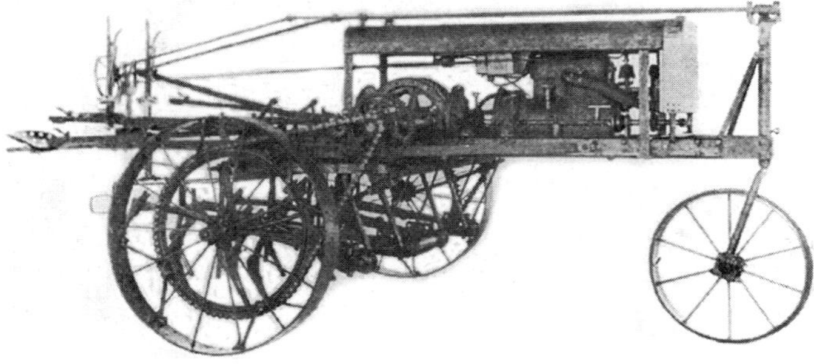

Avery Motor Cultivator

The Avery Motor Cultivator was first announced in the summer of 1916. The engine and drive train were essentially the same as the 5-10 tractor announced earlier in the year. This design was a one-row cultivator, using the same individual beams and control handles that were used on horse-drawn cultivators. This design left the market about 1920, and was replaced with the Model C, six-cylinder motor cultivator.

Avery did not limit its motor cultivator to cultivating alone. Other options included a mounted planter, one of the first such units ever built. The motor cultivator with its tricycle chassis design could certainly have been the basis for a row-crop tractor, but that would not come for about a decade after the 1916 Avery Motor Corn Planter illustrated here was announced.

Avery Motor Cultivator converted into a motor corn planter.

Nebraska Test Data

Model: Avery Motor Cultivator

Test No. 40

Date Tested: July 21 to July 25, 1920

Using the identical engine as the Avery Model C of Test No. 39, the Avery Motor Cultivator was the first such machine ever tested at Nebraska. Several mechanical problems occurred during the test, and of an altogether different sort than the difficulties experienced under Test No. 39. For some reason, the bolts holding the motor to the frame sheared off at various times, and mechanical difficulties plagued the governor. As with the Avery Model C, gasoline was the chosen fuel, but this particular tractor came up with slightly more brake hp, and a slight improvement in fuel economy over the Model C. Test No. 40 indicates that 15.54 brake hp was developed on the rated load test, with 6.22 hp-hours per gallon. On the drawbar, 8.99 maximum hp resulted, at a ground speed of 2.01 mph, for a maximum pull of 1,674 lbs. Three forward speeds were provided: 2, 2-1/2, and 5-1/2 mph. Total weight was 3,450 lbs. Coolant temperatures ranged from 199 to 210 degrees F. throughout the tests.

Avery "Road-Razer"

Avery 5-10 Single Row Cultivator

Nebraska Test Data

Model: Avery 5-10 Single Row Cultivator

Test No. 57

Date Tested: August 25 to September 8, 1920

A small four-cylinder, vertical, L-head engine powered the Avery single row cultivator. Designed and built by Avery, it carried a 3 x 4-inch bore and stroke with a rated speed of 1,200 rpm. Weighing only 2,650 lbs., this little tractor carried a three-speed transmission with speeds of 1-1/2, 2-1/8, and 4-1/4 mph. As with the larger Avery tractors, a Kingston carburetor and K-W magneto were adopted as standard equipment. Total fuel consumption was too small to warrant the expense of adding extra equipment to burn kerosene. The 5-10 went through the tests without any mechanical problems. Using second gear, a 6 hp drawbar load was imposed on the 5-10 for a 10-hour period, giving an average pull of 914 lbs. Fuel economy was nothing sensational on the rated brake hp test, with 5.45 hp-hours per gallon recorded as the final figure. With a 10.11 hp load, fuel consumption totaled 1.86 gph. Just over one additional hp appeared on the maximum brake hp test, although fuel economy improved slightly. The unit is shown here equipped with corn cultivating gangs. Note the unusual chain connection between the steering wheel and the steering column mounted on top of the engine housing.

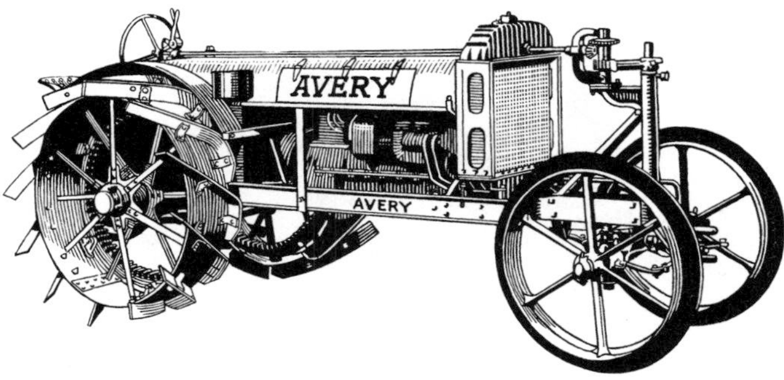

Avery six-cylinder orchard tractor

Late in 1919 Avery introduced its Model C six-cylinder tractor. It replaced the earlier 5-10 model, and permitted the Model C to operate as a two-row cultivator, and to handle a corn planter or other implements. Production of this model ended about 1924.

Introduced alongside the standard version of the Model C tractor was the Avery Six-Cylinder Orchard Special Tractor. The special fenders and smooth hood lines permitted close cultivation in orchard work.

Nebraska Test Data

Model: Avery Model C

Test No. 39

Date Tested: July 12 to August 4, 1920

The Avery Model C was the first six-cylinder tractor ever tested at Nebraska. Using a vertical, L-head design, the engine had a 3 x 4-inch bore and stroke with a rated speed of 1,250 rpm. Three forward speeds were provided: 1-5/8, 2-1/4 and 4-1/2 mph. Total weight was 3,164 lbs. Standard equipment included a K-W Model T magneto and a Kingston Model L carburetor. Several problems occurred during the test including a broken countershaft in the transmission and a broken drive chain and sprocket on the belt pulley drive. Using low gear, the Model C exerted a maximum pull of 1,962 lbs. with a ground speed of 1.74 mph, for a maximum of 8.65 drawbar hp. At rated brake hp, the Model C was not overly impressive on fuel economy—only 6.035 hp-hours per gallon resulted when operating at its rated 14 hp. Total consumption came to 2.33 gallons per hour.

COLLECTOR VALUES	1	2	3	4
MODEL C	$15,000	$12,000	$6,000	$3,000

About 1920 Avery offered a special lawn mowing tractor built over the 5-10. It consisted of a special extended frame and truck unit to carry the mower gangs. This tractor was built especially for maintaining golf courses and large estates. Apparently, sales of this outfit were limited.

Avery lawn mowing tractor

Avery six-cylinder motor cultivator

With the introduction of the Model C six-cylinder tractor in 1919 came the subsequent announcement of a new Avery six-cylinder motor cultivator. This two-row outfit

Avery 25-50

had much more power than the earlier four-cylinder machine. Farmers were not especially excited about motor cultivators, and they sold rather poorly. Production of this model ended by 1924.

Along with the 1919 introduction of the Avery six-cylinder tractor came the Avery "Road-Razer." Built beneath the Model C was a standard road grader blade. It could be completely controlled from the operator's seat. Although suitable for light grader work, the Model C Road Razer lacked the power for heavy grading.

Avery 12-20

Nebraska Test Data

Model: Avery 12-20

Test No. 41

Date Tested: July 22 to August 2, 1920

From data supplied by the manufacturer, it would appear that Avery's 12-20 tractor was a fairly recent introduction, because the test tractor carried an engine serial of No. 2. Yet, the four-cylinder, horizontal, opposed, valve-in-head design had been a hallmark of Avery engines for several years. Rated at 800 rpm, the 12-20 carried a 4-3/8 x 6-inch bore and stroke. Regular equipment included a K-W magneto and Kingston Model E dual carburetor. Total weight of this unit was 5,500 lbs. Using low gear, the 12-20 exerted a 2,608 pound maximum drawbar pull, developing 17.58 hp in the process. Another maximum load test made in high gear revealed a maximum pull of 1,298 lbs. at a speed of 3.98 mph. Fuel economy was quite good in the rated brake hp tests, calculating to 8.98 hp-hours per gallon, with a figure of about half that much on the rated drawbar test. A maximum of 24.26 brake hp was developed at a speed of 800 rpm-fuel consumption on this test totaled 3.8 gph. Kerosene was used throughout the test. Few repairs or adjustments were necessary during the 30 hours of tests. Avery credited this tractor with being able to pull two or three moldboard plows or four or five disc plows.

Avery Track Runner

AVERY
TRACK-RUNNER

Avery Track Runner mark

The Patent Office Gazette provides definite information regarding the Avery Track Runner, noting that this mark was first used on January 8, 1921. The Track Runner was Avery's one and only entry into the crawler tractor business. The design left things to be desired, so this small tractor never achieved any success. It is unknown whether any of the Track Runner tractors still exist.

Nebraska Test Data

Model: Avery Track Runner
Test No. 89
Date Tested: March 16 to April 12, 1923

Leading off the 1923 test season was the Avery Track-Runner. Three forward speeds were provided: 2.43, 2.93, and 3.9 mph. The four-cylinder vertical engine was presumably of Avery design, and featured 16 valves—two intake and two exhaust valves per cylinder. Accessories included a K-W Model TK magneto, Kingston 1-1/2 inch, Model L carburetor and a United whirling vane dry air cleaner. Total weight was 5,600 lbs. No. 89. Rated brake hp tests indicated an economy of 8.24 hp-hours per gallon with a load of 25.1 hp. Under maximum load, 30.6 brake hp appeared. Maximum drawbar hp was observed in second gear, with a pull of 3,280 lbs. at 2.3 mph for a total of 20.13 drawbar hp. Problems abounded with Test No. 89. Test notes indicate that on March 21 the magneto timing was advanced, along with other minor adjustments. On March 29, a number of track rollers lost out, jamming the track and bending the curved track frame. The following day saw further track problems, with 33 additional rollers replaced. A complete set of 352 track rollers was installed April 6, and on April 9, all valves were ground. On the next day the pistons were removed, with all rings showing excessive wear. New rings were installed, even though the cylinders and pistons also evidenced "excessive abrasive action." Some 56 hours were required to complete the test procedures.

Avery 20-35

In 1922 Avery revamped its 20-35, giving it a new cellular radiator. Other changes included a full-length hood, wider fenders and a bigger platform. Apparently the canopy or cab remained during the first year, but for 1923 it, too, was elim-inated. With the new models came a change from the dark red finish of earlier years to a simple gray finish with red wheels.

Nebraska Test Data

Model: Avery 20-35
Test No. 96
Date Tested: June 24 to July 2, 1923

Although its appearance was different than the Avery tractors previously tested, the 20-35 carried the same style horizontal engine. In this case the four-cylinder, opposed, valve-in-head design used a 4-7/8 x 7-inch bore and stroke, with a rated speed of 900 rpm. Regular equipment included a K-W Model TK magneto, Kingston Model E dual carburetor, Modine tubular radiator, and a Madison-Kipp mechanical lubricator. Test notes indicated no air cleaner was used. Minor problems occurred, including several broken valve springs during the tests. Low gear gave a speed of 3 mph, compared to 4 mph in high gear. Using low gear, the 20-35 pulled its rated drawbar load at a speed of 2.94 mph over the 10-hour test time. A maximum pull of 3,080 lbs. was observed with a travel of 2.75 mph, for 22.62 maximum drawbar hp. Throughout the test kerosene fuel was used, and at rated brake hp an economy of 9.07 hp-hours per gallon of fuel was recorded. The 20-35 indicated 37.33 maximum brake hp, burning 6.702 gallons of fuel per hour, and yielding an economy of 5.57 hp-hours per gallon of fuel under maximum load Total weight of this unit was 7,540 lbs.

During 1922 and 1923 Avery revamped its tractor line, including the intermediate 25-50 model. The tubular radiator of past years was gone, replaced with a cellular radiator. This change gave greater cooling capacity but despite the changes, Avery experienced serious financial difficulties, which led to bankruptcy in 1924.

COLLECTOR VALUES	1	2	3	4
25-50	$30,000	$25,000	$15,000	$8,000

Louisville-Avery Motor Plow

Avery 45-65

The big 1923 Avery 45-65 tractor was essentially the same as the earlier 40-80 model. The new hp rating reflected the results of Nebraska Test No. 44. In this test the 40-80 delivered more than 46 drawbar hp, but only 69 belt hp. The company re-rated the tractor as the 45-65. Production virtually came to an end with the bankruptcy of 1924, although a few may have been built after the firm reorganized.

Avery 15-30

About 1921 or 1922 Avery introduced its 15-30 "New Avery" tractor. This model was of conven-tional design, using a four-cylinder engine with a 4-1/2 x 6-inch bore and stroke. The crank was carried on a pair of ball bearings. Despite the modern appearance of the 15-30, sales were far below expectations.

After its 1924 reorganization, Avery concentrated on its thresher and combines, giving little attention to tractors until the 1938 introduction of the Avery Ro-Trak. This small tractor featured a Hercules QXB5, six-cylinder engine. Its design included a 3-1/4 x 4-1/8-inch bore and stroke. Production of the Ro-Trak was halted in 1941, probably because of World War II military requirements.

COLLECTOR VALUES	1	2	3	4
RO-TRAK	$11,000	$9,500	–	–

Avery Ro-Trak

B. F. Avery & Sons Company

LOUISVILLE, KENTUCKY

B.F. Avery & Sons entered the tractor business in 1915 with its Louisville Motor Plow. This 20 hp outfit had removable plows mounted beneath the tractor chassis, permitting the tractor to be used for other farm duties. Production of the Louisville Motor Plow was very limited, apparently ending altogether by the following year.

Beginning about 1942, B. F. Avery offered its Model A tractor, a dead-ringer for the Cletrac General GG tractor. About 1945 the company again announced the Model V tractor, a small one-plow tractor. Early models used a Hercules IXB-3 four-cylinder engine with a 3-1/4 x 4-inch bore and stroke. Later models carried a Hercules 3 x 4 engine. Production ended with the Model R, announced in 1950. It used a Hercules four-cylinder, 133-cid engine, and also featured the Avery Tru-Draft hitch system. Minneapolis-Moline Company bought out B. F. Avery in 1951.

Tru-Draft trademark

COLLECTOR VALUES	1	2	3	4
MODEL A	$2,500	$1,500	$750	$400
MODEL BF	$2,700	$1,800	$1,100	$600
MODEL BFH	$3,200	$2,000	$1,4000	$800
MODEL BG	$3,000	$2,250	$1,200	$800
MODEL V	$2,500	$1,500	$750	$400

[Throughout this section, assume that gasoline was used for fuel unless another fuel source is indicated.]

Backus Tractor Company

ALTON, ILLINOIS

Baby Savidge tractor

In 1917 the Savidge Tractor Company was organized to build the Baby Savidge tractor. It was the work of William Savidge, and was rated at 8 drawbar and 16 belt hp. Subsequent activity was mediocre, and in 1920 the company reappeared as the Backus Tractor Company. The company disappeared after that time. This small tractor weighed about 3,500 lbs. and its retail price was $1,395.

Badley Tractor Company

PORTLAND, OREGON

Angleworm "10" tractor

ANGLEWORM

"Angleworm" trademark

A trademark application filed in 1937 indicated that Joy E. Badley, Portland, Oregon, had been using the "Angleworm" trade name for tractors since January 1934. Coincidentally, in 1934 the Angleworm tractor made its appearance. The Angleworm 10 weighed just 2,600 lbs., and was priced at about $950. It was equipped with a Continental four-cylinder motor with a 3-3/8 x 4 inch bore and stroke. The Angleworm remained on the market until the onset of World War II.

Kultor King Garden Tractor

In 1935 the Kultor King garden tractor was listed by Badley Tractor Company, but it may have made its debut in 1934 or even earlier. Weighing 560 lbs., it was equipped with an automotive transmission and axles. Power came from a single-cylinder engine with a 2-3/4 x 3-1/4-inch bore and stroke.

COLLECTOR VALUES	1	2	3	4
KULTOR KING	$600	$450	$300	$200

Bailor Plow Mfg. Company

ATCHISON, KANSAS

Bailor was organized in 1912 to build plows, cultivators and numerous other tillage implements. By 1919 the company had developed a two-row motor cultivator that looked remarkably like a row crop tractor in its chassis design. It does not appear the company made any efforts toward perfecting its design into a universal farm tractor. By 1920 Bailor was also building a small single-row motor cultivator and, like the two-row model, it used a LeRoi four-cylinder engine.

Bailor two-row motor cultivator

Bailor single-row motor cultivator

COLLECTOR VALUES	1	2	3	4
BAILOR CULTIVATORS	$5,000	$3,000	$1,500	$600

Baines Engineering Company

CANAL DOVER, OHIO

A 1921 article on garden tractors includes mention of the Model A and Model B Baines garden tractors. Both were of the same general design, varying primarily in physical size. The various implements available for the Baines garden tractors were Planet Junior designs from S. L. Allen & Company.

Baird Machine Company

STRATFORD, CONNECTICUT

For 1957, Baird offered its Model H Beaver Riding Tractor in four configurations, with tiller or wheel steering, and with hand or electric starting. It was powered by a Wisconsin BKN engine with a 2-7/8 x 2-3/4-inch bore and stroke and weighed only 500 lbs.

A. D. Baker Company

SWANTON, OHIO

Baker began building steam traction engines in 1898. By 1920 it was obvious that steam was on the way out, as the tractor began to dominate. The company adjusted its efforts accordingly.

Baker 16-30 model

Baker was one of the few companies to attempt a modernized "steam tractor," coming out with its 16-30 model in 1923. (The only one known in existence is in the Ford Museum.) Rated at 16 drawbar and 30 brake hp, this model weighed 9,000 lbs. It used an automatic coal stoker with the "radiator" at the front of the tractor actually the condenser that permitted repeated reuse of the condensed steam. A 20-40 model emerged in 1924 (only one is known to exist today), and it was re-rated as the 22-45 tractor. Production of the steam tractor apparently ended in 1925.

22-40 gasoline tractor

In 1926 Baker introduced the 22-40 gasoline tractor. Initially a Beaver four-cylinder engine was used, but this was changed to a LeRoi four-cylinder. The LeRoi was used until production ended with the onset of World War II. Baker tractors were largely built up of OEM parts, including the transmission, engine, and wheels.

COLLECTOR VALUES	1	2	3	4
22-40	$8,500	$5,000	$3,000	$1,500

Baker 25-50 (43-67)

The Baker 25-50 first appeared late in 1927, and remained in the trade directories until the late 1940s. Production after World War II was probably quite limited. The 25-50 was capable of more than 43 drawbar and 67 belt hp, and was sometimes known as the 43-67 model. It used a LeRoi four-cylinder engine.

Nebraska Test Data

Model: Baker 25-50 (43-67)

Test No. 161

Date Tested: May 16 to May 24, 1929

Originally introduced as the Baker 25-50, this tractor assumed a 43-67 rating shortly after completion of this 1929 test. At rated drawbar load it pulled 4,327 lbs. at 3.82 mph, experiencing slippage of only 4.6 percent. Final calculations revealed 43.57 drawbar hp on this test. Fuel economy came in at 5.58 hp-hours per gallon. Maximum drawbar tests were made in both forward gears, but in low gear the tractor pulled 7,840 lbs. at 2.67 mph with slippage of 9.26 percent, for a total of 55.72 drawbar hp. It was necessary to lock the gears in mesh during the high gear maximum and rated load drawbar tests. The rated brake hp test at 67.37 hp ended with an economy of 9.31 hp-hours per gallon and total consumption of 7.236 gph. The economy rating dropped to 9.18 at maximum load of 75.88 brake hp with fuel consumption in this test was slightly over 8-1/4 gph. A LeRoi four-cylinder vertical engine powered the tractor. Of I-head design, it used a 5-1/2 x 7-inch bore and stroke with a rated speed of 1,100 rpm. Included was an Eisemann G4 magneto, Stromberg M-4 carburetor, and Pomona air cleaner. Total weight was 10,575 lbs.

COLLECTOR VALUES	1	2	3	4
25-50 (WISCONSIN MOTOR)	$15,000	$14,000	$8,000	$5,000
25-50 (LEROI MOTOR)	$12,000	$10,000	$6,500	$4,000

Baker & Baker

ROYAL OAK, MICHIGAN

In 1913 this tractor manufacturer was purchased by Detroit Tractor Company, also of Royal Oak. The following year the latter moved to Lafayette, Indiana where they continued building the "Baker" tractor for a time.

Baker Mfg. Company

SPRINGFIELD, ILLINOIS

Baker heavy crawler tractor

About 1916 Baker introduced a heavy crawler tractor, but very little is known about this machine. The company was active until the late 1930s as a manufacturer of road graders, scrapers, and other road machinery. Often listed as a tractor builder, it seems more logical this reference is to the company's tractor graders built over a Fordson or an IHC 10-20 tractor.

Baker Tractor Corporation

DETROIT, MICHIGAN

The 1919 issue of Power Wagon Reference Book lists the Baker tractors, but aside from this reference, no other information about this company has been located.

Ball Tread Company

DETROIT, MICHIGAN

See: Yuba Mfg. Co.

Organized in 1912, Ball Tread Company specialized in crawler tractors. The company was bought out by Yuba Construction Company of Marysville, California, in 1914. Subsequently the firm was renamed Yuba Mfg. Company; the Ball Tread tractors are referenced under that heading.

Banting Mfg. Company

TOLEDO, OHIO

Greyhound tractor

The Banting brothers operated a repair shop until entering the engine and thresher business about 1918. Only 145 of their steamers were built by the time production ceased in 1922. About 1927 Banting made a deal with Allis-Chalmers to build Greyhound tractors, while A-C would sell Banting's Greyhound thresher line. The tractor had a few visible changes, notably, the top radiator tank has "Greyhound" cast in place of "Allis-Chalmers." The so-called Greyhound tractors were only marketed for a few years. In 1929 the company was reorganized as Allis-Chalmers farm equipment dealers, then remained in existence until 1954.

COLLECTOR VALUES	1	2	3	4
GREYHOUND	$6,000	$4,000	$2,000	$1,200

Barnes-Granger Corporation

KANSAS CITY, MISSOURI

Trade references for this company run between 1947 and 1953. The firm built the Pow-R-Queen garden tractor during this time, but no illustrations or specs on this unit have been located.

Baskins Tractor Company

ILLINOIS; ADDRESS UNKNOWN

A trade reference of the early teens provided the name of the company, and located it in Illinois, but no other information has been found.

Bates Machine & Tractor Company

JOLIET, ILLINOIS

This firm was organized in 1919 through the merger of Joliet Oil Tractor Company and the Bates Tractor Company of Lansing, Michigan. The latter firm was organized in 1911 by Madison F. Bates and others. He was also the moving force in the Bates & Edmonds Motor Company. They were well-known engine builders with their Bulldog engine line. Joliet Oil Tractor Company was organized in 1913 to build wheel-type and crawler tractors. Bates Machine & Tractor Company continued in the tractor business until 1929. The firm then became a division of Foote Bros. Gear & Machine Company. Foote Bros. continued with the Bates line until about 1935, and from then until 1937 the company reappeared as Bates Mfg. Company. After 1937, parts only were available from Foot Bros. Gear & Machine Company.

See: Bates Tractor Company; Foote Bros. Gear & Machine Co.; Joliet Oil Tractor Company

Bates Steel Mule Model D 15-22

Joliet Oil Tractor Company began building its Bates Steel Mule in 1918. A year later Joliet merged with the Bates Tractor Co. to form Bates Machine & Tractor Co. Various changes were made to the Model D in the following years but the 15-22 tractor remained on the market until at least 1920.

Nebraska Test Data

Model: Bates Steel Mule Model D 15-22
Test No. 60
Date Tested: August 30 to September 7, 1920

Widely heralded as the ideal all-around tractor, the Bates Steel Mule debuted with the Nebraska Tractor Test Laboratory in the Fall of 1920. Kerosene was used throughout the test. The tractor featured an Erd four-cylinder engine with a 4-1/4 x 6-inch bore and stroke. Rated at 1,100 rpm, this engine was of vertical, valve-in-head design. Other vendor-supplied items included a Bennett Model J carburetor, Dixie Aero magneto, and a Borg & Beck clutch. In low gear the 15-22 traveled at 3 mph, moving up to 4-1/2 mph in high gear. Minor repairs and adjustments were necessary, including the replacement of a fan bearing at the end of the test. A fuel economy rating of 7.12 hp-hours per gallon resulted from the rated brake hp test. Total fuel consumption during this test came to 3.18 gph, and 22.66 hp was developed. Nearly 25 brake hp resulted from the maximum load test. The maximum test on the drawbar yielded 20.66 hp with a pull of 2,996 lbs. at a speed of 2.59 mph. Slippage was only 3.7 percent on this test.

Nebraska Test Data

Model: Bates Steel Mule 15-22 (gasoline)
Test No. 68
Date Tested: October 12 to October 18, 1920

Weighing 4,600 lbs., the Bates Steel Mule featured a unique halftrack design. The Midwest engine installed as standard equipment yielded a maximum drawbar pull of 3,100 lbs. at a speed of 2.81 mph—this corresponded to a maximum of 23.19 drawbar hp. On the belt, 7.39 hp-hours per gallon was recorded in the rated load test for a total consumption of 3 gph. Under maximum load conditions, 29.78 brake hp was noted. The Midwest engine used in the 15-22 was of four-cylinder vertical, valve-in-head design, and was rated at 1,100 rpm. Bore and stroke dimensions were 4-1/8 x 5-1/4 inches. Two forward speeds of 3 and 4-1/2 mph were provided. Regular equipment included a Bennett Model J carburetor, Dixie Aero magneto, track-laying drivers, and a Borg & Beck clutch. Only minor repairs and adjustments were required during the 32 hours of running time necessary to complete the tests.

Steel Mule Model F 18-25

Introduced in 1921, the Model F apparently replaced the earlier Model D, and featured an 18 to 25 hp rating. This model remained in production until the company quit making tractors in 1937. Initially, a Midwest engine was used in the Model F, but for 1926 to 1928 a Beaver engine was substituted, and from 1929 to the end of production a LeRoi four-cylinder motor was featured.

Steel Mule Model G 25-35

The Model G 25-35 tractor was produced from 1921 to 1928. This model was somewhat larger than the Model F and used a Beaver four-cylinder engine with a 4-1/2 x 6-inch bore and stroke. Capable of a 4,500 lb. drawbar pull, the Model G, like its brothers, made extensive use of ball and roller bearings.

Steel Mule Model H 15-25

Bates was content to focus most of its manufacturing efforts in its unique crawler tractor designs, but in 1921 the company emerged with the Model H 15-25 wheel tractor. It used the same engine as the Model F crawler, a Midwest four-cylinder design with a 4-1/8 x 5-1/4-inch bore and stroke. Production of the Model H ended in 1924.

Steel Mule Industrial 25

The first full-fledged crawler tractor from Bates Machine & Tractor Co. came in 1924 with the Industrial 25 model. Produced until 1929, it featured a Beaver 4-1/4 x 6-inch four-cylinder engine. How well did it sell? Unfortunately, no production figures for the Bates tractors are known to exist.

Steel Mule Model 35

From 1930 to 1936, Bates offered the Steel Mule Model 35, which featured a completely enclosed drive train with all gears running in oil. The engine used a Ricardo head for extra power.

Nebraska Test Data

Model: Bates Steel Mule Model 35

Test No. 186

Date Tested: April 6 to April 18, 1931

A Waukesha six-cylinder L-head engine was featured in the Bates Model 35. Rated at 1,500 rpm, it used a 4-1/4 x 4-3/4-inch bore and stroke. Advertised speeds of 1.9, 2.85, and 3.8 mph were featured, along with an American Bosch U6 magneto and a Schebler HDX carburetor. Gasoline was used throughout the 47 hours of engine time. Weighing 11,218 lbs. the "35" made its maximum pull of 8,375 lbs. in low gear. At a speed of 1.96 mph it experienced slippage of 4.43 percent and developed 43.73 drawbar hp. At its rated 35 hp this tractor delivered fuel efficiency on the drawbar of 6.38 hp-hours per gallon, pulling a 4,368 lb. load at 3.04 mph. Rated brake tests at 45.18 hp revealed a fuel economy of 7.71 hp-hours per gallon. This figure jumped to 8.22 while producing 52.58 hp in the maximum load test. Fuel consumption in the maximum hp test totaled 6.395 gph. No repairs or adjustments were required during the test. This was the first model tested after Foote Bros. of Chicago had taken over the manufacture of Bates tractors in 1929.

Bates Steel Mule Model 40

Production of the Bates Steel Mule Model 40 ran from 1924 to 1929. A Waukesha four-cylinder engine was used in this model. Its four cylinders carried a 5 x 6-1/2-inch bore and stroke. During these years the company was constantly changing and improving its designs.

COLLECTOR VALUES	1	2	3	4
MODEL 40	$10,000	$7,000	$4,000	$1,500

Bates Steel Mule Model 45

The Bates Steel Mule Model 45 was built in the 1930-33 period. It was essentially an upgrade from the Model 40 crawler, and was actually manufactured by Foote Bros. Gear & Machine Co. In order to maintain the continuum of Bates production, the models built by Foote Bros. are also included under this heading.

Nebraska Test Data

Model: Bates Steel Mule Model 45
Test No. 187
Date Tested: April 8 to April 28, 1931

Weighing in at 13,509 lbs., the Bates Model 45 was somewhat heavier than the Model 35 tested under No. 186. Like its smaller cousin, this model used a six-cylinder L-head Waukesha engine rated at 1,500 rpm, but in this case a 4-5/8 x 5-1/8-inch bore and stroke was featured. Ignition remained the same as in Test No. 186, as did the carburetor, with gasoline as the chosen fuel. At its rated 45 drawbar hp, this tractor managed a 5,482 lb. pull at 3.09 mph and slippage of 1.07 percent. Total fuel consumption came to 6.691 gph during this test with an economy of 6.74 hp-hours per gallon. Maximum brake tests at 66.53 hp saw fuel consumption rise to 7.815 gph with an economy of 8.51 hp-hours per gallon. This dropped slightly to 8.14 at rated load of 55.6 hp. After the 55 hours of test time, oil was leaking from the clutch housing, indicating a leaky rear main bearing seal. Otherwise the Model 45 went through its paces without major problems.

Bates Steel Mule Model 50

The Bates Steel Mule Model 50 was on the market from 1934 to 1937. Model 50 crawlers used a six-cylinder Waukesha engine with a Ricardo head, which raised the power level substantially. This engine carried a 4-5/8 x 5-1/8-inch bore and stroke, and rated speed was 1,400 rpm. Total weight of the Model 50 was 14,000 lbs.

Bates Steel Mule Model 80

Bates Steel Mule Model 80 tractors were marketed between 1929 and 1937. This big tractor weighed more than 11 tons, and used a huge Waukesha four-cylinder engine with a 6-1/2 x 7-inch bore and stroke.

The only Bates Steel Mule diesel tractor was the Model 40 Diesel offered in 1937. This $3,100 tractor featured a Waukesha-Hesselman diesel engine with a 4-1/2 x 5-1/4-inch bore and stroke. The unique engine design used a compression of 150 psi, and fuel was injected as with the full diesel, but a conventional spark plug ignited the fuel. The Hesselman enjoyed only limited success, because newer diesel designs were much simpler. After 1937 the company quit production, but continued to supply repair parts for some years.

Bates Steel Mule 40 Diesel

Bates Tractor Company

LANSING, MICHIGAN

Organized in 1911, this firm owed its designs to Madison F. Bates, one of the principals in the Bates & Edmonds Motor Company, also of Lansing. The company merged with Joliet Oil Tractor Co. to form the Bates Machine & Tractor Company in 1919.

See: Bates Machine & Tractor Company

Bates tractor

Rated at 30 belt hp, the Bates tractor had a working drawbar pull of 2,500 lbs., sufficient to pull two or three plows, depending on the circumstances. This tractor weighed 8,000 lbs. The completely hooded engine and the operator's canopy made the design very attractive.

Bates 10-15 tractor

The Bates tractor was built in two sizes of 15 and 30 hp. In 1914 the 10-15 model used a single-cylinder horizontal engine and it weighed 5,000 lbs. The 18-30 carried a two-cylinder opposed engine. Also, by 1914 the cab had been removed and the tractor had been modified slightly from the original design.

Bates 15-25 All-Steel tractor

Near the end of production, Bates came out with its 15-25 All-Steel tractor. One of its new features was automotive-type steering, compared to the stiff axle-and-chain steering then in vogue. It also used a Bates-built four-cylinder engine with a 4-3/8 x 5-1/2-inch bore and stroke. It remained on the market for a short time, eventually being replaced by the Bates Model H 15-25 tractor from Bates Machine & Tractor Company.

Bauroth Bros.

SPRINGFIELD, OHIO

This company began building gasoline engines in the 1890s, and was listed in trade directories as a tractor manufacturer during 1906, 1907, and 1908. Aside from that, no illustrations of its tractors have been found.

Wm. C. Bealmear

EL MONTE, CALIFORNIA

In 1945 this firm was listed as the manufacturer of the Western garden tractor.

Bean Spray Pump Company

SAN JOSE, CALIFORNIA

Bean Trackpull

Initially, this firm built its reputation on spray pumps, beginning business in 1884. About 1914 or 1915 the company introduced the Bean Trackpull. This was an unusual design using a single front-mounted track and two carrier wheels at the rear. Initially the company offered only its 6-10 Trackpull, but by 1920 the company was also building the Trackpull in an 8-16 model. Both were of the same essential design, differing primarily in the power level. Production ended in the early 1920s.

Bear Tractor Company

NEW YORK, NEW YORK

Bear began building its 25-35 crawler tractor in 1923. It was powered with a Stearns four-cylinder engine with a 4-3/4 x 6-1/2-inch bore and stroke. Weighing 6,000 lbs., it was priced at $4,250. The Bear tractor line was taken over by Mead-Morrison Company at East Boston, Massachusetts in 1925.

See: Mead-Morrison Company

Bear 25-35 crawler

Nebraska Test Data

Model: Bear Model B 25-35
Test No. 100
Date Tested: October 4 to October 18, 1923

The Bear 25-35 crawler tractor closed out the 1923 testing season. Problems abounded with Test No. 100—50 hours of running time were required to complete the tests, and the 10-hour rated drawbar test was interrupted before completion, making the final figures slightly inaccurate. Frequent adjustments were necessary, and in an unsuccessful attempt to increase engine power output, the carburetor was cleaned, magneto and spark plugs were cleaned and adjusted, a new cylinder head was installed, and valve timing was advanced by 4 degrees. Bear equipped this tractor with three forward speeds of 2.17, 3.5, and 5.67 mph. A Stearns four-cylinder vertical, valve-in-head engine was used, rated at 1,190 rpm. The rated brake hp test used gasoline fuel, as did all subsequent tests. At rated load of 35.46 hp, fuel economy was recorded at 8.54 hp-hours per gallon for a total consumption of 4.152 gph. Under maximum load, 49.99 brake hp was developed. Drawbar tests revealed an average of 25.11 hp during the rated load test, with the 25-35 pulling a 2,758 pound load at 3.4 mph. In low gear, 27.46 maximum drawbar hp was achieved at a speed of 1.86 mph and a pull of 5,545 lbs.. The 25-35 weighed 6,400 lbs.

Nebraska Test Data

Model: Bear Model B 25-35
Test No. 101
Date Tested: April 1 to April 8, 1924

After the poor showing in Test No. 100, Bear Tractors presented another Model B to launch the 1924 test season. As in Test No. 100, a Stearns four-cylinder vertical, valve-in-head engine was featured, but Bear had increased speed to 1,290 rpm. Specific engine features included Dow-metal magnesium alloy pistons and Lynite aluminum alloy connecting rods. A Pomona air cleaner built by Vortox Manufacturing Company came as standard equipment, as did a Bosch AT-4 magneto and Wheeler-Schebler carburetor. As in Test No. 100, gasoline was the chosen fuel. At rated load the Model B came up with 8.06 hp-hours per gallon, developing 36.53 brake hp. Under maximum load, 55.56 brake hp was recorded, higher than in Test No. 100. A similar situation was found in the drawbar tests, this tractor made a maximum pull of 6,805 lbs. in low gear. Maximum drawbar hp was displayed in second gear, with 44.64 hp recorded, along with a pull of 4,863 lbs. at 3.44 mph. Except for a slight modification to the governor, few repairs or adjustments were necessary. Total weight of the Model B tested in No. 101 was 7,000 lbs.

COLLECTOR VALUES	1	2	3	4
MODEL B 25-35	$8,000	$6,000	$4,000	$2,000

Beaver Mfg. Company

MILWAUKEE, WISCONSIN

Although Beaver is sometimes listed as a tractor manufacturer, the company specialized in building engines for tractors. The Beaver design was frequently specified, with the JA and JB design illustrated here. Both used four cylinders. The JA carried a 4-1/2 x 6-inch bore and stroke, while the large JB used a 4-3/4 x 6-inch bore and stroke.

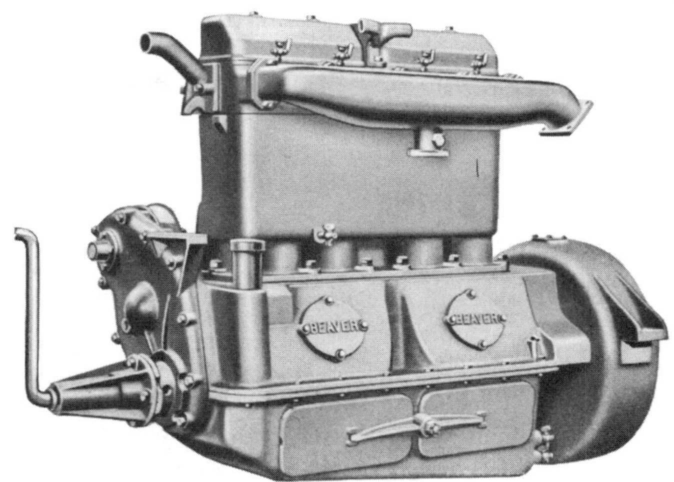

Beaver engine

Beaver Tractor Company

STRATFORD, CONNECTICUT

Beaver garden tractor

Trade directories list this firm as the manufacturer of the Beaver garden tractors between 1948 and 1953 but little information on this small tractor has been found.

COLLECTOR VALUES	1	2	3	4
GARDEN TRACTORS	$750	$450	$250	$150

Bedford Tractor Company

BEDFORD, INDIANA

Except for some correspondence, very little information has been found concerning this company. Late in 1921 the company developed a "universal" style tractor, similar to the Hoke, the Indiana, and the Moline Universal. Bedford apparently applied to Moline for a license to build under that company's patents, but the latter refused to grant a license. Without that, the venture apparently died before production ever began.

Beeman Tractor Company

MINNEAPOLIS, MINNESOTA

Incorporated in 1916, Beeman was one of the early entrants into the garden tractor business. Business continued until the company was reorganized in 1925 as the New Beeman Tractor Company. The firm continued to appear in trade directories until 1945, where it last appeared in Millard's Implement Directory. The small tractor shown here was rated at 2 drawbar and 4 belt hp. Numerous models were built during a long production run.

Beeman garden tractor

Nebraska Test Data

Model: Beeman Model G

Test No. 28

Date Tested: June 22 to July 2, 1920

Compared to some of the behemoths in earlier tests, the Beeman Model G carried the distinction of being the smallest unit tested up to this time. Although the company gave it a rating of 2 drawbar and 4 belt hp, testing illustrated 2.4 brake hp over a two-hour period. Gasoline consumption came to only 0.44 gph, with an economy ratio of 5.43 hp-hours per gallon. Traveling at 2.17 mph, the Beeman exerted a 187.8 lb. maximum drawbar pull for 1.08 drawbar hp. Weighing only 550 lbs., the Beeman featured a single cylinder vertical, L-head engine with a 3-1/2 x 4-1/2-inch bore and stroke. Rated speed varied from 230 to 1,500 rpm. During the test procedures lasting 40 hours, no serious defects were found.

COLLECTOR VALUES	1	2	3	4
GARDEN TRACTORS	$2,500	$2,000	$1,000	$500

Robert Bell Engine & Thresher Company

SEAFORTH, ONTARIO

About 1918 this firm got into the tractor business with its 12-24 model. It is likely a Flour City Junior from Kinnard-Haines Company of Minneapolis, although this one was sold under the Imperial trade name of Robert Bell Engine & Thresher Company.

Model 12-24

Imperial Super-Drive tractor

In 1920 Bell offered an Imperial Super-Drive tractor. It had a special spring-cushioned rear wheel drive system. The Imperial 15-30 used a four-cylinder Climax engine with a 5 x 6-1/2-inch bore and stroke.

COLLECTOR VALUES	1	2	3	4
IMPERIAL SUPER DRIVE 15-30	$20,000	$18,000	$12,000	$10,000
IMPERIAL SUPER DRIVE 22-40	$22,000	$20,000	$15,000	$12,000

Belle City Mfg. Company

RACINE, WISCONSIN

Trackpull crawler

Belle City manufactured numerous farm machines, and was known particularly as a threshing machine builder. In the late 1920s Belle City began offering its Trackpull crawler tractor attachment. Built specifically for the Fordson tractor, this unit enjoyed lots of popularity for several years.

Belsaw Machinery Company

KANSAS CITY, MISSOURI

Belsaw Ride-Trac No. 552

For a time in the late 1950s, Belsaw, the famous sawmill manufacturer, offered the Ride-Trac No. 552 shown here. The buyer supplied an engine of choice, installing it on a universal mounting plate furnished with the tractor.

Beltrail Tractor Company

ST. PAUL, MINNESOTA

Beltrail trademark

This company was organized in 1917 and produced two versions of a crawler tractor through 1920.

Beltrail 12-24 crawler

The Beltrail folks offered a unique crawler design that needed no differential. The steerable front wheels further simplified the design. Their initial model was a 12-24 size. The Beltrail trademark shown was first used in April 1918.

Beltrail Model B

Beltrail was reorganized in 1918, and about this same time the company came out with the Model B. It was nothing more than an improved version of the original 12-24. A Waukesha four-cylinder engine was used and it carried a 3-3/4 x 5-1/2-inch bore and stroke. Production ended during 1920.

Benjaman Tractor Company

DALLAS, TEXAS

In 1918 W. B. Chenoweth filed patent applications on a new tractor design, with Patents No. 1,331,184 and 1,331,185 issued in 1920. The company proposed three sizes—the Handy Ben as a 6-12 model, the Little Ben as a 10-20 tractor, and the Big Ben as a 20-40 style. Like several other tractors of the day, the models used a hinged frame design. In 1920 the 20-40 had a list price of $1,625.

Big Ben 20-40

Besser Mfg. Company

ALPENA, MICHIGAN

Besser tractor

The February 1918 issue of Gas Review Magazine illustrated the Besser tractor. It was rated at 15 drawbar and 30 belt hp. Aside from a few 1918 advertisements, nothing more is known of this tractor. Many, if not most, of the early tractor manufacturers were undercapitalized and simply did not have the financing to launch both a major advertising and manufacturing effort.

C. L. Best Gas Traction Company

SAN LEANDRO, CALIFORNIA

Daniel Best became famous for his huge three-wheeled traction engine of 1889. On this first model, Best became a large manufacturer of steam traction engines, but sold out to a competitor, the Holt Mfg. Company in 1908. A son, C. L. Best, organized the C. L. Best Gas Traction Engine Company in 1910. One of its early crawlers was the Best 75 of 1913 and numerous other sizes and styles followed. Finally, Best merged with Holt on April 25, 1925 to form the Caterpillar Tractor Company.

See: Caterpillar Tractor Co.; Holt Mfg. Co.

Best 75

The Best 75 came onto the market in 1913. Initially it used a large front tiller wheel for steering, but eventually it was discovered this feature was unnecessary, and it was removed. The early models of the 75 featured a full-length canopy, and this too was removed by about 1915.

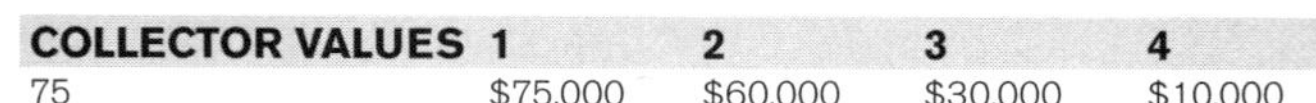

COLLECTOR VALUES	1	2	3	4
75	$75,000	$60,000	$30,000	$10,000

Model 75 40-70 crawler

In 1918 the Best Model 75 40-70 crawler had a list price of $5,750. Weighing 28,000 lbs., it carried a huge four-cylinder engine with a 7-3/4 x 9-inch bore and stroke. Although expensive, this big crawler had its place, and remained in production until about 1919. The company also built a 45-90 Tracklayer model around 1917.

Best 25 Tracklayer

The Best 25 Tracklayer came onto the scene in 1920. This small tractor used a four-cylinder engine with a 4-3/4 x 6-1/2-inch bore and stroke. The cylinders were cast individually, making repair much simpler, even though this increased the total length of the engine by several inches. The Best 25 sold for $2,450.

During 1920 Best introduced the 30 Tracklayer model—that apparently used the same engine as the Tracklayer 25. It has been difficult to determine the exact production period for the Tracklayer 25 and the Tracklayer 30 models, but from all appearances, the Tracklayer 30 survived into the Best-Holt merger of 1925.

Best likely began producing an early version of the Tracklayer 30 by 1914. A year later the company introduced an orchard version called the Humpback Thirty. By redesigning the transmission and drive system, the Humpback Thirty had the low profile needed for orchard work.

Nebraska Test Data

Model: Best 30 18-30 Tracklayer

Test No. 77

Date Tested: May 9 to May 20, 1921

The Best 30 Tracklayer used gasoline throughout the test procedures. Rated speeds were 2 and 3-1/16 mph. The rated drawbar load test was run in high gear and revealed 19.75 drawbar hp at a speed of 2.92 mph. A maximum load test in low gear gave a maximum pull of 4,343 lbs. at a speed of 2.12 mph, for a corresponding 24.53 maximum drawbar hp. At the belt, 30.4 rated hp was delivered at a crankshaft speed of 810 rpm. Total fuel consumption was 4.55 gph or 6.68 hp-hours per gallon. Under maximum load, less than 1/10th-hp was generated above that noted in the rated load test. Prior to the recording of any official data, magneto timing was advanced 5 degrees and the carburetor was enlarged. Minor repairs and adjustments were made prior to beginning the drawbar tests. Best used its own four-cylinder vertical, valve-in-head engine with a 4-3/4 x 6-1/2-inch bore and stroke, and carrying a rating of 800 rpm. Total weight was 7,400 lbs. Some 47 hours of running time was required to complete the tests.

Nebraska Test Data

Model: Best 30 20-30 Tracklayer

Test No. 99

Date Tested: Septembeer 11 to September 24, 1923

Rated as a 20-30, this new version of the Best 30 weighed in at 8,100 lbs. The company used its own four-cylinder vertical, valve-in-head engine, with its own governor and a Bosch ZR4 magneto. Other equipment included an Ensign Model GT carburetor and a Pomona oiled fiber type air cleaner. Two forward speeds were available at 2.03 and 3.1 mph. Minor adjustments were made during the 34 hours of running time. Gasoline was used, with the "30" demonstrating a fuel economy of 7.4 hp hours per gallon at rated brake hp, or a total consumption of 4.107 gph. Slightly more than 32-1/2 maximum brake hp was recorded. At rated drawbar load the "30" pulled a 2,541 lb. load at 3.06 mph for 20.75 hp over the 10-hour run. A maximum of 25.96 drawbar hp was recorded in low gear, with the "30" pulling 4,930 lbs. at 1.98 mph.

Best 30 Tracklayer

Nebraska Test Data

Model: Best "S" 30
Test No. 104
Date Tested: September 15 to September 22, 1924

This tractor was later known as the Caterpillar "30" after Holt and Best merged to form Caterpillar Tractor Company in 1925, but it was tested in 1924 bearing the Best moniker. Using its own four-cylinder vertical, valve-in-head engine, the "30" carried a 4-3/4 x 6-1/2 inch bore and stroke and was rated at 850 rpm. It was built with three forward speeds of 1.75, 2.63, and 3.63 mph. Regular equipment included a Stromberg MP-3 carburetor and a Bosch ZR4 magneto. The "30" delivered a fuel economy of 9.28 hp-hours per gallon at rated brake hp. Under maximum load of 37.80 hp, fuel economy dropped to 7.71 hp-hours per gallon. Rated drawbar tests indicated a 3,796 lb. pull at rated load, with the maximum pull occurring in low gear of 7,563 lbs. recorded at a speed of 1.5 mph. No repairs or adjustments were required through the 36 hour test. Actual weight, including the operator, was 9,065 lbs.

Best 40 Tracklayer

The 1919 version of the Model 40 Tracklayer illustrates the full canopy and, in fact, the same basic designs that the company had been using for several years. The rear-mounted belt pulley came as standard equipment. Sidecurtains were also provided on these machines and they could be rolled down to protect it from the elements.

Best 60 Tracklayer

Production of the Best 60 Tracklayer apparently began about 1919 and continued up to the 1925 merger with Holt that formed Caterpillar Tractor Company. This popular model featured the company's own four-cylinder engine with a 6-1/2 x 8-1/2-inch bore and stroke. The Best 60 weighed more than nine tons.

Nebraska Test Data

Model: Best 60 35-55 Tracklayer
Test No. 76
Date Tested: May 6 to May 24, 1921

Test notes on the Best 60 Tracklayer indicated that prior to recording any official data, the standard equipment air cleaner was removed and was not to be a regular equipment item for units sold in Nebraska. The test data did not indicate the reason for this ruling. Although this model came in with a manufacturer's rating of 60 belt hp, it was re-rated downward to 55 hp. The rated load test revealed 56.09 hp at 656 rpm, slightly higher than the manufacturer's rated speed of 650 rpm. This test recorded a fuel economy rating of 8.05 hp-hours per gallon of gasoline, the fuel used throughout the test. Even on the maximum load test the Best 60 cranked out 56.33 hp, somewhat below its nameplate rating. On the drawbar, a maximum pull of 11,000 lbs. was achieved at a speed of 1.71 mph, corresponding to 50.20 drawbar hp. Ground speeds of 1-7/8 and 2-5/8 mph were provided. Weighing 17,500 lbs., the Best 60 was equipped with the company's vertical four-cylinder, valve-in-head engine, with a 6-1/2 x 8-1/2-inch bore and stroke. Regular equipment included an Ensign Model G carburetor and a Bosch ZR41S magneto.

Nebraska Test Data

Model: Best 60 40-60 Tracklayer
Test No. 98
Date Tested: September 10 to September 14, 1923

Gasoline was the chosen fuel throughout Test No. 98. The 18,580 pound Best 60 delivered 41.26 drawbar hp on the rated load test, pulling 5,969 lbs. at a speed of 2.59 mph In low gear a maximum of 56.78 drawbar hp was observed, with the "60" pulling a load of 11,295 lbs. at a speed of 1.865 mph. Best equipped this model with a three-speed transmission, permitting speeds of 1-7/8, 2-5/8, and 3-6/10 mph. A fuel economy of 7.22 hp-hours per gallon was noted in the rated brake hp test—with total consumption of 8.374 gph delivering 60.45 hp. At maximum load, 65.87 hp was recorded. During this test, coolant temperature rose to 210 degrees F., but for all other tests the temperature ranged from 146 to 189 degrees F. Best equipped the "60" with its own four-cylinder, vertical, valve-in-head engine rated at 650 rpm and carrying a 6-1/2 x 8-1/2-inch bore and stroke. Accessory items included a Bosch ZR4 magneto and a Stromberg M4 carburetor. No repairs or adjustments were made during the test.

COLLECTOR VALUES	1	2	3	4
BEST 60	$20,000	$15,000	$8,000	$5,000

Toward the end of Best tractor production the Best 60 cruiser model appeared. This special tractor was designed for higher ground speeds than the standard tractors and used lower grouser bars than those intended for heavy traction. The special buggy top gave some measure of comfort to the operator.

Best 60 cruiser model

Bethlehem Motors Corporation

EAST ALLENTOWN, PENNSYLVANIA

Bethlehem 18-36 model

Beginning in 1918 Bethlehem attempted to enter the tractor business with an18-36 model. It was powered by a Beaver four-cylinder engine with a 4-3/4 x 6-inch bore and stroke. Weighing 6,200 lbs. this model was sold without fenders, probably to help hold down the price. Adding fenders made the tractor more attractive and shielded the operator from a constant dust storm.

Big Bud Tractors Inc.

HAVRE, MONTANA

Nebraska Test Data

Model: Big Bud 525/50 Diesel

Test No. 1400

Date Tested: June 29 to July 9, 1981

No PTO shaft was provided and no brake hp tests were run. Weighing 51,920 lbs., the 525/50 used dual 30.5L-32 inch tires. Drawbar testing was completed without the use of additional ballast. Repairs and adjustments during 36 hours of operating time were limited to replacement of a hydraulic hose. The Cummins six-cylinder turbocharged and inter-cooled engine was rated at 2,100 rpm and carried a 6.25 inch bore and stroke for an 1,150 cubic inch displacement. The selective gear fixed-ratio transmission included a six-range power shift with a torque converter and automatic lockup. Operating in third gear, the two-hour drawbar test at 406.48 maximum available hp indicated a pull of 26,984 lbs. at 5.65 mph. Slippage totaled 4.04 percent and fuel economy was set at 14.87 hp-hours per gallon. The 10-hour test at 75 percent pull noted an economy of 13.97 hp-hours per gallon with an output of 345.77 drawbar hp. Other data included a pull of 21,462 lbs. at 6.04 mph and slippage totaling 3.06 percent. A low-gear maximum pull of 42,216 lbs. was recorded at 3.55 mph. Slippage in this test totaled 9.2 percent.

Big Farmer Tractor Company

FORT MADISON, IOWA

Aside from a trade reference in the 1916 era noting that the company was being organized, no other information has been located.

Birrell Motor Plow Company

AUBURN, NEW YORK

About 1910 the Birrell Motor Plow appeared, and apparently the manufacturer was looking at the Canadian market with its large expanse of prairie land. It was equipped with a six-bottom Moline plow hung beneath the tractor frame, and used a big four-cylinder engine for power. Little else is known of the Birrell.

Biwer Mfg. Company

CRESCO, IOWA

The 1953 Farm Implement News Buyer's Guide lists this company as a manufacturer of garden tractors, but no further information has been located.

Blazer Mfg. Company

CLEVELAND, OHIO

In the 1948-1953 period, and perhaps longer, this firm is listed as the manufacturer of the Gardenette and Soil Blazer garden tractors.

Blewett Tractor Company

TACOMA, WASHINGTON

Webfoot 53 tractor

Blewett Tractor Company announced its Webfoot 53 tractor in 1920. It was rated as a 28-53 and was equipped with a Wisconsin four-cylinder Model M engine with a 5-3/4 x 7-inch bore and stroke. In 1920 this tractor sold for $5,000. Production ended about 1922.

Priced at $4,000, the Webfoot 40 tractor was built in 1920 and 1921. It weighed 8,900 lbs. Power was provided by a four-cylinder Beaver engine with a 4-3/4 x 6-inch bore and stroke. As shown in the photo, steering was achieved with a single lever.

Webfoot 40 tractor

John Blue Company

HUNTSVILLE, ALABAMA

G-1000 model

John Blue Company was established in 1886 as a farm implement manufacturer. At that time the company was in Laurinburg, North Carolina, but moved to Huntsville, Alabama, in 1945. The firm began building small tractors for market gardeners and nurseries. The photo illustrates the company's G-1000 model from the 1970s.

Blumberg Motor Mfg. Company

SAN ANTONIO, TEXAS

BLUMBERG
STEADY PULL
TRACTOR

Blumberg Steady Pull Tractor trademark

Sometimes the Patent Office Gazette yields valuable clues regarding a firm's origins. In this instance, a trademark application of 1921 illustrates that the company had been using the "Blumberg Steady Pull Tractor" mark since April 1915. A simple deduction would be that the company probably started at least a year earlier, because it would have taken at least that long to develop the design and set up a manufacturing operation.

Steady Pull 12-24

In 1915 the Blumberg Steady Pull tractor appeared. The 12-24 model shown here used a four-cylinder, 4 x 5 engine of the company's own manufacture. The company continued for a few years, but by 1924 disappeared from the scene.

The Steady Pull 9-18 tractor first appeared about 1919. This model was of the same basic design as the 12-24 and used a four-cylinder engine with a 3-3/4-inch bore and stroke. At the time a "square" engine—one with the same bore and stroke—was rather unusual in the tractor industry. For the most part, tractor builders of the time preferred a long-stroke engine with the bore was about 70 to 80 percent of the stroke.

Steady Pull 9-18

Boenker Motor Plow Company

ST. CHARLES, MISSOURI

H. H. Boenker patented this interesting motor plow in 1910 and the following year a company was organized to build it. The 1911 Boenker used an Anderson Model E, two-cylinder engine of the opposed horizontal design. The tractor weighed 2,800 lbs. and was priced at $1,250. After a few notices in the trade papers the company disappeared from the tractor business.

Boenker's Tractor and Motor Plow

Bolens Products Company

PORT WASHINGTON, WISCONSIN

Bolens offered its first garden tractor about 1919. Numerous designs appeared in the years to follow, although accurate production data on the Bolens line has been difficult to document. In the mid-1940s the company became the Bolens Product Division of FMC Corporation.

Bolens garden tractor

This is Bolens' first garden tractor, introduced in 1919. Numerous attachments were available for this tractor including the planter shown in this photo.

COLLECTOR VALUES	1	2	3	4
GARDEN TRACTOR	$650	$450	$300	$200

The Bolens Huski line, which was started in 1946, was among the first of the so-called compact garden tractors. As with farm tractors, the early garden tractor designs were heavy and cumbersome. A Bolens garden tractor of 1948 vintage is shown in the photo.

COLLECTOR VALUES	1	2	3	4
HUSKI	$850	$550	$350	$250

Bolens Huski

Bolens Ridemaster

Nebraska Test Data

Model: Bolens 12BB Ridemaster

Test No. 473

Date Tested: June 9 to June 14, 1952

A Briggs & Stratton single-cylinder engine rated at 3,600 rpm and using a 2-1/4 x 2-inch bore and stroke was featured in the 12BB garden tractor. With a displacement of 7.95 cubic inches, this engine achieved a maximum torque of 8.09 lbs.-ft. at a speed of 2,682 rpm. By governor control and sheave adjustment, speed was variable from 1-1/4 to 3-3/4 mph. With a bare weight of 211 lbs., the 12BB received an additional 77 lbs. of weight on each rear wheel during certain drawbar tests. Standard equipment included 5.00-12 tires. Test H, run at a speed of 3.06 mph yielded an output of 1.3 drawbar hp with a 159-pound drawbar pull under slippage of 6.35 percent. Test H also indicated a fuel economy of 5.75 hp- hours per gallon of fuel. A Test G maximum pull of 210 lbs. was noted in Test G. Belt testing included a fuel economy of 6.1 hp-hours per gallon under a Test D rated load of 1.8 hp. At the Test B 100 percent maximum load of 1.95 hp, fuel economy came in at 6.59 hp-hours per gallon.

Bolens model 20HD Riding Tractor

By 1956 the Bolens line included the Model 20HD riding tractor. It incorporated the Bolens Ride-a-matic design and the Versa-Matic drive and reverse. It used both front- and rear-mounted attachments.

COLLECTOR VALUES	1	2	3	4
RIDING TRACTOR	$750	$550	$350	$250

Bollstrom Motors Company

MARION, INDIANA

A 1918 announcement indicated this company was being organized with a capitalization of $3 million. After this announcement nothing more was heard of the company or its tractors and presumably neither came to fruition.

J.G. Bolte

DAVENPORT, IOWA

Bolte 20-40 tractor

J.G. Bolte began building his tractors by 1918, and was probably in business for several years prior to that. In 1919 the J. G. Bolte Company was organized to build the 20-40 tractor shown here. Weighing 5,000 lbs., it featured a unique steering system the company called "The Square Turn" design. After a few trade announcements in 1919, nothing more was heard of this company or its tractors.

Boring Tractor Corporation

ROCKFORD, ILLINOIS

Boring 12-25 tractor

The Boring tractor was the inventive work of Charles E. Boring, who received Patent No. 1,203,304 for his design in 1916. In 1918 the firm was incorporated to build the Boring 12-25. It was equipped with a four-cylinder Waukesha engine with a 4-1/4 x 5-3/4-inch bore and stroke. For plowing, the right-hand drive wheel ran in the furrow, and the left hand driver could be adjusted upward so that the tractor and plow ran level. This tractor had price of $1,485 in 1919. Production ended about 1922.

Boss Tractor Mfg. Company

DETROIT, MICHIGAN

In 1915 this company was rechristened as the Chief Tractor Mfg. Company at Detroit. At the time they are said to have been building the "Chief 4" tractors, but no other information has surfaced, nor do we know when Boss Tractor Mfg. Co. was originally organized.

Boyett-Brannon Tractor Company

ATLANTA, GEORGIA

Boyett tractor

This company, one of Georgia's few tractor builders, announced a 30-hp model in 1913. The completely hooded design was quite unusual for the time, and the operator's cab was a welcome addition. Roller chain drives were used to power the drivewheels, and the tractor featured auto-guide steering at a time when most tractors were built with a chain steering a stiff front axle.

David Bradley Mfg. Company

BRADLEY, ILLINOIS

Tractors produced by David Bradley Mfg. Company were sold by Sears, Roebuck & Company, which owned the company. See this heading for further information.

Bray Corporation

PASADENA, CALIFORNIA

This firm was listed in 1948 as a garden tractor manufacturer, and apparently manufactured the Tillex 40 garden tractor. This is a walk-behind model with cleated steel wheels, an aluminum clutch housing, and an aluminum transaxle. It has a Wisconsin AK single-cylinder engine.

Bready Tractor & Implement Company

CLEVELAND, OHIO

Details are sketchy regarding this company and its products. Originally called Bready Cultivator Company, it started business in the early 1920s building Cultimotor garden tractors. By the late 1940s the Model A, a 2-1/2-hp model, appeared. A variety of front-mounted Bready implements were available. The company moved from Cleveland to Solon, Ohio, in the late 1940s or early 1950s.

Model A Cultimotor garden

COLLECTOR VALUES	1	2	3	4
MODEL A CULTIMOTOR	$450	$350	$250	$100

Allen Breed Tractor Company

CINCINNATI, OHIO

During 1913 Allen Breed succeeded in perfecting a large 30-hp tractor. This unit had several unique features including three forward speeds, something unheard of in those days. The autoguide steering was also a forward step from the stiff axle-and-chain steering then in vogue. After mid-1914 no further advertising appeared for the Breed, and presumably production ended about that same time.

Brillion Iron Works

BRILLION, WISCONSIN

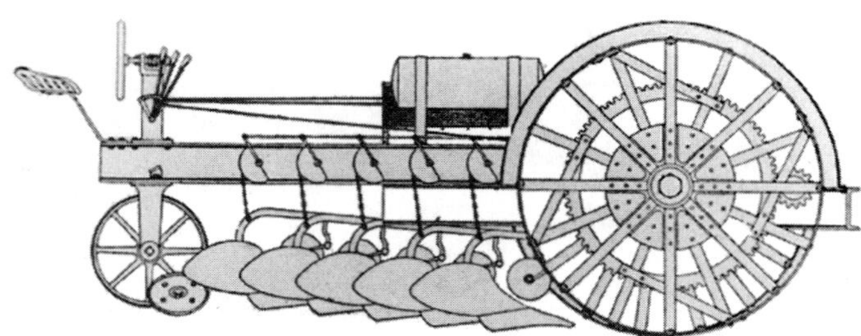

Brillion 24-30 tractor

A line drawing is about all the information that has been located on the Brillion 24-30 tractor, first advertised in 1916. It featured a two-cylinder engine with a 6-3/4 x 8-inch bore and stroke; the engine was built by Brillion. The tractor sold for $1,885. In 1918 the company also offered a 12-24 tractor of the same design. All tractor production ended in 1918 though Brillion Iron Works continues to make farm implements and parts.

British-Canadian Tractors Ltd.

SASKATOON, SASKATCHEWAN

The Canadian Thresherman of 1913 illustrated the British-Canadian 15 hp tractor of the period. The com-

Allen Breed 30 hp tractor

pany name implied the tractor may have been imported to Canada from Great Britain. Unfortunately, this rear view of the tractor is the only image thus far located.

British-Canadian 15 hp tractor

Brockway Tractor Company

BEDFORD, OHIO

Brockway 49G tractor

Beginning in 1949 Brockway offered two models, the 49G two-plow gasoline tractor that used a Continental F-162 engine and the diesel 49D, equipped with a Continental GD-157 engine. Production of the Brockway tractor continued until 1958, then it disappeared from trade directories.

COLLECTOR VALUES	1	2	3	4
BROCKWAY TRACTOR	$11,500	–	–	–

Brown Cultivator Company

MINNEAPOLIS, MINNESOTA

This firm was listed in the 1921 Minneapolis city directories as being organized by M. F. Hewitt, O. K. Brown, and others. In 1922 the company was no longer listed. It is unknown whether the company survived long enough to produce any of its cultivating tractors.

Bryan Harvester Company

PERU, INDIANA

In 1920 Bryan introduced its revolutionary steam tractor design. It employed a small high-pressure water tube boiler operating at a pressure of 550 psi.

Bryan 26-70

Initially, the company offered this 26-70 model. The Bryan was one of the few attempts to market a small high-pressure condensing steam engine to the farm tractor trade. By 1920 the big steam traction engines were on their way out as the smaller gasoline tractors took their place.

Bryan small 20 hp steamtractor

In the mid-1920s Bryan offered this small 20 hp version of its steam tractor. It used a two-cylinder steam engine with a 4 x 5-inch bore and stroke, along with a high-pressure water tube boiler operating at 550 psi. The exhaust steam was condensed for reuse, cutting down the need for extra boiler feed water. Ground speed was variable and was anywhere from 1/8 to 7-1/2 mph. Production ended in the late 1920s.

W. G. Buck

WARREN, OHIO

A note in the American Machinist for 1915 indicated this firm was being organized to build tractors. Aside from this notice, no other information has been located.

Buckeye Mfg. Company

ANDERSON, INDIANA

Buckeye introduced its first tractors in 1912. In 1917 the company rechristened its Buckeye tractors as the Trundaar line. The firm does not appear in the trade directories after 1923.

Buckeye Junior tractor

Buckeye Junior tractors made their first appearance in 1912. This small crawler design was typical of a time when it was thought that "front wheels" were still necessary for steering. There were numerous companies building half-track crawlers. The Buckeye Jr. remained on the market until about 1915.

Buckeye Chain Tread 16-32

The Buckeye Chain Tread tractor appeared in 1917, a year after the company had bought out the Lambert Gas Engine Company, also of Anderson, Indiana. The Chain Tread had a 16-32 hp rating and was powered by a 4-1/2 x 6-3/4-inch four-cylinder engine.

Buckeye introduced a different Chain Tread tractor in 1917, shortly before announcing its Trundaar tractor line. Little is known of this particular model, except it had an entirely different design than its predecessors. A small advertisement of the day simply referred to it as its "Chain Tread Tractor."

Buckeye Chain Tread new model

Trundaar

Trundaar trademark

A trademark application of 1918 illustrated the Trundaar trademark and also noted it was first used on the company's tractors in September 1917.

Trundaar 20-35 crawler

At the same time, Buckeye announced the 20-35 Trundaar crawler. This was a full-fledged crawler of an entirely new design. It used a unique front linkage system that permitted the tracks to oscillate on uneven ground. The 20-35 used a Waukesha four-cylinder engine with a 4-3/4 x 6-3/4-inch bore and stroke.

The Trundaar 25-40 came onto the market in 1920, and seems to have been the replacement for the earlier 20-35 tractor. It was rated to pull 4,000 lbs. at 2-1/2 mph. The 25-40 tractors carried a four-cylinder Waukesha engine with a 5 x 6-1/4-inch bore and stroke.

Trundaar 25-40 tractor

Model 10 Trundaar tractor

Little information has surfaced concerning the Model 10 Trundaar tractor. It was the smallest of the line, and made its debut about 1920. Production of the Model 10, and all Trundaar tractors, was quite limited.

Buckeye Traction Ditcher Company

FINDLAY, OHIO

This company was best known as the manufacturer of the first successful traction ditching machine for laying agricultural tiles. A trade papers noted that Buckeye was announcing a "new outfit" for 1910. Nothing more was heard until the 1919 Power Wagon Reference Book that listed Buckeye as the manufacturer of the Alligator tractor, but no specifications for the tractor have been located.

Buffalo-Pitts Company

BUFFALO, NEW YORK

Buffalo-Pitts had a history going back to 1834, especially with early threshers. By the 1880s the company was building steam traction engines, and in 1910 it came out with the huge 40-70 tractor.

Buffalo-Pitts tractor, early version

Few specs have been found on this tractor, although it remained in the industry listings until at least 1916, despite the fact the company had gone into receivership in 1914. The original 40-70 tractor used a three-cylinder engine, and roller chains connected the rear wheels to the bull pinions.

Buffalo-Pitts 40-70 tractor, late version

The 40-70 retained the three-cylinder engine until about 1914 when the tractor was revamped and given a four-cylinder vertical engine. Weighing 22,000 lbs., the new 40-70 style was listed in the trade directories as late as 1920.

Bull Tractor Company

MINNEAPOLIS, MINNESOTA

Of all companies that paved the way for the small, lightweight farm tractor, Bull was probably the most noticeable. While Bull's designs were unique (to say the least) the company proved a small and lightweight tractor could be a practical machine compared to the heavy and cumbersome tractors then on the market. The Little Bull of 1914 sold for only $335 compared to $2,000 or $3,000 for one of the "big" tractors. Historically, the Bull revolutionized the farm tractor industry and brought the small tractor to the farm. Hundreds of companies came in its wake, all trying to make their mark, and of course, their fortune. Few made it...even the Bull Tractor Company went broke by 1920.

Little Bull tractor

In 1914 Bull Tractor Company was incorporated at Minneapolis. In 1913 the company had displayed the Little Bull at the Minnesota State Fair, where it received wide acclaim. The 1914 model had a 5 to 12 hp rating. Weighing 2,900 lbs., the Little Bull sold for the incredibly low price of $335. More than 3,800 Little Bull tractors were sold between April and December of 1914.

Big Bull tractor

In 1915 the Big Bull emerged, originally with a 7 to 20 hp rating, but by 1917 it became a 12-24 tractor. The 12-24 used a Toro two-cylinder opposed engine with a 5-1/2 x 7-inch bore and stroke. Through 1917 the Bull tractors were made in the shops of Minneapolis Steel & Machinery Co. This contract was canceled, and eventually a deal was made to build them in the Toro Motor Company shops in Minneapolis. Bull merged with Madison Motors Corporation of Anderson, Indiana, in 1919 but by 1920 this venture went broke and the remaining parts and inventory was sold to American Motor Parts Company.

BULL

Bull tractor trademark

COLLECTOR VALUES	1	2	3	4
LITTLE BULL	$65,000	$50,000	$25,000	$10,000
BIG BULL	$65,000	$50,000	$25,000	$10,000

Bull Dog Tractor Company

OSHKOSH, WISCONSIN

Bull Dog 30

The Bull Dog 30 was introduced in 1920. This was a unique four-wheel-drive design was powered by a big Waukesha four-cylinder engine with a 5 x 6-1/2-inch bore and stroke. The Bull Dog 30 was listed only in 1920, so apparently it was built only for a short time. It was priced at $4,250.

Bullock Tractor Company

CHICAGO, ILLINOIS

The Creeping Grip tractor was originally built by Western Implement & Motor Co. at Davenport, Iowa. When this company went broke in 1913, H. E. Bullock, one of the largest stockholders, revived the firm as Bullock Tractor Co.

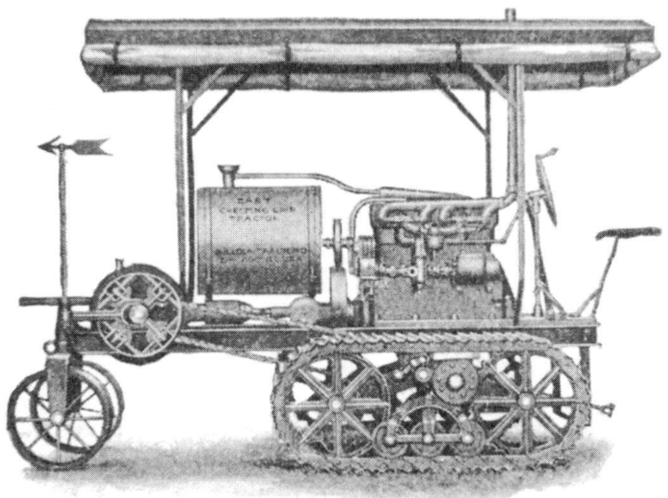

Bullock Baby Creeper

The tractor illustrated here is the Bullock Baby Creeper of 1914. Rated at 20 drawbar and 30 belt hp, the Baby Creeper was essentially the same design that had been built at Davenport.

Bullock Creeping Grip tractor

Creeping Grip tractors underwent numerous changes after 1914. Four new models were introduced that year and in addition to the 20-30, the company offered a 12-20, a 30-40, a 45-60, and the big 55-75. The 12-20 remained in production until the company merged with the Franklin Flexible Tractor Company of Greenville, Ohio, in 1920 to form the Franklin-Bullock Tractor Co. The 20-30 remained in production for several years.

CREEPING GRIP.

Creeping Grip trademark

Bullock Tractor Co. filed a trademark application in 1915 for its Creeping Grip trademark, noting that it had been used since November 9, 1911. This would coincide with the first use of the mark by the predecessor company, Western Implement & Motor Company at Davenport, Iowa.

Burn Oil Tractor Company

PEORIA, ILLINOIS

Burn Oil 15-30

In 1920 Burn Oil Tractor Co. came out with the 15-30 model. At the time, the company was located in Peoria, but 1921 listings indicated the firm had relocated to Warren, Indiana. After that, the company disappeared. The 15-30 used a two-cylinder horizontal engine with a 6-3/4 x 7-inch bore and stroke. Weighing some 5,500 lbs., the Burn Oil 15-30 sold for $1,650.

Burtt Mfg. Company

KALAMAZOO, MICHIGAN

Burtt was building gasoline engines by 1902, but a 1914 trade announcement indicates that the firm was anticipating production of a new three-bottom motor plow. Aside from this note, there is no other information on this company's activities in the tractor business.

[Throughout this section, assume that gasoline was used for fuel unless another fuel source is indicated.]

California Tractor Corporation

SAN FRANCISCO, CALIFORNIA

During the 1930s and the 1940s, this firm was listed as the manufacturer of the Trojan garden tractors. Despite the listings, no specs or photos of this tractor have been located.

COLLECTOR VALUES	1	2	3	4
TROJAN GARDEN TRACTOR	–	–	$3,000	–

W. P. Callahan & Company

DAYTON, OHIO

Callahan was a well known builder of gasoline engines and was listed as a builder of gasoline traction engines in the 1905-1907 period. No illustrations of the company's design have been located. The company remained in the gasoline engine business until about 1910.

Cameron Tractors, Inc.

NEW YORK, NEW YORK

Cameron tractor

In the early 1920s, Cameron offered its small, one-plow tractor. Of rather unique design, it featured the company's own four-cylinder air-cooled engine and used a 3-1/4 x 4-1/2-inch bore and stroke. Also included was a belt pulley, mounted in line with the engine and just below the steering wheel. Production of the Cameron continued for only a short time.

Campco Tractors Inc.

STOCKTON, CALIFORNIA

Campco logo

A trademark application filed in 1925 is the only evidence found on the Campco tractors. According to the application, the Campco mark was first used on December 1, 1919.

Can-A-Ford Company

SPARTA, MICHIGAN

This company was organized in 1917 to build a tractor attachment specifically for the Ford Model T automobiles. No other information has been located.

Canadian Rein Drive Tractors Ltd.

TORONTO, ONTARIO

This firm was incorporated for $1 million in 1917. Aside from this information, no further data has been located.

Canadian-American Gas & Gasoline Engine Company

DUNVILLE, ONTARIO

A 1911 advertisement illustrated the Canadian tractor, available in 6-, 10- and 12-hp sizes. This unusual design used a two-cylinder engine that could be governed either with the "hit-and-miss" method or the volume-governed method. In addition, the spark could come from a conventional spark plug or from a mechanical igniter.

Canadian tractor

Cameco 235 Powershift

Cane Machinery & Engineering Company

THIBODAUX, LOUISIANA

In the early 1960s Cameco was organized to build modern field machinery for the sugar cane industry.

By the 1970s the firm was producing the Cameco 115 shown here. Of four-wheel-drive articulated design, the 115 featured a Caterpillar D3304 engine with 100 flywheel hp.

The Cameco 235 Powershift tractor debuted about 1975. This big four-wheel-drive tractor was equipped with a Caterpillar 3208 V-8 diesel engine. Capable of 135 flywheel hp, the 235 had a working weight of 20,000 lbs. Numerous special features were available that were especially tailored to sugar cane harvest.

Cameco 405

With a Caterpillar 3208 engine, capable of producing 210 flywheel hp, the big Cameco 405 tractor was available with either a standard direct-drive transmission or a powershift transmission. A Caterpillar planetary axle was also featured, along with an elaborate hydraulic system.

Cameco 115

Capp Bros.

STOCKTON, CALIFORNIA

The Pull-Away garden tractors were listed from Capp Bros. in the 1953 trade directories but no other information has been found.

J. I. Case Company

J. I. Case Threshing Machine Company

RACINE, WISCONSIN

Jerome I. Case began in the threshing machine business in 1842. Initially, Case left Oswego County, New York, and settled in the small community of Rochester, Wisconsin. Over the next two years Case perfected his design. About that time, Case moved to nearby Racine, setting up what would be a huge manufacturing operation. In fact, Case built more threshing machines than anyone else.

The dramatic growth of J. I. Case Threshing Machine Company got another boost with the 1869 introduction of a portable steam engine. It was among the first such engines to be offered to the American farmer and was a hallmark in the beginning of farm power. The Case portable led to the development of Case steam traction engines and Case quickly rose to the top. The company built more steam traction engines than any other.

In 1876 J. I. Case got into the plow business, forming a separate company that came to be known as J. I. Case Plow Works. This firm had no connection with the J. I. Case Threshing Machine Company aside from the fact that both were founded by J. I. Case. The J. I. Case Plow Works made an excellent reputation for itself, eventually building the Wallis tractors. In 1928 the Plow Works was sold to Massey-Harris. After the sale, Massey-Harris sold out all rights to the Case name to the Threshing Machine Company. The latter dropped "Threshing Machine" from the company name, simply calling itself J. I. Case Company.

J. I. Case Threshing Machine Company was the first major farm equipment manufacturer to attempt to build a "gasoline traction engine," as they were originally called. In 1892 the company built a "Paterson" tractor, but despite every effort to perfect the machine, constant problems with carburetion and ignition thwarted its success. The idea was abandoned and nearly two decades passed before Case again entered the tractor business.

The first Case tractor appeared in 1911 and had huge dimensions, but served to help the company launch its first line of tractors in 1912. That year the company launched its 20-40 and 30-60 models, continuing to build them for several seasons. The tractors that followed are illustrated and described below.

J. I. Case continued in the farm equipment business until 1984 when the company merged with International Harvester Company to form the present-day Case-IH line. Full details of the J. I. Case implement and tractor line may be found in the author's title, 150 Years of J. I. Case.

Paterson (1892) tractor

Commonly known as the Paterson, the first Case tractor, introduced in 1892, was also the first tractor to be built by any major implement manufacturer of the day. Surprisingly little is known of the 1892 model except that it was plagued with ignition and carburetion problems and the technology of the day was not advanced enough to solve them. It is said the Paterson resided in a Case warehouse for years before being scrapped.

Case 30-60 Prototype

In 1911 J. I. Case came out with a huge 30-60 tractor. This prototype design was somewhat different than the 1912 production model, but it provided designers a chance to field test it prior to full production.

Case 30-60

Full production of the Case 30-60 tractor began in 1912. Like other tractors of the time, it was built over a heavy structural steel chassis. Due to the great weight of the early tractors the frame was exceedingly heavy, but in most cases it was overdesigned as a safety factor. Production of the 30-60 continued into 1916.

COLLECTOR VALUES	1	2	3	4
30-60	–	$155,000	–	–

Case 20-40, early style

The Case 20-40 was a popular model. Introduced in 1912, the tractors built through 1916 were equipped with a large tubular radiator. The engine exhaust was piped to the top of the radiator, terminating in vertical nozzles that exhausted from the small stack atop the radiator. The action of the exhaust created an induced draft through the radiator tubes, cooling the engine automatically.

COLLECTOR VALUES	1	2	3	4
20-40, EARLY	$60,000	$50,000	$32,000	$15,000

Case 20-40, late style

Between 1916 and 1919, the last year of production, the Case 20-40 saw a few modifications. The most noticeable was the elimination of the induced-draft radiator and the addition of a fan-cooled cellular radiator. Case 20-40 tractors used a two-cylinder opposed engine with an 8-3/4 x 9-inch bore and stroke.

Nebraska Test Data

Model: Case 20-40

Test No. 7

Date Tested: April 10 to May 7, 1920

While all previous tests had been made on relatively new tractor designs, the Case 20-40 had an illustrious history, going back several years. Its large, heavyweight design was typical of an earlier stage of tractor development. Despite this, the 20-40 was still firmly entrenched among tractor users, so the Case people sent Serial No. 22518 into Lincoln for testing. Weighing 13,780 lbs., the 20-40 featured two forward speeds of 2 and 3 mph. A two-cylinder opposed engine with an 8-3/4 x 9-inch bore and stroke was used—it was rated at 475 rpm. On the rated drawbar test, which ran for 9-3/4 hours, a drawbar pull of 3,987 lbs. was recorded. On the maximum drawbar test, 24.66 hp was developed, along with a 5,537 lb. drawbar pull. Slightly more than 40 hp was developed on the rated brake hp test, with a fuel consumption of 5.66 hp-hours per gallon of kerosene, or 7.1 gph.

COLLECTOR VALUES	1	2	3	4
20-40, LATE	$65,000	$48,000	$30,000	$15,000

Case 12-25

Introduced in 1914, the Case 12-25 tractor was the company's first move into the small tractor business. Farmers clamored for smaller tractors, because the huge 30-60 tractors were of no use to the average farmer. The 12-25 used a two-cylinder opposed engine with a 7-inch bore and stroke. Production ended in 1918.

COLLECTOR VALUES	1	2	3	4
12-25	--	$34,000	--	--

The 10-20 was an unusual tractor design that appeared in 1915. It sported only three wheels and was powered by a four-cylinder engine. Production of the 10-20 may have ended as early as 1918, but it took another couple of years to sell the remaining inventory. This tractor retailed for $900.

Nebraska Test Data

Model: Case 10-20

Test No. 6

Date Tested: April 9 to May 5, 1920

This was the first three-wheeled style tested at Nebraska, although it actually may have been tested after its production run was over. Test engineers noted "the clutch gave some trouble from sticking so that it could not be disengaged with the engine running. Oil was applied to the friction surface but this did not entirely remedy the trouble." With this exception, only minor adjustments or repairs were made, and even the problems experienced with the clutch were not deemed serious enough to disqualify the tractor. Using a four-cylinder 4-1/4 x 6-inch engine rated at 900 rpm, the 10-20 displayed slightly more than 20 brake hp on the rated load test, and achieved a fuel consumption rating of 8.42 hp-hours per gallon of kerosene fuel. On the drawbar, a maximum pull of 2,631 lbs. was attained at a speed of 2.18 mph. This resulted in 15.28 drawbar hp. Rated speed for the 10-20 was 2-1/4 miles per hour. Total weight was 5,080 lbs.

COLLECTOR VALUES	1	2	3	4
10-20	$25,000	$20,000	$12,000	$8,000

Case 9-18

During 1916, J. I. Case introduced its small 9-18 tractor. This conventional four-wheel design was more popular than the three-wheeled Case 10-20. This tractor heralded the beginning of many new features, including the use of an air cleaner as standard equipment. Production ended in 1918.

COLLECTOR VALUES	1	2	3	4
9-18	$22,000	$17,000	$10,000	–

Production of the 10-18 tractor marked a new era in Case tractor design. This new model was the first Case tractor to use a unit frame. For the 10-18, a single iron casting carried the entire tractor. A four-cylinder Case-built engine was used and it carried a 3-7/8 x 5-inch bore and stroke. Hyatt roller bearings were used throughout the tractor. Production of the 10-18 ended in 1922 when it was replaced with the 12-20 model.

Case 10-20

Case 10-18

Nebraska Test Data

Model: Case 10-18

Test No. 3

Date Tested: April 7 to April 15, 1920

Using a four-cylinder, vertical, valve-in-head engine, the Case 10-18 developed 18.41 belt hp on the dynamometer, keeping it just within the requirements necessary to justify the advertised rating. Nearly 6-1/4 hp-hours per gallon of kerosene fuel resulted from the test. At the drawbar, 11.24 hp was developed on the maximum load test with a drivewheel slippage of 11.4 percent recorded. A drawbar pull of 1,730 lbs. was achieved. Specifications included bore and stroke dimensions of 3-7/8 x 5 inches and a rated engine speed of 1,050 rpm. Two forward speeds of 2-1/4 and 3-1/2 mph were provided. Total weight was 3,760 lbs. Regular equipment included a Kingston Type L carburetor and a Kingston magneto. Except for tightening the friction drive on the fan, no other repairs or adjustments were needed.

COLLECTOR VALUES	1	2	3	4
10-18	$13,000	$10,000	$5,000	$1,500

Case 15-27

Case 15-27 tractors were built between 1919 and 1924. A one-piece, cast iron frame was standard, and removable cylinder sleeves were part of the design. Other innovations included the use of a drilled crankshaft and full-pressure lubrication of important engine parts. The 15-27 was rerated to the 18-32 model in 1925.

Nebraska Test Data

Model: Case 15-27

Test No. 4

Date Tested: April 2 to April 30, 1920

Weighing 6,460 lbs., the Case 15-27 was one of a complete series of new Case models. A cross-mounted, four-cylinder, 4-1/2 x 6-inch engine was the most noticeable feature. The 15-27 was tested using kerosene fuel. Accessory items included a Berling magneto and Kingston carburetor. Two forward speeds of 2-1/4 and 3 mph were provided. During 37 hours of testing, the clutch was adjusted twice, along with fine tuning of the governor and carburetor. On the drawbar a maximum pull of 3,440 lbs. was achieved with a ground speed of 2.05 mph—the resulting calculations gave 18.80 drawbar hp. Nearly 22 drawbar hp resulted on a second test made in high gear, but the drawbar pull dropped to 2,840 lbs. On the belt, 31.23 maximum hp appeared, with fuel consumption coming to 9.9 hp-hours per gallon of kerosene.

COLLECTOR VALUES	1	2	3	4
15-27	$10,000	$7,500	$5,000	$1,200

Case 22-40

A heavy structural iron frame supported the big Case 22-40 tractor. Rated to pull 3,700 lbs. at the drawbar, this four-cylinder tractor used a 5-1/ 2 x 6-3/4-inch bore and stroke. Produced between 1919 and 1925, the 22-40 was priced at $3,100. The tractor's physical size and hefty price limited sales of this model.

Nebraska Test Data

Model: Case 22-40

Test No. 5

Date Tested: April 7 to May 6, 1920

On the rated load test, the Case 22-40 developed 40.06 belt hp, with a fuel consumption of 9.72 hp-hours per gallon of kerosene. A four-cylinder engine powered the 22-40 and it had a rated speed of 850 rpm. Two forward speeds were provided, 2.2 and 3.2 mph. Weighing 9,940 lbs., the 22-40 attained a maximum drawbar pull of 4,965 lbs. at a speed of 2.19 mph, a 29.04 maximum drawbar hp. To attain this maximum pull, engineers recorded a drivewheel slippage of 19.25 percent, compared to only 13-1/2 percent slippage on the rated drawbar load tests. Standard equipment for the test model included a Bosch ZR4 magneto and a Kingston Type E carburetor. During the 53 hours of running time, only minimal repairs and adjustments were necessary.

COLLECTOR VALUES	1	2	3	4
22-40	$18,000	$12,000	$7,500	$2,750

Case 12-20

In 1921 Case introduced the 12-20 tractor, replacing the earlier 10-18 model. The four-cylinder motor used a 4-1/8 x 5-inch bore and stroke, or a quarter inch larger engine bore than the 10-18. The cylinders were cast en bloc and full force feed lubrication was featured. The 12-20 remained in production until 1928 when it was renamed the Case Model A, but that model was also dropped by the following year.

Nebraska Test Data

Model: Case 12-20

Test No. 88

Date Tested: August 14 to August 17, 1922

Weighing 4,450 lbs., the Case 12-20 featured the company's own vertical, four-cylinder, valve-in-head engine. Rated at 1,050 rpm, the 12-20 tested used kerosene fuel throughout the procedures. Special features included removeable cylinder sleeves, plus a governor and a water-type air cleaner of J.I. Case design. Additional equipment included a Berling Model F-41 magneto and a Kingston 13-V carburetor. Two forward speeds of 2.2 and 3.0 mph were provided. On the rated load test, 20.17 brake hp was developed with an economy of 8.58 hp-hours per gallon, or a total consumption of 2.35 gph. Under maximum load conditions the 12-20 managed 22.51 brake hp. The 10-hour rated drawbar test revealed an average load of 13.15 hp with a pull of 1,703 lbs. at 2.91 mph. A maximum pull of 2,225 lbs. was achieved in low gear.

Nebraska Test Data

Model: Case 12-20

Test No. 91

Date Tested: April 6 to April 17, 1923

Major differences between this 12-20 and the version tested a year earlier included a Kingston Model L-3 carburetor instead of the Kingston Model 13-V, and a Bosch AT4 magneto replaced the Berling magneto. Kerosene remained the fuel of choice. Still weighing 4,450 lbs., the 12-20 noted here came up with a maximum drawbar pull of 3,150 lbs. in low gear. This corresponded to 17.52 drawbar hp. Rated drawbar tests in high gear indicated a pull of 1,557 lbs. at a speed of 3.09 mph or 12.83 drawbar hp. Fuel economy improved in the rated brake hp test when compared to Test No. 88: 10.1 hp-hours per gallon was realized with a load of 20.16 hp, and a total consumption of 1.996 gph. Under maximum load, 25.54 brake hp was recorded. Basic specifications remained the same in both tests, but a comparison with No. 88 revealed some differences in the results, probably because of the change in ignition and fuel systems.

COLLECTOR VALUES	1	2	3	4
12-20	$12,000	$9,000	$4,500	$1,200

Case 40-72

The huge Case 40-72 first appeared in 1921, with a few more built in 1922 and 1923. Priced at $4,000, the 40-72 was a huge four-cylinder tractor with a 7 x 8-inch bore and stroke. Capable of more than 90 belt hp, it was a good choice for large threshing machines, sawmills and for plowing.

Nebraska Test Data

Model: Case 40-72

Test No. 90

Date Tested: April 6 to April 29, 1923

During the preliminary limbering-up runs, it was necessary to replace the head gaskets on the 40-72. With this exception, only minor repairs were necessary during the 38 hours of testing. Case used kerosene throughout the test, and at its rated load of 72 hp, an efficiency of 8.08 hp-hours per gallon was attained on the belt. This corresponded to total consumption of 8.959 gph. Under maximum load the 40-72 cranked out 91.42 brake hp with a fuel consumption of 11.37 gph. Drawbar tests indicated a maximum pull of 10,680 lbs. in low gear for 49.87 drawbar hp at 1.75 mph. Another maximum load test in high gear revealed 55.14 drawbar hp by pulling a 7,400 lb. load at 2.79 mph. Case used its own four-cylinder, valve-in-head, vertical engine on the 40-72 with a rated speed of 800 rpm. Also supplied was a J.I. Case governor, a Bosch ZR4 magneto, and a Kingston Model L carburetor. The 40-72 weighed 22,000 lbs.

COLLECTOR VALUES	1	2	3	4
40-72	$150,000	--	--	—

Case 12-20 Industrial

Case Industrial tractors made their debut in 1925, and this one was based on the little 12-20 model. By 1929 this model was dropped from the line and was replaced with an entirely new tractor design.

COLLECTOR VALUES	1	2	3	4
12-20 INDUSTRIAL	$9,000	$6,500	$4,000	$1,500

During 1925, Case revamped the 15-27 tractor and re-rated it as the Case 18-32. It used the same four- cylinder 4-1/2 x 6 engine as had been used in the 15-27. Production of the 18-32 ended in 1927 when the Model K tractor appeared. It was essentially the same tractor, but with a different model designator. By 1929 the Model K had also disappeared.

Nebraska Test Data

Model: Case 18-32

Test No. 109

Date Tested: October 27 to November 4, 1924

Under Serial No. 51320 Case presented the 18-32 tractor—virtually a carbon copy of the 15-27 model listed in Test No. 4. Except for raising the engine speed from 900 to 1,000 rpm, and substituting a Bosch AT4 magneto and a water-type air washer, few changes were made. During the maximum drawbar tests, the clutch was adjusted once, otherwise no repairs or adjustments were required throughout the 36 hours of running time. Using high gear for the rated drawbar test gave a pull of 2,117 lbs. at 3.4 mph for an average of 19.21 drawbar hp during the 10-hour test. A maximum load test in low gear revealed 24.01 drawbar hp, with the 18-32 pulling 3,882 lbs. at 2.32 mph. All tests used kerosene fuel, with the rated brake hp test at 32.08 hp showing a total consumption of 3.080 gph and a fuel economy of 10.417 hp- hours per gallon. Under maximum brake load, 36.73 hp was developed and 9.23 hp-hours per gallon.

COLLECTOR VALUES	1	2	3	4
18-32	$14,000	$10,000	$7,500	$2,500

Case 25-45

Case 18-32

In 1924 Case replaced the 22-40 tractor with the Case 25-45. This model continued until 1927 when it was designated the Model T, although it was essentially the same tractor as before. The 25-45 weighed more than 10,000 lbs. and used a 5-1/2 x 6-3/4-inch engine. Production ended in 1929.

Nebraska Test Data

Model: Case 25-45

Test No. 110

Date Tested: October 28 to November 9, 1924

The Case 25-45 tested here saw few changes from the Case 22-40 of test No. 5 in 1920, so refer to that test for engine data. Apparently, the 22-40 was greatly underrated by the manufacturer, allowing it to qualify for a higher rating without requiring increased engine speed over the earlier model. Even with its new 25-45 rating, the tractor submitted for Test No. 110 made an impressive showing in the drawbar tests. Using high gear, an average of 26.09 hp was delivered over the 10-hour rated load test, giving a pull of 2,966 lbs. at 3.298 mph. In the low gear maximum test, 5,750 lbs. were indicated at a speed of 2.145 mph for 32.96 drawbar hp. Fuel economy came to 8.8 hp-hours per gallon in the rated brake hp test, with kerosene consumption totalling 5.135 gph at 45.18 hp. At maximum load, 52.59 hp was achieved with a fuel economy of 9.14 hp-hours per gallon.

COLLECTOR VALUES	1	2	3	4
25-45	$20,000	$12,000	$7,500	$2,500

Case Model L, 26-40

J. I. Case introduced an entirely new line of tractors in 1929. The first one was the Model L, also known as the 26-40. It was a new design and carried a Case-built four-cylinder engine with a 4-5/8 x 6-inch bore and stroke. Production of Model L tractors continued into 1940 when it was replaced with the Case Model LA.

Nebraska Test Data

Model: Case Model L, 26-40

Test No. 155

Date Tested: March 16 to March 27, 1929

Three advertised speeds of 2-1/2, 3-1/4, and 4 mph were featured in the Case Model L tractor. Kerosene fuel was used throughout the 58 hour test. Rated brake hp testing yielded a fuel economy of 9.76 hp-hours per gallon, while in the maximum load test, 44.01 hp was developed with the economy rating rising slightly to 9.87. Drawbar tests indicated that maximum pull occurred in low gear. Traveling at 2.47 mph the "L" pulled a 4,555 lb. load, although it was at 21.9 percent slippage. Also, this 5,307 lb. tractor pulled nearly 83 percent of its own weight. Final results indicated 30.02 maximum drawbar hp. At rated drawbar load, fuel economy came in at 6.52 hp-hours per gallon. Case used its own four-cylinder vertical, I-head engine in the Model L tractor. It was rated at 1,100 rpm. Standard equipment included a Robert Bosch FU4 magneto, Kingston L-3 carburetor, and the company's own governor, air cleaner, and oil filter.

Case Model L, Updated

Case Model L tractors underwent various modifications during their production run. For instance, in 1934 Case began offering the Model L on full factory rubber tires instead of the usual steel wheels. (Note: The author once owned a 1938 Model L exactly like the one shown here and has always regretted selling it!)

Nebraska Test Data

Model: Case Model L, Updated

Test No. 309

Date Tested: October 10 to October 24, 1938

Equipped with rubber tires, the updated Model L weighed in at 8,025 lbs., compared to only 5,300 lbs. on steel wheels. Three forward speeds of 3.52, 4.48, and 5.58 mph were provided. Test H for rated drawbar load was made on rubber tires. Final results indicated a fuel economy of 10.05 hp-hours per gallon of distillate fuel while pulling 2,768 lbs. at 4.35 mph. Test G for operating maximum load was made on rubber tires and on steel wheels. The low-gear test on rubber tires yielded a pull of 4,474 lbs. at 3.09 mph and slippage of 14.79 percent for a total of 36.81 hp. The same test on steel wheels ended with a pull of 4,472 lbs. at 2.65 mph and slippage of 11.75 percent for an output of 31.64 hp. Fuel economy tests on steel and using second gear gave an economy figure of 7.94 hp-hours per gallon. Test D for rated belt hp yielded 11.2 hp-hours per gallon with a load of 42.1 hp. Operating at maximum load of 45.02 hp, economy was recorded at 11.62. The Model L tested was rated at 1,100 rpm and featured a four-cylinder I-head engine of the company's own design. It used a 4-5/8 x 6-inch bore and stroke, along with a Zenith K6A carburetor and a Case magneto.

Case Model LI Industrial

COLLECTOR VALUES	1	2	3	4
MODEL L (NO UPDATES)	$5,000	$3,000	$1,500	$500
MODEL L (UPDATES)	$3,000	$2,000	$1,000	$500
MODEL L (STARTER/ LIGHTS)	$4,500	$3,500	$1,500	$750
MODEL LA	$3,000	$1,900	$1,100	$500
MODEL LA (LP)	$3,500	$2,250	$1,000	$500
MODEL LA (HYDRAULIC)	$3,500	$2,250	$1,000	$500

Model LI Industrial tractors were available during the same 1929-1940 production run as the Model L farm tractor. It was essentially the same except for special wheel equipment and a modified transmission.

COLLECTOR VALUES	1	2	3	4
LI INDUSTRIAL	$5,000	$3,500	$1,300	$1,000

Case Model C

Model C Case tractors were a smaller version of the Model L, and except for their physical size and characteristics, looked almost identical. Production of this tractor began in 1929, continuing for another decade. The company also built a Model CH tractor; it was a special high-clearance model.

Nebraska Test Data

Model: Case Model C, 17-27

Test No. 167

Date Tested: August 12 to August 19, 1929

This tractor replaced another Model C that was submitted for Test No. 166, but later withdrawn. Using kerosene, the "replacement" Model C ended the 10-hour rated drawbar test with an average pull of 1,856 lbs. at 3.52 mph, and slippage of 8.76 percent. Fuel economy dropped in at 7.02 hp-hours per gallon. Advertised speeds of 2.3, 3.28, and 4.5 mph were provided. The maximum drawbar test in low gear yielded a pull of 3,289 lbs., or 79 percent of the tractor's total weight of 4,155 lbs. Results of this test also indicated 19.6 drawbar hp. Fuel economy at rated brake hp came in at an impressive 11.06 hp-hours per gallon, and an even better figure of 11.36 when operating at maximum load of 29.81 brake hp. During the 35 hours of running time the clutch was adjusted and the fuel line was cleaned; otherwise no repairs or adjustments were necessary. A Case-built engine was featured. Of vertical, I-head design, it was rated at 1,100 rpm and used a 3-7/8 x 5-1/2-inch bore and stroke. A Robert Bosch FU4ARS magneto was featured, along with a Kingston L-3 carburetor, and a Case air cleaner system.

COLLECTOR VALUES	1	2	3	4
C TRACTOR	$4,000	$2,500	$1,250	$500

Case Model CI tractors were simply an industrial version of the Case Model C farm tractor. This model had a production period approximately the same as the Model C and was intended for factories, warehouses, and similar applications where the tractor operated on concrete floors.

COLLECTOR VALUES	1	2	3	4
MODEL CI	$3,750	$2,500	$1,000	$500

Case Model CI

Case Model CO

Although a limited market, the need for orchard tractors brought about the Case Model CO. Built during the same period as the Model C, the Model CO was equipped with special fenders and other accessories needed for this specialized work. All Model C tractors were equipped with a Case-built four-cylinder engine with a 3-7/8 x 5-1/2-inch bore and stroke. Beginning in 1934, Case briefly built a Model CV Vineyard tractor.

COLLECTOR VALUES	1	2	3	4
MODEL CO	$3,850	$2,800	$1,300	$800

Case Model CC

Case Model CC tractors were introduced in 1929. This row-crop version was the same as the Model C standard-tread version in many respects. Production of the Model C, the Model CC and other variations continued into 1939 when they were replaced with a new streamlined series.

Nebraska Test Data

Model: Case Model CC
Test No. 169
Date Tested: September 10 to September 18, 1929

Weighing 4,240 lbs., the Case CC tractor delivered 17.88 drawbar hp on the rated load test, pulling 1,599 lbs. at 4.19 mph. Kerosene was used in this test, and at rated drawbar, economy came in at 7.52 hp-hours per gallon. Three advertised speeds of 2.6, 3.72, and 5.14 mph were provided in the CC tractor. Using low gear, it delivered 22.7 maximum drawbar hp, pulling a load of 2,950 lbs. at 2.88 mph with a slippage of 6.3 percent. As usual, Case built its own engine for the CC. It was of four-cylinder vertical I-head design and featured a 3-7/8 x 5-1/2 inch bore and stroke with a rated speed of 1,100 rpm. Included, too, was a Robert Bosch FU4 magneto, Kingston L3V carburetor, and the company's own air cleaner and oil filter. Rated brake hp testing gave a score of 10.52 hp-hours per gallon while cranking out 27.37 hp. At a maximum load of 28.97 hp, this figure dropped slightly to 10.06 with total fuel consumption of 2.88 gph. No major repairs or adjustments were required during the 40-hour test.

COLLECTOR VALUES	1	2	3	4
MODEL CC				
(1929-1932)	$3,000	$1,500	$700	$500
(1933-1937)	$1,800	$1,200	$800	$300
(1938, STARTER/LIGHTS)	$5,000	$3,500	$1,500	$500

Case Model RC

The Case Model RC tractors first appeared in 1935. This little tractor had a rating of 11 drawbar and 17 belt hp. Like the Model CC, numerous row-crop implements were available and tailored to these models.

Nebraska Test Data

Model: Case Model RC

Test No. 251

Date Tested: April 7 to April 16, 1936

During 52 hours of running time, the Case RC tractor used gasoline. Under Test H for rated drawbar load, fuel economy was recorded at 6.72 hp-hours per gallon; this in addition to an output of 11.61 hp, and a pull of 1,228 lbs. at 3.55 mph. Under Test G for operating maximum load, the RC pulled 2,103 lbs. in low gear. In Test D the RC developed 17.55 rated hp, yielding a fuel economy of 9.87 hp-hours per gallon and a slightly diminished economy figure of 9.69 in Test C for operating maximum load. This tractor featured a Waukesha four-cylinder, L-head engine with a 3-1/4 x 4-inch bore and stroke. Rated at 1,425 rpm, it also featured an American Bosch MJB4 magneto, Zenith carburetor, Case-Waukesha governor, and United air cleaner. Advertised speeds of 2-1/3, 3-1/3, and 4-1/2 mph were provided. Total weight was 3,350 lbs. No repairs or adjustments were noted.

COLLECTOR VALUES	1	2	3	4
MODEL RC				
(OVER TOP STEERING)	$2,500	$2,000	$1,000	$500
(SIDE ARM STEERING)	$2,750	$2,000	$1,000	$300

Case Model RC, Restyled

With the 1939 restyling of the Case tractor line, the Model RC took on a new look that included a heavy cast-iron grille (known as the "sunburst" grille) and the "Flambeau Red" finish instead of the time-honored gray enamel. By this time rubber tires became popular. With the onset of World War II and material shortages, tractor production was limited and many of those built during the war came out on steel wheels.

COLLECTOR VALUES	1	2	3	4
MODEL RC (SUN BURST GRILLE)	$3,000	$2,500	$1,500	$500

Case Model R

Case Model R tractors were introduced in 1938. The Model R had the same general appearance as other models of the Case line and was essentially the standard-tread version of the Model RC row-crop tractor. The company also built this model in RO Orchard and RI Industrial models.

Nebraska Test Data

Model: Case Model R

Test No. 308

Date Tested: October 10 to October 20, 1938

This standard-tread tractor featured 11.25 x 24-inch rear tires and 5.00 x 15-inch front rubber. Weighing in at 4,140 lbs., it included three forward speeds of 2-1/3, 3-1/3, and 4-1/2 mph. Standard equipment included a four-cylinder Waukesha L-head engine. Rated at 1,425 rpm, it used a 3-1/4 x 4-inch bore and stroke. Featured, too, was an American Bosch MJB4A108 magneto, along with a Zenith 193-1/2 carburetor and a United air cleaner. During 43 hours of engine running time, gasoline was used. The rated drawbar load of Test H indicated 14.19 hp, along with a pull of 1,512 lbs. at 3.52 mph and an economy of 8.55 hp-hours per

Case Model LA

gallon. Test G for operating maximum load resulted in a pull of 2,574 lbs. in low gear, along with an output of 15.58 hp. Test D for rated belt load indicated an economy of 10.27 with an output of 18.48 hp. At operating maximum load of 19.25 hp, fuel economy rose slightly to 10.48 hp-hours per gallon. A slight grease leak was noted on the transmission cover, and at one point it was necessary to repair the front wheel dust shield. Otherwise, no repairs or adjustments were required or noted.

COLLECTOR VALUES	1	2	3	4
MODEL R	$3,000	$2,500	$1,500	$500
MODEL R (W/ SUN BURST GRILLE)	$4,000	$3,000	$1,500	$500

Model LA Case tractors first appeared in 1940, replacing the venerable Model L. Rated at 1100 rpm, the Model LA engine was built by Case and used a 4-5/8 x 6-inch bore and stroke. This tractor was also available as the Model LAI Industrial tractor and could be furnished with special rice field equipment when so ordered. Production of the LA continued into about 1952.

Nebraska Test Data

Model: Case Model LA

Test No. 480

Date Tested: August 15 to August 28, 1952

At one point in the test procedures it was necessary to adjust the clutch–otherwise no repairs or adjustments were noted for the LA during 46 hours of engine operating time. This tractor was equipped with a Case-built, four-cylinder, I-head engine rated at 1,150 rpm and carrying a 4-3/8 x 6-inch bore and stroke for a 403.2 cubic inch displacement. Engine torque peaked at 433.1 lbs.-ft. with an engine speed of 801 rpm. Weighing 7,621 lbs., the LA used 15-30 rear and 7.50-18 front tires as standard equipment. Advertised speeds of 2-1/2, 3-1/3, 4-1/3, and 10 mph were provided. During some of the drawbar tests, an additional 1,576 lbs. was added to each rear wheel. Test H, at a rated drawbar load of 41.63 hp, indicated a fuel economy of 10.24 hp-hours per gallon of gasoline. This test also shows a pull of 3,347 lbs. at 4.66 mph under a slippage of 5.05 percent. Test G revealed a low-gear maximum pull of 6,659 lbs. at 2.26 mph with slippage totaling 15.76 percent. Under a Test C operating maximum load of 55.6 belt hp, fuel economy was recorded at 11.76 hp-hours per gallon, with this figure dropping very slightly to 11.71 at a Test D rated belt load of 52.58 hp.

Nebraska Test Data

Model: Case Model LA (Distillate)

Test No. 481

Date Tested: August 18 to August 29, 1952

Although this tractor was virtually identical to the Case LA in Test No. 480, it was equipped to burn distillate or "tractor fuel." Close comparison of these tests indicated that in Test 480 a compression ratio of 5.75:1 was used, while in this test the compression ratio was listed at 4.55:1. Engine speed, cubic inch displacement, ground speeds, and tire equipment were the same in both tests. Using third gear, Test H indicated a rated drawbar load of 34.99 hp and a fuel economy of 9.34 hp-hours per gallon. Also shown was a pull of 2,769 lbs. at 4.74 mph with a slippage of 3.83 percent. Test G yielded a low-gear maximum pull of 6,444 lbs. at 2.36 mph. At a Test C operating maximum load of 46.61 belt hp, fuel economy was noted at 10.76 hp-hours per gallon, dropping to 10.58 at a Test D rated belt load of 43.05 hp.

Nebraska Test Data

Model: Case Model LA (LPG)

Test No. 482

Date Tested: August 21 to September 6, 1952

Once again, the same basic LA tractor was presented, with a major modification being a change in compression ratio to 7.58:1 for use with commercial propane. With this exception, all other specifications remained virtually the same. No repairs or adjustments were noted for this tractor during 53 hours of engine operating time. Test H, at a rated drawbar load of 40.90 hp indicated a fuel economy of 8.14 hp-hours per gallon of propane. Also noted was a drawbar pull of 3,274 lbs. at 4.68 mph with a slippage of 4.49 percent. Test G manifested a low-gear maximum pull of 6,874 lbs. at 2.27 mph. Belt testing came up with a fuel economy of 9.42 hp-hours per gallon under a Test C operating maximum load of 57.89 hp, compared to an economy figure of 9.39 at a Test D rated load of 52.67 belt hp.

Case Model D

As part of a new tractor line, Case introduced its Model D standard-tread tractor in 1939. It was equipped with a Case four-cylinder engine with a 3-7/8 x 5-1/2-inch bore and stroke. Standard-tread tractors are also designated as fixed-width models. In either case, the designator portended a design featuring a wide front axle with no adjustment for varying tread widths. Row-crop tractors have an adjustable tread width to work in various crops.

Nebraska Test Data

Model: Case Model D

Test No. 349

Date Tested: June 18 to June 27, 1940

The Case Model D tractor featured the company's own four-cylinder, I-head engine rated at 1,200 rpm and carrying a 3-7/8 x 5 ½-inch bore and stroke. Case used its own magneto, along with a Zenith 62AXJ9 carburetor. Weighing in at 7,005 lbs., it went through 60 hours of engine operating time with no repairs or adjustments. The test weight included 343 lbs. of water ballast and 763 lbs. of cast-iron weights for each rear wheel, plus another 99 lbs. of cast-iron weight for each front wheel. The test tractor used 12.75 x 24 inch rear rubber and 7.50 x 16-inch front tires. Advertised speeds of 2.75, 4, 5.5, and 11 mph were provided. Second gear was used for Test H. It resulted with a fuel economy of 11.32 hp-hours per gallon of distillate, along with an output of 24.86 rated drawbar hp. Slippage in this test was recorded at 5.34 percent, along with a ground speed of 3.78 mph. A maximum pull of 4,192 lbs. was noted in Test G using low gear. At a speed of 2.4 mph the Model D had a recorded slippage of 14.88 percent along with a total output of 26.78 drawbar hp. Under operating maximum load the Model D produced 33.45 brake hp and yielded a fuel economy of 12.76 hp-hours per gallon, compared to 12.81 under rated brake load of 31.87 hp.

Case Model DO

COLLECTOR VALUES	1	2	3	4
MODEL D	$2,500	$2,000	$1,200	$500
MODEL D (HYDRAULIC)	$2,250	$1,800	$900	$300
MODEL D (HYDRAULIC, FOOT CLUTCH)	$3,000	$2,500	$1,100	$300
MODEL D-1 STANDARD (8,103 BUILT)	$3,000	$2,000	$1,000	$500
MODEL D-1 NT (445 BUILT)	$5,000	$3,500	$2,500	$1,250

With the introduction of the Model D tractor in 1939, Case also announced the Model DO orchard tractor. In addition, Case began to actively promote the use of LP gas as a tractor fuel in the early 1950s. Shown here is a Case DO tractor of 1952 with LP gas equipment.

COLLECTOR VALUES	1	2	3	4
MODEL DO (2,879 BUILT)	$5,500	$4,500	$2,500	$1,500

Case Model DC

Production of the Case Model DC tractors began in 1939. This model was very popular and was widely used as a three-plow tractor. Numerous attachments were available to further broaden their use. In 1952 Case began to furnish the DC tractors with special LP gas equipment as a factory option. By the time production of the Model DC ended in 1955, this tractor had received numerous modifications, including a hydraulic system and, beginning in 1952, the Case Eagle Hitch system.

Nebraska Test Data

Model: Case Model DC

Test No. 340

Test C for operating maximum load indicated a fuel economy of 12.13 hp-hours per gallon with an output of 35.51 brake hp for the Case DC. At rated load under Test D, fuel economy slipped very slightly to 12.07, along with an output of 32.94 brake hp. The DC was equipped with three forward speeds of 2-1/2, 3-1/2, and 5 mph. These speeds were calculated using 9.00 x 36-inch rear tires, although the test model carried 11.25 x 36-inch rear rubber. A maximum drawbar pull of 4,128 lbs. was achieved in low gear as noted in Test G. An output of 24.39 drawbar hp was realized during this pull, along with slippage of 15.88 percent. The 10-hour rated drawbar test indicated a fuel economy of 9.98 hp-hours per gallon. Other data from Test H indicates a pull of 2,730 lbs. at 3.54 mph, slippage of 5.46 percent, and an output of 25.74 drawbar hp. The DC was equipped with a Case-built four-cylinder engine with a 3-7/8 x 5 ½-inch bore and stroke, plus a rated speed of 1,100 rpm. Accessories included a Zenith 62AXJ9 carburetor and a Case magneto. Total weight as tested was 7,010 lbs. During the last few hours of Test H, intermittent missing developed. An inspection at the end of the test revealed an accumulation of lead oxide on the exhaust valve stems, preventing them from seating properly.

COLLECTOR VALUES	1	2	3	4
MODEL DC-3	$3,000	$2,500	$1,600	$700
MODEL DC-4	$3,000	$2,500	$1,500	$700

MODEL DDS(1,206 BUILT)	$15,000	$9,000	$4,500	$2,000
MODEL DE (16,000 BUILT)	$2,500	$1,250	$1,000	$500
MODEL DH (141 BUILT)	$10,000	$8,000	$5,000	$1,500
MODEL DV (582 BUILT)	$8,000	$5,500	$2,500	$1,500

Case Model DI Industrial

Model DI Industrial tractors were a variation of the Model D for factories and warehouses. The DI tractors could be furnished with a special pintle hitch for towing heavy trucks of materials within a factory.

COLLECTOR VALUES	1	2	3	4
MODEL DI INDUSTRIAL	$3,000	$2,000	$1,000	$500

Case Model S

Production of the Model S tractors began in 1940 and ended in 1955. This small tractor used a Case four-cylinder engine with a 3-1/2 x 4-inch bore and stroke. In 1944 the tractor had a list price of $845 yet very few were available because of World War II.

COLLECTOR VALUES	1	2	3	4
MODEL S	$2,800	$2,000	$1,000	$400
MODEL S (HYDRAULIC)	$2,500	$1,800	$800	$300

Case Model SO Orchard

Case Model S tractors initially used a 3-1/2 x 4 engine, but for 1953 the engine bore was increased to 3-5/8- inches for a 15 percent increase in the power level. Shown here is a specially built Model SO Orchard tractor.

COLLECTOR VALUES	1	2	3	4
MODEL SO ORCHARD	$4,000	$3,200	$2,000	$1,000

Model SC row-crop

Production of the Model SC row-crop tractors closely paralleled that of the Model S standard-tread version. Late models of the S and SC tractors could be furnished with live hydraulics. After the power level was raised in 1952, the SC tractors were capable of about 19 drawbar hp.

Nebraska Test Data

Model: Case Model SC

Test No. 367

Date Tested: April 29 to May 16, 1941

Case featured its own four-cylinder I-head engine in the SC tractor. Rated at 1,550 rpm, it carried a 3-1/2 x 4-inch bore and stroke. Four forward speeds of 2-1/2, 3-1/2, 4-3/4, and 9-2/3 mph were provided. Accessories included an Edison-Splitdorf magneto, Zenith carburetor, and brakes built by Auto Specialties Company. Test J tractor weight with no ballast was noted at 4,200 lbs. At an operating maximum load of 21.62 brake hp the SC came through Test C with a fuel economy of 10.55 hp-hours per gallon of distillate. Test D indicates nearly the same economy, in this case totaling 10.05 hp-hours per gallon under a rated load of 20.24 brake hp. An operating maximum load of 19.33 drawbar hp was noted in first gear under Test G. This test also gave a maximum drawbar pull of 3,166 lbs. at 2.29 mph with slippage of 8.88 percent. At rated drawbar output of 16.18 hp, the SC yielded a fuel economy of 9.08 hp-hours per gallon in Test H. Other data of this test included a pull of 1,794 lbs. at 3.38 mph and slippage of 4.8 percent.

Nebraska Test Data

Model: Case Model SC (new engine)

Test No. 496

Date Tested: June 15 to June 20, 1953

This upgraded Model SC tractor was equipped with a four-cylinder, I-head engine with a 3-7/8 x 4-inch bore and stroke, along with a rated speed of 1,600 rpm, and a 165.1 cubic inch displacement. Engine torque peaked at 210 lbs.-ft. with an engine speed of 992 rpm. Advertised speeds of 2-1/2, 3-7/8, 5, and 10 1/3 mph were standard on the SC tractor. Test H was run in second gear. With a rated output of 22.41 drawbar hp, the SC pulled 2,347 lbs. at 3.58 mph with a slippage of 5.67 percent. Fuel economy in this 10-hour run totaled 10.28 hp-hours per gallon. A low-gear maximum pull of 4,072 lbs. at 2.33 mph was achieved in Test G, although each rear tire carried an additional 603 lbs. of ballast over and above the bare tractor weight of 5,007 lbs. Also included with the SC were 11-38-inch rear and 5.50-16-inch front tires. Test C, run at an operating maximum belt load of 29.68 hp, produced a fuel economy of 11.38 hp-hours per gallon with a virtually identical economy figure of 11.39 appearing in the Test D rated belt run made at 28.05 hp. No repairs or adjustments were noted during 44 hours of engine operating time.

Nebraska Test Data

Model: Case Model SC (tractor fuel)

While the SC tractor of Test No. 496 used gasoline, the tractor presented for this test was designated as an "all-fuel" model and was tested using tractor fuel. While the tractor noted in Test No. 496 had a 6.25:1 compression ratio, this version was altered to 4.8:1. Otherwise, all specifications remained the same. Engine torque measured at the dynamometer peaked at 187.3 lbs.-ft. with an engine speed of 798 rpm. Test C, run at an operating maximum belt load of 23.67 hp produced a fuel economy of 10.08 hp-hours per gallon. When run under a Test D rated belt load of 22.25 belt hp, fuel economy increased to 10.42 hp-hours per gallon. Second gear was chosen for the 10-hour run of Test H. At a rated drawbar load of 18.54 hp, the SC pulled 1,904 lbs. at 3.65 mph with a slippage of 3.96 percent. Fuel economy in this test totaled 9.35 hp-hours per gallon. Test G indicated a low-gear maximum pull of 3,226 lbs. at 2.48 mph with slippage of 7.55 percent. No repairs or adjustments were noted during 46 hours of engine operating time.

COLLECTOR VALUES	1	2	3	4
MODEL SC	$2,000	$1,200	$600	$300
MODEL SC (SINGLE WHEEL FRONT–WIDE REAR AXLE, NO HY-DRAULIC)	$2,200	$1,600	$700	$350
MODEL SC (WIDE AD-JUSTABLE FRONT AXLE AND EAGLE HITCH)	$2,750	$2,000	$800	$500
MODEL SC (HYDRAULIC)	$3,000	$2,400	$1,000	$350
MODEL SC-4	$3,000	$2,500	$1,500	$800

Case Model V

Model V tractors first appeared in 1939. This small tractor used a Continental four-cylinder engine with a 3 x 4-3/8-inch bore and stroke. The Model V was also available as the Model VI Industrial tractor, complete with electric starter, lights and a pintle hitch. Production of the Model V and its derivatives continued until 1955.

COLLECTOR VALUES	1	2	3	4
MODEL V	$3,000	$2,500	$1,200	$600

Case Model VC

During 1939 Case introduced its Model VC tractor, a one- or two-plow model. This small tractor was built only until 1942 when it was replaced with the Model VAC. At the time, Case was building an extensive line of small tractors, with the largest model being the Model LA of about 45 belt hp.

Nebraska Test Data

Model: Case Model VC

Test No. 348

Date Tested: June 18 to June 25, 1940

Weighing in at 4,290 lbs., the VC was equipped with four forward speeds of 2.65, 3.64, 4.67, and 10.03 mph. Test H, formerly called "Rated Load," indicated a pull of 1,627 lbs. using second gear and traveling at 3.47 mph. Slippage was recorded at 5.5 percent, along with an output of 15.07 drawbar hp. The maximum low-gear pull of 2,798 lbs. as recorded in Test G notes an output of 17.5 drawbar hp plus a speed of 2.35 mph and slippage of 12.28 percent. This tractor featured a Continental four-cylinder, L-head engine with a 3 x 4 3/8-inch bore and stroke. It was rated at 1,425 rpm for drawbar duty and 1,650 rpm for belt work. Standard equipment included an Edison-Splitdorf magneto and a Schebler TSX43 carburetor. The test model carried 9 x 32-inch rear rubber and 5.00 x 15-inch front tires. Test C yielded a maximum operating load of 23.76 brake hp and a fuel economy of 11.33 hp-hours per gallon. Economy dropped insignificantly to stand at an even 11 hp-hours per gallon under Test D with a rated output of 22.07 brake hp. During 52 hours of engine operating time, a minor oil line leak was the only repair or adjustment noted.

COLLECTOR VALUES	1	2	3	4
MODEL VC	$2,500	$2,000	$1,200	$500

Case Model VA

Model VA tractors were built in the 1942 to 1955 period. The Model VA used a Case-built four-cylinder engine with a 3-1/4 x 3-3/4-inch bore and stroke. It was rated at 1,425 rpm. By about 1952, electric starter and lights had become standard equipment.

COLLECTOR VALUES	1	2	3	4
MODEL VA	$2,500	$2,000	$1,200	$500

Case Model VAC tractors first appeared in 1942 and remained on the market until about 1955, with various modifications. After about 1952 the electric starter and lights came as standard equipment. Prior to that time it was a $50 extra-cost option.

Case Model VAC

Nebraska Test Data

Model: Case Model VAC (tractor fuel)

Test No. 430

Date Tested: October 15 to October 26, 1949

Tractor fuel was selected for the Case VAC in this test. At a Test C operating maximum load of 16.98 hp the VAC achieved a fuel economy of 10.82 hp-hours per gallon, while at the Test D rated belt load of 15.93 hp the economy figure came in at 10.76. The VAC featured a four-cylinder, I-head engine rated at 1,425 rpm and using a 3-1/4 x 3-3/4-inch bore and stroke. Also featured was an Auto-Lite electrical system and a Marvel-Schebler TSX-253 carburetor. During Test A the starter button stuck, causing a short circuit. Otherwise, no repairs or adjustments were noted during 42 hours of engine operating time. Tire equipment included 10-28-inch rear and 5.50-15-inch front rubber. The bare tractor weight of 3,199 lbs. was increased to the tune of 492 lbs. of additional ballast per rear wheel for Tests F, G, and H. Four forward speeds of 2.32, 3.08, 4, and 8.4 were provided, with third gear being used for Test H. At a rated drawbar load of 12.54 hp the VAC pulled 1,183 lbs. at 3.97 mph with a slippage of 4.83 percent and achieved a fuel economy of 9.12 hp-hours per gallon. A low-gear maximum pull of 2,394 lbs. at 2.02 mph was noted in Test G.

Nebraska Test Data

Test No. 431

Date Tested: October 17 to October 26, 1949

The only difference between this and Test No. 430 was that gasoline fueled this tractor. Although test figures indicate a considerable difference in octane ratings, the final results show little variation in fuel economy from one test to the other. The belt pulley was found to be defective and was replaced with a new one, otherwise no repairs or adjustments were noted during 43 hours of operating time. Test C at an operating maximum load of 20.06 belt hp indicated a fuel economy of 10.74 hp-hours per gallon, compared to 10.65 under a Test D rated load of 19.04 hp. Test G produced a low-gear maximum pull of 2,768 lbs. at 2.06 mph. Third gear was used for Test H, and at a rated drawbar load of 15.00 hp the VAC pulled 1,424 lbs. at 3.95 mph with a slippage of 4.2 percent. Fuel economy from this 10-hour run was recorded at 9.02 hp-hours per gallon.

COLLECTOR VALUES	1	2	3	4
MODEL VAC-14	$2,600	$2,000	$1,200	$600

Model VAO Orchard

The Case Eagle Hitch lift system was added to the Model VA tractors as an extra-cost option in 1949. It was available on any of the V-Series tractors, including this special Model VAO (orchard) tractor. The VAO tractors went into production in 1943 and continued until 1955.

COLLECTOR VALUES	1	2	3	4
MODEL VAO ORCHARD	$3,000	$2,500	$1,500	$700

In 1952 Case offered eight different variations of its Model VA tractors, including this Model VAH high-clearance model. It was designed for work in crops where the extra clearance was necessary to avoid damage to the growing plants.

COLLECTOR VALUES	1	2	3	4
MODEL VAH	$3,300	$2,700	$1,500	$700

Case Model VAH

Beginning in 1953, Case initiated a model code for its various tractor models. With some variations, this system continued until 1969. The first digit indicated the tractor series. The second digit indicated fuel type, with "0" being diesel; "1" being spark ignition, either gasoline or propane; and "2" meaning an Industrial model. Tread style was shown by the third digit, with "0" being standard tread; "1" for a general-purpose tractor; "2" indicated special models, such as orchard, Western, or rice; and "3" meant it was a high-clearance model.

Case marketed its first diesel-powered tractor in 1953. The Case 500 Diesel was a six-cylinder, 377-cid model. This big standard-tread tractor was marketed until 1955. A new feature was optional power steering. This would eventually become standard equipment on all models.

COLLECTOR VALUES	1	2	3	4
CASE 500 DIESEL	$4,000	$2,500	$1,000	$600

Case 500 Diesel

Nebraska Test Data

Model: Case 500 Diesel

Test No. 508

Date Tested: October 5 to October 10, 1953

This tractor has the distinction of being the first Case diesel-powered model presented for testing, and also the first Case tractor tested with power steering. Tests B and C at a 100 percent maximum belt load of 63.81 hp produced a fuel economy of 15.79 hp-hours per gallon-fuel economy rose still further to stand at 16.03 under a Test D rated load of 55.14 hp. Engine torque peaked at 411.3 lbs.-ft. at an engine speed of 1,048 rpm. Rated engine speed was 1,350 rpm. This tractor was equipped with a Case-built six-cylinder, I-head engine with a 4 x 5-inch bore and stroke. No repairs or adjustments were noted during 40-1/2 hours of running time. Advertised speeds of 2.69, 3.7, 4.91, and 10.10 mph were featured, along with 15-30-inch rear and 7.50-18-inch front rubber tires. Bare tractor weight was 8,128 lbs., with an additional 1,734 lbs. of weight added to each rear wheel during Tests F, G, and H. Test G, run at 100 percent maximum drawbar load produced a low-gear maximum pull of 7,409 lbs. at 2.42 mph with a recorded slippage of 15.89 percent. The 10-hour run of Test H was made in third gear, and at a rated output of 44.24 hp, fuel economy at the drawbar totaled 14.34 hp-hours per gallon. During this test the 500 Diesel pulled 3,302 lbs. at 5.02 mph with a slippage of 4 percent.

Case 300 Series

In 1955 Case introduced an entirely new series of tractors, characterized by the 300 Series. Case offered these tractors in several chassis versions and they could be equipped with a Case-built spark ignition engine or a Continental four-cylinder diesel. The 300 Series tractors were capable of about 23 drawbar and 29 PTO hp. The 300 Series was built into 1958.

Nebraska Test Data

Model: Case 311

Test No. 613

Date Tested: April 15 to April 23, 1957

Weighing 3,561 lbs., the Case 311 featured 12-28 rear and 5.50-16 inch front rubber tires. During Tests F, G, and H an additional 968 lbs. was added to each rear wheel. This tractor had forward speeds of 2.68, 3.94, 5.18, and 12.8 mph, with third gear being used for the 10-hour run of Test H. At a rated drawbar output of 23.4 hp, the 311 pulled 1,733 lbs. at 5.06 mph with a slippage of 3.46 percent. Fuel economy was posted at 10.07 hp-hours per gallon. Test G elicited a low-gear maximum drawbar pull of 4,186 lbs. at 2.33 mph with a slippage of 14 percent. The 311 featured a Case four-cylinder engine rated at 1,750 rpm. Using a 3-3/8 x 4-1/8-inch bore and stroke, it had 148-cubic inches of displacement. Test L noted that 113 percent of rated-speed torque was available all the way from 70 percent to 60 percent of rated rpm. At a Test D rated belt load of 29.33 hp, fuel economy came in at 11.4 hp-hours per gallon. Economy rose to 11.76 hp-hours per gallon under a Test C operating maximum load of 32.32 belt hp. No repairs or adjustments were noted during 42-1/2 hours of operating time.

Nebraska Test Data

Model: Case 301 Diesel

Test No. 614

Date Tested: April 15 to April 23, 1957

At a Test D rated belt load of 27.1 hp, the 301 Diesel delivered a fuel economy of 14.22 hp-hours per gallon. By comparison, fuel economy slipped to 13.83 at a 100 percent maximum belt load of 30.8 hp. This tractor was equipped with a Continental four-cylinder diesel engine with a 3-3/8 x 4-3/8-inch bore and stroke. Rated at 1,750 rpm, it used a 15.54:1 compression ratio and carried a 157 cubic inch displacement. Other features included 12-28 rear and 5.50-16 inch front tires. Bare tractor weight was 3,743 lbs., to which was added an additional 978 lbs. on each rear wheel during Tests F, G, and H. Advertised speeds of 2.68, 3.94, 5.18, and 12.8 mph were specified, with third gear being used for Test H. At a rated drawbar load of 22.39 hp, the 301 Diesel pulled 1,658 lbs. at 5.06 mph against a slippage of 3.34 percent. Fuel economy came in at 12.77 hp-hours per gallon. Test G yielded a low-gear maximum pull of 4,067 lbs. at 2.31 mph with a slippage of 14.53 percent. No repairs or adjustments were noted during 41 hours of operating time.

COLLECTOR VALUES	1	2	3	4
300	$3,000	$2,500	$1,800	$500
300B, 310B & 320B	$3,000	$2,500	$1,800	$700
300 & 320	$3,000	$2,500	$1,800	$700

Case 350 LP gas model

Numerous fuel options were available for Case tractors, including LP gas as offered for the 350 model illustrated here. Produced 1956-1958, the 350 tractors were a continuation of the earlier 300 Series. The 350 tractors were available only with spark ignition engines fueled by gasoline, distillate, or LP gas.

COLLECTOR VALUES	1	2	3	4
350	$3,200	$2,700	$1,800	$800

Case 400 Series

Case 400 Series tractors made their debut in 1955 and replaced the D Series tractors that had been introduced in 1939. Many different implements were available for the 400 Series tractors. This model was available with a gasoline or a diesel engine and was capable of about 50 PTO hp.

The 400 Series tractors were available in numerous chassis configurations, including a special high-clearance model sold as the 400 Cane Tractor. Because of the limited production of the high-clearance models, they carried a substantially higher price than the comparable row-crop tractors. Case 400 tractors could also be furnished in a conventional standard-tread design. The standard tractor illustrated here was available as the 400 Diesel Standard, the 400 Super Diesel Standard and the 400 Special Super Diesel Standard. 400 Series Orchard tractors were also available.

Case 400 series row-crop tractor

Case 400 Cane tractor

Nebraska Test Data

Model: Case 401 Diesel

Test No. 565

Date Tested: October 17 to October 25, 1955

During 44 hours of running time, no repairs or adjustments were noted for the Case 401 Diesel tractor. Features included 13-38-inch rear and 6.00-16-inch front tires, along with forward speeds of 1.36, 1.94, 2.66, 3.85, 4.84, 6.89, 9.44, and 13.66 mph. Weighing 6,582 lbs., the 401 was burdened with an additional 1,639 lbs. of weight on each rear wheel during Tests F, G, and H. A low gear maximum pull of 6,018 lbs. at 1.2 mph with a slippage of 16.53 percent was noted in Test G. Using fifth gear, the 10-hour run of Test H was made with a rated drawbar output of 33.47 hp. This test also recorded a pull of 2,578 lbs. at 4.87 mph with a slippage of 4.1 percent. Fuel economy was pegged at 13.91 hp-hours per gallon of diesel fuel. This tractor was equipped with a Case four-cylinder, 251-cid, 4 x 5-inch engine. Rated at 1,500 rpm, it reached a maximum engine torque of 328.5 lbs.-ft. with an engine speed of 1,106 rpm. Belt testing indicated a Test D rated load of 43.55 hp, along with a fuel economy of 16.17 hp-hours per gallon. Test B, run at a 100percent maximum belt load of 49.4 hp produced a fuel economy of 15.96 hp-hours per gallon.

Nebraska Test Data

Model: Case 411

Test No. 566

Date Tested: October 17 to October 26, 1955

The 411 had a spark-ignition engine, and was of row-crop design. With a four-cylinder, 4 x 5-inch engine of 1,508 rpm rated speed, this 251-cid tractor attained a peak engine torque of 305 lbs.-ft. at 1,178 rpm. Test G indicated a low gear maximum pull of 6,147 lbs. at 1.22 mph, while Test H, run at a rated drawbar load of 35.8 hp, indicated a pull of 2,764 lbs. at 4.86 mph, slippage of 4.41 percent, and a fuel economy of 10.86 hp-hours per gallon. Test C, under an operating maximum load of 50.49 belt hp, produced a fuel economy of 12.72 hp-hours per gallon. This figure climbed insignificantly to 12.74 at a Test D rated belt load of 46.7 hp. Bare tractor weight was 6,319 lbs.

Nebraska Test Data

Model: Case 411B

Test No. 689

Date Tested: March 20 to April 16, 1959

Using either direct-drive or the torque converter system, this tractor had 16 different speeds ranging from 0 to 11.6 mph. This 4,349-lb. tractor also featured 13-28-inch rear and 5.50-16-inch front tires. Added ballast brought the test weight to 8,193 lbs. Using first gear with the torque converter saw a maximum pull of 5,947 lbs. at 1.46 mph with 14.69 percent slippage. Using fifth gear direct-drive saw 29.72 maximum available drawbar hp, along with a pull of 2,374 lbs. at 4.69 mph and 4.3 percent slippage. Another test, run for 10 hours at 75 percent of maximum pull, indicated an output of 24.04 drawbar hp, a pull of 1,858 lbs. at 4.85 mph and 3.52 percent slippage. Fuel economy in this 10-hour run totaled 7.95 hp-hours per gallon compared to an economy figure of 9.00 under the two-hour maximum load run. The 411-B featured a Case four-cylinder engine with a 3-3/8 x 4-1/8-inch bore and stroke for a 148-cubic-inch displacement. Rated at 2,000 rpm, it developed a maximum of 37.12 PTO hp at this speed, with a resultant fuel economy of 10.7 hp-hours per gallon. No repairs or adjustments were noted during 60 hours of running time.

Nebraska Test Data

At its rated engine speed of 1,750 rpm, a maximum of 33.11 PTO hp was recorded, together with a fuel economy of 11.85 hp-hours per gallon. Case furnished its own engine in this tractor. Using a 3-3/8 x 4-1/8-inch bore and stroke, it carried a 148-cubic-inch displacement. Also featured was a selective gear fixed-ratio transmission with four speeds of 2.49, 3.66, 4.81, and 11.88 mph. As presented for testing, the 441 weighed 3,620 lbs., but additional rear wheel ballast gave a test weight of 6,202 lbs. Using third gear for the drawbar fuel economy runs, the 441 delivered 29.15 drawbar hp in the two-hour maximum load test. Also recorded was a pull of 2,170 lbs. at 5.04 mph, 4.13 percent slippage, and a fuel economy of 10.01 hp-hours per gallon. The economy figure was posted at 10.36 after the 10-hour run made at 75 percent pull. This test indicated an output of 23.68 hp, a pull of 1,638 lbs. at 5.42 mph and 2.52 percent slippage. No repairs or adjustments were recorded during 35-1/2 hours of running time.

Nebraska Test Data

Model: Case 431 Diesel

Test No. 785

Date Tested: April 6 to April 15, 1961

Featuring a four-cylinder engine rated at 1,750 rpm, the 431 Diesel developed a maximum of 34.38 PTO hp with a fuel economy of 16.93 hp-hours per gallon. Using a 3-13/16 x 4-1/8-inch bore and stroke, this was a 188.4-cid engine and was designed with a 17.5:1 compression ratio. The selective gear fixed-ratio transmission entertained four forward speeds of 2.49, 3.66, 4.81, and 11.88 mph. No repairs or adjustments were recorded during 39-1/2 hours of operation. Factory weight was 3,839 lbs., but this figure rose to 6,355 lbs. with the addition of rear wheel ballast. Drawbar performance indicated a fuel economy of 14.5 hp-hours per gallon on the two-hour maximum power test. This run, made at 30.33 drawbar hp, noted a pull of 2,282 lbs. at 4.98 mph with 5.08 percent slippage. The economy figure dipped slightly to stand at 14.16 on a 10-hour drawbar economy test made at 75 percent pull. In this test an output of 24.8 hp was observed, together with a pull of 1,768 lbs. at 5.26 mph and 3.54 percent slippage. Both runs were made in third gear.

COLLECTOR VALUES	1	2	3	4
400	$3,500	$2,500	$2,000	$900
400 CANE	$4,500	$3,200	$2,700	$1,200
400 DIESEL WESTERN SPECIAL WITH HAND CLUTCH	$5,500	$3,000	$1,200	$600

Case 600 series, rear view

In 1957 the Case 600 Series standard-tread tractor appeared and stayed on the market for about a year. The six-cylinder Case diesel engine used a 4 x 5-inch bore and stroke; operating speed was 1500 rpm. This tractor had an operating weight of over 7,600 lbs.

During 1958 Case announced its B-Series tractors. In effect, they were a continuation of the 1955 series, but with a variety of changes and improvements. Illustrated here is a 600-B row-crop model with an adjustable wide-front axle. The Case 600 was also available with a torque converter drive.

Case 600B row-crop tractor

Nebraska Test Data

Model: Case 611B

Test No. 687

Date Tested: March 19 to April 16, 1959

Of the 16 forward speeds available with this tractor, eight could be selected in direct drive, with the remainder being available through a torque converter system. Using second gear with the torque converter gave a maximum drawbar pull of 5,462 lbs. at 2.03 mph and 13.94 percent slippage. Standard features included 13.9-36-inch rear and 6.00-16-inch front tires. Bare tractor weight was 4,885 lbs., with test weight coming to 8,049 lbs. Using fifth gear in direct drive, 37.04 maximum drawbar hp was recorded, along with a pull of 3,233 lbs. at 4.3 mph and 5.87 percent slippage. Fuel economy was posted at 8.4 hp-hours per gallon, with this figure slipping to 7.93 under a 75 percent pull of 2,424 lbs. and an output of 29.44 hp. The 611-B was equipped with a Case four-cylinder engine rated at 2,250 rpm. Using a 3-9/16 x 4-1/8-inch bore and stroke it had a 164.5 cubic inch displacement. PTO testing indicated a fuel economy of 9.78 hp-hours per gallon at rated engine speed and maximum load of 44.56 hp. This test, when run at a PTO speed of 540 rpm yielded an output of 41.14 hp, along with a fuel economy of 9.99 hp-hours per gallon. No repairs or adjustments were noted during 51 hours of running time.

Nebraska Test Data

Model: Case 640C

Test No. 770

Date Tested: October 11 to October 22, 1960

This tractor featured a selective-gear, fixed-ratio transmission together with a torque converter system. Eight forward speeds were provided, ranging from 1.77 to 13.64 mph. After the addition of liquid and cast iron ballast this tractor assumed a test weight of 9,615 lbs., but the bare tractor weight was 4,675 lbs. Using fifth gear in direct-engine drive, a two-hour drawbar fuel economy test made at 43.25 maximum available hp saw a pull of 3,560 lbs. at 4.56 mph and 4.71 percent slippage. Fuel economy totaled 9.89 hp-hours per gallon. The 10-hour economy run made at 75 percent pull indicated an output of 39.79 hp, a pull of 2,675 lbs. at 4.72 mph and 3.91 percent slippage with fuel economy being posted at 9.17 hp-hours per gallon. The 640C was equipped with a Case-built four-cylinder engine rated at 2,250 rpm. Its 188.4-cubic-inch displacement resulted from a 3-13/16 x 4-1/8-inch bore and stroke. During 59-1/2 hours of operating time, no repairs or adjustments were reported. At rated engine speed a maximum of 49.72 PTO hp was observed, together with a fuel economy of 11.39 hp-hours per gallon of gasoline. The economy figure rose slightly to stand at 11.93 under a load of 46.76 PTO hp, a standard 540 rpm speed at the PTO, and a corresponding engine speed of 1,966 rpm.

Nebraska Test Data

Model: Case 640

Test No. 773

Date Tested: October 13 to October 27, 1960

This 640 tractor lacked a torque converter, but still used a 12-speed, selective gear fixed-ratio transmission. Engine specifications remained the same as for the 640C, and both tractors featured 16.9-28-inch rear and 7.50-16-inch front tires. Weighing 4,495 lbs., this model assumed a test weight of 9,485 lbs. by the addition of rear wheel ballast. Using seventh gear, the two-hour economy run made at 41.93 maximum available drawbar hp yielded a pull of 2,911 lbs. at 5.4 mph with 4.07 percent slippage. Fuel economy totaled 10.6 hp-hours per gallon. The economy figure was pegged at 9.96 during a 10-hour economy run made at 75 percent pull. Other statistics from this test include an output of 33.91 hp, a pull of 2,237 lbs. at 5.69 mph and 3.23 percent slippage. Using the rated engine speed of 2,000 rpm for this tractor, a maximum of 50.61 PTO hp was observed, as was a fuel economy of 12.09 hp-hours per gallon. By running at 540 rpm on the PTO shaft and a corresponding crankshaft speed of 1,950 rpm an output of 49.69 hp was recorded, along with a fuel economy of 12.18 hp-hours per gallon.

Nebraska Test Data

Model: Case 630C Diesel

Test No. 787

Date Tested: April 7 to April 21, 1961

This tractor's engine had a rated speed of 2,250 rpm. At this crankshaft speed a maximum output of 48.85 PTO hp was observed, together with a fuel economy of 12.65 hp-hours per gallon. Another run, made at 540 PTO rpm and a corresponding engine speed of 1,966 rpm saw an output of 45.24 hp, together with an economy figure of 12.96. The selective-gear, fixed-ratio transmission also included a torque converter system. In all, eight forward speeds ranging from 1.77 to 13.64 mph were provided. Standard features of this 4,838 lb. tractor also included 16.9-28-inch rear and 7.50-16-inch front tires. Additional rear wheel ballast brought the test weight to 9,725 lbs. Using fifth gear, a two-hour run at 43.71 maximum available hp indicated a pull of 3,615 lbs. at 4.53 mph with 5.23 percent slippage. Also indicated was an economy of 11.34 hp-hours per gallon of diesel fuel. The 10-hour economy run, made at 75 percent pull, noted an economy figure of 11.19, with an output of 35.39 hp, a pull of 2,773 lbs. at 4.79 mph and 3.66 percent slippage.

Nebraska Test Data

Model: Case 630 Diesel

Test No. 788

Date Tested: April 10 to April 22, 1961

Both this tractor and the 630C carried the same 188.4-cid engine, but this model did not feature a torque converter system. A selective-gear, fixed-ratio transmission offering 12 forward speeds ranging from 1.52 to 20.2 mph was used. Also featured were 16.9-28-inch rear and 7.50-16-inch front tires. Bare weight was 4,637 lbs., but additional rear wheel ballast gave a test weight of 9,615 lbs. In seventh gear, a two-hour economy run at 40.68 maximum drawbar hp yielded a fuel economy of 12.79 hp-hours per gallon. This run also noted a pull of 2,836 lbs. at 5.38 mph with 4.21 percent slippage. The 10-hour run, made at 75 percent pull, recorded an economy figure of 12.85. This test manifested an output of 32.24 drawbar hp, a pull of 2,125 lbs. at 5.69 mph and slippage of 3.00 percent. No repairs or adjustments were reported during 40 hours of operating time. At rated engine speed of 2,000 rpm, a maximum PTO output of 48.24 hp was observed, along with a fuel economy of 14.66 hp-hours per gallon. The economy rose slightly to stand at 14.75 when using 540 rpm at the PTO shaft and a corresponding crankshaft speed of 1,951 rpm. Also recorded in this test was an output of 47.4 PTO hp.

COLLECTOR VALUES	1	2	3	4
600 SERIES	$4,000	$2,500	$1,800	$800

Case 800

Case 800 tractors featured the Case-O-Matic drive system. It had the advantages of a torque converter drive, but a lockout lever permitted direct-drive operation as well. The 800 Series tractors were offered in gasoline, diesel and LP gas versions, all delivering approximately 54 PTO hp. This model was first offered in 1958.

Nebraska Test Data

Model: Case 811B

Test No. 679

Date Tested: October 27 to November 17, 1958

This tractor featured a torque converter drive in addition to the usual direct-drive. With this system, eight forward speeds were available, ranging from 0 to 16.64 mph. Weighing 6,772 lbs., it was equipped with 15.5-38 rear tires—each of these were burdened with 1,158 additional lbs. of weight. The 6.00-16-inch front tires received 162 lbs. of iron ballast. Test G, run in second gear, direct-drive yielded a maximum pull of 7,207 lbs. at 1.99 mph with 14.27 percent slippage. Test H, run for two hours at 43.83 observed maximum hp yielded a pull of 3,990 lbs. in fourth gear direct-drive. This test also noted a speed of 4.12 mph and 4.32 percent slippage. Fuel economy came in at 9.74 hp-hours per gallon. The same test, run for two hours using fourth gear and the torque converter achieved an output of 41.47 hp and a pull of 4,481 lbs. at 3.47 mph with 4.76 percent slippage. Drawbar fuel economy in this test totaled 8.93 hp-hours per gallon. The 10-hour run of Test H was made at 75 percent of pull, with a third run being made at 50 percent. Case featured a four-cylinder 4 x 5-inch engine in this tractor. Rated at 1,800 rpm, it carried a 251-engine. Belt testing indicated a fuel economy of 10.49 hp-hours per gallon of gasoline under a Test D rated load of 47.38 hp. This figure rose to 10.94 under a Test C operating maximum load of 51.45 hp. No repairs or adjustments were noted during 79-1/2 hours of operating time.

Nebraska Test Data

Model: Case 801B Diesel

Test No. 680

Date Tested: October 27 to November 14, 1958

Except for the diesel engine, this tractor was virtually identical to the Case 811B noted in the previous test. Like the gasoline model, this diesel version included a torque converter drive that could be locked out if desired. Test D, run at a rated belt load of 48.25 hp yielded a fuel economy of 13.45 hp-hours per gallon of diesel fuel. By comparison, at a 100 percent maximum belt load of 54.42 hp, fuel economy came in at 13.53 hp-hours per gallon. This tractor featured a Case-built four-cylinder engine rated at 1,800 rpm and carrying a 4-1/8 x 5-inch bore and stroke for a 267-cubic-inch displacement. No repairs or adjustments were noted during 60-1/2 hours of engine operating time. Test G, run in low gear direct-drive yielded a maximum pull of 7,888 lbs. at 2 mph with 13.75 percent slippage. The same test, run with the torque converter achieved a maximum pull of 7,963 lbs. at 1.7 mph with 14.85 percent slippage. Test H, when run in fourth gear and at an observed maximum of 51.38 hp produced a fuel economy of 12.5 hp-hours per gallon. This test, run in direct-drive also noted a pull of 4,387 lbs. at 4.39 mph and 4.9 percent slippage. The same test, when run for two hours with the torque converter, saw an output of 46.98 hp, along with a pull of 5,154 lbs. at 3.42 mph and 6.01 percent slippage. Fuel economy in this test was posted at 11.36 hp-hours per gallon.

Nebraska Test Data

Model: Case 811B LPG

Test No. 6695

Date Tested: April 27 to May 16, 1959

At a rated engine speed of 1,800 rpm, this tractor developed a maximum of 55.58 PTO hp, with a resulting fuel economy of 8.98 hp-hours per gallon of propane. Case equipped this tractor with a four-cylinder, 4 x 5-inch engine suitably modified to an 8:1 compression ratio to accommodate the propane fuel. Also featured were 16 forward speeds ranging from 0 to 16.64 mph, using either direct-drive or the torque converter system. A maximum second-gear pull in the torque converter range was recorded at 7,159 lbs. at 1.69 mph against 14.66 percent slippage. Weighing 6,775 lbs., this tractor was burdened with an additional 2,390 lbs. of ballast for a major portion of the drawbar testing. At a maximum of 50.62 drawbar hp, and using fourth gear in direct-drive, this tractor pulled 4,093 lbs. at 4.41 mph with a 5.11 percent slippage. Fuel economy was posted at 8.2 hp-hours per gallon. A 10-hour run made in fourth gear direct-drive, but at 75 percent of maximum power yielded an output of 40.64 hp, along with a pull of 3,268 lbs. at 4.66 mph and 4.06 percent slippage, with a resultant fuel economy of 7.4 hp-hours per gallon. No repairs or adjustments were noted during 56-1/2 hours of running time.

Nebraska Test Data

Model: Case 831C Diesel

Test No. 736

Date Tested: April 5 to April 19, 1960

Rated at 1,900 rpm, the 831C developed a maximum of 63.74 PTO hp and delivered a fuel economy of 13.97 hp-hours per gallon. A similar test, run at 540 PTO rpm and a corresponding engine speed of 1,682 rpm yielded 61.08 hp and 14.46 hp-hours per gallon. Case featured its own four-cylinder diesel engine that used a 4-3/8 x 5-inch bore and stroke for a 301 cubic inch displacement. Eight advertised speeds were provided—these ranged from 1.7 to 17.6 mph. Also featured were 15.5-38-inch rear and 6.00-16- inch front tires. As presented for testing the 831C weighed 7,275 lbs., but 585 lbs. of liquid ballast and 1,265 lbs. of cast iron weight was added to each rear wheel during most of the drawbar testing. Using fourth gear, fuel economy came in at 12.55 hp-hours per gallon under a maximum drawbar output of 58.3 hp. This two-hour run saw a pull of 4,721 lbs. at 4.63 mph and slippage of 5.47 percent. A 10-hour run, made at 75 percent pull, indicated a fuel economy figure of 13.20, along with an output of 46.57 hp, a pull of 3,607 lbs. at 4.84 mph and slippage of 4.47 percent. Because this tractor was equipped with a torque converter, separate runs were made in this range as well as in the direct-drive position previously noted. No repairs or adjustments were noted during 53 hours of running time.

Nebraska Test Data

Model: Case 831 Diesel

Test No. 737

Date Tested: April 5 to April 23, 1960

The 831 Diesel featured a Case-built four-cylinder engine. Rated at 1,700 rpm, it carried a 4-3/8 x 5-inch bore and stroke for a 301 cubic inch displacement. At rated engine speed, 63.76 maximum PTO hp was observed, along with a fuel economy of 14.98 hp-hours per gallon. While the 831C Diesel featured a torque converter system, this tractor was equipped with a selective gear, fixed-ratio transmission with eight forward speeds ranging from 1.5 to 15.7 mph. Fourth gear was selected for the two-hour economy run at maximum available power. With an output of 54.27 hp the 831 Diesel pulled 4,997 lbs. at 4.07 mph with 6.93 percent slippage. Fuel economy in this test totaled 12.92 hp-hours per gallon, compared to 13.61 in the 10-hour run made at 75 percent pull. The latter test evoked an output of 44.3 drawbar hp, a pull of 3,857 lbs. at 4.31 mph and slippage of 4.55 percent. Both this tractor and the 831C of the preceding test used the same tire sizes. The tractor weighed in at 7,145 lbs., but assumed a test weight of 10,920 lbs. with the addition of liquid and cast iron ballast. Repairs and adjustments noted during 42 hours of running time were minor in nature.

Nebraska Test Data

Model: Case 841

Test No. 738

Date Tested: April 5 to April 23, 1960

No repairs or adjustments were recorded for this tractor during 41-1/2 hours of operating time. At its rated engine speed of 1,700 rpm, a maximum of 64.57 PTO hp was observed, along with a fuel economy of 12.73 hp-hours per gallon. Case featured its own four-cylinder engine in this tractor; it carried a 4-1/4 x 5-inch bore and stroke for a 284-cubic-inch displacement. The selective-gear, fixed-ratio transmission offered eight speeds ranging from 1.5 to 15.7 mph. The 841 carried the same tire equipment as the 831 and 831C. Weighing 6,905 lbs., this tractor assumed a test weight of 10,795 lbs. with the addition of suitable ballast. Fuel economy came in at 11.07 hp-hours per gallon at 53.34 maximum available drawbar hp. Using fourth gear, a pull of 4,902 lbs. was recorded at 4.08 mph with 6.49 percent slippage. A 10-hour run made at 75 percent pull indicated a drawbar output of 42.54 hp, a pull of 3,700 lbs. at 4.31 mph and slippage of 4.42 percent. This tractor featured a standard 540 rpm PTO drive and could also be equipped with a belt pulley if desired.

Nebraska Test Data

Model: Case 841 LPG

Test No. 740

Date Tested: April 11 to April 23, 1960

Except for the LP-gas equipment, this tractor was virtually identical in design to the 841 gasoline model noted in Test No. 738, including tires, transmission, and speeds. A notable difference was in engine compression: the gasoline model carried a 7.4:1 ratio, the LPG tractor used an 8.4:1 ratio. Otherwise, both used the same four-cylinder design with a rated engine speed of 1,700 rpm. At rated engine speed, a two-hour run at maximum PTO hp recorded a figure of 63.38 together with a fuel economy of 9.72 hp-hours per gallon. As delivered for testing, the 841 LPG weighed 7,045 lbs.—the addition of rear ballast brought this figure to a test weight of 10,835 lbs. Using fourth gear, fuel economy was recorded at 8.48 hp-hours per gallon under a maximum load of 52.99 drawbar hp. This two-hour run manifested a pull of 4,876 lbs. at 4.08 mph and slippage of 6.63 percent. A 10-hour run made at 75 percent load registered an output of 43.02 drawbar hp, a pull of 3,730 lbs. at 4.33 mph and slippage of 4.23 percent. Fuel economy in the 10-hour run came in at 7.94 hp-hours per gallon. During 40 hours of operating time, no repairs or adjustments were noted.

Nebraska Test Data

Model: Case 841C

Test No. 777

Date Tested: November 2 to November 12, 1960

Eight forward speeds ranging from 1.7 to 17.6 mph were featured on the 841C. In addition to the selective-gear, fixed-ratio transmission, a torque converter was used—it could be engaged or locked out at the will of the operator. Using fourth gear, direct-drive, and at 58.41 maximum available hp, this tractor pulled 4,716 lbs. at 4.64 mph with 4.48 percent slippage, yielding a fuel economy of 9.94 hp-hours per gallon. Another two-hour economy run made with the torque converter engaged illustrated an output of 54.03 hp, a pull of 5,633 lbs. at 3.6 mph and 5.47 percent slippage for a fuel economy of 9.26 hp-hours per gallon. The 10-hour economy run made in direct-drive and at 75 percent pull noted an output of 47.78 hp, a pull of 3,620 lbs. at 4.95 mph and 3.56 percent slippage. Fuel economy was posted at 9.13 hp-hours per gallon. This 7,325 lb. tractor featured 15.5-38-inch rear and 6.00-16-inch front tires. During drawbar testing it assumed a weight of 10,885 lbs. by the addition of rear wheel ballast. Case equipped the 841C with a four-cylinder engine rated at 1,900 rpm. It had a 4-1/4 x 5-inch bore and stroke, delivering a 284-cubic-inch displacement. At rated engine speed, a maximum of 65.64 PTO hp was noted, along with a fuel economy of 11.28 hp-hours per gallon. The same test, when run at 540 rpm on the PTO shaft and a crankshaft speed of 1,682 rpm, observed an output of 63.78 hp with an economy figure of 11.83. No repairs or adjustments were noted during 51 hours of running time.

Nebraska Test Data

Model: Case 841C LPG

Test No. 780

Date Tested: November 4 to November 19, 1960

Except for the type of fuel used, and necessary equipment to use and store propane, this tractor was virtually identical to the 841C gasoline model of Test No. 777. While the gasoline model carried a 7.4:1 compression ratio, this propane-fired version used an 8.37:1 compression ratio. From the standpoint of fuel economy, the 841-C LPG of this test delivered a maximum of 65.96 PTO hp at its 1,900 rpm rated crankshaft speed. In the process it delivered a fuel economy of 9.23 hp-hours per gallon. Another PTO run made at the standard 540 rpm PTO speed noted an output of 62.6 hp and an economy figure of 9.74. Using fourth gear direct-drive, a two-hour economy run at 57.46 maximum available drawbar hp saw a pull of 4,645 lbs. at 4.64 mph with 4.63 percent slippage. Fuel economy came in at 8.1 hp-hours per gallon, compared to a figure of 7.49 in the 10-hour drawbar economy run. The latter test, also made in fourth gear, but at 75 percent pull, noted an output of 47.5 hp, a pull of 3,562 lbs. at 5.00 mph, and 3.59 percent slippage.

Nebraska Test Data

Model: Case 841CK

Test No. 919

Date Tested: October 8 to October 16, 1965

Rated at 1,900 rpm, this tractor yielded an economy of 11.65 hp-hours per gallon against a maximum output of 65.24 PTO hp. A second PTO run at 540 rpm and a corresponding crankshaft speed of 1,682 rpm saw an economy of 12.08 hp-hours per gallon against a load of 62.17 hp. Case equipped this tractor with a four-cylinder engine. Using a 4-1/4 x 5-inch bore and stroke, it had a 284 cubic inch displacement. The chassis design included a selective-gear, fixed-ratio transmission with eight forward speeds ranging from 1.7 to 17.6 mph. Also featured were 15.5-38-inch rear and 7.50-16-inch front tires. Bare tractor weight was 7,830 lbs., but the addition of rear wheel ballast raised this figure to 10,865 lbs. during drawbar testing. Repairs and adjustments reported during 42-1/2 hours of running time were minor. Using fourth gear, and at 58.02 maximum available drawbar hp, a two-hour economy run saw a delivery of 10.33 hp-hours per gallon. This test, made at a pull of 4,730 lbs. was run at 4.6 mph with slippage of 5.17 percent being recorded. A 10-hour run at 75 percent pull saw an economy figure of 9.90 against an output of 46.56 drawbar hp. Other statistics include a pull of 3,606 lbs. at 4.84 mph with 3.61 percent slippage.

Nebraska Test Data

Model: Case 841CK LPG

Test No. 921

Date Tested: October 9 to October 25, 1965

Except for the propane fuel equipment, and the engine's 8.4: 1 compression ratio, the tractor was identical to Case's gasoline-powered 841 CK (which used a 7.4: compression ratio). The engine had a rated speed of 1,900 rpm and 284-cubic-inch displacement. Weighing in at 8,040 lbs., this tractor assumed a test weight of 11,055 lbs. through the addition of front and rear ballast. In fourth gear, the two-hour economy run was made at 58.24 maximum available hp, with fuel economy posted at 7.74 hp-hours per gallon of propane. The two hour run also indicated a pull of 4,741 lbs. at 4.61 mph and slippage of 5.55 percent. A 10-hour run at 75 percent pull saw an economy of 7.48 hp-hours per gallon of propane against an output of 47.04 drawbar hp. Also recorded was a pull of 3,645 lbs. at 4.84 mph and slippage of 3.91 percent. No repairs or adjustments were reported during 47 hours of operating time. At a rated engine speed of 1,900 rpm, and a maximum output of 64.08 PTO hp, fuel economy came in at 8.58 hp-hours per gallon of propane. This figure rose to 9.35 in a PTO run made at an output speed of 540 rpm and a corresponding engine speed of 1,683 rpm. Also indicated in this test was an output of 61.26 PTO hp.

COLLECTOR VALUES	1	2	3	4
800 SERIES	$4,300	$2,700	$1,900	$800

Case 900B, 930, 940 series

The big 900B Case tractors were built from 1957 to 1959. This tractor could be furnished in a diesel or gasoline engine and the latter could also be adapted as an LP gas model. Listing at about $5,900, the 900B used a six-cylinder, 377-cid engine and was capable of about 71 PTO hp.

First built in 1960, the big Case 930 tractor was built only in a standard-tread version. The original 930 model remained on the market until 1964 when it was replaced with the new 930 CK model. The suffix refers to the introduction of the new Case Comfort King line. This model was capable of over 85 pto hp.

Nebraska Test Data

Model: Case 940 LPG

Test No. 739

Date Tested: April 5 to April 23, 1960

The 940 standard-tread model shown here was equipped with special LP-gas equipment. It featured a Case six-cylinder engine using an 8.0:1 compression ratio. Rated at 1,700 rpm, this engine was designed with a 4 x 5-inch bore and stroke. At rated engine speed, 79.64 maximum PTO hp was observed, together with a fuel economy of 9.14 hp-hours per gallon of propane fuel. Another PTO run, made at 540 PTO rpm and 1,476 rpm on the crankshaft revealed 74.60 hp and a fuel economy figure of 9.29. Case equipped this tractor with a selective gear fixed-ratio transmission with six forward speeds ranging from 2.5 to 13.6 mph. Also featured were 18-26-inch rear and 7.50-18-inch front tires. As presented, the 940 LPG weighed 8,755 lbs., but the addition of front and rear ballast raised this figure to 15,335 lbs. during most of the drawbar testing. Using third gear, fuel economy was registered at 8.24 hp-hours per gallon under a maximum load of 69.99 drawbar hp. This two-hour run noted a pull of 5,552 lbs. at 4.73 mph and slippage of 4.38 percent. A 10-hour run made at 75 percent pull noted an output of 56.48 hp, a pull of 4,242 lbs. at 4.99 mph and slippage of 2.7 percent. Fuel economy totaled 7.54 hp-hours per gallon.

Nebraska Test Data

Model: Case 930 Diesel

Test No. 741

Date Tested: April 14 to May 5, 1960

At its rated crankshaft speed of 1,600 rpm the 930 Diesel developed a maximum of 80.65 PTO hp and yielded a fuel economy of 15.18 hp-hours per gallon of diesel fuel. Another PTO run made at 540 rpm and an engine speed of 1,479 rpm noted an output of 79.10 hp together with a fuel economy of 15.29 hp-hours per gallon. Case equipped this tractor with their own six-cylinder engine designed with a 4-1/8 x 5- inch bore and stroke. This 401-cid engine was built with a 15.2:1 compression ratio. Other features included a selective-gear, fixed-ratio transmission with six forward speeds ranging from 2.5 to 13.6 mph. Also included were 18-26 rear and 7.50-18-inch front tires. With ballast the 930 Diesel weighed 15,105 lbs., but removal of this burden gave a total weight of 8,845 lbs. Using third gear, a two-hour drawbar run made at maximum available power yielded a fuel economy of 13.14 hp-hours per gallon. This test also noted an output of 70.93 hp, corresponding to a pull of 5,670 lbs. at 4.69 mph with 4.43 percent slippage. The 10-hour drawbar run, made at 75 percent power, recorded 56.64 hp, a pull of 4,283 lbs. at 4.96 mph, and slippage of 2.92 percent. Fuel economy totaled 13.55 hp-hours per gallon. During 46 hours of running time, no repairs or adjustments were noted.

Nebraska Test Data

Model: Case 931GP Diesel

Test No. 918

Date Tested: October 7 to October 16, 1965

At a rated engine speed of 1,800 rpm, this tractor delivered a maximum output of 85.39 PTO hp, while yielding an economy of 13.6 hp-hours per gallon. A second PTO run at 540 rpm and a corresponding engine speed of 1,683 rpm saw an output of 82.87 hp and an identical fuel economy of 13.6 hp-hours per gallon. This tractor featured a six-cylinder Case-built engine. Its 4-1/8 x 5-inch bore and stroke gave a 401-cubic-inch displacement. The chassis design included a selective-gear, fixed-ratio transmission with eight forward speeds ranging from 1.8 to 14.7

mph. The 18.4-34-inch rear and 7.50-15-inch front tires supported the base weight of 8,915 lbs. During drawbar testing, additional front and rear ballast brought the total weight to 13,240 lbs. Using fourth gear, the two-hour run at 72.98 maximum available hp saw an economy of 11.74 hp-hours per gallon. Other statistics include a pull of 6,036 lbs. at 4.53 mph and slippage of 6.73 percent. The 10-hour run at 75 percent pull indicated an economy of 12.04 hp-hours per gallon against a load of 60.49 drawbar hp. This test was run with a pull of 4,725 lbs. at 4.8 mph. Slippage was recorded at 4.84 percent. No repairs or adjustments were recorded during 44 hours of running time.

Nebraska Test Data

Model: Case 941GP

Test No. 920

Date Tested: October 8 to October 27, 1965

Weighing in at 8,810 lbs., this tractor assumed a test weight of 13,370 lbs. through the addition of front and rear ballast. The chassis design included a selective gear fixed-ratio transmission with eight forward speeds in a range from 1.8 to 14.7 mph. Also featured were 18.4-34-inch rear and 7.50-15-inch front tires. Using fourth gear, and at a maximum load of 69.77 drawbar hp, the two-hour economy run illustrated an economy of 9.4 hp-hours per gallon. Also manifested was a pull of 5,759 lbs. at 4.54 mph with slippage of 5.83 percent. The 10-hour economy run at 75 percent pull saw this figure pegged at 8.79 hp-hours per gallon against a load of 58.95 hp. Other statistics included a pull of 4,503 lbs. at 4.91 mph and slippage of 4.23 percent. Case equipped this tractor with its own six-cylinder, 377-cid engine. Rated at 1,800 rpm, it used a 4 x 5-inch bore and stroke. At rated engine speed, a two-hour run saw a maximum output of 86.21 PTO hp with an economy of 11.37 hp-hours per gallon. This figure rose slightly to stand at 11.60 in a second PTO run made at 83.85 hp, an output speed of 540 rpm, and a corresponding engine speed of 1,682 rpm. No repairs or adjustments were reported during 61-1/2 hours of operating time.

Nebraska Test Data

Model: Case 941GP (LPG)

Test No. 922

Date Tested: October 9 to October 23, 1965

Rather than being a distinctively different model, the 941GP propane version was a derivation of the gasoline model seen in Test No. 920. Both models used the same six-cylinder, 377-cid engine, and both featured the same basic chassis design. Rated speed for this tractor was 1,800 rpm. The 7.5:1 compression ratio of the gasoline model was raised to 8.5:1 in this tractor—a change necessitated by the use of propane. No repairs or adjustments were required during 42 hours of operating time. At rated engine speed, 85.86 maximum PTO hp was developed, together with an economy of 8.82 hp-hours per gallon of propane. Operating at 540 PTO rpm and a corresponding engine speed of 1,683 rpm, 82.98 PTO hp was observed, together with an economy of 9.11 hp-hours per gallon of propane. Weighing 8,975 lbs., this model assumed a test weight of 13,225 lbs. by the addition of front and rear ballast. In fourth gear, a maximum output of 72.63 drawbar hp was observed, along with an economy of 7.55 hp-hours per gallon. This two-hour run also saw a pull of 6,001 lbs. at 4.54 mph and slippage of 6.16 percent. A 10-hour run at 75 percent pull indicated an economy of 7.04 against an output of 60.97 drawbar hp. Other statistics include a pull of 4,666 lbs. at 4.9 mph with 4.29 percent slippage.

COLLECTOR VALUES	1	2	3	4
900 SERIES	$4,000	$3,000	$1,500	$750
900 DIESEL	$4,000	$2,800	$1,000	$750

Case 430 Series

Case 430 tractors first appeared in 1960, with production ending in 1969. This model used a four-cylinder, 188-cid engine and was available in several chassis styles to suit individual needs.

Case 530 Series

The Case-O-Matic drive was a regular feature of the Case 530 Series tractors. Introduced in 1960, the 530 Series models remained in production until 1969. While the Case-O-Matic drive was very popular, it was more expensive and so the company also offered a standard sliding-gear style 530. Gasoline, diesel and LP gas versions were available.

Case 630

Case 630 tractors came onto the market in 1960, remaining there into 1963. Like others of this period, the 630 could be equipped with a standard transmission or the Case-O-Matic torque converter drive. A four-cylinder engine with 188-cubic-inch displacement was used.

COLLECTOR VALUES	1	2	3	4
630 SERIES	$5,000	$3,500	$1,500	$750

Case 730

Another segment of the 30 Series Case tractors was the 730 model. Built 1960-1969, this tractor offered an OEM choice of gasoline, diesel, or LP gas engines. The four-cylinder diesel model had a 301-cubic-inch displacement, resulting from a 4-3/8 x 5-inch bore and stroke.

Case 830 row-crop

Topping the Case row-crop tractor line in the 1960 to 1969 period was the 830 model. This tractor was available in gasoline, diesel and LP gas versions. The four-cylinder, 284-cid spark-ignition engine used a 4-1/4 x 5-inch bore and stroke was capable of 65-plus PTO hp.

Nebraska Test Data

Model: Case 831CK Diesel (also 830CK and 832CK)

Test No. 917

Date Tested: October 7 to October 16, 1965

Weighing 8,070 lbs., the 831CK Diesel featured 15.5-38-inch rear and 7.50-16 inch front tires. During drawbar testing, additional front and rear ballast brought the total weight to 11,055 lbs. Standard chassis features included a selective-gear, fixed-ratio transmission with eight forward speeds ranging from 1.7 to 17.6 mph. Using fourth gear, 57.69 maximum available hp was observed on the two-hour drawbar economy run. This test also indicated a pull of 4,708 lbs. at 4.60 mph with 5.13 percent slippage and an economy of 11.93 hp-hours per gallon. The 10-hour run at 75 percent pull saw an economy of 12.23 hp-hours per gallon against a load of 46.93 hp, a pull of 3,598 lbs. at 4.89 mph and slippage of 3.89 percent. Case equipped this tractor with its own four-cylinder diesel engine. Rated at 1,900 rpm, it used a 4-3/8 x 5-inch bore and stroke for a 301-cubic-inch displacement. No repairs or adjustments were noted during 42-1/2 hours of operating time. At rated engine speed, fuel economy was recorded at 13.46 hp-hours per gallon against a maximum load of 64.26 PTO hp. A second test at 540 PTO rpm and a corresponding crankshaft speed of 1,683 rpm saw an economy of 13.92 hp-hours per gallon against an output of 60.05 PTO hp.

COLLECTOR VALUES	1	2	3	4
830 DIESEL				
(ADJUSTABLE WIDE FRONT)	$4,500	$3,500	$1,500	$700
(WESTERN SPECIAL)	$5,000	$3,000	$1,500	$700

Case 1200 Traction King

Case entered the realm of four-wheel-drive tractors in 1964 with its 1200 Traction King model. It was produced until 1969. This big tractor was capable of more than 120 PTO hp. The engine was a Case-built six-cylinder style with a 451-cubic-inch displacement.

Nebraska Test Data

Model: Case 1200 Diesel

Test No. 868

Date Tested: October 14 to October 23, 1964

The six-cylinder turbocharged engine featured in the 1200 Diesel was rated at 2,000 rpm. Its 4-5/8 x 5- inch bore and stroke gave a displacement of 451 cubic inches. Of four-wheel-drive design, the 1200 Diesel featured a selective-gear, fixed-ratio transmission with six forward speeds from 2.48 to 12.6 mph. Bare tractor weight was 16,585 lbs., carried by four 23.1-26-inch tires. During drawbar testing, front and rear ballast gave a total weight of 19,345 lbs. In third gear, the two-hour run at 106.2 maximum available drawbar hp saw an economy of 12.97 hp-hours per gallon. Revealed, too, was a pull of 8,681 lbs. at 4.59 mph with 3.74 percent slippage. Economy was recorded at 11.81 for the 10-hour drawbar run made at 75 percent pull. This test, run at 84.84 drawbar hp, yielded a pull of 6,622 lbs. at 4.8 mph with 2.76 percent slippage. No repairs or adjustments were recorded during 43-1/2 hours of operating time. At rated engine speed, a maximum of 119.9 PTO hp was observed—this test further indicated an economy of 14.63 hp-hours per gallon of diesel fuel.

Case 770 Series

Case 70 Series tractors first appeared in late 1969. Numerous other models appeared subsequently. In 1984 Case and International Harvester merged to form the Case-IH line.

Nebraska Test Data

Model: Case 770 Power-Shift

Test No. 1032

Date Tested: November 10 to November 22, 1969

This gasoline-powered model used a four-cylinder, 251-cid engine. Rated at 1,900 rpm, it featured a 4 x 5-inch bore and stroke. At rated engine speed, 53.53 maximum PTO hp was observed, as was an economy of 10.65 hp-hours per gallon. No repairs or adjustments were required during 42-1/2 hours of operating time. Weighing in at 8,990 lbs., the standard package included 16.9-34-inch rear and 7.5L-15- inch front tires. Additional front and rear ballast raised the total test weight to 10,780 lbs. The transmission design included partial range power shifting within the selective gear fixed-ratio design. Its 12 forward speeds ranged from 1.8 to 17.0 mph. Operating in the high range of second gear, the two-hour economy run achieved a maximum available output of 46.3 drawbar hp and delivered an economy of 8.94 hp-hours per gallon. In the process, a pull of 4,005 lbs. was recorded at 4.34 mph with slippage totaling 5.83 percent. The 10-hour run at 75 percent pull noted 7.58 hp-hours per gallon against an output of 37.78 hp. Other data included a pull of 3,118 lbs. at 4.54 mph with slippage of 4.36 percent.

Nebraska Test Data

Model: Case 770 Manual Diesel

Test No. 1033

Date Tested: November 11 to November 22, 1969

The four-cylinder, 267-cid, diesel-powered engine of this tractor was rated at 1,900 rpm and used a 4-1/8 x 5-inch bore and stroke. At rated engine speed it developed 56.36 maximum PTO hp and yielded an economy of 15.46 hp-hours per gallon of fuel. Features included a selective gear fixed-ratio transmission with eight forward speeds ranging from 1.9 to 15.0 mph. The 9,050 lb. total weight was carried on 16.9-34-inch rear and 7.5L-15-inch front tires. Additional front and rear ballast boosted the total test weight to 10,820 lbs. No repairs or adjustments were reported during 41 hours of operating time. Using fourth gear, the two-hour economy run at 49.18 maximum available drawbar hp saw an efficiency of 13.2 hp-hours per gallon. Also established was a pull of 4,048 lbs. at 4.56 mph and 5.39 percent slippage. The 10-hour run at 75 percent pull noted an economy of 12.92 hp-hours per gallon against a load of 39.83 hp. Other data from this test includes a pull of 3,118 lbs. at 4.79 mph and 3.72 percent slippage.

Nebraska Test Data

Model: Case 770 Power-Shift Diesel

Test No. 1058

Date Tested: October 28 to November 7, 1970

Weighing in at 9,220 lbs., this model was furnished with 16.9-34-inch rear and 7.5L-15-inch front tires. Additional front and rear ballast raised the total test weight to 10,950 lbs. The selective-gear, fixed-ratio transmission offered partial range power shifting. Its 12 forward speeds ranged from 1.8 to 17.0 mph. Drawbar performance runs included the two-hour test at 50.36 maximum available hp. In addition to establishing an economy of 13.76 hp-hours per gallon, this test recorded a pull of 4,388 lbs. at 4.3 mph with slippage of 6.31 percent. The 10-hour run at 75 percent pull noted an economy of 12.58 hp-hours per gallon with a load of 41.3 hp. Other data included a pull of 3,421 lbs. at 4.53 mph—slippage totaled 4.51 percent. Case equipped this model with its own four-cylinder engine. Rated at 1,900 rpm, it used a 4-1/8 x 5-inch bore and stroke for 267-cubic inch displacement. At rated engine speed, 56.77 maximum PTO hp was observed, as was an economy of 15.08 hp-hours per gallon. No repairs or adjustments were reported during 44 hours of operating time.

Nebraska Test Data

Model: Case 770 Manual

Test No. 1061

Date Tested: November 6 to November 19, 1970

Powered by a four-cylinder, 251-cid gasoline engine, this tractor developed 56.32 maximum PTO hp at its rated speed of 1,900 rpm, achieving an economy of 11.19 hp-hours per gallon. The engine used a 4 x 5 inch bore and stroke. Weighing 8,810 lbs., it was furnished with 16.9-34-inch rear and 7.5L-15-inch front tires. Additional front and rear ballast raised the total test weight to 10,545 lbs. Operating in fourth gear, 49.12 maximum available drawbar hp was witnessed in the two-hour drawbar performance run. This test achieved an economy of 9.83 hp-hours per gallon while pulling 4,022 lbs. at 4.58 mph. Slippage came to 5.34 percent. The 10-hour run at 75 percent pull indicated an economy of 8.17 hp-hours per gallon with a load of 40.27 hp. Also recorded was a pull of 3,115 lbs. at 4.85 mph and 4.28 percent slippage. Case equipped this model with a selective-gear, fixed-ratio transmission. Its eight forward speeds ranged from 1.9 to 15.0 mph. No repairs or adjustments were reported during 38-1/2 hours of operating time.

Nebraska Test Data

Model: Case 770 Manual Diesel

Test No. 1088

Date Tested: November 13 to November 23, 1971

No repairs or adjustments were recorded during 51 hours of operating time. Rated at 2,000 rpm, the 770 Diesel carried a four-cylinder, 267-cid engine with a 4-1/8 x 5-inch bore and stroke. At rated engine speed it developed 63.9 maximum PTO hp and delivered an economy of 14.98 hp-hours per gallon. Operating at 540 PTO rpm and a corresponding engine speed of 1,906 rpm, 15.16 hp-hours per gallon was realized with a load of 62.85 hp. The 770 Diesel featured a selective-gear, fixed-ratio transmission with eight forward speeds ranging from 2.0 to 15.8 mph. Using fourth gear, the two-hour economy run at 56.85 maximum available drawbar hp achieved a pull of 4,200 lbs. at 5.08 mph, with slippage totaling 4.64 percent. Fuel economy was registered at 13.2 hp-hours per gallon. By comparison, fuel economy came in at 12.67 in the 10-hour run made at 75 percent pull. This test, made at 45.43 drawbar hp indicated a pull of 3,194 lbs. at 5.33 mph with slippage totaling 3.38 percent. Bare weight of this model was 10,070 lbs., but additional front and rear ballast gave a total test weight of 12,300 lbs. Standard equipment included 18.4-34-inch rear and 10.00-16-inch front tires.

Nebraska Test Data

Model: Case 770 Power-Shift Diesel

Test No. 1089

Date Tested: November 15 to November 24, 1971

Using the same 267-cid diesel engine as described in Test No. 1088, this tractor differed primarily in its use of a power-shift transmission. In this case, 12 forward speeds were provided in a range from 1.9 to 17.9 mph. Using sixth gear, the two-hour drawbar run at 55.96 maximum available hp saw an economy of 12.62 hp-hours per gallon. Also recorded was a pull of 4,895 lbs. at 4.29 mph and slippage of 5.74 percent. The 10-hour run at 75 percent pull evoked an economy of 12.45 hp-hours per gallon against a load of 45.96 hp. Other statistics included a pull of 3,794 lbs. at 4.54 mph and slippage of 4.38 percent. Weighing 10,160 lbs., this model assumed a total test weight of 12,375 lbs. by the addition of front and rear ballast. No repairs or adjustments were reported during 47-1/2 hours of operating time. At the rated engine speed of 2,000 rpm, 64.56 maximum PTO hp was observed and an economy of 14.51 hp-hours per gallon was achieved. Operating at 540 PTO rpm and a corresponding crankshaft speed of 1,906 rpm, an economy figure of 14.72 presented itself against an output of 61.93 PTO hp.

Case 870 Series

Nebraska Test Data

Model: Case 870 Power-Shift Diesel

Test No. 1030

Date Tested: November 10 to November 19, 1969

No repairs or adjustments were reported for this tractor during 43 hours of operation. Weighing 9,390 lbs., it was equipped with 18.4-34-inch rear and 7.50-16-inch front tires. Additional front and rear ballast raised the total operating weight to 12,010 lbs. during drawbar testing. Features included a selective-gear, fixed-ratio transmission with partial range power shifting. Its 12 forward speeds ranged from 1.8 to 17.0 mph. Using second gear in the high range, the two-hour economy run at 61.38 maximum available drawbar hp saw an economy of 13.02 hp-hours per gallon. This test recorded a pull of 5,127 lbs. at 4.49 mph and also saw slippage of 6.32 percent. The 10-hour run at 75 percent pull noted an economy of 12.93 hp-hours per gallon against a load of 50.36 hp. Other statistics included a pull of 4,015 lbs. at 4.7 mph and 5.28 percent slippage. Case equipped this model with its own four-cylinder, 336-cid diesel engine. Rated at 1,900 rpm, it used a 4-5/8 x 5-inch bore and stroke. At rated engine speed, 70.53 maximum PTO hp was achieved and an economy of 15.13 hp-hours per gallon was established.

Nebraska Test Data

Model: Case 870 Manual Diesel

Test No. 1032

Date Tested: November 10 to November 20, 1969

Differing from the tractor of the previous test only in the transmission style, this version also carried a four-cylinder, 336-cid engine. The selective-gear, fixed-ratio transmission offered eight forward speeds ranging from 1.9 to 15.0 mph. Using fourth gear, 61.77 maximum available drawbar hp was delivered in the two-hour drawbar economy run. This test, with a resultant economy of 14.43 hp-hours per gallon, also saw a pull of 4,886 lbs. at 4.74 mph and slippage of 6.17 percent. The 10-hour run at 75 percent pull noted an economy of 13.37 hp-hours per gallon with a load of 50.18 hp. Other statistics included a pull of 3,751 lbs. at 5.02 mph and 4.63 percent slippage. Weighing in at 9,205 lbs. the tractor shown here used 18.4-34-inch rear and 7.50-16-inch front tires. Additional front and rear ballast raised the total test weight to 11,190 lbs. No repairs or adjustments were reported during 42-1/2 hours of operating time. At its rated speed of 1,900 rpm, 70.67 maximum PTO hp was developed and an economy of 15.67 hp-hours per gallon was achieved.

Nebraska Test Data

Model: Case 870 Power-Shift

Test No. 1059

Date Tested: October 28 to November 17, 1970

Rated at 1,900 rpm, this gasoline model developed 70.65 maximum PTO hp while yielding an economy of 11.24 hp-hours per gallon. Case featured its own four-cylinder, 301-cid engine in this tractor—it used a 4-3/8 x 5-inch bore and stroke. No repairs or adjustments were reported during 49-1/2 hours of operating time. Weighing 9,120 lbs., it was furnished with 18.4-34-inch rear and 7.50-16-inch front tires. Additional front and rear ballast raised the total test weight to 11,910 lbs. Operating in second gear, the two-hour performance run at 58.03 maximum available drawbar hp achieved an economy of 9.47 hp-hours per gallon. This test also recorded a pull of 4,801 lbs. at 4.53 mph and slippage of 5.42 percent. The 10-hour drawbar performance run at 75 percent pull manifested an economy figure of 7.99 against a load of 47.61 hp. Other data includes a pull of 3,697 lbs. at 4.83 mph—slippage totaled 3.68 percent.

Nebraska Test Data

Model: Case 870 Manual

Test No. 1060

Date Tested: October 28 to November 7, 1970

This gasoline-powered 870 used a manual transmission. Rated at 1,900 rpm, it used a 4-3/8 x 5-inch bore and stroke for a 301-cubic inch displacement. At rated engine speed, 71.06 maximum PTO hp was observed, as was an economy of 11.86 hp-hours per gallon. The eight-speed, selective gear fixed-ratio transmission ranged from 1.9 to 15.0 mph. No repairs or adjustments were required during 44 hours of operating time. Using fourth gear, the two-hour drawbar performance run at 62.52 maximum available hp saw an economy of 10.09 hp-hours per gallon. This test likewise indicated a pull of 4,930 lbs. at 4.76 mph and 5.6 percent slippage. The 10-hour run at 75 percent pull noted an economy of 8.76 hp-hours per gallon against a load of 49.91 hp. Other statistics include a pull of 3,697 lbs. at 5.06 mph and slippage of 4.05 percent. Weighing 8,925 lbs., this model was furnished with 18.4-34-inch rear and 7.50-16 inch front tires. The addition of front and rear ballast raised the total test weight to 11,705 lbs.

Nebraska Test Data

Model: Case 870 Power-Shift Diesel

Test No. 1076

Date Tested: September 13 to September 24, 1971

Standard equipment for this model included 18.4-34-inch rear and 10.00-16-inch front tires. Weighing 10,230 lbs., the 870 assumed a total test weight of 13,550 lbs. through the addition of front and rear ballast. The selective gear fixed-ratio transmission included partial range power shifting. Its 12 forward gears ranged from 1.8 to 17.0 mph. Using sixth gear, the two-hour drawbar economy run was made at 66.89 maximum available hp—and this test yielded an economy of 12.13 hp-hours per gallon. Other data included a pull of 5,919 lbs. at 4.24 mph and slippage of 5.51 percent. The 10-hour run at 75 percent pull indicated a fuel economy of 12.41 hp-hours per gallon with a load of 54.53 hp. This was equivalent to a pull of 4,508 lbs. at 4.54 mph and slippage of 4.67 percent. Because the threads on the fuel adjusting screw were damaged, replacement of this part was necessary; otherwise, no repairs or adjustments were required during 55 hours of operating time. Case equipped this model with a four-cylinder, 336-cid engine. Rated at 2,000 rpm, it used a 4-5/8 x 5-inch bore and stroke. At rated engine speed, 77.92 maximum PTO hp appeared, as did an economy of 14.10 hp-hours per gallon. Operating at 1,000 PTO rpm and a corresponding engine speed of 1,870 rpm, an economy of 14.42 hp hours was established against a load of 77.11 PTO hp.

Nebraska Test Data

Model: Case 870 Manual Diesel
Test No. 1077
Date Tested: September 12 to September 24, 1971

Except for a different transmission, this tractor was virtually identical to the 870 Power-Shift of the previous test, including its four-cylinder, 336-cid engine. In this instance, 77.45 maximum PTO hp was observed at the rated speed of 2,000 rpm. This test gave an economy of 15.38 hp-hours per gallon. Operating at 1,000 PTO rpm and a corresponding engine speed of 1,870 rpm, 76.63 PTO hp appeared, as did an economy of 15.46 hp-hours per gallon. An oil seal on No. 4 exhaust valve was replaced during the preliminary PTO runs. This marked the only repair during 58 hours of operating time. Features of this 10,070 lb. model included a selective gear fixed-ratio transmission with eight forward speeds ranging from 2.0 to 15.8 mph. Additional front and rear ballast gave a total test weight of 13,520 lbs. Operating in fourth gear, the two-hour drawbar economy run was made at 69.04 maximum available hp, and achieved an efficiency of 13.35 hp-hours per gallon. Also recorded was a pull of 5,130 lbs. at 5.05 mph and slippage of 5.23 percent. The 10-hour run at 75 percent pull indicated a fuel economy of 13.44 hp-hours per gallon against an output of 56.18 hp. Other data included a pull of 3,949 lbs. at 5.34 mph and slippage of 3.98 percent.

Nebraska Test Data

Model: Case 870 Manual Diesel
Test No. 1149
Date Tested: October 22 to October 31, 1973

This tractor featured a selective-gear, fixed-ratio transmission without a power-shift mechanism. The eight forward speeds ranged from 2.0 to 15.8 mph. Operating in fourth gear, the two-hour economy run at 69.53 maximum available drawbar hp saw a pull of 4,980 lbs. at 5.24 mph, slippage of 6.18 percent, and an economy of 12.42 hp-hours per gallon. By comparison, the economy figure stood at 12.53 in the 10-hour run at 75 percent pull. This test, run at 57.3 drawbar hp, yielded a pull of 3,842 lbs. at 5.59 mph with slippage totaling 4.66 percent. Weighing 10,075 lbs., the 870 was equipped with 18.4-34-inch rear and 10.00-16-inch front tires. Additional front and rear ballast raised the total test weight to 13,510 lbs.. Also featured in this tractor was a four-cylinder, 336-cid engine. Rated at 2,100 rpm, it used a 4-5/8 x 5- inch bore and stroke. At rated engine speed, an economy of 14.12 hp-hours per gallon appeared under a maximum PTO load of 80.2 hp. Operating at 1,000 PTO rpm and a corresponding engine speed of 1,870 rpm, an economy of 14.52 hp-hours per gallon was noted with a load of 77.93 PTO hp. No repairs or adjustments were required during 49-1/2 hours of operating time.

Nebraska Test Data

Model: Case 870 Power-Shift Diesel
Test No. 1150
Date Tested: October 26 to November 6, 1973

Partial range power shifting characterized the major difference between this tractor and the 870 Manual Diesel of Test No. 1149. In this case, 12 forward speeds were provided in a range of 1.8 to 17.0 mph. Weighing 10,095 lbs., additional front and rear ballast gave a total test weight of 13,760 lbs. Operating in sixth gear, the two-hour economy run at 68.9 maximum available hp indicated a pull of 5,840 lbs. at 4.42 mph and slippage of 7.25 percent. Fuel economy was pegged at 11.49 hp-hours per gallon. The 10-hour run at 75 percent pull noted an economy figure of 12.04 under a load of 57.65 drawbar hp. Other statistics include a pull of 4,558 lbs. at 4.74 mph and slippage of 5.51 percent. Using the same 336-cid diesel engine as noted in Test No. 1149, this model developed 80.49 maximum PTO hp at its rated speed of 2,100 rpm. Fuel economy was measured at 13.33 hp-hours per gallon. Operating at 1,000 PTO rpm and a corresponding engine speed of 1,870 rpm, fuel economy came in at 13.64 hp-hours per gallon with a load of 76.52 PTO hp. No repairs or adjustments were required during 48 hours of operating time.

Case 970 Series

Nebraska Test Data

Model: Case 970 Manual Diesel
Test No. 1034
Date Tested: April 7 to April 27, 1970

This six-cylinder, 401-cubic inch model was rated at 1,900 rpm and used a 4-1/8 x 5-inch bore and stroke. At rated engine speed, 85.7 maximum PTO hp was observed, as was an economy of 15.64 hp-hours per gallon. Standard equipment included a selective-gear, fixed-ratio transmission with eight forward speeds in a range from 1.9 to 15.0 mph. Also featured were 18.4-38 rear and 10.00-16-inch front tires. Bare tractor weight was 10,185 lbs. No repairs or adjustments were reported during 56-1/2 hours of operating time. Additional front and rear ballast raised the total test weight to 13,700 lbs. Using fourth gear, the two-hour economy run at 69.63 maximum available drawbar hp saw an economy of 12.79 hp-hours per gallon. This test also noted a pull of 5,557 lbs. at 4.7 mph with slippage of 5.52 percent. The 10-hour run at 75 percent pull recorded an economy of 12.93 hp-hours per gallon against a load of 57.45 drawbar hp and this test likewise indicated a pull of 4,362 lbs. at 4.94 mph and 3.97 percent slippage.

Nebraska Test Data

Model: Case 970 Power-Shift Diesel
Test No. 1037
Date Tested: April 15 to April 28, 1970

Following the same general design already outlined in Test No. 1034, this model featured a selective-gear, fixed-ratio transmission with partial range power shifting. Its 12 forward speeds ranged from 1.8 to 17.0 mph. Using seventh gear, the two-hour economy run at 71.56 maximum available drawbar hp saw an economy of 13.51 hp-hours per gallon of fuel. Other data included a pull of 5,585 lbs. at 4.8 mph with slippage of 5.43 percent. The 10-hour run at 75 percent pull noted an economy of 12.85 hp-hours per gallon against an output of 59.65 hp. Further statistics included a pull of 4,394 lbs. at 5.09 mph and slippage totaling 3.76 percent. Standard equipment for this model included 18.4-38-inch rear and 10.00-16-inch front tires. Weighing 10,335 lbs., this model assumed a test weight of 13,870 lbs. through the additional front and rear ballast. Most of this was rear wheel ballast—only 10 lbs. of cast iron weight was added to each front wheel. No repairs or adjustments were reported during 54-1/2 hours of operating time. The six-cylinder, 401-cid engine carried a 4-1/8 x 5-inch bore and stroke. At its rated speed of 1,900 rpm, 85.31 maximum PTO hp appeared and an economy of 15.71 hp-hours per gallon was achieved.

Nebraska Test Data

Model: Case 970 Power-Shift

Test No. 1038

Date Tested: April 17 to May 5, 1970

Using the same power-shift transmission as featured on the 970 diesel, this tractor differed in its use of a six-cylinder, 377-cid gasoline engine. Rated at 1,900 rpm, it carried a 4 x 5-inch bore and stroke. At rated engine speed, 85.23 maximum PTO hp appeared, as did an economy of 10.15 hp-hours per gallon. No repairs or adjustments were noted during 46-1/2 hours of operating time. Features included 18.4-38-inch rear and 10.00-16-inch front tires. The bare weight of 10,130 lbs. was enhanced with front and rear ballast for a total test weight of 13,665 lbs. Operating in seventh gear, the two-hour economy run at 74.64 maximum available drawbar hp saw an economy of 8.96 hp-hours per gallon. Other statistics included a pull of 5,866 lbs. at 4.77 mph and slippage that totaled 6.38 percent. By comparison, the 10-hour run at 75 percent pull indicated an economy of 8.15 hp-hours per gallon under a load of 61.11 drawbar hp. These figures resulted from a pull of 4,525 lbs. at 5.06 mph, with slippage totaling 4.5 percent.

Nebraska Test Data

Model: Case 970 Manual

Test No. 1039

Date Tested: April 15 to May 5, 1970

Of nearly identical design to the 970 Manual Diesel noted in Test No. 1034, this unit offered a six-cylinder, 377-cid gasoline engine. Rated at 1,900 rpm, it featured a 4 x 5-inch bore and stroke. At rated engine speed, an economy of 10.34 hp-hours per gallon was posted against an output of 85.02 PTO hp. No repairs or adjustments were reported during 43-1/2 hours of operation. The selective gear fixed-ratio transmission offered eight forward speeds ranging from 1.9 to 15.0 mph. At 77.2 maximum available drawbar hp, an economy of 8.99 hp-hours per gallon was recorded in the two-hour economy run. These figures resulted from a pull of 6,203 lbs. at 4.67 mph with slippage totaling 6.55 percent. The 10-hour run at 75 percent pull indicated 8.4 hp-hours per gallon under a load of 63.56 hp. Other statistics included a pull of 4,833 lbs. at 4.93 mph and 4.61 percent slippage. The bare tractor weight of 10,050 lbs. was enhanced with additional front and rear ballast for a total test weight of 13,540 lbs.

Nebraska Test Data

Model: Case 970 Power-Shift Diesel

Test No. 1068

Date Tested: May 6 to May 21, 1971

At its rated engine speed of 2,000 rpm, this model delivered 93.41 maximum PTO hp and achieved an economy of 15.05 hp-hours per gallon. Operating at 1,000 PTO rpm and a corresponding engine speed of 1,870 rpm, 93.47 PTO hp appeared and an economy of 15.11 hp-hours per gallon was observed. Case equipped this tractor with a six-cylinder, 401-cid engine with a 4-1/8 x 5-inch bore and stroke. The selective-gear, fixed-ratio transmission included partial range power shifting. Its 12 forward speeds ranged from 1.8 to 17.0 mph. No repairs or adjustments were reported during 49 hours of operating time. Weighing 11,190 lbs., the 970 featured 18.4-38-inch rear and 10.00-16-inch front tires. Additional front and rear ballast gave a total test weight of 14,510 lbs. Using seventh gear, 79.85 maximum available drawbar hp was observed in the two-hour economy run. Also in evidence was a pull of 5,891 lbs. at 5.08 mph and slippage of 5.11 percent. Fuel economy was recorded at 12.88 hp-hours per gallon. The 10-hour run at 75 percent pull saw an economy figure of 12.37 against an output of 65.04 hp. This test further indicated a pull of 4,534 lbs. at 5.38 mph and slippage of 4.07 percent.

Nebraska Test Data

Model: Case 970 Manual Diesel

Test No. 1078

Date Tested: September 9 to September 21, 1971

The 970 Diesel featured a six-cylinder, 401-cid engine. Rated at 2,000 rpm, it used a 4-1/8 x 5-inch bore and stroke. Operating at rated engine speed, an economy of 15.56 hp-hours per gallon resulted from a maximum output of 93.87 PTO hp. At 1,000 PTO rpm and a corresponding engine speed of 1,870 rpm, 92.11 PTO hp appeared, as did 15.51 hp-hours per gallon. Weighing 11,080 lbs., the 970 used 18.4-38-inch rear and 11.00-16-inch front tires. Additional front and rear ballast raised the total test weight to 14,470 lbs. A selective gear fixed-ratio transmission with eight forward speeds was standard equipment and advertised speeds ranged from 2.0 to 15.8 mph. No repairs or adjustments were reported during 46-1/2 hours of operating time. Operating in fourth gear, 79.90 maximum available drawbar hp was evidenced in the two-hour economy run. At this load, fuel economy was pegged at 13.53 hp-hours per gallon. Other data from this test included a pull of 6,092 lbs. at 4.92 mph, with slippage totaling 6.42 percent. The 10-hour run at 75 percent pull saw 13.26 hp-hours per gallon at a load of 65.4 hp. Other data includes a pull of 4,676 lbs. at 5.24 mph, along with slippage of 4.46 percent .

Case 1070 Series

Nebraska Test Data

Model: Case 1070 Manual Diesel

Test No. 1035

Date Tested: April 6 to May 2, 1970

Weighing 10,310 lbs., this tractor was equipped with 18.4-38-inch rear and 10.00-16-inch front tires. Chassis features included a selective-gear, fixed-ratio transmission. Its eight forward speeds ranged from 1.9 to 15.0 mph. Additional front and rear ballast gave a total test weight of 14,995 lbs. Operating in fourth gear, the two-hour economy run was made at 84.53 maximum available hp, yielding a resultant fuel economy of 13.7 hp-hours per gallon. Also recorded was a pull of 6,444 lbs. at 4.92 mph and 5.94 percent slippage. The 10-hour run at 75 percent pull indicated an economy of 12.82 hp-hours per gallon with a load of 67.29 hp. Other statistics included a pull of 4,894 lbs. at 5.16 mph and 4.42 percent slippage. Case equipped this model with its own six-cylinder, 451-cid engine. Rated at 2,000 rpm, it used a 4-3/8 x 5-inch bore and stroke. At rated engine speed, 100.73 maximum PTO hp was observed and an economy of 15.48 hp-hours per gallon was achieved. Operating at 1,000 PTO rpm and a corresponding engine speed of 1,870 rpm, an output of 96.50 hp resulted in an economy of 15.7 hp-hours per gallon. During 76 total hours of operating time, new fuel injectors were installed because of a loss in PTO hp, and a new fuel shut-off stop cable was installed.

Nebraska Test Data

Model: Case 1070 Power-Shift Diesel

Test No. 1036

Date Tested: April 6 to April 20, 1970

This model featured the same 451-cid engine used in the Case 1070 of Test No. 1035. At its rated speed of 2,000 rpm, 100.21 maximum PTO hp was developed, with economy of 15.56 hp-hours per gallon. At 1,000 PTO rpm and a corresponding engine speed of 1,869 rpm, 98.74 PTO hp appeared, as did an economy of 15.9 hp-hours per gallon. No repairs or adjustments were reported during 49-1/2 hours of operating time. The selective-gear, fixed-ratio transmission featured partial-range power shifting. Its 12 forward speeds ranged from 1.8 to 17.0 mph. Tire equipment included 18.4-38-inch rear and 9.50-20-inch front rubber. The bare weight of 10,480 lbs. was raised to a total test weight of 15,140 lbs. through the use of additional rear wheel ballast. Operating in seventh gear, the two-hour economy run indicated 82.12 maximum available drawbar hp and an economy of 12.93 hp-hours per gallon. This test was made with a pull of 6,108 lbs. at 5.04 mph and slippage of 5.81 percent. During the 10-hour economy run, made at 75 percent, a pull of 4,869 lbs. was recorded at 5.27 mph with slippage totaling 4.54 percent. An economy of 12.98 hp-hours per gallon was recorded with a total load of 68.45 drawbar hp.

Nebraska Test Data

Model: Case 1070 Power-Shift Diesel

Test No. 1066

Date Tested: May 7 to May 21, 1971

At its rated speed of 2,100 rpm, this model developed 108.1 maximum PTO hp and yielded an economy of 14.92 hp-hours per gallon. Operating at 1,000 PTO rpm and a corresponding engine speed of 1,871 rpm, the economy figure stood at 15.44 against an output of 99.92 hp. Case equipped this model with its own six-cylinder, 451-cid engine using a 4.375 x 5-inch bore and stroke. Also featured was a selective-gear, fixed-ratio transmission with partial-range power shifting. Its 12 forward speeds ranged from 1.8 to 17.0 mph. No repairs or adjustments were required during 47 hours of running time. Weighing 11,510 lbs., the 1070 was equipped with 20.8-38-inch rear and 11.00-16-inch front tires. Additional front and rear ballast raised the total test weight to 17,675 lbs. Operating in fifth gear, 90.99 maximum available drawbar hp was evidenced in the two-hour economy run. Also observed was a pull of 7,652 lbs. at 4.46 mph, slippage of 6.57 percent, and an economy of 12.62 hp-hours per gallon. The 10-hour run at 75 percent pull noted an economy figure of 12.68 against an output of 76.17 hp. This test evoked a pull of 6,063 lbs. at 4.71 mph with slippage totaling 4.66 percent.

Nebraska Test Data

Model: Case 1070 Manual Diesel

Test No. 1067

Date Tested: May 6 to May 21, 1971

This model used the same six-cylinder, 451-cubic-inch engine as previously noted in Test No. 1066. The major difference was a selective-gear, fixed-ratio transmission offering eight forward speeds ranging from 2.0 to 15.8 mph. No repairs or adjustments were reported during 54 hours of operating time. Weighing in at 11,410 lbs., this tractor assumed a total test weight of 17,520 lbs. through the addition of front and rear ballast. Operating in fourth gear, the two-hour economy run at 90.77 maximum available drawbar hp saw a pull of 6,158 lbs. at 5.53 mph, slippage of 5.19 percent, and an economy of 13.05 hp-hours per gallon. The 10-hour run at 75 percent pull indicated an economy figure of 12.62 against a load of 72.35 drawbar hp. Also in evidence was a pull of 4,669 lbs. at 5.81 mph and slippage of 3.91percent. At rated engine speed, 107.36 maximum PTO hp was observed, and an economy of 15.10 hp-hours per gallon. Operating at 1,000 PTO rpm and a corresponding engine speed of 1,870 rpm, 103.91 hp was recorded, together with an economy of 15.75 hp-hours per gallon.

Case 1170

Nebraska Test Data

Model: Case 1170 Diesel

Test No. 1062

Date Tested: November 6 to November 19, 1970

A 451-cubic-inch, six-cylinder engine was featured in this model. Rated at 2,100 rpm, it used a 4-3/8 x 5- inch bore and stroke. At rated engine speed, 121.93 maximum PTO hp was observed, as was an economy of 15.76 hp-hours per gallon. At 1,000 PTO rpm and a corresponding engine speed of 1,870 rpm, 118.13 PTO hp appeared and an economy figure of 16.46 was established. No repairs or adjustments were reported during 51 hours of operating time. The selective-gear, fixed-ratio transmission offered eight forward speeds varying from 1.9 to 15.0 mph. Weighing 13,540 lbs., this tractor was furnished with 20.8-38-inch rear and 9.50-20-inch front tires. A total test weight of 18,520 lbs. resulted from the addition of front and rear ballast. Using fourth gear, the two-hour drawbar performance run at 108.15 maximum available drawbar hp saw an economy of 13.94 hp-hours per gallon. Further, this test indicated a pull of 7,765 lbs. at 5.22 mph with slippage of 5.83 percent. The 10-hour run at 75 percent pull noted an economy of 13.09 hp-hours per gallon against a load of 87.73 drawbar hp. Other data from this test included a pull of 5,989 lbs. at 5.49 mph with slippage that totaled 4.47 percent.

Case 1270

Nebraska Test Data

Model: Case 1270 Diesel

Test No. 1103

Date Tested: June 9 to June 16, 1972

Once again Case featured its 451-cid, six–cylinder, turbocharged engine. Rated at 2,100 rpm, it delivered 126.7 maximum PTO hp at this speed and achieved an economy of 14.18 hp-hours per gallon. A second PTO run at 1,000 PTO rpm and a corresponding engine speed of 1,999 rpm saw an economy of 14.52 hp-hours per gallon against a load of 126.6 PTO hp. The selective gear fixed-ratio transmission offered 12 forward speeds ranging from 1.9 to 17.8 mph. Unlike the 1370's dual rear wheels of the previous test, this tractor carried 20.8-38 rear rubber and 9.5-20 front tires. The bare tractor weight of 13,400 lbs. was raised to a total of 17,625 lbs. through the use of front and rear ballast. Operating in sixth gear, 108.45 maximum available drawbar hp was evidenced in the two-hour economy run. This test saw a pull of 8,133 lbs. at 5.00 mph, slippage of 6.72percent, and an economy of 12.13 hp-hours per gallon. The 10-hour drawbar run at 75 percent pull indicated an economy of 11.55 hp-hours per gallon under a load of 89.72 hp. Also recorded was a pull of 6,190 lbs. at 5.44 mph and 4.77 percent slippage. No repairs or adjustments were reported during 46-1/2 hours of running time.

Nebraska Test Data

Model: Case 1270 Diesel

Test No. 1160

Date Tested: June 3 to June 11, 1974

This 1270 featured a Case-built six-cylinder, 451-cid, turbocharged diesel engine. Rated at 2,100 rpm, it used a 4-3/8 x 5-inch bore and stroke. At rated engine speed, 135.39 maximum PTO hp appeared, as did an economy of 13.86 hp-hours per gallon. By comparison, when operating at 1,000 PTO rpm and a corresponding engine speed of 2,000 rpm, an economy figure of 14.23 was achieved under a load of 135.41 PTO hp. No repairs or adjustments were required during 48-1/2 hours of operating time. The selective gear fixed-ratio transmission included 12 forward speeds ranging from 1.9 to 17.7 mph. Also featured was partial range power shifting. Operating in sixth gear, the two-hour economy run at 116.77 maximum available drawbar hp saw a pull of 9,211 lbs. at 4.75 mph with slippage totaling 6.48 percent. Fuel economy was posted at 12.16 hp-hours per gallon. By comparison, the 10-hour run at 75 percent pull set an economy of 11.49 hp-hours per gallon under a load of 95.88 drawbar hp. Also recorded in this test was a pull of 7,141 lbs. at 5.04 mph with slippage totaling 4.88 percent. Dual rear wheels of 18.4-38- inch size were used, as were 10.00-16-inch front tires. Weighing 15,470 lbs., the 1270 assumed a total test weight of 18,910 lbs. through the addition of front and rear ballast.

Nebraska Test Data

Model: Case 1370 Diesel

Test No. 1102

Date Tested: June 10 to June 19, 1972

Case 1370

This tractor featured a six-cylinder turbocharged engine with a 504-cubic-inch displacement. Rated at 2,100 rpm, it carried a 4-3/8 x 5-inch bore and stroke. The drive train included a selective-gear, fixed-ratio transmission with partial range power shifting. Its 12 forward speeds ranged from 1.9 to 17.8 mph. Operating in sixth gear, the two-hour drawbar run at 120.97 maximum available hp yielded an economy of 12.73 hp-hours per gallon with a pull of 9,439 lbs. at 4.81 mph. Slippage was recorded at 5.95 percent, even with the dual 18.4-38-inch rear tires shown in this photograph. A 10-hour run at 75 percent pull noted an economy of 11.82 hp-hours per gallon with a load of 99.90 hp. This test further recorded a pull of 7,230 lbs. at 5.18 mph and slippage of 4.19 percent. Bare tractor weight was 15,290 lbs., but additional front and rear ballast raised this figure to a total test weight of 20,960 lbs. No repairs or adjustments were reported during 44-1/2 hours of operating time. At rated engine speed, 142.51 maximum PTO hp was observed, together with an economy of 14.9 hp-hours per gallon. The economy figure rose to 15.37 under a load of 143.64 PTO hp. This one-hour run was made at 1,000 PTO rpm and a corresponding engine speed of 2,000 rpm.

Nebraska Test Data

Model: Case 1370 Diesel

Test No. 1148

Date Tested: October 31 to November 7, 1973

This tractor used a Case-built six-cylinder, 504-cid turbocharged engine. Rated at 2,200 rpm, it carried a 4-5/8 x 5-inch bore and stroke. At rated engine speed, 155.56 maximum PTO hp was observed, as was an economy of 14.07 hp-hours per gallon. Operating at 1,000 PTO rpm and a corresponding engine speed of 2,001 rpm, an economy figure of 15.01 was established under a PTO load of 156.32 hp. Twelve forward speeds ranging from 2.0 to 18.5 mph were available within the selective gear fixed-ratio transmission. It also offered partial range power shifting. Using sixth gear, the two-hour economy run at 130.93 maximum available drawbar hp yielded an economy of 12.04 hp-hours per gallon. Also recorded was a pull of 9,847 lbs. at 4.99 mph with slippage totaling 6.42 percent. The 10-hour run at 75 percent pull indicated an economy of 10.91 hp-hours per gallon under a load of 107.76 drawbar hp. Other statistics included a pull of 7,568 lbs. at 5.34 mph with slippage totaling 4.71 percent. Weighing in at 15,345 lbs., the 1370 was equipped with dual rear wheels of 18.4-38-inch size, plus 10.00-16 inch front tires. Additional front and rear ballast raised the total test weight to 20,290 lbs. Repairs and adjustments over 49 hours of operating time were relatively minor in nature.

Case 1470

Nebraska Test Data

Model: Case 1470 Diesel

Test No. 1006

Date Tested: April 15 to April 23, 1969

Weighing in at 17,300 lbs., this four-wheel-drive model featured 28.1-26 tires. Although no ballast was used on the rear wheels, front-wheel ballast raised the total test weight to 18,510 lbs. Other features included a selective-gear, fixed-ratio transmission with eight forward speeds ranging from 2.46 to 13.93 mph. Operating in fourth gear, the two-hour drawbar run at 126.86 maximum available hp saw an economy of 15.79 hp-hours per gallon. Also indicated was a pull of 9,225 lbs. at 5.16 mph and slippage of 3.32 percent. The 10-hour run at 75 percent pull noted an economy of 14.39 hp-hours per gallon against a load of 103.41 drawbar hp. Other statistics included a pull of 7,145 lbs. at 5.43 mph with slippage of 2.66 percent. Case equipped this model with its own six-cylinder, 504-cid diesel engine. Rated at 2,000 rpm, it used a 4-5/8 x 5-inch bore and stroke. Operating at rated engine speed, 144.89 maximum PTO hp was observed with a fuel economy of 17.7 hp-hours per gallon. New fuel filter cartridges were installed during the preliminary PTO runs. With this exception, no repairs or adjustments were reported during 58 hours of running time.

Case 1570

Nebraska Test Data

Model: Case 1570 Diesel

Test No. 1218

Date Tested: August 27 to September 3, 1976

Weighing 16,290 lbs., the tractor presented for testing was equipped with dual 20.8-38-inch rear tires and 11.00-16-inch front tires. Additional front and rear ballast gave a total test weight of 20,350 lbs. The selective-gear, fixed-ratio transmission offered partial range power shifting. Its 12 forward speeds ranged from 1.9 to 19.5 mph. Sixth gear was used for the two-hour economy run. Operating at 147.89 maximum available drawbar hp, an economy of 12.72 hp-hours per gallon was achieved. Also recorded in this test was a pull of 11,049 lbs. at 5.02 mph with slippage totaling 6.17 percent. The 10-hour run at 75 percent pull noted an economy of 12.46 hp-hours per gallon under a load of 122.22 drawbar hp. This test likewise saw a pull of 8,571 lbs. at 5.35 mph and slippage totaling 4.38 percent. No repairs or adjustments were required during 46-1/2 hours of operating time. The six-cylinder turbocharged engine was rated at 2,100 rpm. Its 4-5/8 x 5-inch bore and stroke gave a 504-cubic-inch displacement. At rated engine speed, 180.41 maximum PTO hp appeared and an economy of 15.09 hp-hours per gallon was achieved.

Case 2470

Nebraska Test Data

Model: Case 2470 Diesel

Test No. 1114

Date Tested: October 25 to October 31, 1972

Dual 18.4-34-inch tires were on all four corners on the 2470 Diesel. Weighing 20,485 lbs., it was tested without the use of additional ballast. The 2470 carried a selective-gear, fixed-ratio transmission with partial range power shifting. Its 12 forward speeds ranged from 2.0 to 15.0 mph. Using eighth gear, the two-hour economy run at 150.52 maximum available drawbar hp saw a fuel efficiency of 13.3 hp-hours per gallon. Also recorded in this test was a pull of 9.929 lbs. at 5.68 mph with slippage of 4.76 percent. The 10-hour run at 75 percent pull noted an economy of 12.55 hp-hours per gallon against a load of 122.18 drawbar hp. Other statistics included a pull of 7,639 lbs. at 6.00 mph and 3.38 percent slippage. No repairs or adjustments were reported during 45-1/2 total hours of operating time. This tractor featured a six-cylinder turbocharged diesel engine. Rated at 2,200 rpm, it used a 4-5/8 x 5-inch bore and stroke for a 504-cubic-inch displacement. At rated engine speed, the 2470 developed 174.20 maximum PTO hp and achieved an economy of 15.22 hp-hours per gallon.

Case 2670

Nebraska Test Data

Model: Case 2670 Diesel

Test No. 1165

Date Tested: October 23 to October 28, 1974

Dual 20.8-34-inch tires were used on all four corners of the 2670 Diesel. Weighing 20,810 lbs., it gained additional front and rear ballast for a total test weight of 25,260 lbs. The 12-speed, selective-gear, fixed-ratio transmission included partial range power shifting. The speed selection varied from 2.0 to 14.5 mph. A 504-cid turbocharged and intercooled six-cylinder Case engine was rated at 2,200 rpm, and carried a 4-5/8 x 5-inch bore and stroke. At rated engine speed, 219.44 maximum PTO hp appeared, and an economy of 15.29 hp-hours per gallon was observed. No repairs or adjustments were necessary during 42-1/2 hours of operating time. Using eighth gear, the two-hour economy run at 189.35 maximum available drawbar hp saw a pull of 11,885 lbs. at 5.97 mph with slippage totaling 4.14 percent. Fuel economy in this test came to 13.42 hp-hours per gallon. The 10-hour run at 75 percent pull indicated an economy of 12.6 hp-hours per gallon under a load of 154.88 drawbar hp. Also recorded was a pull of 9,095 lbs. at 6.39 mph with slippage totaling 3.01 percent .

Case 2870

Nebraska Test Data

Model: Case 2870 Diesel

Test No. 1241

Date Tested: May 3 to May 12, 1977

Weighing 25,100 lbs., the 2870 gained front and rear ballast for a total test weight of 28,150 lbs. Dual 20.8-34-inch tires were standard equipment for this four-wheel-drive model. Also featured was a selective-gear, fixed-ratio transmission with partial range power shifting. Its 12 forward speeds ranged from 2.0 to 14.9 mph. Operating in eighth gear, the two-hour economy run at 210.64 maximum available drawbar hp saw a pull of 13,784 lbs. at a speed of 5.73 mph. Slippage totaled 5.12 percent, and fuel economy was posted at 12.98 hp-hours per gallon. The 10-hour run at 75 percent pull noted an economy of 12.37 hp-hours per gallon under a load of 174.98 drawbar hp. Also recorded was a pull of 10,552 lbs. at 6.22 mph and slippage of 3.76 percent. No repairs or adjustments were reported during 52-½ hours of operating time. Case equipped this model with a SAAB-Scania six-cylinder turbocharged engine. Rated at 2,200 rpm, it used a 5.00 x 5.71 inch bore and stroke for a 673 cubic inch displacement. At rated engine speed, 252.10 maximum PTO hp was observed, as was an economy of 15.45 hp-hours per gallon.

Case 1190

Nebraska Test Data

Model: Case 1190 Manual Diesel
Test No. 1378
Date Tested: March 27 to April 9, 1981

This tractor weighed in at 4,620 lbs. and additional front and rear ballast gave a total test weight of 6,780 lbs. Standard equipment included 13.6-28-inch rear and 6.00-16-inch front tires. Also featured was a selective-gear, fixed-ratio transmission with twelve forward speeds over a range of 1.1 to 16.1 mph. Operating in eighth gear, the two-hour drawbar run at 34.65 maximum available hp indicated a pull of 2,512 lbs. at 5.17 mph and slippage totaling 6.88 percent. Fuel economy was posted at 12.22 hp-hours per gallon. The 10-hour run at 75 percent pull saw an economy of 12.59 hp-hours per gallon under a load of 28.62 drawbar hp. Other test statistics included a pull of 1,969 lbs. at 5.45 mph and 4.98 percent slippage. No repairs or adjustments were required during 38 hours of operating time. A Case three-cylinder engine was featured. Rated at 2,200 rpm, it carried a 3.939 x 4.500-inch bore and stroke for a 165 cubic inch displacement. At rated engine speed, 43.09 maximum PTO hp was evidenced, as was an economy of 14.70 hp-hours per gallon. Operating at 540 PTO rpm and a corresponding engine speed of 1,827 rpm, an economy of 14.99 hp-hours per gallon was established under a load of 38.54 PTO hp.

Case 1290

Nebraska Test Data

Model: Case 1290 Manual Diesel
Test No. 1379
Date Tested: Marrch 18 to April 13, 1981

The 1290 Diesel submitted for testing included a front-wheel assist option. Using this feature and operating in eighth gear, 44.81 maximum available drawbar hp was evidenced, as was a pull of 3,288 lbs. at 5.11 mph. Slippage totaled 3.88 percent, and fuel economy came in at 12.70 hp-hours per gallon. The same test run without using the front-wheel-assist, but again using eighth gear, indicated an output of 44.66 drawbar hp and a fuel economy of 12.41 hp-hours per gallon. Other statistics included a pull of 3,367 lbs. at 4.98 mph and slippage totaling 5.12 percent. No repairs or adjustments were required during 44-1/2 hours of operation. The selective-gear, fixed-ratio transmission offered 12 forward speeds ranging from 1.0 to 15.0 mph. Other features of this 6,570 lb. tractor included 16.9-14-30-inch rear and 9.5-24-inch front tires. Additional front and rear ballast gave a total test weight of 9,320 lbs. The Case-built four-cylinder engine was rated at 2,200 rpm. Its 3.939 x 4-inch bore and stroke gave a 195 cubic inch displacement. At rated engine speed, 53.73 maximum PTO hp was achieved an economy of 14.86 hp-hours per gallon was observed. Operating at 540 PTO rpm and a corresponding engine speed of 1,827 rpm, an economy of 15.20 hp-hours per gallon was indicated with a load of 47.80 PTO hp.

Case 1390

Nebraska Test Data

Model: Case 1390 Manual Diesel, 12 Speed
Test No. 1380
Date Tested: March 25 to April 10, 1981

At its rated speed of 2,200 rpm, the 1390 developed 60.59 maximum PTO hp while achieving an economy of 15.27 hp-hours per gallon. At 1,000 PTO rpm and a corresponding engine speed of 2,047 rpm, an economy of 15.58 hp-hours per gallon resulted from a load of 58.40 PTO hp. The 1390 featured a four-cylinder engine with a 3.939 x 4.500-inch bore and stroke for a 219-cubic-inch displacement. No repairs or adjustments were necessary during 38 hours of operating time. The selective-gear, fixed-ratio transmission gave 12 forward speeds ranging from 1.0 to 15.0 mph. Using eighth gear, a two-hour drawbar test at 50.38 maximum available hp saw a pull of 3,834 lbs. at 4.93 mph. Slippage totaled 6.1 percent and an economy of 12.89 hp-hours per gallon of fuel was indicated. This test was run without the front-wheel-assist option. Using this feature and operating in eighth gear, a maximum pull of 3,726 lbs. at 5.06 mph was recorded with slippage totaling 4.71 percent . This test saw an economy of 12.69 hp-hours per gallon of fuel under a load of 50.26 drawbar hp. Weighing 6,620 lbs., the 1390 with front-wheel-assist used 16.9-14-30-inch rear and 9.5-24-inch front tires. Additional front and rear ballast gave a total test weight of 9,780 lbs.

Case 1490

Nebraska Test Data

Model: Case 1490 Manual Diesel, 12 Speed
Test No. 1381
Date Tested: March 17 to April 2, 1981

A four-cylinder turbocharged engine was featured in the 1490 tractor. Rated at 2,200 rpm, it carried a 3.939 x 4.5 inch bore and stroke for a 219 cubic inch displacement. At rated engine speed, 70.51 maximum PTO hp was observed with 16.66 hp-hours per gallon. Operating at 1,000 PTO rpm and a corresponding engine speed of 2,047 rpm, an economy figure of 17.18 was recorded under a load of 68.75 PTO hp. No repairs or adjustments were necessary during 45 hours of operating time. A selective-gear, fixed-ratio transmission was used—its 12 forward speeds ranged from 1.1 to 16.1 mph. Using front-wheel-assist and operating in eighth gear, 60.31 maximum drawbar hp was evidenced, as was an economy of 14.04 hp-hours per gallon. This test saw a pull of 4,831 lbs. at 4.68 mph with slippage totaling 4.71 percent. Without this option, but operating in eighth gear, a pull of 4,864 lbs. was indicated at a speed of 4.56 mph with slippage totaling 6.52 percent. Fuel economy came in at 13.82 hp-hours per gallon. Standard equipment for this 7,705 lb. tractor included 18.4-34 rear and 12.4R24 front tires. Additional front and rear ballast gave a total test weight of 11,305 lbs.

Nebraska Test Data

Model: Case 1490 Power-Shift Diesel, 12 Speed
Test No. 1382
Date Tested: March 18 to April 2, 1981

Rated at 2,200 rpm, the 1490 delivered 70.91 maximum PTO hp while achieving an economy of 15.60 hp-hours per gallon. Operating at 1,000 PTO rpm and a corresponding engine speed of 2,048 rpm, an economy of 16.42 hp hours resulted from a load of 70.48 PTO hp. The four-cylinder turbocharged engine carried a 3.939 x 4.500-inch bore and stroke for a 219 cubic inch displacement. No repairs or adjustments were required during 37 hours of operating time. A four-range power shift was featured in the selective-gear, fixed-ratio transmission. Its 12 forward speeds varied from 1.0 x 16.0 mph. Using seventh gear, the two-hour drawbar test at 60.12 maximum available hp saw a pull of 4,656 lbs. at 4.85 mph with slippage totaling 6.61 percent. Fuel economy came in at 13.12 hp-hours per gallon. By comparison, the 10-hour run at 75 percent pull yielded 12.01 hp-hours per gallon under a load of 48.90 drawbar hp. Also evidenced was a pull of 3,569 lbs. at 5.14 mph and slippage totaling 4.89 percent. Standard equipment included 18.4-34-inch rear and 11L-15-inch front tires. Weighing 8,425 lbs., the 1490 assumed a total test weight of 11,060 lbs. with front and rear ballast.

Case 1690

Nebraska Test Data

Model: Case 1690 Manual Diesel
Test No. 1383
Date Tested: March 27 to April 21, 1981

The 1690 featured a selective-gear, fixed-ratio transmission offering 12 forward speeds with a range of 1.0 to 15.1 mph. Using seventh gear and the front-wheel-assist option, this tractor emerged from a two-hour drawbar run with an economy of 13.20 hp-hours per gallon against a maximum output of 72.55 drawbar hp. Also indicated was a pull of 6,302 lbs. at 4.32 mph and slippage totaling 6.39 percent. Without the front-wheel-assist, but using seventh gear, 70.30 maximum available drawbar hp was evidenced, as was a pull of 6,344 lbs. at 4.16 mph. Slippage totaled 8.63 percent, and fuel economy came in at 12.84 hp-hours per gallon. Repairs and adjustments during 53 hours of operation included replacement of all injectors after the 10-hour drawbar run, replacement of the fuel transfer pump, and readjustment of the fuel injection pressure. Standard equipment for this 8,755 lb. tractor included 18.4-34-inch rear and 13.6-24-inch front tires. Additional front and rear ballast gave a total test weight of 12,470 lbs. The six-cylinder engine was rated at 2,300 rpm. Its 3.939 x 4.500-inch bore and stroke gave a 329 cubic inch displacement. At rated engine speed, 15.58 hp-hours per gallon was observed at a load of 90.39 PTO hp.

Case 2090

Nebraska Test Data

Model: Case 2090 Power-Shift Diesel

Test No. 1295

Date Tested: November 6 to November 13, 1978

Weighing 12,030 lbs., this tractor assumed a total test weight of 15,190 lbs. by the addition of front and rear ballast. Standard equipment included 20.8-38 rear and 11.00-16 inch front tires. No repairs or adjustments were required during 36-½ hours of operation. The selective-gear, fixed-ratio transmission offered partial range power shifting. Its 12 forward speeds ranged from 2.0 to 18.8 mph. Using eighth gear, the two-hour economy run at 89.40 maximum available drawbar hp indicated a pull of 5,106 lbs. at 6.57 mph, slippage of 4.89 percent, and an economy of 12.49 hp-hours per gallon. The 10-hour run at 75 percent pull noted an economy of 11.96 hp-hours per gallon under a load of 74.71 drawbar hp. Also recorded was a pull of 4,024 lbs. at 6.96 mph and slippage totaling 3.70 percent. Case equipped this tractor with its own six-cylinder diesel engine. Rated at 2,100 rpm, it used a 4.625 x 5.000-inch bore and stroke for a 504 cubic inch displacement. At rated engine speed, 108.29 maximum PTO hp was observed, as was an economy of 14.94 hp-hours per gallon.

Nebraska Test Data

Model: Case 2090 Manual Diesel, 8-Speed

Test No. 1304

Date Tested: April 11 to April 21, 1979

This tractor used a 504-cid engine lacking a turbocharger. At its rated 2,100 rpm, an economy of 15.4 hp-hours per gallon was reckoned under a maximum load of 108.74 PTO hp. No repairs or adjustments were reported during 34-1/2 hours of operating time. The selective-gear, fixed-ratio transmission offered eight forward speeds ranging from 2.2 to 16.1 mph. Using fifth gear, the two-hour economy run at 93.17 maximum available drawbar hp indicated a pull of 6,288 lbs. at 5.56 mph with slippage totaling 5.64 percent. Fuel economy came in at 13.41 hp-hours per gallon. The 10-hour run at 75 percent pull noted an economy of 12.69 hp-hours per gallon under a load of 75.53 drawbar hp. Other test data included a pull of 4,801 lbs. at 5.9 mph and slippage of 3.94 percent. Standard equipment included 20.8-38-inch rear and 11.00-16-inch front tires. Weighing in at 11,910 lbs., total test weight was 15, 030 lbs. with ballast.

Case 2390

Nebraska Test Data

Model: Case 2390 Power-Shift Diesel

Test No. 1302

Date Tested: April 6 to April 16, 1979

At its rated engine speed of 2,100 rpm, the 2390 Diesel achieved a maximum output of 160.62 PTO hp and delivered an economy of 15.23 hp-hours per gallon. The six-cylinder turbocharged engine used a 4.625 x 5-inch bore and stroke for a 504 cubic inch displacement. Also featured was a selective gear fixed-ratio transmission with partial range power shifting. The 12 forward speeds ranged from 2.0 to 20.1 mph. No repairs or adjustments were required during 38-1/2 hours of operating time. Operating in sixth gear, the two-hour economy run at 137.72 maximum available drawbar hp indicated a pull of 9,946 lbs. at 5.19 mph with slippage totaling 6.04 percent. Fuel economy was posted at 13.20 hp-hours per gallon. Operating for 10 hours at 75 percent pull, an economy of 12.66 was observed under an output of 113.06 drawbar hp. Also indicated was a pull of 7,660 lbs. at 5.53 mph and slippage of 4.25 percent. Standard equipment for this 15,590 lb. tractor included dual 20.8-38-inch rear and 16.5L-16-inch front tires. Additional front and rear ballast gave a total test weight of 18,710 lbs.

Case 2590

Nebraska Test Data

Model: Case 2090 Power-Shift Diesel, 12-Speed

Test No. 1303

Date Tested: April 9 to April 19, 1979

No repairs or adjustments were reported for this tractor during 40-1/2 hours of engine operating time. Its selective-gear, fixed-ratio transmission offered 12 forward speeds ranging from 2.0 to 20.1 mph. Operating in sixth gear, the two-hour drawbar economy run at 153.24 maximum available hp yielded an economy of 13.42 hp-hours per gallon. Also recorded in this test was a pull of 11,111 lbs. at 5.17 mph and slippage totaling 6.62 percent. The 10-hour run at 75 percent pull noted an economy of 13.03 hp-hours per gallon under a load of 125.09 drawbar hp. Other statistics included a pull of 8,495 lbs. at 5.52 mph and slippage of 4.57 percent. Dual 20.8-38 rear and 16.5L-16 inch front tires were standard equipment. Weighing in at 15,740 lbs., the 2590 assumed a total test weight of 20,500 lbs. through the addition of front and rear ballast. The six-cylinder turbocharged engine was rated at 2,100 rpm. Its 4.625 x 5 inch bore and stroke gave a 504 cubic inch displacement. At rated engine speed the 2590 achieved an economy of 15.53 hp-hours per gallon under a maximum PTO load of 180.38 hp.

Case 4490, 4690, 4890

Nebraska Test Data

Model: Case 4490 Diesel, 12-Speed

Test No. 1328

Date Tested: October 15 to October 20, 1979

At its rated engine speed of 2,200 rpm, the 4490 developed 175.20 maximum PTO hp while achieving an economy of 15.27 hp-hours per gallon. A Case-built six-cylinder turbocharged and intercooled engine was featured. Its 4.625 x 5-inch bore and stroke gave a 504 cubic inch displacement. The selective-gear, fixed-ratio transmission featured partial range power shifting. Its 12 forward speeds ranged from 2.0 to 17.5 mph. No repairs or adjustments were required during 35 hours of engine operating time. Using eighth gear, the two-hour economy run at 150.14 maximum available drawbar hp indicated a pull of 9,977 lbs. at 5.64 mph with slippage totaling 4.07 percent. Fuel economy was registered at 13.30 hp-hours per gallon. By comparison, the 10-hour test at 75 percent pull noted an economy of 12.52 hp-hours per gallon under a load of 121.71 drawbar hp. Also witnessed was a pull of 7,639 lbs. at 5.97 mph with slippage totaling 2.78 percent. The 4490 weighed in at 20,840 lbs., but additional front ballast gave a total test weight of 22,450 lbs. Standard equipment included dual 18.4-34-inch tires.

Nebraska Test Data

Model: Case 4690 Diesel, 12-Speed

Test No. 1329

Date Tested: October 18 to October 26, 1979

Partial range power shifting was incorporated into the selective-gear, fixed-ratio transmission used in the 4690 Diesel. The 12 forward speeds varied from 2.0 to 18.2 mph. Using eighth gear, the two-hour economy run at 189.75 maximum available drawbar hp indicated a pull of 11,925 lbs. at 5.97 mph with slippage totaling 3.98 percent. Fuel economy was recorded at 13.39 hp-hours per gallon. The 10-hour run at 75 percent pull saw an economy of 12.84 hp-hours per gallon under a load of 154.65 PTO hp. Also indicated by this test was a pull of 9,226 lbs. at 6.29 mph and slippage totaling 2.87 percent. Weighing 22,310 lbs., the 4690 featured dual 20.8-34-inch tires. Additional front ballast gave a total test weight of 25,320 lbs. No repairs or adjustments were necessary during 34-1/2 hours of operation. The 4690 featured a Case-built six-cylinder turbocharged and intercooled engine. Rated at 2,200 rpm, it carried a 4.625 x 5-inch bore and stroke for a 504 cubic inch displacement. At rated engine speed, 219.62 maximum PTO hp was manifested and an economy of 15.26 hp-hours per gallon was observed.

Nebraska Test Data

Model: Case 4890 Diesel, 12-Speed

Test No. 1330

Date Tested: October 22 to October 29, 1979

The 4890 Diesel featured a six-cylinder Saab-Scania turbocharged engine. Rated at 2,200 rpm, it used a 5 x 5.71-inch bore and stroke. At rated engine speed it developed 253.41 maximum PTO hp while achieving an economy of 16.32 hp-hours per gallon. No repairs or adjustments were required during 35 hours of operating time. The selective-gear, fixed-ratio transmission offered partial range power shifting. Its 12 forward speeds ranged from 2.0 to 18.2 mph. Using eighth gear, the two-hour economy run at 218.68 maximum available drawbar hp indicated an economy of 14.19 hp-hours per gallon. Also revealed by this test was a pull of 13,778 lbs. at 5.95 mph and slippage totaling 3.87 percent. By comparison, the 10-hour run at 75 percent pull indicated 13.27 hp-hours per gallon under a load of 180.71 drawbar hp. Other statistics from this test include a pull of 10,611 lbs. at 6.39 mph and slippage totaling 2.66 percent. Weighing 25,750 lbs., this tractor was equipped with dual 20.8-34-inch tires. Additional front ballast gave a total test weight of 28,460 lbs.

Case 1594

Nebraska Test Data

Model: Case 1594 Synchromesh Diesel

Test No. 1546

Date Tested: October 24 to November 2, 1984

The 1594 featured a Case six-cylinder diesel engine. Rated at 2,300 rpm, it used a 3.939 x 4.5-inch bore and stroke for a 329 cubic inch displacement. Also featured was a 12-speed selective-gear, fixed-ratio transmission with a range of 1.4 to 19.7 mph. Tires included 18.4-

34-inch rear and 10.00-16-inch front rubber. Weighing in at 9,345 lbs., the 1594 assumed a total test weight of 11,100 lbs. through the addition of front and rear ballast. No repairs or adjustments were required during 36-1/2 hours. At 85.90 maximum PTO hp, an economy of 16.59 hp-hours per gallon was recorded. With a PTO speed of 1,000 rpm and a corresponding crankshaft speed of 2,048 rpm, the economy figure stood at 17.04 against a load of 80.83 PTO hp. Drawbar economy indicated 72.17 maximum available hp in the two-hour run. This test saw a pull of 5,113 lbs. at 5.29 mph, slippage of 6.98 percent, and a fuel economy of 14.26 hp-hours per gallon. The 10-hour run at 75 percent pull noted an economy of 13.56 hp-hours per gallon under a load of 58.81 drawbar hp. And there was a pull of 3,911 lbs. at 5.64 mph and slippage of 5.09 percent.

Nebraska Test Data

Model: Case 1594 Power-Shift Diesel
Test No. 1547
Date Tested: October 23 to October 30, 1984

Features of this 1594 included partial range power shifting within the selective-gear, fixed-ratio transmission. Its 12 forward speeds ranged from 1.5 to 16.7 mph. Tire equipment included 18.4-34-inch rear and 10.00-16-inch front rubber. This 9,465 lb. tractor had a test weight of 11,210 lbs. after front and rear ballast was added. No repairs or adjustments were required during 37 hours of operating time. The Case six-cylinder diesel engine was the same used in Test No. 1546. At the rated speed of 2,300 rpm, 85.54 maximum PTO hp was observed yielding 16.35 hp-hours per gallon. Operating at 1,000 PTO rpm and a corresponding crankshaft speed of 2,048 rpm, the economy figure rested at 16.86 against a load of 81.94 PTO hp. Using seventh gear, the two-hour drawbar run at 69.37 maximum available hp noted a pull of 4,766 lbs. at 5.46 mph. Slippage totaled 6.81 percent, and fuel economy was established at 13.59 hp-hours per gallon. The 10-hour run at 75 percent pull established an economy figure of 13.10 against a load of 55.94 drawbar hp. Also shown was a pull of 3,627 lbs. at 5.78 mph and slippage of 4.79 percent.

Case 2094 and 2096

Nebraska Test Data

Model: Case 2094 Power-Shift Diesel
Test No. 1525
Date Tested: May 30 to June 16, 1984

Weighing 14,190 lbs., the 2094 was equipped with dual 18.4-38-inch rear and 11.00-16-inch front tires. Additional front and rear ballast gave a total test weight of 14,750 lbs. No repairs or adjustments were required for this tractor during 40 hours of engine operating time. The selective-gear, fixed-ratio transmission featured three-range power shifting. Its 12 forward speeds ranged from 1.9 to 18.1 mph. Using eighth gear, the two-hour drawbar run at 98.66 maximum available hp indicated a pull of 5,851 lbs. at 6.32 mph. Slippage totaled 4.45 percent, and fuel economy came in at 13.81 hp-hours per gallon. By comparison, the 10-hour run at 75 percent pull noted 12.93 hp-hours per gallon against a load of 79.35 drawbar hp. Also shown was a pull of 4,443 lbs. at 6.7 mph and slippage of 3.26 percent. The 2094 used a Case six-cylinder engine. Rated at 2,100 rpm, it carried a 4.625 x 5-inch bore and stroke for a 504 cubic inch displacement. At rated engine speed, 110.50 maximum PTO hp was observed, as was an economy of 15.40 hp-hours per gallon.

Nebraska Test Data

Model: Case 2096 Power-Shift Diesel
Test No. 1549
Date Tested: October 24 to November 5, 1984

The 2096 was equipped with a six-cylinder turbocharged and inter-cooled engine, a Consolidated Diesel Corporation-Case design. Rated at 2,100 rpm, it used a 4.016 x 4.724-inch bore and stroke for a 359 cubic inch displacement. Weighing 14,180 lbs., the 2096 was equipped with dual 18.4-38 rear and 11.00-16SL front tires. Additional front and rear ballast gave a total test weight of 14,940 lbs. The selective-gear, fixed-ratio transmission featured partial range power shifting. Its 12 forward speeds ranged from 1.9 to 18.1 mph. Using eighth gear, a two-hour drawbar run at 100.56 maximum available hp indicated a pull of 5,915 lbs. at 6.38 mph. Slippage totaled 3.9 percent and fuel economy was posted at 15.21 hp-hours per gallon. The 10-hour run at 75 percent pull saw 13.92 hp-hours per gallon against a load of 79.68 drawbar hp. Other data from this test included a pull of 4,463 lbs. at 6.69 mph and slippage of 2.84 percent. At rated engine speed, 115.67 maximum PTO hp appeared and an economy of 17.38 hp-hours per gallon was achieved. Repairs and adjustments during 32-1/2 hours of operating time included an adjustment of the hydraulic lift control valve linkage.

Case 2294, 2394, 2594

Nebraska Test Data

Model: Case 2294 Power-Shift Diesel
Test No. 1526
Date Tested: June 1 to June 12, 1984

The 2294 carried the same 504-cid engine as the Case 2094, except that this model featured a turbocharger. With this added feature, and operating at the rated engine speed of 2,100 rpm, the two-hour PTO run at 131.97 maximum hp saw an economy of 14.86 hp-hours per gallon. Three-range power shifting was featured in the selective-gear, fixed-ratio transmission. Its 12 forward speeds ranged from 1.9 to 18.1 mph. Using eighth gear, the two-hour run at 115.35 maximum available drawbar hp indicated an economy of 13.11 hp-hours per gallon. Also shown in this test was a pull of 6,877 lbs. at 6.29 mph and slippage of 5.11 percent. The 10-hour run at 75 percent pull was made at 92.28 drawbar hp and evidenced an economy of 12.21 hp-hours per gallon. Other statistics from this test include a pull of 5,191 lbs. at 6.67 mph and slippage totaling 3.51 percent. No repairs or adjustments were necessary during 39 hours of operating time. Weighing in at 14,390 lbs., the 2294 assumed a total test weight of 15,670 lbs. after additional front and rear ballast had been installed. Standard equipment included dual 18.4-38-inch rear and 11.00-16-inch front tires.

Nebraska Test Data

Model: Case 2394 Power-Shift Diesel
Test No. 1527
Date Tested: June 7 to June 23, 1984

Six-range power shifting was featured in the 2394 tractor. Its 24 forward speeds ranged from 1.7 to 20.1 mph. Operating in 16th gear, a two-hour drawbar test at 137.78 maximum available hp saw an economy of 13.42 hp-hours per gallon. Other data from this test included a pull of 8,548 lbs. at 6.04 mph and slippage totaling 4.81 percent. The 10-hour run at 75 percent pull established an economy figure of 12.71 against a load of 110.93 drawbar hp. Likewise indicated was a pull of 6,573 lbs. at 6.33 mph and slippage of 3.51 percent. These tests were run using dual 20.8-38-inch bias-ply tires. A supplemental run on 20.8R38 radial tires indicated an economy of 13.60 hp-hours per gallon under a maximum load of 139.80 drawbar hp. Weighing 16,240 lbs., the 2394 assumed a total test weight of 18,595 lbs. through the addition of front and rear ballast. No repairs or adjustments were necessary during 54 hours of operating time. The six-cylinder turbocharged engine was rated at 2,100 rpm. Its 4.625 x 5-inch bore and stroke gave a 504 cubic inch displacement. At rated engine speed, 162.15 maximum PTO hp was observed, as was an economy of 15.46 hp-hours per gallon.

Nebraska Test Data

Model: Case 2594 Power-Shift Diesel
Test No. 1529
Date Tested: May 31 to June 20, 1984

Six-range power shifting featured within this tractor's selective-gear, fixed-ratio transmission gave a total 24-speed range of 1.9 to 20.8 mph. Operating in 16th gear, the two-hour drawbar test at 159.64 maximum available hp noted a pull of 9,346 lbs. at 6.41 mph. Slippage totaled 5.83 percent, and fuel economy was posted at 13.37 hp-hours per gallon. By comparison, the 10-hour run at 75 percent pull set an economy figure of 12.94 under a load of 128.78 drawbar hp. Other data included a pull of 7,115 lbs. at 6.79 mph and slippage of 4.16 percent. While these tests were run with dual 20.8-38-inch bias-ply tires, a two-hour run using dual 20.8R38-inch radial tires indicated a maximum output of 161.92 drawbar hp, plus a pull of 8,845 lbs. at 6.86 mph. Slippage totaled 2.58 percent, and fuel economy was recorded at 13.76 hp-hours per gallon. Weighing 16,220 lbs., the 2594 assumed a total test weight of 19,790 lbs. through the addition of front and rear ballast. At its rated speed of 2,100 rpm, 182.07 maximum PTO hp was observed plus 15.22 hp-hours per gallon. The six-cylinder turbocharged engine carried a 4.625 x 5-inch bore and stroke for a 504 cubic inch displacement. Repairs and adjustments during 48 hours of operating time included replacing brake shoes.

Case 3294

Nebraska Test Data

Model: Case 3294 Power-Shift Diesel
Test No. 1528
Date Tested: June 12 to June 22, 1984

The 3294 featured an all-wheel drive with a constant-mesh front axle. The test model was equipped with 20.8R38-inch rear and 16.9-28-inch front tires. A total test weight of 17,980 lbs. resulted from additional front and rear ballast, while the bare tractor weight was 17,915 lbs. No repairs or adjustments were required during 38 hours of operating time. Three-range power shifting was featured within the selective gear fixed-ratio transmission. Its 12 forward speeds varied from 2.0 to 18.8 mph. Using seventh gear, a two-hour drawbar run at 140.79 maximum available hp saw a pull of 9,183 lbs. at 5.75 mph. Slippage totaled 3.82 percent, and fuel economy came in at 13.55 hp-hours per gallon. By comparison, the 10-hour run at 75 percent pull established an economy figure of 12.76 under a load of 113.38 drawbar horse-power. Other data from this test included a pull of 7,029 lbs. at 6.05 mph and slippage of 2.6 percent. The Case-built six-cylinder engine was equipped with a turbocharger. Rated at 2,100 rpm, it carried a 4.625 x 5-inch bore and stroke for a 504 cubic inch displacement. At rated engine speed, 162.63 maximum PTO hp was observed, with an economy of 15.32 hp-hours per gallon.

Case 4994

Nebraska Test Data

Model: Case 4994 Power-Shift Diesel
Test No. 1530
Date Tested: June 9 to June 27, 1984

This four-wheel-drive model was equipped with dual 24.5-32-inch tires. Weighing in at 31,315 lbs. it assumed a total test weight of 39,930 lbs. through the addition of front and rear ballast. No repairs or adjustments were noted during 39-1/2 hours of operation. Full range power shifting was featured in the selective-gear, fixed-ratio transmission. Its 12 forward speeds varied from 2.5 to 17.2 mph. Operating in sixth gear, a two-hour drawbar run at 294.24 maximum available hp established an economy of 14.67 hp-hours per gallon. Also revealed during this test was a pull of 18,142 lbs. at 6.08 mph with slippage totaling 3.86 percent. The 10-hour run at 75 percent pull set an economy figure of 13.87 under a load of 244.29 drawbar hp. Other data included a pull of 14,037 lbs. at 6.53 mph and slippage of 2.77 percent. A SAAB-Scania engine was featured. Of turbocharged V-8 design, it was rated at 2,100 rpm. The 5 x 5.51- inch bore and stroke gave an 866 cubic inch displacement. At rated engine speed, a two-hour PTO run saw a maximum output of 344.04 hp, together with an economy of 17.03 hp-hours per gallon.

Case 1896

Nebraska Test Data

Model: Case 1896 Power-Shift Diesel
Test No. 1548
Date Tested: October 24 to November 7, 1984

At its rated engine speed of 2,100 rpm, the 1896 delivered 95.92 maximum PTO hp while achieving an economy of 16.71 hp-hours per gallon. This tractor featured a six-cylinder turbocharged engine by Consolidated Diesel Corporation. Its 4.016 x 4.724-inch bore and stroke gave a 359 cubic inch displacement. Partial range power shifting was featured in the selective-gear, fixed-ratio transmission. The 12 forward speeds ranged from 1.9 to 18.1 mph. Using eighth gear, the two-hour drawbar run at 84.51 maximum available hp saw a pull of 4,914 lbs. at 6.45 mph. Slippage totaled 3.08 percent, and fuel economy was posted at 14.82 hp-hours per gallon. The 10-hour run at 75 percent pull established an economy figure of 13.65 against an output of 66.89 drawbar hp. Other data included a pull of 3,735 lbs. at 6.72 mph and slippage of 2.24 percent. Weighing 13,495 lbs., the 1896 was equipped with dual 18.4-38-inch rear and 11.00-16-inch front tires. Additional front and rear ballast gave a total test weight of 13,925 lbs. Adjustment of the hydraulic lift control valve linkage was noted during 31-1/2 hours of operation.

The Terratrac line of crawler tractors was merged into J. I. Case in 1957 when the latter bought out American Tractor Corporation of Churbusco, Indiana. The following year Case introduced its 310 crawler tractor, following closely on the lines established by American Tractor. Case marketed this model as an agricultural crawler, with a PTO shaft, belt pulley and remote hydraulics all available as optional equipment.

Nebraska Test Data

Model: Case 310C
Test No. 709
Date Tested: July 14 to July 31, 1959

Case featured its own four-cylinder gasoline engine in the 310C tractor. Rated at 1,850 rpm, it carried a 3-3/8 x 4-1/8-inch bore and stroke for a 148-cubic-inch displacement. Also featured was a 12-volt electric system. The transmission carried three forward speeds of 1.74, 2.75,

Case 310 Crawler

and 4.52 mph. The 540 rpm PTO drive was achieved at an engine speed of 1,727 rpm. A belt pulley was also available. Total weight was 6,145 lbs., including 550 lbs. of front counterweight and other accessory items. At rated crankshaft speed of 1,850 rpm, the 310C yielded 33.32 maximum PTO hp with a fuel economy of 11.3 hp-hours per gallon. At a standard PTO speed of 540 rpm, fuel economy was posted at 11.67 against an output of 31.43 hp. Second gear was used for the drawbar testing, with 26.75 hp being derived under maximum load. This test indicated a pull of 3,706 lbs. at 2.71 mph against a slippage of 3.33 percent. Fuel economy came in at 8.49 hp-hours per gallon. Under 75 percent load, an output of 21.68 hp was noted, along with a pull of 2,895 lbs. at 2.81 mph and 2.74 percent slippage. Fuel economy in this 10-hour run came to 8.37 hp-hours per gallon. No repairs or adjustments of major importance were noted during 56 hours of running time.

Nebraska Test Data

Model: Case 310E Diesel

Test No. 805

Date Tested: July 25 to August 16, 1961

At its rated engine speed of 1,850 rpm, the 310E displayed a maximum output of 36.89 PTO hp and garnered a fuel economy of 15 hp-hours per gallon. A one-hour run made a 540 PTO rpm and a corresponding crankshaft speed of 1,727 rpm noted an economy figure of 15.14 while delivering 34.96 PTO hp. This tractor was equipped with a Case-built four-cylinder engine with a 3-13/16 x 4-1/8-inch bore and stroke for a 188.4-cubic-inch displacement. Also featured on this 7,545 lb. tractor was a selective gear fixed-ratio transmission with three forward speeds of 1.74, 2.75, and 4.52 mph. No repairs or adjustments were recorded during 53-1/2 hours of running time except for adjustment of the steering brakes during the 10-hour drawbar run. A two-hour drawbar economy test made at 29.56 maximum available hp used second gear, and indicated a pull of 4,058 lbs. at 2.73 mph with 1.41 percent slippage. Fuel economy was posted at 12.51 hp-hours per gallon. The economy figure slipped slightly to 12.14 in a 10-hour drawbar run made at 75 percent pull. This test noted an output of 25.12 hp, a pull of 3,286 lbs. at 2.87 mph, and 1.06 percent slippage. Also of interest was a low-gear maximum pull of 7,061 lbs. at 1.67 mph, with this test indicating an output of 31.45 drawbar hp.

Case 610 crawler

Case 610 crawlers were built in gasoline and diesel versions, and first appeared in 1960. This model was capable of about 60 PTO hp and continued the Terramatic transmission and torque converter drive that had been developed by American Tractor Corporation. Power steering was also standard equipment for the 610.

Nebraska Test Data

Model: Case 610 Diesel

Test No. 7114

Date Tested: August 19 to August 28, 1959

The 610 Diesel featured a torque multiplier system; forward speeds ranging from 0 to 7.2 mph were attainable in four different gear selections. This model was also equipped for PTO/belt pulley operation, and at a rated engine speed of 2,100 rpm, it delivered 38.58 maximum PTO hp with a fuel economy of 9.29 hp-hours per gallon. A Continental four-cylinder diesel engine was used—it carried a 3-11/16 x 4-7/8-inch bore and stroke with a 208-cubic-inch displacement. The design included a 16.0:1 compression ratio. Second gear was used for the varying drawbar power and fuel consumption tests. At maximum available power, a pull of 4,277 lbs. was recorded at 2.84 mph with 1.84 percent slippage. With 32.4 maximum hp, this two-hour run yielded a fuel economy of 7.93 hp-hours per gallon. A 10-hour run made at 75 percent load indicated 29.33 hp, a pull of 3,336 lbs. at 3.3 mph and slippage of 0.99 percent for a fuel economy of 7.05 hp-hours per gallon. Total tractor weight was 9,510 lbs., including a 1,200 lb. counterweight. Repairs and adjustments were minor in nature during a 40-1/2 hour run.

Case 750 crawler

Nebraska Test Data

Model: Case 750 Diesel

Test No. 865

Date Tested: August 17 to September 8, 1964

This crawler tractor featured a selective-gear, fixed-ratio transmission that also contained a torque converter and partial range power shifting. Through this means, four forward speeds were available from zero up to 6.24 mph. Weighing 14,035 lbs., the 750 Diesel emerged from a two-hour drawbar economy run with a maximum output of 36.25 hp, a pull of 7,155 lbs. at 1.9 mph and slippage of 2.8 percent. Economy in this test came to 8.28 hp-hours per gallon. By comparison, the 10-hour run at 75 percent pull saw an economy figure of 7.65. In this test the 750 accrued an output of 34.45 hp, making a pull of 5,479 lbs. at 2.36 mph with a 2.31 percent slippage. No repairs or adjustments were noted during 42-1/2 hours of operating time. Of interest in this test is a low-gear maximum pull of 10,327 lbs. at 1.35 mph with 3.71 percent slippage. Case equipped the 750 Diesel with its own four-cylinder engine. Rated at 1,900 rpm, it used a 4 x 4-1/8-inch bore and stroke for a 267-cubic-inch displacement.

Case 800 crawler

The Case 800 crawlers were built from 1957 to 1963 and were then followed by the 810C crawler. Weighing 7-1/2 tons, the 800 could pull 20,000 lbs. and was built in 60- or 54-inch track widths.

Nebraska Test Data

Model: Case 810 Diesel

Test No. 713

Date Tested: August 14 to August 28, 1959

A Continental four-cylinder diesel engine rated at 2,250 rpm was featured in the 810 Diesel. Using a 4 x 5 ½-inch bore and stroke, this engine had a 277-cubic-inch displacement. The design also included a 15.9:1 compression ratio. No PTO tests were run on this tractor. Using second gear, and at maximum available power, a two-hour run indicated an output of 38.57 drawbar hp, along with a corresponding pull of 7,240 lbs. at 2 mph and 1.69 percent slippage for a fuel economy of 8.34 hp-hours per gallon. At 75 percent load, fuel economy was noted at 7.93 against an output of 36.94 hp, a pull of 5,564 lbs. at 2.49 mph and slippage of 0.93 percent. The 810 weighed 15,000 lbs. This tractor featured a torque multiplier system, giving a speed range of 0 to 6 mph in four different gear ranges. No repairs or adjustments were noted during 39 hours of running time.

Case 1150 crawlers were first built in 1965 and replaced the Case 1000 crawler that had been built under that title since 1957. In fact, the 1000 came over to Case from the American Tractor Corporation merger of that year. The 1150 boasted 100 flywheel hp and at the time was the largest machine in the Case crawler tractor line. Subsequently, Case continued building numerous sizes and styles of crawler tractors.

Case 1150 crawler

Case 450 crawler

Case 450 crawlers first emerged in 1965 and remained on the market for several years. This tractor weighed nearly five tons and was equipped with a four-speed, dual-range transmission that included a torque converter drive. It was built only with a diesel engine.

J. I. Case Plow Works

RACINE, WISCONSIN

Wallis Tractor Company was organized at Cleveland, Ohio, in the fall of 1912 by H.M. Wallis and others. Wallis was a son-in-law of J. I. Case and was involved with the J. I. Case Plow Works at Racine.

Wallis Bear

About this same time the company was organized, the Wallis Bear tractor appeared. Rated at about 60 belt hp, it was built in small numbers, with the only one known to exist now owned by W. R. Schmidt & Sons at Upper Sandusky, Ohio.

Wallis Cub

By 1913 the Wallis Tractor Co. had moved to Racine and set up shop in the J. I. Case Plow Works. That same year the company announced the Wallis Cub, the first farm tractor with a unit frame design. E. J. Baker Jr., the former editor of Farm Implement News once noted that "this was the frameless construction that lifted the myopic lids from the eyes of Henry Ford and led directly to the design of the revolutionary Fordson tractor." The boiler plate frame of the Wallis was protected under Patent No. 1,205,982 with Clarence M. Eason and Robert O. Hendrickson as the patentees. Eason later moved to the Hyatt Roller Bearing Company.

In 1915 Wallis came out with its Model J, or Cub Junior tractor. This design had a 13-25 hp rating and used a four-cylinder engine with a 4-1/2 x 5-3/4-inch bore and stroke. The rolled boiler plate frame also served as the oil-pan for the engine and terminated at the final drives of the tractor.

COLLECTOR VALUES	1	2	3	4
CUB JUNIOR (MODEL J)	–	–	$8,000	--

Wallis two-row cultivator

Wallis Cub Junior (Model J)

Wallis offered a motor cultivator in 1919. The unit shown here was of two-row design and used an engine of 12 belt hp. Had the company modified the design slightly, it would have anticipated the row-crop design that was soon to come from the Farmall tractor of International Harvester Company.

Wallis Model K

Model K tractors appeared for the first time in 1919. This model had a rating of 15 drawbar and 25 belt hp. This tractor used a four-cylinder engine with a 4-1/4 x 5-3/4-inch bore and stroke. It was rated at 900 rpm. Weighing about 3,500 lbs., the 15-25 was capable of at least 2,700 lbs. on the drawbar.

Nebraska Test Data

Model: Wallis 15-25

Test No. 49

Date Tested: August 7 to August 16, 1920

Rated at 900 rpm, the Wallis 15-25 carried the company's own four-cylinder vertical, valve-in-head engine with a 4-1/4 x 5-3/4-inch bore and stroke. Removable cylinder sleeves were an innovative feature. Two forward speeds were provided of 2.5 and 3.5 mph. Although it weighed only 3,500 lbs., the 15-25 exerted a 2,782 lb. maximum drawbar pull in low gear, or slightly over half its own weight. This test noted a maximum of 18.58 drawbar hp. At rated brake hp, fuel economy came to 7.74 hp-hours per gallon, using kerosene fuel. Two maximum brake hp tests were made. The first one, using kerosene, revealed 27.57 hp-this increased to 29.87 on gasoline. Minor mechanical problems occurred, such as a leak in the fuel tank, plugged fuel lines, and clutch adjustments. Test engineers noted that during the entire test procedure with kerosene, the engine would load up on fuel and slow down, then return to normal. On gasoline, the problem disappeared. Coolant temperatures ranged from 180 to 210 degrees F. throughout the test procedures of about 32 hours.

Production of the Model K tractor ended in 1922, just as production of the Model OK 15-27 model began. The major difference was that the Model OK used an engine speed of 1,000 rpm, compared to 900 rpm for the earlier model. Engine dimensions were the same. Few changes were made in the Model OK 15-27 design until it was replaced with the 20-30 Wallis in 1927.

Wallis Model OK 15-27

Nebraska Test Data

Model: Wallis OK 15-27

Test No. 92

Date Tested: April 26 to May 5, 1923

Prior to recording any official data all valves were ground and the carburetor was cleaned. The report notes further that "These repairs were made in an effort to stabilize the unsteady operation of the motor, but did not improve its performance." Aside from these comments, no repairs or adjustments were required during the test. Weighing 4,020 lbs., the Wallis 15-27 displayed a maximum of 18.15 drawbar hp in low gear, pulling a 2,590 lb. load at a speed of 2.63 mph. In high gear a 1,740 lb. load was pulled at 3.13 mph for 14.53 maximum drawbar hp. Brake hp tests revealed a fuel economy of 8.67 hp-hours per gallon, with gasoline the selected fuel. Consumption during the rated load test came to 3.129 gallons per hour at a 27.13 hp load. Wallis used its own four-cylinder vertical, valve-in-head engine. Rated at 1,000 rpm, it carried a 4-1/4 x 5-3/4-inch bore and stroke. Standard equipment included a Bosch DU4 magneto and a Bennett carburetor.

COLLECTOR VALUES	1	2	3	4
OK 15-27	–	–	$2,700	$800

Wallis Model OK orchard tractor

Wallis began offering an orchard tractor version of its Model OK tractor in the early 1920s. As with other contemporary models, the orchard design had smooth hood-lines with a re-routed air stack and exhaust pipe. Special fenders were provided and the front wheels had enclosed spokes.

Wallis Model 20-30

During 1927 Wallis again revamped its proven design. This time the Model OK was modified so the rated engine speed was raised from 1,000 to 1,050 rpm. Other noticeable changes included a substantial oil bath air cleaner system. Typical of the Wallis designs was the unfortunate placement of the belt pulley inside the left rear wheel. J. I. Case Plow Works sold out to Massey-Harris in 1928. The latter continued building tractors under the Wallis trade name for a few years. The 10-20 Wallis was built by Massey-Harris.

Nebraska Test Data

Model: Wallis 20-30
Test No. 134
Date Tested: April 29 to May 10, 1927

The Wallis OK 15-27 provided the basis for this new model. Using distillate fuel throughout the test, it delivered 7.68 hp-hours per gallon on rated drawbar load, and managed to pull 3,409 lbs. in the maximum drawbar test, using low gear. This test gave a maximum of 27 drawbar hp for the 20-30, and slightly over 26 drawbar hp when using high gear. Slightly over 35 brake hp was exhibited in the maximum load test, while at rated load the 20-30 delivered 10.28 hp-hours per gallon of distillate, consuming 2.942 gph. The company used its own four-cylinder vertical, valve-in-head engine rated at 1,050 rpm and using a 4-3/8 x 5-3/4-inch bore and stroke. Other features included a Kingston carburetor, American Bosch ZR4 magneto, Pickering governor, and a cloth screen air cleaner built by Wallis. Total weight was 4,523 lbs. No repairs or adjustments were made during the 38 hours of running time required to complete the tests.

Caterpillar Tractor Company

PEORIA, ILLINOIS

Caterpillar Tractor Company resulted from a 1925 merger of Holt Mfg. Co. and C.L. Best Company. Both firms had previously come to a dominant position as manufacturers of crawler tractors. The first year of the merger the new company had sales of nearly $14 million. In 1928, three years after the merger, Caterpillar bought out the Russell Grader Company of Minneapolis, Minnesota. This was the beginning of the Caterpillar grader line.

Caterpillar was the first company to offer a crawler tractor powered by a diesel engine. Work on this project began in 1929, with a completed model ready in October of 1931. Within a short time the company was offering several models of diesel-powered Caterpillar tractors, and was the first tractor manufacturer to opt solely for diesel engines in its fleet, doing so in 1942.

It is difficult to document the exact production dates of the early models up to the late 1930s. Once the company began building the R- Series and the D-Series tractors, establishing the production dates is much easier, but several distinct styles of each model were built during the production runs.

Caterpillar made history with its 320 hp D-9 tractor introduced in 1955. At the time, it was the largest tractor ever built.

Although various makes of crawler tractors are oftentimes referred to as "caterpillars" the Caterpillar name and the Cat name are both registered trademarks of Caterpillar Tractor Company. That's why all other crawler tractor manufacturers referred to their machines as crawler tractors, tracklayers and various other names.

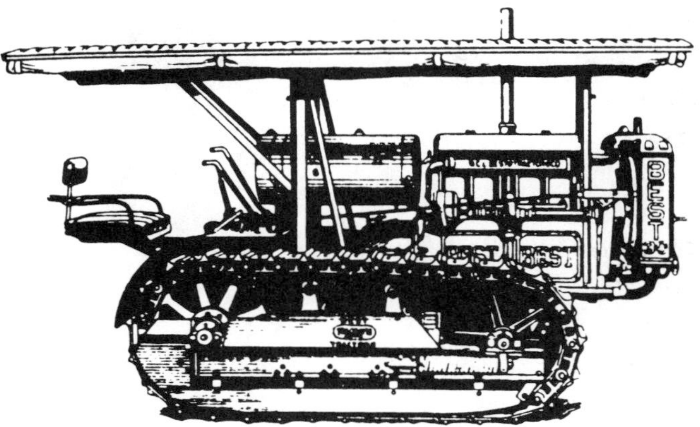

Caterpillar Best 30

Holt and Best merged in 1925 to form Caterpillar Tractor Company. At first the new company selected models from the two different product lines. In 1925, for instance, the new Caterpillar line included the old Best 30. This 8,700 lb. crawler used a four-cylinder engine with a 4-3/4 x 6-1/2-inch bore and stroke. The Thirty was built until 1931.

See: Test No. 104 under C. L. Best heading.

A close look at the Caterpillar 30 and the Caterpillar 60 for 1925 still reveals the "Best" trademark in the side of the radiator. By 1927 the "Holt" and "Best" trade names had disappeared. The Caterpillar 60 weighed 19,000 lbs. and was powered by the company's own four-cylinder engine with a 6-1/2 x 8-1/2-inch bore and stroke. Production of the 60 ended in 1931.

See: Test No. 105 under C. L. Best heading.

Caterpillar 60

COLLECTOR VALUES	1	2	3	4
CATERPILLAR 60	$18,000	$14,000	$7,000	$3,500

Caterpillar 2-Ton

The Caterpillar 2-Ton of 1925 was essentially the same as the Holt 2-Ton previously introduced. This small tractor weighed only 4,700 lbs., or just over two tons. It was equipped with the company's own four-cylinder engine with a 4 x 5-1/2-inch bore and stroke and used an overhead camshaft. Production continued into 1928.

Nebraska Test Data

Model: Caterpillar 2-Ton (formerly T-35)

Test No. 86

Date Tested: July 19 to July 26, 1922

Notes in the official test indicate that the Caterpillar 2-Ton had formerly been known as the T-35, the major difference between them being in name only. Three forward speeds graced this model, permitting a choice of 2.18, 3.04, and 5.23 mph. Weighing only 4,040 lbs., it managed a maximum drawbar pull of 3,275 lbs. at a speed of 1.77 mph. On the rated drawbar load test stretching out over 10 hours, an average of 15.13 drawbar hp was recorded, with a drawbar pull of 1,896 lbs. at a speed of 3 mph. Slippage was 5.55 percent. Brake hp tests revealed a fuel economy of 9.45 hp-hours per gallon of gasoline. Fuel consumption on the rated load test came to 2.685 gph with a load of 25.38 hp. Holt used its own four-cylinder vertical, valve-in-head engine featuring an overhead cam shaft. Rated at 1,000 rpm, it carried a 4-inch bore and a 5-1/2-inch stroke. Also featured was Holt's own built-in governor system. Standard accessories included a Kingston Model L carburetor and an Eisemann Model G4 magneto.

COLLECTOR VALUES	1	2	3	4
2 TON	$10,000	$7,500	$4,000	$2,000

Caterpillar 5-Ton

Weighing 10,400 lbs. the Caterpillar 5-Ton was a carryover from Holt, but remained in the Caterpillar line into 1926. The 5-Ton was a popular intermediate model. It carried a four-cylinder 4-3/4 x 6-inch engine, and like other models, could be equipped with special electric lighting equipment. Production of the 5-Ton ended in 1928.

COLLECTOR VALUES	1	2	3	4
5-TON	$18,000	$14,000	$7,000	$3,000

Caterpillar 10-Ton

The Caterpillar 10-Ton was essentially the same tractor as the Holt 10-Ton built prior to the 1925 Holt-Best merger. Weighing 20,000 lbs.—or 10 tons—this model was furnished with a big 6-1/2 x 7-inch, four-cylinder engine. Ordinarily this model had a top road speed of 3 mph, but with special gearing it could travel up to 4-3/4 mph. The 10-Ton was built until 1928.

COLLECTOR VALUES	1	2	3	4
10-TON	$20,000	$15,000	$8,000	$4,000

Caterpillar Ten

The Caterpillar Ten first appeared in 1928. This model used a four-cylinder L-head engine with the cylinders and crankcase cast en bloc. Rated at 1500 rpm, this engine used a 3-3/8 x 4-inch bore and stroke. Production of the Ten continued until 1933. The Ten was also available in a special high clearance model.

Nebraska Test Data

Model: Caterpillar Ten

Test No. 160

Date Tested: May 6 to May 21, 1929

Weighing only 4,575 lbs., the Caterpillar Ten featured three forward speeds of 2.02, 2.59, and 3.5 mph At its rated 10 drawbar hp, this tractor pulled 1,466 lbs. at a speed of 2.58 mph during the 10-hour rated drawbar test. Results indicate an economy of 5.85 hp-hours per gallon. The low gear maximum load test yielded 14.89 drawbar hp, with the Ten pulling 2,816 lbs. at 1.98 mph and experiencing slippage of only 1.82 percent. At its rated 15 brake hp this tractor came up with 7.93 hp-hours per gallon, while at maximum brake load this figure rose to 8.59. The latter test indicated a maximum of 18.1 brake hp with total fuel consumption of 2.107 gallons per hour. Standard equipment included Caterpillar's own four-cylinder vertical, L-head engine. Rated at 1,500 rpm, it carried a 3-3/8 x 4-inch bore and stroke. Other features included an Eisemann G4 magneto, Ensign carburetor, and Pomona air cleaner. Also featured was an upholstered seat—one of the first crawler tractors to be thus equipped. No repairs or adjustments were required during the 37-hour test run.

COLLECTOR VALUES	1	2	3	4
TEN	$4,000	$3,000	$2,000	$1,000

Caterpillar Fifteen

Caterpillar Fifteen tractors were exactly like the smaller Cat Ten, varying only in physical size. Weighing 5,900 lbs., the Fifteen was capable of 15 drawbar and 20 belt hp. It used a four-cylinder L-head engine with a 3-3/8 x 4-inch bore and stroke. Production of the Fifteen continued into 1933.

Nebraska Test Data

Model: Caterpillar Fifteen

Test No. 207

Date Tested: June 7 to June 29, 1932

Three forward speeds of 2, 2.6, and 3.5 mph were built into the Caterpillar Fifteen tractor. Using second gear, and developing 13.74 drawbar hp, it came out of the rated drawbar test with a fuel economy of 7.08 hp-hours per gallon. In this test the "15" pulled a 2,023 lb. load at 2.55 mph with a slippage of 1.96 percent. The low gear maximum test revealed 16.24 hp, along with a pull of 3,105 lbs. at 1.96 mph. At its rated load of 18.75 brake hp, fuel economy came in at 8.9 hp-hours per gallon, with this figure rising to 9.09 at the maximum load of 20.39 brake hp. The Fifteen used Caterpillar's own four-cylinder L-head engine featuring a 3-3/8 x 4-inch bore and stroke with a rated speed of 1,500 rpm. Included was an Eisemann GV4 magneto and an Ensign carburetor, plus Caterpillar's own air cleaner built under the Vortox patents. During the 45 hours no repairs or adjustments were made to the 4,750 lb. tractor.

COLLECTOR VALUES	1	2	3	4
15, 7C1	$4,000	$3,000	$2,000	$1,000
15HC, 1D1	$4,000	$3,000	$2,000	$1,000
15, PV1	$4,000	$3,000	$2,000	$1,000

Priced at $1,900 the Caterpillar Twenty weighed a hefty 7,500 lbs. Introduced in 1928, the Twenty was built as late as 1933. It was capable of over 27 belt hp and well over 20 horses on the drawbar. This was equivalent to a maximum drawbar pull of over 4,250 lbs. The Twenty used a four-cylinder engine with a 3-3/4 x 5-inch bore and stroke.

Caterpillar Twenty

Nebraska Test Data

Model: Caterpillar Twenty
Test No. 205
Date Tested: May 20 to June 22, 1932

Using gasoline, the Twenty delivered 24.26 brake hp at rated load, squeezing 9.39 hp hours out of each gallon. Economy increased still further to 9.50 when under maximum belt load of 27.43 hp. Its three forward speeds of 2.0, 2.6, and 3.6 mph were all tried out in the maximum drawbar tests, but in low gear a maximum pull of 4,252 lbs. was achieved at a speed of 1.93 mph and slippage of 1.36 percent. This corresponded to 21.88 drawbar hp. Second gear was used for the rated load test. At 2.56 mph the Twenty pulled 2,668 lbs. with a slippage of 1.36 percent for a total of 18.23 drawbar hp. Fuel economy at rated load came in at 7.35 hp-hours per gallon. Weighing 6,325 lbs., the Twenty featured the company's own four-cylinder L-head engine. Rated at 1,250 rpm, it carried a 3-3/4 x 5-inch bore and stroke. Standard equipment included an Eisemann GV4 magneto, Ensign carburetor, and Caterpillar's own air cleaner built under the Vortox patents. During the 41 hours of running time, no repairs or adjustments were required.

COLLECTOR VALUES	1	2	3	4
20, IJ, PL1	$7,000	$5,5000	$2,000	$1,000
10, 8CI	$8,000	$5,000	$3,500	$1,500
22, 2FI, IJI	$5,000	$3,5000	$2,000	$750

Caterpillar Twenty-Five

The Caterpillar Twenty-Five, introduced in 1932, was built only into 1933. It used a 4 x 5-1/2-inch engine of four-cylinder design and rated at 1,100 rpm. Weighing slightly over 8,000 lbs., the "25" was capable of pulling over 6,000 lbs. on the drawbar. Production of the Caterpillar Twenty-Five ended in 1933.

Nebraska Test Data

Model: Caterpillar Twenty-Five
Test No. 203
Date Tested: May 16 to May 23, 1932

Caterpillar's own four-cylinder I-head engine was featured in the Twenty-Five. Rated at 1,100 rpm, it used a 4 x 5-1/2-inch bore and stroke, along with an Eisemann GV4 magneto, and an Ensign carburetor. Three forward speeds of 1.8, 2.6, and 3.6 mph were built into the Twenty-Five. Total weight of this tractor was 8,087 lbs. One hour of this 39-hour test was used in the rated brake hp test. At 29.98 hp, fuel economy was recorded at 9.84 hp-hours per gallon, dropping slightly to 9.65 under maximum brake load of 32.97 hp. The rated drawbar test was made in second gear. With a net output of 22.74 hp, the Twenty-Five pulled 3,366 lbs. at 2.53 mph and yielded an economy of 7.52 hp-hours per gallon. Slippage in this test was 2.25 percent. The low gear maximum drawbar test gave a total of 26.74 hp, along with a pull of 6,011 lbs. at 1.67 mph. No repairs or adjustments were noted.

COLLECTOR VALUES	1	2	3	4
25, 3CI	$8,000	$6,000	$4,000	$2,000

Caterpillar Thirty-Five

Introduced in 1932, the Caterpillar Thirty-Five remained in production until 1933. This model used a four-cylinder engine with a 4-7/8 x 6-1/2- inch bore and stroke. It was rated at 850 rpm. It was capable of nearly 30 drawbar hp and almost 40 hp was delivered at the belt pulley. Caterpillar gave it a 37-41 hp rating.

Nebraska Test Data

Model: Caterpillar Thirty-Five

Test No. 206

Date Tested: June 6 to June 24, 1932

Even though it was not rated by the manufacturer, the Caterpillar had maximum permissible ratings of 29.15 drawbar and 39.58 belt hp under existing tractor rating codes. Using these parameters, the rated brake hp test was made at 39.79 hp. At this load, the Thirty-Five delivered a fuel economy of 9.05 hp-hours per gallon, compared to 8.9 when operating at its maximum of 43.8 hp. Advertised speeds of 1.7, 2.5, 3.2, and 4.6 mph were built into this tractor. The rated drawbar test in second gear indicated 29.37 hp, along with a pull of 4,470 lbs. at 2.46 mph and a fuel economy of 7.75 hp-hours per gallon. In low gear the Thirty-Five developed 35.77 hp, puffing an 8,169 lb. load at 1.64 mph. Using a 4-7/8 x 6-1/2 inch-bore and stroke, the engine was of Caterpillar design, carrying four-cylinders of I-head construction. Rated speed was 850 rpm. Rounding out the power plant was an Eisemann GV4 magneto, and an Ensign carburetor. Total weight was 12,380 lbs.

COLLECTOR VALUES	1	2	3	4
35, 5CI	$8,000	$5,000	$3,000	$2,000

Caterpillar Fifty

The new Caterpillar tractor line of 1932 included the Fifty, a big 17,000 lb. model that retailed for $3,675. The Fifty was equipped with a four- cylinder 5-1/2 x 6-1/2-inch engine rated at 850 rpm.

Nebraska Test Data

Model: Caterpillar Fifty

Test No. 204

Date Tested: May 18 to June 11, 1932

Although not rated by the manufacturer, the Caterpillar Fifty was given a maximum permissible rating of 38.96 drawbar and 51.64 belt hp through the tractor rating codes. Using a 5-1/2x 6-1/2-inch bore and stroke with a rated speed of 850 rpm, the Caterpillar-built engine featured a four-cylinder I-head design. An Ensign KE carburetor and Eisemann GV4 magneto completed this section. At rated belt load of 51.75 hp, the Fifty burned 5.99 gph, yielding 8.64 hp-hours per gallon. Economy dropped slightly to 8.37 under maximum load of 56.14 hp. Advertised speeds of 1.6, 2.4, 3.4, and 4.7 mph were built into the Fifty. Second gear was used for the rated drawbar test, which revealed a fuel economy of 6.86 hp-hours per gallon. During this test 39.23 hp was developed, along with a pull of 6,070 lbs. at 2.42 mph and slippage of 1.34 percent. At a speed of 1.53 mph, the Fifty made its maximum pull of 12,061 lbs. using low gear and developing slightly over 49 drawbar hp. Slippage in this test was only 2.86 percent.

COLLECTOR VALUES	1	2	3	4
50, 5AI	$8,000	$5,000	$3,000	$2,000

Caterpillar Sixty-Five

Production of the Caterpillar Sixty-Five began in 1932. Capable of over 78 belt hp, this big crawler used a four-cylinder engine with a 7 x 8-1/2-inch bore and stroke. Weighing 12-1/2 tons, the Sixty-Five was also capable of delivering a pull of about 6-3/4 tons at the drawbar, or about 68 hp. Production of the Sixty-Five was apparently quite limited, ending by the following year.

Nebraska Test Data

Model: Caterpillar Sixty-Five

Test No. 209

Date Tested: July 5 to July 22, 1932

With a maximum permissible rating of 54 drawbar and 72 belt hp, the Caterpillar Sixty-Five delivered a fuel economy of 8.21 hp-hours per gallon at rated brake hp. A slightly better figure of 8.28 was noted at maximum brake load of 78.41 hp. Caterpillar used its own four-cylinder I-head engine with a 7 x 8-1/2- inch bore and stroke, along with a rated speed of 650 rpm. Like other gasoline models of this series it also carried an Eisemann GV4 magneto and an Ensign K carburetor. Weighing in at 24,965 lbs., the Sixty-Five featured three forward speeds of 1.9, 2.6, and 4.4 mph. Using second gear for the rated drawbar test gave a fuel economy of 6.72 hp-hours per gallon, along with 54.18 hp, a pull of 8,004 lbs. at 2.54 mph, and slippage of 1.85 percent. The low gear maximum test indicated 67.86 hp. In this test the Sixty-Five pulled 13,597 lbs. at 1.87 mph with a recorded slippage of 2.19 percent. No repairs or adjustments were required during the 55 hours of running time.

Caterpillar Diesel

In 1931 Caterpillar became the first company to offer a diesel-powered tractor. Experiments had begun a year earlier and the new design was to become a hallmark of the tractor industry. Caterpillar sent its new "Diesel" to Nebraska's Tractor Test Laboratory in June 1932. Production was limited to a few units for this model, but a number of different Caterpillar diesel tractors were on the horizon.

Nebraska Test Data

Model: Caterpillar "Diesel"
Test No. 208
Date Tested: June 14 to July 20, 1932

Under the S.A.E. and A.S.A.E. tractor rating codes, this tractor had maximum permissible ratings of 54 drawbar and 73.85 belt hp. The diesel engine design added a new dimension to tractor testing. In this case it was Caterpillar's own four-cylinder I-head engine with a 6-1/8 x 9-1/4-inch bore and stroke and a rated speed of 700 rpm. A Robert Bosch fuel system was employed, and three forward speeds were provided of 2.1, 2.8 and 4.7 mph. Total weight was 25,860 lbs. Using second gear, the "Diesel" pulled 7,300 lbs. at 2.76 mph in the rated drawbar test, developing 53.78 hp and experiencing slippage of 1.05 percent. Fuel economy came in at an unheard of 11.66 hp-hours per gallon of fuel oil. The low gear maximum test revealed 65.11 hp with a pull of 11,991 lbs. at 2.04 mph. Rated brake hp tests at 74.73 hp ended with a new economy record of 13.87 hp-hours per gallon. This dropped to 12.9 under a maximum load of 77.08 brake hp. No repairs or adjustments were required during the 54 hours of running time.

Caterpillar Seventy

First built in 1932 the Caterpillar Seventy was a huge 30,000-lb. crawler with a four-cylinder gasoline engine. Rated at 700 rpm, it used a 7 x 8-1/2-inch bore and stroke. It could pull almost 18,000 lbs. on the drawbar and was capable of almost 78 belt hp. The Caterpillar Seventy was built as late as 1936.

Nebraska Test Data

Model: Caterpillar Seventy
Test No. 213
Date Tested: May 15 to June 6, 1933

Weighing 30,800 lbs., the big Caterpillar Seventy featured an impressive four-cylinder engine rated at 700 rpm and carrying a 7 x 8-1/2-inch bore and stroke. Also featured were six forward speeds of 1.7, 2.3, 2.7, 3.1, 3.7, and 5 mph. Accessory items included an Eisemann GV4 magneto and an Ensign carburetor. Near the end of the 51 hour test, an exhaust valve spring failed, but otherwise no repairs or adjustments were required Using gasoline, the Seventy achieved a fuel economy of 6.7 hp-hours per gallon at rated drawbar load of 58.46 hp, pulling a 9,632 lb. load at 2.28 mph. Slippage in this test was only 0.75 percent. The low gear maximum test recorded a pull of 16,796 lbs. at 1.62 mph. With a slippage of 2.17 percent, this translated into 72.73 hp. At its rated 77.58 brake hp the Seventy delivered a fuel economy of 8.13 hp-hours per gallon, with a slightly higher figure of 8.50 being recorded at its maximum load of 82.4 brake hp. In the latter test, fuel consumption totaled 9.698 gallons per hour.

Caterpillar Seventy Diesel

Apparently built only in 1932 and 1933, the Seventy Diesel was priced at $6,250. Weighing 31,000 lbs., this huge tractor used essentially the same engine as the original "Diesel" although the exterior appearance shows obvious changes. Six forward speeds were available, ranging up to 5 mph.

Caterpillar Seventy-Five Diesel

Topping the Caterpillar tractor line for 1933 was the Seventy-Five Diesel crawler. This model weighed more than 16 tons and could pull nearly 9-1/2 tons on the drawbar, equivalent to about 80 hp. Production of this model continued through 1935.

Nebraska Test Data

Model: Caterpillar Seventy-Five Diesel
Test No. 218
Date Tested: October 10 to October 31, 1933

Weighing in at 32,050 lbs., the Caterpillar Sevventy-Five Diesel featured six forward speeds of 1.7, 2.3, 2.7, 3.1, 3.7, and 5 mph. Rated drawbar tests at 63.62 hp were made in second gear. Once again a new fuel economy record was set and this time at 12.31 hp-hours per gallon of fuel oil. Other data from this test included a 10,455 lb. pull at 2.28 mph. In low gear the Seventy-Five Diesel managed a pull of 18,697 lbs. at 1.61 mph for a maximum of 80.51 drawbar hp. At its rated belt load of 83.34 hp the Seventy-Five Diesel also set a new economy record of 14.62 hp-hours per gallon but this figure dropped slightly to 14.26 while developing its maximum of 92.85 brake hp. Caterpillar equipped this tractor with its own six-cylinder I-head diesel engine. Rated at 820 rpm, it carried a 5-1/4 x 8-inch bore and stroke. Caterpillar equipped this engine with its own fuel system, clutch, and governor, but used a Vortox air cleaner. No repairs or adjustments were required during the 57-1/2 hours of running time.

Caterpillar Twenty-Two

Production of the Caterpillar Twenty-Two began in 1934, ending in 1939. It used essentially the same four-cylinder, 4 x 5-inch engine as the Caterpillar R-2 model. Weighing 6,200 lbs., the Twenty-Two was priced at $1,450. It had a standard track gauge of 40 inches, but a special 50- inch wide-gauge style was also available.

Nebraska Test Data

Model: Caterpillar Twenty-Two (distillate)
Test No. 226
Date Tested: September 25 to October 9, 1934

Using basically the same engine but a slightly different chassis, the Twenty-Two was quite similar to the Caterpillar R-2. Included was the same four-cylinder 4 x 5-inch engine, but instead of using gasoline, the Twenty-Two tested here burned distillate. Advertised speeds remained the same, as did accessory items. The Twenty-Two however, carried a 10-inch wide track, compared to 13 inches on the R-2 tractor. Using second gear for the rated drawbar test, fuel economy for the Twenty-Two was recorded at 8.1 hp-hours per gallon, and this while pulling a 2,806 lb. load at 2.55 mph. Slippage was 1.75 percent, with an output of 19.08 hp. A maximum pull of 4,534 lbs. was made in low gear, together with an output of 23.43 hp and a ground speed of 1.94 mph with 2.84 percent slippage. No repairs or adjustments were required during the 48 hours of operating time.

Nebraska Test Data

Model: Caterpillar Twenty-Two (gasoline)
Test No. 226
Date Tested: October 17 to October 30, 1934

Under the same serial number of 2F-1117, the Caterpillar Twenty-Two was once again tested—just as it had been in No. 226—but this time was powered by gasoline. Both tests gave the Twenty-Two a maximum permissible rating of 19.34 drawbar and 27.17 belt hp, even though they were not hp-rated by the manufacturer. At rated load of 27.27 brake hp, fuel economy in this test totaled 9.11 hp-hours per gallon, rising slightly to 9.18 at a maximum load of 30.71 hp. Fuel economy at rated drawbar load in second gear came in at 6.83 hp-hours per gallon, with the Twenty-Two pulling a 2,870 lb. load at 2.55 mph. A maximum pull of 4,900 lbs. was achieved in low gear. Developing 25.26 hp, the Twenty-Two traveled at 1.93 mph and experienced slippage of 3.29 percent. Total operating time was 30 hours, with no repairs or adjustments being noted.

COLLECTOR VALUES	1	2	3	4
22, 2FI, IJI	$5,000	$3,500	$2,000	$1,000

Caterpillar Twenty-Eight

A tread width of 42 inches was standard for the Caterpillar Twenty-Eight, introduced in 1933 and continued into the following year. Also available was a special model with a 55-inch track width. The Twenty-Eight was furnished with a four-cylinder engine with a 4-3/16 x 5-1/2-inch bore and stroke. It weighed nearly 7,900 lbs. and listed at $1,900.

COLLECTOR VALUES	1	2	3	4
28, 4FI	$7,000	$5,000	$3,000	$1,500

Caterpillar Thirty-Five

Caterpillar introduced the Thirty-Five in 1932 and production continued until 1935. The Thirty-Five used a four-cylinder engine with a 4-7/8 x 6-1/2-inch bore and stroke. It weighed 12,500 lbs. and sold for $2,400.

Nebraska Test Data

Model: Caterpillar Thirty-Five
Test No. 206
Date Tested: June 6 to June 24, 1932

Even though it was not rated by the manufacturer, the Caterpillar Thirty-Five had maximum permissible ratings of 29.15 drawbar and 39.58 belt hp under existing tractor rating codes. Using these parameters, the rated brake hp test was made at 39.79 hp. At this load, the Thirty-Five delivered a fuel economy of 9.05 hp-hours per gallon, compared to 8.9 when operating at its maximum of 43.8 hp. Advertised speeds of 1.7, 2.5, 3.2, and 4.6 mph were built into this tractor. The rated drawbar test in second gear indicated 29.37 hp, along with a pull of 4,470 lbs. at 2.46 mph and a fuel economy of 7.75 hp-hours per gallon. In low gear the Thirty-Five developed 35.77 hp, puffing an 8,169 lb. load at 1.64 mph. Using a 4-7/8 x 6-1/2-inch bore and stroke, the engine was of Caterpillar design, carrying four-cylinders of I-head construction. Rated speed was 850 rpm. Rounding out the power plant was an Eisemann GV4 magneto, and an Ensign carburetor. Total weight was 12,380 lbs.

Caterpillar Thirty-Five Diesel

The Caterpillar Thirty-Five Diesel came out in 1933. This tractor used a three-cylinder diesel engine with a 5-1/4 x 8-inch bore and stroke. Rated at 850 rpm, it was capable of about 45 belt hp and could exert a maximum drawbar pull of 9,100 lbs. Production of the Thirty-Five Diesel apparently ended in 1935.

Nebraska Test Data

Model: Caterpillar Thirty-Five Diesel
Test No. 217
Date Tested: October 10 to October 25, 1933

Continuing its line of diesel-powered tractors, the Diesel Thirty-Five featured a three-cylinder I-head engine with a 5-1/4 x 8-inch bore and stroke, along with a rated speed of 850 rpm. Like the Diesel Fifty, this tractor used Caterpillar's own fuel system, and also featured four forward speeds of 1.7, 2.5, 3.2, and 4.6 mph. Weighing in at 14,720 lbs., it mustered a maximum pull of 9,135 lbs. in low gear, traveling at 1.62 mph and with a slippage of 4.07 percent. Second gear was used for the rated drawbar test, and at 30.58 hp this tractor delivered a fuel efficiency of 10.91 hp-hours per gallon while pulling a 4,672 lb. load at 2.45 mph. Rated brake hp tests at 39.43 hp manifested a fuel economy of 13.49 hp-hours per gallon of fuel oil, with a slightly higher figure of 13.75 at maximum load of 44.72 hp. The latter test saw the highest coolant temperature of any test procedure at 164 degrees F. During the 42 hours of running time, no repairs or adjustments were required.

Caterpillar Fifty Diesel

Production of the Fifty Diesel began in 1933 and ended in 1936. This model used the same 5-1/4 x 8-inch bore and stroke as the Thirty-Five Diesel, but while the latter had but three cylinders, the Fifty Diesel carried four. Initially it was rated at 850 rpm, but by raising the speed to 1,000 rpm, the power level increased substantially.

Nebraska Test Data

Model: Caterpillar Fifty Diesel
Test No. 240
Date Tested: August 19 to August 29, 1935

Advertised speeds of 1.6, 2.4, 3.4, and 4.7 mph were built into this tractor. Weighing in at 20,790 lbs., it went through the 10-hour rated drawbar test using second gear, and delivering 42.32 hp. Fuel economy came in at 12.07 hp-hours per gallon, plus a drawbar pull of 6,591 lbs. at 2.41 mph. Slightly over 13,000 lbs. of drawbar pull was demonstrated in the low gear maximum load test. At a speed of 1.45 mph and slippage of 7.68 percent, 50.57 hp was developed. At rated brake load of 54.3 hp fuel economy was charted at 14.24 hp-hours per gallon, with an even better figure of 14.75 being recorded on the two-hour, 100 percent maximum load test. Caterpillar used its own four-cylinder I-head diesel engine in the Fifty. Rated at 850 rpm, it featured a 5 3/4 x 8-inch bore and stroke. Featured too was Caterpillar's own fuel system. No repairs or adjustments were noted during the 48 hours of running time.

Nebraska Test Data

Model: Caterpillar Fifty Diesel (high-speed engine)

Test No. 241

Date Tested: August 29 to September 16, 1935

Using the same tractor as with the previous test, Caterpillar increased the engine speed to 1,000 rpm. A review of both tests indicated a substantial increase in power at the expense of fuel economy. At its rated 48.71 drawbar hp, this tractor achieved 11.29 hp-hours per gallon, pulling a 6,401 lb. load at 2.85 mph. Rated brake tests at 65.01 hp showed an economy figure of 13.93, with a rise to 14.07 hp-hours per gallon at 100-percent maximum load of 71.81 hp. The substantial increase in available hp tended to offset the loss in economy. Running at its rated 65 belt hp, the Caterpillar Fifty of this test consumed 4.668 gph. Coolant temperatures never went above 171 degrees F., and this only on the two-hour, 100-percent maximum load test. Except for the speed change from 850 to 1,000 rpm, all specifications remained the same as in Test No. 240. No repairs or adjustments were noted.

COLLECTOR VALUES	1	2	3	4
50 DSL, 1E1	$10,000	$8,000	$4,500	$2,500

Caterpillar Forty

Equipped with its standard 56-inch track width, the Caterpillar Forty sold for $2,575. This figure rose to $2,775 when the tractor was built with the wide-gauge 74-inch track. The Forty was a gasoline model with a four-cylinder, 5-1/8 x 6-1/2-inch engine. Production began in 1934 and ended in 1936.

Nebraska Test Data

Model: Caterpillar Forty

Test No. 244

Date Tested: September 16 to September 20, 1935

At its rated load of 43.95 brake hp the Caterpillar Forty obtained a fuel economy of 9.24 hp-hours per gallon. At 100 percent maximum load conducted over two hours, fuel economy was recorded at 8.17, along with an output of 48.57 hp. Fuel consumption in the latter test totaled 5.943 gph. Rated drawbar tests in second gear indicated 33.25 hp, along with a 5,151 lb. load at 2.42 mph and fuel efficiency of 7.32 hp-hours per gallon. Maximum drawbar pull came in low gear with 9,496 lbs. at 1.6 mph. Caterpillar equipped this tractor with its own four-cylinder vertical engine. Rated at 850 rpm, it carried a 5-1/8 x 6-1/2-inch bore and stroke. An Eisemann CT-4 magneto and an Ensign K-3 carburetor complemented the basic equipment. Operating weight was 13,625 lbs. No repairs or adjustments were noted during the 48 hours of running time.

Nebraska Test Data

Model: Caterpillar Forty (Zenith carburetor)

Test No. 244

Date Tested: September 18 to September 23, 1935

Operating at 1,000 rpm, this was the same model as noted in Test No. 244, although a different tractor was used. Engine specifications remained the same for both tractors except for a Zenith carburetor replacing the Ensign design. Gasoline was used for both tests, and in this case the rated brake test at 50.6 hp indicated a fuel economy of 9.71 hp-hours per gallon, with a substantially lower figure of 8.14 appearing at 100 percent maximum load of 56.42 hp. Rated drawbar tests were made in second gear. With an output of 38.56 hp, this tractor pulled 5,053 lbs. at 2.86 mph, delivering an economy of 7.5 hp-hours per gallon. At 100 percent maximum load (Test F) and using second gear the Caterpillar Forty delivered 48.91 hp at the drawbar. During 40 hours of operation, no repairs or adjustments were noted.

COLLECTOR VALUES	1	2	3	4
40 5G1	$10,000	$8,000	$4,500	$2,500

Caterpillar Forty Diesel

The Caterpillar Forty Diesel was built from 1934 through 1936. This model weighed in at an impressive 14,700 lbs. and was priced at $3,325. The engine was a three-cylinder design with a 5-1/4 x 8-inch bore and stroke. The Forty Diesel was also built with a four-cylinder engine with a 5-1/8 x 6-1/2-inch bore and stroke.

Nebraska Test Data

Model: Caterpillar Forty Diesel (high-speed engine)
Test No. 242
Date Tested: August 19 to September 9, 1935

This tractor's engine was rated at 1,000 rpm. All other engine and tractor specifications remained the same for this and the following test. Rated at 52 drawbar hp in second gear by Caterpillar, the Diesel Forty yielded 39.83 horses on the 10-hour rated load test. Pulling 5,173 lbs. at 2.89 mph this tractor came in with a fuel economy of 11.77 hp-hours per gallon. Slightly over 50 drawbar hp was noted in the low gear maximum load test—this plus a pull of 9,750 lbs. at 1.93 mph. Nebraska's Test D for rated brake hp indicated 13.55 hp-hours per gallon at a 50.43 hp load. At 56.05 maximum load, economy went still higher to 13.71 hp-hours per gallon. Weighing in at 15,642 lbs. the Diesel Forty went through 51 hours of testing with no repairs or adjustments.

Nebraska Test Data

Model: Caterpillar Forty Diesel
Test No. 243
Date Tested: September 10 to September 12, 1935

Rated by Caterpillar at 44 drawbar hp, this tractor was tested at the original design speed of 850 rpm. As with similar tests previously noted, the diminished hp output yielded an increase in fuel economy. Under Test D for rated brake load, fuel economy was recorded at 14.18 hp-hours per gallon with an output of 44.14 hp. At 100 percent maximum load of 48.6 hp this figure improved to 14.37. Test H for rated drawbar hp was made in second gear, and with an output of 33.15 hp, along with a pull of 5,071 lbs. at 2.46 mph the Diesel Forty produced an economy of 11.51 hp-hours per gallon. A maximum of 42.82 drawbar hp, along with a maximum pull of 9,692 lbs. occurred in low gear. Caterpillar built the Diesel Forty with four speeds of 1.7, 2.5, 3.2, and 4.6 mph. Rated at 850 rpm, it carried a three-cylinder 5-3/4 x 8-inch engine of I-head design. A Caterpillar fuel system was also featured. Total weight was 15,642 lbs.

COLLECTOR VALUES	1	2	3	4
40 DSL, 3G1	$8,000	$6,000	$3,500	$1,500

Caterpillar Thirty

Built only in 1937, the Caterpillar Thirty was in no way related to the earlier Thirty that had been brought in from Best at the time of the 1925 Holt-Best merger. This model weighed about 4-1/2 tons when built with the standard track gauge of 44 inches. Thus built, it was priced at $2,100. The Thirty was designed around a four-cylinder engine with a 4-1/4 x 5-1/2-inch bore and stroke.

Nebraska Test Data

Model: Caterpillar Thirty (distillate)
Test No. 271
Date Tested: October 13 to October 24, 1936

Five forward speeds of 1.7, 2.4, 3, 3.7, and 5.4 mph were featured in the Caterpillar Thirty. Test G for operating maximum load was made in all five forward speeds, but in low gear the maximum pull of 6,120 lbs. appeared. At a speed of 1.64 mph and with slippage of 3.94 percent, the Thirty produced 26.71 drawbar hp. Test H for rated drawbar load saw a pull of 3,968 lbs. at 2.31 mph and an output of 24.46 hp. Fuel economy on the rated drawbar test came in at 7.78 hp-hours per gallon. Second gear was used for Test H. Test D for rated brake load evidenced a fuel economy of 9.01 hp-hours per gallon with an output of 32.64 brake hp. Economy rose to 9.33 at the Test C operating maximum load of 34.13 hp. The four-cylinder

Caterpillar R-2 crawler

I-head, Caterpillar-built engine burned distillate fuel during this test. Rated at 1,400 rpm it featured a 4-1/4 x 5-1/2-inch bore and stroke. Accessories included an Eisemann CM-4 magneto, Zenith K5A carburetor and a Donaldson air cleaner. Operating weight was 9,975 lbs. Only minor adjustments were necessary during 72 hours of motor operating time.

Nebraska Test Data

Model: Caterpillar Thirty (gasoline)
Test No. 272
Date Tested: October 13 to October 23, 1936

This Caterpillar Thirty burned gasoline, but engine specifications remained the same, as did accessory items and chassis specifications. During 47 hours of running time it was necessary to free up a sticky governor mechanism, otherwise no repairs or adjustments were necessary. Test C for operating maximum brake load ended with a recorded 37.81 hp, along with an economy of 8.82 hp-hours per gallon. Economy dropped slightly to 8.59 in rated brake load Test D with an output of 34.9 hp. Test H for rated drawbar load was run for 10 hours in second gear. At 26.59 hp, fuel economy was recorded at 7.16 hp-hours per gallon, along with a pull of 4,346 lbs. at 2.29 mph and slippage of 2.52 percent. Test G maximum operating load results in low gear indicated a pull of 7,211 lbs. at 1.61 mph and slippage of 5.39 percent with an output of 30.99 drawbar hp.

COLLECTOR VALUES	1	2	3	4
30, S1001, PS1	$6,000	$4,000	$2,000	$1,000

Production of the R-2 crawler began in 1934 and continued into 1938, when it was replaced with a new R-2 tractor. This model used a four-cylinder engine with a 4 x 5-inch bore and stroke and operating at 1,250 rpm. The R-2 was capable of more than 32 belt hp.

Nebraska Test Data

Model: Caterpillar R-2
Test No. 225
Date Tested: September 24 to October 16, 1934

Weighing 7,420 lbs., the R-2 carried three advertised speeds of 2, 2.6, and 3.6 mph. Ten hours of the total 52 hours of running time was used in the rated drawbar test. Burning gasoline, an economy of 7.03 hp-hours per gallon was achieved while pulling a 3,216 lb. load at 2.55 mph and developing 21.87 hp. Maximum drawbar pull in low gear came to 5,274 lbs. at 1.93 mph for 27.15 hp. At maximum brake load the R-2 developed 32.47 hp with an efficiency of 8.78 hp-hours per gallon, and a slightly higher 8.93 economy at rated load of 29.2 hp. Caterpillar supplied its own engine—in this case a four-cylinder I-head, 4 x 5 model rated at 1,250 rpm. Accessory items were an Eisemann GT4 magneto and a Zenith K5A carburetor. Due to excessive friction in the tracks they were replaced with new ones before the official drawbar tests were run. Otherwise, no repairs or adjustments were required.

COLLECTOR VALUES	1	2	3	4
R-2, IJ SERIES	$7,500	$4,500	$2,500	$1,000

During 1938 Caterpillar revamped the R-2 crawler, giving it an engine with smaller displacement than the original model, but raising the speed to 1,525 rpm from the original 1,250 rpm. With this change, the engine carried a 3-3/4 x 5-inch bore and stroke. Production of this model continued into 1942.

Caterpillar R-2 (1938)

Nebraska Test Data

Model: Caterpillar R-2 (gasoline)
Test No. 320
Date Tested: July 17 to August 3, 1939

Some 50 hours of engine operating time were required for completion of all testing on the Caterpillar R-2. During that time, no repairs or adjustments were recorded. The R-2 was equipped with five forward speeds of 1.7, 2.5, 3, 3.6, and 5.1 mph. Using second gear, this tractor pulled 2,922 lbs. at 2.42 in Test H. Slippage amounted to only 2.76 percent in this test, and 18.86 rated drawbar hp was the final result. The maximum drawbar pull in first gear was noted in Test G where a 5,676 lb. load was drawn at 1.58 mph for a total 23.84 hp. Caterpillar equipped this tractor with a four-cylinder I-head engine with a 3-3/4 x 5- inch bore and stroke with a rated speed of 1,525 rpm. During this entire test, gasoline was used. Test C for operating maximum load indicated a fuel economy of 8.62 hp-hours per gallon under a load of 28.95 hp. By comparison, Test D for rated load delivered 8.33 hp-hours per gallon with a 26.49 hp load. Accessory items on the R-2 included an Eisemann CM-4 magneto, Zenith K-5A carburetor and Donaldson air cleaner. Operating weight was 6,835 lbs.

Nebraska Test Data

Model: Caterpillar R-2 (distillate)
Test No. 321
Date Tested: July 24 to August 3, 1939

Caterpillar resubmitted the R-2 for testing using distillate instead of gasoline. Specifications remained the same. The R-2 was equipped with a 12-inch diameter belt pulley with a 7-1/2-inch face. Operating at 850 rpm gave a belt speed of 2,670 feet per minute. Unfortunately, early tractors were not all uniform in belt speed at rated load, necessitating a change either in the drive pulley or the driven pulley for a proper match. PTO drives of recent years have undergone far more standardization. In Test H for rated drawbar hp, economy was recorded at 6.77 hp-hours per gallon. This test also showed a pull of 2,898 lbs. at 2.45 mph for an output of 18.95 drawbar hp at rated load. Test G for operating maximum load revealed a maximum pull of 5,379 lbs. at 1.57 mph using first gear, for an output of 22.49 drawbar hp. Test C for operating maximum belt hp showed an economy of 8.99 hp-hours per gallon with a load of 27.78 hp compared to 26.28 hp at rated load (Test D) and an economy of 8.76 hp-hours per gallon.

Caterpillar R-3

Production of the R-3 Caterpillar tractor began in 1934. Rated at 37 belt hp, this tractor was equipped with a four-cylinder engine with a 4-1/2 x 5-1/2-inch bore and stroke. Production of this model was very limited, although there are indications that it was available as late as 1936.

Nebraska Test Data

Model: Caterpillar R-3

Test No. 227

Date Tested: September 26 to October 15, 1934

At its rated load of 37.51 brake hp the R-3 burned 4.147 gph with an economy yield of 9.05 hp-hours per gallon. Economy dropped slightly to 8.51 at full load of 41.99 brake hp. Caterpillar built this tractor with a four-cylinder I-head engine rated at 1,100 rpm and with a 4-1/2 x 5-1/2-inch bore and stroke. Integral equipment included an Eisemann GT4 magneto and an Ensign carburetor. Advertised speeds of 1.8, 2.6, and 3.6 mph were also built into the R-3. Second gear was used for the rated drawbar test, with fuel economy coming in at 6.89 hp-hours per gallon. Statistics also indicated a pull of 4,180 lbs. at 2.49 mph. With a maximum pull of 7,622 lbs., the R-3 pulled slightly over 76 percent of its own weight. This pull, made in low gear, also revealed 33.88 drawbar hp with a ground speed of 1.67 mph and slippage of 7.41 percent. No repairs or adjustments were noted during the 46 hours of running time.

COLLECTOR VALUES	1	2	3	4
R-3, 5E2501	$10,000	$8,000	$3,500	$2,000

Caterpillar R-4

Built from 1935 to 1944, the Caterpillar R-4 was available in a standard track gauge of 44 inches, or a wide-gauge model of 60 inches. This model was also available as a special orchard tractor. A rear PTO shaft was available, as was a belt pulley. The R-4 tractor was capable of 35 drawbar and 40 PTO hp.

COLLECTOR VALUES	1	2	3	4
R-4, 6G1	$7,000	$4,500	$2,500	$1,000

Caterpillar R-5

Production of the R-5 tractor began in 1934 and continued into 1941. After this time the company built diesel-powered tractors exclusively. The R5 weighed nearly seven tons and was capable of over 54 drawbar hp. It could also deliver over 64 hp on the belt or the PTO shaft.

Nebraska Test Data

Model: Caterpillar R-5

Test No. 224

Date Tested: July 12 to July 20, 1934

Designed for gasoline, the R-5 was equipped with Caterpillar's own four-cylinder I-head engine. Rated at 950 rpm, it featured a 5-1/2 x 6-1/2-inch bore and stroke. Regular equipment included an Eisemann GT4 magneto and an Ensign carburetor, along with advertised speeds of 1.9, 2.8, 3.6, and 5.1 mph. Operating at maximum brake load it developed 58.89 hp, consuming 6.112 gph with a yield of 9.64 hp-hours per gallon. A virtually identical figure emerged from the rated brake test at 54.83 hp. Although maximum drawbar load tests were conducted in each forward gear, second gear was used for the rated load test at 41.29 hp. At a speed of 2.74 mph, a pull of 5,649 lbs., and slippage of 1.3 percent, the R-5 yielded a fuel economy of 7.49 hp-hours per gallon. Maximum pull occurred in low gear with this figure totaling 10,384 lbs. at a speed of 1.77 mph and slippage of 5.96 percent for a total of 48.93 hp. Total weight of the R-5 was 13,675 lbs. No repairs were necessary during the 41 hours of running time.

COLLECTOR VALUES	1	2	3	4
R-5, 3R SERIES	$7,500	$5,500	$3,000	$1,500

Caterpillar RD-4

Production of the new RD-4 tractor began in 1936. The "R" was eventually dropped from the model designation. The Caterpillar four-cylinder diesel engine was rated at 1,400 rpm and carried a 4-1/4 x 5-1/2-inch bore and stroke.

Nebraska Test Data

Model: Caterpillar RD-4

Test No. 273

Date Tested: October 14 to October 28, 1936

Later known simply as the D-4, this diesel-powered tractor had a manufacturer's rating of 35 drawbar hp in second gear under standard conditions. Test H for rated drawbar load was run in second gear. At 26.8 hp, it pulled 4,374 lbs. at 2.3 mph with slippage of 2.63 percent. Fuel economy was calculated at 11.75 hp-hours per gallon. A maximum pull of 7,852 lbs. occurred in low gear. At a speed of 1.6 mph the RD-4 developed 33.43 drawbar hp, experiencing a slippage of 6.17 percent. Rated brake hp testing indicated an economy of 13.83 hp-hours per gallon while producing 35.61 hp. Economy dropped insignificantly to 13.80 at 100 percent maximum load of 39.82 hp. No repairs or adjustments were required during 57 hours of running time. Operating weight was 10,100 lbs. Featured was Caterpillar's own four-cylinder diesel engine of I-head design. Rated at 1,400 rpm it carried a 4-1/4 x 5-1/2-inch bore and stroke, and of course used the Caterpillar fuel system.

Caterpillar D-4

Caterpillar D-4 tractors were modified at various times during a long production run ending in 1959. About 1947 the engine was modified to include a 4-1/2 x 5-1/2-inch bore and stroke. This increased the power level substantially. About 1954 the D-4 was again modified, including an increase in the rated speed of 200 rpm. By this time the D-4 was capable of more than 58 belt hp. Eventually, the D-4 had run its course and was replaced with an entirely new model.

Nebraska Test Data

Model: Caterpillar D-4

Test No. 417

Date Tested: July 11 to July 26, 1949

Weighing 11,175 lbs., the Caterpillar D-4 tractor featured forward speeds of 1.7, 2.4, 3, 3.7, and 5.4 mph. Second gear was used for Test H-at a rated load of 33.01 drawbar hp the D-4 pulled a 5,392 lb. load of 2.3 mph with a slippage of 2.6 percent. Fuel economy was scored at 11.37 hp-hours per gallon. A low-gear maximum pull of 9,555 lbs. was noted in Test G, and this while moving at a speed of 1.55 mph with a slippage of 9.17 percent. No repairs or adjustments were noted during 37 hours of engine running time. Like the Caterpillar models noted in Tests 415 and 416, the D-4 used a diesel engine of I-head design, but with four cylinders of 4-1/2 x 5-1/2-inch bore and stroke and a rated speed of 1,400 rpm. Belt testing revealed a fuel economy of 14.49 hp-hours per gallon under the Test D rated load of 46.48 belt hp. Test C and Test B at 100 percent maximum load saw fuel economy sag slightly to 14 hp-hours per gallon.

Nebraska Test Data

Model: Caterpillar D-4
Test No. 554
Date Tested: July 25 to August 10, 1955

Using a four-cylinder, 4-1/2 x 5-1/2-inch bore and stroke engine, the D-4 had displaced 350 cubic inches. Rated at 1,600 rpm, it achieved a maximum torque of 421.4 lbs.-ft. with an engine speed of 1,000 rpm. Also featured was a two-cylinder horizontal opposed starting engine rated at 3,000 rpm and using a 2 3/4 x 3-inch bore and stroke. Total weight was 12,531 lbs. At a Test D rated belt load of 53.2 hp the D-4 scored a fuel economy of 13.94 hp-hours per gallon, with this figure sliding to 13.31 at a Test B, 100 percent maximum load of 58.88 hp. Standard equipment included forward speeds of 1.9, 2.7, 3.4, 4.2, and 6.1 mph. Second gear was selected for the 10-hour run of Test H. At a rated drawbar load of 39.35 hp, the D-4 pulled 5,585 lbs. at 2.64 mph with a slippage of 2.31 percent. Fuel economy was pegged at 11.51 hp-hours per gallon. A low-gear maximum pull of 9.976 lbs. at 1.81 mph and slippage of 7.19 percent was recorded in Test G. Following Test A, track roller guards were installed and the 13-inch track shoes were replaced with 20-inch track shoes. Otherwise, no repairs or adjustments were noted during 50 hours of running time.

Nebraska Test Data

Model: Caterpillar D-4
Test No. 746
Date Tested: June 14 to June 29, 1960

Weighing in at 14,825 lbs., the D-4 entered the two-hour economy run at 49.31 maximum available drawbar hp, using second gear. This test indicated a pull of 8,072 lbs. at 2.29 mph with 2.46 percent slippage. Fuel economy was recorded at 11.82 hp-hours per gallon of diesel fuel. A 10-hour run, also made in second gear, but at 75 percent pull, indicated an output of 39.78 drawbar hp, a pull of 6,129 lbs. at 2.43 mph and slippage of 1.4 percent. This test evoked a drawbar fuel economy of 11.52 hp-hours per gallon. Also, the D-4 made a low gear maximum pull of 11,694 lbs. at 1.56 mph with 4.76 percent slippage. Caterpillar equipped this tractor with its own four-cylinder engine with a 4-1/2 x 5-1/2-inch bore and stroke and a rated speed of 1,600 rpm. This 350-cid engine carried an 18:1 compression ratio. Also featured was a two-cylinder vertical starting engine rated at 15 hp. Five forward speeds ranging from 1.6 to 5.5 mph also were featured. Using the belt pulley attachment, the D-4 delivered a maximum of 56.54 hp at rated engine speed, evoking 13.12 hp-hours per gallon. No repairs or adjustments were noted during 41-1/2 hours of running time.

Caterpillar D-2

The D-2 tractor first appeared in 1938 and was built in various styles until 1957. One early style was furnished with special equipment for orchard work. The D-2 used a four-cylinder engine rated at 1,525 rpm and carrying a 3-3/4 x 5-inch bore and stroke. It was capable of about 30 belt hp.

Nebraska Test Data

Model: Caterpillar D-2
Test No. 322
Date Tested: July 24 to August 4, 1939

Caterpillar featured its own four-cylinder I-head engine on this tractor, along its its own fuel injection system. Rated at 1,525 rpm, the D-2 carried a 3-3/4 x 5-inch bore and stroke. Five forward speeds of 1.7, 2.5, 3, 3.6, and 5.1 mph were built into this 7,420 lb. tractor. No repairs or adjustments were noted during some 41 hours of engine operating time. At 100 percent maximum load over two hours, the D-2 delivered 29.98 belt hp, burning 2.264 gallons of diesel fuel per hour and yielding an economy of 13.24 hp-hours per gallon. At its rated 27.46 hp the D-2 had a slightly better economy figure of 13.32 as noted in Test D. Drawbar tests as noted in Test G show a maximum pull of 5,903 lbs. at 1.6 mph using low gear. Also noted is a slippage of 5.71 percent under this load, with an output of 25.15 drawbar hp. Test H for rated drawbar load manifested a fuel economy of 10.35 hp-hours per gallon, plus a pull of 2,993 lbs. at 2.44 mph with an output of 19.45 drawbar hp over the 10-hour test run.

Nebraska Test Data

Model: Caterpillar D-2
Test No. 418
Date Tested: July 11 to July 26, 1949

The D-2 featured a four cylinder 4 x 5 diesel engine. Of I-head design, it was rated at 1,525 rpm. Weighing in at 7,255 lbs., the D-2 managed a low-gear maximum pull of 6,778 lbs., doing so at a speed of 1.49 mph and with a slippage of 11.39 percent. Advertised speeds of 1.7, 2.5, 3, 3.6, and 5.1 mph were provided, with second gear being used for Test H. In this 10-hour run the D-2 produced 24.13 rated drawbar hp, along with a pull of 3,778 lbs. at 2.4 mph and experiencing a slippage of 3.52 percent. Fuel economy came in at 10.78 hp-hours per gallon of diesel fuel. Under a Test B & C 100 percent maximum load of 36.02 belt hp, fuel economy rested at 13.66 hp-hours per gallon, compared to 13.63 at the Test D rated load of 32.85 belt hp. No repairs or adjustments were noted during 34 hours of engine operation.

Caterpillar D-2 (upgraded)

In 1947 the D-2 was upgraded to a 4 x 5 engine and this increased the power level substantially; the D-2 was now capable of about 47 belt hp. Various other changes were made to the D-2 during its long production run that finally ended in 1957. This tractor weighed about 7,200 lbs.

Nebraska Test Data

Model: Caterpillar D-2
Test No. 553
Date Tested: July 25 to July 30, 1955

At a Test D rated belt load of 38.68 hp, the D-2 yielded a fuel economy of 12.93 hp-hours per gallon of diesel fuel. Fuel economy slipped to 12.3 hp-hours per gallon at a Test B, 100 percent maximum load of 41.86 belt hp. Rated at 1,650 rpm, this tractor achieved a maximum engine torque of 307.8 lbs.-ft. with an engine speed of 1,052 rpm. Weighing in at 8,536 lbs., the D-2 featured a four-cylinder diesel engine carrying a 4 x 5-inch bore and stroke for a displacement of 252 cubic inches. This engine used an 18.5:1 compression ratio. Also included was a Caterpillar-built two-cylinder starting engine with a 2-3/4 x 3- inch bore and stroke. Following Test A, track roller guards were installed. With this exception, no other repairs or adjustments were noted during 42 hours of operation. Advertised speeds of 1.8, 2.7, 3.2, 3.9 and 5.5 mph were provided, with second gear used for the rated drawbar run of Test H. Under a rated output of 29.03 hp, the D-2 pulled 4,147 lbs. at 2.63 mph with a slippage of 2.69 percent, yielding 10.68 hp-hours per gallon. Test G indicated a low-gear maximum pull of 7,413 lbs. at 1.75 mph.

Caterpillar RD-6

Production of the RD-6, later known as the D-6, began in 1935. Initially, the D-6 used a three-cylinder engine with a 5-3/4 x 8-inch bore and stroke. Weighing about 7-1/2 tons, the D-6 had a list price of about $3,600. The RD-6 was earlier built as the Diesel Forty. Production of this style ended in 1941.

Nebraska Test Data

Model: Caterpillar D-6 Diesel
Test No. 374
Date Tested: September 6 to September 13, 1941

Test G of the D-6 indicated a low-gear maximum pull of 16,674 lbs. at 1.36 mph, thus the large parade of load tractors followed. As tested, this tractor weighed in at 17,750 lbs., and featured five forward speeds of 1.4, 2.3, 3.2 4.4, and 5.8 mph. Caterpillar used its own six-cylinder I-head diesel engine with a 4- ¼ x 5-1/2 inch bore and stroke. It was rated at 1,400 rpm. No repairs or adjustments were noted during 64 hours of engine operating time. Test H was run in second gear. With a rated output of 50 drawbar hp, the D -6 pulled 8,510 lbs. at 2.2 mph with slippage of 2.91 percent and a fuel economy of 12.54 hp-hours per gallon. Test C and Test B were run together at a 100-percent maximum load of 78.03 belt hp and yielded 13.72 hp-hours per gallon. Test D at a rated load of 68.66 belt hp produced 14.57 hp-hours per gallon.

Caterpillar D-6 (six-cylinder engine)

During 1941 Caterpillar phased out the three-cylinder D-6 tractor and began using a six-cylinder engine in its place. This new model carried a 4-1/4 x 5-1/2-inch bore and stroke with a rated speed of 1,400 rpm. The D-6 delivered a maximum pull of almost 17,000 lbs. or about 50 drawbar hp. Production of various styles of the D-6 continued until 1959.

Nebraska Test Data

Model: Caterpillar D-6
Test No. 416
Date Tested: July 11 to July 23, 1949

The D-6 Caterpillar delivered 68.48 belt hp as noted in Test D. Fuel economy for this test came in at 14.28 hp-hours per gallon, compared to a figure of 13.88 under the Test B 100-percent maximum load of 76.9 hp. The D-6 featured a Caterpillar-built, six-cylinder, I-head engine. Rated at 1,400 rpm, it used a 4-1/2 x 5-1/2-inch bore and stroke. The starting engine was of two-cylinder horizontal opposed design. Rated at 3,000 rpm, it carried a 3-1/8 x 3-1/2-inch bore and stroke. No repairs or adjustments were noted for this tractor during 33 hours of engine operating time. The D-6 featured forward speeds of 1.4, 2.3, 3.2, 4.4, and 5.8 mph. Second gear was used for Test H, and at a rated load of 49.35 drawbar hp this tractor pulled a load of 8,250 lbs. at 2.24 mph with a slippage of 1.37 percent. Fuel economy was registered at 11.51 hp-hours per gallon. A low gear maximum pull of 16,222 lbs. was achieved at a speed of 1.35 mph and with a slippage of 7.38 percent. Total weight of the D-6 was 18,805 lbs.

Nebraska Test Data

Model: Caterpillar D-6

Test No. 555

Date Tested: July 25 to August 12, 1955

Weighing 20,765 lbs., this D-6 featured forward speeds of 1.7, 2.6, 3.6, 5, and 6.6 mph. The low-gear maximum pull of Test G gave a reading of 17,486 lbs. at 1.56 mph with a slippage of 6.3 percent. Test H, run in second gear, indicated a rated drawbar output of 59.33 hp, along with a pull of 8,668 lbs. at 2.57 mph with a slippage of 1.2 percent. During this test a fuel economy of 11.39 hp-hours per gallon of diesel fuel was recorded. Caterpillar equipped this tractor with a six-cylinder diesel engine with a 4-1/2 x 5-1/2-inch bore and stroke and a 525 cubic inch displacement. Rated at 1,600 rpm, it achieved a maximum engine torque of 534.5 lbs.-ft. with an engine speed of 1,036 rpm. Also featured was a two-cylinder horizontal opposed starting engine rated at 3,000 rpm and using a 3-1/8 x 3-1/2-inch bore and stroke. Test B, run at a 100-percent maximum belt load of 92.52 hp, yielded a fuel economy of 13.75 hp-hours per gallon, with economy rising to 14.13 under a Test D rated belt load of 81.56 hp. Track roller guards and a radiator grille were installed following Test A. The 16-inch track shoes were replaced with 24-inch track shoes. Otherwise, no repairs or adjustments were noted during 48-1/2 hours of running time.

Nebraska Test Data

Model: Caterpillar D-6

Test No. 747

Date Tested: June 14 to June 29, 1960

Only drawbar tests were run on this tractor, since no belt pulley or PTO shaft was provided. Using second gear, a two-hour economy run at maximum available power recorded an output of 74.82 drawbar hp, together with a pull of 10,925 lbs. at 2.57 mph and slippage of 1.26 percent. Fuel economy was posted at 12.19 hp-hours per gallon. The economy figure stood at 11.15 on the 10-hour economy run made at 75 percent pull. This test indicated an output of 59.3 hp, a pull of 8,097 lbs. at 2.75 mph, and slippage of 0.62 percent. A low-gear maximum pull of 17,687 lbs. at 1.56 mph was also recorded, but fuel economy was not calibrated in the maximum power runs made in each individual forward gear. This 20,670-lb. tractor featured a Caterpillar six-cylinder diesel engine of 4-1/2 x 5-1/2-inch bore and stroke. Rated at 1,600 rpm, it displaced 525 cubic inches. Also featured was a two-cylinder vertical starting engine rated at 15 hp. This engine carried a 2-3/8-inch bore and stroke with rated power being developed at 6,000 rpm. No repairs or adjustments were noted during 41-1/2 hours of operating time.

Caterpillar RD-7 and D-7

With the exception of slightly changed specifications, the RD-7 of 1935 was the same as the Caterpillar Diesel Fifty. The four-cylinder engine used a 5-3/4 x 7-inch bore and stroke and was rated at 61 drawbar and 70 belt hp. Weighing over 20,000 lbs., the RD-7 had a maximum drawbar pull of almost 15,000 lbs. Production of this model continued into the late 1950s, albeit with numerous changes along the way.

Nebraska Test Data

Model: Caterpillar RD-7 (61 hp)

Test No. 253

Date Tested: May 5 to May 15, 1936

As submitted by Caterpillar, this tractor had a rating of 61 maximum drawbar hp in second gear, operating under standard conditions. Test D for rated brake hp established this figure at 61.22, with fuel economy being recorded at 14.85 hp-hours per gallon, compared to an economy of 14.56 at 100 percent maximum load of 68.24 hp. Advertised speeds of 1.6, 2.4, 3.4, and 4.7 mph were provided. Second gear was used for Test H covering rated drawbar load. At 46.48 hp, Test H indicated a fuel economy of 11.95 hp-hours per gallon, along with a pull of 7,186 lbs. at 2.43 mph and slippage of 1.07 percent. The low gear maximum indicated in Test G manifested a pull of 14,746 lbs. at 1.53 mph, slippage of 2.7 percent, and an output of 60.32 hp. Caterpillar equipped the RD-7 with a four-cylinder I-head, 5-3/4 x 8-inch engine. Rated at 850 rpm, it featured a Caterpillar fuel system and Donaldson air cleaner. During 45 hours of running time the clutch was adjusted on the starting motor, otherwise no repairs or adjustments were noted. Operating weight was 21,020 lbs.

Nebraska Test Data

Model: Caterpillar RD-7 (69 hp)

Test No. 254

Date Tested: May 16 to May 20, 1936

Using the same tractor as noted in Test No. 253, Caterpillar adjusted the fuel pumps for an output of 69 drawbar hp in second gear. All other tractor specifications remained the same as previously indicated. Test D at 69.96 rated brake hp and 850 rpm gave a recorded fuel economy of 15.09 hp-hours per gallon of diesel fuel. A slightly diminished economy of 14.65 appeared at 100 percent maximum brake load of 77.47 hp. Test H for rated drawbar hp was made in second gear. At an output of 52.34 hp the RD-7 gave a fuel economy of 12.17 hp-hours per gallon, along with a pull of 8,135 lbs. at 2.41 mph and slippage of 1.6 percent. The low gear maximum test at 65.22 hp gave a pull of 16,098 lbs. at 1.52 mph. No repairs or adjustments were noted during the 27 hours of running time for this test.

Nebraska Test Data

Model: Caterpillar RD-7 (high speed)

Test No. 255

Date Tested: May 21 to May 25, 1936

Once again, as in Tests 253 and 254, the same RD-7 tractor was used. But this time, instead of operating at 850 rpm, the speed was increased to 1,000 rpm. All other tractor specifications remained the same. Test D for rated brake load revealed a dramatic increase to 86.31 hp, fuel consumption of 5.983 gph, and an economy of 14.43 hp-hours per gallon. At 100 percent maximum load of 95.97 hp, economy dropped to 10.72. Test H for rated drawbar load indicated a pull of 8,272 lbs. at 2.83 mph and an output of 62.52 hp. Fuel economy was recorded at 12.01 hp-hours per gallon. The low gear maximum load test gave a pull of 16,782 lbs. at 1.72 mph, slippage of 7.24 percent, and an output of 76.89 hp. No repairs or adjustments were noted during the 32 hours of running time for this test.

Nebraska Test Data

Model: Caterpillar D-7

Test No. 358

Date Tested: October 2 to October 11, 1940

Five forward speeds of 1.4, 2.2, 3.2, 4.6, and 6 mph were built into the Caterpillar D-7 tractor. Test G indicated a maximum low gear pull of 21,351 lbs. at a speed of 1.33 mph and slippage of 4.8 percent for an output of 75.83 drawbar hp. At a rated 60.63 drawbar hp the D-7 came through Test H with a fuel economy of 12.81 hp-hours per gallon, pulling a 10,335 lb. load at 2.2 mph with slippage of 1.63 percent. This 24,790 lb. tractor went through 42 hours of engine operating time with no repairs or adjustments recorded. Test C and Test B at 100percent maximum belt hp indicated a fuel economy of 14.86 hp-hours per gallon under an 89.10 hp load. Economy sagged slightly to 14.81 under a load of 78.96 hp as noted in Test D. Brief engine specifications include a four-cylinder I-head design with a 5-3/4 x 8-inch bore and stroke and a rated speed of 1,000 rpm. Caterpillar furnished its own fuel injection equipment.

Nebraska Test Data

Model: Caterpillar D-7

Test No. 582

Date Tested: July 23 to August 6, 1956

At a Test H rated drawbar load of 83.28 hp, the D-7 pulled 14,173 lbs. at 2.2 mph with a slippage of 1.04 percent. Fuel economy came in at 12.15 hp-hours per gallon. Second gear was used during this ten-hour run. The D-7 featured forward speeds of 1.5, 2.2, 3.2, 4.6, and 5.9 mph. Test G delivered a low-gear maximum pull of 26,289 lbs. at 1.45 mph with a slippage of 5.31 percent . This 30,460-lb. tractor used a Caterpillar four-cylinder diesel engine of I-head engine design. Rated at 1,200 rpm, it achieved a peak of 108 percent rated torque at 75 percent rated speed, maintaining this level down to 55 percent of rated speed. With an 831 CID, the engine carried a 5-3/4 x 8 inch bore and stroke. Also featured was a two-cylinder, 25 hp starting engine rated at 2,700 rpm and using a 3-5/8 x 4-inch bore and stroke. During the drawbar tests the tracks were adjusted, otherwise no repairs or adjustments were reported during 56 hours of running time. At a Test D rated belt load of 110,4 hp, the D-7 yielded a fuel economy of 15.39 hp-hours per gallon, with this figure sliding to 12.49 under a Test B & C maximum load of 121.7 hp.

Nebraska Test Data

Model: Caterpillar D-7

Test No. 710

Date Tested: August 3 to August 11, 1959

Five forward speeds of 1.5, 2.2, 3.2, 4.6, and 5.9 mph were featured in this D-7. Standard equipment also included a cable control system for integral or drawn equipment. A two-cylinder starting engine rated at 25 hp was featured—it used a 3-5/8 x 4-inch bore and stroke and was rated at 2,700 rpm. The diesel engine was of four-cylinder turbocharged design, rated at 1,200 rpm and used a 5-3/4 x 8-inch bore and stroke for a displacement of 831 cubic inches. The design included a 15.7:1 compression ratio. This tractor carried no PTO or belt pulley equipment. Weighing 32,035 lbs., the D-7 delivered a maximum drawbar output of 109.79 hp against a pull of 18,959 lbs. at 2.17 mph and a slippage of 2.6 percent. Economy in this test totaled 13.3 hp-hours per gallon. A 10-hour run, made at 75 percent load, yielded 91.4 drawbar hp against a pull of 14,888 lbs. at 2.3 mph and 1.19 percent slippage. This test indicated a fuel economy of 12.34 hp-hours per gallon. No repairs or adjustments were noted during 38-1/2 hours of running time.

Caterpillar RD-8

Production of the Caterpillar RD-8 began in 1935. This tractor used the same 5-3/4 x 8-inch bore and stroke engine as the D-6 and D-7 tractors, but had six cylinders. This gave the D-8 a capability of over 103 belt hp. On the drawbar this tractor was able to pull a load in excess of 20,000 lbs. Total tractor weight was over 33,000 lbs. Various changes and modifications were evident on the RD-8 and D-8 over its long production run that ended in 1955.

Nebraska Test Data

Model: Caterpillar RD-8

Test No. 256

Date Tested: May 7 to May 19, 1936

Weighing 33,690 lbs., the RD-8 featured six forward speeds of 1.7, 2.4, 2.8, 3.2, 3.9, and 5.3 mph. Test H for rated drawbar load used second gear. With an output of 72.26 hp the RD-8 pulled 11,465 lbs. at 2.36 mph, slippage of 1.54 percent, and a fuel economy of 12.02 hp-hours per gallon. A pull of 20,485 lbs. was recorded in the low gear maximum load test—plus 91.75 drawbar hp at a speed of 1.68 mph and slippage of 2.86 percent. Test D at a 92.15-hp brake load yielded 14.41 hp-hours per gallon, with a slight decrease to 14.18 at maximum output of 103.21 brake hp. This tractor was equipped with a huge six-cylinder I-head engine with a 5-3/4 x 8-inch bore and stroke. Rated at 850 rpm, it included a Caterpillar fuel system. During 46 hours of running time no repairs or adjustments were noted.

Nebraska Test Data

Model: Caterpillar RD-8 (high speed)

Test No. 257

Date Tested: May 19 to May 25, 1936

Caterpillar used the same RD-8 tractor as in Test No. 256, but increased the engine speed to 1,000 rpm. Test D for rated brake load indicated 107.89 hp with a fuel consumption of 7.75 gph and a fuel economy of 13.92 hp-hours per gallon. Economy dropped minutely to 13.81 under a maximum load of 118.29 brake hp. As in Test No. 256, maximum drawbar load runs were made in all six forward gears. Low gear yielded an output of 103.95 hp, together with a pull of 19,795 lbs. at 1.97 mph and slippage of 2.93 percent. Test H for rated drawbar load indicated a fuel economy of 11.43 hp-hours per gallon. This occurred while pulling a 10,813 lb. load at 2.78 mph, slippage of 1.32 percent, and an output of 80.25 drawbar hp. No repairs or adjustments were noted during 33 hours of running time.

Nebraska Test Data

Model: Caterpillar D-8

Test No. 357

Date Tested: October 11 to October 16, 1940

Caterpillar rated this tractor to pull 26,200 lbs. in low gear. Test G indicated it did pull 26,208 lbs. at a speed of 1.49 mph with slippage of 6.58 percent and a total output of 104.12 drawbar hp. Test H for rated drawbar hp was run in second gear and yielded 13.05 hp-hours per gallon while pulling a 14,728 lb. load at 2.17 mph under a recorded slippage of 1.67 percent. This test also indicated an output of 85.33 drawbar hp. This photograph illustrated the D-8 during brake hp testing. Test C and Test B for 100 percent maximum load yielded 14.86 hp-hours per gallon with an output of 127.93 hp. At rated load of 111.27 hp under Test D, fuel economy was recorded at 15.02 hp-hours per gallon. The D-8 submitted for this test was equipped with six forward speeds of 1.6, 2.2, 2.6, 3, 3.6, and 4.9 mph. Weighing in at 35,000 lbs., it also featured a six-cylinder I-head diesel engine. Rated at 950 rpm, it carried a 5-3/4 x 8-inch bore and stroke. Caterpillar featured its own fuel injection system and governor. During 32 hours of engine operating time, no repairs or adjustments were noted.

Nebraska Test Data

Model: Caterpillar D-8

Test No. 415

Date Tested: July 11 to July 19, 1949

No belt tests were made on this tractor. Weighing 36,915 lbs., the D-8 featured five forward speeds of 1.7, 2.3, 2.8, 3.7, and 4.8 mph. Second gear was used for the 10-hour run of Test H. At a speed of 2.24 mph the D-8 pulled a load of 16,619 lbs., delivering an output of 99.16 rated drawbar hp in the process. Slippage was 0.98 percent , and fuel economy was recorded at 12.5 hp-hours per gallon of diesel fuel. A low gear maximum pull of 28,664 lbs. was recorded in Test G, and this while traveling at a speed of 1.62 mph with slippage of 4.98 percent. Standard equipment for the D-8 included a six-cylinder Caterpillar engine of I-head design. Rated at 1,000 rpm it used a 5-3/4 x 8-inch bore and stroke. Also featured was a Caterpillar-built fuel injection system, along with the company's own two-cylinder starting engine. No repairs or adjustments were noted during 31 hours of engine operating time.

Nebraska Test Data

Model: Caterpillar D-8

Test No. 583

Date Tested: July 27 to July 30, 1956

Rated at 155 maximum drawbar hp, the D-8 delivered 157.58 hp at 100 percent maximum load using second gear. The low-gear maximum load test indicated a maximum pull of 40,032 lbs. at 1.37 mph with a slippage of 5.86 percent. Total tractor weight was 47,335 lbs. This tractor featured forward speeds of 1.5, 1.9, 2.7, 3.9, and 5.2 mph. Also featured was a Caterpillar six-cylinder diesel engine of I-head design. Rated at 1,200 rpm, this engine carried a 5-3/4 x 8-inch bore and stroke for a 1,246-cubic-inch displacement. A compression ratio of 15.7:1 was used. The starting engine was a Caterpillar-built, two-cylinder vertical model rated at 25 hp and 2,700 rpm. It carried a 3-5/8 x 4 inch bore and stroke. No belt tests were made on this tractor. Test H, run for 10 hours in second gear indicated a rated drawbar output of 124.34 hp. This test also showed a pull of 24,644 lbs. at 1.89 mph with a slippage of 1.31 percent. Fuel economy in this test was scored at 13.09 hp-hours per gallon of diesel fuel.

Nebraska Test Data

Model: Caterpillar D-8 Diesel

Test No. 711

Date Tested: August 3 to August 12, 1959

The D-8's 1,246-cid engine was a six-cylinder design with a 5-3/4 x 8-inch bore and stroke. This turbocharged engine was rated at 1,200 rpm. Also featured was a two-cylinder starting engine. This tractor weighed in at 53,655 lbs. A two-hour drawbar run made at maximum available power using second gear indicated an output of 168.38 drawbar hp. During this run, a pull of 33,452 lbs. was recorded at 1.89 mph and 2.7 percent slippage. Fuel economy was posted at 12.8 hp-hours per gallon. A 10-hour drawbar run made at 75 percent load yielded an output of 140.23 hp, plus a pull of 26,535 lbs. at 1.98 mph and slippage of 1.92 percent. That gave a fuel economy of 12.39 hp-hours per gallon. The complete Test Reports also indicated maximum power with ballast for each tractor tested, and in the case at hand, low gear produced 173.69 drawbar hp, along with a pull of 45,526 lbs. at 1.43 mph and 4.23 percent slippage. No PTO or belt tests were run and no repairs or adjustments were noted during 34 ½ hours of operating time.

Caterpillar D-9

The huge Caterpillar D-9 tractor was first built in 1954. Weighing more than 33 tons, the D-9 was equipped with a six-cylinder turbocharged engine with a 6-1/4 x 8-inch bore and stroke. At the drawbar, the D-9 demonstrated its capability to pull a load of nearly 57,000 lbs. The D-9 had six forward speeds ranging all the way up to 7 mph.

Nebraska Test Data

Model: Caterpillar D-9

Test No. 584

Date Tested: July 31 to August 4, 1956

Weighing 66,025 lbs., the D-9 was not subjected to belt testing due to the limited capacity of the dynamometer. Advertised speeds of 1.7, 2.2, 3, 3.9, 5, and 7 mph were provided. In addition the main clutch and steering clutches were equipped with hydraulic boosters. Caterpillar equipped this tractor with a six-cylinder turbocharged diesel engine of I-head design. Rated at 1,240 rpm, it carried a 6-1/4 x 8-inch bore and stroke for a displacement of 1,473 cubic inches. Also featured was a two-cylinder, 25 hp starting engine similar to that used on the D-8. During the preliminary run the engine temperature gauge was replaced, otherwise no repairs or adjustments were noted during 32 hours of operating time. Test G yielded a maximum output of 252.33 drawbar hp in second gear. During this run the D-9 pulled 44,817 lbs. at 2.11 mph with a slippage of 2.54 percent. A low-gear maximum pull of 56,724 lbs. at 1.6 mph was also recorded. Slippage in this test came to 5.66 percent. Test H, run for 10 hours in second gear, scored a fuel economy of 15.293 hp-hours per gallon of diesel fuel. During this test the D-9 pulled 36,521 lbs. at 2.12 mph with a slippage of 1.44 percent, and delivered 206.84-rated hp in the process.

C-E Tractor Company

TOLEDO, OHIO

See: Cleveland Engineering Company

C-E garden tractor

The C-E garden tractor appeared in the late 1930s. It was powered by a Wisconsin AF-single cylinder engine rated at 5 hp. It used a 3-1/4 x 4-inch bore and stroke. Weighing 950 lbs., the C-E also featured a three-speed automotive transmission. By the late 1940s parts were still available, but the C-E had apparently gone out of production.

Centaur Tractor Corporation

GREENWICH, OHIO

See: Central Tractor Company, Greenwich, Ohio

Now owned by LeRoi, Centaur traced its roots back to the Central Tractor Co., which was founded in Greenwich in 1920.

Centaur tractor

The Centaur tractor first appeared from Central Tractor Company in 1921. Rated at 10 belt hp, the Centaur could be equipped with a wide array of implements built especially for use with this tractor. A 1926 Centaur catalog notes that the Model G, as it was known at the time, weighed 1,220 lbs. and was capable of 6 drawbar hp. In 1928 the company name was changed to Centaur Tractor Corporation.

COLLECTOR VALUES	1	2	3	4
MODEL G	$3,000	$2,000	$1,000	$850

Centaur KV (Klear View) tractors first appear in the 1935 directories, and indicating that production probably

Centaur KV (Klear View)

began in 1934. Rated at 22 belt hp, the KV was equipped with a LeRoi four-cylinder engine with a 3-1/4 x 4-inch bore and stroke. This unstyled version was built until about 1939.

Centaur KV

Production of the Centaur KV tractor began about 1934 and continued with little change until about 1939 when it was given a stylized hood and fenders. Otherwise the tractor was essentially the same as before, continuing with the LeRoi D133 four-cylinder engine. A unique feature of the later models was their capability of traveling up to 25 mph on the road. Production of the KV was suspended during World War II.

Nebraska Test Data

Model: Centaur KV-48

Test No. 402

Date Tested: September 27 to October 6, 1948

Weighing in at 2,824 lbs., the Centaur KV-48 was given a manufacturer's rating of approximately 20 drawbar and 25 belt hp. Test an Test B at 100-percent maximum load indicated an output of 24 hp along with a fuel economy of 9.33 hp-hours per gallon. Under a Test D rated load of 21.34 belt hp, economy rose slightly to stand at 9.47 hp-hours per gallon. Advertised speeds of 2.4, 4.5, 7.4, and 15.9 mph were featured, with second gear chosen for the 10-hour Test H. At a rated load of 16.21 hp, the KV-48 pulled a 1,566 lb. load at 3.88 mph with a slippage of 7.07 percent. Fuel economy was recorded at 8.46 hp-hours per gallon. Test G for 100-percent maximum drawbar load indicated a low-gear maximum pull of 2,109 lbs. at 1.91 mph and slippage of 15.1 percent. This tractor was equipped with 9-24-inch rear and 5.00-15-inch front rubber. Also featured was a LeRoi four-cylinder I-head engine. Rated at 1,500 rpm, it used a 3-1/2 x 3-5/8 inch bore and stroke. Also included was an Auto-Lite electrical system, Zenith 161X7 carburetor, and Vortox air cleaner. No repairs or adjustments were noted during 41-1/2 hours of engine running time.

COLLECTOR VALUES	1	2	3	4
KV	$3,000	$2,000	$1,000	$500

Central Machine Works

INDIANAPOLIS, INDIANA

Late in 1911 Central Machine Works announced its new tractor design that featured a friction-drive transmission, along with a four-cylinder Clifton engine. Weighing 10,000 lbs., the Central is shown here pulling a six-bottom plow. No specifications have been found relative to the size of this tractor, nor in fact, has any other information appeared.

A Central Machine Works tractor

Central Tractor Company Model 6-10

Central Tractor Company

GREENWICH, OHIO

See: Centaur Tractor Corporation

Organized in 1921 Central Tractor Company specialized in building its Centaur garden tractors. The 6-10 model was equipped with a LeRoi two-cylinder engine with a 3-1/8 x 4-1/4-inch bore and stroke. In 1928 Central Tractor Co. became the Centaur Tractor Corporation.

Two different trademark applications illustrate the Centaur trademarks of 1921. Both appeared in the Patent Office Gazette. From these marks it is learned that they were first used on March 3, 1921, and this could very well establish the beginnings of the company at least so far as the Centaur tractor line is concerned.

Centaur logo

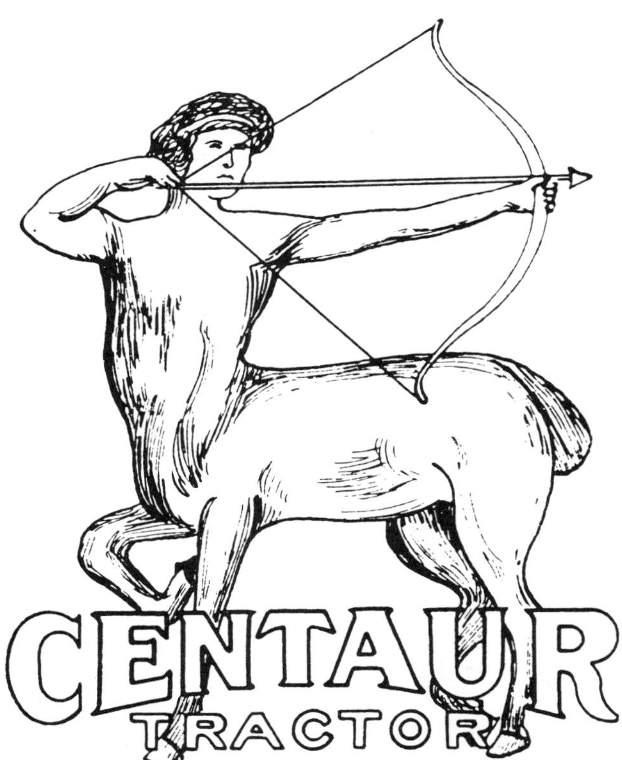

Centaur trademark

Central Tractor Company

GREAT FALLS, MONTANA

This company was incorporated for $25,000 in 1919 to build tractors, but no other information can be found concerning the firm.

Central Machine Company

MINNEAPOLIS, MINNESOTA

Central Auto Tractor

In 1912 the Central Auto Tractor appeared at the Minnesota State Fair and generated considerable interest. It used a four-cylinder engine and featured two forward speeds. Rated at 24 belt hp, the Central Auto Tractor also featured a unique differential lock for extra traction in slippery spots.

Challenge Tractor Company

MINNEAPOLIS, MINNESOTA

Challenge Tractor Company logo

The December 26, 1916 issue of the Patent Office Gazette contained the trademark application of the Challenge Tractor Company, noting that they first used the mark on October 1, 1916. Aside from this, no other information has been located.

Champion Tractor Company

ARGO, ILLINOIS

Champion started business around 1918, manufacturing two different tractor models for about two years, but very little is known about the company.

Probably beginning in 1918, Champion offered its 15-30 tractor. It retailed for $1,465. The Champion was largely built up of OEM components including the engine and transmission. This tractor used a Buda four-cylinder engine with a 4-1/4 x 5-1/2-inch bore and stroke. Production apparently ended by 1920.

Champion Tractor Company 15-30

Champion Tractor Company 17-1/2-32 tractor

For 1919 and 1920 Champion produced the 17-1/2-32 tractor. Like the 15-30 it is shown without fenders, indicating that they were probably an extra-cost option, or that development of the Champion tractors had not yet achieved final completion.

Chandler Motor Car Company

CLEVELAND, OHIO

The 1918 issue of the Farm Implement News Buyer's Guide listed this well-known automobile manufacturer as a tractor builder. No further information has been found regarding its tractors.

Charter Gas Engine Company

STERLING, ILLINOIS

Charter steam traction engine

About 1887 John Charter built and sold the first successful liquid fuel engine. Although this claim would later be a point of contention, Charter always maintained his claim. In 1889 Charter built the first successful gasoline traction engine, using his own stationary engine over the trucks from a steam traction engine. Although this traction engine operated with considerable success and even greater promise, it appears this was the beginning and end of Charter's involvement in the tractor business.

Chase Motor Truck Company

SYRACUSE, NEW YORK

Chase Tractors Corporation Ltd.

TORONTO, ONTARIO

Chase Motor Truck Company tractor

Chase Motor Truck Company began building tractors as early as 1908, but early designs assumed the form of a tractor-roller. The 1908 design shown here was powered by a small air-cooled engine and was intended primarily for use as a roller.

Chase tractor-roller combination

By 1913 the Chase tractor-roller combination had been developed to include a three-cylinder, two-cycle engine of 30 belt hp. Although more suitable for tractive use than the original machine, its application to heavy traction work was very limited.

Chase 40

Chase 8-16

By 1915 Chase had developed a conventional tractor, with this 8-16 using a four-cylinder Waukesha engine. By 1918 the company had upgraded the design to a 9-18 hp rating; the new model was built with a Buda four-cylinder engine.

Little is known of the Chase 40 hp tractor of 1915. Weighing some 6,000 lbs., this tractor had a 1916 list price of $1,750. For reasons now unknown the Chase 40 then disappeared from the market.

Chase 9-18 with Buda Engine

Chase tractors reappear in 1919 at Toronto, Ontario. The 9-18 Buda engine of the 1918 models was replaced with a larger Buda four-cylinder design that carried a 4-1/4 x 5-1/2-inch bore and stroke. All Chase tractor production ended in 1921.

Chief Tractor Company

DETROIT, MICHIGAN

In 1915 this company took over the Boss Tractor Mfg. Company of Detroit. The firm is listed in the Farm Implement News Buyer's Guide as late as 1918, but no other information has been found.

Christensen Engineering Company

MILWAUKEE, WISCONSIN

The Farm Implement News Buyer's Guide lists this company as a tractor builder from 1909 through 1913. Christensen was a gasoline engine manufacturer and also was well known for its developments in railway air brakes and other railway appliances. No information regarding its entry into the tractor business has been located.

Chrysler Corporation

DETROIT, MICHIGAN

Ostensibly, the Dodge Power Wagon was intended to answer the immense popularity of the Willys Jeep. Both were developed as a result of World War II, and the Jeep could be furnished with a belt pulley and other attachments. The concept rested on the premise that one vehicle could do everything on the farm, and on Sunday could become a pleasure vehicle.

Nebraska Test Data

Model: Dodge Power Wagon

Test No. 454

Date Tested: November 13 to November 21, 1950

With eight speeds ranging from 4 to 54 mph, the Dodge Power Wagon featured a four-wheel-drive design and weighed in at 5,809 lbs. During Tests F, G, and H and additional 1,057 lbs. of cast iron was added to each rear wheel, with an additional 594 lbs. of iron added to each front wheel, giving a total operating weight of 9,110 lbs. Test G, run in low gear, produced a maximum pull of 6,480 lbs. at 2.03 mph with a slippage of 12.82 percent. Using second gear, the 10-hour run of Test H produced a rated output of 30.64 drawbar hp, along with a pull of 2,615 lbs. at 4.39 mph against a slippage of 3.59 percent. Fuel economy came in at 7.05 hp-hours per gallon for this test. No repairs or adjustments were recorded during 39 hours of engine operating time. The Power Wagon featured a Chrysler six-cylinder L-head engine. Rated at 1,700 rpm, and using a 3-1/4 x 4-5/8-inch bore and stroke, this engine had a 230.2 cubic inch displacement. Belt testing indicated a fuel economy of 8.63 hp-hours per gallon under a Test B and C 100-percent maximum load of 42.4 hp. Economy slipped to 7.97 hp-hours per gallon against a Test D rated load of 36.77 belt hp. This vehicle proved to be an interesting conclusion to the 1950 testing season.

Dodge Power Wagon

Cizek Mfg. Company

CLUTIER, IOWA

Cizek Little John garden tractor

In the mid-1950s Cizek offered its Little John garden tractor. Shown here with a small trailer, the Little John could be furnished with a variety of different garden tillage implements, lawn sweepers and lawn mowers.

COLLECTOR VALUES	1	2	3	4
	$200	$150	$75	$50

Clarke, Airborne

DETROIT MICHIGAN

A small 3,000 lb. crawler was designed for U.S. military about 1941. This crawler was positioned into a wooden glider and landed in remote areas to build or repair airfields. A small pull-scraper was available from LaPlante-Choate. Clark used a Waukesha engine and shuttle clutch to four forward and reverse gears. The plant closed after WWII and production was taken over by U.S. Tractor Corp., Warren, Ohio.

Cleveland Engineering Company

CLEVELAND, OHIO

In 1934 Cleveland Engineering Co. announced its new "C-E" garden tractor. Weighing 950 lbs., it was furnished with a single-cylinder, air-cooled engine. Numerous attachments were available, including the one-bottom plow shown here. Apparently in the late 1930s the company relocated to Toledo, Ohio, and established the C- E Tractor Company there.

Cleveland Engineering Co. C-E garden tractor

COLLECTOR VALUES	1	2	3	4
C-E GARDEN TRACTOR	$550	$400	$250	$100

Cleveland Horseless Machinery Company

CLEVELAND, OHIO

Various trade references indicate that in 1915 and 1916 this firm was building its Baby Johnson tractor, but no illustrations or other information has been located.

Cleveland Tractor Company

CLEVELAND, OHIO

Cleveland Motor Plow Company

CLEVELAND, OHIO

Cleveland motor plow

By 1912 Rollin H. and Clarence G. White had developed their own motor plow. Early experiments were successful enough to cause the formation of the Cleveland Motor Plow Company. For reasons unknown, they chose not to pursue this design, concentrating instead on crawler tractors. In 1917 the company name was changed to Cleveland Tractor Company. Cletrac was bought out by Oliver in 1944.

In 1916 Cleveland Motor Plow Company introduced its new Model R crawler. Built only in 1916 and 1917, the Cleveland Motor Plow used Buda or Waukesha engines, but no specific data on them has been found.

Model R Crawler

The initial success of the Model R crawler led to the development of the Model H, offered in the 1917-1919 period. This model was equipped with a Weideley engine. Early Cletrac models placed the belt pulley on the front of the tractor.

Cletrac Model R crawler

Cletrac Company Model W crawlers

Cletrac Model F crawler

Model W crawlers emerged in 1919 as the replacement for the Model R. The Model W was also known as the 12-20. This tractor used a Weideley four-cylinder engine with a 4 x 5-1/2-inch bore and stroke. The Model W was the first crawler tractor tested at the Nebraska Tractor Test Laboratory. Model W crawlers were built until about 1925.

Nebraska Test Data

Model: Cletrac Model W 12-20

Test No. 45

Date Tested: July 29 to August 9, 1920

Weighing only 3,300 lbs., the 12-20 exerted a maximum drawbar pull of 1,734 lbs., or about 52 percent of its own weight. Slightly over 15-1/2 drawbar hp was recorded in this test with a ground speed of 3.36 mph. On rated drawbar load, slippage was only 4.3 percent, but 576-square inches of traction surface were on the ground, compared to a much smaller area for conventional tractors. As with the great majority of tractors tested up to this time, kerosene was the chosen fuel. Repairs and adjustments during the test were minor. Slightly over 20 hp was recorded on the rated load test and fuel economy soared to 8.33 hp-hours per gallon, with only 2.42 gph required. Normal speed for the 12-20 was 3-1/2 mph, although this was variable from 1 to 4 mph. A Weidely engine was used and it was of four-cylinder vertical design with overhead valves, and carried a 4 x 5-1/2 inch bore and stroke. Rated speed was 1,265 rpm. Test engineers noted the 12-20 climbed a 45-degree incline easily.

Model F Cletrac tractors were built 1920-1924. This small crawler had a 9-16 hp rating and used a four-cylinder engine with a 3-1/4 x 4-1/2-inch bore and stroke. It sold for the surprisingly low price of $850. The "Cletrac trade-name was first used in 1918. Model F used a distinctive high drive like many modern crawlers.

Nebraska Test Data

Model: Cletrac Model F 9-16

Test No. 85

Date Tested: April 14 to April 20, 1922

Only one forward speed and a reverse were provided in the Cletrac 9-16. This gave a variable range from one to three mph. Test notes indicated no adjustments were made during the 30 hours of running time. Cleveland featured its own four-cylinder vertical, L-head engine with a 3-1/4 x 4-1/2-inch bore and stroke. It was rated at 1,600 rpm, substantially faster than crankshaft speeds indicated on earlier tests. Weighing 1,920 lbs., the 9-16 managed a maximum drawbar pull of 1,780 lbs. while travelling at a speed of 2.77 mph, and recorded a slippage of only 10.11percent while accomplishing this feat. Kerosene fuel was used. On the rated load test, 16.36 brake hp was developed at a crankshaft speed of 1,611 rpm. Cletrac was the first to come up with a fuel economy in excess of 10 hp-hours per gallon, doing so handily with a rating of 10.17. Fuel consumption on this load came to only 1.608 gph. At maximum brake hp, 19.61 was the final figure, but fuel economy dropped dramatically to 6.74 hp-hours per gallon. Regular equipment for the 9-16 included an Eisemann magneto and a Tillotson carburetor.

Between 1925 and 1932 Cletrac offered its Model 20 crawler. This model was equipped with the company's own four-cylinder engine with a 4 x 5-inch bore and stroke. While a sizable number of early Cletrac crawlers were used for construction work, the company's chief market was the farmer. Numerous implements were available for use with the Cletrac crawlers.

Cletrac Model 20 crawler

COLLECTOR VALUES	1	2	3	4
MODEL 20	$5,000	$4,000	$2,500	$1,000

Cletrac Model 30A (30-45 tractor)

The Model 30A tractors were built 1926-1928. Also known as the 30-45 tractor, this one was followed in 1929 and 1930 with an improved Model 30B tractor. Model 30 crawlers used a Wisconsin six-cylinder engine with a 4 x 5-inch bore and stroke.

Nebraska Test Data

Model: Cletrac Model 30A 30-45

Test No. 125

Date Tested: August 27 to September 7, 1926

Two forward speeds of 2.4 and 4.75 mph were featured in the Cleveland Model 30A. Weighing 7,223 lbs., it made a maximum drawbar pull of 6,170 lbs. in low gear, or about 85 percent of its own weight. Slippage of 5.41percent was noted in this test, along with a speed of 2.34 mph and a total of 38-drawbar hp. During this test the shift lever had to be tied in place in order to keep the gears in mesh. Gasoline was used throughout the 36 hours of running time. At rated brake hp, fuel consumption totaled 5.639 gph for 8.01 hp-hours per gallon. Under maximum load 48.62 hp was recorded. The Cletrac 30A featured a six-cylinder Wisconsin valve-in-head engine rated at 1,577 rpm and carried a 4 x 5-inch bore and stroke. Other features included a Pomona air cleaner, Taco governor, Eisemann GS6 magneto, and a Tillotson ST3A carburetor.

COLLECTOR VALUES	1	2	3	4
MODEL 30A	$6,000	$4,000	$2,500	$1,000

Cletrac Model 40 tractor production began in 1928 and ran until 1931. Subsequently, this model was followed by the 55-40—essentially the same tractor but with numerous improvements. The Model 40 had a big six-cylinder Beaver engine with a 4-1/2 x 5-inch bore and stroke. Electric starting was a standard feature.

Cletrac Model 40

Nebraska Test Data

Model: Cletrac Model 40 40-55

Test No. 149

Date Tested: April 24 to May 10, 1928

One of the few problems occurring during the 37 hours of running time for this test was a shorted ignition system due to a bare spot on a battery cable. Rated at 1,575 rpm, this tractor featured a six-cylinder Beaver engine with a 4-1/2 x 5-inch bore and stroke. Along with the Delco-Remy starting and ignition system came a Wheeler-Schebler AT carburetor, Borg & Beck clutch, and a Taco governor. Total weight was 12,038 lbs. Three forward gears gave advertised speeds of 2, 3-1/2, and 5-1/2 mph. At rated brake hp the Model 40 indicated an efficiency of 7.46 hp-hours per gallon, also indicated in the report as 0.874 lbs. per hp hour. At 96.5 percent of maximum load (63 hp) fuel consumption totalled 8.447 gph. The rated drawbar test was run in intermediate gear and indicated 6.54 hp-hours per gallon, while a maximum drawbar test in low gear gave a recorded pull of 9,725 lbs. at 2.14 mph, for a maximum of 55-1/2 drawbar hp.

Cletrac Model 55

Model 55 Cletrac crawlers were built between 1932 and 1936. This tractor was the immediate successor to the Model 55-40 of 1931 and 1932. By this time the Cletrac crawlers were widely known and used and the company was a major manufacturer of crawler tractors.

Cletrac Model 100

In terms of size, the Cletrac Model 100 was one of the largest crawler tractors of its time. Built between 1927 and 1930, the Model 100 used a huge six-cylinder Beaver engine with a 6 x 7-inch bore and stroke. Only about 50 of these huge tractors were built.

Cletrac Model 15 crawler

Cletrac introduced its Model 15 crawler in 1931, with production continuing into 1933. At that time the Model 15 was replaced with the Model 20-C, and the latter was available into 1936.

Nebraska Test Data

Model: Cletrac Model 15
Test No. 196
Date Tested: July 28 to August 13, 1931

Rated at 15 drawbar and 22 belt hp, the Model 15 carried a Hercules four-cylinder, 4 x 4-1/2-inch L-head engine rated at 1,250 rpm. Included also was an Eisemann GL4 magneto, Hercules governor, Tillotson P1A carburetor, and Pomona air cleaner. Advertised speeds of 1.95, 3.05, and 4.37 mph were also built into this model. Weighing 5,700 lbs., the Cletrac 15 made a maximum drawbar pull of 3,927 lbs. at 1.79 mph, and slippage of 8.39 percent. This corresponded to a maximum of 18.69 drawbar hp. At its rated 15.41 hp the Model 15 pulled a load of 1,897 lbs. at 3.05 mph, yielding an economy of 4.71 hp-hours per gallon. At rated brake load of 23.38 hp, fuel economy came in at 7.2 hp-hours per gallon, with a substantially better economy rating of 8.52 appearing at maximum belt load of 25.83 hp. No repairs or adjustments were noted during the 48 hours of running time.

Nebraska Test Data

Model: Cletrac Model 15
Test No. 202
Date Tested: April 9 to May 4, 1932

In the low gear maximum drawbar test this tractor pulled 4,444 lbs. at a speed of 1.77 mph, or nearly 73 percent of its own operating weight of 6,100 lbs. It achieved an economy of 6.35 hp-hours per gallon at rated drawbar load of 18.73 hp. During this test the Cletrac 15 pulled 2,535 lbs. at 2.77 mph. Powered by a Hercules four-cylinder L-head engine, it was equipped with an Eisemann GL4 magneto, Tillotson P1B carburetor, and Vortox air cleaner. The engine was rated at 1,250 and carried a 4 x 4-1/2-inch bore and stroke. No repairs or adjustments were required during the 49 hours of running time. Brake hp tests indicated a fuel economy of 7.89 hp-hours per gallon at rated load of 24.23 hp. Economy rose to 8.79 when under maximum load of 26.94 belt hp. Although not rated by the manufacturer, the Cletrac 15 had a maximum permissible rating of 17.75 drawbar and 24.44 belt hp.

Cletrac Model 20-C

Model 20-C Cletrac crawlers were built between 1933 and 1936. This one carried a four-cylinder Hercules engine with a 4 x 4-1/2-inch bore and stroke. Numerous attachments and accessories were available for special conditions. Cletrac replaced the 20-C in 1936 with the Model AG, and production of this model continued into 1942. Model AG crawlers also used a Hercules four-cylinder engine.

COLLECTOR VALUES	1	2	3	4
MODEL 20-C	$5,000	$3,500	$2,500	$1,000

Cletrac Model 25 tractor

Cletrac 25 tractors came into being during 1932. Weighing more than 3-1/2 tons, the Cletrac 25 was equipped with a Hercules six-cylinder engine with a 3-3/4 x 4-1/4-inch bore and stroke. Model 25 tractors were capable of about 33 belt hp. The Cletrac 40-30 was of similar design, but used a larger engine.

Nebraska Test Data

Model: Cletrac Model 25
Test No. 201
Date Tested: April 9 to April 30, 1932

Delco-Remy battery ignition and electric starting were regular features of the Cletrac 25, along with a Tillotson Y8A carburetor, Hercules governor, and Vortox air cleaner. The six-cylinder Hercules engine was of L-head design and carried a 3-3/4x 4-1/4-inch bore and stroke with a rated speed of 1,250 rpm. Also included were advertised speeds of 1.95, 2.8, and 4 mph. The 10-hour rated drawbar test results indicated a pull of 3,091 lbs. at 2.8 mph, slippage of 0.75 percent and an output of 23.07 hp. Fuel economy came in at 6.94 hp-hours per gallon. The low gear maximum drawbar test revealed 26.22 hp with a 5,206 lb. pull at 1.89 mph and slippage of 3.68 percent, or nearly 72 percent of the 7,275 lb. operating weight. Belt testing at rated load of 30.27 hp gave a fuel economy of 8.58 hp-hours per gallon, with a slightly improved figure of 8.9 under maximum belt load of 33.11 hp. No repairs or adjustments were required during the 54 hours of running time.

Cletrac 35 tractor

The Cletrac 35 tractor was built between 1932 and 1936. Its immediate predecessor was the Cletrac 40-35 and was followed in 1936 with the Cletrac CG crawler; the latter was built until 1942. The three models were so similar that they all used the same parts book.

COLLECTOR VALUES	1	2	3	4
CLETRAC 35	$5,000	$4,000	$2,500	$1,000

Cletrac Model 40-30

Model 40-30 Cletrac crawlers were first built in 1930, with production ending the next year. This model used a Hercules six-cylinder engine with a 4-1/4 x 4-1/2-inch bore and stroke.

Nebraska Test Data

Model: Cletrac Model 40-30
Test No. 195
Date Tested: July 28 to August 17, 1931

Rated by Cletrac at 30 drawbar and 44 belt hp, this tractor featured three forward speeds of 2.06, 3.05, and 4.42 mph. Using low gear, it made a maximum pull of 7,580 lbs.—more than 78 percent of its total 9,700 lb. operating weight. Rated drawbar load of 30.44 hp yielded a pull of 3,741 lbs. at 3.05 mph with slippage of 0.99 percent, and fuel economy came in at 5.55 hp-hours per gallon. Under its maximum of 45.64 brake hp the 40-30 burned 5.588 gph, leaving an efficiency of 8.17 hp-hours per gallon. This figure dropped substantially to 7.12 when under a rated brake load of 44.36 hp. Cleveland Tractor Company featured a Hercules six-cylinder L-head engine in this tractor. Rated at 1,450 rpm, it carried a 4-1/4x 4-1/2-inch bore and stroke. A Delco-Remy electrical system was standard equipment, including electric starting. Other features included a Tillotson Y7A carburetor, Hercules governor, Pomona air cleaner, plus a Borg & Beck clutch. No repairs or adjustments were noted during the 53-hour test.

Cletrac Model 40 Diesel and Model DD

Model 40 Diesel tractors saw first light in 1935 and a year earlier as the Model 35 Diesel. Sometime later in 1935 this became the Model DD Cletrac. Production under this designation continued into 1936. Eventually this model became known as the Oliver-Cletrac. Power came from a Hercules Model DRXH engine.

Nebraska Test Data

Model: Cletrac Model 40 Diesel

Test No. 235

Date Tested: June 13 to June 24, 1935

Not rated by the manufacturer, this tractor had the highest permissible ratings of 45.89 drawbar and 57.55 belt hp. Three forward speeds of 1.8, 3.0, and 4.3 mph were provided, with the 10-hour rated drawbar test run in second gear. At a load of 46.14 hp, the "40" pulled a load of 5,943 lbs. at 2.91 mph and achieved a fuel economy of 12.39 hp-hours per gallon of "dieseline" fuel, weighing 6.99 lbs. per gallon. With an output of 46.83 hp, the "40" made its maximum pull of 11,134 lbs. in low gear while moving at a speed of 1.58 mph. At rated belt load of 57.79 hp this tractor attained an economy of 14.12 hp-hours per gallon, with a slightly diminished economy of 13.14 at maximum load of 63.64 hp. Standard equipment included a Hercules six-cylinder diesel engine rated at 1,200 rpm. Using an I-head design, this engine carried a 4-3/8 x 5-1/4-inch bore and stroke. Also included was an American Bosch fuel system. Total tractor weight was 12,150 lbs.

Cletrac Model 80

The Model 80 Cletrac had its beginnings as the Cletrac 50-60, built from 1930 to 1932. In 1932 the Model 80 appeared and stayed in the line until 1936. This big crawler had a six-cylinder Hercules engine with a 5-3/4 x 6-inch bore and stroke for over 100 belt hp.

Cletrac Model E crawler

Cletrac Model E crawlers first came out in 1934. They were built in several different track widths and were especially designed for farm and field work. In 1938 the Model E was streamlined and this dramatically changed its external appearance. Production of various E-Series crawlers continued until 1940.

Nebraska Test Data

Model: Cletrac Model E

Test No. 261

Date Tested: June 16 to July 9, 1936

Three forward speeds of 2-1/8, 2-3/4, and 4 mph were built into the Cletrac Model E tractor. As in previous tests, a Hercules engine was standard equipment, specifically for the Model E. It was a four-cylinder L-head design-rated at 1,300 rpm and using a 4 x 4-1/2-inch bore and stroke. This engine was equipped with an American Bosch MJB4A magneto, Tillotson PIB carburetor, and a Vortox air cleaner. Operating weight was 6,100 lbs. During 59 hours of engine running time, no repairs or adjustments were noted. Test H for rated drawbar load was made in second gear, and with an output of 16.48 hp the Model E pulled 2,435 lbs. at 2.54 mph with a slippage of 5.5 percent and a fuel economy of 5.18 hp-hours per gallon. Test G for operating maximum load was made in all three forward gears, but in low gear a maximum pull of 3,867 lbs. was achieved at a speed of 1.84 mph and with an output of 19.01 drawbar hp. Test C for operating maximum brake load indicated 28.3 hp with an efficiency of 9.27 hp-hours per gallon, compared to 8.83 at rated load (Test D) of 25.97 hp.

Cletrac BG and BD tractors

Nebraska Test Data

Model: Cletrac Model BG

Test No. 259

Date Tested: June 16 to July 10, 1936

Under Test C for operating maximum load, the Cletrac BG delivered 38.42 brake hp, and yielded an economy of 8.81 hp-hours per gallon. Test D, at a rated load of 35.03 brake hp recorded a slightly lower economy figure of 8.55. Three forward speeds of 1.8, 2.625, and 3.5

mph were featured. Test H for rated drawbar load at 23.03 hp gave a pull of 3,309 lbs. at 2.61 mph, slippage of 1.85 percent, and an economy of 6.13 hp-hours per gallon. A maximum pull of 6,131 lbs. occurred in the low gear maximum test at a speed of 1.66 mph, and slippage of 8.54 percent, with a maximum operating hp of 27.2 noted. Total weight was 8,686 lbs. During 65 hours of running time, it was necessary to clean and polish part of the governor mechanism to restore its action. Otherwise, no repairs or adjustments were noted. The BG was equipped with a Hercules six-cylinder L-head engine. Rated at 1,400 rpm, it used a 3-3/4 x 4-1/4-inch bore and stroke. Accessory items included a Delco-Remy electrical system, Hercules governor, and Vortox air cleaner, plus a Tillotson Y8C carburetor.

Nebraska Test Data

Model: Cletrac Model BD
Test No. 288
Date Tested: September 16 to October 2, 1937

Test D for rated load indicated a fuel economy of 12.7 hp-hours per gallon with an output of 37.65 brake hp. Economy slipped to 12.17 at a maximum load of 41.97 brake hp. The BD was equipped with a Hercules six-cylinder I-head diesel engine. Rated at 1,530 rpm, it used a 3-1/2 x 4-1/2-inch bore and stroke. A Bosch fuel system was featured, as was a Bosch vacuum governor. Also included were three forward speeds of 1.8, 2.625, and 3.5 mph. Second gear was used for Test H. This test indicated a fuel economy of 9.68 hp-hours per gallon with an output of 26.86 drawbar hp. Weighing in at 9,200 lbs., the BD made a maximum pull of 7,537 lbs. in low gear, or nearly 82 percent of its own weight. This test, like all others, contained voluminous data regarding ambient air temperature, coolant temperature, and barometric pressure during each test.

Nebraska Test Data

Model: Cletrac Model BD
Test No. 235
Date Tested: August 10 to August 30, 1939

Weighing in at 9,500 lbs. the Cletrac BD featured three forward speeds of 1.81, 2.64, and 3.46 mph. Second gear was selected for Test H. Results of this test include a fuel economy of 10.98 hp-hours per gallon of diesel fuel, along with a pull of 4.136 lbs. at 2.61 mph, slippage of 1.81 percent, and an output of 28.83 rated drawbar hp. Test G showed a maximum low gear pull of 7,530 lbs. at 1.55 mph and an output of 31.15 hp. The BD tractor was equipped with a Hercules six-cylinder I-head diesel engine. Rated at 1,400 rpm, it carried a 3-3/4 x 4-1/2-inch bore and stroke. Also included was a Bosch fuel injection system, along with a Timken governor and Vortox air cleaner. At the end of the drawbar tests it was observed that two track pins had worked out approximately one-half inch, but otherwise, no repairs or adjustments were recorded during 45 hours of engine running time. Belt hp tests indicate a rated 40.67 hp per Test D. This test also indicated a fuel economy of 13.73 hp-hours per gallon. A slightly diminished economy figure of 13.12 was recorded in Test C-maximum output in this test was 45.37 brake hp.

Cletrac CG tractor

The first Cletrac CG tractor was built in 1936. It was a successor to the Model 35. Capable of nearly 46 drawbar hp, the CG weighed almost six tons. This model was built into 1942.

Cletrac Model D-Series crawler

Nebraska Test Data

Model: Cletrac Model CG
Test No. 258
Date Tested: June 16 to June 24, 1936

Weighing in at 11,800 lbs., the Cletrac CG crawler tractor featured three forward speeds of 1.87, 3.05, and 4.44 mph. Test H used second gear, and at a rated 32.31 drawbar hp the CG delivered a fuel economy of 5.63 hp-hours per gallon, along with a pull of 3,986 lbs. at 3.04 mph and slippage of 1.28 percent. The low gear maximum trial recorded 40.94 hp with a pull of 8,387 lbs. at 1.83 mph. Cletrac equipped the CG with a Hercules six-cylinder L-head engine with a 4-1/4 x 4-1/2-inch bore and stroke. Rated at 1,450 rpm, it also featured an American Bosch MJB6A magneto, Tillotson Y7B carburetor, Hercules governor, and a Vortox air cleaner. Operating weight was 11,800 lbs. No repairs or adjustments were noted during the 47 hours of running time. Test D for rated brake load at 46.03 hp yielded a fuel economy of 7.76 hp-hours per gallon. An improved economy figure of 8.13 appeared at operating maximum load under Test C of 50.07 hp.

Cletrac Model D-Series crawler

Nebraska Test Data

Model: Cletrac Model CG

Test No. 289

Date Tested: September 16 to October 4, 1937

Battery ignition using a Delco-Remy distributor was standard equipment on the Cletrac CG tractor. Also featured was a Tillotson Y7B carburetor, Hercules governor, and Vortox air cleaner. Cletrac embodied this equipment in a Hercules six-cylinder L-head engine rated at 1,565 rpm and using a 4-1/4 x 4-1/2-inch bore and stroke. Weighing 11,700 lbs., the CG also featured three forward speeds of 1.87, 3.05, and 4.44 mph. Second gear was used for the 10-hour rated drawbar load test, known after 1937 as Test H. At 33.98 hp the CG produced a fuel economy of 6.6 hp-hours per gallon, pulling a 4,198 lb. load at 3.04 mph. Slippage in this test came to 0.99 percent. A maximum pull of 9,385 lbs. was achieved in low gear. With an output of 45.79 hp the CG managed this load at 1.83 mph and slippage of 2.29 percent. Test D for rated brake load indicated an economy of 7.6 hp-hours per gallon at a load of 47.28 hp. Economy rose slightly to 8.02 at a 52.6 hp maximum load. No repairs or adjustments were noted during 49 hours of running time.

Model D-Series Cletrac crawlers first came onto the market in 1937. That year the DG (gasoline) crawler appeared, followed the next season with the DD (diesel) crawler. Production of the DG and its variations continued until 1955, while the DD model remained in production until 1958.

Cletrac F-Series crawlers

Beginning in 1936 the F-Series crawlers were built, including the FG gasoline model and the FD diesel tractor. This series replaced the earlier Model 80 tractors. The FG was equipped with a huge Hercules HXE six-cylinder engine with a 5-3/4 x 6-inch bore and stroke. At full load, the engine burned gasoline at 12 gph.

Cletrac Model HG tractors first appeared in 1939 and were built until 1950. The HG was equipped with a Hercules IXA engine capable of about 20 belt hp. This small crawler weighed only 3,500 lbs. After Oliver bought out the Cletrac line in 1944 the HG tractor continued in the line for several more years.

Cletrac Model HG tractor

An innovative development was the rubber-track version of the HG crawler tractors. Cletrac introduced this design in the early 1940s, but due to problems with the rubber tracks, the company retrofitted virtually all of these tractors with steel tracks.

Cletrac HG (Rubber Track Version)

Nebraska Test Data

Model: Cletrac Model HG

Test No. 324

Date Tested: August 12 to August 30, 1939

From all appearances, the Cletrac HG crawler tractor used the same Hercules 3 x 4-inch engine as the Cletrac General GG tractor. As with the GG, no repairs or adjustments were noted for the HG during its 64 hours of engine operating time. Three forward speeds of 2, 3, and 5 mph were built into the HG. Using second gear, it delivered a fuel economy of 7.28 hp-hours per gallon in Test H. This test also indicated an output of 11.14 rated drawbar hp while pulling a 1,415 lb. load at 2.95 mph and recorded a slippage of 4.42 percent. Test G indicated a low gear maximum pull of 2,800 lbs. for this 3,510 lb. tractor, or nearly 80 percent of its own operating weight. Test C for operating maximum load showed 8.85 hp-hours per gallon at 19.36 brake hp. Economy fared slightly better at the rated 17.59 belt hp coming in at 8.93 hp-hours per gallon.

Cletrac Model GG General tractor

In the 1939-1942 period, Cleveland Tractor Company produced its Model GG General tractor. This wheeled version was fairly popular, but because of World War II, production was suspended. Oliver bought out the Cletrac line in 1944, and after the war was over, production of the General never resumed. This little tractor used the same engine as the HG crawler and was capable of 19 belt hp. In 1939 its retail price was $595.

Nebraska Test Data

Model: Cletrac Model GG
Test No. 323
Date Tested: August 10 to August 30, 1939

In a radical departure from its usual tracklayer designs, Cleveland Tractor Co. developed this interesting tricycle model. Three forward speeds of 2-1/4, 3-1/2, and 6 mph were provided. Using second gear the GG emerged from Test H with 10.38 rated drawbar hp, along with an economy of 7.19 hp-hours per gallon. It pulled 1,172 lbs. at 3.32 mph. Test G indicated a maximum pull of 1,699 lbs. in first gear. At a speed of 1.86 mph and slippage of 19.65 percent, an output of 8.44 drawbar hp was recorded. Specifications included a Hercules four-cylinder L-head engine with a 3 x 4-inch bore and stroke, along with a rated speed of 1,400 rpm on the drawbar and 1,700 rpm in the belt. Among the accessory items were a Wico C1113B magneto, Tillotson YC2A carburetor, and a Hercules-Handy governor. Operating weight was 3,115 lbs. Standard equipment also included 9 x 24-inch rear tires and 5.50 x 16-inch front rubber. Test C for maximum belt load ended with an economy of 8.79 hp-hours per gallon against 19.29 brake hp. Test D indicated a rated load of 17.42 hp with fuel economy of 8.20 hp-hours per gallon.

Cluff Ammunition Company

TORONTO, ONTARIO

This firm is listed as a tractor builder in the 1919 trade directories, but no further information is available.

C. O. D. Tractor Company

MINNEAPOLIS, MINNESOTA

Albert O. Espe established a machine shop at Crookston, Minnesota in 1898, and built his first tractor there in 1907. In 1909 the Crookston Mfg. Company was organized to build tractors, but in 1916 the company moved to Minneapolis.

C.O.D. 1916 model

The 1916 model shown here had a 13-25 hp rating. It was equipped with a two-cylinder engine with a 6-1/2 x 7-inch bore and stroke.

C.O.D. Model B tractor

The Model B tractor appeared in 1919. While it had the same 13-25 hp rating as the earlier model, several noticeable changes were made, such as the use of a cellular radiator. A. O. Espe was responsible for numerous tractor designs, notably the "Universal" that was built by Union Iron Works and others. Eventually this design was bought out by Rumely and marketed for a time as its GasPull tractor. Production of the C. O. D. tractors ended in 1919.

COLLECTOR VALUES	1	2	3	4
MODEL B	$26,000	$20,000	$15,000	$8,000

Coates Mfg. Company

LOMA LINDA, CALIFORNIA

For 1948, Coates offered its Little Giant Model A garden tractor. It was equipped with a Lauson RSC single-cylinder engine using a 2 x 1-7/8-inch bore and stroke and capable of 1-1/2 hp. Specific production data has not been located.

COLLECTOR VALUES	1	2	3	4
LITTLE GIANT MODEL A	$350	$250	$150	$75

Coates Little Giant Model A

Cockshutt Farm Equipment Company Ltd.

BRANTFORD, ONTARIO

James G. Cockshutt, a Canadian merchant, started the Brantford Plow Works in 1877. The company was incorporated as the Cockshutt Plow Company in 1882. It became a success in the farm implement business. In the late 1920s the company begain selling Allis-Chalmers and United tractors, but the arrangement was not a satisfactory one. The company then switched to selling Oliver tractors. The tractors—including the 60, 70, 80, 90, and 99 models—were very popular. Many were sold painted in a variation of Oliver green, while others wore the Cockshutt red-and-cream colors. After World War II, Cockshutt started selling its own very popular line of tractors.

Cockshutt Model 30 tractor

Cockshutt Model 30 tractors made their first appearance in 1946 with production running until 1956. The Cockshutt 30G gasoline model used a four-cylinder Buda engine with a 3-7/16 x 4-1/8-inch bore and stroke. A Buda four-cylinder, 153-cid engine was used in the 30D diesel model. This tractor was also marketed in the U.S. as the Model E-3 Co-op tractor and as the Farmcrest 30.

Cockshutt Model 40

Nebraska Test Data

Model: Cockshutt Model 30

Test No. 382

Date Tested: May 21 to June 3, 1947

The Cockshutt 30 was the first Canadian tractor tested at Nebraska. Specifications included a Buda four cylinder I-head engine. Rated at 1,650 rpm, it carried a 3-7/16 x 4-1/8-inch bore and stroke. Also included were 11-38-inch rear and 5.50-16-inch front tires. Bare weight was 3,609 lbs. The throttle lever broke during the varying load tests, otherwise no repairs or adjustments were noted during 58 hours of engine operating time. Advertised speeds of 2.5, 3.6, 5, and 10 mph were standard, with second gear being used for Test H. At a rated load of 21.68 drawbar hp the Model 30 pulled 2,122 lbs. at 3.83 mph with a slippage of 3.6 percent and delivered a fuel economy of 9.49 hp-hours per gallon. A low-gear maximum pull of 3,743 lbs. at 2.36 mph was noted in Test G. Under an operating maximum load of 30.28 belt hp this tractor had a fuel economy of 11.43 hp-hours per gallon, compared to an economy figure of 10.98 when under the Test D rated load of 28.10 belt hp.

COLLECTOR VALUES	1	2	3	4
MODEL 30 (FARMCREST 30)	$3,650	$2,000	$800	$325

Cockshutt Model 20

Model 20 Cockshutt tractors were built between 1952 and 1958. The Model 20 was available with the adjustable-width axle shown here or a conventional tricycle front. Model 20 tractors were built only with gasoline engines. It was sold in the U.S. as the Co-op E-2 and the Black Hawk 20.

Nebraska Test Data

Model: Cockshutt Model 20

Test No. 474

Date Tested: June 16 to June 24, 1952

The Cockshutt 20 featured a Continental four-cylinder L-head engine. Rated at 1,800 rpm, it used a 3-3/16 x 4-3/8-inch bore and stroke with a displacement of 140 cubic inches. No repairs or adjustments were noted for this tractor during 43 hours of engine operation. Using advertised speeds of 2-1/2, 3-3/4, 5-1/4, and 13-1/4 mph, the Cockshutt 20 weighed in at 2,813 lbs., with another 839 lbs. added to each rear wheel during Tests F, G, and H. Third gear was used for the 10-hour run of Test H. Under a rated drawbar load of 20.24 hp, the 20 pulled 1,459 lbs. at 5.2 mph with a slippage of 4.48 percent. Fuel economy was noted at 9.17 hp-hours per gallon. A low-gear maximum pull of 3,266 lbs. emanated from Test G. Maximum engine torque peaked at 185.5 lbs.-ft. at an engine speed of 996 rpm. Test D, under a rated load of 25.94 hp, saw a fuel economy of 10.46 hp-hours per gallon, with this figure climbing to 10.68 under a Test C operating maximum load of 27.4 belt hp.

COLLECTOR VALUES	1	2	3	4
MODEL 20 (BLACK HAWK 20)	$4,300	$3,000	$1,400	$450

The Cockshutt 40 gasoline tractor was built from 1949 to 1957. This model used a six-cylinder Buda engine with the same bore and stroke dimensions as the four-cylinder Cockshutt 30. The diesel model carried a Buda six-cylinder engine of the same displacement as the gasoline model. Cockshutt 40D diesel tractors were built between 1950 and 1957. The 40D was built primarily for the Canadian market, but was available in the U.S. as the Black Hawk 40.

Nebraska Test Data

Model: Cockshutt Model 40

Test No. 442

Date Tested: June 12 to June 17, 1950

During 49 hours of engine operating time, no repairs or adjustments were noted for the Cockshutt 40. This was the first tractor tested at Nebraska with a live PTO system. Also featured was a Buda six-cylinder I-head engine rated at 1,650 rpm and using a 3-7/8 x 4-1/8-inch bore and stroke, for a 230-cubic inch displacement. Featured were forward speeds of 1.6, 2.7, 3.7, 5.25, 6.25, and 12 mph. As presented this tractor weighed 5,305 lbs., with 1,533 lbs. of ballast per wheel being used for a portion of the drawbar testing. At a rated drawbar load of 30.36 hp, the Cockshutt 40 delivered a fuel economy of 9.72 hp-hours per gallon. Test H also indicated a pull of 2,187 lbs. at 5.21 mph with a slippage of 3.53 percent. Test G evoked a low-gear maximum pull of 5,538 lbs. at 1.38 mph. At a Test D rated load of 38.68 belt hp, fuel economy rested at 10.91 hp-hours per gallon, climbing slightly to 11.33 under a Test C operating maximum load of 41.44 belt hp.

COLLECTOR VALUES	1	2	3	4
MODEL 40 (BLACK HAWK 40)	$3,600	$2,300	$1,400	$425

Cockshutt Golden Eagle tractor

Cockshutt Golden Eagle tractors were built for the U.S. market, while the identical 40D4 tractor was built for Canada. These tractors were built only in a diesel version and were manufacturered from 1955 to 1957.

COLLECTOR VALUES	1	2	3	4
GOLDEN EAGLE	$4,200	$3,500	$1,900	$450

Cockshutt Model 35 and Golden Arrow tractors

Model 35 tractors were built from 1955 through 1957 for sale in Canada, while the Golden Arrow was made only in 1957 for U.S. distribution. While similar, the Golden Arrow was not the same as the Model 35. Both tractors shared the same engine, but other parts are different. The Golden Arrow was essentially a "550" with "35" sheet metal. It was also marketed under the Black Hawk brand. The engine was a GO-198 Hercules. There was a derivative of the Model 35 called the "35L." Production of the 35L was low. Several have been seen in Canada and the Eastern U.S. They are a Model 35 with 28-inch tires on the back and a low-profile, non-arched standard front end. It appears that many were equipped with loaders and back hoes and were used for industrial applications. The engine was a GO-198 Hercules.

COLLECTOR VALUES	1	2	3	4
GOLDEN ARROW	$4,750	$4,000	$2,000	$625
MODEL 35	$4,000	$3,000	$1,400	$450

Cockshutt Model 50 tractor

Gasoline and diesel versions were available for the Cockshutt 50 tractors. This 50-hp tractor was made from 1952 to 1957. In addition, the same tractor was sold in the U.S. as the Co-op E-5 tractor.

Nebraska Test Data

Model: Cockshutt Model 50 Diesel

Test No. 487

Date Tested: October 29 to November 6, 1952

A Buda six-cylinder diesel engine of I-head design was featured in the Cockshutt 50 Diesel. Rated at 1,650 rpm, this engine had a 273-cubic inch displacement, with a bore and stroke of 3-3/4 x 4-1/8-inches. Advertised speeds of 1.52, 2.57, 3.53, 4.32, 5.95, and 9.85 mph came as standard design, with 14-34 rear and 7.50-16-inch front rubber also being included among the standard equipment. Weighing 6,163 lbs., this tractor received an additional 2,246 lbs. of weight on each rear wheel during Tests F, G and H. The latter test for rated drawbar hp was run in fourth gear. At a rated load of 35.74 hp, the 50 Diesel pulled 3,048 lbs. at 4.4 mph under a slippage of 7.68 percent. Fuel economy was pegged at 12.8 hp-hours per gallon of diesel fuel. A low-gear maximum pull of 6,319 lbs. at 1.45 mph was noted in Test G. Maximum engine torque measured at the dynamometer came to 338.6 lbs.-ft. with an engine speed of 1,152 rpm. Test D, run at a rated belt load of 44.45 hp yielded a fuel economy of 14.63 hp-hours per gallon. With the Test B & C, 100-percent maximum load run, it produced a fuel economy figure of 14.55. No repairs or adjustments were recorded during 44-1/2 hours of engine operating time.

Nebraska Test Data

Model: Cockshutt Model 50 (gasoline)

Test No. 488

Date Tested: October 29 to November 6, 1952

This tractor was also fitted with a six-cylinder Buda engine, with the same specifications noted above, but was equipped to burn gasoline. No repairs or adjustments were noted for this tractor during 46-1/2 hours of engine operating time. A maximum engine torque of 348.4 lbs.-ft. was recorded with an engine speed of 1,145 rpm. Test D revealed a fuel economy of 11.99 hp-hours per gallon under a rated belt load of 49.24 hp. At a Test C operating maximum load of 52.18 belt hp, fuel economy rose to 12.24 hp-hours per gallon. Although Test G was run in all forward gears at operating maximum drawbar load, low gear evoked a maximum pull of 6,463 lbs. at 1.4 mph. Fuel economy in Test H rested at 10.69 hp-hours per gallon, and this with a rated output of 38.78 drawbar hp. Test H also indicated a pull of 3,246 lbs. at 4.48 mph and slippage of 6.09 percent. This tractor had a bare weight of 6,041 lbs.

COLLECTOR VALUES	1	2	3	4
MODEL 50 (BLACK HAWK)	$4,100	$3,500	$2,000	$550

The new Cockshutt tractor line for 1958 included the 540 two-plow model shown here. This tractor featured a Continental four-cylinder, 162-cid engine plus a dual-range, six-speed transmission. Production continued until 1961.

COLLECTOR VALUES	1	2	3	4
MODEL 540	$4,400	$3,000	$2,000	$600

Cockshutt 540 two-plow model

Cockshutt 550 tractor

For 1958 the Cockshutt tractor line included this 550 model. Available in gasoline and diesel versions, it was equipped with a Hercules engine. Both the gasoline and diesel models were capable of about 35 belt hp.

Nebraska Test Data

Model: Cockshutt Model 550 Diesel

Test No. 681

Date Tested: November 12 to November 26, 1958

The Cockshutt 550 featured a Hercules four-cylinder diesel engine rated at 1,650 rpm. Using a 3-3/4 x 4-1/2-inch bore and stroke, it had a displacement of 198-cubic inches. Also featured were six forward speeds of 1.88, 2.5, 3.5, 4.88, 7, and 13.5 mph, along with 13-38-inch rear and 6.00-16-inch front tires. Although bare tractor weight was 5,695 lbs., this was augmented with 1,020 lbs. on each rear wheel during most of the drawbar testing. Test G, run in low gear, achieved a maximum pull of 6,544 lbs. at 1.7 mph and 14 percent slippage. Using third gear, the 10-hour run of Test H was made at a rated drawbar load of 27.17 hp. This test noted a pull of 2,706 lbs. at 3.77 mph and slippage of 4.15 percent. Drawbar fuel economy came in at 13.42 hp-hours per gallon of diesel fuel. No repairs or adjustments were noted during 39-1/2 hours of running time. Test D, made under a rated belt load of 34.22 hp, produced a fuel economy of 15.49 hp-hours per gallon of diesel fuel, and slipped to 15.14 at a 100-percent maximum belt load of 38.45 hp.

COLLECTOR VALUES	1	2	3	4
MODEL 550	$4,000	$3,000	$1,800	$550

A big Perkins four-cylinder diesel engine powered the Cockshutt 560 tractor. For the U. S. market this tractor was offered only in the diesel version, but was otherwise available with a four-cylinder 198-cid gasoline engine.

Cockshutt 1250 tractor

(Note: The early engine was a Perkins L4, similar to Golden Eagle. Later models used a Perkins 4-2700 engine, diesel only.) The 560 was rated at about 43 belt hp. Production ran from 1958 to 1961.

Cockshutt 560 tractor

Nebraska Test Data

Model: Cockshutt Model 560 Diesel

Test No. 682

Date Tested: November 10 to November 26, 1958

Weighing 7,295 lbs., the 560 Diesel featured 15-34-inch rear and 7.50-18-inch front tires. No ballast was used on the front wheels, but each rear wheel was burdened with 1,075 lbs. of additional weight during most of the drawbar testing. Also featured were six forward speeds ranging from 1.81 to 13.2 mph. Fourth gear was selected for the 10-hour run of Test H. At a rated drawbar load of 35.21 hp, a pull of 2,758 lbs. was recorded at 4.79 mph with 3.23 percent slippage. Fuel economy was posted at 15.16 hp-hours per gallon of diesel fuel. This tractor featured a four-cylinder Perkins Diesel engine rated at 1,650 rpm. Using a 4-1/4 x 4-3/4-inch bore and stroke, it had a displacement of 269.5-cubic inches. No repairs or adjustments were noted during 41 hours of running time. Test D, run at a rated belt load of 42.95 hp, indicated a fuel economy of 17.54 hp-hours per gallon. The economy figure rose to 17.73 at a 100-ercent maximum belt load of 48.42 hp.

COLLECTOR VALUES	1	2	3	4
MODEL 560	$4,200	$2,800	$1,800	$500

Cockshutt 570 tractor

Cockshutt 570 tractors were built from 1958 to 1960; for 1961 and 1962 they were available as the 570 Super Diesel. While sold mainly as a diesel tractor, particularly in the United States, this model was also available with a gasoline engine.

Coleman 10-20 tractor, 1917

Nebraska Test Data

Model: Cockshutt Model 570 Diesel

Test No. 683

Date Tested: November 12 to November 27, 1958

The Cockshutt 570 entered with a bare weight of 7,175 lbs. This tractor used 15-34 rear and 7.50-18 inch front tires. No added weight was placed on the front wheels, but each rear wheel was given an additional 2,090 during a majority of the drawbar tests. Six forward speeds ranging from 1.81 to 13.2 mph were featured, with fourth gear being used for the 10-hour run of Test H. This test, made at a rated load of 39.99 drawbar hp, saw a pull of 3,073 lbs. at 4.88 mph and 3.64 percent slippage. Fuel economy was posted at 13.36 hp-hours per gallon. Test G, run in low gear, achieved a maximum pull of 9,063 lbs. at 1.6 mph with 13.9 percent slippage. The 570 featured a Hercules six-cylinder diesel engine rated at 1,650 rpm. Using a 3-3/4 x 4-1/2-inch bore and stroke, it had a displacement of 298-cubic inches. No repairs or adjustments were noted during 63 hours of running time. At a Test D rated belt load of 53.9 hp, fuel economy came in at 15.65 hp-hours per gallon of diesel fuel. This figure slipped to 15.03 under a 100-percent maximum belt load of 60.84 hp.

COLLECTOR VALUES	1	2	3	4
MODEL 570	$4,600	$3,000	$2,200	$700
MODEL 570 SUPER	$6,500	$3,100	$3,000	$800

White Motors Corporation bought out Cockshutt in 1962 and with the purchase production of Cockshutt tractors ended. For a time, Oliver (another White acquisition) built tractors with red paint and Cockshutt decals, but they were nevertheless Oliver tractors. One example is the Cockshutt 1250 shown here—actually an Oliver 1250. In addition, White bought Fiat tractors and sold them as the 411R and 411 RG Cockshutt tractors from 1961 to 1965.

Coleman Tractor Corporation

KANSAS CITY, MISSOURI

During 1917 Coleman tractors appeared. Rated at 10 drawbar and 20 belt hp, the Coleman distinguished itself with a worm gear final drive system. A Climax four-cylinder engine was featured.

See: Farmer's Mfg. Company

Coleman Model B 16-30 tractor

By 1919 the Coleman tractor had been remodeled and gained a new rating of 16 drawbar and 30 belt hp. In this model a Climax four-cylinder engine was used; it had a 5 x 6-1/2-inch bore and stroke. Production of the Coleman ended in 1920 and the company was acquired by Welborn Corporation at Kansas City. In 1921 the Coleman reappeared for a short time from Farmers Mfg. Company, also of Kansas City.

Nebraska Test Data

Model: Coleman Model B 16-30

Test No. 35

Date Tested: July 16 to July 21, 1920

A maximum drawbar pull of 2,690 lbs. was recorded for the Coleman 16-30. Travelling at a speed of 2.16 mph, this gave an equivalent of 15.47 hp on the drawbar, just slightly below the manufacturer's rating. Kerosene was used throughout the test, and possibly if gasoline had been the chosen fuel, performance might have been somewhat better. Except for problems with spark plug fouling, Nebraska test engineers noted little in the way of repairs or deficiencies. Weighing 5,100 lbs., the 16-30 carried a four-cylinder vertical, L-head engine with a 5 x 6-1 /2-inch bore and stroke. Rated speed varied from 800 to 900 rpm. Two forward speeds of 2 and 3 mph were provided. Regular equipment included a Stromberg carburetor and Splitdorf Model 448 magneto. Only 5.34 hp-hours per gallon were recorded in the rated brake hp tests, with consumption totaling 5.67 gph. On maximum load, the Coleman tractor developed only a tiny fraction more power than the 30.27 recorded in the rated load test. Coolant temperatures ranged from 186 to 212 degrees F. throughout the 32 hours of running time.

Columbus Machine Company

COLUMBUS, OHIO

Columbus Machine Company began building gasoline engines in the late 1890s. In 1905 the company is listed as a manufacturer of "gasoline traction engines" and likely mounted its engines to the Morton Traction Trucks. Nothing further is known of the Columbus traction engines, but in 1911 the company began building the Eastman Cable Tractor designed by C. J. Eastman of Washington, D.C. This venture lasted only a short time.

Columbus Tractor Company

COLUMBUS, OHIO

Columbus Tractor Company Farmer Boy tractor

This company was organized in 1918 from the ashes of McIntyre Tractor Company, also of Columbus. The latter had been organized to build the Farmer Boy tractor in 1915. It used a Waukesha four-cylinder engine with a 3-3/4 x 5-1/4-inch bore and stroke. Columbus Tractor Co. was apparently out of business by 1920.

Combination Saw & Tractor Company

DENTON, TEXAS

Superior Combination Saw and Tractor

In the late 1940s the Superior Combination Saw & Tractor appeared, remaining on the market at least into the early 1950s. Specific production data has not been located. The Superior was intended to be used as a felling or buck saw, as shown here, and the saw could be removed so that the tractor could be adapted to other uses.

Comet Automobile Company

DECATUR, ILLINOIS

Comet 15-30 tractor

Comet Automobile Co. began business in 1917 as an automobile manufacturer. In 1919 the company began building the Comet 15-30 tractor. On the automotive side, the company had fairly good sales, but got the fever to expand and by late in 1920 was in serious financial trouble. About this time the Comet 15-30 tractor production run came to an end and in 1922 the entire factory was sold piece-by-piece at auction.

Common Sense Tractor Company

MINNEAPOLIS, MINNESOTA

Common Sense Tractor Co. was incorporated in 1915 to build a unique three-wheel tractor. The tractor was designed by H. W. Adams who has been identified with several different tractor designs originating in the Minneapolis area.

Common Sense 1915 model

The original model was rated at 15 drawbar and 25 belt hp provided by a four-cylinder engine.

Common Sense V-8 model

Late in 1916 the Common Sense tractor was modified and fitted with a Herschell-Spillman V-8 engine. This was the first tractor ever equipped with a V-8. It had a 3-1/4 x 5-inch bore and stroke for 20 drawbar and 40 belt hp. By late 1919 the Common Sense was being offered by Farm Power & Sales Company of Minneapolis; in another year it disappeared from view.

Commonwealth Tractor Company

CHICAGO, ILLINOIS

An advertisement running about 1918 makes reference to Commonwealth's Thorobred tractor, calling it "America's Pedigreed Tractor." The Thorobred people implored interested parties to write for further information. Beyond this, no additional data has been located.

Community Industries

SULLIVAN, ILLINOIS

The company was started in 1946 and soon developed the walk-behind George Garden tractor, which was supported by a full line of tools. By the late 1950s they also offered the Earth-Bird garden tiller, Snow-Bird snowblower, and Lawn-Bird riding mowers. They remained in business until 1967 when purchased by Yard-Man (today MTD) of Jackson, Michigan.

Community Mfg. Company

LOS ANGELES, CALIFORNIA

See: Allen-Burbank Motor Company

Allen 10-20

The Allen 10-20 was essentially the same tractor as had been formerly built by Allen-Burbank Motor Company. However, the tractor shown here is somewhat different in its exterior appearance, particularly with the addition of a totally enclosed engine compartment and enclosed rear wheels.

Allen Model A 10-20

Allen Model A 10-20 tractors were built during 1923 and 1924 by Community Mfg. Company. They used a Continental four-cylinder engine with a 4-1/8 x 5-1/4-inch bore and stroke. Operating speed was 950 rpm. The Allen 10-20 weighed 3,400 lbs..

Connors Hoe & Tool Company

COLUMBUS, OHIO

This company appeared at various times in the late 1940s and early 1950s as a garden tractor manufacturer, but no further information has been found.

Consolidated Gasoline Engine Company

NEW YORK, NEW YORK

Shortly before 1920 this firm came out with its Do-It-All garden tractor. Rated at 6 belt hp, it was capable of pulling a one-bottom plow, as shown here. Apparently this machine remained on the market for only a few years.

COLLECTOR VALUES	1	2	3	4
DO-IT-ALL GARDEN TRACTOR	$1,250	$650	$450	$250

Continental Cultor Co.

SPRINGFIELD, OHIO

CULTOR

Cultor logo

Continental began building its "Cultor" in 1925. The company endured for at least a few years, but vanished from the trade directories by 1929. The Cultor was designed as an all-around tractor, and to its favor, it was powered by a Ford Model T engine. Since these were in abundance at the time, engine repairs were relatively simple and inexpensive.

Nebraska Test Data

Model: Continental Cultor

Test No. 138

Date Tested: August 6 to August 17, 1927

With a single forward speed of 3 mph, the Continental Cultor developed 4.93 drawbar hp on the rated load test, pulling a 591 lb. load at 3.13 mph. At maximum drawbar load, 8.41 hp was developed, pulling 1,050 lbs. at 3.01 mph. Slippage in this test was only 11.7 percent, even though total tractor weight was only 1,840 lbs. Gasoline powered the Cultor throughout

Cook's Auto Thresher

the test, which required about 25 hours of running time. No brake hp tests were made since this tractor was not equipped with a belt pulley. The four-cylinder, vertical, L-head engine carried a 3-3/4 x 4-inch bore and stroke with a rated speed of 1,050 rpm. Ignition was the standard Ford Model T style, as was the cooling system, radiator and radiator shell and support. A Holley carburetor also came as standard equipment. There was no governor or air cleaner. Except for a broken main drive chain, few problems occurred during the test.

Continental Tractor Company

CONTINENTAL, OHIO

In 1918 this company was organized and incorporated for $100,000. The following year a patent application was filed by O. L. Plettner and W. H. Lowe for the tractor plow shown here. A patent was granted on this application under No. 1,378,196 of May 17, 1921. Meanwhile, Continental attempted to interest other companies in manufacturing the new design, including the then-powerful Moline Plow Company—apparently with little success.

Continental tractor plow

Convertible Tractor Corporation

ST. PAUL, MINNESOTA

Charles F. Megow was an experimental engineer with Ford Motor Company. In 1916 he developed the Megow Convertible Tractor. This was a conversion device that used an automobile engine and chassis, together with suitable traction wheels and gearing. The conversion unit was priced at $325. By 1918 the Me-Go farm tractor was developed, but despite considerable efforts to launch this new tractor, it never reached any sort of production level and disappeared shortly after it was announced.

Megow Convertible Tractor

A.E. Cook

ODEBOLDT, IOWA

A.E. Cook designed and built a motor plow in 1909, ostensibly with ideas of marketing the new machine. The plans did not materialize and no further information has been located.

Herman Cook

SIOUX CITY, IOWA

In 1908 Herman Cook advertised "Cook's Auto Thresher." While not truly a farm tractor in the usual sense of the term, this self-contained threshing machine represented a major forward step in threshing machinery. A separate tractor was not required, nor was it necessary to have a long and troublesome drive belt between tractor and thresher. The idea did not catch on and the Cook lasted only a short time.

Cook & Roberts Machine & Equipment Company

OREGON CITY, OREGON

Track-O-Matic garden tractor

In 1950 this firm began building its Track-O-Matic garden tractors, with a 1953 model being shown here. Apparently the firm did not survive past 1955, since it disappeared from the trade directories by that time. The Track-O-Matic was equipped with a 6 hp Wisconsin AEH engine with a 23.0-cubic inch displacement.

Cooper Engineering Corporation

SUNLAND, CALIFORNIA

About 1947 Cooper began building the Moto-Mule garden tractors. The Model RG-75 was a small outfit powered by a Gladden 75 single-cylinder air-cooled engine with a 2.875 x 3.000-inch bore and stroke. The Moto-Mule disappears from trade listings after 1953.

Co-Operative Mfg. Company

BATTLE CREEK, MICHIGAN

With various companies involved, the history of the Co-op tractor is difficult to untangle. The Co-op tractor line owed its design to Dent Parrett; he had formerly been with the Parrett Tractor Company at Chicago. The original Parrett design went all the way back to 1913. Parrett continued his tractor design work after the company folded about 1922. In 1937 Parrett Tractors appears at Benton Harbor, Michigan, with a Parrett 6 model. In May 1938 Duplex Printing Press Company at Battle Creek was dismissed as the manufacturer of the three Co-op tractor models. In its place came the Co-Operative Mfg. Company, also at Battle Creek.

Co-op No. 1

The Co-op No. 1 shown here weighed only 3,380 lbs. It was powered by a Waukesha four-cylinder engine with a 3-1/4 x 4-inch bore and stroke. Electric starting and lighting came as standard equipment.

COLLECTOR VALUES	1	2	3	4
NO. 1	–	$3,500	$2,300	$1,000

Co-op No. 2

The Co-op No. 2 shown here was a standard-tread design that used a Chrysler Industrial six-cylinder engine; it was built with a 3-1/8 x 4-3/8-inch bore and stroke.

COLLECTOR VALUES	1	2	3	4
NO. 2	–	$3,000	$1,800	$800

Co-Op No. 3 tractors for 1938 were built with a six-cylinder Chrysler Industrial engine using a 3-3/8 x 4-1/2-inch bore and stroke. Weighing 5,000 lbs., this tractor featured electric starting and lighting. The Co-op tractors were also capable of road speeds up to 25 mph. References to the Co-op tractors will also be found under: Arthurdale Farm Equipment Corporation, Arthurdale, West Virginia; Farmers Union Central Exchange, St. Paul, Minnesota; and National Farm Machinery Co-operatives, Shelbyville, Indiana.

Co-op No. 3

COLLECTOR VALUES	1	2	3	4
NO. 3	–	$3,000	$1,800	$800

Corbitt Company

HENDERSON, NORTH CAROLINA

Richard Corbitt organized the Corbitt Automobile Co. in 1913. Eventually the company began a successful run of building heavy trucks. About 1948 the company came out with the Corbitt tractor. The G-50 model used a gasoline engine, the K-50 had a kerosene manifold, and the D-50 was a diesel model. All offered about 31 PTO hp. After Richard Corbitt retired in 1952 the company struggled. During the 1956 and '57 period the company attempted an unsuccessful revival and Corbitt tractors made a brief reappearance. Corbitt was out of business by 1958.

Corbitt tractor

Nebraska Test Data

Model: Corbitt G-50

Test No. 422

Date Tested: August 29 to September 3, 1949

With a base weight of 3,543 lbs., the G-50 featured 11-3F rear and 6.00-16-inch front rubber tires. During Tests F, G, and H an additional 1,067 lbs. of ballast was added to each rear wheel. Advertised speeds of 2.5, 3.6, 5, and 10 mph were available in the G-50, with second gear used for the 10-hour run of Test H. Under a rated drawbar load of 24.58 hp, this tractor pulled 2,205 lbs. at 4.18 mph with slippage of 5.8 percent. Fuel economy was noted at 8.7

Corn Belt tractor

hp-hours per gallon. A low-gear maximum pull of 3,566 lbs. was recorded in Test G, and this at a speed of 2.65 mph with 13.82 percent slippage. The G-50 featured a LeRoi four-cylinder I-head engine with a 3-3/4 x 4-inch bore and stroke, along with a rated speed of 1,800 rpm. Also included was a Delco-Remy electrical system and a Zenith 62AJ9 carburetor. Except for minor problems, no repairs or adjustments were noted during 43 hours of engine operating time. Under a Test C operating maximum load of 33.83 belt hp, fuel economy was noted at 10.18 hp-hours per gallon, compared to a figure of 9.71 recorded under a Test D rated load of 31 hp.

Corn Belt Motor Company

WATERLOO, IOWA

M&K Farm-Auto

During 1915 the M & K Farm-Auto was developed and the company attempted raising the capital for full-scale production the following year. The M & K Farm-Auto was fully equipped with Hyatt roller bearings; this was a great advantage over many competitive models of the day with plain babbitt bearings. Rated as a 12-24 model, it used a four-cylinder engine with a 3-3/4 x 5 inch bore and stroke. Unfortunately, the fund-raising efforts failed and little more is known of the M & K Farm-Auto.

Corn Belt Tractor Company

MINNEAPOLIS, MINNESOTA

Corn Belt announced a new tractor in 1914. Rated at 15 belt hp, it utilized a front-wheel-drive system. The engine, drivewheel and transmission were all a single unit. This permitted the tractor to turn in a four-foot radius. Little else is known about the Corn Belt tractor.

Craig Tractor Company

CLEVELAND, OHIO

Incorporated in 1918 for $35,000 the Craig Tractor Company remained in business until about 1922. The company's 5,500 lb. tractor was powered by a Beaver four-cylinder engine with a 4-3/4 x 6-inch bore and stroke. The tractor sold for $2,385 in 1920. Apparently, Craig built only this single model rated at 15 drawbar and 25 belt hp.

Craig Tractor Company logo

Crockett Bros.

STOCKTON, CALIFORNIA

See: Harris Mfg. Co.

Power Herse four-wheel-drive

The January 10, 1952 issue of Farm Implement News advertises the Power Horse four-wheel-drive tractor from Crockett Brothers. Aside from this advertisement, little else is known of the company and its tractor manufacturing efforts.

Crookston Mfg. Company

CROOKSTON, MINNESOTA

See: C. O. D. Tractor Company.

Crosley Motors

CINCINNATI, OHIO

During 1950 and 1951 Crosley marketed its Farm-O-Road combination vehicle. It was a tractor, a truck, a mobile power plant and a road vehicle. Numerous farm implements were designed especially for the Farm-O-Road, with a front-mounted mower shown here.

COLLECTOR VALUES	1	2	3	4
FARM-O-ROAD	–	$6,250	–	–

Crosley Farm-O-Road combination vehicle

Crown Iron Works

MINNEAPOLIS, MINNESOTA

This firm is listed as a tractor manufacturer in 1921, but no further information can be located.

Cultiller Corporation

NEW BRUNSWICK, NEW JERSEY

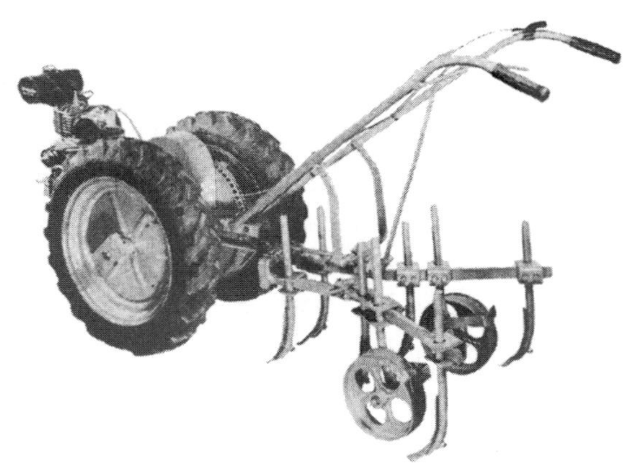

Cultiller garden tractor

The Cultiller garden tractor appeared in the late 1940s, probably about 1948. The company is listed in this business as late as 1953. Cultiller garden tractors were equipped with a Clinton single-cylinder engine. Various attachments were available.

COLLECTOR VALUES	1	2	3	4
CULTILLER GARDEN TRACTOR	$400	$250	$125	$50

Cultitractor Company

MINNEAPOLIS, MINNESOTA

Although this firm was organized in 1918 as a tractor builder, nothing is known of its activities.

Cultor or Continental Cultor Co.

SPRINGFIELD, OHIO

Manufacturer of articulated motor cultivator using ford Model T engines 1918-1930.

James Cunningham, Son & Company

ROCHESTER, NEW YORK

Cunningham garden tractor

Organized in 1838, this company rose to be a major carriage builder, and in 1907 began building automobiles, continuing until 1931. Subsequently Cunningham experimented with aircraft and during World War II was an important defense contractor. In 1947 the company began building a line of garden tractors, apparently continuing until 1955. Most of them used the company's own engines, although one or two models were equipped with Wisconsin air-cooled engines.

COLLECTOR VALUES	1	2	3	4
CUNNINGHAM GARDEN TRACTOR	$450	$250	$125	$50

Curtis Form-A-Tractor Company

CHICAGO, ILLINOIS

About 1918 Curtis was offering this tractor attachment, pricing it at $350. This unusual design used leather straps that buckled to the rear wheels so that power could be transmitted to the drive wheels of the attachment. When it was desired to use the car on the road, the attachment was uncoupled. By 1920, there were more than fifty different companies offering tractor attachments for use with automobiles.

Curtis tractor attachment

Curtis Motor Car Company

LITTLE ROCK, ARKANSAS

This company was in the automobile manufacturing business during 1920 and 1921. Apparently, the firm also had plans to enter the tractor business and was listed as a tractor manufacturer in 1921. It does not appear that the Curtis tractor manufacturing operation ever became more than a fine idea.

Cushman Motor Works

LINCOLN, NEBRASKA

Cushman 10-22

About 1917 Cushman entered the farm tractor business in Canada. Initially the company offered a 10-22 model, but this was re-rated upward to a 12-24 model in 1918. It was sold as the Macdonald tractor. The 12-24 used a Beaver four-cylinder engine with a 4-3/4 x 6-inch bore and stroke. Total weight of the tractor was 5,900 lbs. The venture apparently ended by 1920.

Custom Mfg. Company

SHELBYVILLE, INDIANA

About 1947 the Custom Model C tractor appeared from Custom Mfg. Company. Production continued at Shelbyville into 1949. During the 1950 through '52 period, the Custom was available from Harry A. Lowther Company at Shelbyville. The company then moved briefly to Butler, Indiana. By 1953 the Custom Tractor Mfg. Co. appeared at Hustisford, Wisconsin. The Model C Custom tractor was equipped with a Chrysler six-cylinder engine with a 3-1/4 x 4-3/8-inch bore and stroke.

Custom Model C Tractor

Custom Tractor Mfg. Company

HUSTISFORD, WISCONSIN

See also: Custom Mfg. Company and Harry A. Lowther Company.

Custom tractor

Beginning in 1953 and continuing at least a couple of years, the Custom tractor was offered in two sizes, the 96R and the 98R. Both sizes were available in row-crop or standard-tread designs. The 96R was equipped with a Chrysler six-cylinder engine with a 3-1/4 x 4-5/8-inch bore and stroke, while the 98R used a six-cylinder Chrysler with a 3-7/16 x 4-1/2-inch bore and stroke. Both were equipped with a Gyrol fluid coupling ahead of the transmission.

Cuyahoga Tractor Sales Company

CLEVELAND, OHIO

This firm was organized and incorporated in 1917 to manufacture farm tractors. No additional information has been found.

[Throughout this section, assume that gasoline was used for fuel unless another fuel source is indicated.]

Danielson Mfg. Company

INDEPENDENCE, MISSOURI

The Danielson trade name is listed in the 1919 Power Wagon Reference Book. No information has been located concerning this company or its tractors.

Dart Truck & Tractor Corporation

WATERLOO, IOWA

Wm. Galloway and C. W. Hellen bought Dart Mfg. Co. of Anderson, Indiana, in 1910 and moved the factory to Waterloo. During 1914 the company was reorganized as the Dart Motor Truck Company and in 1918 the name was changed to Dart Truck & Tractor Company. Dart tractors were built from 1918 to 1921. In 1924 the company was again reorganized as Hawkeye-Dart Truck Company at Waterloo. In 1925 the reorganized Dart Truck Company moved to Kansas City, Missouri.

Dart Blue J tractors

The first Dart tractors appeared in 1918. By 1920 the Dart Blue J line included two models. The 12-25 sold for $1,850 and the larger 15-30 model sold for $2,000. Both tractors used the same chassis and both used Buda four-cylinder engines. The 12-25 carried a 4-1/4 x 5-1/2-inch bore and stroke, while the 15-30 used a 4-1/2 x 6-inch bore and stroke.

Nebraska Test Data

Model: Dart 15-30

Test No. 38

Date Tested: Withdrawn August 2, 1920

In many cases, no records or other data exist concerning withdrawn tractor models. Fortunately, that was not the case with the Dart 15-30 tractor. Initial specifications indicate a Buda Model YTU engine was featured in the 15-30 and used a 4-1/2 x 6-inch bore and stroke, with a rated speed of 1,050 rpm. A drilled crankshaft and pressure-feed lubrication were indicative of what tractor engines would adopt as standard procedure within a very few years. Standard equipment included a Dixie Model 46 magneto and a Kingston carburetor. An R-W Parrett water-type air cleaner was also featured, along with a Pierce governor. Dart used its own three-speed transmission, offering speeds of 1.9, 2.8, and 5 mph. Ball and roller bearings were used throughout the tractor. Total weight of the Dart 15-30 was 5,050 lbs. Possibly the tractor was withdrawn because the company was headed into bankruptcy. Withdrawal did not not necessarily imply a serious defect in the tractor.

Dauch Mfg. Company

SANDUSKY, OHIO

J. J. Dauch and others formed the Dauch Mfg. Co. in 1914. This was essentially a takeover of the Sandusky Auto Parts & Motor Truck Co., which built various kinds of motor trucks from 1911 to 1914.

Sandusky 15-35 tractor

In 1914 Dauch announced its Sandusky 15-35 tractor. It featured a Dauch-built four-cylinder engine with cylinders cast separately. The engine used a 5 x 6-1/2-inch bore and stroke. This model was also sold as the Sandusky Model E tractor.

In January 1917 Dauch Mfg. Co. announced the Sandusky 10-20 tractor. Also sold as the Sandusky Model J, it used a four-cylinder Dauch-built engine with a 4-1/4 x 5-inch bore and stroke. Weighing about 4,900 lbs., this tractor was built into about 1920. By 1921 Dauch Mfg. Company no longer appears in the tractor directories.

COLLECTOR VALUES	1	2	3	4
SANDUSKY 10-20	--	$46,000	--	--

Sandusky 10-20 tractor

Davis Gasoline Traction Engine Company

WATERLOO, IOWA

Although this firm was a well established gas engine manufacturer by the mid-1890s, nothing is known of their activities in the "gasoline traction engine" business. Given the size of the company, it seems entirely logical that they may have attempted an entry into the business, but no information has surfaced concerning their activities.

Dayton-Dick Company

QUINCY, ILLINOIS

This firm was organized in 1915 by the amalgamation of Leader Engine Co., Detroit, Michigan, with the Dayton Foundry & Machine Co., and Hayton Pump Co., both of Quincy. Early in 1919 the company was reorganized as Dayton-Dowd Company. All production ceased by 1924.
See: Dayton-Dowd Company

When Dayton-Dick was organized in 1915, it continued building the Leader tractor that had already been established for some time. The Leader was rated at 12 drawbar and 18 belt hp. It used a two-cylinder opposed engine. This tractor weighed about 5,000 lbs. and listed at $890.

Dayton-Dick Leader tractor

Leader 12-18

By 1917 the Leader 12-18 had been redesigned with a cellular radiator to replace the large cooling tank of the first model. By making this change it was possible to shorten the tractor frame considerably. Adding a partial hood over the engine served to improve the aesthetics. At this time the Leader line also included a 15-25 model, but it was only offered in 1917. Two examples of this model are known to exist and condition #1 value would be $20,000.

Leader 25-40 tractor crawler

The 1917 Leader line also included a 25-40 tractor with crawler treads. This model carried a four-cylinder engine with a 6 x 7-inch bore and stroke and could pull about 4,000 lbs. This model remained in production until 1920, but by this time the company was known as Dayton-Dowd.

Dayton-Dowd Company

QUINCY, ILLINOIS

Dayton-Dowd Co. was created in a 1919 reorganization of Dayton-Dick Co. Dayton-Dowd continued building Leader tractors until 1924.

Leader 16-32

Shown here is the Leader 16-32 model that apparently saw first light about 1920, and continued until all production ended four years later. The 16-32 was equipped with a Climax four-cylinder engine with a 5 x 6-1/2-inch bore and stroke. Weighing 5,000 lbs., the 16-32 sold for $1,725.

Leader Model C 25-40

Production of the Leader Model C 25-40 tractor began in 1917 under the auspices of Dayton-Dick Company, and continued with Dayton-Dowd until 1920, when production was suspended. Apparently, this model was followed with the Leader GU-Series crawlers in 1920 or 1921.

Leader GU 16-32

With the end of the Model C 25-40 tractor in 1920 came the Leader GU 16-32 crawler tractor. By 1921, essentially the same tractor was re-rated upward as an 18-35 model. The GU crawler used the same Climax engine as used in the 16-32 wheel-type tractor previously noted. Weighing 7,500 lbs., this tractor was priced at $2,150. Production of this model apparently ended in 1923.

Decker Machine & Tractor Company

CHICAGO, ILLINOIS

A trade note in the American Machinist indicates that this firm was incorporated in Chicago in 1917. Aside from that, no further information has been found on the company.

Melvin tractor

Deere & Company

MOLINE, ILLINOIS

Numerous books have been published about the origins of Deere & Company. John Deere came to Grand Detour, Illinois in 1836, and the following year built the first steel plow. Eventually Deere moved to Moline, Illinois where the company's main offices and numerous manufacturing facilities are located.

By about 1910, Deere & Co. was looking at various tractor designs and engaged some of their engineers in development of a lightweight design. Progress was slow and finally in March 1918 the company bought the Waterloo Gasoline Engine Company for $2.1 million. The venerable Waterloo Boy tractor came into the John Deere line and there has been a steady progression of tractors to the present day.

Deere & Company began serious tractor experiments in 1912 with the Melvin tractor. It was designed by C. H. Melvin, a company engineer. The Melvin closely followed the design of the Hackney tractor. Only a single tractor was built, since the company was not satisfied with the design.

The John Deere Dain tractor appeared in 1914. Joseph Dain had founded the Dain Mfg. Company at Ottumwa, Iowa. Deere bought out the company and Joe Dain became

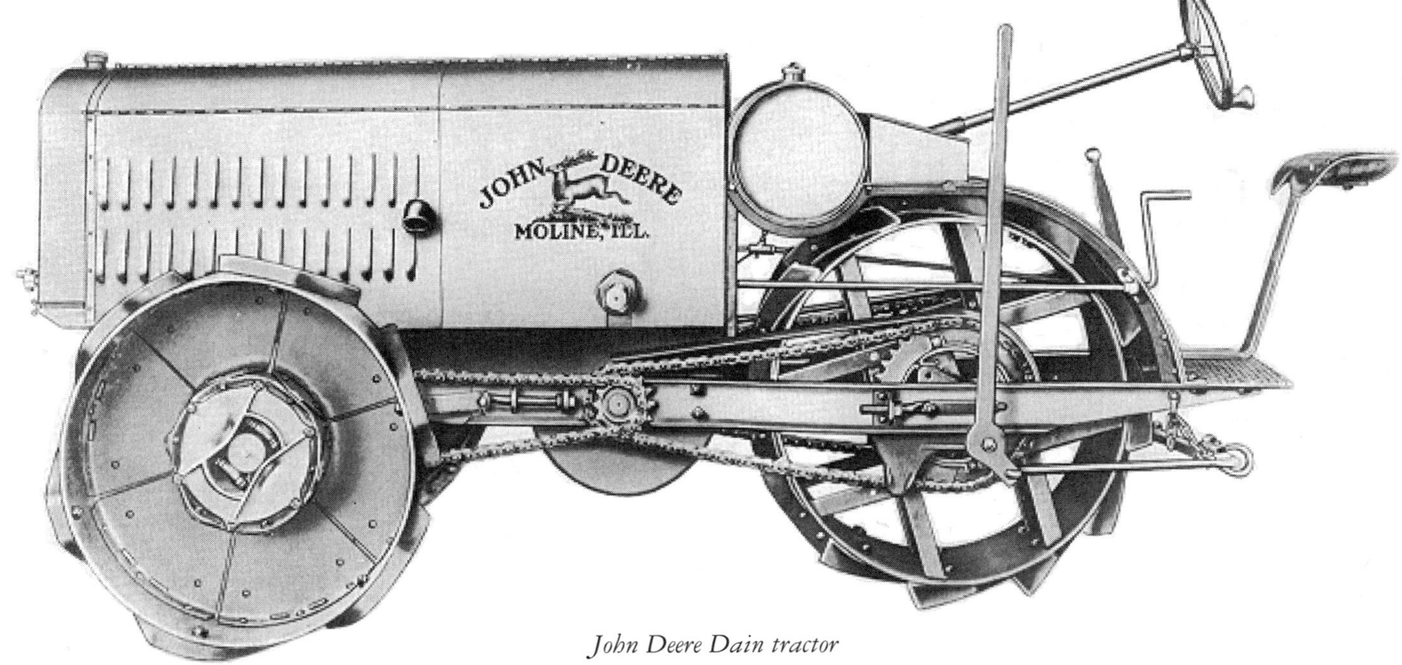

John Deere Dain tractor

B-2 tractor

a design engineer. After several experimental models, the company built 100 Dain tractors for general distribution in 1919, but the death of Joe Dain brought the venture to an end.

During 1915 and 1916 Max Sklovsky designed a new tractor that carried the entire machine in a single frame casting. Mr. Sklovsky is shown here on the seat of a B-2 tractor that was equipped with a four-cylinder Northway engine. World War I intervened and design experiments were abandoned and never resumed.

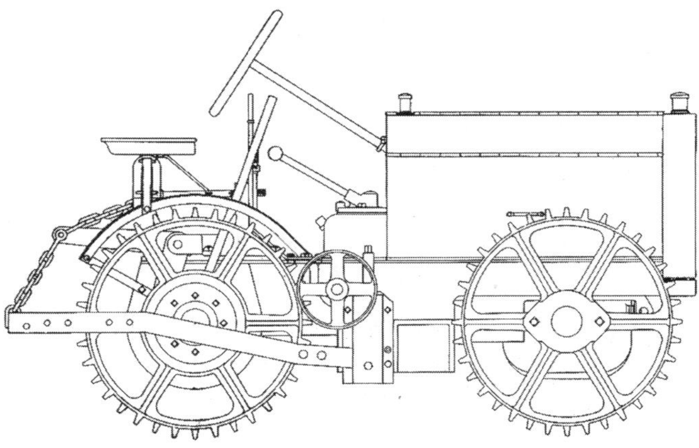

Silver motor cultivator

The Silver motor cultivator was an experiment running from 1916 to 1921. During this time Walter Silver came up with several unique designs, but none of them ever attained production status.

Walter Silver motor cultivator

Apparently Deere & Company had some plans for marketing the Walter Silver motor cultivator design, going so far as to apply for a trademark in July 1917. The new model was to be called the Tractivator and the company claimed first use of the term in June 1917. However, the Tractivator never materialized.

Model R Waterloo Boy tractor

Deere & Company finally got into the tractor business with its 1918 buyout of Waterloo Gasoline Engine Company, Waterloo, Iowa. The latter had begun building the Model R Waterloo Boy tractor in 1914, and it had gained considerable attention in the tractor industry. The Model R was equipped with a two-cylinder engine with a 5-1/2 x 7-inch bore and stroke, but by 1915 the cylinder bore was increased to 6 inches. Deere closed out the Model R in 1918, but by this time the engine bore was raised to 6-1/2 inches. The Waterloo Boy Type R had a single forward speed.

COLLECTOR VALUES	1	2	3	4
WATERLOO BOY, R	--	$45,000	$20,000	$10,000

Waterloo Gasoline Engine Company developed the Waterloo Boy Model N tractor, first building it in 1917. This refined version of the Type R had two forward speeds, but used essentially the same engine. It was of two-cylinder design, using a 6-1/2 x 7-inch bore and stroke. When the Nebraska Tractor Tests began in 1920, the Waterloo Boy was the very first tractor to be tested. Production of the Type N continued into 1924.

Waterloo Boy Model N tractor

Nebraska Test Data

Model: Waterloo Boy Model N

Test No. 1

Date Tested: March 31 to April 9, 1920

Following several years of agitation, party politics, and farmer demands, the Nebraska Tractor Tests got their start with the famous Waterloo Boy as the first example. Slightly over 25 hp was developed on the maximum brake hp test, while the maximum drawbar test yielded 15.98 hp. A drawbar pull of 2,900 lbs. was achieved at a speed of 2.07 mph. In their final report, test engineers noted the governor didn't give close regulation, even with a constant speed. On varying loads, governor action was erratic. This problem did not seem serious enough to disqualify the 12-25 from a passing grade. Fuel consumption came to 3.80 gph (gallons per hour) at maximum brake load with 6.83 hp-hours per gallon of kerosene fuel. A Schebler Model D carburetor was standard, along with a Dixie magneto. Rated speed was 750 rpm. Brief specifications included a valve-in-head engine design. The two-cylinder Waterloo Boy carried a 6-1/2 x 7- inch bore and stroke. Only two forward speeds were provided. Shipping weight came to 6,183 lbs.

Model D, 15-27

COLLECTOR VALUES	1	2	3	4
WATERLOO BOY, N	--	$45,000	$18,000	$10,000
WATERLOO BOY, L & LA	--	$45,000	$20,000	$8,000

John Deere Tractor Company released its first version of the venerable Model D in 1923. Initially, this tractor was known as the 15-27. It featured a two-cylinder engine with a 6-1/2 x 7-inch engine rated at 800 rpm. The tractors built up to 1926 used a spoke flywheel, but a solid flywheel was used after that time. This model had a two-speed transmission.

Nebraska Test Data

Model: John Deere Model D 15-27

Test No. 102

Date Tested: April 11 to April 17, 1924

Weighing 4,260 lbs., the Model D featured the company's own two-cylinder horizontal, valve-in-head engine with a 6-1/2 x 7-inch bore and stroke. Rated speed was 800 rpm. Other equipment included Deere's own governor, a Schebler carburetor, Dixie Aero magneto and a Donaldson air cleaner. Two forward speeds of 2.45 and 3.27 mph were provided in this model. Using kerosene, the Model D came out of the rated brake hp test with a fuel economy of 9.03 hp-hours per gallon, developing 27.11 hp in the process. Under maximum load, 30.4 hp was recorded. Rated drawbar testing was done in high gear, with the Model D pulling 1,786 lbs. at 3.52 mph for 16.75 drawbar hp. A maximum load test taken in low gear showed 3,277 lb. maximum pull and 22.53 hp. Only 3 quarts of oil were added during the 32 hours of test time, and no repairs or adjustments were made during the test.

Model D, 1927-1930 version

For 1927 John Deere modified and improved the Model D, 15-27 tractor. The power level was raised by increasing the cylinder bore to 6-3/4 inches but the rated speed remained at 800 rpm. This change alone boosted the maximum belt hp by about 7 horses to an output of 36.98. At this time the Model D was also redesigned to use a splined flywheel and crankshaft, compared to the keyed shaft formerly used. Production of this model continued into 1930. During the 1927 through 1940 period Deere also built a Model DI Industrial tractor.

Nebraska Test Data

Model: John Deere Model D

Test No. 146

Date Tested: October 24 to October 29, 1927

Two forward speeds of 2-1/2 and 3-1/4 mph were featured in the 1927 Model D tractor. Deere's own two-cylinder horizontal, valve-in-head engine was used. It was rated at 800 rpm and carried a 6-3/4 x 7- inch bore and stroke, slightly larger than the Model D tested under No. 102 of 1924. Regular equipment for this model included a Splitdorf 246C magneto, Schebler DLT carburetor, and Donaldson air cleaner. No repairs or adjustments were required during the 35-hour test. At rated brake hp the 15-27 delivered a fuel economy of 10.74 hp-hours per gallon of kerosene. This fuel was used throughout the test. The maximum load test indicated 36.98 brake hp, substantially higher than was noted in Test No. 102. Similar results may be noted from a comparison of the drawbar tests and in the case at hand, 28.53 maximum drawbar hp was recorded in low gear. At a speed of 2.4 mph the 15-27 pulled 4,462 lbs. Rated drawbar tests indicated 6.69 hp-hours per gallon. Total weight including the operator was 4,917 lbs.

Model D, 1931-34 version

Until 1931 the John Deere D had the steering wheel on the left side, but that year it was moved to the right side. Also in 1931, the governed speed was raised from 800 to 900 rpm. Changes along the way brought the net operating weight of the Model D to 4,878 lbs. Electric lights were available as an extra-cost option.

Model D, 1935-38 version

A major improvement to the John Deere Model D came in 1935 when it was equipped with a three-speed transmission. Other minor changes were also made. By this time,

Model D, 1939-1953 version

the Model D had a rated brake load of about 37-1/2 hp, meaning that it was capable of delivering this load hour-after-hour and day-after-day. At this point the Model D was essentially in its final form from a mechanical viewpoint.

Nebraska Test Data

Model: John Deere Model D

Test No. 236

Date Tested: June 26 to July 2, 1935

This model featured three forward speeds of 2-1/2, 3-1/2, and 5 mph, compared to the two forward speeds of earlier styles. Also included was Deere's two-cylinder horizontal, valve-in-head engine with a 6-3/4 x 7-inch bore and stroke and rated at 900 rpm. Accessory items were a Splitdorf 246T magneto and a Schebler DLTX6 carburetor along with a Donaldson air cleaner. Weighing 5,690 lbs., the "D" went into the rated drawbar test using second gear. With an output of 24.64 hp it pulled 2,357 lbs. at 3.92 mph, achieving a fuel economy of 7.33 hp-hours per gallon of distillate fuel. The low gear maximum test revealed 30.74 hp, along with a pull of 4,037 lbs. at 2.86 mph and slippage of 5.48 percent, for a pull approaching 71 percent of the tractor's own weight. At rated brake load of 37.51 hp, fuel economy came in at 10.48 hp-hours per gallon, while at operating maximum load this figure decreased slightly to 10.14 at a load of 40.11 hp. No repairs or adjustments were noted during the 43 hours of running time.

In 1939 the John Deere was given a styled hood mainly so it would conform to the other styled models in the tractor line. By this time rubber tires had become the preferred choice for most farmers, and in addition, electric starting and lighting became optional equipment. When production finally ended in 1953, the John Deere Model D had achieved the longest production run of any tractor in history.

Nebraska Test Data

Model: John Deere Model D

Test No. 350

Date Tested: July 22 to July 26, 1940

The test weight of 8,125 lbs. shown for this tractor included 556 lbs. of cast iron plus 478 lbs. of calcium chloride solution for each rear wheel. Standard equipment included 13.5 x 28-inch rear tires and 7.50 x 18-inch front rubber. Advertised speeds of 3, 4, and 5-1/4 mph were provided, with the 10-hour run of Test H made in second gear. Traveling at 3.97 mph the Model D pulled 2,907 lbs. with a recorded slippage of 7.3 percent with a total output of 30.77 rated drawbar hp. Fuel economy was registered at 8.78 hp-hours per gallon of distillate. A maximum pull of 4,830 lbs. was achieved in low gear. At a speed of 2.68 mph the Model D experienced slippage of 14.97 percent but produced a low gear output of 34.5 drawbar hp. Belt testing included the operating maximum load results from Test C. At 40.24 brake hp, economy was recorded at 10.14 hp-hours per gallon, compared to 9.85 under Test D rated load of 38.15 brake hp. This tractor was equipped with a two-cylinder horizontal, I-head engine with a 6-3/4 x 7-inch bore and stroke with a rated speed of 900 rpm. Included was an Edison-Splitdorf CD-2 magneto and a Marvel-Schebler DLTX16 carburetor. No repairs or adjustments were noted during 45 hours of engine operating time.

COLLECTOR VALUES	1	2	3	4
D/15-27 SPOKED FLY-WHEEL 26"	--	$15,000	$6,000	$3,000

24"	--	$10,000	$5,000	$2,500
D/15-27 SOLID FLY-WHEEL*	$5,000	$3,500	$1,800	$800
MODEL D 1931-34	$4,500	$3,000	$1,800	$800
MODEL D 1935-38	$4,500	$3,500	$1,800	$800
MODEL D 1939-53	$4,500	$3,500	$1,800	$500

***Note: "Nickel Hole" (small flywheel holes) "D" add $1,000**

John Deere 10-20 (Model GP)

The John Deere 10-20, also known as the Model G, made its debut in 1928. Its immediate predecessor was the Model C tractor, which was built in relatively small numbers during 1927. Between 1928 and 1930 the GP was built with a two-cylinder engine with a 5-3/4 x 6-inch bore and stroke. It was rated at 900 rpm. This tractor was capable of almost 25 belt hp.

Nebraska Test Data

Model: John Deere Model GP 10-20

Test No. 153

Date Tested: October 22 to October 29, 1928

Featuring a two-cylinder horizontal, L-head engine, the Model GP tractor carried a 5-3/4 x 6-inch bore and stroke and was rated at 900 rpm. Operating on kerosene fuel, this 4,265 pound tractor delivered a maximum pull of 2,489 lbs. in low gear. Moving at a speed of 2.6 mph it experienced slippage of 7.3 percent and came up with a maximum of 17.24 drawbar hp. Rated drawbar tests in second gear show an average pull of 1,078 lbs. at 3.55 mph. Fuel economy came in at 4.95 hp-hours per gallon. At rated brake load the Model GP demonstrated 8.55 hp-hours per gallon, with total consumption of 2.362 gph. The maximum load test indicated 24.97 hp, fuel consumption of 2.721 gph, and 9.18 hp-hours per gallon. Only minor repairs were required during the 42-hour test run. Standard accessories for the test tractor included a Fairbanks-Morse magneto, Ensign BJ, 1-1/4 inch carburetor, and a Donaldson-Simplex air cleaner. Tractor No. 200112, the second John

The GP tractor from 1930 to 1935 used an engine with a 6-inch bore and stroke. It also had a governed speed of 950 rpm. This gave the GP about 25-1/2 belt hp. The "GP" stood for "General Purpose" and in fact, the GP could be equipped with numerous implements specially designed for use with this tractor.

Model GP ("General Purpose") tractor

Model GPO

Nebraska Test Data

Model: John Deere Model GP
Test No. 190
Date Tested: May 4 to May 15, 1931

Weighing 4,925 lbs. the "Improved General Purpose" tractor followed an earlier model tested under No. 153 of 1928. Rated at 950 rpm, this model carried a two-cylinder horizontal engine of L-head design, using a 6-inch bore and stroke, A Schebler DLTX5 carburetor was featured, along with a Fairbanks-Morse R-2 magneto built especially for John Deere tractors. Distillate was the chosen fuel and in the rated drawbar test fuel economy came in at 6.32 hp-hours per gallon, along with a 1,702-pound pull at 3.38 mph for 15.34 drawbar hp. Maximum pull of 2,853 lbs. at 2.48 mph gave 18.86 drawbar hp. This tractor carried three advertised speeds of 2-1/4, 3, and 4-1/8 mph. Maximum brake hp tests revealed 25.36 hp and an economy of 9.50 hp-hours per gallon, with this important measure of efficiency dropping slightly to 9.22 in the rated brake test at 24.14 hp. Although not rated by the manufacturer, the General Purpose had a maximum of 15 drawbar and 24 belt hp.

During the 1931-1935 period, the John Deere GP was also available as a special orchard tractor; this model was designated as the GPO. Its low-profile design was further enhanced by the use of special fenders, plus the air intake and exhaust stacks were relocated to permit working under low branches.

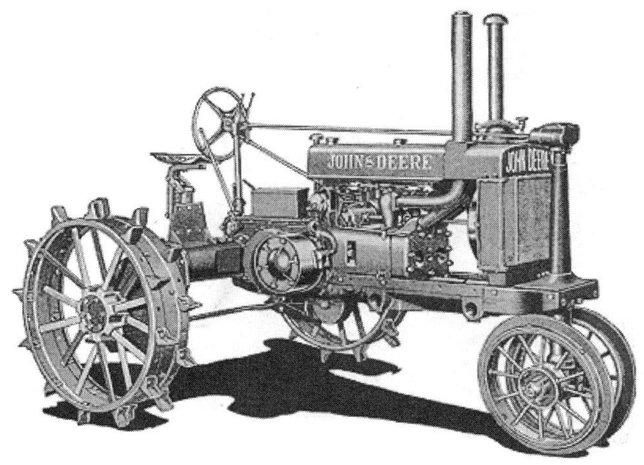

Model GP Wide-Tread

The GP Wide-Tread was the first John Deere row-crop tractor. Its engine was the same as the GP Standard-Tread model. During 1932 the Wide-Tread was given a tapered hood for better visibility. Another advantage of this model was the power lift system that quickly became the idea to copy, and various kinds of power lifts soon appeared on almost all row-crop tractors. Add $1,000 for the model GPs with slant plug heads.

COLLECTOR VALUES	1	2	3	4
MODEL GP STANDARD-TREAD	$5,000	$3,500	$2,000	$1,000
MODEL GP WIDE-TREAD	$10,000	$7,500	$5,000	$2,000
MODEL GPO	$6,000	$4,500	$3,000	$1,500

Model A

John Deere Model A tractors made their first appearance in 1934. The Model A was among the first to offer an adjustable-width wheel tread. Various changes took place in the Model A during its long production run.

Nebraska Test Data

Model: John Deere Model A
Test No. 222
Date Tested: April 19 to April 27, 1934

Although it was not rated by the manufacturer, the John Deere "A" was given a maximum permissible total of 16.22 drawbar and 23.52 belt hp under existing tractor rating codes. Using these parameters, the "A" was operated at 23.63 hp in the rated brake test. Burning distillate fuel, it achieved an economy of 10.5 hp-hours per gallon, a figure that dropped to 10.1 at maximum load of 24.71 hp. Advertised speeds of 2-1/3, 3, 4-3/4, and 6-1/4 mph were built into the "A." Using second gear for the rated drawbar test gave 16.31 hp, along with a pull of 1,839 lbs. at 3.33 mph and slippage of 3.3 percent. Fuel economy was recorded at 7.35 hp-hours per gallon. Pulling 2,923 lbs. at 2.4 mph, and producing 18.72 mph gave the "A" its highest readings on both points in the low gear maximum drawbar test. The "A" was equipped with Deere's own two-cylinder horizontal, I-head engine rated at 975 rpm and featuring a 5-1/2 x 6-1/2- inch bore and stroke. Also included with this 4,059-lb. tractor was a Schebler DLTX8 carburetor and a Fairbanks-Morse DRV-2A magneto. During the 53-hour test, grease leaked from the lefthand rear axle housing, and the exhaust pipe connection to the manifold was tightened. Otherwise, no repairs or adjustments were required.

Model A, 1938-40 version

In 1938 the Model A took on a stylized hood and grille. An important feature of the Model A was the use of differential brakes geared directly to the bull gears.

Nebraska Test Data

Model: John Deere Model A
Test No. 335
Date Tested: November 13 to November 16, 1939

The John Deere A featured a two-cylinder horizontal engine of I-head design. Rated at 975 rpm, it used a 5-1/2 x 6-3/4-inch bore and stroke. Also included was a Wico C-1042 magneto and a Schebler DLTX-24 carburetor. Rubber tires were used in this test with 11 x 38-inch tires on the rear and 5.50 x 16 front rubber. No repairs or adjustments were noted during 50 hours of engine operating time. Test weight was 6,410 lbs. An operating maximum load of 28.93 brake hp was recorded in Test C, along with an economy of 11.3 hp-hours per gallon of distillate. Test D indicates a rated load of 26.36 brake hp. In this test, fuel economy drooped slightly to an even 11 hp-hours per gallon. A maximum first-gear pull of 4,110 lbs. was noted in Test G. This test also noted 24.64 drawbar hp and slippage of 13.03 percent at 2.25 mph. Test H for rated drawbar ended with a fuel economy figure of 9.57 hp-hours per gallon, along with a pull of 1,815 lbs. at 4.23 mph and an output of 20.48 drawbar hp. Advertised speeds of 2-1/3, 3, 4, and 5-1/4 mph were provided.

In 1941 the "styled" Model A was given a power boost by raising the piston stroke from 6-1/2 to 6-3/4 inches. Starting in 1947, the Model A was modified to include electric starting, plus a pressed steel frame that was somewhat different from previous models. By the time production ended in 1951, the John Deere Model A had become the most popular model in the history of the company.

Model A, 1941-1951 version

Nebraska Test Data

Model: John Deere Model A

Test No. 384

Date Tested: June 7 to June 16, 1947

The John Deere A had previously been tested at Nebraska under No. 222 of 1934 and No. 335 of 1939. This version carried the usual two-cylinder I-head engine. Rated at 975 rpm, it featured a 5-1/2 x 6-3/4- inch bore and stroke. Accessory items included a Marvel Schebler DLTX-71 carburetor and a Wico C-1042B magneto. The test model used 11-38-inch rear and 5.50-16-inch front tires-without additional wheel weights this tractor weighed in at 5,228 lbs. Advertised speeds of 2-1/2, 3-1/2, 4-1/2, 5-3/4, 7-3/4, and 13 mph were featured. Test H was run in third gear. Using gasoline, the Model A delivered a fuel economy of 9.74 hp-hours per gallon under a rated load of 26.7 drawbar hp. Other Test H data included a pull of 2,441 lbs. at 4.1 mph with slippage of 6.12 percent. The low-gear maximum pull noted in Test G came to 4,034 lbs. at 2.1 mph. At an operating maximum load of 35.81 belt hp, the Model A delivered a fuel economy of 11.44 hp-hours per gallon. This dropped microscopically to 11.43 at the Test D rated belt load of 33.82 hp. No repairs or adjustments were noted during 47 hours of engine running time.

COLLECTOR VALUES	1	2	3	4
MODEL A	$3,000	$2,000	$1,000	$500
OPEN FANSHAFT A	$5,000	$4,000	$2,000	$1,500

Following the same production period as the regular row-crop models, the AN and BN tractors differed only in their front wheel design. In this instance, a single front wheel was used. This design was especially useful where narrow rows were used. The AN and BN had the same general appearance. These models used a longer rear axle shaft to provide a wider wheel tread, and also provided greater clearance than the regular row-crop model.

John Deere Model BN, 1951

The AW and BW tractors featured an adjustable front axle width, as well as extra-long rear axles. These tractors were designed especially for bedded crops where it was essential to plant and cultivate without splitting the center. Both models were of the same general appearance and both had production runs approximating that of their row-crop counterparts. A 1951 advertisement for the AW and BW

Model AN row-crop

tractors noted, "Except for the front-end assemblies, the 'AW' and 'BW' [tractors] are identical to the single front-wheel type..." Deere also offered a wide variety of integral equipment for both the "N" and "W" models.

Early Model AW

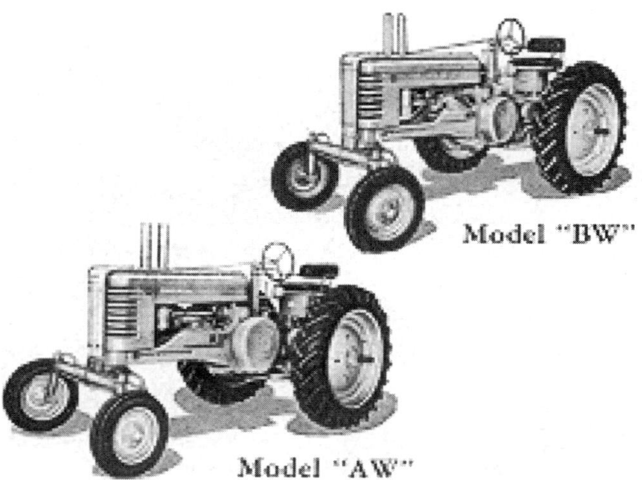

Model AW and BW tractors

Model AH Hi-Crop

During 1951 and 1952 Deere offered the Model AH Hi-Crop model. It was essentially the same tractor as the Model A Row-Crop, but was modified to permit more than 32 inches of ground clearance, as well as 48 inches between the axle housings. In the 1951 through 1953 period Deere offered the Model GH Hi-Crop model. It had the same general appearance but was a modified John Deere Model G row-crop tractor.

COLLECTOR VALUES	1	2	3	4
AH HI-CROP*	$10,000	–	–	–

**For High Clearance models with 42-inch rear tires add $1,000.*

Model AR tractor

From 1935 to 1940 Deere offered the unstyled Model AR tractor shown here. This was a standard-tread version of the Model A row-crop tractor. Like the row-crop, it used an engine with a 5-1/2 x 6-1/2-inch bore and stroke until 1941. At that time the Model A tractors were redesigned with a 6-3/4-inch stroke while the bore remained the same.

Nebraska Test Data

Model: John Deere Model AR

Test No. 378

Date Tested: October 27 to November 3, 1941

This John Deere standard-tread model was equipped with 12-26-inch rear and 6.00-16-inch front tires. Without added ballast, test weight was 4,815 lbs. Four forward speeds of 2, 3, 4, and 6-1/2 mph were featured. Other specifications include a two-cylinder I-head engine rated at 975 rpm and using a 5-1/2 x 6-3/4-inch bore and stroke. A 1042 magneto and Marvel-Schebler DLTX-41 carburetor were among the accessory items. No repairs or adjustments were noted during 44 hours of engine running time. Distillate was used throughout the test. At its rated 26,37 belt hp the AR delivered 11.13 hp-hours per gallon, and a virtually identical figure of 11.12 was noted at the Test C operating maximum load of 28.71 belt hp. Test H at a rated 20.66 drawbar hp yielded 9.66 hp-hours per gallon, along with a pull of 1,861 lbs. at 4.16 mph. Third gear was used for this test. The low-gear maximum pull noted in Test G came to 4,248 lbs. at 1.75 mph with a recorded slippage of 17.56 percent. Because of World War II, this was the last tractor tested at Nebraska until late 1946.

COLLECTOR VALUES	1	2	3	4
AR UNSTYLED	$4,500	$3,000	$2,000	$1,000

Model AR styled

In the 1941-52 period Deere offered the Model AR in a styled version. During this time the AR underwent several changes, although the basic tractor design remained the same. By the time production ended, the AR was equipped with a six-speed transmission and electric starting.

Nebraska Test Data

Model: John Deere Model AR

Test No. 429

Date Tested: October 11 to October 15, 1949

At a Test C, operating at maximum load of 36.13 belt hp, the AR achieved 11.74 hp-hours per gallon. Economy fell slightly to 11.52 under a Test D rated load of 33.28 belt hp. The AR was equipped with a two-cylinder horizontal, I-head engine rated at 975 rpm and carried a 5-1/2 x 6-3/4-inch bore and stroke. Wico magneto ignition was featured, along with a 12-volt Delco-Remy electrical system. Marvel-Schebler furnished their DLTX71 carburetor for this model. No repairs or adjustments were noted during 50 hours of engine operation. Standard equipment also included 13-26-inch rear and 6.00-16-inch front tires. Weighing 5,597 lbs., the AR received an additional 885 lbs. of ballast per wheel during Tests F, G, and H. Advertised speeds of 1-1/4, 2-1/2, 3-1/4, 4-3/8, 6-1/4, and 11 mph were provided, with fourth gear being used for Test H. At a rated drawbar load of 26.24 hp the AR pulled 2,279 lbs. at 4.32 mph with a slippage of 4.71 percent. Records indicated a fuel economy of 9.86 hp-hours per gallon for this test. Test G yielded a low-gear maximum pull of 4,372 lbs. at 1.08 mph with slippage of 18.34 percent.

COLLECTOR VALUES	1	2	3	4
AR STYLED	$4,500	$3,000	$2,000	$1,000

Add $500 with water pump.

Model AI Industrial tractors were available from 1936 to 1941. This style was built with a four-speed transmission and included electric lighting as standard equipment. The AI weighed 4,680 lbs. and had a turning radius of 11-1/2 feet.

Model AI industrial tractor

Model AO orchard tractor

John Deere Model AO orchard tractors were first built in 1935. The following year the design was streamlined, as shown here. This was essentially an AR standard-tread tractor equipped with special grille, hood, and fenders. There were numerous changes to the intake and exhaust stacks, steering wheel and seat location, and other modifications. In 1940 the Model AR was modified to include the added quarter-inch to the original piston stroke of 6-1/2 inches. Its design closely followed the concurrent Model A tractor line. The 1951 version featured a styled hood and was equipped with electric starting as standard equipment.

John Deere Model AO orchard tractor, streamlined

COLLECTOR VALUES	1	2	3	4
MODEL AO	$5,000	$3,100	$2,000	$800
MODEL AO STREAMLINED	$10,000	$7,500	$4,500	$1,500

John Deere Model B

Production of the John Deere Model B began in 1935. The original design with a shorter frame continued until 1937. Model B tractors built into 1938 used a two-cylinder engine with a 4-1/4 x 5-1/4-inch bore and stroke. Like the Model A, it was equipped with a PTO shaft and could also be furnished with a hydraulic power lift system for integral equipment.

Nebraska Test Data

Model: John Deere Model B

Test No. 232

Date Tested: November 15, 1934, to April 19, 1935

Although testing on this tractor began in late 1934, cold weather forced a recess in operations until April of 1935. Featuring a two-cylinder horizontal, I-head engine, the Model B was rated at 1,150 rpm. It carried a 4-1/4 x 5-1/4-inch bore and stroke. Included was a Fairbanks-Morse DRV-2B magneto and a Wheeler-Schebler DLTX-10 carburetor. Distillate was used throughout this test. Total tractor weight was 3,275 lbs. At its 14.3 rated brake hp the Model B delivered an economy of 10.28 hp-hours per gallon. At its operating maximum load of 15.07 hp, this figure dropped minimally to 10.19. Advertised speeds of 2-1/4, 3-1/3, 4-3/4, and 6-3/4 mph were provided. Second gear was used for the rated drawbar test. Economy was recorded at 6.39 hp-hours per gallon, with the "B" pulling a 1,023 pound load at 3.44 mph at a slippage of only 0.77 percent. The low gear maximum load test came up with 1,728 lbs. of pull at 2.57 mph, plus a slippage figure of 2.7 percent and total output of 11.84 hp.

COLLECTOR VALUES	1	2	3	4
MODEL B 1935-37	$3,500	$2,500	$1,500	$1,000
4-BOLT FRONT END	$7,000	–	–	–

Model B, 1938 version

During 1938 the Model B was modified with a longer frame and also during that year was given a stylized hood and grille. It also gained a higher power level with its 4-1/2 x 5-1/2-inch engine. At its rated load, the Model B was capable of about 17 hp.

Nebraska Test Data

Model: John Deere Model B
Test No. 305
Date Tested: September 6 to September 16, 1938

Using a 4-1/2 x 5-1/2-inch bore and stroke, the John Deere B was rated at 1,150 rpm. The two-cylinder horizontal engine was of I-head design and built by Deere. Included was a Wico AP-477-B magneto and a Schebler DLTX10 carburetor. Test records indicated that drawbar trials were made on rubber tires and with steel wheels. Test H for rated drawbar load was conducted with steel wheels. Using second gear, the 10-hour run indicated an output of 10.84 drawbar hp, along with a pull of 1,228 lbs. at 3.31 mph and an economy of 6.82 hp-hours per gallon. A four-hour fuel economy test was run in second gear, but using rubber tires indicated an economy of 9.5 hp-hours per gallon, plus an output of 13.26 hp and a pull of 1,584 lbs. at 3.14 mph. Test G for operating maximum load gave a first gear pull of 2,690 lbs. at 2.22 mph for an output of 15.92 hp on rubber-the same test on steel yielded a pull of 2,088 lbs. at 2.52 mph and an output of 14.03 hp. Belt hp tests pegged fuel economy at 10.19 hp-hours per gallon at rated load of 16.94 hp. At operating maximum load of 18.31 hp, economy increased to 10.56. Except for a leaking joint in the fuel tank outlet flange, no repairs or adjustments were noted during 66 hours of running time.

Model B, 1941 version

When equipped with rubber tires, the Model B of 1941 was equipped with a road gear of 12-1/2 mph. This resulted from the new six-speed transmission installed at that time. Engine dimensions remained the same. Model B tractors were extremely popular on small farms as well as an all-around "go-fer" on larger farms.

During 1947 the Model B was once again modified. The most obvious difference was the use of a pressed steel frame. The engine was also modified to include a bore of 4-11/16 x 5-1/2 inches. This tweaked the power level slightly, and along with a higher rated speed of 1,250 rpm, the Model B was now rated for a load of nearly 25-1/2 belt hp. Production of the Model B ended in 1952. The John Deere BN and BW models in the 1935 through 1940 period are quite similar in appearance to the AN and AW models previously noted.

Model B, 1947 version

Nebraska Test Data

Model: John Deere Model B
Test No. 380
Date Tested: April 28 to May 5, 1947

The tractor featured a two-cylinder I-head engine with a 4-11/16 x 5-1/2-inch bore and stroke. Rated at 1,250 rpm, it featured a Wico C-1042 magneto and a Marvel-Schebler DLTX-67 carburetor. No repairs or adjustments were recorded during 52 hours of engine running time. Test J, conducted without the use of any added ballast, indicated a bare weight of 4,400 lbs. Under an operating maximum load of 25.79 brake hp, the Model B manifested a fuel economy of 11.79 hp-hours per gallon. Test D, at a rated load of 24.46 belt hp produced an economy figure of 11.61. Advertised speeds of 1-1/2, 2-1/2, 3-1/2, 4-1/2, 5-3/4, and 10 mph were standard. Fourth gear was used for Test H. At a rated load of 19.04 drawbar hp the "B" pulled a load of 1,666 lbs. at 4.29 mph with a slippage of 4.78 percent. Fuel economy was recorded at 9.88 hp-hours per gallon. A maximum low-gear pull of 3,353 lbs. was noted in Test G. The test tractor featured 10-38-inch rear and 5.50-16-inch front tires.

Nebraska Test Data

Model: John Deere Model B (all-fuel)
Test No. 381
Date Tested: May 9 to May 15, 1947

For a short time following World War II, "tractor fuel" was offered by most of the major oil companies. It was about two notches above distillate, and fell somewhere between gasoline and kerosene. The idea caught on briefly, and several tractor builders tailored specific models to use it. The John Deere B noted here is a case in point. Engine specifications remained virtually identical to the tractor noted in Test No. 380. Third gear was used for Test H, and under a load of 16.82 hp, the Model B pulled 1,908 lbs. at 3.31 mph with a slippage of 5.83 percent. Fuel economy was noted at 10.16 hp-hours per gallon of tractor fuel. Test G, using low gear, delivered a maximum pull of 3,689 lbs. at 1.33 mph with a slippage of 14.94 percent . At its rated belt load of 20.75 hp, the "B" evoked a fuel economy of 11.07 hp-hours per gallon, compared to an economy figure of 11.487 under the Test C operating maximum load of 22.17 belt hp. No repairs or adjustments were noted during 50 hours of engine operating time.

COLLECTOR VALUES	1	2	3	4
MODEL B	$3,500	$2,300	$1,100	$1,000

Model BR

John Deere Model BR tractors were a standard-tread version of the Model B row-crop models. Design changes, such as the 1938 changeover from a 4-1/4 to a 4-1/2-inch engine, were generally the same as for other models of the B tractor. The four forward speeds ranged from 2 to 6-1/4 mph. Although this model is shown on steel wheels, rubber tires were optional. Production of the Model BR tractors ended in 1947.

COLLECTOR VALUES	1	2	3	4
MODEL BR	$6,500	$4,500	$3,800	$1,500

Model BI industrial

In the 1936-1941 period, John Deere offered a Model BI Industrial version of the Model B tractor series. It was essentially the same tractor as the Model BR standard-tread, but was modified for use in factories and other industrial applications.

COLLECTOR VALUES	1	2	3	4
MODEL BI	$8,000	$6,000	$3,000	$1,500

Production of the Model BO orchard tractor commenced in 1935 and ended in 1947. This model was essentially the same as the Model BR standard-tread tractor, but was equipped with special fenders and other amenities required for use in orchards and groves.

COLLECTOR VALUES	1	2	3	4
MODEL BO	$8,000	$6,500	$4,500	$2,000

Model BO orchard tractor

John Deere Lindemann crawler

Between 1939 and 1947 the Lindemann crawler conversion was used with the Model BO tractor chassis. Lindemann Bros. at Yakima, Washington, mounted these units on their crawler tracks, with the result the John Deere-Lindemann crawlers.

COLLECTOR VALUES	1	2	3	4
LINDEMAN CRAWLER	$10,000	$7,500	$4,000	$2,000

John Deere Model G

In November 1937 the John Deere Model G appeared. It was the largest row-crop tractor in the line and was capable of about 34 belt hp. The Model G used a two-cylinder engine with a 6-1/8 x 7-inch bore and stroke. Rated speed was 975 rpm. In 1941, the Model G was given a six-speed transmission, with numerous other options being available.

Nebraska Test Data

Model: John Deere Model G

Test No. 295

Date Tested: November 15 to November 19, 1937

Using Deere's two-cylinder horizontal, I-head engine the Model G featured speeds of 2-1/4, 3-1/4, 4-1/4, and 6 mph. The tractor used steel wheels, and in Test H it pulled 2,252 lbs. at 3.46 mph with slippage of 3.7percent. Fuel economy was calculated at 7.35 hp-hours per gallon of distillate at its rated 20.75 drawbar hp. A maximum pull of 4.085 lbs. at 2.37 mph resulted in an output of 25.86 hp. Test D indicated 31.51 rated belt hp with a fuel economy of 10.66 hp-hours per gallon. Economy slipped to 10.59 on Test C, operating at a maximum load of 34.09 hp. The Model G engine was rated at 975 rpm and featured a 6-1/8 x 7-inch bore and stroke. Included was an Edison-Splitdorf CD-2 magneto plus a Schebler DLTX-24 carburetor, and a Donaldson air cleaner. During 50 hours of operating time no repairs or adjustments were noted.

Capable of nearly 40 belt hp, the Model G was a full three-plow tractor. By 1947 electric starting was available and this was important for the big two-cylinder engine, especially in cold weather. The Model G was also built in a high clearance design known as the GH Hi-Crop.

Model G, 1947 version

Model H tractor

Nebraska Test Data

Model: John Deere Model G (all-fuel)

Test No. 383

Date Tested: June 5 to June 16, 1947

This tractor was previously tested under No. 295 of 1937. The streamlined model presented for this test featured six forward speeds of 2-1/2, 3-1/2, 4-1/2, 6-1/2, 8-3/4, and 12-1/2 mph. Also included was a two-cylinder I-head engine rated at 975 rpm and using a 6-1/8 x 7-inch bore and stroke. Bare weight was 6,056 lbs. As tested, this tractor carried 12-38-inch rear and 6.00-16-inch front tires. Test H, run for 10 hours at rated drawbar load, delivered 9.43 hp-hours per gallon. Other data from this test included a pull of 2,313 lbs. at 4.39 mph using second gear. Slippage was noted at 5.14 percent, with a net output of 27.08 drawbar hp. Test G, using low gear, gave a maximum drawbar pull of 4,394 lbs. at 2.07 mph with a slippage of 16.9 percent. Under an operating maximum load of 36.03 brake hp the Model G delivered a fuel economy of 10.74 hp-hours per gallon, compared to a virtually identical figure of 10.74 while under the Test D rated load of 34.2 belt hp.

COLLECTOR VALUES	1	2	3	4
MODEL G (HIGH RADIATOR)	$5,000	$4,000	$2,500	$1,000
MODEL G (LOW RADIATOR)	$6,000	$4,500	$3,000	$1,500

Introduced in 1939, the Model H tractor was built until 1947. This small two-cylinder model had a maximum output of about 14 belt hp. Rated at 1400 rpm, the two-cylinder engine had a 3-9/16 x 5-inch bore and stroke. Operating in road gear, the engine speed could be raised to 1800 rpm for a maximum road speed of 7-1/2 mph.

Nebraska Test Data

Model: John Deere Model H

Test No. 312

Date Tested: October 31 to November 10, 1938

Equipped to burn distillate, the model H carried the usual two-cylinder horizontal engine—in this case it used 3-9/16 x 5-inch bore and stroke with a rated speed of 1,400 rpm Standard equipment included an Edison-Splitdorf RM-2 magneto and a Marvel-Schebler DLTX-26 carburetor. Standard equipment also included 7.50 x 32-inch rear tires and 4.00 x 15-inch front rubber. Weight as tested was 3,035 lbs. Three forward speeds of 2-1/2, 3-1/2, and 5-3/4 mph were provided, with second gear used for Test H (rated drawbar). This 10-hour test revealed a fuel economy of 10.16 hp-hours per gallon, along with a pull of 1,065 lbs. at 3.44 mph for an output of 9.77 drawbar hp. Test G for operating maximum hp indicated a low gear maximum pull of 1,839 lbs. at 2.38 mph and slippage of 10.14 percent for a net output of 11.67 drawbar hp. Belt hp tests indicated an impressive fuel economy of 11.72 hp-hours per gallon at rated load of 13.01 hp. This figure improved slightly to 11.95 when under operating maximum load of 14.22 belt hp. No repairs or adjustments were noted during the 43 hours of engine running time.

COLLECTOR VALUES	1	2	3	4
MODEL H	$3,500	$2,500	$1,800	$800

Model HN tractor

Production of the Model HN tractor ran from 1939 to 1947. This small tractor with the single front tire was ideal for crops planted in narrow rows. In addition, Deere built the HWH and HNH special high-clearance models in 1941 and 1942.

Model L tractor

The first John Deere utility tractor was the Model L, introduced in 1937 and built until 1946. Weighing only 2,200 lbs., the L was equipped with a two-cylinder vertical engine designed by Deere and built by Hercules. It was rated at 1,480 rpm and used a 3-1/4 x 4-inch bore and stroke and it was capable of nearly 10 belt hp.

Nebraska Test Data

Model: John Deere Model L

Test No. 313

Date Tested: November 4 to November 16, 1938

The John Deere L was offered with three forward speeds of 2-1/2, 3-3/4 and 6 mph. The two-cylinder vertical engine in the Model L was a John Deere-Hercules design and featured a 3-1/4 x 4-inch bore and stroke with a rated speed of 1,480 rpm. Standard equipment included 6.00 x 22-inch rear tires and 4.00 x 15-inch front rubber. Also featured was an Edison Splitdorf RM series magneto and a Marvel-Schebler TS-13 carburetor. No repairs or adjustments were noted during 39 hours of engine running time. Gasoline was the chosen fuel. In Test H for rated drawbar load, 7.06 hp appeared, along with a pull of 688 lbs. at 3.85 mph and 8.10 hp-hours per gallon. Test C for operating maximum load indicated an economy figure of 9.82 hp-hours per gallon with an output of 10.42 belt hp. Test D for rated load yielded 9.81 hp-hours per gallon with a load of 9.28 hp. Among the extensive data with each test is Test E for varying load. Each 20 minute run was recorded, with an average figure being derived from these totals. For the Model L, fuel economy in the varying load test came to 7.66 hp-hours per gallon.

COLLECTOR VALUES	1	2	3	4
MODEL L	$5,000	$4,500	$2,500	$1,200

Subtract $400 if missing belt pully assembly.

Model LA tractor

Deere introduced the Model LA tractor in 1940. This model featured the company's own two-cylinder vertical engine with a 3-1/2 x 4-inch bore and stroke. Operating at a rated speed of 1,850 rpm, this model displayed a maximum of almost 14-1/2 belt hp. Production of the Model LA ended in 1946. Deere also built the Model LI Industrial version in the 1938-46 period.

Nebraska Test Data

Model: John Deere Model LA

Test No. 373

Date Tested: June 20 to June 28, 1941

With a bare weight of 2,285 lbs., the LA featured 9-24-inch rear and 5.00-15-inch front tires. Also featured were three forward speeds of 2-1/2, 3-1/2, and 9 mph. It carried a Deere-built two-cylinder vertical engine of L-head design. Rated at 1,850 rpm, it carried a 3-1/2 x 4-inch bore and stroke. This was enhanced with an Edison-Splitdorf magneto and a Marvel-Schebler TS-60 carburetor. Minor testing problems included a foreign particle lodged in the main carburetor jet. Also, the rated drawbar load test was halted because of rain. The following day, moisture accumulated in the distributor cap. Aside from these slight nuisances, no repairs or adjustments were noted during 66 hours of engine operation. Test C at 100-percent maximum load indicated 10.47 hp-hours per gallon under a load of 14.34 belt hp. At a Test D rated load of 12.97 hp, economy was noted at 10.35. Test H was run in second gear. At a speed of 3.65 mph the LA pulled 1,091 lbs. at 3.65 mph with a slippage of 4.49percent , an output of 10.62 drawbar hp, and an economy of 8.46 hp-hours per gallon. A low-gear maximum pull of 1,936 lbs. was recorded in Test G.

COLLECTOR VALUES	1	2	3	4
MODEL LA	$4,000	$3,000	$2,000	$800

Subtract $400 if missing belt pully assembly.

Model M tractor

In October 1947 Deere & Company sent one of its new Model M tractors to the Tractor Test Laboratory in Lincoln, Nebraska. The Model M was equipped with a two-cylinder vertical engine with a 4-inch bore and stroke. It was rated at 1,650 rpm. Production of the Model M ended in 1952.

Nebraska Test Data

Model: John Deere Model M

Test No. 387

Date Tested: October 6 to October 16, 1947

Weighing in at 2,695 lbs., the John Deere M feature a two-cylinder vertical engine with a 4-inch bore and stroke. Using an L-head design, it was rated at 1,650 rpm. Also featured was a Delco-Remy electrical system, plus a Marvel-Schebler TSX-245 carburetor. Tire equipment included 9-24-inch rear and 5.00-15-inch front rubber. The Model M was built with four forward speeds of l 5/8, 3-1/8, 4-1/4, and 10 mph. Third gear was used for Test H and indicated a rated drawbar output of 14.65 hp, along with a pull of 1,279 lbs. at 4.3 mph with slippage of 6.8 percent. Fuel economy settled at 9.24 hp-hours per gallon. A low gear maximum pull of 2,329 lbs. was noted in Test G, along with a speed of 1.61 mph and slippage of 16.08 percent. Under a Test C operating maximum load of 19.49 belt hp, the Model M delivered 11.12 hp-hours per gallon, compared to 11.10 at the Test D rated load of 18.23 belt hp. At one point during the test it was necessary to remove the cylinder head and reseat the valves. No other repairs were noted during 29-1/2 hours of operating time.

COLLECTOR VALUES	1	2	3	4
MODEL M	$5,000	$3,500	$2,000	$500

Model MT tractor

Production of the John Deere Model MT tractor ran from 1949 to 1952. It was essentially the same tractor as the Model M, but was of the tricycle chassis design. Despite its small size this tractor could pull more than 1,100 lbs. at its rated load. The M and MT tractors were built at Deere's Dubuque (Iowa) Works.

Nebraska Test Data

Model: John Deere Model M

Test No. 423

Date Tested: September 7 to September 16, 1949

The John Deere MT weighed in at 3,183 lbs., with an additional 343 lbs. of ballast added per wheel for Tests F, G, and H. Advertised speeds of 1-3/4, 3-1/4, 4-1/2, and 11 mph were provided, with third gear being used for Test H. At a rated load of 14.15 drawbar hp, the MT pulled 1,118 lbs. at 4.75 mph with a slippage of 3.77 percent. Fuel economy was recorded at 9.03 hp-hours per gallon. A low-gear maximum pull of 2,385 lbs. at a speed of 1.73 mph was noted in Test G. The MT tractor featured a two-cylinder vertical engine of l-head design. Rated at 1,650 rpm, it used a 4-inch bore and stroke. Also included were a Delco-Remy electrical system and a Marvel-Schebler TSX245 carburetor. Tire equipment included 5.00-15-inch front and 9-34-inch rear rubber. At a Test D rated load of 18.42 belt hp the MT yielded 11.01 hp-hours per gallon, compared to 11.16 under the Test C operating maximum load of 19.8 belt hp.

COLLECTOR VALUES	1	2	3	4
MODEL MT	$4,000	$3,000	$2,000	$500

Model MC crawler

Using the same engine as the Model M and Model MT tractors, the MC crawler model had a displacement of 101 cubic inches. Weighing 4,000 lbs., it could pull over 1,800 lbs. on the drawbar. The MC used three track rollers, and offered four forward speeds ranging from 0.8 to 4.7 mph. Model MC crawlers were built from 1949 to 1952.

Nebraska Test Data

Model: John Deere Model MC

Test No. 448

Date Tested: July 20 to July 26, 1950

Advertised speeds of 0.9, 2.2, 2.9, and 4.7 mph were featured in the MC crawler tractor. Test G yielded a maximum low-gear pull of 1,654 lbs. with a slippage of 5.11 percent. Test H at a rated load of 13.88 drawbar hp was run in third gear. Under a pull of 1,833 lbs. at 2.84 mph, the MC delivered a fuel economy of 8.73 hp-hours per gallon. Test weight was 4,293 lbs. During Test B a decrease in hp occurred. Upon removing the engine head and cleaning out some fuel deposits the test resumed with improved performance. With these exceptions, no repairs or adjustments were noted over 50 hours of engine operating time. Test C at an operating maximum load of 20.12 belt hp yielded 11.36 hp-hours per gallon, with this figure slipping very slightly to 11.13 under a Test D rated load of 18.91 belt hp. The MC featured a two-cylinder vertical, l-head engine with a dispalcement of 101 cubic inches. Rated at 1,650 rpm, it carried a 4-inch bore and stroke.

COLLECTOR VALUES	1	2	3	4
MODEL MC CRAWLER	$9,000	$7,000	$4,000	$2,000

Model R tractor

In 1949 John Deere introduced its first diesel tractor, the Model R. This big two-cylinder model used a two-cylinder engine with a 5-3/4 x 8-inch bore and stroke, with a rated speed of 1,000 rpm. The main engine had a displacement of 416 cubic inches and was designed with a 16 to 1 compression ratio. A two-cylinder gasoline engine was used for starting. At maximum load the Model R could develop approximately 48-1/2 belt hp. It weighed nearly 7,400 lbs. Production of the Model R ended in 1952.

Nebraska Test Data

Model: John Deere Model R
Test No. 406
Date Tested: April 19 to April 28, 1949

Deere's first diesel tractor opened the 1949 testing season at the Tractor Test Laboratory. Featuring a two-cylinder horizontal, I-head engine, this tractor was rated at 1,000 rpm and carried a 5-3/4 x 8-inch bore and stroke. Also featured was a Deere-built two-cylinder starting engine with a 2-6/10 x 2-5/16-inch bore and stroke and a rated speed of 4,000 rpm. A glass sediment bowl broke during the limber-up run, otherwise no repairs or adjustments were noted during 57 hours of engine operating time. Bare weight was 7,603 lbs. Standard equipment included 14-34-inch rear and 7.50-18-inch front tires. Advertised speeds of 2-1/8, 3-1/3, 4-1/4, 5-1/3, and 11-1/2 mph were provided. Third gear was used for Test H. Results indicated a fuel economy of 15.19 hp-hours per gallon, along with a rated output of 34.45 drawbar hp, a pull of 3,140 lbs. at 4.11 mph and slippage of 4.7 percent. A Test G maximum pull in low gear tallied 6,644 lbs. at 1.88 mph with slippage of 15.01 percent. Tests B & C at 100 percent maximum belt load indicated an economy of 17.35 hp-hours per gallon at 48.58 hp, while Test D at a rated load of 43.52 belt hp produced an economy of 17.63 hp-hours per gallon.

COLLECTOR VALUES	1	2	3	4
MODEL R	$5,500	$3,000	$2,000	$800

The John Deere 40 was a continuation of the new numbered series that had been introduced with the 50 and 60 tractors in 1952. The 40 row-crop model shown here had a two-cylinder vertical engine with a 4-inch bore and stroke. Although this model had a bare weight of only 3,200 lbs., it was capable of over 17 drawbar hp. A three-point hitch was standard equipment for the John Deere Model 40 tractors. Rated at 1,850 rpm, the 40 tractors could pull two plow bottoms in most soils. Extra equipment included a belt pulley, electric lights and PTO shaft. Production of the Model 40 row-crop ran from 1953 to 1956.

Model 40 tractors

John Deere 40 row crop

Nebraska Test Data

Model: John Deere Model 40 Row Crop
Test No. 503
Date Tested: September 9 to September 17, 1953

Rated at 1,850 rpm, the John Deere 40 carried a two-cylinder vertical engine of 4-inch bore and stroke with a displacement of 101 cubic inches. Forward speeds of 1-5/8, 3-7/8, 4-1/4, and 12 mph were featured, along with 5.00-15-inch front and 9-34-inch rear tires. Bare weight was 3,219 lbs., to which was added 675 lbs. of ballast on each rear wheel during Tests F, G, and H. No repairs or adjustments were noted during 74 hours of operating time. At a Test C operating maximum load of 23.51 belt hp, fuel economy was registered at 11.16 hp-hours per gallon, with an even better economy figure of 11.31 appearing under a Test D rated load of 21.47 belt hp. Test G produced a low-gear maximum pull of 3,022 lbs. at 1.53 mph Third gear was used for the 10-hour run of Test H. At a rated output of 17.43 drawbar hp the 40 yielded a fuel economy of 9.38 hp-hours per gallon while pulling a 1,475 lb. load at 4.43 mph under a slippage of 5.67 percent.

Nebraska Test Data

Model: John Deere Model 40 Standard

Test No. 504

Date Tested: September 9 to September 23, 1953

Using an identical engine and identical forward speeds, the 40 Standard weighed in at 2,925 lbs. Standard equipment included 5.00-15-inch front and 10-24-inch rear tires. During Tests F, G, and H an additional 638 lbs. of ballast was added to each rear wheel. While engine torque peaked at 153.5 lbs.-ft. at 1,441 rpm in the 40 noted in Test No. 503, a maximum torque of 155.7 lbs.-ft. at 1,343 rpm was recorded for the 40 Standard shown here. Test G yielded a low-gear maximum pull of 2,543 lbs. at 1.59 mph. Third gear was used for Test H, and at a rated output of 17.05 drawbar hp, the 40 Standard pulled 1,364 lbs. at 4.69 mph, and recorded a slippage of 6.22 percent. Fuel economy totaled 10.2 hp-hours per gallon. Under a Test C operating maximum load of 23.21 belt hp the 40 Standard produced a fuel economy of 11.27 hp-hours per gallon, with a slight drop in the economy figure to 11.19 under a Test D rated belt load of 21.14 hp. No repairs or adjustments were noted during 54 hours of operating time.

Nebraska Test Data

Model: John Deere Model 40 S (all-fuel)

Test No. 546

Date Tested: June 3 to June 10, 1955

The 40-S tractor featured a two-cylinder vertical engine with a 4-inch bore and stroke. Rated at 1,850 rpm, this engine had a displacement of 101 cubic inches. Also featured were forward speeds of 1-5/8, 3-1/8, 4-1/4, and 12 mph. Tire equipment included 9-24-inch rear and 5.00-15-inch front rubber. With a bare weight of 3,007 lbs., the 40-S gained an additional 581 lbs. on each rear wheel during Tests F, G, and H. A low-gear maximum pull of 2,511 lbs. was noted in Test G. Run at 1.39 mph. This test indicated a slippage of 15.78 percent. Test H, run in third gear, and with a rated output of 14.35 drawbar hp, yielded a pull of 1,329 lbs. at 4.05 mph and a slippage of 6.1 percent. Fuel economy came to 8.69 hp-hours per gallon of tractor fuel. Engine torque peaked at 132.6 lbs.-ft. with an engine speed of 1,391 rpm. At a Test D rated belt load of 17.8 hp, fuel economy came to 9.8 hp-hours per gallon, while under a Test C operating maximum load of 19.13 hp, the economy figure rested at 10.51 hp-hours per gallon. No repairs or adjustments were noted during 47-1/2 hours of operating time.

COLLECTOR VALUES	1	2	3	4
MODEL 40 SPECIAL	$10,000	$7,500	$4,500	$2,000
MODEL 40 STANDARD	$5,000	$3,500	$2,000	$1,000
MODEL 40 UTILITY	$5,000	$3,500	$2,000	$1,000
MODEL 40 HI-CROP	$10,000	$7,500	$4,500	$2,000
MODEL 40 TRICYCLE	$4,000	$3,000	$2,000	$500
MODEL 40 TWO-ROW UTILITY	$5,000	$3,500	$2,000	$1,000

Like other 40-series tractors, the 40 C crawler was built in the 1953 through 1956 period. It also used the same 101-cid engine that was capable of over 23-1/2 belt hp. Model 40 C crawlers could be furnished with either a four-roller or a five-roller undercarriage, the latter being optional. Four rollers were standard.

Model 40 C crawler

Nebraska Test Data

Model: John Deere Model 40 C

Test No. 505

Date Tested: September 9 to September 23, 1953

Once again Deere featured the same two-cylinder vertical engine noted in Tests 503 and 504. Obviously, the 40 C was of tracklayer design, and featured forward speeds of 0.82, 2.21, 2.95, and 5.31 mph. Weighing in at 4,669 lbs. the 40 C went through 48-1/2 hours of operating time with no recorded repairs or adjustments. Test G produced a low-gear maximum pull of 4,515 lbs. at 0.76 mph with a slippage of 6.49 percent. The 10-hour run of Test H at a rated drawbar load of 15.08 hp came up with a fuel economy of 8.33 hp-hours per gallon. Test H also indicated a pull of 1,938 lbs. at 2.92 mph with a slippage of 1.57 percent. Engine torque at the dynamometer peaked at 158.9 lbs.-ft. with an engine speed of 1,254 rpm. Test C, run at an operating maximum load of 23.64 belt hp yielded a fuel economy of 11.61 hp-hours per gallon. That climbed slightly to 11.66 under a Test D rated belt load of 21.28 hp.

COLLECTOR VALUES	1	2	3	4
MODEL 40C	$9,000	$7,000	$3,500	$1,500

John Deere Model 50

In 1952 the end was at hand for the "letter series" tractors, with the new "number series" models taking their place. The first of these was the John Deere 50. It was available in various styles, although the conventional row-crop design was the most popular. The 50 was designed around a two-cylinder engine with a 4-11/16 x 5-1/2-inch bore and stroke. Rated at 1,250 rpm, it produced nearly 21 drawbar hp. Production of the John Deere 50 ended in 1956. During 1955 and 1956 this model was also available with an LP gas option.

Nebraska Test Data

Model: John Deere Model 50

Test No. 486

Date Tested: October 15 to October 22, 1952

The John Deere 50 presented for this test was equipped with Deere's horizontal two-cylinder I-head engine. Rated at 1,250 rpm, it carried a 4-11/18 x 5-1/2-inch bore and stroke for a 190.4-cubic inch displacement. Compression ratio was 6.10:1. No repairs or adjustments were noted during 52-1/2 hours of operating time. Standard equipment included 11-38 rear and 5.50-16 inch front tires, plus advertised speeds of 1-1/2, 2-1/2, 3-1/2, 4-1/2, 5-3/4, and 10 mph. Bare tractor weight was 4,855 lbs., but this was burdened with an additional 289 lbs. of liquid ballast on each rear wheel during Tests F, G, and H. At a rated drawbar load of 20.89 hp the Model 50 delivered a fuel economy of 10.51 hp-hours per gallon as noted in Test H. This 10-hour run also indicated a pull of 1,747 lbs. at 4.48 mph with a slippage of 5.74 percent. Test G achieved a low-gear maximum pull of 3,504 lbs. at 1.34 mph with a slippage of 18.43 percent. Under Test C, run at an operating maximum load of 28.85 belt hp, fuel economy came in at 11.82 hp-hours per gallon, dropping slightly to 11.79 at a Test D rated belt load of 26.32 hp. Engine torque peaked at 733 rpm with a reading of 183.8 lbs.-ft.

Nebraska Test Data

Model: John Deere Model 50 (all-fuel)

Test No. 507

Date Tested: September 25 to October 2, 1953

During 39-1/2 hours of running time the 50 All-Fuel model was operated on tractor fuel. With this exception the tractor presented here was virtually identical to that shown in Test No. 486. Weighing in at 4,965 lbs., it was equipped with 11-38 rear and 5.50-16-inch front tires. During Tests F, G, and H an additional 281 lbs. of liquid ballast was added to each rear wheel. Advertised speeds of 1-1/2, 2-1/2, 3-1/2, 4-1/2, 5-3/8 and 10 mph were featured. Also included was a two-cylinder horizontal engine rated at 1,250 rpm and carrying a 4-11/16 x 5-5/8, inch bore and stroke for a displacement of 190.4 cubic inches. Engine torque peaked at 158.6 lbs.-ft. with an engine speed of 852 rpm. Test C, run at an operating maximum load of 23.64 belt hp, produced a fuel economy of 11.09 hp-hours per gallon, while this figure dropped very slightly to 11.06 at a Test D rated belt load of 21.89 hp. Test G produced a low-gear maximum pull of 3,583 lbs. at 1.36 mph. Third gear was used for the 10-hour run of Test H. At a rated drawbar load of 17.63 hp the 50 All-Fuel pulled 1,904 lbs. at 3.47 mph against a recorded slippage of 4.68 percent. Fuel economy in this test totaled 10.07 hp-hours per gallon.

Nebraska Test Data

Model: John Deere Model 50 (LP gas)

Test No. 540

Date Tested: May 9 to May 13, 1955

Compared to the John Deere 50 of Test No. 507, the 50 LP tested here differed in external appearance mainly due to the large propane cylinder that replaced the fuel tank. An internal change was an 8:1 compression ratio used in this model, compared to a 5.35:1 ratio for the tractor in Test No. 507. During 39 hours of operating time, no repairs or adjustments were noted. Test C, run at an operating maximum load of 30.18 belt hp, produced a fuel economy of 9.13 hp-hours per gallon, slipping to 9.03 per gallon of propane at a Test D rated belt load of 27.61 hp. Engine torque peaked at 199.9 lbs.-ft. with an engine speed of 916 rpm. Like the 50 All-Fuel previously noted, this tractor was rated at 1,250 rpm. Drawbar testing produced a Test G low-gear maximum pull of 3,466 lbs. at 1.36 mph and a slippage of 16.3 percent. In the 10-hour drawbar run of Test H, it came in at 7.83 hp-hours per gallon of propane fuel. During this test the 50 LP delivered 22.13 drawbar hp, plus a pull of 1,858 lbs. at 4.47 mph and a slippage of 5.12 percent.

COLLECTOR VALUES	1	2	3	4
MODEL 50	$3,500	$2,500	$1,500	$750

Model 60 tractor

The John Deere 60 was built in the 1952 through 1956 period. Weighing 5,300 lbs., it was powered by a two-cylinder engine with a 5-1/2 x 6-3/4-inch bore and stroke. The engine displaced 321 cubic inches and was rated at 975 rpm. This model had a maximum output of approximately 38-1/2 belt hp. The 60 was built in numerous axle configurations.

Nebraska Test Data

Model: John Deere Model 60
Test No. 472
Date Tested: May 26 to June 2, 1952

Advertised speeds of 1-1/2, 2-1/2, 3-1/2, 4-1/2, 6-1/4, and 11 mph were featured in the John Deere 60. Standard tire equipment included 6.00-16-inch front and 12-38-inch rear rubber. Bare tractor weight was 5,911 lbs., to which was added another 747 lbs. of weight on each rear wheel during Tests F, G, and H. At a rated drawbar load of 28.04 hp, Test H indicated a fuel economy of 10.22 hp-hours per gallon under a pull of 2,402 lbs. at 4.38 mph and a slippage of 5.56 percent. Fourth gear was used for this test. A low-gear maximum pull of 4,319 lbs. at 1.23 mph was noted in Test G. Rated at 975 rpm, the two-cylinder horizontal engine developed a maximum torque of 251.3 lbs.-ft. at 653 rpm. A displacement of 321 cubic inches resulted from the 5-1/2 x 6-3/4 inch bore and stroke. No repairs or adjustments were noted during 56 hours of operating time. Test C, at an operating maximum load of 38.58 belt hp, yielded a fuel economy of 11.61 hp-hours per gallon. That figure swelled to 11.64 at a Test D rated belt load of 35.3 hp.

Nebraska Test Data

Model: John Deere Model 60 (all-fuel)
Test No. 490
Date Tested: April 15 to April 21, 1953

In accordance with its "All-Fuel" designation, the tractor presented for this test went through 54-1/2 hours of operation on "tractor fuel." No repairs or adjustments were noted during this period. Standard features included forward speeds of 1-1/2, 2-1/2, 3-1/2, 4-1/2, 6-1/4, and 11 mph. Also included were 12-38-inch rear and 6.00-16-inch front tires. With a bare weight of 5,950 lbs., the 60 was burdened with an additional 420 lbs. of liquid ballast in each rear wheel during Tests F, G, and H. The latter test, run at a rated drawbar load of 22.68 hp, indicated an economy of 9.41 hp-hours per gallon of tractor fuel. During this 10-hour run a pull of 1,918 lbs. at 4.44 mph was recorded, along with a slippage of 4.27 percent. In Test G, run at operating maximum load, the 60 achieved a low-gear maximum pull of 4,499 lbs. at 1.22 mph. Test D, run at a rated belt load of 28.33 hp produced a fuel economy of 10.77 hp-hours per gallon, with this figure increasing to 11.08 at a Test C operating maximum load of 31.09 belt hp. Engine torque peaked at 213.9 lbs.-ft. with an engine speed of 648 rpm. A two-cylinder horizontal engine was featured. Rated at 975 rpm, it carried a 5-1/2 x 6-3/4 inch bore and stroke and displaced 321 cubic inches.

Nebraska Test Data

Model: John Deere Model 60 (LP fuel)
Test No. 513
Date Tested: November 6 to November 12, 1953

Propane fuel was used for this test. The special tank significantly altered the tractor's appearance, compared to the tractors in Tests No. 472 and 490. No repairs or adjustments were noted during 42-1/2 hours of operating time. Basic specifications remained the same for this tractor as noted in the tests previously cited. The 321-cid engine carried a 7.3:1 compression ratio, compared to 6:1 for the gasoline model of Test No. 472 and 4.7:1 for the 60 All-Fuel tractor of Test No. 490. Rated at 975 rpm, the 60 LP achieved its maximum torque of 238.7 lbs.-ft. at an engine speed of 754 rpm. Test C, run at an operating maximum belt load of 38.94 hp, produced an economy of 9.16 hp-hours per gallon, climbing to 9.22 at a Test D rated belt load of 35.95 hp. Test G at an operating maximum drawbar load of 17.11 in low gear produced a pull of 5,258 lbs. at 1.22 mph with a recorded slippage of 17.12 percent. The 10-hour run of Test H was made in fourth gear. With an output of 28.78 hp, the 60 LP pulled 2,443 lbs. at 4.42 mph with a slippage of 4.47 percent. Economy totaled 7.96 hp-hours per gallon of propane fuel.

COLLECTOR VALUES	1	2	3	4
MODEL 60	$3,000	$2,000	$1,000	$500

Model 60 Standard tractor

Two varieties of the Model 60 Standard were built in the 1952-1956 period. Until 1954 the "low-seat" style was built and during 1955 and 1956 the "high-seat" style was built. Except for this, the design remained basically unchanged. The standard-tread style was built especially for those whose farming operations required this kind of chassis as compared to the row-crop tractor. Deere also built a 60 Orchard tractor during the same 1952-1956 period.

Model 70 tractor

COLLECTOR VALUES	1	2	3	4
HIGH-SEAT 60 STANDARD	$3,000	$2,000	$1,000	$500
LOW-SEAT 60 STANDARD	$4,800	$3,400	$2,000	$1,000

Production of the John Deere 70 began in 1953 and continued until 1956. Rated at 975 rpm, the two-cylinder engine had a 5-7/8 x 7-inch bore and stroke. It had a maximum output of about 46 belt hp. John Deere 70 row-crop tractors were available in various configurations, including a special Hi-Crop model.

Nebraska Test Data

Model: John Deere Model 70

Test No. 493

Date Tested: May 15 to May 20, 1953

Rated at 975 rpm, the 70 achieved a maximum torque of 287.9 lbs.-ft. at 805 rpm, maintaining this torque down to 748 rpm. A John Deere two-cylinder horizontal engine was featured. It used a 5-7/8 x 7- inch bore and stroke. Advertised speeds of 2.5, 3.5, 4.5, 6.5, 8.75, and 12.5 mph were used with third gear selected for the rated drawbar run of Test H. Weighing in at 6,617 lbs., the 70 used 13-38 rear and 6.00-16-inch front tires as standard equipment. During Tests F, G, and H an additional 1,030 lbs. of ballast was added to each rear wheel. Test H, run at a rated load of 33.61 drawbar hp, recorded a pull of 2,771 lbs. at 4.55 mph and a slippage of 5.35 percent. Fuel economy came in at 10.33 hp-hours per gallon. A low-gear maximum pull of 5,453 lbs. at 2.18 mph was noted in Test G. Belt testing indicated a fuel economy of 11.7 hp-hours per gallon under a Test D rated load of 43 hp. Fuel economy climbed to 11.92 in Test C, run at an operating maximum load of 45.88 belt hp.

Nebraska Test Data

Model: John Deere Model 70 (all-fuel)

Test No. 506

Date Tested: September 25 to October 1, 1953

Rated at 975 rpm, the all-fuel 70 had a two-cylinder engine with 6-1/8 x 7-inch bore and stroke displacing 412.5 cubic inches. It also featured forward gears of 2.5, 3.5, 4.5, 6.5, 8.75, and 12.5 mph. Standard equipment also included 13-38-inch rear and 6.00-16-inch front tires. Bare tractor weight was 6,655 lbs. Tests F, G, and H used an additional 750 lbs. of weight on each rear wheel. Test G indicated a low-gear maximum pull of 5,102 lbs. at 2.17 mph with a slippage of 16.05 percent. The 10-hour run of Test H was made under a rated drawbar load of 31.06 hp, and resulted in a fuel economy of 9.94 hp-hours per gallon of tractor fuel. During this test the 70 All-Fuel pulled 2,539 lbs. at 4.59 mph with a slippage of 3.93 percent. Under a Test C operating maximum load of 40.9 belt hp, fuel economy was recorded at 11.06 hp-hours per gallon. This figure slipped to 10.90 under a Test D rated belt load of 38.4 hp. A maximum engine torque of 265.3 lbs.-ft. was recorded at 759 rpm. No repairs or adjustments were noted during 41 hours of running time.

Nebraska Test Data

Model: John Deere Model 70 (LP fuel)

Test No. 514

Date Tested: November 6 to November 12, 1953

Of the same general design as the John Deere 70 models tested previously, the 70 LP also used the same 379.5-cid engine as the gasoline. In this case, a compression ratio of 7.3:1 was used to better accommodate propane fuel. Test H, run in third gear, and with an output of 34.95 drawbar hp yielded a pull of 2,878 lbs. at 4.55 mph with a slippage of 4.99 percent. Fuel economy came in at 8.34 hp-hours per gallon of propane. Test G gave a low-gear maximum pull of 6,127 lbs. at 2.16 mph. While this tractor was rated at 975 rpm, a maximum torque of 298.7 lbs.-ft. was registered at a speed of 889 rpm. Belt testing indicated a Test D rated load fuel economy of 9.52 hp-hours per gallon while under a burden of 44.2 hp. At a Test C operating maximum load of 48.18 hp, fuel economy improved slightly to stand at 9.57. No repairs or adjustments were noted during 41 hours of operating time.

COLLECTOR VALUES	1	2	3	4
MODEL 70	$4,000	$3,000	$2,000	$1,000

Model 70 Standard LP

Built during the same 1953 through 1956 production period as the 70 Row-Crop style, the 70 Standard was likewise available for burning LP gas and in an All-Fuel version for burning low-grade fuels. The all-fuel engines were bored out to 6-1/8 inches, while the 7-inch stroke remained the same. This model had a shipping weight of 6,815 lbs.

COLLECTOR VALUES	1	2	3	4
MODEL 70 STANDARD ALL-FUEL	$5,000	$4,000	$3,000	$1,500

Deere's first row-crop diesel came to the market in 1954. The 70 Diesel was available as both a standard-tread and row-crop tractor. This model used a two-cylinder engine with a 6-1/8 x 6-3/8-inch bore and stroke, with a rated speed of 1,125 rpm. Starting was by a Deere-built V-4 gasoline starting engine; the latter was equipped with an electric starter. When tested at Nebraska in 1954, the 70 Diesel set a new fuel economy record that stood for a number of years. This tractor was capable of over 50 belt hp.

Model 70 Diesel

Nebraska Test Data

Model: John Deere Model 70 Diesel
Test No. 528
Date Tested: October 19 to October 22, 1954

The 70 Diesel delivered a fuel economy of 17.72 hp-hours per gallon at a Test D rated load of 44.14 hp. At a Test B, 100 percent maximum belt load of 50.4 hp, fuel economy went still higher to stand at 17.74 hp-hours per gallon. Weighing in at 7,137 lbs., the 70 Diesel was burdened with an additional 940 lbs. of weight on each rear wheel during Tests F and H. As with other diesel models, Tests F and G were one and the same-100 percent maximum drawbar load. A low gear maximum pull of 6,189 lbs. was achieved at a speed of 2.19 mph and slippage of 15.85 percent. Test H yielded a fuel economy of 15.78 hp-hours per gallon over the 10-hour run. This test, made in third gear, showed a rated output of 34.79 hp, along with a pull of 2,831 lbs. at 4.61 mph and a slippage of 4.33 percent. Features included 13-38-inch rear and 6.00-16-inch front tires, along with advertised speeds of 2.5, 3.5, 4.5, 6.5, 8.75, and 12.5 mph. The two-cylinder horizontal diesel engine carried a 6-1/8, x 6-3/8-inch bore and stroke displacing 376-cubic inches. Rated at 1,125 rpm, this tractor was equipped with a four-cylinder starting engine carrying a 2 x 1-1/2-inch bore and stroke, and a displacement of 18.85 cubic inches with a rated speed of 5,500 rpm. During 44 hours of operation, no repairs or adjustments were noted.

COLLECTOR VALUES	1	2	3	4
MODEL 70 DIESEL	$4,000	$3,000	$2,000	$1,000

Model 80 Diesel

Built only during 1955 and 1956, the John Deere 80 was the largest of the line at the time. Weighing 8,500 lbs., the 80 Diesel had a displacement of 471.5 cubic inches from its big two-cylinder engine. It used a 6-1/8 x 8-inch bore and stroke. This tractor was capable of over 65 belt hp, as well as 46-plus horses at the drawbar.

Nebraska Test Data

Model: John Deere Model 80 Diesel
Test No. 567
Date Tested: October 27 to November 1, 1955

Weighing 8,511 lbs., the 80 Diesel carried 15-34-inch rear and 7.50-18-inch front tires. Advertised speeds of 2-1/2, 3-1/2, 4-1/2, 5-1/3, 6-3/4, and 12-1/4mph were provided. During Tests F, G and H an additional 1,492 lbs. was added to each rear wheel. Test G produced a low-gear maximum pull of 7,394 lbs. at 2.06 mph with a slippage of 14.17 percent. Third gear was used for Test H, and with a rated drawbar output of 46.83 hp, this test recorded a pull of 3,979 lbs. at 4.41 mph and a slippage of 6.19 percent. Fuel economy came in at 15.96 hp-hours per gallon. The 80 Diesel was equipped with a two-cylinder horizontal engine rated at 1,125 rpm. It achieved a peak torque of 424.4 lbs.-ft. with an engine speed of 768 rpm. With a 471.5-cid engine, it carried a 6-1/8 x 8-inch bore and stroke. Also included was a four-cylinder "Vee-type" starting engine with a 2 x 1-1/2 inch bore and stroke. Belt testing indicated a fuel economy of 17.58 hp-hours per gallon of diesel fuel under a Test B 100-percent load of 65.33 hp. At a Test D rated belt load of 57.52 hp, fuel economy came in at 17.84 hp-hours per gallon. No repairs or adjustments were noted during 40 hours of operating time.

COLLECTOR VALUES	1	2	3	4
MODEL 80	$6,500	$5,000	$3,000	$1,300

Model 320

Introduced in 1956, the Model 320 was equipped with the same two-cylinder vertical, 4 x 4 engine as many of its predecessors, such as the Model M. In this instance, the engine was rated at 1650 rpm and about 21-1/2 hp. The 320 was built in several chassis configurations.

COLLECTOR VALUES	1	2	3	4
MODEL 320	$10,000	$7,500	$4,500	$1,500

Model 420

Several styles of the 420 tractor were built begining in 1956 and continuing into 1958. The 420-S standard-tread model is shown here and it weighed 2,850 lbs. These tractors were equipped with a 4-1/4 x 4-inch two-cylinder vertical engine rated at 1,850 rpm. It was capable of 26 drawbar and 28 belt hp.

Nebraska Test Data

Model: John Deere Model 420 S

Test No. 600

Date Tested: October 13 to October 25, 1956

This tractor's test weight of 4,311 lbs. included 646 lbs. of weight added to each rear wheel during Tests F, G, and H. Features included 10-24-inch rear and 5.00-15-inch front tires, along with forward speeds of 1-5/8, 3-1/8, 4-1/4 and 12 mph. It featured a two-cylinder, 113-cid engine with a 5.2:1 compression ratio designed into this All-Fuel model. New spark plugs were installed prior to Test B. Otherwise nothing of notice was recorded during 43 hours of operation. Test L indicated a maximum 107 percent of rated torque at 65 percent of the rated 1,850 rpm. At a Test D rated belt load of 19.95 hp, fuel economy came in at 9.05 hp-hours per gallon of tractor fuel. This rose to 9.98 at a Test B & C 100 percent maximum load of 22.73 belt hp. Drawbar fuel economy was posted at 8.1 hp-hours per gallon of tractor fuel in Test H. This run was made in third gear, and with a rated load of 17.07 drawbar hp, a pull of 1,482 lbs. at 4.32 mph was recorded against a slippage of 5.24 percent. Test G yielded a low-gear maximum pull of 2,734 lbs. at 1.54 mph with a slippage of 11.63 percent.

COLLECTOR VALUES	1	2	3	4
MODEL 420	$6,000	$4,000	$2,000	$1,000

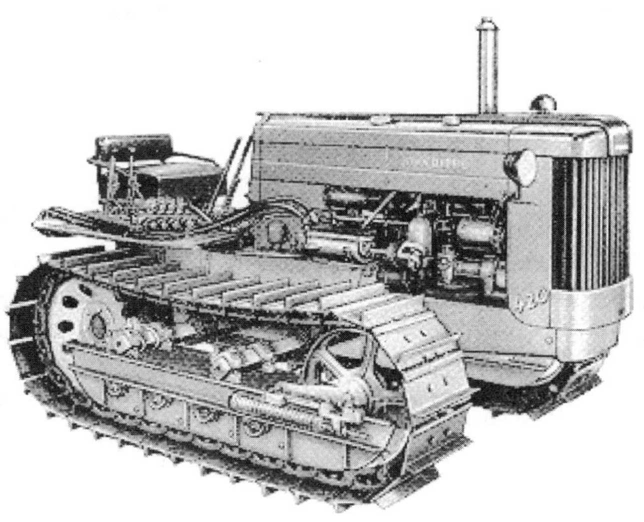

Model 420 C crawler

Weighing slightly over 5,000 lbs., the 420 C crawler was offered in the 1956 through 1958 period. This tractor had the same two-cylinder 4-1/4 x 4 engine as other models in the 420 series. In testing, the 420-C demonstrated a maximum drawbar pull of over 4,800 lbs., although its rated pull was only 2,400 lbs.

Nebraska Test Data

Model: John Deere Model 420 C crawler

Test No. 601

Date Tested: October 15 to October 25, 1956

The 420 C crawler weighed in at 5,079 lbs. At a Test C operating maximum belt load of 27.39 hp, fuel economy was reported at 11.9 hp-hours per gallon, with an even better rating of 11.95 at a Test D rated belt load of 25.36 hp. Rated speed for this tractor was 1,850 rpm, with Test L indicating 107 percent of rated-speed torque was developed at 65 percent of rated engine speed. Prior to Test B, the engine head was removed and combustion chamber cleaned; otherwise no repairs or adjustments were noted during 41-1/2 hours of operating time. Features of the 420-C included forward speeds of 7/8, 2-1/4, 3, and 5-1/4 mph. Also included was a John Deere two-cylinder vertical engine with a 4.250 x 4.00 bore and stroke for a 113 cubic inch displacement. Under a Test G maximum drawbar load using low gear, the 420-C pulled 4,862 lbs. at 0.78 mph with a slippage of 10.08 percent. Third gear was used for Test H. At a rated drawbar output of 18.65 hp, this tractor pulled 2,407 lbs. at 2.91 mph with a slippage of 2.09 percent. Fuel economy in this test totaled 8.97 hp-hours per gallon of gasoline.

COLLECTOR VALUES	1	2	3	4
MODEL 420 C CRAWLER	$7,000	$5,000	$3,000	$1,500

Model 420 W

Like others of the 420 series, the 420 W was built at Deere's Dubuque (Iowa) Works. This model had an adjustable-width front axle, as well as adjustable rear wheel treads. Production of all 420 models ended in 1958. The 420 W had the same general specifications as others of the 420 series.

Nebraska Test Data

Model: John Deere Model 420 W

Test No. 599

Date Tested: October 13 to October 25, 1956

Features of the 420-W included forward speeds of l-5/8, 3-1/8, 4-1/4, and 12 mph. Also included were 12-28-inch rear and 6.00-16-inch front tires. The 5,781-lb. test weight added 1,095 lbs. on each rear wheel, as used in Tests F, G, and H. Prior to Test C the engine head was removed and the combustion chamber cleaned. Otherwise, no repairs or adjustments were noted during 43 hours of operating time. Using third gear, the 420-W went into Test H with a rated drawbar load of 20.82 hp, pulling 1,689 lbs. at 4.62 mph, and recorded a slippage of 4.5 percent. Fuel economy rested at 9.72 hp-hours per gallon. Test G yielded a low-gear maximum pull of 3,790 lbs. at 1.58 mph against a slippage of 14.5 percent. This tractor carried a two-cylinder vertical, 4.250 x 4.00-inch engine with a 113-cubic inch displacement. Rated at 1,850 rpm, it achieved 105 percent of rated torque at 70 percent of rated engine rpm. Belt testing indicated a fuel economy of 11.7 hp-hours per gallon at a Test D rated belt load of 24.9 hp. Fuel economy remained virtually identical, at 11.72 hp-hours per gallon with a Test C operating maximum load of 27.25 belt hp.

COLLECTOR VALUES	1	2	3	4
MODEL 520	$5,000	$3,500	$2,000	$1,000

Model 520 (LPG version)

Many new features were included on the "20" series tractors. An entirely new combustion chamber was featured on the gasoline and LP-gas models. This Model 520 is shown with the LP-gas option. The two-cylinder engine carried a 4-11/16 x 5-1/2 inch bore and stroke. The propane version used a compression ratio of 8.75 to 1, slightly higher than the gasoline model. This model was capable of about 38 belt hp. Production of the 520 tractors ran from 1956 to 1958.

Nebraska Test Data

Model: John Deere Model 520 (LP fuel)

Test No. 590

Date Tested: September 5 to September 11, 1956

One of three different John Deere 520 models presented for testing, this propane version carried most of the features later noted in Tests 592 and 597. Advertised speeds of 1-1/2, 2-1/2, 3-1/2, 4-1/2, 5-3/4, and 10 mph were standard, along with 13.9-36-inch rear and 5.50-16-inch front tires. Bare tractor weight was 5,890 lbs., to which was added an additional 355 lbs. of liquid ballast on each rear wheel during Tests F, G, and H. Test G manifested a low-gear maximum pull of 4,659 lbs. at 1.33 mph with a slippage of 15.8 percent. The 10-hour run of Test H, made in fourth gear, indicated a rated drawbar output of 26.1 hp. Test H also showed a pull of 2,229 lbs. at 4.39 mph and slippage of 3.95 percent. Fuel economy was recorded at 8.87 hp-hours per gallon of propane. This tractor used a two-cylinder horizontal engine with a 4-11/16 x 5-1/2-inch bore and stroke and displaced 189.8 cubic inches. The propane model shown here used an 8.75:1 compression ratio. At a Test C operating maximum load of 35.75 belt hp, the 520 LP yielded a fuel economy of 10.27 hp-hours per gallon of propane, with a slightly lower economy figure of 10.13 appearing under a Test D rated belt load of 32.46 hp. No repairs or adjustments were noted during 43-1/2 hours of operation. Test L showed the 520 LP attained 106 percent of rated speed torque at 70 percent of rated engine speed.

Nebraska Test Data

Model: John Deere Model 520 (All-Fuel)

Test No. 592

Date Tested: September 13 to September 17, 1956

The 520 All-Fuel model burned tractor fuel during the entire 42-1/2-hour procedure. No repairs or adjustments were reported during this time. Compared to the 520 LP model of Test No. 590, this model carried a 4.90:1 compression ratio, but used the same 189.8-cid, two-cylinder engine. Rated engine speed and advertised transmission speeds were also the same. The 5,715-lb. 520 All-Fuel was burdened with an additional 355 lbs. of liquid ballast in each rear wheel during Tests F, G, and H. Using third gear, Test H indicated a rated output of 18.95 hp, along with a pull of 2,087 lbs. at 3.41 mph and slippage of 3.6 percent. Fuel economy was posted at 10.03 hp-hours per gallon of tractor fuel. A low-gear maximum pull of 4,660 lbs. at 1.35 mph and slippage of 13.81percent was recorded in Test G. This tractor recorded 118 percent of rated speed engine torque when operating at 60percent of rated speed. With a Test C operating maximum load of 24.75 belt hp the 520 All-Fuel yielded a fuel economy of 10.94 hp-hours per gallon and slipped slightly to stand at 10.64 under a Test D rated belt load of 22.86 hp.

Nebraska Test Data

Model: John Deere Model 520 (gasoline)
Test No. 597
Date Tested: October 6 to October 10, 1956

The 520 gasoline model was virtually identical to the propane and all-fuel models. All used the same two-cylinder 4-11/16 x 5-1/2-inch engine, with this model carrying a 7.10:1 compression ratio. Total weight of this tractor was 6,505 lbs., including 350 lbs. of liquid ballast added to each rear wheel during Tests F, G, and H. No repairs or adjustments were noted during 38-1/2 hours of operation. Advertised speeds and other brief specifications may be noted under Tests 590 and 592. Test H, run in fourth gear, indicated a rated drawbar load of 26.05 hp. This test also showed a pull of 2,236 lbs. at 4.37 mph and slippage of 3.740. Fuel economy in this test totaled 11.1 hp-hours per gallon. Test G came up with a low-gear maximum pull of 4,695 lbs. at 1.37 mph and slippage of 12.41percent. In Test L, the 520 gasoline version came up with 105 percent of rated torque at 85 percent of the rated 1,325 rpm, repeating this peak again at 65 percent and at 60 percent of rated rpm. Fuel economy was noted at 12.7 hp-hours per gallon at a Test D rated belt load of 36.11 hp, with fuel economy climbing infinitesimally to 12.74 hp-hours per gallon at a Test C operating maximum load of 36.11 hp.

John Deere 620 Standard

John Deere 620 tractors were available in row-crop, standard-tread, orchard and Hi-Crop models. Except for the wheel configuration, all were essentially the same. The 620 used a 5-1/2 x 6-3/8-inch two-cylinder engine and was rated at 1,125 rpm. This gave a rated output of nearly 50 belt hp. Production of the 620 ran from 1956 to 1958.

Nebraska Test Data

Model: John Deere Model 620 (LP fuel)
Test No. 591
Date Tested: October 6 to October 11, 1956

The 620 LP featured a two-cylinder horizontal engine with a 5-1/2 x 6-3/8 inch bore and stroke for a 302.9-cubic inch displacement. Rated at 1,125 rpm, it achieved 103 percent of rated speed torque at 70 percent of rated speed. This propane model carried an 8.10:1 compression ratio. Features of this 5,809-lb. tractor included forward speeds of 1-1/2, 2-1/2, 3-1/2, 4-1/2, 6-1/2, and 11-1/2 mph, along with 13.6-38-inch rear and 6.00-16-inch front tires. During Tests F, G, and H, an additional 845 lbs. was added to each rear wheel. Test H, run in fourth gear, indicated a rated drawbar load of 34.53 hp, along with a pull of 2,916 lbs. at 4.44 mph and slippage of 4.78 percent. Fuel economy was noted at 8.71 hp-hours per gallon of propane. During 44 hours of operation, no repairs or adjustments were reported. Test C, run at an operating maximum load of 48.13 belt hp produced a fuel economy of 9.6 hp-hours per gallon of propane, improving to 9.73 at a Test D rated belt load of 42.85 hp.

Nebraska Test Data

Model: John Deere Model 620 (gasoline)
Test No. 598
Date Tested: October 10 to October 15, 1956

The 620 gasoline model was virtually identical to the propane version previously noted. Using the same 5-1/2 x 6-3/8-inch engine with a displacement of 302.9 cubic inches, it was rated at 1,125 rpm. Test L indicated that 112 percent of rated torque was developed at 70 percent of the rated engine speed. Advertised speeds and other specifications may be noted in the previous test. At a Test C operating maximum load of 44.25 belt hp, the 620 achieved a fuel economy of 12.52 hp-hours per gallon. Economy slipped slightly to stand at 12.49 under a Test D rated load of 41.45 belt hp. During 52-1/2 hours of operating time, no repairs or adjustments were noted. Test G showed a low-gear maximum pull of 6,122 lbs. at 1.3 mph and a slippage of 11.82 percent. The 10-hour Test H run was made in fourth gear, and with a rated drawbar load of 33.59 hp. Test H also showed a pull of 2,834 lbs. at 4.44 mph and a slippage of 4.26 percent. Fuel economy was posted at 11.25 hp-hours per gallon. The 8,655 pound total weight noted for this tractor included 818 lbs. on each rear wheel as used in Tests F, G, and H.

Nebraska Test Data

Model: John Deere Model 620 (all-fuel)
Test No. 604
Date Tested: November 1 to November 8, 1956

Equipped to burn various types of fuel, this unit went through 49-1/2 hours of testing on "tractor fuel." The two-cylinder, 5-1/2 x 6-3/8-inch engine carried a 4.78:1 compression ratio. Rated at 1,125 rpm, it had a 302.9-cubic inch displacement. Other features included 13.6-38 rear and 6.00-16 inch front tires, along with forward speeds of 1-1/2, 2-1/2, 3-1/2, 4-1/2, 6-1/2, and 11-1/2 mph. Weighing 6,855 lbs., it was burdened with an additional 827 lbs. on each rear wheel during Tests F, G, and H. A low-gear maximum pull of 6,107 lbs. at 1.29 mph and slippage of 12.3 percent was noted in Test G. Using fourth gear, this tractor pulled a rated 24.63 belt hp in Test H, with a drawbar pull of 2,065 lbs. at 4.47 mph and slippage of 3.36 percent. Fuel economy came to 9.96 hp-hours per gallon. Test L indicated that 119 percent of rated-speed torque was developed at 70 percent of rated engine speed. Belt testing at a Test D rated load of 30.59 hp yielded 11.21 hp-hours per gallon of tractor fuel, with a slightly improved figure of 11.25 at a Test C operating maximum load of 32.87 belt hp. No repairs or adjustments were required.

COLLECTOR VALUES	1	2	3	4
MODEL 620	$4,500	$3,000	$1,500	$800

Built in the same 1956-1958 period as the other "20" series tractors, the 720 was Deere's largest row-crop tractor of the period. Like others of this series, the 720 featured an independent live PTO shaft. The 720 was capable of over 59 belt hp and could deliver over 53 horses at the drawbar. Model 720 tractors were available in gasoline, all-fuel and LP-gas models.

Model 720 row crop

Nebraska Test Data

Model: John Deere Model 720 (LP fuel)

Test No. 593

Date Tested: September 17 to September 19, 1956

Rated at 1,125 rpm, the 70 LP carried a 7.94:1 compression ratio and featured a two-cylinder engine of horizontal design. The 360.5-cubic inch displacement resulted from the 6 x 6-3/8-inch bore and stroke. Also featured were forward speeds of 1.5, 2.25, 3.5, 4.5, 5.75, and 11.5 mph, along with 15.5-38-inch rear and 6.00-16-inch front tires. Bare tractor weight of this model was 7,717 lbs., to which was added 672 lbs. of liquid ballast for each rear wheel during Tests F, G, and H. Test L shows that a peak 108 percent of rated torque occurred at 80 percent of rated speed. Using low-gear, the 720 LP made a Test G maximum pull of 6,664 lbs. at 1.15 mph with a slippage of 15.72 percent. The 10-hour run of Test H indicated a drawbar fuel economy of 7.96 hp-hours per gallon of propane. This test also showed a rated output of 39.05 hp, a pull of 3,428 lbs. at 4.27 mph and slippage of 5.26 percent. During 45 hours of operation, no repairs or adjustments were noted. Test C, run at an operating maximum load of 55.48 hp, showed a fuel economy of 9.27 hp-hours per gallon of propane, dropping slightly to stand at 9.08 at a Test D rated belt load of 51.1 hp.

Nebraska Test Data

Model: John Deere Model 720 (gasoline)

Test No. 605

Date Tested: November 6 to November 12, 1956

The 720 delivered a Test H rated load of 40.37 hp, pulling 3,499 lbs. at 4.33 mph with a slippage of 3.97 percent. Fuel economy in this test came to 10.93 mph. As with the 620 All-Fuel noted in Test No. 604, fourth gear was used throughout this 10-hour run. Test G delivered a low-gear maximum pull of 6,647 lbs. at 1.24 mph with a slippage of 12.75 percent. This tractor used 15.5-38-inch rear and 6.00-16-inch front tires—during Tests F, G, and H an additional 720 lbs. of liquid ballast was added to each rear wheel. Also featured in this 7,505 lb. tractor were forward speeds of 1.5, 2.25, 3.5, 4.5, 5.75, and 11.5 mph. No repairs or adjustments were noted during 47 hours of operation. Test L indicated that 111 percent of rated-speed torque was available at 70 percent of the 1,125 rpm rated engine speed. Test D, run at a rated belt load of 50.33 hp, yielded a fuel economy of 12.07 hp-hours per gallon, climbing to 12.21 under a Test C operating maximum load of 55.11 hp. The 720 carried a 360.5-cid, two-cylinder engine with a 6 x 6-3/8-inch bore and stroke, and a 6.14:1 compression ratio.

Nebraska Test Data

Model: John Deere Model 720 (all-fuel)

Test No. 606

Date Tested: November 12 to November 19, 1956

The 720 All-Fuel was virtually identical in design to the 720 gasoline model of Test No. 605, using the same 360.5-cid, two-cylinder engine, but featuring a 4.91:1 compression ratio to accommodate the tractor fuel used for this test. Test weight, added weight, and other test specifications remained nearly identical for both tractors. Charted data from this test indicated that using fourth gear, the 720 All-Fuel delivered a Test H rated output of 31.59 drawbar hp. In this test, a pull of 2,708 lbs. was recorded at 4.38 mph with a slippage of 3.03 percent. Fuel economy was scored at 10.03 hp-hours per gallon. Test G yielded a low-gear maximum pun of 6,608 lbs. at 1.21 mph with a slippage of 14.31 percent. Under Test L, the 720 All-Fuel achieved 118 percent of rated-speed engine torque at 69 percent of the rated 1,125 speed. No repairs or adjustments were reported during 48-1/2 hours of operating time. Test C, run at an operating maximum load of 42.38 belt hp, produced a fuel economy of 10.89 hp-hours per gallon, rising to 11.16 at a Test D rated belt load of 38.84 hp.

COLLECTOR VALUES	1	2	3	4
MODEL 720	$4,500	$3,000	$1,500	$800

Model 720 Diesel

The 720 Diesel, like the gasoline models, was built in row-crop and standard-tread designs. This tractor carried a two-cylinder engine with a 6-1/8 x 6-3/8-inch bore and stroke. Starting was by a V-type four-cylinder engine with a 2 x 1-1/2 inch bore and stroke. Production began in 1956 and ended in 1958.

Nebraska Test Data

Model: John Deere Model 720 Diesel

Test No. 594

Date Tested: September 18 to September 22, 1956

Weighing 7,899 lbs., the 720 Diesel was equipped with 15.5-38 inch rear and 6.00-16-inch front tires. During Tests F, G, and H an additional 669 lbs. of liquid ballast was added to each rear wheel. This tractor offered forward speeds of 1-1/2, 2-1/4, 3-1/2, 4-1/2, 5-3/4, and 11-1/2 mph. Using fourth gear, Test H was run at a rated output of 40.41 drawbar hp. With a pull of 3,532 lbs. at 4.29 mph and slippage of 5.12percent, fuel economy was posted at 16.56 hp-hours per gallon of diesel fuel. Test G recorded a low-gear maximum pull of 6,547 lbs. at 1.19 mph and slippage of 16.3 percent. During 45-1/2 hours of running time, no repairs or adjustments were noted. The two-cylinder horizontal diesel engine was rated at 1,125 rpm, and achieved 116 percent of rated torque at 65 percent of rated speed. The 376-cubic inch displacement resulted from a 6-1/8 x 6-3/8-inch bore and stroke-compression ratio was fixed at 16:1. Starting was accomplished by means of a V-type four-cylinder gasoline engine rated at 5,500 rpm and using a 2 x 1-1/2-inch bore and stroke for a displacement of 18.85 cubic inches. Test B & C, run at a 100 percent maximum belt load of 56.66 hp, produced 17.97 hp-hours per gallon. This figure climbed to 18.33 at a Test D rated belt load of 50-16 hp.

Model 820 Diesel

The big John Deere 820 Diesel had a displacement of over 471-cubic inches. This resulted from a two-cylinder engine with a 6-1/8 x 8-inch bore and stroke. Rated speed was 1,125 rpm. Under maximum load, the 820 Diesel could deliver nearly 73 belt hp. Like the 720 Diesel, this model also used a V-type four-cylinder starting engine. Production ran from 1956 to 1958.

Nebraska Test Data

Model: John Deere Model 820 Diesel

Test No. 632

Date Tested: October 14 to October 18, 1957

This tractor used forward speeds of 2.5, 3.5, 4.5, 5.33, 6.75, and 12.25 mph. Weighing in at 8,729 lbs., the 820 carried 15-34-inch rear an 7.50-18-inch front tires. During Tests F, G, and H an additional 1,628 lbs. was added to each rear wheel for a total test weight of 11,995 lbs. At 100-percent maximum drawbar load, this tractor pulled 8,667 lbs. at 2.01 mph with a slippage of 14.76 percent. Test H, run in third gear, and at a rated output of 53.16 drawbar hp, yielded a fuel economy of 16.46 hp-hours per gallon of diesel fuel. This test also noted a pull of 4,553 lbs. at 4.38 mph and slippage of 5.76 percent. The 820 Diesel used a Deere-built two-cylinder horizontal engine rated at 1,125 rpm and carrying a 6-1/8 x 8 inch bore and stroke for a 471.5-cubic inch displacement. Also featured was a four-cylinder V-type gasoline starting engine with a 2 x 1-1/2 inch bore and stroke. At a 100-percent maximum belt load of 72.82 hp, fuel economy was pegged at 17.28 hp-hours per gallon, climbing to 18.03 under a Test D rated belt load of 64.26 hp. During 40-1/2 hours of operating time, no repairs or adjustments were recorded.

COLLECTOR VALUES	1	2	3	4
MODEL 820	$6,000	$4,000	$3,000	$800

Model 330 tractor

The "30" series tractors were essentially the same as the "20" series tractors except for a modified styling. The little 330 shown here was built either as a Standard or as a Utility tractor. Weighing 2,750 lbs. it used a two-cylinder 4 x 4-inch engine with a displacement of 100.5 cubic inches. Production of the 330, like other "30" series tractors ran from 1958 to 1960.

COLLECTOR VALUES	1	2	3	4
MODEL 330	$15,000	$10,000	$5000	$15,000

Model 430

The John Deere 430 was built in several different configurations, with the 430 Standard shown here. The 430 tractors used a two-cylinder, 4-1/4 x 4 inch engine rated at 1,850 rpm. Weighing 3,000 lbs., it was capable of about 27 drawbar hp.

COLLECTOR VALUES	1	2	3	4
MODEL 430	$8,000	$6,000	$4,000	$1,500
MODEL 430C CRAWLER	$10,000	$7,000	$4,000	$2,000

Model 435 Diesel

Built in the 1958-1960 period, the John Deere 435 Diesel was unique in that it used a General Motors two-cylinder diesel engine, vis-à-vis an engine built by Deere & Company. The GM engine was of two-cycle design and used a 3-7/8 x 4-1/2 inch bore and stroke. This engine used a compression ratio of 17 to 1. This tractor had a rated output of nearly 33 PTO hp.

Nebraska Test Data

Model: John Deere Model 435 Diesel

Test No. 716

Date Tested: September 8 to September 18, 1959

Weighing 4,101 lbs., the 435 Diesel acquired a test weight of 6,057 lbs. by the addition of liquid and cast iron ballast. At a rated engine speed of 1,850 rpm, a maximum PTO output of 32.91 hp was noted—this two-hour run yielded a fuel economy of 14.35 hp-hours per gallon. At a standard 540 rpm PTO speed and a corresponding engine speed of 1,784 rpm, an output of 32.13 PTO hp was noted, along with a fuel economy figure of 14.49. This tractor featured a General Motors two-cylinder, two-cycle diesel engine with a blower. Using a 3-7/8 x 4-1/2-inch bore and stroke, it carried a 17:1 compression ratio and had a displacement of 106.1-cubic inches. Standard equipment also included five forward speeds ranging from 1-7/8 to 13-1/2 mph. The test model was equipped with 13.6-28-inch rear and 6.00-16-inch front tires. Third gear was used for the two-hour drawbar fuel economy run at maximum available power. With an output of 27.59 hp, the 435 Diesel pulled 2,044 lbs. at 5.06 mph with a 4.63 percent slippage and registered 12.38 hp-hours per gallon. Under 75-percent load, an output of 22.54 drawbar hp was noted, along with a pull of 1,557 lbs. at 5.43 mph and slippage of 3 percent. This 10-hour run gave a fuel economy of 11.61 hp-hours per gallon. No repairs or adjustments were noted during 49 hours of running time.

COLLECTOR VALUES	1	2	3	4
MODEL 435	$8,000	$6,000	$3,000	$1,500

Model 530

The 530 was a popular John Deere model. Rated at about 39 belt hp, it was widely used on smaller farms and also found a place on larger farms. The independent PTO shaft was an important feature, and the power-adjustable rear wheels were a popular option. Production of the 530 ran from 1958 to 1960.

COLLECTOR VALUES	1	2	3	4
MODEL 530	$7,500	$5,000	$3,000	$1,500

Model 630 LPG hi crop

Numerous designs were available in the 630 series, including this LP-gas 630 Hi-Crop model. Although the

"30" series tractors included many modern features, they also retained much of the popular design developed in the 1930s, including the hand-clutch and the cross-mounted two-cylinder engine. The 630 tractors were capable of nearly 49 belt hp.

COLLECTOR VALUES	1	2	3	4
MODEL 630	$7,000	$4,500	$2,500	$1,500

Model 730 standard tread

The John Deere 730 tractors were built in row- crop, Hi-Crop and standard-tread designs. Shown here is a 730 standard-tread tractor equipped for burning LP-gas for fuel. The 730 tractor could also be made to burn gasoline or tractor fuel; the latter was known as Deere's All-Fuel engine. Production ran from 1958 to 1960.

COLLECTOR VALUES	1	2	3	4
MODEL 730	$7,000	$4,500	$2,500	$1,500

Model 730 Diesel tractor

While the John Deere 720 Diesel was available only with a gasoline starting engine, the 730 Diesel could optionally be furnished with electric starting. The 730 Diesel Standard model shown here weighed in at 7,800 lbs. It was capable of almost 54 hp on the drawbar. Production began in 1958 and ended in 1960.

Model 830 tractor

John Deere 830 tractors were, like the earlier 820, built only in a standard-tread design. This big tractor used a 24-volt electrical system—a requirement to roll over the 471-cid, two-cylinder engine. Production ran from 1958 to 1960. By this time the two-cylinder design had run its course and in 1960 Deere & Company launched a new series of four-cylinder tractors.

COLLECTOR VALUES	1	2	3	4
MODEL 830	$6,500	$5,000	$3,000	$1,500

When evaluating various John Deere models the following features add to the value of tractors on which they are found:
Round-top fenders: $1,000
Clams: $300+
Deluxe flat tops with lights and brackets: $700+
Complete 3-point: $1,000
Round tube wide front: $800+
Square tube wide front: $1,100+
Round-spoke rubber, front and rear: $2,000

John Deere 1010 Series

Nebraska Test Data

Model: John Deere 1010 RU

Test No. 802

Date Tested: June 20 to June 28, 1961

This tractor used a four-cylinder, 115.5-cid engine. At its rated engine speed of 2,500 rpm, a maximum output of 36.13 PTO hp was observed, together with a fuel economy of 10.33 hp-hours per gallon. The economy figure slipped to 10.24 under a standard PTO speed of 540 rpm, an engine speed of 1,946 rpm, and an output of 29.6 PTO hp. Weighing 3,923 lbs., the 1010 RU took on a test weight of 5,711 lbs. through the addition of rear wheel ballast. Standard equipment included 12.4-28-inch rear and 5.00-15-inch front tires. Also featured was a selective gear fixed-ratio transmission with five forward speeds ranging from 2.62 to 16.86 mph. Using second gear, and operating at 30.00 maximum available hp, this tractor displayed a pull of 2,350 lbs. at 4.79 mph with 7.69 percent slippage. Fuel economy was observed at 8.62 hp-hours per gallon. A 10-hour run made at 75 percent pull disclosed an output of 24.58 drawbar hp, a pull of 1,797 lbs. at 5.13 mph and 5.04 percent slippage, giving a net total of 7.99 hp-hours per gallon in the economy section. No repairs or adjustments were required during 39 hours of operation.

Nebraska Test Data

Model: John Deere 1010 RU Diesel

Test No. 803

Date Tested: June 21 to June 29, 1961

This tractor used essentially the same chassis as the 1010 RU gasoline model. In this case, a four-cylinder diesel engine was featured. Rated at 2,500 rpm, it carried a 3-5/8 x 3-1/2-inch bore and stroke for a 144.5-cubic inch displacement. The engine design included an 18:1 compression ratio. No repairs or adjustments were noted for this tractor during 37 hours of running time. At its rated engine speed, a maximum output of 35.99 PTO hp was observed, along with a fuel economy of 11.93 hp-hours per gallon. The economy figure rose to 12.62 under a PTO load of 29.70 hp. This test was run at a standard 540 rpm on the PTO shaft and a corresponding engine speed of 1,946 rpm. Both this tractor and that of the previous test used the same transmission and tire equipment. Weighing in at 4,041 lbs., the 1010 RU Diesel took on a test weight of 5,754 lbs. through the addition of rear wheel ballast. Using second gear, a maximum output of 29.16 drawbar hp was observed in the two-hour economy run. This test noted a pull of 2,304 lbs. at 4.75 mph with 7.93 percent slippage. Also recorded was a fuel economy of 9.89 hp-hours per gallon. The 10-hour economy run, made at 75 percent pull, noted an output of 24.32 hp, a pull of 1,853 lbs. at 4.98 mph, and 5.31 percent slippage. Fuel economy in this test totaled 10.66 hp-hours per gallon.

John Deere 2010 Series

Nebraska Test Data

Model: John Deere 2010 RU Diesel

Test No. 799

Date Tested: June 6 to June 22, 1961

At its rated speed of 2,500 rpm, this tractor developed a maximum of 46.67 PTO hp and accrued a fuel economy of 12.78 hp-hours per gallon. A second PTO run made at 540 PTO rpm and a crankshaft speed of 1,903 rpm indicated an output of 38.64 hp with an economy figure of 13.17. The 2010 RU was equipped with a four-cylinder engine with a 3-7/8 x 3-1/2-inch bore and stroke for a displacement of 165.1 cubic inches. Also included was a selective gear fixed-ratio transmission that provided partial-range syncromesh shifting. Eight forward speeds were available ranging from 2.67 to 19.3 mph. The basic tractor weight of 5,120 lbs. was raised to 6,392 lbs. for testing through the addition of rear wheel ballast. Also featured were 13.6-28-inch rear and 6.00-16-inch front tires. Using third gear, the two-hour economy run at 39.28 maximum available hp yielded 10.78 hp-hours per gallon. Other statistics included a pull of 3,399 lbs. at 4.33 mph with 8.19 percent slippage. A 10-hour run, made at 75 percent pull, posted an economy figure of 10.51, along with an output of 31.94 hp, a pull of 2,599 lbs. at 4.61 mph and 5.48 percent slippage. No repairs or adjustments were noted during 46-1/2 hours of running time.

Nebraska Test Data

Model: John Deere 2010 RU (gasoline)

Test No. 800

Date Tested: June 13 to June 22, 1961

Weighing in at 5,054 lbs., this tractor assumed a test weight of 6,310 lbs. through the addition of rear wheel ballast. The four-cylinder gasoline engine was rated at 2,500 rpm and carried a 3-5/8 x 3-1/2 inch bore and stroke for a 144.5-cubic inch displacement. With this exception the tractor was nearly identical to the 2010 RU Diesel of Test No. 799. Third gear was used for the drawbar fuel economy tests. At 39.12 maximum available hp, fuel economy was posted at 10.06 hp-hours per gallon. Other statistics for this run include a pull of 3,403 lbs. at 4.31 mph with 8.79 percent slippage. The economy figure settled in at 9.34 during the 10-hour run, made at 75 percent pull. This test yielded an output of 32.21 hp, a pull of 2,655 lbs. at 4.55 mph and 5.83 percent slippage. No repairs or adjustments were reported during a total of 41-1/2 hours operating time. At rated engine speed, 46.86 maximum PTO hp was observed, together with an accrued economy of 11.79 hp-hours per gallon. The economy figure rose to 12.11 under an output of 38.45 PTO hp. This test was run at 540 rpm on the PTO shaft with a corresponding crankshaft speed of 1,903 rpm.

2510 Series

Nebraska Test Data

Model: John Deere 2510 Power-Shift
Test No. 913
Date Tested: September 24 to September 30, 1965

Rated at 2,500 rpm, the 2510 delivered a maximum of 49.57 PTO hp at rated speed and yielded an economy of 10.27 hp-hours per gallon. A second PTO run at 1,000 rpm and a corresponding engine speed of 2,066 rpm saw an economy of 10.74 hp-hours per gallon against an output of 45.05 PTO hp. The Deere-built four-cylinder engine carried a 3.86-inch bore and stroke for a displacement of 180.43 cubic inches. No repairs or adjustments were noted during 43-1/2 hours of ranging from 1.67 to 17.49 mph. Standard equipment included 13.6-38 rear and 6.00-16 inch front tires. Bare tractor weight was 6,575 lbs. and this was raised to a test weight of 8,045 lbs. through the addition of rear wheel ballast. Using fourth gear, a two-hour economy run at 42.44 maximum available drawbar hp saw an economy of 8.6 hp-hours per gallon. Also recorded was a pull of 3,533 lbs. at 4.5 mph and slippage of 5.59 percent. The 10-hour drawbar economy run at 75 percent pull set the economy figure at 7.64 against an output of 33.67 drawbar hp. This test saw a pull of 2,665 lbs. at 4.74 mph and slippage of 3.68 percent.

Nebraska Test Data

Model: John Deere 2510 Syncro-Range
Test No. 914
Date Tested: September 24 to October 2, 1965

Except for a different transmission, this tractor was nearly identical to the 2510 Power-Shift model of Test No. 913. Both carried the same 180.43-cid engine, and both were rated at 2,500 rpm. Likewise, tire equipment was identical for both models, but the 6,245-lb. base weight for this model largely reflected the lesser weight requirements of the transmission. Eight forward speeds were provided. These ranged from 1.78 to 15.76 mph. The selective gear fixed-ratio design incorporated partial range syncro-mesh shifting. Using fourth gear, the two-hour economy run yielded an economy of 9.59 hp-hours per gallon against a maximum load of 45.21 drawbar hp. This test saw a pull of 3,834 lbs. at 4.42 mph with 6.85 percent slippage. The 10-hour run at 75 percent pull yielded an output of 37.36 drawbar hp with a pull of 2,981 lbs. at 4.7 mph and slippage of 4.81 percent. Fuel economy was posted at 8.86 hp-hours per gallon. No repairs or adjustments were required for this tractor during 44 hours of operating time. At rated engine speed, 53.74 maximum PTO hp was observed, together with an economy of 11.28 hp-hours per gallon. A second PTO run at 1,000 rpm and a corresponding engine speed of 2,071 rpm saw an economy of 11.63 hp-hours per gallon against an output of 48.28 PTO hp.

Nebraska Test Data

Model: John Deere 2510 Power-Shift Diesel
Test No. 915
Date Tested: September 30 to October 5, 1965

This version of the Deere 2510 was nearly identical to the Power-Shift model of Test No. 913 except it used a Deere-built four-cylinder diesel engine. Other specifications remained unchanged. Weighing 6,745 lbs., it assumed a test weight of 8,215 lbs. by the addition of rear wheel ballast. Using fourth gear, a two-hour run at 43.54 maximum available drawbar hp saw an economy of 12.33 hp-hours per gallon. Also indicated was a pull of 3,604 lbs. at 4.53 mph with 5.22 percent slippage. The 10-hour run at 75 percent pull saw an economy figure of 11.62 against a load of 36.27 hp. This test was made at a pull of 2,812 lbs. with a speed of 4.84 mph and slippage of 3.57 percent. No repairs or adjustments were reported during 41-1/2 hours of operation. At a rated engine speed of 2,500 rpm, 50.66 maximum PTO hp was observed, as was an economy of 14.22 hp-hours per gallon of diesel fuel. A second PTO run at 1,000 rpm and a corresponding engine speed of 2,066 rpm saw an economy of 15.23 hp-hours per gallon against an output of 45.8 hp. The four-cylinder, 202.68-cid engine carried a 3.86 x 4.33 inch bore and stroke.

Nebraska Test Data

Model: John Deere 2510 Syncro-Range Diesel
Test No. 916
Date Tested: September 30 to October 7, 1965

Continuing the series of 2510 tractors was the Syncro-Range Diesel model. It used the same transmission style noted for the gasoline version of Test No. 914, but carried a diesel engine of the same style recorded in Test No. 915. As presented for testing, this tractor weighed 6,525 lbs., but the addition of rear wheel ballast raised this figure to 8,485 lbs. At a rated engine speed of 2,500 rpm, 54.96 maximum PTO hp was observed this yielded an economy of 15.84 hp-hours per gallon. The economy figure stood at 16.43 in a second test run made at 1,000 PTO rpm and a corresponding crankshaft speed of 2,072 rpm. Also indicated was an output of 49.24 PTO hp. Using fourth gear, a two-hour drawbar run at 46.82 maximum available hp saw a pull of 3,966 lbs. at 4.43 mph with 6.55 percent slippage. Economy was pegged at 13.74 hp-hours per gallon. A 10-hour drawbar run at 75 percent pull saw an output of 38.71 hp with an economy figure of 13.27. Also recorded was a pull of 3,129 lbs. at 4.64 mph and slippage of 4.66 percent.

3010 Series

Nebraska Test Data

Model: John Deere 3010 Diesel
Test No. 762
Date Tested: September 19 to September 24, 1960

This tractor featured a selective gear fixed-ratio, partial range syncro-mesh transmission. Eight forward speeds ranging from 1-3/4 to 14-1/2 mph were provided. Also featured were 13.9-36-inch rear and 6.00-14-inch front tires. Bare tractor weight was 6,542 lbs., a figure that climbed to 8,640 lbs. through the addition of rear wheel ballast in the forms of liquid and cast iron. Drawbar fuel economy was posted at 12.94 with 52.77 maximum available hp. This test, run in fourth gear, recorded a pull of 4,256 lbs. at 4.65 mph with 8.12 percent slippage. The 10-hour drawbar economy run made at 75 percent pull evoked a fuel economy of 12.96 hp-hours per gallon with a drawbar output of 43.4 hp. Also recorded in this test was a pull of 3,275 lbs. at 4.97 mph and slippage of 5.18 percent. At rated engine speed, a maximum of 59.44 PTO hp was observed, as was a fuel economy of 14.52 hp-hours per gallon. The economy figure came in at 15.47 at a 1,000 rpm PTO speed and a corresponding engine speed of 1,866 rpm. This test produced 55.29 PTO hp. No repairs or adjustments were noted during 41-1/2 hours of operating time. The 3010 Diesel carried a four-cylinder engine rated at 2,200 rpm, and used a 4-1/8 x 4-3/4-inch bore and stroke for a 254-cubic inch displacement.

Nebraska Test Data

Model: John Deere 3010 Gasoline
Test No. 763
Date Tested: September 24 to September 28, 1960

Tire sizes and the transmission style used in this tractor remained virtually the same as found in the 3010 Diesel. Weighing 6,320 lbs., this tractor assumed a test weight of 8,470 lbs. by the addition of rear wheel ballast. Using fourth gear, 50.98 maximum available hp was observed in a two-hour fuel economy run. With economy standing at 9.83 hp-hours per gallon, this test also came up with a pull of 4,040 lbs. at 4.73 mph and 5.91 percent slippage. A 10-hour drawbar economy run, made at 75 percent pull, and again using fourth gear, set the economy figure at 9.12. This test indicated an output of 41.2 hp, a pull of 3,007 lbs. at 5.14 mph and 4.00 percent slippage. Deere featured its own four-cylinder engine in this tractor. Rated at 2,200 rpm, it carried a 4-inch bore and stroke for a 201-cubic inch displacement. At rated engine speed, 55.09 maximum PTO hp was observed, along with a fuel economy of 10.7 hp-hours per gallon. The economy slipped slightly to stand at 10.62 in a test run at 1,000 PTO rpm and a corresponding crankshaft speed of 1,866 rpm. This test produced 50.54 hp. No repairs or adjustments were noted during 42 hours of operating time.

Nebraska Test Data

Model: John Deere 3010 LPG
Test No. 764
Date Tested: September 24 to September 29, 1960

Weighing in at 6,375 lbs., the 3010 LPG model assumed a test weight of 8,535 lbs. through the addition of rear wheel ballast. Tire sizes and the transmission style remained the same as noted for the 3010 gasoline and diesel models of the two previous tests. A notable difference in addition to the obvious propane equipment was a compression ratio of 9.0:1 for this tractor, compared to 7.5:1 in the gasoline style, and a much higher 16.4:1 for the diesel engine of Test No. 762. At rated engine speed of 2,200 rpm, 55.39 maximum PTO hp was observed, together with a fuel economy of 8.46 hp-hours per gallon of propane. The economy figure improved very slightly to stand at 8.57 with a standard 1,000 rpm PTO speed and an engine speed of 1,866 rpm. This test saw an output of 50.8 hp. No repairs or adjustments were recorded during 41 hours of operating time. The two-hour drawbar economy run, made at 49.22 maximum available hp and using fourth gear, indicated a fuel economy of 7.57 hp-hours per gallon, together with a pull of 3,897 lbs. at 4.74 mph and 6.27 percent slippage. The 10-hour drawbar economy run, made at 75 percent pull, saw an economy figure of 7.34 hp-hours per gallon, a drawbar output of 41.05 hp, a pull of 2,994 lbs. at 5.14 mph and slippage of 4.43 percent .

4010 Series

Nebraska Test Data

Model: John Deere 4010
Test No. 759
Date Tested: September 12 to September 23, 1960

This tractor featured a Deere-built six-cylinder engine rated at 2,200 rpm. Using a 4-inch bore and stroke it carried a 302-cubic inch displacement. At rated engine speed, a maximum of 80.96 PTO hp was observed with a fuel economy of 11.26 hp-hours per gallon. At 1,000 PTO rpm and a crankshaft speed of 1,900 rpm, 73.91 hp was observed, along with a fuel economy of 12.09 hp-hours per gallon. This tractor was equipped with a selective gear fixed-ratio partial range syncro-mesh transmission offering eight speeds ranging from 1-l/2 to 14-1/4 mph. Also featured were 15.5-38-inch rear and 6.00-16-inch front tires. Weighing 7,155 lbs., the 4010 took on a test weight of 9,595 lbs. by the addition of liquid and cast iron ballast on the rear wheels. Using fifth gear, a two-hour economy run made at 71.25 maximum available drawbar hp saw a pull of 4,699 lbs. at 5.69 mph with 5.44 percent slippage. Fuel economy was recorded at 10.03 hp-hours per gallon. The following 10-hour run, made at 75 percent pull, saw an output of 57.39 hp, a pull of 3,464 lbs. at 6.21 mph and slippage of 3.22 percent. This run elicited a fuel economy of 9.26 hp-hours per gallon. No repairs or adjustments were noted during 41 hours of running time.

Nebraska Test Data

Model: John Deere 4010 LPG
Test No. 760
Date Tested: September 12 to September 23, 1960

A 9.0:1 compression ratio was a unique feature of the 4010 LPG tractor. By comparison, the 4010 gasoline model of the previous test used a 7.5:1 compression ratio. Both units carried the same six-cylinder, 302-cid engine, and both used the same transmission and tire equipment. Weighing in at 7,280 lbs., the 4010 LPG assumed a test weight of 9,735 lbs. by the addition of liquid and cast iron ballast to the rear wheels. Using fifth gear, a two-hour drawbar run at 71.77 maximum available hp noted a pull of 4,691 lbs. at 5.74 mph and 5.55 percent slippage. Fuel economy was posted at 7.87 hp-hours per gallon of propane. A 10-hour run, made at 75 percent pull registered the economy figure at 7.59. This test indicated an output of 57.11 hp, a pull of 3,506 lbs. at 6.11 mph and 3.62 percent slippage. No repairs or adjustments were noted during 49 hours of operation. At rated engine speed of 2,200 rpm a maximum output of 80.60 PTO hp was observed, along with a fuel economy of 8.72 hp-hours per gallon of propane. This figure rose to 9.00 at a 1,000 rpm PTO speed and an engine speed of 72.82 hp.

Nebraska Test Data

Model: John Deere 4010 Diesel
Test No. 761
Date Tested: September 19 to September 23, 1960

The 4010 Diesel featured a Deere-built six-cylinder engine rated at 2,200 rpm. Using a 4-1/8 x 4-3/4-inch bore and stroke, it had a displacement of 380 cubic inches. At rated engine speed a maximum of 84 PTO hp was recorded, together with a fuel economy of 14.97 hp-hours per gallon. Using the standard 1,000 rpm PTO speed and a corresponding crankshaft speed of 1,900 rpm, 76.71 PTO hp was noted, together with a fuel economy of 15.67 hp-hours per gallon. The transmission style and tire sizes were virtually identical to those used in the gasoline and propane models of the two previous tests. Weighing in at 7,445 lbs., the 4010 Diesel assumed a test weight of 9,775 lbs. through the addition of liquid and cast iron ballast on the rear wheels. A two-hour economy run, made at 71.93 maximum available drawbar hp, evoked a fuel economy of 13.08 hp-hours per gallon. Other statistics included a pull of 4,737 lbs. at

5.69 mph with 5.8 percent slippage. The 10-hour drawbar economy run made at 75 percent pull noted a fuel economy of 12.38 hp-hours per gallon with an output of 58.8 hp, a pull of 3,560 lbs. at 6.19 mph and 3.72 percent slippage. During 48 hours of running time, no repairs or adjustments were recorded.

John Deere 5010

Nebraska Test Data

Model: John Deere 5010 Diesel

Test No. 828

Date Tested: October 15 to October 20, 1962

Weighing 12,925 lbs., the 5010 Diesel was burdened with rear ballast for a total test weight of 17,175 lbs. This tractor featured 24.5-32 rear and 11.00-16 inch front tires. Using fourth gear, a two-hour drawbar economy run made at 105.92 maximum available drawbar hp yielded a fuel economy of 13.31 hp-hours per gallon. Also recorded was a pull of 7,759 lbs. at 5.12 mph with 5.01 percent slippage. A 10-hour drawbar run made at 75 percent pull noted an economy figure of 12.94. Other statistics included an output of 87.79 hp, a pull of 6,043 lbs. at 5.45 mph and 3.88 percent slippage. This tractor was equipped with a selective gear fixed-ratio transmission that included partial range syncromesh shifting. Eight forward speeds were provided, ranging from 1-3/4 to 15-1/2 mph. The 531-cid, six-cylinder engine was rated at 2,200 rpm, using a 4-3/4 x 5-inch bore and stroke. At rated speed, 121.12 maximum PTO hp was observed, together with an economy of 15.03 hp-hours per gallon. A second PTO run made at 1,000 rpm on the PTO shaft and a corresponding engine speed of 1,880 rpm indicated an output of 108.67 hp plus an economy figure of 15.48. Upon completion of the PTO runs it became evident the hydraulic pump drive discs were failing. After replacing the metal discs the test continued. Otherwise, no repairs or adjustments were recorded during 42-1/2 hours of running time.

Nebraska Test Data

Model: John Deere 1020

Test No. 935

Date Tested: May 2 to May 14, 1966

Weighing 4,730 lbs., this tractor was supplied with front and rear ballast for a total test weight of 5,940 lbs. Standard equipment included 13.6-28-inch rear and 6.00-16-inch front tires. The chassis design included a selective gear fixed-ratio transmission with eight forward speeds ranging from 1.4 to 16.6 mph. Operating in fifth gear, the two-hour drawbar run was made at 31.64 maximum available hp. This test indicated a run of 2,178 lbs. at 5.45 mph, slippage of 4.62 percent, and an economy of 8.99 hp-hours per gallon. The 10-hour run at 75 percent pull revealed an economy figure of 8.08 against an output of 26.85 hp. Also manifested was a pull of 1,739 lbs. at 5.79 mph and 3.86 percent slippage. No repairs or adjustments were required during 42 hours of running time. Deere equipped this model with its own three-cylinder, 135.32-cid engine. Rated at 2,500 rpm, it used a 3.86-inch bore and stroke. PTO testing revealed a maximum output of 38.82 hp at rated engine speed. Also recorded was an economy of 10.49 hp-hours per gallon. At 1,000 PTO rpm and a corresponding engine speed of 2,066 rpm, 10.63 hp-hours per gallon was realized against a load of 35.61 hp.

1020 Series

Nebraska Test Data

Model: John Deere 1020 Diesel

Test No. 937

Date Tested: May 6 to May 17, 1966

During 39 hours of operating time, no repairs or adjustments were reported for this tractor. Weighing in at 4,870 lbs., it was burdened with additional front and rear ballast for a total test weight of 5,955 lbs. Standard equipment, including tires and drive train was nearly identical to the 1020 gasoline model of Test No. 935. Using fifth gear, and operating at 31.81 maximum available drawbar hp, the two-hour economy run delivered a fuel efficiency of 12.05 hp-hours per gallon. Also, a pull of 2,195 lbs. was recorded at 5.43 mph with slippage of 5.12 percent. The 10-hour economy run at 75 percent pull noted an economy of 11.18 hp-hours per gallon against an output of 26.02 hp. Also recorded was a pull of 1,686 lbs. at 5.79 mph and slippage of 3.67 percent. This tractor was equipped with the company's own three-cylinder diesel engine. Rated at 2,500 rpm, it used a 3.86 x 4.33-inch bore and stroke for a 152.01-cubic inch displacement. At the rated engine speed, 38.92 maximum PTO hp was developed, together with an economy of 14.76 hp-hours per gallon. When operating at 1,000 PTO rpm and a corresponding crankshaft speed of 2,066 rpm, 36.02 PTO hp was delivered, with 15.49 hp-hours per gallon.

1520 Series

Nebraska Test Data

Model: John Deere 1520 Diesel

Test No. 991

Date Tested: October 14 to October 22, 1968

At its rated engine speed of 2,500 rpm, the 1520 Diesel delivered an economy of 15.42 hp-hours per gallon against a maximum PTO load of 46.52 hp. Operating at 1,000 PTO rpm and a corresponding engine speed of 2,067 rpm, 42.97 PTO hp was developed and an economy of 15.97 hp-hours per gallon was observed. Deere equipped this tractor with a three-cylinder, 164.9-cid engine with a 4.02 x 4.33-inch bore and stroke. No repairs or adjustments were required during 46-1/2 hours of running time. Features included partial range power shifting within a selective gear fixed-ratio transmission. In all, eight forward speeds were available ranging from 1.46 to 17.05 mph. Weighing in at 5,855 lbs., this tractor was supported on 14.9-28-inch rear and 6.00-16-inch front tires. Additional front and rear ballast raised the total test weight to 6,970 lbs. Using 10th gear, 38.48 maximum available drawbar hp was observed in the two-hour economy run. This test saw a pull of 2,604 lbs. at 5.54 mph, a slippage of 5.38 percent, and an economy of 12.44 hp-hours per gallon. The 10-hour run at 75 percent pull indicated an economy of 11.96 hp-hours per gallon against a load of 30.53 drawbar hp. Other statistics included a pull of 1,970 lbs. at 5.81 mph with slippage totaling 3.81 percent.

Nebraska Test Data

Model: John Deere 1520

Test No. 1004

Date Tested: March 28 to April 2, 1969

Weighing in at 5,770 lbs., this tractor featured 14.9-28-inch rear and 6.00-16-inch front tires. Additional front and rear ballast raised the total weight to 6,665 lbs. Also featured was a selective gear fixed-ratio transmission with partial range power shifting. The eight forward speeds ranged from 1.46 to 17.05 mph. No repairs or adjustments were required during 44 hours of operating time. In 10th gear, this model displayed 37.24 maximum available drawbar hp during the two-hour economy run, and in so doing, achieved an economy of 9.01 hp-hours per gallon. Also recorded was a pull of 2,525 lbs. at 5.53 mph and slippage of 4.73 percent. The 10-hour run at 75 percent pull saw an economy of 8.14 against an output of 31.35 drawbar hp. This test revealed a pull of 1,939 lbs. at 6.06 mph and slippage of 3.16 percent. Deere equipped this model with its own three-cylinder, 164.55-cid engine. Rated at 2,500 rpm, it carried a 4.02 x 4.33-inch bore and stroke. At rated engine speed, 47.86 maximum PTO hp appeared and an economy of 11.23 hp-hours per gallon was achieved. At 1,000 PTO rpm and a corresponding engine speed of 2.066 rpm, the fuel economy stood at 10.89 hp-hours per gallon against an output of 43.95 PTO hp.

John Deere 2020 Series

Nebraska Test Data

Model: John Deere 2020

Test No. 936

Date Tested: May 3 to May 13, 1966

Weighing 5,770 lbs., the 2020 was enhanced with additional front and rear ballast for a total test weight of 7,435 lbs. during drawbar testing. Standard equipment included 14.9-28-inch rear and 6.00-16-inch front tires. The chassis design featured a selective gear fixed-ratio transmission with eight forward speeds in a range from 1.4 to 16.6 mph. Using fifth gear, 43.94 maximum available drawbar hp was present in the two-hour economy run. This test indicated a pull of 2,942 lbs. at 5.6 mph and slippage of 5.55 percent, with fuel economy totaling 9.03 hp-hours per gallon. By comparison, the 10-hour run at 75 percent pull indicated an economy figure of 7.98 against an output of 35.33 drawbar hp. The 10-hour run, made at 75 percent pull, also indicated a pull of 2,257 lbs. at 5.87 mph with slippage of 3.69 percent. No repairs or adjustments were noted during 46-1/2 hours of operating time. Deere equipped this tractor with its own four-cylinder engine—it was rated at 2,500 rpm. Using a 3.86-inch bore and stroke, this engine had a 180.43-cubic inch displacement. At rated engine speed, 53.91 maximum PTO hp was observed, as was an economy of 11.17 hp-hours per gallon. Operating at a crankshaft speed of 2,066 rpm and a PTO speed of 1,000 rpm, 48.32 hp was developed for a yield of 11.89 hp-hours per gallon.

Nebraska Test Data

Model: John Deere 2020 Diesel
Test No. 938
Date Tested: May 7 to May 17, 1966

Except for the diesel engine, this tractor differed little from the gasoline 2020. Deere equipped this model with its own four-cylinder diesel engine. Rated at 2,500 rpm, it carried a 3.86 x 4.33-inch bore and stroke for a 202.68-cubic inch displacment. At rated engine speed, 54.09 maximum PTO hp was observed, as was an economy of 15.33 hp-hours per gallon. The same test when run at 1,000 PTO rpm and a corresponding crankshaft speed of 2,066 rpm saw an economy figure of 16.43 against a load of 49.31 hp. Weighing in at 5,900 lbs., the 2020 Diesel was burdened with additional front and rear ballast for a total test weight of 7,310 lbs. Operating at 45.9 maximum available drawbar hp, the two-hour economy run yielded a fuel efficiency of 12.89 hp-hours per gallon. This test, made in fifth gear, saw a pull of 3,046 lbs. at 5.65 mph with slippage of 4.77percent. By comparison, the 10-hour run at 75 percent pull, yielded a fuel economy of 12.06 hp-hours per gallon. This test, run with an output of 37.56 drawbar hp, saw a pull of 2,378 lbs. at 5.92 mph with slippage of 3.82 percent.

John Deere 2520 Series

Nebraska Test Data

Model: John Deere 2520 Syncro-Range Diesel
Test No. 992
Date Tested: October 22 to October 29, 1968

Partial range syncro-mesh shifting was included within the selective gear fixed-ratio transmission found on this tractor. Its eight forward speeds ranged from 1.78 to 15.76 mph. Operating in fourth gear, the two-hour economy run manifested a pull of 4,482 lbs. at 4.38 mph with slippage of 7.48 percent. These figures converted to a maximum available output of 52.36 drawbar hp, and resulted in an economy of 13.25 hp-hours per gallon. The 10-hour run at 75 percent pull noted an economy of 13.27 hp-hours per gallon against a load of 42.73 hp. Other statistics included a pull of 3,431 lbs. at 4.67 mph with 5.26 percent slippage. Weighing 7,180 lbs., this tractor was carried on 13.6-38 rear and 6.00-16 inch front tires. Additional ballast gave a total test weight of 8,955 lbs. Deere equipped this model with a four-cylinder, 219.8-cid engine. Rated at 2,500 rpm, it featured a 4.02 x 4.33 inch bore and stroke. Operating at rated speed, 61.29 maximum PTO hp was observed, as was an economy of 15.27 hp-hours per gallon. The economy figure stood at 16.08 in a test run at 1,000 PTO rpm, a corresponding engine speed of 2,071 rpm, and a maximum output of 55.86 PTO hp. No repairs or adjustments were reported during 45-1/2 hours of operating time.

Nebraska Test Data

Model: John Deere 2520 Power-Shift Diesel
Test No. 993
Date Tested: October 22 to October 29, 1968

Although this tractor assumed the same general appearance as the 2520 Syncro-Range model of Test No. 992, it instead featured full range power shifting within the selective gear fixed-ratio transmission. Its eight forward speeds ranged from 1.67 to 17.49 mph. Other specifications remained virtually the same as previously noted in Test No. 992. At its rated speed of 2,500 rpm, 56.28 maximum PTO hp appeared, together with an economy of 13.42 hp-hours per gallon. Operating at 1,000 PTO rpm and a corresponding engine speed of 2,067 rpm, 51.98 PTO hp appeared, as did an economy of 14.68 hp-hours per gallon. No repairs or adjustments were noted during 48 hours of operating time. The two-hour drawbar economy test was run at 45.98 maximum available hp, using fourth gear. It indicated a pull of 3,807 lbs. at 4.53 mph with slippage of 5.47 percent, and an economy of 11.43 hp-hours per gallon. The 10-hour run at 75 percent pull saw an economy of 10.83 hp-hours per gallon against a load of 37.61 hp. Also manifested was a pull of 3,013 lbs. at 4.68 mph and 4.61 percent slippage. Bare tractor weight was 7,425 lbs.—additional front and rear ballast raised this figure to a total test weight of 9,040 lbs.

Nebraska Test Data

Model: John Deere 2520 Power-Shift
Test No. 1002
Date Tested: March 12 to March 21, 1969

Opening the 1969 test season came Deere's gasoline powered 2520 model. Featuring full-range power shifting, this model offered eight speeds in a range of 1.67 to 17.49 mph. No repairs or adjustments were reported during 42 hours of running time. Using fourth gear, the two-hour economy run was made at 48.09 maximum available drawbar hp and yielded an economy of 8.51 hp-hours per gallon. Also recorded was a pull of 4,030 lbs. at 4.48 mph and 6.63 percent slippage. The 10-hour run at 75 percent pull saw an economy of 7.15 hp-hours per gallon, an output of 38.46 hp, plus a pull of 3,030 lbs. at 4.76 mph with 4.61 percent slippage. Weighing in at 7,390 lbs., this unit assumed a test weight of 8,990 lbs. through the addition of front and rear ballast. Deere equipped this model with their own four-cylinder, 202.7-cid engine. Rated at 2,500 rpm, it used a 3.86 x 4.33-inch bore and stroke. Operating at rated engine speed, 56.98 maximum PTO hp appeared and an economy of 10.3 hp-hours per gallon was achieved. Operating at 1,000 PTO rpm and a corresponding engine speed of 2,066 rpm, an economy of 10.86 hp-hours per gallon was recorded against an output of 51.96 hp.

Nebraska Test Data

Model: John Deere 2520 Syncro-Range
Test No. 1003
Date Tested: March 13 to March 28, 1969

Using the same four-cylinder, 202.7-cid engine, this model differed from that of the previous test by using an eight-speed, selective gear, fixed ratio transmission with partial range syncro-mesh shifting. Speeds ranged from 1.78 to 15.76 mph. At rated engine speed, this unit delivered 60.16 maximum PTO hp, together with an economy of 10.46 hp-hours per gallon. Operating at 1,000 PTO rpm and a corresponding engine speed of 2,071 rpm, 53.21 PTO hp was delivered and an economy of 10.54 hp-hours per gallon was achieved. A new air cleaner element was installed during the preliminary PTO runs, but with this exception, no repairs or adjustments were required during 57 hours of operating time. Weighing in at 7,130 lbs., this unit assumed a test weight of 8,955 lbs. through the addition of front and rear ballast. Standard equipment for this tractor as well as that of the previous test included 13.6-38-inch rear and 6.00-16-inch front tires. Using fourth gear, the two-hour drawbar economy run was made under a maximum available output of 54.45 hp and yielded an economy of 9.73 hp-hours per gallon. Other statistics included a pull of 4.654 lbs. at 4.39 mph with 7.09 percent slippage. The 10-hour run at 75 percent pull saw an economy of 8.38 hp-hours per gallon against an output of 44.42 hp. This test indicated a pull of 3,597 lbs. at 4.63 mph with slippage of 4.87 percent.

John Deere 3020 Series

Nebraska Test Data

Model: John Deere 3020 Diesel

Test No. 848

Date Tested: September 23 to October 2, 1963

At its rated engine speed of 2,500 rpm a maximum output of 65.28 PTO hp was recorded, as was a fuel economy of 12.71 hp-hours per gallon. A second PTO run made at 1,000 rpm on the output shaft and a corresponding engine speed of 2,067 rpm noted an economy figure of 13.85 and an output of 59.25 hp. The 3020 Diesel carried a 270-cid engine using a 4.25 x 4.75-inch bore and stroke. Also featured was a fixed-ratio transmission with full-range power shifting. Eight forward speeds were available in a range from 1-1/2 to 16-3/8 mph. No repairs or adjustments were recorded during 43 hours of running time. As presented for testing the 3020 Diesel weighed 7,945 lbs., but the addition of rear wheel ballast raised this figure to a test weight of 9,585 lbs. Standard equipment included 15.5-38 rear and 6.00-16-inch front tires. In fourth gear, a two-hour run at 54.77 maximum available drawbar hp yielded an economy of 10.88 hp-hours per gallon. Also manifested was a pull of 4,045 lbs. at 5.08 mph with 5.4 percent slippage. The 10-hour run at 75 percent pull noted an output of 44.71 hp with an economy figure of 10.61. This test was run with a pull of 3,177 lbs. at 5.28 mph against a slippage of 3.9 percent.

John Deere 3020 Series

Nebraska Test Data

Model: John Deere 3020

Test No. 851

Date Tested: September 30 to October 7, 1963

Using fourth gear, the 3020 delivered a maximum output of 54.6 drawbar hp in the two-hour economy run. Recorded too was a pull of 4,006 lbs. at 5.11 mph with 5.01 percent slippage. Economy came in at 8.82 hp-hours per gallon. By comparison, the economy column recorded 7.85 in a 10-hour drawbar run at 75 percent pull. This test saw an output of 43.78 hp, a pull of 3,050 lbs. at 5.38 mph and 3.69 percent slippage. Standard equipment of this 7,695-pound tractor included 15.5-38 rear and 6.00-16-inch front tires. The addition of rear wheel ballast gave a total test weight of 9,495 lbs. The fixed-ratio power-shift transmission offered eight forward speeds ranging from 1-1/2 to 16-3/8 mph. No repairs or adjustments were recorded during 49 hours of running time. Deere equipped this tractor with a 227-cid, four-cylinder engine. Rated at 2,500 rpm, it carried a 4-1/4 x 4-inch bore and stroke. At rated engine speed, 64.14 maximum PTO hp was observed at 10.37 hp-hours per gallon. The economy was recorded at 10.68 during a PTO run made at 1,000 rpm on the output shaft and a corresponding engine speed of 2,067 rpm. This test saw an output of 59.33 hp.

Nebraska Test Data

Model: John Deere 3020 LPG

Test No. 852

Date Tested: October 2 to October 11, 1963

Except for the obvious changes required by the propane storage tank, plus the required engine modifications, this tractor was nearly identical to the 3020 gasoline model. The 7.5 to 1 compression ratio of the gasoline style was changed on this tractor to 9.0:1 for proper accommodation of the propane fuel. No repairs or adjustments were recorded during 43 hours of operating time. At its rated speed of 2,500 rpm, the 3020 LPG delivered 64.7 PTO hp, yielding an economy of 8.13 hp-hours per gallon of propane. A second run at 2,067 rpm on the crankshaft and an output speed of 1,000 rpm noted 56.34 hp with an economy figure of 8.33. Just as in Test No. 851, fourth gear was used for the drawbar economy tests. At 54.5 maximum available hp, a two-hour run recorded the economy at 7.07 hp-hours per gallon. Also recorded in this test was a pull of 4,011 lbs. at 5.10 mph against slippage of 4.76 percent. The 10-hour drawbar run made at 75 percent pull noted 43.64 hp, together with a pull of 3,096 lbs. at 5.29 mph and slippage of 3.27 percent. This test gave an economy of 6.76 hp-hours per gallon of propane. Bare weight was 7,825 lbs. By the addition of rear wheel ballast, the test weight totaled 9,605 lbs.

Nebraska Test Data

Model: John Deere 3020 Syncro-Range Diesel

Test No. 940

Date Tested: May 17 to May 25, 1966

At its rated speed of 2,500 rpm, the 3020 Diesel developed a maximum of 71.26 PTO hp and delivered an economy of 13.87 hp-hours per gallon. A second run made at 1,000 PTO rpm and a corresponding engine speed of 2,071 rpm saw an economy figure of 14.76 hp-hours per gallon with a load of 64.32 hp. No repairs or adjustments were noted during 41-1/2 hours of operating time. Deere equipped this model with a four-cylinder engine with a 4.25 x 4.75-inch bore and stroke for a 270-cubic inch displacement. Standard equipment included 15.5-38 rear and 6.00-16-inch front tires. A selective gear fixed-ratio transmission with partial range syncromesh shifting was also provided—it offered eight speeds ranging from 2.0 to 17.6 mph. Operating in fourth gear, the two-hour economy run was made at 61.47 maximum available drawbar hp. Also indicated was a pull of 4,656 lbs. at 4.95 mph, slippage of 6.63 percent, and a fuel economy of 12.55 hp-hours per gallon. The 10-hour run at 75 percent pull saw an economy of 12.52 hp-hours per gallon against a load of 49.76 hp. Recorded too was a pull of 3,578 lbs. at 5.21 mph and slippage of 4.54 percent.

Nebraska Test Data

Model: John Deere 3020 Syncro-Range

Test No. 941

Date Tested: May 31 to June 7, 1966

Of nearly identical design to the 3020 Diesel of Test No. 940, this model replaced the diesel engine with the company's own four-cylinder gasoline style. Its 227-cubic inch displacement resulted from a 4-1/4 x 4-inch bore and stroke. Rated speed was 2,500 rpm. No repairs or adjustments were required during 39-1/2 hours of operating time. At rated engine speed, 70.59 maximum PTO hp yielded and economy of 10.66 hp-hours per gallon. By comparison, the economy figure stood at 10.79 against a load of 64.74 hp. The latter test was run at a PTO speed of 1,000 rpm and a corresponding engine speed of 2,072 rpm. While this unit had a total test weight of 9,825 lbs., subsequent removal of front and rear ballast gave a bare tractor weight of 7,760 lbs. Fourth gear was used for the drawbar economy runs. At 61.38 maximum available hp, fuel economy was posted at 9.86 hp-hours per gallon. This two-hour test saw a pull of 4,634 lbs. at 4.97 mph with slippage of 6.26 percent. A 10-hour run at 75 percent pull indicated an economy of 8.86 hp-hours per gallon against a load of 50.04 hp. This test gave a pull of 3,568 lbs. at 5.26 mph with slippage of 4.73 percent.

Nebraska Test Data

Model: John Deere 3020 Syncro-Range LPG

Test No. 942

Date Tested: May 31 to June 8, 1966

This tractor carried the basic chassis design already referenced in Tests 940 and 941. Likewise, it carried an engine nearly identical to the gasoline model of Test No. 941. Except for the modifications in exterior design, and with a compression ratio of 9.0:1 compared to 7.5:1 for the gasoline model, both tractors were nearly the same. No repairs or adjustments were noted during 40 hours of running time. Operating at its rated 2,500 rpm, 70.66 maximum PTO hp was observed, together with an economy of 8.62 hp-hours per gallon of propane. Operating at 1,000 PTO rpm and a corresponding engine speed of 2,071 rpm, the output of 62.88 PTO hp gave an economy of 9.33 hp-hours per gallon. Bare weight of this tractor was 7,950 lbs. and additional rear wheel ballast raised this figure to a total test weight of 9,830 lbs. Fourth gear gave 63.13 maximum available drawbar hp in the two-hour economy run. Also evidenced was a pull of 4,785 lbs. at 4.95 mph, slippage of 6.3 percent, and an economy of 7.83 hp-hours per gallon of propane. The 10-hour run at 75 percent pull indicated an economy of 7.8 hp-hours per gallon against a load of 51.19 hp. Also recorded was a pull of 3,691 lbs. at 5.20 mph with slippage of 4.31 percent.

Nebraska Test Data

Model: John Deere 3020 Power-Shift

Test No. 1010

Date Tested: May 13 to June 2, 1969

Weighing in at 8,350 lbs., this tractor used 15.5-38-inch rear and 6.00-16-inch front tires. Additional front and rear ballast gave a total test weight of 10,320 lbs. The fixed-ratio transmission offered full-range power shifting. Eight forward speeds ranged from 1.9 to 19.5 mph. Operating in fourth gear, the two-hour economy run was made at 55.79 maximum available hp and yielded an economy of 8.16 hp-hours per gallon. Also recorded was a pull of 4,125 lbs. at 5.07 mph with slippage of 5.64 percent. The 10-hour run at 75 percent pull saw an economy of 7.49 hp-hours per gallon against a load of 45.87 hp. Other statistics included a run of 3,215 lbs. at 5.35 mph with 4.33 percent slippage. Deere equipped this model with its own four-cylinder, 241-cid engine. Rated at 2,500 rpm, it featured a 4-1/4-inch bore and stroke. At rated engine speed, 67.13 PTO hp was observed, with an economy of 9.77 hp-hours per gallon. Operating at 1,000 PTO rpm and a corresponding engine speed of 2,066 rpm, 10.44 hp-hours per gallon was recorded, as was an output of 62.63 hp. During 42 hours of total operation, the foot throttle was adjusted and oil leakage was noted from the PTO clutch valve.

Nebraska Test Data

Model: John Deere 3020 Syncro-Range
Test No. 1011
Date Tested: May 13 to June 2, 1969

This 3020 offered a Syncro-Range design. It was a selective gear fixed-ratio transmission with partial range power shifting. With this exception, the tractor was nearly identical to that of the previous test, with the same 241-cid engine. At its rated speed of 2,500 rpm, this tractor delivered a maximum of 71.37 PTO hp together with an economy of 10.91 hp-hours per gallon. At 1,000 PTO rpm and a corresponding engine speed of 2,071 rpm, an economy of 11.29 hp-hours per gallon resulted with a load of 66.11 hp. Except for an adjustment to the foot throttle, no repairs or adjustments were reported during 50 hours of operating time. Weighing 8,180 lbs., this unit assumed a total test weight of 10,220 lbs. through the addition of front and rear ballast. Operating in fourth gear, the two-hour economy run was made at 61.26 maximum available hp. This test saw a pull of 4,642 lbs. at 4.95 mph and slippage of 6.28 percent and yielded an economy of 9.4 hp-hours per gallon. The 10-hour run at 75 percent pull noted an economy of 7.94 hp-hours per gallon against a load of 45.03 hp. Other statistics included a pull of 3,213 lbs. at 5.26 mph with slippage of 3.88 percent.

John Deere 4000 Series

Nebraska Test Data

Model: John Deere 4000 Diesel
Test No. 1023
Date Tested: September 30 to October 14, 1969

Features of this model included selective gear, fixed-ratio transmission with partial range syncro-mesh shifting. The eight forward speeds ranged from 1.8 to 16.8 mph. Weighing in at 8,605 lbs., this unit was equipped with 16.9-34-inch rear and 9.5L-15-inch front tires. Additional front and rear ballast raised the total test weight to 10,870 lbs. Operating in fifth gear, the two-hour economy run established this figure at 13.39 hp-hours per gallon of diesel fuel under a maximum available load of 82.59 drawbar hp. Also in evidence was a pull of 5,464 lbs. at 5.67 mph and slippage of 8.24 percent. The 10-hour run at 75 percent pull saw an economy of 13.13 hp-hours per gallon against a load of 69.32 drawbar hp. This test noted a pull of 4,215 lbs. at 6.17 mph with 6.08 percent slippage. No repairs or adjustments were reported during 41 hours of operation. Deere equipped this model with a six-cylinder 404-cid engine. Rated at 2,200 rpm, it used a 4.25 x 4.75-inch bore and stroke. At rated engine speed, 96.89 maximum PTO hp and an economy of 15.65 hp-hours per gallon was observed. With a PTO speed of 1,000 rpm and a corresponding engine speed of 1,894 rpm, 88.88 PTO hp was developed, together with an economy of 16.03 hp-hours per gallon.

John Deere 4020 Series

Nebraska Test Data

Model: John Deere 4020 Diesel
Test No. 849
Date Tested: September 23 to October 2, 1963

At 2,200 rpm rated engine speed the 4020 Diesel developed a maximum of 91.17 PTO hp and achieved a fuel economy of 14.2 hp-hours per gallon. Using an engine speed of 1,895 rpm and a corresponding PTO speed of 1,000 rpm, 83.57 hp was developed with a resultant fuel economy of 14.89 hp-hours per gallon. A six-cylinder engine was used and its 4.25 x 4.75-inch bore and stroke gave a displacement of 404-cubic inches. The fixed-ratio transmission featured full-range power shifting and offered eight forward speeds ranging from 1-1/2 to 15-1/2 mph. In fourth gear, and at 76.36 maximum available drawbar hp, fuel economy was pegged at 11.86 hp-hours per gallon. Also indicated was a pull of 5,848 lbs. at 4.9 mph with 6.01 percent slippage. The economy figure came in at 11.77 against an output of 63.3 drawbar hp. This 10-hour run at 75 percent load also indicated a pull of 4,506 lbs. at 5.27 mph with 3.89 percent slippage. Standard equipment included 18.4-34 rear and 7.50-15-inch front tires. The bare weight of 8,945 lbs. rose to 13,055 lbs. through the addition of rear wheel ballast. No repairs or adjustments were recorded during 47 hours of running time.

Nebraska Test Data

Model: John Deere 4020
Test No. 850
Date Tested: September 30 to October 7, 1963

Except for the gasoline engine, this tractor was virtually identical to the 4020 Diesel. Deere used a six-cylinder engine rated at 2,200 rpm. Its 4-1/4 x 4-inch bore and stroke gave a displacement of 340-cubic inches. At rated engine speed, 88.09 PTO hp was developed, giving a resultant economy of 10.53 hp-hours per gallon. Using 1,000 rpm at the PTO shaft and a corresponding engine speed of 1,895 rpm, the economy came in at 10.99 against a load of 79.95 hp. No repairs or adjustments were noted during 54 hours of operating time. Fourth gear was used for the drawbar economy runs. The two-hour test at 73.06 maximum available hp indicated a pull of 5,553 lbs. at 4.93 mph with 5.86 percent slippage. Fuel economy came in at 8.92 hp-hours per gallon. This figure was 7.79 in a 10-hour run at 75 percent pull. Also recorded was an output of 59.7 hp, a pull of 4,244 lbs. at 5.28 mph and 4.08 percent slippage. By comparison, the 8,645 total lbs. as presented, totaled 13,135 lbs. during testing through the addition of front and rear ballast.

Nebraska Test Data

Model: John Deere 4020 LPG
Test No. 853
Date Tested: October 5 to October 11, 1963

The John Deere 4020 LPG model shown here was nearly identical to the 4020 gasoline, other than raising the compression ratio from 7.5:1 to 9.0:1 and adding propane equipment. This propane-fired version weighed 8,835 lbs., but the addition of rear wheel ballast raised this figure to 13,125 lbs. No repairs or adjustments were recorded during 40-1/2 hours of running time. At rated engine speed, 90.48 PTO hp was observed, along with an economy of 8.95 hp-hours per gallon of propane. Using 1,000 rpm at the PTO shaft and a corresponding engine speed of 1,895 rpm, 81.14 PTO hp was apparent, as was an economy of 9.22 hp-hours per gallon. Drawbar economy testing included a two-hour run at 75.19 maximum available hp. Using fourth gear, this test yielded a pull of 5,716 lbs. at 4.93 mph with 5.67 percent slippage. The economy was pegged at 7.77 hp-hours per gallon. The 10-hour run at 75 percent pull set this figure at 7.42. It saw an output of 63.84 hp, a pull of 4,548 lbs. at 5.26 mph and 3.94 percent slippage.

Nebraska Test Data

Model: John Deere 4020 Syncro-Range Diesel
Test No. 930
Date Tested: November 16 to November 20, 1963

Weighing 8,865 lbs., this tractor was supported on 18.4-34 rear and 7.50-15-inch front tires. Additional front and rear ballast gave a total test weight of 14,265 lbs. Standard features included a selective gear fixed-ratio with partial range syncro-mesh shifting. Eight forward speeds were provided in a range from 1.9 to 17.6 mph. The two-hour drawbar economy run was made under maximum available output of 83.79 hp and yielded an economy of 14.04 hp-hours per gallon. Other statistics included a pull of 6,396 lbs. at 4.91 mph with slippage of 6.13 percent. The 10-hour run at 75 percent pull indicated an economy of 13.38 against an output of 70.68 drawbar hp. Also revealed was a pull of 4,898 lbs. at 5.41 mph and slippage of 4.25 percent. No repairs or adjustments were reported during 47 hours of running time. Deere equipped this tractor with its own four-cylinder, 404-cid engine. Rated at 2,200 rpm, it used a 4.25 x 4.750-inch bore and stroke. Operating at rated speed, 94.88 maximum PTO hp was observed, as was an economy of 15.82 hp-hours per gallon. When operating at 540 rpm on the PTO shaft and a corresponding engine speed of 1,894 rpm, 86.85 hp resulted with a yield of 16.4 hp-hours per gallon.

Nebraska Test Data

Model: John Deere 4020 Syncro-Range LPG
Test No. 934
Date Tested: April 26 to May 2, 1966

Except for the obvious changes required by propane fuel, this tractor differed little from the 4020 gasoline model. Deere featured a six-cylinder, 340-cid engine. Rated at 2,200 rpm, it used a 4-1/4 x 4-inch bore and stroke. The engine design was altered to include a 9.0:1 compression ratio. No repairs or adjustments were reported during 43 hours of running time. At 94.57 maximum PTO hp, and at rated engine speed, the economy came in at 9.24 hp-hours per gallon of propane fuel. This figure increased to 9.45 in a second PTO run at 1,000 PTO rpm and a corresponding engine speed of 1,895 rpm. During this test, 84.22 PTO hp was recorded. Included in the chassis design was a selective gear, fixed-ratio partial range syncro-mesh transmission with eight forward speeds in a range from 1.9 to 17.6 mph. Standard equipment of this 9,180-lb. tractor included 18.4-34 rear and 7.50-15-inch front tires. Additional front and rear ballast gave a total test weight of 14,150 lbs. Operating in fourth gear, the two-hour economy run was made at 83.59 maximum available drawbar hp. Fuel economy was posted at 8.19 hp-hours per gallon in this test. Also indicated was a pull of 6,390 lbs. at 4.91 mph and slippage of 7.2 percent. The 10-hour run at 75 percent pull saw an output of 68.91 hp, a pull of 4,977 lbs. at 5.19 mph, and slippage of 5.44 percent. Fuel economy came in at 7.9 hp-hours per gallon.

Nebraska Test Data

Model: John Deere 4020 Syncro-Range
Test No. 939
Date Tested: May 17 to May 24, 1966

This model's 340-cubic inch displacement resulted from six cylinders with a 4-1/4 x 4-inch bore and stroke. Rated at 2,200 rpm, the 4020 gasoline model developed 95.59 maximum PTO hp at this speed. Fuel economy was recorded at 12.12 hp-hours per gallon. The economy figure stood at 12.52 in a PTO run made at 1,000 rpm and a corresponding engine speed of 1,895 rpm. Also recorded was an output of 85.81 PTO hp. The chassis design included a selective gear, fixed-ratio transmission with partial range syncro-mesh shifting. Eight forward speeds were provided in a range from 1.9 to 17.6 mph. No repairs or adjustments were required or noted during 42 hours of operation. Standard equipment for this 8,910-lb. tractor included 18.4-34 rear and 7.50-15-inch front tires. During drawbar testing, additional front and rear ballast boosted total test weight to 14,030 lbs. The two-hour economy test at 83.28 maximum available drawbar hp saw an economy figure of 10.81. Also recorded was a pull of 6,354 lbs. at 4.91 mph with slippage of 6.73 percent. During the 10-hour run, made at 75 percent pull, fuel economy was posted at 9.99 hp-hours per gallon against an output of 68.28 hp. This test saw a pull of 4,822 lbs. at 5.31 mph with slippage of 4.98 percent.

Nebraska Test Data

Model: John Deere 4020 Power-Shift
Test No. 1012
Date Tested: May 13 to June 4, 1969

Weighing in at 9,240 lbs., this tractor used 18.4-34 rear and 7.50-15-inch front tires. Additional front and rear ballast brought the total test weight to 13,820 lbs. The fixed-ratio transmission included full-range power shifting and offered eight forward speeds ranging from 1.8 to 18.7 mph. Using fourth gear, the two-hour economy run saw a maximum load of 82.57 drawbar hp and a consequent yield of 8.9 hp-hours per gallon. Also indicated was a pull of 6,443 lbs. at 4.81 mph with slippage of 6.86 percent. The 10-hour run at 75 percent pull indicated an economy of 7.98 hp-hours per gallon against a load of 68.71 drawbar hp. Other statistics included a pull of 4,939 lbs. at 5.22 mph with 4.61 percent slippage. Deere equipped this model with a six-cylinder, 362-cid engine. Rated at 2,200 rpm, it used a 4-1/4-inch bore and stroke. At rated engine speed, fuel economy stood at 10.3 hp-hours per gallon against a maximum output of 95.66 PTO hp. At 1,000 PTO rpm and a corresponding engine speed of 1,894 rpm, an economy of 10.76 hp-hours per gallon resulted under a load of 87.52 hp. During 54-1/2 hours of operation, repairs and adjustments included repair of a hydraulic tee fitting on the power steering housing, plus an adjustment of the foot throttle linkage.

Nebraska Test Data

Model: John Deere 4020 Syncro-Range
Test No. 1013
Date Tested: May 13 to June 3, 1969

Of the same general specifications already noted in Test No. 1012, this 4020 gasoline-powered model featured an eight-speed transmission. Of selective gear fixed-ratio design, it offered partial range syncro-mesh shifting. At its rated engine speed of 2,200 rpm, 96.66 maximum PTO hp was observed, as was an economy of 11.71 hp-hours per gallon. Using a PTO speed of 1,000 rpm and a corresponding engine speed of 1,894 rpm, an economy of 12.12 hp-hours per gallon was delivered against a load of 88.15 hp. Except for a foot throttle adjustment, no repairs or adjustments were noted during 58-1/2hours of operation. Weighing in at 9,060 lbs., this unit assumed a test weight of 13,800 lbs. through the addition of front and rear ballast. Operating in fourth gear, the two-hour economy run was made at 84.52 maximum available drawbar hp and yielded an economy of 10.10 hp-hours per gallon of gasoline. Also indicated was a pull of 6,569 lbs. at 4.83 mph with slippage totaling 6.73 percent. The 10-hour run at 75 percent pull saw an economy figure of 9.34 against a load of 71.25 drawbar hp. Other statistics included a pull of 5,096 lbs. at 5.24 mph with 4.83 percent slippage.

Nebraska Test Data

Model: John Deere 4020 Power-Shift Diesel

Test No. 1024

Date Tested: September 30 to October 17, 1969

Rated at 2,200 rpm, this tractor developed 95.83 maximum PTO hp while achieving an economy of 14.77 hp-hours per gallon. At 1,000 PTO rpm and a corresponding crankshaft speed of 1,894 rpm, 89.93 PTO hp was observed, as was an economy of 14.87 hp-hours per gallon. The six-cylinder, 404-cid engine carried a 4.25 x 4.75-inch bore and stroke. Also featured was a fixed-ratio transmission with full range power shifting. Its eight forward speeds ranged from 1.8 to 18.7 mph. Using fourth gear, the two-hour economy run saw 83.09 maximum available drawbar hp and a resultant economy of 12.64 hp-hours per gallon. Also recorded was a pull of 6,446 lbs. at 4.83 mph and slippage of 7.64 percent. The 10-hour run at 75 percent pull indicated an economy of 12.5 hp-hours per gallon against an output of 67.63 hp. Other statistics included a pull of 4,871 lbs. at 5.21 mph and 5.78 percent slippage. Weighing in at 9,560 lbs., this tractor assumed a test weight of 13,980 lbs. through the addition of front and rear ballast. This included 1,260 lbs. of cast iron weight on each rear wheel, an obvious addition. Standard equipment included 18.4-34 rear and 7.5L-15-inch front tires. No repairs or adjustments were reported during 43-1/2 hours of operation.

John Deere 4320 Series

Nebraska Test Data

Model: John Deere 4320 Syncro-Range Diesel

Test No. 1050

Date Tested: September 21 to September 26, 1970

The 4320 Syncro-Range emerged from the two-hour drawbar run with an economy of 12.73 hp-hours per gallon against a maximum available output of 101.71 drawbar hp. This test, run in fourth gear, saw a pull of 7,475 lbs. at 5.1 mph with slippage totaling 6.62 percent. An economy of 11.77 hp-hours per gallon was established under a load of 83.78 hp. These figures, taken from the 10-hour run at 75 percent pull, indicated a pull of 5,784 lbs. at 5.43 mph and 4.94 percent slippage. Weighing in at 10,675 lbs., this unit was equipped with 18.4-38 rear and 11L-15-inch front tires. Additional front and rear ballast raised the total test weight to 14,380 lbs. Features included a selective gear fixed-ratio transmission with partial range syncro-mesh shifting. The eight forward speeds ranged from 2.01 to 18.87 mph. No repairs or adjustments were reported during 47 hours of operation. Deere equipped this model with a six-cylinder turbocharged engine. Rated at 2,200 rpm, it used a 4-1/4 x 4-3/4-inch bore and stroke for displacement of 404-cubic inches. At rated engine speed, an economy of 14.65 hp-hours per gallon was established under a maximum PTO load of 116.55 hp. Running at 1,000 PTO rpm and a corresponding engine speed of 1,894 rpm, 108.02 PTO hp was achieved at 15.35 hp-hours per gallon.

John Deere 4520 Series

Nebraska Test Data

Model: John Deere 4520 Power-Shift Diesel

Test No. 1014

Date Tested: June 3 to June 10, 1969

Using a six-cylinder, 404-cid turbocharged engine, this diesel model was rated at 2,200 rpm and featured a 4-1/4 x 4-3/4-inch bore and stroke. At rated engine speed it developed 122.36 maximum PTO hp and achieved an economy of 15.08 hp-hours per gallon. Operating at 1,000 PTO rpm and a corresponding engine speed of 1,905 rpm an economy figure of 15.64 hp hours was established against a load of 115.44 hp. Deere equipped this model with a selective gear fixed-ratio transmission with full-range power shifting. Its eight forward speeds ranged from 1.72 to 18.47 mph. No repairs or adjustments were reported during 45-1/2 hours of operation. Using fourth gear, the two-hour economy run at 107.76 maximum available drawbar hp yielded an economy of 13.4 hp-hours per gallon. This test recorded a pull of 8,427 lbs. at 4.8 mph with slippage of 6.62 percent. By comparison, the 10-hour run at 75 percent pull achieved an economy of 12.58 hp-hours per gallon against an output of 89.36 hp. Other statistics included a pull of 6,673 lbs. at 5.02 mph with slippage of 5.09 percent. Standard equipment for this model included 20.8-38-inch rear and 10.00-16-inch front tires. Weighing in at 14,175 lbs., it assumed a total test weight of 17,955 lbs. through the addition of front and rear ballast.

Nebraska Test Data

Model: John Deere 4520 Syncro-Range Diesel
Test No. 1015
Date Tested: June 3 to June 10, 1969

The 4520 Syncro-Range model differed from the Power-Shift style only in its somewhat different transmission. In this case, a selective gear fixed-ratio style was used — it offered partial range syncro-mesh shifting. The eight forward speeds ranged from 1.95 to 18.3 mph. Using fourth gear, the two-hour economy run at 111.21 maximum available drawbar hp yielded an economy of 13.6 hp-hours per gallon. This test also established a pull of 8,219 lbs. at 5.07 mph with slippage totaling 6.82 percent. The 10-hour run at 75 percent pull yielded an economy of 12.79 hp-hours per gallon against a load of 89.84 drawbar hp. Other statistics included a pull of 6,223 lbs. at 5.41 mph with slippage of 4.88 percent. No repairs or adjustments were reported during 47 hours of running time. Weighing in at 13,900 lbs., this unit assumed a test weight of 17,850 lbs. through the addition of front and rear ballast. Using the same six-cylinder, 404-cid turbocharged diesel as previously noted for Test No. 1014, the model illustrated here achieved an economy of 15.54 hp-hours per gallon under a maximum load of 123.39 PTO hp while operating at its rated speed of 2,200 rpm. Using a 1,000 PTO rpm and a corresponding engine speed of 1,905 rpm, the economy figure rested at 16.05 hp-hours per gallon against a load of 115.22 PTO hp.

Nebraska Test Data

Model: John Deere 4620 Power-Shift Diesel
Test No. 1064
Date Tested: April 20 to May 4, 1971

Weighing in at 14,930 lbs., this model used 20.80-38 rear and 14L-16-inch front tires. Additional front and rear ballast raised the total test weight to 18,585 lbs. No repairs or adjustments were reported during 48-1/2 hours of operation. The selective gear fixed-ratio transmission offered full-range power shifting. Eight forward speeds were provided in a range from 1.72 to 18.47 mph. Using fourth gear, the two-hour drawbar run at 110.92 maximum available hp set an economy of 12.23 hp-hours per gallon of fuel. Likewise, a pull of 8,823 lbs. at 4.71 mph and 7.68 percent slippage was indicated by this test. A 10-hour drawbar run at 75 percent pull noted an economy of 11.27 hp-hours per gallon with an output of 91.77 hp. Further data includes a pull of 6,822 lbs. at 5.19 mph and slippage of 5.5 percent. Deere equipped this model with a six-cylinder turbocharged engine rated at 2,200 rpm. Its 4-1/4 x 4-3/4 inch bore and stroke yielded a 404 CID. At rated engine speed, 135.62 maximum PTO hp was observed, as was an economy of 14.77 hp-hours per gallon of fuel. Operating at 1,904 crankshaft rpm and a corresponding output speed of 1,000 rpm, 130.79 PTO hp was recorded, as was an economy of 15.7 hp-hours per gallon of diesel fuel.

John Deere 4620 Series

John Deere 5020 Series

Nebraska Test Data

Model: John Deere 5020 Diesel

Test No. 947

Date Tested: September 24 to October 1, 1966

Large hp units became more evident in the 1960s, and testing these tractors required additional equipment. Operating in fourth gear, the two-hour economy run for the 5020 Diesel was made at 113.72 maximum available drawbar hp. This test yielded an economy of 13.85 hp-hours per gallon, and saw a pull of 8,529 lbs. at 5 mph with slippage of 5.26 percent. The 10-hour run at 75 percent pull indicated an economy figure of 13.49 against a load of 94.05 hp. Also recorded in the 10-hour test was a pull of 6,520 lbs. at 5.41 mph with 3.76 percent slippage. Weighing in at 16,045 lbs., additional rear wheel ballast raised this figure to a test weight of 21,360 lbs. Standard equipment included dual 18.4-38 rear wheels and 9.50-20-inch front tires. The chassis design included a selective gear fixed-ratio partial range syncro-mesh transmission of eight forward speeds ranging from 1.9 to 17.9 mph. Deere equipped this tractor with their own six-cylinder, 531-cid engine. Rated at 2,200 rpm, it carried a 4-3/4 x 5-inch bore and stroke. No repairs or adjustments were required during 41 hours of running time. At rated engine speed, 133.25 maximum PTO hp was observed, as was an economy of 16.21 hp-hours per gallon. The economy was pegged at 16.89 in a PTO run made with an output speed of 1,000 rpm and a corresponding engine speed of 1,881 rpm. This test achieved an output of 122.76 PTO hp.

Nebraska Test Data

Model: John Deere 5020 Diesel

Test No. 1025

Date Tested: October 1 to October 16, 1969

Weighing in at 17,350 lbs., this unit was carried on dual rear wheels of 20.8-38-inch size, plus two 11.00-16-inch tires. Additional rear wheel ballast brought the total test weight to 19,630 lbs. Features included a selective gear, fixed-ratio transmission with partial range syncro-mesh shifting. Its eight forward speeds ranged from 1.9 to 17.9 mph. Using fourth gear, the two-hour economy run at 121.86 maximum available drawbar hp saw an economy of 13.6 hp-hours per gallon. Also recorded was a pull of 8,582 lbs. at 5.33 mph and slippage totaling 4.63 percent. The 10-hour run at 75 percent pull achieved an economy of 13.01 hp-hours per gallon against a load of 100.36 drawbar hp. Other data included a pull of 6,673 lbs. at 5.64 mph with 3.24 percent slippage. No repairs or adjustments were required during 45-1/2 hours of operation. Deere equipped this model with a six-cylinder, 531-cid engine. Rated at 2,200 rpm, it featured a 4.75 x 5.00-inch bore and stroke. At rated engine speed, an economy of 15.46 hp-hours per gallon was achieved against a maximum load of 141.34 PTO hp. Operating at 1,000 PTO rpm and a corresponding engine speed of 1,881 rpm, the economy was 16.04 hp-hours per gallon against a load of 128.51 PTO hp.

Nebraska Test Data

Model: John Deere 7020 Diesel

Test No. 1063

Date Tested: April 20 to May 4, 1971

At its rated engine speed of 2,200 rpm, this tractor developed 146.17 maximum PTO hp while delivering an economy of 14.28 hp-hours per gallon. The six-cylinder, turbocharged engine carried a 4.25 x 4.75-inch bore and stroke for a 404-cubic inch displacement. Weighing 18,495 lbs., it was equipped with four dual wheels, each using 18.4-34-inch tires. An additional 23 lbs. of cast-iron weight was added to each rear wheel, plus 246 lbs. on each front wheel for a total test weight of 19,570 lbs. Deere equipped this model with a selective gear fixed-ratio transmission with partial range syncro-mesh shifting. Its 16 forward speeds ranged from 1.99 to 21.4 mph. No repairs or adjustments were reported during 47-1/2 hours of operating time. Operating in seventh gear, the two-hour drawbar performance run at 127.72 maximum available hp saw an economy of 12.82 hp-hours per gallon. This test likewise recorded a pull of 8,969 lbs. at 5.34 mph, with slippage totaling 3.98 percent. The 10-hour run at 75 percent pull indicated an economy of 11.81 hp-hours per gallon with a load of 105.32 hp. This output resulted from a pull of 6,962 lbs. at 5.67 mph—slippage in this test totaled 2.92 percent.

John Deere 7020 Series

John Deere 7520 Series

Nebraska Test Data

Model: John Deere 7520 Diesel
Test No. 1101
Date Tested: May 25 to June 6, 1972

This four-wheel-drive unit was equipped with 23.1-30-inch tires, using a total of eight for the four corners. Weighing 22,320 lbs., this unit was tested without the use of additional ballast. The selective gear fixed-ratio transmission offered partial range syncro-mesh shifting. Its 16 forward speeds ranged from 2.08 to 22.35 mph. Operating in seventh gear, the two-hour drawbar run at 160.46 maximum available hp saw a pull of 10,580 lbs. at 5.69 mph with slippage recorded at 3.21 percent. During this test, fuel economy was recorded at 13.76 hp-hours per gallon. A second run at 75 percent pull saw an economy figure of 12.82 against an output of 129.16 drawbar hp. Also recorded was a pull of 8,159 lbs. at 5.94 mph and slippage of 2.36 percent. Deere equipped this model with its own six-cylinder turbocharged and intercooled diesel engine. Rated at 2,100 rpm, it carried a 4.75 x 5.00-inch bore and stroke for a 531-cubic inch displacement. At rated engine speed, 175.82 maximum PTO hp was observed and an economy of 15.18 hp-hours per gallon was achieved. During the 10-hour drawbar run, it was necessary to stop and reset the hub bolts on one rear wheel before completing the test. With this exception, no repairs or adjustments were recorded during 41-1/2 hours of operation.

Nebraska Test Data

Model: John Deere 830 Diesel
Test No. 1146
Date Tested: September 24 to October 1, 1966

Weighing 4,376 lbs., the 830 was equipped with 13.6-28 rear and 6.50-16-inch front tires. Additional front and rear ballast raised the total test weight to 5,714 lbs. Features included a selective gear fixed-ratio transmission with eight forward speeds in a range from 1.4 to 15.9 mph. Fifth gear was used for the two-hour economy run made at 28.02 maximum available drawbar hp. This test recorded a pull of 2,028 lbs. at 5.18 mph, slippage of 4.54 percent, and a fuel economy of 11.84 hp-hours per gallon. The 10-hour run at 75 percent pull noted an economy of 11.03 hp-hours per gallon under a load of 22.16 drawbar hp. Also recorded was a pull of 1,550 lbs. at 5.36 mph with 3.26 percent slippage. This tractor was equipped with a Deere-built three-cylinder engine. Rated at 2,400 rpm, it used a 3.86 x 4.33-inch bore and stroke for a 152-cubic inch displacement. At rated engine speed, 35.30 maximum PTO hp was observed and an economy of 14.28 hp-hours per gallon was achieved. The economy figure rested at 14.74 in another run made at 540 PTO rpm and a corresponding engine speed of 2,076 rpm. This test recorded an output of 32.62 PTO hp. No repairs or adjustments were required during 46-1/2 hours of operation.

Model 830 Diesel

This tractor was a product of the Mannheim, West Germany, factory.

Model 950 Diesel

The Model 950 was built by Yanmar Diesel Company Ltd., in Osaka, Japan.

Nebraska Test Data

Model: John Deere 950 Diesel
Test No. 1281
Date Tested: June 12 to June 16, 1978

Weighing 2,812 lbs., the 950 was equipped with 12.4-28 rear and 5.50-16-inch front tires. Additional front and rear ballast gave a total test weight of 3,615 lbs. The selective gear fixed-ratio transmission offered eight forward speeds ranging from 0.8 to 12.1 mph. Using sixth gear, the two-hour drawbar test at 22.12 maximum available hp indicated a pull of 1,663 lbs. at 4.99 mph, slippage of 6.45 percent, and an economy of 12.42 hp-hours per gallon. The 10-hour run at 75 percent pull revealed an economy figure of 12.23 under a load of 18.78 drawbar hp. Other data from this test included a pull of 1,332 lbs. at 5.29 mph and slippage totaling 5.01 percent. The 950 Diesel was equipped with a Yanmar three-cylinder engine. Rated at 2,400 rpm, it used a 3.54-inch bore and stroke for a 105-cubic inch displacement. At rated engine speed, 27.36 maximum PTO hp appeared, and an economy of 14.89 hp-hours per gallon was observed. Operating at 540 PTO rpm and a corresponding engine speed of 2,258 rpm, an economy figure of 14.68 was established under a load of 28.05 PTO hp. No repairs or adjustments were required during 35 hours of operating time.

John Deere 1050 Series

The 1050 series was built by Yanmar Diesel Company Ltd., in Osaka, Japan.

Nebraska Test Data

Model: John Deere 1050 Diesel, 8-Speed
Test No. 1327
Date Tested: October 8 to October 12, 1979

With the front-wheel-drive disengaged, and using sixth gear, this tractor developed 27.25 maximum available drawbar hp in the two-hour economy run. Also indicated by this test was a pull of 1,938 lbs. at 5.27 mph and slippage totaling 6.4 percent. By comparison, when running the same test with the front-wheel-drive engaged, a pull of 1,887 lbs. was recorded at 5.43 mph with slippage totaling 4.76 percent. This test saw a maximum output of 27.31 drawbar hp and an economy of 12.57 hp-hours per gallon. The 1050 weighed in at 3,410 lbs. Standard equipment included 13.6-28 rear and 7-16-inch front tires. Additional front and rear ballast gave a total weight of 4,140 lbs. No repairs or adjustments were necessary during 37 hours of operation. A selective gear fixed-ratio transmission was used and its eight forward speeds varied from 0.9 to 12.5 mph. Also featured was a Yanmar three-cylinder diesel engine. With a rated speed of 2,400 rpm, it carried a 3.54-inch bore and stroke for a 105-cubic inch displacement. At rated engine speed, 33.41 maximum PTO hp was observed, as was an economy of 15.14 hp-hours per gallon. Operating at 540 PTO rpm and a corresponding engine speed of 2,258 rpm, an economy of 15.46 hp-hours per gallon resulted from a load of 33.42 PTO hp.

John Deere 1450 Series

The 1450 series was built by Yanmar Diesel Company Ltd., in Osaka, Japan.

Nebraska Test Data

Model: John Deere 1450 Diesel
Test No. 1505
Date Tested: October 31 to November 9, 1983

At its rated crankshaft speed of 2,400 rpm, the 1450 delivered 51.39 maximum PTO hp while establishing a fuel economy of 17.38 hp-hours per gallon of fuel. Operating at 540 PTO rpm and a corresponding engine speed of 2,237 rpm, an economy figure of 17.60 was established against a load of 50.93 PTO hp. This tractor featured a Yanmar four-cylinder diesel engine. Its 3.74 x 4.33-inch bore and stroke gave a 190-cubic inch displacement. Also featured was a nine-speed selective gear fixed-ratio transmission with a total range of 1.3 to 16.0 mph. Tire equipment included 16.9-28 rear and 7.50-16-inch front rubber. Weighing 5,230 lbs., this model assumed a test weight of 6,570 lbs. after the addition of front and rear ballast. No repairs or adjustments were reported during 47 hours of operating time. Using sixth gear, the two-hour drawbar run at 43.17 maximum available hp saw a pull of 2,951 lbs. at 5.49 mph. Slippage totaled 5.35 percent, and fuel economy was established at 14.74 hp-hours per gallon. The 10-hour run at 75 percent pull noted an economy of 13.67 hp-hours per gallon under a load of 34.68 drawbar hp. Likewise indicated was a pull of 2,244 lbs. at 5.79 mph and slippage totaling 3.87 percent.

John Deere 1650 Series

The 1650 series was built by Yanmar Diesel Company Ltd., in Osaka, Japan.

Nebraska Test Data

Model: John Deere 1650 Diesel
Test No. 1506
Date Tested: October 31 to November 11, 1983

The 1650 weighed in at 5,350 lbs. Additional front and rear ballast gave a total test weight of 7,785 lbs. Standard equipment included 18.4-26 rear and 7.50-16-inch front tires. Also featured was a speed range of 1.3 to 15.9 mph in the selective gear fixed-ratio transmission. The four-cylinder Yanmar turbocharged engine used a 3.74 x 4.33-inch bore and stroke for a displacement of 190-cubic inches. No repairs or adjustments were required during 35-1/2 hours of operating time. Operating in sixth gear, the two-hour drawbar run at 53.13 maximum available hp established an economy of 15.96 hp-hours per gallon. Also indicated was a pull of 3,583 lbs. at 5.56 mph and slippage totaling 6.07 percent. The 10-hour run at 75 percent pull noted an economy figure of 14.97 under a load of 42.77 drawbar hp. Other data included a pull of 2,733 lbs. at 5.87 mph with slippage totaling 4.52 percent. At the rated engine speed of 2,300 rpm, 62.22 maximum PTO hp was observed at 18.64 hp-hours per gallon. Operating at 540 PTO rpm and a corresponding crankshaft speed of 2,237 rpm, the economy was 18.81 hp-hours per gallon under a load of 62.70 PTO hp.

John Deere 2150 Series

The 2150 Diesel was built by John Deere Werke in Mannheim, West Germany.

Nebraska Test Data

Model: John Deere 2150 Diesel
Test No. 1469
Date Tested: April 15 to May 9, 1983

Weighing 5,110 lbs., the 2150 featured 16.9-28-inch rear and 7.50-16-inch front tires. Additional front and rear ballast gave a total test weight of 5,930 lbs. No repairs or adjustments were required for this tractor during 45 hours of engine operating time. Features included a John Deere three-cylinder diesel engine. Rated at 2,500 rpm, it carried a 4.19 x 4.33-inch bore and stroke for a 179-cubic inch displacement. At rated engine speed, an economy of 14.46 hp-hours per gallon was observed under a load of 46.47 PTO hp. Operating at 540 PTO rpm and a corresponding engine speed of 2,383 rpm, the economy figure was established at 14.77 under a load of 46.13 PTO hp. Partial range power shifting was featured in the selective gear fixed-ratio transmission. Its 16 forward speeds ranged from 1.6 to 18.3 mph. Using ninth gear, the two-hour drawbar run at 38.11 maximum available drawbar hp indicated a pull of 2,879 lbs. at 4.97 mph. Slippage totaled 6.45 percent, and fuel economy was posted at 11.88 hp-hours per gallon. The 10-hour run at 75 percent pull saw an economy of 11.24 hp-hours per gallon under a load of 30.93 drawbar hp. Also manifested was a pull of 2,203 lbs. at 5.27 mph and slippage totaling 5.03 percent.

John Deere 2350 Series

The 2350 Diesel was built by John Deere Werke in Mannheim, West Germany.

Nebraska Test Data

Model: John Deere 2350 Diesel
Test No. 1470
Date Tested: April 12 to May 5, 1983

The 2350 featured a John Deere four-cylinder diesel engine. Rated at 2,500 rpm, it carried a 4.19 x 4.33-inch bore and stroke for a 239-cubic inch displacement. At rated engine speed, 56.18 maximum PTO hp was observed, as was an economy of 15.31 hp-hours per gallon. Operating at 540 PTO rpm and a corresponding engine speed of 2,382 rpm, the economy figure was established at 15.67 under a load of 55.69 PTO hp. No repairs or adjustments were required during 39-1/2 hours of operating time. Standard equipment included 16.9-30-inch rear and 7.50-16-inch front tires. Also featured was partial range power shifting within the selective gear fixed-ratio transmission. Advertised speeds ranged from 1.5 to 17.8 mph. Operating in ninth gear, the two-hour drawbar test at 46.66 maximum available hp saw a pull of 3,674 lbs. at 4.76 mph and slippage totaling 7.6 percent. Fuel economy was recorded at 12.96 hp-hours per gallon. In contrast, the 10-hour run at 75 percent pull set an economy figure of 11.87 under a load of 37.26 drawbar hp. Other statistics from this test include a pull of 2,789 lbs. at 5.01 mph and slippage of 5.47 percent. Weighing 6,810 lbs., the 2350 assumed a total test weight of 7,190 lbs. through the addition of front and rear ballast.

John Deere 2630 Series

Nebraska Test Data

Model: John Deere 2630 Diesel

Test No. 1157

Date Tested: April 16 to April 25, 1974

The 2630 entered the two-hour economy run at a maximum available output of 57.88 hp. This test revealed a pull of 4,027 lbs. at 5.39 mph with slippage of 6.31 percent. Fuel economy came in at 12.1 hp-hours per gallon. As in the two-hour test, the 10-hour run at 75 percent pull was made using tenth gear. In this test, an economy figure of 10.98 was established under a load of 46.2 drawbar hp. Also recorded was a pull of 3.042 lbs. at 5.7 mph with slippage totaling 4.5 percent. The 2630 weighed in at 5,800 lbs., but additional front and rear ballast raised the total test weight to 8,430 lbs. Standard equipment included 16.9-28-inch rear and 7.50-16-inch front tires. Also featured was a selective gear fixed-ratio transmission with partial range power shifting. Its 16 forward speeds varied from 1.3 to 16.3 mph. No repairs or adjustments were necessary during 49 hours of operating time. At its rated speed of 2,500 rpm, the 2630 developed 70.37 maximum PTO hp and achieved an economy of 14.38 hp-hours per gallon. At 540 PTO rpm and a corresponding engine speed of 2,075 rpm, the economy figure was 16.01 under a load of 69.02 hp. This model was equipped with a four-cylinder, 276-cid engine with a 4.19 x 5.00-inch bore and stroke.

John Deere 4030 Series

Nebraska Test Data

Model: John Deere 4030 Quad-Range Diesel

Test No. 1111

Date Tested: October 9 to October 13, 1972

At its rated engine speed of 2,500 rpm, this tractor developed 80.33 maximum PTO hp and achieved an economy of 14.29 hp-hours per gallon. At a standard PTO speed of 1,000 rpm and a corresponding engine speed of 2,108 rpm, 77.72 PTO hp emerged, with an economy of 15.4 hp-hours per gallon. Deere equipped this model with a six-cylinder diesel engine with a 4.00 x 4.33-inch bore and stroke for a 329-cubic inch displacement. The selective gear fixed-ratio transmission offered power shifting and partial range syncro-mesh shifting. Its 16 forward speeds ranged from 1.9 to 16.4 mph. No repairs or adjustments were recorded during 41-1/2 hours of operating time. The two-hour drawbar economy run was made using seventh gear. At 67.03 maximum available drawbar hp, a pull of 4,805 lbs. was recorded at 5.23 mph and slippage of 7.01 percent. Fuel economy totaled 11.71 hp-hours per gallon. The 10-hour run at 75 percent pull produced an economy of 10.99 hp-hours per gallon against a load of 54.63 drawbar hp. Other data included a pull of 3,670 lbs. at 5.58 mph and 4.98 percent slippage. Weighing 9,180 lbs., the 4030 was equipped with 16.9-34-rear and 7.5L-15-inch front tires. Additional front and rear ballast gave a total test weight of 10,150 lbs.

John Deere 4230 Series

Nebraska Test Data

Model: John Deere 4230 Quad-Range Diesel

Test No. 1112

Date Tested: October 13 to October 24, 1972

Weighing 10,900 lbs., this model featured 20.8-34-inch rear and 9.5L-15-inch front tires. Additional front and rear ballast gave a total test weight of 14,150 lbs. This model used a Quad-Range transmission similar to that noted in the Model 4030. In this case, 16 forward speeds were provided with a range of 1.9 to 16.7 mph. Seventh gear was used for the two-hour drawbar economy run. At 83.95 maximum available drawbar hp, a pull of 5,664 lbs. was noted at a speed of 5.56 mph, while slippage was tallied at 5.75 percent. Fuel economy came to 12.02 hp-hours per gallon. The 10-hour run at 75 percent pull saw an economy of 11.92 hp-hours per gallon against an output of 69.02 drawbar hp. Other statistics of this test included a pull of 4,362 lbs. at 5.93 mph and slippage of 4.19 percent. The 4230 was equipped with a Deere-built six-cylinder, 404-cid engine. Rated at 2,200 rpm, it used a 4.25 x 4.75-inch bore and stroke. At rated engine speed, a maximum output of 100.32 PTO hp was recorded, as was an economy of 14.10 hp-hours per gallon. After more than 42-1/2 hours of operation, a single entry was made under "Repairs and Adjustments:" "Following the Maximum Available Power run the left hand impeller for the pressurizer blower failed and the blower was replaced."

John Deere 4430 Series

Nebraska Test Data

Model: John Deere 4430 Quad-Range Diesel

Test No. 1110

Date Tested: October 5 to October 13, 1972

No repairs or adjustments were reported for this tractor during 41 hours of operating time. Weighing in at 11,350 lbs., it featured 18.4-38-inch rear and 11L-15-inch front tires. Additional front and rear ballast raised the total test weight to 15,060 lbs. The selective gear fixed-ratio transmission featured partial range syncro-mesh shifting, along with a power-shift device. Its 16 forward speeds ranged from 2.0 to 17.8 mph. Operating in seventh gear, 104.99 maximum available drawbar hp was recorded in the two-hour economy run. This test indicated a pull of 7,211 lbs. at 5.46 mph and slippage of 7.07 percent, and also saw an economy of 12.94 hp-hours per gallon. The 10-hour run at 75 percent pull noted an economy of 11.96 hp-hours per gallon under a load of 87.70 drawbar hp. Other statistics included a pull of 5,578 lbs. at 5.9 mph and 4.69 percent slippage. The six-cylinder turbocharged engine was rated at 2,200 rpm. Its 4.25 x 4.75-inch bore and stroke gave a 404-cubic inch displacement. At rated engine speed, 125.88 maximum PTO hp was observed, as was an economy of 15.56 hp-hours per gallon.

John Deere 4630 Series

Nebraska Test Data

Model: John Deere 4630 Power-Shift Diesel

Test No. 1113

Date Tested: October 13 to October 24, 1972

A Deere-built six-cylinder diesel engine was featured in this model. Rated at 2,200 rpm, the turbocharged and intercooled design included a 4.25 x 4.75-inch bore and stroke for a 404-cubic inch displacement. At rated engine speed, 150.66 maximum PTO hp appeared and an economy of 15.68 hp-hours per gallon was achieved. The selective gear fixed-ratio transmission offered full-range power shifting. Its eight forward speeds ranged from 1.7 to 17.7 mph. Standard equipment also included dual rear tires of 18.4-38-inch size, along with 10.00-16-inch front tires. Weighing 16,250 lbs., this tractor was tested without the use of additional ballast. Using fourth gear, the two-hour drawbar economy run at 127.92 maximum available hp saw an economy figure of 13.34 hp-hours per gallon. This test achieved a pull of 10.751 lbs. at 4.46 mph with slippage totaling 7.63 percent. The 10-hour drawbar run at 75 percent pull noted an economy of 12.88 hp-hours per gallon with a load of 102.88 drawbar hp. Also recorded was a pull of 8,047 lbs. at 4.79 mph with 5.77 percent slippage. No repairs or adjustments were recorded during 47 hours of engine operation.

Nebraska Test Data

Model: John Deere 6030 Diesel

Test No. 1100

Date Tested: May 23 to June 2, 1972

This tractor featured a six-cylinder, turbocharged, intercooled diesel engine. Rated at 2,100 rpm, it used a 4.75 x 5.00-inch bore and stroke for a 531-cubic inch displacement. At rated engine speed, 175.99 maximum PTO hp was recorded and an economy of 15.82 hp-hours per gallon. The 6030 Diesel was equipped with a selective gear fixed-ratio transmission with partial range syncromesh shifting. Its eight forward speeds ranged from 2.01 to 18.5 mph. No repairs or adjustments were reported during 41-1/2 hours of operating time. Weighing in at 18,180 lbs., this model went through the entire series of drawbar tests without additional ballast. Standard equipment included dual rear tires of 20.8-38-inch size, plus 14L-16A front tires. Operating in fourth gear, 148.70 maximum available drawbar hp was evidenced in the two-hour economy run. The test showed an economy of 13.52 hp-hours per gallon and indicated a pull of 10,680 lbs. at 5.22 mph, with slippage totaling 7.2 percent. The 10-hour run at 75 percent pull saw an economy of 12.72 hp-hours per gallon with a load of 122.73 drawbar hp. Other data from this test included a pull of 8,276 lbs. at 5.56 mph and 4.72 percent slippage.

John Deere 6030 Series

John Deere 8430 Series

Nebraska Test Data

Model: John Deere 8430 Diesel

Test No. 1179

Date Tested: June 3 to June 10, 1975

The 8430 Diesel featured a Deere-built six-cylinder turbocharged and intercooled engine. Rated at 2,100 rpm, it carried a 4.5625 x 4.750-inch bore and stroke for a 466-cubic inch displacement. At rated engine speed, 178.16 maximum PTO hp was observed, as was an economy of 15.12 hp-hours per gallon. The 16-speed selective gear fixed-ratio transmission included partial range power shifting. Speed selections varied from 2.0 to 20.3 mph. No repairs of adjustments were required during 43-1/2 hours of operating time. Weighing in at 22,810 lbs., the 8430 carried dual 20.8-34-inch tires. Additional front and rear ballast raised the total test weight to 23,100 lbs. Operating in sixth gear, the two-hour economy run at 155.56 maximum available drawbar hp saw a pull of 10,482 lbs. at 5.56 mph with slippage totaling 3.73 percent. Fuel economy was pegged at 13.44 hp-hours per gallon. The 10-hour run at 75 percent pull established an economy of 12.64 hp-hours per gallon under a load of 125.69 drawbar hp. Also recorded in this test was a pull of 8.133 lbs. at 5.8 mph and slippage of 2.82 percent.

John Deere 8630 Series

Nebraska Test Data

Model: John Deere 8630 Diesel

Test No. 1180

Date Tested: June 3 to June 11, 1975

Weighing in at 24,530 lbs., the 8630 assumed a total test weight of 26,480 lbs. through the addition of front wheel ballast. Standard equipment included dual 23.1-30-inch tires. The selective gear fixed-ratio transmission featured partial range power shifting. Its 16 forward speeds ranged from 2.0 to 20.3 mph. No repairs or adjustments were reported during 42-1/2 hours of operating time. Using sixth gear, the two-hour economy run at 198.12 maximum available drawbar hp set an economy of 13.67 hp-hours per gallon.. Also recorded was a pull of 13,681 lbs. at 5.43 mph with slippage totaling 3.49 percent. The 10-hour run at 75 percent pull indicated an economy of 12.8 hp-hours per gallon under a load of 161.70 drawbar hp. Other statistics included a pull of 10,766 lbs. at 5.63 mph with slippage of 2.42 percent. Features of the 8630 included a Deere-built, six-cylinder, turbocharged and intercooled engine. Rated at 2,100 rpm, it used a 5.125 x 5.000-inch bore and stroke for a displacement of 619 cubic inches. At rated engine speed, 225.59 maximum PTO hp was observed, as was a fuel economy of 15.34 hp-hours per gallon.

Wm. Deering & Company

CHICAGO, ILLINOIS

Wm. Deering & Company prototype

In 1902 Wm. Deering & Company, McCormick Harvesting Machine Company, and others merged to form International Harvester Company. Indications are that Deering had begun gas engine experiments as early as 1891 and by late in the decade the company built an engine-powered mowing machine. Although it gained considerable attention, it never got past a few prototypes and few details of the design have been found.

Denning Motor Implement Company

CEDAR RAPIDS, IOWA

Denning Wire & Fence Company was organized at Cedar Rapids, Iowa in 1899. Joseph M. Denning had numerous patents on machinery to weave metal fence. As early as 1908 the company began experimenting with farm tractors, with a marketable design appearing about 1913. The company name was changed to Denning Tractor Company in 1916, reflecting the firm's new emphasis on tractor production. Despite the advantages of Denning's lightweight

Denning 6-12 tractor

tractor designs, the company went into receivership in 1919 whereupon it was sold to National Tractor Company and shortly after this, to General Ordnance Company of New York City. The latter then sold the "National" for a short time and then renamed the tractor as the "G-O" model. By 1922 this firm was also in bankruptcy.

Denning's little 6-12 tractor was first offered in 1913. Equipped with a two-cylinder, four-cycle engine, it featured a lightweight tubular steel frame. Numerous attachments were available for this tractor, including the one-bottom plow shown here. Late in 1913 the design was changed to include a four-cylinder engine for a major increase in the power level.

Denning Model B

Late in 1913 Denning announced the Model B tractor. Of conventional four-wheel design, it used the same tubular steel frame as its predecessor. Rated at 16 drawbar and 24 belt hp, the Model B carried a four-cylinder engine with a 4-3/8 x 5-1/4-inch bore and stroke. Weighing some 3,500 lbs., the Model B sold for $1,200. This model was also known as the Denning Pug Tractor.

Denning Model E 10-18 tractor

During 1916 Denning introduced the Model E, 10-18 tractor. Weighing only 3,600 lbs., it sold for $800. It had many innovative features, including a spring-mounted front axle. Despite its advantages, the Denning saw relatively low production levels, forcing the company into receivership in 1919.

Dependable Truck & Tractor Company

GALESBURG, ILLINOIS

In 1918 this company announced plans for building a factory to make trucks and tractors, but the outcome of the venture is unknown.

Depue Bros. Mfg. Company

CLINTON, IOWA

The Depue tractor resulted from the inventive efforts of C. A. Depue. By 1918 several years of experimental work had delivered a four-wheel-drive tractor.

Depue 20-30

Depue's four-wheel-drive 20-30 tractor was equipped with a Buda four-cylinder engine featuring a 4-1/2 x 6-inch bore and stroke. The 20-30 was built during 1918 and 1919.

Depue redesigned tractor

Depue redesigned its tractor in 1920, with the most obvious changes being different wheels and a new hood. Production of this tractor continued until 1924. Although the tractor was in production several years, little is known about the design, and it does not appear that any Depue tractors remain in existence.

Homer M. Derr

BROOKINGS, SOUTH DAKOTA

Homer M. Derr tractor

Early in 1911, Prof. Homer M. Derr offered this tractor design, though it does not appear that Prof. Derr ever set up a manufacturing operation for this tractor. It is likely that only this single example was ever built.

Detroit Engine Works

DETROIT, MICHIGAN

About 1911 Detroit Engine Works announced its "Amazing Detroit Self-Propelled Portable Outfit." By 1914 the company offered a line of Wadsworth tractors. After 1915 the Wadsworth tractors disappeared from the market.

As the name implies, this was not so much a tractor as a gas engine that could move itself from one place to another. It featured a Detroit two-cycle vertical engine of 6 hp.

Detroit Self-Propelled Portable Outfit

Wadsworth 12 hp chain-drive model

By 1914 the Wadsworth tractors from Detroit Engine Works were available in 6, 8, 12 and 18 hp sizes. The engines were of course, built by Detroit. Shown here is a 12 hp chain-drive model; it was also available in a heavy duty design using gears rather than chains. The model shown here was priced at $800.

Wadsworth 18 hp two-cylinder model

The largest of the Wadsworth tractors was this two-cylinder model with 18 belt hp. Priced at $990, this model used a 5-1/4 x 5-inch bore and stroke. Like other Wadsworth models, it was rated at 750 rpm.

Detroit Harvester Company

DETROIT, MICHIGAN

FARMFORD

Farmford logo

Aside from a trademark application in March 1927, little is known of the Farmford tractor conversion unit from Detroit Harvester Company.

Detroit Line Drive Tractor Company

DETROIT, MICHIGAN

Detroit Tractor Company

DETROIT, MICHIGAN

Detroit Tractor Company

LAFAYETTE, INDIANA

Detroit farm tractor

All of these companies have the same ancestry. Baker & Baker at Royal Oak, Michigan, was organized prior to 1913 to build the Baker farm tractors. In March 1913 Detroit Tractor Co. was organized to build the Baker, but the following year the company moved to Lafayette, Indiana, continuing there for a few years. This was a line-drive tractor of the universal frame design and could be attached to any number of farm implements.

Detroit Tractor Corporation

DETROIT, MICHIGAN

Aside from a 1949 trade listing, little is known of the history surrounding Detroit Tractor Corporation. Beginning in 1947 or 1948 the company offered its Detroit 44-16 four-wheel-drive tractor. Weighing only 1,660 lbs., it was equipped with a Continental N62, four-cylinder engine. Rated at 1,800 rpm, it had a displacement of 62 cubic inches. No references have been found for the company after 1949.

Detroit 44-16 four-wheel-drive tractor

Diamond Iron Works

MINNEAPOLIS, MINNESOTA

American 40-70 model

Diamond 20-36 tractor

Diamond Iron Works had beginnings going back to 1902 as engineers and machinists. In 1911 the company decided to enter the tractor business and entered this American 40-70 model in the 1912 Winnipeg Motor Contest. For reasons now unknown, the company stopped building its own tractors by 1914. Diamond 20-36 tractors were offered in 1913 and 1914. This model used a four-cylinder cross-mounted engine and weighed about 8,000 lbs. Late in 1914, Diamond began building Lion tractors on contract, and when this venture failed the company returned to its former specialties of machine work and engineering.

See: Lion Tractor Company

Diamond Match Company

CHICO, CALIFORNIA

Beginning in 1914, the Diamond Model M crawler tractor came on the market. Rated at 55 drawbar and 75 belt hp, the Diamond M model used a front tiller wheel, as was common practice for large crawlers of the time. Production was apparently of short duration, since the company is listed in various trade directories only for 1914.

Diamond Model M crawler

Diamond Tractor Company

MINNEAPOLIS, MINNESOTA

The Diamond Tractor Company first appeared about 1915, and as facts later came out, was only a company on paper. It was the brainchild of L. A. La Fond, who billed himself as "one of the greatest Tractor Engineering Experts in America." Apparently, Diamond Tractor Company hardly got past anything more than a sign in an office window. It does not appear that a single tractor was built by this company, although it generated some money from the sale of stock certificates.

Dice Engine Company

ANDERSON, INDIANA

This company often appears as a tractor manufacturer, but the company's main effort was in building engines of all kinds, including those that were used in tractors.

Dill Tractor & Mfg. Company

LITTLE ROCK, ARKANSAS

Geo. I. Dill organized a company at Harrisburg, Arkansas, in 1914 to build a tractor for use in rice fields. The company moved to Little Rock, Arkansas in 1920. By the early 1920s many different tractor makers were offering special rice field tractors and this eroded the market to the point that Dill left the tractor business entirely by 1924.

Dill tractor

The Dill tractor's long frame permitted a grain binder to be mounted directly over the tractor. Owing to the wet conditions typical of rice fields, the Dill tractor was designed with extra-wide wheels to provide maximum flotation.

Dill tractor, 1920

Dill produced several tractor models, although they all utilized the same special designs for use in rice fields. This illustration shows a Dill tractor at work plowing in a typical southern rice field.

C. H. A. Dissinger & Bros. Company

WRIGHTSVILLE, PENNSYLVANIA

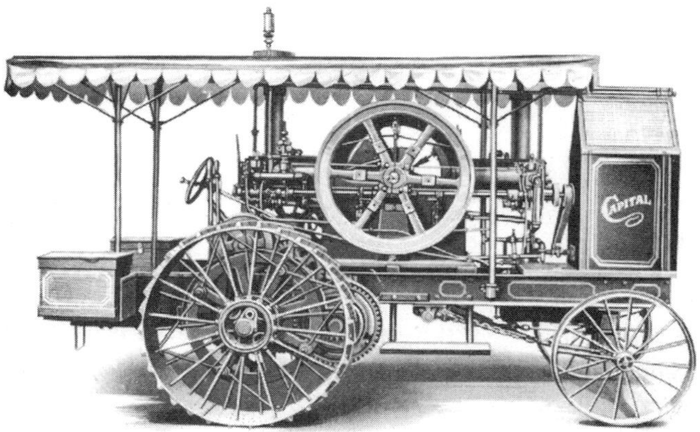

Dissinger 30 hp model

Dissinger began offering tractors at least by 1904, and perhaps earlier. The company's roots go back to 1892 when it began building gas engines. Shown here is the 30 hp model of 1905. Known as the Capital gasoline traction engine, it used the company's own stationary engine as the power source. A unique feature was the two-speed transmission, quite unusual for a 1905 model.

Dissinger 30 hp model

By 1910 the Capital tractors were mounted on springs and pulled on springs. Four different models were available. The 10-20 used an 8 x 12-inch, two-cylinder opposed engine, while the 15- 30 carried a two-cylinder engine with a 9 x 14-inch bore and stroke. A 25-45 model was also available and carried a 6-1/2 x 12-inch bore and stroke. Topping the line was the gigantic 40-80 model with its four cylinders built with a 10 x 15-inch bore and stroke. Capital traction engines disappeared from the market by 1920.

Dixieland Motor Truck Company

TEXARKANA, TEXAS

Dixieland 12-25 tractor

This firm began building the Dixieland tractors in 1918 and continued until 1920. The 12-25 model weighed only 2,800 lbs. Included was a four-cylinder Erd engine with a 4 x 6-inch bore and stroke.

H. C. Dodge Inc.

BOSTON, MASSACHUSETTS

Spry Wheel garden tractor

This company appears in the 1931 issue of Farm Implement News Buyer's Guide as the manufacturer of the Spry Wheel garden tractor, and continues to appear as late as 1946. Actually, the Spry Wheel went back to some time before World War I, but the exact origins of the company are unclear. After 1946 the Spry Wheel appears briefly with B. H. Mott & Company, Huntington, West Virginia. The Spry Wheel shown here is a very early version from about 1915.

COLLECTOR VALUES	1	2	3	4
SPRY WHEEL	$1,750	$750	$550	$350

Do-It-All Tractor Corporation

NEW YORK, NEW YORK

In 1924 this firm is listed as the manufacturer of the Do-It-All garden tractors, but no other information has been found.

P. J. Downes Company

MINNEAPOLIS, MINNESOTA

Patrick J. Downes first appeared as a wholesaler of carriages, wagons, and farm implements in 1900. By 1904 the firm of Downes & Morrison appeared, but by 1910 the company was listed as P. J. Downes Company. The company's Liberty tractor first appeared in 1915. Rated as an 18-32 model, it followed conventional lines and gained at least a slight popularity. However, the company is not listed as a tractor manufacturer after 1916.

Liberty 18-32 tractor

Dubuque Truck & Tractor Company

DUBUQUE, IOWA

Klumb Model F, 16-32 tractor

This company offered the Klumb Model F, 16-32 tractor in 1920. The firm was a continuation of the Liberty Tractor Company, organized at Dubuque in June 1919. The latter had its beginnings as Klumb Engine & Machinery Company at Sheboygan, Wisconsin. The Klumb 16-32 used a Climax four-cylinder engine with a 5 x 6-1/2-inch bore and stroke. Nothing is known of the firm after 1920.

See: Liberty Tractor Company

Duplex Machine Company

BATTLE CREEK, MICHIGAN

Duplex Machine Company was the manufacturer of the Co-op tractors in 1937. Actually, a trademark application indicates that the company first began using the Co-op trademark on September 10, 1935. Various companies manufactured the Co-op tractors, but after 1937 the scepter was passed to Co-operative Mfg. Company at Battle Creek, Michigan.

Co-p No. 1

This model was furnished with a four-cylinder Waukesha engine with a 3-1/4 x 4-inch bore and stroke. Weighing 3,400 lbs., the No. 1 had road speeds up to 22-1/2 mph, a full floating rear axle and full electric starting and lighting system.

COLLECTOR VALUES	1	2	3	4
NO. 1	–	$3,500	$2,500	$1,000

Co-op No. 2

Weighing 4,050 lbs., the Co-op No. 2 was a standard-tread model. It was designed with a Chrysler Industrial engine of six cylinders, each with a 3-1/8 x 4-3/8-inch bore and stroke. The transmission was a combination sliding gear and constant mesh style and was capable of road speeds up to 28 mph. This tractor was later sold by Farmers Union Central Exchange of St. Paul, Minnesota.

Nebraska Test Data

Model: Co-op No. 2

Test No. 275

Date Tested: October 22 to November 10, 1936

The Co-op No. 2 featured a Chrysler Industrial engine featuring a 3-1/8 x 4-3/8-inch bore and stroke with a rated speed of 1,500 rpm. Also featured was an Auto-Lite electrical system, Zenith carburetor, and Pierce governor. Five forward speeds of 2.7, 4.7, 6.8, 14.2, and 21.3 mph were built into the No. 2 tractor. Third gear was used for the rated drawbar test, and at 22.77 rated hp, fuel economy came in at 9.29 hp-hours per gallon. Rubber tires were standard equipment. The operating maximum load tests indicate a maximum pull of 1,980 lbs. in low gear. At a speed of 2.32 mph, the No. 2 developed 12.23 hp along with slippage of 13.81 percent. No repairs or adjustments were noted during 54 hours of test time.

COLLECTOR VALUES	1	2	3	4
NO. 2	–	$3,000	$1,800	$800

Co-op No. 3

Topping the Co-op line was the No. 3. This model used a Chrysler Industrial six-cylinder engine with a 3-3/8 x 4-1/2 inch bore and stroke. As with other Co-op models, electric starting and lighting came as standard equipment. The full-floating rear axle design was an innovative feature that was borrowed from motor trucks and similar applications. This tractor was later produced by Farmers Union Central Exchange of St. Paul, Minnesota.

Nebraska Test Data

Model: Co-op No. 3

Test No. 274

Date Tested: October 22 to November 5, 1936

Weighing 6,065 lbs., the No. 3 was available only on rubber tires, and had five forward speeds of 2.7, 4.6, 6.6, 13, and 20 mph. During preliminary belt testing, the fiber belt pulley failed and was replaced with a cast-iron pulley. Otherwise, no repairs or adjustments were required. At its rated 37.36 brake hp the No. 3 achieved a fuel economy of 10.84 hp-hours per gallon, with an even better 11.07 occurring at the maximum brake load of 40.8 hp. Test H for rated drawbar load was run in third gear. At a speed of 6.37 mph the No. 3 pulled 1,719 lbs., delivering 29.19 hp. The maximum pull of 2,679 lbs. came in low gear at a speed of 2.38 mph and an output of 16.99 hp with slippage of 12.1 percent. This tractor was equipped with a Chrysler Industrial six-cylinder L-head engine. Rated at 1,600 rpm, it featured a 3-3/8 x 4-1/2-inch bore and stroke. Also included was a Zenith carburetor and an Auto-Lite electrical system. Operating weight was 6,065 lbs.

COLLECTOR VALUES	1	2	3	4
NO. 3	–	$3,000	$1,200	$800

See also: Arthurdale Farm Equip.; Co-Operative Mfg. Company; Farmers Union Central Exchange; National Farm Machinery Co-Op.

[Throughout this section, assume that gasoline was used for fuel unless another fuel source is indicated.]

Eagle Mfg. Company

APPLETON, WISCONSIN

Eagle made an initial entry into the tractor business in 1905 with a two-cylinder tractor boasting a rating of 32 belt hp.

Eagle's first tractor, which weighed 12,000 lbs., was built only into 1906, after which production was suspended. The company remained out of the tractor business until 1910. The 32 hp model used a two-cylinder opposed engine with a 9-1/4 x 13-inch bore and stroke. Very few were built.

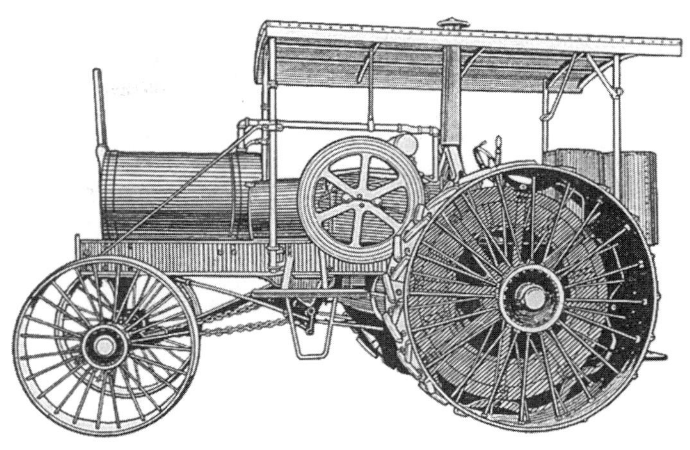

Eagle 56 hp tractor

In the 1910 through 1916 period, Eagle built a four-cylinder tractor in three different sizes. The 16-30 used a 6 x 8-inch bore and stroke; the 25-45 was a 7 x 8-inch design; and the 40-60 carried an 8-inch bore and stroke. Very little is known about the two smaller sizes, but the larger 40-60 model seems to have been successful. The latter model weighed 19,000 lbs. and sold for $2,600.

Note: The value of an early four-cylinder heavyweight model would be very high if one could be found.

Eagle 32 hp tractor

Eagle Model D Series

Eagle began building its two-cylinder tractors in 1913, with the Model D Series remaining on the market until 1916. These were built in three sizes—the 8-16 used a 6 x 8-inch bore and stroke, the 12-22 was a 7 x 8-inch model and the 16-30 carried an 8-inch bore and stroke. All sizes had an operating speed of 450 rpm. The Model D typified the Eagle tractor line until 1930.

COLLECTOR VALUES	1	2	3	4
EAGLE D	$25,000	$22,000	$10,000	$8,000

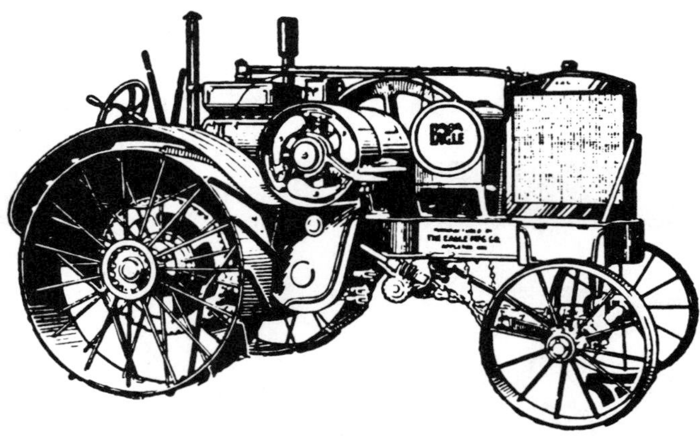

Eagle Model F

Model F Eagle tractors were built from 1916 to 1922. This series included two models, the 12-22, priced at $1,500 and the 16-30, which sold for $1,825. Both continued with the 8-inch stroke; the 16-30 carried an 8-inch bore, while the 12-22 was an inch smaller in its cylinder diameter.

Nebraska Test Data

Model: Eagle Model F 12-22

Test No. 81

Date Tested: August 18 to September 21, 1921

A variety of minor difficulties plagued the Model F. Before taking any official data, the carburetor was readjusted and magneto timing was advanced. The standard pistons were replaced with some higher compression pistons, and these were to be standard for 12-22 tractors sold in Nebraska. Engineers found it nearly impossible to keep the automatic grease cups tight on the connecting rod bearings, and at some point the air intake pipe was replaced with a larger one having two dampers, one for hot air and one for cold air. This was probably necessitated by the use of kerosene fuel. Specifications were the same as the 16-30 model except the 12-22 used a 7 x 8-inch bore and stroke. At rated brake hp, fuel consumption totaled 2.828 gallons per hour (gph) for an economy of 7.92 hp-hours per gallon of kerosene. Two gallons of water were consumed per hour in the fuel mixture on this test. Using low gear, the 12-22 exerted a maximum pull of 2,715 lbs. at a speed of 2.04 mph, corresponding to a maximum of 14.75 drawbar hp. Total weight of the 12-22 was 6,090 lbs..

COLLECTOR VALUES	1	2	3	4
EAGLE F	$22,000	$18,000	$12,000	$8,000

Eagle Model H 13-25 tractor

The Eagle Model H 13-25 tractor was essentially a re-rated version of the Model F 12-22. The Series H tractors were built in the 1922 through 1930 period. Automotive-type steering was adopted in the Model H tractors, along with other refinements. In 1928 this model listed at $1,100. A substantial number were sold in Canada.

COLLECTOR VALUES	1	2	3	4
MODEL H	$21,000	$17,000	$11,000	$8,000

Model H 16-30 tractor

Like other models of the H-Series tractors, the 16-30 was built in the 1922 through 1930 period.

Nebraska Test Data

Model: Model H 16-30

Test No. 80

Date Tested: August 17 to August 25, 1925

Brief specifications of the Eagle 16-30 Model H tractor included an engine built by the company, using a two-cylinder, horizontal, valve-in-head design. Rated at 500 rpm, it carried an 8-inch bore and stroke. The sliding gear transmission permitted two forward speeds of 2 and 3 mph. Total weight was 7,210 lbs. Also included was a Schebler Model A carburetor and a Dixie Model 462 magneto. Kerosene fuel was used throughout the test. A number of repairs and adjustments were necessary. The automatic grease cup on the left-hand connecting rod came off, burning out the rod bearing. It was also necessary to adjust the clutch during the tests. Using low gear, the 16-30 developed a maximum of 19.97 drawbar hp, pulling a 3,615 lb. load at 2.07 mph. A maximum of 31.8 brake hp was displayed. At its rated load of 30 hp, fuel consumption totaled 3.65 gallons of kerosene per hour, for an economy rating of 8.285 hp-hours per gallon of fuel. A dry centrifugal air cleaner was apparently accepted as standard equipment.

Model H 20-40 tractor

Eagle Model H 20-40 tractors were the largest of this series. This two-cylinder model used an 8-inch bore but increased the stroke from 8 to 10 inches. The 20-40 was sold in three different styles, with the 20-40 Regular shown here that listed at $1,875. The 20-40 Improved was priced at $2,175.

COLLECTOR VALUES	1	2	3	4
EAGLE 20-40	$30,000	$24,000	$15,000	$8,000

Model H 20-40 Special

The 20-40 Special came along late in the production period, likely in the late 1920s. Ironically, the 20-40 models became very popular, especially in the Canadian market. While this tractor was built in three different styles, Regular, Improved and Special, the difference was primarily in the chassis, wheels and gearing as the engine was essentially the same throughout.

Model E, 22-45

Closing out production of the Eagle two-cylinder tractors was the Model E, 22-45. This was Eagle's largest tractor in the two-cylinder series and used an engine having an 8-1/2 x 10-inch bore and stroke. Three different chassis and wheel styles were offered. In addition, a number of 20-40 Improved and 20-40 Special models were retrofitted with the larger engine to convert them to 22-45 tractors.

COLLECTOR VALUES	1	2	3	4
EAGLE E, 22-45	$30,000	$27,000	$15,000	$8,000

Model 6A

In 1930 Eagle phased out its two-cylinder tractors and introduced the new six-cylinder Model 6A. During its first two years of production a Hercules six-cylinder engine was used. It carried a 4 x 4-1/2-inch bore and stroke. In 1932 the company changed to a six-cylinder Waukesha engine with similar specifications as the Hercules. Production of the latter style continued until 1937.

Nebraska Test Data

Model: Eagle Model 6A

Test No. 184

Date Tested: October 21 to November 11, 1939

Although not rated by the manufacturer, the Model 6A was given a 22-37 rating under A.S.A.E. and S.A.E. test codes. A Hercules six-cylinder vertical, L-head engine was featured. Rated at 1,416 rpm, it carried a 4 x 4-1/2-inch bore and stroke. Standard items were an American Bosch U6 magneto and a Zenith 96ATO carburetor. Advertised speeds of 2.5, 3.3, and 4.5 mph were provided in this 5,670 lb. tractor. Gasoline was used, and no repairs or adjustments were required during the 50-hour test. At its rated 37 brake hp the Eagle scored an efficiency of 9.18 hp-hours per gallon, with an even higher figure of 9.39 at maximum load of 40.36 brake hp. Fuel consumption in the latter test came to 4.3 gph. Maximum drawbar pull of 4,650 lbs. occurred in low gear. At a speed of 2.25 mph the Eagle developed its maximum of 27.87 drawbar hp. Efficiency on rated drawbar load of 22.2 hp was recorded at 5.24 hp- hours per gallon. This was the first six-cylinder Eagle tractor to be produced. Up until this time, the company had been known for its rather wide range of two-cylinder tractors.

COLLECTOR VALUES	1	2	3	4
EAGLE 6A, 22-37	$7,500	$6,000	$4,000	$1,500

Model 6B and 6C 18-26 tractors

Beginning in 1936 the 6B and 6C tractors made their appearance. The 6B used a tricycle design, while the 6C was a standard-tread version. This design carried a six-cylinder Hercules QXB-5 engine with a 3-1/4 x 4-1/8- inch bore and stroke. Production of this model ended in 1938. As late as 1945 the company is listed as Eagle Division, Four Wheel Drive Auto Company.

COLLECTOR VALUES	1	2	3	4
EAGLE 6B AND 6C	$7,500	$6,000	$4,000	$1,500

R. D. Eaglesfield

INDIANAPOLIS, INDIANA

By 1940 the Unitractor garden tractor was on the market. It was available at least into the early 1950s. The Unitractor is illustrated as both a cultivator and a sickle mower. By 1948 the company was also building the Eaglesfield NR-6 garden tractor and there may have been other models as well.

COLLECTOR VALUES	1	2	3	4
UNITRACTOR	$500	$350	$200	$75

Earthmaster Farm Equipment

HOLLYDALE, CALIFORNIA

This firm is listed with the Hollydale address, as well as being at Burbank, California. It is also listed at times as being a division of Adel Precision Products Corporation. Production of the Earthmaster tractors continued at Burbank until about 1955 when the firm moved to Statesville,

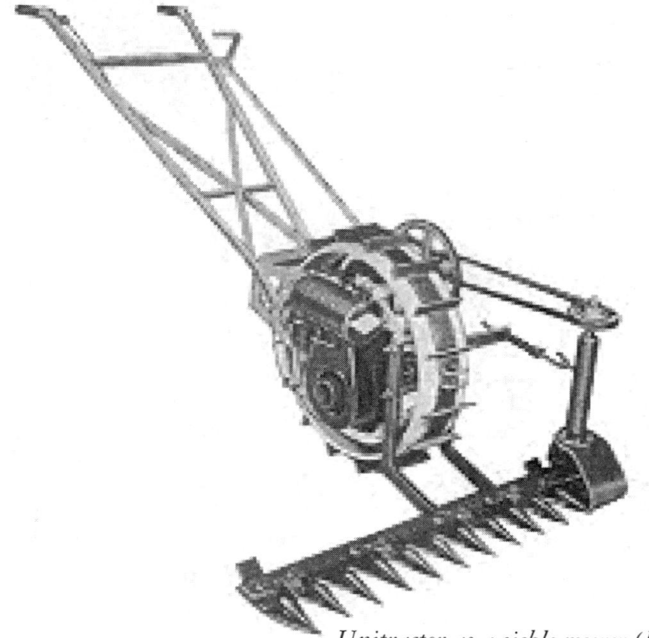

Unitractor as a sickle mower (left), as a cultivator (right)

North Carolina, and operated as the Earthmaster Division of Turner Mfg. Company. The latter kept some Earthmaster models in production until about 1960.

Earthmaster "R" garden tractor

The Earthmaster "R" garden tractor was equipped with a Briggs & Stratton Model N Ultimotor with a 2-inch bore and stroke. Earthmaster also built a Model "S" garden tractor.

COLLECTOR VALUES	1	2	3	4
EARTHMASTER R	$550	$300	$150	$75

Earthmaster Model C tractor

The Earthmaster Model C tractor appeared around 1948. Weighing only 1,520 lbs., it was equipped with a Continental N62 four-cylinder motor. Three forward speeds were provided and disc brakes were standard equipment.

Earthmaster Model CN tractors were essentially the same as the Model C tractors except for a slightly different axle width and other variations. In addition, the Model C tractor was also available in a high-crop design known as the Model CH, and the CN model was also available in a high-crop version known as the Model CNH. All models used the Continental four-cylinder N62 engine.

Earthmaster Model CN tractor

Model D

Model D and Model DH Earthmaster tractors were available as early as 1948, with production continuing for several years thereafter. Like the Model C and its variations, the Model D used a Continental N62 engine.

COLLECTOR VALUES	1	2	3	4
MODEL D	$3,500	–	–	–

Eason-Wysong Company

TOPEKA, KANSAS

Clarence M. Eason built his first tractor in association with Ansel Wysong. Eason later had a distinguished career with Hyatt Roller Bearing Company. None of the Eason-Wysong tractors ever saw anything resembling full production.

Autotractor No. 1

Clarence Eason built his Autotractor No. 1 in Meade County, Kansas, during 1905.

Eason tractor

By 1906 Eason had built a somewhat larger tractor than the Autotractor No. 1. Within a few years Eason was largely responsible for the first unit frame design as employed on the Wallis Cub tractor. For this design, Eason was granted Patent No. 1,205,982.

Eastern Tractor Mfg. Company

KINGSTON, NEW YORK

Production of the Gardenaid garden tractor apparently began about 1947, continuing into the early 1950s. It was equipped with a 2 hp Briggs & Stratton engine. The machine shown here is equipped with a plow, but presumably, there were also other attachments.

COLLECTOR VALUES	1	2	3	4
GARDENAID	$325	$250	$150	$75

Gardenaid garden tractor

C. J. Eastman

WASHINGTON, D. C.

FARMOBILE

Farmobile trademark

A trademark application of January 2, 1908, shows Clyde J. Eastman at Los Angeles, California. This application for the Farmobile claims first use in January of 1902. It was specifically for an "agricultural cable power wagon." Obviously, Eastman spent a number of years developing his Farmobile, but so far as is known, none of his efforts met with ultimate success.

Eastman Cable Tractor

The Eastman Cable Tractor appeared in 1911, but nothing has been found to indicate that it ever got past the prototype stage. Apparently this design intended to emulate the European practice of cable plowing. Aside from an illustration and a reference in a 1911 issue of Gas Power Magazine, little else is known of the tractor.

Eaton Gas Engine Company

EATON, OHIO

Vaughn Gearless tractor

Eaton Gas Engine Company had already been in existence for a few years prior to the 1912 introduction of its Vaughn Gearless tractor. The "Gearless"' reference was not to the traction gearing but to a unique gearless design for the engine itself. The two-cylinder engine normally operated under the four-cycle system, but when more power was needed it could be changed over to operate like a two-cycle engine. In 1913 the company had closed its doors, with the assets being taken over by Hoopeston Gas Engine Company, Hoopeston, Illinois.

Eaton Machine Works

JACKSON, MICHIGAN

This firm is listed as a tractor manufacturer in 1918, but no other information has been located.

Eau Claire Implement Company

EAU CLAIRE, WISCONSIN

This firm was incorporated in 1916 to take over the Opsata Motor Plow Company, also of Eau Claire. No other information has been located.

Ebert Tractor Company

CHICAGO, ILLINOIS

The Ebert tractor was designed for use with a variety of towed or semi-mounted implements. Much like the Moline Universal and other universal designs, the drive wheels were forward. For ordinary drawbar work, a small caster wheel, barely visible here, was mounted to the back of the tractor, directly beneath the operators seat. Announced in 1918, the Ebert disappeared shortly after its birth. There are indications that the company may have had its beginnings at Cleveland, Ohio.

Ebert Tractor

Economic Power Company

ROCHESTER, NEW YORK

Although listed as a tractor manufacturer in a 1900 farm implement directory, no information has been found regarding this company or its tractors.

Eimco Corporation

SALT LAKE CITY, UTAH

Eimco Power Horse

About 1939 Eimco began building the Power Horse tractor. This tractor was developed by Albert Bonham at Clinton, Utah in the 1930s. Eimco built the tractor for a couple of years and then Bonham Company continued until World War II restricted materials. Allis-Chalmers was quite interested in Bonham's design but never pursued it. In 1949 Harris Mfg. Company took over the design and continued with the Harris Power Horse until about 1964.

In the mid-1950s the Eimco crawler tractor appeared in the tractor directories and the Eimco 105 was tested at Nebraska in 1957. This model featured a General Motors 4-71 diesel engine and was capable of about 70 maximum drawbar hp. Eimco crawlers continued in production at least into 1963.

Eimco 105 crawler
Nebraska Test Data

Model: Eimco 105
Test No. 628
Date Tested: July 26 to August 2, 1957

Weighing 29,955 lbs., the EIMCO 105 featured a General Motors 71 two-cycle diesel engine with four cylinders of 4-1/4 x 5-inch bore and stroke. Rated at 2,000 rpm, it had a displacement of 283.7 cubic inches. Also featured was a torque converter system where forward travel speed was automatically controlled by the applied load. No belt pulley was available for this tractor, so no torque or belt tests could be made. In the low range, the 105 had infinitely variable speed from 0 to 2.27 mph, and from 0 to 5.45 mph in the high range. Test G indicated that at 0.75 mph this tractor pulled 27,141 lbs. with a slippage of 10.36 percent, developing a 54.53 drawbar hp in the process. At a speed of 2.23 mph, this tractor pulled 12,146 lbs. with a slippage of 1.93 percent and developed a peak of 72.29 drawbar hp. Test H, run for 10 hours at a rated output of 69.93 hp, indicated a pull of 12,243 lbs. at 2.14 mph with a slippage of 1.85 percent. Fuel economy in this test totaled 8.41 hp-hours per gallon of diesel fuel. Following Test A (the limbering-up run) the generator adjusting bracket broke. During Test A the fan shield was removed to provide better cooling, and during Test F & G (100-percent maximum load) the generator failed. With these exceptions, no other repairs or adjustments were noted during 34-1/2 hours of operating time.

See: Harris Mfg. Co.

Elderfield Mechanics Company

PORT WASHINGTON, LONG ISLAND, NEW YORK

Universal A-20

In 1920 this firm was offering its Universal A-20 garden tractor. It was rated at one drawbar and four belt hp, using a single-cylinder engine with a 3-1/2 x 5 inch bore and stroke. Weighing 900 lbs., it is shown here with a one-bottom plow, although other cultivating equipment was also available.

COLLECTOR VALUES	1	2	3	4
UNIVERSAL A-20	$2,000	$1,000	$500	$200

Electric Tractor Company

CHICAGO, ILLINOIS

This company was organized and incorporated at Chicago in 1916 for $20,000. Aside from the announcement of the firm, no other information has been located.

Electric Wheel Company

QUINCY, ILLINOIS

Electric Wheel Company was incorporated in April 1890. As the name implies, the firm was formed to make steel wheels using an innovative electric welding process. Subsequently the firm saw steady growth and in 1941 EWC merged with Peru Wheel Company of Peru, Illinois. The latter dated back to 1851.

EWC began experimenting with gasoline tractors as early as 1904 and five years later the company was offering a traction truck. This was a complete tractor chassis to which the farmer could fit his own engine. The company began building its own line of tractors in 1911 and continued in the tractor business until about 1930.

Electric Wheel Company became an operating division of Firestone Tire & Rubber Company in 1957.

EWC traction truck

In 1908 and perhaps earlier, EWC was offering its traction truck. With this outfit a farmer could mount his own engine to the chassis for an instant tractor. In the early years of tractor development, traction trucks gained a slight popularity. Electric Wheel Company offered this device for several years.

EWC Quincy Model "O"

During 1911 EWC introduced the Quincy Model "O" tractor. Originally it was rated as a 20-30, but this was soon cut back to a 15-30 hp rating. The auto-guide steering, tubular radiator and three-speed transmission were innovative features for a tractor design of 1911. A four-cylinder engine was standard equipment. There are indications that this model was also offered in a 25 to 45 hp size. Production ended in 1912 or 1913.

EWC No. 1

EWC's No. 1 tractor emerged late in 1912. Rated at 30 drawbar and 45 belt hp, this model weighed nearly five tons. Little information is available for this tractor, although it is assumed that the No. 1 remained in production until about 1917.

EWC Lightweight Allwork tractor

Various EWC advertising indicates that the Allwork design first came out in 1913, undergoing various changes in the following years. In 1915 EWC announced a new lightweight Allwork tractor but few details about this tractor are available. This model was a two-cylinder design, with cylinders opposed, and offered in the range of 20 belt hp.

1915 Allwork tractor

A magazine article in 1920 illustrated a 1915 Allwork tractor noting that it is "still in use on the Gibson Farm, New Brunswick, New Jersey." At the time, getting five years of use from a farm tractor was a meritorious achievement. On the other hand, many of the heavyweight tractors continued in operation for decades with few mechanical problems.

EWC Light Allwork tractor

After announcing the Light Allwork tractor in 1915, EWC made numerous changes, although most of them had little or nothing to do with the essential chassis design. An early style, perhaps from about 1916, included dropped fenders. While this was likely done to minimize dust on the operator's platform, it was also a problem in wet and muddy conditions.

1916 Allwork tractor

For 1916 the Allwork was fitted with a four-cylinder, 5 x 6-inch engine, mounted crosswise, and with the belt pulley on the lefthand side of the tractor.

COLLECTOR VALUES	1	2	3	4
1916 ALLWORK TRACTOR	$35,000	$25,000	$17,000	$10,000

Allwork 14-28 tractor

By late 1916 the Allwork tractor had taken what would essentially be its final form. Initially it was rated as a 12-25 model, but this was raised to a 14-28 rating within a year. Production of this model continued until about 1923. A platform view of the 14-28 tractor illustrated its design. The company kept the 14-28 very simple, but provided the operator with plenty of room. The hood over the engine was of a unique design and was intended primarily to protect the engine from the weather.

For 1917 and continuing until about 1924, the Allwork kerosene tractor followed essentially the same design as shown here. EWC tractors were among the earliest to use the auto-steer design while many tractors were still using the stiff bolster axle as with steam traction engines. In 1918 this model retailed for $1,460.

Nebraska Test Data

Model: EWC Allwork 14-28

Test No. 53

Date Tested: August 16 to September 14, 1920

The complete test required 35 hours of running time to complete and was spread out over several weeks due to mechanical problems. The clutch pin came out after about 20 hours and was replaced. Within another couple of hours it was necessary to regrind one of the valves, and within another two hours all the valves were reground. Finally, after about 26 hours of running time, a larger carburetor was installed, along with a modified hot air intake line. Official data was recorded only after these changes were made. Specifications included the company's own four cylinder vertical, L-head engine with a 5 x 6-inch bore and stroke and rated at 900 rpm. Weighing 5,000 lbs., the 14-28 had two forward speeds of 1-3/4 and 2-1/2 mph. Using low gear, a maximum pull of 3,950 lbs. was recorded for a resultant 19.69 drawbar hp. In the brake tests, 28.41 rated hp consumed 4.21 gallons of fuel per hour and gave an economy of 6.75 hp-hours per gallon. Kerosene fuel was used throughout the test. Rated brake tests ran for two hours, and the rated drawbar test lasted slightly over 10 hours. Kingston was chosen to supply both the magneto and carburetor for this model.

Allwork II, 12-25 tractor

Production of the Allwork II, 12-25 tractor began in 1920, but in 1923 it was re-rated as a 14-28 model. This was the first EWC tractor to use an in-line engine, although a unit frame design was not employed. An unusual feature was the front-mounted belt pulley. By 1923 the Allwork II, 12-25 tractor was slightly modified and then became the Allwork Model G tractor. It used a four-cylinder engine with a 4-3/4 x 6-inch bore and stroke. Weighing 4,800 lbs., it sold for $1,500. Production of the Model G ran until 1927.

COLLECTOR VALUES	1	2	3	4
ALLWORK II/ MODEL G 12-25	–	$10,000	$7,000	$4,000

Allwork 20-38 tractor

Electric Wheel Company offered itsAllwork 20-38 tractor in 1922 and 1923. This model used a four-cylinder EWC crossmounted engine having a 5 x 7-inch bore and stroke. Weighing 6,500 lbs., it sold for $1,695.

Allwork 16-30 tractor

The four-cylinder engine in the Allwork 16-30 tractor used a 5 x 6-inch bore and stroke. Offered in 1925 and 1926, it sold for $1,395. The price reduction compared to the 14-28 G, for example, was probably due to the intense competition in the tractor industry.

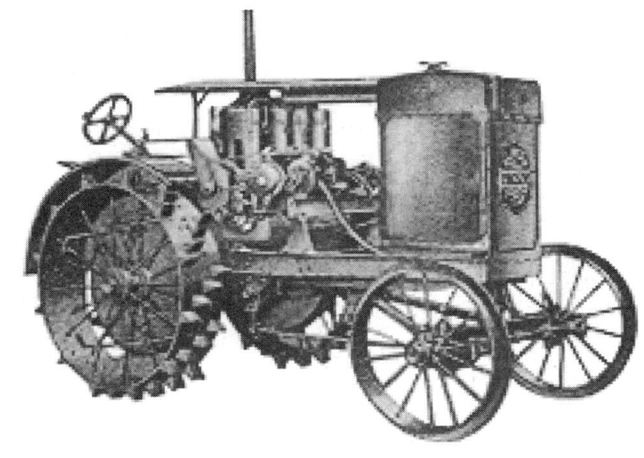

Allwork 20-35

First offered in 1925, the Allwork 20-35 remained in production until the company left the tractor business in 1929. This model used an EWC four-cylinder engine with a 5 x 7-inch bore and stroke. Weighing 6,500 lbs., this model sold for $1,700.

COLLECTOR VALUES	1	2	3	4
20-35	$24,000	$20,000	$12,000	$6,000

Allwork 22-40 tractor

The Allwork 22-40 tractor was first built in 1925. In 1928 it became the Model DA, 22-40 tractor. The 22-40 used an EWC four-cylinder engine with a 5-1/2 x 7-inch bore and stroke. It had a total operating weight of 8,000 lbs. Production ended in 1929.

COLLECTOR VALUES	1	2	3	4
22-40	$24,000	$20,000	$12,000	$6,000

Allwork 25-35 crawler

Electric Wheel Company offered its Allwork 25-35 crawler tractor in 1925 and 1926. This model used the EWC four-cylinder engine with a 5-1/4 x 6-inch bore and stroke. Weighing 9,500 lbs., it could be furnished with electric starter and lights as special equipment. In 1925 EWC also offered a crawler tractor conversion unit for use with the Fordson tractor.

EWC 5-Ton crawler

Weighing over 10,000 lbs., the EWC 5-Ton crawler was a 1926 upgrade from the earlier Allwork 25-35 model. It carried the same 5-1/4 x 6-inch engine as its predecessor. Production of this model ended in 1928.

EWC 80 Crawler

Built between 1926 and 1928, the EWC 80 crawler was the largest of all EWC tractors. This one carried a big Waukesha four-cylinder engine with a 6-3/4 x 8-inch bore and stroke. Weighing 21,000 lbs., the EWC 80 was probably capable of about 80 belt hp. Production of all EWC tractors ended in 1929, probably hastened by the onset of the Great Depression.

Elgin Tractor Corporation

ELGIN, ILLINOIS

Elgin tractor

Waite Tractor Sales Company began marketing the Waite tractor in 1913. The firm was in financial straits by 1916 and was reorganized as Elgin Tractor Corporation at Elgin, Illinois. Within a year the company was again in financial trouble, so the company reorganized and moved to Piqua, Ohio. The Elgin shown here was rated at 9 drawbar and 18 belt hp initially, but this was raised to a 10-20 hp rating about the time the company moved to Ohio.

Elgin Tractor Corporation

PIQUA, OHIO

Elgin 10-20

As noted in the previous listing, Elgin Tractor Corporation moved to Piqua in 1917. By this time the Elgin 9-18 had been re-rated upward to a 10-20 model. Originally the Elgin used a four-cylinder Buda motor, but when the 10-20 model appeared, power came from a Rutenber motor. In 1919 the Elgin was redesigned as a 12-25 model and an Erd motor was used. After 1920 the Elgin disappeared from the scene.

Ellinwood Industries

LOS ANGELES, CALIFORNIA

Bear Cat trademark

A trademark application of March 1946 claimed first use of the Bear Cat tradename on February 11 of that year. This effectively noted the beginning of production for the Bear Cat tractor since it was the first of the Ellinwood line.

Bear Cat tractor

In July 1946 the Nebraska Tractor Test Laboratory at Lincoln resumed tractor testing following World War II and the first tractor to be tested was the Bear Cat. Various Ellinwood advertisements seem to indicate that several different engines were used, including a Continental AA-7, a Lauson TLC, or a Briggs & Stratton Model A. At the same time the company also developed its own Model 44 engine.

Nebraska Test Data

Model: Ellinwood Bear Cat 3000-1

Test No. 379

Date Tested: July 22 to August 8, 1946

The Ellinwood Bear Cat weighed only 316 lbs. It was equipped with a Lauson single-cylinder vertical, L-head engine. Rated at 3,000 rpm, this little engine carried a 2-1/4-inch bore and stroke. Since the Bear Cat had only a single forward speed, drawbar testing was relatively simple. Test H was run with a rated load of 1.33 drawbar hp. Pulling 267 lbs. at 1.87 mph the Bear Cat had a slippage of 3.77 percent and yielded a fuel economy of 5.66 hp-hours per gallon. Test G under an operating maximum load of 1.748 hp yielded a pull of 340 lbs. Belt testing produced a fuel economy of 7.546 hp-hours per gallon under the Test C operating maximum load of 2.128 belt hp, this economy compared favorably to a figure of 7.297 set in Test D with a rated load of 1.942 belt hp. Aside from minor governor problems and frequent replacement of the drive belt, no repairs or adjustments were noted during 69 hours of engine operation.

Bearcat Jr. garden tractor

The Bearcat Jr. garden tractor was a smaller version than the Bearcat and was equipped with a Lauson RSC one-cylinder engine with a 2 x 1-7/8-inch bore and stroke. Production appears to have started in 1947.

COLLECTOR VALUES	1	2	3	4
BEARCAT JR.	$400	$225	$125	$50

Ellinwood Tomcat garden tractors used a single drive wheel and were powered by a Lauson RSC engine like the Bearcat Jr. garden tractor. Production appears to have ended about 1953.

Ellinwood Tiger Cat garden tractor

Nebraska Test Data

Model: Ellinwood Tiger Cat

Test No. 390

Date Tested: November 11 to December 1, 1947, and April 8 to April 14, 1948

The Ellinwood Tiger Cat garden tractor was equipped with the company's own single-cylinder L-head engine. Rated at 3,200 rpm, it featured a 2-5/8 inch bore and stroke, along with a Bendix-Scintilla magneto and a Bendix-Stromberg carburetor. Total weight without ballast was 378 lbs. Rated ground speed was 2-1/2 mph. Test H, at a rated drawbar load of 2.19 hp, indicated a pull of 316 lbs. at 2.6 mph, slippage of 3.76 percent, and a fuel economy of 3.57 hp-hours per gallon. Test G yielded a maximum drawbar pull of 397 lbs. at 2.48 mph under a slippage of 6.35 percent. At its rated belt load of 3.85 hp, the Tiger Cat produced a fuel economy of 6.97 hp-hours per gallon, but this figure rose substantially to 8.02 under the Test C maximum load of 4.3 belt hp. No repairs or adjustments were recorded during 50 hours of engine operating time.

Ellinwood Tomcat garden tractor

COLLECTOR VALUES	1	2	3	4
ALL MODELS	$500	$300	$150	$75

G.W. Elliott & Son

DESMET, SOUTH DAKOTA

Dakota tractor

This firm began building its Dakota tractor in 1913. That year the company offered two models, one with 25 hp and the other 40 hp. The following year saw only the 5-12 model and a 10-20 size. By 1916 the Dakota line included the 7-10 that weighed 2,700 lbs. It sold for $935. Dakota No. 2 tractors weighed 4,300 lbs. and listed at $1,500. This model was rated at 14 drawbar and 18 belt hp. Nothing more is known of the firm after 1916.

Ellis Engine Company

DETROIT, MICHIGAN

Ellis was a well known gasoline engine builder. Its two-cycle models were sold far and wide. At various times the company is listed as a tractor builder, but no images of an Ellis tractor have been located. However, a 1915 catalog illustrates some home-built tractors that used an Ellis engine for power.

Emerson-Brantingham Company

ROCKFORD, ILLINOIS

Emerson-Brantingham dates all the way back to 1852 when the John H. Manny Company was organized to build a grain reaper. After Manny died in 1856, Ralph Emerson and Waite Talcott took over the firm. Eventually Emerson gained complete ownership and christened the company as Emerson Mfg. Co. Charles S. Brantingham entered the firm in the 1890s and in 1909 the Emerson-Brantingham Company was formed, with Brantingham as president.

E-B bought out several companies in 1912. Included were: Reeves & Company, Columbus, Indiana; Rockford Engine Works, Rockford, Illinois; Gas Traction Company, Minneapolis, Minnesota; Geiser Mfg. Company, Waynesboro, Pennsylvania, and several others.

The E-B tractors were initially the same as the Big Four and the Reeves line, but by 1916 Emerson-Brantingham began building tractors of its own design. Owing perhaps to the lack of funds for new tractor development, the E-B designs languished during the 1920s. In August 1928 the company was taken over by J. I. Case Company of Racine, Wisconsin.

Big 4 "30"

When Emerson-Brantingham bought out the Gas Traction Company in 1913, it acquired the company's full line of tractors. The latter had pioneered the Big 4, the first four-cylinder tractor. Until at least 1916 E-B continued marketing the Big 4 line, including the Big 4 "30" tractor. It had drive wheels more than 8 feet high, weighed over 10 tons and sold for $2,300. For another $500 this tractor could be purchased as the Model F tractor with three forward speeds.

COLLECTOR VALUES	1	2	3	4
BIG 4 "30" (1913)	$110,000	$85,000	$50,000	$25,000

Big 4 "20" Model D tractor

The Big 4 "20" Model D tractor made its first appearance in December 1913. Weighing 10,000 lbs., it was powered by a four-cylinder engine with a 5 x 7-inch bore and stroke. It had three forward speeds. Production of the 20-35 Model D continued until about 1920.

Big 4 "45" tractor

Emerson-Brantingham introduced the Big 4 "45" tractor in 1913. Weighing 11-1/2 tons, it used a 6-1/2 x 8-inch engine like the Big 4 "30." Instead of four cylinders for the latter, this big tractor used six cylinders. In 1915 this tractor sold for $3,500. It featured extensive use of Hyatt roller bearings and was probably the only one of the so-called "big tractors" of the day to feature a three-speed transmission.

COLLECTOR VALUES	1	2	3	4
BIG 4 "45" (1914-15)	$160,000	–	–	–

Model 40-65 tractor

Among the 1912 acquisitions of Emerson-Brantingham was the firm of Reeves & Company, Columbus, Indiana. The latter had developed a large 40-65 tractor. E-B made some slight alterations and continued to build it until at least 1920. The four-cylinder 7-1/4 x 9-inch engine was identical to the TC40 engine of Minneapolis Steel & Machinery Company. The latter built the Reeves tractor for E-B.

Model L, 12-20 tractor

During 1916 Emerson-Brantingham introduced its Model L, 12-20 tractor. This unique design utilized a drum drive, as shown here. This eliminated the need for a differential gear, since all power was transmitted to a large traction drum. This model used a four-cylinder motor with a 4-1/2 x 5-inch bore and stroke. It weighed about 5,500 lbs. Production continued into 1917.

COLLECTOR VALUES	1	2	3	4
L 12-20, 3-WHEEL (1915)	$18,000	$13,000	$8,500	$4,000

E-B offered its Model Q, 12-20 tractor in 1917, probably as a followup to the Model L drum-drive tractor. The design was essentially a scaled-down version of the Big Four "20" tractor. In 1918 the Model Q sold for $1,395. Its four-cylinder engine carried a 4-3/4 x 5-inch bore and stroke.

Model Q 12-20 tractor

Nebraska Test Data

Model: Emerson-Brantingham 12-20

Test No. 20

Date Tested: August 27 to September 3, 1920

Featuring its own four-cylinder L-head engine, Emerson-Brantingham Company presented this 12-20 model for testing in the Fall of 1920. Using a 4-3/4 x 5-inch bore and stroke, the 12-20 was rated at 900 rpm. Two forward speeds were provided of 2.1 and 2.77 mph. Other features included a cone clutch, K-W magneto, and Stromberg Model M-3 carburetor. Various problems occurred during the 30-hour test procedure. After 16 hours the valve timing was advanced and new spark plugs were installed. At this time the radiator was replaced, and within a few hours the cylinder heads cracked, requiring replacement. After testing was completed it was discovered that a smaller-than-standard fan was installed—the cause of excessive heating during the test. With this change the tractor was then re-tested and performed much better. Slightly over 27 brake hp was attained using gasoline. This dropped to 25.9 hp on kerosene. A maximum pull of 3,022 lbs. was recorded at the drawbar with a ground speed of 2.18 mph, for a corresponding drawbar hp of 17.55. Total weight was 4,400 lbs.

COLLECTOR VALUES	1	2	3	4
Q 12-20	$15,000	$10,000	$6,500	$4,000

Model G, 12-20 tractor

Through various models, the E-B 12-20 remained in production until the J. I. Case Company takeover of August 1928. Shown here is the Model G, 12-20 tractor. Except for minor improvements, it was the same basic tractor as the earlier Model Q.

E-B 9-18 tractor

In 1918 the E-B 9-18 tractor appeared. This model had the entire transmission and final drives enclosed to eliminate damage from dust and dirt. All shafts were equipped with Hyatt roller bearings. The four-cylinder engine used a 4-1/8 x 4-1/2-inch bore and stroke. Production of this model ended about 1920.

Model AA, 12-20 tractor

The Emerson-Brantingham Model AA 12-20 tractor first appeared in July 1918. The company billed it as a 15-25 for the price of a 12-20. This tractor weighed only 4,700 lbs., almost 2,000 lbs. less than the Model Q 12-20 tractor. This model remained in production until the E-B line ended in 1928.

In 1919 Emerson-Brantingham introduced its 20-35 tractor. It was nothing more than an improved version of the Big 4 "20" that had been on the market since 1913. This five-ton tractor used a four-cylinder engine with a 5 x 7-inch bore and stroke. The 20-35 was off the market by 1920.

E-B No. 101 Motor Cultivator

The E-B No. 101 Motor Cultivator first appeared in 1923. It was designed with a friction-drive transmission that provided infinitely variable ground speeds. The No. 101 was equipped with a LeRoi four-cylinder motor with a 3-1/8 x 4-1/2-inch bore and stroke. Production of the No. 101 continued until 1928.

20-35 tractor

Emerson-Brantingham 16-32 Model

Emerson-Brantingham introduced the 16-32 model in 1921 and continued it in production until the company was bought out by J. I. Case Company in 1928. This model used a four-cylinder engine with a 5-1/4 x 7-inch bore and stroke. When J. I. Case bought out E-B, the tractor line ended, but much of the E-B implement line remained intact for several years.

Empire Tractor Corporation

PHILADELPHIA, PENNSYLVANIA

Empire Tractor Corporation was formed after World War II and built a small tractor using a Willys Jeep engine. There were plenty of these available after the war. Production of the Empire continued only for a few years. Fascination with the rather scarce Empire tractors eventually led to the formation of the Empire Tractor Owners Club with headquarters at Cayuga, New York.

COLLECTOR VALUES	1	2	3	4
EMPIRE TRACTOR	–	–	$3,000	–

Engineering Products Company

WAUKESHA, WISCONSIN

About 1947 the Economy tractor first appeared. The Economy Standard is shown here and is the model usually illustrated in the trade directories. However, the Economy Deluxe, Economy Special, the Jim Dandy and the Power King were also built in the 1947 through 1954 period.

Nebraska Test Data

Model: Economy Special

Test No. 483

Date Tested: September 20 to September 27, 1952

Weighing 1,039 lbs., the Economy Special was equipped with 7-24-inch rear and 3.00-12-inch front tires. The added ballast required for Tests F, G, and H brought total tractor weight to 1,613 lbs. Advertised speeds of 2-1/4, 4-1/2 and 8 mph were standard equipment, as was a single-cylinder Briggs & Stratton L-head engine. Rated at 3,200 rpm, this engine carried a 3 x 3-1/4-inch bore and stroke with a 22.97 cubic-inch displacement. No repairs or adjustments were noted during 38 hours of engine operating time. Engine torque at the dynamometer peaked at 11.91 lbs.-ft. with an engine speed of 2,136 rpm. Tests B & C, at a 100 percent maximum load of 6.23 belt hp, yielded a fuel economy of 7.44 hp-hours per gallon, with this figure dropping to 6.81 under a Test D rated load of 5.55 belt hp. Test H for rated drawbar load was run in second gear. With an output of 4.42 hp, the Economy Special delivered a fuel economy of 6.17 hp- hours per gallon while pulling a 378-lb. load at 4.39 mph under a slippage of 3.92 percent. Test G produced a low-gear maximum pull of 955 lbs. at 2.14 mph.

Economy Standard Tractor

COLLECTOR VALUES	1	2	3	4
STANDARD	$600	$400	$200	$100
DELUXE AND SPECIAL	$3,000	$2,000	$1,500	$500

Enterprise Machine Company

MINNEAPOLIS, MINNESOTA

Enterprise Machine Company was an engine builder at Minneapolis, beginning about 1900. The engines were designed by Emil Westman who held a number of patents. In the 1910 through 1917 period Enterprise Machine Co. is listed as the builder of Westman tractors in various trade directories, but images have not been located. Two sizes of Westman tractors, the 40-45 and the 20-22 (brake hp), are listed as late as 1917.

Erin Motor Plow Company

VAN ETTEN, NEW YORK

This firm is listed as a tractor manufacturer in 1918, but no further references have been found.

A.J. Ersted

SAN FRANCISCO, CALIFORNIA

A trademark application for the Ersted Auto Cat tractor indicates that this mark was first used on November 14, 1933. Aside from this, no further information has been found.

Erwin Power Equipment Company

OMAHA, NEBRASKA

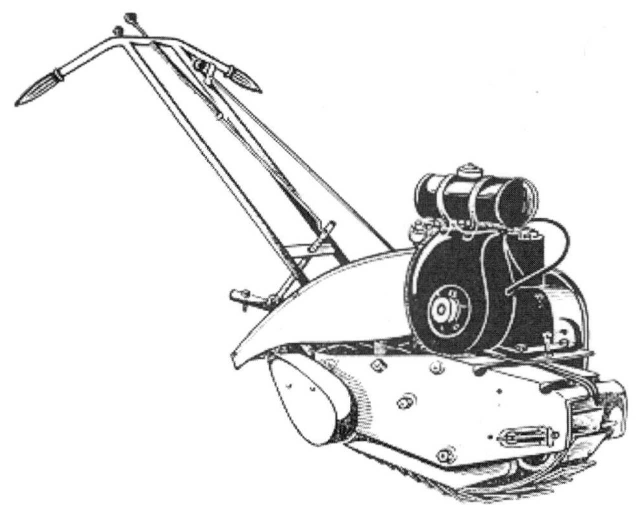

Erwin Pow-R-Trak Model C

The Erwin Pow-R-Trak Model C first appears in the trade directories in 1947. However, there are few other references to this model, leading to the conclusion that it was marketed for only a short time. The Pow-R-Trak Model C weighed only 100 lbs. and was equipped with a Clinton 700 engine capable of 1-1/2 hp.

COLLECTOR VALUES	1	2	3	4
ERWIN POW-R-TRAK "C"	$500	$350	$150	$75

Chester L. Eshelman Company

BALTIMORE, MARYLAND

Eshelman Riding Tractor

By 1954 the Eshelman Riding Tractor was available in 6 and 8 hp sizes. The smaller model was equipped with a Wisconsin AKN engine, while the 8 hp size used a Briggs & Stratton Model 23 engine. The smaller model weighed 425 lbs. and the 8 hp size weighed 490 lbs.

COLLECTOR VALUES	1	2	3	4
RIDING TRACTOR	$850	$500	$300	$150

Essex Tractor Company Ltd.

ESSEX, ONTARIO

Nothing is known of the Essex Tractor Company's beginnings, but by 1919 it was building a two-cylinder Essex tractor with a 10-20 hp rating. Apparently, the company was out of the tractor business by the mid-1920s.

Essex 12-20 tractor

In 1920 the Essex 12-20 tractor appeared. It listed for $1,000 and was equipped with a Waukesha four- cylinder engine.

Essex 15-30 tractor

In the early 1920s Essex began offering its 15-30 tractor. Of four-cylinder design, it used a Waukesha engine. The price was $1,600. After appearing in the trade directories for a few years, the Essex 15-30 disappeared and the company was out of the tractor business.

Evans & Barnhill

SAN FRANCISCO, CALIFORNIA

Aside from a trademark application of 1923, nothing is known of this firm as a tractor builder. Apparently the company was building a wide range of farm machinery, including hay presses, plows, cultivators and other equipment, as well as tractors.

Evans & Barnhill logo

Evans Mfg. Company

HUDSON, OHIO

Evans introduced its first tractor in 1917, and followed with other models over the next few years. However, by 1921 the Evans tractors disappear from the trade directories, and the company quietly left the tractor-building business

Evans 12-20 Model M tractor

In 1917 Evans introduced its 12-20 Model M tractor. This model was equipped with a Buda four-cylinder engine with a 3-3/4 x 5-/12-inch bore and stroke. The 12-20 weighed 3,000 lbs. About 1920 this model was replaced with a 15-30 Evans tractor, which used a Buda engine with a 4-1/2 x 6-inch bore and stroke. Electric starting and lighting were extra-cost options.

Evans 18-30 tractor

About 1918 Evans introduced the 18-30 tractor. For 1919 this model sold at $1,895. During 1920—at roughly the same time the 12-20 was rerated to 15-30—Evans gave the 18-30 a new 20-35 rating.

[Throughout this section, assume that gasoline was used for fuel unless another fuel source is indicated.]

Fageol Motors Company

OAKLAND, CALIFORNIA

See: Great Western Motor Co.

Fageol was organized in 1912 to build luxury automobiles and orchard tractors.

This model was called the Fageol Walking Tractor. Production appears to have ended by 1918, about the same time the company quit making cars.

Fageol 9-12 tractor

Production of the Fageol 9-12 tractors began in 1918 and continued through 1924. A four-cylinder Lycoming engine was featured. It used a 3-1/2 x 5-inch bore and stroke. In 1922 this tractor was priced at $1,525. The hood vents were much like those used on Fageol buses and trucks of the time. In 1932 the company was reorganized as Fageol Truck & Coach Company, functioning under this title until 1939.

Fageol Walking Tractor

Fairbanks, Morse & Company

CHICAGO, ILLINOIS

In 1909 Fairbanks-Morse began tractor experiments. In 1910 the company's efforts yielded the 15-25 tractor shown here.

Fairbanks-Morse 15-25 tractor

The engine of the FM 15-25 tractor was essentially the same as that in the Type N 25 hp stationary engine. Rated speed was 250 rpm, and the engine carried a 10-1/2 x 18-inch bore and stroke. Production continued until 1914.

COLLECTOR VALUES	1	2	3	4
15-25 (1910)	–	$115,000	--	–

Concurrently with the 15-25 experiments, Fairbanks-Morse also began developing a larger 30-60 tractor. Initially, it was of a two-cylinder opposed design, but by 1912 it has taken on the style shown here, using a 10-1/2 x 12-inch bore and stroke. This engine used a crankshaft 5 inches in diameter! Shipping weight was 28,000 lbs. Production ended in 1914. Only two are known to exist in the U.S.

Fair-Mor 10-20 tractor

Production of the Fair-Mor tractors began late in 1917. The Fair-Mor 10-20 shown here was really a Reliable built by Reliable Tractor & Engine Company at Portsmouth, Ohio. Fairbanks-Morse marketed this tractor for only a short time and it disappeared from the price lists after 1918.

Fairbanks-Morse 30-60 tractor

Fair-Mor 12-25 tractor

The Fair-Mor 12-25 tractor was in fact built by Townsend Mfg. Company of Janesville, Wisconsin. Roy C. Townsend was earlier associated with Fairbanks-Morse at Beloit, Wisconsin. Roy C. Townsend was largely responsible for the Fairbanks-Morse tractors, and when production ended in 1914, he set up shop at Janesville the following year to build and market his own design. Although the Fair-Mor 12-25 was only marketed for a short time in the United States, it appears that Canadian Fairbanks sold this model until about 1920. However, all tractor production and sales at the Beloit, Wisconsin, factories ended in 1918. Only one known specimen remains today.

COLLECTOR VALUES	1	2	3	4
FAIR-MOR 10-20	$25,000	--	--	--
FAIR-MOR 12-25 (1917)	$25,000	–	–	–

Fairbanks-Morse garden tractor

In 1948 Fairbanks-Morse made a brief entry into the garden tractor business with this small outfit. It was equipped with a Lauson RSC or Lauson TLC engine, and could be furnished with various attachments. Little is known about this unit. It is unlikely that it was actually built by Fairbanks-Morse, but more likely that it was built on contract by another manufacturer. After World War II, Fairbanks-Morse made a brief but concerted effort to enter various phases of farm and garden equipment lines. The company quickly withdrew from these fields to once again concentrate its efforts on large engines and machinery.

COLLECTOR VALUES	1	2	3	4
GARDEN TRACTOR	$350	$225	$125	$50

Fairbury Windmill Company

FAIRBURY, NEBRASKA

This firm is listed in 1915 as the manufacturers of a 30-60 Auto Tractor. It was designed with a four-cylinder engine and weighed 16,000 lbs. No other information has been found concerning this design.

Fairmont Gas Engine & Railway Car Company

FAIRMONT, MINNESOTA

Fairmont 15-22 tractor

While this company is much better known for its railway motor cars and engines, the company announced its own tractor in 1914. In 1915 this model was listed as the "Mighty Fairmont" 15-22 and the following year the tractor carried a 16-26 hp rating. Nothing more has been found concerning this tractor after 1916.

Famous Mfg. Company

CHICAGO, ILLINOIS

This company was well known for its hay presses and various other farm machinery. The Farm Implement News Buyer's Guide lists this firm as a tractor builder in the 1906 to 1912 period, but no illustrations of the tractor have ever been located.

Little Chief tractor

Farm & Home Machinery Company

ORLANDO, FLORIDA

In 1948 Farm & Home Machinery Co. applied for a trademark to cover its line of agricultural implements, including tractors. The company claimed first use of its FARMCO mark in July 1939. No illustrations of the FARMCO tractor have been found.

Farm Engineering Company

SAND SPRINGS, OKLAHOMA

In 1915 the Patch Bros. Tractor Company was organized by A. J. and O. G. Patch, along with J. P. Burke. The latter had formerly been associated with J. I. Case Threshing Machine Company. The partners designed the Little Chief tractor, and in 1916 the firm was reorganized as Farm Engineering Company. The engine itself was unique with a four-cylinder "V" design that used a 5-1/2 x 5-inch bore and stroke. This gave it about 45 belt hp. For 1916 the Little Chief sold at $1,500 alone, or $1,800 with the plows. Little Chief tractors survived until about 1918.

Farm Horse Traction Works

HARTFORD, SOUTH DAKOTA

Farm Horse Traction Works

GUTTENBERG, IOWA

Organized and incorporated in 1916, Farm Horse Traction Works announced a 15-26 tractor that same year. In 1920 the company moved from South Dakota to Guttenberg, Iowa.

Farm Horse 15-26

Weighing 4,800 lbs, the Farm Horse 15-26 sold for $895 starting in 1916. Apparently the tractor remained in production through 1919.

18-30 Farm Horse tractor

In 1920 Farm Horse Traction Works announced its new 18-30 Farm Horse tractor. This model used a Climax four-cylinder engine with a 5 x 6-1/2-inch bore and stroke. Weighing 5,000 lbs., the 18-30 sold for $1,685. After this date, little more is known about the company.

Farm Motors Company

MINNEAPOLIS, MINNESOTA

In the June 30, 1919, issue of Farm Implements & Tractors, the incorporation of Farm Motors Company was announced. No further information has appeared on this firm.

Farm Tractor Company

INDIANAPOLIS, INDIANA

Farm Tractor Company tractor

In 1913 this firm moved from Indianapolis to Newcastle, Indiana. No information concerning its subsequent activities in Newcastle has been found.

Farm Tractor Company

FOND DU LAC, WISCONSIN

This firm was incorporated in 1917 with a capitalization of $20,000. Its claim to fame was a tractor conversion unit whereby an automobile could be converted for farm tractor purposes. Little is known of the company aside from an occasional advertisement for the conversion unit.

Farm Power Machinery Company

MINNEAPOLIS, MINNESOTA

This company was incorporated in 1912 with a capital of $100,000. Ostensibly, its purpose was to "make gas traction engines in Minneapolis." Beyond this notice, no further information has been found regarding Farm Power Machinery Company.

Farm-Craft Corporation

CLEVELAND, OHIO

Farm-Craft R-4

In 1957 the Farm-Craft R-4 and R-6 garden tractors appeared. These models were the same except for the engines. The R-4 used a Wisconsin ABN engine, while the R-6 was equipped with the Wisconsin AKN engine. Thus, the R-4 was capable of about 4-1/2 hp.

Farm-Craft Model R-8

With a Wisconsin AEN engine, the Farm-Craft Model R-8 was capable of 8-1/4 hp. This model was capable of speeds ranging from 1/2 to 8-1/2 mph. Total weight was 740 lbs.

R-8-E Farm-Craft tractor

The R-8-E Farm-Craft tractor used the same Wisconsin AEN engine as the Model R-8. This model was equipped with electric starter and generator as standard equipment. In addition the R-8 models could also be furnished with a Vexelmatik automatic gear box as an extra-cost option.

COLLECTOR VALUES	1	2	3	4
ALL MODELS	$600	$500	$300	$100

Farm-Ette

MANTUA, OHIO

Farm-Ette 3-wheel rider

In the early 1950s the Farm-Ette appeared, remaining on the market until about 1955. The three-wheel rider shown was one of several different models, but no specifications of the Farm-Ette line have been located.

COLLECTOR VALUES	1	2	3	4
FARM-ETTE	$200	$100	$75	$25

Farmall Tractor Company

CLEVELAND, OHIO

Farmall Tractor Company was incorporated in 1919 with a capitalization of $100,000. No other information has been found.

Farmaster Corporation

CLIFTON, NEW JERSEY

See: Mercer-Robinson Company

The Farmaster FD-33 and FG-33 tractors appeared in the trade directories for 1949 and 1950. Since both tractors were tested at Nebraska in August 1949, it is likely development was under way at least a year before this time.

The FD-33 was a diesel model that featured a Buda four-cylinder engine with a 3-7/16 x 4-1/8-inch bore and stroke. Rated at 1650 rpm, it was capable of nearly 24 belt hp.

Farmaster FD-33

Nebraska Test Data

Model: Farmaster FD-33

Test No. 419

Date Tested: August 3 to August 15, 1949

Replacement of a pulley bearing oil seal, along with a leaky primary fuel filter were the only repairs or adjustments noted for the FD-33 tractor during 36 hours of engine operation. This tractor featured a Buda four-cylinder I-head diesel engine. Rated at 1,650 rpm, it used a 31.6 x 4.6 inch bore and stroke. An Auto-Lite 12-volt electrical system was featured, along with a Bosch fuel injection system. The FD-33 offered speeds of 2.75, 4, 5.5, and 11 mph, with second gear being used for Test H. At a rated load of 17.72 drawbar hp, the FD-33 pulled a load of 1,697 lbs. at 3.92 mph with a slippage of 4.36 percent. Fuel economy was noted at 11.16 hp-hours per gallon in this test. A low-gear maximum pull of 3,055 lbs. was recorded in Test G, but this test included an additional 1,018 lbs. of ballast on each rear wheel over and above the bare tractor weight of 3,526 lbs. At a Test D rated load of 21.46 belt hp the FD-33 delivered a fuel economy of 12.36 hp-hours per gallon, compared to an economy figure of 12.31 when under the Test C maximum load of 23.59 belt hp. A relatively low production machine, the Farmaster appeared for the first time this year, then slowly faded from the scene.

Farmaster FG-33

The Farmaster FG-33 gasoline model used a Buda engine of the same bore and stroke dimensions as the FD-33 diesel version. However, the gasoline model was capable of more than 28 belt hp. The Farmaster FG-33 later became the Mercer 30-CK offered by Mercer-Robinson Company, New York, New York.

Nebraska Test Data

Model: Farmaster FG-33

Test No. 421

Date Tested: August 3 to August 23, 1949

This tractor featured was a Buda four-cylinder I-head engine rated at 1,650 rpm and using 3-7/16 x 4-1/8-inch bore and stroke. Also included was a Delco-Remy electrical system and a Zenith 162J9 carburetor. The FG-33 offered forward speeds of 2.75, 4, 5.5, and 11 mph, with second gear used for Test H. At a rated load of 19.6 drawbar hp , the FG-33 pulled a load of 1,893 lbs. at 3.88 mph with a slippage of 5.04 percent. Fuel economy was registered at 8.03 hp-hours per gallon. For the purposes of Tests F, G, and H, an additional 841 lbs. of ballast was added to each rear wheel, bringing the bare tractor weight of 3,507 lbs. to well over 2-1/2 tons. Test G evoked a low-gear maximum pull of 3,202 lbs. at 2.41 mph with a slippage of 14.75 percent. Except for minor repairs noted in the official report, no other repairs or adjustments were required during 52 hours of engine operation. Test C and Test B at 100-percent maximum load indicated a fuel economy of 9.73 hp-hours per gallon under a load of 28.36 belt hp. At the rated load of 25.44 belt hp, as noted in Test D, fuel economy came to 9.46 hp-hours per gallon.

COLLECTOR VALUES	1	2	3	4
FD-33	$12,000	–	–	–

Farmers Mfg. Company

KANSAS CITY, MISSOURI

Coleman Tractor

Coleman Tractor Company began marketing its tractors in 1918, or perhaps earlier. Production ended in 1920 and the company was taken over by the Welborn Corporation, also of Kansas City. Perhaps Welborn sold manufacturing rights for the Coleman tractor to Farmers Mfg. Company. At any rate, this firm appeared in 1921 as building the same essential Coleman 16-30 design. No subsequent listings have been found.

Farmers Oil Tractor Company

MASON CITY, IOWA

Farmers Oil Tractor Company

WATERTOWN, SOUTH DAKOTA

Farmers Oil Tractor

In early 1913 Farmers Oil Tractor Co. announced its new model at Mason City, Iowa. Before the year ended, the company had moved its operation to Watertown, South Dakota. The latter location was also of short duration, since nothing more can be found concerning the firm. Little is known of the dimensions, but an unusual feature was the cross-mounted engine beneath the tractor chassis.

Farmers Tractor Company

MINNEAPOLIS, MINNESOTA

This firm was incorporated in 1911 as a tractor manufacturer, and appeared as late as 1917 as an exhibitor at the Twin City Tractor Show. No images of the tractor or any other information have been found.

Farmers Tractor Corporation

OSHKOSH, WISCONSIN

MPM 25-40 tractor

The MPM 25-40 tractor first appeared in the 1921 trade directories, and likely was first built in 1920. This model used a four-cylinder 5-1/2 x 6-inch engine. The MPM 25-40 did not appear in the tractor directories after 1921, so production was apparently quite limited.

Farmers Tractor Sales Company

WINNIPEG, MANITOBA

Farmer's Tractor

The "Farmer's Tractor" shown here was the same tractor offered by Sageng Threshing Machine Company of St. Paul, Minnesota. Farmers Tractor Sales Company offered this model in 1912, the same year that Sageng went into bankruptcy. The Farmer's Tractor was rated at 25 drawbar and 35 belt hp.

Farmers Union Central Exchange

ST. PAUL, MINNESOTA

Co-op No. 2 tractor

As noted under the Duplex Machinery Co. heading, the Co-op tractor line is difficult to follow. After Duplex came Co-Operative Mfg. Co. at Battle Creek, and then came Farmers Union Central Exchange. Also involved was Arthurdale Farm Equipment at Arthurdale, West Virginia. Still later came the National Farm Machinery Co-Operative at Shelbyville, Indiana. Despite the changing company names, the Co-op No. 2 shown here remained essentially the same as shown under the Duplex heading.

Co-op No. 3 tractor

The Farmers Union Central Exchange was listed as the manufacturer in 1940, continued until 1945. First the tractors were built at Battle Creek, then at Arthurdale, then Shelbyville, and finally South St. Paul, Minnesota in 1948. Tractor production ended at this plant in 1950. Both the No. 2 and the No. 3 were tested at Nebraska by Duplex Machinery Co.

See also: Co-Operative Mfg. Company; Arthurdale Farm Equipment; Farmers Union Central Exchange; National Farm Machinery Cooperative; Indiana Farm Bureau Co-Op.

Farmobile Mfg. Company

COLUMBUS, OHIO

This firm began business in 1909, and there are reports that it demonstrated its tractor at the Winnipeg tractor trials that year. However, no illustrations of the tractor have been found.

A.B. Farquhar Company

YORK, PENNSYLVANIA

Farquhar had beginnings going back to 1856 and the Pennsylvania Agricultural Works. Eventually the company took the name of A. B. Farquhar Company. This firm built a wide range of farm implements during its long history. Included were an extensive array of threshing machines, stationary steam engines, steam traction engines and tractors. The company also made a reputation for itself with a line of sawmill machinery. In 1952 the plant was sold to the Oliver Corporation.

Farquhar 4-40

By 1913 Farquhar was listed in the trade directories as a tractor builder. By 1915, and perhaps earlier, its 4-40 tractor was available. This big tractor had a four-cylinder engine with 7 x 8-inch cylinders, and apparently was rated at 40 belt hp . The rear wheels were 84 inches in diameter with a 24-inch face. Production of this model apparently ended by 1918, with the introduction of the Farquhar 25-50.

The Farquhar 4-30 appeared to come onto the market about 1913. About 1918 it became the Farquhar 18 or the Farquhar 18-35. The model designator varied from time to time. Like the 4-40 tractor, it used the company's own engine, but in this instance, the four cylinders carried a 6 x 8-inch bore and stroke. Both tractors used essentially the same chassis, but the diminished size of the 4-30 gave it a total weight of 16,000 lbs., or 3,500 lbs. less than the 4-40 tractor.

Farquhar 18-35

In 1918 the Farquhar 4-30 was named the Farquhar 18 and also the Farquhar 18-35. This model used the same engine as the earlier 4-30, and was apparently of the same essential design. Production of the 18-35 ended about 1924.

Farquhar 4-30

Farquhar 25-50

In 1918 the Farquhar 4-40 became the 25-50. It was essentially the same tractor as before, but with an increased hp rating. A canopy top was standard equipment on the Farquhar tractors, and the 25-50 could be furnished with power steering attachment as an extra-cost option. Production ended about 1924.

Farquhar 15-25

The Farquhar 15-25 tractor made its debut in 1918. This model was furnished with a Buda four-cylinder engine with a 4-1/2 x 6-inch bore and stroke. Rated speed was 900 rpm. Total weight of this model was 6,300 lbs. Although regular production of the Farquhar tractor line ended about 1924, it is possible a few were built to order after that time.

Farwick Tractor Company

CHICAGO, ILLINOIS

A 1917 trade note indicates that this company was being organized to manufacture tractors, but no further information has been found.

Fate-Root-Heath Company

PLYMOUTH, OHIO

See: Mountain States Engineering

F-R-H tractor (Plymouth 10-20)

Introduced in 1933, the F-R-H tractor was also known as the Plymouth 10-20. Standard equipment included a Hercules four-cylinder Model IXA engine with a 3 x 4-inch bore and stroke. The revolutionary lightweight design was also capable of speeds up to 25 mph. By 1935 the Plymouth tractors became known as the Silver King. That came after a legal dispute with Chrysler. Since the original Plymouth company had built some trucks and one Plymouth car, the court ruled that Chrysler had to purchase the Plymouth name.

Silver King Model SR38

The Silver King Model SR38 and the R44 tractors were available during the 1937 to 1939 period. Both were essentially the same, with the SR38 being set up for 38-inch tread width and the R44 with a 44-inch tread. Through 1935 these tractors used a Hercules IXA 3 x 4 engine, but in 1936 this was changed to a Hercules IXB four-cylinder engine with a 3-1/4 x 4-inch bore and stroke.

This model used the Hercules IXB, 3-1/4 x 4 engine. Late in 1936 this model was given the designation of Model R66, even though it was the identical tractor. The R66 was redesigned with a new hood and grille in 1938.

Nebraska Test Data

Model: Silver King 3-Wheel

Test No. 250

Date Tested: March 23 to April 20, 1936

Test D for rated brake hp indicated a fuel economy of 9.42 hp-hours per gallon while cranking out 17.35 hp. At 100-percent maximum load of 19.74 hp, fuel economy remained virtually identical. Two sets of drawbar tests were run—first with steel wheels, and then with rubber tires. Using steel, Test H for rated drawbar load gave an output of 10.51 hp, an economy of 5.46 hp-hours per gallon, and a pull of 1,045 lbs. at 3.77 mph. The company equipped this tractor with four speeds of 2.25, 3.35, 5.5, and 14.5 mph, with the latter ranging up to 25 mph, depending on engine speed. Fourth gear was definitely not recommended for tractors equipped with steel wheels! A fuel economy test run in third gear indicated 4.37 hp-hours per gallon on steel wheels, compared to 7.41 on rubber tires. Standard equipment included a Hercules four-cylinder L-head engine. Rated at 1,400 rpm, it carried a 3-1/4 x 4-inch bore and stroke. Accessory items included a Fairbanks-Morse RV-4 magneto, Zenith 193-1/2 carburetor, Borg & Beck clutch, Hercules governor, and Air-Maze air cleaner. During the preliminary tests the motor overheated since the radiator core was painted aluminum and had no shroud. An unpainted radiator and addition of a shroud solved the problem.

Silver King 3-Wheel

Silver King 380 tractor

By 1940 the R38 and R44 models were slightly redesigned and became known as the 380 and 440 tractors. Aside from the new hood and grille, there was little different from the earlier versions. These tractors gained a big reputation with their capability of attaining a 25 mph road speed.

Silver King 340 tricycle model

During 1940 Fate-Root-Heath changed engines in the 340 tricycle model. Instead of the Hercules IXB came a four-cylinder engine designed by F-R-H engineers and built by Continental. It used a 3-7/16 x 4-3/8-inch bore and stroke, and was classified as the F-R-H No. 41 engine. This design was continued until about 1943. The Hercules IXB engine reappeared in the 340 during 1944.

During 1945 the Silver King 340 took the new designation of Model 345. Included now was a Continental F-162 engine with a displacment of 162-cubic inches. Rated at 1,800 rpm, the Model 345 could travel at speeds up to 20 mph. Except for minor changes and new model designators each year, the 345 continued in production until the company closed out the tractor business in 1953.

Silver King Model 345 tractor

Nebraska Test Data

Model: Silver King Model 345

Test No. 424

Date Tested: September 19 to September 22, 1949

No repairs or adjustments of major consequence were noted for the Silver King during 37 hours of engine operating time. Weighing in at 3,789 lbs., the Silver King was adorned with an additional 665 lbs. of ballast on each rear wheel during Tests F, G, and H. Test H, run in second gear, indicated a fuel economy of 9.62 hp-hours per gallon under a rated load of 22.4 drawbar hp. During this 10-hour run the Silver King pulled 2,107 lbs. at 3.99 mph with a slippage of 6.81 percent. A low gear maximum pull of 3,004 lbs. at a speed of 2.32 mph was recorded in Test G. This tractor featured forward speeds of 2.67 4.1, 5.93, and 19.1 mph. Also featured was a Continental F-M four-cylinder, L-head engine. Rated at 1,800 rpm, this engine used a 3-7/16 x 4-3/8-inch bore and stroke. Under a Test D rated load of 29.3E belt hp, 10.95 hp-hours per gallon emerged as the fuel economy, with this figure increasing slightly to stand at 11.20 under a Test C operating maximum load of 31.17 belt hp .

Silver King Model 445 tractor

Production of the Model 445 tractor continued essentially the same as the tractor shown here until all production ended in 1953. It used the same Continental F-162 engine as the 3-wheel design. After F-R-H closed out production in 1953, Mountain State Fabricating Company at Clarksburg, West Virginia, built the Silver King tractors from 1955 through 1957.

Federal Foundry Supply Company

CLEVELAND, OHIO

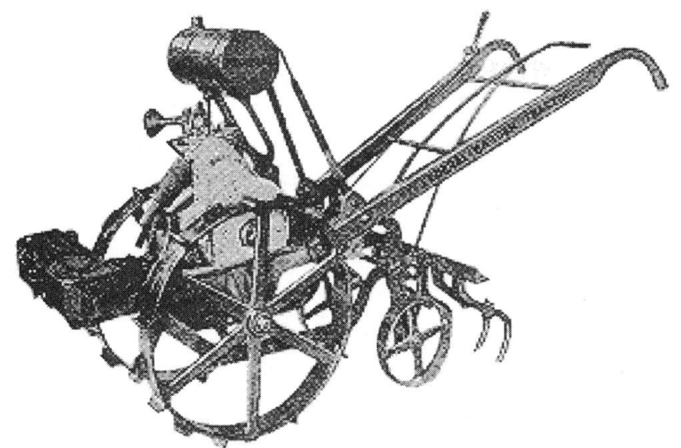

Merry Garden tractor

In the early 1920s, Federal Foundry Supply Co. was the successor to Atlantic Machine & Mfg. Company, also of Cleveland. The Merry Garden tractor that had been built by Atlantic became the Federal Model A garden tractor. This model remained on the market, virtually unchanged, at least until the late 1930s.

Federal Machine & Welder Company

WARREN, OHIO

USTRAC crawler

This company was a successor to the U.S. Tractor Corporation, also of Warren, Ohio. The latter had begun building the USTRAC crawler about 1947; in 1949 or 1950 Federal became the manufacturer. The USTRAC 10A weighed only 3,425 lbs. and was powered by a Continental F124 engine. Production continued for only a short time.

COLLECTOR VALUES	1	2	3	4
USTRAC CRAWLER	$3,000	$2,000	$1,000	$500

Federal Tractor Company

MINNEAPOLIS, MINNESOTA

Tom Thumb tractor

In 1917 Federal took over the Tom Thumb Tractor Company, previously established at Minneapolis. The Tom Thumb used an interesting chassis design consisting of a single track at the rear and it was steered by two rather large front wheels. It was equipped with a four-cylinder engine capable of 12 drawbar and 20 belt hp. The Tom Thumb appeared in 1918, but eventually drifted from view, probably leaving the market by 1920.

Harry Ferguson Inc.

DETROIT, MICHIGAN

Harry Ferguson began experimenting with plows in 1919. Using a unique linkage system, the Ferguson plow could be connected to a Fordson tractor. In the early 1920s Ferguson contracted with Roderick Lean Company at Mansfield, Ohio, to build his plows. The latter went broke in 1924, and the following year, Ferguson-Sherman Inc. was organized at Evansville, Indiana. Ferguson supplied the design and the Sherman brothers furnished the manufacturing facilities and the money. When American production of the Fordson ceased in 1928, so did production of the plows.

Ferguson continued his experiments, and in 1933 he and his associates built the Black tractor (named thus because it was painted black). At this juncture the three-point system was essentially developed and included a draft-responsive hydraulic control. Eventually Ferguson persuaded David Brown in England to form David Brown Tractors Ltd., with Harry Ferguson Ltd. as the sales organization. The new tractor was known by various names, including the Ferguson-Brown and the Irish Ferguson.

In a relatively short time Ferguson and Brown were at odds. Ferguson then contacted the Sherman brothers and they in turn were instrumental in introducing Henry Ford to the Ferguson three-point system. Ferguson first demonstrated his design at Ford's home in 1938, and in 1939 the Ford 9N tractor was fitted with the Ferguson system. Ferguson-Sherman Mfg. Corporation was formed on July 1, 1939, to market the new tractor, with Ford actually building the tractor and supplying the capital. In 1942 the sales organization was renamed as Harry Ferguson Inc.

Ford and Ferguson operated on the basis of a verbal agreement made in 1939. Especially after World War II, Ford executives opined the company should be building and marketing its own tractor. In late 1946 Dearborn Motors was organized as a Ford subsidiary, and began building the 8N Ford tractors.

Now that the Ford-Ferguson agreement was vacated, Ferguson went back to England and began building Ferguson tractors there. In October 1948 the first Ferguson tractor was completed at Ferguson Park in Detroit. The Ferguson TE-20 was built in England, and the TO-20 was built at Detroit. In August 1951 a larger engine was installed, and the new tractor was known as the TO-30. The TO-35 appeared in 1954. It was of similar design to its predecessors, but had a slightly larger engine bore.

Massey-Harris-Ferguson Limited was announced in August 1953. In 1958 the company changed its name to Massey-Ferguson Ltd.

The Ford 9N, 2N, and others will be found under the Ford Motor Company heading.

Ferguson TE-20 and TO-20

Initially, the Ferguson TE-20, built in England, was shipped to the United States. By October 1948 the TE-20 was being built at Detroit. The TE-20 of 1948 used a Continental four-cylinder engine. The TO-20 of later that year was essentially the same tractor. Production of this model continued into 1951.

Nebraska Test Data

Model: Ferguson TE-20

Test No. 392

Date Tested: April 26 to May 10, 1948

During 67-1/2 hours of testing, no repairs or adjustments were recorded except replacing the fan belt, and removing and cleaning the cylinder head. The TE-20 featured a Continental four-cylinder I-head engine rated at 1,750 and 2,000 rpm. It carried a 3-3/16 x 3-3/4-inch bore and stroke. Accessories included a Lucas coil and starter, Delco-Remy distributor, and Marvel-Schebler TSX-312 carburetor. Standard equipment also included 10-28 rear and 4.00-19-inch front tires. Advertised speeds of 2.9, 3.99, 5.5, and 11.49 mph were used, with second gear being selected for Test H. This test revealed a rated drawbar load of 16.35 hp at 4.42 percent. Fuel economy at rated drawbar load was 8.99 hp along with a pull of 1,666 lbs. at 3.68 mph. Test C for operating maximum load yielded an economy of 10.57 hp- hours per gallon at a load of 24.02 belt hp. At a rated brake load of 22.59 hp, fuel economy was recorded at 10.34 hp hours per gallon. Also, the TE-20 made a maximum low-gear pull of 2,650 lbs. in Test G, but with 754 lbs. of added weight for each rear wheel. Bare tractor weight was 2,760 lbs.

Ferguson TO-30

Production of the TO-30 began in August 1951 and continued into 1954. The TO-30 used a Continental four-cylinder engine with a 3-1/4 x 3-7/8-inch bore and stroke. Except for this slightly larger engine there was little difference between this and the TE-20. The Massey-Harris-Ferguson merger of 1953 effectively ended the Ferguson tractor as a distinct entity.

Nebraska Test Data

Model: Ferguson TO-30

Test No. 466

Date Tested: October 5 to October 11, 1951

A Continental four-cylinder I-head engine was featured in the TO-30 tractor. Rated at 1,750 on the drawbar and 2,000 rpm in the belt, this engine used a 3-1/4 x 3-7/8-inch bore and stroke for a 129-cubic inch displacement. A six-volt battery was standard equipment. Weighing 2,843 lbs., this tractor used 11-28-inch rear and 6.00-16-inch front tires as standard equipment. Advertised speeds of 2.9, 4, 5.5, and 11.48 mph were provided, with second gear used for Test H. During this test, as well as in Test F and G, an additional 684 lbs. of ballast was added to each rear wheel. The 10-hour run of Test H was made at a rated drawbar load of 19.26 hp, with the TO-30 pulling 1,842 lbs. at 3.92 mph under a slippage of 7.02 percent. Fuel economy for this test was pegged at 9.98 hp-hours per gallon. Test D, under a rated belt load of 27.96 hp, indicated a fuel economy of 10.85 hp-hours per gallon, improving slightly to 11.31 under a Test C operating maximum load of 27.96 belt hp. No repairs or adjustments were noted during 51 hours of engine operating time.

Ferguson TO-35
Nebraska Test Data

Model: Ferguson TO-35

Test No. 564

Date Tested: October 10 to October 17, 1955

Standard equipment for the TO-35 included 11-28-inch rear and 6.00-16-inch front tires, along with advertised speeds of 1.23, 1.84, 3.37, 4.9, 7.36, and 13.49 mph. During Tests F, G, and H an additional 947 lbs. of ballast was added to each rear wheel of this 3,093-lb. tractor. Test H, run in fourth gear, indicated a rated drawbar output of 23.67 hp , along with a pull of 1,922 lbs. at 4.62 mph and slippage of 6.34 percent. Fuel economy in this test came to 9.32 hp-hours per gallon. Test G produced a low-gear maximum pull of 3,409 lbs. at 1.01 mph with a slippage of 17.29 percent. The TO-35 featured a Continental four-cylinder engine rated at 2,000 rpm. It delivered a peak engine torque of 221.6 lbs.-ft. at 1,490 rpm. With a 134-cubic inch displacement, this engine carried a 3-5/16 x 3-7/8-inch bore and stroke. No repairs or adjustments were noted during 41-1/2 hours of running time. Belt testing indicated a fuel economy of 11.14 hp-hours per gallon with a Test D rated load of 29.29 hp. Economy rose to 11.52 hp- hours per gallon with a Test C operating maximum load of 31.82 hp.

COLLECTOR VALUES	1	2	3	4
TE-20	$3,000	$2,300	$1,550	$1,000
TO-20	$3,500	$2,400	$1,500	$1,000
TO-30	$3,500	$2,400	$1,600	$1,000
TO-35	$4,200	$2,800	$2,000	–

Ferguson Mfg. Company

BELLEVILLE, KANSAS

Ferguson Automobile Thresher being loaded onto railcar for demonstration, 1906

In 1906 the Ferguson Automobile Thresher appeared, essentially a self-propelled threshing machine. Although it was not designed for drawbar power, it was an early demonstration of the possibilities and the potential for gas power.

Flinchbaugh Mfg. Company

YORK, PENNSYLVANIA

Flinchbaugh was an early entrant into tractors and used its own engines. The company was building engines by 1900, and commenced tractor experiments shortly after.

Flinchbaugh tractor

By 1905 Flinchbaugh was offering this small traction engine with 2 drawbar and 4 belt hp. It was equipped with a single-cylinder engine with a 4-1/2 x 6-inch bore and stroke. Few are known to exist.

COLLECTOR VALUES	1	2	3	4
FLINCHBAUGH	--	$30,000	--	--

York Little Pet 2 hp

Production of the York traction engines continued until the company went broke in 1915. The York Little Pet 2 hp model remained throughout the entire production run. Later models of the 2 hp size utilized a much larger water hopper on the engine to provide better cooling, as shown here. This model sold for $340.

York 5 and 8 hp tractors

The 5- and 8-hp sizes were capable of 10 and 15 belt hp respectively. A 5 hp York tractor is shown here. This model used a two-cylinder engine with a 5 x 7-inch bore and stroke. The 8 hp York carried a 6-1/2 x 9-inch double cylinder engine, weighed 6,000 lbs. and sold for $1,425. The smaller 5 hp York was priced at $980. It weighed 4,000 lbs.

York 10 hp tractor

Production of the 10 hp York tractor ended sometime prior to the 1915 dissolution of the company. This model was equipped with a single cylinder engine with a 7-3/4 x 13-inch bore and stroke. It was capable of 14 belt hp. The 10 hp size weighed 10,000 lbs. and sold for $1,375.

York 12, 16 and 20 hp tractors

The 12, 16, and 20 hp York tractors were all of two-cylinder design. Priced at $1,985 the 12 hp model used a 7-1/2 x 12-inch bore and stroke; it was capable of 22 belt hp. The 16 hp model could deliver 32 belt hp, using an engine with a 7-3/4 x 13-inch bore and stroke. This tractor weighed 16,500 lbs. and listed at $2,290. An 8-1/2 x 14 double-cylinder engine was used in the 20 hp model. It could deliver 45 belt hp. This size sold for $2,290 and it weighed 20,000 lbs.

Flinchbaugh 25-65 and 40-90 tractors

Flinchbaugh built 25-65 and 40-90 tractors through about 1913. The 25-65 was designed around a two-cylinder engine with a 10 x 16-inch bore and stroke. This tractor sold for $3,160 and weighed an impressive 24,000 lbs. The big 40-90 style illustrated above carried a four-cylinder engine with an 8-1/2 x 14-inch bore and stroke. Priced at $4,650, it weighed 32,000 lbs. All sizes of 12 hp and larger tractors could be furnished with power steering as an extra-cost option, and all models featured two forward speeds.

York 10-Ton Road Roller

The York 10-Ton Road Roller was essentially built over the 16-32 traction engine. Since the ordinary tractor weighed 8-3/4 tons by itself, the addition of special wheels and auxiliary equipment boosted the total weight to ten tons or more. Production of this model apparently ended about 1913.

York tractor with locomotive cab

All York tractors of 8 hp and larger could be specially equipped with a locomotive cab and shielded gearing at extra cost. Another option was the use of oil coolant when the engine was going to be operated in cold climates during freezing weather. The York tractors were built in heavy proportions. For example, the big 40-90 tractor had a 5-inch crankshaft. After the company went broke in 1915 the buildings were sold to Landis Tool Company for $42,500.

Foos Gas Engine Company

SPRINGFIELD, OHIO

Foos Gas Engine Company developed a successful series of gasoline engines during the 1890s. Subsequently the company began developing its own gasoline traction engine, and in fact, the firm is listed as a traction engine manufacturer as late as 1905. No illustrations of its efforts have been found.

Foote Bros. Gear & Machine Company

JOLIET, ILLINOIS

Bates Machine & Tractor Company was taken over by Foote Bros. Gear & Machine Co. in 1929. The latter continued the Bates Steel Mule tractor line until 1935 when Bates Mfg. Company reemerged briefly, then left the business in 1937. Two Foote Bros. models were the Bates Steel Mule "35" and the Bates Steel Mule "45" with the latter shown here. This model was equipped with a Waukesha six-cylinder engine capable of 45 drawbar hp.

See: Bates Machine & Tractor Company

Bates Steel Mule "45"

Ford Tractor Company

MINNEAPOLIS, MINNESOTA

Ford Tractor Company owed much of its impetus to W. Baer Ewing. The latter organized numerous companies, one of which was the Federal Securities Company at Minneapolis, which sold securities in the Power Distribution Company. When the bonds fell due, bondholders had problems getting their money.

The Ford Tractor Company was another of Ewing's enterprises. Allegedly, the concept was to capitalize on the name of Henry Ford. In 1916, virtually anything that had "Ford" on the nameplate found a ready market. In order to legitimize the plan, one Paul B. Ford was employed and was billed as the designer.

Initially the Ford Tractor Co. was organized as a South Dakota corporation. In November 1916 this company went bankrupt, but while this case was still in litigation, Ewing organized the Ford Tractor Co. as a Delaware corporation. Sale of $3 million in stock was arranged on a sliding scale so that of the total sale $850,000 went to Ford Tractor Company, and the remaining $2.15 million went to the stockbrokers, Robert P. Matches & Company.

A few Ford tractors were built, and a very few still exist. In July 1917, the case of the Ford Tractor Co. came before a United States Grand Jury convened in New York. The company went into receivership in December of that year, and on October 21, 1918 the company was sold at auction. Matches was convicted and sentenced in 1917 on a charge of conspiracy to defraud investors in another case, and Ewing was reported to have organized another tractor company in Canada.

Ford Model B tractor

The Ford tractor made its first appearance in 1916, and in December 1917 the company went into receivership. During this relatively short time a few tractors were built. The Ford was of the three-wheel design, with two front drivers and a small rear tail wheel. The design itself was relatively poor compared to many other tractors on the 1917 market. Tractors with poor design, little or no aftermarket service, and inadequate performance led to the establishment of the Nebraska Tractor Test law in 1919.

COLLECTOR VALUES	1	2	3	4
FORD	$22,500	$15,000	$10,000	$5,000

Ford Motor Company

DETROIT, MICHIGAN

Henry Ford began experimenting with gasoline engines in 1890 and completed his first automobile in 1896. In 1903 the first "Ford" appeared and this led to the introduction of the world-famous Model T in 1908. Over 15 million Model T Ford automobiles were built between 1908 and 1927.

Ford's success with the Model T reinforced his belief that American farmers wanted a small, lightweight, inexpensive tractor. By 1907 Ford was experimenting with various designs. This led to the 1917 introduction of the Fordson tractor. Over 700,000 Fordsons were built before U. S. production ended in 1928.

Henry Ford was forced to use the Fordson name for his tractors because the rights to the Ford name, as applied to tractors, had already been taken by the Ford Tractor Company at Minneapolis, Minnesota. (See the previous listing.) Ford was not deterred in the least with the Fordson name. The new tractors were built by a subsidiary called Henry Ford & Son. The company was chartered on July 27, 1917, the same day production began on Ford trucks. With the charter came exclusive rights to "Fordson" as applied to tractors.

In 1939 Ford began building the 9N tractor. It used the Ferguson three-point hitch system. Henry Ford and Harry Ferguson sealed their deal with a handshake, and this would lead to a host of difficulties for both parties. The result was that the Ford-Ferguson arrangement was terminated in 1946 and Ford began building and marketing its own tractors and implements under the Dearborn Motors Company subsidiary.

Henry Ford's early tractor experiments led to the 1907 automobile plow. It used the engine from a 1905 Model B automobile, with the chassis and other parts coming from a Ford Model K. This model was never put into production.

1907 automobile plow

Henry Ford himself is seated on this version. Ford would spend money by the hundreds of thousands over the next decade in his quest for the ideal small tractor.

Experimental Ford tractor

A 1915 magazine article illustrated two different views of the experimental Ford tractor, noting that Ford intended to market a new tractor by the fall of 1916 and that it would sell in the neighborhood of $300. Although Henry came close to a full-fledged production model by late 1916, the price was slightly higher than was originally announced.

Fordson F tractor (1917-1919)

Production models of the Fordson tractor used the same vibrator spark coils as the inimitable Model T. The unusual carburetion system caused starting problems in cold weather. By the time the atomized fuel left the carburetor, went through the multi-pass vaporizer and into the cylinders, it was too late to do much good—mostly wind and little fuel. An old farmer once compared this to calling in the cows from the back 40—it took time. Actual production of the Fordson began on October 8, 1917. On that day the first Fordson came off the assembly line at Ford's Brady Street Plant in Dearborn. The first Fordsons (and an eventual total of more than 7,000) were shipped to the British Isles. Ford wanted to be sure there was an adequate supply of tractors there, so he purchased land for a tractor factory in Ireland's County Cork, the family's ancestral home.

Fordson (1918-1928) with fenders

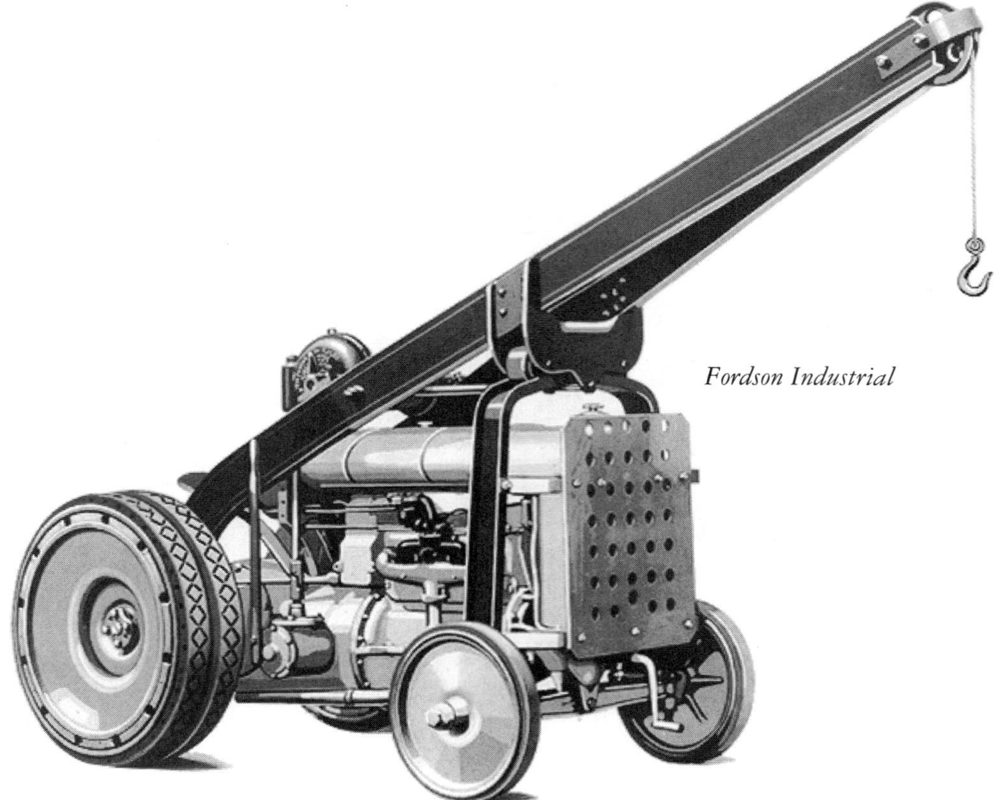

Fordson Industrial

About 1923 the Fordson sprouted fenders, although most advertising does not show this style until 1925. Already in 1918 various editorial writers and agricultural engineers were making negative comments about the Fordson, noting it had a tendency to tip over backwards under certain conditions. Notable and sensational was The Suppressed Report of Prof. Yerkes, sent by the United States Department of Agriculture to the factory, in response to complaints about the tractor tipping over backwards. Some engineers noted that the weight of the tractor had not been properly distributed and this was the cause of the problem. Adding the fenders aided greatly in minimizing the problem, because the front end couldn't rear back very far before the fenders interfered with terra firma. The final drive system was of worm gear design, making it impossible to start the tractor by pulling it. The friction within the gear case also created lots of heat, and like many tractors of the day, the engine ran at the boiling point. Farmers sometimes commented they didn't know how anything could get so hot in summer and still freeze up in the winter.

Nebraska Test Data

Model: Fordson

Test No. 18

Date Tested: June 2 to June 12, 1920

Despite many complaints about the Fordson tractor, it came through Test No. 18 reasonably well, with test engineers noting that "Repairs necessary during this test do not indicate any important mechanical defect." Ford's little four-cylinder L-head engine used a 4 x 5 inch bore and stroke with a rated speed of 1,000 rpm. Total weight of the Fordson was only 2,710 lbs. Three forward gears were provided of 1.34, 2.7, and 6.83 mph. About 12 hours into the test it was necessary to regrind the valves, and during the procedure it was also necessary to replace one spark coil. In the rated brake test, 18.16 hp was developed during the two hour run, with fuel consumption totaling 2.48 gph and fuel economy coming to 7.32 hp hours per gallon of kerosene. During all the brake and drawbar tests, coolant temperatures ranged at or near the boiling point. Since the Fordson was not equipped with a governor it was necessary to adjust the throttle by hand to give approximately the right speed for each load. A maximum of 2,187 lbs. drawbar pull was attained at a ground speed of 1.6 mph, for a yield of 9.34 drawbar hp.

Nebraska Test Data

Model: Fordson

Test No. 124

Date Tested: June 21 to June 28, 1926

Few changes were apparent between the Fordson tractor presented for this test and the one in the previous test. Still present was the four-cylinder, L-head engine of before, along with a 4 x 5-inch bore and stroke and a rated speed of 1,000 rpm. Like the earlier test model this tractor had no governor, but featured a Fordson Special magneto and a Holley Special "235" carburetor. Kerosene fuel was used. At rated load, fuel economy came in at 9.63 hp-hours per gallon with a total consumption of 2.097 gallons per hour (gph) and a recorded figure of 20.19 hp. At maximum load, 22.28 hp was noted, along with 8.95 hp hours per gallon of fuel. Maximum drawbar load tests were run in all three forward gears, with maximum drawbar hp appearing in intermediate gear. In this test, 12.325 drawbar hp was derived, with a load of 2,142 lbs. at a speed of 2.16 mph. Total weight, including the operator, was 3,175 lbs. No repairs or adjustments were made during the test.

Shortly after the Fordson appeared, various modifications became available. One was an industrial version, and in this case, a front-mounted crane is evident. Several companies built crawler attachments for the Fordson, effectively converting it into a small crawler tractor. Numerous companies built implements and machines especially tailored for use with the Fordson, and Ford Motor Company went so far as to produce a small book called Fordson Farming that detailed the products of various manufacturers. U. S. production of the Fordson ended in 1928.

COLLECTOR VALUES	1	2	3	4
FORDSON 1918-1919 LADDER SIDE RADIATOR	$4,200	$3,200	$1,500	$700
FORDSON 1920-1928 (US)	$3,200	$2,200	$1,200	$500

Note: A restored 1918 Fordson recently sold at auction for $8,000.

Fordson "N" tractor

Starting in 1929 and continuing until 1933 a revamped Fordson tractor—the "N"—was built in Cork, Ireland. Production was then shifted to Dagenham, England, and continued until 1938.

Nebraska Test Data

Model: Fordson "N"

Test No. 173

Date Tested: March 11 to April 8, 1930

This was an entirely new Fordson tractor compared to those in earlier tests. Although it carried no manufacturer's hp rating, test engineers noted it should be limited under A.S.A.E. and S.A.E. rules to 11 drawbar and 21 belt hp. Using kerosene, the "F" pulled 1,212 lbs. at 3.3 mph on the rated drawbar test, developing 10.67 hp, and yielding an economy of 4.4 hp-hours per gallon. Although this test was conducted in second gear, maximum drawbar tests were made in all three forward speeds, with the maximum pull coming in low gear. At a speed of 1.55 mph the Fordson pulled 3,289 lbs. with a slippage of 19.85 percent and a total of 13.6 drawbar hp. At maximum load this tractor produced 23.24 brake hp with an economy of 7.07 hp-hours per gallon, while at rated load of 21.05 hp this figure increased to 7.83. Total fuel consumption on the rated brake test was 2.689 gph. Brief specifications included a four-cylinder vertical L-head engine with a 4-1/8 x 5-inch bore and stroke with a rated speed of 1,100 rpm. Also included was a Robert Bosch FU4 magneto, Kingston MD2 carburetor, and Ford's own governor and air cleaner systems. Total weight was 3,820 lbs. Few repairs were required during the 65-hour test.

Nebraska Test Data

Model: Fordson "N" (gasoline)

Test No. 174

Date Tested: March 20 to April 10, 1930

Although no profound differences existed between this tractor and the one noted above, the test results were quite different. Using gasoline instead of kerosene, this tractor delivered 5.91 hp-hours per gallon at its rated 15.52 drawbar hp. Both models featured three advertised speeds of 2-1/8, 3-1/8, and 7-3/4 mph. Rated brake hp tests ended with an efficiency of 9.53 hp-hours per gallon, with total consumption of 3.059 gph while delivering 29.09 hp. At rated load of 26.12 hp, fuel efficiency increased slightly to 9.53 hp-hours per gallon. Along with the change in fuel came Zenith IN5F carburetor instead of the Kingston carburetor found on the kerosene model. Some 25 hours of running time was required to complete the test procedures. No major repairs or adjustments were required. Test notes indicate that in order to conform to existing codes this tractor was not to be rated above 14 drawbar and 26 belt hp .

COLLECTOR VALUES	1	2	3	4
FORDSON N 1929-1933 (IRELAND)	$4,500	$3,500	$1,200	$600
FORDSON N 1934-1938 (ENGLAND)	$3,500	$2,700	$900	$600

Fordson All-Around: Rubber Tires or Steel Wheels Available

In 1936 the Fordson Allaround appeared as Ford's first entry with a tricycle-style row-crop tractor. This model used the same engine as the standard-tread model. A noticeable improvement in the All-Around was the addition of a rear PTO shaft. Production of the All-Around ended in 1940.

Nebraska Test Data

Model: Fordson All-Around

Test No. 282

Date Tested: May 17 to June 10, 1937

This was the first British-built tractor tested at Nebraska. Drawbar tests on the All-Around were run first with steel wheels and then on rubber tires. This tractor featured three forward gears of 1.92, 2.91, and 5.13 mph. Second gear was used for Test H, formerly the RATED LOAD test, and with an output of 11.88 hp, this tractor pulled a load of 1,409 lbs. at 3.16 mph with a slippage of 5.78 percent and a fuel economy of 4.32 hp-hours per gallon of distillate. Four-hour fuel economy tests were made in third gear. On steel wheels, with an output of 11.59 hp, the All-Around pulled 757 lbs. at 5.74 mph and yielded 3.049 hp-hours per gallon. The same test on rubber tires indicated an economy of 6.53 hp hours, along with an output of 16.51 hp, and a pull of 1,193 lbs. at 5.19 mph. Test C indicated a rating of 20.31 belt hp, with economy coming to rest at 7.84 hp-hours per gallon, and a slight economy drop to 7.72 at operating maximum load of 21.69 hp. The All-Around was equipped with the company's own four-cylinder L-head engine rated at 1,100 rpm and carrying a 4-1/8 x 5-inch bore and stroke. Also included was an American Bosch U4 magneto and a Kingston carburetor bearing some modifications by Ford. On steel, this tractor weighed in at 4,020 lbs., compared to 5,030 lbs. for the rubber-tired model.

Nebraska Test Data

Model: Fordson All-Around (gasoline)

Test No. 299

Date Tested: May 9 to May 20, 1938

This is the same tractor tested previously, this time using gasoline instead of distillate fuel. Test D elicited a fuel economy of 9.22 hp-hours per gallon at the rated 25.46 hp. At its operating maximum load of 27.69 hp, fuel economy, by comparison, rose to 9.34. Advertised speeds of 1.92, 2.91, and 5.13 mph were featured. Dual test runs were made on steel wheels as well as on 9.00 x 36 rubber tires. Four-hour economy tests show this figure to be 4.59 hp-hours per gallon on steel wheels compared to 6.9 on rubber tires. Test H was made in second gear, and after 10 hours the calculations indicated a fuel economy of 5.71 hp-hours per gallon with a rated output of 15.05 drawbar hp. Ford featured its own four-cylinder

L-head engine. Rated at 1,100 rpm it carried a 4-1/8 x 5-inch bore and stroke. A Robert Bosch FU4B magneto, Handy governor, and Zenith carburetor complemented the basic engine. On steel the All-Around weighed in at 3,965 lbs., compared to 4,970 lbs. on rubber tires. During 68 hours of running time no repairs or adjustments were noted.

Ford-Ferguson 9N

The first Ford 9N tractor was built in 1939. It used the company's own four-cylinder engine, which carried a 3-3/16 x 3-3/4-inch bore and stroke. The unique feature of the 9N tractor was the fact that it was equipped with Harry Ferguson's unique three-point-hitch system. Although Ford built the tractor, marketing was carried out initially by Ferguson-Sherman Mfg. Corporation of Detroit. Production ended in 1942.

Nebraska Test Data

Model: Ford-Ferguson 9N

Test No. 339

Date Tested: April 9 to April 18, 1940

Weighing only 3,375 lbs., the Ford 9N was equipped with three forward speeds of 2.51, 3.23, and 7.48 mph. The test model was furnished with 8.00 x 32 rear tires plus 4.00 x 19 front rubber. For added weight, 151 lbs. of calcium chloride solution was added to each rear tire. Test G indicated a low-gear maximum operating load of 12.61 hp with a maximum pull of 2,236 lbs. at 2.11 mph plus slippage of 17.33 percent. Test H for rated drawbar load indicated an output of 12.8 hp , along with a pull of 1,568 lbs. at 3.06 mph and slippage of 6.7 percent. Fuel economy from this 10-hour test came to 7.95 hp-hours per gallon. The Ford 9N was equipped with the company's own four-cylinder L-head engine with a 3-3/16 x 3-3/4-inch bore and stroke. It was rated at 1,400 rpm for drawbar work and 2,000 rpm for belt duty. Standard equipment included a Marvel-Schebler TSX-33 carburetor, Novi governor, and the company's own electric generator and starting system. At an operating speed of 2,001 rpm, the 9N delivered 23.07 maximum brake hp in Test C and yielded a fuel economy of 9.74 hp-hours per gallon. Economy slipped to 8.76 at rated load of 20.24 brake hp as noted in Test D. No repairs or adjustments were noted during some 64 hours of engine operating time.

COLLECTOR VALUES	1	2	3	4
FORD 9-N	$3,000	$2,250	$1,750	$700

(Note: For the earliest 1939 models with aluminum hoods and grills, add $1,000-$2,000. For V-8 and 6-cylinder conversions, add $1,000-$2,000.)

Ford 2N

Numerous changes had taken place on the Ford 9N subsequent to its introduction in 1939, and many of these changes were embodied in the Ford 2N, introduced in 1942. The onset of World War II was responsible for the introduction of this new model, due to the restrictions imposed by the war effort. Initially the 2N was offered without an electrical system and without rubber tires. However, the 2N had the electrical system back by the end of 1942, and rubber tires were available, at least occasionally. The 2N was the same as the 9N except for steel wheels and magneto ignition. Production of the 2N ended in 1947.

COLLECTOR VALUES	1	2	3	4
FORD 2N	$3,000	$2,250	$1,750	$900

Ford 8N

Ford 8N tractors made their debut in 1947, with production continuing until 1952. This model used a Ford-built four-cylinder engine with a 3-3/16 x 3-3/4-inch bore and stroke. It was rated at 1,500 rpm on the drawbar, and 2,000 rpm for belt work. The 8N was tested at Nebraska three different times. A fourth test, No. 444, used the same 119.7-cubic inch engine, but burned "tractor fuel" instead of gasoline, and the model was classified as the Ford 8NAN.

Nebraska Test Data

Model: Ford 8N

Test No. 385

Date Tested: September 8 to September 19, 1947

Four forward speeds of 2.75, 3.54, 4.87, and 10.16 mph were featured in the Ford 8N tractor. It was equipped with a Ford-built four-cylinder engine. Rated at 1,500 on the drawbar and 2,000 rpm for belt work, this L-head design carried a 3-3/16 x 3-3/4-inch bore and stroke. Also included was a Marvel-Schebler TSX-33 carburetor, Novi governor, Oakes air cleaner, and a Ford battery and ignition system. Tire equipment included 10-28 rear and 4.00-19-inch front rubber. Bare weight without additional ballast was 2,714 lbs. During 88 hours of engine operating time the transmission slipped out of mesh on three occasions while operating in first gear. Other noted items included adjustment of the belt pulley shaft bearing and replacement of the original six-blade fan with a four-blade style. Second gear was used for Test H. During this 10-hour run the 8N yielded a fuel economy of 6.74 hp-hours per gallon under a rated drawbar load of 13.62 hp. Other data included a pull of 1,571 lbs. at 3.25 mph with slippage of 5.68 percent. A Test G maximum pull in low gear came to 2,550 lbs. at 2.38 mph. Belt testing indicated a Test D rated load of 18.35 hp with 7.23 hp-hours per gallon, compared to 7.79 under the operating maximum load of 21.06 belt hp.

Nebraska Test Data

Model: Ford 8N

Test No. 393

Date Tested: May 11 to May 18, 1948

The 8N featured a Ford-built four-cylinder L-head engine. Using a 3-3/16 x 3-3/4-inch bore and stroke, it operated at 1,750 rpm on the drawbar and 2,000 rpm for belt work. Ford also featured its own electrical system on this tractor, along with a Marvel-Schebler TSX-33 carburetor. Bare weight was 2,600 lbs. with tire equipment that included 4.00-19-inch front and 10-28-inch rear rubber. During Tests F, G, and H, 670 lbs. of weight was added to each rear wheel. Following Test B it was necessary to clean the combustion chamber and touch up the valves, otherwise no repairs or adjustments were noted during 67-1/2 hours of engine operating time. The 8N featured forward speeds of 2.97, 3.83, 5.27, and 10.97 mph. Second gear was chosen for Test H. At a rated load of 17.43 drawbar hp , the 8N pulled 1,753 lbs. at 3.73 mph with slippage of 6.73 percent. Fuel economy came in at 9.52 hp-hours per gallon. At an operating maximum load of 25.77 belt hp was noted in Test C, a fuel economy of 10.75 hp-hours per gallon was recorded. By comparison, economy slipped to 10.03 at the Test D rated load of 22.57 belt hp.

Nebraska Test Data

Model: Ford 8N

Test No. 443

Date Tested: June 16 to June 27, 1950

Weighing in at 2,717 lbs., the 8N received an additional 663 lbs. of weight on each rear wheel during Tests F, G, and H. Tire equipment included 10-28-inch rear and 4.00-19-inch front rubber. Also featured were forward speeds of 3.23, 4.16, 5.72, and 11.92 mph. Test G indicated a low-gear maximum pull of 2,810 lbs. at 2.77 mph with a slippage of 10.74 percent. Second gear was used for Test H, and at a rated load of 17.65 drawbar hp, the 8N pulled 1,759 lbs. at 3.76 mph against a slippage of 5.46 percent. Fuel economy was noted at 10.13 hp-hours per gallon. This tractor featured the company's own four-cylinder L-head engine. It was rated at 2,000 rpm on the belt and 1,750 rpm on the drawbar. With a 3 7/16 x 3-3/4-inch bore and stroke, it had a displacement of 119.7-cubic inches. Test C at an operating maximum load of 25.49 belt hp yielded a fuel economy of 11.18 hp-hours per gallon, dropping slightly to 11.03 under a Test D rated belt load of 23.24 hp. No repairs or adjustments were noted during 39 hours of engine operating time.

Nebraska Test Data

Model: Ford 8NAN

Test No. 444

Date Tested: June 22 to June 29, 1950

The Ford 8NAN noted here was designed especially for use with "tractor fuel." With this exception, the tractor appears to have been virtually identical to the 8N, including the 119.7-cid engine. No repairs or adjustments were recorded for the 8NAN during 42 hours of engine operating time. The rated drawbar run of Test H was run in second gear. At a rated load of 14.9 hp , the 8NAN produced a fuel economy of 8.8 hp-hours per gallon of tractor fuel. Under this load a pull of 1,477 lbs. was recorded at a speed of 3.78 mph with a slippage of 4.8 percent. Test G produced a low-gear maximum pull of 2,355 lbs. at 2.72 mph. Belt testing at a Test C operating maximum load of 21.51 hp yielded a fuel economy of 9.6 hp- hours per gallon of tractor fuel, with this figure dropping slightly to reside at 9.39 at a Test D operating load of 19.52 belt hp .

COLLECTOR VALUES	1	2	3	4
FORD 8-N	$3,000	$2,500	$2,000	$800

(Note: For 1951 and later with side distributors, add $200.)

For 1953 Ford introduced a new tractor, the Model NAA, also known as the Jubilee model. Ford Motor Company celebrated its 50th anniversary in 1953, thus the title. The new NAA used a slightly larger engine than its predecessor, the 8N. The four-cylinder motor carried a 3.4375 x 3.60 inch bore and stroke for a displacement of 134-cubic inches. Live hydraulics were standard equipment, and a live PTO was available as an option. Production of the NAA continued into 1954. By this time Dearborn Motors had been merged into the new Tractor & Implement Division of Ford Motor Company. Ford was now ready to enter the tractor and implement business as a major contender.

Ford Model NAA (Jubilee)

Nebraska Test Data

Model: Ford NAA

Test No. 494

Date Tested: May 22 to June 1, 1953

At a Test C, operating under maximum load of 30.15 belt hp, the NAA delivered a fuel economy of 11.24 hp-hours per gallon. Fuel economy sagged to 10.55 under a Test D rated belt load of 27.61 hp. This tractor featured a four-cylinder I-head engine rated at 2,000 rpm in the belt and 1,750 rpm on the drawbar. Its 3.4375 x 3.60 bore and stroke yielded a displacement of 134-cubic inches. No repairs or adjustments of consequence were noted during 55 hours of operating time. Standard equipment included 10-28-inch rear and 5.50-16-inch front tires, along with advertised speeds of 3.13, 4.02, 5.54, and 11.55 mph. The NAA "Jubilee" model illustrated here produced a fuel economy of 10.08 hp-hours per gallon under a Test H rated drawbar load of 20.21 hp . Also recorded in this 10-hour run was a pull of 2,055 lbs. at 3.69 mph under a slippage of 6.46 percent. Test G produced a low-gear maximum pull of 3,232 lbs. at 2.66 mph. The NAA weighed in at 2,841 lbs., but an additional 774 lbs. of cast iron was added to each rear wheel during certain drawbar tests. A maximum engine torque of 191.3 lbs.-ft. was recorded at an engine speed of 1,124 rpm.

COLLECTOR VALUES	1	2	3	4
NAA/JUBILEE	$3,750	$3,000	$2,200	$1,000

Fordson Dexta Diesel

This tractor was built by Ford Motor Company Ltd. in Dagenham, England.

Nebraska Test Data

Model: Fordson Dexta Diesel

Test No. 684

Date Tested: February 28 to March 16, 1959

Weighing 3,393 lbs., the Fordson Dexta Diesel featured 12.4-28-inch rear and 5.50-16-inch front tires. Additional ballast brought the test weight to 6,000 lbs., including the operator. Also featured were six forward speeds ranging from 1.56 to 17.33 mph. Third gear was used for the drawbar fuel economy tests, with this tractor achieving 12.54 hp-hours per gallon of diesel fuel under 75 percent of maximum pull. This test was run at 23.03 hp, with a pull of 1,654 lbs. at 5.22 mph and 3.62 percent slippage. Using first gear, a maximum pull of 4,362 lbs. was attained at 1.69 mph with 12.99 percent slippage. This tractor used a Ford three-cylinder diesel engine rated at 2,000 rpm. Its 3.50 x 5.00-inch bore and stroke gave a 144-cubic inch displacement. Power Take-off Performance runs indicated 31.41 maximum hp at rated engine speed and a fuel economy of 15.47 hp-hours per gallon. This test, when run at the standard PTO speed of 540 rpm, indicated 26.07 hp and 16.24 hp-hours per gallon. No repairs or adjustments were noted during 43-1/2 hours of running time.

Fordson Major tractor

These tractors were built by Ford Motor Company Ltd. in Dagenham, England.

Nebraska Test Data

Model: Fordson Major Diesel

Test No. 500

Date Tested: August 17 to August 27, 1953

The four-cylinder diesel engine featured in this tractor was rated at 1,600 rpm. Using a 3.938 x 4.524 inch bore and stroke it had a 220-cubic inch displacement and a compression ratio of 16:1. Advertised speeds of 2.07, 2.92, 3.73, 5.25, 7.32, and 13.16 mph were standard, as were 14-30-inch rear and 7.50-16-inch front tires. Bare tractor weight was 5,308 lbs., but an additional 1,292 lbs. of weight was added to each rear wheel during certain drawbar tests. Test D, run at a rated belt load of 34.6 hp, yielded 15.44 hp-hours per gallon of diesel fuel, climbing slightly to 15.50 under a Test B & C 100-percent maximum belt load of 38.49 hp. Engine torque peaked at 220.7 lbs.-ft. with an engine speed of 959 rpm. Test H, run in third gear, and with an output of 27.74 drawbar hp, produced 13.93 hp-hours per gallon. This 10-hour run was made at a speed of 3.51 mph with a pull of 2,966 lbs. and slippage of 7.02 percent. Test G came up with a low-gear maximum pull of 5,315 lbs. at 1.73 mph. No repairs or adjustments were noted over 44-1/2 hours of operating time.

Nebraska Test Data

Model: Fordson New Major

Test No. 501

Date Tested: August 17 to August 26, 1953

Using gasoline, the New Fordson Major delivered 29.46 hp at a Test D rated belt load. Fuel economy in this test came to 9.43 hp-hours per gallon, compared to 10.05 under a Test B 100-percent maximum belt load of 33.56 hp. Engine torque peaked at 212.5 lbs.-ft. with an engine speed of 1,155 rpm. Rated tractor speed was 1,600 rpm. This tractor featured a four-cylinder I-head engine with a 3.740 x 4.524-inch bore and stroke and a 199-cubic inch displacement. Advertised speeds of 2.07, 2.92, 3.73, 5.25, 7.32, and 13.16 mph were provided. No repairs or adjustments were noted during 43 hours of operating time. Standard equipment included 7.50-16-inch front and 14-30-inch rear tires. Bare tractor weight was 5,165 lbs., but 1,058 lbs. was added to each rear wheel during Tests F, G, and H. A low-gear maximum pull of 5,016 lbs. was secured in Test G. The 10-hour run of Test H was made in third gear. Fuel economy in this drawbar run totaled 8.19 hp-hours per gallon. Other data from Test H included a rated output of 23.91 drawbar hp, along with a pull of 2,509 lbs. at 3.57 mph and slippage of 6.59 percent.

Ford 640, 650, 660 Series

Nebraska Test Data

Model: Ford 640

Test No. 560

Date Tested: September 19 to October 4, 1955

Weighing 3,031 lbs., the Ford 640 featured 11-28-inch rear and 5.50-15-inch front tires. Also included were forward speeds of 3.13, 4.02, 5.54, and 11.55 mph. During Tests F, G, and H an additional 579 lbs. of cast-iron weight was added to each rear wheel. At a Test H rated drawbar load of 22.39 hp, the 640 pulled 1,873 lbs. at 4.48 mph with an 8.05 percent slippage. Fuel economy totaled 9.87 hp-hours per gallon. Test G yielded a low-gear maximum pull of 3,008 lbs. at 3.18 mph with a slippage of 16.13 percent. The 640 used a Ford four-cylinder engine with a 3.4375 x 3.60 bore and stroke for a displacement of 134-cubic inches. Rated at 2,000 rpm, it achieved a maximum engine torque of 197.9 lbs.-ft. with an engine speed of 1,125 rpm. No repairs or adjustments were noted during 42 hours of operating time. Under a Test D rated belt load of 27.64 hp, fuel economy was scored at 10.73 hp-hours per gallon, climbing to 10.99 at a Test C operating maximum load of 29.46 belt hp.

Nebraska Test Data

Model: Ford 660

Test No. 561

Date Tested: September 21 to October 7, 1955

At a Test C operating maximum load of 32.34 belt hp, the Ford 660 came up with a fuel economy of 11.29 hp-hours per gallon. Economy came in at 11.08 with a Test D rated belt load of 30.19 hp. This tractor was equipped with a four-cylinder engine with a 3.4375 x 3.6 inch bore and stroke for a 134-cubic inch displacement. Rated at 2,200 on the belt and 2,000 rpm at the drawbar, the 660 achieved a maximum engine torque of 234.5 lbs.-ft. with an engine speed of 1,150 rpm. Standard equipment included forward speeds of 2.22, 3.52, 4.72, 6.48, and 11.75 mph. Also featured were 11-28-inch rear and 5.50-16-inch front tires. Bare tractor weight was 3,095 lbs. This was increased to 4,917 lbs. with the additional ballast used during Tests F, G, and H. A low-gear maximum pull of 3,859 lbs. at 1.97 mph was recorded in Test G. Fuel economy came in at 10.04 hp-hours per gallon during the 10-hour rated drawbar run of Test H. This test saw a rated output of 22.36 hp, along with a pull of 1,782 lbs. at 4.7 mph and slippage of 4.79 percent. During 39 hours of operating time, no repairs or adjustments were recorded.

Ford 841 tractor

Nebraska Test Data

Model: Ford 841

Test No. 653

Date Tested: June 2 to June 10, 1958

Twelve forward speeds, ranging from 2.46 to 15.47 mph, were featured in this diesel tractor. Also included were 13.6-28-inch rear and 6.00-16-inch front tires. No front wheel ballast was used during testing, but 1,350 lbs. was added to each rear wheel, bringing the total test weight with operator to 6,259 lbs. Test H, run in fifth gear, was made with a rated drawbar load of 28.91 hp. This test recorded a pull of 2,451 lbs. at 4.42 mph with 5.51 percent slippage. Drawbar fuel economy resulting from this 10-hour run came in at 13.49 hp-hours per gallon of diesel fuel. A low-gear maximum pull of 4,705 lbs. at 2.12 mph against a slippage of 11.7 percent was recorded in Test G. No repairs or adjustments were noted during 40 hours of running time. Ford used its own four-cylinder engine in the 841 tractor. Rated at 2,000 rpm, it carried a 3.90 x 3.60-inch bore and stroke for a displacement of 172-cubic inches. The design also featured a 16.8:1 compression ratio. Test D, run at a rated belt load of 35.35 hp, yielded 14.48 hp-hours per gallon. At a 100-percent maximum belt load of 39.88 belt hp the Ford 841 achieved 14.2 hp-hours per gallon.

Ford 681 Series

Nebraska Test Data

Model: Ford 681

Test No. 702

Date Tested: June 11 to June 20, 1959

The Ford 681 was equipped with a power-shifting, fixed-ratio transmission and 10 forward speeds, ranging from 1.01 to 16.94 mph. During 40 hours of running time, no repairs or adjustments were required for this tractor. Drawbar performance was noted at 26.81 maximum available hp over a two-hour run in sixth gear. In this test, the 681 pulled 2,274 lbs. at 4.42 mph with 6.15 percent slippage, yielding a fuel economy of 9.51 hp-hours per gallon. A 10-hour run made at 75 percent of maximum load indicated an output of 22.18 hp, a pull of 1,728 lbs. at 4.81 mph and 8.63 hp-hours per gallon. Weighing 3,395 lbs., the 681 was burdened with 839 lbs. of additional ballast on each rear wheel during the varying drawbar tests. In other tests, a run made without ballast indicated an output of 24.27 hp, along with a pull of 2,087 lbs. at 4.36 mph and 9.25 percent slippage. The 681 was equipped with a four-cylinder engine carrying a 3.44 x 3.90 inch bore and stroke for a 134-cubic inch displacement. It carried a 2,000 rpm rating for drawbar work and 2,200 rpm for PTO service. At rated engine speed, the 681 delivered a maximum of 34.33 PTO hp, yielding a fuel economy of 10.98 hp-hours per gallon. By comparison, fuel economy was posted at 10.91 at a standard (1,000 rpm) PTO speed, along with an output of 28.29 hp.

Nebraska Test Data

Model: Ford 681-L

Test No. 704

Date Tested: June 18 to June 25, 1959

Except for the propane fuel used in this model, there was virtually no difference in engine and chassis specifications with the previous tractor. Both models used a 7.5:1 compression ratio. Standard equipment, common to both styles, included 12.4-28-inch rear and 5.50-16-inch front tires. Except for minor repairs, the 681-L went through 40 hours of operating time without incident. At its rated speed of 2,200 rpm, the 681-L delivered a maximum of 32.57 PTO hp, yielding 8.06 hp-hours per gallon of propane. When running at a 1,000 PTO rpm and a corresponding engine speed of 1,730 rpm, fuel economy was noted at 8.36 hp-hours per gallon of propane against a load of 27 hp. At a maximum available drawbar load of 25.52 hp, a pull of 2,162 lbs. was noted at 4.43 mph against a slippage of 5.71 percent. At 75 percent, a pull of 1,666 lbs. was recorded at 4.79 mph with a slippage of 4.37 percent and a fuel economy of 6.51 hp-hours per gallon—somewhat lower than the 7.18 economy figure derived at maximum available power.

Nebraska Test Data

Model: Ford 681-D

Test No. 706

Date Tested: June 20 to June 26, 1959

Completing this series of tests, Ford presented the 681 Diesel, another variation of the models previously noted. Once again, specifications remained virtually identical for all three models, except that Ford used its own four-cylinder, 144-cid diesel engine. With a 3.562 x 3.600-inch bore and stroke, this engine featured a 16.8:1 compression ratio. No repairs or adjustments were noted during 45 hours of running time. At a standard PTO speed of 1,000 rpm and a corresponding engine speed of 1,734 rpm, the 681 Diesel recorded an output of 26.3 hp, along with a fuel economy of 13.61 hp-hours per gallon. By contrast, at a rated engine speed of 2,200 rpm, output totaled 31.56 PTO hp, and a recorded fuel economy of 13.32 hp-hours per gallon. Sixth gear was again chosen for the varying drawbar power and fuel consumption tests. In the case at hand, at 25.52 maximum available hp , the 681 Diesel pulled 2,162 lbs. at 4.43 against a slippage of 5.28 percent. Fuel economy was posted at 11.69 hp-hours per gallon. By comparison, fuel economy rose to 12.10 under a 75 percent load, corresponding to 21 drawbar hp and a pull of 1,629 lbs. at 4.84 mph. The 681 Diesel weighed in at 3,490 lbs., but with additional ballast, a test weight of 5,485 lbs. was recorded.

Ford 841 and 851 Series
Nebraska Test Data

Model: Ford 841

Test No. 641

Date Tested: March 14 to March 31, 1958

Twelve forward speeds ranging from 2.46 to 15.47 mph were featured in the 841 gasoline model shown here. Standard equipment also included 13.6-28-inch rear and 6.00-16-inch front tires. Bare tractor weight was 3,393 lbs., with 1,397 lbs. of ballast added to each rear wheel during all drawbar testing except for Test J. Test rules indicated this operating maximum test was conducted without any additional weight over and above the base operating weight. Test G, run in low gear, indicated a maximum drawbar pull of 4,631 lbs. at 2.14 mph and slippage of 10.95 percent. Using fifth gear, Test H was run at a rated drawbar output of 32.10 hp, displaying a pull of 2,588 lbs. at 4.65 mph and slippage of 5.68 percent. Fuel economy came in at 9.76 hp-hours per gallon. The 841 used a four-cylinder, 3.90 x 3.60-inch engine with a 172-cubic inch displacement and a 7.50:1 compression ratio. Test C, run at an operating maximum load of 43.1 belt hp, indicated 11.66 hp-hours per gallon, dropping to 10.37 under a Test D rated belt load of 39.54 hp. During 41-1/2 hours of operation, no repairs or adjustments were noted.

Ford 850-L tractor
Nebraska Test Data

Model: Ford 850-L (LPG)

Test No. 626

Date Tested: June 24 to July 12, 1957

Advertised speeds of 2.3, 3.66, 4.87, 6.72, and 11.96 mph were featured in the 850-L. Standard equipment also included 12-28-inch rear and 6.00-16-inch front tires. Weight was 3,425 lbs., but an additional 1,483 lbs. was added to each rear wheel during Tests F, G, and H. Using low gear, Test G elicited a maximum pull of 5,170 lbs. at 1.96 mph with a slippage of 13.34 percent. Test H yielded a drawbar fuel economy of 7.6 hp-hours per gallon of propane. This test, run in third gear, recorded a pull of 2,329 lbs. at 4.55 mph with a slippage of 4.67 percent. During 46-1/2 hours of operating time, no repairs or adjustments were recorded. Ford equipped this tractor with its own four-cylinder engine using a 3.9 x 3.6 inch bore and stroke for a 172-cubic inch displacement. Designed specifically for propane, it featured an 8:1 compression ratio, and was rated at 2,200 rpm on the belt and 2,000 rpm for drawbar work. Test L noted an operating maximum torque of 112 percent rated-speed torque in a range of 75 percent down to 70 percent of rated rpm. Under a Test C operating maximum belt load of 38.22 hp, fuel economy was 8.27 hp-hours per gallon of propane, declining to 8.06 at a Test D rated belt load of 35.5 hp.

Ford 860 series
Nebraska Test Data

Model: Ford 860

Test No. 562

Date Tested: September 21 to October 6, 1955

Weighing 3,255 lbs., the Ford 860 was burdened with an additional 1,346 lbs. of ballast during Tests F, G, and H. Standard features included 12-28-inch rear and 6.00-16-inch front tires, along with forward speeds of 2.22, 3.52, 4.72, 6.48, and 11.75 mph. Test H, run in third gear, yielded a fuel economy of 10.28 hp-hours per gallon, along with a rated output of 30.51 drawbar hp , a pull of 2,559 lbs. at 4.47 mph and slippage of 6.76 percent. Test G indicated a low-gear maximum pull of 4,514 lbs. at 1.89 mph with a slippage of 16.98 percent. The 860 was equipped with a Ford four-cylinder, 172-cid engine with a 3.90 x 3.60 inch bore and stroke. Rated at 2,200 on the belt on 2,000 rpm at the drawbar, it gave a peak engine torque of 315 lbs.-ft. with an engine speed of 1,144 rpm. Under a Test D rated belt load of 39.97 hp, fuel economy came in at 11.53 hp-hours per gallon, climbing to 11.82 under a Test C operating maximum load of 43.04 belt hp. During 40 hours of operation, no repairs or adjustments were noted.

Ford 881 Series

Nebraska Test Data

Model: Ford 881

Test No. 701

Date Tested: June 6 to June 17, 1959

Rated at 2,200 PTO rpm and 2,000 rpm at the drawbar, the 881 carried a four-cylinder, 172-cid engine with a 3.90 x 3.60-inch bore and stroke. A six-volt electrical system was standard equipment, along with 10 forward speeds ranging from 1.06 to 16.36 mph. Also featured were 13-26-rear and 6.00-16-inch front tires. Total weight without ballast was 3,563 lbs. At rated engine speed of 2,200 rpm, the 881 delivered a maximum of 46.16 PTO hp and yielded 12.10 hp-hours per gallon. When run with a standard PTO speed of 1,000 rpm, an output of 39.04 hp was indicated, along with a fuel economy of 12.49 hp-hours per gallon. Using sixth gear, maximum available drawbar hp was noted at 37.02. Other data from this two-hour test included a pull of 3,347 lbs. at 4.15 mph and slippage of 8.26 percent. Fuel economy was recorded at 10.68 hp-hours per gallon. A 10-hour run made at 75 percent of maximum pull indicated a fuel economy of 8.94 hp-hours per gallon. Only a minor repair was required during 44-1/2 hours of running time. The 881 was equipped with an operator-controlled power-shifting, full-range, fixed-ratio transmission. During the varying drawbar load tests, an additional 1,406 lbs. of weight was added to each rear wheel, along with 176 lbs. for each front wheel.

Nebraska Test Data

Model: Ford 881-L (LPG)
Test No. 703
Date Tested: June 16 to June 24, 1959

While the Ford 881 gasoline model of Test No. 701 carried a 7.5:1 compression ratio, it was altered for the 881-L to 8.65:1. With this exception, specifications remained virtually the same. Except for tightening the fan belt during the test, no repairs or adjustments were noted during 42-1/2 hours of running time. A two-hour run made at rated engine speed and maximum PTO load indicated an output of 43.61 hp, along with an economy of 8.72 hp-hours per gallon of propane. The same test, when run at the standard PTO speed of 1,000 rpm noted an economy figure of 8.92 with an output of 39.31 hp. Again, sixth gear was used for the varying drawbar tests, with a maximum output of 34.28 hp indicated in a two-hour run. This test noted a pull of 3,076 lbs. at 4.18 mph and slippage of 7.89 percent. Fuel economy was posted at 7.31 hp-hours per gallon of propane. A 10-hour drawbar run, made at 75 percent of maximum, delivered 29.37 hp, along with a pull of 2,373 lbs. at 4.64 mph and slippage of 5.76 percent. Fuel economy came in at 6.45 hp-hours per gallon. Without ballast, this tractor weighed in at 3,683 lbs., but with added ballast, the figure jumped to 6,950 lbs.

Nebraska Test Data

Model: Ford 881-D (diesel)
Test No. 705
Date Tested: June 28 to July 2, 1959

Weighing 3,635 lbs., the 881 Diesel carried a test weight of 6,955 lbs. when additional ballast was added. Standard equipment also included 13.6-28-inch rear and 6.00-16-inch front tires. Like the various 881 models noted in previous tests, this tractor also carried a dual speed rating—2,200 engine rpm for PTO work, and 2,000 rpm at the drawbar. Unlike gasoline or propane versions that used a 6-volt electrical system, the 881 diesel was equipped with a 12-volt battery. Ford equipped this tractor with a four-cylinder engine carrying a 3.90 x 3.60-inch bore and stroke and a 16.8:1 compression ratio. No repairs or adjustments were noted during 40 hours of running time. At maximum available drawbar hp of 33.60, a drawbar pull of 3,005 lbs. was recorded at a speed of 4.19 mph and slippage of 6.37 percent. Fuel economy in this two-hour run calculated to 12.72 hp-hours per gallon. That figure ascended to 12.86 under 75 percent of pull at maximum power. This 10-hour run noted a drawbar load of 28.05 hp, along with a pull of 2,275 lbs. at 4.62 mph and slippage of 4 percent. At rated engine speed of 2,200 rpm, the 861 Diesel yielded an output of 41.36 PTO hp, and 13.86 hp-hours per gallon. When run at the standard 1,000 PTO rpm, and a corresponding engine speed of 1,730 rpm, fuel economy was 14.48 hp-hours per gallon against a load of 33.93 PTO hp .

Ford 6000 Series

Nebraska Test Data

Model: Ford 6000 Diesel
Test No. 783
Date Tested: March 25 to April 4, 1961

Featuring an operator-controlled, full range, power-shifting, fixed-ratio transmission, the Ford 6000 was equipped with 10 forward speeds ranging from 1.2 to 18.2 mph. Weighing 7,405 lbs., it took on additional rear wheel ballast for a test weight of 9,545 lbs. Standard equipment included 15.5-38-inch rear and 6.50-16-inch front tires. Using sixth gear at 59.24 maximum available hp, the two-hour economy run saw a pull of 4,512 lbs. at 4.92 mph with 5.74 percent slippage. Also recorded was a fuel economy of 10.95 hp-hours per gallon of diesel fuel. The 10-hour drawbar run, made at 75 percent pull, yielded an economy figure of 11.68, along with an output of 49.12 hp, a pull of 3,463 lbs. at 5.32 mph and 3.9 percent slippage. Ford equipped this tractor with its own six-cylinder engine rated at 2,400 rpm. Using a 3.62 x 3.90-inch bore and stroke, it had a 241.7-cubic inch displacement. At rated engine speed, 66.17 maximum PTO hp was observed, yielding a fuel economy of 12.75 hp-hours per gallon. The figure slipped slightly to 12.66 when operating at 540 PTO rpm and a corresponding engine speed of 2,227 rpm. This test saw an output of 65.35 hp. During the PTO runs the engine speed became unstable. Replacement of the governor cured the problem and testing continued. With this exception, no repairs or adjustments were reported during 62-1/2 hours of running time.

Nebraska Test Data

Model: Ford 6000 Gasoline
Test No. 784
Date Tested: April 1 to April 8, 1961

At its rated crankshaft speed of 2,400 rpm, the 6000 gasoline model delivered a maximum of 66.86 PTO hp, plus a corresponding economy of 10.32 hp-hours per gallon. Using a 1,000 rpm PTO speed and a corresponding engine speed of 2,227 rpm, 63.12 PTO hp was observed, together with an economy figure of 10.37. This 7,225 lb. tractor was equipped with a Ford six-cylinder engine carrying a 3.62 x 3.60-inch bore and stroke for a displacement of 223-cubic inches. Also featured was a full range power shifting, fixed-ratio transmission with 10 forward speeds ranging from 1.2 to 18.2 mph. Tire equipment was identical to that already noted in Test No. 783. Additional front and rear ballast brought the test weight to 9,535 lbs. Using sixth gear, a two-hour economy run at 59.34 maximum available hp indicated a pull of 4,473 lbs. at 4.98 mph with 5.21 percent slippage. Also manifested was a fuel economy of 9.08 hp hours per gallon of gasoline. The economy figure slipped to 7.66 in a 10-hour drawbar run made at 75 percent pull. This test noted an output of 49.45 hp, a pull of 3,470 lbs. at 5.34 mph and 3.92 percent slippage. During the drawbar tests it was necessary to readjust the high idle speed, but with this exception the 6000 went through 55 hours of operating time without incident.

Nebraska Test Data

Model: Ford 5000 8-Speed Diesel
Test No. 96
Date Tested: October 30 to November 25, 1968

Weighing in at 5,795 lbs., this tractor featured 16.9-30-inch rear and 7.50-16-inch front tires. Additional front and rear ballast gave a total test weight of 9,690 lbs. The eight-speed transmission was of the selective gear fixed-ratio type and offered a range of 1.5 to 16.8 mph. Using fourth gear, the two-hour economy test was run at 59.92 maximum available drawbar hp. A pull of 5,344 lbs. at 4.2 mph was recorded, as was slippage of 8.52 percent, and a fuel

Ford 5000 Series

economy of 13.25 hp-hours per gallon. The economy figure stood at 13.40 in the 10-hour run at 75 percent pull. This test manifested an output of 48.98 hp, a pull of 3,950 lbs. at 4.65 mph and slippage of 6.07 percent. Ford equipped this model with its own four-cylinder, 256-cid diesel engine. Rated at 2,100 rpm, it used a 4.4 x 4.2-inch bore and stroke. At rated engine speed, 67.23 maximum PTO hp was observed, together with 15.47 hp-hours per gallon. Operating at 540 PTO rpm and a corresponding engine speed of 1,901 rpm, 64.16 PTO hp was recorded and an economy of 16.06 hp-hours per gallon was achieved. During the preliminary PTO runs the fuel injectors were removed and cleaned, after which testing continued. With this exception, no repairs or adjustments were required during 55 hours of operating time.

Nebraska Test Data

Model: Ford 5000 Selecto-O-Speed

Test No. 997

Date Tested: November 7 to November 25, 1968

This tractor differed from the 5000 diesel model in the previous test by the substitution of a gasoline engine. Replacing the diesel was a Ford-built four-cylinder, 256-cid gasoline engine. Rated at 2,100 rpm, it carried a 4.4 x 4.2-inch bore and stroke. At rated engine speed, 65.64 maximum PTO hp was observed, as was an economy of 11.6 hp-hours per gallon. Operating at 540 PTO rpm and a corresponding engine speed of 1,901 rpm, 61.97 PTO hp appeared and an economy of 11.71 hp-hours per gallon was recorded. Another difference between this tractor and that of the previous test was the transmission style. The tractor shown here featured a selective gear fixed-ratio transmission with full-range power shifting. Its 10 forward speeds varied from 1.0 to 16.4 mph. Using sixth gear, the two-hour economy run was made at 54.53 maximum available hp and yielded 9.98 hp-hours per gallon. Likewise, this test noted a pull of 4,895 lbs. at 4.18 mph with slippage of 7.82 percent. The 10-hour run indicated an economy of 9.1 hp hours per gallon against an output of 44.46 hp. Other statistics included a pull of 3,695 lbs. at 4.51 mph and 5.79 percent slippage. Bare tractor weight was 5,110 lbs. and additional front and rear ballast raised this figure to a test weight of 9,700 lbs. During the preliminary PTO runs it was twice necessary to remove the cylinder head and clean the combustion chamber. New spark plugs and ignition points were also installed. These constituted the necessary repairs or adjustments during 57 hours of operating time.

Nebraska Test Data

Model: Ford 5000 8-Speed Diesel

Test No. 998

Date Tested: November 7 to November 25, 1968

This tractor featured the same four-cylinder, 256-cid gasoline engine as noted in Test No. 997. Rated at 2,100 rpm, it developed a maximum output of 67.31 PTO hp with an observed economy of 11.58 hp hours per gallon of fuel. At 540 PTO rpm and a corresponding engine speed of 1,901 rpm, 63.73 PTO hp appeared, as did an economy of 11.75 hp-hours per gallon. The major difference between this model and that of Test No. 997 was an eight-speed transmission for this tractor. Of the selective gear fixed-ratio design, it offered a range from 1.5 to 16.8 mph. Using fourth gear, 57.87 maximum available hp was demonstrated in the two-hour economy run - this test also saw a pull of 5,125 lbs. at 4.23 mph, slippage of 8.1 percent, and an economy of 9.70 hp-hours per gallon was achieved. The 10-hour run at 75 percent pull indicated an economy of 9.48 hp-hours per gallon against a load of 47.1 hp. Also manifested was a pull of 3,854 lbs. at 4.58 mph and 6.06 percent slippage. Weighing in at 5,730 lbs., this unit assumed a total test weight of 9,690 lbs. through the addition of front and rear ballast. During the preliminary PTO runs the cylinder head was removed twice for cleaning the combustion chambers. New spark plugs were also installed. This constituted the repairs and adjustments required during 51 hours of running time.

Ford 4000 Series

Nebraska Test Data

Model: Ford 4000 8-Speed

Test No. 891

Date Tested: April 21 to May 5, 1965

Rated at 2,200 rpm, this tractor featured a three-cylinder gasoline engine with a 4.4 x 4.2-inch bore and stroke for a displacement of 192-cubic inches. Operating at rated speed, a maximum of 46.31 PTO hp was observed, together with an economy of 11.07 hp-hours per gallon. This figure rose to 11.95 in another PTO run made at 540 rpm on the output shaft and a corresponding engine speed of 1,809 rpm. Also recorded was an output of 42.63 hp. The eight forward speeds ranged from 1.3 to 16.8 mph. Featured too were 14.9-30-inch rear and 7.50-16-inch front tires. Bare tractor weight was 4,766 lbs., but the use of front and rear ballast raised this to a test weight of 8,410 lbs. The two-hour drawbar economy run was made at 41.09 maximum available hp and achieved 9.52 hp-hours per gallon. Also recorded was a pull of 3,718 lbs. at 4.14 mph with 6.81 percent slippage. The 10-hour run at 75 percent pull saw an economy of 9.37 hp-hours per gallon against an output of 33.34 drawbar hp. Other statistics from this test included a pull of 2,793 lbs. at 4.48 mph with 4.67 percent slippage. During 45-1/2 hours of operation, no repairs or adjustments were recorded.

Nebraska Test Data

Model: Ford 4000 Select-O-Speed Diesel

Test No. 892

Date Tested: April 23 to May 6, 1965

No repairs or adjustments were reported for this tractor during 51-1/2 hours of operating time. Featuring a three-cylinder, 201-cid engine, it used a 4.4-inch bore and stroke with a rated speed of 2,200 rpm. At rated engine speed, 45.62 maximum PTO hp was observed, as was an economy of 13.9 hp-hours per gallon. Another test made at 540 PTO rpm and a corresponding engine speed of 1,809 rpm saw an economy of 15.19 hp-hours per gallon with an output of 41.68 hp. The full-range power-shift transmission offered 10 forward speeds ranging from 1.1 to 17.6 mph. Bare tractor weight was 4,895 lbs. By the addition of front and rear ballast this was raised to a test weight of 8,215 lbs. Standard equipment included 14.9-30-inch rear and 7.50-16-inch front tires. Using sixth gear, a two-hour drawbar run at 38.22 maximum available hp saw an economy of 11.72 hp-hours per gallon. Also evidenced was a pull of 3,242 lbs. at 4.42 mph and slippage of 5.85 percent. The 10-hour run at 75 percent pull achieved a fuel economy of 10.69 against an output of 31.58 hp. Also recorded was a pull of 2,491 lbs. at 4.75 mph and slippage of 5.85 percent.

Nebraska Test Data

Model: Ford 4000 8-Speed Diesel

Test No. 893

Date Tested: April 26 to May 12, 1965

At its rated 2,200 rpm, this tractor developed a maximum of 46.71 PTO hp, achieving 14.6 hp-hours per gallon. A second PTO run at 540 rpm on the output shaft, together with a corresponding engine speed of 1,810 rpm, saw an output of 41.75 hp balanced against 15.42 hp-hours per gallon. Standard features included a Ford-built three-cylinder, 201-cid engine with a 4.4-inch bore and stroke. Also featured were 14.9-30-inch rear and 7.50-16-inch front tires, plus an eight-speed transmission with a range from 1.3 to 16.8 mph. No repairs or adjustments were required during 43 hours of running time. The total test weight of 8,165 lbs. included 1,490 lbs. of ballast for each rear wheel plus 175 lbs. of cast iron for each front wheel. In fourth gear, 39.35 maximum drawbar hp was observed in a two-hour test, which also saw 12.44 hp-hours per gallon. Other statistics included a pull of 3,539 lbs. at 4.17 mph and slippage of 5.91 percent. At 75 percent pull, the 10-hour drawbar run indicated 12.27 hp-hours per gallon against an output of 33.57 hp. Recorded too was a pull of 2,851 lbs. at 4.42 mph and 4.9 percent slippage.

Ford 3000 Series

Nebraska Test Data

Model: Ford 3000 8-Speed Diesel

Test No. 881

Date Tested: March 29 to April 6, 1965

Although using an engine of the same 4.2-inch bore and stroke as noted for the Ford model of Test No. 880, this tractor featured a 175-cid, three-cylinder engine. Rated at 2,000 rpm, it featured a 16.5:1 compression ratio. Eight forward speeds were provided by the selective gear fixed-ratio transmission. The speeds ranged from 1.4 to 17.4 mph. Standard equipment included 14.9-24-inch rear and 6.00-16-inch front tires. The bare weight of 4,141 lbs. was augmented with rear wheel ballast for a total test weight of 6,885 lbs. Using fourth gear, 34.88 maximum available drawbar hp was demonstrated in a two-hour run. This load evoked 13.74 hp-hours per gallon. Also revealed was a pull of 2,798 lbs. at 4.68 mph with 4.78 percent slippage. The 10-hour run at 75 percent pull noted 13.25 hp hours per gallon against a load of 29.1 drawbar hp. This test recorded a pull of 2,173 lbs. at 5.02 mph with 3.89 percent slippage. No repairs or adjustments were required during 53 hours total operating time. At rated engine speed, 39.2 maximum PTO hp was observed, together with 16.19 hp-hours per gallon. This figure rose to 16.74 in a second run made at 540 PTO rpm and a corresponding engine speed of 1,810 rpm. This test saw an output of 37.34 PTO hp.

Nebraska Test Data

Model: Ford 3000 Select-O-Speed Diesel

Test No. 882

Date Tested: March 24 to April 9, 1965

Except for the transmission, this tractor was identical to the Ford 3000 8-Speed model. As the name implies, the Select-O-Speed transmission offered full-range power shifting. Ten speeds were provided, ranging from 1.0 to 16.4 mph. No repairs or adjustments were reported during 58-1/2 hours of running time. A comparison with Test No. 881 clearly indicated some variation existed in test results, even between two tractors of identical engine design. A study of the test reports also showed a difference in humidity, temperature, and barometric pressure during these two tests. At rated engine speed, this model exerted a maximum output of 38.06 PTO hp with an economy of 15.04 hp-hours per gallon. The same test, run at 540 PTO rpm and a corresponding engine speed of 1,811 rpm, indicated an economy of 15.49 while delivering 35.96 hp. The usual two-hour drawbar economy run was made at 30.6 maximum available hp. A pull of 2,577 lbs. at 4.45 mph resulted, with a slippage of 5.34 percent. Economy was pegged at 12.36 hp-hours per gallon. The 10-hour run at 75 percent pull noted 11.89 hp-hours per gallon against an output of 25.44 hp. Also recorded was a pull of 2,051 lbs. at 4.65 mph with 4 percent slippage.

Nebraska Test Data

Model: Ford 3000 4-Speed Diesel

Test No. 883

Date Tested: March 27 to April 7, 1965

In this Ford 3000 there were only four forward speeds provided by the selective gear fixed-ratio transmission. Starting at 4.0 mph, the speed range continued through 4.8, 7.0, and 14.8 mph. Within each of these speed ranges came the choice of under, direct, or over-drive. All three models of this and previous tests used the same tire equipment and the same three-cylinder diesel engine. Using fifth gear (2nd direct), the two-hour drawbar run was made at 35.43 maximum available hp. This run saw an economy of 13.6 hp-hours per gallon. Also revealed was a pull of 2,876 lbs. at 4.62 mph with 5.62 percent slippage. During the 10-hour run, made at 75 percent pull, economy was recorded at 12.9 hp-hours per gallon against an output of 28.97 drawbar hp. Other statistics included a pull of 2,188 lbs. at 4.97 mph with 4.03 percent slippage. Repairs and adjustments reported during 44 hours of operation were minor. At rated engine speed of 2,000 rpm, 39.46 PTO hp was observed, as was 15.59 hp-hours per gallon. The economy figure stood at 16.43 against an output of 31.81 PTO hp. This test was made at 540 PTO rpm and a corresponding engine speed of 1,484 rpm.

Ford 2000 Series

The Super Dexta Diesel was manufactured in Dagenham, England, while the other Ford 2000s were built in Ford's Birmingham, Michigan, Plant.

Nebraska Test Data

Model: Ford 2000 Super Dexta Diesel

Test No. 844

Date Tested: June 19 to July 2, 1963

This tractor featured a Ford-built three-cylinder diesel engine. Using a 3.6 x 5.0-inch bore and stroke it carried a 152.7-cubic inch displacement and was rated at 2,250 rpm. At rated engine speed a maximum of 38.83 PTO hp was developed, together with an observed fuel economy of 14.32 hp-hours per gallon. A second PTO run at 540 rpm and a corresponding engine speed of 1,810 rpm indicated an economy figure of 15.50, together with an output of 34.31 hp. The selective gear fixed-ratio transmission offered six forward speeds ranging from 1.61 to 19.53 mph. Using third gear, the two-hour drawbar economy run was made at 32.25 maximum available hp. In this test an economy of 12.30 hp-hours per gallon was recorded. Also indicated was a pull of 2,744 lbs. at 4.41 mph with 7.97 percent slippage. Using third gear, the 10-hour run at 75 percent pull noted an output of 26.17 hp, a pull of 2,102 lbs. at 4.67 mph, and 5.24 percent slippage. Fuel economy was 12.45 hp hours per gallon. No repairs or adjustments were required during 44 hours of running time. Standard equipment on this 3,510-lb. tractor included 12.4-28-inch rear and 5.50-16-inch front tires. Test weight came to 6,030 lbs. by the addition of front and rear wheel ballast.

Nebraska Test Data

Model: Ford 2000 4-Speed

Test No. 884

Date Tested: April 5 to April 21, 1965

Rated at 1,900 rpm, the Ford 2000 carried a three-cylinder engine similar to that featured in the Ford 3000 series. A notable change was the 4.2 x 3.8-inch bore and stroke, which resulted in a displacement of 157.95 cubic inches. At rated engine speed, fuel economy was recorded at 10.96 hp-hours per gallon against a maximum output of 30.57 PTO hp. Another test made at 540 PTO rpm and a corresponding engine speed of 1,484 rpm gave an output of 26.35 hp and a resultant fuel economy of 11.08 hp-hours per gallon. The four-speed transmission was also equipped with over, under, and direct-drive ranges for an actual total of 12 forward speeds. Using second gear in direct-drive, the two-hour economy run was made at 27.17 maximum available hp and yielded an economy of 9.78 hp-hours per gallon. Also recorded in this test was a pull of 2,367 lbs. at 4.30 mph with 6.31 percent slippage. The 10-hour run at 75 percent pull set an economy figure of 9.52 against an output of 22.18 hp. This test saw a pull of 1,816 lbs. at 4.58 mph with 4.69 percent slippage. Standard equipment on this model included 12.4-28-inch rear and 5.50-16-inch front tires. The bare weight of 3,770 lbs. was raised to 6,015 lbs. through the addition of front and rear ballast. No repairs or adjustments were reported during 47 hours of operation.

Nebraska Test Data

Model: Ford 2000 8-Speed

Test No. 894

Date Tested: May 1 to May 11, 1965

Weighing 3,895 lbs., this tractor was supported by 12.4-28-inch rear and 5.50-16-inch front tires. During drawbar testing, additional rear wheel ballast gave a total test weight of 5,955 lbs. The selective gear fixed-ratio transmission offered speeds ranging from 1.3 to 16.8 mph. Using fourth gear, and at 26.49 maximum available drawbar hp, a two-hour drawbar economy test observed an economy of 9.38 hp- hours per gallon. Also noted was a pull of 2,290 lbs. at 4.34 mph and 6.25 percent slippage. Fuel economy slipped to 9.22 hp-hours per gallon in a 10-hour run made at 75 percent pull. This test, run at 22.03 drawbar hp, saw a pull of 1,788 lbs. at 4.62 mph and an identical 4.62 percent slippage. Rated at 1,900 rpm, the three-cylinder, 157.95-cid engine carried a 4.2 x 3.8-inch bore and stroke. At rated speed it delivered an economy of 10.79 hp-hours per gallon against a maximum output of 30.85 PTO hp. Another run made at 540 PTO rpm and an engine speed of 1,810 rpm saw 10.79 hp-hours per gallon with a total output of 30.04 hp. During 43 hours of running time, no repairs or adjustments were reported.

Ford FW Series

These tractors were manufactured by Steiger Tractor, Inc., of Fargo, North Dakota.

Nebraska Test Data

Model: Ford FW-30 Diesel

Test No. 1288

Date Tested: September 25 to October 14, 1978

Weighing 31,310 lbs., this tractor was equipped with dual 24.5-32-inch tires. Additional front ballast gave a total test weight of 31,720 lbs. A selective gear fixed-ratio transmission was used—its 20 forward speeds ranged from 2.2 to 21.8 mph. Operating in ninth gear, the two hour economy run at 205.20 maximum available drawbar hp indicated a pull of 13,131 lbs. at 5.86 mph with slippage totaling 3.95 percent. Fuel economy was recorded at 13.71 hp-hours per gallon. The 10-hour run at 75 percent pull noted an economy of 12.24 hp-hours per gallon under a load of 170.59 drawbar hp. Also indicated was a pull of 10,127 lbs. at 6.32 mph and slippage totaling 3.11 percent. Except for replacement of a hose assembly and a control switch, no repairs or adjustments were required during 58-½ hours of operating time. The FW-30 featured a Cummins V-8 diesel engine with a 5.5 x 4.75-inch bore and stroke for a 903-cubic inch displacement. The hydrostatic PTO system was designed for a rated load of 105.31 PTO hp. Under this load an economy of 9.65 hp-hours per gallon was recorded.

Nebraska Test Data

Model: Ford FW-60 Diesel

Test No. 1289

Date Tested: September 28 to October 10, 1978

No PTO shaft was provided on the tractor and no brake hp tests were run. The FW-60 was equipped with a Cummins V-8 turbocharged diesel engine. Rated at 2,600 rpm, it used a 5.5 x 4.75-inch bore and stroke for a 903-cubic inch displacement. The selective gear fixed-ratio transmission offered 20 forward speeds ranging from 2.2 to 21.8 mph. Using 10th gear, the two-hour economy run at 270.87 maximum available drawbar hp indicated a pull of 15,469 lbs. at 6.57 mph with slippage totaling 4.61 percent. Fuel economy was posted at 14.9 hp-hours per gallon. The 10-hour run at 75 percent pull indicated an economy of 13.38 hp-hours per gallon under 229.62 drawbar hp. Other tests included a pull of 12,068 lbs. at 7.14 mph and slippage of 3.57 percent. The FW-60 made a fourth gear maximum pull of 29,304 lbs. at 2.94 mph with slippage of 14.91 percent. Standard equipment for this 31,100-lb. tractor included dual 24.5-32-inch tires. Additional front and rear ballast gave a total test weight of 33,970 lbs. Repairs and adjustments required during 33 ½ hours of operating time consisted of replacing a single gasket.

Nebraska Test Data

Model: Ford FW-40 Diesel

Test No. 1290

Date Tested: October 10 to October 16, 1978

Weighing 30,630 lbs., the FW-40 was equipped with dual 24.5-32 tires. Additional front and rear ballast gave a total test weight of 32,950 lbs. A selective gear fixed-ratio transmission was used—its 20 forward speeds ranged from 2.2 to 21.8 mph. Using 10th gear, the two-hour drawbar run at 227.48 maximum available hp witnessed a pull of 12,897 lbs. at 6.61 mph, slippage of 3.77 percent, and an economy of 13.83 hp-hours per gallon. By comparison, the 10-hour run at 75 percent pull noted an economy figure of 12.84 under a load of 194.11 drawbar hp . Also recorded was a pull of 10,174 lbs. at 7.15 mph and 3.25 percent slippage. Using third gear, a maximum drawbar pull of 28,245 lbs. was recorded at 2.65 mph. Slippage in this instance totaled 14.99 percent. No repairs or adjustments were required during 29-½ hours of operating time. The FW-40 was equipped with a Cummins V-8 diesel engine. Rated at 2,600 rpm, it carried a 5.5 x 4.75-inch bore and stroke for a 903-cubic inch displacement. No brake hp tests were run on this tractor.

Nebraska Test Data

Model: Ford FW-20 Diesel

Test No. 1291

Date Tested: October 5 to October 12, 1978

No PTO shaft was provided on this tractor and no brake hp tests were run. The FW-20 was equipped with a Cummins V-8 diesel engine. Its 4.625 x 4.125-inch bore and stroke gave a 555-cubic inch displacement. Rated speed was 2,850 rpm. A selective gear fixed-ratio transmission was featured. Its 20 forward speeds ranged from 2.0 to 20.3 mph. Standard equipment of this 29,615-lb. tractor also included dual 23.1-30-inch tires. Additional front ballast gave a total test weight of 31,000 lbs. Using 10th gear, the two-hour economy test at 150.51 maximum available drawbar hp indicated a pull of 9,157 lbs. at 6.16 mph. Slippage totaled 2.35 percent, and fuel economy was 12.12 hp-hours per gallon. The 10-hour run at 75 percent pull indicated 11.69 hp-hours per gallon under a load of 125.47 drawbar hp. Also recorded was a pull of 7,131 lbs. at 6.6 mph and slippage totaling 1.8 percent. Of further interest, the FW-20 made a low-gear maximum pull of 27,155 lbs. at 1.87 mph. Slippage totaled 14.78 percent. No repairs or adjustments were required during 30 hours of operating time.

Four Drive Tractor Company

BIG RAPIDS, MICHIGAN

John Fitch developed a unique four-wheel-drive tractor by 1913 and organized a company at Ludington, Michigan to manufacture it. The firm was incorporated in 1915, and about that time, moved to Big Rapids, Michigan.

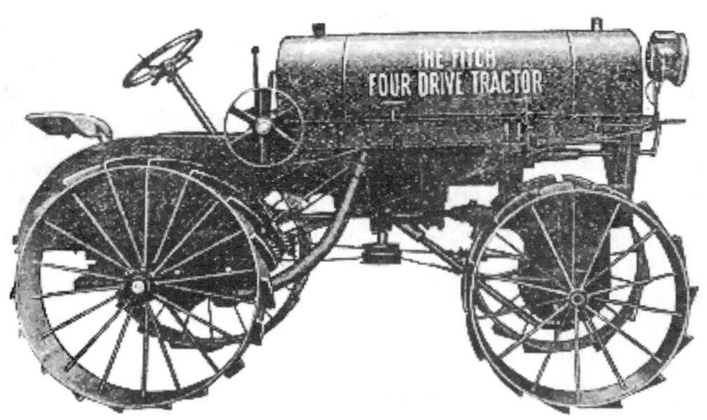

Four-wheel-drive 20-30 tractor

Initially the company built only a 20-30 model. Equipped with a four-cylinder engine, the 20-30 weighed 3,000 lbs.

COLLECTOR VALUES	1	2	3	4
20-30	$17,000	$10,000	$6,500	$4,000

By 1918 the Fitch Four-Drive had undergone obvious changes. Included in the line was the 15-30 tractor. This model was equipped with a Waukesha four-cylinder engine with a 4-1/4 x 5-3/4-inch bore and stroke. Priced at $2,000, the 15-30 weighed 5,100 lbs.

The Fitch Four-Drive 20-35 saw little change after about 1918 until production ended in 1930. It featured a Climax four-cylinder engine with a 5 x 6-1/2-inch bore and stroke. The standard tractor weighed 6,000 lbs., but the Model D was also available with special tamping grousers for packing and rolling. Thus equipped, the 20-35 weighed 10,000 lbs. It could also be furnished with hard rubber tires if so desired.

Fitch Four-Drive 15-30 tractor

Fitch Four-Drive 20-35 tractor

Model E 15-30 Cat tractor

The Model E, 15-30 Cat tractor first appeared about 1927, and was marketed until the company left the tractor business about 1930. This model was tested at Nebraska in 1929. The 15-30 Cat used a Waukesha four-cylinder engine with a 4-3/8 x 5-3/4-inch bore and stroke. Weighing 5,800 lbs., it was capable of speeds up to 6 mph. By the late 1920s all Fitch tractors were equipped with ball and roller bearings, as well as Alemite lubrication.

Four-Wheel Tractor Company

CLINTONVILLE, WISCONSIN

This firm was incorporated in 1916 by D. S. Stewart, Charles Topp, and others. In 1917 the company name was changed to Topp-Stewart Tractor Company. The reader is directed to the latter heading.

Four Wheel Traction Company

NEW YORK, NEW YORK

Super 4 Drive trademark

Aside from a 1930 trademark application, little is known about the Four-Wheel Traction Company. The company claimed first use of its "Super 4 Drive" trademark on July 3, 1930.

Fox River Tractor Company

APPLETON, WISCONSIN

20-40 Fox tractor

In 1919 the Fox River Tractor Co. was incorporated at Appleton. Ostensibly the first product was to be the 20-40 Fox tractor. This four-cylinder design carried a 5-1/2 x 7-1/2-inch bore and stroke. The postwar depression and intense competition within the tractor industry caused the company to change its direction from tractor production to forage harvesting machines. Less than a dozen Fox tractors were built.

Franklin Tractor Company

GREENVILLE, OHIO

Organized in 1919, Franklin Tractor Co. offered two different crawler models.

Franklin 15-30 and 18-30 crawlers

The Franklin 15-30 shown here was a small 5,500-lb. machine equipped with an Erd four-cylinder engine with a 4-1/4 x 6-inch bore and stroke. The larger 18-30 crawler weighed 8,000 lbs. and was powered by a Climax four-cylinder, 5 x 6-1/2-inch engine.

Franklin crawler with front-mounted winch system

Franklin Tractor Co. offered several variations of its crawler tractors, including this one with a front-mounted winch system. The company applied for a trademark in February 1920 and only remained in business for a short time. It apparently entered some type of merger with the Bullock Tractor Company of Chicago.

Franks Tractor Cultivator Company

OWENSBORO, KENTUCKY

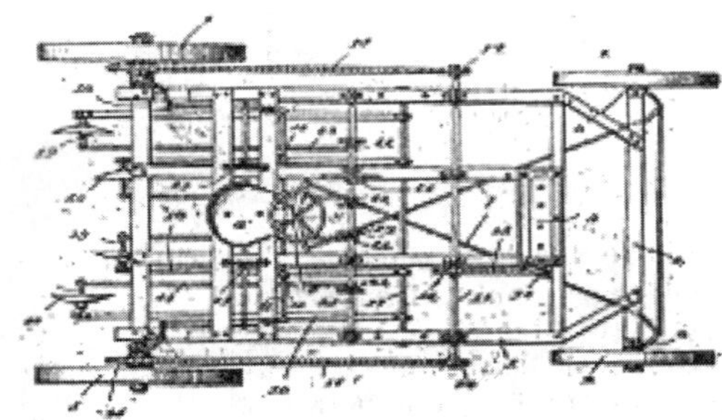

Franks Tractor Cultivator

Numerous inventors developed motor cultivators in the 1915 through 1925 period. Few of them were successful, and all of them disappeared with the coming of the row-crop tractors. Franks was organized in 1917 to build this machine, but aside from a few articles announcing the machine, little more is known of either the tractor or the company. Patent No. 1,174,842 was issued for this design.

Franks Welding Service

ESCONDIDO, CALIFORNIA

This company was listed as a garden tractor manufacturer in 1948, but no other information has been found.

Frazer Farm Equipment Corporation

YORK, PENNSYLVANIA

Frazer Farm Equipment tractor

For 1948 Frazer Farm Equipment was offering this small tractor capable of pulling one 12-inch plow. Power was furnished by a Simar-Swiss single-cylinder engine with a 3 x 3-1/4-inch bore and stroke. It featured six forward speeds ranging up to 4.78 mph in high gear. Production lasted for only a few seasons.

Frazer Rototiller B1-6

The Frazer Rototiller B1-6 shown here was very popular among market gardeners. It used the company's own two-cycle B1-6 engine with a 3 x 3-1/4-inch bore and stroke. By 1953 the Rototiller is listed with Frazer Farm Equipment Company at Auburn, Indiana.

COLLECTOR VALUES	1	2	3	4
FRAZER ROTOTILLER B1-6	$600	$400	$200	$100

C.E. Freeman Tractor Company

LITTLE ROCK, ARKANSAS

This firm was incorporated for $25,000 in 1919. Beyond this bit of trade information, no other data has been located.

Frick Company

WAYNESBORO, PENNSYLVANIA

Frick Company was one of the so-called old-line thresher manufacturers. Established in 1853, the company had roots back to 1843 when George Frick built his first grain thresher. Frick began selling steam engines in the 1870s and entered the refrigerating machine business in 1882.

The company announced in early 1913 that it would be selling the tractors produced by Ohio Tractor Company at Columbus, Ohio. This continued for a time, but by 1917 the company had perfected its own tractor design. Production of farm tractors continued until about 1928.

The Frick 12-20 first emerged in 1918 as the 12-25. It was equipped with an Erd four-cylinder engine with a 4 x 6-inch bore and stroke. After its Nebraska Test in 1920, the 12-25 was re-rated downward as the 12-20 tractor. Weighing 5,800 lbs., the 12-20 was built over 7-inch structural steel channels. Production continued until about 1928.

Nebraska Test Data

Model: Frick Model A 12-20

Test No. 47

Date Tested: August 2 to August 10, 1920

The Frick Model A entered Test No. 47 with a nominal manufacturer's rating of 25 belt hp. Subsequent to this test, the rating was lowered by 5 hp to stay within the test results. In the official test scores, 22.4 brake hp was developed on the rated load test. Fuel economy was slightly lower for the 12-20 than for its larger brother noted in Test No. 46, coming to 6.69 hp-hours per gallon. Fuel consumption totaled 3.35 gallons per hour (gph) of kerosene. This fuel was used throughout the tests. A maximum of 22.31 brake hp was produced with only a slight increase in fuel consumption. Using low gear, a maximum of 14.37 drawbar hp was recorded, with a pull of 2,340 lbs. An Erd motor was featured in the 12-20 and it carried a 4 x 6-inch bore and stroke with a rated speed of 900 rpm. Like the larger 15-28, it was of vertical, four-cylinder, valve-in-head design. Two forward speeds of 2.3 and 3.8 mph were provided. Regular equipment included a Kingston Model L magneto and a Kingston carburetor.

COLLECTOR VALUES	1	2	3	4
12-20	$12,000	$9,000	$6,500	$3,500

Frick Model A 12-20

Frick Model C 15-28 tractor

Weighing 6,100 lbs., the Frick 15-28 tractor made its first appearance about 1919. This model was powered by a Beaver four-cylinder engine with a 4-3/4 x 6 -inch bore and stroke. It was rated at 900 rpm. As with the 12-20, production ended about 1928.

Nebraska Test Data

Model: Frick Model C 15-28
Test No. 46
Date Tested: August 2 to August 6, 1920

A Beaver four-cylinder vertical, valve-in-head engine was featured in the Frick 15-28 tractor. Using a 4-3/4 x 6-inch bore and stroke, it was rated at 900 rpm. Two forward speeds of 2.3 and 3.8 mph were provided, and shipping weight was 6,100 lbs. During the 32-hour test, minor repairs and adjustments were made. In addition, the differential spider gear broke and was replaced without further incident. Kerosene was used for fuel throughout the tests except for a second run of the maximum brake hp test. Exactly 30 hp was recorded, with fuel consumption of 3.91 gph and a fuel economy of 7.66 hp-hours per gallon. The same test, using kerosene, revealed 29.72 hp with consumption totaling 5.21 gph and a fuel economy of 5.71 hp-hours per gallon. Using low gear, a maximum drawbar pull of 3,264 lbs. was achieved, resulting in 19.48 drawbar hp. The 15-28 managed the rated drawbar test at 15.24 hp without difficulty. Regular equipment included a Dixie Model 46 magneto and a Bennett Model J carburetor.

COLLECTOR VALUES	1	2	3	4
15-28	$12,000	$9,000	$6,500	$3,500

Friday Tractor Company

HARTFORD, MICHIGAN

Beginning about 1947 the Friday O-48 Orchard tractor appeared, and remained on the market into the late 1950s. It featured a Chrysler Industrial IND-5 six-cylinder engine with a 3-1/4 x 4- 3/8-inch bore and stroke for a displacement of 217.7-cubic inches. It featured nine forward speeds ranging from 1.9 to 32.4 mph. The company is listed as building the O-48 tractor as late as 1957.

Friday O-48 Orchard tractor

COLLECTOR VALUES	1	2	3	4
O-48	$5,000	$3,000	$1,000	$500

Fulton Mfg. Company

ST. LOUIS, MISSOURI

Do-More garden tractor No. 36CF

Do-More garden tractor No. 50

By 1946 Fulton was building its Do-More garden tractor. By 1950 the line expanded to include the No. 36CF and the Fulton No. 50. The 36CF was equipped with a Wisconsin ABN single-cylinder engine with a 2-1/2 x 2-3/4-inch bore and stroke, and rated at 3.7 hp. The smaller No. 50 was built with a Briggs & Stratton Model N engine. The latter had a 2-inch bore and stroke and was rated at 1.68 continuous hp. Production continued at least into the early 1950s.

COLLECTOR VALUES	1	2	3	4
BOTH MODELS	$650	$500	$350	$150

Fulton Tractor Company

ANDERSON, INDIANA

Fulton was incorporated in 1918 with a maximum capitalization of $1 million. It was part of the Madison Motors Corporation, a major player in the engine and tractor business at that time. Aside from a trade note announcing the incorporation of the company, no further data has been found.

FWD Wagner Inc.

PORTLAND, OREGON

FWD Wagner

Advertising of the early 1960s relates that the FWD Wagner was the "first successful all wheel drive agricultural tractor." Wagner Tractor Company was the original firm, and was later acquired by FWD Corporation of Clintonville, Wisconsin. The latter was eminently successful in four-wheel-drive truck designs going back to 1909.

[Throughout this section, assume that gasoline was used for fuel unless another fuel source was indicated.]

Gaar, Scott & Company

RICHMOND, INDIANA

Gaar-Scott 40-70

Gaar-Scott first announced in 1909 that it was planning to enter the tractor business. Early in 1911 the company's first tractor appeared, the Gaar-Scott 40-70. Weighing 28,000 lbs., this $3,900 tractor featured a four-cylinder engine with a 7-3/4 x 10-inch bore and stroke. Gaar-Scott was an old company that went back to 1849 as a thresher manufacturer. The saga of the Gaar-Scott tractor lasted but a few months after its introduction. Late in 1911 the company was acquired by M. Rumely Company, LaPorte, Indiana. Rumely sold the few remaining tractors as the Gaar-Scott TigerPull. Once the parts inventory was used, production ended. Only one specimen is known to exist today.

William Galloway Company

WATERLOO, IOWA

William Galloway Company was incorporated at Waterloo, Iowa, in 1906. From the beginning, the Galloway line included gasoline engines as part of an extensive offering of farm equipment. In 1916 the Galloway Farmobile tractor appeared, continuing in production until 1919. The company sought bankruptcy protection in 1920 and reemerged as The Galloway Company Inc. under different management that did not include William Galloway. In 1927 the latter began business again as William Galloway & Sons, and remained in the farm equipment business for some years after. Mr. Galloway died in 1952.

Farmobile tractor

The Farmobile tractor was first marketed in 1916. Rated at 12 drawbar and 20 belt hp, it used a four-cylinder engine with a 4-1/2 x 5-inch bore and stroke. Galloway made a deal with Great Britain after World War I to sell a substantial number of tractors in the British Isles. History has it that many of the tractors never left the Port of New Orleans where they were to be loaded onto ships for export. Legend has it that Galloway didn't get paid, and as a result, went into bankruptcy. Various factors contributed to Galloway's failure, with the tractor being one of several causes.

COLLECTOR VALUES	1	2	3	4
FARMOBILE (1916)	$15,000	$11,000	$8,000	$6,000

Gamble-Skogmo, Inc.

MINNEAPOLIS, MINNESOTA

See: Cockshutt Farm Equipment Company Ltd.

In June 1930 the Cockshutt 30 was tested at Nebraska (Test No. 382). Subsequently this tractor was sold in the United States as the Co-op E-3 tractor or as the Farmcrest sold by the Gamble Stores. Gamble apparently began selling the Farmcrest in 1948, continuing into the early 1950s. This model featured a Buda four-cylinder engine with a 3-7/16 x 4-1/8-inch bore and stroke. Capable of about 30 belt hp, it also featured a four-speed transmission, 3500 psi hydraulics, and a live PTO shaft.

COLLECTOR VALUES	1	2	3	4
FARMCREST/E-3	$2,500	$1,700	$800	$200

The Gamer Company

FORT WORTH, TEXAS

In 1913 the Gamer tractor was announced. Designed especially for grubbing and breaking land in one operation, this huge tractor was built around a four-cylinder engine with a 10 x 12-inch bore and stroke. The crankshaft was 3-1/2-inches in diameter. The tractor frame consisted of two 12-inch beams weighing 40 lbs. per foot. Despite the potential for this tractor, nothing more has been found subsequent to its initial announcement.

Garden-All Tractor Inc.

LIBERTY, INDIANA

Production of the Cultivette tractors apparently began about 1947 and continued at least into the mid-1950s.

Cultivette D garden tractors

Co-op E3

Gamer tractor

Cultivette E garden tractors

The Cultivette D (above left) and the Cultivette E (above right) were essentially the same garden tractor. Both used a Briggs & Stratton NPR-6 engine with a 2-inch bore stroke. However, the "D" had smaller physical dimensions and was set up for a 14- to 18-inch wheel tread, while the "E" was capable of an 18- to 28-inch wheel tread.

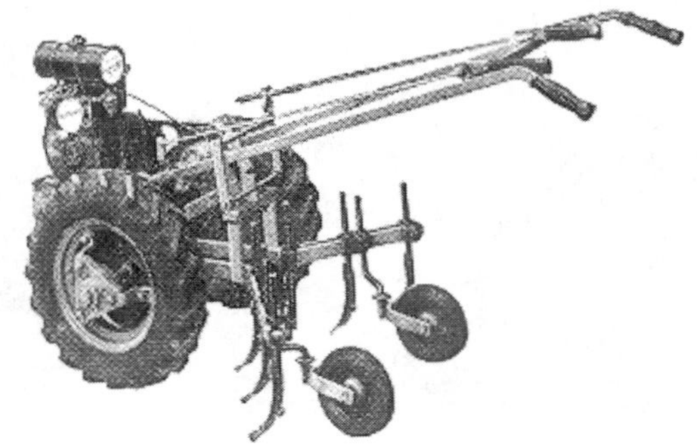

Cultivette S garden tractor

Although the Cultivette S garden tractor used the same Briggs & Stratton engine as the D and E models, the "S" used larger tires and was of a somewhat different design. The heavier frame gave it a weight of 277 lbs., compared to 186 lbs. for the two smaller models.

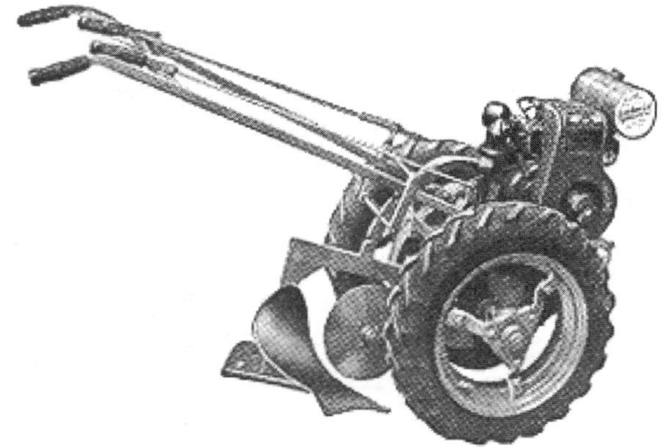

Garden-All S2, S3 and S5 garden tractors

The Garden-All S2 and S3 tractors were of similar appearance. The S2 (shown above) carried a Clinton 1100 engine with a 2-3/8 x 1-7/8-inch bore and stroke for about 3 hp. This model weighed 277 lbs. The S3 model used a Wisconsin ABN engine of 4.6 hp. Garden-All also built an S5 garden tractor. This model used a Wisconsin AKS engine with a 2-7/8 x 2-3/4-inch bore and stroke, for 5 hp.

Gard'n Mast'r garden tractor

Gard'n Mast'r garden tractors featured a Briggs & Stratton Model 23 engine with 8-1/4 hp. It used a 3 x 3-1/4-inch bore and stroke. This model was capable of pulling one 10-inch plow, and various other attachments were also available. Total weight of this unit was 810 lbs.

COLLECTOR VALUES	1	2	3	4
ALL MODELS	$650	$500	$350	$150

Garden Equipment Company

PORTLAND, OREGON

This firm is listed as a manufacturer of garden tractors in 1953, but no further information has been found.

Garden King Tractor Sales

STRATFORD, CONNECTICUT

Garden King GRT-3 tractor

The Garden King GRT-3 tractor appeared in the late 1940s. This unit was powered by a Wisconsin AB-3 single-cylinder, 3 hp engine. Aside from a 1948 trade listing, little else has been found on the Garden King line.

COLLECTOR VALUES	1	2	3	4
GRT-3	$650	$500	$350	$150

Garden Tractor & Equipment Company

WINDSOR, ONTARIO

This firm is first listed in 1946 offering the Empire garden tractor. It was built in 3 hp and 6 hp models, both using a Briggs & Stratton engine. No photographs of this unit have been located.

COLLECTOR VALUES	1	2	3	4
EMPIRE GARDEN TRACTORS	$650	$500	$350	$150

Garden Tractor Sales & Service

LOS ANGELES, CALIFORNIA

This company is listed as a garden tractor manufacturer in 1953, but no other information has been found.

Garvar Tractor Corporation

NEW YORK, NEW YORK

Garver Model L-20

The Garvar Model L-20 made its first appearance in the early 1950s, probably about 1952. This 13 hp tractor was equipped with a Wisconsin Model TF two-cylinder engine with a 3-1/4-inch bore and stroke. Weighing 1,200 lbs., the L-20 was available with various options, including a rear PTO shaft. Aside from a few 1953 trade references, little else is known of this company.

Gas Traction Company

MINNEAPOLIS, MINNESOTA

See: Emerson-Brantingham

The Big Four tractor of Gas Traction Company owed its beginnings to D. M. Hartsough. In 1899 he built a

Big 4 "30"

small one-cylinder tractor of 8 hp, but soon abandoned this design. The following year he built a 15 hp model. Convinced of the possibilities for tractor power, Hartsough built a two-cylinder model in 1901. During 1904 a fourth model was built using a four-cylinder engine with a 4 x 5-inch bore and stroke. This was a dramatic departure in tractor design and was the first successful tractor to be built with a four-cylinder engine.

Hartsough gained the attention of Patrick J. Lyons in 1906, and the Transit Thresher Company was organized to build the tractor. In 1908 the company name was changed to Gas Traction Company.

Emerson-Brantingham Company, Rockford, Illinois, bought out Gas Traction Company in 1912 and continued Big 4 models for several years.

Gas Traction Engine

Transit Thresher Company operated from 1906 to 1908. Shown here is one of the early models of the Gas Traction Engine. The plow guide eased the work of the operator, but this model had only inside wheel guards, and no fenders. Apparently the first production model was built in 1905. The early models were rated at 25 drawbar and 60 belt hp. The four-cylinder engine carried a 6 x 8-inch bore and stroke.

Big 4

By 1910 Gas Traction Company had billed its tractor as the Big 4. Also, the engine was given a power boost by increasing the bore to 6-1/2 inches from the earlier 6-inch bore. The cylinders were cast singly, and mounted to a massive crankcase. The huge rear wheels were 96-inches in diameter with a 24-inch face.

Sometime during 1910 the Big 4 "30" gained a new look with a modified radiator and new fenders. The famous Big 4 trademark, consisting of the number "4" within a circle was first used in December 1910. By this time the company billed itself as the "first and largest builders of four-cylinder farm tractors." James J. Hill, the famous railroad magnate, bought a Big 4 in 1910. The company noted this in its advertising, saying "...on July 23rd (1910) Gas Traction Engine Number 452 was delivered to the James J. Hill Farm at Northcote, Minnesota."

COLLECTOR VALUES	1	2	3	4
BIG 4 "30"	$55,000	$40,000	$25,000	–

Gasoline Thresher & Plow Company

STERLING, KANSAS

Hockett tractor

In 1896 J. A. Hockett and others announced its "new gasoline traction engine." The tractor shown here used a two-cylinder tandem engine. According to magazine articles of the day, the machine was built at St. Louis, although the company had its offices in Sterling, Kansas. Few details of the "Hockett" tractor remain. It survived for only a short time, and there are no indications that anything more than a few prototypes were built. The Hockett is significant in that it was the first "gasoline traction engine" to be advertised for sale in the trade papers of the day.

Gasport Motor Company

GASPORT, NEW YORK

Gasport tractor

By 1911 the Gasport tractor had been developed. Although built especially for orchard work, it was also suitable for other tractor uses. The Gasport used a two-cylinder vertical engine of four-cycle design, and with a 6 x 8-inch bore and stroke. This gave the Gasport about 25 belt hp. An interesting feature of the Gasport was the three-speed transmission giving a speed range of 1-1/2 to 3-1/2 mph. It was priced at $1,500. The company remained in business only a short time and few references can be found after the initial 1911 announcement.

Gehl Bros. Mfg. Company

WEST BEND, WISCONSIN

Gehl 12-25 tractor

Gehl introduced its 12-25 tractor in 1916, continuing with it until 1918. This model used a single drive drum for traction. Initially priced at $1,150 it was equipped with a Waukesha four-cylinder engine with a 4-1/2 x 6-3/4-inch bore and stroke. For 1919 the 12-25 was re-rated as a 15-30 model, although it used the same engine as before, and even retained the same rated speed of 900 rpm. After 1919 the Gehl tractor disappeared from the trade listings.

Geiser Mfg. Company

WAYNESBORO, PENNSYLVANIA

Geiser 20-25 tractor

Peter Geiser began building grain threshers in 1850 and organized Geiser Company in 1855. Geiser Mfg. Co. was incorporated in 1869, and the company built its first steam

GMC Samson Sieve-Grip tractor

traction engine in 1881. In 1909 the company announced it was introducing a gasoline tractor and it emerged the following year. This model was a 20 (drawbar) hp machine that used a four-cylinder engine with a 7-inch bore and stroke. Induced draft cooling was featured. The engine exhaust was directed upward into the stack, creating an induced draft over the cooling tubes within the radiator.

Emerson-Brantingham Company of Rockford, Illinois, bought out Geiser in 1912. E-B continued building the Geiser tractor for about one more year until the parts inventory was depleted.

COLLECTOR VALUES	1	2	3	4
20-25 HP (1912)	$40,000	$30,000	$10,000	$5,000

GI garden tractor

General Implement Corporation

CLEVELAND, OHIO

In the 1920s there was a "General" garden tractor built in Cleveland by General Implement. All values below are for this model only. In 1947 the GI garden tractor took the form shown here. It was equipped with a Wisconsin air-cooled engine of 2-1/2 x 2-3/4-inch bore and stroke, and capable of 3 hp. In 1948 the GI 3 hp model took on a slightly different appearance, but still used the same Wisconsin engine. In addition, it could be furnished with a Gladden engine of the same size. Curiously, the 1948 line also included the GI 4 hp model, but it used the same Wisconsin 2-1/2 x 2-3/4 engine as the 3-hp size.

COLLECTOR VALUES	1	2	3	4
GENERAL (1920S)	$500	$350	$200	$100

General Motors Corporation

PONTIAC, MICHIGAN

By 1917 Henry Ford had nearly cornered the automobile market with the inimitable Model T. Then in 1918 Ford introduced his Fordson tractor which became an instant success. Bill Durant, chairman of General Motors Corporation was determined to meet this latest Ford challenge with a GMC tractor.

Samson Tractor Works of Stockton, California, was purchased and GMC moved the operation to a new plant at Janesville, Wisconsin. Initially GMC continued building the Samson Sieve-Grip tractor, but in December 1918 GMC announced its Samson Model M, priced at only $650. Early in 1919 the Samson Model A was announced, but this larger three-plow tractor never went into production.

During January 1919 GMC announced its Model D Iron Horse. GMC had bought out the rights to the Jim Dandy (later Jerry) motor cultivator, modified its design, and produced the Model D. However, this model was poorly designed and was too limited in its versatility to become popular with farmers. Thus, the Iron Horse did little more than incur huge losses.

Financial losses, an intensely competitive tractor market, and changes in corporate direction were among the reasons that GMC left the tractor market in 1922. The Janesville plant was then converted into a Chevrolet assembly operation.

The GMC Samson Sieve-Grip tractor had originally been developed by Samson Tractor Works, Stockton, California. GMC bought out Samson in early 1918 and set up a tractor factory at Janesville, Wisconsin. The original Samson design was modified to include a GM-built four-cylinder engine with a 4-3/4 x 6-inch bore and stroke. It was capable of 12 drawbar and 25 belt hp. The Samson Sieve-Grip was built into 1919.

Samson Model M tractor

General Motors announced the Samson Model M tractor in December 1918. This tractor used a 276-cid, four-cylinder Northway engine with a 4 x 5-1/2-inch bore and stroke. Priced at $650, the Model M was complete with fenders, governor, belt pulley, and other items not furnished as regular equipment on the competing Fordson. Production of the Model M continued until 1922 when General Motors left the tractor business. The tractor was marketed by Samson Tractor Company, Janesville, Wisconsin.

Nebraska Test Data

Model: Samson Model M

Test No. 27

Date Tested: June 19 to June 30, 1920

The ever-popular Kingston carburetor was featured as standard equipment on Samson Model M tractors, specifically the Model L-2. At least for the purposes of Nebraska Test No. 27, a Simms K4 magneto was also furnished as standard equipment. Rated at 1,100 rpm, the Model M carried a four-cylinder, vertical, L-head engine with a 4 x 5-1/2-inch bore and stroke. Rated speeds were 2.3 mph in low gear and 3.19 mph in high. Total weight of the Model M was 3,300 lbs. Test No. 27 is the first to indicate the use of an air cleaner. A note in the final report states that "A new air washer with an improved style of filler opening was put on to replace the washer first installed which could not be filled with the engine running under load." Slightly over 11-1/2 maximum drawbar hp was recorded, with drawbar pull coming to 1,670 lbs. at a speed of 2.6 mph. More than 19 brake hp was noted on the maximum load test, with fuel consumption totaling 2.79 gallons of kerosene per hour or an economy rating of 6.94 hp-hours per gallon. Except for replacing the air washer unit, few repairs or adjustments were necessary.

COLLECTOR VALUES	1	2	3	4
SAMSON M	$5,000	$4,000	$2,000	$1,000

Samson Model D Iron Horse

In January 1919 General Motors decided to enter the motor cultivator business, doing so with its Model D Samson Iron Horse. This design originated with the Jerry motor cultivator. The hastily contrived Model D was steered somewhat like a crawler tractor—or more accurately, like today's skid-steer loaders. Belts and pulleys were used on each side of the tractor. Weighing 1,900 lbs. the Iron Horse was equipped with a Chevrolet four-cylinder 3-11/16 x 4-inch engine. It sold for $450.

General Ordnance Company

CEDAR RAPIDS, IOWA

G-O tractor

In May 1919 General Ordnance Co., with offices in New York City, bought out the bankrupt Denning Tractor Company at Cedar Rapids, Iowa. For a few months General Ordnance sold a slightly modified version of the Denning under the National Tractor trademark. By early 1920 the G-O tractor appeared. Two models were offered, the 12-22 and the 14-28. The smaller one used a four-cylinder engine with a 4-1/4 x 5-3/4-inch bore and stroke. This 4,200 pound tractor listed at $1,375. The 14-28 used a four-cylinder 4-1/2 x 5-3/4-inch engine, listed at $1,485, and weighed 4,300 lbs. The G-O was built for only a short time. Advertisements for this tractor disappeared by late 1920. Six specimens are known to exist today.

COLLECTOR VALUES	1	2	3	4
G-O (1919)	$17,000	$12,500	$8,000	$3,500

General Tractor Company

CLEVELAND, OHIO

General 10-12 tractor

The General 10-12 tractor first appeared about 1927. It was of the front-wheel-drive or "universal" design. Power was derived from the company's own two-cylinder engine with a 3-1/2 x 5-1/4-inch bore and stroke. It was also equipped with the company's own planetary transmission that offered speeds from 1 to 3 mph. Weighing 1,600 lbs., the 10-12 sold for $550. About 1927 the 10-12 became known as the 9-12 Model D. After 1932 the 9-12 disappeared from the trade listings. For some years after, repairs were available from Cleveland Tractor Company, Cleveland, Ohio.

COLLECTOR VALUES	1	2	3	4
10-12	$4,000	$3,000	$2,000	$900

General Tractor Company

SEATTLE, WASHINGTON

WESTRAK

WESTRAK trademark

Aside from a trademark application, no other information has been found on the WESTRAK design, or General Tractor Co. The mark was first used in April 1948.

General Tractors Inc.

CHICAGO, ILLINOIS

General Tractors 20-12

See: Monarch Tractor Company

Monarch Tractor Company began business at Watertown, Wisconsin, in 1913. In 1919 the company reorganized and moved to Chicago, Illinois, and operated under the title of General Tractors Inc. The company moved to Springfield, Illinois, in 1925 and organized as Monarch Tractor Company. During the time in Chicago, General built the Model M 9-16 crawler, as well as a 20-12 model and the popular Model N 30-18 crawler. Curiously, when the Model N was tested at Nebraska in 1920 (Test No. 56), the company was listed in the test report at Monarch Tractors Inc., Watertown, Wisconsin. The comings and goings of Monarch in the 1919-1925 period are not well documented, but it is a certainty that the firm moved to Springfield in 1925. Allis-Chalmers bought out Monarch in February 1928.

Genesee Tractor Company

HILTON, NEW YORK

Genesee Tractor Company was organized and incorporated in 1915, but no further information has been found.

Geneva Tractor Company

GENEVA, OHIO

ADAPTO-TRACTOR

Adapt-O-Tractor trademark

Geneva Tractor Co. was organized by Frank E. Jacobs in 1917. By the following year the company had adopted the Adapt-O-Tractor trademark. This covered a conversion unit whereby an automobile could be converted into a tractor.

George Tractor Division

MEMPHIS, TENNESSEE

George Garden Tractor

In 1948 the George Tractor Division offered its George Garden Tractor. This small 250-pound unit was available with numerous attachments, including the sickle mower shown here. Power was furnished by a single-cylinder, 2-1/2-hp Ultimotor engine.

COLLECTOR VALUES	1	2	3	4
GEORGE GARDEN TRACTOR	$350	$225	$125	$50

GFH Corporation

LOCATION UNKNOWN

In 1921 GFH Corporation filed its "Jerry" trademark application for "gas, gasoline, oil, and steam tractors." The company claimed to have first used this mark in May 1920. Aside from this application, no further information has appeared on the company or its tractors.

GFH Corporation "Jerry" trademark

Giant Gas Tractor Mfg. Company

MINNEAPOLIS, MINNESOTA

H. H. Kryger and others organized the Giant Gas Tractor Mfg. Co. in 1914. Some of their advertising noted that the company was "the mfgr's. of the Kryger gas tractor and Kryger rotary harrow and seeder combined; the best gas tractor on the market; sells on its own merits." The company was listed in the Minneapolis city directories until 1917. Further information has not been found.

Gibson Mfg. Corporation

LONGMONT, COLORADO

Gibson trademark

In 1949 Gibson filed a trademark application for its tractors and farm implements. Curiously, the mark claims to have been first used in April 1943. However, the Gibson Model D tractor first appeared in the 1948 trade directories. It likely appeared sometime in 1947, or perhaps earlier.

The Gibson Model D tractor first appeared in the 1948 tractor directories, though it may have been in production as early as 1943. This model used a single-cylinder engine—a Wisconsin Model AEH with a 3 x 3-1/4-inch bore and stroke. It had three forward speeds of 2, 4, and 7 mph. The Model D was likely out of production by 1949.

COLLECTOR VALUES	1	2	3	4
GIBSON D	$2,000	$1,200	$500	$200

Gibson Model D tractor

Gibson Model H tractor

Weighing 4,100 lbs., the Model H was equipped with a Hercules IXB-3 four-cylinder engine with a 3-3/4 x 4-inch bore and stroke. This model was capable of about 23 belt hp. Production of the Model H continued until 1956. In 1957 the Gibson tractors were listed under Western American Industries of Longmont, Colorado.

Nebraska Test Data

Model: Gibson Model H

Test No. 407

Date Tested: May 2 to May 7, 1949

Advertised speeds of 2, 3.5, 5.1, and 14.7 mph were featured in the Gibson Model H tractor. Standard equipment also included 11-38-inch rear and 5.50-15-inch front tires. Bare weight was 4,079 lbs., to which was added 867 lbs. of weight per wheel for Tests F, G, and H. Third gear was chosen for Test H. At a rated load of 18.44 drawbar hp, a pull of 1,632 lbs. was recorded at 4.24 mph, along with a slippage of 5.16 percent. Economy was noted at 9.12 hp-hours per gallon. A maximum low-gear pull of 3,583 lbs. resulted from Test G. This tractor featured a Hercules IXB3, four-cylinder, L-head engine. Rated at 1,800 rpm, it carried a 3-3/4x4-inch bore and stroke. Also featured was a Delco-Remy electrical system and a Marvel-Schebler TSX388 carburetor. At a Test C operating maximum load of 23.32 belt hp, fuel economy rested at 10.17 hp-hours per gallon, with an identical economy figure resulting from the 22.12 rated hp load imposed by Test D. Routine inspection at the end of the test revealed small areas of bearing metal flaked from two connecting rod bearings. Otherwise, no repairs or adjustments were noted during 37 hours of engine operating time.

COLLECTOR VALUES	1	2	3	4
GIBSON H	$7,500	$6,200	$5,000	$1,500

Gibson Model I tractor

A Hercules six-cylinder engine was featured in the Gibson Model I tractor. It was rated at 1,800 rpm and used a 3-7/16 x 4-1/8-inch bore and stroke. This model was capable of nearly 40 belt hp. Production began about 1948 and continued until about 1956. No serial number lists or specific production data has been located for the Gibson tractor line.

Nebraska Test Data

Model: Gibson Model I

Test No. 408

Date Tested: May 8 to May 12, 1949

A Hercules six-cylinder L-head engine was featured in the Gibson Model I tractor. Rated at 1,800 rpm, it used a 3-7/16 x 4-1/8-inch bore and stroke. Also featured was a Delco-Remy electrical system, along with a Marvel-Schebler TSX389 carburetor. Tire equipment included 12-38-inch rear and 5.50-16-inch front rubber. Bare weight was 4,512 lbs. No repairs or adjustments were noted during 44 hours of engine running time. Test C at an operating maximum load of 39.5 belt hp yielded a fuel economy of 10.08 hp-hours per gallon. A nearly identical economy figure of 10.12 was derived from Test D under a rated belt load of 36.82 hp. Test G produced a low-gear maximum pull of 4,572 lbs. at 1.63 mph and slippage of 15.27 percent. Advertised speeds were identical to those of the Gibson Model H of Test No. 407. Third gear was chosen for Test H, and at a rated drawbar load of 29.12 hp, fuel economy came in at 8.98 hp-hours per gallon. Other Test H data included a pull of 2,682 lbs. at 4.07 mph with a slippage of 4.63 percent.

COLLECTOR VALUES	1	2	3	4
GIBSON I	$10,000	$8,500	$6,500	$3,000

Gile Tractor & Engine Company

LUDINGTON, MICHIGAN

Information on the Gile tractors is elusive, but production of the Gile tractors seems to have started in 1913, and ended by about 1920.

Gile Model L tractor

The Gile Model L, first built about 1913, was a simple three-wheel design. Rated at 10 drawbar and 20 belt hp, it used a Gile-built two-cylinder engine with a 5-1/2 x 6-1/2-inch bore and stroke.

COLLECTOR VALUES	1	2	3	4
MODEL L	$18,000	$14,000	$10,000	$6,000

Gile Model XL tractor

The Gile Model XL tractor was identical to the Model L except this one had two front wheels, compared to the single front wheel of the Model L. Gile built the Stinson tractor in 1917, and perhaps for a time after that.

Gile Model K crawler

The Gile Model K crawler tractor emerged in 1916. This tractor used a slightly larger engine than the Model L—two cylinders with a 6 x 6-1/2- inch bore and stroke. This gave the Model K a rating of 12 drawbar and 24 belt hp.

Gile Model Q 15-35 tractor

By 1918 the Gile Model Q,15-35 tractor had emerged. This one used a four-cylinder Gile engine with a 4-3/4 x 6-1/2-inch bore and stroke.

Gilson Mfg. Company

PORT WASHINGTON, WISCONSIN

See: Bolens Products Co.

Gilson Mfg. Company was established at Port Washington in the 1850s. In 1905 the company began building gasoline engines, and shortly after they established a factory at Guelph, Ontario. The Gilson tractors emerged from the Guelph factory in 1918. Offered in 11-20, 12-25, and 15-30 sizes, the Gilson was built for only a short time. H. W. Bolens, a Gilson stockholder, bought out the company in 1916 and began building the Gilson-Bolens garden tractors. Late-model Gilson garden tractors are generally valued at $100 in No. 2 condition.

Globe Tractor Company

STAMFORD, CONNECTICUT

Globe is listed as a tractor manufacturer in 1919 but no illustrations of its tractors have been found.

Goodfield Tractor Company

GOODFIELD, ILLINOIS

The 9-18 Goodfield tractor made its debut in 1918. This small tractor had three forward speeds ranging up to 7 mph. Power was derived from a Gray four-cylinder engine with a 3-3/4 x 5-inch bore and stroke. Apparently the Goodfield remained on the market until 1921 or 1922.

Goold, Shapley & Muir Company Ltd.

BRANTFORD, ONTARIO

Goold, Shapley & Muir began building gasoline engines in the early 1900s. In 1909 they entered the tractor business with two models, one of which was the 45-30. The company apparently left the tractor business about 1922.

Goold, Shapley & Muir 45-30 tractor

The Goold, Shapley & Muir 45-30 tractor featured a big two-cylinder opposed engine, also built by Goold, Shapley & Muir.

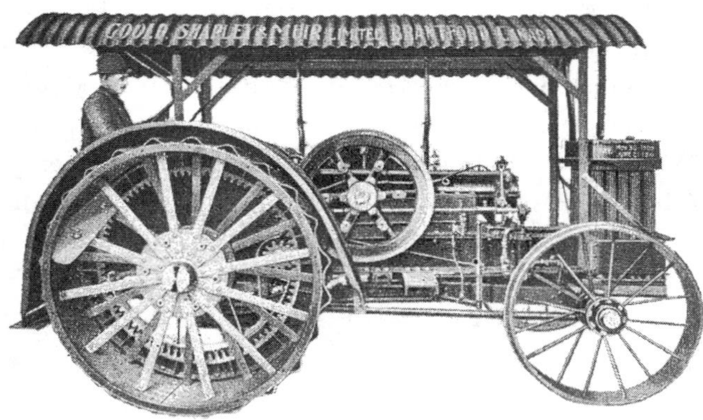

Goold, Shapley & Muir 28-20 tractor

The Goold, Shapley & Muir 28-20 tractor was a smaller version of the big 45-30. It also used a two-cylinder opposed engine of the company's own design and manufacture. These tractors had a special appeal to the Canadian market, but few, if any, were shipped to the United States.

A new tractor design emerged from Goold, Shapley & Muir in 1912. This new Ideal model was much more compact than its predecessors, and even went so far as to use a cellular radiator, much like automotive design. Few details of this model have been found.

Goold, Shapley & Muir Ideal tractor

Goold, Shapley & Muir Ideal Kerosene tractor

The Ideal Kerosene Tractor made its appearance in 1917. This one maintained the use of opposed cylinders, as in previous models. Instead of a cellular radiator, the tractor shown here used hopper-cooled cylinders. Advertising of the day noted "The Ideal Kerosene Tractor drew crowds of interested farmers at the Brandon Plowing Demonstration." This model was rated at 15 drawbar and 30 belt hp.

Goold, Shapley & Muir Beaver tractor

Goold, Shapeley and Muir 45-30 tractor

In the 1918-1921 period Goold, Shapley & Muir offered its 12-24 and 15-30 Beaver tractor. It was built with a Waukesha four-cylinder engine with a 4-1/2 x 6-3/4-inch bore and stroke. Operating weight was 5,800 lbs. The Beaver used a friction-drive transmission that offered seven speeds forward or reverse.

COLLECTOR VALUES	1	2	3	4
BEAVER	$20,000	$18,000	$12,000	$8,500

Graham-Paige Motors Corporation

DETROIT, MICHIGAN

The Graham-Bradley 32 hp tractor was developed in 1937 and was presented to the market in 1938. Advertising stated the tractor was "built by Graham, equipped by Bradley, and proved at Graham Farms." The 1940 trade listings showed the David Bradley Mfg. Works at Bradley, Illinois, as the manufacturer, although Graham actually built the tractor. (Bradley Works was owned and operated by Sears, Roebuck & Company).

With the onset of World War II, the company apparently ended production of the tractors in favor of military contracts. This likely happened when the company ceased automobile production in November 1941. In 1947, the Graham-Paige manufacturing entity was sold to Kaiser-Frazer. The Graham-Bradley tractors offered numerous features, including an adjustable drawbar, PTO shaft, belt pulley, power lift system, and a wide variety of David Bradley implements.

The 32 hp tractor was equipped with the company's own "103" six-cylinder engine. Rated at 1,500 rpm, it used a 3-1/4 x 4-3/8-inch bore and stroke.

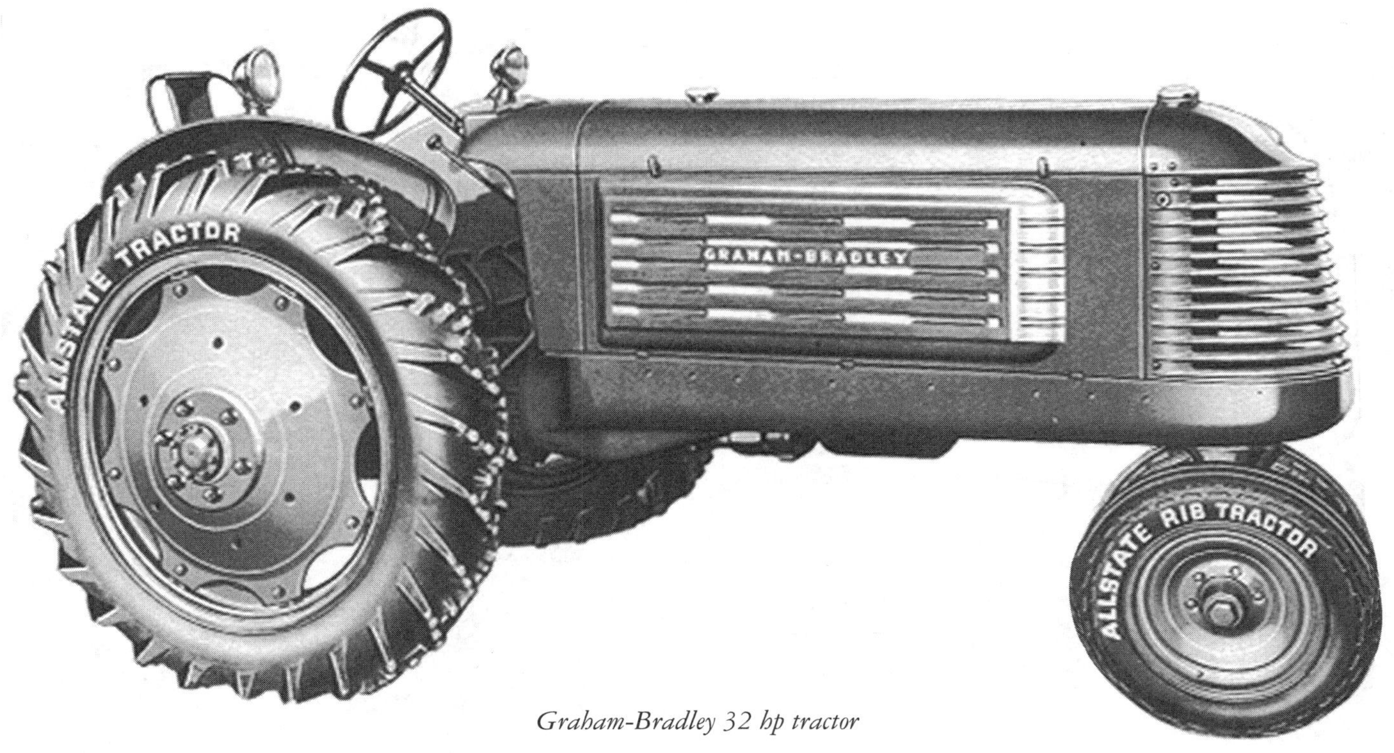

Graham-Bradley 32 hp tractor

Nebraska Test Data

Model: Graham-Bradly 32 hp

Test No. 296

Date Tested: April 6 to April 14, 1938

This 4,955-lb. unit featured four speeds of 2.77, 4.42, 5.67, and 19.8 mph. It was equipped with a Graham-Paige six-cylinder L-head engine. Rated at 1,500 rpm, the engine used a 3-1/4 x 4-3/8-inch bore and stroke. A Delco-Remy electrical system was featured, along with a Schebler TRX-15 carburetor, Handy governor, and a Donaldson air cleaner. No repairs or adjustments of consequence were noted during 43 hours of operating time. Test D manifested a fuel economy of 10.06 hp-hours per gallon while producing 27.06 rated brake hp. Test C for operating maximum load pegged the economy at a slightly improved 10.39 with a 28.27 hp output. Test H data indicated 20.03 rated drawbar hp, along with a 1,751 pull at 4.29 mph and slippage of 6.35 percent. Fuel economy was noted at 8.3 hp-hours per gallon. Using low gear, the Test C operating maximum load gave a pull of 3,013 lbs. with an output of 19.11 drawbar hp.

COLLECTOR VALUES	1	2	3	4
32 HP	$6,500	$5,000	$2,500	$1,200

Graham-Bradley Model 104

The Graham-Bradley Model 104 tractor was a standard-tread version of the 32 hp unit. Apparently, this model saw first light in 1939.

COLLECTOR VALUES	1	2	3	4
MODEL 104	$8,000	$6,500	$4,500	$2,000

Grain Belt Tractor Company

MINNEAPOLIS, MINNESOTA

Grain Belt Tractor Co. 15-35

Grain Belt Tractor Co. began operations at Minneapolis in 1917. Its first model was a 15-35. Weighing about 7,000 lbs., it used a Waukesha four-cylinder engine with a 4-3/4 x 6-3/4-inch bore and stroke. The 15-35 sold for $1,800. Grain Belt initially built its tractors in Minneapolis, but by mid-1917 moved the factory to St. Cloud, Minnesota. Production of this model continued until about 1919.

By October 1918, the Grain Belt Mfg. Company had been incorporated at Fargo, North Dakota. For reasons now unknown, the company left its Minnesota roots and reorganized at Fargo. The 15-35 continued for a time, but by 1920 the company was building the Grain Belt 18-36, a redesigned version of the 15-35 tractor. It used the same Waukesha engine. The company remained in the tractor business at least until 1921.

Gramont Traction Plow

Gramont Traction Plow Company

SPRINGFIELD, OHIO

In January 1913 the Gramont Traction Plow was announced. A. W. Grant and Paul A. Montanus developed this machine and equipped it with a 35-hp two-cylinder engine. The drive wheels were 2 feet wide and 5-1/2 feet high. Later that year the company announced a larger traction plow...it carried five bottoms and used a 50-hp engine. After the initial announcements, nothing more is known of the company or its traction plows.

Grand Forks Tractor Company

FARGO, NORTH DAKOTA

Grand Forks Tractor Co. was incorporated in 1918 for $250,000. Aside from this, no other information has been found.

Grand Haven Stamped Products Company

GRAND HAVEN, MICHIGAN

Beginning about 1947 Grand Haven offered several different models of garden tractors. The BC model was equipped with a Briggs & Stratton ZZ engine capable of about 6-1/2 belt hp, and the CC model was capable of 8 hp. These tractors were designed for truck gardeners and could be furnished with numerous attachments, including seeders, cultivators, and sprayers. Production apparently continued for only a short time.

COLLECTOR VALUES	1	2	3	4
GRAND HAVEN	$850	$450	$250	$150

S. A. Grant

THOMPSONVILLE, CONNECTICUT

Squirrel cage garden tractor

Grand Haven BC model

In 1915 S. A. Grant announced his squirrel cage garden tractor. The engine and gearing operated inside the large drive wheel, and a plow can be seen to the rear. Although it does not appear that this particular design made any great headway, various modifications of the squirrel cage design have been offered from time to time.

Gravely Motor Plow & Cultivator Company

DUNBAR, WEST VIRGINIA

Gravely Garden 2 garden tractor

About 1927 the Gravely Garden 2 garden tractor appeared. It used a single drive wheel and derived power from the company's own single cylinder engine. The latter used a 2-1/2 x 3-inch bore and stroke. Various attachments were available. Gravely continued to produce this same unit until about 1944.

Gravely Garden 2 redesigned

In about 1945 the Gravely Garden 2 was redesigned to include a somewhat larger engine of 3-1/4 x 3-1/2- inch bore and stroke. As with the earlier model, Gravely built its own engine. Although shown here with a sickle mower, the Gravely Garden 2 could be equipped with various attachments. Production of this model continued until 1947.

Gravely Model D garden tractor

In 1947 or 1948 Gravely introduced its Model D garden tractor. This one used the same basic engine as the earlier Gravely Garden 2 model, that is, with a 2-1/2 x 3-inch bore and stroke. In fact, the Model D was essentially the same as the early style that began production already in the 1920s.

COLLECTOR VALUES	1	2	3	4
MODEL D	$1,200	$800	$400	$200

Gravely Model L

The Gravely Model L was essentially the same as the Gravely Garden 2 that had emerged in 1945 or 1946. This style used a 3-1/4 x 3-1/2-inch engine that was capable of over 4 hp on a continuous basis. Production of the Model D and Model L tractors continued at least into the late 1950s.

COLLECTOR VALUES	1	2	3	4
MODEL L	$1,000	$600	$300	$100

Gray Company Inc.

MINNEAPOLIS, MINNESOTA

In the 1948-53 period, and perhaps for a longer time span, this firm is listed as the manufacturer of the Gardeneer garden tractors. No other information has been found. Specimens would be valued at $800 in any condition.

Gray Tractor Company

MINNEAPOLIS, MINNESOTA

See also: W. Chandler Knapp

Gray 1908 tractor

In 1908 W. Chandler Knapp built this small two-cylinder tractor. It used a single rear drive wheel. Knapp was from Rochester, New York, but eventually he helped form the Gray Tractor Company in Minneapolis.

Knapp Farm Locomotive

By 1909 the 'Knapp Farm Locomotive' used two drive wheels set close together to eliminate the need for a differential. Knapp's early design was one of the first to use the drum-drive principle that would later be a salient feature of the Gray tractors.

Gray tractor, 1914

The tractors up to 1914 used a two-cylinder engine, but in this year the tractor underwent numerous modifications, including the use of a four-cylinder engine. The previous year, 1913, the Wide Drive Drum was first used. Gray Tractor Company was organized at Minneapolis in 1914.

Gray tractor, 1916

Gray 18-36 tractor

By 1916 the Gray tractor had taken on its essential form that would remain throughout production. A Gray tractor was present at the Power Farming Demonstration held at Fremont, Nebraska in 1914. No doubt the favorable reviews of the Gray were good news to the owners of the company.

The Gray tractor of 1918 would remain virtually unchanged until the company was reorganized in 1925. Different sizes were built, but the Gray 18-36 seems to have been the most popular. The 18-36 was equipped with a Waukesha four-cylinder engine with a 4-3/4 x 6-3/4-inch bore and stroke. From its beginnings, all gears were enclosed with the exception of the drive chains to the drum. By 1918 the two drive chains were enclosed, an important feature compared to other tractors of the day. After the company reorganized in 1925 its 22-40 Canadian Special was the only model built. The company closed its doors in 1933.

Nebraska Test Data

Model: Gray 18-36

Test No. 22

Date Tested: June 11 to July 3, 1920

Although it was assigned an official test number, the Gray 18-36 had many problems during the 43 hours of running time required to complete various test sections. Initially, the manufacturer's representative was dissatisfied with the tractor's performance and was permitted to install new cylinders and pistons. During the limbering-up run, the Bennett carburetor shipped with the tractor was replaced with a Stromberg M-3 style, and it was used for all test procedures. When the governor was set to give rated speed and 30 hp, it had no control of the engine when the load was removed, and the engine speed had to be controlled by hand. The Gray 18-36 was the first tractor tested entirely on gasoline. During the maximum load test it developed 32.2 brake hp with a fuel consumption of 4.83 gph, for an equivalent of 6.67 hp-hours per gallon. A maximum pull of 3,390 lbs. was noted with a ground speed of 2.12 mph so 19.15 maximum drawbar hp was recorded. Although the Gray Drum-Drive design was touted as ideal, a slippage of 25.21 percent was recorded on the maximum drawbar load test. Regular equipment of the 6,500-pound Gray 18-36 included a four-cylinder vertical L-head engine with a 4-3/4 x 6-3/4-inch bore and stroke, and a rated speed of 950 rpm. Two forward speeds of 2-1/4 and 2-3/4 mph were provided.

COLLECTOR VALUES	1	2	3	4
18-36	$15,000	$9,500	$7,200	$3,000

Great Lakes Tractor Company

ROCK CREEK, OHIO

By 1947 the Chief garden tractors were available in three sizes of 1-1/2, 2, and 2-1/2 hp. Apparently, all three models used the same basic chassis, but the engines used were Briggs & Stratton, Continental, and Ultimotor respectively. Numerous attachments were available for these tractors.

COLLECTOR VALUES	1	2	3	4
CHIEF	$375	$250	$150	$100

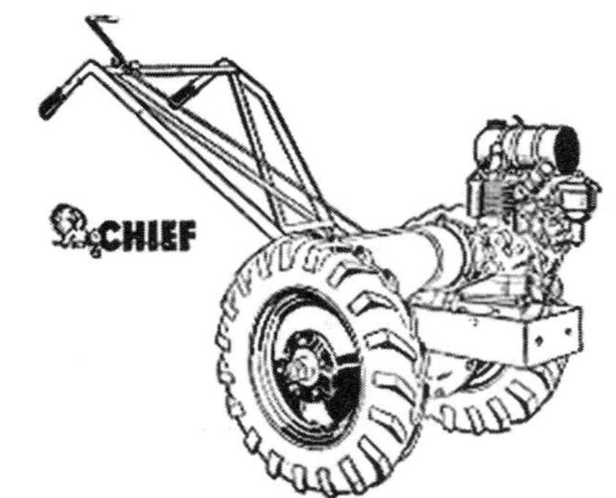

Chief garden tractor

Great Lakes Jr. garden tractor

For 1953 Great Lakes offered its "Jr." garden tractor. Priced at $147, it was equipped with a Briggs & Stratton NPR6 or a Kohler K7-2 engine, both rated at 2 hp.

COLLECTOR VALUES	1	2	3	4
GREAT LAKES JR.	$350	$250	$125	$75

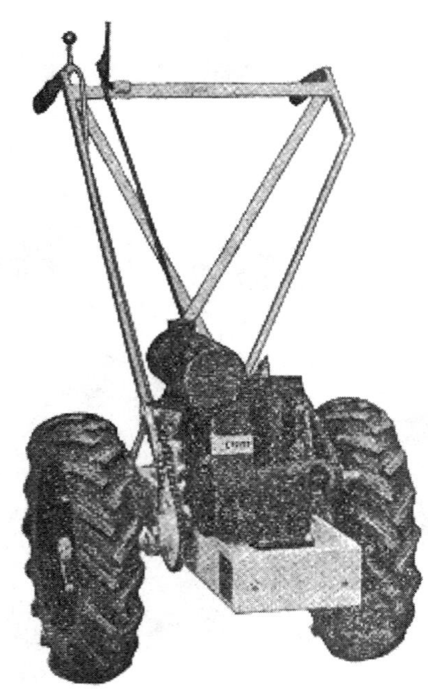

Great Lakes Economy Chief garden tractor

The Economy Chief was only slightly larger than the Great Lakes Jr. model and its engine was only rated at 2.2 hp. Briggs & Stratton or Kohler engines were used. Priced at $174, the Economy Chief used two drive wheels, compared to only one on the Jr. Both the Jr. and the Economy Chief were built at least into the 1950s.

Big Chief garden tractor

Two different models of the Big Chief were offered in 1953. The "251" used either the Kohler K7-2 engine or the Briggs & Stratton 8R6 engine, both capable of 7 hp. The Big Chief "303" was the largest, with over 12 hp coming from a Kohler K12-2 engine. The "251" sold for $218, while the Big Chief "303" was priced at $268.

COLLECTOR VALUES	1	2	3	4
ALL MODELS	$800	$600	$200	$100

Great Western Motor Company

SAN JOSE, CALIFORNIA

Great Western 10-15

See: Fageol Motors Company

After Fageol Motors Company left the tractor business in 1924, Great Western offered this Fageol 10-15 in 1925, and for perhaps a short time afterward. The 10-15 was equipped with a Lycoming four-cylinder engine with a 3-3/4 x 5- inch bore and stroke. Priced at $1,320, this tractor weighed 3,800 lbs. The 10-15 had only a single speed forward and reverse of 2-1/2 mph.

Great Western Tractor Company

COUNCIL BLUFFS, IOWA

Great Western Sr. 20-30 tractor

About 1919 Great Western was organized at Omaha, Nebraska. Within a few months the company moved to Council Bluffs, Iowa. For two years this firm built the Great Western Sr. tractor, a 20-30 model. The 20-30 was furnished with a Beaver four-cylinder engine with a 4-3/4 x 6-inch bore and stroke. Weighing 4,900 lbs., the 20-30 sold for $1,750.

Ground Hog Tractor Company

DETROIT, MICHIGAN

This company was incorporated with a maximum capitalization of $275,000 in 1920. No other information has been located.

Guardian Motors Company

NORFOLK, VIRGINIA

In 1918 this firm announced a "new truck garden tractor." For reasons unknown, these plans did not materialize.

[Throughout this section, assume that gasoline was used for fuel unless another fuel source is indicated.]

Haas Foundry Company

RACINE, WISCONSIN

Haas Model D tractor

This company was a major manufacturer of parts for many automotive and tractor companies during World War II, providing parts for Rolls Royce engines and P-51 fighter planes. The president of the company was Edward P. Haas. The company built two smaller model tractors, the A and B, and a larger model, the Model D. All were equipped with a three-point hitch. Of the smaller models, none are known to exist. The tractor in the photo is thought to be the only remaining Model D.

Hackney Mfg. Company

ST. PAUL, MINNESOTA

The Hackney Auto Plow was first marketed in 1911. Hackney Mfg. Co. continued until 1914 when it was sold to Standard Motor Co., Mason City, Iowa. The latter failed after a short time. Subsequently the Hackney Auto Plow Company was organized in 1917, but a fire wiped out the factory the following year. Within another year or so the Hackney disappeared from the market.

The Hackney was finished in bright red and yellow colors, and included a fully upholstered seat, similar to luxury automobiles of the day. For plowing the drivers were forward, but for road work the tractor was operated with the single steering wheel forward. This was achieved with a unique seat and steering wheel arrangement that permitted the operator to face either direction.

Hackney Corn-Planter 12-20 tractor

The Hackney Corn-Planter 12-20 tractor first appeared in 1917. It was not a "corn planter" but was designed for

Hackney Auto Plow

the corn grower. Curiously, the design had great similarities to the true row-crop design that would soon be developed by IHC and its Farmall tractor. At this point, Hackney's chief engineer was John Froehlich, the same man who had developed the Froehlich tractor at Waterloo Gasoline Traction Engine Company in Waterloo, Iowa. Froehlich left the firm, and eventually the company was bought out by Deere & Company.

No. 5 Hackney Auto Plow

The No. 5 Hackney Auto Plow of 1917 was rated at 15 drawbar and 30 belt hp. The design was similar to that of the original Hackney Auto Plow. Although the Hackney did not become a well-known, high-production model, the company persevered in the tractor business for nearly seven years. A disastrous fire in January 1918 completely destroyed the Hackney factory and took the company out of the tractor market.

Hadfield-Penfield Steel Company

BUCYRUS, OHIO

In the early 1920s this company came out with its 25-40 crawler tractor. It was equipped with a Stearns four-cylinder engine with a 5 x 6-1/2-inch bore and stroke. Weighing 8,500 lbs., the 25-40 offered three forward speeds, enclosed gearing, and a belt pulley. Little is known of the H-P 25-40 crawler. Virtually no advertising has been found, and none of these tractors are known to exist. A 1925 trademark application for its "Rigid Rail" tractor indicated this model name was first used in December 1921. In 1926 the company filed a trademark application for its "crawlerized" tractors. A few months later it applied for the trade name "Road Hog" for its tractors and road machinery.

Hagan Gas Engine & Mfg. Company

WINCHESTER, KENTUCKY

This company was organized by Louis T. and Charles Hagan about 1903 to build gasoline engines.

In the 1906 through 1908 period Hagan offered "gasoline traction engines" in sizes from 14 to 50 hp. The company's own stationary engines were adapted to this purpose. Few specifics have been found on these traction engines.

Hagan gasoline traction engine

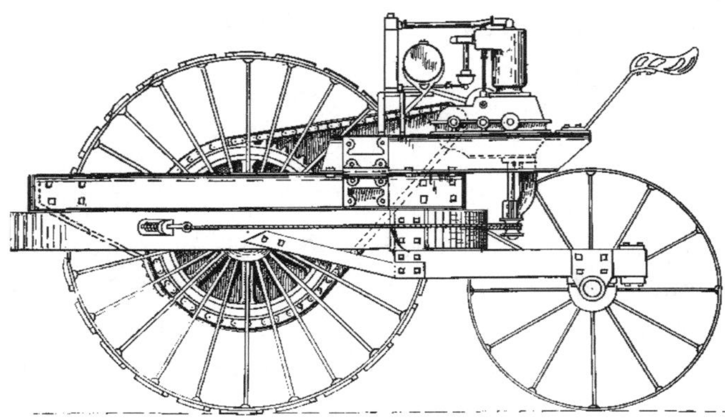

Hagan lightweight tractor

Hagan continued with engine production until 1918. Somewhere during the 1908 through 1918 period the company developed a prototype of its new lightweight tractor design, as shown in this drawing. This design never achieved regular production, and it is not known whether or not a prototype was ever built.

Paul Hainke Mfg. Company

HUTCHINSON, KANSAS

In early 1950, Hainke applied for a trademark protecting its Multivator trade name. No illustrations of the Multivator garden tractor line have been located.

Hamlin Mfg. Company

GREENSBORO, NORTH CAROLINA

Various references have been found to this company and its garden tractors in the 1947 to 1953 period, but no photos or specifications have been located.

Handt Tractor Company

WATERLOO, IOWA

In 1913 it was announced that this company was being taken over by the National Engine Company, also of Waterloo, Iowa, but no other references to either firm have been located.

Han-D-Trac Company

KANSAS CITY, MISSOURI

The Han-D-Trac garden tractor appeared in 1946. Advertising of the time noted that it featured a "monotube chassis, adjustable handles, power take-off and simplified maintenance." Little information has been found on this small 5-hp unit.

Han-D-Trac

COLLECTOR VALUES	1	2	3	4
HAN-D-TRAC	$400	$275	$125	$75

Haney Corporation

PHILADELPHIA, PENNSYLVANIA

Haney Bull Terrier garden tractor

In 1947 Haney was offering its Bull Terrier garden tractor. It was equipped with a 12-1/2 hp air-cooled engine. Little else is known about the company or its tractors.

COLLECTOR VALUES	1	2	3	4
BULL TERRIER	$3,500	$2,300	$1,500	$850

Happy Farmer Tractor Company

MINNEAPOLIS, MINNESOTA

See: LaCrosse Tractor Co.

Happy Farmer tractor

Organized at Minneapolis in November 1915, the Happy Farmer Tractor Co. began producing tractors by January of the following year. LaCrosse Tractor Company was organized at LaCrosse, Wisconsin, in late 1916, and was the direct successor to the short-lived Happy Farmer Tractor Company. Rated at 16 belt hp, the Happy Farmer used a two-cylinder opposed-cylinder engine with a 5 x 6-1/2-inch bore and stroke.

COLLECTOR VALUES	1	2	3	4
HAPPY FARMER	$15,000	$12,500	$10,000	$6,000

A.W. Harpstrite

MOWEQUA, ILLINOIS

Harpstrite Motor Plow

In 1907 A. W. Harpstrite designed this motor plow. It was equipped with a Westerfield two-cylinder opposed engine with a 7-inch bore and stroke. By 1908 the machine showed enough promise that plans were made for Union Iron Works, Decatur, Illinois, to manufacture the new design. For reasons unknown, this venture did not materialize.

Harris Mfg. Company

STOCKTON, CALIFORNIA

See: Eimco; Crockett Brothers

The Harris Power Horse 53 made its appearance in 1952, with one of them being sent to the Nebraska Tractor Test Laboratory in July of that year. Few details are known about Harris, though apparently the Power Horse was manufactured until 1964.

Weighing some 5,300 lbs., the Power Horse 53 was equipped with a Chrysler Industrial six-cylinder engine with a 3-7/16 x 4-1/2-inch bore and stroke.

Harris Power Horse 53

Nebraska Test Data

Model: Harris Power Horse 53

Test No. 479

Date Tested: July 27 to August 9, 1952

No brake hp tests were run on this tractor, since it was not equipped with a belt pulley. Weighing 5,375 lbs., the Power Horse was of four-wheel-drive design, and used 13-24-inch rubber tires. During Tests F, G, and H, this tractor was burdened with another 839 lbs. of weight on each rear wheel, and an additional 1,266 lbs. of ballast on each front wheel. Four forward speeds of 2.4, 3.79, 5.33, and 15.4 mph were provided. Third gear was used for the 10-hour rated drawbar run of Test H. In this test the Power Horse pulled 2,930 lbs. at 5.04 mph with a slippage of 5.13 percent for an output of 39.41-rated drawbar hp. Fuel economy was recorded at 6.95 hp-hours per gallon. Test J, run in third gear, and under an operating maximum load of 44.51 hp, produced a pull of 3,670 lbs. at 4.55 mph and a slippage of 14.43 percent. This test was run without any additional wheel weights, and using standard tire equipment as noted above. Test G yielded a low-gear maximum pull of 6,160 lbs. at 2.01 mph. The Power Horse was equipped with a Chrysler 8A Industrial engine. Of six-cylinder, L-head design, it was rated at 2,000 rpm and carried a 3-7/16 x 4-1/8-inch bore and stroke for 250.6-cubic inch displacement. No repairs or adjustments were noted during 30-1/2 hours of engine operating time.

COLLECTOR VALUES	1	2	3	4
	$6,500	$3,700	$2,500	$1,000

Harris FDW-C tractor

Nebraska Test Data

Model: Harris FDW-C (GM engine)

Test No. 519

Date Tested: May 18 to May 22, 1954

A General Motors two-cylinder, two-cycle diesel engine was featured in this Harris tractor. Rated at 1,800 rpm, it carried a 4-1/4 x 5-inch bore and stroke with a displacement of 142-cubic inches. Since no belt pulley was available, neither is any data regarding brake hp economy or maximum engine torque. Standard equipment for this tractor included four 13-24-inch tires, along with forward speeds of 2.16, 3.41, 4.79, and 13.86 mph. While the bare tractor weighed 6,173 lbs., additional weight was added to both the front and rear wheels for a total tractor weight of 10,445 lbs. during Tests F, G, and H. The latter test, run in third gear, indicated a rated drawbar output of 34.33 hp, along with a pull of 2,788 lbs. at 4.62 mph and a slippage of 5.07 percent. Fuel economy in this test came to 10.26 hp-hours per gallon. A low-gear maximum pull of 6,528 lbs. was recorded in the combined Test F and Test G. No repairs or adjustments were noted during 28 hours of operating time.

Nebraska Test Data

Model: Harris FDW-C (Continental engine)

Test No. 523

Date Tested: August 2 to August 16, 1954

This version of the FDW-C was equipped with a Continental four-cylinder diesel engine rated at 1,800 rpm and carrying a 3-7/8 x 5-1/2-inch bore and stroke for a 260-cubic inch displacement. The compression ratio was 15:1. Weighing 6,089 lbs., this tractor used four 13-24-inch tires and featured forward speeds of 2.16, 3.41, 4.79, and 13.86 mph. Since no power-take-off or belt pulley was available, no data can be secured concerning brake hp economy or maximum engine torque. During Test A the fuel tank began to leak and was replaced with a new one. Otherwise, no repairs or adjustments were noted during 41 hours of operating time. Test G gave a low-gear maximum pull of 6,999 lbs. at 1.85 mph, but during this test and Test H, an additional 4,376 lbs. of weight was distributed over the four drive wheels. Test H was run in third gear, and with a rated load of 33.95 drawbar hp, a pull of 2,789 lbs. was achieved at 4.56 mph against a slippage of 3.61 percent. Fuel economy in this test came to 11.67 hp-hours per gallon of diesel fuel.

A.T. Harrow Tractor Company

DETROIT, MICHIGAN

In December 1915 this firm took over the Michigan Tractor Company, also of Detroit. The latter had been organized earlier in the year. Apparently the company had developed an all-wheel drive tractor using a three-wheel design.

Hart-Parr Company

MADISON, WISCONSIN

Hart-Parr Company was organized to build gasoline engines in 1896 at Madison, Wisconsin. In 1901 the firm moved to Charles City, Iowa, and established the first company to solely build tractors. The first model appeared in 1902, and in fact, a "Hart-Parr" trademark application notes that its mark was first used on tractors in July of that year.

Although the company moved slowly at first, the new Hart-Parr tractors gained ready acceptance, and by 1906 the firm was well established in the tractor business. Various styles of heavyweight tractors appeared, ranging up to a gigantic 60-100 model. Although a few of these were built, little is known about them, and none are known to exist.

Hart-Parr Company underwent an internal upheaval in 1917, with C. W. Hart leaving the company. Subsequently, Hart relocated to Montana. He developed various enterprises, including the Hart Refineries. Charles H. Parr remained with the firm until his retirement.

The New Hart-Parr tractor of 1918 had been largely the design of C. W. Hart, but had not yet begun production when Hart left the company. Subsequently a whole family of Hart-Parr two- and four-cylinder tractors appeared. They remained on the market until 1930 when they were replaced with new unit frame designs.

Hart-Parr merged with others to form the Oliver Farm Equipment Corporation in 1929. From the legacy of C. W. Hart and C. H. Parr came an entirely new family of Oliver farm tractors.

Hart-Parr No. 1 tractor

The first Hart-Parr tractor, often referred to as Hart-Parr No. 1, was built during 1901 and 1902. Rated at 17 drawbar and 30 belt hp, No. 1 used a two-cylinder engine with a 9 x 13-inch bore and stroke. Oil cooling was used. Using an oil coolant eliminated the problems of freezing and, in addition, a higher cylinder temperature could be maintained. (None are known to exist.)

Hart-Parr (No. 2) 22-45 tractor

In December 1902 Hart-Parr placed its first advertisement for its tractors. The Hart-Parr 22-45, also known as Hart-Parr No. 2, gained considerable attention and enabled the company to continue with its tractor developments. (None are known to exist.)

Hart-Parr No. 3 emerged in 1903. It was sold in August of that year to a farmer near Charles City, Iowa. This tractor remained active for more than 20 years, and in 1924 the Hart-Parr Company bought the tractor back from the original owner for advertising purposes. This No. 3 finally went to the Smithsonian Institution. Certain research indicates that No. 3 may in fact be Hart-Parr No. 4.

Hart-Parr No. 3 tractor

COLLECTOR VALUES	1	2	3	4
NO. 3, 18-30	$150,000	--	--	--

Hart-Parr 17-30 tractor

Weighing almost 7-1/2 tons, the Hart-Parr 17-30 was the first full-fledged production model. Built in the 1903-1906 period, this tractor used a two-cylinder engine with a 9 x 13-inch bore and stroke. Hart-Parr tractors of this era used extra-heavy parts and many were used for traction work such as plowing.

Hart-Parr 17-30 model

By 1906 Hart-Parr was offering its 17-30 and 22-40 models. Both were of the same general design, but varied substantially in the proportions. The 22-40 weighed 8-1/2 tons and used a big two-cylinder engine with a 10 x 15-inch bore and stroke. These models developed their rated power at 300 rpm.

Production of the 17-30 and 22-40 tractors ran from 1903 to 1906. Along the way, various changes were made to the design, including a redesigned differential and a revised fuel system that were included in 1905. Hart-Parr made heavy use of steel forgings and steel castings in its tractors. This provided greater strength without the added weight required by cast iron components.

Hart-Parr 22-40 tractor

COLLECTOR VALUES	1	2	3	4
17-30	$125,000	$100,000	$80,000	$35,000
22-40	$90,000	$80,000	$60,000	$25,000

Over 4,100 copies of the Hart-Parr 30-60 tractor were built in the 1907 to 1918 period. This famous tractor took the name of "Old Reliable" and quickly became the most famous of the early Hart-Parr models. Rated at 300 rpm, the 30-60 used a 10 x 15-inch bore and stroke. It had a road speed of 2-1/2 mph.

COLLECTOR VALUES	1	2	3	4
30-60	$90,000	$75,000	$50,000	$30,000

Hart-Parr 30-60 tractor ("Old Reliable")

Hart-Parr 40-80 tractor

Between 1908 and 1914 Hart-Parr offered its big 40-80 tractor. About 300 were built during this time. A unique feature of the 40-80 was the heavy use of steel castings and forgings. The engine cylinders, flywheel, and belt pulley were the only major parts made of cast iron. The big four-cylinder engine was located beneath the operator's platform with two large exhaust stacks to the rear. The engine used a 9 x 13-inch bore and stroke. (None are known to exist.)

Hart-Parr 15-30 tractor

Hart-Parr began building a 15-30 tractor in 1909. Initially, it used an opposed-cylinder engine, but by 1910 the familiar vertical two-cylinder design was selected. The heavy steel canopy was a familiar feature that protected the operator from the elements, as well as providing a measure of protection for the engine in rainy weather. Production of this model ended in 1912.

COLLECTOR VALUES	1	2	3	4
15-30	$100,000	--	--	--

Hart-Parr 60-100 tractor

A few copies of the Hart-Parr 60-100 tractor were built in 1911 and 1912. Weighing more than 25 tons, this model was powered by a huge four-cylinder engine. Unfortunately, no specifications for this tractor have been located. A few of these tractors were shipped, but nothing in the company records indicated whether they were successful. The 60-100 remains as one of the largest wheel-type tractors ever built. (None are known to exist.)

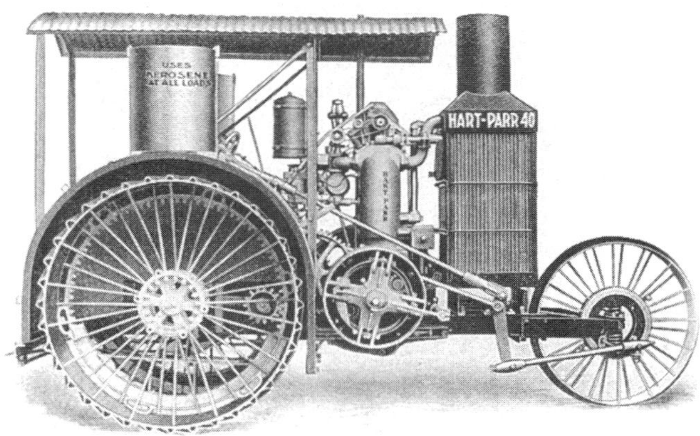

Hart-Parr 20-40 tractor

In the 1912-1914 period, Hart-Parr offered its 20-40 tractor as a direct successor to the earlier 15-30 model. This tractor had the unique feature of two forward speeds, something rather unusual on a tractor of this size, and built during this time. About 600 of these tractors were built.

COLLECTOR VALUES	1	2	3	4
20-40	$90,000	--	--	--

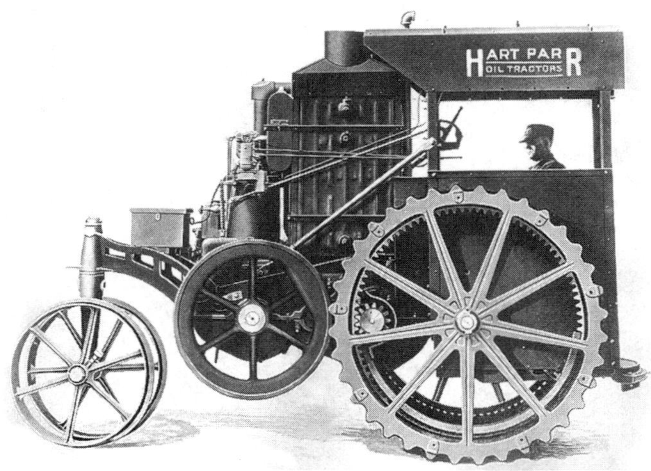

Hart-Parr 12-27 and 18-35 tractors

Hart-Parr introduced its 12-27 tractor in 1914. The following year it was superseded by the 18-35 Oil King, little more than a rerated version of the earlier model. In its 1915-1918 production run, more than 2,000 of the 18-35 Oil King tractors were built, making it one of the most popular of the Hart-Parr line up to this time.

COLLECTOR VALUES	1	2	3	4
12-27	$70,000	$50,000	$35,000	$15,000
18-35	$66,000	$50,000	$35,000	$15,000

In late 1914 Hart-Parr developed its "Little Red Devil" tractor. It was an entire departure from the previous Hart-Parr tractor line, and was an obvious effort to capture the developing market for small tractors. The Little Red Devil used a two-cylinder, two-cycle engine. The two-speed transmission had no reverse. To back up, the engine was reversed, as in marine practice. Only 700 were built.

Hart-Parr "Little Red Devil" tractor

COLLECTOR VALUES	1	2	3	4
RED DEVIL	$40,000	$35,000	$20,000	$10,000

Hart-Parr Company introduced the New Hart-Parr 12-25 tractor in 1918. The 12-25 had an open governor. This model had been developed primarily by C. W. Hart and C. H. Parr during 1917. Hart left (or was forced from) the company in 1917 and this model would be his enduring legacy to the company he had founded with Parr. After a short time this tractor became known as the 15-30 Type A tractor.

COLLECTOR VALUES	1	2	3	4
12-25	$18,000	$10,000	$7,000	$5,000

New Hart-Parr 12-25 tractor

Hart-Parr 30

Hart-Parr 30 tractor

Between 1918 and 1922 more than 10,000 of the Hart-Parr 30 tractors were built. Initially, it was known as the Type A 15-30 model, an upgrade of the New Hart-Parr. Originally, the two-cylinder engine used a 6 x 7- inch bore and stroke, but this was raised to 6-1/2 inches. Essentially, the tractor design remained the same for a decade. An interesting feature was the use of a one-way oiling system. Lubricant was pumped through a force-feed lubricator to significant engine parts and was eventually discharged through overflow tubes to the ground. The Hart-Parr 30 was immensely popular with farmers, particularly in the Midwestern states.

Nebraska Test Data

Model: Hart-Parr 30

Test No. 26

Date Tested: June 17 to June 22, 1920Kerosene was used throughout the various tests on the Hart-Parr 30 tractor. As with many early tractor designs, lubricating oil made a one-way trip through the engine. In the subject tractor, 5-3/4 gallons of three different oil viscosities were used during a 30-hour test run. Hart-Parr featured its own two-cylinder, horizontal, valve-in-head engine with a 6-1/2 x 7-inch bore and stroke. Two forward speeds were available of 1.98 and 2.88 mph. Rated engine speed was 750 rpm, and total weight of the tractor was 5,450 lbs. An impressive fuel economy of 8.04 hp-hours per gallon was achieved in the rated brake hp test, but this figure dropped to 6.62 on maximum load. Fuel consumption totaled 4.74 gallons per hour (gph) on the maximum brake hp test with 31.37 hp recorded. Nearly 3,500 lbs. of drawbar pull was recorded on the maximum load test. At a ground speed of 1.67 mph, an equivalent of 15.56 drawbar hp was developed. By using high gear, 19.65 hp was recorded with a ground speed of 2.64 mph, but the drawbar pull dropped to 2,788 lbs.

COLLECTOR VALUES	1	2	3	4
15-30 MODEL A	$8,500	$6,500	$3,500	$2,000
15-30 MODEL C	$7,500	$4,500	$3,500	$2,000

Hart-Parr 16-30 tractor

In October 1924 Hart-Parr submitted its new 16-30 tractor for testing at Nebraska. This was the 16-30 Type E tractor; it was built from 1924 to 1926. Almost 25 drawbar hp was demonstrated, and at the belt, the 16- 30 "E" delivered slightly over 37 hp.

Nebraska Test Data

Model: Hart-Parr 16-30

Test No. 106

Date Tested: October 14 to October 23, 1924

Weighing 6,000 lbs., the Hart-Parr 16-30 came through the drawbar tests with a 2,097 lb. pull at rated load. Using high gear, 16.97 drawbar hp was developed at a speed of 3 mph. Under maximum load, 24.79 drawbar hp was observed in high gear with a pull of 3,320 lbs. at a speed of 2.8 mph. In low gear only 18.66 drawbar hp was noted, with a maximum pull of 4,913 lbs. at 1.42 mph. Slippage in this test exceeded 30 percent. At its rated brake hp load, the 16-30 gave a fuel economy of 9.13 hp-hours per gallon, developing 30.33 hp. Under maximum load, 37.03 brake hp was observed. Kerosene was used throughout the 38 hours of test time. Hart-Parr used its own two-cylinder horizontal, valve-in-head engine rated at 750 rpm. It carried a 6-1/2 x 7-inch bore and stroke. Also included was the company's own governor, along with a Stromberg MB-3 carburetor and a K-W Type T magneto. A United whirling vane-type dry air cleaner was also furnished. The 16-30 went through Test No. 106 without incident except that during the maximum drawbar test in low gear, the shift gear would not stay in mesh unless held there by the operator. Adjustments to remedy this problem were unsuccessful.

COLLECTOR VALUES	1	2	3	4
16-30 MODEL E & F	$7,000	$4,000	$3,000	$2,000

Hart-Parr 20 tractor

Production of the Hart-Parr 20 tractor began in 1921. First it was the 10-20 "B" during 1921 and 1922. In the latter year, this model was modified slightly and became the 10-20 "C" model. Production of the Type C ran into 1924. The 10-20 "C" used a 5-1/2 x 6-1/2-inch bore and stroke in its two-cylinder engine. Rated at 800 rpm, it was capable of about 23 belt hp. Only one Model C is known to exist.

Nebraska Test Data

Model: Hart-Parr 20

Test No. 79

Date Tested: June 11 to June 17, 1921

Weighing only 3,990 lbs., the Hart-Parr 20 went through Test No. 79 with only minor repairs required. These included cleaning the fuel line once and filing the magneto breaker points. At its rated load of 20 brake hp, fuel consumption totaled 2.27 gph of kerosene or 8.86 hp-hours per gallon. At a maximum of 23.01 brake hp, fuel economy rose to 9 hp-hours per gallon. Two forward speeds of 2 and 3 mph were provided on the "20." Using low gear, a maximum pull of 2,500 lbs. was achieved at a speed of 2.11 mph. This corresponded to a maximum of 14.08 drawbar hp. Hart-Parr used its own two-cylinder, horizontal, valve-inhead engine featuring a 5-1/2 x 6-1/2-inch bore and stroke, and rated at 800 rpm. Accessories included a K-W Model TK magneto and a Stromberg Model MB-3 carburetor. The final test report noted "The clutch on this tractor grabbed, making smooth gradual starting practically impossible."

COLLECTOR VALUES	1	2	3	4
10-20 MODEL B	$18,000	$14,000	$8,000	$6,000
10-20 MODEL C	$18,000	$14,000	$8,000	$6,000

Hart-Parr 40 tractor

As with other Hart-Parr models, the Hart-Parr 22-40 used an engine designed and built within the Hart-Parr factory. In this case, two of the Hart-Parr "20"engines were coupled to yield a four-cylinder engine with a 5-1/2 x 6-1/2-inch bore and stroke. The "40" was built in the 1923 through 1927 period.

Nebraska Test Data

Model: Hart-Parr 40

Test No. 97

Date Tested: July 10 to July 19, 1923

Hart-Parr used its own engine in the "40." It used two sets of cylinders from the Hart-Parr 20, giving it four barrels with a 5-1/2 x 6-1/2-inch bore and stroke. Two Schebler Model D carburetors were used — one for each pair of cylinders. Also featured was a K-W Model TK magneto, and Hart-Parr's own governor. No air cleaner was used, although a high intake pipe was included. Weighing 8,300 lbs., the "40" exerted a maximum drawbar pull of 4,830 lbs. at 1.9 mph for a total of 24.71 maximum drawbar hp. Another maximum load test in high gear revealed 28.23 drawbar hp with a dynamometer reading of 3,750 lbs. at 3.75 mph. Kerosene was used on the rated brake hp trials, with the "40" displaying an economy of 8.2 hp-hours per gallon, or a total consumption of 4.959 gph. Water injected into the intake air stream totaled 5 gph during this test. This figure was not always recorded, since many tractors were so designed that accurate measurement was impossible. On maximum load the Hart-Parr "40" delivered 46.4 brake hp. During the test a larger water pump was installed, along with a few minor repairs.

COLLECTOR VALUES	1	2	3	4
22-40	$9,500	$7,500	$6,000	$3,000

Hart-Parr 12-24 tractor

Production of the Hart-Parr 12-24 began in 1924. This tractor replaced the earlier Hart-Parr 20. Initially the 12-24 was built with the same 5-1/2 x 6-1/2 engine as was used in the "20." This changed in 1926 with the use of a 5-3/4 x 6-½-inch engine. The power level was raised from about 17 maximum drawbar hp to 22 drawbar hp. The 12-24 remained in the line until 1928.

Nebraska Test Data

Model: Hart-Parr 12-24

Test No. 107

Date Tested: October 14 to October 23, 1924

Weighing only 4,675 lbs., the Hart-Parr 12-24 pulled 1,326 lbs. in the 10-hour rated drawbar test, or about 29 percent of its own weight. Slightly over 11-1/2 drawbar hp was indicated. Using low gear, a maximum pull of 3,054 lbs. was achieved, with the 12-24 delivering 16.99 drawbar hp. As with the 16-30 shown under No. 106, kerosene was used throughout the test. In the rated brake hp tests, an impressive fuel economy of 9.44 hp-hours per gallon was derived with a load of 24.24 hp and total consumption of 2.567 gph. The 12-24 delivered 26.97 hp in the maximum load test, with economy dropping slightly to 8.58 hp-hours per gallon. Except for cleaning one spark plug, no repairs or adjustments were made during the entire 32 hour test. The 12-24 carried the company's own two-cylinder horizontal, valve-in-head engine rated at 800 rpm and using a 5-1/2 x 6-1/2-inch bore and stroke. Regular equipment included a Madison-Kipp lubricator, United dry air cleaner, Stromberg MB-3 carburetor and a K-W Type T magneto.

Nebraska Test Data

Model: Hart-Parr 12-24

Test No. 129

Date Tested: October 18 to October 28, 1926

A two-cylinder horizontal, valve-in-head engine was featured in the Hart-Parr 12-24. Rated at 850 rpm, it used a 5-3/4 x 6-1/2-inch bore and stroke. A Robert Bosch ZE4/2 magneto was standard equipment, as was a Stromberg MB3 carburetor, Donaldson air cleaner, and Madison-Kipp lubricator. Low gear gave a ground speed of 2 mph, compared to 3-1/3 mph in high gear. During the low-gear maximum drawbar tests, it was necessary to tie the gear shift in place to hold the gears in mesh. Otherwise the 12-24 went through Test No. 129 without major repairs or adjustments. At rated drawbar load, fuel economy was 4.6 hp-hours per gallon on distillate fuel. The maximum drawbar pull occurred in the low gear maximum test where 2,950 lbs. were recorded at a speed of 2.77 mph, and gave a total of 21.77 maximum drawbar hp. At rated brake hp, the 12-24 burned 2.381 gallons of distillate per hour, giving an economy of 10.12 hp-hours per gallon. When called on for a maximum load, the 12-24 came up with 31.99 brake hp. Total weight was 5,440 lbs.

COLLECTOR VALUES	1	2	3	4
12-24	$8,000	$6,000	$4,000	$2,500

Hart-Parr 18-36 tractor

Production of the Hart-Parr 18-36 ran from 1926 until 1930. This model replaced the Hart-Parr "30" and was substantially larger than its predecessor. The 18-36 was vastly underrated, delivering over 32 maximum drawbar hp in Nebraska Test No. 128. This 7,300-lb. tractor was also capable of nearly 43 belt hp.

Nebraska Test Data

Model: Hart-Parr 18-36

Test No. 128

Date Tested: October 18 to October 25, 1926

Using distillate fuel, the Hart-Parr 18-36 went through Test No. 128 without a hitch except for adjusting the spark plug gap midway through the procedure. Hart-Parr supplied its own two-cylinder horizontal, valve-in-head engine in this model. It was rated at 800 rpm and carried a 6-3/4 x 7-inch bore and stroke. Standard equipment included a Robert Bosch ZU4/2 magneto, Stromberg MB3 carburetor, Madison-Kipp lubricator, and a Donaldson dry centrifugal air cleaner. Two forward speeds of 2 and 3 mph were provided, and in high gear the 18-36 yielded 32.25 maximum drawbar hp, pulling 4,075 lbs. at 2.97 mph. Fuel economy at rated drawbar load came to 6.5 hp-hours per gallon, compared to 9.74 hp-hours per gallon on the rated brake hp test. Operating at maximum load, the 18-36 delivered 42.85 brake hp, burning 5.029 gallons of distillate per hour and yielding 8.52 hp-hours per gallon. Total weight, as tested, with operator, was 7,325 lbs..

COLLECTOR VALUES	1	2	3	4
18-36 MODEL G	$7,000	$4,500	$3,250	$1,700
18-36 MODEL H	$7,000	$4,500	$3,250	$1,700

Hart-Parr 28-50 tractor

Almost 44 drawbar hp was manifested for the Hart-Parr 28-50 as shown in Nebraska Test No. 140. The 28-50, built in the 1927 through 1930 period, was a four-cylinder design using a 5-3/4 x 6-1/2-inch bore and stroke. This big tractor was capable of nearly 65 belt hp. On April 1, 1929 the Hart-Parr Company merged with others to form the Oliver Farm Equipment Corporation. The Hart-Parr name remained for a few years, but with the merger came the end of Hart-Parr as a manufacturing entity. Henceforth, the Oliver name would be a dominant force in the farm tractor industry.

Nebraska Test Data

Model: Hart-Parr 28-50

Test No. 140

Date Tested: August 17 to August 31, 1927

This tractor was originally entered as Test No. 133, but was withdrawn for unknown reasons. Using distillate fuel, the 28-50 came out of the rated drawbar test pulling a 2,967 lb. load at 3.6 mph and consuming 4.79 gallons of fuel per hour (gph) for an economy of 5.95 hp-hours per gallon. Maximum load tests were made in both forward gears, but low gear saw the best pull with 7,347 lbs. recorded on the dynamometer at a speed of 2.22 mph for 43.58 hp. Slippage was 16.89 percent on this test. Total tractor weight was 10,394 lbs. Hart-Parr featured its own four-cylinder horizontal, valve-in-head engine using a 5-3/4 x 6-1/2-inch bore and stroke. Rated at 850 rpm, it had a compression of 70 psi at this speed. Standard equipment included a Robert Bosch ZU4 magneto and Schebler Model D carburetor. At rated brake hp this tractor scored 10.73 hp-hours per gallon, and consumed 4.694 gph. At maximum load, 64.56 brake hp was noted with consumption rising to 7.94 gph. Only minor repairs were necessary, although the water passage between the cylinder head and engine block was enlarged to provide better circulation. This change was to be made standard on all future tractors of this model.

COLLECTOR VALUES	1	2	3	4
28-50 HART-PARR	$9,000	$7,500	$5,250	$2,500
18-27 (SINGLE WHEEL ROW CROP)	$4,250	$2,500	$1,800	$1,000
18-27 (DUAL WHEEL ROW ROP)	$3,500	$2,500	$1,800	$1,000
18-28 (2-3 PLOW TRAC-TOR)	$4,200	$3,000	$2,000	$1,500
28-44 (3-5 PLOW TRAC-TOR)	$4,250	$3,200	$2,500	$1,800
70 OLIVER HART PARR*	$3,700	$2,400	$2,000	$1,000
70 OLIVER**	$2,800	$2,200	$1,800	$800

(Note: Oliver-Hart Parr 70 was built from 1935-1937 when the Hart-Parr name was dropped.)

*****(Note: 70 Oliver add $700+ for tiptoe rears and cast fronts.)***

Hart tractor

Hart tractor

C. W. Hart

WAUWATOSA, WISCONSIN

After C. W. Hart left Hart-Parr Company in 1917 he spent time in Montana and Wauwatosa, Wisconsin. Hart continued working on tractor design with his friend and chief engineer at Charles City, Conrad E. Frudden. The latter went on to be a tractor engineer at Allis-Chalmers for many years. About 1918 the Hart tractor appeared and was patented under No. 1,509,293. Three of these tractors were built, and Hart eventually shipped them to Montana for use on his wheat ranch. The lure of wheat ranching and the oil refinery business brought an end to Hart's active work in tractor design, with the Hart tractor being the last example.

Hebb Motors Company

LINCOLN, NEBRASKA

In 1918, Hebb Motors Co. filed a trademark application for its "Patriot" tractor, claiming that it had first used this mark on October 1, 1917. Aside from this, no other information on this company has been found.

Heer Engine Company

PORTSMOUTH, OHIO

See: Morton-Heer Company and Reliable Tractor and Engine Company

Heer four-wheel-drive tractor

Chris Heer announced his new tractor in 1912. At the time, it was the only four-wheel-drive tractor on the market. By 1914 it was being built in three sizes: 16-24, 20-28, and 24-32. Apparently they used Heer stationary engines, or modifications of it, for the power plant. Heer had previously pioneered the development of two-cylinder opposed engines in sizes up to 40 hp. The company endured until 1916 when it was reorganized as Reliable Tractor & Engine Company.

Heider Mfg. Company

CARROLL, IOWA

John Heider announced his first tractor in 1911. With it, Heider made the friction drive system famous as a method of power transmission.

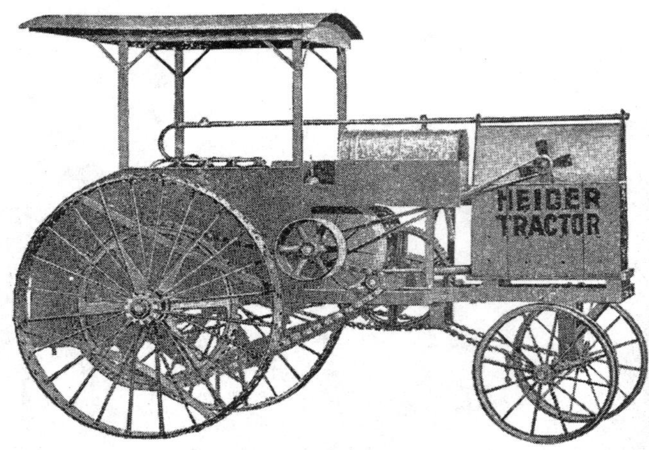

Heider tractor, 1911

Weighing only 4,500 lbs., the Heider tractor was equipped with a four-cylinder Waukesha engine with a 4-3/4 x 5-inch bore and stroke. This was one of the first successful tractors of lightweight design.

Improved Heider tractor, 1912

By 1912 the Heider tractor had been substantially improved. This model caught the attention of Rock Island Plow Company. As a result, the latter began selling the Heider tractors by the hundreds in 1914. In January 1916, Rock Island bought out the Heider tractor line and continued selling them under the Heider name until 1927.

COLLECTOR VALUES	1	2	3	4
SCREEN COOLED	$32,000	$25,000	$12,000	$7,000
HEIDER C	$17,000	$13,000	$10,000	$5,000
HEIDER D	$12,500	$10,000	$6,500	$2,500

Heinss Motor Plow Company

FORT WAYNE, INDIANA

This firm was organized in 1916 but no other information has been found.

Heinz & Munschauer

CLEVELAND, OHIO

This firm was apparently the antecedent of the Leader Tractor Company of Cleveland. The latter began building tractors in 1948. Heinz & Munschauer appear in a trademark application for the "Leader" trademark dated February 5, 1948. In the application the company claims to have first used the "Leader" trademark on January 21, 1945.

Frank Held Tractor Company

COLUMBUS, OHIO

Gro-Mor Cultivator

In 1927 the Gro-Mor Cultivator was listed from this firm. It was equipped with a Briggs & Stratton engine with a 2-1/2-inch bore and stroke. Priced at $175, it weighed 200 lbs.

COLLECTOR VALUES	1	2	3	4
GRO-MOR	$850	$650	$450	$200

Joshua Hendy Iron Works

SUNNYVALE, CALIFORNIA

In 1912 M. Rumely Company at LaPorte, Indiana, bought out an orchard tractor design from Hendy. This became the Rumely ToeHold tractor. In 1919 the firm is listed as the manufacturer of the Paragon tractor, but no additional information regarding this model has been located.

Henneuse Tractor Company

SACRAMENTO, CALIFORNIA

About 1920 Henneuse began offering its Rigid-Rail crawler tractor. It was rated at 25 drawbar and 40 belt hp. A Stearns four-cylinder engine with a 5 x 6-1/2-inch engine powered this model. The Rigid-Rail was advertised in 1921, but no other listings or specifications have been located.

Rigid-Rail crawler

Henry, Millard & Henry Company

YORK, PENNSYLVANIA

In 1911 Henry, Millard & Henry advertised this single-cylinder tractor. It was apparently available in several different horsepower sizes, and used the company's own stationary engines for power. Few specific details regarding this tractor have been found.

In 1914 H. M. & H. was still advertising its single-cylinder tractors. Initially, they had been offered under the "Advance" trade name, but by 1914 they were sold as the "HM & H" tractors. Shortly after this time the company left the tractor business, concentrating instead on its line of stationary engines.

Henry, Millard & Henry tractor

Herbert Tractor Company

DETROIT, MICHIGAN

In 1917 this company was listed as the manufacturer of the Herbert 16-32 tractor. No other information has been found.

Hercules Tractor Company

EVANSVILLE, INDIANA

This company was incorporated in 1916 for $300,000. Ostensibly, the firm was organized to build farm tractors, but apparently this did not materialize.

HM&H tractor

The company was involved with the Hercules Gas Engine Works and the Hercules Buggy Works, also of Evansville.

Hero Mfg. Company

WINNIPEG, MANITOBA

Hero tractor

In 1911 Hero announced its first tractor. It was designed by Albert O. Espe. The latter had previously designed the Universal tractor, built first by Crookston Mfg. Company, and then by the Northwest Thresher Company of Stillwater, Minnesota. Hero apparently bought out all of Espe's plans, patents, and foundry patterns as it prepared to put the tractor into production. The plans apparently came to naught, since nothing more can be found regarding the company or its tractors.

Hession Tractor & Tiller Corporation

BUFFALO, NEW YORK

Hession tractor

See: Wheat Tiller & Tractor Company

Hession Tractor & Tiller Corporation was incorporated for $10 million in 1917. Its Hession tractor was available with ordinary steel wheels for farm work, but could also be furnished with hard rubber tires for road work, as shown here. The tractor was sold as the "Hession" up to 1919, but during that year the company sold it as the "Wheat" tractor. Rated as a 12-24, it used an Erd four-cylinder engine with a 4 x 6-inch bore and stroke. After 1920 the firm was known as Wheat Tiller & Tractor Corporation.

COLLECTOR VALUES	1	2	3	4
HESSION	–	$15,000	–	–

Hicks Tractor Company

MINNEAPOLIS, MINNESOTA

Hicks 12-25 crawler tractor

This firm was incorporated at Minneapolis in 1916. Late the following year the company relocated to Harvey, Illinois, and by 1918 was situated at Milwaukee, Wisconsin. The company built the Hicks 12-25 crawler tractor, and as shown here, it was a half-track design with front steering wheels.

Highway Tractor Company

JACKSON, MICHIGAN

This company was incorporated for $2 million in 1917. No other details have been found.

Hiller Engineering Corporation

REDWOOD CITY, CALIFORNIA

Hiller Yard Hand Model 100 garden tractor

Hiller Yard Hand Model 100 garden tractors appear in trade directories in 1954. The model shown here used a Power Products Model 170 single-cylinder two-cycle motor with a 1-3/4 x 1-1/2-inch bore and stroke. Various attachments were available, including a mower, sweeper, cart, roller, and spreader. An interesting attachment was a 10-inch circular saw.

COLLECTOR VALUES	1	2	3	4
YARD HAND 100	$800	$600	$200	$150

J. A. Hockett

STERLING, KANSAS

See: Gasoline Thresher & Plow Company

J. A. and P. Hockett, R. A. Steward, P. P. Truehart, and W. W. Webb formed the Gasoline Thresher & Plow Company at Sterling in 1893. This company was organized to develop the Sterling gasoline traction engine under development by J. A. Hockett. Given the state of the art in the gas engine business at the time, the venture failed.

Hoke Mfg. Company

NEW CARLISLE, INDIANA

In 1948 this company was listed as a garden tractor manufacturer, but no other references or photographs have been located.

Hoke Tractor Company

SOUTH BEND, INDIANA

Hoke 12-24 tractor

John I. Hoke announced his first tractor in 1912. At the time, Hoke was located at Washington, Indiana. His "universal" tractor design prompted him to apply for a patent—No. 1,073,490 was eventually issued. During 1913 the new company set up a factory at South Bend, Indiana.

Hoke 12-24 tractor

The Hoke tractor was built only in one size with a 12-24 hp rating. It featured a Waukesha four-cylinder engine with a 4-1/4 x 5-3/4-inch bore and stroke. Despite the quality features of the Hoke tractor, it disappeared from the market after 1917.

COLLECTOR VALUES	1	2	3	4
HOKE 12-24	$14,500	–	$7,500	–

Hollis Tractor Company

PITTSBURGH, PENNSYLVANIA

Hollis first appeared with its Type M, 15-25 tractor in 1916 or 1917. This unusual design placed two driving and steering wheels at the front, and support wheels at the rear. A Light four-cylinder engine was used and it had a 3-1/4 x 4- ½-inch bore and stroke. The Hollis tractor only remained on the market until about 1920.

Hollis Type M, 15-25 tractor

J. S. Holmes

BELOIT, WISCONSIN

Holmes tractor

In 1906, J. S. Holmes began experimenting with a small, lightweight tractor design. By 1908 he had perfected the small tractor shown here. It used a two-cylinder vertical engine, and two forward speeds were provided. Considerable notice was given to the Holmes design, and plans were made to set up a factory for this purpose, but this did not materialize.

Holmes Mfg. Company

PORT CLINTON, OHIO

In 1912 Holmes announced its new Holmes Little Giant Tractor. It was rated at 12 brake hp and weighed 4,500 lbs. In 1913 the company name was changed to Holmes Tractor Co. Little else is known of the company or its venture into the tractor business, since it disappears from the tractor directories in 1914.

Holmes Little Giant Tractor

Holt Mfg. Company

STOCKTON, CALIFORNIA

Benjamin Holt demonstrated his first steam-powered tracklayer tractor in 1890. Various steam tracklayers were built in the following years. Holt bought out Daniel Best in 1908 and began building a gasoline-powered tracklayer that year. In 1909 the company bought the Peoria, Illinois, facility of Colean Mfg. Company and established a second factory there. C. L. Best emerged as one of Holt's strongest competitors. In 1925 the two companies merged to form Caterpillar Tractor Company.

Holt tracklayer tractor

In the 1890s Benjamin Holt perfected the idea of a tracklayer tractor. For several years, it was steam powered, mainly because gasoline engines were not yet perfected and were very heavy and somewhat unreliable. This large steam powered tracklayer was especially designed to work in soft and mucky soil that was otherwise untouchable with conventional plowing methods.

Holt gasoline-powered crawler

In 1908 Holt publicly demonstrated the company's first gasoline-powered crawler tractor. Initially, and for several years to come, a front tiller wheel was used for steering. It was eventually discovered that the crawler could be steered on its own tracks and the tiller wheel quickly disappeared.

Holt-Illinois tractor

In 1911 the Holt-Illinois tractor appeared for a short time, and was one of the very few entries Holt made into the wheel tractor business. Little is known of this tractor except that it used Holt's 45 hp four-cylinder engine, along with the heavy construction that typified all the tractors built by Holt.

Holt Caterpillar crawler

By 1912 Holt's Caterpillar tractors had become well known and were popular in Canada. At this time they were offered in 45 and 60 hp sizes, both using a four-cylinder engine. With their tremendous tractive force, these machines were virtually unstoppable, especially when compared with other methods then in use.

Holt Caterpillar 18 crawler

In 1914 Holt Mfg. Company placed the Caterpillar 18 on the market. It was the smallest of the Caterpillar line, and was designed specifically to work in orchards, vineyards, and small ranches. The "18" was only 53 inches wide and 53 inches high. Weighing 5,900 lbs., it sold for $1,600.

Holt Caterpillar 25-45 crawler

For 1918 Holt offered its Caterpillar 25-45 model. It weighed 6-3/4 tons, and was equipped with Holt's own four-cylinder engine with a 6 x 7-inch bore and stroke. The canopy and sidecurtains were standard equipment intended to protect the engine from the elements. Note the front-mounted belt pulley.

Holt Caterpillar 40-75 crawler

A huge four-cylinder engine with a 7-1/2 x 8-inch bore and stroke was used in the Caterpillar 40-75 tractor. This 1918 model was 104 inches wide, 10 feet high, 20 feet long and weighed almost 12 tons. At this point in time the front steering wheel remained for the larger Caterpillar models, but would shortly disappear.

Holt Caterpillar 70-120 crawler

A 1918 offering was the Caterpillar 70-120. It was one of the largest tractors on the market at the time (if not the largest) and weighed an impressive 24,800 lbs.. Power came from a six-cylinder engine with a 7-1/2 x 8- inch bore and stroke. A rear-mounted belt pulley came as standard equipment.

Holt Caterpillar Two-Ton crawler

By 1923 the Caterpillar Two-Ton tractor was on the market. This little crawler only weighed 4,000 lbs. It was equipped with a four-cylinder engine with a 4 x 5-1/2-inch bore and stroke. Three forward speeds were provided, ranging from 2 to 5-1/4 mph. A belt pulley came as standard equipment.

COLLECTOR VALUES	1	2	3	4
TWO-TON	$10,000	$7,500	$4,000	$2,000

The Caterpillar Five-Ton model was also built as the 25-40 tractor. Weighing 9,400 lbs., it was designed around a four-cylinder engine with a 4-3/4 x 6-inch bore and stroke. This model was still in production at the time of the 1925 Holt-Best merger that formed Caterpillar Tractor Company.

Holt Caterpillar Five-Ton (25-40) crawler

Nebraska Test Data

Model: Holt 25-40

Test No. 59

Date Tested: August 30 to September 17, 1920

Compared to previous crawler tractor tests, the Holt 25-40 was by far the largest unit tested. Weighing 9,400 lbs., it carried a big four-cylinder engine with a 4-3/4 x 6-inch bore and stroke. Designed and built by Holt, the engine was a vertical, valve-in-head style, and was rated at 1,050 rpm Three forward speeds were provided of 1.5, 3, and 5.7 mph. After running about 14 hours, the engine was dismantled, new piston rings were installed and the valves were ground. Only after these repairs were made did official tests begin. Previous tests indicated kerosene was chosen for nearly all tractor models, but the 25-40 used gasoline throughout the test. Drawbar performance indicated a maximum pull of 5,558 lbs. in low gear. Using second gear, a pull of 3,546 lbs. resulted, with 33.34 hp calculated. Slippage was only 2 percent. The rated load test was taken at 30.24 hp, with fuel consumption at 3.81 gph and fuel economy of 7.94 hp-hours per gallon. Slightly more than 35-1/2 brake hp was developed on the maximum load test.

Holt Caterpillar Ten-Ton (40-60) crawler

COLLECTOR VALUES	1	2	3	4
FIVE-TON	$18,000	$14,000	$7,500	$3,500

Caterpillar Ten-Ton tractors were easily capable of pulling six plows under virtually any conditions. Weighing 19,000 lbs., the Ten-Ton like its contemporaries, was furnished with a rear-mounted belt pulley as standard equipment. Power came from a four-cylinder engine with a 6-1/2 x 7-inch bore and stroke.

Nebraska Test Data

Model: Holt 40-60

Test No. 61

Date Tested: September 2 to September 20, 1920

Three forward speeds were standard equipment on Holt's 40-60 crawler tractor. Low gear gave a ground travel of 1.77 mph, with 3.21 and 5.13 being the respective speeds in second and third gears. On the rated load test, 55.25 hp was noted, with an economy of 7.16 hp-hours per gallon and fuel consumption of 7.72 gph. On maximum load, 57.21 brake hp was indicated. At rated drawbar load, 42.76 hp was apparent, with only 0.6 percent slippage, a ground speed of 3.23 mph, and a pull of 4,963 lbs. At maximum load in second gear, 5,250 lbs. were indicated on the traction dynamometer, with slippage still at an impressive 1.3 percent. By shifting to low gear, a 9,756 lb. drawbar pull was achieved, but with a slippage of 15.3 percent. Regular equipment included a Kingston Model E carburetor and a K-W magneto. Total weight was 18,500 lbs. The engine was designed and built by Holt. It was a four-cylinder vertical, valve-in-head model with a 6-1/2 x 7-inch bore and stroke. Rated speed was 750 rpm. Engineer's notes from the test indicate that the 40-60 was brought to Lincoln with an air cleaner, but it was removed prior to the brake tests "and it was agreed that same would not be sold as regular equipment."

COLLECTOR VALUES	1	2	3	4
TEN-TON	$20,000	$15,000	$8,500	$4,000

Holton Tractor Company

INDIANAPOLIS, INDIANA

This firm announced it was building a new factory in 1915. From it came the Holton 10-16 tractor. This model used a four-cylinder LeRoi engine with a 31/8 x 4-1/2-inch bore and stroke. (The same engine was used in numerous small tractors of the day.) Holton advertised this engine into the early 1920s. While this model demonstrated many of the salient features of the row-crop tractor, it was not designed and built as such—the single front wheel was simply a part of the design. Apparently the manufacturer did not consider the potential of using a front-mounted cultivator.

Homestead Tractor Corporation

NEW YORK, NEW YORK

Homestead Tractor likely built the Auto-Tiller 12 sometime in the 1920s, but no other information has been located on this tractor.

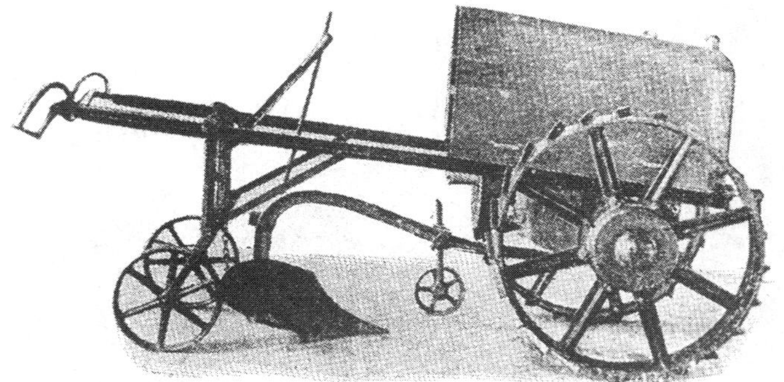

Autotiller "12" from Homestaed Tractor Corporation

Hoosier Wheel & Tractor Company

FRANKLIN, INDIANA

The Hoosier 20-35 tractor appeared about 1920 and remained on the market for only a short time. It was equipped with a four-cylinder Midwest engine with a 4-1/2 x 6-inch bore and stroke.

Hoyse Tractor Company

SOUTH BEND, INDIANA

This company was incorporated in 1914 with a capitalization of $90,000, but no other information has been found.

Huber Mfg. Company

MARION, OHIO

Edward Huber established a small factory in Marion, Ohio, in 1865. By 1880 the company was recognized as a significant builder of steam traction engines and threshing machines. In 1898 the firm built a gasoline tractor using a VanDuzen gasoline engine. Various problems kept this project from further development, but in 1911 the company returned with the "Farmer's Tractor." The company continued producing tractors until suspended during World War II. Tractor production never resumed after the war ended.

In 1898 Huber Mfg. Company produced its first tractor. The company bought out Van Duzen Gasoline Engine Company, Cincinnati, Ohio. The latter had been in the engine business for several years. Using a Van Duzen engine, the company proceeded to build a tractor mounted on wheels and gearing from the Huber steam traction engines. The experiment met with poor success and the entire project was abandoned.

Huber gasoline traction engine

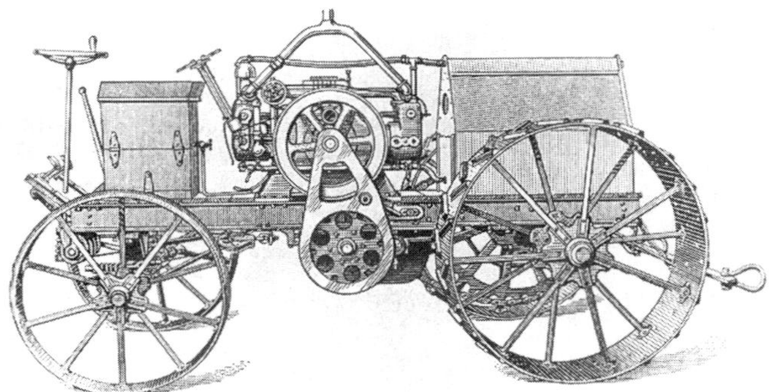

Huber Farmer's Tractor

During 1910 and 1911 Huber developed its Farmer's Tractor. It used a two-cylinder engine with a 5-3/4 x 6-inch bore and stroke. Tower cooling was used, that is, cooling water was pumped over inclined screens at the top of the tank for evaporative cooling. This model apparently was marketed for only a couple of years.

Huber 13-22 Farmer's Tractor

The 1912 Huber tractor line included a new 13-22 Farmer's Tractor. It may have been no more than an upgrade from the previous Farmer's tractor, but a few magazine advertisements of the day point to it as being a 'new' model. A two-speed transmission was featured, and everything was enclosed but the final drives. Power came from a two-cylinder engine with a 7-inch bore and stroke. Like the original Farmer's Tractor, this one used evaporative cooling with a large tank mounted to the front of the radiator.

Huber 30-60 tractor

In 1912 the Huber 30-60 tractor appeared. This big tractor had a four-cylinder engine with a 7 x 8-inch bore and stroke. To give some idea of the physical size of this tractor, the rear wheels stood 8 feet tall. The huge tubular radiator carried 95 gallons of water and cooling air was drawn through 175 two-inch tubes. Production continued until 1916 when it was superseded by the big four-cylinder 35-70 model. The 35-70 was closed out in 1917.

COLLECTOR VALUES	1	2	3	4
30-60	$55,000	$40,000	$32,500	$20,000

Huber 20-40 tractor

About 1914 Huber introduced its 20-40 tractor. It was built along the same general lines as the larger 30-60. The 20-40 used a two-cylinder engine. Like the 30-60, production continued until about 1917. Very little data has been found for the 20-40.

Huber Light Four tractor

During 1916 the Huber Light Four tractor appeared. This model weighed 5,200 lbs. Power came from a four-cylinder Waukesha engine with a 4-1/2 x 5-3/4-inch bore and stroke. This model was very popular, even with an initial price tag of $1,085. The Light Four was built until about 1929. Adding to the confusion, the company also built a Super Four 15-30 model in the 1921-25 period.

Nebraska Test Data

Model: Huber Light Four 12-25

Test No. 12

Date Tested: May 18 to June 3, 1920

During a total running time of about 45 hours, Huber representatives had their share of problems with the 12-25. None were of major consequence, but included such things as replacing the original carburetor, adjusting and readjusting the magneto, replacing the fan belt, replacing a leaky water tank, and regrinding the valves. A Waukesha four-cylinder vertical, L-head engine was featured. It used a 4 x 5-3/4-inch bore and stroke and had a rated speed of 1,000 rpm. Weighing only 5,550 lbs., the Light Four offered two forward speeds of 2.7 and 4.15 mph. Although none of the testing problems disqualified the Light Four, test engineers noted that frequent governor adjustments were necessary during the various tests. Quite possibly, Huber rectified these problems in later versions. On the belt, a maximum of 25.7 hp was achieved with an efficiency of 5.77 hp-hours per gallon of kerosene. Slightly over 2,500 lbs. of pull was delivered at the drawbar, and this at a speed of 2 mph. This equated to 16.7 drawbar hp. The very popular Kingston Model L carburetor was featured, along with a Kingston magneto.

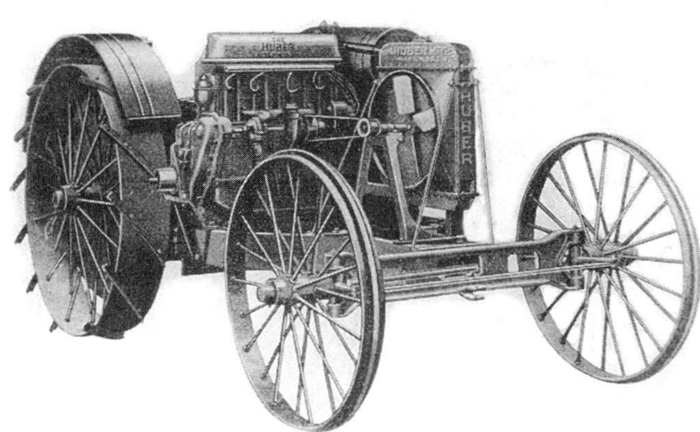

Huber Super Four 15-30 tractor

Huber introduced its Super Four 15-30 tractor in 1921. A copy was sent to Nebraska's Tractor Test Laboratory that year where it demonstrated a maximum of almost 45 belt hp. This model was equipped with a Midwest four-cylinder engine with a 4-1/2 x 6-inch bore and stroke. By 1923 though, the engine was changed to a four-cylinder Waukesha with a 4-1/2 x 5-3/4-inch bore and stroke. Production of this model continued into 1925. By 1926 Huber was building the Super Four 18-36 tractor. It used the same Midwest four-cylinder engine as the earlier Super Four 15-30 tractor. There is considerable confusion about some of the Huber models, especially since some of the crossmotor tractors and some of those with in-line engines used the same model designation although they were entirely different tractors.

Nebraska Test Data

Model: Huber Super Four 15-30

Test No. 74

Date Tested: April 11 to April 20, 1921

Using low gear, the Huber 15-30 made a maximum drawbar pull of 3,645 lbs. at a speed of 2.76 mph, for a corresponding maximum of 26.85 drawbar hp. This somewhat underrated tractor came up with a maximum of 44.68 brake hp, far in excess of the manufacturer's rating. At rated load, a fuel economy of 9.23 hp-hours per gallon was recorded. Gasoline was used throughout the 32-hour test procedure. Total fuel consumption on the rated brake hp test totaled 3.287 gph. The 15-30 carried a Midwest four-cylinder vertical, valve-in-head engine with a 4-1/2 x 6-inch bore and stroke. Rated speed was 1,000 rpm. Regular equipment included a two-speed transmission with a choice of 2.7 or 4.15 mph. Also included was a Kingston Model LD4 magneto and a Kingston Model L carburetor. Except for changing spark plugs and other minor items, few repairs or adjustments were necessary during the test. Total weight of the 15-30 was 6,090 lbs.

COLLECTOR VALUES	1	2	3	4
SUPER FOUR 15-30	$12,000	--	--	--

Huber Master Four 25-50 tractor

In 1922 Huber introduced the Master Four 25-50 tractor. This model used a Hinkley four-cylinder engine with a 5-1/2 x 6-inch bore and stroke. Rated speed was 1,000 rpm. This model used a drilled crankshaft for full pressure lubrication of the crank journals, and also used drilled connecting rods for perfect lubrication of the wrist pins. Despite the quality features of the 25-50, it was marketed for only a short time.

COLLECTOR VALUES	1	2	3	4
LIGHT FOUR/SUPER FOUR/ MASTER FOUR	$10,000	$7,000	$4,000	$1,500

Huber Super Four 18-36 tractor

In 1926 Huber began building its new Super Four 18-36 tractor. This unit frame design carried a four-cylinder Stearns engine with a 4-3/4 x 6-1/2-inch bore and stroke. Delivering over 43 belt hp in Nebraska Test No. 123, the 18-36 was also capable of 27 drawbar hp. By 1929 this model became the Super 4, 21-39 tractor.

Nebraska Test Data

Model: Huber Super Four 18-36

Test No. 123

Date Tested: June 7 to June 12, 1926

Two forward speeds of 2.2 and 3.8 mph were built into the Huber 18-36. A maximum drawbar load test taken in low gear indicated 27.02 hp with a load of 5,419 lbs. at a speed of 2.21 mph. Slippage was in excess of 27 percent for this test, compared to slightly over 12 percent when operated at rated drawbar hp. As with the drawbar tests, gasoline was used in the brake hp trials. At rated load of 36 hp, 7.9 hp-hours per gallon appeared, with total consumption of 4.577 gph. Under maximum brake load, 43.15 hp was recorded with total fuel consumption of 5.857 gph. Huber used a Steams four-cylinder valve-in-head engine in the 18-36. Rated at 1,000 rpm, it carried a 4-3/4 x 6-1/2-inch bore and stroke. Standard accessory items included a Pomona Vortox oil-type air cleaner, Kingston governor, Eisemann GS4 magneto, and a Kingston L-3 carburetor. Total weight was 8,595 lbs.

In 1926 the Huber Super Four 20-40 tractor appeared. This model was tested at Nebraska in September of that year. In 1929 the company rerated it as a 32-45 tractor. Power came from a four-cylinder Stearns engine with a 5-1/8 x 6-1/2-inch bore and stroke.

Nebraska Test Data

Model: Huber Super Four 20-40

Test No. 126

Date Tested: September 7 to September 16, 1926

Weighing 9,336 lbs., the Huber 20-40 made such an impressive showing in this test that Huber later gave it a 32-45 rating, and during the 1930s marketed virtually the same tractor as the Huber Model "HK." Using gasoline fuel, the 20-40 came out of the rated brake hp test with an economy of 8.23 hp-hours per gallon. In the maximum load test, 50.05 hp was recorded, along with 7.07 hp-hours per gallon. Drawbar tests indicated a maximum of 40.79 hp in low gear, with the 20-40 pulling a 5,932-lb. load at 2.57 mph. Slippage came in at an unusually low 6.305 percent during this test. A maximum load test in high gear yielded a 3,931-lb. pull at 3.605 mph. The 20-40 featured a Stearns four-cylinder, valve-in-head engine rated at 1,100 rpm and using a 5-1/8 x 6-1/2-inch bore and stroke. Standard accessories included a Pomona Vortex air cleaner, Eisemann GS4 magneto, Kingston governor, and a Kingston L-3 carburetor. Except for a broken fan belt, no repairs or adjustments were necessary during the 47-hour test.

COLLECTOR VALUES	1	2	3	4
20-40	$7,500	$5,000	$2,500	$1,000

Huber Four 20-40 tractor

Huber Light Four 20-36 tractor

Advertising for Huber's Light Four 20-36 model first appeared in 1928. The 20-36 was equipped with a Waukesha four-cylinder engine with a 4-3/4 x 6-1/4-inch bore and stroke. A unique feature of this engine was the use of a Ricardo head. Its unique design added extra power, lowered exhaust temperatures, and reduced spark plug fouling. The 20-36 remained on the market through 1935.

Nebraska Test Data

Model: Huber Light Four 20-36

Test No. 168

Date Tested: August 19 to August 24, 1929

Advertised speeds of 2.32 and 3.08 mph were built into the Huber 20-36. Using high gear for the rated load tests gave an average pull of 2,191 lbs. at 3.48 mph, along with an economy of 5.04 hp-hours per gallon. The maximum drawbar load test in low gear yielded a pull of 4,483 lbs. at 2.28 mph for 27.25 drawbar hp. Huber powered the 20-36 with a Waukesha four-cylinder vertical, L-head engine rated at 1,150 rpm and using a 4-3/4 x 6-1/4-inch bore and stroke. It was equipped with a Donaldson air cleaner, Waukesha governor, Stromberg M-3 carburetor, and an Eisemann GV4 magneto. Rated brake hp tests concluded with an economy of 7.79 hp-hours per gallon—fuel consumption totaled 4.625 gph. Under maximum load, economy rose to 8.12 hp-hours per gallon. Total weight of the 20-36 was 6,725 lbs. During the 36-hour test the clutch was adjusted once, otherwise no repairs or adjustments were necessary.

The Huber 25-50 Super Four appeared in 1926. This powerful tractor was capable of nearly 70 belt hp, and nearly 50 hp on the drawbar. It weighed nearly five tons. Power was derived from a Stearns four-cylinder engine with a 5-1/2 x 6-1/2-inch bore and stroke. This tractor was later rerated as the Huber 40-62.

Nebraska Test Data

Model: Huber 40-62 (25-50)

Test No. 135

Date Tested: May 17 to June 24, 1927

Although the 40-62 was introduced as a 25-50 model, it appears to have carried this rating only prior to this test. Weighing 9,910 lbs., the 40-62 delivered 40.62 drawbar hp in the rated load test, pulling 4,442 lbs. at a speed of 3.4 mph. This yielded an economy of 6.58 hp-hours per gallon. Although maximum load tests were made both in low and in high gear, the low-gear test came up with a pull of 7,607 lbs. at 2.43 mph and 9.15 percent slippage for 49.44 drawbar hp. A recorded 69.76 brake hp came from the maximum load test, with the 40-62 delivering 9.29 hp-hours per gallon at rated load. Total fuel consumption in this test was 6.45 gph. A Stearns four-cylinder vertical, valve-in-head engine powered the 40-62-it was rated at 1,100 rpm and used a 5-1/2 x 6-1/2-inch bore and stroke. Also included was a Pomona air cleaner, Ensign "A" carburetor, Eisemann G4 magneto, and a Kingston governor.

Huber Super Four 32-45 tractor

Huber Super Four 25-50

This model was originally known as the Super Four 20-40 tractor and was equipped with a four-cylinder Stearns engine with a 5-1/8 x 6-1/2-inch bore and stroke. In 1935 the Huber HK tractor was introduced and it was described in some publications as the "Huber HK 32-45" tractor. This was an entirely different model than the Huber Super Four 32-45 tractor. About this time the company began offering rubber tires as an extra-cost option. Production of the Super Four 32-45 continued until being suspended by World War II. After the war, tractor production was not resumed.

Huber 40-62 tractor

During 1929 the Huber 25-50 took on a new 40-62 hp rating. As noted previously, this tractor was capable of nearly 70 belt hp, so the new 62 hp rating on the belt was still quite conservative. Production of the 40-62 continued until the onset of World War II.

COLLECTOR VALUES	1	2	3	4
40-62	$12,000	$10,000	$6,000	$2,500

Huber 27-42 tractor

Production of the Huber HS 27-42 tractor continued until World War II. This model was a continuation of the Super Four 18-36 that had been introduced in 1925. In 1929 this model was rerated as the Huber 21-39 and by 1936 was designated as the Huber HS 27-42 tractor.

The Huber Modern Farmer probably made its first appearance in 1933 or 1934. Weighing less than two tons, it used a Waukesha four-cylinder engine with a 4-1/4 x 5-inch bore and stroke. By 1936 it had been replaced by the more powerful Huber L.

Huber Modern Farmer tractor

Huber Modern Farmer SC tractor

The Huber Modern Farmer SC tractor appeared in 1935 and stayed on the market only a short time. This tractor used a four-cylinder Waukesha engine with a 4-1/8 x 5-1/4-inch bore and stroke. In 1936 this tractor was apparently replaced by the Modern Farmer LC tractor with slightly more hp.

Huber L tractor

By 1936 the Huber L tractor appeared. The "L" used a 4-1/2 x 5-1/4 engine for slightly more hp, and the most obvious change is the use of solid disk wheels, both front and rear. Production of the Model L continued until suspended by World War II. The Modern Farmer and the larger "L" tractors were both standard-tread design, while the "SC" and "LC" were both tricycle designs.

Huber Modern Farmer LC tractor

The Modern Farmer LC tractor of 1936 was an improved model over the original "SC" tractor of 1935. This one weighed 3,900 lbs. and was powered by a Waukesha engine with a 4-1/2 x 5-1/4-inch bore and stroke. Rubber tires were optional equipment, and electric starting and lights could be furnished when ordered, but as an extra-cost option. Production of this model ended with the beginning of World War II.

Nebraska Test Data

Model: Huber LC

Test No. 291

Date Tested: October 11 to October 28, 1937

Problems abounded during the 77 hours of operating time required for this test. The off pressure gauge line broke, requiring a replacement. During the third gear maximum drawbar pull the transmission slipped out of gear several times, but the problem was rectified. Also the main fuel tank began leaking, requiring both end seams to be completely resoldered. The LC was tested both with rubber tires and with steel wheels. Fuel economy tests on steel, and using third gear show an efficiency of 6.83 hp-hours per gallon of distillate, compared to an economy of 9.21 when the same test was run on rubber tires. Test H for rated drawbar was made on steel. It indicated an output of 23.34 hp with an efficiency of 7.28 hp-hours per gallon. Test D gave an economy of 10.35 hp-hours per gallon at a load of 37.73 hp and an even better economy of 11.25 at maximum load of 42.24 hp. The LC was equipped with a Waukesha four-cylinder I-head engine. Rated at 1,200 rpm, it carried a 4-1/2 x 5-1/4-inch bore and stroke. Regular equipment included an American Bosch MJB4A magneto and Zenith 455 carburetor. Three speeds were provided of 2.4, 3.5, and 4.5 mph. Operating weight was 5,300 lbs. on steel wheels and 5,500 lbs. on rubber tires.

COLLECTOR VALUES	1	2	3	4
MODERN FARMER LC	--	--	$2,500	--

The Huber Model B came onto the market in 1936 and was built until 1943. This model included a streamlined hood and rubber tires as standard equipment. Electric starting and lights also came as standard equipment. A four-cylinder Buda engine was used in this model; it carried a 3-13/16 x 4-1/2-inch bore and stroke.

Huber Model B tractor

Nebraska Test Data

Model: Huber B

Test No. 292

Date Tested: October 13 to November 8, 1937

Huber used a Buda four-cylinder engine in this tractor model. Rated at 1,300 rpm, it featured an L-head design and carried a 3-13/16 x 4-1/2-inch bore and stroke. An American Bosch MJC4A magneto, Zenith TU4VP carburetor, and Pierce governor were among the accessory items. Several repairs were necessary during the test, including reseating of the valves and repairing the fuel tank. Like the Huber tractor noted in Test No. 291, the Model B was also tested with steel wheels and with rubber tires. Four-hour economy tests in third gear indicate 5.49 hp-hours per gallon on steel wheels, with a substantially better 7.06 economy rating being recorded on rubber tires. Test H on steel wheels indicated an economy of 5.58 hp-hours per gallon and an output of 16.29 rated drawbar hp. Test D results show 8.69 hp-hours per gallon at rated load of 24.15 hp, and an economy of 9.09 at maximum operating load of 27.5 hp. On steel, the Model B weighed in at 3,745 lbs., compared to 4,465 lbs. on rubber tires. A total of 75 hours running time was required for completion of the tests.

COLLECTOR VALUES	1	2	3	4
MODEL B	$4,000	$2,500	$1,500	$800

Huber Model OB orchard tractor

Huber began building its Model OB orchard tractor about 1937. It was simply a standard-tread version of the "B" row-crop tractor, plus the addition of the necessary modifications and the special fenders needed for orchard

Huber road grader

work. It is unlikely that any great number were built, since all tractor production ceased at the beginning of World War II.

By 1920 Huber Mfg. Company had developed an undermounted road grader that was integrated with a specially modified Light Four tractor. This was the beginning of Huber's entry into the road machinery business. Occasionally this machine was illustrated in Huber's farm machinery catalogs. After World War II, Huber once again resumed building road machinery and continued building a specially modified Model B tractor with an extended frame and an undermounted road grader. The tractor shown here is also equipped with a hydraulically-operated front bulldozer blade, and it could be fitted with a scarifier and other devices.

Huber Model B tractor with road grader

Hudkins Tractor Company

SALINA, KANSAS

This company was incorporated for $100,000 in 1918. Aside from this, no other information has been found.

Huffman Traction Engine Company

KENTON, OHIO

Master Huffman tractor

The Master Huffman tractor first appeared in 1913. This massive tractor had an 8-foot drive wheel, and was powered by a huge two-cylinder engine of 70 hp. It also featured two forward speeds, a feature not often found on large, heavyweight tractors. Aside from the initial announcement, little else is known about the company.

Little Oak tractor

Humber-Anderson Mfg. Company

ST. PAUL, MINNESOTA

See: Willmar Tractor Co.

The Little Oak tractor first appeared in 1913 with the incorporation of Humber-Anderson. Originally, it was rated at 25 drawbar and 47 belt hp. A four-cylinder engine was used that it had a 5-5/8 x 7-1/2- inch bore and stroke. It weighed 9,500 lbs., and could be furnished with a four-bottom mounted plow. For exceptional conditions the rear bottom could be hinged upward if needed. Each plow bottom was furnished with a break pin in case a stone or other object was encountered. In August 1914 the company was reorganized as Willmar Mfg. Company at Willmar, Minnesota. In December 1916 the company was again reorganized as Standard Tractor Company at Stillwater, Minnesota.

COLLECTOR VALUES	1	2	3	4
LITTLE OAK	–	–	$9,000	–

Hume Mfg. Company

HUME, ILLINOIS

Hume was organized in 1913 and eventually received Patent No. 1,068,517 for its design. This tractor was rated at 20 drawbar and 30 belt hp, using a four-cylinder engine. Weighing 7,000 lbs., it sold for $1,350. About 1916 a Hume Jr. tractor appeared, but our research has found little information on this model. About 1917 the company was bought out by Lyons-Atlas Company of Indianapolis, Indiana, which built the same tractor under the Atlas name for a short time.

Hume Jr. tractor

Hunter Tractor Company

LOS ANGELES, CALIFORNIA

Hunter tractor

The Hunter was a short-lived tractor that apparently made its first appearance about 1918 or 1919. It was a four-wheel-drive design and featured hard rubber tires. Weighing three tons, it was capable of speeds from 1-1/2 to 12 mph. Power came from a Barker six-cylinder horizontally opposed engine. In 1920, the last year it was listed in the trade directories, the Hunter 15-25 sold for $5,500.

Huron Engineering Company

BELLEVILLE, MICHIGAN

Huron Model A-2 garden tractor

The Huron Model A-2 garden tractor appears in the 1948 trade directories. No other references to this model have been found. Powered by a Clinton 1-1/2-hp engine, the A-2 rode on 4.00x18 implement tires with the wheel spacing adjustable from 23 to 30 inches. Shipping weight was 270 lbs.

COLLECTOR VALUES	1	2	3	4
MODEL A-Z	$500	$350	$150	$45

Huron Tractor Company

DETROIT, MICHIGAN

The Boyer Four, 12-25 tractor appeared in the 1917 trade directories, the only year in which it is listed. It was equipped with a Waukesha four-cylinder engine with a 4-1/4 x 5-3/4-inch bore and stroke. Little else is known of the Boyer Four, probably because it was marketed for only a short time.

Boyer Four, 12-25 tractor

H. L. Hurst Mfg. Company

GREENWICH, OHIO

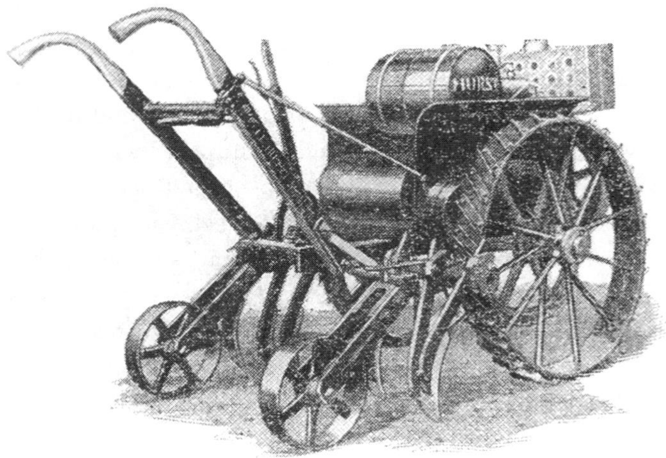

Hurst 2-4 garden tractor

In 1920 the Hurst 2-4 garden tractor appeared. Rated at 2 drawbar and 4 belt hp, it was equipped with a single-cylinder engine. This outfit weighed 600 lbs. and was priced new at $355. It was also known as the Hurst Culti-Plow. The Hurst 2-4 is currently valued at $2,000 to $3,000 in any condition.

[Throughout this section, assume that gasoline was used for fuel unless another fuel source is indicated.]

Illinois Tractor Company

BLOOMINGTON, ILLINOIS

The Illinois Motor Cultivator made its appearance in 1916. At the time the company was known as Illinois Silo Company, and by the following year the name was changed to Illinois Silo & Tractor Company.

Illinois Motor Cultivator

The motor cultivator was available with a single-cylinder 4 hp engine as shown here, or it could be supplied with an 8 hp two-cylinder engine if so desired.

Illinois Motor Cultivator, 1917 model

The 1917 Illinois Motor Cultivator was vastly improved over the original 1916 model. Power now came from a four-cylinder engine of 16 brake hp and it used a 3 x 3-1/4-inch bore and stroke. Through a unique clutch system built into each drive wheel, the motor cultivator could literally turn in its own tracks. Front caster wheels were used to permit short turns. No Motor Cultivators are known to exist.

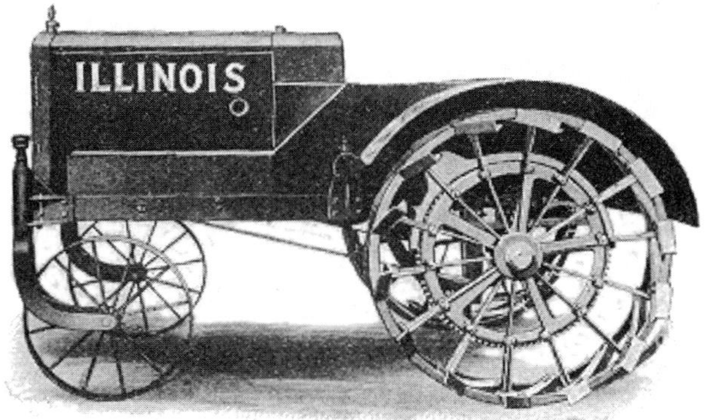

Illinois 12-30 tractor

Sometime in 1917 the Illinois 12-30 tractor appeared. Weighing 3,700 lbs., it was priced at $1,200. Power came from a Waukesha four-cylinder engine with a 4-1/2 x 5-3/4-inch bore and stroke. A friction drive transmission provided infinitely variable speeds up to 6 mph. This model remained on the market through 1918.

Illinois Super-Drive 18-30 tractor

By 1918 the company had once again changed its name to Illinois Tractor Company. The following year the Illinois Super-Drive 18-30 tractor appeared. It was powered by a Climax four-cylinder engine with a 5 x 6-1/2-inch bore and stroke. The 18-30 weighed 5,500 lbs. and sold for $2,250. This tractor used a unique drive system with springs between the rear wheels and the spokes. It was intended to minimize unwanted strain for both the engine and the load.

COLLECTOR VALUES	1	2	3	4
SUPER DRIVE 18-30	$8,000	$6,000	$4,000	$2,200

Illinois Super-Drive 22-40 tractor

By 1920 Illinois Tractor Company was offering its Illinois Super-Drive 22-40 tractor. This model was likely built for only a short time, since the company disappeared from the trade directories after 1921. The 22-40 used a four-cylinder Climax engine and weighed 6,200 lbs. Illinois Super-Drive tractors were sold in Canada by Robert Bell Engine & Thresher Company of Seaforth, Ontario, under the name of Imperial Super-Drive.

Imperial Mfg. Company

MINNEAPOLIS, MINNESOTA

Imperial 40-60 tractor

The Imperial 40-60 tractor first appeared in 1910 from this firm, although they were previously built in 1908 by Valentine Bros., also of Minneapolis. The latter merged with the Shock & Hay Loader Co. of Minneapolis to form Imperial in 1910. The 40-60 tractor was actively built as late as 1914, but the company continued to build them on a limited basis as late as 1920. The 40-60 used a four-cylinder horizontally opposed engine with a 7-1/2 x 9-inch bore and stroke. In 1920 the Imperial tractor was offered at a price of $4,500. Three specimens are known to exist today.

COLLECTOR VALUES	1	2	3	4
40-60 (1910)	$100,000	–	–	–

Independent Harvester Company

PLANO, ILLINOIS

Independent was fairly well known as an implement builder, but little is know about its efforts in the tractor business.

Independent Tractor Company

MINNEAPOLIS, MINNESOTA

In 1917 this firm was listed as the manufacturer of the Independent Drive Tractor. No other information has been located.

Indiana Farm Bureau Co-Op

SHELBYVILLE, INDIANA

Co-Op Model C tractor

In 1945 the Indiana Farm Bureau Co-Op at Shelbyville, Indiana, produced a Co-Op Model C tractor. It is believed that only 66 units were built. It used a Continental F124 flathead engine. In 1985 an article in Gas Engine magazine suggested that only three of these exist. At this point it seems two more have surfaced. It is believed that of those extant only two (or maybe three) are complete and have been restored. The PTO was operated by a roller chain drive. Also of interest is the fact that an ordinary hex-shaped salt shaker glass was used as a sediment bowl. The

Co-op emblem on the front of the tractor was made of cast iron. At the 1999 Ed Speiss Classic Tractor Auction, a Co-Op C Narrow Front sold for $10,000 and a Wide Front sold for $11,000, both in No. 1 restored condition.

Indiana Silo & Tractor Company

ANDERSON, INDIANA

Indiana 5-10 tractor

The Indiana tractor first appeared in 1918 and remained on the market into the early 1920s. Weighing 2,200 lbs., it was powered by a LeRoi four-cylinder engine with a 3-1/8 x 4-1/2-inch bore and stroke. Much of the design for the Indiana tractor came from C. A. Schubert of Findlay, Ohio. It was also sold as the Indiana All 'Round Tractor.

Nebraska Test Data

Model: Indiana 5-10

Test No. 62

Date Tested: September 13 to September 17, 1920

Designed as an all-purpose tractor, the Indiana 5-10 featured the same LeRoi 3-1/8 x 4-1/2-inch, four-cylinder engine found in many other small tractors of the period. As used in the 5-10, it was equipped with a Kingston Model L carburetor and an Atwater-Kent Model K-3 ignition system. Rated speed was 1,000 rpm. During the entire 28 hours of running time, few repairs or adjustments were necessary, although the small sprocket on the final drive showed considerable wear at the end of the test. Total weight of the Indiana 5-10 was 2,400 lbs. This photograph illustrates a grain drill coupled to the 5-10 and many other implements could be similarly attached, as could a set of trailer wheels with seat. Gasoline was the chosen fuel, with 8.52 hp-hours resulting from the rated brake hp test. With 10.20 hp developed, fuel consumption during the two-hour test totaled 1.2 gallons per hour (gph). Rated speed was variable from one to four mph, and at rated drawbar, 5 hp was developed at 2.21 mph, yielding a pull of 849 lbs. A second maximum load test at 1.79 mph gave a maximum pull of 1,189 lbs. and 5.66 drawbar hp.

COLLECTOR VALUES	1	2	3	4
5-10	$8,000	$5,000	$3,000	$1,000

Inexco Tractor Corporation

NEW YORK, NEW YORK

Inexco started offering its Tiger garden tractors in 1948. By 1950 the Piedmont Tractor Division of Inexco was building the Tiger tractors at its plant in Fort Lee, New Jersey. In 1951 the Tiger tractor line was being built by Tiger Tractor Corporation at Keyser, West Virginia.

Inexco Tiger 12 garden tractor, Model IXA-12

In 1948 Inexco offered its Tiger 12 garden tractor, Model IXA-12. It was powered by a Wisconsin Model TF single-cylinder engine with a 3 x 3-1/4-inch bore and stroke. Various implements were available, and a belt pulley came as standard equipment.

Inexco Tiger 3 Motor Cultivator

The 1948 Inexco line also included the Tiger 3 Motor Cultivator. Weighing 440 lbs., this outfit used a sliding motor base to add or release tension on the drive belt as the clutch mechanism. Power came from a choice of a 3-1/2 hp Lauson engine, or Wisconsin or Clinton engines. Two forward speeds were provided.

Inexco Tiger 5

Tiger tractor PTD6

The 1950 Tiger tractor line included the PTD6 shown here. This one is equipped with optional dual rear tires, plus a plow attachment and a sickle mower attachment. Briggs & Stratton or Clinton engines could be specified. The PTD5 shown here was quite similar to the concurrent PTD6 model. Numerous attachments were available, as was the choice of a Clinton or a Briggs & Stratton engine.

COLLECTOR VALUES	1	2	3	4
ALL MODELS	$1,200	$800	$400	$250

Inland-American Tractor Company

EAU CLAIRE, WISCONSIN

This firm was listed as a tractor builder in 1921, but no further information has been found.

Intercontinental Mfg. Company

GARLAND, TEXAS

The Intercontinental C-26 was apparently developed during 1946 and 1947, and was on the market by 1948. The company continued building tractors throughout the 1950s, but for unknown reasons disappeared from the market after 1960.

Intercontinental C-26 tractor

This model used a Continental four-cylinder gasoline engine with a 3-7/16 x 4-3/8-inch bore and stroke. This model was tested at Nebraska and demonstrated a rated output of 20 drawbar hp.

Nebraska Test Data

Model: Intercontinental C-26

Test No. 400

Date Tested: August 28 to September 9, 1948

During 43 hours of engine operating time, Nebraska Test engineers noted that at one point the battery was discharged due to a faulty voltage regulator and also that the radiator shroud came loose from the radiator during testing. No other repairs or adjustments were noted. This tractor featured forward speeds of 2.7, 3.8, 5.3, and 10.7 mph. Second gear was used for Test H. This 10-hour test indicated a fuel economy of 8.74 hp-hours per gallon. Also noted was a rated output of 20.19 drawbar hp, along with a pull of 1,978 lbs. at 3.83 mph and a slippage of 3.85 percent. A low-gear maximum pull of 3,441 lbs. at 2.34 mph was recorded in Test G. Standard equipment for the C-26 included 11-38-inch rear and 5.50-16- inch front tires. Also featured was a Continental four-cylinder L-head engine rated at 1,650 rpm and that carried a 3-7/16 x 4-3/8-inch bore and stroke. Accessories included an Auto-Lite electrical system and Marvel-Schebler TSX338 carburetor. Under a Test C operating maximum load of 28.16 belt hp, the C-26 produced 10.87 hp-hours per gallon of fuel. A comparable figure of 10.70 was manifested under a Test D rated belt load of 26.69 hp. This was the first Texas-built tractor to be tested at Nebraska.

COLLECTOR VALUES	1	2	3	4
C-26	$18,000	–	–	–

Intercontinental D-26 diesel tractor

Production of the Intercontinental D-26 diesel tractor began in late 1948 or early 1949. This model was quite similar to the gasoline-powered C-26, but used a Buda four-cylinder diesel engine. Rated at 1,800 rpm, it carried a 3-7/16 x 4-1/8-inch bore and stroke.

Nebraska Test Data

Model: Intercontinental D-26 (diesel)

Test No. 420

Date Tested: August 4 to August 13, 1949

Weighing in at 3,578 lbs., the D-26 featured 11-38-inch rear and 5.50-16-inch front rubber. For the purposes of Tests F, G, and H an additional 148 lbs. of liquid ballast plus 900 lbs. of cast-iron weight was added to each rear wheel, for a total test weight of 6,091 lbs. Test H, run in second gear, manifested a rated output of 21.07 drawbar hp, along with a pull of 1,852 lbs. at 4.27 mph and a slippage of 3.48 percent. A fuel economy of 11.1 hp-hours per gallon of diesel fuel was recorded. In addition, a maximum low-gear pull of 3,406 lbs. was achieved at a speed of 2.78 mph under a slippage of 8.94 percent. This tractor featured a Buda four-cylinder diesel engine of I-head design. Rated at 1,800 rpm, it carried a 3-7/16 x 4-1/8-inch bore and stroke. Also included was an Auto-Lite 12-volt electrical system and Bosch fuel injection equipment. Except for a fuel line leak, no repairs or adjustments were noted during 43 hours of engine operating time. This tractor featured forward speeds of 2.5, 3.5, 4.9, and 9.8 mph. Tests B and C at a 100 percent maximum load of 28.86 belt hp indicated 10.96 hp-hours per gallon of diesel fuel, compared to an economy figure of 12.14 at the Test D rated load of 26.05 hp.

Cultrac crawler

In 1950 the Cultrac crawler appeared. This interesting design weighed only 1,750 lbs., and was equipped with a Waukesha four-cylinder engine with a displacement of 61 cubic inches. Designed primarily as a cultivating tractor, it could be used for other jobs as well. Production continued for only a short time.

Model DF tractor

The largest tractor of the Intercontinental line was the Model DF. It first appeared in 1952 or 1953. It had a maximum output of 34 belt hp. A four-cylinder Buda diesel engine was used and it carried a 3-3/4 x 4-1/8-inch bore and stroke. This tractor was also designated as the Federal DF.

International Cultivator Company

OSHKOSH, WISCONSIN

During 1921 International Cultivator Co. was listed as a tractor manufacturer. Further details are yet to be found.

International Gas Engine Company

CUDAHY, WISCONSIN

Ingeco tractor

In late 1914 or early 1915 the Ingeco tractor appeared. Rated at 10 drawbar and 20 belt hp, it used a two-cylinder opposed engine. It weighed 5,000 lbs., and the retail price was $700. The company remained in the tractor market until a merger created Worthington Pump & Machinery Company. The latter continued to build the tractor for only a short time.

International Harvester Company

CHICAGO, ILLINOIS

Few companies of any sort, and especially in the farm machinery industry, can boast the history associated with International Harvester Company. Cyrus Hall McCormick invented the reaper in 1831, and since that time his name has carried a special mystique shared by few others in the history of agricultural mechanization. Deering Harvester Company began operations in 1880, although the company had roots going back to the 1850s. By 1900 Deering was also a huge manufacturer of harvesting machinery.

McCormick, Deering, and several other companies merged in 1902 to form International Harvester Company. Within a couple of years IHC began experimenting with gasoline tractors. This in itself is interesting, since the company never seems to have had much fascination with steam power, even though in 1902 and for another 20 years steam power reigned supreme on American farms.

To its credit, IHC probably poured more money into research and development of the farm tractor than any of its competitors, at least in the early years. The gamble paid off, because IHC quickly rose to the forefront in the tractor industry. The challenge of the Fordson tractor only goaded the company into accelerated research on a truly practical row-crop tractor. Full production of the Farmall row-crop tractor began in 1924. It revolutionized thinking about what a row-crop tractor should look like, and how it should perform!

By 1930 the IHC tractor line was already the most extensive of any American manufacturer. Farm tractors were available in row-crop and standard-tread designs. The IHC crawler tractor line was developing, and several styles of IHC Industrial tractors were available. Curiously, the company did not enter the garden tractor business. With the huge dealer network and product loyalty enjoyed by IHC, the odds are garden tractors would have been very successful.

Despite the quality of the IHC tractor and equipment lines, the company veered into financial problems due in part to the depressed agricultural economy of the 1980s. It eventually merged with J. I. Case to form today's Case-IH product line.

International Harvester Company Auto-Mower

International Harvester Company began building tractors in 1906. One of the predecessors, McCormick Harvesting Machine Company, began developing an "Auto-Mower" a decade earlier. Although it was not well accepted, and never got past a small production, it certainly indicated the mindset of company engineers. Gasoline power would be the coming thing in the mechanization of agriculture.

Deering Harvester Company mower

Deering Harvester Company began experimenting with a self-powered mowing machine as early as 1891. One of these machines even went to the Paris Exhibition of 1900. Although it attracted considerable attention, it was impractical for a variety of reasons and never went into full production.

International Harvester gasoline tractor

By 1906 International Harvester was producing gasoline tractors. Already in 1889 S. S. Morton's friction drive traction trucks were attracting attention. With this chassis almost any gasoline engine could be mounted as the power unit. International Harvester did so with its newly designed gasoline engines. Various styles of friction-drive tractors were built in the following years.

IHC Type A tractor

For 1907 the International Harvester gasoline tractor was given an improved appearance over the initial offering. This model showed a 15-hp IHC Famous engine mounted on the frame, along with an evaporative cooling tank mounted to the front. In 1908, IHC sold almost 630 of these tractors. The 15-hp Type A used a single-cylinder engine with an 8 x 14-inch bore and stroke. A larger 20-hp model had a 9 x 15-inch bore and stroke. Type A tractors continued in production through 1916.

COLLECTOR VALUES	1	2	3	4
15 HP	–	$70,000	$50,000	$20,000
20 HP	$125,000	–	–	–

By 1908 International Harvester was looking past the single-cylinder tractors that comprised the line. This three-cylinder experimental tractor emerged. Rated at 40 hp, it used a 7 x 9-inch bore and stroke. It was entered in the 1908 Winnipeg tractor trials and performed fairly well, but apparently IHC engineers weren't impressed because nothing more was heard of the tractor after that time.

IHC Type B tractor

The IHC Type B tractors were similar to the Type A. The 20-hp size was the most popular. The Type B was built between 1910 and 1917. In addition, a Type B, two-speed model was also built in the 1910 through 1917 period.

IHC three-cylinder tractor

IHC Type C Mogul tractor

The 20-hp IHC Type C Mogul tractor first appeared in 1909. Beginning about this time, and for some years to come, Mogul engines were sold by McCormick implement dealers, and Titan tractors were sold by Deering dealers. This separation of models was the result of a long, convoluted anti-trust suit that spurred by the 1902 merger. In 1911 IHC added the 25 hp Mogul to the line and both styles went out of production in 1914.

IHC Mogul 45 tractor

In 1911 IHC introduced the Mogul 45 tractor. This big two-cylinder model was among the first to leave Harvester's new Chicago Tractor Works and the IHC Titan tractors were mostly produced at Milwaukee Works. Initially at least, the Mogul 45 used the cooling system shown here and it would change by 1912.

COLLECTOR VALUES	1	2	3	4
MOGUL 45	--	$121,000	--	–

IHC Mogul 30-60 tractor

By 1912 the IHC Mogul 45 had taken the form shown here. Late that year the company revised the tractor slightly and called it the Mogul 30-60. More than 2,400 IHC Mogul 45 and Mogul 30-60 tractors were built between 1911 and 1917. This model used a big two-cylinder opposed engine with a carburetor for each cylinder. A small 1-hp engine was used to turn the big flywheels for starting.

COLLECTOR VALUES	1	2	3	4
MOGUL 30-60	--	--	$90,000	–

With the 1911 introduction of the Mogul 45 came the single-cylinder Mogul Jr. 25 hp tractor. It was quite similar in design to the Mogul 45. During late 1912 or early 1913 this tractor was given a 15-30 hp rating. Production of the 15-30 continued into 1915. During 1912 and 1913 IHC produced a similar 10-20 model, but little information is available on this tractor.

COLLECTOR VALUES	1	2	3	4
MOGUL JR.	--	--	$80,000	–

IHC Mogul Jr. tractor

IHC Mogul 12-25 tractor

The Mogul 12-25 actually first saw light in 1911, but was then built as the Mogul 10-20 (no relation to the Mogul 10-20 of a few years later). In 1912 it was christened the Mogul 12-25 and was the first of the IHC production models to actually look like a lightweight design. Production of this model continued into 1918.

COLLECTOR VALUES	1	2	3	4
12-25	$35,000	$25,000	$15,000	–

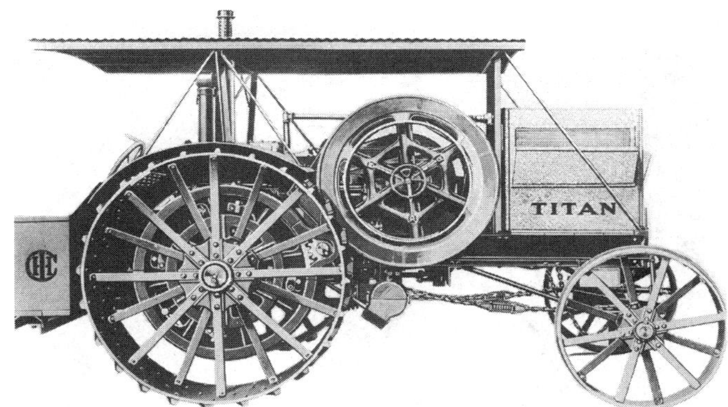

IHC Type D Titan tractor

Production of the IHC Type D Titan 25-hp tractor began in 1910 and ended in 1914. The model was originally sold as a 20-hp tractor, but was upgraded about 1912. A single-cylinder engine was used that had an 8-3/4 x 15-inch bore and stroke.

COLLECTOR VALUES	1	2	3	4
MOGUL 30-60	--	--	$80,000	–

IHC Titan 12-25 tractor

IHC Titan 45 tractor

While McCormick farm machinery dealers were busy selling Mogul tractors, the Deering dealers were geared up to sell the Titan tractor line. For a number of years the various components of IHC were forced by government edict to operate as separate companies, under the IHC corporate umbrella. The Titan 45 first appeared in 1911. It was sold under this rating until 1913 when it was revamped and rerated as the Titan 30-60. The last reported sale of an early Titan 45, in 1999, was for $116,000.

IHC Titan 30-60 tractor

About 1913 the Titan 45 became the Titan 30-60 tractor. Its outward appearance changed slightly, but in 1915 the 30-60 took on an entirely new appearance with an enclosed cab and a cellular radiator. A friction-drive starting engine was used to roll over the flywheels of the big engine for starting. Production of the Titan 30-60 ended in 1917. The last reported sale, in 1998, was for $120,000.

The first 12-25 Titan tractor appeared at Milwaukee Works in 1915. This model remained in production until 1916 when it was re-rated as the 15-30 Titan. Production continued through 1917; then, it was slightly altered and became known as the International Titan 15-30. On these tractors, each cylinder had its own mixer and needle valve, so it required some careful adjustment to get each cylinder properly tuned.

International Titan 15-30 tractor

Production of the International Titan 15-30 tractor began in 1918 and continued into 1921. This model used a four-cylinder engine with a 5-1/4 x 8-inch bore and stroke. For 1918 this model had a list price of $1,900. Despite this, more than 5,500 of these tractors were built in the 1918 through 1921 period.

Nebraska Test Data

Model: International 15-30

Test No. 24

Date Tested: June 14 to June 19, 1920

Weighing 8,990 lbs., the International 15-30 featured a four-cylinder horizontal, valve-in-head engine with a 5-1/4 x 8-inch bore and stroke. Rated speed was 575 rpm. Standard equipment included a K-W magneto and a carburetor of Harvester's own design—indeed the over-design of the 15-30 carburetor typified early IH tractors. Two forward speeds were provided of 1.85 and 2.48 mph. Further proof of its excellent design is shown in an evaluation of Test No. 24 that indicated the clutch was adjusted once, but otherwise no repairs or adjustments were necessary. Nearly 26 hp was recorded in the maximum drawbar test, with the 15-30 pulling a 4,210 lb. load at 2.31 mph. Kerosene was used throughout the test procedures, with fuel economy calculating to 6.88 hp-hours per gallon on the rated load test. A maximum of 36.98 brake hp was achieved but fuel consumption rose to 7.29 gph. Coolant temperature varied from 207 to 212 degrees F. throughout the tests.

COLLECTOR VALUES	1	2	3	4
TITAN 15-30	$40,000	--	–	–

IHC Titan Type D 18-35 tractor

The IHC Titan Type D 18-35 tractor was produced between 1912 and 1915. This model was essentially built over the Titan 30-60 chassis, but with a smaller engine. Production of this model was very limited. Less than 300 left the production line. Two specimens are known to exist.

COLLECTOR VALUES	1	2	3	4
TITAN 18-35 D	–	$100,000	–	–

Titan 15-30 tractor

International 8-16

IHC Mogul 8-16 tractor

IHC got into the tractor business in a big way with its 1914 introduction of the IHC Mogul 8-16 tractor. It used a single-cylinder engine of hopper-cooled design for the ultimate in simplicity. The 8-16 engine had an 8 x 12-inch bore and stroke. Production of the 8-16 continued into 1917. During that time the company built over 14,000 of the 8-16 Mogul tractors. The 8-16 was replaced with the similar, improved, Mogul 10-20.

COLLECTOR VALUES	1	2	3	4
MOGUL 8-16				
TIN HOPPER	$30,000	$22,000	$17,000	$7,000
CAST HOPPER	$28,000	$20,000	$15,000	$5,000

IHC Mogul 10-20 tractor

Harvester began building the Mogul 10-20 in late 1916, with both the 8-16 and the 10-20 available late that year, and early into 1917. The Mogul had a single-cylinder engine with an 8-1/2 x 12-inch bore and stroke. New features included two forward speeds and the addition of fenders. Over 8,900 of these tractors were built in the 1916 through 1919 period.

COLLECTOR VALUES	1	2	3	4
MOGUL 10-20	--	$35,000	--	--

IHC Motor Cultivator

International Harvester introduced its motor cultivator in 1916 and continued building them into 1918. Contrary to expectations, this machine did not become popular, and it took two years after production ended to sell the last of them. Harvester modified this machine extensively, hoping it could be adapted to a variety of farm machines and become the basis for a universal tractor. This finally happened when the company built 200 of its new 1924 Farmall row-crop tractors. (Only a few are known to exist.)

IHC Titan 10-20 tractor

Between 1916 and 1922 IHC built over 78,000 of the IHC Titan 10-20 tractors. From its introduction, the Titan 10-20 was phenomenally popular, and was the first tractor for many farmers. It was powered by a two-cylinder engine with a 6-1/2 x 8-inch bore and stroke. In 1919 the 10-20 got full-length rear fenders, and the rated speed was raised from 500 to 575 rpm. About this time an Ensign carburetor replaced the simple mixer used on earlier models.

Nebraska Test Data

Model: International Titan 10-20

Test No. 23

Date Tested: June 14 to June 19, 1920

Throughout some 30 hours of running time it was necessary to clean one spark plug and adjust the magneto breaker points. Otherwise no repairs or adjustments were noted in Test No. 23. The 10-20 Titan featured a twin-cylinder engine with parallel cranks. Rated at 575 rpm, it used a 6-1/2 x 8-inch bore and stroke. At its rated load of 20.18 hp, the 10-20 delivered an economy of 7.86 hp-hours per gallon of kerosene, but economy slipped to 6.06 when at the maximum brake load of 28.15 hp. Two forward speeds of 2.15 and 2.9 mph were provided Low gear was used for the rated drawbar test, and at 9.94 hp the 10-20 pulled 1,827 lbs. at 2.04 mph with slippage of 11.7 percent. Fuel economy was registered at 3.31 hp-hours per gallon. The maximum drawbar trials in low gear elicited a pull of 2,660 lbs. at 1.93 mph with slippage recorded at 14.4 percent and a maximum output of 13.67 drawbar hp. Standard equipment included a K-W TK magneto and Harvester's own carburetor. Operating weight was 5,708 lbs.

COLLECTOR VALUES	1	2	3	4
TITAN 10-20	$16,000	$14,000	$8,000	$4,000

International 8-16 tractor

First built in 1917, the International 8-16 was a four-cylinder lightweight model. It followed the 8-16 Mogul tractor production, and despite numerous changes the International 8-16 remained in production until 1922. Early in production, Harvester also adapted this tractor as an industrial model by replacing the steel wheels with hard rubber tires. The 8-16 was equipped with the company's own four-cylinder engine with a 4-1/4 x 5-inch bore and stroke. It marked the company's entry into the design and production of lightweight tractors.

Nebraska Test Data

Model: International 8-16

Test No. 25

Date Tested: June 16 to June 21, 1920

Featuring Harvester's own four-cylinder vertical, valve-in-head engine, the 8-16 weighed in at 3,660 lbs. Rated speed was 1,000 rpm with a bore and stroke of 4-1/4 x 5-inches. Three forward speeds were provided of 1.81, 2.81, and 4.1 mph. An Ensign carburetor and Dixie Model 46 magneto served as standard equipment. Kerosene was used throughout the test procedures, which required 32 hours of running time. Except for a broken governor spring, no repairs or adjustments were necessary. Slightly over 18-1/2 brake hp was developed on the maximum load test with a fuel consumption of 3.24 gph. At rated load this figure dropped to 2.19 gph, with a fuel economy of 7.32 hp-hours per gallon. Nearly 2,600 lbs. was recorded on the maximum drawbar test at a ground travel of 1.59 mph, for an equivalent of 11.00 drawbar hp. Drive wheel slippage rose to 18.2 percent on the maximum load test. Coolant temperatures ranged from 209 to 211 degrees F. throughout the test procedures.

COLLECTOR VALUES	1	2	3	4
8-16				
FIRST YEAR	$11,000	$9,000	$7,000	$3,500
LATER	$9,000	$7,500	$3,500	$2,500

International 15-30 tractor

In 1921 IHC began producing its 15-30 tractor. It marked the end for heavyweight designs and was the first IHC tractor to use the unit-frame design. All parts were enclosed, and a single casting ran from the radiator to the bull gears. The engine crankshaft was carried by two massive ball bearings. Numerous options were available, including a rear PTO shaft. The tractor used the company's own four-cylinder engine, which carried a 4-1/2 x 6-inch bore and stroke. About 1926 the rated engine speed was raised from 1,000 to 1,050 rpm and it gave the 15-30 nearly 35 belt hp.

Nebraska Test Data

Model: International 15-30

Test No. 87

Date Tested: August 9 to August 14, 1922

No adjustments or repairs were necessary during the 31 hours of running time. This new International model featured Harvester's own four-cylinder vertical, valve-in-head engine. It was the first tractor ever tested at Nebraska to feature ball bearing main crankshaft bearings. Using a 4-1/2 x 6-inch bore and stroke, it was rated at 1,000 rpm. Standard equipment included a Dixie Model 46-C Aero magneto and an Ensign 1-1/2-inch Style J.T.W. carburetor. The sliding gear transmission permitted speeds of 2.3, 2.92, and 4.46 mph. Total weight was 6,000 lbs. On the rated brake hp test, 30.18 hp was developed, consuming 2.96 gallons of kerosene per hour, for 10.19 hp-hours per gallon. Under maximum load conditions 32.86 belt hp was noted, with fuel economy coming in at 9.78. On the drawbar, rated load tests were taken in second gear. Travelling at 2.74 mph the 15-30 pulled a load of 2,107 lbs. over 10 hours, for an average of 15.35 drawbar hp. Shifting to low gear in the maximum load test gave a maximum pull of 2.790 lbs. and 19.87 drawbar hp.

Nebraska Test Data

Model: McCormick-Deering 15-30

Test No. 130

Date Tested: October 26 to November 2, 1926

Shortly after the conclusion of Test No. 87, IHC started using the McCormick-Deering brand name on this tractor. Featuring Harvester's own "E4A" magneto and an Ensign RW carburetor, the higher-speed version of the 15-30 was also equipped with a Pomona air cleaner, along with a governor system designed and built by International Harvester. The four-cylinder vertical, valve-in-head engine was rated at 1,050 rpm and carried a 4-1/2 x 6-inch bore and stroke. Low gear gave a speed of 2 mph, compared to 4 mph in high gear. Total tractor weight was 6,982 lbs. No repairs or adjustments were necessary during the test. At rated drawbar load the 15-30 delivered 7.21 hp-hours per gallon of kerosene for substantially better fuel economy at the drawbar than was usually the case. A maximum pull of 4,190 lbs. in low gear, along with a speed of 2.39 mph and slippage of 9.17 percent gave a maximum of 25.545 drawbar hp. The rated brake hp test indicated 10.32 hp-hours per gallon of kerosene, with consumption totaling 2.928 gph. Under maximum load, 34.91 brake hp was recorded.

McCormick-Deering 15-30 tractor

The McCormick-Deering 15-30 was modified in 1929. A major change was the use of a 4-3/4-inch engine bore, compared to 4-1/2 inches in earlier tractors. This model was known as the 15-30, the New 15-30, and the 22-36, depending on where it was sold. (A former company official once noted export tractors were taxed on the basis of hp. Obviously, a nameplate bearing 15-30 was taxed less than one reading 22-36.) Production of this model ended in 1934. Nearly 100,000 were built during its 1921 through 1934 production run.

Nebraska Test Data

Model: McCormick-Deering 15-30

Test No. 156

Date Tested: March 30 to April 9, 1929

The 15-30 noted in this test carried bore and stroke dimensions of 4-3/4 x 6 inches. Rated speed was 1,050 rpm. Harvester supplied its own E4A magneto along with a Pomona air cleaner and an oil filter of its own design. Advertised speeds of 2-1/2, 3-1/4, and 4-1/8 mph were featured. Kerosene fuel was used throughout the 48-hour test. Weighing 7,486 lbs., the 15-30 gave a maximum pull of 3,912 lbs. at 2.88 mph, developing slightly over 30 drawbar hp in the process. At rated drawbar load of 22.78 hp, this tractor yielded 6.18 hp-hours per gallon of kerosene, pulling 2,258 lbs. at 3.78 mph. The rated brake test indicated 36.15 hp while consuming 3.898 gallons of kerosene per hour and producing 9.27 hp-hours per gallon. The latter figure rose to 9.99 while operating at maximum load and producing 40.66 hp. No repairs or adjustments were made during the test.

COLLECTOR VALUES	1	2	3	4
15-30	$3,500	$1,900	$1,200	$900

McCormick-Deering 10-20 tractor

Introduced in 1923, the McCormick-Deering 10-20 tractor remained in production until 1939. Over 215,000 were built during this period. This tractor was tested at Nebraska in 1923, with specifications showing the four-cylinder, 4-1/4 x 5-inch engine operating at 1,000 rpm. In 1927 the 10-20 returned, with the only major difference being a rated speed of 1,025 rpm. Numerous variations were available for the 10-20, along with a variety of special equipment. Pneumatic tires became optionally available in the late 1930s.

Nebraska Test Data

Model: McCormick-Deering 10-20

Test No. 95

Date Tested: September 25 to October 3, 1923

Weighing only 4,010 lbs. and using a four-cylinder, 4-1/4 x 5-inch engine, the 10-20 was rated at 1,000 rpm and carried a Splitdorf Aero 46-C magneto and an Ensign JH, 1-1/4-inch carburetor. Harvester provided its own governor and water-type air cleaner. Low gear gave a ground speed of 2.17 mph, with intermediate and high gears with respective speeds of 3.21 and 4.25 mph. No repairs or adjustments were made during the test. Using kerosene throughout the test, the 10-20 showed an economy of 10.15 hp-hours per gallon or total consumption of 1.978 gph. A maximum drawbar load test run in low gear gave a value of 15.54 drawbar hp, with the 10-20 pulling a 2,640-lb. load at 2.21 mph. Much of the 10-20 design was a scaled down version of the earlier 15-30 tractor noted in Test No. 87.

Nebraska Test Data

Model: McCormick-Deering 10-20

Test No. 142

Date Tested: October 3 to October 8, 1927

The McCormick-Deering previously tested under No. 95 had a rated speed of 1,000 rpm, while the tractor submitted for this test had a 1,025 rpm speed rating. Another minor change was the use of Harvester's "E4A" magneto on this tractor. Otherwise the tractors were virtually identical. Using kerosene throughout the test, rated drawbar trials indicated a fuel economy of 6.11 hp-hours per gallon. Maximum load tests were made in all three forward gears, but low gear yielded the highest pull with 2,955 lbs. recorded. Total tractor weight was 5,028 lbs. At rated brake hp the 10-20 burned 2.035 gph of fuel, yielding 10.05 hp-hours per gallon. Maximum load tests indicated 24.81 hp with an economy of 9.12 hp-hours per gallon and total consumption of 2.721 gph. No repairs or adjustments were made throughout the 35 hours of running time required for the complete test.

Nebraska Test Data

Model: McCormick-Deering Industrial 20

Test No. 194

Date Tested: July 20 to July 27, 1931

This industrial tractor, also known as the I-20, was in many respects identical to the McCormick-Deering 10-20 tractor tested in 1927. Gasoline was used for this test, and at rated drawbar load of 17.77 hp the I-20 pulled 1,679 lbs. at 3.97 mph with a fuel economy of 6.09 hp-hours per gallon. Low gear gave both the maximum pull and maximum drawbar hp of 3,144 and 23.01 respectively, at a speed of 2.74 mph. At its maximum load of 29.87 brake hp, the I-20 yielded 9.07 hp-hours per gallon, with a slightly higher economy of 9.26 appearing at its rated 27.03 hp. This 5,415-lb. tractor featured Harvester's own four-cylinder vertical, I-head engine with a 4-1/4 x 5-inch bore and stroke. Rated at 1,150 rpm, it also featured three forward speeds of 2-1/2, 3-1/2, and 5 mph. Accessory items included Harvester's own air cleaner, governor, and its own E4A magneto, plus a Zenith C5FE carburetor. No repairs or adjustments were required during the 50 hour test.

COLLECTOR VALUES	1	2	3	4
10-20 HP	$3,000	$1,500	$1,000	$750

McCormick-Deering Farmall (Regular) tractor

The Farmall became the third of IHC's famous tractor brands (along with International and McCormick-Deering), the first launched as part of McCormick-Deering. Farmall ultimately became the most important to the success of the company. Limited production of the Farmall began in 1924, with full production beginning the following year. This light design offered a high power-to-weight ratio, and its narrow front with a single guide wheel made it the first row-crop tractor tested at Nebraska. Rated at 1,200 rpm, the Farmall used a four-cylinder engine with a 3-3/4 x 5-inch bore and stroke. Many attachments were designed for the Farmall (Regular) tractor, and numerous modifications were made during a production run that ended in 1932.

Nebraska Test Data

Model: McCormick-Deering Farmall
Test No. 117
Date Tested: September 14 to September 19, 1925

Having the distinction of being the first true row-crop tractor to be tested at Nebraska, the Farmall went through 39 hours of running time with no repairs or adjustments required. Three forward speeds were provided of 2, 3, and 4 mph. Harvester used its own four-cylinder vertical valve-in-head engine with removable sleeves. Rated at 1,200 rpm, the Farmall engine carried a 3-3/4x 5-inch bore and stroke. Kerosene was used throughout this test, and the rated brake hp trials revealed a fuel economy of 9.64 hp-hours per gallon. Total fuel consumption came to 1.87 gph, with 18.03 hp delivered. At maximum load, 20.05 hp was developed with 9.39 hp-hours per gallon. On the rated drawbar test made in second gear, 9.35 hp was noted, with a pull of 1,113 lbs. at 3.15 mph. A maximum test in low gear gave 12.7 hp with a run of 2,727 lbs. The Farmall weighed in at 4,100 lbs.

COLLECTOR VALUES	1	2	3	4
FARMALL (REGULAR)	$2,200	$1,500	$1,000	$500

Production of the Farmall F-20 began in 1932 and ended in 1939, with almost 149,000 units produced. The F-20 was first tested at Nebraska in 1934. In this test it demonstrated over 23 belt hp using kerosene fuel. In 1936 the F-20 delivered almost 27 belt hp using distillate fuel.

Farmall F-20 tractor

For many farmers the F-20 was their first row-crop tractor, and indeed for many it was their only tractor. Numerous axle and chassis designs were available, along with a wide range of implements.

Nebraska Test Data

Model: Farmall F-20
Test No. 221
Date Tested: April 3 to April 16, 1934

As submitted, this tractor was equipped to burn kerosene, and at its rated 22.16 brake hp, it burned 2.112 gph for 10.49 hp-hours per gallon. A tiny decrease to 10.41 appeared under maximum load of 23.11 hp. Advertised speeds of 2-1/4, 2-3/4, 3-1/4, and 3-3/4 mph were built into the F-20, and in second gear, fuel economy came in at 6.62 hp-hours per gallon, developing 12.61 hp while pulling a 1,524 lb. load at 3.1 mph. Some 15.38 drawbar hp was evidenced in the low gear maximum load test, along with a pull of 2,334 lbs. at 2.47 mph. Harvester equipped this tractor with its own four-cylinder vertical engine with a 3-3/4 x 5-inch bore and stroke. It was rated at 1,200 rpm. Accessory items for this 4,545 lb. tractor included Harvester's own E4A magneto, plus a Zenith K5 carburetor. No repairs or adjustments were required during the 45 hours of running time.

Nebraska Test Data

Model: Farmall F-20
Test No. 264
Date Tested: July 20 to July 29, 1936

The Farmall F-20 was previously tested using kerosene. This test differed in that distillate was chosen instead. Featured was Harvester's own four-cylinder I-head engine with a 3-3/4 x 5-inch bore and stroke with a rated speed of 1,200 rpm Also included was Harvester's own F-4 magneto and a Zenith K-5 carburetor. Four forward speeds of 2-1/4, 2-3/4, 3-1/4, and 3-3/4 mph were provided. Total weight was 4,400 lbs. Only one minor repair was made during the 50-hour test run. Test C for operating maximum load indicated 26.78 brake hp with an economy of 9.82 hp-hours per gallon. A slightly lower economy of 9.67 occurred in Test D for rated load at 25.72 hp. Fuel consumption figures indicated an economy of 6.57 hp-hours per gallon at rated drawbar load of 16.6 hp. The test yielded a pull of 1,668 lbs. at 3.73 mph and slippage of 5.12 percent. Test G made maximum operating load runs in all four forward gears, but in low gear the highest drawbar pull of 2,799 lbs. occurred. At a speed of 2.51 mph and with slippage of 12.14 percent, some 18.76 hp was developed.

Nebraska Test Data

Model: Farmall F-20
Test No. 276
Date Tested: November 5 to November 12, 1936

Previously tested under No. 264, the F-20 presented for this test was almost identical in design. A notable exception was that in the earlier test, valve port diameter was 1.562 inches compared to 1.4375 inches in this tractor. Distillate fuel was used for both tractors, and accessory items were identical. Test D for rated load indicated a fuel economy of 10.51 hp hours with an output of 24.13 brake hp. Economy dropped to an even 10.50 at operating maximum load of 26.67 hp. Third gear was used for the rated drawbar test-with an output of 16.12 hp and the economy was recorded at 7.14 hp-hours per gallon. In this test the F-20 pulled a load of 1,619 lbs. at 3.73 mph with a slippage of 6.02 percent. Test G for operating maximum drawbar load indicated a maximum pull of 2,927 lbs. in low gear. Other data from this test include a speed of 2.51 mph, slippage of 12.53 percent, and an output of 19.6 maximum drawbar hp. During 45 hours of tests, no repairs or adjustments were noted.

COLLECTOR VALUES	1	2	3	4
F-20	$2,300	$1,700	$1,000	$500

Farmall F-30 tractor

Late in 1931 International Harvester introduced its F-30 tractor. Production of the F-30 continued until 1939. The four-cylinder engine carried a 4-1/4 x 5-inch bore and stroke. By the mid-1930s the F-30 was also available with rubber tires as an extra-cost option; steel wheels were still the standard equipment at this time.

Nebraska Test Data

Model: Farmall F-30

Test No. 198

Date Tested: October 9 to October 23, 1931

With a maximum permissible rating of 20.27 drawbar and 30.29 belt hp, the F-30 made its Nebraska tests debut using kerosene. Harvester supplied its own four-cylinder I-head engine with a 4-1/4 x 5-inch bore and stroke and a rated speed of 1,150 rpm. Also included was the company's own governor, air cleaner, and the ever-famous E4A magneto. Completing the accessories was a Zenith K5 carburetor. Advertised speeds of 2, 2-3/4, 3-1/4, and 3-3/4 mph were built into the F-30. Using low gear, 24.85 maximum drawbar hp was developed. This converted into a pull of 4,157 lbs. at 2.24 mph and drive wheel slippage of 9.7 percent. At its rated 20.88 drawbar hp, fuel economy came in at 6.62 hp-hours per gallon, along with a pull of 2,520 lbs. at 3.11 mph over the 10-hour test run. Rated belt hp of 30.31 indicated a fuel economy of 9.11 hp-hours per gallon of kerosene. A slightly higher figure of 9.61 was recorded at the maximum of 32.8 hp. A pin holding the splined end of the steering rod in the splined sleeve sheared off twice, and was replaced. Otherwise, no repairs or adjustments were necessary.

COLLECTOR VALUES	1	2	3	4
F-30	$3,500	$2,700	$1,600	$900

The W-30 was a standard-tread version of the F-30 row-crop tractor. Rated at 19 drawbar and 31 belt hp, the W-30 was comparable in size to the McCormick-Deering 10-20, yet it had a power level akin to the McCormick-Deering 15-30. Production of this model ran into 1938, and by 1935 it was available with pneumatic rubber tires as an extra-cost option. The W-30 was also available as a special Orchard Tractor; this option included special fenders and other accessories.

Nebraska Test Data

Model: McCormick-Deering W-30

Test No. 210

Date Tested: July 26 to August 10, 1932

This tractor appeared as a standard-tread version of the F-30 model noted in Test No. 198. It carried the same IH four-cylinder, 4-1/4 x 5-inch engine, along with the same accessories. Advertised speeds of 2-1/2, 3-1/4, and 3-3/4 mph were built into the W-30, and its total weight was 5,575 lbs. Kerosene was the chosen fuel for this test, just as it was for the F-30 previously noted. Using intermediate gear and its rated load of 20 drawbar hp, the W-30 went through the rated load test with a pull of 2,008 lbs. at 3.78 mph and achieved a fuel economy of 7.05 hp-hours per gallon. The maximum load test in low gear indicated a pull of 3,118 lbs. at 2.92 mph with a slippage of 6.58 percent. At its rated brake load of 31.62 hp, the W-30 burned kerosene at 3.018 gph and yielded 10.48 hp-hours per gallon, a figure that dropped slightly to 10.17 when under the maximum load of 33.26 brake hp. No repairs or adjustments were required during 43 hours of running time.

COLLECTOR VALUES	1	2	3	4
W-30	$2,500	$1,700	$1,100	$800

McCormick-Deering W-30 tractor

A four-cylinder engine with a 3 x 4-inch bore and stroke was used in the Farmall F-12 tractor. Production of this model began in 1932 and ended in 1938. By 1934 the F-12 was available on pneumatic tires as an extra-cost option, making it one of the first IHC tractors to offer rubber tires.

Nebraska Test Data

Model: Farmall F-12
Test No. 212
Date Tested: May 1 to May 10, 1933

To launch the 1933 testing season, Harvester presented the little F-12 tractor. Equipped for burning gasoline, the F-12 developed 14.61 hp at rated brake load, yielding 9.47 hp-hours per gallon. At its maximum of 16.2 brake hp, this figure rose slightly to 9.54. Three advertised speeds of 2-1/4, 3, and 3-3/4 mph were built into the F-12. Using intermediate gear for the rated drawbar test, it developed 10.09 hp, pulling a 1,172-lb. load at 3.23 mph with a slippage of 2.61 percent. Fuel economy on this test came in at 6.27 hp-hours per gallon. The maximum load test in low gear gave the maximum pull of 1,870 lbs. at 2.34 mph. Harvester equipped this 3,280 lb. tractor with its own four-cylinder L-head engine. Using a 3 x 4-inch bore and stroke, it was rated at 1,400 rpm. Standard equipment included an IH E4A magneto, and Harvester's own A-10 carburetor. Only a minor adjustment was required during 47 hours of testing.

Nebraska Test Data

Model: Farmall F-12 (kerosene)
Test No. 220
Date Tested: November 1 to November 16, 1933

This tractor was previously tested using gasoline, while the test at hand chose to use kerosene. Engine specifications remained virtually identical. In the interim between the two tests, Harvester replaced the E4A magneto with the newer F-4 style. At its rated 13.59 brake hp, the F-12 delivered 9.5 hp-hours per gallon, with an improved figure of 10.01 appearing at maximum brake load of 14.59 hp. Advertised speeds of 2-1/4, 3, and 3-3/4 mph were provided, and maximum drawbar load tests were made in all three forward gears. These indicated a low gear output of 11.81 hp with a pull of 1,814 lbs. at 2.44 mph. Second gear yielded 11.01 hp with a 1,278 lb. load at 3.23 mph, while in third gear a 956 lb. load was pulled at 4.17 mph for 10.63 hp. The rated drawbar load test in second gear gave results of 9.71 hp, along with a pull of 1,122 lbs. at 3.25 mph and slippage of 2.69 percent. During this 10-hour test, fuel economy settled in at 7.18 hp-hours per gallon of kerosene.

COLLECTOR VALUES	1	2	3	4
F-12	$2,000	$1,500	$1,000	$300
F-12 WAUKESHA	$3,500	$2,200	$1,500	$800

McCormick-Deering W-12 tractor

A standard-tread version of the Farmall F-12 was the W-12 tractor. Built in the 1934 through 1938 period, this model displayed over 12-1/2 drawbar hp in Nebraska Test No. 229. This model was also built as the I-12 Industrial model as well as the Fairway-12, a special tractor built for use on golf courses and large estates.

Nebraska Test Data

Model: McCormick-Deering W-12
Test No. 229
Date Tested: October 23 to November 9, 1934

The McCormick-Deering W-12 noted in this test was a standard-tread version of the Farmall F-12 tractor. It featured the same IHC four-cylinder, 3 x 4-inch engine as noted in No. 220, with accessory items including an IHC F-4 magneto and the IHC A-10 carburetor. Advertised speeds of 2-1/4, 2-3/4, and 3-3/4 mph were also provided. No repairs or adjustments to this 3,360 lb. tractor were required during 57 hours of running time. The second gear rated drawbar test revealed fuel economy of 4.98 hp-hours per gallon of kerosene, along with a pull of 1,195 lbs. at 3.11 mph, a slippage of 2.19 percent and an output of 9.9 drawbar hp. Slightly more than 12-1/2 drawbar hp was demonstrated in the low gear maximum load test, along with a pull of 1,998 lbs. at 2.36 mph. Maximum brake tests at 15.28 hp yielded an economy of 10.12 hp-hours per gallon, with a slightly diminished figure of 9.87 appearing on the rated load test at 13.99 hp.

Nebraska Test Data

Model: McCormick-Deering W-12 (gasoline)
Test No. 231
Date Tested: November 12 to November 16, 1934

Using the same tractor as Test No. 229, further tests were run with gasoline. All specifications remained identical. This tractor was not rated by the manufacturer, but was given maximum permissible ratings of 10.46 drawbar and 16.07 belt hp under existing tractor rating codes. At its rated brake load of 16.17 hp the W-12 elicited an economy of 9.78 hp-hours per gallon, with a slight improvement to 10.07 when under a maximum load of 17.65 hp. Using second gear for the rated drawbar test gave 6.33 hp-hours per gallon as the final result, along with a pull of 1,250 lbs. at 3.16 mph and an output of 10.52 hp. Maximum drawbar tests indicated the greatest pull coming in low gear with 2,140 lbs. at 2.37 mph, slippage of 3.53 percent, and an output of 13.52 hp.

COLLECTOR VALUES	1	2	3	4
W-12	$3,500	$2,200	$1,500	$800
I-12	$4,500	$3,200	$2,500	$1,200
O-12	$5,000	$4,000	$2,800	$1,800

International O-12 Orchard tractor

Between 1935 and 1938 IHC built almost 2,400 copies of the O-12 Orchard Tractor. It was especially designed for use in orchards, groves, and vineyards. Retailing at about $800, it was normally equipped with rubber tires. It had a top speed of 7-1/2 mph, considerably faster than was possible with steel wheels.

Farmall F-14 tractor

Production of the Farmall F-14 tractor began in 1938 and ended the following year. This model evolved from the earlier F-12, and was nearly identical. The major change was raising the rated engine speed from 1,400 rpm to 1,650 rpm. The F-14 is shown here with the optional wide-front axle. Various chassis designs were available, as with the former F-12. This basic design was also available as the W-14 Wide-Tread model, the O-14 Orchard, and the I-14 Industrial.

Nebraska Test Data

Model: Farmall F-14
Test No. 297
Date Tested: April 19 to April 27, 1938

Using 9.00 x 40 rear tires, the F-14 exited the 10-hour rated drawbar test (Test H) with a fuel economy of 8.56 hp-hours per gallon of distillate. Other data from this test included 11.57 rated drawbar hp, a pull of 1,451 lbs. at 2.99 mph, and slippage of 5.25 percent. Test G for operating maximum load was conducted in all three forward gears, but in low gear a maximum pull of 2,369 lbs. was recorded at a speed of 2.1 mph and an output of 13.24 hp. Test D at 15.54 rated brake hp yielded an economy of 10.26 hp-hours per gallon, and a slightly better economy of 10.86 at an operating maximum load of 17 hp (Test C). The 4,900 lb. F-14 was equipped with an IH-built four-cylinder engine. Using 3 x 4-inch cylinders, it was rated at 1,650 rpm. Also featured was an IHC F-4 magneto, IHC A-10 carburetor, and the company's own air cleaner. No repairs or adjustments were noted during 44 hours of running time.

COLLECTOR VALUES	1	2	3	4
F-14	$2,250	$1,750	$1,200	$900
W-14	$4,000	$3,100	$2,400	$1,000
I-14	$6,200	$5,100	$3,000	$1,500
O-14	$6,800	$5,500	$3,500	$2,500

International W-40/McCormick-Deering WK-40 tractor

In the 1934 through 1940 period International Harvester built its W-40 tractor. This standard-tread design saw total production of about 6,500 units during that time. This was the first tractor from Harvester to use a six-cylinder engine—in this case it carried a 3-3/4 x 4-1/2-inch bore and stroke. The McCormick-Deering WK-40 was the same tractor with a pre-heater manifold for burning kerosene (distillate). The WA-40 had a gasoline engine.

Nebraska Test Data

Model: McCormick-Deering WK-40
Test No. 268
Date Tested: August 25 to September 3, 1936

Rated at 1,600 rpm, the WK-40 tractor submitted for this test was equipped to burn distillate fuel. Harvester used its own six-cylinder I-head engine featuring a 3-3/4 x 4-1/2-inch bore and stroke, and included its own F-6 magneto, along with a Zenith 50-AY12 carburetor. Test C for operating maximum load revealed 43.39 brake hp along with a fuel economy of 9.88 hp-hours per gallon. Economy dropped to 9.61 at the rated brake load of 41.06 hp noted in Test D. Three forward speeds of 2.4, 3.1, and 3.6 mph were provided, and second gear was used for Test H to determine rated drawbar load performance. At 25.94 hp the WK-40 pulled 2,807 lbs. at 3.47 mph with a slippage of 5.43 percent and yielded a fuel economy of 6.52 hp-hours per gallon. Test G for operating maximum load came up with a recorded pull of 4,399 lbs. in low gear. At a speed of 2.57 mph the WK-40 experienced slippage of 10.49 percent, but produced 30.11 drawbar hp. Operating weight was 7,600 lbs. No repairs or adjustments were noted during 50 hours of running time.

Nebraska Test Data

Model: McCormick-Deering WK-40 (high speed)
Test No. 269
Date Tested: September 3 to September 15, 1936

This tractor carried a rated speed of 1,750 rpm. Test C for operating maximum brake load resulted in an output of 48.53 hp, together with a fuel economy of 10.16 hp-hours per gallon of distillate. Economy slipped to 9.87 at the rated load of 45.11 hp recorded under Test D. Standard equipment was an IH six-cylinder, 3-3/4 x 4-1/2-inch engine rated as noted above, and carrying the same accessories as indicated in Test No. 268. Of the three forward speeds, second gear was chosen for the rated drawbar test. At 28.50 hp, Test H concluded with a fuel economy of 6.69 hp-hours per gallon while pulling a 3,117-lb. load at 3.43 mph. Some 4,982 lbs. of drawbar pull was recorded in the low gear operating maximum load test, along with a speed of 2.62 mph, a slippage of 7.7 percent and an output of 34.86 drawbar hp.

McCormick-Deering WD-40

The first wheel-type tractor in America to use a diesel engine was the McCormick-Deering WD-40, introduced in 1934. The WD-40 used a four-cylinder engine with a 4-3/4 x 6-1/2-inch bore and stroke. It was rated at 1,100 rpm. By the time production ended in 1940, almost 3,400 of these tractors had been built. A unique starting system was used in the WD-40. In simple terms, the engine started as an ordinary gasoline engine, and through an automatic system, changed over to diesel operation after several engine revolutions.

Nebraska Test Data

Model: McCormick-Deering WD-40
Test No. 246
Date Tested: September 23 to September 27, 1935

Although several diesel-powered crawler tractors had already been tested at Nebraska, the WD-40 was the first diesel wheel-type tractor to be submitted. Rated at 1,100 rpm, it featured a four cylinder 4-3/4 x 6-1/2-inch engine. A unique feature was the gasoline starting system whereby the engine was started using a conventional carburetor and magneto. After switching over to diesel operation, these accessories were deactivated. The tractor submitted for testing was equipped with steel wheels with 32 spade lugs per side, plus 6-inch wide extension rims with 16 lugs each. No repairs or adjustments were noted during 47 hours of testing. Advertised speeds of 2.6, 3.4, and 3.9 mph were provided, and in second gear the rated drawbar test at 28.09 hp evidenced a fuel economy of 10.06 hp-hours per gallon, plus a pull of 2,783 lbs. at 3.79 mph. Rated load results (Test D) indicated an output of 44.1 hp with an economy of 14.69 hp-hours per gallon. This figure diminished slightly to 14.56 at the maximum load of 48.79 brake hp. Operating weight was 8,450 lbs.

COLLECTOR VALUES	1	2	3	4
WK-40	$5,500	$3,500	$2,800	$1,000
WA-40, WD-40	$10,000	$8,000	$6,000	$1,500

Farmall A tractor

In 1939 International Harvester Company launched an entire new series of streamlined tractors. Included was the Farmall A. This small tractor used a four-cylinder engine of 3 x 4-inch bore and stroke. While most of these tractors were sent out with electric starting, it remained a $31 option over the base price of $575. Production of the Farmall A ended in 1947.

Nebraska Test Data

Model: Farmall A (gasoline)

Test No. 329

Date Tested: September 28 to October 6, 1939

Four forward speeds of 2-1/4, 3-5/8, 4-3/4, and 10 mph were built into the Farmall A tractor. Standard equipment also included 9 x 24-inch rear and 4.00 x 15-inch front tires. Operating weight was 3,570 lbs. This tractor was tested using gasoline. Second gear was used for Test H, with this 10-hour rated drawbar test indicating a fuel economy of 9.6 hp-hours per gallon, along with an output of 13.11 drawbar hp. Traveling at a speed of 3.43 mph the Farmall A pulled a load of 1,434 lbs. Test G for operating maximum load yielded a maximum pull of 2,387 lbs. in low gear. At a speed of 1.93 mph this tractor developed 12.27 drawbar hp and experienced slippage of 17.49 percent. Test D for rated brake load indicated an economy of 11.64 hp-hours per gallon with an output of 16.34 hp. At operating maximum load (Test C) of 16.86 hp economy came in at 11.97 hp-hours per gallon.

Nebraska Test Data

Model: Farmall A (distillate)

Test No. 330

Date Tested: October 9 to October 16, 1939

This Farmall A used distillate, but was equipped identically as the tractor in Test No. 329 with a four-cylinder I-head engine with a 3 x 4-inch bore and stroke and a rated speed of 1,400 rpm. Also included was an IHC H-4 magneto and a Zenith 61AX7 carburetor. This tractor required replacement of a defective cylinder head prior to running the official belt test. During the preliminary tests it was necessary to replace a broken radiator shutter control rod. Test C for operating maximum load indicated 15.18 brake hp with an economy of 11.9 hp-hours per gallon. Test D for rated brake load revealed a tiny reduction in economy to 11.63 with an output of 14.58 brake hp. A maximum pull of 2,360 lbs. was achieved in low gear as noted in Test G. During this pull the Farmall A developed a 15.17 drawbar hp as it moved along at 1.97 mph. Slippage was recorded at 16.01 percent. Test H for rated drawbar load indicated an economy of 9.28 hp-hours per gallon with a pull of 1,211 lbs. at 3.52 mph and slippage of 5.77 percent for an output of 11.37 drawbar hp. Some 66 hours of engine operating time were recorded upon completion of the test.

COLLECTOR VALUES	1	2	3	4
A	$2,700	$2,000	$1,500	$700

Farmall B tractor

Farmall B tractors were built in the 1939 through 1947 period. This model used the basic Farmall A engine but was capable of greater tread width adjustment. For the Farmall B, this ranged from 64 to 92 inches, compared to a range of 40 to 68 inches for the Farmall A. In 1940 the Farmall B sold for about $600.

Nebraska Test Data

Model: Farmall B (gasoline)

Test No. 331

Date Tested: September 25 to September 29, 1939

The Farmall B carried a tricycle-type chassis. Rear tires were of 9 x 24 size with 6 x 12-inch front rubber. Test weight was 3,740 lbs. Advertised speeds of 2-1/4, 3-5/8, 4-3/4, and 10 mph were built into this tractor. Test H for rated drawbar load used second gear. The Farmall B displayed an economy of 9.58 hp-hours per gallon, along with a pull of 1,420 lbs. at 3.44 mph for an output of 13.04 drawbar hp. Slippage in this test totaled 7.05 percent. A maximum low-gear pull of 2,377 lbs. was recorded in Test G-at a speed of 3.39 mph and slippage of 18.87 percent, the Farmall B delivered 12.06 drawbar hp. Belt testing at operating maximum load in Test Q ended with a fuel economy of 11.89 hp-hours per gallon and an output of 16.82 hp. At rated load of 16.41 hp, economy dropped insignificantly to 11.51 hp-hours per gallon. No repairs or adjustments were noted during 46 hours of engine operation.

Nebraska Test Data

Model: Farmall B (distillate)

Test No. 332

Date Tested: October 9 to October 13, 1939

This Farmall B was tested using distillate fuel. During more than 53 hours of engine running time no repairs or adjustments were noted except for replacing the governor thrust pin that had been improperly assembled and caught in the governor at the end of Test H. As in No. 331, Test H was run in second gear. Economy was pegged at 9.6 hp-hours per gallon of distillate, along with a pull of 1,242 lbs. at 3.49 mph for an output of 11.55 rated drawbar hp. Test G recorded a maximum low-gear pull of 2,463 lbs. at 1.83 mph and slippage of 21.68 percent for a net of 12.02 maximum drawbar hp. This tractor, like that noted in No. 331, used a four-cylinder I-head engine rated at 1,400 rpm and carried a 3 x 4-inch bore and stroke. A Zenith 61AX7 carburetor was featured, along with an IHC H-4 magneto. Under Test C the Farmall B delivered an operating maximum of 15.36 brake hp and yielded a fuel economy of 11.82 hp-hours per gallon. By comparison, fuel economy dropped slightly to 11.21 with an output of 14.31 rated brake hp as noted in Test D.

COLLECTOR VALUES	1	2	3	4
B	$2,500	$1,700	$1,200	$500

Farmall AV tractor

Farmall Model AV tractors were simply a high-clearance version of the ordinary Farmall A. Except for the special parts needed to raise the tractor profile, the same basic engine and chassis was used. Production also ran during the 1939 through 1947 period as the Farmall A.

COLLECTOR VALUES	1	2	3	4
AV	$3,200	$2,300	$1,700	$900

Between 1948 and 1954 IHC built the Farmall Super A tractor. It continued to use the same four-cylinder, 3 x 4-inch engine as was used in the Farmall A, and was rated at 1,400 rpm.

COLLECTOR VALUES	1	2	3	4
SUPER A	$3,200	$2,500	$1,700	$900

Farmall Super A tractor

The Farmall H and Farmall M tractors both featured adjustable rear wheel treads. In addition, both tractors had the same wheelbase for better implement interchangeability. The Farmall H used a four-cylinder engine with a 3-3/8 x 4-1/4-inch bore and stroke. Production of the Farmall H ran until 1953 when it was replaced with the Farmall Super H tractor.

Farmall H tractor

Nebraska Test Data

Model: Farmall H (gasoline)
Test No. 333
Date Tested: October 5 to October 11, 1939

Rated at 1,650 rpm, the Farmall H presented for this test carried Harvester's own four-cylinder I-head engine with a 3-3/8 x 4-1/4-inch bore and stroke. Also included was an IHC H-4 magneto and an IHC D-10 carburetor. Tire equipment for the test model included 10 x 36-inch, 6-ply rear tires and 5.50 x 16-inch front rubber. No repairs or adjustments were made during 43 hours of engine operating time. Test C for operating maximum load pegged fuel economy at 11.7 hp-hours per gallon with an output of 24.28 brake hp. Test D indicated a rated load of 23.83 hp, along with an economy figure of 11.46. Throughout this test as in all others, accurate measurement of coolant temperature, air temperature, and barometric pressure was also recorded. Test H for rated drawbar load was made in second gear. At a speed of 3.25 mph the Farmall H pulled a load of 2,211 with a slippage of 4.83 percent and delivered 19.14 drawbar hp plus a yield of 9.48 hp-hours per gallon. The highest maximum drawbar pull as noted in Test G, came in low gear. At a speed of 2.06 mph the tractor pulled 3,603 lbs., delivering 19.84 drawbar hp.

Nebraska Test Data

Model: Farmall H (distillate)
Test No. 334
Date Tested: November 6 to November 11, 1939

Using distillate, a different Farmall H was enlisted. Although Harvester used almost all of its own accessories, these tractors were equipped with a Rockford single-plate clutch, but used its own carburetor and magneto as indicated under Test No. 333. Weighing in at 5,550 lbs., the Farmall H offered a choice of five forward speeds of 2-5/8, 3-1/2, 4-1/4, 5-1/8, and 16-3/8 mph. Second gear was chosen for Test H. It manifested a fuel economy of 10.14 hp-hours per gallon of distillate, compared to a figure of 9.48 when using gasoline. Test G indicated a first-gear maximum pull of 3,169 lbs., along with a recorded slippage of 7.75 percent and a total output of 19.38 drawbar hp. Test D for rated brake load showed a fuel economy of 11.11 hp-hours per gallon, along with an output of 20.80 brake hp. At its operating maximum load as recorded in Test C, the Farmall H delivered 22.14 brake hp and a fuel economy of 11.75 hp-hours per gallon.

Farmall Super H tractor

During 1953 and 1954 International Harvester built the Farmall Super H tractor. This model used a four-cylinder IH C-164 engine with a 3-1/2 x 4-1/4-inch bore and stroke. Rated at 1,650 rpm it delivered slightly over 31 belt hp.

Nebraska Test Data

Model: Farmall Super H
Test No. 492
Date Tested: April 27 to May 13, 1953

Standard equipment for this tractor included 11-38-inch rear and 5.50-16-inch front tires. Weighing in at 4,389 lbs., the Super H was burdened with another 1,162 lbs. of ballast on each rear wheel during certain drawbar tests. No repairs or adjustments were noted during 39 hours of engine operating time. Advertised speeds of 2-5/8, 3-3/4, 5, 6-5/8, and 16-1/4, mph were provided, with third gear being used for Test H. At a rated drawbar load of 23.48 hp, the Super H pulled 1,807 lbs. at 4.87 mph, with a recorded slippage of 3.8 percent. Fuel economy came in at 10.27 hp-hours per gallon. Test G manifested a low-gear maximum pull of 4,178 lbs. at 2.33 mph. The Super H carried an IH-built C-164, four-cylinder engine. Rated at 1,650 rpm, it used a 3-7/8 x 4-1/4 inch bore and stroke with a 164-cubic inch displacement. A maximum engine torque of 266.9 lbs.-ft. was recorded at 1,046 rpm. Test C, run at an operating maximum load of 31.3 belt hp produced a fuel economy of 11.69 hp-hours per gallon, sagging to 11.55 at a Test D rated load of 29.48 belt hp.

COLLECTOR VALUES	1	2	3	4
H, SUPER H	$2,500	$1,500	$1,100	$600

Farmall M

From the time of its introduction in August 1939 the Farmall M was one of the most popular farm tractors in America. By the time production ended in 1952, more than 288,000 of these tractors had been sold. Nebraska Test No. 328 demonstrated over 34 drawbar hp, and nearly 40 belt hp. These power levels made the Farmall M the ideal size for its time. Rated at 1,650 rpm, the Farmall M carried a four-cylinder engine with a 3-7/8 x 5-1/4-inch bore and stroke. The Farmall M was available in several configurations, including the MV High Clearance model. A host of attachments were built especially for the Farmall M and Farmall H tractors. Both used the same frame and the same wheelbase to provide better interchangeability of mounted implements.

Nebraska Test Data

Model: Farmall M (distillate)
Test No. 327
Date Tested: September 5 to September 17, 1939

Harvester's new Farmall M tractor was equipped with 11.25 x 36-inch rear tires and 6.00 x 16-inch front tires when presented for Test No. 327. Also included was Harvester's own four-cylinder I-head engine rated at 1,450 rpm and using a 3-7/8 x 5-1/4-inch bore and stroke. An IH H-4 magneto and an E-12 carburetor complemented the accessory items. Weighing in at 6,770 lbs., the Model M featured five forward speeds of 2-5/8, 3-1/2, 4-1/4, 5-1/8, and 16-3/8 mph. Second gear was used for Test H, and burning distillate fuel, the Model M delivered an economy of 8.99 hp-hours per gallon with an output of 24.89 drawbar hp. In this test a pull of 2,941 lbs. was recorded at 3.17 mph. A low gear maximum pull of 4,365 lbs. at 2.19 mph was noted in Test G. No repairs or adjustments were required during 57 hours of engine operating time. Test D for rated brake load indicated a fuel economy of 12.16 hp-hours per gallon of distillate with an output of 31.38 hp. Under Test C for operating maximum load, hp was recorded at 34.16, with a fuel economy of 12.5 hp-hours per gallon.

Nebraska Test Data

Model: Farmall M (gasoline)
Test No. 328
Date Tested: September 11 to September 20, 1939

This tractor was virtually identical to that in Test No. 327, but this tractor burned gasoline. A comparison of these two tests indicates only slight differences in hp output and fuel economy using either distillate or gasoline. Test H for rated drawbar load recorded a fuel economy of 10.51 hp-hours per gallon, compared to 8.99 in Test No. 327. Horsepower output totaled 26.23 for Test No. 328, along with a pull of 3,102 lbs. at 3.17 mph. The low gear maximum pull noted in Test G came to 4,233 lbs. at 2.17 mph with slippage of 15.57percent and an output of 24.49 drawbar hp. Test D for rated brake load showed 33.46 hp with an economy of 11.81 hp-hours per gallon. At operating maximum load (Test C) the Farmall M delivered 36.07 hp with an economy of 12.16 hp-hours per gallon. During 53 hours of engine running time no repairs or adjustments were noted except for the temperature gauge becoming inoperative.

Farmall MD tractor

Introduced in 1941, the Farmall MD was one of the first row-crop diesel-powered tractors in America. It used an engine similar to that pioneered by the WD-40, and with the same 3-7/8 x 5-1/4-inch cylinder dimensions as the gasoline-powered Farmall M. Production of the Farmall MD continued until 1952 when it was replaced with the Farmall Super MD model.

Nebraska Test Data

Model: Farmall MD Diesel
Test No. 368
Date Tested: May 21 to June 18, 1941

Five forward speeds of 2-5/8, 3-1/2, 4-1/4, 5-1/8, and 16-3/8 mph were featured in the Farmall MD tractor. Test G was run in the four lowest forward gears, with a low-gear maximum pull of 4,541 lbs. being recorded. The rated drawbar load of Test H was run in second gear. At a speed of 3.29 mph and slippage of 6.89 percent the MD pulled a 2,893 lb. load and developed 25.4 drawbar hp. Fuel economy landed at 12.95 hp-hours per gallon. This test was run on 12 x 38-inch rubber tires with 415 lbs. of liquid ballast plus 720 lbs. of cast iron weight on each rear wheel. Test C at 100 percent maximum load of 35.02 brake hp yielded an economy of 14.57 hp-hours per gallon of diesel fuel, compared to an economy of 14.7 at the Test D rated load of 31.17 belt hp. Harvester equipped with MD with its own four-cylinder diesel engine with a 3-7/8 x 5-1/4-inch bore and stroke. Rated speed was 1,450 rpm. Standard equipment included a Bosch fuel injection system.

Nebraska Test Data

Model: Farmall MD Diesel
Test No. 460
Date Tested: June 1 to June 16, 1951

The Farmall MD of Test No. 368 carried the same 3-1/8 x 5-1/4-inch bore and stroke, along with the same rated speed of 1,450 rpm, as the tractor presented for this test. A comparison of these two tests indicated somewhat different results. With a bare weight of 5,861 lbs., the MD was enhanced with another 1,347 lbs. of ballast on each rear wheel during a portion of the drawbar tests. This tractor featured forward speeds of 2-5/8, 3-1/2, 4-1/4, 5-5/8, and 16-1/4 mph, along with 12-38 rear and 6.00-16-inch front tires. Using third gear, Test H indicated a pull of 2,485 lbs. at 4.16 mph with a slippage of 4.91 percent, and an output of 27.54 drawbar hp. Fuel economy was noted at 12.44 hp-hours per gallon of diesel fuel. At a Test D rated load of 34.12 belt hp, fuel economy came in at 14.12 hp-hours per gallon, with a slightly lower economy figure of 14.09 under a Test B maximum load of 38.21 belt hp. No repairs or adjustments were noted during 37 hours of operating time.

Farmall Super M tractors

During 1953 and 1954 International Harvester built its Super M and Super M-TA tractors. This model boasted 43 drawbar hp due to an increased engine bore which went from 3-7/8 to 4-inches. Other new features included faster field speeds, double-disc brakes and direct-power hydraulic control. The Torque Amplifier system permitted on-the-go shifting in tough conditions for greater operating efficiency.

Nebraska Test Data

Model: Farmall Super M

Test No. 475

Date Tested: June 25 to July 2, 1952

With a 264 cubic inch displacement, the Super M featured a four-cylinder, 4 x 5-1/4-inch engine rated at 1,450 rpm. Advertised speeds were 2-1/2, 3-7/8, 5, 6-5/8 and 16-3/4 mph. Standard tire equipment included 6.00-16-inch front and 13-38-inch rear rubber. Basic tractor weight was 5,603 lbs., with 1,663 lbs. of added weight per rear wheel being used during a portion of the drawbar testing. Fuel economy totaled 10.3 hp-hours per gallon under a Test H rated load of 33.33 drawbar hp. During this test the Super M pulled 2,520 lbs. at 4.69 mph, using third gear. Slippage was recorded at 4.24 percent. Test G achieved a low-gear maximum pull of 5,676 lbs. at 2.45 mph. Engine torque peaked at 362.8 lbs.-ft. with an engine speed of 991 rpm, remaining the same at 845 rpm, and falling to 355.3 lbs.-ft. at 770 rpm. Under a Test D rated load of 41.33 belt hp, fuel economy was noted at 11.78 hp-hours per gallon, with this figure climbing to stand at 12.01 hp-hours per gallon under a Test C operating maximum load of 43.92 belt hp. No repairs or adjustments were noted during 45 hours of engine operating time.

Nebraska Test Data

Model: Farmall Super M (LPG)

Test No. 484

Date Tested: October 1 to October 10, 1952

Although this tractor used the same 264 CID engine as the Super M gasoline model of Test No. 475, the 5.9:1 compression ratio of that test was changed to 6.75:1 for the LP-gas model shown here. With this exception, basic tractor specifications were virtually identical for both models. In this test, engine torque peaked at 371.2 lbs.-ft. with an engine speed of 920 rpm. Test C, run at an operating maximum load of 45.66 belt hp yielded a fuel economy of 8.76 hp-hours per gallon of propane, with this figure dropping slightly to stand at 8.61 under a Test D rated belt load of 41.54 hp. Test G, at an operating maximum drawbar load of 39.54 hp yielded a 6,115 lb. pull in low gear. The 10-hour run of Test H produced a fuel economy of 7.86 hp-hours per gallon of propane. This test was made against a rated drawbar load of 33.95 hp, with the Super M pulling 2,541 lbs. at 5.01 mph and experiencing a slippage of 3.66 percent. No repairs or adjustments were noted during 42-1/2 hours of engine operating time.

The Farmall Super MV and the Farmall Super MDV were high-clearance versions of the regular models. With this style there was over 30 inches of clearance under the front axle. High-clearance tractors were used for certain

Farmall Super MV tractor

Farmall Super MD tractor

crops where the extra height was needed to prevent damage to growing plants. Aside from the altered specifications required by the high-clearance equipment, there was virtually no difference between the MV models and the Super M tractors.

Farmall Super MD diesel tractors were built during 1953 and 1954. This model used a 264-cubic inch, four-cylinder engine with a 4 x 5-1/4-inch bore and stroke. Rated at 1,450 rpm, it delivered almost 47 belt hp. The basic tractor weighed about 6,000 lbs.

Nebraska Test Data

Model: Farmall Super MD

Test No. 477

Date Tested: July 7 to July 11, 1952

Engine torque for the Super MD peaked at 350 lbs.-ft. at an engine speed of 1,154 rpm. The torque remained at this figure when engine speed was pulled to 1,080 rpm, but fell to 344.8 lbs.-ft. when engine speed dropped to 1,004 rpm. Harvester used its four-cylinder I-head diesel engine in this tractor. With a 264-cubic inch displacement, it was rated at 1,450 rpm and carried a 4 x 5-inch bore and stroke. A 12-volt electrical system was standard equipment. Tire equipment included 6.00-16 front and 13-38-inch rear tires. Advertised speeds of 2-5/8, 3 percent, 5 or 6 percent, and 16 percent, mph were provided. Basic tractor weight was 6,034 lbs.—with 1,652 lbs. of ballast added to each rear wheel during a portion of the drawbar testing. Using third gear, Test H displayed a rated drawbar output of 33.03 hp, with the Super MD pulling 2,483 lbs. at 4.99 mph under a slippage of 3.84 percent. Test H fuel economy was noted at 13.13 hp-hours per gallon. Test G manifested a low-gear maximum pull of 5,772 lbs. of 2.45 mph. As with other diesel engine test runs, Test C and Test B were the same, and in the case of the Super MD, fuel economy in this trial at 100 percent maximum belt load came to 13.93 hp-hours per gallon at a load of 46.73 hp. At a Test D rated load of 41.08 hp, fuel economy was noted at 14.57 hp-hours per gallon.

COLLECTOR VALUES	1	2	3	4
M	$3,200	$2,250	$1,200	$800
SUPER M	$3,500	$2,500	$1,600	$1,000
MD	$4,200	$3,000	$1,900	$900

Farmall C tractor

Between 1948 and 1951 International Harvester offered the Farmall C tractor. During this relatively short production run, almost 80,000 units were sold. The Farmall C demonstrated nearly 19 belt hp at its rated load. The four-cylinder IH engine used a 3 x 4-inch bore and stroke. In 1951 this model was replaced with the Farmall Super C.

Nebraska Test Data

Model: Farmall C

Test No. 395

Date Tested: June 7 to June 17, 1948

Under a Test C operating maximum load of 19.91 belt hp, the Farmall C recorded a fuel economy of 11.24 hp-hours per gallon. This figure sagged to 10.88 at the Test D rated load of 18.82 belt hp. IH equipped this tractor with its own four-cylinder I-head engine rated at 1,650 rpm and using a 3 x 4-inch bore and stroke. Also featured was an IH magneto and a Zenith 161X7 carburetor. During the test procedures it was necessary to remove the head and clean the combustion chamber. Since the generator and hydraulic pump were listed as special equipment, testing was done without these items. Otherwise, no repairs or adjustments were noted during some 61-1/2 hours of engine operating time. Tire equipment included 4.00-15-inch front and 9-36-inch rear rubber. Advertised speeds of 2-3/8, 3-3/4, 5, and 10-1/4 mph were featured, with second gear being chosen for Test H. At a rated drawbar load of 15 hp, Test H indicated a fuel economy of 9.47 hp-hours per gallon, along with a pull of 1,568 lbs. at 3.59 mph and slippage of 4.41 percent. A maximum low-gear pull of 2,902 lbs. occurred in Test G, along with a speed of 2.05 mph and slippage of 12.89 percent. Tests F, G, and H used 222 lbs. of liquid ballast plus 560 lbs. of cast-iron weight on each rear wheel for a total tractor weight of 4,409 lbs.

Farmall Super C tractor

The Farmall Super C was marketed in the 1951 through 1954 period. During that time about 98,000 units were built. This model was essentially the same tractor as the "C" but had a slightly larger engine. While the earlier model had a four-cylinder, 3 x 4 engine, the Super C had a 3-1/8 x 4-inch bore and stroke. In Nebraska Test No. 458 the Super C delivered almost 23 maximum belt hp.

Nebraska Test Data

Model: Farmall Super C

Test No. 458

Date Tested: May 31 to June 9, 1951

With a 122.7-cubic inch displacement, the Super C featured a four-cylinder engine rated at 1,650 rpm and using a 3-1/8 x 4-inch bore and stroke. During 40-1/2 hours of engine operating time, no repairs or adjustments were recorded. Although the Super C had a bare weight of 3,209 lbs., an additional 916 lbs. of ballast was added per wheel during Tests F, G, and H. Standard equipment included 10-36-inch rear and 5.00-15-inch front tires. Also featured were forward speeds of 2-1/2, 3-7/8, 5, and 10-1/4 mph. Using second gear, Test H indicated a fuel economy of 8.88 hp-hours per gallon under a rated output of 16.29 drawbar hp. This 10-hour run was made at a speed of 3.73 mph, pulling a 1,637-lb. load at a slippage of 4.36 percent. Fuel economy at a Test D rated belt load of 20.83 hp came in at 10.5 hp-hours per gallon, climbing slightly to 10.78 at a Test C operating maximum load of 22.92 belt hp.

COLLECTOR VALUES	1	2	3	4
C, SUPER C	$3,000	$2,100	$1,500	$500

Farmall Cub tractor

The smallest of the IH tractor line was the Farmall Cub. Introduced in 1947, it remained virtually unchanged for a decade. The Cub delivered about 9-1/4 maximum belt hp, using a four-cylinder engine with a 2-5/8 x 2-3/4-inch bore and stroke. Thousands of these tractors were sold, and a substantial number remain in use today, a half century after they were introduced.

Nebraska Test Data

Model: Farmall Cub

Test No. 386

Date Tested: September 29 to October 9, 1947

No repairs or adjustments were noted for the Farmall Cub during 68 hours of engine operating time. Equipped with three forward speeds of 2.14, 3.12, and 6.4 mph, the Cub used second gear for Test H. Under a rated load of 6.75 drawbar hp, it pulled an 837-lb. load of 3.02 mph with a slippage of 5.69 percent, yielding a fuel economy of 8.6 hp-hours per gallon. A maximum low-gear pull of 1,596 lbs. was recorded in Test G. This test also indicated a speed of 1.96 mph and slippage of 10.98 percent. At an operating maximum load of 9.23 belt hp, the Cub delivered a 10.94 hp-hours per gallon, compared to a virtually identical figure of 10.27 at the Test D rated load of 8.32 belt hp. This tractor was equipped with 6-24-inch rear and 4.00-12-inch front tires without additional ballast. It included a McCormick-Deering four-cylinder, L-head engine rated at 1,600 rpm and carrying a 2-5/8 x 2-3/4-inch bore and stroke. Also featured on this model was an IHC J-4 magneto and an IHC carburetor.

Nebraska Test Data

Model: McCormick Farmall Cub
Test No. 575
Date Tested: May 18 to June 3, 1956

Advertised speeds of 2.44, 3.25, and 7.3 mph were featured in the Farmall Cub tractor. Standard equipment also included 8-24-inch rear and 4.00-12-inch front rubber. Weighing in at 1,895 lbs., the Cub was burdened with an additional 498 lbs. of weight on each rear wheel during Tests F, G, and H. During 35-1/2 hours of running time, no repairs or adjustments were noted. Test G yielded a low-gear maximum pull of 1,605 lbs. at 2.25 mph with a slippage of 6.73 percent. The 10-hour run of Test H was made in second gear at a rated drawbar load of 7.86 hp. During this test the Cub pulled 957 lbs. at 3.08 mph with a slippage of 4.01 percent. Fuel economy totaled 8.54 hp-hours per gallon. This tractor used an International four-cylinder, I-head engine with a 2-5/8 x 2-3/4-inch bore and stroke for a displacement of 59.5-cubic inches. Rated at 1,800 rpm, Test L indicated 105 percent of rated torque at 84 percent of rated engine speed. Test B, run at a 100 percent maximum belt load of 10.39 hp, yielded a fuel economy of 9.38 hp-hours per gallon and this figure dropped to 9.15 at a Test D rated load of 9.19 hp.

COLLECTOR VALUES	1	2	3	4
CUB	$3,200	$2,500	$1,500	$750

McCormick-Deering W-4 and Super W-4 tractor

The McCormick-Deering W-4 tractor was simply a standard-tread version of the Farmall H row-crop tractor. Introduced in 1940, it remained on the market until 1953. W-4 tractors used the same IH-built C-152 four-cylinder engine as on the Farmall H. Steel wheels or rubber tires were available for this model, although the latter was far more popular. In 1953 and 1954 Harvester built a slightly improved Super W-4 tractor.

Nebraska Test Data

Model: McCormick-Deering W-4 (distillate)
Test No. 342
Date Tested: May 9 to May 25, 1940

During 59 hours of engine operating time, no repairs or adjustments were noted for the McCormick-Deering W-4 tractor. This particular unit was equipped to burn distillate, and under Test D for rated brake load, the W-4 yielded a fuel economy of 11.32 hp-hours per gallon with an output of 21.18 brake hp. An operating maximum load of 22.16 brake hp was noted in Test C, along with a fuel economy of 11.63 hp-hours per gallon. Harvester equipped the W-4 with its own four-cylinder I-head engine with a 3-3/8 x 4-1/4-inch bore and stroke. Rated at 1,650 rpm, this engine also featured an IHC H-4 magneto along with Harvester's D-10 carburetor. The test tractor carried 12.75 x 24-inch rear rubber and 6.00 x 16-inch front tires. Test weight was 5,690 lbs. Advertised speeds of 2-3/8, 3-1/4, 4, and 5-1/8 mph were built into the W-4 tractor. Using second gear for Test H, the W-4 produced 16.92 drawbar hp, pulling 2.004 lbs. at 3.17 mph with a noted slippage of 4.8 percent. Test G indicated a low-gear maximum pull of 3,297 lbs. at 2.21 mph for 19.46 drawbar hp.

Nebraska Test Data

Model: McCormick-Deering W-4 (gasoline)
Test No. 353
Date Tested: September 16 to September 20, 1940

Advertised speeds of 2-3/8, 3-1/4, and 5-1/8 mph were featured in the W-4 tractor. This particular model was equipped to burn gasoline, and in test H for rated drawbar load it yielded an economy of 9.90 hp-hours per gallon. This 10-hour test was run in second gear. Other Test H data includes a pull of 2,362 lbs. at 3.09 mph with slippage of 5.75 percent and an output of 19.43 drawbar hp. The low-gear maximum load trial as recorded in Test G indicated a pull of 3,671 lbs. at 2.16 mph with slippage of 10.2 percent and an output of 21.12 drawbar hp. Belt testing included Test C for operating maximum load. With an output of 24.3 brake hp, the W-4 yielded an economy of 11.65 hp-hours per gallon, slightly higher than the figure of 11.55 recorded in Test D. The latter test was run at a rated belt load of 23.77 hp. The IH four cylinder I-head engine used in this tractor carried a 3-3/8 x 4-1/4-inch bore and stroke with a rated speed of 1,650 rpm. Also included was an IH-built H-4 magneto and its own D-10 carburetor. The test tractor was equipped with 12.75 x 24-inch rear tires and 6.00 x 16-inch front rubber. No repairs or adjustments were noted during 52 hours of engine operating time.

Nebraska Test Data

Model: McCormick-Deering Super W-4
Test No. 491
Date Tested: April 27 to May 13, 1953

International featured a four-cylinder I-head engine in the Super W-4. Rated at 1,650 rpm, it carried a 3-1/2 x 4-1/4-inch bore and stroke with a 164 CID and a 6.1:1 compression ratio. Also featured were forward speeds of 2-1/2, 3-1/2, 4-5/8, 6-1/4, and 15 mph. Tire equipment included 13-26-inch rear and 5.50-16-inch front rubber. As presented for testing, this tractor weighed 4,219 lbs., with an additional 1,347 lbs. of ballast being added to each rear wheel during certain drawbar tests. Test C, run at an operating maximum belt load of 31.49 hp produced a fuel economy of 11.67 hp-hours per gallon of gasoline, with this figure dropping to 11.55 at a Test D rated load of 29.58 belt hp. A maximum engine torque of 266 lbs.-ft. was noted under an engine speed of 951 rpm. Test G, run at operating maximum load, produced a low-gear pull of 4,501 lbs. at a speed of 2.19 mph. At a Test H rated drawbar load of 23.1 hp the Super W-4 pulled 1,869 lbs. at 4.63 mph under a slippage of 3.74 percent. Fuel economy in this test was pegged at 10.12 hp-hours per gallon. Test H was run in third gear. No repairs or adjustments were noted during 46 hours of engine operating time.

COLLECTOR VALUES	1	2	3	4
W-4	$2,700	$2,200	$1,500	$750

McCormick-Deering W-6 tractor

Rated at about 33 drawbar hp, the W-6 tractor came onto the market in 1940 and remained in production until 1952. That year it was replaced with the Super W-6 and the latter continued until 1954. The W-6 used a four-cylinder engine with a 3-7/8 x 5-1/4-inch bore and stroke. This tractor was also available as an O-6 orchard design with special fenders and other accessories.

Nebraska Test Data

Model: McCormick-Deering W-6 (distillate)

Test No. 354

Date Tested: September 16 to September 23, 1940

No repairs or adjustments were noted for the W-6 tractor during some 51 hours of engine operating time. Distillate was used for this test, with basic tractor specifications being almost identical to those for Test No. 355. Four forward speeds were provided of 2-3/8, 3-1/8, 4, and 4-7/8 mph. Second gear was used for the rated load trials (Test H). Results indicate a fuel economy of 10.37 hp-hours per gallon of distillate, along with a 3,149 lb. pull at 2.95 mph for a rated output of 24.77 drawbar hp. Test G for operating maximum load was run in all four forward gears, but he maximum pull of 4,755 lbs. was achieved in low gear. At a speed of 1.96 mph the W-6 experienced a slippage of 7.24 percent and produced 24.84 drawbar hp. Test C and Test B for 100-percent maximum belt load ran for two hours, yielding a fuel economy of 12.2 hp-hours per gallon at a load of 34.23 brake hp. Test D for rated belt load was run at 31.23 hp and delivered a fuel economy of 12.09 hp-hours per gallon. The W-6 was equipped with 13.50 x 24-inch rear and 6.50 x 16-inch front tires.

Nebraska Test Data

Model: McCormick-Deering W-6 (gasoline)

Test No. 355

Date Tested: September 16 to September 27, 1940

Weighing in at 7,610 lbs., this W-6 was virtually identical to the tractor noted in Test No. 354 except gasoline was used. Brief engine specifications include an IH-built four-cylinder I-head engine with a 3-7/8 x 5-1/4-inch bore and stroke and a rated speed of 1,450 rpm. Also included was Harvester's H-4 magneto and E-12 carburetor. Other data regarding the W-6 gasoline model may be noted in Test No. 354. Also of interest is the comparative fuel economy of these tractors when using different fuels. Test H was run in second gear and gave a recorded fuel economy of 10.09 hp-hours per gallon. Other data from this test includes a rated load of 25.48 drawbar hp, a pull of 3,238 lbs. at 2.95 mph and slippage of 6.84 percent. The maximum drawbar pull as recorded in Test G occurred in low gear with a total of 4,777 lbs. at 1.97 mph and slippage of 17.23 percent. Test C was run with an operating maximum load of 36.15 brake hp and yielded a fuel economy of 12.49 hp-hours per gallon. By comparison, the rated 33.11 hp of Test D produced an economy of 12.04 hp-hours per gallon. No repairs or adjustments were noted during 45 hours of engine operating time.

Nebraska Test Data

Model: McCormick-Deering Super W-6

Test No. 476

Date Tested: June 25 to July 7, 1952

Standard equipment included 15-30-inch rear and 6.00-16-inch front tires on the Super W-6. Weighing 5,515 lbs., this tractor was burdened with another 1,823 lbs. of ballast on each rear wheel during Tests F, G, and H. Advertised speeds of 2-5/8, 3-5/8, 4-3/4, 6-5/8, and 16-1/8 mph were provided—third gear was used for the rated drawbar run of Test H. Under an output of 32.97 drawbar hp, the Super W-6 pulled 2,458 lbs. at 5.03 mph with a slippage of 3.95 percent. Test H fuel economy settled in at 9.87 hp-hours per gallon. Engine torque peaked at 370 lbs.-ft. at a speed of 997 rpm. A low-gear maximum pull of 5,663 lbs. was noted in Test G. Harvester used a four-cylinder I-head engine in this tractor. With a 264-cubic inch displacement, this engine was rated at 1,450 rpm and carried a 4 x 5-1/4-inch bore and stroke. Over 41 hours of engine operating time, no repairs or adjustments were noted. Test C, at an operating maximum belt load of 44.2 hp, produced a fuel economy of 11.83 hp-hours per gallon. This figure dropped slightly to stand at 11.61 under a Test D rated belt load of 41.47 hp.

Nebraska Test Data

Model: McCormick-Deering Super W-6 (LPG)

Test No. 485

Date Tested: October 1 to October 13, 1952

A compression ratio of 6.75:1 was used in this tractor, compared to 5.9:1 found in the Super W-6 gasoline version noted in Test No. 476. With this exception, basic tractor specifications remained virtually identical except of course, for the special LP-gas equipment shown in this photograph. Fuel economy was pegged at 7.62 hp-hours per gallon of propane fuel in Test H. This 10-hour rated drawbar run also saw an output of 33.59 hp, plus a 2,490-lb. pull at 5.06 mph and a slippage of 4.21 percent. In Test G a low-gear maximum pull of 5,775 lbs. was achieved at a speed of 2.51 mph and a recorded slippage of 11.75 percent. Test C, at an operating maximum load of 46.37 belt hp, produced a fuel economy of 8.71 hp-hours per gallon of propane, with the economy figure dropping to 8.52 under a Test D rated belt load of 41.82 hp. Engine torque measured at the dynamometer reached its peak of 373.8 lbs.-ft. with an engine speed of 918 rpm. No repairs or adjustments were noted during 39 hours of operating time.

COLLECTOR VALUES	1	2	3	4
W-6	$3,200	$2,500	$1,700	$800

McCormick-Deering WD-6 Diesel tractor

Production of the WD-6 Diesel tractor ran concurrently with the W-6 and Super W-6 gasoline models, that is, from 1940 until 1954. In Nebraska Test No. 356 the WD-6 delivered nearly 35 belt hp. Rated at 1,450 rpm, the four-cylinder engine used a 3-7/8 x 5-1/4-inch bore and stroke. WD-6 tractors used the same gasoline starting system as the WD-40 introduced some years earlier.

Nebraska Test Data

Model: McCormick-Deering WD-6
Test No. 356
Date Tested: September 20 to September 27, 1940

Harvester's own four-cylinder diesel engine was featured in the WD-6 tractor. Of I-head design it was rated at 1,450 rpm and used a 3-7/8 x 5-1/4-inch bore and stroke. A Bosch fuel injection system was featured, along with a gasoline starting system similar in design to that used on the WD-40 noted in Test No. 246. Standard equipment included 13.50 x 24-inch rear tires and 6.50 x 16-inch front rubber. Advertised speeds of 2-3/8, 3-1/8, 4, and 4-7/8 mph were also featured. No repairs or adjustments were noted during 39 hours of engine operation. The 7,995-lb. test weight included rear wheel weights consisting of 970 lbs. of cast iron plus 393 lbs. of water ballast per wheel, along with 80 lbs. of cast-iron front wheel weights. Test H was run in second gear, and at a rated output of 23.43 drawbar hp the WD-6 pulled a 2,948 lb. load at 2.98 mph with a slippage of 6.23 percent. Economy was registered at 13.02 hp-hours per gallon of diesel fuel. Under Test G a maximum pull of 4,806 lbs. was achieved in low gear. At 1.97 mph and with slippage of 18.03 percent, the WD-6 yielded 25.25 drawbar hp in this test. Test C and Test B at 100 percent maximum belt load of 34.75 hp produced 14.85 hp-hours per gallon, and an even higher economy of 14.94 under rated load of 30.98 brake hp as noted in Test D.

Nebraska Test Data

Model: McCormick-Deering WD-6
Test No. 459
Date Tested: June 1 to June 14, 1951

Featuring a 12-volt starting system, the WD-6 carried a four-cylinder diesel engine with a displacement of 247.7-cubic inches. Rated at 1,450 rpm, this engine used a 3-7/8 x 5-1/4-inch bore and stroke. Standard equipment included forward speeds of 2-1/2, 3-3/8, 4-3/8, 5-1/4, and 15-3/4. Tires included 14-30 rear and 6.00-16-inch front rubber. Bare tractor weight was 5,789 lbs., with an additional ballast of 1,533 lbs. added on each rear wheel during a portion of the test procedures. No repairs or adjustments were noted during 42 hours of engine operating time. Test H, run in third gear, yielded a fuel economy of 12.23 hp-hours per gallon of diesel fuel. This run was made against a rated drawbar load of 26.46 hp, along with a pull of 1,450 lbs. at 4.44 mph with a slippage of 3.96 percent. Test G revealed a low-gear maximum pull of 5,095 lbs. at 2.06 mph. Belt testing came up with a Test D rated load fuel economy of 13.72 hp-hours per gallon against an output of 33.52 hp. By contrast, the Test B, 100-percent maximum belt load test at 37.64 hp delivered a fuel economy of 13.9 hp-hours per gallon.

Nebraska Test Data

Model: McCormick-Deering Super WD-6
Test No. 478
Date Tested: July 8 to July 17, 1952

With more than 39-1/2 hours of engine operating time, no repairs or adjustments were noted for this tractor. Weighing 6,011 lbs., the Super WD-6 was equipped with 15-30-inch rear and 6.00-16-inch front tires. During Tests F, G, and H an additional 1,817 lbs. of ballast was added to each rear wheel. Advertised speeds of 2-5/8, 3-5/8, 4-3/4, 6-5/8, and 16-1/8 mph were provided with third gear used for the rated drawbar run of Test H. At 33.1 hp, the Super WD-6 pulled 2,475 lbs. at 5.01 mph under a slippage of 3.36 percent. Under these parameters, fuel economy came in at 12.77 hp-hours per gallon of diesel fuel. A low gear maximum pull of 5,857 lbs. was achieved in Test G with a ground speed of 2.44 mph. This tractor carried an International four-cylinder I-head engine rated at 1,450 rpm that carried a 4 x 5-1/4-inch bore and stroke for a 264-cubic inch displacement. Engine torque peaked at 364.5 lbs.-ft. at an engine speed of 1,152 rpm. Test B, at a 100-percent maximum belt load of 46.84 hp saw 14.25 hp-hours per gallon, with this figure climbing slightly to 14.49 under a Test D rated load of 41.24 hp.

COLLECTOR VALUES	1	2	3	4
WD-6	$3,400	$2,700	$1,700	$800

W-9 tractor

Topping the IHC tractor line was the W-9 tractor. This standard-tread model was capable of 52 belt hp. The IHC-335 four-cylinder engine was used. It was the same engine as was used in the T-9 crawler tractor with a 4.4 x 5.5-inch bore and stroke. This 1940 model is shown with steel wheels, but rubber tires were far more popular. Production continued until 1953.

Nebraska Test Data

Model: McCormick-Deering W-9 (gasoline)
Test No. 369
Date Tested: May 21 to June 17, 1941

The W-9 had a bare weight of 6,350 lbs. when equipped with 13.50 x 32-inch rear and 7.50 x 18-inch front tires. Regular features included forward speeds of 2-3/8, 3-1/8, 4-2/3, 5-

3/8, and 15-3/8 mph. Featured too was an IH-built four-cylinder I-head engine rated at 1,500 rpm and carrying a 4.4 x 5.5-inch bore and stroke. This package was complemented with an IH H-4 magneto and an III Model E-13 carburetor. No repairs or adjustments were noted during 46 hours of engine operating time. Test C at operating maximum load of 48.5 brake hp yielded an economy of 11.75 hp-hours per gallon of gasoline compared to an economy figure of 11.36 under the Test D rated load of 44.66 belt hp. Test H, formerly called the Rated Drawbar Test, was run in third gear. At a speed of 4.17 mph and with slippage of 5.36 percent, the W-9 yielded a fuel economy of 9.8 hp-hours per gallon of fuel while pulling a 3,244-lb. load and producing 36.11 drawbar hp. The low-gear maximum pull noted in Test G was 6,414 lbs. at 1.95 mph with an output of 33.28 drawbar hp.

Nebraska Test Data

Model: McCormick-Deering W-9 (distillate)

Test No. 371

Date Tested: June 4 to June 17, 1941

No repairs or adjustments were noted during 57 hours of engine operating time on the W-9 distillate model. Virtually identical to the tractor tested in No. 369, this model differed primarily in the type of fuel used, and carried a slightly different manifold. Test H for rated drawbar hp was run in third gear. At the end of 10 hours, fuel economy stood at 9.37 hp-hours per gallon of distillate. Other data from this test includes a pull of 3,022 lbs. at 4.22 mph under a slippage of 4.69 percent and with an output of 33.97 drawbar hp. Test G, using low gear, gave a maximum drawbar pull of 6,577 lbs. at 2.02 mph with a slippage of 13.56 percent for an output of 35.36 drawbar hp. Test C for operating maximum load yielded an economy of 11.04 hp-hours per gallon of distillate while under a load of 45.40 belt hp. Test D at a rated load of 41.79 hp indicated a slight reduction to 10.57 hp-hours per gallon of distillate.

McCormick-Deering WD-9 tractor

Production of the IHC WD-9 paralleled that of the gasoline-powered W-9 tractor. It used a four-cylinder IH engine with a 4.4 x 5.5-inch bore and stroke. At its rated speed of 1,500 rpm this tractor delivered over 46 belt hp. In 1953 this model was replaced with the Super WD-9. The latter used a 4.5 x 5.5-inch bore and stroke, but the same rated speed of 1,500 rpm that was used in its predecessor. This model remained in production until 1956.

Nebraska Test Data

Model: McCormick-Deering WD-9

Test No. 370

Date Tested: May 21 to June 18, 1941

Of the same basic design as the W-9s of Test Nos. 369 and 371, this tractor featured an IH-built diesel engine. This four-cylinder, I-head style carried a 4.4 x 5.5-inch bore and stroke with a rated speed of 1,500 rpm and featured a Bosch fuel injection system. As with earlier IH-diesels, a unique gasoline starting system, complete with magneto and carburetor, was also featured. It was automatically deactivated during the starting cycle. Test C and Test B indicated a 100-percent maximum load of 46.43 belt hp with an economy of 14.7 hp-hours per gallon. At a rated load of 41.84 belt hp as noted in Test D, fuel economy stood at 14.6 hp-hours per gallon. Test H, formerly called "Rated Load," was run in third gear. At a speed of 4.2 mph, and with slippage of 5.25 percent, the WD-9 pulled a load of 3,073 lbs. with an output of 34.43 drawbar hp. The operating maximum load of Test G and using low gear gave a pull of 6,367 lbs. at 1.98 mph and an output of 33.55 hp. No repairs or adjustments were noted during 57 hours of engine operating time.

Nebraska Test Data

Model: McCormick-Deering WD-9

Test No. 441

Date Tested: May 31 to June 7, 1950

An IH four-cylinder diesel engine was featured in the WD-9. Rated at 1,500 rpm, it carried a 4.4 x 5.5- inch bore and stroke with a 334.5-cubic inch displacement. A 12-volt electrical system was standard equipment as were the 14-34-inch rear and 7.50-18-inch front tires. Weighing 7,221 lbs., the WD-9 received an additional 1,882 lbs. of weight on each rear wheel during Tests F, G, and H. Advertised speeds of 2-3/8, 3-1/4, 4-5/8, 5-5/8, and 16-1/4 mph were provided with third gear being used for Test H. This test indicated a fuel economy of 12.86 hp-hours per gallon of diesel fuel against a rated drawbar load of 36.61 hp. At this load the WD-9 pulled 3,147 lbs. at 4.36 mph with a slippage of 4.7 percent. A low-gear maximum pull of 6,727 lbs. was noted in Test G. Tests B and C at a 100-percent maximum load of 51.27 belt hp yielded a fuel economy of 14.62 hp-hours per gallon, compared to an economy figure of 14.39 at a Test D rated load of 45.36 belt hp. Repairs and adjustments noted during 45-1/2 hours of running time were of little consequence.

Nebraska Test Data

Model: McCormick-Deering Super WD-9

Test No. 518

Date Tested: May 10 to May 19, 1954

During 42-1/2 hours of running time, no repairs or adjustments were noted for the Super WD-9. Weighing 9,027 lbs., it was equipped with 18-26-inch rear and 7.50-18-inch front tires. During Tests F, G, and H an additional 1,884 lbs. of weight was added to each rear wheel. Test H, run in third gear, revealed a rated drawbar output of 44.72 hp, along with a pull of 3,779 lbs. at 4.44 mph and slippage of 4.66 percent. Fuel economy came to 12.58 hp-hours per gallon of diesel fuel. Test G delivered a low-gear maximum pull of 8,416 lbs. at 2.06 mph. Harvester equipped this tractor with a four-cylinder I-head engine with a 4.5 x 5.5-inch bore and stroke. Rated at 1,500 rpm, it had a 350-cubic inch displacement. Engine torque peaked at 530.3 lbs.-ft. with an engine speed of 1,039 rpm, remaining at this level at an engine speed of 968 rpm. Standard equipment included forward speeds of 2-3/8, 3-1/8, 4-1/2, 5-1/2, and 15-3/4 mph. Tests B and C, run at 100 percent maximum belt load, indicated a fuel economy of 14.62 hp-hours per gallon under a burden of 65.19 hp. Economy rose slightly to stand at 14.71 under a Test D rated belt load of 57.24 hp.

COLLECTOR VALUES	1	2	3	4
W-9	$3,500	$2,700	$1,800	$800
WD-9	$3,750	$3,000	$2,200	$800

Farmall 100 tractor

Nebraska Test Data

Model: Farmall 100

Test No. 537

Date Tested: April 18 to April 29, 1955

Weighing in at 3,038 lbs., the Farmall 100 was equipped with 11-24 rear and 5.00-15 front tires. Also featured were forward speeds of 2.32, 3.68, 4.84, and 10.05 mph. During Tests F, G, And H an additional 650 lbs. of weight was added to each rear wheel. Test H, run in second gear, produced a fuel economy of 9.06 hp-hours per gallon. This run was made at a rated drawbar load of 14.52 hp, along with a 1,376-lb. pull at 3.96 mph and slippage of 4.41 percent. Test G produced a low-gear maximum pull of 2,503 lbs. at 2.36 mph and slippage of 9.47 percent. The Farmall 100 was equipped with a four-cylinder I-head engine rated at 1,400 rpm and with a 3-1/8 x 4-inch bore and stroke for a displacement of 123-cubic inches, just as noted for the Farmall 200 of Test No. 536. Both engines carried a 6.5:1 compression ratio. Engine torque for this tractor reached a maximum of 146.7 lbs.-ft. with an engine speed of

1,025 rpm. At a Test D rated belt load of 17.95 hp, fuel economy was scored at 10.44 hp-hours per gallon, climbing to 10.95 at a Test C operating maximum load of 18.34 hp. No repairs or adjustments were noted during 46 hours of operating time.

Farmall 200 tractor

Nebraska Test Data

Model: Farmall 200

Test No. 536

Date Tested: April 18 to April 29, 1955

At a Test C operating maximum load of 22.09 belt hp the Farmall 200 achieved 10.83 hp-hours per gallon. The economy figure slipped to 10.35 at a Test D rated belt load of 20.76 hp. This tractor featured a four-cylinder I-head engine rated at 1,650 rpm. Using a 3-1/8 x 4-inch bore and stroke, it had a 123-cubic inch displacement. Engine torque peaked at 159.6 lbs.-ft. with an engine speed of 1,054 rpm. Features included speeds of 2-1/2, 2-7/8, 5-1/8, and 10-5/8 mph. Also included as standard equipment were 10-36-inch rear and 5.00-15-inch front tires. Bare tractor weight was 3,541 lbs., to which an additional 895 lbs. of weight was added on each rear wheel during certain drawbar tests. Test G, run at operating maximum drawbar load in all forward gears, produced a low-gear maximum pull of 3,166 lbs. at 2.26 mph with a slippage of 9.85 percent. Fuel economy came to 8.78 hp-hours per gallon in Test H. This test, run in second gear, revealed a rated drawbar output of 16.85 hp, along with a pull of 1,675 lbs. at 3.77 mph and slippage of 4.97 percent. Following completion of the drawbar tests, the engine head was removed and the combustion chambers cleaned. Testing resumed with improved performance. Otherwise no repairs or adjustments were noted during 49-1/2 hours of operating time.

Farmall 300 series

Nebraska Test Data

Model: Farmall 300

Test No. 538

Date Tested: April 29 to May 2, 1955

Rated at 1,750 rpm, this tractor achieved a maximum torque of 283.2 lbs.-ft. with an engine speed of 1,050 rpm. The Farmall 300 used a four-cylinder I-head engine with a 3-9/16 x 4-1/4-inch bore and stroke for a displacement of 169-cubic inches. During 38-1/2 hours of operating time, no repairs or adjustments were noted. Advertised speeds of 2.5, 3.82, 5.15, 6.6, and 16.11 mph were provided. The integral torque amplifier gave another five speeds about 33 percent slower than direct-drive. Weighing in at 5,361 lbs., the Farmall 300 gained an additional 1,448 lbs. on each rear wheel during Tests F, G, and H. A low-gear maximum pull of 4,852 lbs. was noted in Test G. Run at a speed of 2.32 mph, slippage in this test totaled 11.67 percent. Fuel economy was pegged at 9.58 hp-hours per gallon in Test H. Run at a rated drawbar load of 26.97 hp, this test indicated a pull of 1,933 lbs. at 5.23 mph and a slippage of 3.43 percent. Test H was run in third gear. Belt testing produced a Test D rated load fuel economy of 11.59 hp-hours per gallon against a load of 33.89 belt hp. Economy rose slightly to stand at 11.81 at a Test C operating maximum load of 35.99 belt hp. During 38-1/2 hours of operating time, no repairs or adjustments were noted.

Nebraska Test Data

Model: Farmall 300 (LPG)

Test No. 573

Date Tested: May 9 to June 4, 1956

Using a 169-cubic inch, four-cylinder, 3-9/16 x 4-1/4 inch engine, the Farmall 300 propane model was essentially the same tractor as the gasoline version of Test No. 538. Tire sizes and advertised speeds were the same in both cases. Since Test L, effective with 1956, listed comparative percentage values of engine torque, comparison of these tests with torque recorded in lbs.-ft. is difficult. The comparative percentage does perhaps provide a better picture when viewed from an overall perspective. In this case, engine torque remained at rated speed levels through 90 percent of rated engine speed, steadily dropping thereafter. No repairs or adjustments were noted during 54-1/2 hours of operation. Test C, under an operating maximum load of 36.74 hp yielded a fuel economy of 9.31 hp-hours per gallon of propane. Economy slipped to 9.16 at a Test D rated load of 33.75 belt hp. A low-gear maximum pull of 4,965 lbs. at 2.3 mph and slippage of 11.34 percent was noted in Test G. Using third gear, Test H delivered a fuel economy of 8.16 hp-hours per gallon with a rated drawbar load of 27.59 hp. This test also indicated a pull of 1,999 lbs. at 5.18 mph and slippage of 3.78 percent.

International 300 Utility series

Nebraska Test Data

Model: International 300 Utility

Test No. 539

Date Tested: May 5 to May 10, 1955

Advertised speeds of 2.6, 3.97, 5.36, 6.86, and 16.74 mph were featured in the 300 Utility tractor. The integral Torque Amplifier gave an additional range of speeds at 67.3 percent of direct-drive. Weighing 4,413 lbs., this standard-tread version was equipped with 5.50-16-inch front and 12.28-inch rear tires. With these and other minor exceptions, the 300 Utility model was virtually identical to the Farmall 300 noted in Test No. 538. No repairs or adjustments were noted during 42 hours of operation. Test H was run in third gear. At a rated drawbar load of 29.87 hp, this tractor pulled 2,194 lbs. at 5.11 mph with a slippage of 6.18 percent. Fuel economy was posted at 9.46 hp-hours per gallon. Test G gave a low-gear maximum pull of 4,379 lbs. of 2.19 mph with a slippage of 16.93 percent. Although the 169-cid engine was rated at 2,000 rpm, and maximum torque was achieved at 1,212 rpm with a reading of 286 lbs.-ft. Belt testing produced a Test D rated load of 36.44 hp with a fuel economy of 11.23 hp-hours per gallon. This figure climbed to 11.42 at a Test C operating maximum load of 38.78 belt hp.

Nebraska Test Data

Model: International 300 Utility (LPG)

Test No. 574

Date Tested: May 16 to June 1, 1956

Once again, Harvester presented a propane version of a previously tested gasoline model—in this case the 300 Utility tractor of Test No. 539. The four-cylinder, 169-cid propane-fueled engine carried an 8.75:1 compression ratio, compared to 6.8:1 for the gasoline model. Reference to the earlier test included brief specifications, advertised speeds, and other data. As with other propane models, including this data once again would be redundant. Test H, run in third gear, indicated a fuel economy of 8.06 hp-hours per gallon of propane fuel. During this 10-hour run made at a rated drawbar load of 30.39 hp, a pull of 2,193 lbs. was recorded at 5.2 mph with a slippage of 5.11 percent. Test G yielded a low-gear maximum pull of 4,467 lbs. at 2.27 mph with a slippage of 14.24 percent. No repairs or adjustments were noted during 40 hours of running time. Test L indicated that 106 percent of rated speed torque was present at 66 percent of the rated 2,000 rpm engine speed. At a Test C operating maximum load of 40.77 belt hp, fuel economy came in at 9.42 hp-hours per gallon, dropping to 9.24 at a Test D rated belt load of 37.76 hp.

Farmall 400 series

Nebraska Test Data

Model: Farmall 400

Test No. 532

Date Tested: March 28 to April 4, 1955

Weighing 6,519 lbs., the Farmall 400 featured 13-38-inch rear and 6.00-16-inch front tires as standard equipment. During Tests F, G, and H an additional 1,575 lbs. of weight was added to each rear wheel. Also featured were forward speeds of 2.5, 3.85, 4.83, 6.71, and 16.7 mph. Using the Torque Amplifier, speeds of 1.69, 2.6, 3.26, 4.53, and 11.27 mph were available. Test G produced a low-gear maximum pull of 6,508 lbs. at 2.18 mph under a slippage of 16.63 percent. The 10-hour run of Test H indicated a rated drawbar output of 35.6 hp, along with a 2,769-lb. pull of 4.82 mph and slippage of 4.8 percent. Run in third gear, this test yielded a fuel economy of 9.53 hp-hours per gallon. The Farmall 400 was equipped with a four-cylinder I-head engine carrying a 4 x 5-1/4-inch bore and stroke. With a rated speed of 1,450 rpm, it achieved a maximum torque of 412.5 lbs.-ft. at a speed of 924 rpm. Belt testing gave a fuel economy of 12.11 hp-hours per gallon at a Test C operating maximum load of 48.7 hp. Economy slipped slightly to 11.67 at a Test D rated belt load of 44.89 hp. No repairs or adjustments were noted during 42 hours of operating time.

Nebraska Test Data

Model: Farmall 400 Diesel

Test No. 534

Date Tested: April 8 to April 16, 1955

This 400 carried a 264-cid engine of the same general specifications as previously noted. In this case, a 16.5:1 compression ratio was used, compared to the 6.3:1 ratio found in the gasoline models. Other specifications, such as advertised speeds and tire equipment, were virtually identical to those noted in Test No. 532. Test B & C, run at a 100-percent maximum belt load of 46.73 hp, produced a fuel economy of 13.9 hp-hours per gallon of diesel fuel, improving to 14.1 under a Test D rated belt load of 41.22 hp. Although the engine was rated at 1,450 rpm, engine torque peaked at 371.4 lbs.-ft. with an engine speed of 997 rpm. Using direct-drive, Test G yielded a low-gear maximum pull of 6,415 lbs. at 2.19 mph against a slippage of 16.1 percent. A complete series of maximum load tests was also made using the Torque Amplifier system. Test H gave a fuel economy of 12.31 hp-hours per gallon at a rated drawbar load of 33.58 hp. During this 10-hour run the 400 Diesel pulled 2,610 lbs. at 4.83 mph with a slippage of 4.43 percent. During 46-1/2 hours of operation, no repairs or adjustments were noted.

Nebraska Test Data

Model: Farmall 400 (LPG)

Test No. 571

Date Tested: May 7 to May 28, 1956

Except for the necessary propane equipment, this tractor was virtually identical to the Farmall 400 gasoline model of Test No. 532. The four-cylinder, 264-cid engine in this tractor carried an 8.35:1 compression ratio, compared to 6.3:1 for the gasoline style. During Tests F, G, and H an additional 1,480 lbs. of ballast was added to each rear wheel. Effective with this test, operating maximum torque readings were categorized under Test L. In this case, Test L indicated 107 percent of rated speed torque occurred at 65 percent of rated engine speed (1,450 rpm). Test C, run at an operating maximum belt load of 49.69 hp, yielded 9.78 hp-hours per gallon of propane, sagging to 9.69 at a Test D rated belt load of 46.36 hp. A low-gear maximum pull of 6,374 lbs. at 2.25 mph was attained in Test G. Slippage totaled 14.43 percent. The 10-hour rated drawbar run of Test H was made in third gear. With an output of 37.21 hp, the 400 pulled 2,892 lbs. at 4.83 mph with a slippage of 4.9 percent. Fuel economy came to 8.51 hp-hours per gallon of propane. No repairs or adjustments were noted during 49 hours of operating time.

International W-400 series

Nebraska Test Data

Model: International W-400

Test No. 533

Date Tested: March 28 to April 8, 1955

Using the same 264-cid engine as the Farmall 400 of Test No. 532, the W-400 was a standard-tread version that also featured the Torque Amplifier previously noted. Standard equipment included 15-30-inch rear and 6.50-18-inch front tires. Bare tractor weight was 6,328 lbs., but an additional 1,872 lbs. was added to each rear wheel during Tests F, G, and H. During 45 hours of operation, no repairs or adjustments were noted. The operating maximum drawbar load test was run in all forward gears, including the Torque Amplifier range. A low-gear maximum pull of 6,361 lbs. at 2.2 mph was achieved using direct-drive. Test H gave a fuel economy of 9.92 hp-hours per gallon at a rated drawbar load of 35.73 hp. This test also indicated a pull of 2,755 lbs. at 4.86 mph and slippage of 4.3 percent. Test D, run at a rated 45.64 belt hp, yielded 11.81 hp-hours per gallon. The economy was pegged at 12.23 under a Test C operating maximum load of 48.48 belt hp.

Nebraska Test Data

Model: International W-400 Diesel

Test No. 535

Date Tested: April 8 to April 20, 1955

This standard-tread version was virtually identical to the W-400 gasoline model of Test No. 533, and carried the same 264-cid engine used in the Farmall 400 Diesel of Test No. 534. The "400" series was available in four basic styles—standard tread or row-crop design, and using either gasoline or diesel engines. While the Farmall 400 Diesel of the previous test had a bare weight of 6,898 lbs., this standard-tread model weighed in at 6,699 lbs., with 1,879 lbs. of ballast added to each rear wheel during Tests F, G, and H. The latter test, run for 10 hours at a rated drawbar load of 33.58 hp, produced a pull of 2,586 lbs. at 4.87 mph with a slippage of 3.51 percent. Fuel economy totaled 12.17 hp-hours per gallon of diesel fuel. Test G gave a low-gear maximum pull of 6,476 lbs. at 2.24 mph with a slippage of 14.32 percent. Engine torque peaked at 388.5 lbs.-ft. with an engine speed of 1,073 rpm. The engine carried a rated speed of 1,450 rpm. At a Test B & C 100-percent maximum belt load of 46.61 hp, 13.63 hp-hours per gallon was recorded. That crept upward slightly to 13.89 at a Test D rated belt load of 41.63 hp.

Nebraska Test Data

Model: International W-400 (LPG)

Test No. 572

Date Tested: May 9 to May 25, 1956

Except for the propane gas equipment, this tractor was virtually identical to the W-400 gasoline model noted in Test No. 533. An International four-cylinder, 264-cid engine was used with a 4 x 5-1/4-inch bore and stroke. Rated speeds was 1,450 rpm using propane fuel, it developed 107 percent of rated speed torque at 70 percent of rated engine speed in Test L. At a Test C operating maximum load of 48.58 belt hp, the W-400 scored a fuel economy of 9.64 hp-hours per gallon, dropping to 9.47 at a Test D rated load of 44.97 hp. Test G, run in low gear, yielded a maximum pull of 6,684 lbs. at 2.33 mph with a slippage of 13.5 percent. Using third gear, the 10-hour Test H run was made with a rated output of 37.73 drawbar hp. At a speed of 5.02 mph, a pull of 2,820 lbs. was noted with a slippage of 3.66 percent. Fuel economy was 8.39 hp-hours per gallon of propane. During 40 hours of running time, no repairs or adjustments were noted.

International 500 series

These tractors were built by International Harvester of Canada in Hamilton, Ontario.

Nebraska Test Data

Model: International 500

Test No. 950

Date Tested: October 24 to November 2, 1966

Weighing 7,970 lbs., this tractor went through 37-1/2 hours of operating time with no reported repairs or adjustments. The selective-gear fixed-ratio transmission included partial range power shifting. Ten forward speeds were provided, ranging from 1.53 to 6.52 mph. The International 500 was equipped with a four-cylinder, 145.3-cid engine. Rated at 2,000 rpm, it used a 3-3/8 x 4-1/16-inch bore and stroke. The PTO shaft operated at 980 rpm with an engine speed of 2,000 rpm. Operating at rated engine speed, 37.22 maximum PTO hp was observed, and an economy of 11.73 hp-hours per gallon. Drawbar economy testing was done in fourth gear. At 31.24 maximum available hp, a pull of 5,345 lbs. was recorded at 2.19 mph—slippage was 2.99 percent, and economy was 9.72 hp-hours per gallon. The 10-hour run at 75 percent pull saw an economy of 8.75 hp-hours per gallon against a load of 24.74 hp. Also revealed was a pull of 3,975 lbs. at 2.33 mph with 1.9 percent slippage. Of further interest, this unit made a low-gear maximum pull of 7,988 lbs. while traveling at 1.44 mph and experiencing slippage of 6.06 percent.

Nebraska Test Data

Model: International 500 Diesel

Test No. 951

Date Tested: October 24 to November 2, 1966

Except for the diesel engine, this tractor was nearly identical to the gasoline version. An International four-cylinder diesel engine was featured—its 3-1/2 x 4-inch bore and stroke gave a 153.9-cubic inch displacement. Rated speed was 2,000 rpm. Operating at rated engine speed, 36.65 maximum PTO hp was observed, as was an economy of 13.96 hp-hours per gallon. No repairs or adjustments were noted during 53 hours of total running time. In fourth gear, the two-hour economy run at 30.55 maximum available hp gave a fuel efficiency of 11.34 hp-hours per gallon. Also recorded was a pull of 5,237 lbs. at 2.19 mph with slippage of 3.34 percent. In the 10-hour run, made at 75 percent pull, fuel economy was at 11.03 hp-hours per gallon with a load of 24.63 drawbar hp. The 10-hour run saw a pull of 4,023 lbs. at 2.3 mph with slippage of 1.94 percent. Weighing 1,970 lbs., this unit achieved a low-gear maximum pull of 7,957 lbs. at 1.44 mph with 6.09 percent slippage.

Farmall 130 and 230 tractors

Nebraska Test Data

Model: McCormick Farmall 130

Test No. 617

Date Tested: April 25 to May 7, 1957

The Farmall 130 tractor carried the same C-123 International engine as the Farmall 230 "tricycle" model. Also featured were 11-24-inch rear and 5.00-15-inch front tires, along with forward speeds of 2.3, 3.7, 4.8, and 10 mph. Weighing in at 3,015 lbs., it was given another 800 lbs. of weight on each rear wheel during Tests F, G, and H, Test G, run in low gear, recorded a maximum pull of 2,956 lbs. at 2.34 mph and slippage of 8.73 percent. The 10-hour run of Test H was made in second gear, with fuel economy in this test totaling 10.57 hp-hours per gallon of gasoline. During this test the 130 pulled 1,534 lbs. at 3.93 mph with a slippage of 3.65 percent. During 43 hours of operating time, no repairs or adjustments were noted. Test L indicated that 106 percent of rated-speed torque was available all the way from 75 percent down to 65 percent of rated engine rpm. At a Test C operating maximum load of 21.38 belt hp, fuel economy was recorded at 12.42 hp-hours per gallon, dropping to 11.76 against a Test D rated belt load of 19.69 hp.

Nebraska Test Data

Model: McCormick Farmall 230
Test No. 616
Date Tested: April 25 to May 7, 1957

Using a C-123 International four-cylinder engine, the 230 carried a 3-1/8 x 4-inch bore and stroke for a 123-cubic inch displacement. Rated at 1,800 rpm, it achieved a Test L maximum of 111 percent rated-speed torque at 65 percent of rated engine rpm. Other features included forward speeds of 2.7, 4.3, 5.6, and 11.7 mph, along with 11.2-36-inch rear and 5.00-15-inch front tires. Bare tractor weight was 3,481 lbs., to which was added 925 lbs. of weight on each rear wheel during Tests F, G, and H. Test H, run in second gear, and at a rated load of 20.05 drawbar hp yielded a pull of 1,835 lbs. at 4.1 mph and slippage of 4.4 percent. Fuel economy totaled 10.61 hp-hours per gallon. Test G gave a low-gear maximum pull of 3,574 lbs. at 2.43 mph against a slippage of 10.21 percent. During 42 hours of operation, no repairs or adjustments were noted. At a Test D rated belt load of 24.95 hp, fuel economy was posted at 11.87 hp-hours per gallon, rising to 12.16 at a Test C operating maximum load of 26.71 belt hp.

Farmall 350 series

Nebraska Test Data

Model: McCormick Farmall 350 Diesel
Test No. 609
Date Tested: March 18 to April 5, 1957

The 350 Diesel featured a Continental four-cylinder engine rated at 1,750 rpm and that used a 3-3/4 x 4-3/8-inch bore and stroke for a 193-cubic inch displacement. This tractor used direct-drive in addition to the Torque Amplifier, thus giving 10 forward speeds ranging from 1.7 to 16.1 mph. Standard equipment of this 5,365 lb. unit also included a 13.6-38-inch rear and 5.50-16-inch front tires. During Tests F, G, and H an additional 1,462 lbs. of weight was added to each rear wheel. Test G, using low gear in the Torque Amplifier drive yielded a maximum pull of 6,039 lbs. at 1.51 mph with a slippage of 14.53 percent. Using third gear, Test H indicated a rated drawbar output of 27.76 hp. Also indicated was a pull of 2,006 lbs. at 5.19 mph and slippage of 4 percent for a fuel economy of 12.76 hp-hours per gallon. Test L gave 123 percent of rated-speed torque at 74 percent of rated engine rpm. At a Test D rated belt load of 34.28 hp, fuel economy was recorded at 14.48 hp-hours per gallon of diesel fuel. This figure rose to 14.79 at a 100 percent maximum belt load of 38.65 hp. No repairs or adjustments were noted during 44-1/2 hours of operating time.

Nebraska Test Data

Model: McCormick Farmall 350
Test No. 611
Date Tested: April 1 to April 13, 1957

Although the chassis design of this tractor was nearly identical to the Farmall 350 Diesel model, this unit featured an International four-cylinder gasoline engine with a displacement of 175 cubic inches. Rated at 1,750 rpm, it carried a 3-5/8 x 4-1/4-inch bore and stroke. Like other series models, the Torque Amplifier system was featured—this plus direct-drive gave 10 forward speeds ranging from 1.7 to 16.1 mph. The model presented for testing weighed 5,331 lbs. and was equipped with 13.6-38-inch rear and 5.50-16-inch front tires. During Tests F, G, and H an additional burden of 1,504 lbs. was added to each rear wheel. At a Test C operating maximum load of 39.31 belt hp the 350 achieved a fuel economy of 12.17 hp-hours per gallon of gasoline—this figure dropped to 11.66 at a Test D rated belt load of 36.21 hp. Test L indicated that 115 percent of rated-speed engine torque was available at 65 percent of rated rpm. During 52 hours of operating time, no repairs or adjustments were noted. Test G, using low gear in the Torque Amplifier range, yielded a maximum pull of 6,457 lbs. at 1.5 mph and slippage of 14.7 percent. Third gear was used for Test H. This test noted a rated output of 28.76 drawbar hp, a pull of 2,073 lbs. at 5.2 mph and slippage of 3.29 percent. Fuel economy in this test totaled 10.08 hp-hours per gallon.

Nebraska Test Data

Model: McCormick Farmall 350 (LPG)
Test No. 622
Date Tested: May 22 to May 29, 1957

Like the Farmall 350 of Test No. 611, this tractor was nearly identical except for the propane storage tank and accessory equipment. An unseen change was a 9:1 compression ratio used on this tractor compared to 7:1 for the gasoline model previously noted. Both models used an International C175 engine, and both had the same forward speeds, tires, and other equipment. Weighing 5,475 lbs. the tractor shown here was given another 1,348 lbs. of ballast on each rear wheel during Tests F, G, and H. Test G yielded a low-gear, Torque Amplifier range maximum pull of 6,395 lbs. at 1.5 mph against a slippage of 14.68 percent. The 10-hour run of Test H noted a rated drawbar load of 30.07 hp. Using third gear, this run also achieved a pull of 2,164 lbs. at 5.21 mph against a slippage of 3.11 percent. Fuel economy was noted at 8.33 hp-hours per gallon of propane fuel. Test L indicated that 100 percent of rated-speed torque was available down to 90 percent of rated rpm, dropping to a figure of 92 percent at 55 percent of rated rpm. No repairs or adjustments were noted during 44-1/2 hours of running time. Test C evoked a fuel economy of 9.6 hp-hours per gallon at a load of 39.34 hp, while Test D, run at a rated belt load of 36.36 hp produced a fuel economy of 9.38 hp-hours per gallon.

Nebraska Test Data

Model: International 350 Utility Diesel
Test No. 610
Date Tested: March 26 to April 15, 1957

This tractor and the Farmall 350 Diesel of Test No. 609 both carried a Continental D193 four-cylinder engine, but this tractor used a 2,000 rpm rated speed. As with other models of this series, the transmission was equipped with five forward speeds, using either direct-drive or the Torque Amplifier system, thus giving 10 speed choices ranging from 1.8 to 16.7 mph. During 49-1/2 hours of operating time, no repairs or adjustments were noted. Standard equipment also included 13-28-inch rear and 5.50-16-inch front tires. Weighing in at 4,655 lbs., the 350 Utility Diesel was burdened with another 1,620 lbs. of weight on each rear wheel during Tests F, G, and H. In the Torque Amplifier range, and using low gear, this tractor made a maximum pull of 5,835 lbs. at 1.58 mph with a slippage of 14.28 percent. The 10-hour run of Test H was made in third gear. At a rated output of 31.15 drawbar hp, a pull of 2,154 lbs. was recorded at

5.42 mph with a slippage of 3.8 percent. Fuel economy was registered at 12.45 hp-hours per gallon of fuel. Test L indicated that 121 percent of rated-speed engine torque was available at 70 percent of rated engine rpm. At a 100 percent maximum belt load of 42.89 hp, fuel economy was recorded at an even 14 hp-hours per gallon. This figure came to 113.7 under a Test D rated belt load of 37.5 hp.

Nebraska Test Data

Model: International 350 Utility

Test No. 615

Date Tested: April 24 to May 1, 1957

An International four-cylinder gasoline engine featured in this tractor emerges as the major difference between this model and the 350 Utility Diesel. With this exception, all other specifications remained virtually the same. Rated at 2,000 rpm, the engine used in this tractor carried a 3-5/8 x 4-1/4-inch bore and stroke for a 175-cubic inch displacement. During 44 hours of operating time, no repairs or adjustments were noted. Standard features included 13-28-inch rear and 5.50-16-inch front tires—and the bare tractor weight was 4,595 lbs. During Tests F, G, and H and additional 1,550 lbs. of weight was added to each rear wheel. Test G, using low gear and the Torque Amplifier drive yielded a maximum drawbar pull of 6,029 lbs. at 1.61 mph and slippage of 11.71 percent. The 10-hour run of Test H, made in third gear, indicated a rated drawbar load of 31.24 hp, along with a pull of 2,157 lbs. at 5.43 mph and slippage of 2.92 percent. Drawbar fuel economy per Test H came to 9.53 hp-hours per gallon. Test L indicated that 120 percent of rated-speed torque was available at 65 percent of rated rpm. Fuel economy totaled 11.35 hp-hours per gallon at a Test D rated belt load of 38.32 hp, while at a Test C operating maximum load of 41.11 hp, fuel economy was noted at 11.63 hp-hours per gallon.

Nebraska Test Data

Model: International 350 Utility (LPG)

Test No. 619

Date Tested: May 7 to May 28, 1957

This tractor was virtually identical to the gasoline 350 Utility of Test No. 615 except for the necessary modifications required for burning propane. Both tractors carried an international C175 engine, with this propane style using a 9:1 compression ratio, compared to 7:1 for the gasoline model. Rated at 2,000 rpm the 350 LPG developed 105 percent of rated-speed torque in a range from 75 percent to 66 percent or rated engine rpm, per Test L. Under a Test D rated belt load of 39.68 hp, fuel economy was scored at 9.41 hp-hours per gallon of propane, while at a Test C operating maximum load of 41.98 belt hp, fuel economy stood at 9.54 hp-hours per gallon. During 50-1/2 hours of engine running time, no repairs or adjustments were noted. Test G indicated a low-gear maximum pull of 6,357 lbs. using low gear in the Torque Amplifier range. Using third gear, Test H was run at a rated drawbar load of 32.74 hp. Under this load, a pull of 2,263 lbs. was recorded at 5.43 mph with a slippage of 3.42 percent. Fuel economy in this test totaled 8.34 hp-hours per gallon.

Farmall 450 series

Nebraska Test Data

Model: McCormick Farmall 450 Diesel

Test No. 608

Date Tested: March 18 to April 1, 1957

Weighing 6,877 lbs., the 450 Diesel was equipped with 15.5-38-inch and 6.00-16-inch front tires. During Test F, G, and H and additional 1,193 lbs. of weight was added to each rear wheel. Using either direct-drive or Harvester's Torque Amplifier system gave 10 forward speeds ranging from 1.7 to 16.6 mph. Third gear was used for the 10-hour run of Test H. At a rated output of 34.68 drawbar hp, the 450 Diesel pulled 2,750 lbs. at 4.73 mph with a slippage of 3.8 percent. Fuel economy was pegged at 12.75 hp-hours per gallon of fuel. Test G yielded a low-gear pull of 6,634 lbs. at 1.47 mph with a slippage of 14.96 percent. This particular test was run in the Torque Amplifier range. Rated at 1,450 rpm, the 450 Diesel developed 103 percent of rated-speed torque at 85 percent of rated engine speed per Test L. Standard equipment included an International four-cylinder diesel engine with a 4-1/8 x 5-1/4-inch bore and stroke for a displacement of 281-cubic inches. During 45 hours of operating time, no repairs or adjustments were noted. Test B & C, run at 100 percent maximum belt load of 48.78 hp produced a fuel economy of 13.57 hp-hours per gallon. This figure improved to 14.1 at a Test D rated belt load of 43.16 hp.

Nebraska Test Data

Model: McCormick Farmall 450

Test No. 612

Date Tested: April 9 to April 14, 1957

The Farmall 450 featured an International four-cylinder gasoline engine with a 281-cubic inch displacement. Rated at 1,450 rpm, it carried a 4-1/8 x 5-1/4-inch bore and stroke. With the exception of the gasoline engine, all other specifications remained virtually identical to those noted for the Farmall 450 Diesel. Test L noted 115 percent of rated-speed engine torque to be available at 65 percent of rated engine rpm. At a Test C operating maximum load of 51.55 belt hp, fuel economy was scored at 12.47 hp-hours per gallon and this figure dropped slightly to stand at 12.22 under a Test D rated belt load of 48.58 hp. No repairs or adjustments were noted during 41-1/2 hours of operating time. Using low gear in the Torque Amplifier range, the 450 achieved a Test G maximum pull of 7,318 lbs. at 1.44 mph under a slippage of 15.3 percent. The 10-hour run of Test H, made in third gear, indicated a rated drawbar load of 38.55 hp. This test recorded a pull of 3,079 lbs. at 4.7 mph and slippage of 4.04 percent. Fuel economy came in at 10.46 hp-hours per gallon of gasoline. Bare tractor weight was 6,519 lbs.

Nebraska Test Data

Model: McCormick Farmall 450 (LPG)

Test No. 620

Date Tested: May 7 to May 29, 1957

Except for its much different exterior appearance, the 450 LPG model was identical to the 450 gasoline style noted in Test No. 612. Both models had the same forward speeds and tire sizes, with the major difference in engines resting with an 8.35:1 compression ratio for the propane style, compared to 6.6:1 for the gasoline model. Weighing in at 6,635 lbs., the 450 LPG was burdened with an additional 1,218 lbs. of weight on each rear wheel during Tests F, G, and H. Using low gear in the Torque Amplifier range achieved a maximum drawbar pull of 7,333 lbs. at 1.47 mph with slippage of 14.18 percent per Test G. The 10-hour rated drawbar run of Test H revealed a fuel economy of 8.58 hp-hours per gallon of propane. This test also noted a rated output of 38.01 hp, a pull of 3,025 lbs. at 4.71 mph, and slippage of 3.85 percent. No repairs of adjustments were recorded during 54 hours of running time. Test D, run at a rated belt load of 48.26 hp noted a fuel economy of 9.73 hp-hours per gallon of propane fuel, with this figure climbing to 9.84 under a Test C operating maximum load of 50.5 belt hp.

International 650 series

Nebraska Test Data

Model: International 650

Test No. 618

Date Tested: May 3 to May 21, 1957

This standard-tread model featured forward speeds of 2.4, 3.2, 4.5, 5.5, and 15.7 mph, along with 18-26-inch rear and 7.50-18-inch front tires. Weighing 8,925 lbs., it was given an additional 1,840 lbs. of weight on each rear wheel during Tests F, G, and H. The rated drawbar run of Test H indicated a fuel economy of 9.8 hp-hours per gallon. Run in second gear, this test also noted a rated output of 44.66 hp, along with a pull of 3,722 lbs. at 4.5 mph and slippage of 4.09 percent. Test G elicited a low-gear maximum pull of 8,564 lbs. at 2.19 mph and slippage of 11.38 percent. The 650 featured an International four-cylinder C-350 gasoline engine. Rated at 1,500 rpm, it carried a 4.5 x 5.5-inch bore and stroke for a displacement of 350 cubic inches. Test L indicated an operating maximum of 113 percent rated-speed torque at 65 percent of rated rpm. No repairs or adjustments were noted during 52 hours of operation. At a Test D rated belt load of 55.43 hp, fuel economy settled in at 11.43 hp-hours per gallon, with this figure rising slightly to stand at 11.56 under a Test C operating maximum load of 58.96 belt hp.

Nebraska Test Data

Model: International 650 (LPG)

Test No. 621

Date Tested: May to May 27, 1957

The 650 LPG tractor was nearly identical to the 650 gasoline version tested under No. 618. Both models carried the same range of forward speeds, both used the same tires, and both carried an International C350 four-cylinder engine. A notable difference was the 8.25:1 compression ratio featured in this model, compared to the 6.12:1 ratio found in the 650 gasoline version. Test L indicated that 102 percent of rated-speed torque was available at 90 percent of rated rpm. Belt testing also indicated that under a Test D rated load of 56.8 hp, fuel economy came in at 8.72 hp-hours per gallon of propane, improving to 8.94 at a Test C operating maximum load of 61.33 hp. Test H, run in third gear, noted a rated drawbar output of 46.22 hp, along with a pull of 3,841 lbs. at 4.51 mph and slippage of 3.95 percent. Fuel economy was posted at 7.74 hp-hours per gallon of propane. Test G achieved a low-gear maximum pull of 8,867 lbs. at 2.17 mph against a slippage of 11.92 percent. No repairs or adjustments were noted during 47 hours of operating time.

Farmall 140, 240, and 340 Tractors

Nebraska Test Data

Model: IHC Farmall 140

Test No. 666

Date Tested: September 3 to September 18, 1958

During preliminary belt testing the carburetor was dismantled and cleaned, with a new high speed jet and load needle installed. Otherwise, no repairs or adjustments were recorded for this tractor during 49-1/2 hours of running time. At a Test C operating maximum load of 21.16 hp, fuel economy came in at 12.29 hp-hours per gallon. Test D, run at a rated belt load of 20.61 hp, yielded a fuel economy of 11.84 hp-hours per gallon. The 140 was equipped with an International four-cylinder engine with a 3-1/8 x 4-inch bore and stroke. Rated at 1,400 rpm, it also was designed with a 6.94:1 compression ratio and a 122.7- cubic inch displacement. Standard equipment also included four forward speeds of 1.9, 3.7, 4.8, and 12.8 mph. Weighing 3,000 lbs., it featured 11-24-inch rear and 5.00-15-inch front tires. During a portion of the drawbar testing, 818 lbs. was added to each rear wheel, plus another 95 lbs. of iron weight on each front tire. Test G achieved a low-gear maximum pull of 3,611 lbs. at 1.84 mph with 13.89 percent slippage. Using second gear, Test H was run at a rated drawbar output of 16.41 hp. This test noted a pull of 1,486 lbs. at 4.14 mph with 3.62 percent slippage. Drawbar fuel economy was 10.61 hp-hours per gallon.

Nebraska Test Data

Model: IHC Farmall 240

Test No. 667

Date Tested: September 5 to September 20, 1958

This tractor carried the same four-cylinder C-123 engine as used in the Farmall 140 tractor. The most obvious change was a rated speed of 2,000 rpm for this tractor, compared to 1,400 rpm for the Farmall 140. Also included in this 3,763-lb. unit were forward speeds of 2.2, 4.2, 5.6, and 14.7 mph, along with 12.4-36-inch rear and 5.00-15-inch front tires. During Tests F, G, H, and K an additional 1,056 lbs. of weight was added to each rear wheel, along with 105 lbs. of cast-iron weight on each front tire. A low-gear maximum pull of 4,343 lbs. at 2 mph with 14.06 percent slippage was noted in Test G. Using second gear, Test H was run at a rated drawbar load of 21.55 hp. This test indicated a pull of 1,861 lbs. at 4.34 mph and 4.24 percent slippage, with drawbar fuel economy pegged at 10.23 hp-hours per gallon. At a Test C operating maximum load of 28.32 belt hp, the 240 scored a fuel economy of 12.01 hp-hours per gallon. By comparison, the economy figure sagged to 11.74 under a Test D rated belt load of 27.41 hp. During 45 hours of running time, no repairs or adjustments were recorded.

Nebraska Test Data

Model: International 240 Utility
Test No. 668
Date Tested: September 6 to September 20, 1958

As in Tests 666 and 667, International Harvester used a four cylinder, 3-1/8 x 4 engine in the 240 Utility model. Rated at 2,000 rpm, it carried a displacement of 122.7-cubic inches. Standard equipment included 12-24-inch rear and 5.50-16-inch front tires, along with forward speeds of 1.8, 3.4, 4.5, and 11.8 mph. During most of the drawbar testing this 3,637-lb. tractor was burdened with another 964 lbs. of ballast on each rear wheel and 90 lbs. of cast-iron weight on each front wheel. Test H, run in third gear, was made at a rated drawbar load of 21.93 hp. This test indicate a fuel economy of 10.07 hp-hours per gallon with statistics noting a 1,709 lb. pull at 4.81 mph with 3.69 percent slippage. Test G recorded a low-gear maximum pull of 4,380 lbs. at 1.68 mph with 12.32 percent slippage. During 41-1/2 hours of operating time, no repairs or adjustments were recorded. Test I, run at a rated belt load of 27.45 hp, produced a fuel economy of 11.89 hp-hours per gallon, while Test C, run at an operating maximum load of 28.55 hp, yielded 12.2 hp-hours per gallon of fuel.

IHC Farmall 340

Nebraska Test Data

Model: IHC Farmall 340
Test No. 665
Date Tested: September 3 to September 25, 1958

Using a 3-1/4 x 4-1/16-inch bore and stroke, this four-cylinder tractor was rated at 2,000 rpm and had a 135-cubic inch displacement. Using either direct-drive or the Torque Amplifier system gave a total of 10 forward speeds ranging from 1.2 to 16.6 mph. Weighing in at 4,735

Farmall 460 and 560 tractors

lbs., the 340 carried 13.9-36-inch rear and 5.00-15-inch front tires. Some 870 lbs. of ballast was added to each rear wheel, plus another 143 lbs. for each front wheel. Test G, when run in low gear yielded a maximum pull of 5,142 lbs. at 1.64 mph with 12.1percent slippage. Test H, run in third gear at a rated load of 24.87 drawbar hp, noted a pull of 1,695 lbs. at 5.5 mph with 2.94 percent slippage. Fuel economy was posted at 10.75 hp-hours per gallon. During Test H the differential casting failed, damaging several bearings, gears, and other parts. The complete differential and all damaged parts were replaced and the test continued. Following the belt test, the voltage regulator malfunctioned. With these exceptions, no other repairs or adjustments were noted during 59 hours of running time. Belt testing indicated a fuel economy of 12.03 hp-hours per gallon at a Test D rated load of 30.7 hp. Fuel economy scored at 12.45 hp-hours per gallon at a Test C operating maximum load of 32.3 hp.

Nebraska Test Data

Model: IHC Farmall 140 Diesel

Test No. 775

Date Tested: October 26 to November 3, 1960

Using third gear, the 340 Diesel came out of the two-hour drawbar economy run with a maximum output of 36.14 hp, a pull of 2,666 lbs. at 5.08 mph and 4.79 percent slippage. Fuel economy was posted at 13.08 hp-hours per gallon. The 10-hour run, made at 75 percent pull, noted an economy figure of 11.90, along with an output of 27.95 hp, a pull of 1,959 lbs. at 5.35 mph and 3.6 percent slippage. Standard equipment for this tractor included 13.9-36-inch rear and 5.50-16-inch front tires. Bare tractor weight was 5,195 lbs., a figure that rose to a test weight of 7,579 lbs. Also featured was a selective gear fixed-ratio partial range power shift transmission providing 10 forward speeds ranging from 1.2 to 16.6 mph. Due to the failure of a bearing in the limber-up run the planet carrier assembly was replaced. With this exception, no repairs or adjustments were recorded during 45 hours of operating time. Harvester equipped this tractor with a four-cylinder diesel engine rated at 2,000 rpm and carrying a 3-11/16 x 3-7/8-inch bore and stroke for a displacement of 166-cubic inches. At rated engine speed 38.93 maximum PTO hp was developed, together with an apparent fuel economy of 13.81 hp-hours per gallon of diesel fuel. The economy figure was placed at 13.44 on a PTO run made at a standard 540 rpm output speed and a corresponding engine speed of 1,776 rpm. This run had an output of 37.39 PTO hp.

Nebraska Test Data

Model: IHC Farmall 460

Test No. 670

Date Tested: September 22 to October 3, 1958

At a Test C operating maximum load of 46.94 belt hp, the 460 gasoline model yielded a fuel economy of 12.23 hp-hours per gallon. By comparison, under a Test D rated belt load of 43.92 hp, fuel economy stood at 11.61 hp-hours per gallon. The 460 featured an International six-cylinder engine with a 3-9/16 x 3-11/16-inch bore and stroke. Rated at 1,800 rpm, it had a 221-cubic inch displacement. No repairs or adjustments were noted during 46-1/2 hours of operation. Standard equipment for this 5,835 lb. tractor included 13.6-38-inch rear and 6.00-16-inch front tires, along with 10 forward speeds ranging from 1.7 to 16.6 mph. Five of these speeds were in direct drive, with five more available using the Torque Amplifier, During drawbar testing, 1,420 lbs. of weight was added to each rear wheel, along with an additional 128 lbs. for each front wheel. Test G, run in first gear and using the Torque Amplifier gave a maximum pull of 6,734 lbs. at 1.54 mph and 13.89 percent slippage. The 10-hour run of Test H was made in third gear. At a rated drawbar load of 35.95 hp the 460 pulled 2,432 lbs. at 5.54 mph with 3.27 percent slippage. Fuel economy in this test totaled 10.12 hp-hours per gallon.

Nebraska Test Data

Model: IHC Farmall 460 Diesel

Test No. 672

Date Tested: September 30 to October 11, 1958

The 460 Diesel featured a six-cylinder IHC engine using a 3-11/16-inch bore and stroke. Rated at 1,800 rpm, it had a 236-cubic inch displacement. With this exception, the 460 Diesel was virtually identical to the 460 gasoline model. Basic tractor weight was 6,055 lbs. Drawbar testing indicated a fuel economy of 12.35 hp-hours per gallon of diesel fuel at a Test H rated load of 36.19 hp. This test noted a pull of 2,476 lbs. at 5.48 mph with 4.03 percent slippage. Maximum load tests were run in all 10 forward gears, as with all other tests, but the low gear run using the Torque Amplifier indicated a pull of 6,846 lbs. at 1.57 mph with 13.35 percent slippage. No repairs or adjustments were noted during 42-1/2 hours of operating time. Test D, run at a rated belt load of 44.4 hp achieved a fuel economy of 13.91 hp-hours per gallon of diesel fuel. This figure rose to 14.04 at a 100percent maximum belt load of 50.1 hp.

Nebraska Test Data

Model: International 460 Utility Diesel

Test No. 673

Date Tested: October 2 to October 9, 1958

Weighing 5,255 lbs., this tractor featured 14.9-28-inch rear and 6.00-16-inch front tires as standard equipment. Also featured were 10 forward speeds ranging from 1.2 to 16.5 mph. Five speeds were available in direct-drive, with another five available through the Torque Amplifier system. During a portion of the drawbar testing, 1,505 lbs. was added to each rear wheel, and an additional 158 lbs. was used on each front wheel. Test H, run for 10 hours in third gear, was made under a rated drawbar load of 36.44 hp. This test indicated a pull of 2,440 lbs. at 5.6 mph with 3.02 percent slippage. Fuel economy was posted at 12.38 hp-hours per gallon of diesel fuel. Test G, run in low gear with the Torque Amplifier achieved a maximum pull of 6,437 lbs. at 1.14 mph and 13.81 percent slippage. IH used a D-236, six-cylinder engine rated at 1,800 rpm and carrying a 3-11/16-inch bore and stroke for a 236-cubic inch displacement. At a Test D rated belt load of 44.58 hp, fuel economy was 13.88 hp-hours per gallon. By comparison, at a 100 percent maximum belt load of 50.01 hp, fuel economy was recorded at 13.73 hp-hours per gallon. No repairs or adjustments were noted during 42-1/2 hours of operating time.

Nebraska Test Data

Model: International 460 Utility

Test No. 674

Date Tested: October 6 to October 18, 1958

This tractor was virtually identical to the 460 Utility Diesel, varying primarily through the use of six-cylinder gasoline engine. Rated at 1,800 rpm, it carried a 3-9/16 x 3-11/16-inch bore and stroke for a 221-cubic inch displacement. Bare weight was 5,015 lbs., to which was added 1,485 lbs. on each rear wheel plus 255 lbs. on each front wheel during most of the drawbar testing. At this point in the history of the Nebraska Tests, Test J was run at operating maximum drawbar load without any added weight. For all other tests, additional ballast was used. Test when run in low gear with the Torque Amplifier noted a maximum pull of 6,485 lbs. at 1.12 mph and 14.39 percent slippage. The 10-hour run of Test H was made in third gear with a rated load of 35.28 hp. This test indicated a pull of 2,261 lbs. at 5.85 mph and 2.64 percent slippage. Fuel economy was posted at 9.2 hp-hours per gallon. Except for replacing the high-speed carburetor needle, no repairs or adjustments were noted during 45 hours of running time. Test D, run at a rated belt load of 43.89 hp produced a fuel economy of 11.39 hp-hours per gallon. By comparison, the economy figure climbed to 12.22 at a Test C operating maximum load of 46.69 hp.

Nebraska Test Data

Model: IHC Farmall 460 (LPG)
Test No. 676
Date Tested: October 20 to October 25, 1958

Chassis design for the 460 LPG was virtually identical to the gasoline style noted in Test No. 670. Weighing 6,670 lbs., it was burdened with 1,235 lbs. of ballast on each rear wheel, and 88 lbs. of cast-iron weight on each front wheel. Test G, run in low gear with the Torque Amplifer, yielded a maximum pull of 6,903 lbs. at 1.58 mph with 12.03 percent slippage. The 10-hour run of Test H was made in third gear and under a rated drawbar load of 36.17 hp. This test indicated a pull of 2,461 lbs. at 5.51 mph with a slippage of 2.89 percent. Fuel economy came in at 8.08 hp-hours per gallon of propane. A major difference between this tractor and the gasoline version was the 7.2:1 compression ratio on gasoline, compared to an 8.75:1 compression ratio for this tractor. Both tractors carried an International six-cylinder C-221 engine rated at 1,800 rpm. During 44 hours of running time, no repairs or adjustments were noted. At a Test C operating maximum load of 46.86 hp, fuel economy was registered at 9.29 hp-hours per gallon of propane, with this figure slipping to 9.07 under a Test D rated load of 44.21 hp.

Nebraska Test Data

Model: International 460 Utility (LPG)
Test No. 677
Date Tested: October 17 to October 25, 1958

Fuel economy was scored at 9.14 hp-hours per gallon of propane under a Test C operating maximum load of 45.34 belt hp. With a Test D rated belt load of 43.08 hp, fuel economy was posted at 8.95 hp-hours per gallon of propane. This tractor carried a C-221 engine with an 8.75:1 compression ratio. With this exception, plus the necessary propane equipment, there was virtually no difference between this tractor and the 460 Utility gasoline model of Test No. 674. Weighing in at 5,205 lbs., it was burdened with 1,460 lbs. of weight on each rear wheel, plus 210 lbs. of weight on each front wheel during most of the drawbar testing. Test G, run in low gear with the Torque Amplifier, indicated a maximum pull of 6,560 lbs. at 1.13 mph and 13.98 percent slippage. Test H, run in third gear, was made at a rated drawbar load of 35.77 hp. This test noted a pull of 2,333 lbs. at 5.75 mph and 3.02 percent slippage. Fuel economy was recorded at 8.09 hp-hours per gallon of propane. No repairs or adjustments were noted during 40 hours of running time.

Farmall 560 series

Nebraska Test Data

Model: IHC Farmall 560 Diesel
Test No. 669
Date Tested: September 18 to September 25, 1958

Using either direct-drive or the Torque Amplifier system, this tractor had 10 forward speeds ranging from 1.5 to 16.6 mph amd weighed 6,785 lbs. During most of the drawbar testing, an additional burden of 1,203 lbs. was added to each rear wheel, plus another 135 lbs. on each front wheel, bringing the total test weight, including the operator, to 9,460 lbs. Test G, run in low gear and direct drive, yielded a maximum pull of 7,347 lbs. at 1.91 mph and 13.75 percent slippage. The 10-hour run of Test H was made in third gear. At a rate output of 44.38 hp, the 560 Diesel pulled 3,036 lb. at 5.48 mph with 3.57 percent slippage. Fuel economy was recorded at 13.57 hp-hours per gallon. The 560 Diesel feature an International six-cylinder engine with a 3-11/16 x 4-25/64-inch engine. Rated at 1,800 rpm, it had a displacement of 281-cubic inches. No repairs or adjustment were noted during 43 hours of operating time. Test D, run at a rated belt load of 53.21 hp, noted a fuel economy of 14.79 hp-hours per gallon of diesel fuel. This figure slipped slightly to stand at 14.46 under a 100 percent maximum belt load of 58.48 hp.

Nebraska Test Data

Model: IHC Farmall 560
Test No. 671
Date Tested: September 24 to October 6, 1958

This tractor carried the identical tire equipment, used the same chassis, and featured the same forward speeds as previously noted. The major difference was a C-263 gasoline engine in this model, compared to the 560 Diesel. Weighing 6,563 lbs., this tractor was weighted to virtually the same degree as the diesel model. Test H, run in third gear, was made at a rated output of 44.83 hp. With a pull of 3,063 lbs. at 5.49 mph, slippage was recorded at 2.81 percent. Fuel economy came in at 10.73 hp-hours per gallon. Test G, when run in first gear and the Torque Amplifier, gave a maximum pull of 7,588 lbs. at 1.28 mph with 14.07 percent slippage. No repairs or adjustments were noted during 42-1/2 hours of running time. At a Test C operating maximum load of 61.04 belt hp, fuel economy was pegged at 12.65 hp-hours per gallon, slipping to 11.91 under a Test D rated belt load of 55.47 hp. The C-263 engine used in the 560 gasoline model was a six cylinder and featured a 3-9/16 x 4-25/64-inch bore and stroke. Rated at 1,800 rpm it had a 263-cubic inch displacement.

Nebraska Test Data

Model: IHC Farmall 560 (LPG)
Test No. 675
Date Tested: October 8 to October 20, 1958

Weighing 5,910 lbs., the 560 LPG was virtually identical in chassis design to the 560 gasoline and diesel models. Using a C-263, six-cylinder engine of 3-9/16 x 4-25/64-inch bore and stroke, the 560 LPG was rated at 1,800 rpm and carried a 263-cubic inch displacement. While the gasoline model was designed with a 7.2:1 compression ratio, this tractor carried an 8.75:1 compression ratio to better accommodate the propane fuel. At a Test C operating maximum load of 57.06 hp, fuel economy was recorded at 9.73 hp-hours per gallon of propane—a figure that slipped to 9.49 under a Test D rated belt load of 53.44 hp. No repairs or adjustments were noted during 44 hours of operation. Test H, run in third gear for the 10-hour duration, was made with a rated drawbar load of 43.96 hp. Fuel economy came in at 8.55 hp-hours per gallon of propane. Test H also indicated a pull of 2,968 lbs. at 5.55 mph and 3.49 percent slippage. Using the Torque Amplifier and first gear, Test G noted a maximum pull of 7,524 lbs. at 1.28 mph and 14.34 percent slippage.

International 660 series

Nebraska Test Data

Model: International 660 Diesel

Test No. 715

Date Tested: August 31 to September 5, 1959

Using either a fixed ratio drive or the Torque Amplifier system, this tractor featured a total of 10 forward speeds ranging from 1.35 to 15.39 mph. Standard equipment also included a belt pulley and/or 540 rpm PTO drive. At its rated 2,400 rpm, the 660 Diesel achieved a maximum of 78.78 PTO hp with a fuel economy of 14.23 hp-hours per gallon. Harvester featured its own six-cylinder engine with a 3-11/16 x 4-25/64-inch bore and stroke for a displacement of 281-cubic inches. The design also included an 18.2:1 compression ratio and a 12-volt electrical system. Tire equipment for this test consisted of 18-26-inch rear and 7.50-18-inch front tires. With a bare weight of 9,875 lbs., the 660 Diesel assumed a weight of 15,255 lbs. for most of the drawbar testing. Drawbar fuel economy was posted at 12.35 hp-hours per gallon under a maximum available output of 64.43 hp. This test yielded a pull of 5,254 lbs. at 4.96 mph with 4.52 percent slippage. Under 75 percent loading, 56.88 hp was noted, along with a pull of 4,033 lbs., at 5.29 mph and 3.15 percent slippage for a total economy of 12.72 hp-hours per gallon in this 10-hour test. No repairs or adjustments were noted during 45-_ hours of running time.

Nebraska Test Data

Model: International 660

Test No. 721

Date Tested: October 1 to October 12, 1959

This big standard-tread tractor featured 18-26-inch rear and 7.50-18-inch front tires as standard equipment. With a bare weight of 9,635 lbs., it assumed a total weight of 15,075 lbs. after suitable front and rear ballast was installed. The 660 featured an International six-cylinder engine with a 3-9/16 x 4-25/64-inch bore and stroke. Rated at 2,400 rpm, it had a 263-cubic inch displacement. At rated engine speed the 660 developed 81.39 PTO hp, yielding a fuel economy of 12.76 hp-hours per gallon. Also featured was a Torque Amplifier system giving two speeds for each of five speed ranges, or a total of 10 speeds ranging from 1.35 to 15.39 mph. Third gear was used in the two-hour fuel consumption run at maximum available power. With an output of 70.21 drawbar hp, the 660 pulled 5,262 lbs. at 5 mph with 3.88 percent slippage and gave a fuel economy of 11.17 hp-hours per gallon. Under a 75 percent load of 55.40 hp a pull of 3,956 lbs. was observed at 5.25 mph and slippage was recorded at 2.63 percent. Fuel economy came to 10.33 hp-hours per gallon. No repairs or adjustments were noted during 47-1/2 hours of operating time.

Nebraska Test Data

Model: International 660 (LPG)

Test No. 722

Date Tested: October 3 to October 12, 1959

Except for additional propane equipment, this tractor differed very little from the International 660 of Test No. 721. One notable difference is while the gasoline model used a 7.2:1 compression ratio, this propane model carried an 8.75:1 compression ratio. This tractor also used 15-34-inch rear tires, compared to the 18-26-inch tires of Test No. 721. At a rated engine speed of 2,400 rpm, the 660 LPG model produced a maximum of 80.63 PTO hp with a fuel economy of 9.01 hp-hours per gallon. Using third gear, the two-hour economy run at maximum available power yielded an output of 69.66 drawbar hp, together with a pull of 4,933 lbs. at 5.33 mph and slippage of 5.2 percent for a net fuel economy of 7.89 hp-hours per gallon. The 10-hour drawbar run, made at 75 percent load, ended with a drawbar output of 55.35 hp, a pull of 3,778 lbs. and slippage of 3.38 percent. Fuel economy was posted at 7.55 hp-hours per gallon. No repairs or adjustments were noted during 42 hours of operating time.

Farmall 404 tractor

Nebraska Test Data

Model: Farmall 404

Test No. 818

Date Tested: May 21 to June 4, 1962

The Farmall 404 test model carried a loaded weight of 6,645 lbs. through the addition of front and rear ballast. By comparison, the bare tractor weighed 4,115 lbs. Four forward speeds were available in each of two speed ranges. This provided a total of eight possible choices ranging from 2.23 to 21.03 mph. Also featured were 11.2-36 rear and 5.50-16 inch front tires. Using the low range of third gear, a two-hour drawbar economy run set this figure at 10.83 hp-hours per gallon under a maximum available output of 32.97 hp. Also recorded was a pull of 2,356 lbs. at 5.25 mph with 5.31 percent slippage. The economy figure dipped slightly to stand at 10.10 in a 10-hour drawbar run made at 75 percent pull. This test noted an output of 27.5 hp, a pull of 1,795 lbs. at 5.74 mph and 2.99 percent slippage. Harvester designed this tractor with its own four-cylinder engine rated at 2,000 rpm. Using a 3 _ x 4-1/16-inch bore and stroke, it had a 134.8-cubic inch displacement. No repairs or adjustments were noted during 46-_ hours of operating time. At rated engine speed, 36.70 maximum PTO hp was observed, together with a fuel economy of 12.34 hp-hours per gallon.

Nebraska Test Data

Model: Farmall 504 Diesel
Test No. 816
Date Tested: May 3 to May 16, 1962

The selective-gear fixed-ratio transmission used in this tractor also included partial range power shifting using Harvester's Torque Amplifier system. A total of 10 forward speeds were thus available, ranging from 1.32 to 17.64 mph. Also featured were 13.6-38-inch rear and 6.00-16-inch front tires. The bare weight of 5,605 lbs. was raised to a test figure of 8,075 lbs. through the addition of front and rear ballast. Using third gear, a two-hour drawbar run made at 38.9 maximum available hp yielded a fuel economy of 12.96 hp-hours per gallon. This test also indicated a pull of 2,671 lbs. at 5.46 mph with 4.69 percent slippage. The 10-hour drawbar run, made at 75 percent pull, produced an economy figure of 12.30, along with an output of 31.95 hp, a pull of 2,076 lbs. at 5.77 mph and 3.59 percent slippage. Harvester equipped this tractor with its own four-cylinder diesel engine rated at 2,200 rpm. Using a 3-11/16 x 4.390-inch bore and stroke it had a 187.5-cubic inch displacement. At rated engine speed, a maximum output of 45.99 PTO hp was observed, together with a fuel economy of 14.89 hp-hours per gallon. Economy slipped by a small degree to stand at 14.65 in a PTO run made at 540 rpm on the PTO shaft and a corresponding engine speed of 1,970 rpm. This test manifested an output of 44.94 PTO hp. During 49 hours of operation, no repairs or adjustments were noted.

Nebraska Test Data

Model: Farmall 504
Test No. 819
Date Tested: May 17 to June 6, 1962

During 43-1/2 hours of operating time, no repairs or adjustments were reported on the Farmall 504 tractor. Weighing 5,285 lbs., it was burdened to 7,870 lbs. during drawbar testing with added front and rear ballast. Standard equipment included 13.6-38-inch rear and 6.00-16-inch front tires. Also featured was a five-speed transmission that included the Torque Amplifier system for a total of 10 forward speeds ranging from 1.32 to 17.64 mph. In third gear, direct-drive, a two-hour run made at 40.41 maximum available drawbar hp yielded a fuel economy of 10.93 hp-hours per gallon. Also indicated in this test was a pull of 2,787 lbs. at 5.44 mph with 4.43 percent slippage. The 10-hour run, made at 75 percent pull, noted an economy figure of 9.89. Other test statistics included a pull of 2,129 lbs. at 5.76 mph, 3.21 percent slippage, and an output of 32.7 drawbar hp. The 504 was equipped with an International four-cylinder 152.1-cid gasoline engine rated at 2,200 rpm. It used a 3-3/8 x 4-1/4-inch bore and stroke. At rated engine speed a maximum of 46.2 PTO hp was observed, along with a fuel economy of 12.33 hp-hours per gallon. The economy figure was posted at 12.13 in another PTO run at 540 rpm on the output shaft, with a corresponding engine speed of 1,970 rpm. This test indicated an output of 44.05 PTO hp.

Nebraska Test Data

Model: Farmall 504 LPG
Test No. 820
Date Tested: May 17 to June 9, 1962

Chassis design and tire sizes for this tractor were identical to those given for the 504 gasoline model. This propane version also used a four-cylinder, 152.1-cid engine but the propane-fired tractor used an 8.0:1 compression ratio. At its rated engine speed of 2,200 rpm, a maximum of 44.36 PTO hp was recorded, together with an economy of 8.99 hp-hours per gallon of propane. A second run made at 540 PTO rpm and a corresponding engine speed of 1,969 rpm yielded 9.41 gph, together with an output of 41.21 hp. No repairs or adjustments were required during 43-_ hours of operation. Using third gear, and under 40.17 maximum available drawbar hp, fuel economy was recorded at 8.03 hp-hours per gallon of propane. Also noted was a pull of 2,793 lbs. at 5.39 mph with 5.05 percent slippage. A 10-hour drawbar run made at 75 percent pull produced an economy figure of 7.95, and also recorded an output of 32.91 hp, a pull of 2,164 lbs. at 5.7 mph and 3.00 percent slippage. Bare tractor weight was 5,385 lbs. and this increased to a test weight of 7,895 lbs. through the addition of front and rear ballast.

International B-414 series

Nebraska Test Data

Model: International B-414
Test No. 817
Date Tested: May 3 to May 18, 1962

At its rated engine speed of 2,000 rpm, the B-414 developed a maximum of 36.46 PTO hp, yielding a fuel economy of 12.06 hp-hours per gallon. Using an International four-cylinder engine, this tractor carried a 3-3/8 x 4-inch bore and stroke for a 143.1-cubic inch displacement. Also featured was a selective-gear fixed-ratio transmission with four forward speeds in each of two ranges, for a total speed range of 1.5 to 15.5 mph. Standard equipment for this 3,965-lb. model also included 13.6-28-inch rear and 6.00-16-inch front tires. During drawbar testing, additional front and rear ballast brought the total weight to 6,625 lbs. No repairs or adjustments were noted during 48-1/2 hours of operating time. Using the low range of fourth gear, a two-hour drawbar run at 30.86 maximum available hp produced a fuel economy of 10.23 hp-hours per gallon. This test also indicated a pull of 2,249 lbs. at 5.15 mph with 5.44 percent slippage. A 10-hour run made at 75 percent pull yielded a fuel economy figure of 9.24. Other statistics included a pull of 1,732 lbs. at 5.57 mph, slippage of 3.78 percent, and an output of 25.74 drawbar hp.

Nebraska Test Data

Model: International B-414 Diesel
Test No. 827
Date Tested: September 27 to October 12, 1962

Except for the diesel engine, this tractor was nearly identical to the B-414 gasoline model. The International four-cylinder engine was rated at 2,000 rpm, and carried a 3-1/2 x 4-inch bore and stroke for a displacement of 154 cubic inches. Also of interest, this engine was designed with a 22.6 : 1 compression ratio. At its rated speed a maximum of 35.99 PTO hp was recorded, together with a fuel economy of 14.32 hp-hours per gallon. Eight forward speeds ranging from 1.5 to 15.5 mph were provided, with the low range of fourth gear being used for the drawbar economy runs. A two-hour test made at 31.73 maximum available hp yielded a fuel economy of 12.13 hp-hours per gallon while making a pull of 2,297 lbs. at 5.18 mph with 5.04 percent slippage. The 10-hour economy run, made at 75 percent pull, noted an output of 25.39 hp, a pull of 1,777 lbs. at 5.36 mph, and 3.52 percent slippage. No repairs or adjustments were recorded during 38 hours of operating time. Standard equipment included 13.6-28-inch rear and 6.00-16-inch front tires. Without ballast the B-414 Diesel weighed 4,050 lbs., but front and rear ballast gave a total test weight, including the operator, of 6,715 lbs.

International 424 series

Nebraska Test Data

Model: International 424
Test No. 908
Date Tested: September 8 to September 15, 1965

This standard-tread tractor was equipped with 13.6-28-inch rear and 6.00-16 inch front tires. Weighing 3,955 lbs., it was burdened with additional front and rear ballast for a test weight of 6,715 lbs. The selective gear fixed-ratio transmission offered eight forward speeds ranging from 1.5 to 15.5 mph. No repairs or adjustments were reported during 44 hours of operating time. Using fifth gear, 31.44 maximum available drawbar hp was recorded in a two-hour economy run. This test indicated a fuel economy of 10.54 hp-hours per gallon of gasoline. The 10-hour run at 75 percent pull saw an output of 26.07 drawbar hp, a pull of 1,756 lbs. at 5.57 mph and slippage of 3.64 percent. This test posted an economy of 9.57 hp-hours per gallon. Harvester equipped the 424 with a four-cylinder engine rated at 2,000 rpm. Its 3-3/8 x 4-1/16-inch bore and stroke gave a 145.3-cubic inch displacement. At rated engine speed, fuel economy was recorded at 12.34 hp-hours per gallon against a maximum output of 36.97 PTO hp.

Nebraska Test Data

Model: International 424 Diesel
Test No. 911
Date Tested: September 16 to September 23, 1965

Weighing 4,055 lbs., the 424 Diesel was carried on 13.6-28-inch rear and 6.00-16-inch front tires. During drawbar testing, additional front and rear ballast raised this figure to 6,825 lbs. The selective gear fixed-ratio transmission offered eight forward speeds ranging from 1.5 to 15.5 mph. A two-hour drawbar economy run made at 31.9 maximum available hp saw a pull of 2,317 lbs. at 5.16 mph and slippage of 4.31 percent. Fuel economy was posted at 11.55 hp-hours per gallon. A second economy run for 10 hours and at 75 percent pull indicated an economy of 11.57 hp-hours per gallon against an output of 25.81 hp. Also recorded was a pull of 1,749 lbs. at 5.53 mph and 3.27 percent slippage. Harvester equipped this tractor with its own four-cylinder diesel engine rated at 2,000 rpm. Using a 3-1/2 x 4-inch bore and stroke, it had a displacement of 154-cubic inches. No repairs or adjustments were reported during 36-1/2 hours of operating time. At rated engine speed, a maximum output of 36.91 PTO hp was observed, together with an economy of 13.97 hp-hours per gallon.

Nebraska Test Data

Model: Farmall 706 Diesel
Test No. 856
Date Tested: October 21 to November 8, 1963

Using Harvester's Torque Amplifier system, the 706 Diesel featured partial range power shifting within the selective-gear fixed-ratio transmission. In all, 16 speeds were provided in a range from 1.17 to 18.43 mph. Standard equipment included 15.5-38-inch rear and 6.50-16-inch front tires. The bare weight of 8,530 lbs. was raised to a test figure of 10,011 lbs. through the addition of rear wheel ballast. Using second gear and the Torque Amplifier range, a two-hour drawbar run at 65.12 maximum available hp yielded a pull of 4,701 lbs. at 5.19 mph with 5.88 percent slippage. Economy was posted at 11.97 hp-hours per gallon. By comparison, the 10-hour run at 75 percent pull posted the economy at 12.01. The latter test included an output of 54.46 hp, a pull of 3,668 lbs. at 5.57 mph and 4.28 percent. Harvester equipped this model with its own six-cylinder, 282-cid diesel engine. Rated at 2,300 rpm, it used a 3-11/16 x 4-25/64-inch bore and stroke. At rated engine speed a maximum of 72.42 PTO hp was observed, along with an economy of 13.15 hp-hours per gallon. The economy figure was recorded at 13.19 in a second run made at 1,000 rpm on the PTO shaft with a corresponding engine speed of 2,072 rpm. This test indicated an output of 67.26 hp. Except for replacement of the three-point-hitch vertical stabilizer lockout bracket, no repairs or adjustments were reported during 62-1/2 hours of operation.

Nebraska Test Data

Model: Farmall 706
Test No. 858
Date Tested: October 30 to November 20, 1963

Weighing 8,285 lbs., this gasoline version of the 706 was burdened with rear wheel ballast for a total test weight of 9,895 lbs. Using tenth gear and operating at 66.18 maximum available drawbar hp, the 706 delivered a fuel economy of of 11.17 hp-hours per gallon. Other statistics from this two-hour run included a pull of 4,783 lbs. at 5,19 mph, with 6.25 percent slippage. The 10-hour drawbar run, made at 75 percent pull, noted an economy figure of 10.45. Also recorded was an output of 54.29 hp, a pull of 3,593 lbs. at 5.67 mph and 4.46 percent slippage. Harvester equipped this model with its six-cylinder, 263-cid engine. Rated at 2,300 rpm, it used a 3-11/16 x 4-25/64-inch bore and stroke. No repairs or adjustments were required during 42 hours of operating time. PTO testing indicated a maximum output of 73.82 hp at rated engine speed—also recorded was an economy of 12.86 hp-hours per gallon. A second PTO run made at 1,000 PTO rpm and corresponding engine speed of 2,071 rpm saw an output of 68.77 hp, together with an economy of 13.16 hp-hours per gallon.

Nebraska Test Data

Model: Farmall 706 LPG

Test No. 860

Date Tested: November 8 to November 25, 1963

This model used the same gear train, chassis, and tire sizes as other Farmall 706s tested. Likewise, this tractor was equipped with the same 263-cubic inch engine as used in the 706 gasoline model. To accommodate the propane fuel, this tractor carried an 8.8:1 compression ratio compared to 7.6:1 in the gasoline model. During the limber-up run, a core hole plug came out of the engine block. It was replaced and the test continued without further incident during 41 total hours of running time. Tenth gear was used for the drawbar economy tests. At 66.06 maximum available hp, a two-hour run saw a resultant economy of 8.95 hp-hours per gallon of propane. Also indicated was a pull of 4,747 lbs. at 5.22 mph with 5.8 percent slippage. The 10-hour run at 75 percent pull revealed an economy of 8.02 hp-hours per gallon while delivering 52.13 hp. Other statistics include a pull of 3,576 lbs. at 5.47 mph with 4.38 percent slippage. The bare weight of 8,475 lbs. was raised to a figure of 9,865 lbs. through the addition of rear wheel ballast. PTO testing indicated an economy of 9.88 against a maximum load of 73.66 hp and at rated engine speed.

Nebraska Test Data

Model: Farmall 706 Diesel

Test No. 955

Date Tested: November 14 to November 28, 1966

At its rated engine speed of 2,300 rpm, the 706 Diesel delivered a fuel economy of 15.08 hp-hours per gallon against a maximum PTO load of 76.09 hp. Operating at 2,072 crankshaft rpm and a corresponding PTO speed of 1,000 rpm, 15.37 hp-hours per gallon were achieved with a load of 71.84 hp. This tractor featured an International six-cylinder engine with a 3.875 x 4.375-inch bore and stroke for a 309.6-cubic inch displacement. Also featured was a selective gear fixed-ratio transmission with partial range power shifting. Sixteen forward speeds were available ranging from 1-1/4 to 18-1/2 mph. No repairs or adjustments were reported during 48 hours of running time. Bare tractor weight was 9,160 lbs., but additional rear wheel ballast boosted this figure to a test weight of 10,710 lbs. Using tenth gear, 67.46 maximum available drawbar hp was delivered in the two-hour economy run. This test yielded an economy of 13.4 hp-hours per gallon and indicated a pull of 4,392 lbs. at 5.76 mph with slippage of 4.86 percent. A 10-hour economy run at 75 percent pull achieved a fuel economy figure of 12.47 hp-hours per gallon while developing 53.27 hp. Other statistics included a pull of 3,314 lbs. at 6.03 mph and slippage of 3.86 percent.

Nebraska Test Data

Model: Farmall 706 LPG

Test No. 956

Date Tested: November 14 to November 28, 1966

This tractor carried the same chassis as its 706 counterparts. All three models used 15.5-38-inch rear and 6.50-16-inch front tires, and all featured the same transmission style. This propane-fired version carried a 290.8-cubic inch, six-cylinder engine, suitably modified for propane fuel. Contrary to most propane models, this one used the same 7.5:1 compression ratio as the gasoline style. At its rated speed of 2,300 rpm, 76.3 maximum PTO hp was observed, as was an economy of 9.1 hp-hours per gallon of propane. Operating at 70.98 PTO hp, and at 2,072 crankshaft rpm, the economy figure was pegged at 9.29 with an output shaft speed of 1,000 rpm. No repairs or adjustments were required during 44-1/2 hours of operating time. Using tenth gear, 66.53 maximum available drawbar hp was demonstrated in the two-hour economy run. Also evidenced was a pull of 4,298 lbs. at 5.8 mph, slippage of 4.8 percent, and an economy of 8.05 hp-hours per gallon. The 10-hour run at 75 percent pull saw an economy figure of 7.47 hp-hours per gallon against a load of 55.97 hp. This test indicated a pull of 3,353 lbs. at 6.26 mph with slippage of 3.31 percent. Bare tractor weight was 8,840 lbs. and additional rear wheel ballast raised this figure to a total test weight of 10,410 lbs.

Nebraska Test Data

Model: Farmall 706

Test No. 957

Date Tested: November 16 to November 28, 1966

At the gasoline-powered Farmall 706's rated 2,300 rpm, 76.56 maximum PTO hp was observed, as was an economy of 12.16 hp-hours per gallon. At 1,000 PTO rpm and a corresponding engine speed of 2,071 rpm, the economy figure was posted at 12.46 against an output of 71.8 hp. The six-cylinder, 290.8-cubic inch engine carried a 3.75 x 4.39-inch bore and stroke. It was similar to the six-cylinder engine featured in the 706 LPG model. No repairs or adjustments were noted during 42 hours of operating time. Using tenth gear, the two-hour economy run achieved a fuel efficiency of 10.39 hp-hours per gallon against a maximum load of 65.67 drawbar hp. Also recorded was a pull of 4,270 lbs. at 5.77 mph and slippage of 4.89 percent. Fuel economy came in at 9.5 hp-hours per gallon in a 10-hour run made at 75 percent pull. This test revealed an output of 55.58 drawbar hp, a pull of 3,310 lbs. at 6.3 mph and 3.46 percent slippage. Bare tractor weight was 8,700 lbs. but 730 lbs. of liquid ballast in each rear wheel gave a total test weight of 10,230 lbs.

Farmall 806 series

Nebraska Test Data

Model: Farmall 806

Test No. 859

Date Tested: October 28 to November 22, 1963

The 806 gasoline version was nearly identical in exterior appearance to the 806 Diesel model. Instead of the diesel engine however, this tractor featured a C-301 six-cylinder gasoline engine rated at 2,400 rpm. Using a 3-13/16 x 4-25/64-inch bore and stroke it had a displacement of 301 cubic inches. No repairs or adjustments were recorded for this tractor during 43-1/2 hours of operating time. At rated engine speed, 93.27 PTO hp was observed, along with an economy of 12.58 hp-hours per gallon. When run at 1,000 PTO rpm and a corresponding engine speed of 2,071 rpm, 83.99 PTO hp was recorded, as was an economy figure of 12.81. Transmission speeds and tire sizes of this model were the same as noted in Test No. 857. Using tenth gear, and operating at 80.70 maximum PTO hp, economy was pegged at 10.83 hp-hours per gallon. Also recorded was a pull of 5,412 lbs. at 5.59 mph with 6.71 percent slippage. The 10-hour run at 75 percent pull noted an economy figure of 10.13. This test was made with an output of 66.02 hp, a pull of 4,123 lbs. at 6.00 mph and slippage of 4.97 percent.

Nebraska Test Data

Model: Farmall 806 Diesel

Test No. 857

Date Tested: October 22 to October 30, 1963

Rated at 2,400 rpm, the 806 Diesel achieved a maximum output of 94.93 PTO hp, together with an economy of 14.96 hp-hours per gallon. The economy rested at 15.15 in a second run made at 1,000 PTO rpm and a corresponding engine speed of 2,067 rpm. Also indicated was an output of 89.04 hp. The 361-cid, six-cylinder engine carried a 4-1/8 x 4-1/2-inch bore and stroke. Like the 706 Diesel of the previous test, Harvester's Torque Amplifier System was featured, and in all, 16 forward speeds were available ranging from 1.26 to 19.84 mph. The 9,290-lb. weight was supported by 18.4-34-inch rear and 7.50-15-inch front tires. Additional rear wheel ballast increased this figure to 11,895 lbs. Using tenth gear in the Torque Amplifier range, a two-hour test at 84.77 maximum available drawbar hp saw an economy of 13.25 hp-hours per gallon. Also revealed was a pull of 5,708 lbs. at 5.57 mph with 7.6 percent slippage. Economy was posted at 13.13 during the 10-hour run made at 75 percent pull. Using the same transmission speed, this test evoked an output of 67.26 hp, a pull of 4,345 lbs. at 5.8 mph and slippage of 5.68 percent. Failure and subsequent replacement of the 3-point hitch horizontal stabilizer was the only problem during 57 hours of running time.

Nebraska Test Data

Model: Farmall 806 LPG

Test No. 861

Date Tested: November 6 to November 26, 1963

Except for the obvious changes required by the use of propane, the 806 LPG was nearly identical to the others of this series. The 301-cubic inch engine featured an 8.71:1 compression ratio compared to 7.7:1 in the gasoline model. Operating at its rated 2,400 rpm, the 806 LPG developed a maximum of 93.42 PTO hp while delivering an economy of 9.72 hp-hours per gallon of propane. Operating at 1,000 PTO rpm and a corresponding engine speed of 2,072 rpm saw an economy figure of 9.94 while giving up 83.20 PTO hp. Without ballast, this unit weighed 8,815 lbs., but additional rear wheel ballast gave a test weight of 11,055 lbs. Using tenth gear, a two-hour run at 81.53 maximum available drawbar hp saw an economy of 8.58 hp-hours per gallon of propane. Also evident was a pull of 5,500 lbs. at 5.56 mph against a slippage of 7.3 percent. At 75 percent pull, the 10-hour economy run evidenced an output of 65.13 hp, plus an economy figure of 7.87. This test indicated a pull of 4,112 lbs. at 5.94 mph with 5.94 percent slippage. No repairs or adjustments were recorded during 48-1/2 hours of running time.

Farmall 656 series

Nebraska Test Data

Model: Farmall 656 Diesel

Test No. 912

Date Tested: September 16 to September 23, 1965

The 656 Diesel emerged from a two-hour drawbar test run at 52.98 maximum available hp with an economy of 12.7 hp-hours per gallon of diesel fuel. Also recorded was a pull of 4,182 lbs. at 4.75 mph with 5.87 percent slippage. Like the two-hour run, the 10-hour run at 75 percent pull was made in seventh gear. It indicated an economy of 12.63 hp-hours per gallon against an output of 43.83 hp. The 10-hour economy run saw a pull of 3,250 lbs. at 5.06 mph against a slippage of 4.61 percent. This 7,230-lb. tractor was carried on 15.5-38-inch rear and 6.00-16-inch front tires, but the addition of front and rear ballast raised this figure to 9,235 lbs. No repairs or adjustments were recorded during 40-1/2 hours of running time. The selective-gear fixed-ratio transmission featured partial range power shifting and offered 10 forward speeds ranging from 1.7 to 15.9 mph. Harvester equipped the 656 Diesel with its own six-cylinder, 281.3-cubic inch engine. Rated at 1,800 rpm, it used a 3-11/16 x 4.390-inch bore and stroke. Operating at rated engine speed, 61.52 maximum PTO hp was observed and 14.38 hp-hours per gallon.

Nebraska Test Data

Model: Farmall 656 Hydrostatic Diesel

Test No. 967

Date Tested: October 31 to November 29, 1967

During 70 hours of operating time, no repairs or adjustments were reported for this tractor. Weighing in at 7,480 lbs., it featured an infinitely variable drive using a variable displacement hydraulic pump and motor. Sliding gears were provided to give high and low ranges. Thus, within low range the speed was infinitely variable from 0 to 7-3/4 mph or from 0 to 21 mph in the high range. Standard equipment included 14.9-38-inch rear and 6.00-16-inch front tires. At a speed setting of 4.0 mph, and in low range, the two-hour economy run was made at 50.50 maximum available drawbar hp—this test gave a resultant economy of 9.39 hp-hours per gallon. Recorded also was a pull of 4,681 lbs. at 4.05 mph and slippage of 6.23 percent. Again, using 4.0 mph, but operating at 75 percent pull, the 10-hour economy run saw an economy of 9.06 hp-hours per gallon against a load of 42.75 hp. Other statistics include a pull of 3,633 lbs. at 4.41 mph and slippage of 4.56 percent. Additional front and rear ballast boosted the total test weight to 10,010 lbs. Harvester equipped this tractor with its own six-cylinder, 281.3-cid diesel engine. Rated at 2,300 rpm, it carried a 3-11/16 x 4.390-inch bore and stroke. At rated engine speed, a two-hour PTO run at 66.06 maximum hp delivered an economy of 12.21 hp-hours per gallon. The economy stood at 12.5 in a PTO run made with an output speed of 540 rpm and a corresponding engine speed of 1,989 rpm. Total output was 62.18 hp.

Nebraska Test Data

Model: Farmall 656 Hydrostatic

Test No. 968

Date Tested: October 31 to November 29, 1967

With the exception of the gasoline engine, this model was nearly identical to the 656 Hydro Diesel tractor. Harvester equipped this tractor with its own six-cylinder, 263-cid engine. Rated at 2,300 rpm, it used a 3-9/16 x 4.390-inch bore and stroke. Operating at rated engine speed, 65.8 maximum PTO hp was attained, with 10.41 hp-hours per gallon. At a 540 rpm PTO speed and a corresponding crankshaft speed of 1,989 rpm, the economy was registered at 10.88 hp-hours per gallon against an output of 60.81 hp. A defective thermostat was replaced during the limbering-up run, but otherwise, no repairs or adjustments were noted during 85-1/2 hours of operating time. Tire equipment and the transmission design were the same for both this model, and that of the previous test. At a speed setting of 4.0 mph, 50.09 maximum available drawbar hp was manifested in the two-hour economy run—this test saw a pull of 4,697 lbs. at 4.00 mph with 6.11 percent slippage. Fuel economy came in at 7.85 hp-hours per gallon. The economy figure slumped to 6.89 hp-hours per gallon on the 10-hour run at 75 percent pull. Also recorded was an output of 42.55 hp, a pull of 3,569 lbs. at 4.47 mph and slippage of 4.44 percent. Weighing 7,215 lbs., the gasoline model was burdened with additional front and rear ballast for a total test weight of 9,995 lbs.

Farmall 856 Diesel tractor

Nebraska Test Data

Model: Farmall 865 Diesel
Test No. 970
Date Tested: April 15 to April 30, 1968

The 856 Diesel was equipped with a six-cylinder, 406.9-cid engine, rated at 2,400 rpm. It used a 4.321 x 4.625-inch bore and stroke. At rated engine speed, 100.49 maximum PTO hp was observed, as was an economy of 15.15 hp-hours per gallon. At 1,000 PTO rpm and a corresponding crankshaft speed of 2,872 rpm, 94.29 PTO hp gave 15.59 hp-hours per gallon. No repairs or adjustments were reported during 45 hours of operating time. Standard equipment included 18.4-38-inch rear and 7.50-16 inch front tires. The bare tractor weight of 10,290 lbs. was augmented with 850 lbs. of liquid ballast for each rear wheel, giving a total test weight of 12,035 lbs. Features included a selective gear fixed-ratio transmission with 16 forward speeds with a range of 1-1/4 to 18-3/4 mph. Operating in eighth gear, the two-hour economy run was made at 87.17 maximum available drawbar hp and yielded an economy of 13.13 hp-hours per gallon. Also recorded was a pull of 7,127 lbs. at 4.59 mph with slippage of 8.68 percent. The 10-hour run at 75 percent pull noted an output of 70.6 hp with an economy of 12.78 hp-hours per gallon. Other statistics included a pull of 5,398 lbs. at 4.9 mph with slippage of 6.35 percent.

Nebraska Test Data

Model: International 444
Test No. 985
Date Tested: September 10 to September 27, 1959

Features of the 444 included an eight-speed, selective gear, fixed-ratio transmission with choices ranging from 1.5 to 15.5 mph. Standard equipment included 13.6-28 rear and 6.00-16 inch front tires. Weighing in at 4,130 lbs., it emerged from the two-hour drawbar economy run with an economy of 9.62 hp-hours per gallon against a maximum available output of 32.94 hp. This two-hour test saw a pull of 2,384 lbs. at 5.18 mph with slippage of 4.25 percent. A 10-hour run at 75 percent pull indicated an economy of 8.47 hp-hours per gallon against a load of 26.85 hp. Also recorded was a pull of 1,814 lbs. at 5.55 mph and 3.21 percent slippage. While bare tractor weight was 4,130 lbs., additional front and rear ballast raised this figure to a total test weight of 6,880 lbs. Harvester equipped the 444 with a four-cylinder, 152.1-cubic inch engine. Rated at 2,000 rpm, it carried a 3.375 x 4.25-inch bore and stroke. At rated engine speed, 38.09 maximum PTO hp was observed, as was an economy of 11.17 hp-hours per gallon. No repairs or adjustments were reported during 45-1/2 hours of operating time.

International 4100 tractor

Nebraska Test Data

Model: International 4100 Diesel
Test No. 931
Date Tested: November 19 to November 24, 1965

Since this tractor was equipped with neither a PTO shaft nor a belt pulley, no brake hp testing was done. Harvester equipped the 4100 with an International six-cylinder engine rated at 2,400 rpm. Using a 4-1/2- inch bore and stroke it carried a displacement of 429-cubic inches. The chassis design included a selective gear fixed-ratio transmission with eight forward speeds ranging from 2.0 to 20.25 mph. Also featured on this four-wheel-drive unit were 18.4-30-inch, eight-ply tires. The factory weight of 15,175 lbs. was raised to a test weight of 19,100 lbs. using additional front and rear ballast. No repairs or adjustments were noted during 35-1/2 hours of running time. Operating in fourth gear, a two-hour economy run at 110-82 maximum available drawbar hp saw an economy of 12.61 hp-hours per gallon of fuel. Also manifested was a pull of 7,137 lbs. at 5.82 mph with slippage of 3.58 percent. The 10-hour run at 75 percent pull noted an economy of 11.52 hp-hours per gallon against a load of 93.77 hp. In this test a pull of 5,625 lbs. was made at 6.25 mph with slippage recorded at 2.89 percent. This tractor made a low-gear maximum pull of 16,365 lbs. at 1.79 mph, with slippage totaling 14.79 percent.

Farmall 544 series

Nebraska Test Data

Model: Farmall 544 Diesel

Test No. 983

Date Tested: September 7 to September 20, 1968

Rated at 2,200 rpm, the 544 Diesel featured a four-cylinder, 238.6-cubic inch engine using a 3.875 x 5.06- inch bore and stroke. At rated engine speed, 52.95 PTO hp was observed, as was an economy of 15.98 hp-hours per gallon. Operating at 540 PTO rpm and a corresponding crankshaft speed of 1,987 rpm, 49.66 PTO hp was delivered and 16.32 hp-hours per gallon was achieved. This 7,195-lb. tractor featured a selective gear fixed-ratio transmission with partial range power shifting. Its 10 forward speeds ranged from 1.75 to 18.00 mph. No repairs or adjustments were reported during 46 hours of running time. Using seventh gear, 44.56 maximum available drawbar hp was observed in the two-hour economy run. This test, yielding an economy of 13.44 hp-hours per gallon, saw a pull of 3,577 lbs. at 4.67 mph with slippage of 5.73 percent. At 75 percent pull, the 10-hour run indicated 12.79 hp-hours per gallon with a load of 37.34 drawbar hp. Other statistics included a pull of 2,742 lbs. at 5.11 mph with slippage of 3.83 percent. Total test weight, including 620 lbs. of liquid ballast in each rear wheel, was 8,470 lbs.

Nebraska Test Data

Model: Farmall 544

Test No. 984

Date Tested: September 7 to September 20, 1968

Rated at 2,200 rpm, this tractor delivered an economy of 11.97 hp-hours per gallon against a maximum load of 52.84 PTO hp. Operating at 540 PTO rpm and a corresponding engine speed of 1,988 rpm, 50-29 PTO hp was observed with an economy of 12.35 hp-hours per gallon. This tractor featured an International four-cylinder gasoline engine. Its 200.3-cubic inch displacement resulted from a 3.813 x 4.39-inch bore and stroke. The remainder of the tractor design was virtually identical to that already noted for the 544 Diesel. No repairs or adjustments were required during 44-1/2 hours of operating time. Operating in seventh gear, 44.74 maximum available drawbar hp was demonstrated in the two-hour economy run, as was an economy of 10.14 hp-hours per gallon. This test further indicated a pull of 3,596 lbs. at 4.67 mph with slippage of 5.95 percent. The 10-hour economy run at 75 percent pull noted an economy of 9.53 hp-hours per gallon against a load of 36.77 hp. Other test statistics included a pull of 2,724 lbs. at 5.06 mph with 4.03 percent slippage. An additional 680 lbs. of liquid ballast in each rear tire brought the total test weight to 8,310 lbs.

Nebraska Test Data

Model: Farmall 544 Hydrostatic (also International 544 Hydrostatic and International 2544 Hydrostatic)

Test No. 1007

Date Tested: April 23 to May 5, 1969

This test covered three different versions of the gasoline-powered Farmall 544 tractor. Harvester equipped this model with its own four-cylinder, 200.3-cubic inch engine. Rated at 2,400 rpm, it used a 3-13/16 x 4.390-inch bore and stroke. At rated engine speed, 53.87 PTO hp appeared, and an economy of 9.71 hp-hours per gallon was achieved. Operating at 540 PTO rpm and a corresponding engine speed of 1,987 rpm, an economy of 10.33 hp-hours per gallon resulted under a load of 49.11 PTO hp. No repairs or adjustments were noted during 56 hours of operating time. Features included an infinitely variable hydrostatic drive using a variable displacement pump and motor. Sliding gears were used for the high and low ranges. Low range gave speeds from 0 to 8-1/2 mph, while high range broadened the option to 0 to 21-1/2 mph. Using the low range and with a speed setting of 4 mph, the two-hour economy run was made at 40.33 maximum available drawbar hp and yielded 7.29 hp-hours per gallon. Other statistics included a pull of 3,727 lbs. at 4.06 mph with slippage of 5.18 percent. The 10-hour run at 75 percent pull yielded an economy of 6.3 hp-hours per gallon against a load of 33.6 hp. Also recorded was a pull of 2,834 lbs. at 4.45 mph with 3.71 percent slippage. Weighing 6,875 lbs., this unit assumed a test weight of 9,710 lbs. through additional front and rear ballast. Standard equipment included 14.9-38-inch rear and 6.00-16-inch front tires.

Nebraska Test Data

Model: Farmall 544 Hydrostatic Diesel (also International 544 Hydrostatic Diesel and International 2544 Hydrostatic Diesel)

Test No. 1029

Date Tested: November 1 to November 7, 1969

Weighing in at 7,215 lbs., this tractor assumed a test weight of 9,890 lbs. through the addition of front and rear ballast. Standard equipment included 14.9-38-inch rear and 6.00-16-inch front tires. No repairs or adjustments were required during 45-1/2 hours of operating time. Features included an infinitely variable hydrostatic drive using a variable displacement pump and motor. Sliding gears provided high and low ranges. This tractor was capable of any speed from 0 to 21-1/2 mph. Using a speed setting of 4.0 mph, the two-hour economy run at 41.58 maximum available drawbar hp saw a pull of 3,895 lbs. at 4.00 mph with slippage of 4.98 percent. Fuel economy was 9.88 hp-hours per gallon. The 10-hour run at 75 percent pull noted an economy of 9.29 hp-hours per gallon against a load of 33.91 hp. Also recorded was a pull of 2,939 lbs. at 4.33 mph with slippage of 3.6 percent. Harvester equipped this model with its own four-cylinder, 239-cubic inch diesel engine. Rated at 2,400 rpm, it used a 3.875 x 5.06-inch bore and stroke. At rated engine speed, an economy of 13.37 hp-hours per gallon was established against a load of 55.52 PTO hp. Operating at 540 PTO rpm and a corresponding engine speed of 1,988 rpm, the economy was recorded at 14.13 hp-hours per gallon against a 50.06 PTO hp load.

International 666 series

Nebraska Test Data

Model: International 666 Diesel

Test No. 1151

Date Tested: November 3 to November 11, 1973

At its rated speed of 2,000 rpm, the IHC 666 developed 66.29 maximum PTO hp and achieved an economy of 14.24 hp-hours per gallon. The six-cylinder, 312-cubic inch engine carried a 3.875 x 4.410-inch bore and stroke. Ten forward speeds ranging from 1.8 to 16.5 mph were provided in the selective-gear fixed-ratio transmission. Its design included partial range power shifting. Operating in seventh gear, the two-hour drawbar run at 58.01 maximum available hp saw an economy of 12.6 hp-hours per gallon. Also recorded was a pull of 4,240 lbs. at 5.13 mph with slippage totaling 5.73 percent. The 10-hour run at 75 percent pull noted an output of 46.8 drawbar hp with a resultant economy of 11.98 hp-hours per gallon. Other test statistics included a pull of 3,208 lbs. at 5.47 mph and slippage totaling 4.15 percent. Weighing 8,200 lbs., the IHC 666 was equipped with 18.4-34-inch rear and 9.5L-15-inch front tires. Additional rear wheel ballast raised the total test weight to 10,330 lbs. No repairs or adjustments were required during 42-1/2 hours of operating time.

Nebraska Test Data

Model: International 666

Test No. 1152

Date Tested: November 5 to December 3, 1973

Virtually identical to the 666 Diesel, this tractor carried instead a six-cylinder, 290.8-cubic inch gasoline engine. Rated at 2,000 rpm, it used a 3.75 x 4.39-inch bore and stroke. At rated engine speed, 66.3 maximum PTO hp was observed, and an economy of 11.95 hp-hours per gallon was achieved. Weighing in at 7,690 lbs., the 666 gained additional front and rear ballast for a total test weight of 10,050 lbs. Operating in seventh gear, the two-hour economy run at 57.29 maximum available drawbar hp saw a pull of 4,180 lbs. at 5.14 mph with slippage totaling 5.58 percent. The 10-hour run at 75 percent pull noted an economy of 9.04 hp-hours per gallon against an output of 47.77 drawbar hp. Also recorded was a pull of 3,218 lbs. at 5.57 mph and slippage of 47.1 percent. No repairs or adjustments were reported during 53 hours of operating time.

Farmall 766 series

Farmall 966 series

Nebraska Test Data

Model: Farmall 766

Test No. 1094

Date Tested: April 20 to May 10, 1972

The Farmall 766 used IHC's own six-cylinder, 290.8-cubic inch engine with a 3.75 x 4.39-inch bore and stroke. At its rated speed of 2,400 rpm, the 766 developed 79.73 maximum PTO hp, achieving an economy of 11.29 hp-hours per gallon. At 1,000 PTO rpm and a corresponding engine speed of 2,071 rpm, an economy of 11.78 hp hours resulted with a load of 73.96 PTO hp. No repairs or adjustments were required during 44 hours of running time. Standard equipment included 18.4-34-inch rear and 9.5L-15 inch front tires. Also featured was a selective gear fixed-ratio transmission with partial range power shifting. The 16 forward speeds ranged from 1-_ to 19-_ mph. Using eighth gear, the two-hour economy run at 71.32 maximum available drawbar hp saw an economy of 9.77 hp-hours per gallon. Other data included a pull of 5,609 lbs. at 4.77 mph with slippage of 7.06 percent. The 10-hour run at 75 percent pull elicited an economy of 8.68 hp-hours per gallon under a load of 57.07 hp. This test likewise indicated a pull of 4,236 lbs. at 5.05 mph and 5.01 percent slippage. Weighing in at 10,400 lbs., the 766 gained additional front and rear ballast for a total test weight of 11,880 lbs.

Nebraska Test Data

Model: Farmall 766 Diesel

Test No. 1117

Date Tested: November 10 to December 5, 1972

At its rated engine speed of 2,600 rpm, the 766 Diesel developed 85.45 maximum PTO hp while delivering an economy of 13.87 hp-hours per gallon. Using a standard PTO speed of 1,000 rpm and a corresponding engine speed of 2,269 rpm, 85.66 PTO hp appeared, with 14.85 hp-hours per gallon. The six-cylinder engine used a 3.875 x 5.085-inch bore and stroke for a displacement of 360-cubic inches. Also featured in this model was a selective gear fixed-ratio transmission with partial range power shifting. Its 16 forward speeds ranged from 1-1/2 to 19-3/4 mph. No repairs or adjustments were reported during 481/2 hours of operation. Standard equipment also included 18.4-34-inch rear and 9.5L-15-inch front tires. Weighing 11,340 lbs., the 766 Diesel gained additional front and rear ballast for a total test weight of 12,720 lbs. Operating in eighth gear, the two-hour economy run at 73.37 maximum available drawbar hp saw an efficiency of 12.08 hp-hours per gallon. Also recorded was a pull of 5,755 lbs. at 4.78 mph with slippage of 6.28 percent. The 10-hour drawbar run at 75 percent pull noted 11.05 hp-hours per gallon under an output of 59.25 drawbar hp. Other statistics included a pull of 4,377 lbs. at 5.08 mph and 4.75 percent slippage.

Nebraska Test Data

Model: Farmall 966 Diesel

Test No. 1082

Date Tested: October 5 to October 19, 1971

This tractor was not equipped with a turbocharger. At its rated 2,400 rpm, the 966 Diesel developed 96.01 maximum PTO hp and achieved 14.85 hp-hours per gallon. By comparison, when running at 1,000 PTO rpm and a corresponding engine speed of 2,072 rpm, 93.50 PTO hp was developed and an economy of 15.74 hp-hours per gallon was achieved. No repairs or adjustments were required during 47-_ hours of operating time. The selective gear fixed-ratio transmission offered partial range power shifting. Its 16 forward speeds ranged from 1-1/4 to 18-1/4 mph. The two-hour economy run was made in eighth gear. At 80.4 maximum available drawbar hp, fuel economy stood at 12.57 hp-hours per gallon in this test. Other data includes a pull of 6,804 lbs. at 4.43 mph and slippage of 8.87 percent. The 10-hour run at 75 percent pull saw an economy of 12 hp-hours per gallon against an output of 67.26 hp. Further statistics included a pull of 5,273 lbs. at 4.78 mph and slippage of 5.83 percent. Weighing 11,625 lbs., this tractor assumed front and rear ballast for a total test weight of 13,500 lbs. Standard equipment included 16.9-38-inch rear and 9.5L-15-inch front tires.

Nebraska Test Data

Model: Farmall 966 Hydro Diesel

Test No. 1095

Date Tested: April 28 to May 12, 1972

Weighing in at 11,700 lbs., this model featured an infinitely variable hydrostatic transmission using a variable displacement pump and motor. The two separate speed ranges gave speed options ranging from 0 to 18 mph. Standard equipment for this model also included 16.9-38-inch rear and 9.5L-15-inch front tires. Additional rear wheel ballast gave a total test weight of 12,875 lbs. With a speed setting of 5.4 mph, the two-hour economy run at 68.08 maximum available drawbar hp saw an economy of 9.63 hp-hours per gallon of fuel. Also indicated was a pull of 4,730 lbs. at 5.4 mph with slippage totaling 5.93 percent. The 10-hour run at 75 percent pull indicated a fuel efficiency of 9.19 hp-hours per gallon with a load of 58.72 drawbar hp. Other data includes a pull of 3,631 lbs. at 6.06 mph and 4.18 percent slippage. Following one of the drawbar runs a hydraulic power tube for the power steering was replaced due to leakage. With this exception, no repairs or adjustments were noted during 47 hours of running time. Harvester equipped this model with a six-cylinder, 414-cid engine. Rated at 2,400 rpm, it used a 4.30 x 4.75-inch bore and stroke. At rated engine speed, 91.38 maximum PTO hp was observed, as was an economy of 12.76 hp-hours per gallon. With a 1,000 rpm speed on the PTO shaft and a corresponding crankshaft speed of 2,073 rpm, an economy of 13.8 hp-hours per gallon was achieved with a load of 88.29 hp.

Farmall 1066

Nebraska Test Data

Model: Farmall 1066 Turbo Diesel
Test No. 1081
Date Tested: October 1 to October 21, 1971

Weighing in at 12,145 lbs., this tractor assumed additional front and rear ballast for a total test weight of 15,170 lbs. Standard equipment included 18.4-38 rear and 11L-15 inch front tires. Sixteen forward speeds were provided in a range from 1-1/2 to 20-1/4 mph. The selective-gear fixed-ratio transmission included partial range power shifting. Using eighth gear, the two-hour economy run at 100.5 maximum available drawbar hp saw a pull of 7,839 lbs. at 4.81 mph, slippage of 8.14 percent, and an economy of 13.16 hp-hours per gallon. The economy figure stood at 12.02 in a 10-hour run at 75 percent pull. This test, with an output of 83.14 drawbar hp, indicated a pull of 6,008 lbs. at 5.19 mph with slippage totaling 6.07 percent. Standard equipment included an International six-cylinder turbocharged engine. Rated at 2,400 rpm, it used a 4.30 x 4.75 inch bore and stroke for a 414-cubic inch displacement. At rated engine speed, 15.16 hp-hours per gallon was the economy figure under a maximum load of 116.23 PTO hp. Operating at 1,000 PTO rpm and a corresponding engine speed of 2,071 rpm, 112.18 PTO hp resulted and an economy of 16.52 hp-hours per gallon was achieved. Except for adjustment of valve tappet clearance on one cylinder, no repairs or adjustments were noted during 55-1/2 hours of operating time.

Nebraska Test Data

Model: Farmall 1066 Hydro Turbo Diesel
Test No. 1083
Date Tested: October 7 to October 25, 1971

Once again the six-cylinder, 414-cubic inch turbocharged diesel engine appeared, but in this instance it was coupled to an infinitely variable hydrostatic transmission. Two speed ranges provided any speed from 0 to 17 mph. Weighing 12,320 lbs., this tractor gained suitable front and rear ballast for a total test weight of 13,190 lbs. At a speed setting of 5.4 mph, 84.88 maximum available drawbar hp was evidenced in the two-hour economy run. Also recorded was a pull of 5,906 lbs. at 5.39 mph and slippage of 6.95 percent. Fuel economy came in at 10.64 hp-hours per gallon. By comparison, the 10-hour run at 75 percent pull was made at a 5.4 mph setting—with 10.07 hp-hours per gallon against an output of 73.73 hp. This test indicated a pull of 4,514 lbs. at 6.12 mph with slippage at 4.72 percent. No repairs or adjustments were reported during 51-_ hours of running time. At the rated engine speed of 2,400 rpm, 113.58 PTO hp was observed and an economy of 14.32 hp-hours per gallon. At 1,000 PTO rpm and a corresponding engine speed of 2,071 rpm, 15.54 hp-hours per gallon and an output of 109.32 PTO hp was observed.

Nebraska Test Data

Model: International 1066 Turbo Diesel
Test No. 1124
Date Tested: April 20 to May 17, 1973

Features of this tractor included a six-cylinder, 414-cubic inch, turbocharged engine. Rated at 2,600 rpm, it used a 4.30 x 4.75-inch bore and stroke. At rated speed, 125.68 maximum PTO hp was observed, with an economy of 14.93 hp-hours per gallon. With a 1,000 rpm PTO speed and a corresponding engine speed of 2,270 rpm, an economy of 16.37 hp-hours per gallon was evidenced against a load of 119.2 PTO hp. Using a similar drive train to the 966 Diesel, it entered the two-hour economy run operating in eighth gear. At 105.95 maximum available drawbar hp, economy was pegged at 12.78 hp-hours per gallon. Also recorded was a pull of 7,351 lbs. at 5.1 mph with slippage of 5.16 percent. The 10-hour run at 75 percent pull noted an economy of 11.97 hp-hours per gallon against a load of 87.62 drawbar hp. Other statistics included a pull of 5,721 lbs. at 5.7 mph and 3.94 percent slippage. Weighing in at 13,345 lbs., this model used dual rear tires of 18.4-38 size, along with 11L-15-inch front tires. Additional rear wheel ballast raised the total test weight to 15,260 lbs. No repairs or adjustments were reported during 54 hours of operating time.

Farmall 1256 tractor

Nebraska Test Data

Model: Farmall 1256 Turbo Diesel
Test No. 971
Date Tested: April 15 to April 30, 1968

Weighing 10,405 lbs., the 1256 Turbo Diesel gained additional front and rear ballast for a total test weight of 13,810 lbs. Standard equipment included 18.4-38-inch rear and 7.50-16-inch front tires. The 16-speed transmission was of the selective-gear fixed-ratio type and included Harvester's Torque Amplifier to provide partial-range power shifting. In all, speed selections ranged from 1-1/2 to 19-1/2 mph. Using eighth gear, the two-hour drawbar economy run was made at 102.03 maximum available hp and yielded an economy of 13.38 hp-hours per gallon. This test also indicated a pull of 8,353 lbs. at 4.58 mph with slippage of 8.4 percent. The 10-hour economy run at 75 percent pull indicated an output of 86.19 drawbar hp with an economy of 12.27 hp-hours per gallon. Other statistics included a pull of 6,466 lbs. at 5 mph and slippage of 5.7 percent. No repairs or adjustments were noted during 49-1/2 hours of operating time. Harvester equipped this tractor with its own six-cylinder, 406.9-cid turbocharged engine. Rated at 2,400 rpm, it carried a 4.321 x 4.625-inch bore and stroke. Operating at rated engine speed, 116.12 maximum PTO hp was observed with 15.55 hp-hours per gallon. At the standard PTO speed of 1,000 rpm and a corresponding engine speed of 2,071 rpm, 113.33 maximum PTO hp was developed and 16.68 hp-hours per gallon was achieved.

Farmall 1456, 1466, and 1468 tractors

Nebraska Test Data

Model: Farmall 1456 Diesel
Test No. 1048
Date Tested: June 8 to June 27, 1970

This model, rated at 2,400 rpm, delivered 131.8 maximum PTO hp with an economy of 15.81 hp-hours per gallon. Operating at 1,000 PTO rpm and a corresponding engine speed of 2,071 rpm, an economy of 16.67 was established under a load of 127.27 PTO hp. Harvester equipped this tractor with a six-cylinder, turbocharged diesel engine. Its 4.321 x 4.625-inch bore and stroke gave a 407-cubic inch displacement. No repairs or adjustments were reported during 48 hours of operating time. Features included a selective gear fixed-ratio transmission with partial range power shifting. Its 16 forward speeds ranged from 1-1/2 to 20-1/4 mph. Weighing 12,800 lbs., the 1456 was equipped with dual 18.4-38-inch rear tires in addition to 11L-15-inch front rubber. Additional front and rear ballast raised the total test weight to 17,350 lbs. Using eighth gear, the two-hour economy run at 114.69 maximum available drawbar hp yielded 13.46 hp-hours per gallon. The performance figures also included a pull of 8,633 lbs. at 4.98 mph and slippage of 5.81percent. An economy of 12.53 hp-hours per gallon was achieved under a load of 95.41 drawbar hp. The 10-hour run at 75 percent pull also recorded a pull of 6,648 lbs. at 5.38 mph with slippage totaling 4.23 percent.

Nebraska Test Data

Model: Farmall 1466 Turbo Diesel
Test No. 1080
Date Tested: October 2 to October 19, 1971

At its rated 2,400 rpm, this model developed 133.4 maximum PTO hp and achieved an economy of 15.95 hp-hours per gallon. At 1,000 PTO rpm and a corresponding engine speed of 2,071 rpm, an economy of 16.86 hp-hours per gallon appeared against a load of 125.17 hp. Harvester equipped this model with its own six-cylinder turbocharged engine. Its 436-cubic inches resulted from a 4.30 x 5.00-inch bore and stroke. The selective-gear fixed-ratio transmission offered partial range power shifting. Its 16 forward speeds ranged from 1-1/2 to 20-1/4 mph. No repairs or adjustments were reported during 47 hours of operating time. Weighing 13,480 lbs. the 1466 used 18.4-38-inch rear and 11L-15-inch front tires. Additional front and rear ballast raised the total test weight to 16,230 lbs. Operating in eighth gear, the two-hour economy run at 115.74 maximum available drawbar hp saw a pull of 8,637 lbs. at 5.02 mph with slippage of 5.77 percent. Economy was posted at 13.92 hp-hours per gallon. By comparison, the 10-hour run at 75 percent pull saw an economy of 12.85 hp-hours per gallon with a load of 93.98 drawbar hp. Other data included a pull of 6,589 lbs. at 5.35 mph.

Nebraska Test Data

Model: Farmall 1468 Diesel
Test No. 1118
Date Tested: November 9 to December 7, 1972

Harvester's V-8 Diesel engine was featured in this model. Rated at 2,600 rpm, it carried a 4-1/2 x 4-5/16-inch bore and stroke for a 550-cubic inch displacement. At rated engine speed, 145.49 maximum PTO hp was observed and an economy of 15.6 hp-hours per gallon was achieved. With a PTO speed of 1,000 rpm and a corresponding engine speed of 2,269 rpm, an economy of 15.93 hp-hours per gallon emerged under a load of 136.85 PTO hp. The selective-gear fixed-ratio transmission offered partial range power shifting. Its 16 forward speeds ranged from 1-1/2 to 22 mph. No repairs or adjustments were recorded during 60 hours of operating time. Weighing 13,460 lbs., the 1468 Diesel was equipped with dual 18.4-38-inch rear tires, plus 11L-16-inch front tires. Additional front and rear ballast raised the total test weight to 16,310 lbs. Using eighth gear, the two-hour run at 127.70 maximum available drawbar hp saw 13.87 hp-hours per gallon. Also recorded was a pull of 8,813 lbs. at 5.43 mph with slippage of 5.49 percent. The 10-hour run at 75 percent pull noted a pull of 6,861 lbs. at 5.86 mph with 4.52 slippage. This test was run with an output of 107.23 drawbar hp and a fuel economy of 13.22 hp-hours per gallon.

International 1566 tractor

Nebraska Test Data

Model: International 1566 Turbo Diesel
Test No. 1174
Date Tested: May 3 to May 15, 1975

Weighing 15,195 lbs., this tractor was equipped with a selective-gear, fixed-ratio transmission with partial-range power shifting. Its twelve forward speeds ranged from 1.9 to 17.6 mph. The test model used dual 20.8-38-inch rear tires, plus 10.00-16-inch front tires. Additional front and rear ballast raised the total test weight to 18.260 lbs. Operating in seventh gear, 137.00 maximum available drawbar hp was manifested in the two-hour economy run. Also indicated was a pull of 9,105 lbs. at 5.64 mph, slippage of 5.76 percent, and a fuel economy of 12.55 hp-hours per gallon. The 10-hour run at 75 percent pull indicated an economy of 11.69 hp-hours per gallon under a load of 110.79 drawbar hp. Other data includes a pull of 7,012 lbs. at 5.12 mph and slippage totaling 4.41 percent. The 1566 Turbo featured an International six-cylinder turbocharged engine rated at 2,600 rpm. Its 436-cubic inch displacement resulted from a 4.30 x 5.00-inch bore and stroke. At rated engine speed, 161.01 maximum PTO hp was observed, as was an economy of 14.55 hp-hours per gallon of fuel. Operating at 1,000 PTO rpm and a corresponding engine speed of 2,269 rpm, an economy of 16.16 hp-hours per gallon was recorded under a load of 162.31 PTO hp. No repairs or adjustments were reported during 48-1/2 hours of operating time.

International 4366 tractor

Nebraska Test Data

Model: International 4366 Turbo Diesel

Test No. 1153

Date Tested: November 8 to November 29, 1973

Weighing 21,690 lbs., this four-wheel-drive model used dual 23.1-30-inch tires on all four corners. Additional front and rear ballast raised the total test weight to 23,000 lbs. A selective-gear fixed-ratio transmission offered 10 forward speeds ranging from 2-1/2 to 20-1/2 mph. Operating in fourth gear, the two-hour economy run at 163.17 maximum available drawbar hp witnessed a fuel economy of 12.54 hp-hours per gallon. Also recorded was a pull of 11,426 lbs. at 5.36 mph with slippage totaling 2.9 percent. The 10-hour run at 75 percent pull noted an economy of 11.98 hp-hours per gallon under a load of 134.43 drawbar hp. Other statistics included a pull of 8,834 lbs. at 5.71 mph and slippage of 2.11 percent. No repairs or adjustments were required during 41 hours of operation. The 4366 Turbo was equipped with an International Harvester six-cylinder turbocharged engine. Rated at 2,600 rpm, it used a 4.30 x 5.35- inch bore and stroke for a 466-cubic inch displacement. No PTO tests were run on this model.

International 3088 tractor

This model represented the final chapter of International Harvester Company's career in the farm equipment industry.

Nebraska Test Data

Model: International 3088 Diesel

Test No. 1551

Date Tested: November 8 to November 13, 1984

Rated at 2,400 rpm, the 3088 featured an International six-cylinder engine. Its 3.875 x 5.062-inch bore and stroke gave a 358-cubic inch displacement. At rated engine speed, 81.35 maximum PTO hp appeared, as did an economy of 14.88 hp-hours per gallon. Partial-range power shifting was featured in the selective-gear fixed-ratio transmission. The 16 forward speeds ranged from 1.5 to 19.1 mph. Operating in eighth gear, the two-hour drawbar run at 70.31 maximum available hp saw a pull of 5,100 lbs. at 5.17 mph. Slippage totaled 4.63 percent, and fuel economy was reported at 12.84 hp-hours per gallon. In comparison, the 10-hour run at 75 percent pull saw 11.59 gph against a load of 55.56 drawbar hp. Further indicated was a pull of 3,841 lbs. at 5.42 mph and slippage totaling 3.50 percent. No repairs or adjustments were necessary during 35 hours of operation. Weighing 11,940 lbs., the 3088 was equipped with dual 18.4-34-inch rear and 9.5L x 15-inch front tires. Additional front and rear ballast gave a total test weight of 12,500 lbs.

International 3288 tractor

Nebraska Test Data

Model: International 3288 Diesel

Test No.1438

Date Tested: June 4 to June 11, 1982

Weighing 11,760 lbs., the 3288 was equipped with dual 18.4-34-inch rear and 9.5L-15-inch front tires. Additional front and rear ballast gave a total test weight of 13,560 lbs. Partial range power shifting was offered in the selective gear fixed-ratio transmission. Its 16 forward speeds ranged from 1.5 to 19.1 mph. No repairs or adjustments were reported during 38-1/2 hours of operation. Using eighth gear, a two-hour drawbar run at 79.71 maximum available hp established 13.16 hp-hours per gallon. Also recorded was a pull of 5,792 lbs. at 5.16 mph and slippage of 4.36 percent. By contrast, fuel economy came in at 12.31 hp-hours per gallon in the 10-hour run at 75 percent pull. This test indicated an output of 64.36 drawbar hp, a pull of 4,391 lbs. at 5.5 mph, and slippage of 3.37 percent. The 3288 used an International six-cylinder engine rated at 2,400 rpm. Its 3.875 x 5.062-inch bore and stroke gave a 358-cubic inch displacement. At rated engine speed, 90.46 maximum PTO hp was observed with 14.92 hp-hours per gallon. Operating at 1,000 PTO rpm and a corresponding engine speed of 2,071 rpm, fuel economy was 15.94 hp-hours per gallon under a load of 88.33 PTO hp.

International 3388 tractor

Nebraska Test Data

Model: International 3388 Diesel

Test No. 1319

Date Tested: August 21 to August 27, 1979

At its rated engine speed of 2,400 rpm, the 3388 Diesel achieved an output of 130.61 PTO hp and delivered 15.58 hp-hours per gallon. Operating at 1,000 PTO rpm and a corresponding engine speed of 2,070 rpm, an economy of 16.85 hp-hours per gallon was recorded under a load of 128.59 PTO hp. This tractor featured an International six-cylinder turbocharged engine. Its 4.300 x 5.000-inch bore and stroke gave a 436-cubic inch displacement. Also incorporated into this four-wheel-drive design was a selective-gear fixed-ratio transmission with partial-range power shifting. Its 16 forward speeds varied from 1.8 to 20.7 mph. No repairs or adjustments were required during 37 hours of operation. Using eighth gear, the two-hour drawbar test at 111.75 maximum available hp indicated a pull of 6,864 lbs. at 6.1 mph and slippage of 2.3 percent. Fuel economy was 13.52 hp-hours per gallon. The 10-hour run at 75 percent pull manifested an economy of 12.17 hp-hours per gallon under a load of 89.92 drawbar hp. This test also evoked a pull of 5,232 lbs. at 6.44 mph with slippage totaling 1.75 percent. Weighing 17,420 lbs., the 3388 was equipped with 18.411 38 radial tires. Additional front and rear ballast gave a total test weight of 17,850 lbs.

International 3488 tractor

Nebraska Test Data

Model: International 3488 Hydro Diesel

Test No. 1439

Date Tested: June 8 to June 14, 1982

This tractor featured a hydrostatic transmission with infinitely variable speed selection in two ranges—0 to 8.0 mph and 0 to 17.8 mph. With a speed setting of 6.20 mph, the two-hour drawbar run at 80.50 maximum available hp indicated a pull of 4,848 lbs. at 6.23 mph, slippage of 3.01 percent, and an economy of 10.00 hp-hours per gallon. The 10-hour run at 75 percent pull noted an economy of 9.73 hp-hours per gallon under a load of 69.15 drawbar hp. Also recorded was a pull of 3,761 lbs. at 6.89 mph and 2.25 percent slippage. Standard equipment included dual 18.4-38-inch rear and 11L-15-inch front tires. Weighing 12,880 lbs., the 3488 Hydro assumed a total test weight of 13,940 lbs. by the addition of front and rear ballast. The 466-cid, six-cylinder engine used a 4.30 x 5.35-inch bore and stroke. At its rated speed of 2,400 rpm, 112.56 maximum PTO hp was observed and an economy of 14.12 hp-hours per gallon was achieved. Operating at 1,000 PTO rpm and a corresponding engine speed of 2,072 rpm, the economy was 15.28 hp-hours per gallon under a load of 107.11 PTO hp. Repairs and adjustments during 51 hours of operating time included replacement of a fuel injector line during the preliminary PTO tests.

International 3588 tractor

Nebraska Test Data

Model: International 3588 Diesel, 16 Speed

Test No. 1320

Date Tested: August 22 to August 29, 1979

Weighing 17,620 lbs., the 3588 was equipped with 18.4R38 radial tires. Additional front and rear ballast gave a total test weight of 18,890 lbs. Partial-range power shifting was featured in the selective-gear fixed-ratio transmission. The 16 forward speeds varied from 1.8 to 20.7 mph. Using eighth gear, the two-hour drawbar run at 126.15 maximum available hp saw a pull of 7,777 lbs. at 6.08 mph and slippage totaling 6.08 percent. Fuel economy came in at 13.13 hp-hours per gallon. The 10-hour run at 75 percent pull noted an economy of 12.20 hp-hours per gallon against a load of 101.71 drawbar hp. Other statistics included a pull of 5,994 lbs. at 6.36 mph and slippage totaling 1.83 percent. No repairs or adjustments were required during 36-1/2 hours of operation. The 3588 used an International six-cylinder turbocharged diesel engine. Rated at 2,400 rpm, it carried a 4.300 x 5.350-inch bore and stroke for a 466-cubic inch displacement. At rated engine speed it developed 150.41 maximum PTO hp while achieving an economy of 15.68 hp-hours per gallon. At a speed of 1,000 PTO rpm and a corresponding engine speed of 2,071 rpm, an economy of 16.98 hp-hours per gallon was evidenced under a load of 152.07 PTO hp.

International 3688 tractor

Nebraska Test Data

Model: International 3688 Diesel

Test No. 1440

Date Tested: May 26 to June 7, 1982

At its rated speed of 2,400 rpm, the 3688 developed 113.72 maximum PTO hp while achieving an economy of 15.10 hp-hours per gallon. Operating at 1,000 PTO rpm and a corresponding engine speed of 2,071 rpm, an economy of 15.75 hp-hours per gallon was established under a load of 112.48 PTO hp. This tractor was equipped with an International six-cylinder engine. Its 4.30 x 5.00-inch bore and stroke gave a displacement of 436 cubic inches. No repairs or adjustments were reported during 46 hours of operation. Partial-range power shifting was provided in the selective-gear fixed-ratio transmission. Its 16 forward speeds varied from 1.6 to 20.4 mph. Using eighth gear, the two-hour drawbar test at 99.21 maximum available hp saw an economy of 13.30 hp-hours per gallon. Also witnessed was a pull of 6,813 lbs. at 5.46 mph and slippage of 4.81 percent. The 10-hour run at 75 percent pull indicated an economy of 12.35 hp-hours per gallon under a load of 78.92 drawbar hp. Further data included a pull of 5,157 lbs. at 5.74 mph and slippage of 3.55 percent. Weighing 13,200 lbs., the 3688 assumed a total test weight of 14,355 lbs. adding front and rear ballast. Standard equipment included dual 18.4-38-inch rear and 11L-15-inch front tires.

International 3788 tractor

Nebraska Test Data

Model: International 3788 Diesel

Test No. 1377

Date Tested: November 5 to November 17, 1980

Of four-wheel-drive design, the 3788 featured partial-range power shifting within the selective-gear fixed-ratio transmission. Its 12 forward speeds ranged from 2.3 to 17.7 mph. Standard equipment included 20.8R38-inch tires. Weighing 18,620 lbs., the 3788 took on a test weight of 20,820 lbs. through the addition of front and rear ballast. Using sixth gear, the two-hour economy run at 142.05 maximum available drawbar hp indicated a pull of 8,635 lbs. at 6.17 mph and slippage totaling 1.49 percent. Fuel economy was posted at 13.24 hp-hours per gallon. In contrast, the 10-hour run at 75 percent pull saw an economy figure of 12.25 under a load of 114.49 drawbar hp. Also indicated by this test was a pull of 6,653 lbs. at 6.45 mph and slippage totaling 1.14 percent. No repairs or adjustments were necessary during 38 hours of operation. An International six-cylinder turbocharged engine was featured—rated at 2,500 rpm and carried a 4.300 x 5.350-inch bore and stroke for a 466-cubic inch displacement. At rated engine speed, 170.57 maximum PTO hp was observed, at 15.61 hp-hours per gallon. Operating at 1,000 PTO rpm and a corresponding engine speed of 2,071 rpm, 17.12 hp-hours per gallon was established a load of 166.39 PTO hp.

International 5288 tractor

Nebraska Test Data

Model: International 5288 Diesel

Test No. 1420

Date Tested: November 13 to November 24, 1981

The 5288 emerged from the two-hour PTO run with an economy of 16.07 hp-hours per gallon under a load of 162.60 PTO hp. The 5288 carried an International six-cylinder turbocharged engine. Rated at 2,400 rpm, it used a 4.30 x 5.35-inch bore and stroke for a 466-cubic inch displacement. No repairs or adjustments were reported during 40-1/2 hours of operating time. Partial-range power shifting was featured within the selective-gear fixed-ratio transmission. Its 18 forward speeds ranged from 1.5 to 18.4 mph. Weighing 17,055 lbs., the 5288 featured dual 20.811-38-inch rear and 14L-16-inch front tires. Additional front and rear ballast gave a total test weight of 18,585 lbs. Operating in ninth gear, the two-hour drawbar test at 137.63 maximum available drawbar hp indicated a pull of 9,801 lbs. at 5.27 mph, slippage of 3.07 percent, and 13.70 hp-hours per gallon. The 10-hour run at 75 percent pull saw 12.77 hp-hours per gallon under a load of 111.43 drawbar hp. Other data included a pull of 7,605 lbs. at 5.49 mph and slippage totaling 2.3 percent.

International 5488 tractor

Nebraska Test Data

Model: International 5488 Diesel

Test No. 1441

Date Tested: May 26 to June 8, 1982

Standard equipment for the 5488 included dual 20.8R38-inch rear and 14L-16-inch front tires. Weighing 17,240 lbs., it assumed a total test weight of 20,005 lbs. by the addition of front and rear ballast. The selective-gear fixed-ratio transmission featured partial-range power shifting. Its 18 forward speeds ranged from 1.5 to 18.5 mph. Using ninth gear, the two-hour drawbar test at 163.44 maximum available hp saw a pull of 11,642 lbs. at 5.26 mph and slippage of 3.69 percent. Fuel economy was 14.16 hp-hours per gallon. The 10-hour run at 75 percent pull saw 13.15 hp-hours per gallon under a load of 130.87 drawbar hp. Also recorded was a pull of 8,798 lbs. at 5.58 mph and 2.57 percent slippage. No repairs or adjustments were required during 38-1/2 hours of operation. The six-cylinder International diesel engine was turbocharged and inter-cooled. Rated at 2,400 rpm, it carried a 4.30 x 5.35-inch bore and stroke for a 466-cubic inch displacement. At rated engine speed, 187.22 maximum PTO hp was observed, and an economy of 16.20 hp-hours per gallon of fuel was achieved.

T-20 TracTracTor crawler

The T-20 TracTracTor saw first light in 1931. For several years previously the company had experimented with various designs built around the 10-20 and 15-30 tractors. A few of these saw limited production. This model used the same basic engine as found in the Farmall F-20 tractor. Production of the T-20 continued into 1939.

Nebraska Test Data

Model: McCormick-Deering TracTracTor
Test No. 199
Date Tested: October 10 to October 26, 1931

The TracTracTor weighed 7,010 lbs., and was given 18.33 drawbar and 25.31 belt hp under the tractor rating codes. Rated drawbar hp of 18.04 translated into a pull of 2,528 lbs. at 2.68 mph, with 7.27 hp-hours per gallon of kerosene. Advertised speeds of 1-3/4, 2-3/4, and 3-3/4 mph were built into the TracTracTor. Using low gear, a maximum of 23.33 drawbar hp was achieved, along with a pull of 5,156 lbs. at 1.7 mph and slippage of 3.12 percent. At its maximum of 26.59 belt hp a fuel economy of 10.04 hp-hours per gallon was noted, but dropped slightly to 9.84 at the rated load of 25.12 hp. The TracTracTor was equipped with Harvester's own four-cylinder I-head engine with a 3-3/4 x 5-inch bore and stroke and rated at 1,250 rpm. The magneto, governor, and air cleaner were all built by the company, but the carburetor was a Zenith Model K5. No repairs or adjustments were noted during the test.

COLLECTOR VALUES	1	2	3	4
T-20	$8,000	$6,000	$3,000	$1,000

International Harvester T-35 crawler

International Harvester introduced its T-35 (gasoline) and TD-35 (diesel) crawlers in 1936. Both remained in production until 1939. The T-35 was built with a six-cylinder IH engine with a 3-5/8 x 4-1/2-inch bore and stroke. TD-35 tractors used a four-cylinder IH diesel with a 4-1/2 x 6-1/2-inch bore and stroke. In Nebraska Test No. 279 the T-35 yielded nearly 36 drawbar hp.

Nebraska Test Data

Model: McCormick-Deering T-35 (distillate)
Test No. 278
Date Tested: April 19 to May 10, 1937

Five forward speeds of 1-3/4, 2-1/4, 2-3/4, 3-1/4, and 4 mph were built into the T-35 tractor. Weighing 10,600 lbs., it featured a six-cylinder, Harvester-built engine. Using an I-head design, this engine was rated at 1,750 rpm and carried a 3-5/8 x 4-1/2-inch bore and stroke. The T-35 tested was equipped to burn distillate fuel. Test H (formerly called "Rated Load") disclosed a fuel economy of 8.18 hp-hours per gallon with an output of 27.79 drawbar hp. In this test the T-35 was operated in third gear, pulling a load of 3,756 lbs. at 2.78 mph and experiencing a slippage of 1.44 percent. Test G for operating maximum load was made in all five forward gears, but in first gear a maximum pull of 7,267 lbs. was achieved at l.75 mph and with an output of 33.85 hp. Test D, formerly known as "Rated Belt Hp," indicated a fuel economy of 9.73 hp-hours per gallon of distillate with an output of 37.29 hp. Test C for operating maximum load disclosed an economy figure of 9.58 with hp rising to 40.37.

Nebraska Test Data

Model: McCormick-Deering T-35 (gasoline)
Test No. 279
Date Tested: April 19 to May 10, 1937

The identical tractor noted in Test No. 278 was used in this test, but gasoline was used as fuel and all specifications remained the same. Test D for rated brake hp indicated a fuel economy of 9.38 hp-hours per gallon plus an output of 39.64 hp. Economy rose minimally to 9.4 when under operating maximum load of 43.23 hp. Test B for 100 percent maximum load indicated an output of 44.44 hp, with an average of 24.09 hp appearing in Test E covering the varying load test at six different loads. Test F for 100 percent maximum drawbar load was run in third gear and delivered 35.91 hp, while Test G for operating maximum load was run in all five forward gears. The highest drawbar pull occurred in low gear with 8,053 lbs. at 1.7 mph, slippage of 5.05 percent and an output of 36.58 hp. Test H, formerly known as the "Rated Drawbar Load," was run in third gear. At a speed of 2.8 mph the T-35 pulled 2,896 lbs. with a slippage of 0.62 percent and an output of 29.07 hp. Fuel economy was recorded at 7.35 hp-hours per gallon. No repairs or adjustments were noted during 48 hours of running time.

Nebraska Test Data

Model: McCormick-Deering TD-35

Test No. 277

Date Tested: April 5 to April 27, 1937

The TD-35 was quite similar to the TD-40 tractor, using the same unique gasoline starting system as before. This tractor however, carried a four-cylinder engine of 4-1/2 x 6-1/2-inch bore and stroke with a rated speed of 1,100 rpm. A hand-operated Rockford clutch was also featured, along with five forward speeds of 1.75, 2.25, 2.75, 3.25, and 4 mph. Operating weight was 11,245 lbs. During the preliminary tests kerosene was used to limber up the track joints. No repairs or adjustments were noted during 62 hours of running time. Test H for rated drawbar load now was derived at 75 percent of calculated maximum hp. At 27.02 hp and a speed of 2.72 mph the TD-35 pulled 3,725 lbs. with a slippage of 1.24 percent and 11.59 hp-hours per gallon. Test D for rated brake load was calculated as 75 percent of permissible maximum, and at 37.35 hp the TD-35 delivered an economy of 14.66 hp-hours per gallon, with a higher economy of 14.81 at 100 percent maximum load of 42.2 brake hp.

COLLECTOR VALUES	1	2	3	4
T-35, TD-35	$8,000	$6,000	$3,000	$1,000

T-40 TracTracTor crawler

Production of the T-40 TracTracTor began in 1932 an d continued into 1939. This model was capable of over 44 drawbar hp. Power came from a six-cylinder IH engine with a 3-3/4 x 4-1/2-inch bore and stroke. The engine was rated at 1,750 rpm. Total weight was nearly 13,000 lbs.

Nebraska Test Data

Model: McCormick-Deering T-40

Test No. 211

Date Tested: October 11 to October 20, 1932

Featuring a six-cylinder IH-built, I-head engine, the T-40 carried a 3-5/8 x 4-1/2-inch bore and stroke with a rated speed of 1,600 rpm. Standard equipment included a Robert Bosch FU6 magneto and a Zenith K5S carburetor, along with five forward speeds of 1-3/4, 2-1/4, 2-3/4, 3-1/4, and 4 mph. Weighing 10,790 lbs., this tractor was operated on gasoline fuel throughout the test. The maximum drawbar pull of 9,399 lbs. occurred in low gear-at a speed of 1.67 mph and slippage of 4.38 percent, the T-40 developed 41.78 drawbar hp. Rated drawbar testing was done in third gear, and over the 10-hour test, fuel economy was of 7.71 hp-hours per gallon, along with 33.69 hp and a pull of 4,668 lbs. at 2.71 mph. Rated brake hp tests at 43.33 hp indicated 9.41 hp-hours per gallon, with this figure dropping ever so little to an even 9 hp-hours per gallon at a maximum load of 46.48 belt hp.

Nebraska Test Data

Model: McCormick-Deering T-40 (distillate)

Test No. 280

Date Tested: April 7 to April 29, 1937

At 85 percent of calculated maximum brake hp, the T-40 delivered a fuel economy of 9.77 hp-hours per gallon of distillate with an output of 44.45 hp. Economy rose to 10.17 at operating maximum load of 48.15 hp. The T-40 featured an IH-built six-cylinder I-head engine. Rated at 1,750 rpm, it used a 3-3/4 x 4-1/2-inch bore and stroke. Also included was an IHC F-6 magneto and a Zenith 50-AY12 carburetor. During 92 hours of motor operating time, no repairs or adjustments were required. Total weight with the operator was 12,770 lbs. Five forward speeds of 1-3/4, 2-1/4, 2-3/4, 3-1/4, and 4 mph were provided. Test H for rated drawbar load of 33.95 hp revealed 7.98 hp-hours per gallon along with a pull of 4,599 lbs. at 2.77 mph and slippage of 1.85 percent. Test G was run in all five forward gears, but in low gear a maximum pull of 9,023 lbs. was recorded at a speed of 1.73 mph, slippage of 3.85 percent, and 41.53 drawbar hp.

Nebraska Test Data

Model: McCormick-Deering T-40 (gasoline)

Test No. 281

Date Tested: May 4 to May 14, 1937

This test used the same tractor as Test No. 280, but it was fueled by gasoline this time. All tractor specifications remained the same. During 77 hours of testing, no repairs or adjustments were noted. Third gear was selected for Test H, and at a load of 35.19 hp the T-40 pulled 4,771 lbs. at 2.77 mph with a slippage of 1.88 percent. Fuel economy was recorded at 7.07 hp-hours per gallon. Test G for operating maximum load indicated a pull of 9,553 lbs. in low gear with an output of 44.06 hp. The latter figure came in at 42.74 when using fifth gear-at a speed of 4.02 mph the T-40 pulled a load of 3,984 lbs. Belt testing indicated 50.07 hp in the operating maximum load of Test C, along with an economy of 9.26 hp-hours per gallon. A slightly lower economy of 8.94 was noted in Test D where a rated load of 46.12 was developed.

TD-40 TracTracTor crawler

The TD-40 TracTracTor used the same engine as the WD-40 wheel tractor. Rated at 1,200 rpm, it was capable of over 48 drawbar hp. Like the WD-40, this model had the unique starting system, whereby the engine was started as a gasoline engine, complete with magneto and carburetor. After 900 revolutions the engine automatically converted over to diesel operation. Production of this model ran from 1933 and ended in 1939.

Nebraska Test Data

Model: McCormick-Deering TD-40
Test No. 230
Date Tested: October 25 to November 13, 1934

With the TD-40, International Harvester Company entered the tractor field with its first diesel model. Operating at its rated load of 43.56 brake hp, it set a new economy record of 15.18 hp-hours per gallon of No. 3 furnace oil. This dropped by only .05 of a gallon when operating at a maximum load of 48.26 hp. The 10-hour rated drawbar test in third gear revealed a fuel economy of 12.86 hp-hours per gallon, along with a pull of 4,663 lbs. at 2.72 mph and an output of 33.79 hp. Drawbar pull reached its maximum in low gear. At a speed of 1.69 mph the T-40 Diesel pulled 9,528 lbs. with a slippage of 2.87 percent, or slightly over 75 percent of its own weight, and developed 43.05 maximum drawbar hp. This tractor was equipped with an IH-built four-cylinder I-head engine rated at 1,100 rpm, and featured a 4-3/4 x 6-1/2-inch bore and stroke. A magneto and carburetor were furnished also, but these were for starting purposes only. Also included were advertised speeds of 1-3/4, 2-1/4, 2-3/4, 3-1/4, and 4 mph. No repairs or adjustments were made during the 51 hours of running time.

Nebraska Test Data

Model: McCormick-Deering TD-40
Test No. 298
Date Tested: April 20 to April 30, 1938

Five forward speeds of 1-3/4, 2-1/4, 2-3/4, 3-1/4, and 4 mph were available in the TD-40. Test H was run in third gear, and over 10 hours the test results indicated 11.69 hp-hours per gallon of diesel fuel with a pull of 5,051 lbs. at 2.76 mph and slippage of 1.48 percent. This test also resulted in a rated 37.15 drawbar hp. Maximum load tests were made in all five forward gears, but 48.53 hp was recorded in low gear, with a pull of 10,487 lbs. at 1.74 mph and slippage of 2.87 percent. The TD-40 pulled approximately 80 percent of its own 13,080 lb. operating weight. Rated at 1,200 rpm, the TD-40 diesel engine was built by III and carried a 4-3/4 x 6-1/2-inch bore and stroke. Like previous International Harvester diesel engines, it also featured a unique gasoline starting system with a magneto and carburetor that were deactivated after the engine was running. Test D for rated brake hp set this figure at 48.33 with 14.26 hp-hours per gallon. Economy increased minimally to 14.32 under a 100 percent maximum load of 53.46 brake hp. No repairs or adjustments were noted during 54 hours of running time.

COLLECTOR VALUES	1	2	3	4
T-40	$48,000	$6,000	$3,000	$1500

A new line of IH crawlers emerged in late 1938 with the introduction of the TD-18. This model remained in production until 1949 when it was replaced with the TD-18A. The latter was built until 1955. The TD-18 delivered over 72 drawbar hp. However, the big TD-18A demonstrated almost 84 hp on the drawbar. The engine was of six-cylinder design, using a 4-3/4 x 6-1/2-inch bore and stroke.

TD-18 and TD-18A crawlers

Nebraska Test Data

Model: International TD-18 TracTractor (wide tread)
Test No. 315
Date Tested: March 27 to April 14, 1939

This six-cylinder diesel model featured Harvester's own engine rated at 1,200 rpm and carried a 43/4 x 6-1/2-inch bore and stroke. It used the same unique starting system noted on the TD-40 and WD-40 tractors noted in Tests 230 and 246. A Bosch fuel injection system was featured, along with a Purolator oil filter and Dole thermostat. No repairs or adjustments were recorded during 72 hours of engine running time. This 23,360 lb. tractor featured six forward speeds of 1-1/2, 2-1/2, 3-1/4, 4-5/8, and 5-3/4 mph. Test H for rated drawbar load indicated a pull of 7,943 lbs. at 2.51 mph with an output of 53.22 hp and a fuel economy of 12.63 hp-hours per gallon. Test G for 100 percent maximum load revealed a first-gear maximum pull of 18,973 lbs. at 1.43 mph and an output of 72.38 drawbar hp with slippage of only 3.27 percent. Brake hp test under Test C for 100 percent maximum load show 80.32 hp with an economy of 15.4 hp-hours per gallon. That dropped slightly to 15.31 at the rated brake load of 72.56 hp.

Nebraska Test Data

Model: International TD-18A
Test No. 446
Date Tested: June 27 to July 18, 1950

Test B indicated that at a 100 percent maximum belt load the TD-18A produced 97.83 hp, with 14.7 hp-hours per gallon of diesel fuel. At a Test D rated load of 86.74 belt hp, that dropped infinitesimally to 14.67 hp-hours per gallon. Weighing in at 25,995 lbs., the TD-18A achieved a low-gear maximum pull of 20,234 lbs. per Test G. Test H, run in second gear, indicated a pull of 11,825 lbs. at 2.13 mph with a slippage of 2.77 percent. This 10-hour run revealed an output of 67.04 drawbar hp with a fuel economy of 12.24 hp-hours per gallon. No repairs or adjustments were noted during 46 hours of engine running time. This tractor was equipped with a 681.1-cid engine with six-cylinder of 4-3/4 x 6-1/2-inch bore and stroke. Of I-head design, this engine was rated at 1,350 rpm. Advertised speeds of 1.7, 2.2, 2.7, 3.5, 4.6, and 5.7 mph were featured.

Nebraska Test Data

Model: International TD-18
Test No. 588
Date Tested: August 10 to August 15, 1956

Weighing 30,285 lbs., the TD-18 achieved a low-gear maximum pull of 25,143 lbs. at 1.48 mph with a slippage of 7.75 percent, as reported in Test G. This tractor featured forward speeds of 1.6, 2.1, 2.6, 3.4, 4.5, and 5.5 mph, with second gear used for the 10-hour rated drawbar run of Test H. With an output of 81.81 hp, the TD-18 pulled 14,769 lbs. at 2.08 mph with a slippage of 1.78 percent. Fuel economy was scored at 11.73 hp-hours per gallon. Rated at 1,450 rpm, the TD-18 gave a peak 107 percent or rated torque at 85 percent of rated speed, and reached this torque level once again at 70 percent of rated engine speed. An International six-cylinder engine was featured-with a 4-3/4 x 6-1/2-inch bore and stroke and a 691-cubic inch displacement. No repairs or adjustments were noted during 45 hours of operation. Test B & C, run at a 100 percent maximum belt load of 121.62 hp, yielded 13.5 hp-hours per gallon, climbing to 14.14 at a Test D rated belt load of 110.07 hp.

Nebraska Test Data

Model: International TD-18
Test No. 629
Date Tested: September 3 to September 14, 1957

Since no belt pulley was available for this tractor, no torque tests or belt tests were performed. Weighing 30,955 lbs., the TD-18 featured forward speeds of 1.6, 2.1, 2.6, 3.4, 4.4, and 5.5 mph. Also included was a single-plate hand-operated clutch connected to an international six-cylinder TD-182M diesel engine. Rated at 1,550 rpm, it carried a 4-3/4 x 6-1/2-inch bore and stroke for a displacement of 691-cubic inches. This engine was designed with a 15.04:1 compression ratio. Using low gear, a 100 percent maximum pull of 26,751 lbs. was recorded at 1.48 mph with a slippage of 6.96 percent and an output of 105.79 hp. Second gear gave a maximum output of 106.66 hp, along with a pull of 19,490 lbs. at 2.05 mph and slippage of 2.34 percent. Test H, run in second gear, noted an economy of 11.28 hp-hours per gallon. This test also recorded a rated output of 83.25 hp, with a pull of 15,279 lbs. at 2.04 mph and 2.44 percent slippage. During 44-1/2 hours of operating time, no repairs or adjustments were reported.

COLLECTOR VALUES	1	2	3	4
T-18	$7,000	$5,000	$3,000	$1,000

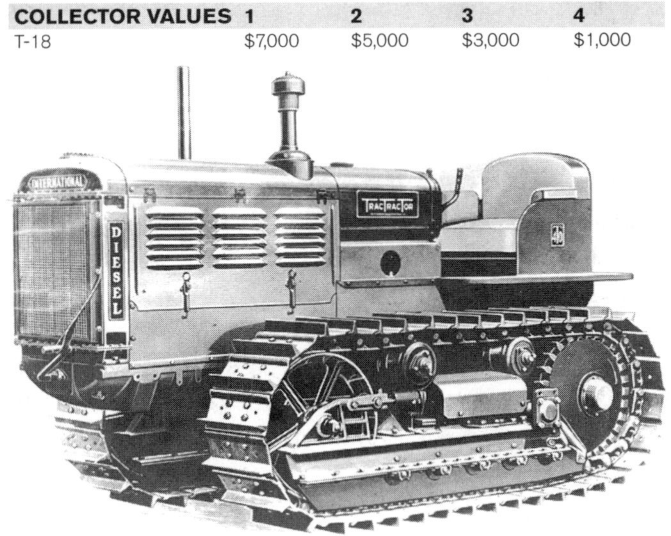

International T-6 and TD-6 crawlers

The International T-6 and TD-6 tractors were introduced in 1939 and remained in production until 1956. Both were virtually identical except that the T-6 used a gasoline engine, and the TD-6 was equipped with a diesel. Both the gasoline and diesel engines were of four-cylinder design and used a 3-7/8 x 5-1/4-inch bore and stroke.

Nebraska Test Data

Model: International T-6 (gasoline)
Test No. 346
Date Tested: May 14 to June 6, 1940

Equipped to burn gasoline, this tractor featured Harvester's four-cylinder I-head engine with a 3-7/8 x 5-1/4-inch bore and stroke with a rated speed of 1,450 rpm. Also included was an IH Model H-4 magneto and an IH Model E-12 carburetor. No repairs or adjustments were noted during 65 hours of engine operation. Advertised speeds of 1.5, 2.2, 3.1, 3.8, and 5.4 mph were provided. Test G for operating maximum load was run in all five forward gears, but the maximum pull of 7,652 lbs. occurred in low gear. At a speed of 1.4 mph the T-6 delivered this pull with a slippage of 8.59 percent and an output of 28.52 drawbar hp. Test H was run in second gear and indicated a pull of 4,266 lbs. at 2.16 mph and slippage of 2.72 percent for an output of 24.63 rated drawbar hp and a fuel economy of 9.34 hp-hours per gallon. Test C for operating maximum load yielded 12.09 hp-hours per gallon under a load of 36.06 brake hp. Test D for rated load recorded a slight drop in economy to 11.97, with an output of 33.04 hp.

Nebraska Test Data

Model: International T-6 (distillate)
Test No. 347
Date Tested: May 22 to June 10, 1940

International Harvester presented an entirely differed T-6 tractor for this test than was used in Test No. 346. Although basic specifications remained the same, this tractor was specifically equipped for use with distillate fuel. Test G was run in all five forward gears, with the first-gear maximum pull being recorded at 7,434 lbs., a speed of 1.44 mph, slippage of 6.02 percent and an output of 28.45 drawbar hp. Test H was run in second gear. This 10-hour test yielded 9.7 hp-hours per gallon, compared to 9.34 in Test No. 346. Test H also indicated an output of 24.63 rated drawbar hp, along with a load of 4,266 lbs. at 2.16 mph. Test C for operating maximum load ended with a fuel economy of 12.3 hp-hours per gallon of distillate at a load of 34.22 brake hp. Economy slipped to 11.59 at 31.21 rated brake hp as noted in Test. D. This test indicated an output of 31.21 hp.

Nebraska Test Data

Model: International T-6
Test No. 589
Date Tested: August 21 to August 23, 1956

Weighing 9,190 lbs., this tractor was a gasoline-powered version of the TD-6 diesel model noted in Test No. 587. It was equipped with an International C-264 engine with a 4 x 5-1/4-inch bore and stroke, rated speed of 1,550 rpm, and a displacement of 264-cubic inches. The T-6 carried the same speed range as noted for the TD-6 diesel model. A low-gear maximum pull of 8,714 lbs. at 1.51 mph and slippage of 6.42 percent was recorded in Test G. Second gear was used for Test H. With a rated drawbar output of 31.32 hp, the T-6 pulled 5,212 lbs. at 2.25 mph with a slippage of 3.98 percent. Fuel economy came in at 8.6 hp-hours per gallon. Test L indicated a maximum 114 percent of rated speed engine torque occurring at 65 percent of rated engine speed. Test D, run at a rated belt load of 43.37 hp, ended with a fuel economy of 11.28 hp-hours per gallon. The same test run at 100 percent maximum load produced a fuel economy of 11.63 hp-hours per gallon. No repairs or adjustments were noted during 39 hours testing.

Nebraska Test Data

Model: International TD-6

Test No. 345

Date Tested: May 6 to June 1, 1940

Advertised speeds of 1.5, 2.2, 3.1, 3.8, and 5.4 mph were built into the TD-6 crawler tractor. Weighing in at 7,950 lbs., it went through 47 hours of engine operating time for completion of the tests. During the varying load belt test, the belt pulley jaw clutch disengaged. After adjusting the clutch, testing resumed and no other repairs or adjustments were noted. Test G recorded a maximum low gear pull of 7,160 lbs. at 1.4 mph, along with a slippage of 8.24 percent and an output of 26.75 drawbar hp. Test H was run in second gear and indicated an economy of 12.21 hp-hours per gallon of diesel fuel, plus an output of 22.28 hp, a pull of 3,818 lbs., and slippage of 1.77 percent at 2.19 mph. Fuel economy rested at 14.23 hp-hours per gallon at an operating maximum load of 34.54 brake hp per Test C. Economy rose slightly to 14.54 hp-hours per gallon in Test D. This test was run at 30.82 brake hp. The TD-6 used a four-cylinder IH engine featuring an I-head design and using a 3-7/8 x 5-1/4-inch bore and stroke with a rated speed of 1,450 rpm. A Bosch fuel injection system was standard equipment.

Nebraska Test Data

Model: International TD-6

Test No. 462

Date Tested: June 25 to July 10, 1951

At a Test D rated belt load of 34.38 hp, the TD-6 tractor delivered an economy of 14.16 hp-hours per gallon of diesel fuel. That figure rose slightly to 14.24 under a Test B maximum belt load of 38.2 hp. This tractor weighed in at 8,585 lbs., and featured forward speeds of 1.5, 2.2, 3.1, 3.8, and 5.4 mph. Second gear was used for the 10-hour rated drawbar run of Test H. At 25.45 hp, the TD-6 pulled 4,406 lbs. at 2.17 mph with a slippage of 2.27 percent. Fuel economy came in at 11.73 hp-hours per gallon. No repairs of consequence were noted during 65 hours of test operating time. The TD-6 featured an International four-cylinder diesel engine rated at 1,450 rpm, and using a 3-7/8 x 5-1/4-inch bore and stroke for a 247.7-cubic inch displacement. This I-head design engine was equipped with a 12-volt electrical system.

Nebraska Test Data

Model: International TD-6

Test No. 587

Date Tested: August 17 to August 22, 1956

At a Test D rated belt load of 43.7 hp, the TD-6 came in with an economy of 13.96 hp-hours per gallon of diesel fuel. By comparison, fuel economy slipped to 13.5 hp-hours per gallon at a Test B & C maximum belt load of 48.99 hp. This 9,410-lb. tractor featured forward speeds of 1.6, 2.3, 3.3, 4.1, and 5.7 mph, with second gear used for the 10-hour run of Test H. This test, made at 31.91 drawbar hp, yielded a pull of 5,315 lbs. at 2.25 mph and slippage of 4.03 percent. Fuel economy was pegged at 11.13 hp-hours per gallon. The TD-6 achieved a low-gear maximum pull of 8,769 lbs. at 1.51 mph with slippage of 6.7 percent in Test G. Standard features included a four-cylinder, 4 x 5-1/4-inch engine with a 264-cubic inch displacement. Test L indicated that 109 percent of rated engine torque was available at 80 percent of the rated 1,550 rpm. During 37-1/2 hours of operation, no repairs or adjustments were recorded.

Built in the 1939-1956 period, the T-9 and TD-9 crawlers were virtually identical except for the style of engine. The IH-built four-cylinder gasoline engine of the T-9 was the same four-cylinder engine used in the W-9 tractor with a 4.4 x 5.5-inch bore and stroke. Capable of about 44 brake hp, the diesel TD-9 used a four-cylinder IH engine with the same 4.4 x 5.5-inch bore and stroke as its gasoline-fired counterpart. Rated speed was 1,400 rpm.

T-9 and TD-9 crawlers

Nebraska Test Data

Model: International T-9

Test No. 372

Date Tested: May 27 to June 18, 1941

Five forward speeds of 1-1/2, 2-1/4, 3-1/4, 3-7/8, and 5-1/4 mph were built into the T-9 crawler tractor. Also featured was an IH-built four-cylinder, I-head engine with a 4.4 x 5.5-inch bore and stroke as used in the W-9 tractors noted in Tests 369 and 371. The T-9 weighed in at 10,830 lbs. During 49 hours of engine operation no repairs or adjustments were noted except for the inconsequential replacement of a missing bolt in one of the track shoes. Test H for rated drawbar load was run in second gear. At a speed of 2.13 mph and with a slippage of 3.03 percent, the T-9 pulled a load of 5,677 lbs. and delivered 32.29 drawbar hp with an economy of 9.1 hp-hours per gallon. Test G was run in all five forward gears, with a low-gear maximum pull of 9,868 lbs. at 1.49 mph and an output of 39.11 drawbar hp. Belt testing, done under the maximum operating load of Test C, indicated a fuel economy of 11.97 hp-hours per gallon with a load of 46.03 brake hp. At rated load of 41.49 hp under Test D, fuel economy came to 11.49 hp-hours per gallon.

Nebraska Test Data

Model: International TD-9

Test No. 344

Date Tested: June 10 to June 12, 1940

Only 28 hours of engine operation was required to complete this test, and no repairs or adjustments were noted. Under Test C the TD-9 developed a maximum operating load of 43.93 brake hp. Its diesel engine yielded 14.78 hp-hours per gallon. Test D at a rated load of 39.15 brake hp gave an economy figure of 14.76, virtually identical to the Test C results. This tractor was equipped with Harvester's own four-cylinder I-head engine carrying a 4.4 x 5.5-inch bore and stroke with a rated speed of 1,400 rpm. A Bosch fuel injection system was standard equipment. Advertised speeds of 1.5, 2.2, 3.2, 3.9, and 5.3 mph were standard equipment. Second gear was used for Test H, and at a rated load of 28.97 drawbar hp the TD-9 pulled a 4,971-lb. load at 2.19 mph with a slippage of 0.81 percent. Test G for maximum drawbar load was run in all forward gears, but in low gear the maximum pull of 9,014 lbs. was recorded. Test data also indicates an output of 34.28 drawbar hp, a speed of 1.43 mph, and slippage of 8.07 percent.

Nebraska Test Data

Model: International TD-9

Test No. 461

Date Tested: June 25 to July 10, 1951

Weighing in at 11,660 lbs., the TD-9 achieved a low-gear maximum pull of 9,909 lbs. at 1.49 mph against a slippage of 4.17 percent. Stated another way, the TD-9 pulled approximately 85 percent of its own weight. Advertised speeds of 1.5, 2.2, 3, 3.9, and 5.3 mph were featured, with second gear used for Test H. This 10-hour rated load run was made at 31.32 drawbar hp, along with a pull of 5,440 lbs. at 2.16 mph and a slippage of 2.45 percent. Fuel economy was pegged at 11.59 hp-hours per gallon. The TD-9 featured a 334.5-cid International diesel engine. Of I-head design, it was rated at 1,400 rpm, and used a 4.4 x 5.5-inch bore and stroke. Belt testing indicated an economy of 14.11 hp-hours per gallon under a Test D rated load of 41.59 hp, with the economy figure rising slightly to 4.24 under the Test B maximum belt load of 46.69 hp. No repairs or adjustments were noted during 47-1/2 hours of engine operation.

Nebraska Test Data

Model: International TD-9

Test No. 586

Date Tested: August 16 to August 21, 1956

Advertised speeds of 1.7, 2.5, 3.4, 4.3, and 5.9 mph were featured in this TD-9 crawler tractor. Test L indicates that this model achieved 113 percent of rated speed torque at 75 percent of its rated 1,550 rpm engine speed. Using first gear, Test G shows a maximum pull of 11,721 lbs. at 1.6 mph with a slippage of 8.63 percent. The rated drawbar run of Test H was made in second gear. At a load of 42.67 hp the TD-9 pulled 6,676 lbs. at 2.4 mph with a slippage of 3.17 percent. Fuel economy came to 11.73 hp-hours per gallon of diesel fuel. Weighing 12,830 lbs., the TD-9 featured an International four-cylinder diesel engine with a 4-1/2 x 5-1/2-inch bore and stroke. Using a 15.64:1 compression ratio, this engine had a 350-cubic inch displacement. During Test F & G the fan belt was tightened, and during Test H a new fuel filter was installed. Otherwise, no repairs or adjustments were noted during 42 hours of operation. Belt testing indicated a fuel economy of 14.48 hp-hours per gallon at a Test D rated load of 55 hp. At a 100 percent maximum belt load of 62.69 hp, fuel economy was registered at 14.54 hp-hours per gallon.

Nebraska Test Data

Model: International TD-9

Test No. 751

Date Tested: August 2 to August 17, 1960

This tractor featured Harvester's own six-cylinder turbocharged engine rated at 1,700 rpm. Using a 3-11/16 x 4.39-inch bore and stroke, it had a displacement of 282-cubic inches and an 18.08:1 compression ratio. PTO testing indicated a maximum output of 69.11 hp at rated engine speed, together with a fuel economy of 14.82 hp-hours per gallon. Another PTO run, made at the standard output shaft speed of 1,000 rpm and a corresponding crankshaft speed of 1,499 rpm, yielded 66.36 hp and 14.26 hp-hours per gallon. Weighing 13,645 lbs., the TD-9 featured five forward speeds ranging from 1.7 to 6.0 mph. A low-gear maximum pull of 13,156 lbs. was recorded at 1.65 mph with 5.86 percent slippage. Drawbar fuel economy was pegged at 12.42 hp-hours per gallon under a maximum load of 56.26 hp. This test, run in second gear, also noted a pull of 8,647 lbs. at 2.44 mph and slippage of 1.78 percent. A 10-hour run, also made in second gear, but at 75 percent pull, noted an output of 44.21 hp, a pull of 6,581 lbs. at 2.52 mph with 1.45 percent slippage, and a resultant fuel economy of 11.79 hp-hours per gallon. No repairs or adjustments were required during 46 hours of operating time.

International T-340 crawler

Nebraska Test Data

Model: International T-340

Test No. 725

Date Tested: October 21 to October 29, 1959

Five forward speeds of 1.5, 2.2, 3.0, 4.3, and 5.8 mph were featured in the T-340 tractor. Weighing 6,695 lbs., this unit delivered 28.33 hp in a two-hour run that saw a fuel economy of 8.71 hp-hours per gallon at maximum available power. This test also yielded a pull of 4,913 lbs. at 2.16 mph with a slippage of 3.07 percent. The 10-hour run, made at 24.28 drawbar hp, indicated a pull of 4,011 lbs. at 2.27 mph with 2.99 percent slippage and 8.13 hp-hours per gallon. The T-340 was equipped with an International four-cylinder engine with a 3-1/4 x 4-1/16-inch bore and stroke for a 135-cubic inch displacement. Rated at 2,000 rpm, it delivered 36.49 PTO hp at this crankshaft speed and yielded 11.65 hp-hours per gallon. A one-hour run made at 540 PTO rpm and 1,747 engine rpm, indicated 32.83 PTO hp and a fuel economy of 11.78 hp-hours per gallon. Repairs and adjustments noted during a 53 hour run were minor.

International T-4 crawler

Nebraska Test Data

Model: International T-4

Test No. 754

Date Tested: August 18 to September 3, 1960

Like the T-5, this model also featured a selective transmission that was augmented by the Torque Amplifier system. Within the five selective speeds, another five were available for an actual total of 10 speeds forward. Weighing 6,995 lbs., the T-4 went into the two-hour fuel economy run using second gear. At 26.99 maximum available hp, a pull of 4,599 lbs. was recorded at 2.22 mph with 2.2 percent slippage. The resultant fuel economy was posted at 10.63 hp-hours per gallon. By comparison, fuel economy sagged to 9.77 in the 10-hour run made at 75 percent pull. This test indicated an output of 21.13 drawbar hp, a pull of 3,453 lbs. at 2.29 mph and slippage of 1.49 percent. Harvester equipped this tractor with a four-cylinder engine rated at 2,000 rpm and carrying a 3-1/8 x 4-inch bore and stroke for a displacement of 122.7-cubic inches. At rated engine speed a maximum of 32.54 PTO hp was observed, with 12.3 hp-hours per gallon. No repairs or adjustments were recorded during 51 hours of running time.

International T-5 and TD-5 crawlers

Nebraska Test Data

Model: International T-5

Test No. 753

Date Tested: August 18 to September 3, 1960

At its 2,000 rpm rated crankshaft speed the T-5 delivered a maximum of 36.01 PTO hp with a fuel economy of 12.28 hp-hours per gallon. This 7,005-lb. tractor was equipped with an International Harvester four-cylinder gasoline engine featuring a 3-1/4 x 4-1/16-inch bore and stroke. These dimensions produced a 134.8-cubic inch displacement. The fixed-ratio transmission was augmented with Harvester's Torque Amplifier. Five forward speeds ranging from 1.48 to 6.54 mph were available in direct-engine drive. Using second gear, a two-hour run at 28.59 maximum available hp yielded 9.86 hp-hours per gallon. This test also indicated an output of 28.59 hp, a pull of 4,858 lbs. at 2.21 mph and slippage of 2.8 percent. The 10-hour economy run, made at 75 percent pull, noted an economy figure of 9.13 while delivering 23.56 drawbar hp. Other statistics included a pull of 3,781 lbs. at 2.34 mph with 1.71 percent slippage. Some 44-1/2 hours of running time saw no reported repairs or adjustments.

Nebraska Test Data

Model: International TD-5 Diesel

Test No. 755

Date Tested: August 24 to September 3, 1960

This tractor featured an International four-cylinder engine with a rated speed of 2,000 rpm, a 3-3/8 x 4-inch bore and stroke, and a 144-cubic inch displacement. The engine had a 21.1:1 compression ratio. At rated engine speed, a maximum output of 35.25 PTO hp was observed, with a fuel economy of 14.06 hp-hours per gallon. This unit was equipped with a selective-speed transmission and the Torque Amplifier. In this case, a total of 10 speeds were available, ranging from 1.00 to 6.54 mph. Total tractor weight was 7,155 lbs. A two-hour fuel consumption run, made in second gear, noted a maximum of 29.61 drawbar hp plus a pull of 5,006 lbs. at 2.22 mph and 1.45 percent slippage. Fuel economy settled in at 11.89 hp-hours per gallon. This figure dropped slightly to 11.48 in the 10-hour economy run made at 75 percent pull. The latter test indicated an output of 23.49 drawbar hp, a pull of 3,759 lbs. at 2.34 mph and slippage of 1.32 percent. During 47-1/2hours of operation, no repairs or adjustments were reported.

International TD-14 and TD-14A crawlers

Nebraska Test Data

Model: International TD-14

Test No. 343

Date Tested: May 6 to May 31, 1940

Weighing 17,595 lbs., the TD-14 carried advertised speeds of 1-1/2, 2, 2-1/2, 3-3/8, 4-3/4, and 5-3/4 mph. The four-cylinder I-head diesel engine was built by IH and carried 4-3/4 x 6-1/2-inch bore and stroke with a rated speed of 1,350 rpm. This tractor maintained the gasoline starting system found on the WD-40 and similar designs of this engine series. No repairs or adjustments were noted during 51 hours of engine operating time. Test C for operating maximum load yielded 61.56 brake hp, along with an economy of 15.71 hp-hours per gallon of diesel fuel. Test D results included a fuel economy figure of 15.6, with an output of 54.61 brake hp. Test G included maximum drawbar load tests in all six forward gears, but in low gear a maximum pull of 13,426 lbs. was achieved, about 76 percent of operating weight. This test was run at a speed of 1.44 mph. Other data included a slippage of 7.18 percent and an output of 51.43 drawbar hp. Test H was run in third gear, with a pull of 6,178 lbs. noted at a speed of 2.48 mph, slippage of 5.16 percent, and an output of 40.81 drawbar hp.

Nebraska Test Data

Model: International TD-14A

Test No. 445

Date Tested: June 26 to July 1, 1950

Advertised speeds of 1.6, 2, 2.6, 3.4, 4.4, and 5.7 were featured in the TD-14A tractor. Test G revealed a low-gear maximum pull of 14,652 lbs. at 1.49 mph with a slippage of 5.52 percent. Total tractor weight was 18,445 lbs. Test H at a rated drawbar load of 49.5 hp produced a 9,244-lb. pull at 2.01 mph with a slippage of 2.41 percent. Economy came in at 13.03 hp-hours per gallon of diesel fuel. This tractor was equipped with Harvester's own four-cylinder diesel engine. Of I-head design, it was rated at 1,400 rpm, and using a 4-3/4 x 6-1/2-inch bore and stroke with a displacement of 460.7-cubic inches. No repairs or adjustments were recorded during 44 hours of engine operation. Tests B and C at a 100 percent maximum belt load of 71.79 hp indicated a fuel economy of 15.4 hp-hours per gallon, while at a rated load of 64.02 belt hp, per Test C, fuel economy was noted at 15.32 hp-hours per gallon.

Nebraska Test Data

Model: International TD-14

Test No. 585

Date Tested: August 11 to August 17, 1956

Under a Test D rated belt load of 82.51 hp, the TD-14 achieved an economy of 13.73 hp-hours per gallon of diesel fuel. By comparison, economy was scored at 13.61 at a 100 percent maximum belt load of 91.33 hp. Rated at 1,650 rpm, the TD-14 peaked at 113 percent of rated torque at 60 percent of rated engine speed. Weighing 23,345 lbs., the TD-14 featured forward speeds of 1.6, 2.1, 2.7, 3.5, 4.5, and 5.8 mph. Second gear was used for the 10-hour rated drawbar run of Test H. With an output of 61.13 hp, this tractor pulled 10,994 lbs. at 2.09 mph with a slippage of 1.52 percent. Test H also saw a fuel economy of 11.43 hp-hours per gallon. A low-gear maximum load test indicated 17,762 lbs. of pull at 1.56 mph with a slippage of 4.04 percent. This tractor featured an International four-cylinder engine with a 4-3/4 x 6-1/2-inch bore and stroke for a 460.7-cubic inch displacement. During 38 hours of operation, no repairs or adjustments were noted.

International TD-15 crawler

Nebraska Test Data

Model: International TD-15 Diesel

Test No. 750

Date Tested: July 30 to August 17, 1960

No PTO hp tests were run on this tractor. Using second gear, a two-hour economy run recorded a maximum output of 76.97 hp, a pull of 15,341 lbs. at 1.87 mph and slippage of 2.18 percent, with fuel economy of 9.84 hp-hours per gallon. A 10-hour run at 75 percent pull noted an economy figure of 9.92. This test also indicated an output of 62.76 drawbar hp, a pull of 12,014 lbs. at 1.96 mph and slippage of 1.5 percent. A maximum pull of 21,275 lbs. at 1.41 mph with 5.44 percent slippage was recorded in low gear. Total weight was 24,555 lbs. The TD-15 Diesel was equipped with Harvester's own six-cylinder engine rated at 1,650 rpm, and using a 4-5/8 x 5-1/2-inch bore and stroke for a 554-cubic inch displacement. A 12-volt electrical system was also featured. International Harvester equipped this tractor with a selective-gear fixed-ratio transmission with six forward speeds ranging from 1.5 to 5.8 mph. No repairs or adjustments were recorded during 54 hours of running time.

International TD-20 crawler

Nebraska Test Data

Model: International TD-20 Diesel

Test No. 806

Date Tested: October 2 to October 18, 1961

Rated by the manufacturer at 113 drawbar hp, this tractor was not equipped with an external PTO shaft, and no brake hp tests were run. The TD-20 was equipped with an IH-built six-cylinder turbocharged engine rated at 1,550 rpm. Using a 4-3/4 x 6-1/2-inch bore and stroke, it carried a displacement of 691- cubic inches and featured a 15.06:1 compression ratio. Also featured was a selective gear fixed-ratio transmission with six forward speeds ranging from 1.6 to 7.3 mph. As presented for testing, the TD-20 weighed 32,485 lbs. Second gear was used for the drawbar economy runs. At a maximum available output of 110.48 hp, the two-hour run recorded a pull of 20,656 lbs. at 2.01 mph with 2.64 percent slippage. Fuel economy was posted at 10.44 hp-hours per gallon, and slipped to 9.77 in the 10-hour economy run. The latter test, made at 75 percent pull, noted an output of 91.54 hp, a pull of 16,241 lbs. at 2.11 mph and 1.88 percent slippage. A low gear maximum pull of 28,326 lbs. was recorded at 1.5 mph with 5.46 percent slippage. No repairs or adjustments were noted during 60-_ hours of operation.

TD-24 crawler

Production of the huge TD-24 crawler began in 1947. Weighing over 20 tons, it was powered by an IH six-cylinder diesel engine with a 5-3/4 x 7-inch bore and stroke for a displacement of 1,090-cubic inches. Production continued until 1959. This big tractor boasted 148 drawbar hp, and for a time, was the largest crawler tractor on the market.

Nebraska Test Data

Model: International TD-24
Test No. 447
Date Tested: June 29 to July 18, 1950

Weighing 40,595 lbs., the gigantic TD-24 tractor was not tested for belt hp owing to the limited capacity of the dynamometer. Tests F and G at 100 percent maximum drawbar load were made in all forward gears, with the TD-24 producing a low-gear maximum pull of 33,714 lbs. at 1.54 mph. Slippage in this test was 3.79 percent, and total output was 138.13 drawbar hp. The 100 percent maximum pull in eighth gear was 4,892 lbs. at 7.96 mph with no slippage recorded. Output was 103.81 hp. Advertised speeds of 1.6, 2, 2.4, 3.1, 4, 5.2, 6.1, and 7.8 mph were featured and third gear was used for the rated drawbar run of Test H. Under an output of 111.81 hp the TD-24 pulled 17,322 lbs. at 2.42 mph with a slippage of 1.16 percent. Fuel economy totaled 12.315 hp-hours per gallon, or a total consumption of 9.079 gph. This tractor was equipped with Harvester's own six-cylinder I-head engine with a 1090.6-cubic inch displacement. Rated at 1,375 rpm, it used a 5-3/4 x 7-inch bore and stroke. No repairs or adjustments were noted over 37 hours of engine operating time.

Nebraska Test Data

Model: International TD-24
Test No. 529
Date Tested: October 22 to October 29, 1954

This TD-24 carried an International six-cylinder engine with a 5-3/4 x 7-inch bore and stroke. Rated at 1,400 rpm, this was a 1090.6-cid engine. Eight forward speeds were provided of 1.6, 2, 2.5, 3.2, 4.1, 5.3, 6.3, and 8 mph. Due to the limited dynamometer capacity, no belt tests were run. During 32-1/2 hours of operation, no repairs or adjustments were noted. Weighing 42,211 lbs., the TD-24 managed a low-gear maximum pull of 37,160 lbs. at 1.48 mph with 9.93 percent slippage. The TD-24 delivered 146.28 hp to the drawbar. A maximum drawbar output of 154.05 hp was achieved in third gear. At 2.47 mph, and with slippage of 1.56 percent, the TD-24 pulled 23,416 lbs. Test H, the 10-hour rated drawbar run, was also made in third gear. With an output of 120.72 drawbar hp, a pull of 18,282 lbs. was recorded at 2.48 mph with a slippage of 0.98 percent. Fuel economy came to 12.61 hp-hours per gallon.

Nebraska Test Data

Model: International TD-24
Test No. 630
Date Tested: September 3 to September 14, 1957

From Test H it was revealed that using third gear, and with a rated output of 131.96 drawbar hp, the TD-24 achieved 11.8 hp-hours per gallon of diesel fuel. During this test a pull of 20,767 lbs. was recorded at 2.38 mph with a slippage of 1.18 percent. Weighing 46,375 lbs., the TD-24 made a low-gear maximum pull of 41,130 lbs. at 1.49 mph with a slippage of 4.95 percent, and with a recorded output of 163.27 drawbar hp. This figure peaked at 168.06 in the third-gear maximum load test with a pull of 26,600 lbs. at 2.37 mph and slippage of 1.56 percent. The TD-24 used forward speeds of 1.5, 2, 2.4, 3, 4.1, 5.2, 6, and 7.7 mph. Also featured was an International six-cylinder diesel engine rated at 1,500 rpm, and carrying a 5 3/4 x 7-inch bore and stroke for a displacement of 1,091-cubic inches. No repairs or adjustments were noted during 31-1/2 hours of operating time.

International TD-25 crawler

Nebraska Test Data

Model: International TD-25 Diesel
Test No. 752
Date Tested: August 6 to August 17, 1960

Weighing 52,495 lbs., the TD-25 made a low gear maximum pull of 47,244 lbs. at 1.47 mph with 6.53 percent slippage. This gave a maximum low-gear drawbar output of 184.68 hp. The TD-25 was equipped with a synchro-mesh selective-gear fixed-ratio transmission with eight forward speeds ranging from 1.5 to 7.7 mph. Using third gear, a two-hour fuel consumption run at 186.85 maximum available hp yielded a pull of 30,049 lbs. at 2.33 mph with 2.52 percent slippage. Fuel economy was 14.21 hp-hours per gallon. A 10-hour run, made in third gear, but at 75 percent pull, registered an economy figure of 13.43. This test, made with an output of 151.87 hp, elicited a pull of 22,749 lbs. at 2.5 mph with 1.34 percent slippage. Harvester equipped this tractor with a six-cylinder turbocharged engine rated at 1,500 rpm. Using a 5-3/8 x 6-inch bore and stroke, it had an 817-cubic inch displacment. Also featured was a 24-volt electric starting system. During 41-1/2 hours of operation no repairs or adjustments were noted.

International TD-340 crawler

Nebraska Test Data

Model: International TD-340 Diesel
Test No. 776
Date Tested: October 29 to November 2, 1960

Weighing 7,135 lbs. this crawler tractor made a low-gear maximum pull of 6,801 lbs., and traveled 1.43 mph with 6.71 percent slippage. The TD-340 was equipped with a selective-gear fixed-ratio transmission capable of five forward speeds ranging from 1.46 to 5.83 mph. Using second gear, a two-hour fuel economy run recorded 31.64 drawbar hp, plus a pull of 5,592 lbs. at 2.12 mph and 4.97 percent slippage. This run resulted in a fuel economy of 11.06 hp-hours per gallon. A slightly higher figure of 11.22 was noted in the 10-hour drawbar fuel economy run. This test, also made in second gear, but at 75 percent pull, noted an output of 25.6 hp, a pull of 4,260 lbs. at 2.25 mph and 3.56 percent slippage. The TD-340 was equipped with an International four-cylinder diesel engine rated at 2,000 rpm. Its 3-11/16 x 3-7/8- inch bore and stroke gave a 166-cubic inch displacement. No repairs or adjustments were reported during 41 hours of running time. At rated engine speed a maximum of 39.8 PTO hp was observed, with 13.1 hp-hours per gallon. Using 540 rpm at the PTO shaft and a corresponding crankshaft speed of 1,775 rpm, an output of 36.15 PTO hp was observed, with 13.17 hp-hours per gallon.

Interstate Engine & Tractor Company

WATERLOO, IOWA

In 1915 the Board of Directors for Sandy McManus Inc. of Waterloo opted for a more conservative approach. The company was reorganized as Interstate Engine & Tractor Company, and started building tractors. By 1919 the financially-troubled company was reorganized as the Plow Man Tractor Company, but the latter firm remained in business for only a short time.

Plow Boy 10-20 tractor

One of the new tractor models from this firm was the Plow Boy 10-20 tractor. It was equipped with a Waukesha four-cylinder engine with a 3-1/2 x 5-1/4-inch bore and stroke. The tractor retailed for $675.

Plow Man "30"

The Plow Man "30" from Interstate was also rated at 13 drawbar hp and about 1916 it was given a 15-30 hp rating. Power came from a Buda four-cylinder engine with a 4-1/4 x 5-1/2-inch bore and stroke.

Iron Horse Tractor Company

KANSAS CITY, MISSOURI

See: Sweeney Tractor Company

Iron Horse Tractor Company

MINNEAPOLIS, MINNESOTA

This company was organized in 1916, with one of its principals having been formerly associated with the Lion Tractor Company, also of Minneapolis. No further information has been found, leading to the conclusion that the company never materialized except perhaps for a prototype model.

Iron Horse Sales Company

LOS ANGELES, CALIFORNIA

Iron Horse

The small Iron Horse tractor emerged from this firm in 1920. Aside from a single advertisement, no other information has emerged. From all appearances, the engine was something less than 10 hp.

Isaacson Iron Works

SEATTLE, WASHINGTON

FARM DOZER

"Farm Dozer" trademark

In 1940 this firm applied for protection of its "Farm Dozer" trademark, claiming first use of the mark in November 1939. Aside from this, no other information has emerged on the company or its tractors.

[Throughout this section, assume that gasoline was used for fuel unless another fuel source is indicated.]

W. S. Jardine

OMAHA, NEBRASKA

Van Nostrand Rotary Plow

In 1913 Jardine announced the Van Nostrand Rotary Plow. The large drum was adorned with curved spikes, similar to a machine from Allis-Chalmers. Little is known about the Van Nostrand and it does not appear that it was ever put into production, except for a few prototypes.

Jenson Mfg. Company

ALHAMBRA, CALIFORNIA

Farmaster 150 tractor

In 1948 the Jenson and J. M. C. garden tractors were listed in some farm directories, although no illustrations of these models have been found. A 1955 directory illustrated the Farmaster 150 tractor from Jenson located at Burbank, California. The Farmaster 150 was equipped with a two-cylinder Wisconsin Model TFU engine and with a total displacement of 54-cubic inches.

Jewell Tractor & Truck Company

BOSTON, MASSACHUSETTS

This company appeared as a tractor builder in a 1918 trade directory, but no other information has been found.

Jiffy Till

LA MESA, CALIFORNIA

Magic Hoe

In 1950 and 1951 the Magic Hoe appeared from Jiffy Till. This was a dedicated design and does not appear to have been a multiple-use tractor. The Magic Hoe is shown here and it used a 2-1/2 hp Briggs & Stratton engine. The Model 2A was equipped with a 5 hp Clinton engine; a larger 3B model was built with an 8-1/4 hp motor.

COLLECTOR VALUES	1	2	3	4
MAGIC HOE	$375	$250	$125	$50

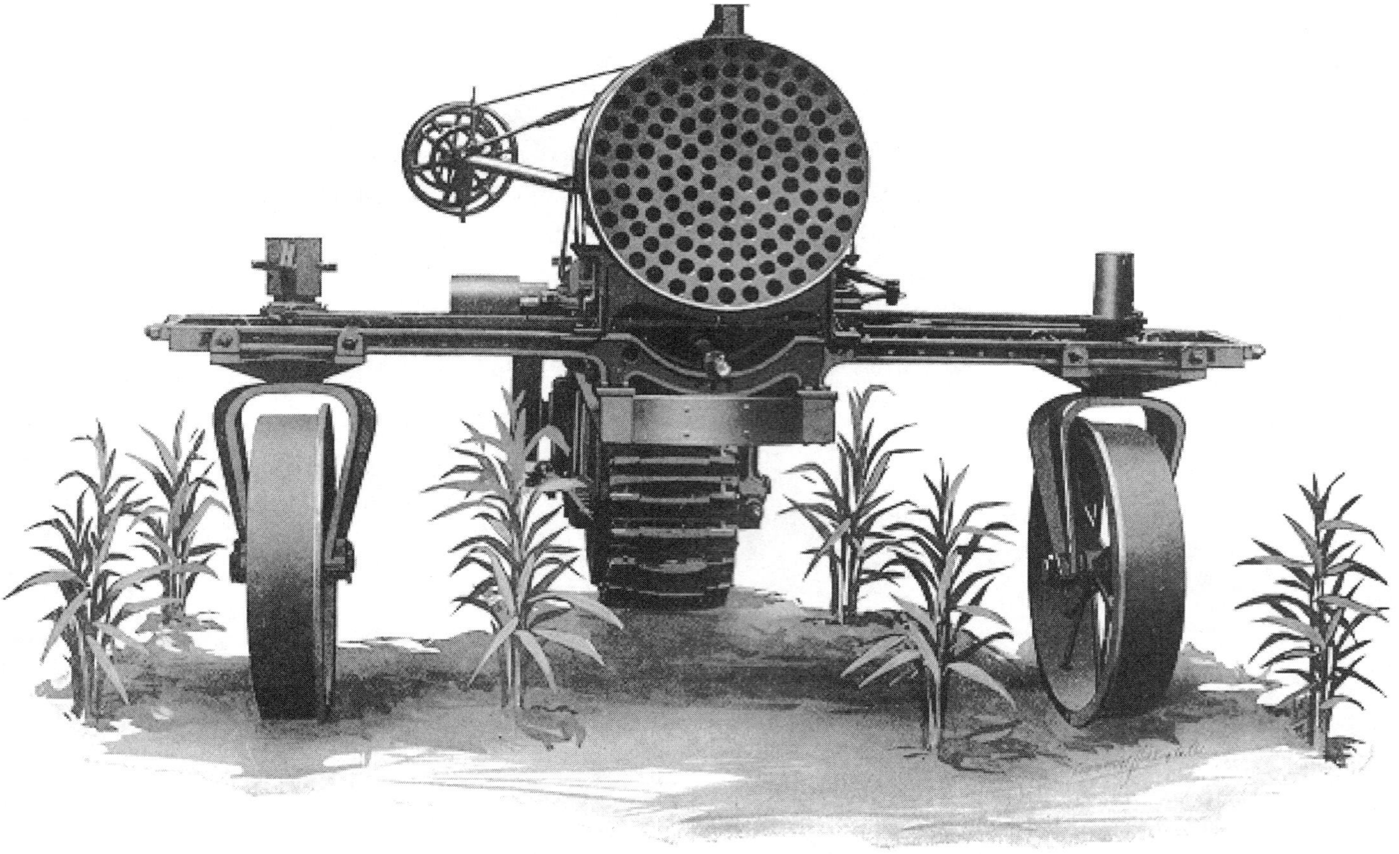

Steel Mule tractor

Johnson Farm Equipment Company

STREATOR, ILLINOIS

This firm was listed as the manufacturer of the Johnson garden tractors in the 1948 through 1953 period, but no other information has been located.

Joliet Oil Tractor Company

JOLIET, ILLINOIS

See: Bates Machine & Tractor Company

Joliet introduced its first tractor late in 1913. By June of the following year the company had adopted the "Steel Mule" trademark.

Rated at 13 drawbar and 30 belt hp, the Steel Mule carried a four-cylinder engine with a 4 x 6-inch bore and stroke. It weighed 5,800 lbs and had two forward speeds. The single rear crawler track was 15 inches wide. Production of the Steel Mule continued into the 1919 merger of Joliet with the Bates Tractor Company.

In 1914 Joliet introduced its 22-40 wheel tractor. Although no specifications have been found, the 22-40 was equipped with a four-cylinder engine. This was a unique design, with both axles spring mounted, much like a large truck. It was also unique with its top road speed of 10 mph, unusually fast for its time. Production of the 22-40 continued for only a short time.

Joliet 22-40 wheel tractor

Jones Mfg. Company

COLBY, KANSAS

Jones Mfg. Company was organized in 1909 and built the first Colby Plow Boy tractor that year. Several were

Colby Plow Boy tractor

built and sold during 1910, and the design gained the attention of the farm press that year. For reasons unknown, nothing more was heard from the company after that time. Little is known of the tractor specifications except it carried a big four-cylinder engine capable of 30 drawbar hp. Designed specifically for drawbar work, the Colby Plow Boy was double-geared.

Joy-McVicker Company

MINNEAPOLIS, MINNESOTA

See: McVicker Engineering Company

J-T Tractor Company

CLEVELAND, OHIO

Tracing the history of this company is difficult, because the only information that has been found consists of magazine advertisements. The firm first used its "J-T" trademark in December 1917, about the same time it introduced its first crawler tractor.

J-T 16-30 crawler

The 16-30 crawler was J-T's first tractor and was introduced in about 1917. Weighing 7,000 lbs, the 16-30 used a four-cylinder Chief engine.

J-T crawler 16-32

By the early 1920s the J-T crawler tractor had been upgraded slightly to a 16-32. It also showed evidence of a redesigned hood and radiator, along with a front-mounted belt pulley. Three large carrier rollers were used on each side and apparently no top roller was needed.

J-T crawler, 1925 model

In 1925 the J-T crawler was again modified. A fully hooded engine was now used, along with protection for the bottom track rollers. The engine was now a Model KU Climax with four cylinders and a 5 x 6-1/2-inch bore and stroke. The J-T tractors disappeared from the directories after 1930.

Jumbo Steel Products

AZUSA, CALIFORNIA

Jumbo Steel Products tractor

By late 1947 this tractor was available from Jumbo Steel Products. It used a 217-cid Chrysler six-cylinder engine. Five forward speeds were available, ranging from 5 to 20 mph. Very little information has been found on this tractor, and presumably, it was built for only a short time.

[Throughout this section, assume that gasoline was used for fuel unless another fuel source is indicated.]

Kanawaha Mfg. Company

CHARLESTON, WEST VIRGINIA

Aside from the test shown here, little is known about this firm or its products.

Nebraska Test Data

Model: Scott Six

Test No. 178

Date Tested: June 16 to June 19, 1930

After completing 9 hours and 25 minutes of the preliminary test, the Scott Six was withdrawn. A copy of the original log sheet indicated overheating was a continuous problem. The log sheet also commented, "Runs made while checking motor performance. Checked by Durant mechanic." The significance of this comment is unknown, but possibly there was a connection with Durant Motors, a firm which was attempting to reestablish itself in the automobile business at the time.

Kansas City Hay Press Company

KANSAS CITY, MISSOURI

Kansas City Hay Press Company moved into the tractor market with the 1908 K-C Traction Gasoline Engine. In 1919 the company name was changed to Kansas City Hay Press & Tractor Company, reflecting a push in the tractor market with its Prairie Dog Model L. The company disappeared from the tractor trade directories by 1922. No Kansas City Hay Press Tractors are known to exist today.

The K-C Gasoline Traction engine used the K-C Lightning gasoline engine, already in production. This unique engine used opposed pistons. While one piston was connected to the crankshaft in the usual manner, the other was connected by extended rods to a pair of outer cranks. Production lasted only a short time.

K.C. Prairie Dog

The K.C. Prairie Dog made its appearance about 1914 or 1915. This tractor used a single rear drive wheel. Power came from a Waukesha four-cylinder engine with a 4-1/4 x

K-C Gasoline Traction Engine

5-inch bore and stroke. This gave the tractor a rating of 12 drawbar and 25 belt hp. This model remained in production until about 1917.

Prairie Dog Model L 9-18 tractor

Production of the Prairie Dog Model L 9-18 tractor began in 1917 and continued until 1920. The 9-18 used a four-cylinder Waukesha engine with a 3-3/4 x 5-1/4-inch bore and stroke and was rerated as a 10-18 model in 1920.

15-30 Model D Prairie Dog tractor

In 1920 Kansas City Hay Press announced its new 15-30 Model D Prairie Dog tractor, built with a Waukesha four-cylinder engine with a 4-1/2 x 6-1/4-inch bore and stroke. This model was built for only about one year.

Kansas Mfg. Company

WICHITA, KANSAS

This company was incorporated in 1913, ostensibly to build tractors, but no other information has been found.

Kardell Truck & Tractor Company

ST. LOUIS, MISSOURI

In 1917 Kardell announced its Four-in-One tractor. The company remained in the tractor business until about 1921 when it was bought out by Oldsmar Tractor Company of Oldsmar, Florida.

Four-in-One tractor

Shown here as a motor plow, the Four-in-One tractor could also be used for other farming operations. In addition, a separate chassis was available whereby it could be converted to a truck if desired. This tractor used a four-cylinder Waukesha engine with a 4-1/2 x 5-3/4-inch bore and stroke. Weighing some 5,100 lbs. the 20-32 retailed at $1,600. Production continued into 1918 or perhaps slightly later.

Kardell Utility tractor

About 1918 the Kardell Utility tractor with an 8-16 hp rating appeared. By the following year it was rerated as a 10-20 tractor. A Wisconsin four-cylinder engine was used and it had a 4 x 5-inch bore and stroke.

Kaws Tractor Company

INDIANAPOLIS, INDIANA

This firm was incorporated in 1919 to build tractors, but no other information has been found.

Kaywood Corporation

BENTON HARBOR, MICHIGAN

Kaywood Model D tractors first appeared in the 1936 tractor directories, and the company was listed as a tractor manufacturer until 1946. This model weighed in at 3,000 lbs. and was equipped with a four-cylinder Hercules IXB engine. It had a 3-1/4 x 4-inch bore and stroke. Little other information has been found on the Kaywood tractors.

Kaywood Model D tractors

COLLECTOR VALUES	1	2	3	4
MODEL D	–	–	$9,750	–

Horace Keane Aeroplanes Inc.

NEW YORK, NEW YORK

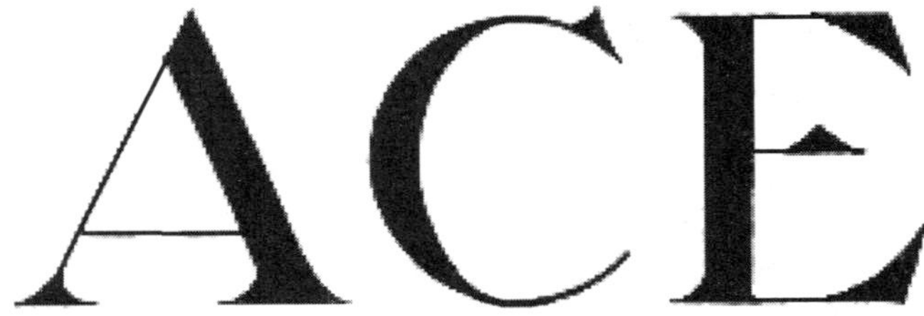

"Ace" trademark

In November 1920 this company filed the "Ace" trademark shown here, claiming first use of the mark a year earlier, as applied to tractors. No further information was found.

Keck-Gonnerman Company

MT. VERNON, INDIANA

Keck-Gonnerman Company began business in 1873 as a steam engine and thresher manufacturer. In 1917 the company entered the tractor business with its 12-24 model, and continued building tractors for more than two decades. Full production of the K-G tractors was suspended during World War II. A single model was offered in 1946, but that appeared to be the end of the line.

Keck-Gonnerman 12-24 tractor

The 12-24 used a two-cylinder engine with a 6-1/2 x 8-inch bore and stroke. This model was modified in 1920 with the use of a larger 7-1/4 x 8-inch engine and a new 15-30 power rating. Production of this tractor continued into the late 1920s.

K-G 18-35 tractor

In 1928 Keck-Gonnerman introduced its K-G 18-35 tractor. This model used a Buda four-cylinder engine with a 4-1/2 x 6-inch bore and stroke. This tractor has a remarkable resemblance to the Rock Island 18-35 introduced about the same time, and used the same Buda four-cylinder engine. Curiously, Keck-Gonnerman increased the engine bore to 4-3/4 inches by 1931, keeping this new size until 1935.

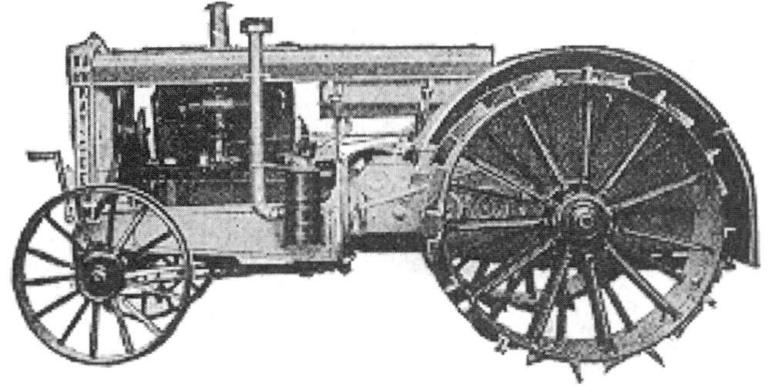

K-G 25-50 tractor

Kenison 12-24 tractor

Introduced in 1928, the K-G 25-50 tractor remained in production into the early 1930s. This 9,800-lb. tractor retailed for $2,850. Originally sold as a 22-45 tractor, it carried a LeRoi four-cylinder engine with a 5-1/4 x 7-inch bore and stroke.

K-G 30-60 tractor

Rounding out the 1928 Keck-Gonnerman line was the big 30-60 tractor. Originally billed as a 27-55, this model used a four-cylinder LeRoi engine with a 5-1/2 x 7-inch bore and stroke. Active production of the 30-60 continued until the late 1930s, and it is possible a few were built after that time.

18-36 tractor

In 1946 the Keck-Gonnerman tractors were listed for the last time. Back in 1935 the 18-35 was revamped to include a four-cylinder Waukesha engine with a 5-1/8 x 6-1/4-inch bore and stroke. It also had four forward speeds of 2, 4, 7, and 10 mph.

Kenison Mfg. Company

SOLOMON, KANSAS

Kenison advertised its 12-24 tractor for a brief period in 1919. Aside from this, no other information has surfaced on the company or the tractor. It is shown here at a plowing demonstration, but even the location of this event is unknown.

Kenney-Colwell Tractor Company

NORFOLK, NEBRASKA

See: Square Turn Tractor Company

In 1913 A. J. Colwell patented a tractor and joined with Albert Kenney to build it. Efforts continued until 1916 when Albaugh-Dover Company, Chicago, Illinois bought the firm. The company then continued at Norfolk as the Square Turn Tractor Company; see this heading for more information.

Keystone Iron & Steel Works

LOS ANGELES, CALIFORNIA

Keystone offered its crawler tractor in the 1920 through 1925 era. The unique track design used two idlers with a

"Strait's Tractor"

large drive sprocket in the center. The latter also served as a track carrier. A Waukesha four-cylinder engine was used for power and was built with a 5 x 6-1/2-inch bore and stroke.

Keystone crawler tractor

Keystone Model 30

By 1923 the Keystone Model 30 had gained a 20-35 hp rating, although the engine remained essentially the same. In addition, the fenders and hood saw a slight redesign. After 1924 the Keystone slips from view.

Killen-Strait Mfg. Company

Killen-Walsh Mfg. Company

APPLETON, WISCONSIN

In 1913 Killen-Walsh Mfg. Company was organized to build "Strait's Tractor." The company name was changed to Killen-Strait in 1914. The company survived until 1917, or a short time longer.

This tractor initially had a rating of 40 brake hp, but soon became the 30-50 model. "Strait's Tractor" was equipped with a four-cylinder Doman engine with a 6 x 7-inch bore and stroke.

Shortly after the 1914 name change to Killen-Strait Company, the Model 3 15-30 tractor appeared. This model was nearly identical in appearance to the larger size, but used a four-cylinder, 30-hp engine with a 4-1/2 x 5-3/4-inch bore and stroke.

Model 3 15-30 tractor

Kimble & Dentler Company

VICKSBURG, MICHIGAN

Kimble & Dentler tractor

In 1913 Kimble & Dentler attempted to enter the tractor business with a 40-hp model. It had several unique features, including a specially designed front axle that permitted short turns. The tractor venture appears to have gone no further than the prototype stage. Kimble & Dentler was a scion of Dentler Bagger Company. The latter had a long career manufacturing tally boxes and other thresher accessories.

King-Wyse Inc.

ARCHBOLD, OHIO

King-Wyse garden tractor

In 1950 and '51 the King-Wyse garden tractor was advertised. It used either a Clinton or a Wisconsin air-cooled single-cylinder engine of about 4-1/2 hp. Little other information has been found.

COLLECTOR VALUES	1	2	3	4
KING-WYSE GARDEN TRACTOR	$350	$225	$125	$50

Kinkead Tractor Company

MINNEAPOLIS, MINNESOTA

Kinkead tractor

Production of the Kinkead tractor began in April 1915. Production ended when R. S. Kinkead, the moving force in the company, was drafted into the military during World War I. The Kinkead was of three-wheel design and used a single drivewheel in the rear. It was equipped with a four-cylinder crossmounted engine with a 4-1/4 x 5-3/4-inch bore and stroke. It was rated at 12 drawbar and 25 belt hp. Operating weight was 5,000 lbs.

Kinnard & Sons Mfg. Company

Kinnard-Haines Company

MINNEAPOLIS, MINNESOTA

This company had a long history going back to 1882 as the Kinnard Press Company. At that time the primary product was a hay press.The first Flour City Gasoline Traction Engine was built in 1900. Kinnard Press Company built its first gasoline engine in 1896. In 1918 the company name was changed to Kinnard & Sons Mfg. Company.

Flour City Gasoline Traction Engine

Through 1907 the Flour City tractors were of this general design, adapting the company's own stationary engines to the tractor chassis.

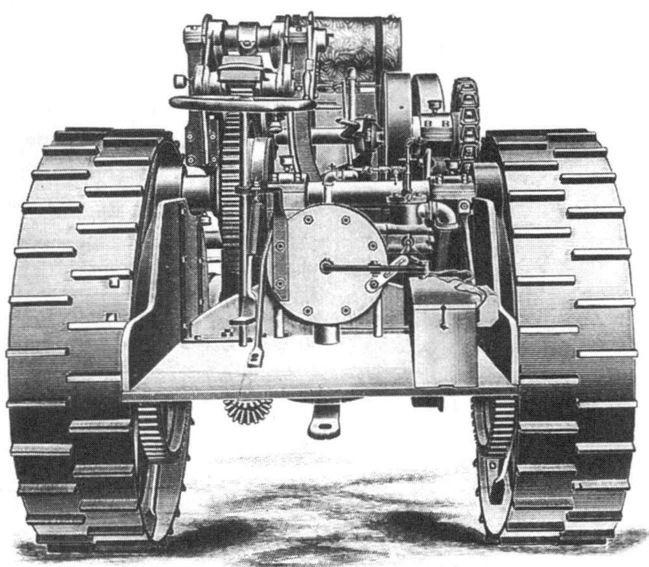

Flour City tractor

A platform view showed the first design of the Flour City tractors. They were built in 8, 12, and 16 hp sizes with a single-cylinder engine. They were also available in 20 and 25 hp models using a two-cylinder engine. The 8 hp model weighed 5,500 lbs, while the 25 hp size weighed 15,000 lbs.

Kinnard-Haines tractor

In 1908 an entirely new tractor design was unveiled. Rated at 30 drawbar hp, it used the company's own four-cylinder engine and had a 6-1/4 x 7-inch bore and stroke. Ground speed was 2-1/2 mph. Production of this model continued until about 1910.

Flour City 40-70 tractor

The Flour City 40-70 emerged in 1911, and remained available until 1927. Weighing about 21,000 lbs, the 40-70 used a four-cylinder engine with a 7-1/2 x 9-inch bore and stroke.

Kinnard-Haines 40-70 Flour City

Nebraska Test Data

Model: Flour City 40-70
Test No. 52
Date Tested: August 1920

Although two forward speeds were provided in the Flour City 40-70, it made little difference, since low gear moved along at 2 mph, with high gear being only one-half mile an hour faster. It took a long while to get from one place to another. Kinnard's own four-cylinder vertical, valve-in-head engine was featured and it used a 7 1/2 x 9-inch bore and stroke. Rated speed was 575 rpm. Included as standard equipment on this 21,000 lb. unit were a Schebler Model A carburetor and K-W magneto. Throughout the entire test run, kerosene was used for fuel. At rated load, 70.81 brake hp was noted, with fuel consumption of 9.35 gph and a fuel economy of 7.57 hp-hours per gallon. Only few more hp was derived in the maximum load test, so reserve power was virtually nonexistent. Slightly over 8,400 lbs. was recorded as the maximum drawbar pull, resulting in a recorded value of 52.84 maximum drawbar hp. Coolant temperatures varied from 173 to 212 degrees F. throughout the test. Ambient air temperatures ranged from 77 to 95 degrees F.

COLLECTOR VALUES	1	2	3	4
FLOUR CITY 40-70	$110,000	$85,000	$60,000	$25,000

Flour City Junior tractor

The Flour City Junior was announced at the same time as the 40-70. This model used a two-cylinder engine that was apparently of the same dimensions as the larger four-cylinder size. The Flour City Junior remained in the line until 1919 when it was replaced with an improved version.

Flour City 20-35 tractor

A four-cylinder engine with a 5-1/4 x 6-inch bore and stroke powered the Flour City 20-35 tractor. Introduced in 1911, it remained in the line until 1927. Total weight of this tractor was about 10,000 lbs.

Nebraska Test Data

Model: Flour City 18-35
Test No. 50
Date Tested: August 9 to August 25, 1920

Featuring the company's own four-cylinder, vertical, valve-in-head engine, the 18-35 made it through 30 hours of running time without major difficulties. Problems occured with the countershaft bearing, a result of improper lubrication. Spark plug fouling was also a problem, and several plugs were replaced during the test. Using a 5-1/2 x 6-inch bore and stroke, the 18-35 was rated at 800 rpm. Provided were two forward speeds of 2-1/4 and 3 mph. Total weight was 10,000 lbs. A Schebler Model A carburetor and K-W Model TK magneto came as standard equipment. Kerosene was used throughout the test. Virtually no reserve power was demonstrated on the brake hp test. At rated load, 35.23 hp was developed—and it was only fractionally higher on the maximum load test. At rated load, an economy of 7.68 hp hours per gallon resulted, with fuel consumption totaling 4.59 gallons per hour (gph). A similar situation occurred on the drawbar test—19.51 maximum drawbar hp was recorded, only 1.5 hp above the nominal rating. A maximum drawbar pull of 4,116 lbs. was recorded at 1.71 mph.

COLLECTOR VALUES	1	2	3	4
FLOUR CITY 20-35	--	$55,000	--	--

Flour City 30-50 tractor

Three sizes of Flour City tractors were introduced in 1911 and continued to be available until 1927. They were the 40-70, the 20-35, and the 30-50 shown here. This model was equipped with a four-cylinder engine with a 6-1/4 x 7-inch bore and stroke. Rated speed was 800 rpm. All three models used engines built by Kinnard-Haines Company, later known as Kinnard & Sons Mfg. Company.

Flour City Junior 14-24 tractor

The Flour City Junior was a two-cylinder tractor built until 1919. At that point it was replaced with the Flour City Junior 14-24 tractor. The latter was built with a four-cylinder engine with a 5-inch bore and stroke. This tractor weighed 6,700 lbs. It remained in the Flour City line until 1927.

Kinnard Four-Plow Tractor

In 1915 the Kinnard Four-Plow Tractor was introduced, and was offered through 1917. It used two drivewheels with a narrow space between, and was essentially a three-wheel tractor—though four were on the ground.

Kinnard 15-25 tractor

The Kinnard 15-25 tractor was built for only a short time. It used a four-cylinder 5 x 5-inch engine as did the Flour City Junior of 1919. Kinnard four-cylinder engines used a two-piece crankshaft coupled in the center—the obvious space between the two sets of engine cylinders.

Klumb Engine & Machine Company

SHEBOYGAN, WISCONSIN

Klumb 10-20 Model C tractor

In 1918 Klumb offered its 10-20 Model C tractor. It used a two-cylinder opposed engine with a 6 x 6-1/2-inch bore and stroke. Total weight of this tractor was 4,000 lbs. The firm was organized in 1913, and was incorporated in 1916. By June 1919, it moved to Dubuque, Iowa, and reorganized as Liberty Tractor Company. The firm again reorganized as Dubuque Truck & Tractor Company. The latter firm remained in the tractor business for only a short time.

W. Chandler Knapp

ROCHESTER, NEW YORK

Knapp's Farm Locomotive

By the time this 1912 model of Knapp's Farm Locomotive appeared, Knapp had built tractors for several years. This one, with a single rear drivewheel, typified the Knapp design. By 1917 the Gray Tractor Company was organized at Minneapolis, Minnesota, to build a tractor that closely followed the design shown here. The Gray Tractor Company continued in business for several years.

See: Gray Tractor Company

Knickerbocker Motors Inc.

POUGHKEEPSIE, NEW YORK

Kingwood Model 5-10 tractor

Knickerbocker Motors began building a tractor conversion outfit already in 1909. In 1917 the company started building its Kingwood Model 5-10 tractor. It used a LeRoi four-cylinder engine with a 3-1/8 x 4-1/2-inch bore and stroke. Numerous attachments were available so that the tractor could be driven from various implements. The Kingwood tractor disappeared from the market after 1920.

Wm. Knudsen

FREMONT, NEBRASKA

The Knudsen tractor of 1920 carried a 25-40 hp rating and used a four-cylinder engine with a 5 x 9- inch bore and stroke. The engine was of Knudsen's design and manufacture. For reasons unknown, this tractor was advertised for only a short time, and apparently only a few were built.

Kohl Tractor Company

CLEVELAND, OHIO

The Power Wagon Reference Book of 1919 listed this firm as the manufacturer of the Kohl 17-35 tractor. No other information has been found.

Kreider Machine Company

LANCASTER, PENNSYLVANIA

Lancaster Traction Engine

Knudsen 25-40 tractor

Kreider Machine Co. advertised its 1907 Lancaster Traction Engine for $150. It consisted of a small engine mounted on a suitable chassis, and was able to pass through a door or gate only 31 inches wide. It is listed in various directories as late as 1911. No other information has been found.

Kroyer Motors Company

SAN PEDRO, CALIFORNIA

The Wizard 4-Pull tractor made its debut in 1919. Of four-wheel-drive design, it was steered by clutches on each side of the machine, much like today's skid-steer loaders. Wizard Tractor Corporation, Los Angeles, California acquired the 4-Pull in 1924.

See: Wizard Tractor Corporation

Wizard 4-Pull tractor

Kuhnert & Ryde Utility tractor

Kruger Mfg. Company

MARSHALLTOWN, IOWA

In the 1946 through 1953 period, the Superior garden tractors from Kruger were listed in various directories, but no other information has been found.

L. C. Kuhnert & Company

Kuhnert & Ryde Company

CHICAGO, ILLINOIS

L. C. Kuhnert & Company was organized in 1913 to build Kuhnert's Vanadiumized Tractor. The fancy title was a reference to the fairly recent discovery of vanadiumized steel which was a new high-strength alloy. In 1915 the company changed its name to Kuhnert & Ryde Company. Kuhnert tractors disappeared from the market by 1920.

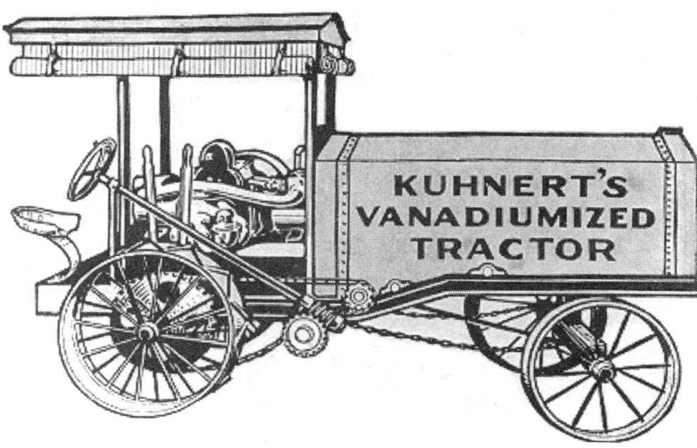

Kuhnert's Vanadiumized Tractor

The company advertised this small tractor as the "Lightest Weight [and] lowest price per horse power in the world." It was also sold on a free trial basis direct from the manufacturer.

The company's 1916 catalog showed the Utility tractor. It used a four-cylinder engine with a 4-1/2 x 6-3/4- inch bore and stroke. Its total weight was 5,500 lbs. The tractor was not rated in the conventional manner but was said to have a pull "equal to 8 to 10 horses."

Kultor King Mfg. Company

PORTLAND, OREGON

This company is listed in the 1946 through 1948 period as building the Kultor King garden tractor, but no illustrations or specifications have been located.

COLLECTOR VALUES	1	2	3	4
KULTOR KING	$750	$600	$400	$200

Kut-Kwick Tool Corporation

BRUNSWICK, GEORGIA

Kut-Kwick J-5 garden tractor

In 1951 the Kut-Kwick J-5 garden tractor appeared. It was powered by a Wisconsin AKN single-cylinder, air-cooled engine capable of about 5-1/2 hp. Numerous attachments were available, ranging from various kinds of plows and cultivators to a hay rake and a sprayer.

COLLECTOR VALUES	1	2	3	4
KUT-KWICK J-5	$350	$250	$150	$75

[Throughout this section, assume that gasoline was used for fuel unless another fuel source is indicated.]

L.A. Auto Tractor Company

LOS ANGELES, CALIFORNIA

About 1919 the Little Bear tractor appeared. It was largely built from Ford Model T parts, including the steering wheel. Weighing only 1,600 lbs., it was designed as a low-priced unit, and given the ample supply of Model T parts then available, servicing should never have presented a problem. Production continued until about 1921.

La Crosse Boiler Company

LA CROSSE, WISCONSIN

See: Fairbanks-Morse and Townsend

La Crosse Boiler Company acquired the Townsend Tractor Company in 1931. La Crosse continued building this 12-25 model until about 1939. It was a two-cylinder model using a 6 x 8-inch bore and stroke. By 1935, electric starting and lighting equipment was an extra-cost option.

Model 12-25

Townsend 20-40 tractor

The earlierTownsend 20-40 tractor became the La Crosse 20-40 after 1931. This model carried a two-cylinder engine with a 7-1/2 x 9-inch bore and stroke. Engine speed ranged from 400 to 480 rpm.

Little Bear

La Crosse 30-60 tractor

A two-cylinder engine with a 9-1/2 x 12-inch bore and stroke was used in the La Crosse 30-60 tractor. This model had a speed range of 375 to 450 rpm, for a ground speed of 2 to 2-1/4 mph. La Crosse continued building these tractors until 1939 or 1940. Production was halted by World War II, if not sooner.

La Crosse Tractor Company

LA CROSSE, WISCONSIN

Late in 1916, the La Crosse Tractor Co. was organized, a consolidation of the Happy Farmer Tractor Company of Minneapolis and the Sta-Rite Engine Co. of La Crosse.

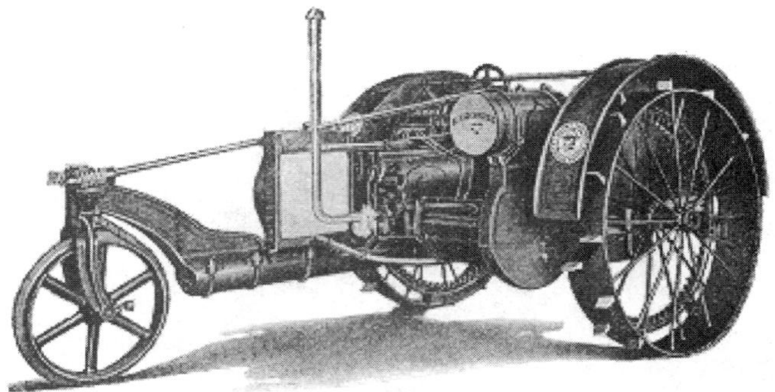

8-16 Model A

Between 1916 and 1918, the company offered the 8-16 Model A and the 12-24 Model B. Both were designed with a two-cylinder engine. The 8-16 had a 5 x 6-1/2-inch bore and stroke.

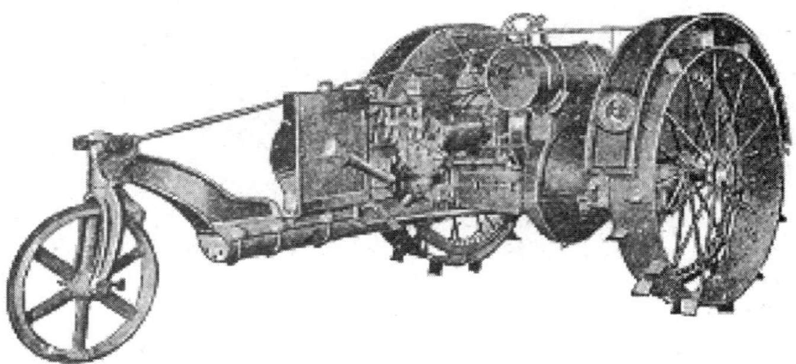

Model F La Crosse-Happy Farmer tractor

Model F La Crosse-Happy Farmer tractors were built in the 1918 to 1920 period. The Model F used a single front wheel as formerly, and carried a two-cylinder engine with a 5-3/4 x 7-inch bore and stroke. Weighing 3,800 lbs., it was priced at $975. It offered only a single speed forward and reverse of 2-1/2 mph.

COLLECTOR VALUES	1	2	3	4
MODEL F	$17,000	$12,000	–	–

Model G 12-24 tractor

The Model G 12-24 tractor was built in the same time frame as the Model F. The only difference between them was the Model G used a conventional four-wheel chassis, while the Model F was a three-wheel design. Both could be equipped in the field with a line drive system to permit operation of the tractor from a wagon, a grain binder or other attached implement.

Nebraska Test Data

Model: La Crosse Model G 12-24

Test No. 29

Date Tested: August 2 to August 5, 1920

Featuring an Atwater-Kent K-3 magneto and dry battery system, the La Crosse was among the first tractors tested at Nebraska to use some automotive industry technology. Another feature was a Stromberg Model MB-3 carburetor, although the tractor was not originally shipped to Nebraska with this style. This model had the distinctive feature of being the only unit ever tested at Nebraska as a "linedrive" tractor. It was operated with line drive control and equipped with four lines: two for guiding, one for starting and one for stopping. Upon completion of the tests, Nebraska's engineers said that a careful operator could safely use the line drive control. On the rated load test, 24.23 brake hp was developed with an economy rating of 6.56 hp-hours per gallon of kerosene fuel, and a total consumption of 3.69 gallons per hour (gph). Throughout the brake and drawbar tests, coolant temperatures varied from 170 to 201 degrees F. A maximum pull of 2,155 lbs. was achieved on the drawbar with a ground speed of 3.1 mph, for a maximum of 17.83 drawbar hp. Specifications included a two-cylinder horizontal, valve-in-head engine rated at 900 rpm and carrying a 6 x 7-inch bore and stroke. Shipping weight was 4,670 lbs.

COLLECTOR VALUES	1	2	3	4
MODEL G	$16,000	$11,000	–	–

Model M, 7-12 line drive tractor

In 1921 La Crosse brought out its Model M, 7-12 line drive tractor. In 1921 it sold for $900, but a year later the price had dropped to $650. Concurrently the company produced the Model H, 12-24 tractor. It was an upgraded version of the earlier Model G. Oshkosh Tractor Co. purchased the assets of the tractor division in 1921, and planned to move the factory to Oshkosh, Wisconsin. The plan fell through in 1922 and La Crosse announced they would continue building the tractor. These plans never materialized.

COLLECTOR VALUES	1	2	3	4
MODEL M 7-12	$20,000	–	–	–

Lambert Gas Engine Company

ANDERSON, INDIANA

Lambert was an early gasoline engine builder with a career going back to 1890. Apparently, the company already had built a tractor in 1894, but it was not a commercial success. About 1904, the firm began mounting its engines on the Morton traction trucks and sold these tractors on a regular basis for a number of years.

Lambert Steel Hoof tractor

The Lambert Steel Hoof tractor emerged in 1912. It had a unique drivewheel design with retractable pads that functioned much like a horse's hoof. No specifications have been found for this tractor. It was produced until about 1916 when the company was taken over by Buckeye Mfg. Company.

Lambert tractor

Lang tractor

Lambert Mfg. Company

LOS ANGELES, CALIFORNIA

This company is listed as a tractor manufacturer in 1914, and probably before. No other information has been found.

Lamson Truck & Tractor Company

WAUSAU, WISCONSIN

From various sources it is learned that this company was organized in 1917 to manufacture tractors, but no other information has been located.

Lang Tractor Company

MINNEAPOLIS, MINNESOTA

The Lang tractor made its appearance in 1917. This design used a four-cylinder Waukesha engine with a 4-1/4 x 5-3/4-inch bore and stroke. It featured two forward speeds of 2-1/2 and 5 mph. While the company made a serious effort to become a force in the tractor business, it appeared they left the market by 1920.

Lapeer Tractor Company

LAPEER, MICHIGAN

Lapeer Tractor Co. was organized in 1917, with plans to begin tractor production by July 1918. After the initial announcement, nothing further was heard of the company.

Homer Laughlin Engineers Corporation

LOS ANGELES, CALIFORNIA

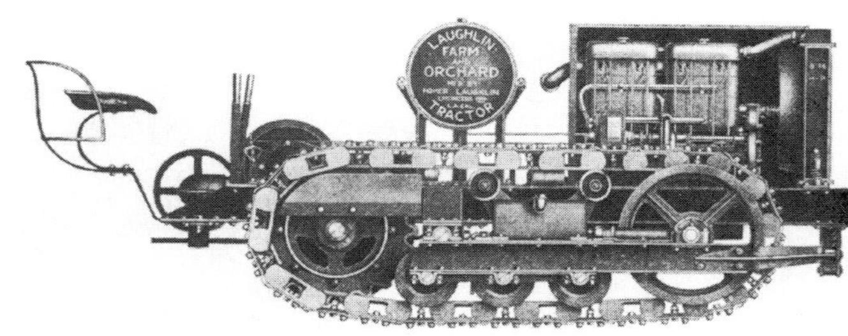

Laughlin Little Husky tractor

In 1919 the Laughlin Little Husky tractor appeared. It was also sold as the Laughlin Farm & Orchard Tractor. Originally it carried an 8-16 hp rating, but by 1920 it was being sold as a 10-20 model. The company used its own four-cylinder engine with a 4-3/8 x 5-1/2-inch bore and stroke. Total weight was 6,000 lbs. The Laughlin disappeared from the directories in the early 1920s.

Laughlin Tractor Company

MARSHALL, TEXAS

The Laughlin Row Crop appeared in the 1948 tractor directories. This was apparently the only model. It used a Continental four-cylinder, 162-cid engine with a 3-7/16 x 4-3/8-inch bore and stroke. Four forward speeds were available, ranging from 2-1/2 to 9-3/4 mph.

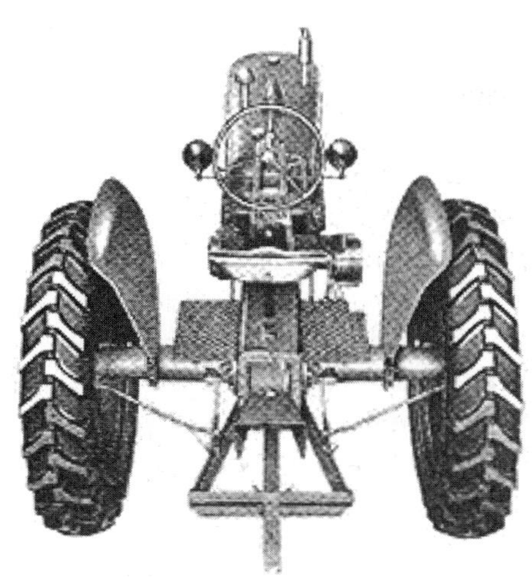

Laughlin Row Crop

Laurel Mfg. Company

DENVER, COLORADO

Laurel Series L tractor

By 1955 the Laurel Series L tractor was on the market. This $700 outfit featured a Briggs & Stratton 23R6 engine and was available with numerous attachments, including a dozer blade and sickle bar mower. The Series L weighed 960 lbs. After 1955 it disappeared from the industry listings.

COLLECTOR VALUES	1	2	3	4
SERIES L	$2,000	$1,500	$1,000	$800

Stephen Laurenchick & Company

TOLEDO, OHIO

In 1953 this firm is listed as the manufacturer of the C-E garden tractor, but no specifications have been found.

See: C-E Tractor Company; Cleveland Engineering Company

C. P. & J. Lauson

MILWAUKEE, WISCONSIN

This famous gasoline engine manufacturer apparently sold gasoline tractors for a time, probably using its own modified engine as the power unit. The company was listed as a tractor manufacturer in trade directories of the 1905 through 1908 period, but in 1908 the company was purchased by Christensen Engineering Company of Milwaukee.

John Lauson Mfg. Company

NEW HOLSTEIN, WISCONSIN

Lauson entered the tractor business in late 1915 offering both a 15-25 and a 20-35. Over the next two decades, the company manufactured a variety of different models.

Lauson 15-25 or 20-35

Lauson tractors disappeared from tractor directories after 1937.

Both the 15-25 and 20-35 tractors had the same external appearance and the chassis was similar for both. The 15-25 used an Erd four-cylinder engine with a 4 x 6-inch bore and stroke, while the 20-35 carried an Erd engine with a 4-3/4 x 6-inch engine.

Lauson 15-25 model

By 1918 the Lauson tractors had lost the operator's cab of the original design. A Beaver engine replaced the Erd motor formerly used in the 15-25 model. It was a four-cylinder design and carried a 4-1/2 x 6-inch bore and stroke. By this time, the "24 Jeweled" tradename had been associated with the Lauson tractors.

In 1919 Lauson upgraded the 15-25 tractor and gave it a new 15-30 rating. This resulted from replacing the earlier 4-1/2 x 6-inch Beaver engine with a 4-3/4 x 6-inch motor. This model weighed 6,500 lbs.

Nebraska Test Data

Model: Lauson 15-30

Test No. 51

Date Tested: August 13 to September 6, 1920

About 31 hours of running time were required to certify the Lauson 15-30 tractor. After about 20 hours of running time, the fuel heating system was changed so the governor would automatically control the hot and cold air. Test documents stipulated this change would become standard equipment on future models. A Beaver four-cylinder vertical, valve-in-head engine was featured, using a 4-3/4 x 6-inch bore and stroke. Rated speed was 950 rpm. Ground speeds of 1-3/4 and 2-1/2 mph were available with the two-speed transmission. Kerosene fuel was used throughout the test. The 15-30 easily handled the rated drawbar test, delivering 17.68 hp, a pull of 2,512 lbs. at a speed of 2.64 mph, and drive wheel slippage of 6.76 percent. On rated brake hp, 30.14 was officially recorded, with 8.19 hp hours per gallon of kerosene and total fuel consumption of 3.68 gph. Slightly over 2 additional hp appeared in the maximum brake hp test, giving the 15-30 a very slight power reserve. The Dixie Model 46 magneto was standard equipment, as was a Kingston Model L carburetor. Total tractor weight was 6,500 lbs.

Lauson Road Model

Lauson 15-30 model

Lauson High-Powered 12-25

The 15-30 Lauson was available in several configurations, including a Lauson Road Model shown here. It was essentially the same tractor, but was equipped with heavy cast rear wheels to provide additional weight for soil compaction. The 15-30 was also built in a special Ricefield design.

In late 1920 or early 1921, the Lauson High-Powered 12-25 tractor appeared. It was designed around a Midwest four-cylinder engine with a 4-1/8 x 5-1/4-inch bore and stroke, and was rated at 1,200 rpm. This tractor carried a list price of $1,295.

Nebraska Test Data

Model: Lauson 12-25

Test No. 75

Date Tested: April 30 to May 6, 1920

A Midwest four-cylinder vertical, valve-in-head engine powered the Lauson 12-25 tractor. Using a 4-1/8 x 5-1/4-inch bore and stroke, it was rated at 1,200 rpm. An internal expanding shoe clutch was featured. Other accessory items included a Kingston Model L carburetor and a Dixie Model 46 magneto. Forward speeds of 2 and 3 mph were provided. At rated brake hp load, an economy rating of 8.53 hp hours per gallon was recorded, with consumption totaling 2.96 gph. Well over 37 brake hp was noted in the maximum load test, but fuel consumption rose to 5.17 gph. On the drawbar, 20.91 maximum hp was recorded with the tractor running in high gear. At a speed of 2.63 mph, it pulled a load of 2,985 lbs. Few repairs or adjustments were necessary during the 32 hours of running time for Test No. 75. Just as the test concluded, the clutch throw-out shoe broke, apparently because of a factory defect. Total weight of the Lauson 12-25 was 4,500 lbs.

Lauson 20-40 model

Lauson came out with a new series of tractors in 1926. Included was the 20-40 model. It was equipped with a Beaver four-cylinder engine with a 4-3/4 x 6-inch bore and stroke. Rated at 1,040 rpm, the 20-40 was easily capable of its load rating. This model disappeared by 1930.

Nebraska Test Data

Model: Lauson 20-40

Test No. 132

Date Tested: March 28 to April 22, 1927

Although this tractor entered Test No. 132 with a 20-40 rating, and indeed lived up to this figure, Nebraska test engineers noted the belt rating should not exceed 37 hp in order to conform to the A.S.A.E. and S.A.E. tractor rating code. A Beaver four-cylinder vertical, valve-in-head engine was used in the 20-40. It had a 4-3/4 x 6-inch bore and stroke and was rated at 1,040 rpm. A Taco governor, Taco air cleaner, American Bosch ZR4 magneto and Kingston L-3 carburetor all came as standard equipment. Total weight was 7,914 lbs. At rated drawbar load the 20-40 displayed 5.51 hp-hours per gallon and at 32.02 maximum drawbar hp, the 20-40 pulled 5,049 lbs. at 2.44 mph, using low gear. In high gear, 31.92 hp was recorded. Maximum brake hp tests revealed fuel consumption of 6.126 gph, developing 41.87 hp in the process. Rated brake tests at 40.4 hp indicated 7.49 hp-hours per gallon for a total of 5.39 gph.

Lauson 20-40 Thresherman's and Roadbuilder's Special

Along with the 20-40 farm tractor, Lauson also built the 20-40 Thresherman's and Roadbuilder's Special. This model developed over 50 belt hp, and used extra heavy wheels. For instance, the drive wheels on this model used one-inch spokes and could be furnished with 16- or 20-inch rims, as desired. With 20-inch road wheels, this model weighed 8,650 lbs.

COLLECTOR VALUES	1	2	3	4
20-40 SPECIAL	$12,500	$9,000	$6,000	$2,500

Lauson 20-35 tractor

Lauson 20-35 tractors first appeared in 1927. Weighing 7,580 lbs., this model was furnished with Bosch lighting equipment as a standard feature. A Beaver four-cylinder engine was featured, and the sun canopy was standard equipment.

Nebraska Test Data

Model: Lauson "S12" 20-35

Test No. 148

Date Tested: April 2 to April 16, 1928

While the 16-32 Lauson of Test No. 131 used a four-cylinder Beaver engine, the 20-35 carried a LeRoi four-cylinder vertical, I-head motor. Rated at 1,100 rpm, it used a 4-1/2 x 6-inch bore and stroke, identical in dimensions to that used in Test No. 131. Despite these similarities, the two engines performed quite differently as a comparison will show. Using gasoline, the 20-35 delivered 40.88 brake hp on the maximum load test, while at rated load of 35 hp, the figures indicated an economy of 7.97 hp-hours per gallon. Drawbar tests showed 5.09 hp-hours per gallon at rated load, and maximum tests, both in low and in high gear, were performed. Using low gear, the 20-35 pulled 5,140 lbs. at 2.06 mph for 28.53 drawbar hp. Effective with this first test of 1928, all tests were conducted with one carburetor setting, which remained unchanged throughout the test. Test reports also included fuel consumption in lbs. per hp hour as another method of judging fuel economy. Standard equipment for the 20-35 included an American Bosch ZR4 magneto and a Tillotson R2 carburetor.

Lauson 16-32

Emerging in 1926, the Lauson 16-32 was tested at Nebraska the following year. Test No. 131 revealed a maximum of nearly 37 belt hp for this model. It was built with a Beaver four-cylinder engine with a 4-1/2 x 6-inch bore and stroke and rated speed was 1,100 rpm.

Nebraska Test Data

Model: Lauson 16-32

Test No. 131

Date Tested: March 28 to April 8, 1927

Weighing 5,890 lbs., the 16-32 Lauson delivered a maximum of 28.9 hp on the drawbar, pulling a 4,975-lb. load at 2.18 mph. Under rated drawbar load, it was able to squeeze 5.48 hp-hours out of each gallon of gasoline. At 3-1/4 mph, high gear was exactly 1 mph faster than low gear. A Beaver four-cylinder valve-in-head engine was featured. It carried a 4-1/2 x 6-inch bore and stroke and was rated at 1,100 rpm. Regular accessories included a Kingston 1.3 carburetor, American Bosch ZR4 magneto, Taco water-type air cleaner and Taco governor. On the maximum brake test, 36.97 hp was delivered, with fuel consumption totaling 5.34 gph and a fuel economy of 6.92 hp-hours per gallon. This figure rose to 8.5 on the rated load test, with total consumption dropping to 3.81 gph. No repairs or adjustments were necessary once the official test began.

Lauson 25-45 tractor

The Lauson 25-45 emerged in 1929. This was a six-cylinder tractor with a LeRoi 4-1/2 x 6-inch engine. It was available with Bosch electric starting and lighting equipment by the mid-1930s. Total weight of this tractor was 9,060 lbs. Production ended about 1937.

Lauson 65 tractor

Lauson 65 tractors carried a 22-35 hp rating. The six-cylinder engine was a Wisconsin, and it used a 3-7/8 x 5-inch bore and stroke. Like the 25-45, it came onto the market in 1929. During the 1930s, the company continued offering the 20-35 and the 25-45 models in addition to the Lauson 65 shown here

Lawter Tractor Company

ST. MARYS, OHIO

1914 Model

In 1913 Lawter Tractor Company was incorporated at Newcastle, Indiana. Later that year, the company purchased the Universal Tractor Mfg. Co., also at Newcastle. The following year the company moved to St. Marys, Ohio. The 1914 model was rated at 20 drawbar and 40 belt hp. By 1916 the tractor was given an 18-38 rating. Production of the Lawter continued for several years, apparently ending about 1918. Weighing 6,500 lbs., it retailed at $1,750.

Leader tractor

Leader Engine Company

DETROIT, MICHIGAN

Leader Engine Company operated at Detroit, Michigan, as well as at Grand Rapids, Michigan. In 1913 the Sintz-Wallin Co. of Grand Rapids merged with Midland Tractor Co. at Detroit to form Leader Engine Co. Rated at 12 drawbar and 18 belt hp, the Leader used a two-cylinder opposed engine of the company's own design and manufacture. Production ended by 1915.

Leader Tractor Mfg. Company

CLEVELAND, OHIO

Leader Model B tractor

By 1946 the Leader tractor was on the market. The 1947 Model B shown here was furnished with a Hercules four-cylinder engine with a 3-1/4 x 4-inch bore and stroke. Total tractor weight was 2,500 lbs. A belt pulley and a PTO shaft both came as standard equipment. Production of the Leader tractors continued into the early 1950s.

COLLECTOR VALUES	1	2	3	4
MODEL B	$2,900	$1,800	$1,100	$400

Leader Tractor Mfg. Company

DES MOINES, IOWA

12-25 Rex tractor

Leader emerged in 1918 with its 12-25 Rex tractor. Weighing 5,600 lbs., the Rex sold for $1,800. The company was apparently a successor to the defunct Ohio Tractor Mfg. Company of Marion, Ohio. The latter went broke in 1916 and was acquired by others to build motor trucks. Perhaps the new owners sold the tractor business to Leader. The Rex tractor did not remain on the market for any length of time, and was out of business by 1920. The Rex 12-25 was powered by a Waukesha four-cylinder engine with a 4-1/4 x 5-3/4-inch bore and stroke.

Harry W. Leavitt

WATERLOO, IOWA

Harry Leavitt was in the tractor business for a time. Without a doubt, he was involved with Waterloo Gasoline Engine Co. for several years in the design of various tractors. Once the company was sold to Deere & Co., Leavitt continued with them for a time as well. At any rate, any tractor production from Leavitt was very limited.

LeClaire Mfg. Company

LECLAIRE, IOWA

Handy Dandy "K" garden cultivator

In the 1950 through 1952 period, the Handy Dandy "K" garden cultivator appeared from LeClaire Mfg. Company. Weighing only 107 lbs., it was powered by various makes of small air-cooled engines. Very few specific details have been found regarding this small garden tractor.

COLLECTOR VALUES	1	2	3	4
K GARDEN CULTIVATOR	$300	$200	$100	$50

Leland Detroit Mfg. Company

DETROIT, MICHIGAN

Terra-Tiller No. 47

Beginning about 1950 and continuing until about 1953, the Terra-Tiller No. 47 was offered by Leland Detroit. This 256-lb. garden tractor was available with numerous attachments and was powered by a Briggs & Stratton 2-hp engine with a 2 x 2-1/4-inch bore and stroke.

COLLECTOR VALUES	1	2	3	4
TERRA-TILLER NO. 47	$250	$125	$75	$50

Lenox Motor Car Company

HYDE PARK, MASSACHUSETTS

Lenox American Model 20, 22-30 tractor

The Lenox American Model 20, 22-30 tractor came out in 1916. Priced at $2,500, this four-wheel-drive tractor was powered with a Wisconsin four-cylinder engine. It used a 4-3/4 x 5-1/2-inch bore and stroke. Specific information has been difficult to locate on this company, but it appears production ended about 1920.

Leonard Tractor Company

GARY, INDIANA

Leonard four-wheel-drive

Built in the 1918-1922 period, the Leonard was a four-wheel-drive design. Initially, it was built with a 12-35 hp rating, but about 1920, this was raised to 20 drawbar hp, while the belt rating remained constant. The company operated at Joliet, Illinois, and Jackson, Michigan, as well in Indiana.

Levene Motor Company

PHILADELPHIA, PENNSYLVANIA

Levene is often referred to as a tractor manufacturer. Levene often bought out failing or bankrupt tractor manufacturers and continued to supply repair parts. The tractors the company built and/or sold were leftover stocks from the companies they purchased.

Liberty Tractor Company

DUBUQUE, IOWA

Liberty tractor

Liberty began business in 1919. The company began in 1913 as Klumb Engine & Machinery Co. in Sheboygan, Wisconsin. Within months after beginning operations at Dubuque, the company name was again changed to Dubuque Truck & Tractor Company. Few tractors were built before the company went out of business.

Liberty Tractor Company

HAMMOND, INDIANA

Although it was organized and incorporated in 1918, no further information has been located relative to this company's activities in the tractor business.

Liberty Tractor Company

MINNEAPOLIS, MINNESOTA

Liberty tractor

Organized in 1917, Liberty did not begin making any large number of tractors until the following year. A large distributing house, P. J. Downes & Co., sold the tractor, and when Downes went broke, Liberty lost its sales organization. Downes reorganized and Liberty came to life again, but the second attempt was not successful. Initially, the tractor was built as a 15-30, but late in production, it was sold as an 18-32 model. Power came from a Climax Model K four-cylinder engine with a 5 x 6-1/2-inch bore and stroke.

Lincoln Steel Works

LINCOLN, NEBRASKA

Lincoln Kitty Krawler

In the mid-1950s Lincoln offered its Kitty Krawler. This was a small track-laying tractor that weighed only 1,500 lbs. It was powered by a Wisconsin air-cooled single-cylinder engine with a 3 x 3-1/4-inch bore and stroke, and capable of about 8-1/2 hp. Three forward speeds were available. Little other information has been found on the Kitty Krawler.

Lincoln Tractor & Farm Implement Company

SANDUSKY, OHIO

After Dauch Mfg. Company went broke, Lincoln was organized to build a new tractor design. Organized in November 1921, the company announced plans to begin tractor production by February of the following year. By October 1922, the company announced plans to begin production in February of 1923. None of the plans materialized, and only a few tractors were made.

Lincoln Tractor Company

LOS ANGELES, CALIFORNIA

Lincoln garden tractor

The Lincoln garden tractor was on the market by 1947. This model used a Salsbury single-cylinder engine of 6-1/2 hp. Weighing 750 lbs., it was available with various options including several different cultivators. It was also equipped with a PTO shaft, both to the front and to the rear of the tractor. Nothing is known of the Lincoln after 1948.

COLLECTOR VALUES	1	2	3	4
LINCOLN GARDEN TRACTOR	$850	$125	$75	$50

Line Drive Tractor Company

MILWAUKEE, WISCONSIN

Line Drive Tractor

The Line Drive Tractor first appeared about 1915. It was designed for operation with a pair of leather lines, just like driving a team of horses. The company persisted in business until 1917 when it was taken over by Automotive Corporation, Fort Wayne, Indiana. Curiously, a trademark application from The Line Drive Tractor Company, Chicago, Illinois, appeared that year, claiming first use of this mark on March 3. Whether the two companies are connected in any way is unknown.

Linn Mfg. Company

MORRIS, NEW YORK

Linn Mfg. Company came out with its tractor-truck in 1916. For a time the firm attempted to enter the tractor market with its machine, but it was better suited to construction and other rough terrain uses than to farming. Initially, the Linn Tractor-Truck was powered by a Continental four-cylinder engine. As it evolved, larger engines were used. The company remained in operation until 1950.

COLLECTOR VALUES	1	2	3	4
LINN 6-CYLINDER TRACTOR	--	$31,000	--	--

Lion Tractor Company

MINNEAPOLIS, MINNESOTA

"King of the Farm" Lion tractor

Billed as "King of the Farm," the Lion tractor made its first appearance in 1914. It was designed by D. M. Hartsough who had also designed the popular Bull tractor made in Minneapolis. Rated at 8 drawbar and 16 belt hp, the Lion used a two-cylinder engine with a 5 x 6-1/2-inch bore and stroke. The company sold a substantial number of tractors for a time but vanished from the market in 1918.

Linn tractor

Litchfield Mfg. Company

WATERLOO, IOWA

In 1912 and 1913 this firm is listed as a farm tractor manufacturer. The company actively built numerous farm machines, and for a time, also built gasoline engines. No information on its farm tractor has been found.

Little Dilly Tractor Works

WICHITA FALLS, TEXAS

The Little Dilly Jr. and Little Dilly Sr. garden tractors are listed in 1947 and 1948, but no illustrations have been found. The Jr. was equipped with a Lauson 2-1/4 hp-engine, and the Sr. used a Briggs & Stratton or Wisconsin engine of 3 hp. Both models had an optional belt pulley drive.

Little Giant Company

MANKATO, MINNESOTA

Mayer Bros. Company began building tractors in 1913, and in June 1918 changed the company name to Little Giant Company.

Model B, 16-22 tractor

By 1918 two tractor models were available, the smallest of which was the Model B, 16-22. This 5,200-lb. tractor retailed at $1,650 in 1918. The engine was a four-cylinder design built by Little Giant and used a 4-1/2 x 5-inch bore and stroke. Toward the end of production in 1927 the bore was raised to 4-1/2 inches.

Little Giant tractors maintained the same general design throughout their production run ranging from 1913 to 1927. The Model A, 26-35 tractor carried the company's own four-cylinder engine. It used a 5-1/4 x 6-inch bore and stroke. For the sake of convenience, the cylinders were cast in pairs. The Model A weighed 8,700 lbs. and sold for $2,500 in 1918.

Little Giant Model A, 26-35 tractor

COLLECTOR VALUES	1	2	3	4
LITTLE GIANT MODEL A 26-35 TRACTOR	--	$34,000	--	--

Little Oak

See: Humber-Anderson; and Willmar Tractor Co.

C.M. Livingston & Son

TULSA, OKLAHOMA

Livy "5hp" garden tractor

Beginning about 1950 and continuing for about 5 years, the Livy "5hp" garden tractor was available. It is shown here with a rotary brush cutter that could also be used for felling small trees. Power came from a Briggs & Stratton Model 14 engine with a 2-5/8-inch bore and stroke. It was capable of about 5 hp. Various attachments were available.

COLLECTOR VALUES	1	2	3	4
LIVY 5HP GARDEN TRACTOR	$375	$225	$125	$75

Lobb Bros.

FAIRMONT, MINNESOTA

This company is listed in a 1918 tractor directory as a tractor manufacturer, but no other information has been found.

Lodge & Shipley Company

CINCINNATI, OHIO

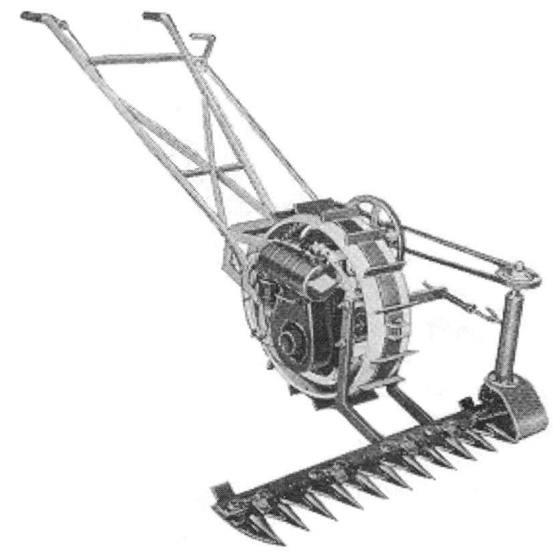

Choremaster garden tractor

Beginning about 1947, the Special Products Division of Lodge & Shipley started producing its Choremaster garden tractor. The simple design was equipped with a Clinton 700 engine with a 2 x 1-7/8-inch bore and stroke. A perusal of the tractor directories leads to the conclusion the Choremaster was built for only a short time.

COLLECTOR VALUES	1	2	3	4
CHOREMASTER GARDEN TRACTOR	$450	$375	$225	$100

Lombard Auto-Tractor-Truck Corporation

NEW YORK, NEW YORK

Lombard tractor-truck

Alvin O. Lombard organized this company in 1901 to build a steam log hauler. In 1917 the company was incorporated and began building a tractor-truck. Power came from a six-cylinder engine with a 5-1/2 x 6-3/4-inch bore and stroke for 140 hp. Two forward speeds were available of 4 and 6 mph. Under suitable conditions, it had a drawbar pull of 15,000 lbs. The company endured until 1920.

London Motor Plow Company

SPRINGFIELD, OHIO

London motor plow

Little company history has been found, but as late as 1923, the firm offered its motor plow. Rated at 12 drawbar and 25 belt hp, it used a Midwest four-cylinder engine with a 4-1/8 x 5-1/4-inch bore and stroke. The tractor weighed 4,600 lbs. and detachable plows added considerably to that figure.

Long Mfg. Company

TARBORO, NORTH CAROLINA

Long Model A tractor

By 1948 the Long Model A tractor was marketed. In the late 1970s, Long again entered the tractor market with several different tractor models built by Universal Tractor Brasov (UTB), Brasov, Romania. Additional details for these tractors may be found in Nebraska Tractor Tests 1108, 1109, 1193, 1298, 1415, 1416, and 1417.

Nebraska Test Data

Model: Long Model A
Test No. 410
Date Tested: May 18 to May 31, 1949

Weighing 3,618 lbs., the Long was another of several new tractor makes to appear after WW II. It featured a Continental four-cylinder, L-head engine. Rated at 1,800 rpm, it used a 3-7/16 x 4-3/8-inch bore and stroke. Also included was an Auto-Lite electrical system and a Marvel-Schebler TSX-338 carburetor. Four forward speeds of 3.34, 4.82, 6.46, and 13.27 were provided. Second gear was used for the 10-hour run on Test H. At a rated load of 20.64 drawbar hp, the Model A pulled 2.015 lbs. at 4.19 mph with a slippage of 5.41 percent. Fuel consumption totaled 9.06 hp-hours per gallon during this test. A low-gear maximum pull of 3,179 lbs. was noted in Test G, but with the aid of another 900 lbs. of weight per each rear wheel. Under a Test C operating maximum load of 30.32 belt hp, the Model A yielded 10.45 hp-hours per gallon, comparing very favorably to the economy figure of 10.36 noted under a Test D rated load of 28.22 belt hp. After 41 hours of engine operation, a hood hold-down bolt broke and a generator support bolt. Otherwise, no repairs or adjustments were necessary.

A.H. Loomis

BELLEVILLE, KANSAS

A. H. Loomis appears in the annals of tractor history as a manufacturer, but no information has been found.

Los Angeles Motor Car Company

LOS ANGELES, CALIFORNIA

No information on this firm has been found regarding tractors it may have built, even in the automobile directories we checked. The company title certainly suggested that automobiles were part of the scene.

Louisville Motor Plow Company

LOUISVILLE, KENTUCKY

No specific information has been located regarding this firm. It seems plausible that it was connected with B. F. Avery Company of the same city. The latter built and sold a motor plow for a short time.

Love Tractor Company

EAU CLAIRE, MICHIGAN

Beginning about 1950 and continuing through the decade, Love offered several tractor models.

Love J51 tractor

The J51 was a small two-plow tractor. This one was built with a Willys CJ2A engine. Much of the tractor was built up of OEM parts. A belt pulley was standard equipment. Total weight of the tractor was 2,650 lbs.

Love C51 or CP51 tractor

While production of the J51 ended in the early 1950s, the C51 and CF51 tractors were available through the decade. Three distinct "51" models were built. The C51 used a Chrysler 217-cid engine. The CF51 used a Chrysler 230.5-cid engine and had a slightly longer wheel base. The F51 tractor was virtually the same, but used a Ford 7HNN5H engine with a 226-cid displacement.

COLLECTOR VALUES	1	2	3	4
C51, CP51	$5,000	$3,500	$1,500	$750

Harry A. Lowther Company

SHELBYVILLE, INDIANA

Custom Model C tractor

The Custom Model C emerged from Custom Mfg. Co. at Shelbyville in 1948. By 1950, what appeared to be the same tractor was being built by Lowther. By 1953, the Custom reappeared at Hustisford, Wisconsin. For 1950, the Custom was built in two sizes. The ER and EW designators were for tricycle or adjustable wide-front axles. This model used a Chrysler Industrial 8 engine with a 250.6-cubic inch displacement. The HR and HW models used a Chrysler Industrial 6 engine with a 230.2-cubic inch displacement. Both models offered five forward speeds and Fluid Drive drive couplings.

Lyons Atlas Company

INDIANAPOLIS, INDIANA

In 1917 Lyons Atlas bought Hume Mfg. Company, Hume, Illinois. The latter developed the Hume tractor, and Lyons Atlas continued to build it under its own name for a short time. The Lyons Atlas had a 16-26 hp rating, and through its special design had a turning radius of only 9 feet. The four-cylinder engine used a 4-1/4 x 5-3/4-inch bore and stroke and was rated at 1,000 rpm. Weighing 5,100 lbs., it was priced at $1,465. When Lyons Atlas went broke, Midwest Engine Company was formed.

Lyons Atlas 16-26 tractor

[Throughout this section, assume that gasoline was used for fuel unless another fuel source is mentioned.]

McCadden Machine Works

ST. CLOUD, MINNESOTA

McCadden was building gasoline engines by 1904. In March 1916 the company incorporated and announced plans to build a tractor. Whether it got past the prototype stage is unknown, since no other information has been found.

S. McChesney

PIPESTONE, MINNESOTA

For a brief time in 1911, S. McChesney offered his E-Z Built Tractor. It was essentially a set of traction trucks, and appeared to have been little more than the essential gearing and accessories. The buyer furnished wheels, frame and a stationary engine. Little else is known of this machine.

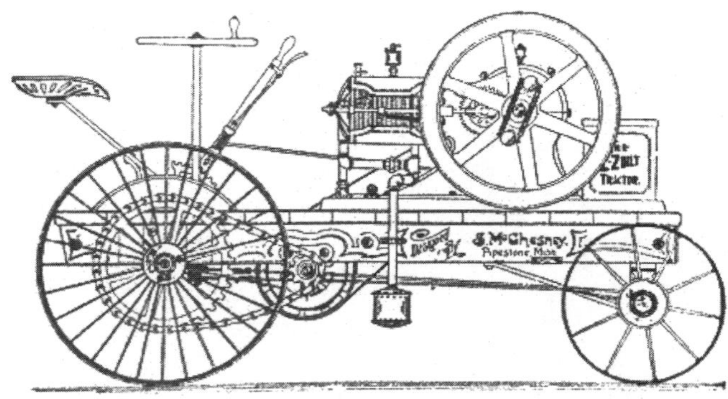

McChesney E-Z Built Tractor

McCormick Harvesting Machine Company

CHICAGO, ILLINOIS

See: International Harvester Company

McCormick Tractor Company

DENVER, COLORADO

In 1918 the McCormick Tractor Company was induced to change its name, admitting it had adopted the name partly because of the advertising value that had been established by International Harvester Company. The company announced that it would choose a new name, but no further information has been found regarding the venture, nor is it known whether any tractors were built.

Tyler McDonald

LA MESA, CALIFORNIA

About 1956 this firm offered its Jiffy-Cart 4-Wheel-Drive garden tractor. It was powered by a Kohler K-90 engine of about 3-1/2 hp. It used a 2-3/8 x 2-1/4-inch bore and stroke. Little else is known of the Jiffy Cart, and no illustrations have been found.

McDougall-Duluth Company

DULUTH, MINNESOTA

This company has been identified as a tractor manufacturer but no other information has been found.

McFarland & Westmont Tractor Company

SAUK CITY, WISCONSIN

See: Wisconsin Farm Tractor Company

McIntyre Mfg. Company

COLUMBUS, OHIO

Farmer Boy tractor

The Farmer Boy tractor was developed in 1915 and appeared on the market the following year. From various advertising, it appears two models were built, including a small 10-20 size and the larger 18-30 model. Both models used four-cylinder engines. Few details of the Farmer Boy tractors have been found. In 1918 the company was reorganized as Columbus Tractor Company.

McKinney Traction Cultivator Company

ST. LOUIS, MISSOURI

Organized at Gainesville, Georgia, in 1910, the McKinney Traction Cultivator Company moved to St. Louis, Missouri, the following year.

D. M. McLaughlin Company

EMERYVILLE, CALIFORNIA

Although this company is listed as a tractor manufacturer, no information has been found regarding what was built or when it was built.

McKinney traction cultivator

The initial design used an 8-hp gasoline engine for power. The 1910 model was equipped with a single lever to control all functions of forward, reverse and steering.

After the move to St. Louis in 1911, McKinney offered two different motor cultivators of 18 and 25 brake hp, with the largest model being shown here. Power came from a two-cylinder, two-cycle engine, and steering was achieved through friction wheels working on the countershafts. Nothing more is known of the firm after its 1911 announcements.

McKinney motor cultivator

McVicker Engineering Company

MINNEAPOLIS, MINNESOTA

McVicker Engineering Company tractor

McVicker Engineering Company began offering a tractor through Joy-Wilson Sales Company in 1909. By the following year, the firm was building three sizes of 40, 70 and 140 brake hp. The latter had a four-cylinder engine with a 10 x 10-1/2-inch bore and stroke for a 3,300 cubic-inch displacement. Walter J. McVicker was a prominent mechanical engineer and designed several different tractors, most notably the early Twin City models of Minneapolis Steel & Machinery Company. The company's career in tractor manufacturing ended after 1910.

M&M Tractor Company

MINNEAPOLIS, MINNESOTA

In 1914 this company announced it would be starting production of a new tractor, and claimed great things for its prototype. After initial announcements, nothing more was heard of the company.

Macultivator Company

SANDUSKY, OHIO

Macultivator Motor Cultivator

This example of the Motor Cultivator was gleaned from an unknown magazine, the date of which is also unknown. Given the design of this garden tractor and the style of engine, it would seem to be of pre-1920 vintage. Perhaps additional information might be found for a later edition of this book.

COLLECTOR VALUES	1	2	3	4
MACULTIVATOR MOTOR CULTIVATOR	$1,250	$800	$500	$200

Magnet Tractor Company

MINNEAPOLIS, MINNESOTA

Magnet Tractor Co. 14-28 model

Incorporated in 1919, Magnet Tractor Co. offered its 14-28 model in 1920 and 1921. Priced at $1,875, this tractor weighed 4,400 lbs. Power came from a Waukesha Model DU four-cylinder engine with a 4-1/2 x 6-1/4-inch bore and stroke. The 14-28 used a worm gear final drive.

Manitoba Universal Farm Tractor Company Ltd.

WINNIPEG, MANITOBA

This company was incorporated in 1915 to build farm tractors, but no other information has been found.

Manley Engineering & Machine Works

COPLEY, OHIO

Various references are found regarding the Blue Ox Garden Tractor built by Manley in the 1948 through 1953 period. However, no illustrations or specifications have been found.

Marine Iron Works

TACOMA, WASHINGTON

By 1947 the Farm Equipment Division of Marine Iron Works had developed the Mighty Man Garden Tractor.

Mighty Man Garden Tractor

In 1950 the line included three models, including the Mighty Man "5" shown here. This model used a Clinton Model 700 air-cooled engine capable of about 1-1/2 hp.

Mighty Man "7" model

The 1950 line of Mighty Man garden tractors included the Mighty Man "7" model shown here, along with the Mighty Man "10" garden tractor. These two were essentially the same, but used different wheels, and on the "10," a four-speed belt reduction was available. This was not used on the Mighty Man "7" tractor. Both styles used a Wisconsin ABN engine capable of over 4 hp. It carried a 2-1/2 x 2-3/4-inch bore and stroke. Numerous attachments were available. The Mighty Man line continued at least into the mid-1950s.

COLLECTOR VALUES	1	2	3	4
MIGHTY MAN "7"	$500	$350	$200	$75

Market Garden Tractor Company

MINNEAPOLIS, MINNESOTA

Market Garden Tractor

Organized and incorporated in 1918, this firm continued until mid-1921. At that point, the company name was changed to Aro Tractor Company. Priced at $295, the Market Garden Tractor was set up especially for garden and orchard cultivating and spraying. Power came from a single-cylinder, two-cycle engine with a 4-inch bore and stroke, capable of about 4-1/2 belt hp.

***Note:** In any condition complete, the Market Garden Tractor is worth between $1,500 and $3,000.*

Maroa Motor Plow Company

MAROA, ILLINOIS

Although the company was organized in 1911 to build the Maroa Motor Plow, little other information has been located.

Marschke Motor Plow Company

VALLEY CITY, NORTH DAKOTA

By 1908 R. B. Marschke had developed the Marschke Motor Plow. That year a company was organized to manufacture the machine. The company lasted at least into 1909 when it tried to promote it. After that time, further references to the company have not been found.

Marschke Motor Plow

Martin Tractor Company

INDIANAPOLIS, INDIANA

During 1912, this firm was organized and incorporated to manufacture tractors, but no further information has been found.

Martin Tractor Company

SPRINGFIELD, MASSACHUSETTS

This firm was incorporated in 1913 to build farm tractors. It is unknown whether there was a connection to the company of the same name, organized a year earlier at Indianapolis, Indiana.

Marvel Tractor Company

COLUMBUS, OHIO

In 1921 Marvel applied for this trademark, noting that it had been first used August 20, 1920. While it is known that Marvel built at least a few tractors, production did not come up to expectations and lasted for only a short time.

Marvel trademark

Massey-Harris Company

TORONTO, ONTARIO AND RACINE, WISCONSIN

Massey-Harris was organized at Toronto in 1891, and was a merger of Massey Mfg. Company and A. Harris & Son. Until about 1910 the company was primarily a Canadian firm and catered mainly to the Canadian trade. With the purchase of Deyo-Macey Co. of Binghamton, New York in 1910 the company began a serious attempt to enter the U.S. market as well.

By 1917 the company had entered the tractor business, first selling the Bull tractor made in Minneapolis. The following year Massey-Harris contracted with Parrett Tractor Company of Chicago, Illinois to design and build the Massey-Harris No. 1. Three different models were produced, and production was entirely suspended in 1923.

During 1927 Massey-Harris began selling the Wallis tractor of J. I. Case Plow Works, and the following year M-H bought out this company for $1.3 million in cash, and guaranteed another $1.1 million in bonds. Massey-Harris Company was organized and incorporated at Racine, Wisconsin, and the company now was able to successfully penetrate the U. S. tractor market.

In 1953 Massey-Harris acquired Harry Ferguson Inc. to form Massey-Harris-Ferguson. In March 1958 the name was abbreviated to Massey-Ferguson. Massey-Harris-Ferguson and Massey-Ferguson tractors may be found under the Massey-Ferguson heading.

Bull tractor

In 1917 Massey-Harris entered the tractor market as a sales wing for the Bull Tractor Company of Minneapolis. The Bull had phenomenal sales when it first came on the market, but by 1917 it had already reached its zenith. The company's first entry into farm tractors was a failure.

Parrett Tractor

During 1918 Massey-Harris made an agreement with Parrett Tractors of Chicago, Illinois. Under this plan, Parrett designed and built the tractor for M-H. Before production ended in 1923, three different models were built, and at least some of them were built at the company's Weston (Ontario) plant.

Wallis 20-30

From 1923 to 1927, Massey-Harris abstained from the tractor business, but in the latter year it contracted with J. I. Case Plow Works to sell its Wallis tractor. The following year Massey-Harris bought out the Racine, Wisconsin, factory of J. I. Case Plow Works and set up its own Massey-Harris Company plant at Racine. The 20-30 Wallis was its first model. The 20-30 was tested at Nebraska (No. 134) in 1927 and displayed well over its rated power.

Nebraska Test Data

Model: Wallis 20-30

Test No. 134

Date Tested: April 29 to May 10, 1927

The Wallis OK, 15-27 tested under No. 92 provided the basis for this new model. Using distillate fuel throughout the test, it delivered 7.68 hp-hours per gallon on rated drawbar load, and managed to pull 3,409 lbs. in the maximum drawbar test, using low gear. This test gave a maximum of 27 drawbar hp for the 20-30, and slightly over 26 drawbar hp when using high gear. Slightly over 35 brake hp was exhibited in the maximum load test, while at rated load, the 20-30 delivered 10.28 hp-hours per gallon of distillate, consuming 2.942 gallons per hour (gph). The company used its own four-cylinder vertical, valve-in-head engine rated at 1,050 rpm and using a 4-3/8 x 5-3/4-inch bore and stroke. Other features included a Kingston carburetor, American Bosch ZR4 magneto, Pickering governor and a cloth screen air cleaner built by Wallis. Total weight was 4,523 lbs. No repairs or adjustments were made during the 38 hours of running time required to complete the tests.

COLLECTOR VALUES	1	2	3	4
WALLIS 20-30	$9,500	--	--	--

J. I. Case Plow Works had developed the 20-30 Orchard tractor in the late 1920s, and after the 1928 Massey-Harris takeover, the latter continued to offer this specialized model. Aside from the special fenders and other accessories, it was essentially the same as the ordinary 20-30.

20-30 Industrial tractor

Several of the larger tractor manufacturers developed industrial models during the 1920s. This brought tractor power to factories and assembly plants. The 20-30 Industrial was equipped with solid rubber tires and different transmission gearing, but it was otherwise a conversion of the farm model.

20-30 Orchard tractor

Massey-Harris Model 25 tractor

Massey-Harris introduced the Model 25 tractor in 1931. It replaced the earlier 20-30 model. The Model 25 was also known as the Massey-Harris 26-41. Its four-cylinder engine carried a 4-3/8 x 5-3/4 inch bore and stroke, and was rated at 1,200 rpm. The PTO shaft shown on this model was an extra equipment item. The Model 25 continued the unit frame design using a boiler plate frame; it went back to the Wallis Cub of 1913.

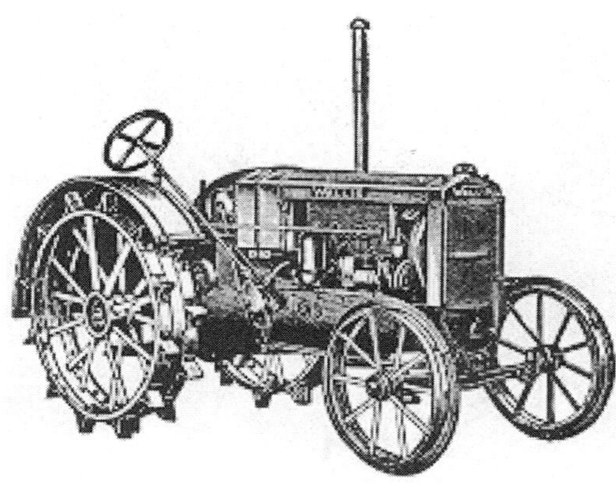

Massey-Harris 12-20 tractor

In late 1928 or early 1929, Massey-Harris introduced its 12-20 tractor. It was a companion to the 20-30 and later, the Model 25 tractor. This model used a four-cylinder engine with a 3-7/8 x 5-1/4-inch bore and stroke. The 12-20 was capable of well over 24 belt hp.

Nebraska Test Data

Model: Wallis 12-20

Test No. 164

Date Tested: June 18 to June 27, 1929

Rated at 1,000 rpm, the 12-20 four-cylinder, I-head engine carried a 3-7/8 x 5-1/4-inch bore and stroke. Complementing the basic engine was an American Bosch U4 magneto and a Kingston L3V carburetor along with the company's own air cleaner. Advertised speeds of 2-1/3, 3-1/3 and 4-1/2 mph were provided. Using intermediate gear for the rated drawbar test, the 12-20 delivered a pull of 1,232 lbs. at 3.76 mph. Distillate fuel was used throughout this test, and the resultant fuel economy at rated drawbar came in at 5.94 hp-hours per gallon. Maximum drawbar hp came in low gear with a pull of 3,018 lbs. at 2.24 mph and slippage of 18-3/4 percent. In this test, the 3,893-lb. 12-20 pulled nearly 78 percent of its own weight. Brake hp trials revealed an economy of 9.79 hp-hours per gallon of distillate at 24.16 maximum hp. This dropped to 8.92 at rated load of 20.32 hp, with fuel consumption totaling 2.277 gph for the rated load test. About midway through the 48 hours of running time, it was necessary to thoroughly clean the fuel system, otherwise no repairs or adjustments were necessary.

Massey-Harris 12-20 Industrial

Besides the regular farm version, the Massey-Harris 12-20 was also available in orchard and industrial models. No major changes were made to the tractor chassis or the engine, but special fenders and relocated air stack and exhaust were all necessary. Production of the 12-20 continued until about 1936.

Massey-Harris General Purpose

Rated as a 15-22, this tractor was equipped with a four-cylinder Hercules engine with a 4 x 4-1/2-inch bore and stroke. Production of this model continued for several years, but no specific production data was located.

Nebraska Test Data

Model: Massey-Harris General Purpose
Test No. 177
Date Tested: May 5 to May 27, 1930

Using gasoline throughout the test procedures, this four-wheel-drive tractor scored 6.06 hp-hours per gallon on the rated drawbar test. Pulling 1,622 lbs. at 3.62 mph, it delivered 15.64 drawbar hp with a slippage of 2.75 percent. Standard equipment included three forward speeds of 2.2, 3.2 and 4 mph. Using low gear, a maximum pull of 3,247 lbs. was recorded at a speed of 2.3 mph, developing 19.91 hp in the process, and experiencing a slippage of 8.26 percent. At rated brake hp, fuel economy came in at 8.16 hp-hours per gallon while cranking out 22.1 hp. At maximum load of 24.84 hp, this tractor scored 8.26 on the hp-hours-per-gallon ledger. Standard equipment included a Hercules four-cylinder vertical, L-head engine with a 4 x 4-1/2-inch bore and stroke and a rated speed of 1,200 rpm. Also included was an American Bosch U4 magneto, Zenith carburetor and Hercules governor. No repairs or adjustments were required during the entire test.

Nebraska Test Data

Model: Massey-Harris General Purpose
Test No. 191
Date Tested: May 22 to June 12, 1931

The only major difference between this test and No. 177 of 1930 is this test was conducted using distillate. AU specifications remained virtually identical, and although this tractor was not given a manufacturer's rating, it was limited to 13 drawbar and 20 belt hp under existing tractor rating codes. The 10-hour rated drawbar test at 12.63 hp revealed a pull of 1,326 lbs. at 3.57 mph and slippage of 2.67 percent for an economy of 5.1 hp-hours per gallon. A maximum test in low gear gave 16.79 hp and a pull of 2,764 lbs. at 2.28 mph, or 67 percent of the tractor's own weight. Maximum brake tests at 22.5 hp showed 7.76 hp-hours per gallon, with a substantially higher 8.14 appearing at the rated 20.11 hp load. During the 68 hours of engine operating time, coolant temperatures varied from 181 to 197 degrees F, which was substantially lower than many tractors of the early 1920s.

Massey-Harris Challenger

The Massey-Harris Challenger first appeared in February 1936. It marked the company's entry into row-crop tractors, and it continued to use the boiler plate unit frame design that had been pioneered on the Wallis Cub of 1913. The engine was built by Massey-Harris; its four-cylinder design carried a 3-7/8 x 5-1/4-inch bore and stroke. The Challenger was capable of 20 drawbar hp. Production of this model ended in 1938.

Nebraska Test Data

Model: Massey-Harris Challenger
Test No. 265
Date Tested: August 10 to August 18, 1936

At its rated 26.21 brake hp, the Challenger delivered a fuel economy of 9.96 hp-hours per gallon of distillate. An even better economy of 10.07 appeared under Test C, with an operating maximum load of 27.16 hp. The Challenger featured four speed choices of 2.4, 3.3, 4.1 and 8.5 mph. Test G for operating maximum load on the drawbar was run in all four speeds, but 20.01 hp appeared using low gear. At a speed of 2.6 mph, this tractor pulled a load of 2,883 lbs., or about 69 percent of its 4,200-lb. operating weight. The rated drawbar run (Test H) at 16.29 hp yielded a pull of 1,638 lbs. at 3.73 mph and an economy of 6.65 hp-hours per gallon. Accessories included an American Bosch U4 magneto, Kingston carburetor and Handy governor. Massey-Harris featured its own four-cylinder I-head engine. Rated at 1,200 rpm, it carried a 3-7/8 x 5-1/4-inch bore and stroke. No repairs or adjustments were noted during some 44 hours of operating time.

Twin Power Challenger

Late model Challenger tractors sported a streamlined hood and grille. Emerging in 1937, the Twin Power Challenger was rated at 1,200 and 1,400 rpm. At the higher speed, this model delivered over 36 belt hp. Essentially, this tractor was the same as the original Challenger design that it replaced. The Twin Power Challenger performance data may be found in Nebraska Test No. 293. The Challenger remained in production until about 1942.

Nebraska Test Data

Model: Massey-Harris Twin Power Challenger
Test No. 293
Date Tested: October 25 to November 16, 1937

The Twin Power Challenger carried an operating weight of 4,570 lbs. on steel wheels, compared to 5,900 lbs. on rubber tires. Massey-Harris featured its own four-cylinder I-head engine. Rated at 1,200 and 1,400 rpm, it carried a 3-7/8 x 5-1/4-inch bore and stroke. Standard equipment included an American Bosch MJB4A magneto, Zenith 62-AX9 carburetor and Kingston governor. Only one minor repair was necessary during 74 hours of running time. Brake tests at 1,200 rpm indicated an economy of 10.08 hp-hours per gallon against a rated load of 31.76 hp. The same test at 1,400 rpm balanced 36.27 rated hp against a fuel economy of 9.72 hp-hours per gallon. Drawbar economy tests indicated 6.62 hp-hours per gallon at 1,200-rpm engine speed and on steel wheels. The economy rose to 8.51 at the same engine speed, but using rubber tires. Test H (on steel wheels only) was run in second gear, with a resultant economy of 6.61 hp-hours per gallon and an output of 19.63 drawbar hp. Test G for operating maximum load indicated a low gear maximum pull of 4,009 lbs. on rubber tires with an output of 23.9 drawbar hp.

Massey-Harris Pacemaker

The Massey-Harris Pacemaker first appeared in 1936. It used the same four-cylinder engine as the Challenger, namely, with a 3-7/8 x 5-1/4-inch bore and stroke. Total weight was about 4,000 lbs. This model was built into 1937 when it was replaced with the Twin Power Pacemaker.

Nebraska Test Data

Model: Massey-Harris Pacemaker
Test No. 266
Date Tested: August 10 to August 19, 1936

Weighing 4,050 lbs., the Massey-Harris Pacemaker used distillate fuel throughout its 40 hours of running time in this test. No repairs or adjustments were noted throughout the various trials. At its rated 26.69 brake hp, fuel economy assumed a figure of 10.27 hp-hours per gallon, with a micro improvement to 10.39 under operating maximum load of 27.52 hp, as noted in Test C. Maximum drawbar pull in low gear was 2,878 lbs. at a speed of 2.4 mph and an output of 18.45 hp. Test H for rated drawbar load was run in second gear. It manifested 16.21 hp, a fuel economy of 6.65 hp-hours per gallon, and a load of 1,658 lbs. at 3.67 mph. Massey-Harris used its own four-cylinder I-head engine of 3-7/8 x 5-1/4-inch bore and stroke with a rated speed of 1,200 rpm. The same accessories were included as noted under Test No. 265, and in addition, a hand-operated, single-plate Twin Disc clutch was used.

Massey-Harris PA Orchard tractor

In addition to the regular standard-tread Pacemaker, Massey-Harris also offered a special Model PA Orchard tractor. It was identical to the regular model but had a 40-inch tread width, special hood and fenders, and no belt pulley. Production of the Pacemaker ended in 1937 when it was replaced with the Twin Power Pacemaker models.

Twin Power Pacemaker

Production of the Twin Power Pacemaker began in 1937. This model had a streamlined hood and grille. The engine was virtually identical to that of the original 1936 Pacemaker but had a dual rating of 1,200 and 1,400 rpm, thus the "Twin Power" tradename. The Twin Power Pacemaker exhibited nearly 42 belt hp. Production apparently continued until about 1942.

Nebraska Test Data

Model: Massey-Harris Twin Power Pacemaker
Test No. 294
Date Tested: October 25 to November 16, 1937

Like the Twin Power Challenger of Test No. 293, the Pacemaker went through brake hp tests both at 1,200- and 1,400-rpm engine speeds. Economy at rated load of 31.94 hp and 1,200 rpm came in at 10.62 hp-hours per gallon, compared to 10.45 with a 1,400-rpm speed and an output of 36.88 hp. Test C for operating maximum load at 1,400 rpm yielded 41.51 brake hp. Test H was run on steel wheels and an economy of 6.67 hp-hours per gallon resulted. Test H also revealed an output of 20.26 drawbar hp, along with a pull of 2,048 lbs. at 3.71 mph, engine speed of 1,200 rpm, and slippage of 5.5 percent. Fuel economy tests in third gear gave 6.45 and 8.36 hp-hours, respectively, to steel wheels and rubber tires. This standard-tread version of the Challenger noted in Test No. 293 offered the same forward speeds of 2.4, 3.3, 4.1 and 8.5 mph.

Massey-Harris Model 81 and Model 82 Standard-Tread tractors

Production of the Massey-Harris Model 81 and Model 82 Standard-Tread tractors began in 1941 and ended in 1946. This two-plow tractor was capable of about 27 belt hp and used a Continental four-cylinder engine with a 3 x 4-3/8 inch bore and stroke. Production of this model was seriously limited by World War II.

COLLECTOR VALUES	1	2	3	4
81 STANDARD	$2,500	$1,750	$1,200	$650
82 STANDARD	$2,500	$1,750	$1,200	$650

Massey-Harris Model 81 Row-Crop tractor

In Nebraska Test No. 376 of 1941, the Massey-Harris Model 81 Row-Crop tractor delivered nearly 21 drawbar hp. Like others of this series, it had a dual-speed rating. For belt work and for road gear, it could be operated at 1,800 rpm, while for drawbar work it was rated at 1,500 rpm. The Model 81 Row-Crop used the same four-cylinder engine as the 81 Standard. Production of the Model 81 and 82 tractors ended in 1946.

Nebraska Test Data

Model: Massey-Harris "81" R

Test No. 376

Date Tested: September 29 to October 20, 1941

Massey-Harris "81" went through 48 hours of engine running time without repairs or adjustments (except that during Test H the temperature gauge failed). Test H was run in third gear. With an output of 16.41 drawbar hp, this tractor pulled 1,330 lbs. at 4.63 mph with a slippage of 4.51 percent and yielded 9.6 hp-hours per gallon. Test G produced a maximum drawbar pull of 2,898 lbs. using low gear. Standard equipment included 9-32 rear and 4.00-15 front rubber with advertised speeds of 2.5, 3.6, 4.7 and 16 mph. A Continental four-cylinder, L-head engine powered this tractor. Rated at 1,500 and 1,800 rpm, it carried a 3 x 4-3/8-inch bore and stroke. Also featured was a Marvel-Schebler TSX-28 carburetor and an Auto-Lite electrical system. Test weight without additional ballast was 2,895 lbs. Test C for operating maximum belt load indicated 11.39 hp-hours per gallon under a load of 26.08 hp. At a rated load of 24.17 belt hp, fuel economy settled in at 10.91 hp-hours per gallon with a 24.17 belt hp load.

COLLECTOR VALUES	1	2	3	4
81/82 ROW-CROP	$2,100	$1,550	$1,000	$400

Twin Power 101 Standard

No Nebraska test was run on the 101 Jr. or 102 Jr. standard-tread tractors. Initially, the Twin Power 101 Standard was equipped with a 3-1/4 x 4-3/8-inch, four-cylinder engine, but this was later changed to a 3-5/16-inch bore. The 102GS Junior was a 2-3 plow tractor that used a four-cylinder Continental engine with a 3-7/16 x 4-3/8-inch bore and stroke. Production of the 101 Jr. and 102 Jr. tractors began in 1939.

Massey-Harris 101 Junior tractor

This tractor was capable of over 30 belt hp from the 162-cid, four-cylinder, Continental engine. It used a 3-7/16 x 4-3/8-inch bore and stroke. The 102 Junior was of similar design. Production of these models ended in 1946. Primary differences between the 81/82 models and the 101/102 models were that the 82 and 102 models were Canadian built and usually had larger displacement engines, as the Canadian output was meant for the use of kerosene and distillate fuels, which required larger displacement engines in order to keep the hp ratings commensurate with the gas engine models.

Nebraska Test Data

Model: Massey-Harris 101 R Junior

Test No. 318

Date Tested: May 22 to May 26, 1939

A four-cylinder Continental MFA engine was featured in the 101 Junior presented for this test. Of L-head design, it was rated at 1500-1800 rpm and carried a 3 x 4-3/8-inch bore and stroke. A complete Auto-Lite electrical system was standard equipment, along with a Schebler TSX-28 carburetor and Pierce governor. The rear tires were 10 x 36-inches, with 5.00 x 15-inch front rubber. Test weight was 4,612 lbs. Four forward speeds of 2.6, 3.6, 4.9 and 17.4 mph were provided (1,800 rpm was used for fourth gear; all other speeds used the standard 1,500-rpm engine speed). Test H was run in third gear. It revealed a pull of 1,384 lbs. at 4.45 mph with slippage of 4.98 percent. Output totaled 16.44 hp during this 10-hour test, while fuel economy was 9.75 hp-hours per gallon. Test D for rated belt hp indicated an economy of 11.17 hp-hours per gallon with an output of 23.78 hp. Economy rose to 11.26 at operating maximum load of 25.39 hp. All belt tests were run at 1,800 rpm, while all the drawbar tests were made at 1,500 rpm. No repairs or adjustments were reported during some 45 hours of engine running time.

Nebraska Test Data

Model: Massey-Harris 101 R Junior
Test No. 359
Date Tested: October 7 to October 12, 1940

This tractor featured a Continental MFA four-cylinder engine. Of L-head design, it carried a 3-3/16 x 4-3/8-inch bore and stroke. A rated speed of 1,500 rpm was selected for drawbar use and 1,800 rpm for belt work. An Auto-Lite electrical system was standard equipment, along with a Schebler TSX28 carburetor. Also included were 10 x 36 rear and 4.75 x 15-inch front tires. Test weight was 4,825 lbs. Advertised speeds of 2.6, 3.6, 4.9 and 17.4 mph were provided, with the highest gear requiring an engine speed of 1,800 rpm. Third gear was used for Test H. After this 10-hour run, fuel economy was recorded at 10.22 hp-hours per gallon. Other data included a pull of 1,648 lbs. at 4.42 mph with a slippage of 4.94 percent and an output of 19.44 rated drawbar hp. The low gear maximum pull as extracted from Test G indicates 3,278 lbs. at 2.09 mph with slippage of 16.18 percent and an output of 18.3 drawbar hp. Test C for operating maximum load yielded 30.15 brake hp and 11.75 hp-hours per gallon. This dropped slightly to 11.59 under Test D rated brake load of 27.57 hp.

COLLECTOR VALUES	1	2	3	4
101/102 JR. STANDARD	$2,300	$1,350	$800	$400
101/102 JR. ROW-CROP	$2,200	$1,200	$600	$300

Production of the 101 Senior tractors began in 1938. The row-crop model was equipped with a Continental six-cylinder engine with a 3-5/16 x 4-3/8-inch bore and stroke. This tractor had a dual speed rating of 1,500 rpm for drawbar work and 1,800 rpm for road and belt work. The PTO shaft and power lift system both came as extra equipment. Production of the 101 Senior tractors continued into 1945.

Nebraska Test Data

Model: Massey-Harris 101 R
Test No. 307
Date Tested: September 9 to September 30, 1938

As with the 101 Standard noted in Test No. 306, the 101 Row-Crop model was tested first on rubber tires, then on steel wheels. In addition, belt tests were made first with an engine speed of 1,500 rpm and secondly with an 1,800-rpm engine speed. Gasoline was used during 85 hours of engine operating time. Test D at 1,500 rpm indicated 31.4 hp and an economy of 11.32 hp-hours per gallon. Raising the speed by 300 rpm revealed 36.34 hp and an economy figure of 11.17. Test C for operating maximum load at 1,800 rpm indicated 38.65 hp and 11.67 hp-hours per gallon. Using rubber tires for Test H (rated drawbar) pegged fuel economy at 9.96 while developing 24.79 hp and pulling 1,936 lbs. at 4.8 mph. A 4-hour economy test on steel gave a pull of 2,138 lbs. in second gear, along with an output of 20.76 hp. Test G for operating maximum drawbar load ended with a maximum pull of 3,233 lbs. in second gear (3.39 mph) and an output of 29.2 hp. This test was made on rubber tires. Chassis design was the only major difference between this tractor and that of Test No. 306.

101 Senior Row-Crop

Nebraska Test Data

Model: Massey-Harris 101 R

Test No. 377

Date Tested: September 30 to October 20, 1941

Standard equipment for this tractor included 11-38-inch rear tires and 5.00-15-inch front rubber. Weighing in at 3,865 lbs., it featured a Chrysler six-cylinder, L-head engine. Rated at 1,500 and 1,800 rpm, this engine carried a 3-1/4 x 4-3/8-inch bore and stroke. The 1,800-rpm speed was used only for belt work and in road gear. The 1,500-rpm setting was used for drawbar work. Also featured in the 101 were four forward gears of 2.68, 3.74, 5 and 17.85 mph. Third gear was used for Test H, and at a rated load of 28.08 drawbar hp, the 101 pulled a 2,204-lb. load at 4.78 mph with slippage of 4.91 percent. Fuel economy was recorded at 10.05 hp-hours per gallon. A maximum low-gear pull of 3,905 lbs. was noted in Test G. Brake hp testing was conducted with an engine speed of 1,800 rpm. Test C for an operating maximum load of 44.11 hp yielded 11.92 hp-hours per gallon, compared to 11.56 when under a rated load of 40.9 belt hp as noted in Test D. No repairs or adjustments were noted during 46 hours of engine running time.

COLLECTOR VALUES	1	2	3	4
101 SENIOR STANDARD	$2,600	$1,875	$1,300	$700
101 SENIOR ROW-CROP	$2,500	$1,700	$1,200	$600
101 SUPER WITH CHRYSLER ENGINE	$4,500	$3,000	$2,000	$1,200

The standard-tread version of the 101 Senior tractors was virtually identical in design, except of course for the chassis itself. Both tractors used a six-cylinder 226-cid Continental engine. While the 101 Senior tractors were rated in the three-plow class, no specific hp data was generally published. Production of the 101 Senior Standard and Row-Crop models ran from 1938 to 1946. The 102 Senior Standard and Row-Crop tractors were built from 1941 to 1946.

Nebraska Test Data

Model: Massey-Harris 101 S

Test No. 306

Date Tested: September 8 to September 30, 1938

The Massey-Harris 101 Standard featured a six-cylinder Chrysler T57-503 engine. It was an L-head design, along with a 3-1/8 x 4-3/8-inch bore and stroke with a rated speed of 1,500 rpm on the drawbar and 1,500 to 1,800 rpm on the belt. This tractor was tested for economy on rubber tires and steel wheels. Test H for rated drawbar load was made on rubber tires. It indicated a pull of 1,987 lbs. at 4.52 mph. With an output of 23.94 hp, economy came in at 9.85 hp-hours per gallon. A 4-hour economy test on steel wheels indicated a second-gear economy of 7.46, along with an output of 18.29 hp and a pull of 1,862 lbs. at 3.68 mph. Belt tests were first made at 1,500-rpm engine speed. At rated load of 31.5 hp, the 101 delivered 11.86 hp-hours per gallon during the 1-hour test. The same test made at an engine speed of 1,800 rpm indicated an economy figure of 10.89 with an output of 36.15 belt hp. Standard features of the 101 included an Auto-Lite electrical system with electric starting. Total weight was 3,805 lbs. on steel and 5,725 lbs. on rubber tires.

COLLECTOR VALUES	1	2	3	4
102 SENIOR STANDARD	$2,550	$1,700	$1,200	$800
102 SENIOR ROW-CROP	$2,500	$1,700	$1,250	$850

Massey-Harris 201

The Massey-Harris 201 was built in 1942 and '43 and used a Chrysler T-100 six-cylinder engine.

COLLECTOR VALUES	1	2	3	4
201	$3,800	$2,500	$1,500	$1,200

101 Senior standard-tread tractor

Massey-Harris 202

The Massey-Harris 202 (223 units were built) used a Continental M-290 six-cylinder engine.

COLLECTOR VALUES	1	2	3	4
202	$6,200	$4,400	$3,200	$1,500

Massey-Harris 203 Distillate tractor

Production of the Massey-Harris 203 Distillate tractor began in 1940, followed the next year by the 203 Gasoline model. Both remained in production until 1947. The 203 used a six-cylinder Continental engine with a 4 x 4-3/8-inch bore and stroke. It was rated at 1,700 rpm for drawbar work and 2,000 rpm for belt and road work.

COLLECTOR VALUES	1	2	3	4
203 DISTILLATE	$3,700	$2,700	$2,000	$900
203 GASOLINE	$6,000	$4,000	$3,500	$2,000

Massey-Harris 20

The Massey-Harris 20 saw first light in 1946 and remained in production until 1948. A Continental F124 engine was used in the M-H 20. It was designed with a 3 x 4-3/8-inch bore and stroke, like its predecessor, the Massey-Harris 81 tractor.

Although M-H advertising noted the row-crop 20 and the standard-tread 20 differed "only in the front axle design," at least one 1947 industry listing showed the 20-K standard-tread model with a Continental F140 engine with a 3-3/16 x 4-3/8-inch bore and stroke. Since the 20-K was designed for use with kerosene, perhaps the larger engine bore was needed to deliver the same hp as the gasoline engine. The 20-K was built only in 1947 and 1948 with a 20 Gas Standard offered only in 1948.

Massey-Harris 20-K

COLLECTOR VALUES	1	2	3	4
20 GAS ROW-CROP	$2,100	$1,550	$1,000	$400
20 GAS STANDARD	$2,500	$1,750	$1,200	$650
20-K ROW-CROP	$2,100	$1,550	$1,000	$400
20-K STANDARD	$2,500	$1,750	$1,200	$650

Massey-Harris "30" tractor

In 1946 Massey-Harris introduced the "30" tractor. It was built in standard-tread and row-crop designs, with several versions of the latter being available. Included was this single-front wheel design, along with the standard tricycle and the high-arch, adjustable-width front axle. The Model 30 used a Continental F-162 four-cylinder engine with a 3-7/16 x 4-3/8-inch bore and stroke. The Model 30 yielded in excess of 33 belt hp. This popular design was built into 1952 when it was replaced with the M-H "33" tractor.

Model 11 Pony tractor

Nebraska Test Data

Model: Massey-Harris 30 RT

Test No. 409

Date Tested: May 12 to May 25, 1949

Under a Test C operating maximum load of 33.03 belt hp, shown here, the Massey-Harris 30 yielded 11.09 hp-hours per gallon, compared to 10.84 at a Test D-rated load of 30.09 hp. This tractor featured a Continental Red Seal four-cylinder, L-head engine. Rated at 1,500 rpm on the drawbar and 1,800 rpm in the belt, it carried a 3-7/16 x 4-3/8-inch bore and stroke. Auto-Lite electrical equipment was specified, as was a Marvel-Schebler TSX308 carburetor. No repairs or adjustments were noted during 47 hours of engine operation. Standard tire equipment included 10-38-inch rear and 5.00-15-inch front rubber. Advertised speeds of 2.58, 3.61, 4.51, 6.31 and 12.63 mph were provided. Third gear was used for the rated drawbar run of Test H. At a load of 20-64 hp, the 30 pulled a 1,817 lbs. at 4.26 mph, experiencing a slippage of 4.6 percent, but yielding a fuel economy of 9.72 hp-hours per gallon. A low-gear maximum pull of 3,273 lbs. was recorded in Test G. For Tests F, G and H, an additional 799 lbs. of weight was added to each rear wheel. The basic tractor weighed in at 3,667 lbs. plus added ballast.

COLLECTOR VALUES	1	2	3	4
30 GAS ROW-CROP	$2,500	$1,800	$1,300	$700
30 GAS STANDARD	$2,600	$1,900	$1,350	$750
30-K ROW-CROP	$2,500	$1,800	$1,300	$700
30-K STANDARD	$2,600	$1,900	$1,350	$750

The Model 11 Pony tractor first appeared in 1948 and was built until 1957. Smallest in the Massey-Harris line, it was powered by a Continental four-cylinder engine with a 2-3/8 x 3-1/2-inch bore and stroke. It was capable of nearly 11 belt hp.

Nebraska Test Data

Model: Massey-Harris Pony

Test No. 401

Date Tested: September 14 to September 22, 1948

Featuring a Continental four-cylinder L-head engine, the Massey-Harris Pony was rated at 1,800 rpm and carried a 2-3/8 x 3-1/2-inch bore and stroke. An Auto-Lite electrical system was featured, as was a Marvel-Schebler TSV-24 carburetor. Three forward speeds of 2.74, 3.59 and 7 mph were provided. Tire equipment included 8-24 rear and 4.00-15 inch front rubber. No repairs or adjustments were noted during 46-1/2 hours of engine operating time. Test D at a rated belt load of 10.38 hp yielded 10.07 hp-hours per gallon, compared to an economy of 10.33 under the Test C operating maximum belt load of 10.71 hp. A maximum Test G drawbar pull of 1,432 lbs. was recorded in low gear, while at a rated load of 8.36 drawbar hp, a pull of 891 lbs. was recorded at 3.52 mph. Second gear was used for this 10-hour test. Fuel economy came in at 9.02 hp-hours per gallon. Other data from Test H included a recorded slippage of 4.96 percent. Without additional wheel weights, the Pony weighed 1,890 lbs.

COLLECTOR VALUES	1	2	3	4
MODEL 11 PONY	$3,000	$2,300	$1,250	$500

Production of the Massey-Harris Model 22 row-crop and standard-tread tractors began in 1948 and continued until 1952. It used the Continental F-140 four-cylinder engine with a 3-3/16 x 4-3/8-inch bore and stroke. The row-crop model was tested at Nebraska in 1948 under Test No. 403. It demonstrated nearly 24 maximum drawbar hp.

Massey-Harris Model 22

Nebraska Test Data

Model: Massey-Harris 22 RT

Test No. 403

Date Tested: October 15 to October 21, 1948

No repairs or adjustments were noted for the Massey-Harris 22 during some 46 hours of engine running time. The test report noted that testing was done without a hydraulic pump, since the company considered that special equipment. Weighing in at 2,928 lbs., the 22 featured 10.28 rear and 4.00-15-inch front rubber. Also featured were speeds of 2.45, 3.51, 4.62 and 13.02 mph. Third gear was chosen for the rated drawbar testing, and during the 10-hour run, Test H indicated 17.95 hp, along with a pull of 1,530 lbs. at 4.4 mph and slippage of 4.9 percent. Fuel economy came in at 9.91 hp-hours per gallon. A maximum operating pull of 2,803 lbs. occurred in Test G using low gear. This test was benefited with the addition of some 475 lbs. of added cast iron for each rear wheel, plus an additional 322 lbs. of liquid ballast in each rear tire. The 22 featured a Continental Red Seal engine of L-head design. Rated at 1,800 rpm on the belt and 1,500 rpm on the drawbar, it used a 3-3/16 x 4-3/8-inch bore and stroke. Auto-Lite electrical equipment was specified, along with a Marvel-Schebler TSX34 carburetor. At a rated belt load of 26.92 hp, Test D yielded 11.33 hp-hours per gallon, compared to 11.65 under a Test C operating maximum load of 29.94 hp.

COLLECTOR VALUES	1	2	3	4
MODEL 22 ROW-CROP	$3,300	$2,450	$1,400	$900
MODEL 22 STANDARD	$3,500	$2,500	$1,500	$1,000

Massey-Harris "33" Row-Crop

Massey-Harris "33" tractors used the company's own Model E-201 four-cylinder engine. It had a 3-5/8 x 4-7/8-inch bore and stroke for a 201-cubic inch displacement. Live hydraulics and a live PTO system came as standard equipment. The row-crop model was available in several configurations, such as tricycle front, single front, and adjustable wide-front axles.

Nebraska Test Data

Model: Massey-Harris 33 RT

Test No. 509

Date Tested: October 10 to October 24, 1953

Features of the 33 RT tractor included 12-38 rear and 5.50-16 front rubber, along with advertised speeds of 2.75, 3.84, 4.8, 6.72 and 13.46 mph. Bare tractor weight was 5,191 lbs., with 910 lbs. of additional weight used on each rear wheel during certain drawbar tests. The rated drawbar load run of Test H was made in third gear. Under an output of 28.02 hp, the 33 RT produced 10.78 hp-hours per gallon. During this 10-hour run, the tractor pulled 2,288 lbs. at 4.59 mph with a slippage of 5.51 percent. Test G produced a low-gear maximum pull of 4,456 lbs. at 2.32 mph. The 33 RT was equipped with the company's own four-cylinder I-head engine. Rated at 1,500 rpm, it developed its maximum torque of 258.1 lbs.-ft. with an engine speed of 924 rpm. The 201-cid engine used a 3-5/8 x 4-7/8-inch bore and stroke. No repairs or adjustments were noted during 51-1/2 hours of running time. Test C, at an operating maximum load of 36.23 belt hp, yielded 12.25 hp-hours per gallon, dropping slightly to 12.10 under a Test D rated load of 34.39 hp.

COLLECTOR VALUES	1	2	3	4
MODEL 33 ROW-CROP	$3,500	$2,500	$1,100	$600

Massey-Harris "33" Standard

All models of the Massey-Harris "33" tractors were built in the 1952 through 1955 period. All used a 201-cid, four-cylinder engine, capable of over 36 belt hp. The "33" row-crop was tested at Nebraska under No. 509 of October 1953 (see above). The standard-tread model was not tested, but was capable of similar performance.

COLLECTOR VALUES	1	2	3	4
MODEL 33 STANDARD	$3,800	$2,800	$1,400	$1,000

Massey-Harris "44" tractor

Production of the Massey-Harris "44" tractor began in 1947 and continued until 1955. This four-cylinder tractor used the company's own engine that carried a 3-7/8 x 5-1/2-inch bore and stroke. It was tested under No. 389 at Nebraska in October 1947 and demonstrated 44 maximum belt hp.

Nebraska Test Data

Model: Massey-Harris 44 RT
Test No. 389
Date Tested: October 29 to November 12, 1947

The Massey-Harris 44 featured five forward speeds of 2.48, 3.75, 4.98, 6.47 and 13.8 mph. Third gear was used for the rated drawbar load of Test H. With an output of 31.24 hp, this tractor pulled a 2,472-lb. load at 4.74 mph with a slippage of 5.23 percent. Fuel economy was registered at 10.19 hp-hours per gallon. Standard equipment included 12-38-inch rear and 5.50-16-inch front tires. A low-gear maximum drawbar pull of 4,612 lbs. was noted in Test G. During this test, 544 lbs. of liquid ballast, plus another 701 lbs. of cast-iron weight was added to each rear wheel, for an overall tractor weight of 6,925 lbs. Test weight without ballast was 4,274 lbs. At an operating maximum load of 44.07 belt hp, this tractor delivered 11.9 hp-hours per gallon, compared to 11.78 at a Test D rated load of 40 hp. During 56 hours of engine operating time, no repairs or adjustments were noted. Features included the company's own four-cylinder I-head engine. Rated at 1,350 rpm, it carried a 3-7/8 x 5-1/2-inch bore and stroke. Also featured was an Auto-Lite battery and ignition system, along with a Zenith 62AJIO carburetor.

Massey-Harris "44" standard-tread model

In addition to several row-crop styles, the Massey-Harris "44" was also built in a standard-tread model. It was essentially the same as the row-crop, except for the modified chassis. Standard-tread models were popular in certain areas, although the row-crop was sold in far greater numbers.

Nebraska Test Data

Model: Massey-Harris 44K Standard
Test No. 427
Date Tested: September 29 to October 14, 1949

If not identical, tractor fuel and distillate appeared to have been quite similar in content. During the 45-1/2 hours of engine running time for this test, tractor fuel was used. No repairs or adjustments were noted. The 44K used the same chassis as the 44 Diesel noted in Test No. 426. A four-cylinder I-head engine rated at 1,350 rpm and using 3-7/8 x 5-1/2-inch bore and stroke was featured, along with a six-volt Auto-Lite electrical system and a Zenith 62AJ10 carburetor. Test H was run in third gear. It revealed 10.42 hp-hours per gallon of tractor fuel under a rated drawbar load of 27.7 hp. This test was run at a speed of 4.29 mph with a slippage of 4.4 percent. Under Test G, a low-gear maximum pull of 4,692 lbs. at 1.91 mph was achieved. Belt testing indicated 11.3 hp-hours per gallon under a Test C operating maximum load of 35.66 hp. The economy figure sagged to 11.19 under a Test D-rated load of 33.64 hp.

COLLECTOR VALUES	1	2	3	4
MODEL 44 ROW-CROP	$2,500	$1,500	$800	$400
MODEL 44 STANDARD	$2,300	$1,300	$700	$400

Massey-Harris "44" tractor LP gas version

For a time during its 1946 through 1955 production run, the "44"was available in an LP gas version with an 8.7-to-1 compression ratio. During the 1950s, LP gas as tractor fuel gained considerable popularity, and many companies responded with specially equipped LP gas tractor models.

COLLECTOR VALUES	1	2	3	4
MODEL 44 LP ROW-CROP	$3,500	$2,500	$2,000	$1,500

Massey-Harris "44" Orchard/Vineyard model

Orchard and Vineyard models of the Massey-Harris "44" were available during its entire production run. These tractors were built over the "44" standard-tread model, and included the special hood and fenders required for this duty. In addition, the air stack and exhaust were placed low, and a special shield helped protect the operator. The Vineyard was built on a narrower chassis than the Orchard and used 44 Standard sheet metal.

COLLECTOR VALUES	1	2	3	4
MODEL 44 ORCHARD/ VINEYARD	$8,000	–	–	–

The 44 Special Cane tractor was yet another version adapted to specific crop needs. This high-clearance model was also used for other growing crops. Production of these models only came to a small fraction of all "44" models that were built.

COLLECTOR VALUES	1	2	3	4
MODEL 44 SPECIAL CANE	$8,000	–	–	–

"44" Diesel standard-tread tractor

Production of the "44" Diesel standard-tread tractor began in 1948 and continued until 1955. The following

44 Special Cane tractor

year, the "44" Diesel row-crop tractor emerged and it remained in production until 1955. This model used a four-cylinder engine with a 3-7/8 x 5-1/2-inch bore and stroke. It featured a Bosch fuel injection system. In Nebraska Test No. 426 of 1949, the "44" Diesel delivered nearly 42 belt hp.

Nebraska Test Data

Model: Massey-Harris 44 Diesel Standard
Test No. 426
Date Tested: September 28 to October 1, 1949

Featuring the company's own four-cylinder I-head diesel engine, the 44 Standard was rated at 1,350 rpm and used a 3-7/8 x 5-1/2-inch bore and stroke. Also included was a Bosch fuel injection system and 12-volt Auto-Lite electrical equipment. No repairs or adjustments were noted for this tractor during 35 hours of engine running time. The bare tractor weighed 5,085 lbs. and Tests F, G and H were run with an additional 1,116 lbs. of ballast on each rear wheel. Advertised speeds of 2.21, 3.33, 4.45, 5.75 and 12.28 mph were provided, with Test H being run in third gear. This test indicated 14.13 hp-hours per gallon of diesel fuel under a rated drawbar load of 29.64 hp. This 10-hour test averaged a pull of 2,608 lbs. at 4.26 mph with slippage of 5.5 percent. Test G delivered a maximum pull of 4,351 lbs. in low gear. Belt testing indicated 15.88 hp-hours per gallon while under a 100 percent maximum load of 41.82 hp per Test C. At its Test D-rated load of 36.67 belt hp, the 44 Standard delivered 16.08 hp-hours per gallon.

COLLECTOR VALUES	1	2	3	4
MODEL 44 DIESEL	$3,500	$2,500	$1,300	$900

In 1947 Massey-Harris introduced its "44-6" tractor as a companion to the four-cylinder Model 44. The "44-6" was intended for those who preferred six-cylinder smoothness, but had no distinct advantage over the four-cylinder model. A Continental F-226 engine was used and it had a 3-5/16 x 4-3/8-inch bore and stroke. Production of the "44-6" standard-tread model ended in 1948; the row-crop style survived until 1951.

COLLECTOR VALUES	1	2	3	4
MODEL 44-6	$3,500	$2,750	$1,500	$800

"44" Special

Massey-Harris "44-6" tractor

Built in the 1953 through 1955 period, the "44" Special used a four-cylinder engine with a 4 x 5-1/2-inch bore and stroke for a displacement of 277-cubic inches. A "44" Special Diesel model was also built.

Nebraska Test Data

Model: Massey-Harris 44 Special
Test No. 510
Date Tested: October 10 to October 24, 1953

Although a 44 Special of regular row-crop design is shown here, the tractor actually tested was a standard-tread model. Massey-Harris catalogs also showed this tractor in a high-clearance row-crop design. The standard-tread model used 14-30 rear and 7.50-16-inch front rubber. Bare weight was 5,789 lbs., to which was added another 1,316 lbs. of ballast on each rear wheel during certain drawbar tests. The standard-tread design featured forward speeds of 2.24, 3.39, 4.5, 5.85 and 12.5 mph, with third gear being used for Test H. At a rated drawbar load of 34.71 hp, the 44 Special pulled 2,948 lbs. at 4.41 mph with a slippage of 5.34 percent. Fuel economy was registered at 11.06 hp-hours per gallon. Test G delivered a low-gear maximum pull of 5,341 lbs. at 1.94 mph. A four-cylinder 4 x 5-1/2, 277-cid engine was featured. Rated at 1,350 rpm, it achieved a maximum torque of 308.9 lbs.-ft. with an engine speed of 968 rpm. Test C, run at an operating maximum load of 45.23 belt hp, indicated a fuel economy of 12.46 hp-hours per gallon. This figure dropped slightly to 12.34 under a Test D-rated load of 42.81 hp. The gear shift lever broke at a welded joint following Test H, otherwise no repairs or adjustments were noted during 48 hours of running time.

COLLECTOR VALUES	1	2	3	4
44 SPECIAL STANDARD	$3,300	$2,500	$1,900	$1,200
44 SPECIAL ROW-CROP	$3,000	$2,200	$1,600	$1,000

Massey-Harris "55"

When the Massey-Harris "55" was introduced in 1946, it was the largest wheel-type farm tractor on the market. This model used a four-cylinder engine with a 4-1/2 x 6-inch bore and stroke. In Nebraska Test No. 394 of 1948, the "55"delivered nearly 56 belt hp. The "55" gasoline model was again tested at Nebraska in 1951 under No. 455. In this test, it delivered 63-1/2 belt hp. Production of the 55 ran until 1955. It was only built as a standard tractor.

Nebraska Test Data

Model: Massey-Harris 55
Test No. 394
Date Tested: May 18 to May 27, 1948

Weighing 7,223 lbs., the Massey-Harris 55 got an additional 811 lbs. of liquid ballast and 420 lbs. of cast iron weights for each rear wheel during Tests F, G and H. Tire equipment included 14-34 rear and 7.50-18-inch front rubber. This tractor featured advertised speeds of 2.96, 4.22, 5.22 and 12.07 mph. Third gear was used for Test H, and at a rated load of 41.1 drawbar hp, the 55 pulled 3,101 lbs. at 4.97 mph with a slippage of 5.09 percent. Fuel economy was 10.09 hp-hours per gallon. At a Test C operating maximum load of 55.72 belt hp, 11.78 hp-hours per gallon was noted, and slipped to 11.37 at the Test D-rated load of 52.22 belt hp. This tractor was equipped with the company's four-cylinder I-head engine. Rated at 1,350 rpm, it carried a 4-1/2 x 6-inch bore and stroke. Also featured was an Auto-Lite electrical system and a Zenith 62AJ10 carburetor. No repairs or adjustments were recorded during 44 hours of engine operation.

Nebraska Test Data

Model: Massey-Harris 55K Standard
Test No. 428
Date Tested: October 3 to October 14, 1949

During Test D, two spark plugs were replaced on this tractor, otherwise no repairs or adjustments were noted during 40 hours of engine operation. The 55K featured the company's own four-cylinder I-head engine rated at 1,350 rpm and used a 4-1/2 x 6-inch bore and stroke. Also featured were an Auto-Lite electrical system and a Zenith 62AJ10 carburetor. Without additional ballast, the 55K weighed 7,265 lbs., but 1,120 lbs. of liquid and cast iron ballast was added to each rear wheel for a portion of the tests. Included with the 55K were forward speeds of 2.96, 4.22, 5.22 and 12.07 mph, with third gear used for Test H. As with Test No. 427, tractor fuel was selected, and under a rated drawbar load of 37.25 hp, a fuel economy of 10.16 hp-hours per gallon was achieved. A Test G low-gear maximum pull of 5,546 lbs. was also noted. Fuel economy, using tractor fuel, came to 11.07 hp-hours per gallon under a Test D-rated load of 46.44 belt hp, and climbed to 11.46 under a Test C operating maximum load of 49.09 hp.

Nebraska Test Data

Model: Massey-Harris 55
Test No. 455
Date Tested: April 16 to May 7, 1951

Using the same 1,350 rpm and the same 382-cubic inch displacement as the 55 Diesel of Test No. 452, this gasoline model opened the 1951 testing season. Other basic specifications, including test weight, tire size and advertised speeds were virtually identical. No repairs or adjustments were noted during 42 hours of engine running time. At a Test C operating maximum load of 63.5 belt hp, the 55 delivered a fuel economy of 12.15 hp-hours per gallon. Fuel economy rested at 12.07 hp-hours per gallon under a Test D-rated belt load of 58.05 hp. Drawbar testing produced a Test G low-gear maximum pull of 6,377 lbs. at 2.63 mph under a slippage of 16.42 percent. Tests F, G and H saw an additional 1,460 lbs. of weight on each rear wheel in addition to the tractor's basic weight of 7,520 lbs. Test H, at a rated drawbar load of 45.66 hp, saw 10.38 hp-hours per gallon with a pull of 3,252 lbs. at 5.05 mph. Slippage in Test H was noted at 4.63 percent. As in Test No. 455, this run was made in third gear.

"55" Diesel tractor

Production of the "55" Diesel began in 1949 and continued until 1955. This model used a 382-cid four-cylinder engine with a 4-1/2 x 6-inch bore and stroke, and delivered almost 60 belt hp. The "55" was built only in a standard-tread design, but variations included a "55" Rice tractor and a "55" Wheatland tractor.

Nebraska Test Data

Model: Massey-Harris 55 Diesel

Test No. 452

Date Tested: October 17 to October 26, 1950

Standard equipment included 15-34 rear and 7.50-18-inch front tires. Weighing in at 7,793 lbs., the 55 Diesel received an additional 1,181 lbs. of ballast for each rear wheel during Tests F, G and H. Advertised speeds of 2.96, 4.22, 5.22 and 12.07 mph were featured, with third gear used for the rated drawbar run of Test H. In this test, the 55 Diesel delivered 41.32 hp with a pull of 2,967 lbs. at 5.22 mph and slippage of 5.44 percent. Fuel economy was registered at 13.95 hp-hours per gallon. Under Test G, a low-gear maximum pull of 5,865 lbs. at 2.62 mph was recorded. Massey-Harris furnished its own four-cylinder, I-head diesel engine for this tractor. Using a 4-1/2 x 6-inch bore and stroke with a rated speed of 1,350 rpm, it had a 382-cubic inch displacement. No repairs or adjustments were recorded during 50 hours of engine operation. At a Test D-rated load of 51.35 belt hp, the 55 Diesel achieved 15.47 hp-hours per gallon. Under the Test B and C 100 percent maximum load of 59.04 hp, fuel economy stood at an even 15 hp-hours per gallon.

Built only during 1952 and 1953, the Massey-Harris Colt was a two-plow tractor. Shown here is the standard-tread design. The Colt was equipped with a Continental F-124 four-cylinder engine with a 3 x 4-3/8 inch bore and stroke. The engine was rated at 1,500 rpm for drawbar work and 1,800 rpm on the belt.

COLLECTOR VALUES	1	2	3	4
21 COLT	$4,850	$3,600	$2,550	$1,980

Massey-Harris Colt standard-tread

Massey-Harris Colt Row-Crop

Colt and Mustang tractors were both available in a row-crop design in lieu of the standard-tread model. The row-crop models could be purchased with standard tricycle front end, single-wheel front, or an adjustable-width, high-arch front axle. All tractors of this series included live hydraulics as standard equipment.

Nebraska Test Data

Model: Massey-Harris No. 16 Pacer
Test No. 531
Date Tested: November 10 to November 15, 1954

Closing out the 1954 testing season, the Pacer came in weighing 2,299 lbs., to which was added an additional 585 lbs. on each rear wheel during Tests F, G and H. This tractor featured forward speeds of 3.02, 3.98 and 7.8 mph, with Test H run in second gear. At a rated drawbar load of 13.03 hp, the Pacer pulled 1,269 lbs. at 3.85 mph against a slippage of 15.12 percent. Fuel economy totaled 9.33 hp-hours per gallon. Test G came up with a low-gear maximum pull of 2,118 lbs. at 2.77 mph and a slippage of 10.3 percent. The Pacer was equipped with a Continental four-cylinder L-head engine rated at 1,800 rpm. Its 91-cubic inch displacement came from a 2-7/8 x 3-1/2-inch bore and stroke. Standard equipment also included 10-24 rear and 4.00-15 front tires. Belt testing yielded 10.54 hp-hours per gallon under a Test C operating maximum load of 17.88 hp. This figure sagged to 10.39 at a Test D-rated belt load of 16.35 hp. Engine torque peaked at 120.4 lbs.-ft. with an engine speed of 1,102 rpm. During 44 hours of operating time, no repairs or adjustments were recorded.

Massey-Harris Model 23 Mustang

Massey-Harris built the Model 23 Mustang tractor between 1952 and 1955. This model followed the M-H 22 tractor, and used the same Continental F-140 four-cylinder engine. The Mustang was available in row-crop design, with the choice of dual-front wheels, single-front wheel, or a high-arch adjustable wide-front axle. This tractor was also built in a standard-tread design.

COLLECTOR VALUES	1	2	3	4
23 MUSTANG	$4,500	$3,400	$2,200	$1,700

Massey-Ferguson "333" tractor

Massey-Harris and Ferguson joined in October 1953 to form Massey-Harris-Ferguson Inc. The "Harris" name was dropped in 1958, thus, Massey-Ferguson. In 1956 production of the "333" tractors began. They were an updated version of the Model 33. The "333"was built in gasoline, distillate, LP gas and diesel models, with the latter being shown here. In Nebraska Test No. 577 of June 1956, the "333" diesel delivered over 37 belt hp. This model used a 3-11/16 x 4-7/8-inch bore and stroke in its four-cylinder engine. The "333" gasoline model appears in Nebraska Test No. 603. It had a similar hp rating. Production of the "333" series ended in 1957.

Nebraska Test Data

Model: Massey-Harris 333 Diesel

Test No. 577

Date Tested: June 8 to June 13, 1956

At a Test D-rated belt load of 32.79 hp, the 333 Diesel scored a fuel economy of 14.78 hp-hours per gallon, with this figure standing at 14.08 under a Test B, 100 percent maximum belt load of 37.15 hp. Rated at 1,500 rpm, the 333 Diesel achieved a Test L operating maximum torque of 106 percent at 75 percent of rated engine speed. Standard equipment of this 6,005-lb. tractor included 12-38 rear and 6.50-16-inch front rubber. Also featured was a Massey-Harris four-cylinder engine. Using a 3-11/16 x 4-7/8- inch bore and stroke, it had a displacement of 208-cubic inches. Five forward speeds were available in two different speed ranges, giving 10 forward speeds ranging from 1.47 to 14 mph. Following Test A, a leak developed at the hydraulic reservoir. After repair, the test continued. Otherwise, no repairs or adjustments were noted during 45 hours of running time. During Tests F, G and H, an additional 858 lbs. was added to each rear wheel. Test H, run in the high range of third gear, indicated a rated drawbar load of 26.53 hp, along with a pull of 2,017 lbs. at 4.93 mph and slippage of 3.7 percent. Fuel economy was posted at 13.26 hp-hours per gallon of diesel fuel. Test G, run in the low range of first gear, produced a maximum pull of 5,262 lbs. at 1.29 mph with a slippage of 13.48 percent.

Nebraska Test Data

Model: Massey-Harris 333

Test No. 603

Date Tested: October 25 to November 3, 1956

Weighing 5,920 lbs., the 333 was equipped with 12-38 rear and 6.50-16-inch front tires. During Tests F, G and H, an additional 1,028 lbs. of weight was added to each rear wheel. The 333 featured two speed ranges, each with five different choices, for a total of 10 different speeds from 1.47 to 14 mph. Using first gear, low range, Test G elicited a maximum pull of 5,407 lbs. at 1.31 mph with a slippage of 12.58 percent. High range in third gear was used for the rated drawbar run of Test H. With an output of 29.71 hp, the 333 pulled 2,262 lbs. at 4.93 mph with a slippage of 3.76 percent. Fuel economy totaled 10.69 hp-hours per gallon. This tractor's features included a Massey-Harris four-cylinder engine with a 3-11/16 x 4-7/8-inch bore and stroke for a displacement of 208-cubic inches. Rated at 1,500 rpm, it developed a Test L operating maximum torque of 107 percent at 56 percent of rated engine speed. The rated belt load test (D) indicated a fuel economy of 12.33 hp-hours per gallon with a load of 37.11 hp. At a Test C operating maximum load of 39.84 hp, fuel economy was 12.37 hp-hours per gallon. During 43-1/2 hours of operating time, no repairs or adjustments were recorded.

COLLECTOR VALUES	1	2	3	4
333-ROW CROP GAS	$6,000	$4,500	$3,000	$1,800
STANDARD GAS	$6,000	$4,500	$3,000	$1,800
ROW CROP DIESEL	$6,300	$4,800	$3,300	$2,000
STANDARD DIESEL	$6,500	$5,000	$3,500	$2,200
ROW CROP LP	$6,500	$5,000	$4,000	$2,500
STANDARD LP	$7,000	$5,500	$4,300	$2,500

Massey-Harris "444" tractor

Massey-Harris "444" tractors were built in gasoline, LP gas distillate, and diesel versions. In addition, there were several different chassis and axle styles available. Live hydraulics and a live pto were standard equipment. These tractors used an engine designed by M-H-F and built by Continental. The four-cylinder design carried a 4 x 5-1/2-inch bore and stroke. This model delivered a maximum of 47 belt hp. Production of the "444"tractors ran from 1956 to 1958. Until the latter date, the company was known as Massey-Harris-Ferguson Inc., with headquarters at Racine, Wisconsin.

Nebraska Test Data

Model: Massey-Harris 444 Diesel

Test No. 576

Date Tested: June 2 to June 14, 1956

Using two speed ranges, each with five forward speeds, the 444 Diesel gave 10 choices ranging from 1.52 to 14.4 mph. Weighing in at 6,499 lbs., the 444 Diesel used 13-38-inch rear and 6.50-16-inch front tires. During Tests F, G and H, an additional 1,533 lbs. of weight was added to each rear wheel. Test G, using the first gear in low range, gave a maximum drawbar pull of 6,463 lbs. at 1.34 mph with a slippage of 13.77 percent. Test H, run in the high range of third gear, indicated a rated drawbar load of 35.07 hp, along with a pull of 2,591 lbs. at 5.08 mph and slippage of 4.14 percent. Fuel economy was pegged at 13.93 hp-hours per gallon. The 444 Diesel used a Massey-Harris four-cylinder diesel engine with a 4 x 5-1/2-inch bore and stroke for a 277-cubic inch displacement. Rated at 1,500 rpm, it achieved 109 percent of rated torque at 70 percent of rated speed, and maintained this torque level through 65 percent of rated speed. Test D, run at a rated belt load of 43.29 hp, indicated a fuel economy of 15.59 hp-hours per gallon, slipping slightly to 15.06 at a Test B, 100 percent maximum belt load of 48.21 hp. No repairs or adjustments were noted during 54-1/2 hours of running time.

Nebraska Test Data

Model: Massey-Harris 444 LP

Test No. 602

Date Tested: October 25 to November 3, 1956

This tractor featured five forward speeds in each of two speed ranges, providing a total of 10 different selections, from 1.52 to 14.4 mph. Also featured was a Massey-Harris four-cylinder, 4 x 5-1/2-inch engine with a 277-cubic inch displacement. The propane model shown here carried an 8.98:1 compression ratio. Weighing 6,385 lbs., it also featured 13-38 rear and 6.50-16-inch front tires. During Tests F, G and H, an additional 1,558 lbs. was added to each rear wheel. Using first gear in the low range, the 444-LP made a Test G maximum pull of 6,534 lbs. at 1.33 mph with slippage of 14.04 percent. Using third gear in the high range, Test H indicated a rated output of 35.11 drawbar hp, along with a pull of 2,596 lbs. at 5.07 mph and slippage of 3.96 percent. Fuel economy came to 8.32 hp-hours per gallon of propane. During 50-1/2 hours of operating time, no repairs or adjustments were noted. Test L indicated that 111 percent of rated-speed torque occurred at 76 percent of the rated 1,500 rpm. At a Test D-rated belt load of 43.84 hp, fuel economy came in at 9.73 hp-hours per gallon, and was pegged at 9.96 at a Test C operating maximum load of 47.54 belt hp.

COLLECTOR VALUES	1	2	3	4
444-ROW CROP GAS	$4,500	$3,500	$2,500	$1,600
STANDARD GAS	$4,300	$3,300	$2,300	$1,400
ROW CROP DIESEL	$4,800	$3,800	$2,800	$1,500
STANDARD DIESEL	$4,500	$3,500	$2,700	$1,400
ROW CROP LP	$5,000	$4,000	$3,000	$2,000
STANDARD LP	$5,000	$4,000	$3,000	$2,000

Production of the Massey-Harris "555" tractor began in 1955 and continued into 1958. These tractors were built in gasoline, LP gas, distillate and diesel-powered versions. All were essentially the same except for the power plant. The big four-cylinder engine had a displacement of 382-cubic inches and used a 4-1/2 x 6-inch bore and stroke. These tractors were rated at about 58 belt or pto hp.

COLLECTOR VALUES	1	2	3	4
555-GAS	$5,000	$4,000	$2,500	$1,500
DIESEL	$4,500	$3,800	$2,300	$1,700
LP	$5,000	$4,200	$2,700	$2,000

Massey-Harris "555" tractor

MH-50 tractor

When the "Harris" part of the corporate name was dropped in 1958, the end came for Massey-Harris tractors. From this point on, the Massey-Ferguson name would predominate. The stage was set for a new line of tractors with the 1956 introduction of the MH-50. This was an entirely new design, and was followed in 1958 with the MF-50 tractor. Its four-cylinder engine used a 3-5/16 x 3-7/8-inch bore and stroke, and delivered nearly 30 belt hp.

Nebraska Test Data

Model: Massey-Harris 50

Test No. 595

Date Tested: September 25 to October 4, 1956

At a Test C operating maximum load of 31.36 belt hp, the M-H 50 yielded 11.47 hp-hours per gallon. This figure slipped to 10.97 at a Test D-rated belt load of 29.4 hp. Features included a Continental four-cylinder engine with a 3-5/16 x 3-7/8-inch bore and stroke with a 134-cubic inch displacement. Rated at 2,000 rpm, this tractor achieved an operating maximum torque of 121 percent at 59 percent of rated engine speed. The spark plugs were cleaned prior to Test H, otherwise no repairs or adjustments were reported during 58-1/2 hours of operating time. Weighing 3,432 lbs., the M-H 50 featured forward speeds of 1.22, 1.99, 3.65, 5.3, 7.96 and 14.59 mph. Also featured were 11-28-inch rear and 6.00-16-inch front tires. During tests F, G and H, an additional 920 lbs. was added to each rear wheel. Test G produced a low-gear maximum pull of 3,525 lbs. at 1.14 mph with a slippage of 15.23 percent. Fuel economy at rated drawbar load came to 9.74 hp-hours per gallon per Test H. This test indicated a rated load of 24.09 hp with a pull of 1,766 lbs. at 5.12 mph and slippage of 4.33 percent.

Massey-Ferguson Inc.

DETROIT, MICHIGAN

In 1953 Massey-Harris bought out Harry Ferguson Inc. and formed Massey-Harris-Ferguson. Until 1958, tractors were sold under the M-H-F trademark. Due to the new vernacular term of Massey-Ferguson, the company dropped "Harris" in 1958, becoming simply Massey-Ferguson.

Nebraska Test Data

Model: Massey-Ferguson TO-35 Diesel
Test No. 690
Date Tested: April 3 to April 13, 1959

At its rated 2,000 rpm, the TO-35 Diesel developed 32.93 maximum PTO hp and achieved 14.64 hp-hours per gallon of diesel fuel. This tractor carried a Standard Motor 23-C diesel engine of four-cylinder design, using a 3-5/16 x 4-inch bore and stroke for a displacement of 137.8-cubic inches. Also featured were six forward speeds ranging from 1.33 to 14.57 mph, along with 11-28-inch rear and 6.00-16-inch front tires. With added ballast, test weight came to 5,775 lbs., although the bare tractor weighed 3,565 lbs. No repairs or adjustments were noted during 51-1/2 hours of operation. Using low gear, a maximum pull of 3,877 lbs. was recorded at 1.88 mph with 14.23 percent slippage. The varying drawbar load tests included a two-hour run at a maximum load of 30.49 hp. This test revealed a pull of 2,282 lbs. at 5.01 mph, using fourth gear. Slippage was 6.44 percent, with an economy totaling 13.18 hp-hours per gallon of diesel fuel. A 10-hour run, made at 75 percent of the maximum pull, noted an output of 24 drawbar hp, a speed of 5.26 mph and slippage of 5.29 percent for a final figure of 12.26 hp-hours per gallon.

Massey-Ferguson 35 tractor

Nebraska Test Data

Model: Massey-Ferguson MF-35 Diesel
Test No. 744
Date Tested: May 16 to May 23, 1960

At its rated engine speed of 2,000 rpm, the MF-35 Diesel delivered 37.04 PTO hp and yielded 15.69 hp-hours per gallon. This tractor was equipped with a Perkins three-cylinder engine. Using a 3.6 x 5-inch bore and stroke, it had a 152.7-cubic inch displacement. The selective-gear fixed-ratio transmission featured six forward speeds ranging from 1.33 to 14.57 mph. Other equipment included 11-28-inch rear and 6.00-16-inch front tires. This tractor weighed 3,559 lbs., but added ballast during the drawbar testing raised this figure to 5,909 lbs. A two-hour economy run at maximum available power elicited 32.13 drawbar hp, a pull of 2,410 lbs. at 5 mph and slippage of 6.52 percent. Fuel economy was 13.75 hp-hours per gallon. The economy figure rose to 13.88 during a 10-hour drawbar run made at 75 percent pull. The latter test indicated 25.82 hp, a pull of 1,855 lbs. at 5.22 mph and slippage of 4.75 percent. Test No. 744 also included runs for maximum power with and without ballast, and varying drawbar pull and travel speed with ballast. Specific data for all tests noted in this volume may be found in the original Test Reports.

Massey-Ferguson 50 tractor

Nebraska Test Data

Model: Massey-Ferguson MF-50 Diesel
Test No. 807
Date Tested: October 23 to November 3, 1961

A three-cylinder Perkins diesel engine was featured in this tractor. Rated at 2,000 rpm, it used a 3.6 x 5.0- inch bore and stroke for a displacement of 152.7-cubic inches. Also featured was a 17.4:1 compression ratio. Operating at rated engine speed, a maximum of 38.33 PTO hp was observed, along with 15.72 hp-hours per gallon. Another test, run at 540 rpm on the PTO shaft and a corresponding crankshaft speed of 1,499 rpm, noted an output of 31.08 hp, with an economy figure of 16.16. Also featured in the MF-50 Diesel was a selective-gear fixed-ratio transmission with six forward speeds ranging from 1.33 to 14.57 mph. Tires were 12.4-28-inch rear and 6.00-16-inch front rubber. The bare tractor weight of 3,933 lbs. rose to 6,017 lbs. through the addition of front and rear ballast. Drawbar fuel economy was posted at 13.42 hp-hours per gallon in a two-hour run that indicated a maximum output of 32.42 hp. This test yielded a pull of 2,436 lbs. at 4.99 mph with 6.2 percent slippage. Economy remained virtually identical, coming in at 13.43 during a 10-hour drawbar run made at 75 percent pull. Statistics included a pull of 1,929 lbs. at 5.18 mph with 4.82 percent slippage. No repairs or adjustments were noted during 44 hours of operation.

Nebraska Test Data

Model: Massey-Ferguson 65 (LPG)
Test No. 657
Date Tested: June 16 to June 27, 1958

Repeated attempts to locate a photograph of the MF65 propane version have been unsuccessful, as even the company advertising submitted with the test illustrated the gasoline model. This tractor used a Continental four-cylinder engine rated at 2,000 rpm. Its 3.578 x 4.375-inch bore and stroke yielded a 176-cubic inch displacement. An 8.1:1 compression ratio was also part of the special propane design. At a 100 percent maximum belt load of 42.6 hp, this tractor achieved 8.23 hp-hours per gallon of propane, slipping to 7.69 under a Test D-rated belt load of 38.15 hp. Other features included six forward speeds ranging from 1.29 to 14.23 mph, along with 13-28-inch rear and 6.00-16-inch front tires. Bare tractor weight was 4,185 lbs., to which was added 1,980 lbs. on each rear wheel and an additional 485 lbs. for each front wheel during the drawbar test runs. Under the "Repairs and Adjustments" section of the test report, this entry appears: "During Test 'H' the wheel weights used on each rear wheel fell off." Other than this statement, no repairs or adjustments were made during four hours of running time. Test H, run in fourth gear and at a rate output of 31.24 hp, noted a pull of 2,078 lbs. at 5.6 mph and 3.2 percent slippage. Fuel economy was recorded at 6.6 hp-hours per gallon of propane. Test G yielded a low-gear maximum pull of 6,825 lbs. at 1.14 mph with 14.69 percent slippage.

Nebraska Test Data

Model: Massey-Ferguson MF-65 Diesel
Test No. 745
Date Tested: May 16 to May 24, 1960

The selective-gear fixed-ratio transmission used in this tractor offered six forward speeds of 1.29, 1.94, 3.56, 5.18, 7.76 and 14.23 mph. Also featured were 13-28-inch rear and 6.00-16-inch front tires. Weighing 4,485 lbs., the MP-65 took on a test weight of 9,275 lbs. with the addition of cast iron and liquid ballast. The 10-hour economy run, made at 75 percent pull, indicated 13.42 hp-hours per gallon of diesel fuel. This test also recorded 33.82 hp, a pull of 2,382 lbs. at 5.33 mph and slippage of 3.95 percent. A two-hour run, made at maximum available power, produced 42.13 drawbar hp, a pull of 3,077 lbs. at 5.13 mph and slippage of 5.45 percent. Fuel economy was 13.72 hp-hours per gallon. Both runs were made in fourth gear. The MF-65 boasted a Perkins four-cylinder engine rated at 2,000 rpm. Using a 3.6 x 5-inch bore and stroke, it had a displacement of 203.5-cubic inches. At rated engine speed, a maximum of 48.59 PTO hp was observed, with 15.64 hp-hours per gallon. Another PTO run, made at the standard 540 rpm shaft speed and corresponding engine speed of 1,499 rpm, indicated 39.67 hp and 16.33 hp-hours per gallon. No repairs or adjustments were noted during 49-1/2 hours of operating time.

Massey-Ferguson 85 series

Nebraska Test Data

Model: Massey-Ferguson 85
Test No. 726
Date Tested: November 2 to November 13, 1959

A Continental four-cylinder engine was featured in the MF-85 tractor. Rated at 2,000 rpm, it carried a 3-7/8 x 5-1/8-inch bore and stroke for a 242-cubic inch displacement. At rated engine speed, a maximum of 61.23 PTO hp was observed, with an economy of 11.64 hp-hours per gallon. Another PTO run, made a 540 PTO rpm and a corresponding engine speed of 1,477 rpm, indicated an output of 52.89 hp and a fuel economy of 11.02 hp-hours per gallon. Standard features of this tractor included eight forward speeds ranging from 1.48 to 18.76 mph. Also featured were 15-30-inch rear and 7.50-16-inch front tires. Bare tractor weight was 5,737 lbs., but total weight after ballast came to 11,245 lbs. Drawbar fuel economy was 10.46 using third gear and delivering a maximum of 50.76 hp. This test also indicated a pull of 5,194 lbs. at 3.66 mph and slippage of 7.55 percent. A 10-hour run at 42.55 drawbar hp yielded a pull of 3,951 lbs. at 4.04 mph against slippage of 5.23 percent. Fuel economy totaled 9.48 hp-hours per gallon. Except for a failed bearing on the PTO shaft, no repairs or adjustments were recorded during 47 hours of operation.

Nebraska Test Data

Model: Massey-Ferguson 85 LPG
Test No. 727
Date Tested: November 2 to November 13, 1959

While the MF-85 gasoline model of Test No. 726 used a 7.35:1 compression ratio, the LPG model carried an 8.8:1 compression ratio. With this exception, both tractors used basically the same engine design. Advertised speeds, tire equipment and other accessories remained virtually identical for both tractors. This model weighed 5,753 lbs., but after ballast was added to the front and rear wheels, the test weight totaled 11,260 lbs. Using third gear, under a load of 55.23 drawbar hp, a pull of 5,101 lbs. was recorded at 4.05 mph with 7.37 percent slippage. Fuel economy was 8.39 hp-hours per gallon of propane. A 10-hour run, at 75 percent pull, yielded an economy figure of 7.30 against an output of 46.25 hp, a pull of 3,965 lbs. at 4.38 mph and slippage of 5.28 percent. At a maximum load of 62.21 PTO hp and rated engine speed of 2,000 rpm, fuel economy was 9.49 hp-hours per gallon of propane. This figure slipped to 8.97 with an output of 52.49 hp, a standard PTO speed of 540 rpm and a corresponding engine speed of 1,477 rpm. During 57 hours of operating time, no repairs or adjustments were noted.

Massey-Ferguson 90 tractor

Nebraska Test Data

Model: Massey-Ferguson Super 90 Diesel
Test No. 822
Date Tested: June 12 to June 21, 1962

At its rated engine speed of 2,000 rpm, 68.53 maximum PTO hp was observed, together with 15.83 hp-hours per gallon. A second run made at 540 PTO rpm and a corresponding engine speed of 1,497 rpm saw the Super 90 develop 57.71 hp and yield 16.47 hp-hours per gallon. Standard equipment included a Perkins four-cylinder diesel engine with a 4.500 x 4.750-inch bore and stroke for a 302.2-cubic inch displacement. Also featured was a selective-gear fixed-ratio transmission, which provided eight forward speeds ranging from 1.7 to 21.59 mph. During preliminary PTO runs, a loss of power occurred. After replacing the fuel transfer pump, fuel filters, injectors and injection pump, testing resumed without further incident during 71 hours of operation. Tire equipment included 18.4-30-inch rear and 7.50-18-inch front rubber. The bare tractor weighed 7,245 lbs. and was augmented with rear wheel ballast for a total test weight of 12,575 lbs. Using third gear, and at 59.8 maximum available drawbar hp, a two-hour economy run yielded 13.82 hp-hours per gallon. Other test statistics included a pull of 5,492 lbs. at 4.08 mph with 6.77 percent slippage. A 10-hour run at 75 percent pull noted an economy figure of 13.21. Other test data included an output of 48.45 hp, a pull of 4,102 lbs. at 4.43 mph, and slippage of 4.89 percent.

Massey-Ferguson MF-135 tractor

Nebraska Test Data

Model: Massey-Ferguson MF-135 Diesel

Test No. 895

Date Tested: May 13 to May 26, 1965

Using a Perkins three-cylinder diesel engine, this tractor had a rated speed of 2,000 rpm. The 152.7-cubic inch displacement resulted from a 3.6 x 5-inch bore and stroke. At rated speed, 37.82 maximum PTO hp was observed, with 17.04 hp-hours per gallon. Another run, made at 540 PTO rpm and an engine speed of 1,705 rpm, saw an output of 34.86 hp, and 17.58 hp-hours per gallon. Massey-Ferguson featured a selective-gear, fixed-ratio transmission that also provided partial range power shifting. The 12 forward speeds ranged from 1.31 to 18.8 mph. Standard equipment for this 3,645-lb. tractor also included 14.9-24-inch rear and 6.00-16-inch front tires. Using seventh gear, 33.06 maximum available drawbar hp was observed in a two-hour run that witnessed 15.03 hp-hours per gallon. Other test statistics included a pull of 2,437 lbs. at 5.09 mph and slippage of 6.38 percent. The 10-hour run, at 75 percent pull, saw 26.21 hp and a yield of 14.26 hp-hours per gallon. Also indicated was a pull of 1,849 lbs. at 5.32 mph and 5.09 percent slippage. No repairs or adjustments were reported during 37-1/2 hours of operating time.

Massey-Ferguson MF-150 tractor

Nebraska Test Data

Model: Massey-Ferguson MF-150 Diesel

Test No. 901

Date Tested: May 25 to June 9, 1965

Weighing 4,805 lbs., the MF-150 was encumbered with front and rear ballast for a total test weight of 6,605 lbs. Standard equipment included 12.4-38-inch rear and 6.00-16-inch front tires. Also featured was a selective-gear fixed-ratio transmission with partial range power shifting. A total of 12 speeds were available ranging from 1.38 to 18.62 mph. No repairs or adjustments were required during 39-1/2 hours of operating time. Using seventh gear, the two-hour drawbar economy run yielded 33.07 maximum available hp, with a pull of 2,514 lbs. at 4.93 mph and 5.59 percent slippage. This test evoked a fuel economy of 15.37 hp-hours per gallon. The economy figure stood at 15.02 after a 10-hour run made at 75 percent pull. Also recorded was an output of 26.31 hp, a pull of 1,931 lbs. at 5.11 mph and 4.22 percent slippage. Massey-Ferguson equipped this tractor with a Perkins three-cylinder diesel engine rated at 2,000 rpm. Using a 3.6 x 5-inch bore and stroke, it carried a 152.7-cubic inch displacement. At rated engine speed, 37.88 maximum PTO hp was observed, with 17.83 hp-hours per gallon. An even higher economy of 18.15 resulted in a second PTO run. Using a standard PTO speed of 540 PTO rpm and a corresponding engine speed of 1,705 rpm, this test recorded an output of 35.38 hp.

Massey-Ferguson MF-165 series

Nebraska Test Data

Model: Massey-Ferguson MF-165 Diesel

Test No. 896

Date Tested: May 13 to May 22, 1965

This tractor used an engine design similar to that noted for Test No. 895, but in this case, four-cylinders of 3.6 x 5-inch bore and stroke were featured. Rated at 2,000 rpm, this engine had a 203.5-cubic inch displacement. Also in the design was a partial range power shift transmission with 12 forward speeds in a range from 1.28 to 18.54 mph. Tire equipment for this 5,085-lb. tractor included 14.9-28-inch rear and 6.00-16-inch front rubber. For the tests, additional front and rear ballast raised the test weight to 7,625 lbs. Using seventh gear, a two-hour run at 44.93 maximum available drawbar hp achieved 14.96 hp-hours per gallon. Also recorded was a pull of 3,428 lbs. at 4.91 mph and 6.62 percent slippage. The slippage fell to 4.9 percent in a 10-hour run made at 75percent pull. Economy was 14.74 hp-hours per gallon against an output of 37.02 hp. The 10-hour run also saw a pull of 2,706 lbs. at 5.13 mph. No repairs or adjustments were required during 40-1/2 hours of operation. Operating at 540 PTO rpm and a corresponding engine speed of 1,705 rpm, 47.4 PTO hp was observed, with 17.1 hp-hours per gallon. Fuel economy was pegged at 16.82 in a two-hour run at rated engine speed and against a maximum load.

Nebraska Test Data

Model: Massey-Ferguson MF-165

Test No. 898

Date Tested: May 18 to May 29, 1965

Standard equipment for the MF-165 included 14.9-28-inch rear and 6.00-16-inch front tires. Weighing 5,005 lbs., this tractor assumed a test weight of 7,345 lbs. through the addition of front and rear ballast. Also featured was a selective-gear fixed-ratio transmission that included partial range power shifting. In all, 12 forward speeds were available in a range from 1.28 to 18.54 mph. Using seventh gear, the two-hour drawbar economy run at 39.89 maximum available hp manifested 9.95 hp-hours per gallon. Also recorded was a pull of 3,034 lbs. at 4.93 mph against 7.35 percent slippage. The 10-hour run at 75 percent pull was conducted at 33.24 drawbar hp and yielded 9.43 hp-hours per gallon. This test saw a pull of 2,391 lbs. at 5.21 mph and 5.58 percent slippage. No repairs or adjustments were reported during 40-1/2 hours of operation. Massey-Ferguson equipped this tractor with a Continental four-cylinder gasoline engine. Rated at 2,000 rpm, it used a 3.578 x 4.375-inch bore and stroke for a 176-cubic inch displacement. At rated engine speed, 46.92 maximum PTO hp was observed, with 11.62 hp-hours per gallon. This figure stood at 11.77 in a second run made with 540 PTO rpm and a corresponding engine speed of 1,705 rpm. This test saw an output of 43.64 PTO hp.

MF-135 (left), MF-150 Wide Row-crop (center), and MF165 Wide Row-Crop

Nebraska Test Data

Model: Massey-Ferguson MF-165 (Also MF-30 Industrial)
Test No. 1008
Date Tested: April 28 to May 12, 1969

At its rated speed of 2,000 rpm, this tractor developed 51.91 maximum PTO hp while yielding 10.85 hp-hours per gallon. This model featured a Perkins four-cylinder engine. Using a 3-7/8 x 4-1/2-inch bore and stroke, it had a displacement of 212-cubic inches. At 540 PTO rpm and a corresponding engine speed of 1,683 rpm, an economy of 11.06 hp resulted against a load of 48.2 hp. Features included a selective-gear fixed-ratio transmission with partial range power shifting. The 12 forward speeds ranged from 1.36 to 19.65 mph. Also featured were 16.9-28-inch rear and 6.50-16-inch front tires. Weighing 5,830 lbs., this unit assumed a test weight of 7,760 lbs. through the addition of front and rear ballast. Using seventh gear, the two-hour economy run at 44.44 maximum available drawbar hp yielded 9.16 hp-hours per gallon. Also indicated was a pull of 3,173 lbs. at 5.25 mph with slippage totaling 6.04 percent. The 10-hour run at 75 percent pull noted 8.26 hp-hours per gallon against a load of 37.99 hp. This output resulted from a pull of 2,479 lbs. at 5.75 mph and slippage of 4.52 percent. During the preliminary PTO runs, the fixed carburetor jet was replaced with an adjustable jet. During the 10-hour run, adjustment of the control valve for the hydraulic steering power assist mechanism was required. No other repairs or adjustments were noted during 59 hours of operating time.

Massey-Ferguson 175 series

Nebraska Test Data

Model: Massey-Ferguson MF-175 Diesel
Test No. 897
Date Tested: May 17 to May 29, 1965

Weighing 6,125 lbs., this tractor assumed a test weight of 9,555 lbs. through the addition of front and rear ballast. Standard equipment included 16.9-28-inch rear and 6.50-16-inch front tires. Also featured was a selective-gear, fixed-ratio transmission with partial range power shifting. The 12 forward speeds ranged from 1.32 to 19.08 mph. No repairs or adjustments were required during 42-1/2 hours of running time. Using seventh gear, the two-hour economy run at 53.51 maximum available drawbar hp saw 14.37 hp-hours per gallon. This test revealed slippage of 6.13 percent while pulling 3,894 lbs. at 5.15 mph. The 10-hour economy run at 75 percent pull saw 14.22 hp-hours per gallon against a load of 43.55 hp. A pull of 3,053 lbs. at 5.35 mph and 4.67 percent slippage was also recorded. This tractor carried a four-cylinder Perkins engine rated at 2,000 rpm. Its 236-cubic inch displacement resulted from a 3.875 x 5-inch bore and stroke. At rated engine speed, 63.34 maximum PTO hp gave 16.68 hp-hours per gallon. An even higher economy figure of 16.93 resulted from a second run made at 540 PTO rpm and a corresponding engine speed of 1,684 rpm. This test saw an output of 55.46 PTO hp.

Nebraska Test Data

Model: Massey-Ferguson MF-175
Test No. 1020
Date Tested: September 11 to September 25, 1969

Dwarfed by the test car, the MF-175 is shown on the course during actual test procedures. Operating in seventh gear, this unit delivered 48.3 maximum available drawbar hp in the two-hour economy run and established a fuel efficiency of 9.8 hp-hours per gallon. Also recorded was a pull of 3,484 lbs. at 5.2 mph and slippage of 6.19 percent. The 10-hour run at 75 percent pull noted 8.33 hp-hours per gallon against a load of 41.75 hp. Other statistics included a pull of 2,783 lbs. at 5.63 mph with slippage totaling 4.76 percent. Weighing 5,925 lbs., the MF-175 assumed a test weight of 9,185 lbs. through added front and rear ballast. Standard equipment included 16.9-28-inch rear and 6.50-16-inch front rubber. No repairs or adjustments were reported during 44 hours of operation. This model featured a selective-gear fixed-ratio transmission with partial range power shifting. Its 12 forward speeds ranged from 1.32 to 19.08 mph. A Perkins four-cylinder, 236-cid engine was used, rated at 2,000 rpm and it used a 3-7/8 x 5-inch bore and stroke. At rated engine speed, 61.89 maximum PTO hp was developed and an economy of 11.12 hp-hours per gallon of gasoline was established. Operating at 540 PTO rpm and a corresponding engine speed of 1,683 rpm, the economy figure stood at 11.52 against a load of 58.06 hp.

Massey-Ferguson MF-180 Row Crop

Nebraska Test Data

Model: Massey-Ferguson MF-180 Diesel
Test No. 900
Date Tested: May 25 to June 9, 1965

Beginning with Test No. 895, several MF diesel models in this series featured Perkins engines. The MF-180 illustrated here was no exception. Rated at 2,000 rpm, it used a 3.875 x 5-inch bore and stroke for a 236-cubic inch displacement. At the rated engine speed, 63.68 maximum PTO hp was recorded and an economy of 16.76 hp-hours per gallon was achieved. An even higher fuel economy of 17.26 was noted in another PTO run made at 540 PTO rpm and a corresponding engine speed of 1,684 rpm. This test saw an output of 57.11 hp. Weighing 6,755 lbs., the MF-180 Diesel was carried on 15.5-38-inch rear and 7.50-15-inch front tires. During drawbar testing it assumed a weight of 8,665 lbs. through the addition of front and rear ballast. Twelve forward speeds were provided ranging from 1.34 to 19.15 mph. Using seventh gear, the two-hour drawbar economy run was made at 53.84 maximum available hp, with an achieved economy of 14.75 hp-hours per gallon. Also recorded was a pull of 3,973 lbs. at 5.08 mph with 6.4 percent slippage. The 10-hour economy run set 14.78 hp-hours per gallon against an output of 42.95 hp. Other statistics include a pull of 3,059 lbs. at 5.26 mph and 4.55 percent slippage.

Massey-Ferguson MF-205 tractor

Nebraska Test Data

Model: Massey-Ferguson MF-205 Diesel, 6-Speed
Test No. 1363
Date Tested: September 18 to October 3, 1980

Weighing 1,905 lbs., this tractor was equipped with 8-3/8-24-inch rear and 4.00-12-inch front tires. Additional front and rear ballast gave a total test weight of 2,840 lbs. Features included a selective-gear fixed-ratio transmission with six forward speeds ranging from 1.1 to 7.0 mph. Using fifth gear, the two-hour drawbar test at 12.87 maximum available hp saw a pull of 1,101 lbs. at 4.38 mph with slippage totaling 7.55 percent. Fuel economy was recorded at 9.98 hp-hours per gallon. The 10-hour run at 75 percent pull noted 9.65 hp-hours per gallon under a load of 10.69 drawbar hp. Other test data included a pull of 866 lbs. at 4.63 mph and 5.51 percent slippage. No repairs or adjustments were necessary during 35 hours of operation. The MF-205 featured a Toyosha two-cylinder diesel engine. Rated at 2,400 rpm, it carried a 3.46-inch bore and stroke for a 65.2-cubic inch displacement CID. At rated engine speed, 16.56 maximum PTO hp was observed, and an economy of 12.86 hp-hours per gallon of fuel was achieved.

Massey-Ferguson MF-210 tractor

Nebraska Test Data

Model: Massey-Ferguson MF-210
Test No. 1365
Date Tested: September 15 to September 24, 1980

With a rated engine speed of 2,500 rpm, the MF-210 delivered 21.96 maximum PTO hp while achieving 13.31 hp-hours per gallon. Operating at 540 PTO rpm and a corresponding engine speed of 2,326 rpm, an economy of 13.61 hp-hours per gallon was evidenced under a load of 21.23 PTO hp. Features included a Toyosha two-cylinder engine. Its 3.62 x 3.74-inch bore and stroke gave a 77.1-cubic inch displacement. Except for replacing the battery, no repairs or adjustments were necessary during 40 hours of engine operation. Weighing 2,460 lbs., the MF-210 was equipped with 11.2/10-24-inch rear and 5.00-15-inch front tires. Additional front and rear ballast gave a total test weight of 3,550 lbs. A selective-gear fixed-ratio transmission was used and its 12 forward speeds ranged from 0.3 to 12.4 mph. Using 10th gear, the two-hour economy run at 17.28 maximum available hp saw a pull of 1,113 lbs. at 5.82 mph and slippage totaling 10.84 percent. Fuel economy was 10.84 hp-hours per gallon. The 10-hour run at 75 percent pull saw 10.53 hp-hours per gallon under a load of 14.30 drawbar hp. Other test statistics included a pull of 877 lbs. at 6.12 mph and slippage totaling 5.43 percent.

Massey-Ferguson MF-220 tractor

Nebraska Test Data

Model: Massey-Ferguson MF-220
Test No. 1367
Date Tested: September 15 to September 26, 1980

A Toyosha two-cylinder, 90.3-cid engine was featured in the MF-220 tractor. Rated at 2,500 rpm, it used a 3.82 x 3.94-inch bore and stroke. At rated engine speed, an economy of 12.69 hp-hours per gallon was observed under a maximum load of 26.37 PTO hp. Operating at 540 PTO rpm and a corresponding engine speed of 2,327 rpm, 13.36 hp-hours per gallon was achieved against a load of 25.52 PTO hp. No repairs or adjustments were required during 41 hours of operation. The 12-speed selective-gear fixed-ratio transmission offered choices varying from 0.3 to 14.0 mph. Using ninth gear, the two-hour drawbar test at 22.73 maximum available hp indicated a pull of 1,965 lbs. at 4.34 mph and slippage totaling 8.3 percent. Fuel economy was 11.22 hp-hours per gallon. The 10-hour run at 75 percent pull indicated 11.60 hp-hours per gallon against a load of 19 drawbar hp. Other statistics included a pull of 1,551 lbs. at 4.59 mph and slippage totaling 6.36 percent. Standard equipment for this 2,765-lb. tractor included 12.4-24-inch rear and 5.00-15-inch front tires. Front and rear ballast gave a test weight of 4,220 lbs.

Massey-Ferguson MF-230 series

Nebraska Test Data

Model: Massey-Ferguson MF-230 Diesel

Test No. 1214

Date Tested: June 1 to June 9, 1976

This tractor was equipped with a selective-gear fixed-ratio transmission offering six forward speeds with a range of 1.4 to 14.5 mph. Using fourth gear, the two-hour economy run at 28.36 maximum available drawbar hp saw a pull of 2,093 lbs. at 5.08 mph with slippage totaling 6.87 percent. Fuel economy was posted at 15.06 hp-hours per gallon. The 10-hour run at 75 percent pull noted 14.74 hp-hours per gallon under a load of 23.32 drawbar hp. Also recorded was a pull of 1,640 lbs. at 5.33 mph and 5.06 percent slippage. Standard equipment for this 4,000-lb. tractor included 12.4-28-inch rear and 5.50-16-inch front tires. Additional front and rear ballast gave a total test weight of 5,110 lbs. A Perkins three-cylinder diesel engine was featured. Rated at 2,000 rpm, it used a 3.6 x 5.0-inch bore and stroke for a 153-cubic inch displacement. At rated engine speed, 34.53 maximum PTO hp appeared and 17.74 hp-hours per gallon was achieved. Operating at 540 PTO rpm and an engine speed of 1,684 rpm, 18.18 hp-hours per gallon was observed under a load of 30.80 PTO hp. No repairs or adjustments were necessary during 43-1/2 hours of operating time.

Nebraska Test Data

Model: Massey-Ferguson MF-230 Gasoline

Test No. 1215

Date Tested: June 1 to June 10, 1976

The primary difference between this tractor and that of Test No. 1214 was the Continental four-cylinder gasoline engine. Rated at 2,000 rpm, the gasoline model had a 145-cubic inch displacement, which resulted from a 3.375 x 4.062-inch bore and stroke. At rated engine speed, 34.34 maximum PTO hp appeared, with an economy of 11.63 hp-hours per gallon. Operating at 540 PTO rpm and a corresponding engine speed of 1,684 rpm, 11.85 hp-hours per gallon was noted with a load totaling 31.29 PTO hp. Tire equipment and chassis design remained virtually identical to that noted in Test No. 1214. Operating in fourth gear, 28.24 maximum available drawbar hp was observed in the two-hour economy run. Also indicated was a pull of 2,086 lbs. at 5.08 mph, slippage of 6.97 percent, and an economy of 9.89 hp-hours per gallon. The 10-hour run at 75 percent pull noted 7.85 hp-hours per gallon under a load of 23.61 drawbar hp. Other data included a pull of 1,640 lbs. at 5.4 mph and slippage of 5.14 percent. Weighing 3,840 lbs., this tractor assumed a total test weight of 4,870 lbs. through the addition of front and rear ballast. Repairs and adjustments reported during 43 hours of operating time were minor. Specific details of this, as well as all other tests recorded in this volume can be obtained from the Official Test Report, available at nominal cost from the Tractor Test Laboratory.

Massey-Ferguson MF-235 tractor

Nebraska Test Data

Model: Massey-Ferguson MF-235 Diesel

Test No. 1187

Date Tested: September 4 to September 18, 1975

The three-cylinder Perkins engine featured in this tractor was rated at 2,250 rpm. Its 153-cubic inch displacement resulted from a 3.6 x 5-inch bore and stroke. At rated engine speed, 42.39 maximum PTO hp appeared and an economy of 16.39 hp-hours per gallon was observed. When operating at 540 PTO rpm and a corresponding engine speed of 1,683 rpm, an economy figure of 16.78 hp-hours per gallon emerged from a load of 35.29 PTO hp. Other features included a selective-gear fixed-ratio transmission with eight forward speeds ranging from 1.6 to 20.8 mph. Except for replacing an oil seal, no repairs or adjustments were necessary during 45 hours of engine operation. Weighing 4,135 lbs., the MF-235 used 13.6-28-inch rear and 6.00-16-inch front tires. Additional front and rear ballast raised the total test weight to 5,860 lbs. Operating in fourth gear, the two-hour economy run at 34.95 maximum available drawbar hp saw a pull of 2,776 lbs. at 4.72 mph with slippage totaling 8.97 percent. Fuel economy was 13.8 hp-hours per gallon. The 10-hour run at 75 percent pull noted 13.39 hp-hours per gallon under a load of 27.99 drawbar hp. Also recorded was a pull of 2,123 lbs. at 4.94 mph and slippage of 6.82 percent.

Massey-Ferguson MF-255 series

Nebraska Test Data

Model: Massey-Ferguson MF-255 Diesel
Test No. 1189
Date Tested: September 4 to September 24, 1975

Weighing 5,970 lbs., the MF-255 was encumbered with additional rear wheel ballast for a total test weight of 7,130 lbs. Standard equipment included 16.9-28-inch rear and 7.5L-15-inch front tires. The selective gear fixed-ratio transmission offered partial range power shifting and featured 12 forward speeds ranging from 1.4 to 19.0 mph. Using seventh gear, the two-hour economy run at 42.07 maximum available drawbar hp saw a pull of 2,986 lbs. at 5.28 mph and 6.63 percent slippage. Fuel economy was pegged at 13.44 hp-hours per gallon. The 10-hour run at 75 percent pull noted 13.36 hp-hours per gallon under a load of 34.45 drawbar hp. Also recorded was a pull of 2,328 lbs. at 5.55 mph and slippage totaling 4.88 percent. A Perkins four-cylinder diesel engine was featured. Rated at 2,000 rpm, it carried a 3.6 x 5-inch bore and stroke for a 203-cubic inch displacement. At rated engine speed, 50.69 maximum PTO hp was achieved and 15.73 hp-hours per gallon was observed. Operating at 540 PTO rpm and a corresponding engine speed of 1,683 rpm, 15.88 hp-hours per gallon resulted with a load of 45.55 PTO hp.

Nebraska Test Data

Model: Massey-Ferguson MF-255 Gasoline
Test No. 1190
Date Tested: September 4 to September 25, 1975

Virtually identical in outward appearance to the MF-255 Diesel of the previous test, this gasoline model featured a Perkins four-cylinder, 212-cid engine. Rated at 2,000 rpm, it carried a 3.875 x 4.500-inch bore and stroke. At rated engine speed, 50.01 maximum PTO hp was recorded and an economy of 10.6 hp-hours per gallon was observed. Operating at 540 PTO rpm and a corresponding engine speed of 1,684 rpm, 10.91 hp-hours per gallon resulted with a load of 47.14 PTO hp. Repairs and adjustments over 45 hours of operating time consisted of replacing a carburetor fuel jet. Using the same drive train as noted in the previous test, this model entered the two-hour drawbar economy run using seventh gear. At 42.22 maximum available hp, 8.94 hp-hours per gallon was achieved. Also recorded was a pull of 3,007 lbs. at 5.26 mph with slippage of 6.66 percent. The 10-hour run at 75 percent pull noted an economy of 8.54 hp-hours per gallon with a load of 35.31 drawbar hp. Other statistics included a pull of 2,324 lbs. at 5.7 mph and slippage of 4.91 percent. Weighing 6,140 lbs., the MF-255 assumed a test weight of 7,280 lbs. by the addition of rear wheel ballast. Tire sizes remained the same as previously noted in Test No. 1189.

Massey-Ferguson MF-265 tractor

Nebraska Test Data

Model: Massey-Ferguson MF-265 Diesel
Test No. 1188
Date Tested: September 4 to September 23, 1975

Weighing 6,385 lbs., the MF-265 was equipped with 16.9-28-inch rear and 7.5L-15-inch front tires. Additional front and rear ballast raised the test weight to 8,200 lbs. The selective-gear fixed-ratio transmission offered partial range power shifting and provided 12 forward speeds ranging from 1.4 to 19.0 mph. Seventh gear was used for the two-hour drawbar economy run. This test, made at 50.38 maximum available drawbar hp, saw a pull of 3,627 lbs. at 5.21 mph, slippage of 7.47percent, and 13.52 hp-hours per gallon. The 10-hour run at 75 percent pull indicated 13.51 hp-hours per gallon under 41 drawbar hp. Also recorded was a pull of 2,791 lbs. at 5.51 mph and slippage of 5.41 percent. No repairs or adjustments were required during 44-1/2 hours of operation. The Perkins four-cylinder diesel engine was rated at 2,000 rpm. Its 236-cubic inch displacement resulted from a 3.875 x 5-inch bore and stroke. At rated engine speed, 60.73 maximum PTO hp was observed, with an economy of 15.9 hp-hours per gallon. Operating at 540 PTO rpm and a corresponding engine speed of 1,683 rpm, 15.88 hp-hours per gallon resulted under a load of 54.76 PTO hp.

Massey-Ferguson MF-275 tractor

Nebraska Test Data

Model: Massey-Ferguson MF-275 Diesel
Test No. 1193
Date Tested: October 24 to November 4, 1975

Features of the MF-275 Diesel included a four-cylinder Perkins engine. Rated at 2,000 rpm, it carried a 3.975 x 5-inch bore and stroke for a 248-cubic inch displacement. At rated engine speed, 67.43 maximum PTO hp was observed with 14.64 hp-hours per gallon. At 540 PTO rpm and a corresponding engine speed of 1,683 rpm, an economy of 14.18 hp-hours per gallon was achieved under a load of 61.76 PTO hp. No repairs or adjustments were required during 53-1/2 hours of operating time. The selective-gear fixed-ratio transmission offered partial range power shifting. Its 12 forward speeds ranged from 1.3 to 19.2 mph. Weighing 6,610 lbs., the MF-275 used 15.5-38-inch rear and 7.5L-15-inch front tires. Additional front and rear ballast gave a total test weight of 9,330 lbs. Using seventh gear, the two-hour drawbar run at 59.73 maximum available hp saw 13.04 hp-hours per gallon. This test saw a pull of 4,341 lbs. at 5.16 mph with slippage totaling 6.25 percent. The 10-hour run at 75 percent pull saw 13.22 hp-hours per gallon at an output of 48 drawbar hp. Also recorded was a pull of 3,241 lbs. at 5.55 mph with slippage of 4.48 percent.

Massey-Ferguson MF-285 tractor

Nebraska Test Data

Model: Massey-Ferguson MF-285 Diesel Standard MP

Test No. 1171

Date Tested: April 2 to April 24, 1975

Weighing 7,650 lbs., this model featured a Perkins four-cylinder, 318-cid diesel engine. Rated at 2,000 rpm, it carried a 4.5 x 5.0-inch bore and stroke. At rated engine speed, 81.96 maximum PTO hp was observed, with an economy of 14.98 hp-hours per gallon. The selective-gear fixed-ratio transmission included partial range power shifting. Its 12 forward speeds ranged from 1.4 to 19.6 mph. No repairs or adjustments were reported during 48-1/2 hours of operating time. Standard equipment included 18.4-34 rear and 9.5L-15 inch front tires. Additional front and rear ballast raised the total test weight to 11,760 lbs. Using seventh gear, the two-hour economy run at 69.46 maximum available hp saw a pull of 5,061 lbs. at 5.15 mph with slippage of 7.44 percent. Fuel economy was posted at 12.85 hp-hours per gallon. By comparison, the 10-hour run at 75 percent pull saw 12.9 hp-hours per gallon under a load of 56.08 drawbar hp. Other test data included a pull of 3,831 lbs. at 5.49 mph with slippage of 5.24 percent.

Massey-Ferguson MF-670 tractor

Nebraska Test Data

Model: Massey-Ferguson MF-670 Diesel (Also MF-270 Multi-power Diesel)

Test No. 1538

Date Tested: September 5 to September 20, 1984

Weighing 8,720 lbs., the 670 was equipped with 16.9-30-inch rear and 11.2-24-inch front tires. Additional front and rear ballast gave a total test weight of 9,200 lbs. Standard equipment included a selective-gear fixed-ratio transmission with advertised speeds ranging from 1.3 to 18.3 mph. Also featured was a Perkins four-cylinder engine. Rated at 2,000 rpm, it carried a 3.875 x 5-inch bore and stroke for a 236-cubic inch displacement. Repairs and adjustments during 42-1/2 hours of operating time included replacement of a hydraulic valve gasket during the limber-up run. At rated engine speed, 55.62 maximum PTO hp was observed, with an economy of 15.54 hp-hours per gallon. Operating at 1,000 PTO rpm and a corresponding engine speed of 1,692 rpm, an economy figure of 16.39 was established under a load of 51.44 hp. Using seventh gear, plus the front-wheel drive, a two-hour run at 46.28 maximum available drawbar hp indicated a pull of 3,459 lbs. at 5.02 mph. Slippage totaled 4.45 percent, and fuel economy was pegged at 13.10 hp-hours per gallon. A two-hour drawbar run, using seventh gear but without the front-wheel assist, established a figure of 12.93 against a maximum load of 45.52 drawbar hp. Other data from this test included a pull of 3,503 lbs. at 4.87 mph and slippage of 6.44 percent.

Nebraska Test Data

Model: Massey-Ferguson MF-690 Diesel

Test No. 1539

Date Tested: September 14 to September 25, 1984

Rated at 2,200 rpm, the 690 featured a four-cylinder Perkins engine. Its 3.975 x 5-inch bore and stroke gave a 248-cubic inch displacement. At rated engine speed, 65.68 maximum PTO hp was observed, as was an economy of 14.56 hp-hours per gallon. Operating at 540 PTO rpm and a corresponding engine speed of 1,893 rpm, the economy figure rested at 15.51, against a load of 62.25 PTO hp. Using seventh gear, but with the front-wheel assist disengaged, a two-hour drawbar run at 53.36 maximum available hp saw a pull of 4,192 lbs. at 4.77 mph. Slippage totaled 6.47 percent, and fuel economy was 12.01 hp-hours per gallon. Another two-hour run with the front-wheel assist engaged saw 11.81 hp-hours per gallon against a load of 52.38 drawbar hp. Also noted was a pull of 3,960 lbs. at 4.96 mph with slippage totaling 4.87 percent. The selective-gear fixed-ratio transmission offered 12 speeds ranging from 1.2 to 18.1 mph. Also featured were 18.4-30 rear and 13.6-24 inch front tires. Weighing 8,020 lbs., the 690 assumed a total test weight of 10,295 lbs. through additional front and rear ballast. No repairs or adjustments were required during 41-1/2 hours of operating time.

Nebraska Test Data

Model: Massey-Ferguson MF-698 Diesel

Test No. 1540

Date Tested: September 11 to September 19, 1984

Using seventh gear, and with the front-wheel drive engaged, a two-hour drawbar test at 65.83 maximum available hp manifested 12.42 hp-hours per gallon. Also shown was a pull of 5,214 lbs. at 4.73 mph with slippage totaling 5.28 percent. The same two-hour test run with the front-wheel assist disengaged revealed an economy figure of 12.55 against a load of 66.72 drawbar hp. Other statistics of this test included a pull of 5,470 lbs. at 4.57 mph and slippage of 6.86 percent. Standard features of the 698 included a selective-gear fixed-ratio transmission with a 12-speed range of 1.2 to 17.6 mph. Also featured were 18.4-34-inch rear and 14.9-24-inch front tires. Weighing 9,940 lbs., the 698 had a total test weight of 12,125 lbs., including front and rear ballast. No repairs or adjustments were necessary during 39-1/2 hours of operation. The Perkins four-cylinder engine was rated at 2,000 rpm. Its 4.5 x 5.0-inch bore and stroke gave a 318-cubic inch displacement. At the rated engine speed of 2,000 rpm, 78.83 maximum PTO hp was observed, and an economy of 14.76 hp-hours per gallon. Operating at 540 PTO rpm and a corresponding engine speed of 1,687 rpm, the economy figure stood at 15.91 against 74.41 PTO hp.

Nebraska Test Data

Model: Massey-Ferguson MF-699 Diesel

Test No. 1541

Date Tested: September 6 to September 28, 1984

At its rated engine speed of 2,200 rpm, the 699 delivered 85.79 maximum PTO hp while achieving 16.05 hp-hours per gallon. Operating at 540 PTO rpm and a corresponding engine speed of 1,894 rpm, the economy figure rested at 16.96 against a load of 78 PTO hp. The 699 featured a Perkins six-cylinder engine. Its 3.875 x 5-inch bore and stroke gave a displacement of 354-cubic inches. Also featured was a selective-gear fixed-ratio transmission with a 12-speed range of 1.2 to 17.5 mph. Tires included 18.4-34 rear and 14.9-24-inch front rubber. The bare tractor weight of 10,325 lbs. was raised to 12,935 lbs. by the addition of front and rear ballast. No repairs or adjustments were necessary during 51-1/2 hours of operation. Using seventh gear, but without the front-wheel assist, the 698 delivered 70.52 maximum available drawbar hp in a two-hour run. This test established an economy of 13.51 hp-hours per gallon with the test noting a pull of 5,632 lbs. at 4.7 mph and 7.42 percent slippage. Another two-hour run, again in seventh gear plus the front-wheel assist, saw 13.32 hp-hours per gallon under a load of 69.33 drawbar hp. Further data included a pull of 5,328 lbs. at 4.88 mph with a 5.75 percent slippage.

Massey-Ferguson MF-1100 tractor

Nebraska Test Data

Model: Massey-Ferguson MF-1100 Diesel

Test No. 923

Date Tested: October 27 to November 1, 1965

A six-cylinder Perkins Diesel engine was featured in this tractor. Rated at 2,200 rpm, it used a 3.875 x 5.00-inch bore and stroke for a 354-cubic inch displacement. At rated engine speed, 93.94 maximum PTO hp was observed, with 15.41 hp-hours per gallon. Operating at 1,000 PTO rpm and a corresponding crankshaft speed of 2,000 rpm, 88.74 PTO hp was evidenced and an economy of 15.85 hp-hours per gallon. This 11,435-lb. tractor was equipped with a selective-gear fixed-ratio transmission with partial range power shifting. In all, 12 forward speeds were available, ranging from 2.18 to 17.16 mph. The addition of rear wheel ballast brought a total test weight of 14,920 lbs. This included 1,295 lbs. of liquid and 388 lbs. of cast iron ballast on each rear wheel. Using fifth gear, 84.61 maximum available drawbar hp was observed, with 13.6 hp-hours per gallon. This two-hour run also saw a pull of 6,886 lbs. at 4.61 mph and slippage of 5.36 percent. A 10-hour run at 75 percent pull indicated 13.19 hp-hours per gallon against an output of 66.55 hp. Other statistics included a pull of 5,172 lbs. at 4.83 mph and slippage of 3.9 percent. No repairs or adjustments were reported during 43-1/2 hours of operating time.

Massey-Ferguson MF-1800 tractor

Nebraska Test Data

Model: Massey-Ferguson MF-1800 Diesel

Test No. 1087

Date Tested: November 4 to November 17, 1971

A 636-cid Caterpillar V-8 Diesel engine was featured in this model. Rated at 2,800 rpm, it used a 4.5 x 5.0-inch bore and stroke. Since this tractor was not submitted with a PTO shaft, no brake hp economy runs were made. Weighing in at 17,330 lbs., the MF-1800 featured 23.1-30 tires. Additional front and rear ballast raised the total test weight to 21,760 lbs. A selective-gear fixed-ratio transmission offered 12 forward speeds ranging from 2.11 to 19.81 mph. Using fifth gear, the two-hour drawbar run at 171.37 maximum available hp set an economy of 13.27 hp-hours per gallon. Also recorded was a pull of 13,242 lbs. at 4.85 mph and the slippage totaled 6.15 percent. The 10-hour drawbar economy, run at 75 percent pull, saw 13.49 hp-hours per gallon with an output of 143.47 hp. Other statistics included a pull of 10.475 lbs. at 5.14 mph and slippage of 4.36 percent. A maximum pull of 18,432 lbs. was recorded in third gear. This test saw an output of 156.06 drawbar hp. Due to excessive slippage, maximum power tests were not made in first and second gears.

Nebraska Test Data

Model: Massey-Ferguson MF-1805 Diesel

Test No. 1173

Date Tested: April 3 to April 23, 1975

At its rated engine speed of 2,800 rpm, the 1805 Diesel developed 192.65 maximum PTO hp and achieved 14.79 hp-hours per gallon. At 1,000 PTO rpm and a corresponding engine speed of 2,765 rpm, an economy figure of 14.79 appeared under a load of 191.6 PTO hp. Features of the 1805 included a Caterpillar 3208 eight-cylinder vee-design engine. Its 4.5 x 5.0 inch bore and stroke gave a 636-cubic inch displacement. Also featured was a selective-gear fixed-ratio transmission offering 12 forward speeds ranging from 2.1 to 19.8 mph. Weighing 18,000 lbs., this tractor assumed a total test weight of 22,790 lbs. through additional front and rear ballast. Standard equipment included 23.1-30 tires. Using fifth gear, the two-hour economy run at 162.95 maximum available hp saw a pull of 12,763 lbs. at 4.79 mph with slippage totaling 6.7 percent. Fuel economy was 12.76 hp-hours per gallon. The 10-hour run at 75 percent pull noted an economy figure of 12.41 under 131.41 drawbar hp. Also recorded was a pull of 9,743 lbs. at 5.06 mph with slippage of 4.46 percent. During 59 hours of operation, it was reported the shifting fork lock screw came loose and the transmission was locked in second gear. This was corrected.

Massey-Ferguson MF-1805

Massey-Ferguson MF-2640

Nebraska Test Data

Model: Massey-Ferguson MF-2640 Diesel

Test No. 1481

Date Tested: May 9 to May 18, 1983

Partial range power shifting was featured in the selective-gear fixed-ratio transmission used in the 2640 tractor. Its 16 forward speeds ranged from 1.3 to 18.2 mph. Using eighth gear, plus the front-wheel assist, a two-hour drawbar run at 74.77 maximum available hp indicated a pull of 6,498 lbs. at 4.32 mph. Slippage totaled 5.34 percent, and fuel economy was posted at 12.44 hp-hours per gallon. The same two-hour run with the front-wheel drive disengaged saw 73.48 maximum available hp, plus a pull of 6,611 lbs. at 4.17 mph. This test saw slippage totaling 7.79 percent, and established an economy of 12.15 hp-hours per gallon. Standard equipment for this 12,435-lb. tractor included 18.4-38-inch rear and 13.6-28-inch front tires. Additional front and rear ballast gave a total test weight of 16,380 lbs. No repairs or adjustments were required during 46-1/2 hours of operation. The Perkins six-cylinder diesel engine was rated at 2,400 rpm. Its 354-cubic inch displacement resulted from a 3.875 x 5.00-inch bore and stroke. At rated engine speed, 90.95 maximum PTO hp was observed, with an economy of 14.62 hp-hours per gallon. Operating at 1,000 PTO rpm and a corresponding engine speed of 2,091 rpm, an economy of 15.81 hp-hours per gallon resulted from a load of 87.60 PTO hp.

Massey-Ferguson MF-2745 tractor

Nebraska Test Data

Model: Massey-Ferguson MF-2745 Diesel

Test No. 1311

Date Tested: May 7 to May 16, 1979

At its rated engine speed of 2,600 rpm, the 2745 Diesel developed 143.40 maximum PTO hp and achieved an economy of 13.96 hp-hours per gallon. Operating at 1,000 PTO rpm and a corresponding engine speed of 2,092 rpm, an economy of 15.40 hp-hours per gallon was observed under a load of 132.21 PTO hp. The 2745 was equipped with a Perkins V-8 diesel engine. Its 4.25 x 4.75-inch bore and stroke gave a 539-cubic inch displacement. The 24-speed transmission was a selective-gear, fixed-ratio design and included partial range power shifting. Speeds ranged from 1.2 to 21.3 mph. Except for replacement of two fuel injectors during the preliminary PTO test, no repairs or adjustments were required during 38-1/2 hours of operation. Fourteenth gear was used for the two-hour drawbar economy test. At 122.28 maximum available drawbar hp, a pull of 8,352 lbs. was recorded at 5.49 mph with slippage totaling 5.97 percent. Fuel economy was 11.96 hp-hours per gallon. The 10-hour run at 75 percent pull indicated 11.13 hp-hours per gallon under a load of 100.07 drawbar hp. Other statistics included a pull of 6,395 lbs. at 5.87 mph and slippage of 4.18 percent. Standard equipment for the 15,190-lb. tractor included dual 18.4-38 rear and 11.00-16 inch front tires. Additional front and rear ballast gave a total test weight of 19,490 lbs.

Massey-Ferguson MF-4800

Nebraska Test Data

Model: Massey-Ferguson MF-4800 Diesel
Test No. 1342
Date Tested: April 17 to May 3, 1980

A Cummins V-8 diesel engine was featured in this tractor. Rated at 2,600 rpm, it used a 5.50 x 4.75-inch bore and stroke for a displacement of 903-cubic inches. At rated engine speed, 179.31 maximum PTO hp was observed, at 14.14 hp-hours per gallon. Operating at 1,000 PTO rpm and a corresponding engine speed of 2,348 rpm, 15.10 hp-hours per gallon was recorded under a load of 172.88 PTO hp. No repairs or adjustments were necessary during 48-1/2 hours of operation. Weighing 30,520 lbs., this tractor was tested without additional ballast. Standard equipment included 23.1-34 tires. The selective gear fixed-ratio transmission offered partial range power shifting. Its 18 speeds varied from 2.4 to 19.2 mph. Using seventh gear, the two-hour drawbar test at 153.78 maximum available hp saw a pull of 11,958 lbs. at 4.82 mph with slippage totaling 4.82 percent. Fuel economy totaled 12.13 hp-hours per gallon. By comparison, the 10-hour run at 75 percent pull emerged with 10.73 hp-hours per gallon under a load of 126.43 drawbar hp. Also recorded was a pull of 9,289 lbs. at 5.1 mph with slippage totaling 2.36 percent.

Master Tractor Company

MINNEAPOLIS, MINNESOTA

Master Jr. 6-12 garden tractor

Master Tractor Co. was incorporated in Minneapolis in 1918. By 1920 the company appeared as Master Truck & Tractor Co., but by 1922 the original title was once again assumed. F. A. Valentine, who was associated with tractor manufacturing in previous years, was a business partner. The company built an 18-35 tractor, but no illustrations have been found. During 1921 the company offered the Master Jr. 6-12 garden tractor. This unique design used a four-cylinder LeRoi engine with a 3-1/8 x 4-1/2-inch bore and stroke.

COLLECTOR VALUES	1	2	3	4
MASTER JR. 6-12	$2,500	$1,200	$750	$500

Masterbilt Truck & Tractor Company

DECATUR, ILLINOIS

Although this firm was incorporated in 1918, no other information has been located.

Matthews Tractor Company

BROCKPORT, NEW YORK

See: Wheat Tiller & Tractor Company

Matthews tractor

Hession Tractor & Tiller Company began building the Wheat tractor in 1917. By 1920 or 1921, the company was reorganized as Wheat Tractor & Tiller Corporation. In the 1922 to 1924 period, the Wheat tractor was built by Matthews Tractor Company. The 12-24 Wheat tractor was equipped with an Erd four-cylinder engine with a 4 x 6-inch bore and stroke and disappeared from trade listings after 1924.

Maxfer Truck & Tractor Company

HARVEY, ILLINOIS

This offered the Maxfer Tractor-Truck in 1918. It was apparently more of a truck than a tractor, and the latter term seems to have applied more to an industrial tractor than to one built for farm use. No other information has been found.

Maxim Munitions Corporation

NEW YORK, NEW YORK

Maxim Model A, 12-24 tractor

The Maxim Model A, 12-24 tractor was offered only in 1919. Industry listings make no other mention of this model. Maxim used its own four-cylinder engine in the 12-24. It carried a 4-1/4 x 5-1/2-inch bore and stroke. The Model A was priced at $1,685.

Maxwell Motor Sales Corporation

DETROIT, MICHIGAN

In 1918 Maxwell started with a tractor known previously as the "Chief" which was then renamed as "Flanders." The Flanders automobile was controlled by Studebaker. At this point, it is not known whether Maxwell Motor Sales was connected with the famous Maxwell automobile, or whether the choice of corporate name was a mere coincidence.

Mayer Brothers Company

MANKATO, MINNESOTA

This firm went back to 1876 when Louis and Lorenz Mayer opened a machine shop at Mankato, Minnesota. About 1911, the company began experimenting with tractors, and by 1914 the company was building tractors exclusively.

Mayer Brothers Model A 26-35 tractor

Included in the Mayer Brothers offerings was the Model A 26-35 tractor that sold for $2,000 in 1916.

Little Giant tractor

The Little Giant tractors were built in two sizes, the Model A 26-35 and the Model B 16-22. Both used engines built in the Mayer Bros. shops. These tractors had a rather advanced design, notably that ball and roller bearings were used exclusively in an age when plain bearings were still used to a great extent. In 1918 the corporate name was changed to Little Giant Company. Further information may be found under that heading.

Mayrath Incorporated

DODGE CITY, KANSAS

Mayrath Mobile tractor

Two sizes of the Mayrath Mobile Tractor were offered, namely, the "5 HP" and the "8-1/4 HP." Few specifics have been found, but apparently these tractors were built in the 1950 through 1952 period. Trade directory information shows both used the same chassis, varying only in their engines.

Maytag Company

NEWTON, IOWA

Maytag 12-25 tractor

This famous home appliance manufacturer made a brief entry into the tractor business during 1916. Rated as a 12-25, the Maytag tractor was a 5,000-lb. machine powered by a four-cylinder Waukesha engine. Very few specifics have been found because it was only marketed for a few months.

M. B. M. Mfg. Company

MILWAUKEE, WISCONSIN

Red-E garden tractor

The Red-E garden tractor first appeared under that title in September 1923. Through 1927, it was built by M.B.M. Mfg. Company, but late in 1927, the Red-E appears from Modern Machine Works, also of Milwaukee. By 1928, the Red-E, with its original design, appeared under Pioneer Mfg. Company of nearby West Allis. Priced at $275, the Red-E used a single-cylinder engine of 3-3/4 x 4-inch bore and stroke. It was built by M.B.M and was named the Red-E because "it was always READY to go to work" according to the company.

COLLECTOR VALUES	1	2	3	4
RED-E	$1,500	$1,000	$750	$350

Mead-Morrison Mfg. Company

BOSTON, MASSACHUSETTS

Mead-Morrison Bear "55" tractor

Beginning about 1924 and continuing until about 1930, the Mead-Morrison Bear "55" was offered. Obvious is the unique front suspension system. Weighing 8,700 lbs., the

Bear "55" used a Stearns four-cylinder engine with a 4-3/4 x 6-1/2-inch bore and stroke. Also, the Bear "55" used a conventional steering wheel to handle the machine.

COLLECTOR VALUES	1	2	3	4
BEAR "55"	$10,000	$7,500	$5,000	$2,250

Mead Specialties Company Inc.

CHICAGO, ILLINOIS

Mead Mighty Mouse Model M-6 crawler tractor

Beginning about 1951 and continuing for several years, Mead offered its Mighty Mouse Model M-6 crawler tractor. Weighing 1,250 lbs., the Mighty Mouse sold for $1,180. It was equipped with either a Briggs & Stratton 14FB or a Wisconsin AKN engine, either of which was capable of 5 to 6 hp.

COLLECTOR VALUES	1	2	3	4
M-6	$3,200	$1,800	$1,500	–

Megow Tractor Company

ST. PAUL, MINNESOTA

Megow was organized in 1916, ostensibly to manufacture farm tractors, but no other information has been found.

Melin Industries

CLEVELAND, OHIO

By 1950 Melin Industries was offering its Garden-Craft "15" and its Soil-Craft "30" garden tractors. The "15" and "30" were of similar design, with the smaller model using a Kohler K7 2-hp engine, while the "30" was equipped with a Kohler K12 3-hp motor. Kohler advertising noted that "over 22 different attachments" were available.

Garden-Craft "15" garden tractor

Farmcraft "45" garden tractor

The Melin line included the Farmcraft "45", Farmcraft "60" and Farmcraft "75"models. All were of similar design and utilized the "Unitool" carriage system for use with various implements. All three sizes used Wisconsin engines. For the "45", it was the ABN 4-hp model. The "60" used the AKN 6-hp motor and the "75" used the AEN 7 1/2-hp engine. Production of these tractors continued at least into the mid-1950s.

COLLECTOR VALUES	1	2	3	4
FARMCRAFT 45	$450	$250	$125	$75

Mellinger Mfg. Company

WILLOW STREET, PENNSYLVANIA

The Garden Spot garden tractor was listed from Mellinger in 1953, but no other information was located.

Mercer-Robinson Company Inc.

NEW YORK, NEW YORK

By 1952 the Mercer "30" tractor was on the market. Two models were offered; the BD was a diesel version, and the CK was powered with a gasoline engine. These tractors originated about 1948 as the Farmaster FD-33 and the Farmaster FG-33, both from Farmaster Corporation at Clifton, New Jersey. These models appeared in Nebraska Test

Numbers 419 and 421, respectively. Both were equipped with 153-cid Buda four-cylinder engines. Mercer production continued at least into the late 1950s.

Merry Mfg. Company

EDMONDS, WASHINGTON

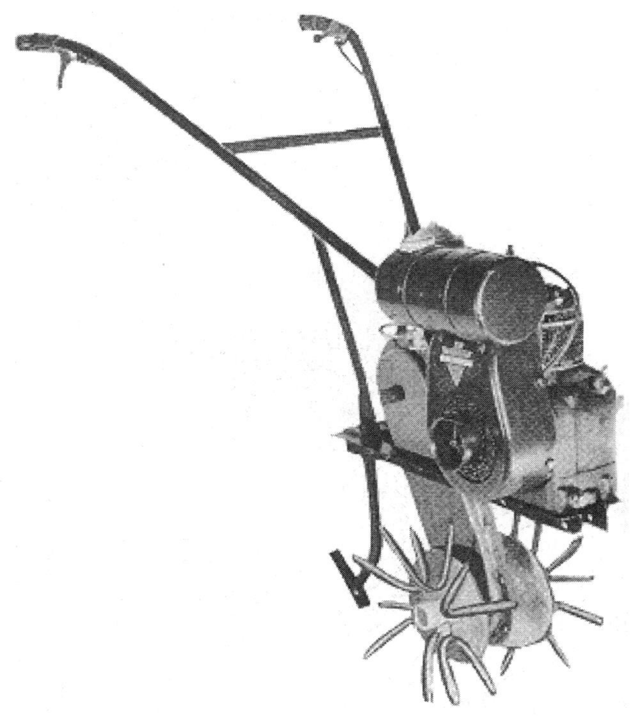

Merry "Tiller"

By 1950 the Merry "Tiller" was on the market. Power came from a Briggs & Stratton Model N engine capable of 2 hp. Numerous attachments were available for this unit, including a sickle bar and a reel mower. Little other information has been found after 1951.

COLLECTOR VALUES	1	2	3	4
MERRY TILLER	$225	$125	$75	$50

Messinger Mfg. Company

TATAMY, PENNSYLVANIA

Various sources indicate that Messinger Mfg. Co. built garden tractors for a time, but the meager information available is conflicting.

Metal Products Corporation

RACINE, WISCONSIN

See: Haas Foundry Company

W.E. Metzler Company

AZUSA, CALIFORNIA

This firm is listed as manufacturing garden tractors in the 1948 through 1953 period, but no other information has been found.

J.J. Meyer

SHEPARD, MICHIGAN

J.J. Meyer is listed for 1920 as the builder of the Chippewa Chief tractors. No other information has been found.

M. F. M. Combination Saw & Machinery Company

DENTON, TEXAS

M.F.M. Combination Saw

By 1950 the M.F.M. Combination Saw had been put on the market. Shown here with its mounted saw, it was also available with several other attachments to further extend its usefulness. Weight of this unit was 680 lbs. Relatively little is known about the machine.

Michigan Tractor Company

DETROIT, MICHIGAN

Organized in 1915, Michigan Tractor Co. developed a unique all-wheel-drive machine. As shown in this illustration, the tractor had a very short turning radius because the powered front steering wheel could be turned virtually upon itself. By late 1915, the company was taken over by the A. T. Harrow Tractor Company, but very little is known of the latter venture.

All-wheel-drive machine

Middletown Machine Company

MIDDLETOWN, OHIO

This firm was well known as the manufacturer of the Woodpecker gasoline engines, and is listed as a tractor manufacturer in trade directories for 1911, 1912 and 1913. No information regarding these tractors has been located. It is assumed that any Middletown tractor production was quite limited.

Midget Tractor Company

MINNEAPOLIS, MINNESOTA

Midget small cultivating tractor

Organized in 1918, Midget produced a small cultivating tractor designed for one-row cultivation. From this firm, Shaw-Enochs Tractor Company was organized in November 1919. Few specifics have been found regarding the Midget tractor.

Midland Company

MILWAUKEE, WISCONSIN

Dandy Boy "Town & Country" model

Beginning about 1950 and continuing for several years, Midland offered several sizes of garden tractors. Typical of the line was the Dandy Boy "Town & Country" model. This one used a Briggs & Stratton 3-hp engine. Other models included the Dandy Boy Clipper, a 2-hp size, and the Dandy Boy "Super," which was equipped with a 5-hp Briggs & Stratton motor.

COLLECTOR VALUES	1	2	3	4
DANDY BOY TOWN & COUNTRY	$425	$225	$125	$75

Midland Tractor Company

DETROIT, MICHIGAN

Midland Tractor

Midland Tractor Co. was organized in 1912 and built a medium-size tractor that weighed 4,800 lbs., and retailed for $1,250. In 1913, the company was bought out by Leader Engine Company, Grand Rapids, Michigan.

Midwest Company

MINNEAPOLIS, MINNESOTA

In 1948 this firm is listed as a garden tractor manufacturer, but no other information has been found.

Midwest Engine Company

INDIANAPOLIS, INDIANA

Midwest Utilitor garden tractor

Midwest first adopted the Utilitor tradename in June 1919. For some years to follow, the company offered the Midwest Utilitor garden tractor. This was a 750-lb. machine equipped with a single-cylinder engine with a 3-1/2 x 4-1/2-inch bore and stroke. Numerous attachments were available, including plows, cultivators and a planter. The basic tractor unit was priced at $295.

COLLECTOR VALUES	1	2	3	4
MIDWEST UTILITOR	$2,500	$2,000	$1,700	$1,500

Milwaukee Equipment Company

MILWAUKEE, WISCONSIN

Beginning about 1946, the Milwaukee rotary tillers appeared in several models. Shown here is the JR16, a new model that first appeared about 1950. It used a Wisconsin 4-1/2-hp engine. The JR12 was the smallest of the line and was powered by a Clinton 3-hp motor. Other models included the G18 with a Wisconsin 7-1/2-hp engine. The big G26 machine was available with a Wisconsin 7-1/2-hp engine or an Onan 10-hp motor.

JR16 tiller

COLLECTOR VALUES	1	2	3	4
ALL MODELS	$600	$500	$200	$100

Minneapolis-Moline Company

MINNEAPOLIS, MINNESOTA

In 1929 three companies merged to form Minneapolis-Moline. Included were the Moline Plow Company, Moline, Illinois; Minneapolis Threshing Machine Company, Hopkins, Minnesota; and Minneapolis Steel & Machinery Company, Minneapolis, Minnesota. Moline Plow Company went back to 1870, and over its career developed an extensive line of tillage tools. Minneapolis Threshing Machine Company began operations in 1887 as a manufacturer of steam engines and threshers. Subsequently, the company developed a substantial tractor line. Minneapolis Steel & Machinery Company was organized in 1902, and subsequently developed the Twin City tractor line.

Minneapolis-Moline was taken over by White Farm Equipment Company in 1963.

The Minneapolis-Moline tractor line had unusual production patterns that sometimes overlapped one another. Model designators are sometimes difficult to decipher and conflicts appear even within the company's own serial number listings. Thus, it is entirely possible that certain M-M models are inadvertently omitted from the following series of illustrations.

See: White Farm Equipment Company

The M-M Twin City 17-28 had previously been developed and marketed by Minneapolis Steel & Machinery Company. It was carried into the 1929 merger, and M-M continued to produce it until 1935. The 17-28 was first built in 1926 and was a rerated version of the Twin City 12-20 model introduced about 1919. This model used a four-cylinder, 4-1/4 x 6-inch engine. This 5,900-lb. tractor was capable of over 22 drawbar hp.

M-M Twin City 17-28

COLLECTOR VALUES	1	2	3	4
17-28	$7,250	$6,000	$4,000	$1,000

17-30 Type A tractor

Minneapolis Threshing Machine Co. introduced its 17-30 Type A tractor about 1920. This model carried on into the 1929 merger and remained in production until 1934. Nebraska Test No. 70 of 1921 notes that this model was equipped with a four-cylinder, 4-3/4 x 7-inch engine and was capable of nearly 32 belt hp.

17-30 Type B tractor

About 1925, Minneapolis Threshing Machine Co. released the 17-30 Type B tractor. It was quite similar to the 17-30 Type A, but had a longer chassis and a slightly larger engine of 4-7/8 x 7-inch bore and stroke. The Type B delivered almost 35 belt hp. Production of the 17-30 Type B ended in 1934.

Nebraska Test Data

Model: Minneapolis "B" 17-30

Test No. 118

Date Tested: October 21 to November 12, 1925

After the limbering-up run prior to taking official data, it was necessary to grind all the valves in the 17-30. During the entire test run, it was necessary to stop periodically and clean the fuel line which became clogged with foreign material. With these exceptions, no repairs or adjustments were required during the test. Throughout the 40 hours of running time, kerosene was used. At rated brake hp load, the 17-30 gave an economy of 9.45 hp-hours per gallon, burning 3.269 gph. The maximum load test indicated 34.76 hp although fuel economy dropped to 6.65 hp-hours per gallon. At the drawbar, maximum load tests were made both in low and high gears in addition to the rated load test. A maximum pull of 4,374 lbs. was achieved in low gear with a speed of 1.92 mph and a resultant 22.37 maximum drawbar hp. Minneapolis used its own four-cylinder vertical valve-in-head engine mounted crosswise to the tractor frame. Rated at 825 rpm, it carried a 4-7/8 x 7-inch bore and stroke. Total weight of the 17-30 was 7,550 lbs. Accessories included a Bosch magneto and a Wheeler-Schebler Model A carburetor.

M-M Twin City KT tractor

The M-M Twin City KT tractor was developed in 1929 and was marketed until 1934. The KT stood for Kombination Tractor. This model had a rating of 11 drawbar and 20 belt hp. Subsequent to Test No. 175 below, the KT was sometimes billed as a 14-23 model.

Nebraska Test Data

Model: Twin City "KT" 11-20

Test No. 175

Date Tested: March 24 to April 12, 1930

Three forward speeds of 2.1, 3.13 and 4.14 mph were advertised for the Twin City KT tractor. Weighing 5,060 lbs., it pulled 1,327 lbs. at 3.35 mph in the rated drawbar load test, for an economy of 5.4 hp-hours per gallon of kerosene, while developing 11.87 hp. Maximum drawbar pull occurred in low gear. With a total of 18.8 drawbar hp, the KT pulled 3,334 lbs. at 2.12 mph with a 13.61 percent slippage. Under operating maximum load, this tractor gave 9.99 hp-hours per gallon of kerosene, developing 25.83 brake hp and consuming 2.585 gph. At rated load of 19.99 hp, economy dropped slightly to 9.81 hp-hours per gallon. Standard engine equipment included an American Bosch U4 magneto, Stromberg LUT1 carburetor and Donaldson air cleaner. The engine was built by Minneapolis, featuring a four-cylinder, vertical, I-head design. Rated at 1,000 rpm, it used a 4-1/4 x 5-inch bore and stroke.

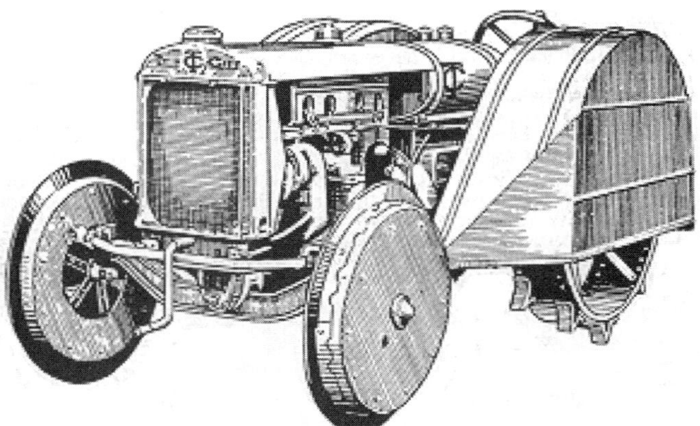

KT Orchard tractor

By 1932 Minneapolis-Moline was marketing the KT Orchard tractor, a specially designed model built over the regular KT chassis. The major difference was the special hood and fender design. M-M also built the KT Industrial tractor in the 1932 through 1935 period.

Model KT-A tractor

During 1934, the improved Model KT-A tractor was introduced, replacing the earlier KT model. The KT-A continued to use the four-cylinder, 4-1/4 x 5-inch engine that was featured in the earlier KT tractor. Various improvements and modifications prompted the change to a new model designation.

Nebraska Test Data

Model: M-M Twin City KT-A

Test No. 247

Date Tested: October 2 to October 9, 1935

Using distillate fuel, the KT-A emerged from Test D for rated brake load with an economy of 10.25 hp-hours per gallon with an output of 30.27 hp. At 100 percent maximum load (Test B), fuel economy dropped to 8.19, although hp increased to 33.65. Three speeds of 2.1, 3.1 and 4.1 mph were provided, with second gear chosen for the rated drawbar tests. At 19.29 hp, this tractor pulled 2,169 lbs. at 3.34 mph over the 10-hour test run, achieving 7.25 hp-hours per gallon. Maximum drawbar pull in low gear yielded 3,931 lbs. at 2.24 hp and a recorded total of 23.51 hp. Standard equipment included the M-M four-cylinder I-head engine with a 4-1/4 x 5-inch bore and stroke. Rated at 1,150 rpm, it also included an American Bosch U-4 magneto and a Schebler TTX-15 carburetor. Operating weight was 5,135 lbs. After running the belt tests, the pulley shaft cracked requiring a replacement and subsequent re-running of the tests. During the preliminary drawbar tests, the air stack broke off, but was repaired by welding.

Nebraska Test Data

Model: M-M Twin City KT-A

Test No. 249

Date Tested: March 30 to April 10, 1936

Inaugurating the 1936 test season, Minneapolis-Moline again offered the KT-A tractor previously noted in 1935 under No. 247. Instead of using distillate fuel, gasoline was chosen. Also, this tractor was tested using rubber tires and steel wheels in dual test runs. Test D for rated brake load indicated that while delivering 37.22 hp this model produced 11.24 hp-hours per gallon, and an even better 11.6 at 41.6 hp, its 100 percent maximum load. Rated drawbar load (Test H) was made in second gear, and on steel wheels. It indicated 23.95 hp, along with a pull of 2,601 lbs. at 3.45 mph and 7.71 hp-hours per gallon. A fuel economy test using third gear indicated 7.05 hp-hours per gallon with an output of 21.76 hp. The same test on rubber tires gave an output of 19.64 hp with 8.46 hp-hours per gallon on the drawbar. This steel-wheeled model had an operating weight of 5,225 lbs., compared to 6,230 lbs. for the rubber-tired model.

COLLECTOR VALUES	1	2	3	4
KT-A TRACTOR	$4,750	$3,000	$1,800	$900

M-M Row-Crop Model 13-25

The first M-M row-crop model was the Universal 13-25. Introduced in 1931, it remained in production until 1934. Nebraska Test No. 197 indicated the Universal was capable of nearly 27 belt hp. The 13-25 was equipped with a four-cylinder engine with a 4-1/4 x 5-inch bore and stroke.

Nebraska Test Data

Model: M-M Universal "MT"

Test No. 197

Date Tested: September 30 to October 9, 1931

During 59 hours of running time, no repairs or adjustments were necessary on the Moline MT tractor. Featuring three forward speeds of 2.1, 3.13 and 4.15 mph, this tractor weighed in at 5,235 lbs. Although it carried no manufacturer-designated hp rating, existing codes gave it 13.81 drawbar and 25.17 belt hp. Burning kerosene, the MT developed 26.68 brake hp at maximum load, consuming 2.608 gph and an economy of 10.23 hp-hours per gallon. This rose to 10.45 at rated load of 25.09 hp. Rated drawbar tests at 13.77 hp yielded an economy of 5.64 hp-hours per gallon while the MT pulled a 1,460-lb. load at 3.54 mph and slippage of an even 2 percent. In low gear, 18.17 maximum drawbar hp was noted, with a pull of 2,889 lbs. at 2.36 mph and slippage of only 5.14 percent. Features of this tractor included the M-M four-cylinder I-head engine with a 4-1/4 x 5-inch bore and stroke, and a rated speed of 1,000 rpm. Included also was an American Bosch U4 magneto, a Schebler TT carburetor, and Donaldson air cleaner.

Nebraska Test Data

Model: M-M Twin City MTA

Test No. 248

Date Tested: October 2 to October 17, 1935

While not rated by the manufacturer, the MTA had maximum permissible ratings of 19.37 drawbar and 29.63 belt hp under existing rating codes. Along with the four-cylinder 4-1/4 x 5-inch engine was an American Bosch U-4 magneto and a Schebler TTX-15 carburetor. Pressed steel drive wheels with 20 spade lugs per wheel were standard equipment. Distillate fuel was used throughout the test. In Test D for rated brake hp, fuel economy came in at 9.92 hp-hours per gallon under a 29.77 hp load. Test B at 100 percent maximum hp gave a lower fuel economy of 8.74 but hp came in at 33.23. Advertised speeds of 2.1, 3.1 and 4.1 mph were provided. Using second gear for rated drawbar load (Test H) gave a fuel economy of 6.99 hp-hours per gallon under a load of 2,140 lbs. at 3.4 mph and an output of 19.43 hp. Test G for operating maximum load indicated a pull of 4,171 lbs. in low gear, nearly 76 percent of the tractor's 5,495-lb. operating weight. No repairs or adjustments were noted during 48 hours of motor operation.

Production of the M-M Universal "J" tractor began in 1934 and continued until 1938. In addition to the row-crop model, a standard-tread tractor was also produced. This small tractor weighed only 3,450 lbs. and was equipped with a four-cylinder engine with a 3-5/8 x 4-3/4-inch bore and stroke. It was available on steel wheels or rubber tires.

COLLECTOR VALUES	1	2	3	4
JT	$3,000	$2,500	$1,800	$800

M-M Universal "J" tractor

M-M Universal "M" tractor

Production of the Universal "M" tractor began in 1934, following the introduction of the Universal "MT" model in 1931. The latter model was tested at Nebraska under No. 197 of October 1931 (see above). It demonstrated nearly 27 belt hp, using a four-cylinder engine with a 4-1/4 x 5-inch bore and stroke. Production of the Universal "M" continued until 1939.

COLLECTOR VALUES	1	2	3	4
MT	$2,200	$1,500	$800	$600

FT 21-32 tractor

An improved version of the FT 21-32 tractor came along in 1935. The new FT-A was essentially the same and continued to carry the same 21-32 hp rating. Slight changes in styling and accessory items were the main differences over the earlier model. Production of the FT-A continued until 1938.

Nebraska Test Data

Model: M-M Twin City FT-A

Test No. 270

Date Tested: September 10 to September 18, 1936

Weighing 6,920 lbs., the FT-A featured three forward speeds of 2.36, 3.17 and 4.05 mph. The 10-hour rated drawbar load test was run in second gear at 3.58 mph, and the FT-A pulled a load of 2,867 lbs. with slippage of 2.23 percent for a total output of 27.34 drawbar hp. Fuel economy was 7.96 hp-hours per gallon of distillate. Test G for operating maximum load evidenced a pull of 4,724 lbs. using first gear. At 2.63 mph, slippage was recorded at 3.66 percent with an output of 33.18 hp. The FT-A was equipped with the company's own four-cylinder I-head engine. Rated at 1,075 rpm, it featured a 4-5/8 x 6-inch bore and stroke. Also included was an American Bosch MJB4A magneto, Schebler TTX-16 carburetor and Donaldson air cleaner. Test D for rated brake load over one hour indicated 41.26 hp, 11.37 hp-hours per gallon, and a slightly diminished economy of 11.01 under maximum operating load of 44.09 hp, as noted in Test C. Only minor repairs and adjustments were necessary during 49 hours of running time.

COLLECTOR VALUES	1	2	3	4
FT	$6,250	$5,000	$3,000	$1,000

Type R streamlined tractor

Production of the Type R streamlined tractors began in 1939 and continued until 1947. The R-Series tractors used a M-M Model EE engine with four-cylinders and a 3-5/8 x 4-inch bore and stroke. The "N" suffix apparently denoted a single-front wheel design.

COLLECTOR VALUES	1	2	3	4
RTN	$1,950	$1,500	$1,000	$350

Minneapolis-Moline RTU tractor

The Minneapolis-Moline RTU tractor was tested at Nebraska in May 1940. This small tractor was capable of 20 drawbar hp and over 23 belt hp. The engine design was unique with its unusual side-valve arrangement.

Nebraska Test Data

Model: M-M Twin City RTU

Test No. 341

Date Tested: April 29 to May 10, 1940

Advertised speeds of 2.3, 3.3, 4.2 and 12 mph were built into the Twin City RTU tractor. Weighing 4,135 lbs., it was equipped with 8 x 36-inch rear tires and 4.00 x 15-inch front tires. Some 339 lbs. of cast-iron wheel weight was added to each rear tire, plus 105 lbs. of water ballast. Test H indicated a rated drawbar output of 15.66 hp, plus a pull of 1,477 lbs. at 3.98 mph and slippage of 5.32 percent. Test H was run in third gear. Test G indicated a maximum drawbar pull of 2,666 lbs. using low gear. This test phase noted an output of 13.47 hp and a speed of 1.89 mph with 17.47 percent slippage. M-M equipped the RTU with its own four-cylinder engine, positioning the valves in the block horizontally over the piston. A Schebler TSX-30 carburetor and Fairbanks-Morse K4B magneto complemented the basic engine. Test C for operating maximum load indicated 10.14 hp-hours per gallon and 21.63 brake hp. At rated load of 20.52 hp, as noted in Test D, economy slipped a few points to 9.97 hp-hours per gallon. No repairs or adjustments were noted during some 55 hours of engine operating time.

COLLECTOR VALUES	1	2	3	4
RTU	$1,800	$1,400	$900	$350

Minneapolis-Moline RTS standard-tread tractor

Minneapolis-Moline RTS standard-tread tractors were another version of the Model R series. Production of the R-Series tractors began in 1939 and continued until 1947, with production hampered during World War II.

COLLECTOR VALUES	1	2	3	4
RTS	$2,250	$1,800	$1,200	$650

Minneapolis-Moline ZTU Row-Crop

Minneapolis-Moline tractors were sold under the M-M Twin City tradename into the early 1940s. The M-M ZTU Row-Crop model was introduced in 1936 and was produced until 1948. In Nebraska Test No. 352 of 1940, the ZTU demonstrated nearly 28 belt hp under its rated load. Power came from a four-cylinder engine with a 3-5/8 x 4-1/2-inch bore and stroke. In 1949, M-M revamped the Z-Series tractors with the ZA series.

Nebraska Test Data

Model: M-M Twin City ZT

Test No. 290

Date Tested: October 4 to October 12, 1937

Although this tractor was tested and rated on steel wheels, rubber tires were available as a factory option. Five forward speeds of 2.18, 2.62, 3.13, 4.57 and 14.3 mph were provided, with fifth gear not recoM-Mended for the steel-wheel version. Third gear was used for Test H, and at a rated load of 15.98 drawbar hp, fuel economy was recorded at 7.45 hp-hours per gallon of distillate. At maximum operating load under Test G, a maximum pull of 3,262 lbs. was shown in low gear. Moving at 2.28 mph, slippage was recorded at 8.31 percent with an output of 19.82 drawbar hp. The ZT featured the M-M four-cylinder engine with the valves mounted in the block horizontally over the pistons. Rated at 1,500 rpm, it carried a 3-5/8 x 4-1/2-inch bore and stroke. Also included was a Fairbanks-Morse RV-4 magneto and a Schebler TRX-12 carburetor. Test D evidenced 10.06 hp-hours per gallon at a rated load of 23.62 brake hp. Economy increased minimally to 10.1 at operating maximum load of 25.2 hp per Test C. Operating weight of the ZT was 4,280 lbs. No repairs or adjustments were made during 46 hours of running time.

Nebraska Test Data

Model: M-M Twin City ZTU

Test No. 352

Date Tested: September 3 to September 7, 1940

Advertised speeds of 2.2, 2.7, 3.7, 4.7 and 14.6 mph were provided in the ZTU tractor. Using fourth gear, this model emerged from Test H with 8.53 hp-hours per gallon. Pulling 1,748 lbs. at 4.51 mph, the ZTU recorded a 4.05 percent slippage and delivered a rated output of 21.04 drawbar hp. Low gear maximum testing gave a pull of 3,254 lbs. at 1.86 mph under slippage of 18.47 percent as noted in Test G. Tire equipment included 9 x 38-inch rear and 5.50 x 16-inch front rubber. Test C for operating maximum load gave an output of 30.55 brake hp and 10.94 hp-hours per gallon, sagging to 10.06 under Test D-rated load of 27.94 brake hp. The ZTU was equipped with the company's own four-cylinder vertical I-head engine with a 3-5/8 x 4-1/2-inch bore and stroke. Rated speed was 1,500 rpm. Also included was a Fairbanks-Morse FMK4B magneto and a Schebler TRX12 carburetor. Although no repairs or adjustments were recorded, it was noted the engine side covers were raised during the belt tests to facilitate cooling. Some 56 hours of engine operating time was recorded for this test.

COLLECTOR VALUES	1	2	3	4
ZAE	$2,800	$2,350	$1,650	$1,000
ZAN	$2,600	$2,000	$1,600	$800
ZAS	$3,000	$2,600	$1,800	$900
ZBE	$2,150	$1,800	$1,000	$600
ZBN	$2,150	$1,800	$1,200	$600
ZBU	$2,100	$1,800	$1,200	$600
ZTU	$2,500	$1,650	$1,350	$650

Minneapolis-Moline ZTN tractor

Built in the same 1936-1948 period as the ZTU row-crop tractor was this ZTN with a single-front-wheel design. In all other respects, it was the same tractor but the single-front design was essential for certain crops.

COLLECTOR VALUES	1	2	3	4
ZTN	$2,500	$1,650	$1,350	$650

Minneapolis-Moline Model ZTS tractor

Between 1937 and 1947, Minneapolis-Moline produced its Model ZTS tractor. It was the standard-tread version of the Z-Series. In the 1936 through '39 period, M-M also built the ZTI, an industrial tractor especially set up for factory and warehouse work. All models used the same engine and the same basic chassis design.

M-M GT Standard-Tread tractor

Topping the M-M line in the 1938 through 1941 period was the GT Standard-Tread tractor. It was equipped with the company's own Model LE engine, a four-cylinder design with a 4-5/8 x 6-inch bore and stroke. With some minor changes, like sheet metal work, the GT-A appeared in 1942 and was in production until 1947.

Nebraska Test Data

Model: M-M Twin City GT

Test No. 317

Date Tested: May 1 to May 12, 1939

Although a steel-wheel version of the M-M GT tractor is illustrated, the tractor actually tested under No. 317 was equipped with 13.5 x 32-inch rear tires and 7.50 x 18-inch front rubber. Test weight was 9,445 lbs. M-M featured four forward speeds of 2.7, 3.8, 5.8 and 9.6 mph in the GT tractor. Second gear was chosen for the rated drawbar trials (Test H). At 36.96 drawbar hp, the GT pulled 3,849 lbs. at 3.6 mph and delivered 9.43 hp-hours per gallon. Test G indicated a maximum first-gear pull of 5,068 lbs. at 2.34 mph for an output of 31.6 drawbar hp. Test D for rated brake hp indicated 11.4 hp-hours per gallon under a 49.02 hp load. At an operating maximum load of 53.99 hp, the GT delivered 11.62 hp-hours per gallon per Test C. Accessory items for the four-cylinder I-head engine included a Fairbanks-Morse FM-4 magneto and a Schebler TTX23 carburetor. Rated at 1,075 rpm, this M-M-built engine carried a 4-5/8 x 6-inch bore and stroke. During 52 hours of engine running time, no repairs or adjustments were noted.

COLLECTOR VALUES	1	2	3	4
GT TRACTOR	$3,500	$2,800	$2,100	$1,400
GTA TRACTOR	$3,500	$2,800	$2,100	$1,400

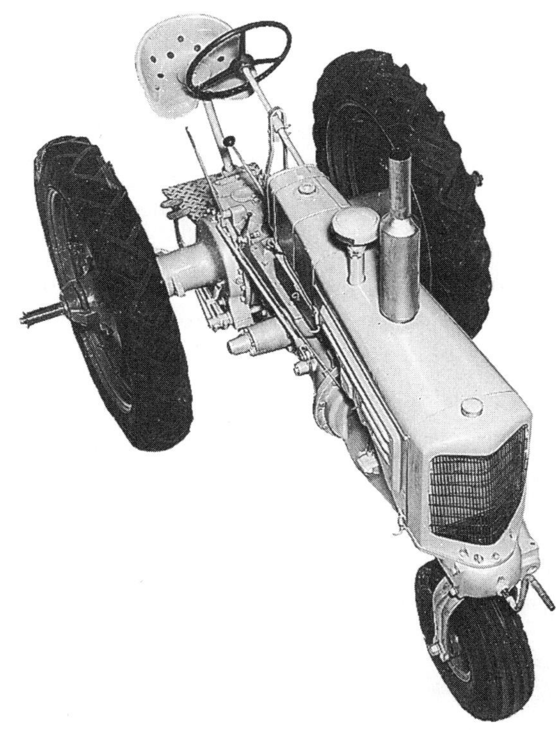

Minneapolis-Moline YT tractor

During 1937, Minneapolis-Moline built a few copies of its YT tractor. This two-cylinder design was essentially one half of the Model R. The YT was never put into production, with assembly ending after a couple dozen were sent into the field. Fourteen specimens exist today.

COLLECTOR VALUES	1	2	3	4
YT TRACTOR	$28,500	–	–	–

UTU row-crop tractor

Production of the U-Series tractors began in 1938 and extended into 1948. The UTU shown here was the ordinary row-crop style. Weighing about 6,700 lbs., it used the company's own Model KEF four-cylinder engine and it had a 4-1/4 x 5-inch bore and stroke. In Nebraska Test No. 319, it yielded nearly 43 belt hp.

COLLECTOR VALUES	1	2	3	4
UB SPECIAL	$3,250	$3,000	$1,850	$1,000
ALL OTHER U-SERIES MODELS	$2,400	$1,800	$1,950	$1,000

UTS tractor

The UTS tractor had a maximum drawbar pull of nearly 5,000 lbs. It was equipped with the same KEF engine as the UTU tractor and delivered 39 drawbar hp. U-Series production continued into 1948.

COLLECTOR VALUES	1	2	3	4
UTS	$2,650	$2,000	$1,400	$900

Minneapolis-Moline UDLX (U-Deluxe) tractor

In 1938 Minneapolis-Moline introduced its UDLX (U-Deluxe) tractor. It was essentially the same as the remainder of the U-Series tractors but was equipped with a special cab, headlights, radio and other accessories. Unfortunately, the concept was ahead of its time. Farmers weren't ready to accept an enclosed tractor cab and production ended in 1939.

COLLECTOR VALUES	1	2	3	4
UDLX TRACTOR	$90,000	$65,000	--	--

Minneapolis-Moline RTU row-crop model

Minneapolis-Moline revamped its R-Series tractors in 1948. The RTU row-crop model continued in production until 1954, while the RTN single-front-wheel style was built in the 1948 through 1951 period. Other styles included the RTE, built from 1948 to 1953, and the RTI Industrial style shown here. It was offered only in 1953. It was equipped with the M-M Model EE four-cylinder engine with a 3-5/8 x 4-inch bore and stroke.

Nebraska Test Data

Model: Minneapolis-Moline R

Test No. 468

Date Tested: October 20 to November 1, 1951The four-cylinder engine used in this tractor had a 165-cubic inch displacement. Rated at 1,500 rpm, it used a 3-7/8 x 4-inch bore and stroke. No repairs or adjustments were noted during 48 hours of engine running time. Standard tires included 5.00-15-inch front and 10-34-inch rear rubber. Basic tractor weight was 3,414 lbs., with an additional 753 lbs. of ballast added to each rear wheel during a portion of the drawbar tests. Advertised speeds of 2.6, 3.6, 4.7 and 13.2 mph were provided, and third gear was used for the rated drawbar load run of Test H. With an output of 18.29 drawbar hp, the Model R pulled 1,550 lbs. at 4.43 mph with a slippage of 5.55 percent. Fuel economy was 7.95 hp-hours per gallon. In Test G, a low-gear maximum pull of 2,801 lbs. at 2.16 mph was recorded. Test C fuel economy at operating maximum of 25.92 belt hp came to 10.07 hp-hours per gallon, while a figure of 9.43 appeared under a Test D-rated belt load of 23.81 hp.

GTB standard-tread model

Introduced in 1947, the GTB standard-tread model was built until 1954. In Nebraska Test No. 437 of 1950, the GTB delivered almost 56 belt hp. The M-M 403A-4 engine had a 4-5/8 x 6-inch bore and stroke. This big tractor weighed 6,400 lbs. During 1953 and 1954, Minneapolis-Moline also offered its GTB Diesel model.

UTS standard-tread tractor

Beginning in 1948, Minneapolis-Moline introduced new and improved models of the U-Series tractors. The UTS standard-tread came along in 1948 and continued until 1957. Weighing 5,500 lbs., it was equipped with a four-cylinder, 283-cid engine. In Nebraska Test No. 310, it delivered 39 drawbar hp. This tractor was also tested at Nebraska using propane fuel under No. 411. M-M pioneered the use of propane for tractors during the 1940s and remained active in this field for at least 20 years.

Nebraska Test Data

Model: M-M Twin City UTS (Gasoline)
Test No. 310
Date Tested: October 24 to November 16, 1938

Rubber tires were featured on the UTS presented for this test. On the rear, 12.75 x 32 tires were standard equipment, along with 7.50 x 16 on the front. During 55 hours of engine running time, gasoline was used. Five forward speeds of 2.7, 3.5, 4.7, 6.2 and 20.2 mph were provided. Using third gear for the rated drawbar trials (Test H), economy was registered at 8.8 hp-hours per gallon, with a pull of 2,559 lbs. at 4.53 mph and an output of 30.9 drawbar hp. A maximum drawbar pull of 4,959 lbs. was recorded in Test G, using low gear. Belt hp tests indicated a maximum operating load of 41.67 hp under Test C, with 11.19 hp-hours per gallon. A slightly lower 10.26 was noted at the rated load of 38.31 hp. M-M used its own four-cylinder I-head engine in the UTS tractor. Using a 4-1/4 x 5-inch bore and stroke, it was rated at 1,275 rpm. Included was a Fairbanks-Morse FM4B magneto and a Schebler TTX-17 carburetor. Test weight was 7,940 lbs.

Nebraska Test Data

Model: M-M Twin City UTS (Distillate)
Test No. 311
Date Tested: November 21 to November 25, 1938

M-M used the same identical tractor with Engine Serial 540560 for both this test and Test No. 310. Distillate was chosen for the test at hand. All tractor specifications remained the same. Under the belt hp tests, Test B at 100 percent maximum load indicated 36.48 hp over the two-hour trial, with a fuel consumption of 9.42 hp-hours per gallon. Test C for operating maximum load indicated 10.33 hp-hours per gallon and an output of 35.19 hp at rated load (Test D), the UTS developed 31.47 hp with economy at 10.54. Test H for rated drawbar load was run in third gear. Developing 24.51 hp, the UTS pulled 2,018 lbs. at 4.55 mph and yielded 9.18 hp-hours per gallon. A maximum pull of 4,773 lbs. was indicated in Test G, using low gear. No repairs or adjustments were noted in this particular test.

Minneapolis-Moline UTU row-crop

The Minneapolis-Moline UTU row-crop of the 1948 through 1955 period was greatly updated from the original UTU model. It was capable of 38 drawbar and 45 belt hp. Details are found in Nebraska Test No. 319. M-M also offered the UTC in 1954 and 1955, the UTE from 1951 to 1954 and the UTN from 1950 to 1952.

Nebraska Test Data

Model: M-M Twin City UTU
Test No. 319
Date Tested: June 13 to June 17, 1939

While delivering 28.32 drawbar hp, the UTU pulled 2,620 lbs. at 4.05 mph in Test H for rated drawbar load. During this test, fuel economy was recorded at 8.7 hp-hours per gallon. Test G for operating maximum load pegged the UTU at a 4,496-lb. pull in low gear. Traveling at 2.06 mph during this test, the UTU experienced slippage of 17.52 percent and yielded 24.65 drawbar hp. The rear tires of this tractor were 11 x 36 six-ply design, along with 6.00 x 16-inch front rubber. M-M listed five speeds for the UTU of 2.5, 3.2, 4.3, 5.7 and 18.5 mph. Standard equipment for this 6,773-lb. tractor included a Fairbanks-Morse FM4B magneto, Schebler TTX17 carburetor, and thermostat-type temperature control. M-M used its own four-cylinder I-head engine. Rated at 1,275 rpm, it featured a 4-1/4 x 5-inch bore and stroke. Test C for operating maximum belt hp manifested 11.13 hp-hours per gallon while under a 41.51 hp load. At rated load of 38.77 hp (Test D), fuel economy sagged to 10.59 hp-hours per gallon. During 55 hours of engine operating time, no repairs or adjustments were indicated.

M-M ZAU row-crop tractor

An improved series of M-M "Z" tractors appeared in 1949 and continued until 1952. Typical of the line was the ZAU row-crop style. It was a 206-cid, four-cylinder engine. Along with the row-crop model, the Z-Series tractors were offered in numerous other chassis configurations.

Nebraska Test Data

Model: Minneapolis-Moline Z

Test No. 438

Date Tested: May 6 to May 15, 1950

Using the company's own four-cylinder engine, the Z featured a 3-7/8 x 5-inch bore and stroke with a rated speed of 1,500 rpm. Displacement totaled 206-cubic inches. During 37 hours of operation, no repairs or adjustments were noted. The Z had forward speeds of 2.4, 3.6, 4.6, 6.3 and 13.1 mph. Third gear was chosen for Test H, and at a rated drawbar load of 25.18 hp, this tractor pulled 2,147 lbs. at 4.4 mph with a 5.27 percent slippage and delivered 8.55 hp-hours per gallon. Test G achieved a low-gear maximum pull of 3,498 lbs. at 2.09 mph. Standard tire equipment included 11-38-inch rear and 5.50-16- inch front rubber. Bare tractor weight was 4,290 lbs., with an additional 760 lbs. of ballast added to each rear wheel during Tests F, G and H. At a Test C operating maximum load of 34.77 belt hp, the Z achieved 10.74 hp-hours per gallon, dropping slightly to 10.16 at a Test D rated load of 31.85 hp.

COLLECTOR VALUES	1	2	3	4
GB TRACTOR	$3,200	$2,000	$1,685	$1,000
GB LP	$3,500	$2,500	$2,000	$1,000

Avery BF tractor

B. F. Avery Company at Louisville, Kentucky, brought out its Avery BF tractor in 1945. Minneapolis-Moline bought out Avery in 1951 and continued to market the BF until 1955. This small tractor was capable of about 26 belt hp. It was equipped with a four-cylinder Hercules engine with a 3-1/4 x 4-inch bore and stroke for a displacement of 133 cubic inches.

Nebraska Test Data

Model: Minneapolis-Moline BF

Test No. 469

Date Tested: October 22 to October 27, 1951

Weighing 2,894 lbs., the BF offered 10-28 rear and 5.50-16 front tires as standard equipment. Also featured were forward speeds of 2.42, 3.67, 5.23 and 13.12 mph. Third gear was used for Test H, and at a rated drawbar load of 19.12 hp, the BF pulled 1,414 lbs. at 5.07 mph, experiencing a slippage of 5.21 percent. Fuel economy totaled 9.1 hp-hours per gallon. During Tests F, G and H an additional 825 lbs. of ballast was added to each rear wheel. Test G evoked a low-gear maximum pull of 2,725 lbs. at 2.1 mph. The BF tractor used a Hercules four-cylinder L-head engine rated at 1,800 rpm and a 3-1/4 x 4 inch bore and stroke for a 133-cubic inch displacement. The repairs and adjustments section included an adjustment of the governor spring tension during 46 hours of engine operating time. Test C, run at an operating maximum load of 26.85 belt hp, revealed 10.33 hp-hours per gallon. A comparable figure of 10.19 was manifested under a Test D-rated belt load of 23.53 hp.

COLLECTOR VALUES	1	2	3	4
AVERY BF	$3,000	$2,400	$1,500	$800
AVERY BG	$3,800	$2,750	$2,500	$1,200
AVERY BH	$3,600	$2,700	$1,600	$1,200

M-M-Avery Model V tractor

Production of the M-M-Avery Model V tractor paralleled the Model BF. The Model V was half the size of the BF, using a Hercules ZXB-3 four-cylinder engine with a 2-5/8 x 3 inch bore and stroke for a displacement of 65-cubic inches. Production of this model was rather limited.

COLLECTOR VALUES	1	2	3	4
AVERY V	$3,000	$2,500	$2,050	$1,000

Minneapolis-Moline G tractor

Nebraska Test Data

Model: Minneapolis-Moline G

Test No. 437

Date Tested: April 21 to May 16, 1950

Shown here during the actual belt tests, the M-M G delivered 11.43 hp-hours per gallon while under a Test C operating maximum load of 55.94 belt hp. Test D at a rated load of 50.64 hp saw fuel economy sag slightly to 11.07 hp-hours per gallon. Advertised speeds of 2.5, 3.5, 4.1, 6 and 13.8 mph were provided, with third gear used for the rated drawbar load of Test H. With 39.2 drawbar hp, the G pulled 3,715 lbs. at 3.96 mph under a slippage of 6 percent. Fuel economy totaled 9.72 hp-hours per gallon. A low-gear maximum pull of 6,410 lbs. was recorded in Test G. As set up from the factory, the G weighed in at 7,230 lbs., but for Tests F, G and H, an additional 1,777 lbs. of ballast was added to each rear wheel. No repairs or adjustments were noted during the 44-1/2 hours of engine running time. The M-M G used the company's own four-cylinder L-head engine. Rated at 1,100 rpm, it carried a 4-3/8 x 6-inch bore and stroke with a 403.2-cubic inch displacement.

Minneapolis-Moline GB tractor

Nebraska Test Data

Model: Minneapolis-Moline GB (LPG)

Test No. 545

Date Tested: May 31 to June 7, 1955

Weighing 7,506 lbs., the GB tractor shown here was equipped with 15-34 rear and 7.50-18-inch front tires. During Tests F, G and H, an additional 2,134 lbs. was added to each rear wheel. Features included forward speeds of 2.7, 3.8, 4.4, 6.3 and 14.7 mph. Third gear was used for Test H. This 10-hour run, made at a rated load of 49.68 drawbar hp, saw a pull of 4,350 lbs. at 4.28 mph and a slippage of 6.1 percent. Fuel economy was 8.25 hp-hours per gallon of propane. A Test G low-gear maximum pull of 7,094 lbs. at 2.31 mph was also recorded. The GB was equipped with a four-cylinder I-head engine rated at 1,300 rpm and carried a 4-5/8 x 6-inch bore and stroke for a 403.2-cubic inch displacement. At an engine speed of 1,298 rpm, the GB achieved a maximum torque of 4,419 lbs.-ft. Test D, run at a rated belt load of 63.75 hp, produced 9.68 hp-hours per gallon of propane, climbing to 9.89 at a Test C operating maximum load of 68.48 hp. The GB gasoline model may be found under Test No. 547.

Nebraska Test Data

Model: Minneapolis-Moline GB

Test No. 547

Date Tested: June 8 to June 15, 1955

During 48-1/2 hours of operation, no repairs or adjustments were noted for the GB tractor. This gasoline model was virtually identical to the propane version in Test No. 545. The large propane cylinder and related equipment for the conventional fuel tank made an obvious exterior difference. Internally, a 5.74:1 compression ratio was used in the tractor shown here, compared to 8.37:1 for the propane version of Test 545. Tire equipment and advertised speeds remained the same for both models. Rated at 1,300 rpm, this tractor achieved a maximum torque of 454.1 lbs.-ft. with an engine speed of 847 rpm. Drawbar testing yielded a Test G low-gear maximum pull of 6,718 lbs. at 2.3 mph and a 16.47 slippage. Test H scored drawbar fuel economy at 10.1 hp-hours per gallon with a rated drawbar load of 46.26 hp. This test also showed a pull of 4,046 lbs. at 4.29 mph and 6.25 percent slippage. Belt testing yielded a Test C operating maximum load of 63.08 hp and 11.71 hp-hours per gallon. This slipped to 11.42 at a Test D-rated belt load of 58.51 hp.

Nebraska Test Data

Model: Minneapolis-Moline GBD

Test No. 568

Date Tested: November 1 to November 7, 1955

The GBD featured a M-M six-cylinder diesel engine rated at 1,300 rpm and carried a 4-1/4 x 5-inch bore and stroke for a displacement of 425.5-cubic inches. Engine torque peaked at 427.9 lbs.-ft. with a speed of 948 rpm. No repairs or adjustments were noted during 39 hours of running time. Features included 15-34-inch rear and 7.50-18-inch front tires, with forward speeds of 2.7, 3.8, 4.4, 6.3 and 14.7 mph. Bare tractor weight was 8,170 lbs., with an additional 2,198 lbs. added to each rear wheel during Tests F, G and H. A low-gear maximum pull of 7,333 lbs. at 2.3 mph and a slippage of 15.24 percent was noted in Test G. The 10-hour run of Test H was made in third gear. With a rated drawbar load of 43.7 hp, the GBD pulled 3,846 lbs. at 4.26 mph with 5.24 percent slippage. Fuel economy was pegged at 13.44 hp-hours per gallon. Test B, run at a 100 percent maximum belt load of 62.78 hp, gave a reading of 15.38 hp-hours per gallon. An identical economy figure appeared under the Test D-rated belt load of 55.9 hp.

Minneapolis-Moline 5-Star series

Nebraska Test Data

Model: Minneapolis-Moline 5-Star (LPG)
Test No. 651
Date Tested: May 13 to May 24, 1958

This tractor featured a Minneapolis-Moline four-cylinder engine designed for use with propane, as evidenced by the 8.3:1 compression ratio. Rated at 1,500 rpm, it carried a 4-1/4 x 5-inch bore and stroke for a 283-cubic inch displacement. Other features included 15.5-38-inch rear and 6.00-16-inch front tires, along with 10 forward speeds ranging from 1.65 to 17.37 mph. Weighing 6,655 lbs., it was burdened with 1,221 lbs. of ballast on each rear wheel, plus another 62 lbs. of cast iron on each front tire. Test G achieved a low-gear maximum pull of 6,023 lbs. at 2.88 mph with 9.6 percent slippage. The 10-hour run of Test H was made in second gear. At a rated drawbar load of 39.57 hp, the 5-Star pulled 3,032 lbs. at 4.89 mph with a slippage of 3.76 percent. Fuel economy was 8.01 hp-hours per gallon of propane. During Test D, the throttle linkage was adjusted, but otherwise no repairs were noted during 43-1/2 hours of operating time. At a Test C operating maximum load of 53.47 hp, fuel economy came in at 9.43 hp-hours per gallon of propane, slipping to 9.29 under a Test D-rated load of 48.58 hp.

Nebraska Test Data

Model: Minneapolis-Moline 5-Star Diesel
Test No. 652
Date Tested: May 13 to May 21, 1958

This M-M 5-Star model featured a Minneapolis-Moline four-cylinder diesel engine with a 4-5/8 x 5-inch bore and stroke. Rated at 1,450 rpm, it had a 336-cubic inch displacement and was designed with a 15:1 compression ratio. Features also included 15.5-38-inch rear and 6.00-16-inch front tires, along with 10 forward speeds ranging from 1.6 to 16.79 mph. Under a Test H rated drawbar load of 38.51 hp, a pull of 3,080 lbs. was recorded at 4.69 mph with 4.03 percent slippage. The drawbar fuel economy was 12.6 hp-hours per gallon of diesel fuel. Test G, using low gear in the Ampli-Torc drive, yielded a maximum pull of 7,247 lbs. at 1.37 mph with a 14.02 percent slippage. Bare tractor weight was 6,689 lbs. to which was added 1,243 lbs. of rear wheel ballast and 62 lbs. of cast-iron weight on each front wheel, for a total test weight of 9,295 lbs., including the operator. No repairs or adjustments were recorded during 52 hours. At a Test D-rated belt load of 48.69 hp, fuel economy came in at 14.54 hp-hours per gallon of diesel, climbing to stand at 14.63 under a 100 percent maximum belt load of 54.68 hp.

Minneapolis-Moline 4-Star series

Nebraska Test Data

Model: Minneapolis-Moline 4-Star
Test No. 789
Date Tested: April 20 to May 4, 1961

Using its Ampli-Torc system, Minneapolis-Moline designed this tractor with a fixed-ratio operator-controlled partial-range power-shifting transmission. Within this unit were 10 forward speeds ranging from 1.7 to 17.8 mph. Also featured were 13.6-38-inch rear and 6.00-16-inch front tires. With a factory weight of 5,245 lbs., the 4-Star's test weight was 8,495 lbs. with the added front and rear wheel ballast. Using second gear for the drawbar fuel economy runs, the 4-Star delivered 38.58 maximum available hp during a two-hour test. This run accrued 9.81 hp-hours per gallon. Other statistics included a pull of 3,013 lbs. at 4.8 mph with 4.49 percent slippage. A 10-hour run, made at 75 percent pull, noted 32.61 hp, a pull of 2,321 lbs. at 5.27 mph, and 3.55 percent slippage. Fuel economy was 9.65 hp-hours per gallon. Standard equipment included a four-cylinder M-M-designed engine. Rated at 1,750 rpm, its 3-5/8 x 5-inch bore and stroke translated into a 206.5-cubic inch displacement. At rated engine speed, a maximum of 44.57 PTO hp was observed, together with 10.75 hp-hours per gallon. New spark plugs were installed prior to the PTO runs, but otherwise no repairs or adjustments were recorded during 55 hours of running time.

Nebraska Test Data

Model: Minneapolis-Moline 4-Star (LPG)
Test No. 790
Date Tested: April 20 to May 5, 1961

Of the same basic design as the 4-Star gasoline model of Test No. 789, this propane-fired tractor featured an 8.75:1 compression ratio, compared to the 7.5:1 ratio in the gasoline model. Except for this difference and the obvious external changes required for the propane storage and handling equipment, both tractors were virtually identical. At rated engine speed of 1,750 rpm, it delivered 45.54 maximum PTO hp, with a fuel economy of 8.91 hp-hours per gallon. Another run, at 540 PTO rpm and a corresponding engine speed of 1,524 rpm, indicated 9.18 while delivering 42.19 PTO hp. Except for adjustment of the governor linkage, no repairs or adjustments were recorded during 42-1/2 hours of operation. Using second gear, 40.96 maximum available hp was developed in a two-hour economy run. This test, yielding 7.78 hp-hours per gallon, also recorded a pull of 3,219 lbs. at 4.77 mph with 4.79 percent slippage. A 10-hour economy run, made at 75 percent pull, noted an economy of 7.23 at 32.75 drawbar hp. This test recorded a pull of 2,411 lbs. at 5.09 mph with 3.81 percent slippage. With a factory weight

Minneapolis-Moline Gvi series

of 5,303 lbs., the 4-Star LPG model took on a test weight of 8,620 lbs. through added front and rear wheel ballast.

Nebraska Test Data

Model: Minneapolis-Moline Gvi (LPG)
Test No. 791
Date Tested: April 24 to May 9, 1961

Weighing 8,155 lbs., this tractor assumed a test weight of 12,615 lbs. through the addition of 1,090 lbs. of liquid and 1,140 lbs. of cast-iron ballast on each rear wheel. Standard equipment included 18.4-34-inch rear and 7.50-18-inch front tires. A selective-gear fixed-ratio transmission providing five forward speeds of 3.1, 4.4, 5.1, 7.4 and 17.1 mph. At 69.92 maximum available hp, and using third gear, a pull of 5,406 lbs. was recorded at 4.85 mph with 6.09 percent slippage. Fuel economy was 8.11 hp-hours per gallon of propane. The 10-hour economy run saw an accrued 7.64 hp-hours per gallon. This test, at 75 percent pull, noted an output of 58.77 hp, a pull of 4,058 lbs. at 5.43 mph and 4.92 percent slippage. The Gvi LPG tractor was equipped with a 425.5-cid six-cylinder engine with a rated speed of 1,500 rpm, and a 4-1/4 x 5-inch bore and stroke. This propane model carried an 8.3:1 compression ratio. At rated engine speed, a maximum output of 78.44 PTO hp was observed at 9.17 hp-hours per gallon. The economy figure slipped to 9.09 at 540 PTO rpm and a crankshaft speed of 1,200 rpm. This test indicated a maximum output of 66.58 hp. No repairs or adjustments were recorded during 42-1/2 hours of running time.

Nebraska Test Data

Model: Minneapolis-Moline Gvi Diesel
Test No. 792
Date Tested: April 24 to May 9, 1961

The company's own six-cylinder engine rated at 1,500 rpm was used in this tractor. Its 4-1/4 x 5-inch bore and stroke gave a 425.5-cubic inch displacement. At rated engine speed, a maximum of 78.49 PTO hp was developed, yielding 14.48 hp-hours per gallon. At standard 540-rpm speed on the PTO shaft, and a corresponding crankshaft speed of 1,999 rpm, economy was 14.79, with an output of 67.09 hp. No repairs or adjustments were recorded during 40-1/2 hours of operating time. Tire equipment and transmission specifications remained the same as recorded in Test No. 791. The factory weight of 8,335 lbs. assumed a total test weight of 12,695 lbs. through additional rear wheel ballast. Using third gear, a two-hour run at 66.06 maximum available hp saw 12.47 hp-hours per gallon. Also recorded was a pull of 5,116 lbs. at 4.84 mph with 6.24 percent slippage. The economy was posted at 12.25 in a 10-hour run at 75 percent pull. This test noted an output of 54.21 drawbar hp, a pull of 3,966 lbs. at 5.13 mph and 4.51 percent slippage.

Minneapolis–Moline M-5 series

Nebraska Test Data

Model: Minneapolis-Moline M-5
Test No. 756
Date Tested: August 31 to September 10, 1960

Weighing 6,765 lbs., the M-5 assumed a test weight of 9,615 lbs. by adding front and rear wheel ballast. Standard equipment included 15.5-38-inch rear and 6.00-16-inch front tires. Using a fixed-ratio operator-controlled partial-range power-shifting transmission, 10 forward speeds were available, ranging from 1.65 to 17.37 mph. Minneapolis-Moline called it the Ampli-Torc system. Fuel economy was 9.49 hp-hours per gallon in a two-hour run made at 52.51 maximum available hp. This test also indicated a pull of 4,331 lbs. at 4.55 mph and 6.41 percent slippage. The economy figure dipped slightly to 9.21 on the 10-hour drawbar run made at 75 percent pull. This test evoked 42.68 drawbar hp, a pull of 3,264 lbs. at 4.9 mph and slippage of 4.65 percent. The M-5 was equipped with a Minneapolis-Moline four-cylinder engine rated at 1,500 rpm. Using a 4-5/8 x 5-inch bore and stroke, it had a 336-cubic inch displacement. Operating at rated engine speed, a maximum of 61.01 PTO hp was observed, with 11.45 hp-hours per gallon. A similar run, at 540 PTO rpm and a corresponding crankshaft speed of 1,365 rpm, gave 57.45 PTO hp and 11.75 hp-hours per gallon. It was necessary to readjust the high idle speed during the drawbar runs, but with this exception, the M-5 went through 43-1/2 hours of running time without incident.

Nebraska Test Data

Model: Minneapolis-Moline M-5 (LPG)
Test No. 757
Date Tested: August 31 to September 10, 1960

With one major exception, this tractor was identical to the M-5 gasoline model noted in Test No. 756. While the previous unit used a 6.5:1 compression ratio, this propane-fired version carried a 7.9:1 compression ratio to accoM-Modate the fuel. The comparison is a direct one between two virtually identical tractors using different types of fuel. At its rated crankshaft speed of 1,500 rpm, a maximum output of 61.26 PTO hp was observed, with 9.00 hp-hours per gallon of propane. Using a standard 540-rpm PTO speed and a corresponding 1,365 rpm at the crankshaft, 57.34 hp was recorded with 9.31 hp-hours per gallon of propane. Drawbar fuel economy was pegged at 8.06 hp-hours per gallon at 54.47 maximum available hp. Statistics from this two-hour run included a pull of 4,458 lbs. at 4.58 mph with 6.94 percent slippage. A 10-hour run made at 75 percent pull recorded 43.84 hp, a pull of 3,265 lbs. at 5.04 mph and slippage of 4.87 percent. Fuel economy totaled 7.4 hp-hours per gallon of propane. No repairs or adjustments were recorded during 40-1/2 hours of operation. Basic engine data was noted in Test No. 757. Despite repeated efforts, an actual photograph of the M-5 LPG version has not been located and the standard gasoline model is illustrated.

Nebraska Test Data

Model: Minneapolis-Moline M-5 Diesel
Test No. 758
Date Tested: September 6 to September 10, 1960

In addition to the M-5 Diesel noted here, Minneapolis-Moline presented a gasoline and a propane version concurrently. This tractor carried a Minneapolis-Moline four-cylinder diesel engine rated at 1,500 rpm and a 4-5/8 x 5-inch bore and stroke. This 336-cid engine was designed with a 14.8:1 compression ratio. At rated engine speed, a maximum of 58.15 PTO hp was observed, with 15.14 hp-hours per gallon. A second PTO run made at 540 rpm and 1,365 crankshaft rpm noted 53.82 hp and a fuel economy of 15.39. The fixed-ratio portion of the transmission provided five speeds ranging from 13.14 to 17.37 mph. Use of the Ampli-Torc power shift provided five more speeds, from 1.65 to 9.12 mph. Weighing 6,965 lbs., the M-5 Diesel was equipped with 15.5-38-inch rear and 6.00-16-inch front tires. Using second gear, a two-hour economy run at 51.37 maximum available hp yielded 51.37 hp, a pull of 4,235 lbs. at 4.55 mph and slippage of 6.78 percent. Fuel economy was 13.3 hp-hours per gallon. The 10-hour economy run, at 75 percent pull, noted an output of 41.02 drawbar hp, a pull of 3,167 lbs. at 4.86 mph and slippage of 4.51 percent. Fuel economy totaled 12.94 hp-hours per gallon. During 41 hours of operating time, no repairs or adjustments were noted.

Minneapolis-Moline U-302 series

Nebraska Test Data

Model: Minneapolis-Moline U-302
Test No. 862
Date Tested: April 10 to April 24, 1964

Weighing 5,475 lbs. without ballast, the U-302 assumed a test weight of 9,245 lbs. through the addition of liquid and cast-iron ballast on the rear wheels. Standard equipment included 15.5-38-inch rear and 6.00-16-inch front tires. Also featured was a selective-gear fixed-ratio transmission that offered partial range power shifting. In all, 10 forward speeds were available with a range of 1.8 to 19.4 mph. In second gear, and under a maximum load of 46.89 drawbar hp, this tractor delivered 9.83 hp-hours per gallon. Also recorded in this two-hour test was a pull of 3,369 lbs. at 5.22 mph with 4.54 percent slippage. At 75 percent pull, and with an output of 38.37 hp, the U-302 delivered 9.56 hp-hours per gallon in a 10-hour run. Statistics included a pull of 2,620 lbs. at 5.49 mph with 3.41 percent slippage. Minneapolis-Moline equipped the U-302 with a four-cylinder engine rated at 1,900 rpm. Using a 3-3/4 x 5-inch bore and stroke, it carried a 221.1-cubic inch displacement. At rated engine speed, and against a maximum load of 55.82 PTO hp, fuel economy was posted at 11.42 hp-hours per gallon. This rose to 11.55 in a second PTO run made at 540 rpm on the output shaft and a corresponding engine speed of 1,525 rpm. During this test, 48.51 PTO hp was developed. Four bolts on a rear wheel hub failed during the drawbar runs. Otherwise no repairs or adjustments were required during 48-1/2 hours of running time.

Nebraska Test Data

Model: Minneapolis-Moline U-302 (LPG)
Test No. 863
Date Tested: April 13 to April 24, 1964

While a 7.60 to 1 compression ratio was used in the U-302 gasoline model of Test No. 862, this propane version carried a 9.8 to 1 compression ratio. Aside from this change and the obvious modifications required for the storage and handling of propane fuel, both tractors were nearly identical in design. In over 39 hours of operating time, no repairs or adjustments were reported for this tractor. Operating at its rated speed of 1,900 rpm, a maximum output of 55.69 PTO hp was observed, together with an economy of 9.58 hp-hours per gallon of propane. A second PTO run made at 540 PTO rpm and a corresponding engine speed of 1,525 rpm saw an economy of 10.12 hp-hours per gallon against an output of 48.32 hp. Using second gear, the two-hour drawbar run at 48.41 maximum available hp indicated 8.57 hp-hours per gallon of propane. Also evidenced was a pull of 3,492 lbs. at 5.2 mph with 4.66 percent slippage. The economy came in at 8.03 in a 10-hour run made at 75 percent pull and with an output of 39.19 drawbar hp. Recorded too was a pull of 2,651 lbs. at 5.54 mph with 3.7 percent slippage. Through the addition of rear wheel ballast, the test weight was 9,385 lbs., compared to a bare weight of 5,635 lbs.

Minneapolis-Moline 445 series

Nebraska Test Data

Model: Minneapolis-Moline 445 Universal

Test No. 578

Date Tested: June 23 to June 30, 1956

Using direct engine drive, the 445 featured speeds of 2.78, 4.26, 6.48, 10.5 and 15.4 mph. With the M-M Ampli-Torc, another five speeds, ranging from 1.46 to 8.09 mph, were provided. Standard equipment included 12-38-inch rear and 5.50-16-inch front tires. Test H, run in second gear and direct drive, indicated a fuel economy of 10.89 hp-hours per gallon with a rated drawbar load of 30.86 hp. This test also showed a pull of 2,732 lbs. at 4.24 mph with a 5.03 percent slippage. Using second gear in Ampli-Torc drive, a maximum drawbar pull of 5,240 lbs. was attained with a speed of 1.98 mph and slippage of 15.03 percent. The 445 Universal carried an M-M four-cylinder I-head engine with a 3-5/8 x 5-inch bore and stroke for a 206-cubic inch displacement. Rated at 1,550 rpm, it achieved a peak 108 percent of rated torque at 70 percent of rated engine speed. Test D, run at a rated belt load of 37.95 hp, achieved 11.87 hp-hours per gallon. This figure rose to 11.96 at a Test C operating maximum load of 39.87 hp. No repairs or adjustments were noted during 43 hours of running time.

Nebraska Test Data

Model: Minneapolis-Moline 445 Utility

Test No. 579

Date Tested: June 24 to July 2, 1956

Except for the standard-tread design of this model, compared to the Universal style shown in Test No. 578, these tractors were virtually identical. Weighing 4,471 lbs. the 445 Utility featured 12-28-inch rear and 5.50-16-inch front tires. During Tests F, G and H, an additional 976 lbs. of weight was added to each rear wheel. Test H, run in second gear, yielded an economy of 10.58 hp-hours per gallon at a rated drawbar load of 31.21 hp. Test H also indicated a pull of 2.952 lbs. at 3.96 mph with a 6.85 percent slippage. Like the 445 Universal of Test No. 578, five forward speeds were available in direct drive, and a like number with the Ampli-Torc system. Test G, using low gear and direct drive, yielded a maximum drawbar pull of 4,229 lbs. at 2.37 mph with a 14.78 percent slippage. Rated at 1,550 rpm, this tractor achieved 107 percent of rated torque at 85 percent of rated speed, per Test L. The fuel gauge did not function during the test. Otherwise, no repairs or adjustments were noted during 44-1/2 hours of operating time. Test C, at an operating maximum belt load of 39.94 hp, yielded 12.12 hp-hours per gallon. This figure slipped to 11.84 under a Test D-rated load of 37.7 hp.

Minneapolis-Moline G-704

Nebraska Test Data

Model: Minneapolis-Moline G-706 Diesel

Test No. 833

Date Tested: April 6 to April 17, 1963

Standard equipment for this tractor included a selective-gear fixed-ratio transmission with five forward speeds ranging from 3.3 to 18.3 mph. Also featured were 23.1-26-inch rear and 9.5-24-inch front tires. Pre-test weight was 9,165 lbs., but the test weight came to 16,145 lbs. by the addition of rear wheel ballast. No repairs or adjustments were reported during 52 hours of operation. Using third gear, and at 87.83 maximum available hp, a two-hour economy run indicated a drawbar pull of 6,553 lbs. at 5.03 mph with 4.79 percent slippage. Economy was recorded at 11.81 hp-hours per gallon. The 10-hour run made at 75 percent pull recorded a drawbar output of 70.44 hp, a pull of 5,013 lbs. at 5.27 mph and 3.68 percent slippage. Fuel economy came to 12.05 hp-hours per gallon. The G-706 featured the company's own six-cylinder engine rated at 1,600 rpm. Using a 4-5/8 x 5-inch bore and stroke, it had a 504-cubic inch displacement. At rated engine speed, 101.68 maximum PTO hp was recorded, along with an observed fuel economy of 13.49 hp-hours per gallon. A second PTO run made at 540 PTO rpm and a corresponding engine speed of 1,200 rpm noted an output of 81.68 hp and 13.95 hp-hours per gallon.

Nebraska Test Data

Model: Minneapolis-Moline G-706 (LPG)
Test No. 834
Date Tested: April 8 to April 23, 1963

At its rated engine speed of 1,600 rpm, this tractor developed a maximum of 101.44 PTO hp, yielding 8.92 hp-hours per gallon of propane fuel. A second PTO run made at 540 PTO rpm and a corresponding engine speed of 1,200 rpm noted an output of 82.29 hp, together with an economy figure of 9.24. The G-706 propane model was equipped with the company's own six-cylinder engine. Using a 4-5/8 x 5-inch bore and stroke, it had an 8.0:1 compression ratio and a 504-cubic inch displacement. Also featured was a selective-gear fixed-ratio transmission of five forward speeds ranging from 3.3 to 18.3 mph. Tires were identical to those already noted in Test No. 833. In the repairs and adjustments section, it was noted that, replacement of several shafts and countershafts was necessary due to failure of the transmission lower countershaft during the preliminary PTO runs. Additionally, a dampening device was installed to control governor hunting. Some 49-1/2 hours were required to complete the test procedures. Using third gear, a two-hour run at 86.24 maximum available hp indicated a pull of 6,452 lbs. at 5.01 mph with 4.88 percent slippage. Fuel economy was 7.82 hp-hours per gallon of propane. The 10-hour run made at 75 percent pull noted an identical economy figure. The latter test also recorded 72.06 hp, a pull of 5,063 lbs. at 5.34 mph and 3.65 percent slippage.

Nebraska Test Data

Model: Minneapolis-Moline G-705 Diesel (Also Massey-Ferguson MF-97 Diesel)
Test No. 835
Date Tested: April 19 to April 30, 1963

As noted in the heading, this tractor was tested as the G-705, but through an arrangement with Massey-Ferguson, the same tractor was marketed through the latter as the MF-97, or in Canada as the MF-95. This tractor carried a Minneapolis-Moline six-cylinder diesel engine rated at 1,600 rpm. Using a 4-5/8 x 5- inch bore and stroke, it had a displacement of 504-cubic inches. Operating at rated speed, a maximum of 101.01 PTO hp was observed, together with 13.63 hp-hours per gallon. A second PTO run made at 540 PTO rpm noted a figure of 14.19, along with an output of 81.47 hp. No repairs or adjustments were required during 41-1/2 hours of operation. Standard features included 23.1-26-inch rear and 7.50-18-inch front tires. Also featured was a selective-gear fixed-ratio transmission with five forward speeds ranging from 3.3 to 18.3 mph. Bare tractor weight was 8,155 lbs. This was raised to 15,110 lbs. by the addition of rear wheel ballast. Using third gear, and at 90.8 maximum available drawbar hp, fuel economy was posted at 12.35 hp-hours per gallon in a two-hour test. Also noted was a pull of 6,899 lbs. at 4.94 mph with 5.98 percent slippage. A 10-hour run at 75 percent pull noted an output of 73.5 hp, a pull of 5,258 lbs. at 5.24 mph and 4.25 percent slippage. Fuel economy came to 12.63 hp-hours per gallon.

Nebraska Test Data

Model: Minneapolis-Moline G-705 LPG (Also Massey-Ferguson MF-97 LPG)
Test No. 836
Date Tested: April 24 to May 1, 1963

Chassis design and tire equipment on this tractor was virtually identical to that given for the G-705 Diesel model of Test No. 835. Furthermore, Minneapolis-Moline marketed this unit as noted in the above model listing, while Massey-Ferguson sold this tractor as the MF-97 LPG model. Weighing 7,985 lbs., it assumed a test weight of 14,875 lbs. through the addition of rear wheel ballast. Using third gear, a two-hour economy run at 90.08 maximum available drawbar hp yielded 7.89 hp-hours per gallon of propane. Also recorded was a pull of 6,845 lbs. at 4.94 mph with 6.31 percent slippage. The 10-hour drawbar run at 75 percent pull indicated an economy of 7.91 hp-hours per gallon. Other test statistics included an output of 74.83 hp, a pull of 5,345 lbs. at 5.35 mph and 4.63 percent slippage. This tractor was equipped with a Minneapolis-Moline six-cylinder engine rated at 1,600 rpm. Using a 4-5/8 x 5-inch bore and stroke, it carried 504-cubic inch displacement and featured an 8.0:1 compression ratio. At 101.05 maximum PTO hp and at rated engine speed, fuel economy was recorded at 8.77 hp-hours per gallon of propane. This figure rose to 9.09 in a second PTO run made at 540 rpm on the PTO shaft and a corresponding engine speed of 1,300 rpm. Also indicated was an output of 82.12 hp.

Minneapolis-Moline M-670 series

Nebraska Test Data

Model: Minneapolis-Moline M-670 (LPG) (Also Minneapolis-Moline M-670 Super (LPG))
Test No. 924
Date Tested: November 1 to November 9, 1965

Weighing 7,545 lbs., this tractor was equipped with 18.4-34-inch rear and 6.00-16-inch front tires. The selective-gear fixed-ratio transmission included partial range power shifting. Ten forward speeds were provided in a range from 1.6 to 17.2 mph. The addition of front and rear ballast gave a total test weight of 12,515 lbs. Operating in sixth gear, the two-hour economy run saw 63.45 maximum available drawbar hp, along with 8.36 hp-hours per gallon of propane fuel. During this test, a pull of 5,187 lbs. was recorded at a speed of 4.59 mph against a 6.24 percent slippage. The 10-hour run at 75 percent pull noted 8.27 hp-hours per gallon against a load of 52.67 hp. Other statistics included a pull of 3,941 lbs. at 5.01 mph and 4.14 percent slippage. Minneapolis-Moline equipped this tractor with its own specially design LPG engine. Rated at 1,600 rpm, its four cylinders of 4-5/8 x 5-inch bore and stroke gave a displacement of 336-cubic inches. Special to the propane design was a 9.3:1 compression ratio. No repairs or adjustments were required during 48-1/2 hours of operation. At rated engine speed, 74.16 PTO hp was observed, with an economy of 9.64 hp-hours per gallon. A run at 540 PTO rpm and a corresponding engine speed of 1,366 rpm saw an output of 66.1 hp with 10.29 hp-hours per gallon of propane fuel.

Nebraska Test Data

Model: Minneapolis-Moline M-670 (Also Minneapolis-Moline M-670 Super)

Test No. 925

Date Tested: November 1 to November 9, 1965

Like the M-670 LPG model of Test No. 924, this tractor carried a four-cylinder, 336-cid engine. It was nearly identical in design, suitably built for gasoline. A 7.0:1 compression ratio was used (by comparison, the propane version of the previous test used a 9.3:1 compression ratio). Chassis specifications of both models were virtually identical. The bare tractor weight of 7,395 lbs. was enhanced with front and rear ballast for a total test weight of 12,445 lbs. Operating in sixth gear, 62.15 maximum drawbar hp was observed, with an economy of 9.89 hp-hours per gallon. Also noted was a pull of 5,065 lbs. at 4.6 mph, with slippage totaling 6.26 percent. The 10-hour run at 75 percent pull noted an output of 51.82 drawbar hp and 9.23 hp-hours per gallon. This test indicated a pull of 3,960 lbs. at 4.91 mph and slippage of 4.41 percent. At the rated engine speed of 1,600 rpm, 73.02 maximum PTO hp was observed, together with of 11.43 hp-hours per gallon. By comparison, the economy stood at 11.66 against a load of 66.10 PTO hp. This test was run at 540 PTO rpm and a corresponding engine speed of 1,365 rpm. No repairs or adjustments were reported during 43 hours of operation.

Nebraska Test Data

Model: Minneapolis-Moline M-670 Diesel (Also Minneapolis-Moline M-670 Super Diesel)

Test No. 926

Date Tested: November 4 to November 10, 1965

Once again, the M-670 tractor appeared but a diesel engine replaced the gasoline style of the previous test. Other specifications remained virtually intact as previously noted in Tests 924 and 925. In this case, the company's own four-cylinder diesel engine was featured. Rated at 1,600 rpm, it used a 4-5/8 x 5-inch bore and stroke for a displacement of 336-cubic inches. No repairs or adjustments were required during 41 hours of running time. At its rated speed, the diesel delivered a maximum of 71.01 PTO hp, together with 14.09 hp-hours per gallon. Operating at 540 rpm and a corresponding engine speed of 1,366 rpm, 62.51 observed PTO hp was recorded, with an economy figure of 14.56. Weighing 7,575 lbs., additional front and rear ballast boosted the total test weight to 12,505 lbs. Sixth gear was used for the drawbar economy runs. At 64.08 maximum available hp, fuel economy came in at 12.63 hp-hours per gallon. Also indicated in this two-hour test was a pull of 5,205 lbs. at 4.62 mph and 5.71 percent slippage. A 10-hour run at 75 percent pull saw 12.42 hp-hours per gallon against an output of 50.46 drawbar hp. Other statistics included a pull of 3,883 lbs. at 4.87 mph with slippage of 4.37 percent.

Minneapolis-Moline G-900 series

Nebraska Test Data

Model: Minneapolis-Moline G-900 Diesel
Test No. 978
Date Tested: June 4 to June 20, 1968

Weighing 10,330 lbs., this tractor was burdened with additional rear wheel ballast for a total test weight of 15,145 lbs. Standard equipment included 23.1-30-inch rear and 7.50-16-inch front tires. Partial range power shifting was featured in the selective-speed fixed-ratio transmission. Its 10 forward speeds ranged from 2.16 to 17.44 mph. Operating in fifth gear, the two-hour drawbar economy run was made at 83.29 maximum available drawbar hp and yielded 12.25 hp-hours per gallon. This test indicated a pull of 6,206 lbs. at 5.03 mph with 4.3 percent slippage. The 10-hour run at 75 percent pull noted 12.04 hp-hours per gallon against a load of 69.69 drawbar hp. Also recorded was a pull of 4,945 lbs. at 5.29 mph with 3.48 percent slippage. During the maximum power drawbar runs, the fan support failed and was replaced. During the 10-hour economy run, it was necessary to adjust the pressure regulating screw for the transmission-differential lubrication system. These were the only repairs and adjustments reported during 43-1/2 hours of operating time. Minneapolis-Moline equipped the G-900 Diesel with its own six-cylinder, 451-cid engine. Rated at 1,800 rpm, it used a 4.375 x 5.00-inch bore and stroke. At rated engine speed, 97.78 maximum PTO hp was observed, with an economy of 14.03 hp-hours per gallon.

Nebraska Test Data

Model: Minneapolis-Moline G-900 (LPG)
Test No. 979
Date Tested: June 4 to June 20, 1968

This tractor carried the same basic chassis design as previously noted for the G-900 Diesel model of Test No. 978. A Minneapolis-Moline six-cylinder engine was featured in this tractor. Rated at 1,800 rpm, it used a 4.250 x 5.00-inch bore and stroke for a 425-cubic inch displacement. Also featured was a 9.0:1 compression ratio. At rated engine speed, 97.57 PTO hp appeared and yielded 9.72 hp-hours per gallon of propane. The 42 hours of operating time included problems with the distributor shaft following the PTO tests. After replacement of several parts, the test continued. As in the previous test, fifth gear was used for the drawbar economy runs. The two-hour test at 84.12 maximum available hp saw a pull of 6,319 lbs. at 4.99 mph, slippage of 4.83 percent, and 8.54 hp-hours per gallon. At 75 percent pull, the 10-hour run indicated 7.86 hp-hours per gallon against a load of 69.98 hp. Other statistics included a pull of 4,898 lbs. at 5.36 mph with a 3.63 percent slippage. Weighing 10,160 lbs., additional front and rear ballast gave a total test weight of 15,100 lbs.

Minneapolis-Miline G-1000 Vista Diestl

Nebraska Test Data

Model: Minneapolis-Moline G-900

Test No. 980

Date Tested: June 11 to June 20, 1968

Using the same chassis as the G-900 models of the two previous tests, this gasoline version carried the same basic engine as previously noted in Test No. 979. While the propane model used a 9.0:1 compression ratio, this gasoline style carried a 7.1:1 compression ratio. Weighing 10,090 lbs., the tractor shown here assumed a test weight of 15,075 lbs. through added front and rear ballast. In fifth gear, the two-hour economy run at 87.78 maximum available drawbar hp indicated 10.45 hp-hours per gallon. Also indicated was a pull of 6,585 lbs. at 5 mph with slippage totaling 5.49 percent. The 10-hour run at 75 percent pull elicited 9.22 hp-hours per gallon against an output of 72.02 hp. This test recorded a pull of 5,048 lbs. at 5.35 mph and 4.1 percent slippage. No repairs or adjustments were reported during 41-1/2 hours of running time. At rated engine speed, 97.81 maximum PTO hp was observed, with the G-900 gasoline model achieving 11.64 hp-hours per gallon.

Minneapolis-Moline G-1000 series

Nebraska Test Data

Model: Minneapolis-Moline G-1000 Vista Diesel

Test No. 974

Date Tested: May 13 to May 24, 1968

In fifth gear, this tractor delivered 96.38 maximum available drawbar hp and achieved an economy of 11.82 hp-hours per gallon. These statistics, taken from the two-hour drawbar economy run, also included a pull of 6,840 lbs. at 5.28 mph and slippage of 4.33 percent. The 10-hour drawbar economy test at 75 percent pull evoked 11.95 hp-hours per gallon against an output of 81.6 hp. The 10-hour run also indicated a pull of 5,429 lbs. at 5.64 mph with slippage of 3.76 percent. No repairs or adjustments were reported for this unit during 45 hours of operating time. Weighing 12,230 lbs., it assumed a test weight of 18,365 lbs. through additional rear wheel ballast. Standard equipment included 23.1-34-inch rear and 10.00-16-inch front tires. Also featured was a 10-speed selective-gear fixed-ratio transmission with partial range power shifting. Speeds ranged from 2.25 to 18.05 mph. At rated engine speed, 111.00 maximum PTO hp was observed, with an economy of 13.88 hp-hours per gallon. Minneapolis-Moline equipped the G-1000 Vista with its own six-cylinder diesel engine. Rated at 1,800 rpm, it carried a 4.625 x 5.00-inch bore and stroke for a 504-cubic inch displacement.

Nebraska Test Data

Model: Minneapolis-Moline G-1000 Vista (LPG)

Test No. 975

Date Tested: May 13 to May 24, 1968

No repairs or adjustments were reported during 46 hours of operation. The chassis design was virtually identical to that previously noted in Test No. 974. A major difference was the use of the company's own six-cylinder engine, specially modified for propane fuel. Rated at 1,800 rpm, its 4.625 x 5.00-inch bore and stroke gave a 504-cubic inch displacement. An 8.8:1 compression ratio was used to better accommodate propane. At rated engine speed, 110.94 maximum PTO hp was observed with 9.76 hp-hours per gallon of propane fuel. Equipped with the same transmission system as the diesel model of Test No. 974, this unit went into the two-hour drawbar economy run using fifth gear. At 96.55 maximum available drawbar hp, a pull of 6,871 lbs. was recorded at 5.27 mph with 4.83 percent slippage. Fuel economy was posted at 8.33 hp-hours per gallon. The 10-hour economy run saw a figure of 7.78 against an output of 79.8 hp. Other statistics included a pull of 5,248 lbs. at 5.7 mph with slippage of 3.24 percent. Although this tractor weighed 11,960 lbs., an additional 1,605 lbs. of liquid ballast and 1,500 lbs. of cast-iron weight was added to each rear wheel for a total test weight of 18,150 lbs.

Minneapolis-Moline G-1355 tractor

Nebraska Test Data

Model: Minneapolis-Moline G-1355 Diesel

Test No. 1141

Date Tested: September 4 to September 17, 1973

Rated at 2,200 rpm, the G-1355 delivered 142.62 maximum PTO hp while achieving 15.21 hp-hours per gallon of fuel. Using the company's own six-cylinder, 585-cid engine, this model carried a 4.75 x 5.50-inch bore and stroke. The selective-gear fixed-ratio transmission included partial range power shifting. Its 18 forward speeds varied from 1.5 to 16.9 mph. Operating in 11th gear, the two-hour drawbar economy run at 125.66 maximum available hp saw a pull of 8,491 lbs. at 5.55 mph and slippage of 5.96 percent. Fuel economy was posted at 13.61 hp-hours per gallon. The 10-hour run at 75 percent pull noted an economy of 12.85 under a load of 101.89 drawbar hp. This test further indicated a pull of 6,573 lbs. at 5.81 mph with slippage totaling 4.49 percent. Standard equipment included dual rear wheels of 18.4-38-inch size, along with 11.00-16-inch front tires. Weighing 17.096 lbs., this model gained additional front and rear wheel ballast for a total test weight of 18,070 lbs. No repairs or adjustments were reported during 45 hours of operating time.

Minneapolis Steel & Machinery Company

MINNEAPOLIS, MINNESOTA

Organized in 1902, Minneapolis Steel & Machinery Co. entered the tractor business in 1910. The following year the company registered its "Twin City" trademark. Numerous models were built in the following years. In 1929 Minneapolis Steel merged with Moline Plow Co. and the Minneapolis Threshing Machine Co. to form Minneapolis-Moline Power Implement Co.

Twin City "40" tractor

In January 1910, Minneapolis Steel & Machinery Co. developed a four-cylinder tractor, with the Twin City "40" emerging late in 1911. Initially, the tractor used a four-cylinder engine with a 7 x 10-inch bore and stroke, but by late 1911, the engine bore was increased to 7-1/4 inches.

By 1913 the Twin City "40" had achieved its final form. This model was rated as a 40-65, meaning it was capable of 40 drawbar and 65 belt hp. It was underrated. In Nebraska Test No. 48, this tractor delivered nearly 66 belt hp and almost 50 hp on the drawbar. Production of the 40-65 continued until 1924.

Nebraska Test Data

Model: Twin City 40-65

Test No. 48

Date Tested: August 5 to August 14, 1920

Designed for power rather than speed, the Twin City 40-65 zoomed along at a top speed of 1.9 mph, forward or reverse. Weighing 25,500 lbs., it made a maximum drawbar pull of 10,820 lbs., or about 42 percent of its own weight. This calculated to 49.71 maximum drawbar hp. The rated brake hp test revealed 65.96 hp, just within the requirements of the manufacturer's nominal rating. To obtain this power, 7.88 gallons of kerosene were consumed per hour, with an economy of 8.38 hp-hours per gallon. No major mechanical difficulties were experienced, but after 18 hours of running time, the carburetor venturi was changed from 1-5/8 to 1-3/4 inches. Either size was standard, depending on the locality and engine performance. Standard equipment included a Holley Model 257 carburetor and a K-W Model HK magneto. Twin City built its own four-cylinder vertical engine, using a 7-1/4 x 9-inch bore and stroke. Rated speed was 535 rpm. Two clutches were used—one for the belt pulley and one for ground travel.

COLLECTOR VALUES	1	2	3	4
TWIN CITY 40-65	--	$45,000	--	--

Twin City "40" 40-65 tractor

Twin City "40" road roller model

The Twin City "40" was available in several variations, including this special road roller model. Designed especially for road work, it had a heavy front steering drum, with special heavy rear wheels. Production of this model was probably measured in rather small numbers.

Twin City "40" crawler model

It is unknown whether the Twin City "40" crawler model ever went into production, or whether it was strictly a special-order tractor. At least one was built, and a few catalogs illustrated or mentioned this special model.

Minneapolis Steel & Machinery Co. 60-90 tractor

During the 1913-1920 period, Minneapolis Steel & Machinery Co. built its 60-90 tractor. Weighing 28,000 lbs., this was one of the largest tractors built and sold for $6,000 in 1917. The 60-90 had the same 7-1/4 x 9-inch bore and stroke as the 40-65, but had a huge six-cylinder engine.

Twin City "25" tractor

Production of the Twin City "25" tractor ran from 1913 to 1920. This model used a four-cylinder engine with a 6-1/4 x 8-inch bore and stroke. Weighing 16,000 lbs., the "25" sold for $3,850. Aside from physical size, the design was virtually identical to the Twin City "40" tractor.

Twin City "25" special road roller tractor

Little is known of the Twin City "25" special road roller tractor. Presumably, production was rather limited, and few, if any, of these special tractors exist. The road roller model was the same as the regular Twin City "25" except for the modifications needed for this special duty.

Twin City "15" tractor

Between 1913 and 1917 there were three different models of the Twin City "15" tractor. Shown here is the earliest version, with a complete hood over the engine. This model has all the appearances of the larger Twin City tractors except for the physical size.

Perhaps the most popular of the Twin City "15"models was this one, a virtual clone of the larger sizes. These tractors were equipped with a four-cylinder engine with a 4-3/4 x 7-inch bore and stroke. As with all other Twin City models, the engine was built by Minneapolis Steel & Machinery Co.

Twin City "15" with cellular radiator

Toward the end of production in 1917, Minneapolis Steel modified the Twin City "15" to include a cellular radiator. This was a much more efficient method of cooling and greatly reduced the weight of the tractor and the required amount of water. Another change was the use of a sun canopy instead of the heavy canopy of previous years.

In 1918 the Twin City 16-30 tractor appeared, probably as a replacement for the Twin City "15" model. The 16-30 used a four-cylinder engine with a 5 x 7-1/2-inch bore and stroke. Early models included a canopy over the operator's platform. Production of this model ended in 1920.

Twin City "15"

Twin City 16-30 tractor

Twin City 12-20 tractor

During 1919 Minneapolis Steel & Machinery Co. announced its little 12-20 Twin City tractor. It used the unit frame design and had all the gearing enclosed. The four-cylinder engine was unique with four valves per cylinder for better performance and increased power, the first farm tractor to use this design. In 1927 the 12-20 was rerated as the 17-28 tractor.

Nebraska Test Data

Model: Twin City 12-20
Test No. 19
Date Tested: June 3 to June 12, 1920

Although Nebraska Tractor Test records indicated the 12-20 was submitted for testing by Twin City Company, the same model had entered production a year before under direction of Minneapolis Steel & Machinery Company. Its compact, unit frame design was indicative of a new farm tractor era: lightweight models without the burdensome weight of earlier years. A four-cylinder, valve-in-head engine was featured, using a 4-1/4 x 6-inch bore and stroke. Rated at 1,000 rpm, this engine used 16 valves—two intake and two exhaust valves per cylinder. Two forward speeds of 2.2 and 2.9 mph were provided. Regular equipment included a Holley carburetor and Bosch DU4 magneto. On the drawbar, a maximum pull of 3,476 lbs. was achieved by this 5,000-lb. tractor traveling at 1.99 mph. A resultant drawbar hp of 18.43 was recorded. In the belt, a maximum of 27.93 hp was noted, with fuel economy reaching 8.77 hp-hours per gallon of kerosene or 3.18 gph. Little or no water was added to the kerosene fuel mixture.

Type FT 21-32 tractor

During 1926 Minneapolis Steel & Machinery Co. introduced its Type FT 21-32 tractor. In Nebraska Test No. 127 of 1926, this model developed nearly 36 belt hp. The 21-32 was rated at 1,000 rpm and used a four-cylinder engine with a 4-1/2 x 6-inch bore and stroke. Minneapolis-Moline continued building the 21-32 tractor until 1934. At that time the FT designation was used, minor changes were made, and the tractor continued in production until 1937.

Twin City 20-35

Nebraska Test Data

Model: Twin City "FT" 21-32

Test No. 152

Date Tested: October 1 to October 8, 1928

Test No. 127 of 1926 on a Twin City 21-32 indicated that kerosene was the chosen fuel, while in the case at hand gasoline was used. Also, the rated engine speed of Test No. 127 was 1,000 rpm, compared to 1,075 for this test. Except for adjusting the clutch, only minor repairs were necessary. Advertised speeds of 2.36, 3.17 and 4.45 mph were provided. Intermediate gear was used for the rated drawbar test. At 22.58 hp, the 21-32 pulled 2,499 lbs. at 3.39 mph and delivered 6.56 hp-hours per gallon. Maximum drawbar pull of 4,716 lbs. at a speed of 2.32 mph in low gear gave a maximum of 29.16 drawbar hp. Operating under maximum load, the 21-32 yielded 39.14 brake hp, and at rated load, it produced 9.15 hp-hours per gallon. Specifications included a four-cylinder vertical I-head engine of 4-1/2 x 6-inch bore and stroke. Accessory items included a Robert Bosch FU4 magneto, Stromberg M-3 carburetor, and Donaldson air cleaner. Test weight with operator was 6,463 lbs.

Weighing 8,100 lbs., the Twin City 20-35 made its debut in 1919. This model used a four-cylinder engine with a 5-1/2 x 6-3/4-inch bore and stroke. This model was built until 1927 when it was rerated and sold as a 27-44 tractor. The 27-44 used a four-cylinder engine with a 5-1/2 x 6-3/4-inch bore and stroke. Production of the 27-44 continued until 1935.

Nebraska Test Data

Model: Twin City 20-35

Test No. 67

Date Tested: October 5 to October 9, 1920

The Twin City 12-20 tested under No. 19 marked the beginning of a new tractor series by the Twin City people. It was followed in the Nebraska Tests by the Twin City 20-35, a much larger model weighing in at 8,100 lbs. Two forward speeds of 2.2 and 2.9 mph were available. Like the 12-20, the 20-35 engine featured two intake and two exhaust valves per cylinder, for a total of 16 valves in the 5-1/2 x 6-3/4- inch, four-cylinder engine. The additional area afforded by the double valving increased performance, and certainly did nothing to hamper fuel economy. At rated load of 35 brake hp the 20-35 yielded 8.39 hp-hours per gallon of kerosenel, consuming 4.2 gph. At maximum brake load, 46.88 hp was developed, with fuel economy dropping slightly to 7.81 hp-hours per gallon of kerosene. At rated drawbar load of 20 hp, fuel consumption figures tallied 4.55 hp-hours per gallon. Under the maximum drawbar load test, using low gear, the 20-35 pulled to within a fraction of its nominal belt hp rating, yielding 34.12 drawbar hp and a maximum pull of 5,730 lbs. Standard equipment included the company's own engine, rated at 900 rpm. Also included was a Holley Model 257 carburetor and a Bosch Model DU magneto.

Nebraska Test Data

Model: Twin City 27-44, Model AT

Test No. 122

Date Tested: May 20 to May 27, 1926

Although this tractor was originally submitted for testing by Minneapolis Steel & Machinery Company, the same model was built in later years by Minneapolis-Moline Power Implement Company subsequent to a merger by Minneapolis Steel and several other firms. The 27-44, like the 17-28 of Test No. 121, had was previously tested in 1920 at a lower rating. Test No. 67 provided virtually identical specifications. Kerosene was used throughout the 38 hours of running time required for Test No. 122. At rated drawbar load of 27 hp, an average pull of 4,367 lbs. was made at 2.33 mph. Maximum load tests were made in low and high gear, and the first test revealed a maximum pull of 5,640 lbs. at a speed of 2.3 mph. Rated brake hp testing indicated a total consumption of 4.69 gph for an economy of 9.38 hp-hours per gallon. Under maximum brake load, 49.05 hp was developed with an economy of 8.89 hp-hours per gallon. The 27-44 used a Schebler Model A carburetor compared to the Holley " 257 " noted for the 20-35 of Test No. 67. Bore and stroke specifications, along with rated engine speed were the same for both models.

COLLECTOR VALUES	1	2	3	4
TWIN CITY 20-35	$8,000	$6,000	$4,000	–

Twin City 17-28 Model TY tractor

In 1926 the 12-20 tractor was again submitted for testing at Nebraska. In Test No. 121 the new 17-28 Model TY tractor delivered 22-1/2 drawbar hp. Production continued into the 1929 merger that formed Minneapolis-Moline.

Nebraska Test Data

Model: Twin City 17-28, Model TY

Test No. 121

Date Tested: May 17 to May 21, 1926

The 17-28 Twin City in this test was apparently a rerated version of the 12-20 Twin City tested under No. 19 of 1920. Brief specifications included a Twin City four-cylinder engine of vertical valve-in-head design. Using a 4-1/4 x 6-inch bore and stroke, it was rated at 1,000 rpm. Regular accessories included a Holley "257" carburetor and a Bosch ZR4 magneto. Few repairs or adjustments were required during the test, but during the drawbar tests, two small bolts were placed in the gear shift lock in order to keep the gears in mesh. Frequent governor adjustments were also required. Kerosene was used throughout the 39 hours of running time. At rated brake hp load, fuel consumption totaled 2.963 gph for 9.58 hp-hours per gallon. Under maximum load, 30.91 brake hp was developed. The rated drawbar test was made in low gear, along with the first maximum test. The latter indicated 22.5 drawbar hp with a 3,777-lb. pull at 2.235 mph. Total weight of the 17-28 was 5,895 lbs.

COLLECTOR VALUES	1	2	3	4
TWIN CITY 17-28	$6,000	$4,000	$2,000	$1,000

Twin City 27-44 tractor

Nebraska Test No. 122 was run on the Twin City 27-44 tractor in May 1926. This tractor was simply an updated version of the 20-35 that saw first light in 1919. Production of the 27-44 continued into the 1929 Minneapolis-Moline merger.

COLLECTOR VALUES	1	2	3	4
TWIN CITY 27-44	$8,000	$6,000	$4,000	–

Twin City FT 21-32 tractor

During 1926, Minneapolis Steel & Machinery Co. introduced its Twin City FT 21-32 tractor. This model used a four-cylinder engine with a 4-1/4 x 6-inch bore and stroke. In Nebraska Test No. 127 of October 1926, this model produced almost 36 belt hp. The 21-32 weighed about 6,200 lbs. Production continued into the 1929 Minneapolis-Moline merger.

Nebraska Test Data

Model: Twin City "FT" 21-32

Test No. 127

Date Tested: October 7 to October 13, 1926

As in earlier tests, the gear-shift lever was locked in place during maximum drawbar tests on the 21-32. With this exception, it came through 36 hours without anything more than minor adjustments. Two forward speeds of 2.2 and 2.9 mph were provided. A maximum drawbar test in low gear indicated 31.05 hp, with the tractor pulling a 5,092-lb. load at 2.28 mph. At rated brake hp, fuel consumption totaled 3.3545 gph for 9.64 hp-hours per gallon. At maximum load, the 21-32 developed 35.875 hp, still maintaining 8.31 hp-hours per gallonl. Featured was the company's own four-cylinder valve-in-head engine. Rated at 1,000 rpm, it used a 4-1/2 x 6-inch bore and stroke. Also included was an American Bosch ZR4 magneto, Zenith U-6 carburetor and a Bennett air cleaner. Total weight was 6,189 lbs.

COLLECTOR VALUES	1	2	3	4
TWIN CITY 21-32	$3,400	$2,800	$2,000	$1,200

Minneapolis Threshing Machine Company

HOPKINS, MINNESOTA

Minneapolis Threshing Machine Co. had an ancestry going back to 1874. That year, Fond du Lac Threshing Machine Co. was organized at Fond du Lac, Wisconsin. In 1887 John S. McDonald left Fond du Lac and organized Minneapolis Threshing Machine Co.

Traction engines became a part of the Minneapolis line in 1891, and by 1897, the company was investigating the gasoline engine as tractor power. MTM became interested in gasoline tractors in 1910, and built a few in 1911, with full production coming the following year.

MTM built several tractor models in the following years, but never marketed a row-crop design. The company was a part of the Minneapolis-Moline merger of 1929.

Minneapolis 20 hp Universal tractor

Minneapolis Threshing Machine Co. (MTM) entered the tractor business in 1911 by marketing the 20-hp Universal tractor. Built by Universal Tractor Co., Stillwater, Minnesota, this model was offered under such names as Universal, Skibo, and the Rumely GasPull. MTM continued to offer this model as late as 1913.

COLLECTOR VALUES	1	2	3	4
UNIVERSAL	$60,000	$40,000	$28,000	$15,000

Minneapolis Farm Motor

The first Minneapolis Farm Motor was designed by McVicker Engineering Company in 1910 and 1911. During 1911, MTM contracted with Northwest Thresher Company at Stillwater, Minnesota, to build 25 of these tractors.

Minneapolis 25-50 tractor

Built in 1912 through 1914, the Minneapolis 25-50 was the immediate successor to the Minneapolis Farm Motor of 1911. The 1912 production run of 48 tractors was built by Northwest Thresher Company, but by 1913, MTM was building its own tractors.

Minneapolis 40-80 tractor

During 1912, MTM perfected its 40-80 tractor. This huge four-cylinder model carried a 7-1/4 x 9-inch bore and stroke. The impressive operator's cab could be furnished with windows for cold weather operation. Production continued until 1920 when it was rerated as a 35-70 tractor.

COLLECTOR VALUES	1	2	3	4
35-70 AND 40-80	$70,000	$55,000	$30,000	$12,000

In late 1913 or early 1914, MTM introduced its 20-40 tractor. This one used a four-cylinder engine with a 5-3/4 x 7-inch bore and stroke. This model used an L-head engine, while the 40-80 and many other MTM tractors carried a valve-in-head engine. Production continued until 1919 when it was replaced with the slightly larger 22-44 tractor.

Minneapolis 20-40 tractor

COLLECTOR VALUES	1	2	3	4
20-40 AND 22-44	--	--	$30,000	--

Minneapolis Threshing Machine made its entry into the small tractor market in late 1915. The "15" used a 4-1/2 x 7-inch four-cylinder engine and was built until 1920 when it was rerated downward to a 12-25 model.

Nebraska Test Data

Model: Minneapolis 12-25

Test No. 13

Date Tested: May 17 to June 3, 1920

A brand new Minneapolis "All Purpose" design was announced in 1920. It was a takeoff of the Minneapolis 15-30 model introduced several years before. In their final report, Nebraska test engineers noted: "The tractor of this model first submitted for test failed to come up to the manufacturer's expectations and since the manufacturer thought that the tractor had some defects not coM-Mon to this model of tractor, a second tractor was accepted for test and results secured as reported above." Success apparently followed the second attempt, since a maximum brake hp of 26.24 was recorded, with fuel economy at 6.20 hp-hours per gallon of kerosenel, or 4.24 gph. Drawbar tests of the 6,600-lb. 12-25 Minneapolis indicated a maximum pull of 2,852 lbs. at 2.14 mph, for a maximum of 16.26 drawbar hp. Two forward speeds of 2.21 and 2.98 mph were provided. For many years, the drawbar tests were conducted on a dirt track, making accurate readings difficult due to constantly changing soil conditions.

Minneapolis 40-80 tractor

In Nebraska Test No. 15 of 1920, the Minneapolis 40-80 tractor developed slightly more than 74 belt hp. The company rerated it as a 35-70, even though it was capable of nearly 50 drawbar hp. This tractor used a four-cylinder, 7-1/4 x 9 inch engine and was rated at 550 rpm. Production ended with the 1929 Minneapolis-Moline merger.

COLLECTOR VALUES	1	2	3	4
MINNEAPOLIS 40-80	--	$45,000	--	--

Nebraska Test Data

Model: Minneapolis 35-70

Test No. 15

Date Tested: May 21 to June 4, 1920

Weighing 22,500 lbs., the Minneapolis 35-70 tractor carried a huge four-cylinder, valve-in-head engine with a 7-1/4 x 9-inch bore and stroke and a rated speed of 550 rpm. Indications are the 35-70 was simply a rerated version of the earlier 40-80 model. Despite the change in

Minneapolis "15" tractor

Minneapolis 22-44 model

nameplate ratings, the 35-70 proved itself very well in the Nebraska Tests. A maximum drawbar pull of 10,998 lbs. was achieved at 1.79 mph. This corresponded to 52.55 drawbar hp. On the belt, a maximum of 74.01 hp was noted, with fuel consumption totaling 9.97 gph. A respectable 7.42 hp-hours per gallon of kerosene was achieved in this test. A single forward speed of 2.1 mph was provided. With the 35-70, as with many other tractors of the time, the fan belt was replaced during the tests. Flat belts had a tendency to stretch and/or glaze, but taken in context with existing technology of the 1920s, this was not taken as a serious tractor defect.

About 1919, the Minneapolis 22-44 appeared as a replacement for the earlier 20-40 model. The 22-44 used a 6 x 7-inch four-cylinder engine. In Nebraska Test No. 14 of 1920, this model delivered over 46 belt hp. Production of the 22-44 ended in 1927.

Nebraska Test Data

Model: Minneapolis 22-44
Test No. 14
Date Tested: May 18 to June 3, 1920

Although it closely resembled a series of Minneapolis tractors that had been on the market for several years, the 22-44 had its birth and christening via the Nebraska Tests during 1920. As with the majority of heavyweight designs, few repairs or adjustments were necessary during the test procedure. Slightly over 46 brake hp was developed on the maximum load test with a fuel economy of 6.83 hp-hours per gallon of kerosene. This corresponded to 6.74 gph. The manufacturer's nominal drawbar rating of 22 hp gave a great margin of reserve power, since in the maximum load test, over 33 hp was achieved, pulling 5,104 lbs. at a speed of nearly 2-1/2 mph. A four-cylinder horizontal, valve-in-head engine was featured, with a 6 x 7-inch bore and stroke. Rated speed was 700 rpm. Total weight of the 22-44 was 12,410 lbs.

COLLECTOR VALUES	1	2	3	4
MINNEAPOLIS 22-44	$25,000	--	--	--

Minneapolis 12-25 tractor

Had it not been for snow and cold weather, the Minneapolis 12-25 tractor would have been the first tractor tested at Nebraska. It was initially presented as a 15-30 model but failed to come up to MTM expectations, and was then rerated as the 12-25. This model was built until 1926.

Minneapolis 17-30 tractor

MTM announced its 17-30 tractor in 1920. It was an entirely new lightweight design and was the first tractor tested at Nebraska in 1921 (Test No. 70). The 17-30 used a four-cylinder engine with a 4-3/4 x 7-inch bore and stroke. In testing, the 17-30 was capable of nearly 20 drawbar hp. About 1926, this model became known as the 17-30 A tractor. This designation was primarily to prevent confusion with the newly released 17-30 B model.

Nebraska Test Data

Model: Minneapolis 17-30

Test No. 70

Date Tested: March 28 to April 2, 1921

To begin the 1921 testing season, Minneapolis presented the 17-30 model. The company used its own four-cylinder vertical, valve-in-head engine featuring removable cylinder sleeves. Rated speed was 750 rpm, with a 4-3/4 x 7-inch bore and stroke. Also featured was a Dixie Model 46 magneto and a Kingston carburetor. Only two forward speeds were used—low gear of 2.06 mph and high gear, moving along at 2.7 mph. Total weight was 6,000 lbs. Using low gear, the 17-30 made a maximum drawbar pull of 3,921 lbs. with at 1.88 mph and slippage of 14.3 percent. This corresponded to a maximum of 19.69 drawbar hp. Static weight on the drive wheels was 4,400 lbs. Under the maximum brake hp tests, 31.95 hp was recorded at an engine speed of 828 rpm. Fuel economy was 8.7 hp-hours per gallon on the rated load test for a total consumption of 3.456 gph. Kerosene was used throughout the tests. Few repairs or adjustments were made during the 35 hours of tests. Engineers noted the tractor didn't guide readily under load due to light weight on the front wheels.

Minneapolis 17-30 A tractor

Specifications for the 17-30 A tractor were essentially the same as for the original 17-30. Minor changes were made during production, and the 17-30 A continued in the Minneapolis-Moline lineup until 1934. The 17-30 A used the same 4-3/4 x 7-inch bore and stroke that had been used on the original 17-30 tractor.

COLLECTOR VALUES	1	2	3	4
17-30 A	$7,200	$5,500	$3,900	$1,000

Minneapolis 17-30 B tractor

About 1925 Minneapolis Threshing Machine Company introduced its 17-30 B tractor. This model had a slightly longer chassis, and the engine bore was increased to 4-7/8 inches. The two tractors were virtually identical. Production of the 17-30 B continued into 1934, several years after the Minneapolis-Moline merger.

Nebraska Test Data

Model: Minneapolis "B" 17-30
Test No. 118
Date Tested: October 21 to November 12, 1925

After the limbering-up run and prior to taking any official data, it was necessary to grind all the valves in the 17-30. During the entire test run, it was necessary to stop periodically and clean the fuel line, which became clogged with foreign material. With these exceptions, no repairs or adjustments were required. Throughout the 40 hours of running time, kerosene was used. At rated brake hp load, the 17-30 gave an economy of 9.45 hp-hours per gallon, burning 3.269 gph. The maximum load test indicated 34.76 hp although fuel economy dropped to 6.65 hp-hours per gallon. At the drawbar, maximum load tests were made both in low and high gears in addition to the rated load test. A maximum pull of 4,374 lbs. was achieved in low gear with a speed of 1.92 mph and a resultant 22.37 maximum drawbar hp. Minneapolis used its own four-cylinder vertical valve-in-head engine mounted crosswise to the tractor frame. Rated at 825 rpm, it carried a 4-7/8 x 7-inch bore and stroke. Total weight of the 17-30 was 7,550 lbs. Regular accessories included a Bosch magneto and a Wheeler-Schebler Model A carburetor.

COLLECTOR VALUES	1	2	3	4
17-30 B	$6,750	$5,000	$3,500	$800

Minneapolis 27-42 tractor

Shortly before the Minneapolis-Moline merger of 1929, MTM announced its 27-42 tractor. It used an engine with the same 4-7/8 x 7-inch bore and stroke as the 17-30 B tractor. The 17-30 B was rated at 825 rpm, and the 27-42 had a rated speed of 925 rpm. This model was capable of nearly 34 drawbar hp. Production ended in 1934.

Nebraska Test Data

Model: Minneapolis 27-42
Test No. 162
Date Tested: May 28 to June 11, 1929

Gasoline was used throughout the 29 hours of running time required for Test No. 162. Operating at maximum load, the 27-42 developed 48.42 brake hp, yielded 9.43 hp-hours per gallon, and consumed 5.133 gph. Operating at a rated load of 42.3 hp, the economy rating rose to 9.98, and fuel consumption dropped to 4.24 gph. This tractor was equipped with the company's four-cylinder vertical, I-head engine with a 4-7/8 x 7-inch bore and stroke. Rated speed was 925 rpm. Advertised speeds were 2.69 and 3.42 mph. Total weight was 8,373 lbs. Accessories included a Donaldson air cleaner, Stromberg URT carburetor and American Bosch ZR4 magneto. At rated drawbar load, the 27-42 pulled 2,956 lbs. at 3.53 mph with slippage of 4.78 percent. Fuel economy was 6.63 hp-hours per gallon. The maximum load tests in low gear ended with a pull of 4,918 lbs. at 2.59 mph and only 6.98 percent slippage for 33.99 drawbar hp. No repairs or adjustments were required.

Production of the M-M 27-42 tractor ended in 1934. This model originated with Minneapolis Threshing Machine Co. about 1928. The 27-42 used a four-cylinder cross-mounted engine with a 4-7/8 x 7-inch bore and stroke. In Nebraska Test No. 162 of 1929, the 27-42 delivered nearly 35 drawbar hp.

Minneapolis 39-57 tractor

During 1928, MTM developed its 39-57 tractor. The Minneapolis-Moline merger occurred in 1929, and when the tractor was tested at Nebraska that June, it was under the auspices of Minneapolis-Moline Power Implement Company. The 39-57 carried a huge four-cylinder engine with a 5-1/2 x 6-1/2-inch bore and stroke. Rated at 1,000 rpm, it was capable of nearly 48 drawbar hp. Production of this model ended shortly after the Minneapolis-Moline merger.

Nebraska Test Data

Model: Minneapolis 39-57
Test No. 163
Date Tested: June 5 to June 14, 1929

A Stearns four-cylinder vertical, I-head engine was featured in the 39-57 tractor. Rated at 1,000 rpm, it used a 5-1/2 x 6-1/2-inch bore and stroke. Also included with this 9,695-lb. tractor was an American Bosch ZR4 magneto, Stromberg M-4 carburetor and Donaldson air cleaner. Pressure lubrication was also featured. Using gasoline, the 39-57 pulled 3,723 lbs. at rated drawbar load, traveled at 4.01 mph and lost 4.03 percent to slippage. The economy side of the ledger indicated 6.78 hp-hours per gallon. Low gear gave an advertised speed of 3 mph, compared to 3.9 in high gear. Maximum drawbar hp and maximum pull both occurred in low gear where the 39-57 came up with a pull of 5,959 lbs. at a speed of 3.01 mph for 47.77 maximum drawbar hp. Operating at maximum load, 64.55 brake hp was manifested. Fuel economy was 10.14 hp-hours per gallon, with total consumption of 6.367 gph. Economy dropped to 8.9 in the rated load test, while fuel consumption rose to 6.445 gph. The fan belt was tightened once during the test, and in the low gear maximum drawbar test, it was necessary to block the gearshift lever in place to keep the gears in mesh.

Minnesota-Nilson Corporation

MINNEAPOLIS, MINNESOTA

See: Nilson Tractor Company

Minnesota Farm Tractor Company

ST. CLOUD, MINNESOTA

In August 1915, it was announced that Minnesota Farm Tractor Co. had been organized and incorporated at St. Cloud to build a three-plow tractor. Aside from this information, nothing else is known of the company.

Minnesota Tractor Company

MINNEAPOLIS, MINNESOTA

Minnesota 18-36 tractor

During 1919, the Minnesota 18-36 tractor appeared. It was advertised for only a short time and then disappeared. It used a two-cylinder engine with a 7-1/2 x 8-inch bore and stroke.

Mitchell Motor Plow Company

PUEBLO, COLORADO

Mitchell Motor Plow Co. was organized and incorporated in 1918, ostensibly to manufacture motor plows. No other information on this company has been found.

Mobile Tractor Company

MOBILE, ALABAMA

Organized in 1919, Mobile launched a major stock sale early the following year. The Mobile tractor was a one-man outfit driven by leather lines, much like driving a team. After a few brief notices in 1920, nothing more was found.

Mobile tractor

Model Gas Engine Works

PERU, INDIANA

Model Gasoline tractor

Model had an ancestry in the gasoline engine business going back to the 1890s. By 1906, the company was making engines in single-cylinder models from 2 to 125 hp. Two- and four-cylinder stationary and marine engines were built in sizes from 15 to 500 hp. The Model Gasoline and Kerosene Traction Engine was available in sizes from 16 to 60 hp. Aside from a few advertisements, no specific information has been found.

Modern Machine Works

MILWAUKEE, WISCONSIN

Red-E garden tractor

The Red-E garden tractor appeared only in the 1927 directories from Modern Machine Works. In the 1923 to 1927 period, it was built by M.B.M. Mfg. Company of Milwaukee. From 1928 onward, it was built by Pioneer Mfg. Company. The Red-E used the company's own single-cylinder engine with a 3-3/4 x 4-inch bore and stroke.

COLLECTOR VALUES	1	2	3	4
RED-E	$1,500	$1,000	$750	$350

Donald K. Moe Company

PORTLAND, OREGON

This company is listed in 1948 as the manufacturer of the Garden Pal garden tractors, but no other information has been located.

COLLECTOR VALUES	1	2	3	4
GARDEN PAL	$500	$400	$250	$100

Moline Plow Company

MOLINE, ILLINOIS

This famous plow and implement manufacturer has roots going back to 1852 as the firm of Candee, Swan & Company. After steady growth, the company reorganized as Moline Plow Company in 1870. Subsequently, the firm acquired numerous other companies, and by 1900 had become a formidable competitor in the farm equipment business.

In 1915, the company bought out the Universal Tractor Company at Columbus, Ohio, and continued to develop its design. Into 1918, Moline Plow Company built a two-cylinder "universal" tractor with a two-cylinder engine, but then changed over to a larger four-cylinder style.

Production of the Moline Universal tractor continued until 1923. In 1929 Moline Plow Co. merged with Minneapolis Steel & Machinery Co. and Minneapolis-Threshing Machine Co. to form Minneapolis-Moline.

Moline two-cylinder motor cultivator

When Moline Plow Company bought out Universal Tractor Co. in 1915, the latter had already developed a small cultivating tractor. This two-cylinder design was built into 1917. The Moline Universal tractor could be equipped with a variety of implements, all of which became an integral part of the tractor.

COLLECTOR VALUES	1	2	3	4
B AND C, 2-CYLINDER OPPOSED ENGINE	$12,000	$10,000	$6,000	$3,000

Model D Moline Universal tractor

During the 1918 through 1923 period, Moline Plow Company built the Model D Moline Universal tractor. The four-cylinder design was rated at 9 drawbar and 18 belt hp. The engine carried a 3-1/2 x 5-inch bore and stroke and operated at 1,800 rpm. It included many features, including electric starter and lights, and an electric governor. Moline Plow Co. offered numerous implements and hitches for the Model D Universal tractor.

Nebraska Test Data

Model: Moline Universal Model D 9-18

Test No. 33

Date Tested: July 14 to July 17, 1920

Throughout the tests, gasoline was the chosen fuel for the Moline Universal tractor. This innovative machine featured a Remy electric governor-generator combination, Holley carburetor, and a four-cylinder vertical engine. Rated at 1,800 rpm, the Model D carried a 3-1 /2 x 5-inch bore and stroke. Rated speed was 3.58 mph. The first tractor submitted for testing was damaged when the rear carrying truck turned over when a short turn was made with the tractor pulling a load. Due to this damage, and a faulty governor, a second tractor was submitted. Aside from this, little mechanical trouble was experienced. Fuel economy on the rated load test (18 hp) came to 8.15 hp-hours per gallon. This dropped significantly to 5.7 on maximum brake hp testing. However, 27.45 brake hp was recorded. Since 17.4 drawbar hp was developed, the 9-18 went far past the manufacturer's nominal rating of 9 drawbar hp. Maximum drawbar pull was 1,778 lbs. at 3.67 mph. Total weight was 3,590 lbs.

COLLECTOR VALUES	1	2	3	4
D	$9,000	$6,000	$4,000	$2,000

Moline Pump Company

MOLINE, ILLINOIS

In 1910 it was announced that Moline Pump Co. would be bringing out a new line of farm tractors. The plan apparently did not materialize, since no other information has been found.

Monarch Iron Works

SAN FRANCISCO, CALIFORNIA

No information has been found regarding this company.

Monarch Machinery Company

NEW YORK, NEW YORK

Monarch Gasoline Traction Engine

Aside from a single advertisement, virtually nothing is known of the Monarch Gasoline Traction Engine of 1904. This particular design consisted of an unknown make of engine mounted on a set of Morton traction trucks. The latter was rather popular at this time, since it permitted virtually any engine manufacturer to instantly enter the tractor business.

Monarch Tractor Company

SPRINGFIELD, ILLINOIS

Monarch Tractor Co. was organized at Watertown, Wisconsin in 1913. Little is known about the company until 1916 when its Lightfoot 6-10 tractor appeared. Following the history of the Monarch tractor line is extremely difficult. Monarch literature is difficult to find, and many Monarch models were not listed in the farm tractor directories since they were intended primarily for heavy construction work. Allis-Chalmers bought out the company in 1927.

Monarch Lightfoot 6-10 tractor

This small tractor was ostensibly intended for farm and light construction work. It was powered by a Kermath four-cylinder engine with a 4-inch bore and stroke. Production apparently ended about 1918.

Monarch 12-20 Neverslip tractor

The Monarch 12-20 Neverslip tractor debuted in 1916 and continued in production for several years. This model weighed 6,200 lbs. and was powered by an Erd four-cylinder engine with a 4 x 6-inch bore and stroke. It sold for $1,650.

Monarch 18-30 tractor

By 1919 the Monarch 18-30 had appeared and by 1920 it had a new rating of 20 drawbar and 30 belt hp. In 1924 this model was revamped, speeded up, and became the Model C, 25-35 crawler. In Nebraska Test No. 56 of 1920 the 18-30 delivered over 21 drawbar hp. It was equipped with a Beaver four-cylinder engine with a 4-3/4 x 6-inch bore and stroke.

Nebraska Test Data

Model: Monarch 18-30

Test No. 56

Date Tested: August 21 to August 27, 1920

Weighing 8,100 lbs., the Monarch 18-30 Neverslip was the second crawler tractor tested at Nebraska. It featured three forward speeds of 1-1/2, 2-1/4, and 3-1/2 mph. Included was a Beaver four-cylinder, valve-in-head, vertical engine carrying a 4-3/4 x 6-inch bore and stroke. Rated speed was 950 rpm. Regular equipment included a Kingston carburetor and K-W magneto. A Bennett air cleaner was supplied as standard equipment, but was modified to include a shroud and hot-air shutoff damper. No other repairs or adjustments were made during the test. Just over 21 drawbar hp was recorded on the maximum load test, with a 4,670-lb. drawbar pull and a speed of 1.69 mph. At rated brake hp, 8.43 hp-hours per gallon was noted, for a total fuel consumption of 3.625 gph. Nearly 31-1/2 hp appeared on the maximum load test. Obviously the tractor's cooling system showed signs of improvement over many others in the earlier tests, as coolant temperatures ranged from 175 to 202 degrees F throughout the test. This was well below the boiling point experienced by many of the previous test tractors.

COLLECTOR VALUES	1	2	3	4
18-30	$15,000	$13,000	$5,000	$2,000

Monarch 20-30 tractor

Production of the Monarch 20-30 continued until about 1924 or early 1925 when it was superceded by the Monarch Model C, 25-35 tractor. The increased power level came from raising the rated speed to 1,200 rpm, compared to 950 rpm for the 20-30. The Model C was capable of about 38 belt hp.

Nebraska Test Data

Model: Monarch C, 25-35
Test No. 113
Date Tested: April 16 to April 24, 1925

A Beaver four-cylinder vertical, valve-in-head engine was featured in the Monarch Model C tractor. Using a 4-3/4 x 6-inch bore and stroke, it was rated at 1,200 rpm. Duralumin connecting rods and Dow metal magnesium pistons were used. Accessory items included a Bennett air cleaner, Pharo governor, Bosch DU4 magneto, and a Stromberg M-4 carburetor. Total weight was 10,630 lbs. Maximum drawbar load tests were made in all three forward gears. The highest drawbar pull occurred in low gear. At 2.11 mph, the Model C pulled 6,680 lbs. with only 5.15 percent slippage for a total of 37.59 drawbar hp. Gasoline was used throughout the 34 hours of running time. No repairs or adjustments were made during this period. In the rated brake hp tests, 4.039 gph were used for 8.83 hp-hours per gallon. Under maximum brake load, 43.67 hp was developed over the one-hour test, with fuel consumption totalling 5.731 gph and an economy rating of 7.62 hp-hours per gallon.

COLLECTOR VALUES	1	2	3	4
20-30	$15,000	$10,000	$6,000	$2,000

Monarch 6-60 tractor

In 1924 Monarch introduced its 6-60 tractor. It was powered by a Beaver six-cylinder engine with a 4-3/4 x 6-inch bore and stroke. Weighing over 8-1/2 tons, the 6-60 was capable of over 70 belt hp and in excess of 51 hp at the drawbar. This tractor became part of the AC-Monarch line when Allis-Chalmers bought out Monarch in 1927.

Nebraska Test Data

Model: Monarch D, 6-60
Test No. 108
Date Tested: October 24 to November 1, 1924

Featuring a Beaver six-cylinder vertical, valve-in-head engine, the Monarch 6-60 weighed 16,789 lbs. Regular equipment included a Bosch electric starter and generator, making this the first test tractor so equipped. Standard accessories with this 4-3/4 x 6-inch engine included a Stromberg M-4 carburetor and a Bosch AT6 magneto. Except for replacing some cotter pins and other minor repairs, the 6-60 went through 38 hours of testing with no major problems. Maximum drawbar load tests were taken in all three forward speeds, with maximum pull occurring in low gear. At a speed of 1.5 mph, 12,922 lbs. of pull was indicated for 51.51 drawbar hp. At its rated speed of 1,200 rpm, the 6-60 delivered 8.98 hp-hours per gallon on the rated brake hp test, using 6.71 gph. At maximum load, 70.74 brake hp was recorded with an economy of 7.59 hp-hours per gallon and total consumption of 9.327 gph.

Model F, 10-Ton Monarch

The Model F, 10-Ton Monarch came onto the market in 1926, with production ending in February 1928. At this time, it was replaced with the Model F, "75" tractor. Allis-Chalmers continued building this model until 1931. The Model F pulled over 20,000 lbs. in low gear. Power came from a LeRoi four-cylinder engine with a 6-3/4 x 7-inch bore and stroke.

Nebraska Test Data

Model: Monarch 10-Ton Model "F"
Test No. 139
Date Tested: August 15 to August 26, 1927

Since the Monarch 10-Ton was not equipped with a belt pulley, no brake hp tests were conducted. The rated drawbar tests demonstrated a 9,023-lb. pull at 2.48 mph. With slippage of 1.43 percent, the final results gave 59.56 drawbar hp. This gave 6.89 hp-hours per gallon as an indication of fuel economy. Maximum tests were conducted in all three forward gears. Second gear gave the highest hp rating, with the 10-Ton pulling 11,960 lbs. at 2.45 mph for 78.17 hp. High gear gave the least slippage—only 1.11 percent was recorded, even though the tractor pulled a 7,550-lb. load at 3.28 mph. Low gear yielded 74.85 drawbar hp, along with a 20,050-lb. pull at 1.4 mph and 4.83 percent slippage. Weighing 21,700 lbs., this translated into a pull of over 92 percent of the tractor's own weight. Specifications included a Beaver-LeRoi four-cylinder valve-in-head engine with a 6-3/4 x 7-inch bore and stroke. Rated at 850 rpm, the engine also featured a Zenith L7T carburetor, American Bosch ZR4 magneto and a United air cleaner.

COLLECTOR VALUES	1	2	3	4
MODEL F, 10-TON	$15,000	$12,000	$6,000	$3,000

Monroe Motors

PONTIAC, MICHIGAN

Monroe Motors was in the automobile business in the 1914 to 1923 period, operating at Pontiac from 1916 to 1918. The company planned to enter the tractor business, but no information on this venture has been found.

Montana Tractor Company

MINNEAPOLIS, MINNESOTA

Montana tactor

Developed in 1916, the Montana tractor was marketed in 1917. After that time, it dropped out of sight. Virtually nothing is known of the company nor is it known whether this company was connected with a firm of the same name at Oconto, Wisconsin, or another at Tinley Park, Illinois.

Montana Tractor Company

OCONTO, WISCONSIN

Montana 15-20 tractor

Only during 1921 was the Montana 15-20 tractor listed in some of the tractor directories. Rated at 15 drawbar and 20 belt hp, it was equipped with a two-cylinder Reliable engine. Power was applied to all three wheels of this machine. The Montana 15-20 weighed 5,200 lbs.

Montana Tractor Company

TINLEY PARK, ILLINOIS

Montana 15-20 model

During 1920, Montana Tractor Co. offered its 15-20 model. The hp rating leads to the assumption that this tractor may have been the predecessor of the one built the following year at Oconto, Wisconsin. Unfortunately, no specific information has been found.

Moon Tractor Company

SAN FRANCISCO, CALIFORNIA

Moon Pathmaker 12-25 crawler

About 1920, the Moon Pathmaker 12-25 crawler made its way into some of the tractor listings. Nothing is known of the company before or after that time. The 12-25 weighed 7,500 lbs. and retailed for $2,875. It was powered by a Buda XTU four-cylinder engine with a 4-1/4 x 6-inch bore and stroke.

Tom Moore Tractor Inc.

MANTUA, OHIO

Moore Farm-Ette garden tractor

Beginning about 1950, Moore offered its Farm-Ette garden tractors in four different models, all with the same general design. The Farm-Ette "B" used a single drive wheel and all others were of two-wheel design. This model was equipped with a Kohler 2-hp motor. The Farmette "A" used a 3-1/2-hp Ultimotor, as did the Farmette "D." Farmette "C" garden tractors were furnished with a 2-hp Kohler engine. The firm was active into the mid-1950s.

COLLECTOR VALUES	1	2	3	4
FARM-ETTE GARDEN TRACTOR	$350	$275	$125	$75

Geo. W. Morris

RACINE, WISCONSIN

Geo. W. Morris had begun with tractor development in 1909 and was building a four-cylinder model with an 8 x 10-inch bore and stroke. Also in the works was a six-cylinder model with a 7-1/2 x 9-inch bore and stroke. It does not appear that any of these models ever went into production.

Few details can be found regarding this 60-hp, four-cylinder tractor developed in 1910 by Geo. W. Morris.

Morris tractor

Morris 60-hp tractor

Another Geo. W. Morris tractor of the 1909 and 1910 period was this huge four-cylinder model with a cross-mounted engine. No details have been found regarding the size of the tractor, but as with other Morris tractors, it doesn't appear that any number were built. Prior to his work at Racine, Morris founded the Morris Threshing Machine Company at Brantford, Ontario.

Otho A. Morris

WICHITA FALLS, TEXAS

Aside from a single listing, no other information has been found for this individual or his efforts at tractor building.

S. S. Morton

YORK, PENNSYLVANIA

In 1904 Morton Traction Company was listed as a tractor manufacturer. To be more precise, Morton built a special tractor chassis. A variety of "stationary" engines were fitted to this chassis for power. Numerous companies did so, with the best known example being the early International Harvester designs. The company thrived for a few years, but as the tractor evolved, there was little need to use a huge single-cylinder engine with an unfavorable weight-to-hp ratio.

Morton-Heer Company

PORTSMOUTH, OHIO

Organized in 1910, this firm was incorporated the following year. It was an alliance of Chris Heer and the Morton interests at Ohio Mfg. Company. When the tractor finally came onto the market in 1912, it was under the auspices of Heer Engine Company. The latter operated until 1916 when it was reorganized as Reliable Tractor & Engine Co. The tractor is illustrated under the Heer Engine Company heading.

Morton Motor Plow Company

COLUMBUS, OHIO

Morton Motor Plow

Little is known of the Morton Motor Plow. Introduced in 1914, it remained on the market for only a short time. Its salient feature was the two-bottom plow mounted to the rear of the tractor. Briefly, the company appeared at Galion, Ohio.

Morton Tractor Company

FREMONT, OHIO

Morton Tractor Co. four-wheel-drive tractor

During 1911, Morton Tractor Co. announced its four-wheel-drive tractor, the same one offered by Heer Engine Company and by Morton-Heer Company. All were connected, and by 1912, Heer Engine Company won out as the sole manufacturer of the Heer tractor.

Morton Truck & Tractor Company

HARRISBURG, PENNSYLVANIA

Morton "60 h.p. four-wheel double worm drive tractor"

Morton billed this model as its "60 h.p. four wheel double worm drive tractor." Weighing 12,000 lbs., it was equipped with a four-cylinder engine with a 5-3/4 x 7-inch bore and stroke. This 1912 model had three forward speeds ranging from 2-1/2 to 8-1/4 mph. This firm was of the same Morton family involved in other tractor building ventures going back to 1899.

Motor Driven Implement Company

GALION, OHIO

Although it was incorporated in 1916 to build tractors and implements, no other information has been found.

Motor Macultivator Company

TOLEDO, OHIO

Motor Macultivator

Our research has not determined the origins of Motor Macultivator Company. It appears the firm was taken over by American Swiss Magneto Co. about 1925. This 1924 model was equipped with a Briggs & Stratton engine with a 2-1/2-inch bore and stroke. It was priced at $162.50.

See: Macultivator Company

Motor Truck & Tractor Company

KNOXVILLE, TENNESSEE

Although it was organized and incorporated in 1918 to build tractors, nothing further can be found regarding this firm.

B. H. Mott Company

HUNTINGTON, WEST VIRGINIA

Utilitor Model 25

The Utilitor Company was taken over by B. H. Mott Co. about 1945. The latter continued advertising the Utilitor until about 1950. A Wisconsin single-cylinder engine was used on the Utilitor Model 25 shown here. It carried a 3 x 3-1/4-inch bore and stroke.

COLLECTOR VALUES	1	2	3	4
UTILITOR MODEL 25	$850	$600	$400	$250

Mountain State Fabricating Company

CLARKSBURG, WEST VIRGINIA

See: Fate-Root-Heath; Plymouth; Silver King

Silver King Model 370

Fate-Root-Heath Company at Plymouth, Ohio, closed out its tractor line in 1954, sending all parts and tooling to Mountain State Fabricating Company. The following year, the Silver King Model 370 appeared from Mountain State Fabricating Company. This model weighed 3,550 lbs. and was equipped with a Continental F-162 four-cylinder engine. This tractor was capable of road speeds up to 19 mph.

Silver King tractor Model 371

The Silver King Model 371 was a standard-tread version of the Model 370 and used the same Continental F-162 engine. Mountain State built fewer than 75 tractor before closing its doors in 1956.

M-R-S A-100

M-R-S Mfg. Company

FLORA, MISSISSIPPI

The first origins of M-R-S Mfg. Co. are unknown, but the company began building four-wheel-drive tractors in the late 1950s, continuing for several years. The tractors were sold primarily in specialty markets and there was no indication the M-R-S was widely sold into the grain country of the western and midwestern states. Several sizes were built, including the A-100 shown here. It was capable of 265 maximum brake hp and was powered by a GM 6V-7IN diesel engine.

Mulsifier Corporation

DETROIT, MICHIGAN

No illustrations have been found for the Mulsifier garden tractor. It was a 225-lb. unit equipped with a Wisconsin Model ABS engine with a 2-1/2 x 2-3/4-inch bore and stroke. This machine is listed in the trade directories about 1947, but no information regarding the firm's history has been located.

COLLECTOR VALUES	1	2	3	4
MULSIFIER GARDEN TRACTOR	$350	$250	$150	$75

Multi-Tractor Company

LINCOLN, NEBRASKA

1914 Motor plow

In 1914 this tractor was displayed at the Fremont Tractor Demonstration. It was essentially a motor plow powered by a two-cylinder Cushman engine, a firm also located at Lincoln, Nebraska. Very little information is available on this tractor, and it is likely only a few were built.

Golden West tractor

Multonomah Mfg. Company

PORTLAND, OREGON

In 1909 it was announced that this firm would build a 35-hp tractor equipped with a six-cylinder engine. Since no other references were found, the tractor was only produced for a short time.

Muscatine Motor Company

MUSCATINE, IOWA

The Golden West tractor was advertised in a 1910 issue of Canadian Thresherman Magazine. No other references have been found to this tractor. It is shown here with an automatic plow guide and a canopy, so it must have been intended as a plowing tractor.

Mustang Motorcycle Corporation

GLENDALE, CALIFORNIA

A trademark application of 1953 indicates that the "Mustang" trademark was first applied to "Tractors" on February 9, 1952. No other references to this "tractor" have been found.

[Throughout this section, assume that gasoline was used for fuel unless another fuel source is indicated.]

Napco Industries

MINNEAPOLIS, MINNESOTA

Napco "Crab" tractor

In early 1958, the Napco "Crab" tractor was announced. It featured front wheel steering, front and rear steer, or oblique steering. This tractor was also equipped with four-wheel power steering, hydraulic brakes, and a mechanical PTO shaft. No other information has been found.

National Brake and Electric Company

MILWAUKEE, WISCONSIN

No information was available about this company.

National Engine Company

WATERLOO, IOWA

This firm was organized in 1913 to "...take over the business of the Handt Tractor Company." No other information has been found on either company.

National Equipment Co. of Texas

MARSHALL, TEXAS

This tractor was the Nateco Laughlin C-24 tractor of 1946 and became the Intercontinental tractor. No specifications for the Nateco have been found.

1946 Nateco Laughlin C-24 tractor

National Farm Equipment Company

NEW YORK, NEW YORK

In 1947 this firm advertised its National Garden King garden tractor. It was a 500-lb. outfit and was powered by a Wisconsin AB single-cylinder engine. The engine was rated at 3 hp and used a 2-1/2 x 2-3/4-inch bore and stroke. Apparently, this machine was built as late as 1953, perhaps later. No illustrations have been found.

National Farm Machinery Cooperative

BELLEVUE, OHIO

About 1945 National Cooperatives began selling the Cockshutt tractors in the United States. This continued into the late 1950s. The Cockshutt "20" was sold as the Co-op E-2, the Cockshutt "30" was sold as the Co-op E-3, and the Cockshutt "40" was sold as the Co-op E-4. These tractors are illustrated under the Cockshutt heading in this book. In 1947 National Cooperatives was selling the Blackhawk Model C garden tractor through its Ohio Cultivator Division at Bellevue. This model was equipped with a Briggs & Stratton Model B engine rated at 2-3/4 hp. No illustrations of this model have been found.

National Pulley & Mfg. Company

CHICAGO, ILLINOIS

National Pulley 10-20 Paramount tractor

The 10-20 Paramount tractor from National Pulley made its debut in 1916. Production of this tractor was probably very limited, since it does not appear in the tractor directories in subsequent years. No information has been found indicating the type of engine used, or other specifications. Operating weight was 4,000 lbs.

National Steel & Shipbuilding Corporation

SAN DIEGO, CALIFORNIA

Lincoln tractor

In the early 1950s, the Lincoln tractor was offered and was listed during 1953 and 1954 but may have been built for a longer period. This tractor was equipped with a Wisconsin AEH single-cylinder engine rated at 6-1/2 hp. Shipping weight was 800 lbs.

National Track-Tractor Company

MILWAUKEE, WISCONSIN

Apparently, the National crawler tractors were built only in the 1930 to 1931 period. No other references to these tractors have been found.

National 20-25 crawler

In 1931 the Tractor Field Book illustrates the National 20-25 crawler tractor. Weighing 5,400 lbs., it was powered by a Continental S12, four-cylinder engine that used a 4-1/4 x 5-inch bore and stroke.

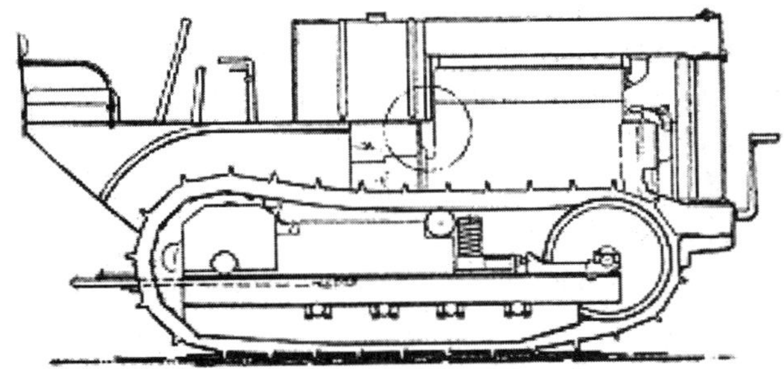

National 25-35 crawler

The National 25-35 shown here in a line drawing was powered by a Continental four-cylinder engine with a 4-3/4 x 6-inch bore and stroke. Both National crawler models were equipped with a rear PTO shaft.

National Tractor Company

WICHITA, KANSAS

Although this company was organized and incorporated in December 1916, no other information has been found on National Tractor Co. or its activities.

National Tractor & Machinery Company

CHICAGO, ILLINOIS

This firm was organized and incorporated early in 1918 to build the Uncle Sam farm tractors. That April, the company name was changed to U. S. Tractor & Machinery Company at Menasha, Wisconsin. The Uncle Sam tractor is illustrated under the latter heading.

National Tractor Company

CEDAR RAPIDS, IOWA

National tractor

National Tractor Company was the reorganized version of the former Denning Tractor Company. National was a subsidiary of General Ordnance Co. with offices in New York City. Denning took bankruptcy in late 1919, with National tractors built under this title until 1920 when the G-O tractor appeared from General Ordnance Co. The tractors were all essentially the same as the former Denning models. The Model E was rated as a 9-16 model, and the Model F was rated at 12 drawbar and 22 belt hp.

Natvik & Company

COLUMBUS, WISCONSIN

Natvik Little Giant garden tractor

Beginning about 1946, Natvik produced its Little Giant garden tractor. It remained in the tractor directories until at least 1953, but any specific history of the firm has not been found. The Little Giant was available with numerous attachments, but few details have been found.

COLLECTOR VALUES	1	2	3	4
LITTLE GIANT	$500	$400	$250	$100

Nelson Blower & Furnace Company

BOSTON, MASSACHUSETTS

Nelson four-wheel-drive tractor

The Nelson four-wheel-drive tractor was introduced in 1919 and remained on the market for a couple of years. It was built in three sizes: 15-24, 20-28, and 35-50. All models were of the same general design, and all used four-cylinder Wisconsin engines. The 15-24 had a 4 x 5-inch bore and stroke; the 20-28 used a 4-3/4 x 5-1/2-inch bore and stroke; and the 35-50 had a 5-3/4 x 7-inch bore and stroke. Operating weight was 5000, 7000, and 10,000 lbs., respectively.

Nevada Auto Plow

Nelson Machine Works

SEATTLE, WASHINGTON

In 1948 this company was listed as the manufacturer of the Mity Midget garden tractor. No details, photographs or specifications have been found.

Nevada Auto Plow Company

Nevada Truck & Tractor Company

NEVADA, IOWA

The Nevada Auto Plow first appeared in 1912. This machine was rated at 12 drawbar and 25 belt hp. Shortly after it was organized, the firm changed the name to Nevada Truck & Tractor Co. The machine shown here was equipped with a three-bottom plow. Within a couple of years, the Nevada quietly disappeared from the market.

New Age Tractor Company

MINNEAPOLIS, MINNESOTA

New Age 10-18 tractor

First built in 1915, the New Age tractor was designed by Alex W. Sutherland. Early in development the company was known as Sutherland Manufacturing Co. In 1917 New Age Tractor Co. was incorporated, and it continued building the 10-18 model shown here. It carried a two-cylinder engine with a 5 x 6-1/2-inch bore and stroke. During 1919, the New Age tractor was remodeled and began using a Beaver four-cylinder engine with a 4-1/2 x 6-inch bore and stroke. That same year the company was renamed Sutherland Machinery Company. By 1921 the New Age tractor disappeared.

New Beeman Tractor Company

MINNEAPOLIS, MINNESOTA

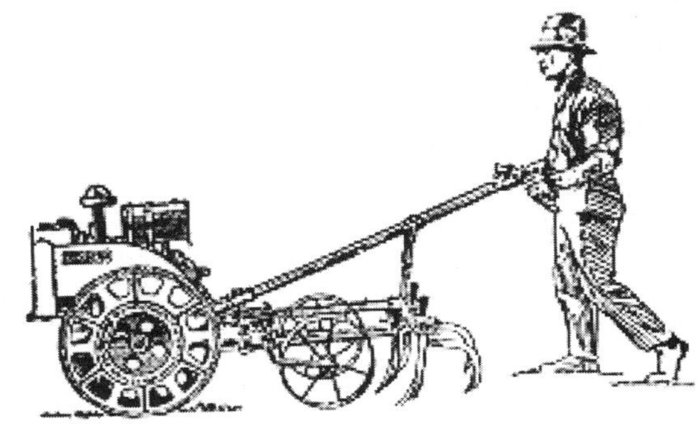

Beeman garden tractor

This firm was incorporated in 1916 as the Beeman Garden Tractor Company. Three years later, in 1919, the name was changed to Beeman Tractor Company. In 1925 the name was again changed to New Beeman Tractor Company. The firm continued at least into the late 1940s.

COLLECTOR VALUES	1	2	3	4
BEEMAN GARDEN TRACTOR	$2,000	$1,500	$750	$350

New Britain Machine Company

NEW BRITAIN, CONNECTICUT

New Britain tractor-cultivator

About 1919, New Britain began building two sizes of its tractor-cultivator. Both used a water-cooled two-cylinder engine with a 2-3/4 x 4-inch bore and stroke. The NB No. 1 retailed at $400, while the NB No. 2 sold for $450. This machine was rated at 6 hp. NB No. 2 had an adjustable left wheel for varying row width. Both models used many Fordson and Model T engine parts. The New Britain disappeared from the trade directories after 1925. Only four are known to exist today.

COLLECTOR VALUES	1	2	3	4
NB NO. 1	$2,000	$1,800	$1,000	$750

New Deal Tractor Company

WYOMING, MINNESOTA

During the 1930s, this company built a limited number of tractors, but little information has been found regarding New Deal tractors.

New Way Machinery Company

EAU CLAIRE, WISCONSIN

This company is listed as a tractor manufacturer in 1918, but no other information has been found.

New Way Motor Company

LANSING, MICHIGAN

New Way was a well-known engine builder. Various references pointed to this firm as a tractor manufacturer. In a 1911 trademark application, New Way claimed first use of its trademark on traction engines as February 1, 1905. The firm is also listed in various trade directories as a tractor manufacturer as late as 1911. No illustrations of the New Way tractors have been found.

Nichols & Shepard Company

BATTLE CREEK, MICHIGAN

Nichols & Shepard Company had its beginnings in 1848, and in the early 1850s, the partnership of John Nichols and David Shepard began building grain threshers. The partnership was incorporated in 1886 as Nichols & Shepard Company. By this time, the company was a major manufacturer of threshing machines and steam traction engines. The Red River Special line appeared about 1900 and continued through the remaining years of the company. Tractor development began about 1911, and at least one model was built as late as 1927. In 1929 Nichols & Shepard became a part of the merger that formed Oliver Farm Equipment Company.

Nichols & Shepard prototype

By December 1911, Nichols & Shepard had developed a large tractor. The prototype is shown here pulling 10 plows. A limited number of these tractors were built in 1912. The Nichols & Shepard design was extremely heavy, and from the beginning, the largest model was rated at 35 drawbar and 70 belt hp.

35-70 tractor

The big 35-70 tractor came into full production in 1913. This huge tractor had a two-cylinder engine with a 10-1/2 x 14-inch bore and stroke. The crankshaft had a diameter of 4-3/4 inches! Various tests run at the time indicated over 90 belt hp at rated engine speed of 375 rpm. Production of the 35-70 was fairly small. Active production continued until 1920, although this model was a special order into the late 1920s.

COLLECTOR VALUES	1	2	3	4
35-70	$100,000	$85,000	–	–

Nichols & Shepard 25-50 model

With the 1913 introduction of the 35-70 tractor, Nichols & Shepard also announced its 25-50 model. Although modified over the years, it remained in production until 1927. The 25-50 was probably underrated since it appeared to be capable of well over 60 belt hp. This model used a two-cylinder engine with a 9 x 12- inch bore and stroke. Among other things, Nichols & Shepard claimed its tractors to have the heaviest gearing of anything on the market.

25-50 tractor

About 1920 the 25-50 tractor was modified to some degree. The basic specifications remained the same, but the radiator was changed, the fuel tanks were relocated, and the canopy was modified. Production of this model continued until 1927.

COLLECTOR VALUES	1	2	3	4
20-40 OR 25-50	--	$65,000	--	--

Nichols & Shepard 18-36 tractor

About 1918, Nichols & Shepard developed its 18-36 tractor. Within a year, it was re-rated as the 20-42 tractor. The latter continued on the market until 1925. The same general design was used in the 18-36 as in the larger models. N & S tractor designs were mastered by R. P. Hawthorne who had formerly been associated with Fairbanks, Morse & Company.

Nichols & Shepard 20-42 tractor

The Nichols & Shepard 20-42 tractor was built from 1919 until about 1925. Like the earlier 18-36, it used a two-cylinder engine with an 8 x 10-inch bore and stroke. The company advertised its tractors very little outside of its annual catalogs, accounting in part for the low production of the various models. None of the Nichols & Shepard tractors were tested at Nebraska. Today, four 20-42s remain in existence.

COLLECTOR VALUES	1	2	3	4
20-42	$55,000	$45,000	--	--

Nichols & Shepard 20-40 Thresherman's Special

Beginning about 1927, Nichols & Shepard supplemented its tractor line with three models from the John Lauson Company at New Holstein, Wisconsin. The 20-40 Thresherman's Special typified the line, although this model had heavier drive wheels and other features not found on regular farm tractors. Also included in the series was the 20-40 farm tractor, along with a smaller 20-35 model. The Nichols & Shepard line was amalgamated into Oliver Farm Equipment Company in a 1929 merger.

See also Lauson Tractors

Nichols Tractor & Equipment Company

EL CAJON, CALIFORNIA

Nichols "410" garden tractor

During the 1946-1948 period, the Nichols "410" garden tractor was listed in various directories. No listings have been found after that time, although this does not mean that the "410" went out of production at that time. Weighing 500 lbs., this garden tractor was powered by a Wisconsin AK single-cylinder engine with a 2-7/8 x 2-3/4-inch bore and stroke. Various tools and implements were also available.

COLLECTOR VALUES	1	2	3	4
NICHOLS 410	$500	$350	$225	$100

Nilson Tractor Company

MINNEAPOLIS, MINNESOTA

Nilson Agricultural Machine Co. was incorporated in March 1913. A few months later, the name was changed to Nilson Farm Machine Co. Late in 1915, the company announced plans to move to Waukesha, Wisconsin, but eventually it moved into a factory of the former Bull Tractor Company in Minneapolis. In December 1916 the company was reorganized as Nilson Tractor Company. Nilson Tractor Company went into receivership in late 1918 and the assets were sold the following year. In February 1920 the Minnesota-Nilson Company was organized, and it again built the Nilson tractors. Production continued through the 1920s, but the company was dissolved in 1929. Repair parts were available for the Nilson tractors as late as 1936.

Nilson Farm Machine Co. tractor

During 1915, the company introduced its first tractor. It had two steering wheels in the front and a single drive wheel in the rear.

Nilson 20-40 tractor

By 1916 the Nilson tractor had been streamlined somewhat and was given a 20-40 hp rating. Retailing at $1,485, this tractor weighed 5,250 lbs.

Nilson 20-40 tractor

Late in 1916, the Nilson 20-40 took on a new look. The single driver of earlier models gained two smaller drivers outside the chassis. This provided better stability and increased traction.

Nilson Junior 16-25 tractor

Production of the Nilson Junior 16-25 tractor began in 1917. However, it had an initial rating of 15 drawbar and 30 belt hp. The new rating did not come until 1918.

Nilson Senior 24-36 tractor

During 1918, the Nilson Senior 24-36 tractor appeared and replaced the original 20-40 models. The 24-36 took on a 20-40 hp rating in 1920. This model used a Waukesha four-cylinder engine with a 4-3/4 x 6-3/4- inch bore and stroke. Production of this model continued until about 1925.

Nilson tractor

In the late 1920s, Shotwell-Johnson Company attempted to sell stock in the Nilson Company. The newest tractor design was illustrated in its literature, although no details or specifications were included. Apparently, this venture did not have great success.

Noble Automatic Company

KANSAS CITY, MISSOURI

No information can be found regarding this company or the tractors it may have built.

Northwest Thresher Company

STILLWATER, MINNESOTA

During 1911, Northwest Thresher Co. and Universal Tractor Co., both of Stillwater, consolidated their interests. The following year, M. Rumely Company of LaPorte, Indiana, bought out Northwest, and its Universal tractor. The latter was then marketed as the Rumely GasPull for a short time.

Northwest Universal tractor

[Throughout this section, assume that gasoline was used for fuel unless another fuel source is indicated.]

Ogburn Tractor Company

INDIANAPOLIS, INDIANA

This firm was organized in 1917 by A. R. and H. R. Ogburn and others. No other information has been found.

Ohio Cultivator Company

BELLEVUE, OHIO

In the late 1940s, this firm is listed as the manufacturer of the Blackhawk garden tractor, but little other information has been found.

Ohio General Tractor Company

CLEVELAND, OHIO

Ohio General crawler

About 1919, the Ohio General crawler came onto the market. It was rated at 25 drawbar and 30 belt hp. It was on the market for only a short time, perhaps as little as a year. No specifications or details regarding this tractor have been located.

Morton Traction Truck

Marion 45-hp tractor

Ohio Mfg. Company

UPPER SANDUSKY, OHIO

This company entered the tractor business in the 1890s with its Traction Truck. In 1916 the company introduced the Whitney tractor. In 1921 the corporate name was changed to Whitney Tractor Company, which continued in business only a short time.

In the late 1890s the Morton Traction Truck first appeared. As shown here in a 1906 advertisement, it was simply a chassis and gearing—any engine from 6 to 50 hp could be fitted to the Morton trucks. Numerous engine manufacturers offered tractors using their own engines and the Morton traction trucks. They were available as late as 1913.

Whitney 9-18 tractor

In 1916 the Whitney 9-18 tractor appeared. Retailing at $1,175, it was equipped with a Gile two-cylinder engine with a 5-1/2 x 6-1/2-inch bore and stroke. Ohio Manufacturing Co. continued building the 9-18 until about 1921.

Ohio Steel Wagon Company

WAPOKONETA, OHIO

In 1911 this firm bought out the Smith Tractor Mfg. Company at Harvey, Illinois. The company was moved to Ohio, and late in 1911, the firm name was changed to Thompson-Breese Company. The tractor is illustrated under that heading.

Ohio Tractor Mfg. Company

MARION, OHIO

This firm began building tractors in 1908, and in 1910 bought out the Marion Mfg. Company, builders of Leader steam traction engines. The Ohio tractors were built in four sizes of 20, 30, 45, and 70 hp. The 45-hp model is shown here, although all were of the same general design. Production continued until 1915 when the company took bankruptcy. No specific details have been found for the Ohio tractors.

Ohio Tractor Company

COLUMBUS, OHIO

Ohio 15-30 tractor

About 1920 the Ohio 15-30 tractor appeared. This model was powered by a Wisconsin four-cylinder engine with a 4-1/2 x 6-inch bore and stroke. Weighing 4,500 lbs., it had a list price of $2,800. This tractor was of modern design for its time and a 12-volt electrical system was available as a factory option. Production of the Ohio 15-30 continued until about 1922.

Oklahoma Auto Mfg. Company

MUSKOGEE, OKLAHOMA

This firm is listed as a tractor manufacturer in 1919, but no other information has been found.

Olds Gas Engine Works

LANSING, MICHIGAN

Olds tractor

In 1905, Olds was listed as a tractor manufacturer, and a catalog from 1908 illustrated its design. It was powered by a single-cylinder Olds stationary engine. It was available in several sizes, but few specific details have been found.

Oldsmar Tractor Company

OLDSMAR, FLORIDA

Oldsmar garden tractor

Organized in 1917, Oldsmar Tractor Company was a brainchild of R. E. Olds of automobile fame. Olds bought out the Kardell Truck & Tractor Company, St. Louis, Missouri, as a start to the project. The Oldsmar garden tractor was rated at 2-1/2 drawbar and 4-1/2 belt hp. Its single-cylinder engine had a 5 x 5-1/2-inch bore and stroke. Production continued until about 1920.

Olin Gas Engine Company

BUFFALO, NEW YORK

Olin was a well known manufacturer of gasoline engines. About 1915, the company developed the Olin–7 garden tractor. This rather heavy design was built somewhat like a "universal" tractor with its hinged frame. Rated at 7 belt hp, the Olin left the market by 1920 or before.

Oliver Farm Equipment Company

CHICAGO, ILLINOIS

On April 1, 1929, four companies merged to form Oliver Farm Equipment Company. Oliver Chilled Plow Works at South Bend, Indiana, had roots going back to 1855. Nichols & Shepard Company at Battle Creek, Michigan, originated in 1848, as did the American Seeding Machine Company. The Hart-Parr Company at Charles City, Iowa, began in 1897 and was the first company devoted exclusively to manufacturing tractors.

Various acquisitions followed, but in 1969, Oliver Corporation, Minneapolis-Moline and Cockshutt merged its interests into White Farm Equipment.

Specific details on these companies and their products can be found in the author's title, Oliver Hart-Parr.

COLLECTOR VALUES	1	2	3	4
900 INDUSTRIAL	$5,000	$3,500	$2,000	$1,500
18 INDUSTRIAL	–	–	$12,000	–
35 INDUSTRIAL	$4,000	$3,000	$2,500	$1,500
44 INDUSTRIAL	$4,250	$3,500	$3,000	$2,000
50 INDUSTRIAL	$4,500	$3,000	$2,000	$1,000

Oliver-Hart-Parr 18-28

In 1930, only a few months after the merger, Oliver came out with its new 18-28 tractor. It marked a new epoch in Oliver tractor design with its unit frame and lightweight design. The 18-28 was available in Standard, Western, Ricefield and Orchard versions. Production continued until 1937. This model used a four-cylinder engine with a 4-1/8 x 5-1/4-inch bore and stroke.

Nebraska Test Data

Model: Oliver Hart-Parr 18-28

Test No. 180

Date Tested: July 7 to July 15, 1930

Coming into Test No. 180, this tractor was not given a hp rating by the manufacturer, but in order to conform to tractor rating codes, the 18-28 designation was the highest permissible hp for this model. Using kerosene, this 4,420-lb. tractor pulled 3,241 lbs. in low gear, and developed 23.56 drawbar hp in the process. Rated drawbar hp tests were done in intermediate gear, and at 3.51 mph, the 18-28 pulled 2,031 lbs. at 3.51 mph while developing 18.99 hp. Fuel consumption totaled 7.8 hp-hours per gallon and 2.436 gallons per hour (gph). At its rated 28 brake hp, fuel economy was recorded at 10 hp-hours per gallon. Economy dropped by a miniscule 0.004 when developing its maximum of 30.29 brake hp. A 4-1/8 x 5-1/4-inch bore and stroke was featured in the four-cylinder vertical, I-head engine. Rated at 1,190 rpm, it also featured an American Bosch U4 magneto, Ensign KZ carburetor, and Donaldson air cleaner. Advertised speeds were 2.6, 3.2, and 4.15 mph.

COLLECTOR VALUES	1	2	3	4
18-28 TRACTOR	$3,750	$2,200	$1,500	$800
18-28 ORCHARD	–	–	–	$1,000

Oliver Hart-Parr 28-44 tractor

Like the 18-28 tractor, the big 28-44 was built in the 1930 through 1937 period. This model used a four-cylinder engine with a 4-3/4 x 6-1/4-inch bore and stroke. Rated speed was 1,125 rpm. The 28-44 weighed in at 5,600 lbs.

Nebraska Test Data

Model: Oliver Hart-Parr 3-5 Plow (28-44)

Test No. 183

Date Tested: October 13 to October 27, 1930

Originally submitted as the Oliver Hart-Parr 3-5 Plow tractor, this model was subsequently known as the Oliver 28-44, and later as the Oliver 90. All three manufacturer designations were marketed under Test No. 183. On maximum brake load, this tractor developed 49.04 hp with a fuel efficiency of 10.00 hp-hours per gallon of kerosene. Economy rose slightly higher to

10.42 at rated load of 44.29 hp. Drawbar economy came in at 7.16 on the rated load test, again using kerosene. While developing 28.44 hp on this test, a 2,940-lb. pull was made at 3.63 mph. Maximum pull of 5,116 lbs. came in low gear, along with 28.36 drawbar hp. Oliver advertised three forward speeds of 2.23, 3.3, and 4.33 mph. Weighing 6,415 lbs., the 28-44 featured Oliver's own four-cylinder I-head engine rated at 1,125 rpm and used a 4-3/4 x 6-1/4-inch bore and stroke. Featured too was an Ensign Model K carburetor and an American Bosch U4 magneto.

COLLECTOR VALUES	1	2	3	4
28-44 TRACTOR	$4,000	$2,500	$1,500	$800

18-27 row-crop model

Another new tractor design for 1930 was the 18-27 row-crop model. A unique feature was the single front wheel of this style. Oliver used its own four-cylinder engine; it had a 4-1/8 x 5-1/4-inch bore and stroke. Rated at 1,150 rpm, the engine in the 18-27 was essentially the same as in the 18-28 standard-tread model. Production of the 18-27 single-wheel model ended in 1931.

Nebraska Test Data

Model: Oliver Hart-Parr Row Crop

Test No. 176

Date Tested: April 14 to April 24, 1930

Although Oliver did not ascribe a horsepower rating to this tractor, the highest permissible rating under A.S.A.E. and S.A.E. rating codes was 18 drawbar and 27 belt hp. As with all tests beginning with the 1928 season, one carburetor setting was used for all tests. Oliver equipped this 4,650-lb. tractor with a four-cylinder, vertical, I-head engine rated at 700 rpm and featuring a 4-1/8 x 5-1/4-inch bore and stroke. Included too was an American Bosch U4 magneto, Donaldson air cleaner, and Ensign Model K carburetor. Standard equipment also included three forward speeds of 2.6, 3.2, and 4.15 mph. At its rated 18-drawbar hp, an average pull of 2,067 lbs. at 3.28 mph was recorded over the 10-hour test. Fuel economy came in at 7.7 hp-hours per gallon of kerosene. Maximum drawbar pull in low gear totaled 3,664 lbs. at 2.32 mph. Rated brake tests indicated a fuel efficiency of 9.86 hp-hours per gallon of kerosene while developing 27.11 hp. Under maximum load, 29.72 brake hp was developed, along with 9.7 hp-hours per gallon of kerosene. No repairs or adjustments were made during the test. The Oliver company was formed in 1929 via a merger of four agricultural companies, including Hart-Parr.

COLLECTOR VALUES	1	2	3	4
18-27 SINGLE	$4,500	$3,000	$1,500	$1,000

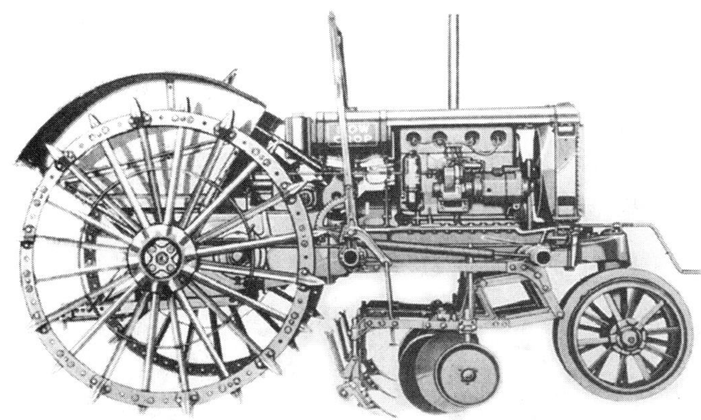

18-27 dual-front design

Replacing the 18-27 single-front wheel design was the 18-27 dual-front-wheel design in 1931. This model continued until 1937. This tractor used the same engine as the 18-28 model. In Nebraska Test No. 176 of April 1930, the 18-27 demonstrated nearly 30 belt hp using kerosene fuel.

COLLECTOR VALUES	1	2	3	4
18-27 DUAL	$3,500	$1,700	$1,000	$500

Oliver "28" tractor

The Oliver "28" Industrial tractor was the first Oliver to use pneumatic tires. It was simply a rubber-tired version of the 28-44 on steel wheels. For industrial purposes, this model had regular features that included an upholstered seat, headlights and many more optional features. Production of this model ran from 1931 to 1937. A similar model was the Oliver Hart-Parr 80 Industrial. Its roots were also with the 18-28 tractor.

Oliver Hart-Parr 99 Industrial tractors were essentially the same as the 28-44 Industrial model. Built in the 1932 through 1947 period, this tractor underwent some cosmetic changes along the way, but the engine and chassis were changed but little. Originally it was sold as the Oliver Special High-Compression 28-44.

Oliver Hart-Parr 99 Industrial

Oliver Hart-Parr 70 Row-Crop tractor

During 1935, Oliver introduced its Oliver Hart-Parr 70 Row-Crop tractor. It was the first Oliver tractor to use a six-cylinder engine. Rated at 1,500 rpm, the engine was designed with a 3-1/8 x 4-3/8-inch bore and stroke. In Nebraska Test No. 252 of 1936, this model demonstrated nearly 17 drawbar hp and approximately 27 belt hp. Production of this model continued until 1937. At that point it was dressed up with a streamlined hood and other niceties. Production of the streamlined model continued until 1948.

Nebraska Test Data

Model: Oliver Hart-Parr Row Crop 70
Test No. 252
Date Tested: April 13 to April 24, 1936

Weighing only 3,500 lbs., the Oliver 70 made a remarkable low gear maximum pull of 3,120 lbs., or slightly over 89 percent of its own weight. As noted in Test G, slippage was 19.11 percent at a speed of 2.17 mph and an output of 18.03 hp. Rated load (Test H) in third gear recorded an output of 16.94 hp, a pull of 1,440 lbs. at 4.41 mph, and a fuel economy of 7.58 hp-hours per gallon. Test C for operating maximum load ended with 26.57 brake hp along with an economy of 11.07 hp-hours per gallon. This figure dropped slightly to 10.87 at rated load of 25.33 hp as indicated in Test D. Oliver equipped this tractor with its own six-cylinder I-head engine. Rated at 1,500 rpm, it carried a 3-1/8 x 4-3/8-inch bore and stroke, featuring an American Bosch MJB6A magneto, Zenith 124 1/2 EX carburetor, Handy governor, and Donaldson air cleaner as accessories. Also featured were speeds of 2.44, 3.32, 4.33, and 5.88 mph. A welded connection on the seat frame broke during the test. Other repairs and adjustments were of a minor nature.

Nebraska Test Data

Model: Oliver Hart-Parr Row-Crop 70 KD
Test No. 267
Date Tested: August 20 to August 31, 1936

Under Test D, the Oliver 70 achieved 10.4 hp-hours per gallon of distillate while developing its rated 24.8 brake hp. Test C for operating maximum load achieved an economy figure of 10.3 while delivering 26.09 hp. Transmission speeds of 2.44, 3.32, 4.33, and 5.88 mph were available. Third gear was used for Test H. At its rated 16.45 drawbar hp in this test, the Oliver 70 pulled 1,363 lbs. at 4.53 mph with a slippage of 4.4 percent. Fuel economy settled in at 7.25 hp-hours per gallon. From Test G, it was noted that an operating maximum load of 15.02 hp was recorded in low gear, along with a pull of 2,523 lbs. at 2.23 mph. Oliver equipped this tractor with its own six-cylinder vertical engine of I-head design. Rated at 1,500 rpm, it carried a 3-1/8 x 4-3/8-inch bore and stroke. An American Bosch MJB6A magneto, Zenith 124-1/2 carburetor, and Handy governor also came as standard equipment. Operating weight was 3,900 lbs. Before running the official belt tests, it was discovered that one bevel pinion tooth was broken in the pulley gear. It was replaced before official test data was taken. Before the testing procedures ended, the radiator temperature indicator became inoperative. Otherwise, no repairs or adjustments were required.

COLLECTOR VALUES	1	2	3	4
70 HART-PARR	$3,600	$2,500	$750	$300
70 HART-PARR ORCHARD	$7,500	–	–	–

Oliver 70 Row-Crop

Few basic changes were made to the Oliver 70 Row-Crop from the time it was introduced in 1935 until production finally ended in 1948. In 1940 an entirely new hood and grille were introduced, but these changes were mainly cosmetic in nature. The unusual skeleton wheels were called "Power on Tiptoe" and were a salient feature until pneumatic tires took over.

Nebraska Test Data

Model: Oliver Row Crop 70 HC
Test No. 351
Date Tested: August 23 to August 29, 1940

Oliver featured its own six-cylinder I-head engine in the "70". Rated at 1,500 rpm, it carried a 3-1/8 x 4-3/8-inch bore and stroke. A Zenith 61AXJ7 carburetor and an American Bosch MJC magneto also came as standard equipment. Although a steel-wheel version is illustrated here, the model actually tested was equipped with 11 x 40-inch rear rubber and 5.50 x 16-inch front tires. To the rear wheels were added 775 lbs. of cast-iron weight plus another 432 lbs. of calcium chloride solution for a total of 2,400 lbs. of ballast included in the operating weight of 6,770 lbs. No repairs or adjustments were noted in 49 hours of engine operating time. Six forward speeds of 2.56, 3.47, 4.55, 6.17, 7.61, and 13.44 mph were provided. Third gear was selected for Test H. In this 10-hour run, the "70" came away with a fuel economy of 9.81 hp- hours per gallon, pulling a 1,986-lb. load at 4.29 mph and delivering 22.72 rated drawbar hp. The low gear maximum test indicated a pull of 4,170 lbs. at 2.23 mph. Test C noted 30.37 brake hp under maximum operating load with an economy of 11.28 hp-hours per gallon. This figure dropped an insignificant 0.04 to 11.24 at the rated load of 28.46 hp as noted in Test C.

Oliver 70 Standard series

Numerous variations of the Oliver Row-Crop 70 tractor were built. An example is the Oliver Hart-Parr 70 Standard model, built in the 1935 through 1937 period. The chassis and engine were virtually the same as in the row-crop tractor, but special features included expanding differential disk brakes. A live PTO was an optional feature.

Nebraska Test Data

Model: Oliver Hart-Parr Standard 70 HC
Test No. 283
Date Tested: June 14 to June 22, 1937

Four forward speeds of 2.44, 3.32, 4.33, and 5.88 mph were built into this Oliver model. Third gear was selected for the 10-hour run of Test H. Delivering 15.92 drawbar hp, the 70 Standard pulled 1,233 lbs. at 4.84 mph while delivering 6.92 hp-hours per gallon. Test G trials for maximum operating load evoked a maximum pull of 2,493 lbs. in low gear, along with an output of 16.17 drawbar hp, together with a speed of 2.43 mph and slippage of 15.81 percent. Oliver equipped the 70 Standard with its own six-cylinder I-head engine with a 3-1/8 x 4-3/8-inch bore and stroke, along with a rated speed of 1,500 rpm. American Bosch supplied its MJB6A magneto, and Zenith furnished its Model 124 1/2-EX carburetor. A lug bolt was lost during the test, otherwise no repairs or adjustments were noted during 61 hours of engine operating time. The tractor weighed in at 3,500 lbs. Belt tests at operating maximum load requirements of Test C indicate an output of 26.58 hp with 10.9 hp-hours per gallon. A slightly lower economy of 10.54 was noted at a rated load of 25.14 hp.

Nebraska Test Data

Model: Oliver Hart-Parr Standard 70 KD
Test No. 284
Date Tested: June 24 to June 30, 1937

This photograph illustrates an Oliver 70 Standard Grove Tractor of slightly later vintage than the subject of this test, but carrying the same basic specifications. The tractor used for this test was the identical unit of Test No. 283 with the exception of distillate used for fuel. Test H for rated drawbar load indicated an output of 15.92 hp, along with a pull of 1,230 lbs. at 4.85 mph and slippage of 5.39 percent. Economy came in at 6.53 hp-hours per gallon. The test model was equipped with steel wheels. The rubber tires as noted on this photograph came later. Test G, using first gear, gave a maximum pull of 2,634 lbs. at 2.26 mph and slippage of 22.15 percent. Rated brake hp as extracted from Test D indicated an output of 24.19 hp and 10.48 hp-hours per gallon. Economy rose minimally to 10.61 at a maximum operating load of 25.67 hp. During the rated drawbar load test, the center steering shaft dropped out of the front steering arm. This was put back in place, and no other repairs or adjustments were noted during 49 hours of operating time.

COLLECTOR VALUES	1	2	3	4
70 INDUSTRIAL	$4,250	$2,500	$1,800	$800
70 ROW-CROP	$2,900	$1,500	$750	$500
70 STANDARD	$4,500	$2,750	$1,200	$750
70 ROW-CROP WIDE FRONT	$3,500	$2,000	$1,250	$1,000

Oliver 80 Row-Crop tractor

In 1937 the Oliver 80 Row-Crop tractor appeared, with production continuing until 1948. In 1940 the 80 Diesel Row-Crop was introduced. Initially, it used a Buda-Lanova engine, but later, an Oliver diesel engine was installed. The 80 Diesel Row-Crop is shown here and the 80 Gasoline model was virtually identical except for its engine.

Nebraska Test Data

Model: Oliver Row-Crop 80 KD

Test No. 300

Date Tested: May 16 to May 26, 1938

Apparently, the tractor submitted for this test was equipped only with steel wheels, as no mention was made of rubber tires. Three forward speeds of 2.7, 3.33, and 4.33 mph were available. Of these, second gear was chosen for the 10-hour rated drawbar test (Test H). Using distillate, the 80 delivered a fuel economy of 8.01 hp-hours per gallon while cranking out 23.32 rated drawbar hp. Test G for operating maximum load revealed a pull of 3,785 lbs. in low gear and a high of 27.13 drawbar hp. Weighing 4,930 lbs., the 80 was equipped with Oliver's own four-cylinder I-head engine. Rated at 1,200 rpm, it featured a 4-1/2 x 5-1/4-inch bore and stroke. Standard equipment included an American Bosch MJB4A magneto, Schebler TTX-18 carburetor, Borg & Beck clutch and a Donaldson air cleaner. Test D at rated brake hp issued 11 hp-hours per gallon with an output of 35.24 hp. At its operating maximum load of 36.33 hp, the 80 gave a virtually identical economy figure of 11.03. No repairs or adjustments were mentioned over 48 hours of operating time.

Nebraska Test Data

Model: Oliver 80 Standard HC

Test No. 365

Date Tested: November 4 to November 8, 1940

Standard equipment for this tractor included 12.75 x 28-inch rear and 7.50 x 18-inch front tires. Also featured were four forward speeds of 2.78, 3,71, 4.79, and 6.44 mph. Oliver furnished its own four-cylinder I-head engine rated at 1,200 rpm and using a 4-1/4 x 5-1/4-inch bore and stroke. Accessories included an American Bosch MJB4A magneto and a Schebler TT X carburetor. During 40 hours of engine operating time, no repairs or adjustments were noted for this 8,145-lb. tractor. Test C for an operating maximum load of 38.11 belt hp yielded 11.51 hp-hours per gallon. At a rated load of 36.25 hp, Test D gave a nearly identical economy figure of 11.53. Test H was run in second gear. With a rated output of 27.64 drawbar hp, the 80 pulled 3,002 lbs. at 3.45 mph under a slippage of 6.31 percent and yielded a fuel economy of 9.5 hp-hours per gallon. Test G for operating maximum drawbar load was run in all four forward gears, but in low gear the maximum drawbar pull of 5,079 lbs. was noted. This phase of testing also reveals a slippage of 13.07 percent, a ground speed of 2.41 mph and an output of 32.67 drawbar hp.

Another style in the 80-Series tractors was the 80 Standard. This model was built in the same 1937 through 1948 time period as the Row-Crop model and was essentially the same tractor except for the chassis configuration. A very few of these tractors were also offered with a diesel engine.

Nebraska Test Data

Model: Oliver 80 Standard KD

Test No. 301

Date Tested: May 16 to May 28, 1938

Spade lugs and steel wheels were used for testing the Oliver Standard 80. Nothing in the records of Test No. 301 indicated this tractor was tested using the rubber tires shown here. As tested, it weighed 4,950 lbs., virtually identical to the row-crop model noted under Test No. 300. Specifications remained almost identical except for the standard tread design of this model, com-

Oliver 80 Standard

pared to the 80 Row-Crop previously noted. Using distillate, the 80 Standard delivered 11.41 hp-hours per gallon under Test D or rated brake load, with an output of 35.2 hp. At its maximum of 37.03 brake hp, the 80 Standard recorded 11.29 hp-hours per gallon. Test H, formerly called rated drawbar load, revealed an economy of 7.78 hp hours per gallon while pulling 2,246 lbs. at 3.7 mph and delivering 22.13 drawbar hp. Maximum pull of 3,596 lbs. was achieved using low gear. Test G also revealed a maximum output of 27.97 drawbar hp.

COLLECTOR VALUES	1	2	3	4
80 INDUSTRIAL	$3,400	$2,000	$1,600	$800
80 ROW-CROP	$3,000	$1,700	$1,000	$600
80 STANDARD	$3,200	$2,200	$1,500	$700
80 ROW-CROP DIESEL	$10,000	–	–	–

Oliver 90 tractor

Oliver 90 tractors were a continuation of the original 28-44 series. The four-cylinder engine used a 4-3/4 x 6-1/4-inch bore and stroke. The same Nebraska Test No. 183 was used for the 28-44 as well as for the Oliver 90. Electric starting was an important feature for these tractors. Production ran from 1937 to 1953.

Oliver 99 tractor

The Oliver 99 tractors were essentially a continuation of the earlier 90-Series tractors. However, the 99 used a high-compression four-cylinder engine designed for 70-octane fuel. In Nebraska Test No. 451, the Oliver 99 delivered over 62 belt hp. Production of this model ended in 1957.

Nebraska Test Data

Model: Oliver 99

Test No. 451

Date Tested: September 29 to October 9, 1950

No repairs or adjustments were recorded during 44-1/2 hours of engine operating time. With a bare weight of 7,281 lbs., the 99 was enhanced with another 2,912 lbs. of ballast on each rear wheel during Tests F, G and H. Advertised speeds of 2-1/2, 3-7/8 and 13-1/2 mph were featured. Second gear was used for the rated drawbar run of Test H. Results indicated that with an output of 41.18 hp, the 99 pulled 4,036 lbs. at 3.83 mph under a 6.03 percent slippage. Fuel economy was noted at 9.74 hp-hours per gallon. Standard equipment included 15-30-inch rear and 7.50-18-inch front tires. A low-gear maximum pull of 7,594 lbs. at 2.29 mph was achieved in Test G. The 99 was equipped with an Oliver-built, four-cylinder, I-head engine. Using a 443-cubic inch displacement, this engine was rated at 1,125 rpm and carried a 4-3/4 x 6-1/4-inch bore and stroke. At a Test D-rated load of 54.52 belt hp, the 99 yielded 11.49 hp-hours per gallon, a figure that increased slightly to 11.74 under a Test C operating maximum load of 58.98 belt hp.

COLLECTOR VALUES	1	2	3	4
90 & 99	$4,100	$2,500	$1,800	$800
99 SUPER GAS OR DIESEL	$6,000	$3,000	$2,200	$100

Oliver 60 Row-Crop

Oliver 60 Row-Crop tractors were built between 1940 and 1948. This model used a four-cylinder engine with a 3-5/16 x 3-1/2-inch bore and stroke. Rated speed was 1500 rpm. It was capable of about 18 belt hp.

Nebraska Test Data

Model: Oliver Row-Crop 60 HC

Test No. 375

Date Tested: September 10 to September 23, 1941

With no added ballast, the Oliver 60 weighed 2,450 lbs. Standard equipment included 9-32 rear and 5.00-15 front tires. Although this tractor was tested with rubber tires, steel wheels apparently were still available as an option. Advertised speeds of 2.58, 3.45, 4.57 and 6.1 mph were featured. Also included was an Oliver four-cylinder, I-head engine rated at 1,500 rpm and it carried a 3-5/16 x 3-1/2-inch bore and stroke. This was complemented with a Wico Type J magneto and a Marvel-Schebler TSX carburetor. No repairs or adjustments were noted during 64 hours of engine operation. Test C, at an operating maximum load of 18.35 belt hp, yielded 12.19 hp-hours per gallon, compared to 11.9 when under the Test D-rated belt load of 16.62 hp. Test H was run in third gear and included an additional 795 lbs. of ballast added to each wheel. At 4.34 mph, the Model 60 pulled 1,179 lbs. with a slippage of 4.94 percent, delivering 13.64 hp with an economy of 10.13 hp-hours per gallon. The low-gear maximum pull as recorded in Test G indicated an output of 15.17 drawbar hp with a pull of 2,496 lbs. and a slippage of 11.75 percent.

Oliver 60 Standard-tread model

A standard-tread model of the Oliver 60 was also built in the 1940 through 1948 period. It was virtually identical to the Row-Crop tractor except for the chassis configuration. The Oliver 60 was also available in an Industrial style.

COLLECTOR VALUES	1	2	3	4
60 INDUSTRIAL	$3,800	$2,000	$1,200	$600
60 ROW-CROP	$3,500	$2,000	$1,200	$400
60 STANDARD OR ADJUSTABLE	$4,200	$2,500	$1,400	$500

Oliver 88 tractors made their debut in 1948, with production continuing until 1954. The Oliver 88 Diesel was introduced in 1949. A six-cylinder engine powered the Oliver 88. It used a 3-1/2 x 4-inch bore and stroke. In Nebraska Test No. 388 of October 1947, the Oliver 88 delivered a maximum of 41 belt hp.

Oliver 88 tractor (high clearance version)

Nebraska Test Data

Model: Oliver Row-Crop 88 HC

Test No. 388

Date Tested: October 20 to October 31, 1947

At a Test C operating maximum load of 41.07 belt hp, the Oliver 88 delivered 11.55 hp-hours per gallon. This figure sagged slightly to 11.07 under the Test D-rated load of 38.02 belt hp. This Oliver used six forward speeds of 2.62, 3.39, 4.5, 5.83, 7.17 and 12.32 mph. Third gear was chosen for Test H, and under a rated load of 28.96 drawbar hp, the Oliver 88 pulled 2,328 lbs. at 4.66 mph with a recorded slippage of 3.57 percent. Under this load, fuel economy came in at 9.47 hp-hours per gallon. A low-gear maximum pull of 5,173 lbs. was noted in Test G. This test also showed a speed of 2.51 mph and slippage of 11.08 percent. The Oliver 88 featured 13.38-inch rear and 6.00-16-inch front tires and without additional ballast, it weighed 5,285 lbs. No repairs or adjustments were noted during 52 hours of engine operation. Features included an Oliver-built six-cylinder engine. Rated at 1,600 rpm, it carried a 3-1/2 x 4-inch bore and stroke. Also featured was a Delco-Remy electrical system and a Marvel-Schebler TSX-181 carburetor.

Nebraska Test Data

Model: Oliver Row-Crop 88 Diesel

Test No. 450

Date Tested: September 25 to October 9, 1950

With a displacement of 230.9-cubic inches, the Oliver 88 Diesel featured a six-cylinder I-head engine rated at 1,600 rpm, using a 3-1/2 x 4-inch bore and stroke. Also included was a 12-volt electrical system. At a bare weight of 5,680 lbs., the 88 Diesel included 13-38-inch rear and 6.00-16-inch front tires. During Tests F, G and H, an additional 1,959 lbs. of weight was added to each rear wheel, with a portion of the added weight visible in this photograph. No repairs or adjustments were noted during 42 hours of engine operating time. Advertised speeds of 2.5, 3.25, 4.25, 5.5, 6.75 and 11.75 mph were provided, with Test H being run in third gear. At a rated drawbar load of 29.42 hp, the 88 Diesel pulled 2,581 lbs. at 4.28 mph with a slippage of 4.31 percent. Fuel economy rested at 12.91 hp-hours per gallon of diesel fuel. A Test G, low-gear maximum pull of 5,869 lbs. was made at 2.27 mph with a 13.01 percent slippage. Belt testing indicated 14.87 hp-hours per gallon under a Test B and C maximum load of 43.53 hp. Economy dropped slightly to 14.80 hp-hours per gallon at a Test D-rated belt load of 38.47 hp.

Nebraska Test Data

Model: Oliver 88 Standard HC

Test No. 391

Date Tested: November 14 to November 30, 1947 and April 19 to April 30, 1948

Testing of this Oliver could not be completed in 1947, so it was placed in storage until testing resumed on April 19, 1948. Because of this, 87 hours of engine operating time was recorded. Featuring a six-cylinder I-head engine, it was equipped with a Delco-Remy electrical system and a Marvel-Schebler carburetor. The engine was rated at 1,600 rpm and carried a 3-1/2 x 4-inch bore and stroke. Also featured were six forward speeds of 2.51, 3.25, 4.31, 5.58, 6.87 and 11.80 mph. Standard equipment also included 14-26 rear and 6.00-16 inch front rubber. Third gear was used for Test H. At a rated load of 29.08 drawbar hp, the "88" pulled 2,430 lbs. at 4.49 mph with a slippage of 3.71 percent. Fuel economy was recorded at 9.66 hp-hours per gallon. A maximum low-gear pull of 5,270 lbs. was noted in Test G. At operating maximum load per Test C, fuel economy was 11.53 hp-hours per gallon under a load of 40.96 hp. Test D, at a rated load of 38.39 hp, yielded 11.26 hp-hours per gallon. Bare tractor weight was 4,863 lbs.

Oliver Super 88

The Oliver Super 88 was the last of this series. It was built between 1954 and 1958. The gasoline model was tested at Nebraska under No. 525, and it displayed almost 37 drawbar hp. It used a six-cylinder engine with a 3-3/4 x 4-inch bore and stroke. Test No. 527 for the Super 88 Diesel revealed nearly 38 drawbar hp. Both of these tests were run in October 1954.

Nebraska Test Data

Model: Oliver Super 88 HC

Test No. 525

Date Tested: September 27 to October 16, 1954

Rated at 1,600 rpm, the Super 88 achieved a maximum torque of 347.7 lbs.-ft. with an engine speed of 1,096 rpm. The six-cylinder, Oliver-built engine carried a 265-cubic inch displacement with a 3-3/4 x 4- inch bore and stroke. Standard features included 13-38-inch rear and 6.00-16-inch front tires, along with advertised speeds of 2.49, 3.22, 4.28, 5.55, 6.82 and 11.75 mph. The 10-hour run of Test H was made in third gear. With an output of 36.84 drawbar hp, the Super 88 pulled 3,220 lbs. at 4.29 mph against a slippage of 5.35 percent. Fuel economy in Test H was pegged at 10.3 hp-hours per gallon. Test G produced a low-gear maximum pull of 6,354 lbs. at 2.24 mph. Although the Super 88 weighed in at 5,513 lbs., an additional 1,914 lbs. of weight was added to each rear wheel during Tests F, G and H. Belt testing indicated a fuel economy of 12.24 hp-hours per gallon at a Test D-rated load of 49.59 hp. Economy increased to 12.67 at a Test C operating maximum belt load of 53.14 hp. Through 40-1/2 hours of operating time, no repairs or adjustments were noted.

Nebraska Test Data

Model: Oliver Super 88 Diesel

Test No. 527

Date Tested: October 4 to October 13, 1954

Like the Super 88 gasoline model noted in Test No. 525, this diesel style featured a six-cylinder, 265-cid engine. Except for the modifications necessary for the two different engine styles, both tractors were virtually identical. The tractor shown here carried a 15.5:1 compression ratio, compared to 7:1 for the gasoline model previously noted. Test H, run in third gear, produced an economy of 13.41 hp-hours per gallon of diesel fuel. This 10-hour run was made at a rated drawbar load of 37.93 hp, with a pull of 3,319 lbs. at 4.29 mph and a slippage of 5.23 percent. Test G produced a low-gear maximum pull of 6,287 lbs. at 2.2 mph with a slippage of 15.69 percent. Test D, run at a rated belt load of 47.7 hp, came in with a fuel economy of 15.37 hp-hours per gallon, compared to 15.23 under a Test B & C maximum load of 54.88 hp. Bare weight of the Super 88 Diesel was 5,606 lbs., with 1,920 lbs. of weight added to each rear wheel during Tests F, G and H. Advertised speeds and other data may be noted under Test No. 525.

COLLECTOR VALUES	1	2	3	4
88 STANDARD	$3,800	$2,200	$1,500	$900
88 ROW CROP	$3,500	$1,800	$900	$500
88 SUPER STANDARD	$6,000	$4,000	$2,000	$1,500
88 SUPER	$3,800	$2,200	$1,500	$900

In 1948 the Oliver 77 tractor appeared and it remained in production until 1954. Late in 1948, this tractor was tested (Nebraska No. 404) and indicated a maximum of over 37 belt hp. This tractor was available in many different configurations, including an LP-gas model. The Oliver 77 Standard was a popular model. Oliver 77 tractors were also available in diesel-powered models.

Nebraska Test Data

Model: Oliver Row-Crop 77 HC

Test No. 404

Date Tested: October 21 to November 9, 1948

When it was equipped with pressed steel rear wheels, the Oliver 77 weighed 3,831 lbs., compared to 4,828 lbs. when it was equipped with cast disc rear wheels. Standard equipment included 12-38 rear and 5.50-16-inch front tires. Some 63 hours of engine operating time was required to complete all the tests, and test notes indicated slight leakage of grease around the right rear axle seal. Six forward speeds of 2-5/8, 3-1/2, 4-1/2, 6, 7 and 12-1/4 mph were provided. Third gear was used for Test H. Results indicated a fuel economy of 8.82 hp-hours per gallon under a rated drawbar load of 22.57 hp, along with a pull of 1,801 lbs. at 4.7 mph and slippage of 2.94 percent. A Test G operating maximum load in low gear produced a pull of 4,079 lbs. at 2.56 mph with 7.57 percent slippage. The 77 was equipped with Oliver's own six-cylinder I-head engine. Rated at 1,600 rpm, it carried a 3-5/16 x 3-3/4-inch bore and stroke. Also included were a Delco-Remy electrical system, Marvel-Schebler TSX-363 carburetor and Donaldson

Oliver 77 tractor

air cleaner. Test D, at a rated belt load of 29.9 hp, indicated 11.11 hp-hours per gallon, while Test C at an operating maximum load of 33.65 hp produced 11.52 hp-hours per gallon.

Nebraska Test Data

Model: Oliver Standard 77 HC

Test No. 405

Date Tested: October 31 to November 6, 1948

Engine specifications of this tractor were identical to those for the Oliver 77 Row Crop model of Test No. 404. The major difference was the standard-tread design of this model, compared to the row-crop construction of the previously noted tractor. Weighing 4,036 lbs., the Oliver Standard 77 underwent the complete battery of tests during 45 hours of engine operating time with no repairs or adjustments noted. Third gear was used for the 10-hour run of Test H. At a rated drawbar load of 22.64 hp, a pull of 1,766 lbs. was recorded at 4.81 mph with a 2.74 percent slippage. Fuel economy settled in at 9.05 hp-hours per gallon. A maximum drawbar pull of 3,802 lbs. was recorded in Test G, using low gear and traveling at a speed of 2.61 mph with slippage of 7.93 percent. Standard equipment for this model included 13-26-inch rear and 5.50-16-inch front tires. At a Test C operating maximum load of 32.61 belt hp, the 77 Standard delivered 11.58 hp hours per gallon, compared to 11.25 under the Test C rated belt load of 30.03 hp.

Nebraska Test Data

Model: Oliver Row-Crop 77 HC

Test No. 425

Date Tested: September 23 to September 29, 1949

Although this tractor model had previously been tested under No. 404 of 1948, it was once again submitted in 1949. No repairs or adjustments were recorded during 45 hours of engine operating time. Featured were forward speeds of 2-1/2, 3-1/4, 4-1/4, 5-5/8, 6-5/8 and 11-1/2 mph. The basic weight of 4,866 lbs. included 12-38-inch rear and 5.50-16-inch front tires. For testing purposes, 1,573 lbs. of weight was added to each rear wheel during Tests F, G and H. Third gear was selected for Test H, and at a rated drawbar load of 25.75 hp, the 77 pulled a 2,260-lb. load at 4.27 mph with a slippage of 4.12 percent. A low-gear maximum pull of 4,714 lbs. at 2.29 mph was noted in Test G. Test D indicated a fuel economy of 11.39 hp hours per gallon under a rated load of 33.02 hp, with economy rising slightly to 11.72 under a Test C operating maximum load of 34.34 belt hp. The basic tractor specifications were virtually identical to those given in Test No. 404.

Nebraska Test Data

Model: Oliver Row-Crop 77 Diesel

Test No. 457

Date Tested: May 21 to May 28, 1951

Advertised speeds of 2-1/2, 3-1/4, 4-1/4, 5-5/8, 6-5/8 and 11-1/2 mph were featured in the Oliver 77 Diesel. Test G achieved a low-gear maximum pull of 4,818 lbs. at 2.16 mph at a slippage of 15.04 percent. This tractor's bare weight was 4,932 lbs., but 1,139 lbs. of cast iron were added to each rear wheel during Tests F, G and H. Standard equipment included 12-38-inch rear and 5.50-16-inch front rubber. No repairs or adjustments were noted during 40 hours of operation. Test H was run in third gear. At a rated output of 25.14 drawbar hp, the 77 Diesel pulled 2,225 lbs. at 4.24 mph with a slippage of 4.25 percent. Fuel economy was noted at 12.41 hp-hours per gallon of diesel fuel. Oliver featured its own six-cylinder diesel engine in this model. Of I-head design, it had a 193.9-cubic inch displacement with a 3-5/16 x 3-3/4-inch bore and stroke, along with a rated speed of 1,600 rpm. At a Test D-rated load of 31.61 belt hp, the 77 Diesel achieved 14.27 hp-hours per gallon. A slightly higher figure of 14.51 occurred under a Test B 100 percent maximum load of 35.79 belt hp.

Nebraska Test Data

Model: Oliver 77 (LPG)

Test No. 470

Date Tested: April 28 to May 10, 1952

Commercial propane gas was the featured fuel for this tractor. Other than this exception, made obvious by the tank atop the cowl area, there was little difference between the 77 shown here and the model tested under No. 425 of 1949. Advertised speeds of 2-1/2, 3-1/4, 4-1/3, 5-3/4, 6-5/8 and 11-5/8 mph were provided. Bare tractor weight was 4,670 lbs., and standard tires included 6.00-16-inch front and 12.38-inch rear rubber. Power was furnished by an Oliver six-cylinder I-head engine with a 193.9-cubic inch displacement. Rated at 1,600 rpm, this engine carried a 3-5/16 x 3-7/8-inch bore and stroke. During the limber-up run (Test A), a new heat exchanger was installed, otherwise no repairs or adjustments were noted during 58-1/2 hours of operation. Fuel economy was 7.32 hp-hours per gallon in Test H. Run at a rated drawbar load of 25.79 hp, this test manifested a pull of 2,240 lbs. at 4.32 mph with a 4.49 percent slippage. During this test and several other drawbar runs, an additional 1,420 lbs. of cast-iron ballast was added to each rear wheel. Test G delivered a low-gear maximum pull of 4,778 lbs. at 2.26 mph. Belt testing evoked 8.2 hp-hours per gallon of propane under a Test D-rated load of 32.51 hp, with the economy figure resting at 8.46 under a Test C operating maximum load of 34.49 hp.

Oliver Super 77 series

Oliver Super 77 tractors were built between 1954 and 1958. The high-clearance design is shown here, but the Super 77 was available in many different configurations, depending on customer needs. The six-cylinder, 216-cid engine used a 3-1/2 x 3-3/4-inch bore and stroke.

Nebraska Test Data

Model: Oliver Super 77 HC

Test No. 542

Date Tested: May 18 to May 24, 1955

At a Test C operating maximum load of 41.48 belt hp, the Super 77 achieved 11.67 hp-hours per gallon. This figure rested at 11.29 when under a Test D-rated belt load of 39.3 hp. Rated at 1,600 rpm, the Super 77 attained a peak torque of 269.9 lbs.-ft. at a speed of 899 rpm. Standard equipment included a six-cylinder, 216-cid engine with a 3-1/2 x 3-3/4-inch bore and stroke. With a bare weight of 5,131 lbs., the Super 77 was regularly equipped with 12-38 rear and 6.00-16-inch front tires. During Tests F, G and H, additional 1,706 lbs. of weight was used on each rear wheel. Test G, when run in low gear, yielded a maximum drawbar pull of 5,366 lbs. at 2.14 mph with a 17.1 percent slippage. At a Test H-rated drawbar load of 30.24 hp, the Super 77 pulled 2.006 lbs. at 5.65 mph, using fourth gear. Slippage was recorded at 4.32 percent, and fuel economy was 9.79 hp-hours per gallon. This tractor featured forward speeds 2-1/2, 3-1/4, 4-1/4, 5-5/8, 6-5/8 and 11-1/2 mph. During 47-1/2 hours of operating time, no repairs or adjustments were noted.

Nebraska Test Data

Model: Oliver Super 77 Diesel

Test No. 543

Date Tested: May 16 to May 26, 1955

This tractor, like the Super 77 gasoline model of Test No. 542, used a 216-cid engine of the same bore and stroke dimensions. Unlike the 7:1 compression ratio noted for the gasoline model, the diesel featured a 16:1 compression ratio. Advertised speeds and tire sizes were virtually identical for both tractors. Rated at 1,600 rpm, the Super 77 Diesel achieved a maximum 294.9 lbs.-ft. of torque with an engine speed of 1,215 rpm. Test D, run at a rated belt load of 39.14 hp, gave 15.09 hp-hours per gallon of diesel fuel. The combined Test B & C, run at a 100percent maximum belt load of 44.05 hp, gave a fuel economy of 14.78 hp-hours per gallon. A low-gear maximum pull of 5,659 lbs. was noted in Test G. Run at 2.17 mph, this test also indicated a slippage of 15.74 percent. At a Test H-rated drawbar load of 30.2 hp, a pull of 2,006 lbs. was recorded at 5.65 mph under a slippage of 4.23 percent. Fuel economy came in at 13.21 hp-hours per gallon of diesel fuel. During 45 hours of operation, no repairs or adjustments were noted.

COLLECTOR VALUES	1	2	3	4
77 ROW-CROP	$3,100	$1,700	$1,000	$500
77 STANDARD	$3,800	$2,200	$1,500	$900
77 SUPER	$3,800	$2,200	$1,500	$900

Production of the Oliver 66 tractor ran from 1949 to 1954. In the 1951 through 1954 period, it was available with a diesel engine, in addition to the gasoline and LP-gas models. In Nebraska Test No. 412, the Oliver 66 delivered nearly 25 belt hp. Test No. 467 was run on the diesel version. Shown here is the standard-tread model, just one of many different available styles.

Oliver 66 tractor

Nebraska Test Data

Model: Oliver Row-Crop 66 Diesel

Test No. 467

Date Tested: October 12 to October 18, 1951

Tests B & C, run at a 100 percent maximum load of 25.03 belt hp, yielded an economy of 14.21 hp-hours per gallon for the 66 Diesel tractor. When run at a Test D load of 22.45 belt hp, fuel economy came in at an almost identical figure of 14.22 hp-hours per gallon. Advertised speeds of 2-1/2, 3-1/4, 4-1/4, 5-5/8, 6-5/8 and 11-3/8 mph were featured, with Test H for rated drawbar load run in third gear. This 10-hour run indicated an economy of 12.09 hp-hours per gallon of diesel fuel with a load of 17.7 drawbar hp. During this test, the 66 Diesel pulled 1,587 lbs. at 4.18 mph with a 4.78 percent slippage. A low-gear maximum pull of 3,571 lbs. was noted in Test G. Standard tire equipment included 10-38-inch rear and 5.00-15-inch front rubber. The 3,795-lb. basic tractor weight was increased by 961 lbs. on each rear wheel during a portion of the drawbar tests. An Oliver diesel engine of I-head design was used. Its four cylinders carried a 3-5/16 x 3-3/4-inch bore and stroke with a rated speed of 1,600 rpm, giving a displacement of 129.3-cubic inches. No repairs or adjustments were noted during 40 hours of engine operating time.

Nebraska Test Data

Model: Oliver Row Crop 66 HC

Test No. 412

Date Tested: June 6 to June 24, 1949

Weighing 3,193 lbs., the Oliver 66 received another 1,184 lbs. of ballast on each rear wheel for Tests F, G and H. Standard equipment included 10-38-inch rear and 5.00-15-inch front rubber. The Oliver 66 was equipped with forward speeds of 2-1/2, 3-1/4, 4-1/4, 5-5/8, 6-5/8 and 11 mph. Third gear was used for Test H. At a rated load of 16.81 drawbar hp, the 66 pulled 1,517 lbs. at 4.16 mph with a 3.84 percent slippage. Fuel economy was registered at 9.89 hp-hours per gallon. A low-gear maximum pull of 3,207 lbs. was noted in Test G. Standard equipment included Oliver's own four-cylinder I-head engine with a rated speed of 1,600 rpm and a 3-5/16 x 3-3/4-inch bore and stroke. Also included were a Delco-Remy electrical system and a Marvel-Schebler TSX363 carburetor. No repairs or adjustments were noted during 55 hours of engine operating time. Under a Test C operating maximum load of 23.92 belt hp, the 66 delivered 11.99 hp-hours per gallon, compared to 11.81 under the Test D-rated load of 22.14 belt hp.

Oliver Super 66 Diesel tractor

Nebraska Test No. 544 was run on the Oliver Super 66 Diesel tractor and demonstrated nearly 30 drawbar hp for this model. A 12-volt electrical system came as standard equipment on this model. The four-cylinder engine used a 3-5/16 x 3-3/4-inch bore and stroke. Production of the Super 66 ran from 1954 to 1958.

Nebraska Test Data

Model: Oliver Super 66 HC

Test No. 541

Date Tested: May 16 to May 19, 1955

Standard equipment for this tractor included 10-38-inch rear and 5.00-15-inch front rubber. Weighing 3,943 lbs., the Super 66 was burdened with an additional 1,340 lbs. on each rear wheel during Tests F, G and H. Advertised speeds of 2.14, 3.08, 3.68, 5.31, 6.27 and 10.81 mph were featured. Fourth gear was used for the 10-hour run of Test H. With a rated drawbar output of 22.36 hp, this tractor pulled 1,615 lbs. at 5.19 mph with a slippage of 4.1 percent. Fuel economy was 9.83 hp-hours per gallon. Test G achieved a low-gear maximum pull of 4,309 lbs. at 1.89 mph with a slippage of 13.39 percent. The Super 66 was equipped with an Oliver six-cylinder I-head engine with a 3-1/2 x 3-3/4-inch bore and stroke. Rated at 1,750 on the drawbar and 2,000 rpm in the belt, this engine had a 144-cubic inch displacement. Engine torque peaked at 242.6 lbs.-ft. with an engine speed of 1,119 rpm. Under a Test D-rated belt load of 30.31 hp, the Super 66 delivered 10.95 hp-hours per gallon, rising to 11.38 at a Test C operating maximum load of 32.83 hp.

Nebraska Test Data

Model: Oliver Super 66 Diesel

Test No. 544

Date Tested: May 19 to May 26, 1955

Like the Super 66 gasoline model of Test No. 541, this diesel model carried a 144-cid engine with the same bore and stroke dimensions, as well as the same rated speed. With the exception of the engine itself, both tractors were virtually identical. Weighing 4,050 lbs., the Super 66 Diesel was burdened with an additional 1,338 lbs. of weight on each rear wheel during Tests F, G and H. At a Test H-rated drawbar load of 22.49 hp, the Super 66 Diesel pulled 1,622 lbs. at 5.2 mph with a slippage of 3.64 percent and produced an economy of 12.65 hp-hours per gallon of diesel. This tractor also achieved a Test G low-gear maximum pull of 4,393 lbs. at 1.91 mph under a slippage of 12.17 percent. Although rated at 2,000 rpm in the belt, engine torque peaked at 222.3 lbs.-ft. with an engine speed of 1,617 rpm. The combined Test B & C, run at a 100 percent maximum belt load of 33.69 hp, yielded 14.17 hp-hours per gallon. This figure increased to 14.28 under a Test D-rated belt load of 30.14 hp. No repairs or adjustments were noted during 38-1/2 hours of running time.

COLLECTOR VALUES	1	2	3	4
66 ROW-CROP	$5,500	$3,000	$1,000	$400
66 ROW-CROP (ADJUSTABLE WIDE FRONT)	$6,300	$3,800	$1,800	$1,000
66 STANDARD OR DIESEL	$5,750	$3,300	$1,300	$500
66 SUPER	$5,500	$3,000	$1,000	$400

Oliver Super 55 tractor

Introduced in 1954, the Oliver Super 55 was the company's first utility tractor. It remained on the market until 1958. In Nebraska Test No. 524 of 1954, the Super 55 gasoline model demonstrated almost 31 maximum drawbar hp, using a four-cylinder engine with a 3-1/2 x 3-3/4-inch bore and stroke. The Super 55 was also available with a diesel engine.

Nebraska Test Data

Model: Oliver Super 55 HC

Test No. 524

Date Tested: September 27 to October 12, 1954

Weighing 3,369 lbs., the Super 55 was furnished with 11-28-inch rear and 6.00-16-inch front tires. Also featured were forward speeds of 1.69, 2.58, 3.46, 5.33, 6.39 and 13.18 mph. During Tests F, G and H, an additional 1,066 lbs. were added to each rear wheel. Drawbar fuel economy was pegged at 10.08 hp- hours per gallon in Test H. This 10-hour rated drawbar run was made with an output of 23.37 hp, a pull of 1,722 lbs. at 5.09 mph, and slippage of 6.82 percent. A low-gear maximum pull of 3,539 lbs. was recorded in Test G. The Super 55 was equipped with an Oliver-built four-cylinder I-head engine with a 3-1/2 x 3-3/4-inch bore and stroke for a 144-cubic inch displacement. It was rated at 2,000 rpm for belt work and 1,750 rpm on the drawbar. At 981 rpm, a maximum engine torque of 228.9 lbs.-ft. was recorded. Test C, at an operating maximum load of 32.65 belt hp, produced 11.4 hp-hours per gallon, and slid to 10.91 at a Test D-rated load of 30.58 hp. During 43-1/2 hours of operating time, no repairs or adjustments were noted.

Nebraska Test Data

Model: Oliver Super 55 Diesel

Test No. 526

Date Tested: September 27 to October 14, 1954

The differences between this tractor and the Super 55 gasoline model noted in Test No. 524 were confined mainly to the different engine design. In the tractor illustrated here, a 144-cid engine with a 15.75:1 compression ratio was used. Weighing in at 3,467 lbs., the Super 55 Diesel was fitted with an additional 341 lbs. of liquid ballast and 720 lbs. of cast-iron weight on each rear wheel during Tests F, G and H. A maximum engine torque of 224.9 lbs.-ft. was achieved at 1,616 rpm. Test G yielded a low-gear maximum pull of 3,641 lbs. at 1.43 mph. The rated drawbar run of Test H produced 12.75 hp-hours per gallon of diesel fuel. This 10-hour run was made at 22.34 drawbar hp, along with a pull of 1,654 lbs. at 5.07 mph and slippage of 4.97 percent. The combined Test B and Test C, run at 100 percent maximum belt load, indicated a 14.12 hp-hours per gallon with a load of 33.71 hp, and slipped to 14.04 at a Test D-rated load of 28.97 belt hp. Some 46-1/2 hours of operating time was required for this test, with no repairs or adjustments being noted.

COLLECTOR VALUES	1	2	3	4
55 SUPER	$4,500	$2,700	$1,800	$800
44 SUPER	$8,000	$5,000	$3,500	$1,500

Oliver Super 99 tractor

Production of the Oliver Super 99 began in 1954, a continuation of the Oliver 99 that went back to 1937. These tractors were available with gasoline or diesel engines, the latter being the most popular. One variation was the Super 99–GM. This model was equipped with a General Motors diesel, although the 99 was also available with Oliver's own diesel model.

Nebraska Test Data

Model: Oliver Super 99 GM

Test No. 556

Date Tested: August 22 to August 27, 1955

A General Motors 3-71, three-cylinder, two-cycle supercharged engine was featured in this tractor. With a 4-1/4 x 5-inch bore and stroke, it had a 213-cubic inch displacement. Engine torque peaked at 504.2 lbs.-ft. with an engine speed of 1,309 rpm. The engine had a rated speed of 1,675 rpm. Weighing 10,155 lbs., the Super 99 GM featured 18-26-inch rear and 7.50-18-inch front tires. During Tests F, G and H, an additional 2,450 lbs. were added to each rear wheel. Advertised speeds of 2.63, 3.45, 4.66, 6.13, 7.7 and 13.68 mph were used. Third gear was used for the rated drawbar run of Test H. This test, made at a rated drawbar load of 58.69 hp, saw a pull of 5,299 lbs. at 4.15 mph with a slippage of 6.1 percent. Fuel economy was pegged at 12.38 hp-hours per gallon of diesel fuel. Test G manifested a low-gear maximum pull of 10,075 lbs. at 2.08 mph with a slippage of 16.47 percent. During 47-1/2 hours of operating time, no repairs or adjustments were noted. Belt testing indicated 13.75 hp hours per gallon at a Test D-rated load of 71.55 hp. Economy slipped to 13.28 at a Test B 100 percent maximum belt load of 78.74 belt hp.

Nebraska Test Data

Model: Oliver Super 99 D

Test No. 557

Date Tested: August 29 to September 3, 1955

Unlike the Oliver 99 GM of Test No. 556, this tractor carried Oliver's own six-cylinder diesel engine with a 4-inch bore and stroke. Rated at 1,675 rpm, it had a 302-cubic inch displacement. A peak engine torque of 405.7 lbs.-ft. was achieved with an engine speed of 1,226 rpm. Standard equipment included 18-26 rear and 7.50-18 front tires, along with advertised speeds of 2.46, 3.23, 4.37, 5.74, 7.22 and 12.81 mph. Bare tractor weight was 9,615 lbs., to which was added an additional 1,848 lbs. of ballast on each rear wheel during Tests F, G and H. Using third gear, the 10-hour run of Test H yielded an economy of 13.53 hp hours per gallon of diesel fuel. This test also indicated a pull of 4,156 lbs. at 4.17 mph and slippage of 4.06 percent. A low-gear maximum pull of 9,212 lbs. at 2.05 mph and slippage of 16.16 percent was recorded in Test G. During 39 hours of operating time, no repairs or adjustments were recorded. Test B, run at a 100 percent maximum belt load of 62.39 hp, produced an economy of 14.1 hp-hours per gallon of diesel fuel, while the Test D-rated load run at 55.41 ended with 14.75 hp-hours per gallon.

COLLECTOR VALUES	1	2	3	4
99-GM	--	$10,000	$5,000	$2,200

Oliver 550 series

Nebraska Test Data

Model: Oliver 550

Test No. 697

Date Tested: May 11 to May 26, 1959

At its rated engine speed of 2,000 rpm, the Oliver 550 delivered a maximum of 41.39 PTO hp and achieved 12.54 hp-hours per gallon. This tractor was equipped with an Oliver four-cylinder engine. Using a 3-5/8 x 3-1/4-inch bore and stroke, it had a displacement of 155-cubic inches. Standard features included 12-26-inch rear and 6.00-16-inch front tires, with six forward speeds ranging from 1.92 to 14.88 mph. The right brake was adjusted during the maximum drawbar runs, but no other entries were made in the "Repairs and Adjustments" section during 46-1/2 hours of running time. Using second gear, the 550 made a maximum pull of 5,149 lbs. at 2.29 mph with 14.61 percent slippage. Fourth gear was selected for the varying power drawbar and fuel consumption runs. At a maximum load of 35.36 drawbar hp, this tractor pulled 2,632 lbs. at 5.04 mph with 5.55 percent slippage. This two-hour run delivered 10.81 hp-hours per gallon. A 10-hour run, made at 75 percent of maximum pull, elicited 28.3 drawbar hp, a pull of 1,986 lbs. at 5.34 mph and slippage of 4.61 percent. Fuel economy was 10.01 hp-hours per gallon. Weighing 3,655 lbs., the 550's test weight was 6,815 lbs. through additional front and rear wheel ballast.

Nebraska Test Data

Model: Oliver 550 Diesel

Test No. 698

Date Tested: May 13 to May 26, 1959

Using an Oliver four-cylinder diesel engine, this tractor was virtually identical to the 550 gasoline style noted in Test No. 697. With a displacement of 155-cubic inches, the 550 Diesel carried a 3-5/8 x 3-3/4-inch bore and stroke. Weighing 3,730 lbs., it assumed a test weight of 6,835 lbs. with added ballast. All drawbar runs except one, titled "Maximum Power Without Ballast," were made with the added burden of additional front and/or rear cast-iron wheel weights or liquid ballast. Using second gear, a maximum pull of 5,110 lbs. was noted at 2.3 mph with 14.62 percent slippage. A two-hour run in fourth gear and at maximum available drawbar power noted an output of 35.09 hp with a pull of 2,643 lbs. at 4.98 mph and 6.25 percent slippage. Fuel economy totaled 12.51 hp-hours per gallon of diesel fuel. A 10-hour run, made at 75 percent of maximum pull and using fourth gear, indicated 28.33 drawbar hp plus a pull of 2,006 lbs. at 5.3 mph and 3.89 percent slippage. This test yielded 11.86 hp-hours per gallon. No repairs or adjustments were reported during 45 hours of running time. At its rated 2,000 rpm, the 550 Diesel delivered a maximum of 39.21 PTO hp, achieving 13.95 hp-hours per gallon in the process

Nebraska Test Data

Model: Oliver 770

Test No. 648

Date Tested: April 21 to May 7, 1958

Under a Test C operating maximum load of 47.59 belt hp, the 770 yielded 12.44 hp hours per gallon, compared to an economy figure of 11.64 at a Test D-rated belt load of 43.89 hp. Oliver used a six-cylinder, 3-1/2 x 3-3/4-inch engine in this tractor. Rated at 1,750 rpm, it carried a 216.48-cubic inch displacement. Features also included six forward gears ranging from 2.11 to 10.8 mph, along with 15.5-38 rear and 6.00-16-inch front tires as standard equipment. Bare tractor weight was 5,945 lbs., rising to 9,145 lbs. during most of the drawbar testing due to additional front and rear wheel ballast. Test G, when run in low gear, yielded a maximum pull of 7,000 lbs. at 1.88 mph against a slippage of 14.02 percent. At a Test H-rated drawbar load of 34.8 hp, the 770 pulled 2,375 lbs. at 5.49 mph with a slippage of 3.11 percent and ended this 10-hour run with a fuel economy of 10.45 hp-hours per gallon. During 42 hours of operating time, no repairs or adjustments were recorded.

Nebraska Test Data

Model: Oliver 770 Diesel

Test No. 649

Date Tested: April 23 to May 7, 1958

Weighing 5,565 lbs., the 770 Diesel featured 15.5-38-inch rear and 6.00-16-inch front tires. For testing purposes, 1,595 lbs. was added to each rear wheel, plus another 180 lbs. on each front wheel. This tractor used six forward speeds ranging from 2.11 to 10.8 mph. Fourth gear was selected for the 10-hour run of Test H. This test, run at a rated drawbar load of 34.92 hp, yielded a pull of 2,442 lbs. at 5.36 mph with a slippage of 2.55 percent. Fuel economy at the drawbar was posted at 12.85 hp-hours per gallon of diesel fuel. The low-gear run of Test G noted a maximum pull of 7,137 lbs. at 1.86 mph with a slippage of 14.87 percent. During 44 hours of operation, no repairs or adjustments were noted. The 770 Diesel featured an Oliver six-cylinder engine with a 3-1/2 x 3-3/4-inch bore and stroke. Rated at 1,750 rpm, it had a 216-cubic inch displacement. At a Test D-rated belt load of 43 hp, fuel economy was 14.12 hp-hours per gallon. A slightly higher economy figure of 14.31 appeared under a 100 percent maximum belt load of 48.8 hp.

Oliver 880 series

Nebraska Test Data

Model: Oliver 880

Test No. 647

Date Tested: April 21 to May 1, 1958

Two fan pulleys were replaced during testing, otherwise no repairs or adjustments were noted during 50 hours of operating time. The 880 was equipped with a six-cylinder engine with a 3-3/4 x 4-inch bore and stroke for a 265.07-cubic inch displacement. Rated speed was 1,750 rpm. Also featured were six forward speeds of 2.07, 2.94, 3.57, 5.06, 6.22 and 10.7 mph. Tires included 14-34-inch rear and 6.50-16-inch front. Weighing 5,631 lbs., the 880 was burdened with an additional 641 lbs. of liquid ballast and 1,595 lbs. of cast-iron weight during much of the drawbar testing. In addition, the front wheels carried 79 lbs. of liquid ballast plus 269 lbs. of iron weights for a total test weight of 10,799 lbs. Test G, run in low gear, yielded a maximum pull of 7,998 lbs. at 1.79 mph against a slippage of 14.11 percent. Fourth gear was used during the 10-hour run of Test H. This test, made at a rated load of 42.89 drawbar hp, noted a pull of 3,103 lbs. at 5.18 mph and a slippage of 3.52 percent. Fuel economy came in at 10.21 hp-hours per gallon. Belt testing indicated 12.07 hp hours per gallon at a Test D-rated load of 54.68 hp, while under a Test C operating maximum load of 57.43 hp, fuel economy was registered at 12.20 hp-hours per gallon.

Nebraska Test Data

Model: Oliver 880 Diesel

Test No. 650

Date Tested: April 23 to May 7, 1958

Although the advertising photograph noted that 12 forward speeds were available, the tractor submitted for testing indicated six speeds of 2.07, 2.94, 3.57, 5.06, 6.22 and 10.7 mph. Also featured were 14-34-inch rear and 6.50-16-inch front tires. Without added ballast, the 880 Diesel weighed 5,735 lbs., although 2,215 lbs. were added to each rear wheel, along with another 340 lbs. on each front wheel, giving a total test weight of 10,485 lbs., including the operator. Test H, run in fourth gear, was made at a rated drawbar load of 41.74 hp. In this run, a pull of 3,014 lbs. was recorded at 5.19 mph with a slippage of 3.02 percent. Economy was 12.75 hp-hours per gallon of diesel fuel. The low-gear run of Test G elicited a maximum pull of 8,118 lbs. at 1.8 mph with 12.64 percent slippage. The 88 Diesel carried a six-cylinder, 3-3/4 x 4-inch engine rated at 1,750 rpm for a displacement of 265.07-cubic inches. No repairs or adjustments were noted during 41-1/2 hours of running time. At a 100 percent maximum belt load of 59.4 hp, fuel economy was 14.75 hp-hours per gallon, and slipped to 14.37 under a Test D-rated belt load of 52.63 hp.

Oliver 950 Diesel

Nebraska Test Data

Model: Oliver 950

Test No. 660

Date Tested: July 7 to July 17, 1958

This standard-tread diesel tractor featured Oliver's own four-cylinder engine rated at 1,800 rpm and used a 4-inch bore and stroke for a 302-cubic inch displacement. Also included were six forward speeds ranging from 2.43 to 12.68 mph, along with 18-26-inch rear and 7.50-18-inch front tires. Bare tractor weight was 10,415 lbs., but was augmented with 1,485 lbs. of liquid ballast in each rear tire, plus 117 lbs. of ballast for each front wheel, for a total test weight, including the operator, of 13,620 lbs. Test D, run at a rated belt load of 59.75 hp, indicated 13.45 hp-hours per gallon of diesel fuel. At a 100 percent maximum load of 67.23 hp, fuel economy was an even 14 hp-hours per gallon. Drawbar testing included 100 percent maximum load in all forward gears under Test G. This test, when run in low gear, achieved a maximum pull of 10,011 lbs. at 2.16 mph with 11.26 percent slippage. Test H, run in third gear and at a rated drawbar load of 48.76 hp, achieved 12.32 hp-hours per gallon. During this test, a flexible oil line leading to the engine oil filter leaked. This was replaced and the test continued. With this exception, no repairs or adjustments were noted during 41 hours of operating time.

Oliver 990 series

Nebraska Test Data

Model: Oliver 990 GM

Test No. 661

Date Tested: July 7 to July 18, 1958

Featured in this tractor was a General Motors 3-71 two-cycle diesel engine with a blower. Rated at 1,800 rpm, it used a 4-1/4 x 5-inch bore and stroke for a 213-cubic inch displacement. The 990 GM had six forward speeds ranging from 2.33 to 12.19 mph. Tire equipment included 18-26-inch rear and 7.50-18- inch front rubber. Bare tractor weight was 10,980 lbs., to which was added 2,625 lbs. on each rear wheel, plus another 218 lbs. for each front wheel, bringing total test weight, including the operator, to 16,665 lbs. Test H, run in third gear, was made at a rated drawbar load of 61.46 hp. This test indicated a pull of 5,361 lbs. at 4.3 mph and slippage of 3.7 percent. Fuel economy was 12.24 hp hours per gallon of diesel fuel. Test G, when run in low gear, yielded a maximum pull of 12,629 lbs. at 2.08 mph with 14.65 percent slippage. Belt testing indicated an economy of 13.37 hp-hours per gallon at a 100 percent maximum load of 84.10 hp. Test D noted 13.61 hp-hours per gallon at a rated load of 75.46 hp. No repairs or adjustments were noted during 38 hours of operating time.

Nebraska Test Data

Model: Oliver 995 GM Lugmatic

Test No. 662

Date Tested: July 7 to July 23, 1958

This tractor was equipped with a hydraulic torque converter, which automatically loaded the engine by controlling the forward travel according to the applied load. This was the major difference between the 995 GM Lugmatic shown here and the 990 GM of Test No. 661. Another difference was, while the previous test tractor was rated at 1,800 rpm, the speed was raised to 2,000 rpm for the tractor illustrated in this test. The torque converter drive permitted a speed range of 0.9 to 13.8 mph. Standard equipment included 18-26-inch rear and 7.50-18-inch front tires. Weighing 11,245 lbs., an additional 2,530 lbs. was added to each rear wheel, along with 220 lbs. for each front wheel, bringing total test weight to 16,745 lbs. The 10-hour Test H run was made at 75 percent pull at observed maximum hp, and using third gear. This test indicated 61.06 drawbar hp, along with a pull of 4,871 lbs. at 4.7 mph and 3.25 percent slippage. Economy was 10.19 hp-hours per gallon of diesel fuel. Test G, run in low gear, gave a pull of 12,538 lbs. at 1.88 mph with 13.1 percent slippage. No repairs or adjustments of consequence were recorded during 50 hours of running time. Test D, run at a rated belt load of 76.13 hp, yielded 12.35 hp-hours per gallon, and climbed to 12.6 at a 100 percent maximum belt load of 85.37 hp.

Nebraska Test Data

Model: Oliver 1600 Diesel

Test No. 840

Date Tested: May 29 to June 13, 1963

Rated at 1,900 rpm, the Oliver 1600 Diesel carried a six-cylinder engine with a 3-3/4 x 4-inch bore and stroke for a 265-cubic inch displacement. Operating at rated engine speed, 57.95 maximum PTO hp was observed, together with an economy of 13.88 hp-hours per gallon. A second run made at 540 PTO rpm and a corresponding engine speed of 1,740 rpm noted an output of 54.79 hp, together with an economy figure of 14.08. This tractor featured six forward speeds in direct-drive with another six available using the Hydra-Power system. A total speed range of 1.85 to 13.57 mph was provided. No repairs or adjustments were noted during 37 hours of running time. Standard equipment for this 7,180-lb. unit included 16.9-34-inch rear and 6.50-16-inch front tires. Adding front and rear ballast, test weight came to 11,020 lbs. Fourth gear in the Hydra-Power range delivered a maximum of 46.9 drawbar hp, and yielded 11.76 hp-hours per gallon. Also indicated was a pull of 3,915 lbs. at 4.49 mph with 4.63 percent slippage. The 10-hour drawbar run at 75 percent pull noted an output of 38.65 hp, a pull of 3,087 lbs. at 4.7 mph and 3.63 percent slippage. Fuel economy totaled 10.76 hp-hours per gallon.

Oliver 1600 series

Nebraska Test Data

Model: Oliver 1600

Test No. 841

Date Tested: June 3 to June 13, 1963

Using fourth gear in the Hydra-Power range, this tractor delivered 9.08 hp-hours per gallon under a maximum available output of 47.09 drawbar hp. Also indicated in this two-hour test was a pull of 3,942 lbs. at 4.48 mph with 5.14 percent slippage. The 10-hour drawbar run made at 75 percent pull noted an economy figure of 8.36 with an output of 38.55 hp. Other statistics included a pull of 3,074 lbs. at 4.7 mph with 3.81 percent slippage. Chassis design and tire sizes were the same for this tractor as previously noted in Test No. 841. The test weight of 10,935 lbs. included 888 lbs. of liquid ballast and 725 lbs. of cast-iron weight on each rear wheel. In addition, each front wheel carried 190 lbs. of cast-iron weight. Featured in the 1600 gasoline model was a six-cylinder, 231-cid engine with a 3-1/2 x 4-inch bore and stroke and a rated speed of 1,900 rpm. At rated speed, 56.5 maximum PTO hp was observed, with an economy of 10.44 hp-hours per gallon. At 540 PTO rpm and a corresponding engine speed of 1,740 rpm, 54.18 hp was noted, with 10.26 hp-hours per gallon. No repairs or adjustments were required during 44-1/2 hours of operating time.

Nebraska Test Data

Model: Oliver 1800

Test No. 766

Date Tested: October 3 to October 11, 1960

The Oliver 1800 featured the company's own six-cylinder engine rated at 2,000 rpm. Using a 3-3/4 x 4- inch bore and stroke, it had a 265-cubic inch displacement. Also featured was a selective-gear fixed-ratio transmission with six forward speeds ranging from 1.59 to 14.3 mph. The rear tires were 18.4-34-inch size, with 7.50-15-inch front tires. As presented for testing, the 1800 weighed 8,410 lbs., but additional front and rear ballast gave a test weight of 14,335 lbs. Using fourth gear, and at a maximum available load of 61.66 drawbar hp, this tractor delivered 11.71 hp-hours per gallon. Other test statistics included a pull of 4,427 lbs. at 5.22 mph and 4.33 percent slippage. The 10-hour drawbar economy run, made at 75 percent pull, indicated an output of 50.32 hp, a pull of 3,485 lbs. at 5.41 mph and 3.51 percent slippage. This test revealed an economy of 10.99 hp-hours per gallon. At rated engine speed, the 1800 delivered a maximum of 73.92 PTO hp and 13.18 hp-hours per gallon. No repairs or adjustments were required during 45 hours of operating time.

Nebraska Test Data

Model: Oliver 1800 Diesel

Test No. 767

Date Tested: October 4 to October 12, 1960

Transmission specifications and tire sizes for this tractor remained virtually identical to the 1800 gasoline model of Test No. 766. A major difference was the Oliver-built six-cylinder diesel engine. Rated at 2,000 rpm, it carried a 3-7/8 x 4-inch bore and stroke for a 283-cubic inch displacment. At rated engine speed, a fuel economy of 14.18 hp-hours per gallon resulted with a PTO output of 70.15 hp. Weighing 8,585 lbs., the 1800 Diesel assumed a test weight of 14,345 lbs. with additional front and rear ballast. Using fourth gear, 62.55 maximum available hp was observed in a two-hour economy run. This test yielded a pull of 4,472 lbs. at 5.25 mph with 4.33 percent slippage. A 10-hour economy run, made at 75 percent pull, noted an output of 49.01 hp, a pull of 3,340 lbs. at 5.5 mph and 3.12 percent slippage. Fuel economy in this test totaled 12.29 hp-hours per gallon. During 40 hours of running time, no repairs or adjustments were required.

Nebraska Test Data

Model: Oliver 1800 Series B Diesel

Test No. 831

Date Tested: November 6 to November 15, 1962

Oliver featured its own six-cylinder diesel engine in this tractor. Rated at 2,200 rpm, it used a 3-7/8 x 4-3/8-inch bore and stroke for a 310-cubic inch displacement. Also featured was a 16.25:1 compression ratio. At rated engine speed, 77.04 maximum PTO hp was observed. Also recorded was an economy of 13.93 hp-hours per gallon. During the preliminary PTO run, a new secondary fuel filter was installed, but with this exception, no repairs or adjustments were required during 54 hours of operation. The selective-gear fixed-ratio transmission also featured partial range power shifting. This gave a total of 10 forward speeds, ranging from 1.17 to 14.37 mph. Tire equipment included 18.4-34-inch rear and 7.50-15-inch front rubber. With front and rear ballast, test weight totaled 11,345 lbs., although bare tractor weight was 9,205 lbs. Using fourth gear in the low range (Hydra-Power Drive), a two-hour drawbar economy run made at 64.53 maximum available hp yielded 11.84 hp hours per gallon. The two-hour run also noted a pull of 6,479 lbs. at 3.74 mph with 6.8 percent slippage. A 10-hour run at 75 percent pull manifested an output of 53.19 drawbar hp, a pull of 5,004 lbs. at 3.99 mph and slippage of 4.91 percent. Fuel economy totaled 11.26 hp-hours per gallon.

Nebraska Test Data

Model: Oliver 1800 Series B Four-wheel Drive Diesel

Test No. 832

Date Tested: November 16 to December 1, 1962

Extensive tests were made on this tractor using both direct-drive and Hydra-Power, with further combinations of the front-wheel-drive engaged and disengaged. Full details of these extensive tests may be found in the complete report on Test No. 832, available from the Tractor Test Laboratory at nominal cost. The same 310-cid engine was featured here as found in the 1800 Series B model of Test No. 832. At its rated speed, a maximum of 76.97 PTO hp was observed, with a fuel economy of 13.94 hp-hours per gallon. Using fourth gear Hydra-Power, a two-hour run at 64 maximum available hp indicated a pull of 6,282 lbs. at 3.82 mph with 4.7 percent slippage. Fuel economy was pegged at 11.65 hp-hours per gallon. This test was run with the front-wheel-drive in gear. The same test when run without the front-wheel-drive noted an output of 61.56 hp, a pull of 6,173 lbs. at 3.74 mph and 6.56 percent slippage. Economy came in at 11.48 hp-hours per gallon. A 10-hour economy run, made at 75 percent pull and with the front wheels in gear, indicated 52.35 drawbar hp, a pull of 4,803 lbs. at 4.09 mph and 3.23 percent slippage. Economy was posted at 10.94 hp-hours per gallon. Following this run came a two-hour test at 75 percent pull with the front-wheel-drive disengaged. Shown here was an output of 50.45 hp, a pull of 4,707 lbs. at 4.02 mph and 4.59 percent slippage. As presented for testing, this tractor weighed 10,675 lbs. and was equipped with 18.4-34-inch rear and 13.6-24-inch front tires. Using additional front and rear ballast, the test weight totaled 17,002 lbs.

Nebraska Test Data

Model: Oliver 1800 Series B

Test No. 839

Date Tested: May 22 to June 4, 1963

This tractor featured a selective-gear fixed-ratio transmission that included partial range power shifting through Oliver's Hydra-Power system. In all, 12 forward speeds were available, ranging from 1.17 to 14.37 mph. The test weight of 14,435 lbs. included front and rear ballast. The bare tractor weighed 8,980 lbs. Standard equipment also included 18.4-34-inch rear and 7.50-15-inch front tires. Using fourth gear with Hydra-Power engaged, a two-hour run at 67.81

Oliver 1800 Series B

maximum available drawbar hp yielded 9.86 hp-hours per gallon. Also recorded was a pull of 6,839 lbs. at 3.72 mph with 7.16 percent slippage. The 75 percent run for 10 hours saw an economy figure of 9.19. This test yielded 55.47 drawbar hp, a pull of 5,275 lbs. at 3.94 mph and 5.27 percent slippage. Oliver equipped this tractor with its own six-cylinder, 283-cid engine. Rated at 2,200 rpm, it used a 3-7/8 x 4-inch bore and stroke. At rated engine speed, a maximum output of 80.16 PTO hp was observed, with a fuel economy of 12.14 hp-hours per gallon.

Nebraska Test Data

Model: Oliver 1800 Series B, Four-Wheel-Drive

Test No. 846

Date Tested: September 10 to September 19, 1963

A selective-gear fixed-ratio transmission with partial range power shifting was featured on this tractor. Using either direct-drive or the Hydra-Power system, 12 forward speeds were available in a range from 1.17 to 14.37 mph. Standard equipment included 18.4-34 rear and 13.6-24-inch front tires. Weighing in at 10,155 lbs., this unit was enhanced with front and rear ballast for a total test weight of 17,755 lbs. Fourth gear in the Hydra-Power range gave 68.40 maximum available drawbar hp with an economy of 10.45 hp-hours per gallon. Also noted in this test was a pull of 6,700 lbs. at 3.83 mph with 4.95 percent slippage. The same gear selection at 75 percent pull recorded 54.98 hp over a 10-hour run. Test economy came to 9.83 hp-hours per gallon. The 10-hour economy test saw a pull of 5,079 lbs. at 4.06 mph with 3.5 percent slippage. Minor governor repairs were made during the preliminary PTO runs, but otherwise no repairs or adjustments were recorded during 40-1/2 hours of operation. This tractor was equipped with a 283-cid, six-cylinder engine. Rated at 2,200 rpm, it featured a 3-7/8 x 4-inch bore and stroke. At rated engine speed, 80.72 maximum PTO hp was observed, with 12.3 hp-hours per gallon.

Nebraska Test Data

Model: Oliver 1900 Diesel

Test No. 768

Date Tested: October 3 to October 8, 1960

At its rated engine speed of 2,000 rpm, the Oliver 1900 delivered a maximum of 89.35 PTO hp with a fuel economy of 14.4 hp-hours per gallon. This tractor was equipped with a General Motors four-cylinder two-cycle engine complete with blower. The 3-7/8 x 4-1/2-inch bore and stroke gave a 212.4-cubic inch displacement. A selective-gear fixed-ratio transmission provided six forward speeds ranging from 1.49 to 13.35 mph. Also featured were 18-26-inch rear and 7.50-18-inch front tires. As presented, the 1900 weighed 11,925 lbs., but the addition of rear wheel ballast brought the test weight to 16,665 lbs. In fourth gear, a two-hour economy run made at 82.85 maximum available drawbar hp saw a pull of 6,282 lbs. at 4.95 mph with 3.77 percent slippage. This test yielded 13.04 hp-hours per gallon. The 10-hour drawbar economy run, made at 75 percent pull, indicated an output of 62.89 hp, a pull of 4,599 lbs. at 5.13 mph and 2.99 percent slippage. This test registered 12.52 hp-hours per gallon. No repairs or adjustments were noted during 44 hours of operation.

Oliver 1900 and 1900 Series B

Nebraska Test Data

Model: Oliver 1900 Series B Diesel

Test No. 824

Date Tested: September 17 to September 25, 1962

At its rated engine speed of 2,000 rpm, the 1900-B yielded 14.97 hp-hours per gallon while delivering a maximum PTO output of 98.54 hp. This tractor was equipped with a General Motors four-cylinder two-cycle blower-equipped engine. Its 3-7/8 x 4-1/2-inch bore and stroke gave a 212.4-cubic inch displacement. Also featured was a selective-gear fixed-ratio transmission that included partial range power shifting. Using either direct or Hydra-Power drive, 12 forward speeds were available with a range from 1.08 to 13.19 mph. Also featured were 23.1-26-inch rear and 7.50-18-inch front tires. Weighing 11,955 lbs., this unit assumed a test weight of 18,355 lbs. through additional rear wheel ballast. Using fourth gear, a 2-hour run made at 84.44 maximum available hp yielded a pull of 6,409 lbs. at 4.94 mph with 4.21 percent slippage. Fuel economy came to 12.95 hp-hours per gallon. The 10-hour drawbar run, made at 75 percent pull, observed an economy of 12.21. This test also showed an output of 67.27 hp, a pull of 4,876 lbs. at 5.17 mph and 3.29 percent slippage. Hydraulic oil leakage occurred from the remote cylinder couplings during the PTO runs. After replacing the couplings with pipe plugs, the test continued. With this exception, no repairs or adjustments were noted during 39 hours of operating time.

Nebraska Test Data

Model: Oliver 1900 Series B, Four-Wheel-Drive Diesel

Test No. 847

Date Tested: September 13 to September 20, 1963

The General Motors four-cylinder, two-cycle supercharged engine used in this tractor was rated at 2,200 rpm. Its 212.4-cubic inch displacement resulted from a 3-7/8 x 4-1/2-inch bore and stroke. At rated engine speed, a maximum of 100.62 PTO hp was observed, together with 13.48 hp-hours per gallon. Weighing 12,905 lbs., it used 24.5-32 rear and 13.6-24-inch front tires. The addition of front and rear ballast brought the test weight to 20,385 lbs. Also featured in this tractor was a selective-gear fixed-ratio transmission that offered partial range power shifting through the Hydra-Drive system. In all, 12 forward speeds were available with a range from 1.71 to 15.34 mph. A two-hour drawbar run using fourth gear in the Hydra-Power range indicated a maximum output of 88.27 hp. A pull of 7,905 lbs. at 4.19 mph with 3.76 percent slippage was noted. Economy was pegged at 12.25 hp-hours per gallon. This figure slipped to 12.03 in a 10-hour run made at 75 percent pull. The latter test indicated an output of 70.66 hp, a pull of 6,007 lbs. at 4.41 mph and 2.86 percent slippage. Except for replacement of minor governor parts, no repairs or adjustments were noted during 44-1/2 hours of operating time.

Nebraska Test Data

Model: Oliver 1550 Diesel

Test No. 943

Date Tested: June 8 to June 15, 1966

Weighing in at 7,020 lbs., this unit received 698 lbs. of liquid ballast and 140 lbs. of cast-iron weight on each rear wheel for a total test weight of 8,730 lbs. Standard equipment included 15.5-38-inch rear and 6.00-16-inch front tires. Also featured was a selective-gear fixed-ratio transmission with partial range power shifting. In all, 12 forward speeds were available in a range from 1.93 to 13.57 mph, using either direct-drive or Oliver's Hydra-Power system. Using fourth gear in the Hydra-Power range gave 45.72 maximum available drawbar hp in the two-hour economy run. This test yielded 10.43 hp-hours per gallon, recorded a pull of 3,800 lbs. at 4.51 mph and slippage of 5.57 percent. The 10-hour run at 75 percent pull saw an output of 36.88 hp with 10.10 hp-hours per gallon. Also recorded in the 10-hour test was a pull of 2,848 lbs. at 4.86 mph with slippage of 4.1 percent. No repairs or adjustments were reported during 41-1/2 hours of running time. Oliver equipped this tractor with its own six-cylinder diesel engine rated at 2,200 rpm. Using a 3-5/8 x 3-3/4-inch bore and stroke, it had a 232-cubic inch displacement. At rated engine speed, it developed a maximum of 53.5 PTO hp while yielding 12.35 hp hours per gallon.

Nebraska Test Data

Model: Oliver 1550

Test No. 944

Date Tested: June 8 to June 16, 1966

Except for using a gasoline engine, it was nearly identical to the Oliver 1550 Diesel of the previous test. In this case, Oliver featured its own six-cylinder gasoline engine with a rated speed of 2,200 rpm. Its 232-cubic inch displacement resulted from a 3-5/8 x 3-3/4-inch bore and stroke. Operating at rated speed, 53.34 PTO hp was evidenced, with a fuel economy of 10.08 hp-hours per gallon. The bare tractor weight of 6,840 lbs. was enhanced with rear wheel ballast for a total test weight of 8,530 lbs. As in the previous test, fourth gear's Hydra-Power range was

Oliver 1550 series

used for the drawbar economy runs. At 45.37 maximum available drawbar hp, a resultant 9.25 hp-hours per gallon was recorded. This two-hour test also recorded a pull of 3,782 lbs. at 4.5 mph with 5.79 percent slippage. Operating at 37.33 hp, the 10-hour economy run achieved 8.54 hp-hours per gallon. Also indicated was a pull of 3,895 lbs. at 4.93 mph with 3.13 percent slippage. No repairs or adjustments were made during 44 hours of operating time.

Oliver 1650

Nebraska Test Data

Model: Oliver 1650 Diesel

Test No. 873

Date Tested: November 4 to November 16, 1964

An Oliver-built six-cylinder diesel engine was featured in the tractor shown here. Rated at 2,200 rpm, it carried a 3-7/8 x 4-inch bore and stroke for a displacement of 283-cubic inches. At rated engine speed, 66.28 maximum PTO hp was observed, with 13.35 hp-hours per gallon. Using either direct-drive or the Hydra-Power system, 12 forward speeds were available from 1.86 to 13.66 mph. Standard equipment for this 7,815-lb. tractor included 15.5-38-inch rear and 6.50-16-inch front tires. During drawbar testing, the addition of front and rear ballast raised the weight to 11,035 lbs. The drawbar fuel economy runs were made in fourth gear's Hydra-Power range. With a maximum output of 56.51 drawbar hp, a two-hour run indicated a pull of 4,660 lbs. at 4.55 mph with 5.25 percent slippage. Economy came in at 11.69 hp-hours per gallon. The 10-hour drawbar run at 75 percent pull saw an economy of 10.45. The latter test, run at an output of 45.61 hp, indicated a pull of 3,564 lbs. at 4.8 mph with 4.12 percent slippage. No repairs or adjustments were reported during 44-1/2 hours of operating time.

Nebraska Test Data

Model: Oliver 1650

Test No. 874

Date Tested: November 6 to November 23, 1964

Nearly identical in chassis design to the Oliver 1650 Diesel of Test No. 873, this gasoline version differed primarily in the engine itself. A 265-cid, six-cylinder engine was featured in this tractor. Rated at 2,200 rpm, it used a 3-3/4 x 4-inch bore and stroke. At rated engine speed, 66.72 maximum PTO hp was recorded, along with an economy of 11.71 hp-hours per gallon. Weighing 7,575 lbs., the 1650 gasoline model was burdened with rear wheel ballast for a total test weight of 9,755 lbs. Fourth gear in the Hydra-Power range was used for the drawbar economy tests. At 58.67 maximum available drawbar hp, a pull of 4,887 lbs. was recorded at 4.5 mph with 6.02 percent slippage. This two-hour test saw an economy of 10.09 hp-hours per gallon. The 10-hour run at 75 percent pull yielded an economy figure of 9.32. Also recorded in the 10-hour economy test was an output of 48.29 hp, a pull of 3,751 lbs. at 4.83 mph and slippage of 4.56 percent. The complete test reports showed drawbar fuel economy at maximum power, 75 percent pull and 50 percent pull. Maximum power runs with ballast were made for each tractor, using various forward gears, but fuel economy wasn't recorded in these tests. Another test was run at maximum power without ballast, and drawbar testing also included a series of varying drawbar pull and travel speed runs. This and additional data on each tractor may be found in the complete test report issued by the Tractor Test Laboratory.

Oliver 1750 series

Nebraska Test Data

Model: Oliver 1750

Test No. 961

Date Tested: May 22 to June 20, 1967

Rated at 2,400 rpm, this model featured a six-cylinder, 283-cid engine with a 3-7/8 x 4-inch bore and stroke. At rated engine speed, 80.31 maximum PTO hp was developed and an economy of 11.55 hp- hours per gallon was achieved. Other features included a selective-gear fixed-ratio transmission with partial range power shifting. In all, 12 forward speeds were available, ranging from 1.18 to 14.45 mph. No repairs or adjustments were reported during 53-1/2 hours of operation. Using sixth gear, 67.05 maximum available drawbar hp was demonstrated in the two-hour economy run. This test achieved a fuel economy of 9.53 hp-hours per gallon. Also recorded was a pull of 6,859 lbs. at 3.67 mph and slippage of 7.98 percent. The 10-hour run at 75 percent pull noted 8.71 hp-hours per gallon against a load of 54.72 hp. Other statistics included a pull of 5,204 lbs. at 3.94 mph and slippage of 5.37 percent. While the bare tractor weight was 9,760 lbs., this was raised to a test weight of 12,150 lbs. by additional front and rear ballast. Standard equipment included 18.4-34-inch rear and 7.50-15-inch front tires.

Nebraska Test Data

Model: Oliver 1750 Diesel

Test No. 962

Date Tested: May 22 to June 12, 1967

The chassis design of this tractor closely followed the pattern previously illustrated in Test No. 961. A major exception was the six-cylinder, Oliver-built diesel engine. Rated at 2,400 rpm, this 310-cid model used a 3-7/8 x 4-3/8-inch bore and stroke. Operating at rated engine speed, 80.05 maximum PTO hp was observed, as was an economy of 14.75 hp-hours per gallon. No repairs or adjustments were required during 48-1/2 hours of operation. Since the drawbar economy runs were made in sixth gear, just as noted for the gasoline model of Test No. 961, interesting comparisons may be made between the gasoline and diesel models. In the two-hour economy run, made at 65.28 maximum available drawbar hp, fuel economy was 12.22 hp-hours per gallon. Also recorded was a pull of 6,637 lbs. at 3.69 mph with slippage of 7.43 percent. The 10-hour run at 75 percent pull indicated 12.42 hp-hours per gallon against a load of 54.12 drawbar hp. Other statistics included a pull of 5,230 lbs. at 3.88 mph with slippage of 5.85 percent. Weighing in at 9,990 lbs., this unit carried a test weight of 12,515 lbs. through the addition of front and rear ballast.

Nebraska Test Data

Model: Oliver 1850 Four-Wheel-Drive Diesel

Test No. 869

Date Tested: October 26 to November 3, 1964

A Perkins six-cylinder diesel engine was featured in this tractor. Rated at 2,400 rpm, it developed a maximum of 92.92 PTO hp while delivering 14.74 hp-hours per gallon. Its 3-7/8 x 5-inch bore and stroke gave a 352-cubic inch displacement. Other features included 23.1-34 rear and 13.6-24 front tires to carry the total tractor weight of 10,965 lbs. A selective-gear fixed-ratio transmission with partial range power shifting provided 12 forward speeds ranging from 1.28 to 15.62 mph, using either direct-drive or the Hydra-Power system. No repairs or adjustments were noted during 40 hours of operation. Using fourth gear in the Hydra-Power range saw a maximum output of 83.55 drawbar hp with an accrued economy of 13.23 hp-hours per gallon. This 2-hour run also indicated a pull of 7,458 lbs. at 4.2 mph with 4.52 percent slippage. Running at 75 percent pull, a 10-hour drawbar economy run set this figure at 12.54 against an output of 65.90 hp. Other statistics included a pull of 5,706 lbs. at 4.33 mph with 3.16 percent slippage. The addition of front and rear ballast brought the tractor test weight to 16,145 lbs.

Nebraska Test Data

Model: Oliver 1850 Diesel

Test No. 870

Date Tested: October 26 to November 5, 1964

The 1850 Diesel tractor carried the same Perkins six-cylinder, 352-cid engine as previously noted for the Oliver 1850 4 x 4 tractor of Test No. 869. Using either direct-drive or the Hydra-Power system, 12 forward speeds were available in a range from 1.18 to 14.45 mph. Standard equipment for this 9,265-lb. unit included 18.4-34-inch rear and 7.50-15-inch front tires. The addition of front and rear ballast raised the test weight to 14,305 lbs. Fourth gear in the Hydra-Power range yielded a maximum output of 80.04 drawbar hp with 13.09 hp-hours per gallon. Also noted in this 2-hour run was a pull of 8,188 lbs. at 3.67 mph with 8.93 percent slippage. The following 10-hour run at 75 percent pull saw an economy of 12.59 hp-hours per gallon against an output of 65.58 drawbar hp. Also evidenced was a pull of 6,361 lbs. at 3.87 mph and slippage of 6.69 percent. No repairs or adjustments were noted on this tractor during 44-1/2 hours of running time. At rated engine speed, PTO testing indicated an economy of 14.74 hp-hours per gallon against a maximum output of 92.94 PTO hp.

Oliver 1850 series

Nebraska Test Data

Model: Oliver 1850

Test No. 875

Date Tested: November 12 to November 24, 1964

Using the same chassis design as the Oliver 1850 Diesel illustrated in test No. 870, this gasoline version used a six-cylinder, 310-cid engine. Rated at 2,400 rpm, it carried a 3-1/8 x 4-3/8-inch bore and stroke. Operating at rated engine speed, the 1850 delivered a maximum of 92.43 PTO hp and yielded 12 hp-hours per gallon. During 44 hours of running time, no repairs or adjustments were recorded. The bare tractor weight of 8,935 lbs. was increased to a test weight of 13,965 lbs. through the use of front and rear ballast. As previously recorded for the 1850 Diesel, this tractor went through the drawbar economy runs using the Hydra-Power range of fourth gear. At 76.66 maximum available drawbar hp, fuel economy came in at 9.83 hp-hours per gallon. This two-hour run also indicated a pull of 7,801 lbs. at 3.69 mph with 8.59 percent slippage. A 10-hour run at 75 percent pull noted an economy of 9.21 while delivering 64.01 drawbar hp. Other statistics included a pull of 5,992 lbs. at 4.01 mph with 6.74 percent slippage.

Nebraska Test Data

Model: Oliver 1850 Four-Wheel-Drive (Gasoline)

Test No. 876

Date Tested: November 16 to November 24, 1964

Closing out the 1964 testing season, the 1850 F-W-D gasoline model was a twin of the 1850 F-W-D Diesel depicted in Test No. 869. Obviously, a gasoline engine replaced the diesel style of the earlier test, and in this case, the same engine style of Test No. 875 was used. This 310-cid engine was rated at 2,400 rpm and used a 3-7/8 x 4-1/8-inch bore and stroke. Operating at rated engine speed, a maximum of 92.92 PTO hp was observed, together with an economy of 11.47 hp-hours per gallon. The bare tractor weight of 10,605 lbs. was raised to 16,225 lbs. by additional front and rear ballast. The two-hour drawbar economy run at 84.52 maximum available hp saw a pull of 7,534 lbs. at 4.21 mph with 4.31 percent slippage. Fuel economy was recorded at 10.37 hp-hours per gallon. The 10-hour run, made at 75 percent pull, indicated 9.22 hp-hours per gallon against an output of 66.93 drawbar hp. Also recorded was a pull of 5,756 lbs. at 4.36 mph with 3.25 percent slippage. No repairs or adjustments were noted during 40 hours of running time.

Nebraska Test Data

Model: Oliver 1950 Diesel

Test No. 871

Date Tested: October 30 to November 11, 1964

The 212.4-cid, four-cylinder, two-cycle engine used in the 1950 Diesel was built by General Motors Corporation. Rated at 2,400 rpm, this blower-equipped engine carried a 3-7/8 x 4-1/2-inch bore and stroke. Operating at rated speed, PTO testing indicated 15.14 hp-hours per gallon against a maximum output of 105.79 hp. The 11,955-lb. base weight was supported by 23.1-34 rear and 11.00-16 inch front tires. Additional rear wheel ballast gave a test weight of 15,855 lbs. Features included a selective-gear fixed-ratio transmission offering five speeds each in direct drive or in the Hydra-Power drive. A range from 1.28 to 15.62 mph was available. The 2-hour drawbar economy run at 98 maximum available hp was made in the Hydra-Power range of fourth gear. Yielding 13.56 hp-hours per gallon, this test also provided a pull of 8,996 lbs. at 4.09 mph with 3.32 percent slippage. Using the same gear selection as before, the 10-hour run at 75 percent pull gave 13.03 hp-hours per gallon against an output of 78.26 hp. This test indicated a pull of 6,942 lbs. at 4.23 mph with 4.56 percent slippage.

Nebraska Test Data

Model: Oliver 1950 Four-Wheel-Drive Diesel

Test No. 872

Date Tested: October 30 to November 23, 1964

Both this tractor and the 1950 Diesel of Test No. 871 used the same General Motors engine. At its rated 2,400 rpm, the tractor developed 105.78 maximum PTO hp while yielding 14.89 hp-hours per gallon. The selective-gear fixed-ratio transmission included partial range power shifting. In all, 12 forward speeds were provided in a range from 1.28 to 15.62 mph. The 12,975-lb. net weight was carried on 23.1-34-inch rear and 13.6-24-inch front tires. During drawbar testing, additional front and rear ballast gave a total weight of 19,925 lbs. Fourth gear in the Hydra-Power range delivered a maximum of 93.24 drawbar hp in a two-hour economy run. This output resulted in 12.71 hp-hours per gallon, together with a pull of 8,368 lbs. at 4.18 mph and 4.45 percent slippage. At 75 percent pull, the 10-hour economy run saw an economy of 12.51 hp-hours per gallon against an output of 76.05 drawbar hp. The pull of 6,596 lbs. was made at 4.32 mph with slippage of 3.36 percent. The "Repairs and Adjustments" section of the test noted: "During the drawbar runs it became apparent that the gear ratio in the front axle was not correct for this tractor. Another front axle, with a more suitable gear ratio, was installed and test continued." Total operating time was 56 hours.

Nebraska Test Data

Model: Oliver 1950-T Diesel Row-Crop

Test No. 969

Date Tested: November 13 to November 18, 1967

Closing out the 1967 testing season, this tractor delivered 105.24 maximum PTO hp at its rated speed of 2,400 rpm. Economy was 16.2 hp-hours per gallon of diesel fuel. Oliver equipped this model with its own six-cylinder, 310-cid, turbocharged engine, using a 3-7/8 x 4-5/9-inch bore and stroke. No repairs or adjustments were reported during 48 hours of running time. Standard equipment included 23.1-34-inch rear and 11.00-16-inch front tires. Also featured was a selective-gear fixed-ratio transmission with a total of 12 forward speeds in a range from 1.48 to 17.21 mph. Bare tractor weight was 10,460 lbs., but additional front and rear ballast raised this to a test weight of 15,780 lbs. Operating in fourth-gear under-drive, the two-hour economy run was made at 90.07 maximum available drawbar hp, with a fuel economy of 14.19 hp-hours per gallon. This test saw a pull of 7,047 lbs. at 4.79 mph with slippage of 4.77 percent. The 10-hour run at 75 percent pull indicated 12.72 hp-hours per gallon against an output of 75.77 hp. This output gave a pull of 5,476 lbs. at 5.19 mph and slippage of 3.61 percent.

Nebraska Test Data

Model: Oliver 1950-T Four-Wheel-Drive Diesel

Test No. 972

Date Tested: April 29 to May 7, 1968

Rated at 2,400 rpm, this tractor developed 105.11 maximum PTO hp and delivered 16.22 hp-hours per gallon. The six-cylinder, 310-cid turbocharged engine carried a 3-7/8 x 4-3/8-inch bore and stroke. Partial range power shifting was included with the selective-gear fixed-ratio transmission. Its 18 speeds ranged from 1.48 to 17.21 mph. Also featured were 23.1-34-inch rear and 14.9-26-inch front tires. No repairs or adjustments were noted during 47 hours of operating time. Weighing in at 11,490 lbs., this unit received front and rear ballast for a total test weight of 20,220 lbs. Using third gear, direct-drive, the two-hour economy run was made at 89.10 maximum available hp, and yielded 13.55 hp-hours per gallon. Other test statistics included a pull of 7,629 lbs. at 4.38 mph and a 3.89 percent slippage. Fuel economy was posted at 12.52-hp hours per gallon against a load of 73.27 drawbar hp in the 10-hour economy run. This test, performed at 75 percent pull, indicated a pull of 5,835 lbs. at 4.71 mph with 3.03 percent slippage.

Oliver 2050

Nebraska Test Data

Model: Oliver 2050 Row-Crop Diesel

Test No. 987

Date Tested: September 23 to October 7, 1968

This tractor carried its 14,540-lb. base weight on dual rear tires of 18.4-38-inch size, plus the usual 11.00-16-inch front tires. Additional ballast, both front and rear, raised the total test weight to 18,890 lbs. The chassis design included partial range power shifting within the selective-gear fixed-ratio transmission. Its 18 forward speeds ranged from 1.49 to 16.72 mph. Using fourth gear, under-drive, the two-hour economy run saw a maximum output of 96.36 drawbar hp with a pull of 7,718 lbs. at 4.68 mph, slippage of 6.72 percent, and an economy of 12.6 hp-hours per gallon. By comparison, the 10-hour run at 75 percent pull indicated an economy figure of 12.15 against an output of 80.85 hp. Other test statistics included a pull of 6,050 lbs. at 5.01 mph and slippage of 5.21 percent. Oliver equipped this tractor with a six-cylinder, 478-cid engine. Rated at 2,400 rpm, it used a 4-9/16 x 4-7/8-inch bore and stroke. At rated engine speed, 118.78 maximum PTO hp was observed, as was an economy of 15.33 hp-hours per gallon. During drawbar testing, the fuel injector for No. 4 cylinder was replaced. With this exception, no repairs or adjustments were noted during 55-1/2 hours of running time.

Oliver 2150

Nebraska Test Data

Model: Oliver 2150 Row-Crop Diesel

Test No. 986

Date Tested: September 27 to October 7, 1968

A turbocharger was featured on the six-cylinder, 478-cubic inch engine used in this tractor. Rated at 2,400 rpm, it carried a 4-9/16 x 4-7/8-inch bore and stroke. Also featured was a selective-gear fixed-ratio transmission with partial range power shifting. Its 18 forward speeds ranged from 1.5 to 16.83 mph. Standard equipment included dual 24.5-32-inch rear and single 11.00-16-inch front tires. Bare tractor weight was 12,990 lbs., but additional front and rear ballast raised this figure to a total test weight of 21,275 lbs. During drawbar testing, the fuel injectors were replaced, but otherwise, no repairs or adjustments were noted during 61-1/2 hours of running time. Using fourth gear, under-drive, 109.51 maximum available drawbar hp appeared in the two-hour economy run. Also evidenced was a pull of 8,590 lbs. at 4.78 mph, a slippage of 5.19 percent, and an economy of 12.75 hp-hours per gallon. The 10-hour run at 75 percent pull manifested 11.64 hp-hours per gallon against a load of 87.73 hp. These figures resulted from a pull of 6,560 lbs. at 5.01 mph with slippage of 3.8 percent. At its rated engine speed, the 2150 Diesel developed a maximum of 131.48 PTO hp and delivered 15.24 hp-hours per gallon.

Oliver 1655 series

Oliver 1950 series

Nebraska Test Data

Model: Oliver 1655 Diesel
Test No. 1041
Date Tested: May 5 to May 22, 1970

At 70.57 maximum PTO hp, this tractor achieved an economy of 14 hp-hours per gallon of diesel fuel. This test was made at the rated engine speed of 2,200 rpm. White equipped this model with an Oliver six-cylinder, 283-cubic-inch engine using a 3-7/8 x 4 inch bore and stroke. No repairs or adjustments were reported during 45 hours of operating time. A selective-gear fixed-ratio transmission was used and it featured three-range power shifting in under-, direct- or over-drive. The 18 speeds ranged from 2.19 to 17.02 mph. Also featured were 18.4-34-inch rear and 7.50-16-inch front tires. Weighing 8,070 lbs., this model took on a total test weight of 11,100 lbs. through the addition of front and rear ballast. Operating in seventh gear, an economy of 12.32 hp-hours per gallon was realized against a maximum available output of 60.07 drawbar hp. This test was run with a pull of 5,434 lbs. at 4.15 mph and the slippage totaled 7.63 percent. The 10-hour run at 75 percent pull saw 12.54 hp-hours per gallon against a load of 49.42 hp. Also established was a pull of 4,200 lbs. at 4.41 mph and 5.4 percent slippage.

Nebraska Test Data

Model: Oliver 1655
Test No. 1042
Date Tested: May 7 to May 22, 1970

The Oliver 1655 gasoline model illustrated here was virtually identical to the diesel style noted in the previous test, except, of course, for a six-cylinder, 265-cid gasoline engine for this test model. Rated at 2,200 rpm, it used a 3-3/4 x 4-inch bore and stroke. At rated engine speed, the 1655 gasoline version achieved 10.61 hp-hours per gallon against a maximum output of 70.27 PTO hp. No repairs or adjustments were required during 47-1/2 hours of running time. This model carried the same chassis design as previously noted in Test No. 1041. Eighteen forward speeds were available. Weighing in at 7,780 lbs., a total test weight of 10,850 lbs. was established through the addition of front and rear ballast. Using seventh gear, and at a maximum available output of 57.44 drawbar hp, the 1655 gasoline version achieved 8.84 hp-hours per gallon in the two-hour economy run. These figures resulted from a pull of 5,147 lbs. at 4.19 mph and slippage totaled 7.44 percent. The 10-hour run at 75 percent pull recorded 8.12 hp-hours per gallon with an output of 46.08 hp. Other statistics included a pull of 3,930 lbs. at 4.4 mph and slippage of 5.35 percent.

Nebraska Test Data

Model: Oliver 1755
Test No. 1056
Date Tested: October 15 to October 26, 1970

At its rated 2,400 rpm, this tractor achieved 11.37 hp-hours per gallon of gasoline under a maximum PTO load of 86.98 hp. White equipped this model with an Oliver six-cylinder, 283-cubic-inch engine with a 3-7/8 x 4-inch bore and stroke. Other features included a selective-gear fixed-ratio transmission with three-range power shifting. The 18 forward speeds varied from 1.3 to 17.2 mph. No repairs or adjustments were required during 42-1/2 hours of running time. Weighing 9,490 lbs., the 1755 was furnished with 18.4-34-inch rear and 7.5L-15-inch front tires. Additional front and rear ballast raised the total test weight to 13,070 lbs. Using eighth gear, the two-hour economy run at 72.45 maximum available drawbar hp gave a fuel efficiency of 9.45 hp-hours per gallon. Also recorded was a pull of 6,669 lbs. at 4.07 mph and slippage of 8.42 percent. The 10-hour run at 75 percent pull noted an economy of 8.34 hp hours per gallon under a load of 59.67 hp. Other statistics of this performance run included a pull of 5,163 lbs. at 4.33 mph. Slippage totaled 6.38 percent.

Nebraska Test Data

Model: Oliver 1755 Diesel
Test No. 1057
Date Tested: October 14 to October 27, 1970

No repairs or adjustments were reported for this model during 45-1/2 hours of operating time. At its rated speed of 2,400 rpm, it developed 86.93 maximum PTO hp and achieved 13 hp-hours per gallon. The selective-gear fixed-ratio transmission featured partial range power shifting. Its 18 forward speeds varied from 1.3 to 17.2 mph. White equipped this model with a six-cylinder, 310-cid diesel engine carrying a 3-7/8 x 4-3/8-inch bore and stroke. Weighing 9,690 lbs., this model was furnished with 18.4-34-inch rear and 7.5L-15-inch front tires. Additional front and rear ballast boosted the total test weight to 13,250 lbs. Using eighth gear, the two-hour drawbar performance run at 73.87 maximum available hp saw an economy of 11.14 hp-hours per gallon. This test indicated a pull of 6,805 lbs. at 4.07 mph with slippage of 8.61 percent. The 10-hour run at 75 percent pull recorded 12.05 hp-hours per gallon under a load of 61.58 hp. Other statistics included a pull of 5,293 lbs. at 4.36 mph and 6.19 percent slippage.

Oliver 1855

Nebraska Test Data

Model: Oliver 1855 Diesel
Test No. 1040
Date Tested: May 5 to May 22, 1970

Weighing 11,140 lbs., this tractor assumed a total test weight of 14,800 lbs. through additional front and rear ballast. Tire equipment included 23.1-34-inch rear and 11L-15-inch front rubber. The selective-gear fixed-ratio transmission included three-range power shifting. Its 18 forward speeds were spread between 1.44 to 18.58 mph. Using eighth gear (third-direct), the two-hour economy run delivered 13.3 hp-hours per gallon against an output of 82.65 maximum available drawbar hp. Also recorded was a pull of 6,680 lbs. at 4.64 mph and slippage of 6.79 percent. An economy figure of 12.23 was established in the 10-hour run. At 75 percent pull, it represented an output of 68.51 hp and developed a pull of 5,100 lbs. at 4.87 mph with 4.87 percent slippage in this case. The six-cylinder Oliver diesel engine was rated at 2,400 rpm. Its 310-cubic inch displacement resulted from a 3-7/8 x 4-3/8-inch bore and stroke. At rated engine speed, an economy of 15.84 hp-hours per gallon was established under a maximum load of 98.6 PTO hp. No repairs or adjustments were noted during 49 hours of running time.

Oliver 1955

Nebraska Test Data

Model: Oliver 1955 Diesel

Test No. 1055

Date Tested: October 15 to October 24, 1970

A six-cylinder, 310-cubic-inch turbocharged diesel was featured in this model. Rated at 2,400 rpm, it used a 3-7/8 x 4-3/8-inch bore and stroke. At rated engine speed, 108.16 maximum PTO hp was observed, with an economy of 15.78 hp-hours per gallon. No repairs or adjustments were reported during 38-1/2 hours of operating time. Features included a selective-gear fixed-ratio transmission with partial range power shifting. This system employed under-, direct- and over-drive within six separate speed ranges. The 18 forward speeds were spread between 1.5 and 17.2 mph. Weighing 11,245 lbs., the 1955 Diesel was furnished with 20.8-38-inch rear and 11L-15-inch front tires. Additional front and rear ballast raised the total test weight to 16,220 lbs. Using eighth gear, 90.32 maximum available horsepower was developed in the two-hour drawbar economy run. This test yielded 12.99 hp-hours per gallon and recorded a pull of 7,919 lbs. at 4.28 mph with slippage totaling 7.81 percent. The 10-hour run at 75 percent pull saw 12.62 hp-hours per gallon with a load of 72.97 drawbar hp. Other statistics included a pull of 5,915 lbs. at 4.63 mph and 5.22 percent slippage.

Nebraska Test Data

Model: Oliver 2255 Diesel

Test No. 1140

Date Tested: September 4 to September 17, 1973

Rated at 2,600 rpm, the 2255 delivered a rated speed load of 146.72 PTO hp and achieved 15.59 hp- hours per gallon of fuel. At 1,000 PTO rpm and a corresponding engine speed of 2,542 rpm, an economy of 15.66 hp-hours per gallon was derived under a load of 147.65 hp. This tractor was equipped with a Caterpillar 573-cubic-inch V-8 engine using a 4.5-inch bore and stroke. Eighteen forward speeds were provided in the selective-gear fixed-ratio transmission. The design also included partial range power shifting. Operating in 11th gear, 123.72 maximum available drawbar hp was evidenced in the two-hour economy run, with 13.43 hp-hours per gallon. This test noted a pull of 8,143 lbs. at 5.7 mph with slippage of 5.98 percent. The 10-hour run at 75 percent pull yielded 12.95 hp-hours per gallon under a load of 100.53 drawbar hp. Also recorded was a pull of 6,245 lbs. at 6.04 mph with 4.16 percent slippage. Weighing 16,407 lbs., the 2255 used dual rear wheels of 18.4-38 inch size, along with 11.00-16- inch front tires. Additional front and rear ballast raised the total test weight to 17,990 lbs. No repairs or adjustments were required during 46 hours of operating time.

Oliver 2255

Oliver Cletrac HG crawler

Oliver Corporation bought out the Cletrac line in 1944. Cletrac had already introduced several small farm crawlers, including the HG. The latter was available in several track widths to accommodate various farming practices. Numerous implements were tailored especially for the HG tractors, and special cab equipment could be furnished for cold weather operations.

Nebraska Test Data

Model: Oliver HG

Test No. 434

Date Tested: November 11 to November 21, 1949

Weighing 4,183 lbs., this crawler tractor used a Hercules four-cylinder L-head engine rated at 1,700 rpm and carried a 3-1/4 x 4-inch bore and stroke. Wico magneto ignition was featured, with a Delco-Remy electrical system and a Marvel-Schebler TSX403 carburetor. No repairs or adjustments were required during a 44-hour run. Advertised speeds of 2.01, 3.19 and 5.24 mph were provided. At a rated drawbar load of 16.53 hp, noted in Test H, the HG pulled 2,029 lbs. at 3.05 mph with a slippage of 5.03 percent, recording 8.47 hp-hours per gallon in the process. Under Test G, a low-gear maximum pull of 3,940 lbs. was achieved. Fuel economy came at 11.06 hp-hours per gallon at a Test C operating maximum load of 24.7 belt hp. Under a Test D-rated belt load of 22.54 hp, fuel economy settled in at 10.86 hp-hours per gallon. This unit was, in effect, a close relative to the old Cletrac tractor, as Oliver had bought the Cleveland Tractor Co. in 1944 and continued production of Crawler tractors under the Oliver name.

Nebraska Test Data

Model: Oliver DG

Test No. 435

Date Tested: November 8 to November 21, 1949

During 46 hours of engine operating time, no repairs or adjustments were noted for this tractor. Weighing 14,645 lbs., it featured forward speeds of 1.45, 2.28, 3.04 and 4.85 mph. Also featured was a six-cylinder, L-head Hercules engine. Rated at 1,300 rpm, it used a 4-5/8 x 5-1/4-inch bore and stroke. A Delco-Remy 12-volt electrical system was standard equipment. Test G yielded a low-gear maximum pull of 14,582 lbs. at 1.4 mph under a slippage of 4.25 percent. Drawbar fuel economy as noted in Test H came in at 7.98 hp-hours per gallon. Other test data included a rated 45.62 drawbar hp, along with a pull of 5,662 lbs. at 3.02 mph and slippage of 1.56 percent. Belt testing indicated 10.78 hp-hours per gallon at a Test C operating maximum load of 66.58 hp. While under a Test D-rated load of 60.88 hp, fuel economy was 10.32 hp-hours per gallon.

Oliver DD and DG crawlers

Nebraska Test Data

Model: Oliver DD

Test No. 436

Date Tested: November 8 to November 22, 1949

Closing out the 1949 testing season, the Oliver DD came through Test D with an economy of 14.77 hp hours per gallon of diesel fuel under a rated belt load of 63.27 hp. At a 100 percent maximum belt load of 73.3 hp, the economy was recorded at 15.5 hp-hours per gallon. Weighing in at 15,515 lbs., this diesel tractor featured a Hercules six-cylinder engine with a 4-3/8 x 5-1/4-inch bore and stroke. Rated at 1,300 rpm, it also featured a Bosch fuel injection system and Delco-Remy electrical equipment. No repairs or adjustments were noted during 44 hours of engine operating time. The DD offered forward speeds of 1.45, 2.28, 3.04 and 4.85 mph, with third gear chosen for Test H. During this 10-hour run, the DD pulled a load of 5,634 lbs. at 3.04 mph with a slippage of 1.16 percent. Fuel economy was noted at 11.03 hp- hours per gallon. In Test G, a low-gear maximum drawbar pull of 14,735 lbs. was achieved at 1.42 mph under a slippage of 3.39 percent.

COLLECTOR VALUES	1	2	3	4
1916-1936	$4,500	$2,500	$1,500	$500
MODEL 20-C	$5,000	$4,000	$2,500	$1,000
MODEL 25	$3,500	$2,500	$1,500	$500
MODEL 30 DIESEL	$3,500	$2,500	$1,500	$500
MODEL 30 GAS	$3,500	$2,500	$1,500	$500
MODEL 35	$5,000	$4,000	$2,500	$1,000
MODEL 35 DIESEL	$3,500	$2,500	$1,500	$500
MODEL 40	$3,500	$2,500	$1,500	$500
MODEL 40/30	$3,500	$2,500	$1,500	$500
MODEL 80/60	$5,000	$4,000	$1,500	$300
MODEL 80 DIESEL	$5,000	$4,000	$1,500	$300
MODEL AD	$2,500	$2,000	$1,500	$300
MODEL AD-2	$2,500	$2,000	$1,500	$500
MODEL AG	$4,000	$3,000	$2,000	$500
MODEL AG-6	$3,000	$2,000	$1,500	$500
MODEL B-30	$3,500	$2,500	$1,500	$300
MODEL BD	$3,500	$2,500	$1,500	$300
MODEL BD-2	$3,500	$2,500	$1,500	$300
MODEL BG	$4,500	$3,000	$2,000	$500
MODEL BGS	$3,500	$2,500	$1,500	$300
MODEL CG	$3,500	$2,500	$1,500	$300
MODEL DD	$3,000	$2,500	$1,500	$300
MODEL DG	$3,000	$2,500	$1,500	$500
MODEL E	$3,000	$2,000	$1,500	$500
MODEL E-38	$3,000	$2,000	$1,500	$500

MODEL E-42	$3,000	$2,000	$1,500	$500
MODEL ED-2	$3,000	$2,000	$1,500	$500
MODEL ED-38	$3,000	$2,000	$1,500	$500
MODEL ED2-38	$3,000	$2,000	$1,500	$500
MODEL ED-42	$3,000	$2,000	$1,500	$500
MODEL ED2-42	$3,000	$2,000	$1,500	$500
MODEL EHD-2	$3,000	$2,000	$1,500	$500
MODEL EHG	$3,500	$2,500	$1,500	$500
MODEL EN	$3,500	$2,500	$1,500	$500
MODEL FD	$8,000	$6,000	$3,000	$1,500
MODEL FDE	$8,000	$3,500	$2,500	$500
MODEL FDLC	$8,000	$3,500	$2,500	$500
MODEL FG	$8,000	$3,500	$2,500	$500
MODEL GG (WHEEL TRACTOR)	$2,000	$1,500	$1,000	$400
MODEL HG	$4,500	$3,000	$2,500	$500
MODEL HGR	$10,000	$7,500	$5,000	$500
MG-1	$8,000	$6,000	$3,000	$1,500

HG crawler on rubber tracks

During the 1940s, the HG crawler could be furnished with special rubber tracks. The idea was far ahead of its time. Unfortunately, the rubber tracks were unable to stand the stress of heavy work and inevitably stretched beyond usefulness. These and other problems prompted the company to retrofit these machines with ordinary steel tracks. Only a very few of these machines still exist.

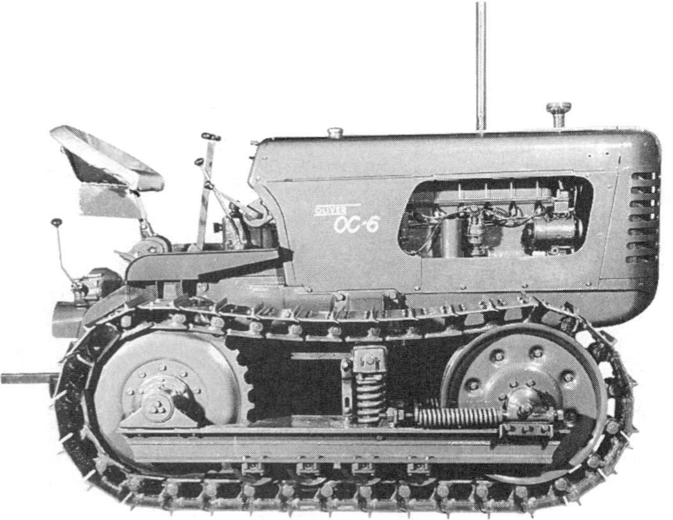

Oliver OC-4 and OC-6 crawlers

Oliver OC-6 crawler tractors used the same engine as the Oliver 66 row-crop model. In Nebraska Test No. 516, the gasoline-powered OC-6 delivered almost 33 hp at the drawbar. Test No. 517 indicated over 34 hp for the diesel model. Oliver built many different crawler tractors, and for additional reference, the reader is referred to the author's title, Oliver Hart-Parr. Oliver abruptly ended production of crawler tractors in 1965.

Nebraska Test Data

Model: Oliver OC-6 (Gasoline)
Test No. 516
Date Tested: April 15 to April 28, 1954

This tractor wasn't equipped with a belt pulley, so no brake hp tests, fuel economy runs or maximum torque figures are available. Weighing 6,600 lbs., the OC-6 gasoline model came with forward speeds of 1.88, 2.44, 3.23, 4.19, 5.15 and 8.86 mph. A direct-drive PTO was fitted with an independent hand clutch. Also featured was an Oliver six-cylinder I-head engine rated at 1,600 rpm and carrying a 3-5/16, x 3-3/4-inch bore and stroke for a 193.9-cubic inch displacement. Test F, run at 100 percent maximum load, was made in second gear. With an output of 31.92 drawbar hp, the OC-6 pulled 4,962 lbs. at 2.41 mph with a slippage of 1.54 percent. Test G yielded a low-gear maximum pull of 6,215 lbs. at 1.83 mph under a slippage of 3.03 percent. During Test F, the 14-inch track pads were replaced with 12-inch pads due to soil conditions. Otherwise no repairs or adjustments were noted during 57-1/2 hours of running time. The 10-hour run of Test H was made in second gear. With an output of 24.75 hp, the OC-6 pulled 3,857 lbs. at 2.41 mph with a 1.7 percent slippage. Fuel economy came to 8.96 hp-hours per gallon.

Nebraska Test Data

Model: Oliver OC-6 (Diesel)
Test No. 517
Date Tested: April 17 to May 7, 1954

Like the OC-6 gasoline model of Test No. 516, the diesel tractor shown here was not equipped with a belt pulley so no brake hp or engine torque data is available. With the exception of the diesel engine used in this model, this tractor and the model shown in Test No. 516 were virtually identical, with this diesel style weighing 6,742 lbs. It was equipped with an Oliver six-cylinder diesel engine using the same dimensions and 193.9-cubic inch displacement of Test No. 516, but featured a compression ratio of 15.75:1, compared to 6.75:1 for the gasoline model. The maximum load tests revealed a low-gear maximum pull of 6,779 lbs. at 1.83 mph with a 3.41 percent slippage. Total test output was 33.01 drawbar hp. Test J, run at operating maximum load in second gear, produced an output of 33.19 drawbar hp, along with a pull of 5,193 lbs. at 2.4 mph and slippage of 2.34 percent. The 10-hour Test H run was made in second gear. With an output of 26.21 hp, the OC-6 diesel tractor pulled 4,066 lbs. at 2.42 mph against a slippage of 1.42 percent. Fuel economy was 12.14 hp-hours per gallon of diesel fuel. No repairs or adjustments of major consequence were recorded during 37-1/2 hours of running time.

Nebraska Test Data

Model: Oliver OC-4 Diesel

Test No. 655

Date Tested: June 5 to June 16, 1958

The OC-4 diesel featured a Hercules three-cylinder engine of I-head design. Rated at 1,700 rpm, it carried a 3-1/2 x 4-1/2-inch bore and stroke for a displacement of 130-cubic inches. The design included a 15:1 compression ratio. Total weight as tested was 5,345 lbs. This tractor featured forward speeds of 1.56, 1.37, 3.37 and 5.27 mph. Test H was run in second gear. At a rated drawbar load of 18.55 hp, the OC-4 diesel pulled 2,776 lbs. at 2.51 mph with 2.57 percent slippage. Fuel economy came in at 10.61 hp-hours per gallon. A 100 percent maximum pull of 5,124 lbs. at 1.41 mph against a 9.99 percent slippage was noted in low gear. During 39 hours of operating time, no repairs or adjustments were required. Test D, run at a rated belt load of 23.26 hp, achieved 12.68 hp-hours per gallon of diesel fuel. This figure slipped to 11.58 under a 100 percent maximum load of 26.08 hp.

Nebraska Test Data

Model: Oliver OC-4

Test No. 656

Date Tested: June 5 to June 16, 1958

Oliver's OC-4 gasoline-powered crawler tractor featured a three-cylinder Hercules engine with a 3-1/2 x 4-1/2-inch bore and stroke. Rated at 1,700 rpm, it carried a 130-cubic inch displacement and a 6.5:1 compression ratio. Weighing 5,255 lbs., it featured speeds identical to the OC-4 Diesel tractor noted in Test No. 655. The tractor shown here was virtually identical except for the engine. No repairs or adjustments were recorded during 44-1/2 hours of operation. Test G elicited a low-gear maximum pull of 4,986 lbs. at 1.41 mph against a slippage of 10.09 percent. Using second gear, Test H was run at a rated drawbar load of 17.99 hp. This test indicated a pull of 2,716 lbs. at 2.48 mph and a slippage of 2.46 percent. Fuel economy was noted at 8.51 hp-hours per gallon. Test D, run at a rated belt load of 22.52 hp, produced a fuel economy of 10.04 hp-hours per gallon. This figure climbed to 10.75 under a Test C operating maximum load of 24.34 hp.

Oliver OC-12 crawler

Nebraska Test Data

Model: Oliver OC-12

Test No. 548

Date Tested: June 15 to June 28, 1955

Using a Hercules JXLD six-cylinder, L-head engine, the OC-12 carried a rated speed of 1,750 rpm. Engine torque peaked at 371.9 lbs.-ft. with a speed of 943 rpm. Using a bore and stroke of 4 x 4-1/2 inches, this engine had a displacement of 339-cubic inches. No repairs or adjustments were noted during 42-1/2 hours of operating time. Features included forward speeds of 1.53, 2.24, 3.2 and 5.04 mph. Total weight of the OC-12 was 11,259 lbs. In Test G, a maximum pull of 10,399 lbs. was made in low gear. Test H, run at a rated drawbar load of 39.98 hp, saw a pull of 6,496 lbs. at 2.31 mph and slippage of 1.59 percent. Fuel economy was 8.89 hp-hours per gallon. Under a Test C operating maximum belt load of 54.64 hp, fuel economy was pegged at 10.52 hp-hours per gallon. Test D, run at a rated belt load of 51.45 hp, saw a fuel economy rating of 10.26 hp-hours per gallon.

Nebraska Test Data

Model: Oliver OC-12 Diesel

Test No. 549

Date Tested: June 15 to June 28, 1955

Weighing 11,771 lbs., the OC-12 Diesel tractor exited from Test H with an economy of 10.65 hp-hours per gallon of diesel fuel. During this test, a rated drawbar load of 40.55 hp was recorded, along with a pull of 6,582 lbs. at 2.31 mph and a slippage of 1.59 percent. Test G produced a low-gear maximum pull of 11,333 lbs. at 1.5 mph with a slippage of 6.36 percent. The OC-12 Diesel was equipped with a Hercules JXLD, six-cylinder, I-head diesel engine. Rated at 1,750 rpm, it achieved a maximum torque of 371 lbs.-ft. with an engine speed of 1,153 rpm. With a 298-cubic inch displacement, this engine carried a 3-3/4 x 4-1/2-inch bore and stroke. Test B, run at a 100 percent maximum belt load of 56.55 hp, noted a fuel economy of 11.72 hp-hours per gallon of diesel fuel. This rose to 12.51 under a Test D-rated belt load of 50.33 hp. Prior to Test B, the fuel injection line to No. 6 cylinder was replaced. Otherwise, no repairs or adjustments were noted during 40-1/2 hours of operating time.

Oliver OC-15 and OC-18 crawlers

Nebraska Test Data

Model: Oliver OC-18

Test No. 489

Date Tested: November 10 to November 24, 1952

Closing out the 1952 testing season, the OC-18 came through with an economy of 10.66 hp-hours per gallon of diesel fuel under a rated drawbar load of 101.62 hp. Test H also indicated a pull of 14,265 lbs. at 2.61 mph and slippage of 0.79 percent. Weighing 35,090 lbs., the OC-18 managed a low-gear maximum pull of 31,028 lbs. in Test G. Due to the limited capacity of the dynamometer, no belt tests were run. Prior to Test H, a fuel injection line was replaced, otherwise no repairs or adjustments were noted during 43 hours of operating time. The OC-18 was equipped with a Hercules DFXE six-cylinder engine. Of I-head design, it was rated at 1,500 rpm and used a 5-3/8 x 6-inch bore and stroke. Displacement was 895-cubic inches, with a 1.8:1 compression ratio. A 12-volt electrical system was standard equipment.

Nebraska Test Data

Model: Oliver OC-15

Test No. 633

Date Tested: November 4 to November 9, 1955

From the heavy winter wear used by the operator, it appeared that early November 1957 was chilly in the Lincoln, Nebraska, area. A look at the test report indicated that during Test H the mercury dropped to 36 degrees! Weighing 19,005 lbs., the OC-15 featured forward speeds of 1.67, 2.64, 3.76 and 5.6 mph. Using second gear, Test H noted a rated output of 71.64 drawbar hp, with a pull of 10,315 lbs. at 2.6 mph and slippage of 1.56 percent. Fuel economy was 12.68 hp-hours per gallon of diesel fuel. Test G noted a low-gear maximum pull of 17,278 lbs. at 1.55 mph with a 7.13 percent slippage. The OC-15 carried a Hercules DRXC six-cylinder diesel engine rated at 1,500 rpm and used a 4-5/8 x 5-1/4-inch bore and stroke for a 529-cubic inch displacement. Test L noted that 103 percent of rated-speed torque was available at 75 percent of rated rpm. During the preliminary belt test, a leak in the pulley gear box was repaired, and during Tests F & G, an oil pressure line was replaced. No other repairs or adjustments were required during 40 hours of running time. Test D, run at a rated belt load of 89.02 hp, yielded 14.53 hp-hours per gallon, slipping to 13.59 under a 100 percent maximum belt load of 101.97 hp.

COLLECTOR VALUES	1	2	3	4
OLIVER OC-3	$7,000	$4,500	$2,500	$1,000
OLIVER OC-4	$7,000	$4,500	$2,500	$1,000
OLIVER OC-4-3G	$7,000	$4,500	$2,500	$1,000
OLIVER OC-6G	$6,000	$9,000	$2,500	$1,000
OLIVER OC-9	$6,000	$4,000	$2,500	$1,000
OLIVER OC-12D	$8,000	$6,000	$3,000	$1,500
OLIVER OC-12G	$8,000	$6,000	$3,000	$1,500
OLIVER OC-15	$10,000	$6,000	$3,500	$1,500
OLIVER OC-18	$12,000	$7,500	$3,500	$1,500

Oliver Tractor Company

KNOXVILLE, TENNESSEE

During 1919, Oliver offered two crawler tractor models. The Model B 12-20 used a Buda four-cylinder engine with a 4-1/2 x 5-1/2-inch bore and stroke. A 15-30 hp rating was given the Model A crawler. The latter carried a Chief four-cylinder engine with a 4-1/2 x 6-inch bore and stroke. Little is known of the company, and it doesn't appear they were in the tractor business for more than a short time.

Olmstead Gas Traction Company

GREAT FALLS, MONTANA

Olmstead four-wheel-drive tractor

During 1912, Olmstead developed its four-wheel-drive tractor. Although plans were made to market the machine, less than 40 were actually built. In 1914 the company announced plans to move to Decatur, Illinois, but apparently this did not materialize and the firm faded into obscurity. Few details have been found regarding this tractor.

COLLECTOR VALUES	1	2	3	4
4WD	$95,000	–	–	–

Omaha-Park Tractor Company

OMAHA, NEBRASKA

No information concerning this company or its tractors has been found.

Omaha Tractor & Engine Company

OMAHA, NEBRASKA

Omaha Tractor was incorporated in 1913, ostensibly to manufacture engines and tractors. No other information has been found.

Once Over Tiller Corporation

NEW YORK, NEW YORK

Once Over Tiller tractor

About 1920, the 15-25 Once Over Tiller tractor appeared. This 4,000-lb. machine was powered by a Buda four-cylinder engine. The plows were equipped with special rotary units that pulverized the soil as it came from the moldboards. Apparently the Once Over was marketed for only a short time.

One Wheel Truck Company

ST. LOUIS, MISSOURI

In 1917 this firm developed the Autohorse; it was apparently a self-powered conversion unit for pulling various vehicles or wagons. No other information has been found.

Oneman Tractor Company

ANN ARBOR, MICHIGAN

This firm was organized in 1917 to build the Oneman Tractor Plow. No other information has been found.

Opsata Motor Plow Company

EAU CLAIRE, WISCONSIN

This firm was organized in 1913 by Martin S. Opsata to build a motor plow he had developed. In 1916, the company was taken over by Eau Claire Machine Company. No illustrations of the Opsata Motor Plow have been located.

Orchard Machinery Mfg. Company

GASPORT, NEW YORK

A 1913 catalog illustrates the 20-hp tractor. Its low profile design was especially suited for orchard work, although the tractor was equally capable of general farm work. A two-cylinder vertical engine was used in this model. It had a top-rated speed of 600 rpm and used a 6-1/4 x 8-inch bore and stroke. The tractor weighed 6,000 lbs.

Osco Motors Corporation

PHILADELPHIA, PENNSYLVANIA

Osco "65" garden tractor

About 1947, the Osco "65" garden tractor appeared, remaining on the market into the early 1950s. It was equipped with a Wisconsin AEN 7-1/2-hp engine. A PTO shaft was standard equipment, as was a belt pulley. Numerous tools were available.

COLLECTOR VALUES	1	2	3	4
OSCA 65 GARDEN TRACTOR	$1,250	$850	$450	$250

Orchard 20-hp tractor

Oshkosh Tractor Company

OSHKOSH, WISCONSIN

In September 1921, this firm was to have bought the La Crosse Tractor Company, La Crosse, Wisconsin. The announced intention was to move the factory to Oshkosh and continue manufacturing tractors there. From all appearances, little or nothing came of this venture.

Ostenburg Mfg. Company

SALINA, KANSAS

In 1953 this company is listed as the manufacturer of the OMC garden tractors. No other information has been found.

Otto Gas Engine Works

PHILADELPHIA, PENNSYLVANIA

Otto Gas Engine Works was the American equivalent to the German company founded by N. A. Otto. The latter was the inventor of today's four-cycle engine. Otto Gas Engine Works is not listed as a tractor manufacturer after 1913.

The first Otto traction engine was this big 42-hp model. Weighing 15,000 lbs., it was powered by a single-cylinder Otto engine with a 12 x 18-inch bore and stroke. This engine was built in 1896 and 1897.

Otto Gas Engine Works 42-hp model

Otto 1897 tractor

By 1897 the Otto tractor had been redesigned, and the tractor was showing commercial promise. It was scheduled for shipment to Hope, North Dakota, for field trials. No other information has been found regarding this tractor.

The Otto gas tractor of 1904 was a rather attractive looking machine, complete with a canopy. Of course, these tractors were powered with an Otto stationary engine. At this time they were available in sizes from 6 to 25 hp.

For 1912, the Otto gasoline tractor was built in sizes of 8, 10, 12, 15 and 21 hp. This tractor varied but little from the 1904 model, although the engine itself was somewhat improved, of course.

Owatonna Tractor Company

OWATONNA, MINNESOTA

During 1912, this company was organized and incorporated to build tractors, but no other information has been found.

Otto 1904 tractor

Otto 1912 tractor

[Throughout this section, assume that gasoline was used for fuel unless another fuel source is indicated.]

Pacific Coast Tractor Company

LOS ANGELES, CALIFORNIA

This firm was organized and incorporated in 1918 to manufacture tractors, but no other information has been found.

Pacific Iron & Machine Company

SAN DIEGO, CALIFORNIA

Pacific H6 garden tractor

The Pacific H6 garden tractor appeared about 1950. It used an articulated chassis and steering brakes for steering of the machine. Power came from a Wisconsin AEH engine capable of about 5 hp. Few other details have been found for this unit.

Pacific Power Implement Company

OAKLAND, CALIFORNIA

Only in 1921 did the All-in-One 12-25 tractor appear in the trade directories. This interesting design was an all-wheel-drive tractor. Weighing 4,800 lbs., it was powered by a Weidely four-cylinder engine with a 3-3/4 x 5-1/2-inch bore and stroke. Few other details were found on this tractor.

COLLECTOR VALUES	1	2	3	4
PACIFIC ALL-IN-ONE 12-25	$1,250	$650	$400	$200

Page Dairy & Farm Equipment Company

MILWAUKEE, WISCONSIN

This firm appears in 1948 as the manufacturer of the Page garden tractors, but no other details have been located.

COLLECTOR VALUES	1	2	3	4
PAGE GARDEN TRACTORS	$550	$400	$250	$125

Pan Motor Company

ST. CLOUD, MINNESOTA

Pan 12-24 tractor

Pan Motor Company was established at St. Cloud in 1916, and by May 1918 about 40 cars had been built. In December 1917, the Pan tractor was announced, and a non-working prototype was displayed at several fairs in 1918. Late in 1919, the prototype operated under its own power. Never-ending legal difficulties plagued Pan Motor Company, and the much-heralded Pan 12-24 tractor never went into production.

Panther Tractor Corporation

GARLAND, TEXAS

Panther tractor

In 1948 the Panther tractor appeared. Presumably, it had been developed during 1947. The Panther was built with a four-cylinder Waukesha engine with a 2-1/2 x 3-1/8-inch bore and stroke. It was rated at 16 hp. By special order, the engine could be secured with the manifold, carburetor and auxiliary fuel tank required for burning kerosene. Numerous attachments were available for the Panther tractors.

Park Tractor Company

CHICAGO, ILLINOIS

James D. Park apparently organized this firm in 1918. The following year he filed a trademark application noting that he had first used the "Park" tradename on tractors in May 1918. No other information was found.

Parker Motor Plow Company

BEDFORD CITY, VIRGINIA

By 1913 Parker Bros. had developed a heavy duty motor plow. It was powered by a two-cylinder engine of 9 hp. Various implements were available. The company was incorporated in 1915, but no other information has been found regarding the Parker Motor Plow.

Parrett Motors Corporation

CHICAGO, ILLINOIS

Parrett Motor Cultivator

About 1919, this firm was organized as a totally separate entity from Parrett Tractor Company. Its purpose was to build the Parrett Motor Cultivator. Rated at 6 drawbar and 12 belt hp, this machine was powered by the well-known LeRoi four-cylinder engine with a 3-1/8 x 4-1/2-inch bore and stroke. A great many small tractors were equipped with this engine. The Parrett Cultivator is listed only during 1920 and 1921.

Parrett Tractor Company

CHICAGO, ILLINOIS

In 1913, Dent and Henry Parrett built their first tractor. Initially they set up a small plant at Ottawa, Illinois,

Parrett tractor

and the first 25 tractors were built at the Plano, Illinois, factory of Independent Harvester Company. Parrett Tractor Company wasn't found in the trade listings after 1922.

The Parrett tractor was compact and lightweight for its time, and it soon became very popular.

10-20 Parrett tractor

Early in 1915, Parrett Tractor Co. moved to Chicago and began building the 10-20 Parrett tractor. Within a short time the Parrett became a very popular design, with thousands sold. The 10-20 was sold between 1915 and 1917.

Between 1918 and 1920 Parrett sold the 12-25 Model H tractor. Among its features was a three-speed transmission. Power came from a Buda four-cylinder engine with a 4-1/4 x 5-1/2-inch bore and stroke. In 1918, this tractor retailed at $1,450.

Parrett Model K 15-30 tractor

During 1919, Parrett developed its Model K 15-30 tractor. Its design was virtually the same as its predecessors except for the increased power level. The company was experiencing financial problems by this time, and it does not appear that the Model K experienced the sales of its ancestors.

Nebraska Test Data

Model: Parrett Model D 15-30

Test No. 37

Date Tested: July 19 to August 17, 1920

Some 54 hours of running time were required to complete testing of the Parrett 15-30. A maximum of 2,988 lbs. drawbar pull was recorded at 2.63 mph, giving an equivalent of 20.94 drawbar hp. In the belt, slightly over 31 hp was the best that could be mustered, although the Parrett came through with an impressive 9.04 hp-hours per gallon of kerosene and fuel consumption of 3.46 gph. A number of minor problems occurred during the test. The fan belt broke three times, and the clutch was adjusted a like number. A new carburetor of the same size and make was installed, and a larger cooling fan replaced the original one. Weighing 5,250 lbs., the 15-30 carried Parrett's four-cylinder vertical, overhead-valve engine with a 4-1/2 x 6-inch bore and stroke. Rated speed was 1,000 rpm. Two forward speeds of 2.75 and 4.07 mph were provided.

Parrett 12-25 Model H tractor

Regular equipment included an Eisemann Model G4 magneto and Stromberg Model M-2 carburetor. During the entire test, coolant temperatures never rose above 200 degrees F, despite the fact that atmospheric temperatures on the test track often ranged as high as 99 degrees F.

Hicks-Parrett 18-30 crawler

Hicks-Parrett Tractor Co. offered its 18-30 crawler model in 1921. The firm was an attempt at a new life, since Parrett Tractor Co. was experiencing financial difficulties. The company had been reorganized in 1918, even though they were building 50 tractors per day. Little is known of the Hicks-Parrett 18-30.

Parrett Tractors Inc.

BENTON HARBOR, MICHIGAN

Parrett tractor

During 1935, Dent Parrett introduced a new lightweight tractor design. This design weighed only 2,600 lbs. and came with electric starter and lights as standard equipment. Power came from a four-cylinder Hercules IXB engine. This tractor was capable of road speeds up to 20 mph. Within a short time, this tractor design was taken over by Co-operative Mfg. Company.

Bert B. Parrott

JACKSON, MICHIGAN

This individual was listed as a tractor manufacturer in 1917, and was the moving force behind the Highway Tractor Company incorporated at that time. No other information has been found.

Patch Bros. Tractor Company

SAND SPRINGS, OKLAHOMA

Patch Bros. was organized in 1915, and the following year, they changed the company name to Farm Engineering Company. The latter built tractors during 1916 and 1917.

Peco Mfg. Company

PHILADELPHIA, PENNSYLVANIA

In 1948 the Peco Model TR47 garden tractor was listed in the directories, but no illustrations of this machine were found. Few details of this machine have been located.

COLLECTOR VALUES	1	2	3	4
MODEL TR47	$850	$650	$400	$250

Peerless Motor Tractor Works

FREEPORT, ILLINOIS

Peerless tractor

In 1911 the Peerless tractor was developed. The front-wheel-drive system could be engaged with a separate clutch and was intended mainly to facilitate short turns and as a power boost in poor conditions. A two-cylinder horizontal opposed engine was used and was capable of 20 belt hp. Little else is known of the Peerless, as nothing was found subsequent to the 1911 announcements.

Pennsylvania Tractor Company

PHILADELPHIA, PENNSYLVANIA

Pennsylvania Tractor Company was in operation for only a short time. The company offered two models in 1920, but does not appear in the 1921 directories.

Morton Four-Wheel-Drive 40 tractor

In 1920 Pennsylvania Tractor Co. offered the Morton Four-Wheel-Drive 40 tractor. Priced at $3,000, the "40" used a 40-hp Buda four-cylinder engine. This tractor followed the designs of the Morton Truck & Tractor Company, Harrisburg, Pennsylvania.

Morton Four-Wheel-Drive model

In addition to the Four-Wheel-Drive 40, Pennsylvania Tractor Company also offered the Morton Four-Wheel-Drive model in 1920. This huge four-drive outfit was equipped with a six-cylinder engine with a 5-1/2 x 7-inch bore and stroke. It was priced at $5,000.

Peoria Tractor Company

PEORIA, ILLINOIS

Peoria offered its first tractor in 1914, and then built four different models over the next several years. The company disappeared from the tractor directories after 1921. Through its relatively short lifespan, Peoria Tractor Company was reorganized several times.

In 1914 Peoria introduced its three-wheeled 8-20 tractor. By 1916 it had been re-rated as a 10-20, although the tractor was essentially unchanged. The Peoria used a Beaver four-cylinder engine with a 3-3/4 x 5-inch bore and stroke. Its total weight was 3,950 lbs. and in 1916 it sold for $685.

Peoria 12-25 tractor

By 1917, the Peoria 12-25 replaced the original 10-20 model. The 12-25 used a Climax four-cylinder engine with a 5 x 6-1/2-inch bore and stroke. An important feature was full-pressure lubrication through a drilled crankshaft. Weighing 4,750 lbs., the 12-25 was priced at $1,585.

Peoria three-wheeled 8-20 tractor

Peoria Model J 12-25 tractor

About 1919, the Peoria Model J 12-25 tractor replaced the original 12-25. This tractor was nearly identical to its immediate ancestor but used a fully hooded design. Also, a conventional two-wheel standard-tread front axle was used instead of the original one-wheel design.

Peoria Model L 12-25 tractor

The Peoria Model L 12-25 tractor first appeared about 1920 and was apparently the last Peoria tractor model, since the firm was not listed after 1921. The Peoria L tractor was similar to the earlier style, although the main frame was changed and heavier wheels were used.

Perkins Tractor Company

BOSTON, MASSACHUSETTS

This firm was incorporated in 1915 to manufacture tractors, but no other information has been found.

Ray Perrin Tractor Company

PORTLAND, OREGON

In 1948 this company was listed as the manufacturer of the Perrin tractor, apparently a machine in the garden-tractor class. No other information has been found.

Petro-Haul Mfg. Company

CHICAGO, ILLINOIS

Petro-Haul tractor

Petro-Haul tractors first appeared in 1913 and remained on the market a couple of years. The Petro-Haul used a unique drive-wheel design with retractable lugs. Weighing 5,400 lbs., it was equipped with a 24-hp Waukesha four-cylinder engine.

Phillips-Palmer Tractor Company

KANSAS CITY, MISSOURI

Incorporated in 1916, Phillips-Palmer apparently intended to build farm tractors, but no other information has been found.

Phoenix Tractor Company

WINONA, MINNESOTA

Phoenix tractor

The Phoenix tractor appeared in 1912. Rated at 20 drawbar and 30 belt hp, it weighed some 7,000 lbs. Within a year of its appearance, the Phoenix tractor was bought out by American Gas Engine Company at Kansas City, Missouri, which marketed this design as the Weber tractor.

Piasa Tractor Company

JAYTON, TEXAS

This company was incorporated in 1913 to build tractors, but no other information has been found.

Piedmont Motor Car Company

LYNCHBURG, VIRGINIA

This company is listed as a tractor manufacturer in 1919, but no other information is available.

Pioneer Mfg. Company

MILWAUKEE, WISCONSIN

Pioneer Red-E 12 garden tractor

In 1946 Pioneer appeared as the manufacturer of the Red-E garden tractors, with the Red-E 12 shown here. This model used the company's own single-cylinder vertical engine, designed with a 3-3/4 x 4-inch bore and stroke. Rated speed was from 500 to 1,500 rpm. The company was also listed as the manufacturer of the Page Model Z garden tractor.

See: Red-E; Page; MBM

Pioneer Tractor Mfg. Company

WINONA, MINNESOTA

Pioneer was incorporated in April 1909 as Pioneer Tractor Company. A year later, Pioneer Tractor Mfg. Co. was organized at Winona, and by the summer of 1910, the Pioneer 30 tractor was on the market. The company persevered in the tractor business until 1925 when it was reorganized as Pioneer Tractors Inc., but the reorganized venture only lasted for a short time.

Pioneer 30 tractor

The Pioneer 30 used a four-cylinder horizontal opposed engine with a 7 x 8-inch bore and stroke. The drive wheels were 96 inches high. An enclosed cab featured removable windows and a back curtain. The Pioneer 30 was listed in the directories as late as 1927, apparently the last year the company was in the tractor business.

COLLECTOR VALUES	1	2	3	4
30 (1910)	–	–	$40,000	$30,000

Pioneer 45-90 tractor

In 1912 the Pioneer 45 appeared. This huge 45-90 tractor carried a six-cylinder engine with a 7 x 8-inch bore and stroke. Three forward speeds were available on the 30 and 45 models, ranging from 2 to 6 mph. Production of this model continued into 1914 and it is likely that it was also available on special order after that time. The company also built a four-cylinder Pioneer Jr. tractor but no illustrations of this model have been located.

Pioneer Pony tractor

About 1916, the Pioneer Pony tractor appeared and was advertised for a short time. This model had a 15-30 hp rating, but few specific details of it have been found. In 1916 it listed at $765.

Pioneer Special 15-30 tractor

During 1917, the Pioneer Special appeared. Rated as a 15-30, it used a four-cylinder engine with a 5-1/2 x 6-inch bore and stroke. In Canada the Pioneer Special was sold as the Winona Special, even though it was the same tractor. Production of this model continued into 1919.

Pioneer 18-36 model

Sometime in 1919, Pioneer replaced its "Special" with a new 18-36 model. This tractor was equipped with a four-cylinder horizontal opposed engine with a 5-1/2 x 6-inch bore and stroke. The 18-36 weighed 6,000 lbs. This model remained active until the company left the tractor business in 1927.

Plano Tractor Company

PLANO, ILLINOIS

12-24 Motox tractor

The 12-24 Motox tractor first appeared in 1917. It initially had a list price of $1,850. Power came from a Buda four-cylinder engine with a 4-1/4 x 5-1/2-inch bore and stroke. There was only one forward speed and reverse. Sometime in 1919, the Motox was taken over by Wabash Tractor Company.

Plowman 15-30 tractor

Plantation Equipment Company

VALLEY PARK, MISSOURI

For 1916 this company is listed as the manufacturers of the Ultimate tractor line. Included was the Ultimate 8-16, the Ultimate 12-25 and the Ultimate 16-32. No illustrations of these tractors were found.

Plowboy Tractor Company

PHOENIX, ARIZONA

This company was organized in 1913 to manufacture the Plowboy tractors, but no other information has been found.

Plowman Tractor Company

WATERLOO, IOWA

The Plowman 15-30 tractor appeared in 1920. It was actually the same tractor that had been offered previously by Interstate Tractor Company, also of Waterloo. The Plowman 15-30 was equipped with a Buda YTU four-cylinder engine with a 4-1/2 x 6-inch bore and stroke. The Plowman 15-30 was marketed for only a short time.

Pocahontas Mfg. Company

CHARLES CITY, IOWA

This firm was organized at Minneapolis in 1917, and shortly afterwards, it bought out the Charles City Engine Company in Charles City, Iowa. The latter had been building the Armstrong gasoline engines, formerly of Waterloo, Iowa. At this same time, the company announced its Poco tractor, but no illustrations or other information were found. The Poco was listed as late as 1919.

Geo. D. Pohl Mfg. Company

VERNON, NEW YORK

This famous gasoline engine manufacturer was also listed as a tractor manufacturer as late as 1913. No illustrations of the Pohl tractor have been found.

Pond Garden Tractor Company

RAVENNA, OHIO

Harold Pond first used the Speedex garden tractor name in 1935, but no illustrations of the earliest machines have been located. The Speedex Model B garden tractor was fitted with a Briggs & Stratton Model ZZ engine with a 3 x 3-1/4-inch bore and stroke.

COLLECTOR VALUES	1	2	3	4
SPEEDEX MODEL B	$450	$350	$250	$100

Pontiac Tractor Company

PONTIAC, MICHIGAN

Pontiac 15-30 tractor

The Pontiac 15-30 tractor was developed during 1918 and marketed into 1919. This tractor used a single-cylinder engine with a 9 x 12-inch bore and stroke. Unfortunately, very little else is known about the company or its tractors.

Pony Tractor Company

LAPORTE, INDIANA

A 1919 trade note indicated that Pony Tractor Co. was incorporated that year, ostensibly to manufacture tractors. No other information has been found.

Pope Mfg. Company

WATERTOWN, SOUTH DAKOTA

Dakota 15-27 tractor

The Dakota 15-27 tractor was offered in 1920 by Pope Mfg. Co. It was a takeoff from the earlier Dakota tractors built by G. W. Elliott & Son at DeSmet, South Dakota. Power for this tractor came from a Doman four-cylinder engine with a 4-3/4 x 6-inch bore and stroke.

Port Huron Engine & Thresher Company

PORT HURON, MICHIGAN

Port Huron 12-25 tractor

Port Huron had an ancestry going back to the 1850s as a small grain thresher manufacturer. The company continued to grow, and in 1890, the name was changed from Upton Mfg. Co. to Port Huron. The company offered its gas tractor between 1918 and 1922. Rated as a 12-25, the Port Huron used a four-cylinder Chief engine with a 4-3/4 x 6-inch bore and stroke. The tractor weighed 6,200 lbs. and was priced at $1,700. The Port Huron used an infinitely variable drive system much like the Heider tractors.

Nebraska Test Data

Model: Port Huron 12-25

Test No. 69

Date Tested: October 20 to October 27, 1920

Test No. 69 indicated the Port Huron 12-25 had either been in production for only a short time prior to October 1920, or else it had not been selling very well. The engine carried Serial No. 1258 and the chassis carried Serial No. 316. A friction drive transmission gave forward speeds ranging from 1-7/8 to 4 mph. Total weight was 6,750 lbs. Regular equipment included a Chief four-cylinder vertical, valve-in-head engine with a 4-3/4 x 6-inch bore and stroke. Rated speed was 900 rpm. It was equipped with a Kingston Model L carburetor and an Eisemann magneto. Test engineers noted that during the limbering-up run the governor was replaced, and that the engine blew out four spark plugs. These were replaced with a different make. Using kerosene, the 12-25 had a fuel economy of only 5.43 hp-hours per gallon at rated brake hp. Under a maximum load of 28.46 brake hp, fuel economy rose to 6.69 hp-hours per gallon. At 1.85 mph, the Port Huron made a maximum pull of 4,144 lbs., corresponding to 20.42 drawbar hp.

Porter Tractor Company

DES MOINES, IOWA

In 1919 the Porter Tractor Co. began operations at Colfax, Iowa. Within a few months, the firm moved to nearby Des Moines. Rated as a 20-40, the Porter tractor featured a Waukesha engine with a 4-3/4 x 6-3/4-inch bore and stroke. A unique feature was the special extension attachment whereby many different implements could be operated from the seat of the connected machine, such as a grain binder. The Porter disappeared after 1920.

Post Tractor Company

CLEVELAND, OHIO

Post Tractor Company was organized and incorporated in 1918. By the following year, the Post 12-20 tractor was

Porter 20-40 tractor

on the market. This unique design used two centrally-placed drive wheels, with an outrigger support wheel on each side. Power came from a four-cylinder Waukesha engine with a 4-1/4 x 5-3/4-inch bore and stroke. Weighing 3,300 lbs., the Post 12-20 sold for $1,250. Production apparently ended during 1920.

Post 12-20 tractor

Powell Tractor Company

ELWOOD, INDIANA

During 1919, the Powell 16-30 appeared. Few details are available for this model except it offered two forward speeds of 2-1/2 and 5 mph. This tractor had many similarities to the Elgin tractor, built earlier at Elgin, Illinois.

Power Garden Cultivator Company

MINNEAPOLIS, MINNESOTA

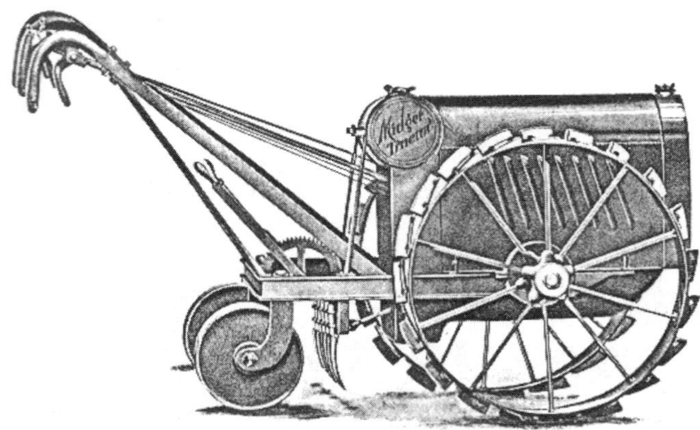

Midget tractor

In 1918 this company appeared, and its advertising brochure led to the conclusion that the company was in full operation. Apparently, the company was operating on a shoestring, and whether the Midget tractor ever became more than a figment of the artist's imagination is unknown.

Power King Tractor Company

MILWAUKEE, WISCONSIN

The Power King appeared in the 1953 directories, but no information was found to determine the career of the

Powell 16-30 tractor

company or its tractors. The 1953 model was capable of about 8 hp and used either a Briggs & Stratton or a Wisconsin engine. Numerous attachments were available.

Power King tractor

COLLECTOR VALUES	1	2	3	4
POWER KING	$1,200	$900	$750	$500

Power Truck & Tractor Company

DETROIT, MICHIGAN

During 1919, Power Truck & Tractor Co. offered this 15-32 tractor. Power came from a single-cylinder engine with a 9 x 12-inch bore and stroke. This tractor is quite similar to the Pontiac 15-30, a tractor offered a year earlier by Pontiac Tractor Co.

Powerall Farm Tools Company

CHULA VISTA, CALIFORNIA

The Powerall garden tractor was listed in 1948, but no illustrations or specifications have been found.

Pow-R-Trak Company

WICHITA, KANSAS

During 1948, the Pow-R-Trak garden tractor was on the market, but no photographs or specifications on this unit have been located.

Prairie Queen Tractor Mfg. Company

TEMPLE, TEXAS

Prairie Queen 8-16 tractor

Power Truck & Tractor Company 15-32 tractor

In the early 1920s, the Prairie Queen 8-16 tractor appeared. This small tractor was priced at only $765. For reasons unknown, it left the market during 1922. No details about the company or its tractor have been located.

Progressive Machinery Company

MINNEAPOLIS, MINNESOTA

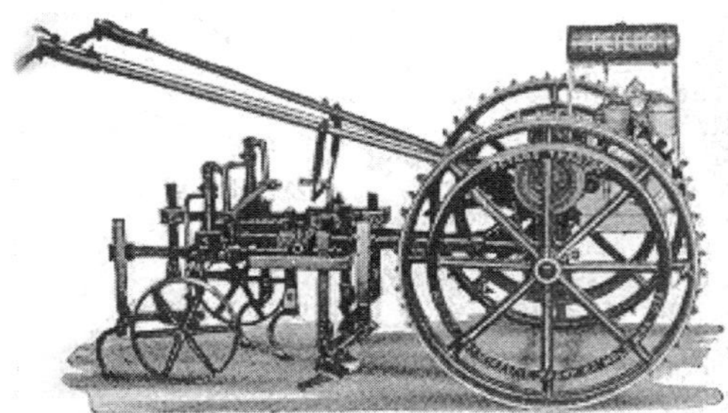

Peters garden tractor

In 1931 the Peters garden tractor was built by Progressive Machinery Co. This model was powered by a Briggs & Stratton Model PB engine with a 2-1/2-inch bore and stroke. Alternatively, a Toro Model ME engine was used and it was slightly larger with its 2-5/8 x 3-1/4-inch bore and stroke.

COLLECTOR VALUES	1	2	3	4
PETERS GARDEN TRACTOR	$2,500	$2,000	$1,000	$650

Providence Engineering Works

PROVIDENCE, RHODE ISLAND

In early 1914, the Providence tractor was announced, and was probably developed the previous year. An interesting feature was that the body of the tractor was of a single iron casting. Power came from a 20-hp three-cylinder engine. After the initial announcements, nothing more was known of the Providence tractor.

Pull-Away Garden Tractor Company

STOCKTON, CALIFORNIA

During 1948, this firm was listed as the builder of the Pull-Away Garden Tractor, but no other information has been found.

Providence tractor

Pullford conversion attachment

Pullet Tractor Company

MINNEAPOLIS, MINNESOTA

A trademark application of 1918 noted the Pullet trademark had first been applied to tractors in October 1917. In 1919 the Pullet tractor with a 40-hp belt rating was displayed at several demonstrations, and the company was listed as a tractor manufacturer as late as 1921. No illustrations or specifications regarding this tractor were found.

Pullford Company

QUINCY, ILLINOIS

Hundreds of companies built conversion units to make a tractor out of a car. One of the most successful of these was the Pullford attachment. By 1917, it was available for the Model T Ford and priced at only $135. It continued on the market into the 1930s, and during that decade was also available for the Model A Ford.

Puritan Machine Company

DETROIT, MICHIGAN

New Elgin 12-25 tractor

During 1920, Puritan offered the New Elgin 12-25 tractor. It was apparently the immediate successor to the Waite and Elgin tractors found elsewhere in this volume. The New Elgin 12-25 used a four-cylinder Erd engine with a 4 x 6-inch bore and stroke.

[Throughout this section, assume that gasoline was used for fuel unless another fuel source is indicated.]

Quick Mfg. Company

SPRINGFIELD, OHIO

Springfield garden tractor

During 1953 Quick Mfg. offered its Springfield 2001, 2002 and 2003 garden tractors. The 2001 was furnished with a Briggs & Stratton NPR-6 engine capable of 2 hp. Model 2002 and 2003 tractors were equipped with a Briggs & Stratton 8R6 engine or a Clinton D1162 engine, both capable of 2-1/2 hp.

COLLECTOR VALUES	1	2	3	4
ALL MODELS	$850	$600	$300	$100

Quincy Engine Company

QUINCY, PENNSYLVANIA

By 1912, Quincy Engine Company entered the tractor business.

This small tractor was capable of about 6 or 8 belt hp. The engine was simply a Quincy portable mounted to the company's own chassis.

The Quincy 10-20 tractor shown here was powered by a Quincy 20-hp single-cylinder engine. This model came onto the market in 1912 and remained as late as 1916. At that time it sold for $1,200. This tractor weighed 10,000 lbs.

1912 Quincy tractor

Quincy 10-20 tractor

R & P Tractor Company

ALMA, MICHIGAN

R & P 12-20 tractor

Between 1918 and 1920 the R & P 12-20 appeared. A unique feature was the unique track-pad wheels. They were originally developed in Italy as military tractors. The R & P was designed with a Waukesha four-cylinder engine with a 3-3/4 x 5-½-inch bore and stroke. At least one R & P tractor remains in existence in Australia.

S. W. Raymond Tractor Company

ADRIAN, MICHIGAN

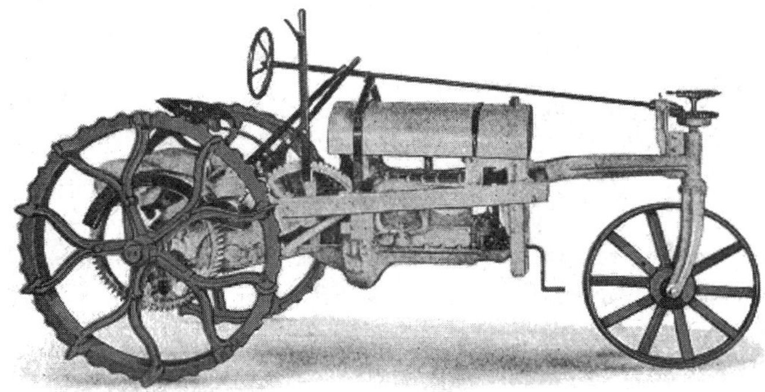

Raymond tractor

About 1922 the Raymond tractor appeared. It had a unique chassis design and was powered by a Ford Model T engine. The Raymond used individual rear brakes and also featured a unique mechanical lift system for the plow. A cultivator could be mounted directly to the tractor frame. After using the engine, transmission, radiator and fuel tank for the tractor, the remaining parts could be used for making a four-wheel trailer.

Redden Truck & Tractor Company

HARVEY, ILLINOIS

Redden Farmer-Tractor-Truck

By 1919, the Redden Farmer-Tractor-Truck appeared. This combination machine was intended as a tractor and a two-ton truck. A Buda four-cylinder engine powered this machine and used a 4-1/4 x 5-1/2-inch bore and stroke. Standard features included a belt pulley. This machine had a list price of $2,600.

Red-E-Tractor Company

RICHFIELD, WISCONSIN

See: M.B.M. Mfg. Co.

In 1953 this firm is listed as the manufacturer of the M.B.M. garden tractor. No other information is available.

Reed Foundry & Machine Company

KALAMAZOO, MICHIGAN

Reed 12-25 tractor

About 1916, the Reed 12-25 tractor appeared. The 12-25 initially used a Waukesha four-cylinder engine with a 3-1/2 x 5-3/4-inch bore and stroke, but within a year, the engine bore was increased to 4 inches. This model sold at about $1,650. Production of the 12-25 ended in 1920.

Reed 12-25 tractor

A redesigned Reed 12-25 appeared in 1921. The new tractor featured a Doman four-cylinder engine of the same size as the Waukesha used in the original model. Shortly after it appeared on the market, this new tractor was known as the Model A 15-30 tractor. The company also developed a tractor using a Doman 5 x 6-inch, four-cylinder motor, but mounted in the same chassis. By the following year the Reed tractor disappeared.

Reeves & Company

COLUMBUS, INDIANA

Reeves "40" tractor

Reeves began building grain threshers in 1874 and began building steam traction engines about 10 years later. The Reeves tractor was developed in 1910 and came out the following year. In 1912 Emerson-Brantingham Company bought out Reeves and continued building the tractor for several years. The Reeves "40" was rated at 40 drawbar and 65 belt hp, and was the same engine used in the Twin City 40-65 model. It was of four-cylinder design and used a 7-1/4 x 9-inch bore and stroke.

Rein Drive Tractor Company Ltd.

TORONTO, ONTARIO

Rein Drive tractor

During April 1917, the Rein Drive tractor was developed. As the name implied, it was intended to be driven by reins, just like driving a team of horses. For reasons unknown, the company succeeded for only a short time. The Rein Drive was advertised into 1918. After that, it disappeared from the scene.

Reliable Tractor & Engine Company

PORTSMOUTH, OHIO

10-20 Reliable tractor

In 1915 Reliable Tractor & Engine Co. was organized to take over the assets of Heer Engine Company, also of Portsmouth. The 10-20 Reliable was equipped with a two-cylinder engine with a 6 x 7-inch bore and stroke. It weighed 3,800 lbs. and sold for $985. This tractor was also sold by Fairbanks, Morse & Company as its Fair-Mor tractor for several years. Production of this model ended about 1921. *See: Morton Tractor Company; Morton-Heer; Heer Engine Co.*

Remy Bros. Tractor Company

KOKOMO, INDIANA

In 1917 this firm was incorporated by Remy Brothers of magneto fame and Elwood Haynes of automotive fame to build a tractor. The Remy 15-30 tractor was announced in 1918, but no other information about the company or its tractors has been located.

Renno-Leslie Motor Company

PHILADELPHIA, PENNSYLVANIA

This firm was organized and incorporated in 1917 to build tractors, but no other information has been located.

Rexroth Industries

RIVERSIDE, CALIFORNIA

Rexroth Bobbette Model L garden tractor

In the late 1950s, the Rexroth Bobbette Model L garden tractor appeared. It was powered with a Wisconsin Model AKN engine with a 2-7/8 x 2-3/4-inch bore and stroke. This produced over 6 hp. Numerous attachments were available, and features included three forward speeds. Total weight was 520 lbs.

COLLECTOR VALUES	1	2	3	4
ALL MODELS	$850	$675	$450	$250

Ripley Cultivator & Motor Tractor Mfg. Company

AURORA, ILLINOIS

This firm was organized in 1920 to manufacture tractors, but no other information has been found.

Rock Island Plow Company

ROCK ISLAND, ILLINOIS

Rock Island Plow Co. began in the plow business in 1855. The company prospered and took the Rock Island name in 1882. By 1912 the firm offered one of the largest lines of tillage implements in the entire industry.

During 1914 and 1915, Rock Island Plow Co. expanded its line with the addition of the Heider tractor built at Car-

Heider Model C 10-20

roll, Iowa. In January 1916, Rock Island bought out the Heider tractor line and launched themselves permanently into the tractor business. This continued until Rock Island Plow Co. was taken over by J. I. Case Company in 1937.
See: Heider Mfg. Company

Rock Island Plow Co. entered the tractor business in 1914 by contracting to sell the output of the Heider Tractor Co., Carroll, Iowa. The Heider proved to be very popular, and in 1916 Rock Island bought out the Heider tractor line. The original 10-20 Model C Heider gave way to a 12-20 Model C in 1916.

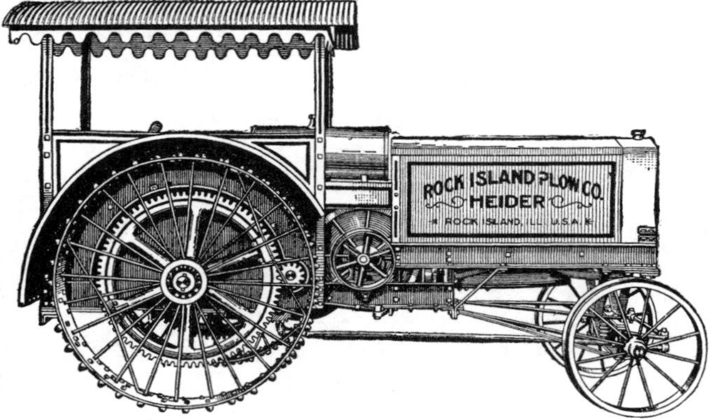

Heider Model C 12-20

During 1916, the 12-20 Model C Heider tractor appeared. It remained on the market until 1924 when it was replaced with the improved 15-27 Model C. A Waukesha four-cylinder engine was used in the 12-20. It carried a 4-1-2 x 6-3/4-inch bore and stroke. Total weight was 6,000 lbs. The salient feature of the Heider tractor was the use of a friction drive system that permitted seven different speeds, forward or reverse.

Nebraska Test Data

Model: Heider Model C 12-20
Test No. 16
Date Tested: May 28 to June 8, 1920

A unique friction-drive transmission gave the Heider 12-20 the distinction of being the first tractor tested at Nebraska to feature more than one or two forward speeds. A total of eight different rated speeds were indicated in the test reports. It would be many years until this speed range was offered by other builders. Like all prior tests, the 12-20 used kerosene in its four-cylinder 4-1/2 x 6-3/4-inch engine. Rated at 900 rpm, it was of vertical, L-head design. Regular equipment included a Kingston Model 13 carburetor and the ever-popular Dixie Model 46 magneto. On the rated brake hp test, 20.18 bhp was indicated, with fuel consumption coming to 2.96 gph. Fuel economy amounted to 6.81 hp-hours per gallon of kerosene. Nearly 25-1/4 hp was developed in the maximum brake hp test, with fuel economy dropping to only 4.24 hp-hours per gallon. At the drawbar, a maximum pull of 2,223 lbs. was recorded at slightly over 2-1/4 mph for a maximum of 13.43 drawbar hp.

Heider Model C, 15-27 tractor

The Heider Model C, 15-27 tractor was built in the 1924 through 1927 period. This model used a Waukesha four-cylinder engine with a 4-3/4 x 6-3/4-inch bore and stroke. In Nebraska Test No. 114 of 1925, the 15-27 proved itself with over 17 drawbar hp and 30 hp on the belt pulley.

Nebraska Test Data

Model: Heider 15-27
Test No. 114
Date Tested: May 7 to May 13, 1925

The Heider 15-27 handily proved itself to be capable of the manufacturer's rating by developing 17.06 drawbar hp in the rated load test. Final results indicated a pull of 2,461 lbs. at 2.6 mph over the 10-hour test run. The friction-drive transmission provided infinitely variable speed, with three different maximum drawbar load tests being run at speeds from 2.45 to 3.15 mph. At the lowest speed, the 15-27 gave a pull of 3,302 lbs. for 21.54 maximum drawbar hp. During the 36 hours required for test completion, kerosene was used. In the brake hp tests, 7.62 hp-hours per gallon was calculated in the rated load test, with an even 30 hp appearing in the maximum load trial. At this load, fuel economy dropped to 6.51 hp-hours per gallon with a total consumption of 4.608 gallons per hour (gph). The 15-27 weighed 6,290 lbs. and carried a Waukesha four-cylinder vertical, L-head engine. Using a 4-3/4 x 6-3/4-inch bore and stroke, it was rated at 900 rpm. Standard equipment also included a Waukesha governor, United whirling vane air cleaner, Dixie 46 magneto and a Kingston Model L carburetor. Minor problems occurred during the test due to a defective ball bearing, but no other repairs or adjustments were necessary.

Heider Model D, 9-16

Rock Island Model F 18-35 tractor

Introduced in 1916, the Heider Model D 9-16 tractor remained on the market until 1929. Weighing 4,000 lbs., the 9-16 featured a Waukesha four-cylinder engine with a 4-1/4 x 5-3/4-inch bore and stroke. In Nebraska Test No. 17 of 1920, the 9-16 delivered nearly 12 drawbar hp. When the 9-16 was taken out of production in 1929, the Heider trade name was dropped.

Nebraska Test Data

Model: Heider Model D, 9-16

Test No. 17

Date Tested: June 1 to June 9, 1920

According to Rock Island Plow Company's own advertising literature, "It (the Model D) is ... an exact duplicate of the Model C, 12-20 except for size." It is apparent that the same transmission, a similar Waukesha engine, and other features followed very closely, model for model. During Test No. 17, which consisted of about 33 hours running time, only minor repairs or adjustments were necessary. A four-cylinder 4-1/4 x 5-3/4 engine powered the 9-16. Total weight of the tractor was 4,100 lbs., compared to 6,200 lbs. for the 12-20 of Test No. 16. In the drawbar tests, a maximum pull of 1,900 lbs. was exerted by the 9-16, at a speed of 2.32 mph, for a corresponding maximum drawbar hp of 11.76. In the belt, a maximum of 19.54 hp was recorded. Fuel consumption came to 2.89 gph in this test for an equivalent of 6.75 hp-hours per gallon of kerosene.

Rock Island Plow Co. introduced its Heider 6-10 cultivator in 1920. It was sold as the M-1 (one-row) or the M-2 (two-row) cultivator. Power came from a four-cylinder Le-Roi engine with a 3-1/8 x 4-1/2-inch bore and stroke. This unit was available through 1926.

Heider 6-10 Motor Cultivator

Production of the Rock Island Model F 18-35 tractor began in 1927. This tractor was furnished with a Buda four-cylinder engine with a 4-1/2 x 6-inch bore and stroke. In Nebraska Test No. 144 of 1927, the 18-35 demonstrated over 30 drawbar hp. Production of this model continued until the firm was bought out by J. I. Case Co. in 1937. A Model FA was also available. The only difference was that the transmission was geared more slowly than the Model F.

Nebraska Test Data

Model: Rock Island 18-35

Test No. 144

Date Tested: October 12 to October 19, 1927

Featuring a Buda four-cylinder vertical, L-head engine, the 18-35 Rock Island went through some 37 hours of running time without any repairs or adjustments. The engine was rated at 1,100 rpm and carried a 4-1/2 x 6-inch bore and stroke. Also included was a Dixie Model 46C magneto, with a Stromberg M3 carburetor and a United air cleaner. Total weight was 5,740 lbs. Two forward speeds gave the choice of either 3 or 4-1/2 mph. Using distillate fuel, the 18-35 delivered 7.07 hp-hours per gallon on the rated drawbar test, burning 2.656 gph. A maximum load test taken in low gear revealed a pull of 3,190 lbs. at 3.58 mph for 30.42 drawbar hp. Maximum brake hp tests resulted in an economy of 7.7 hp-hours per gallon while delivering 36.5 hp. At rated load, economy rose to 9.02 hp-hours per gallon with total consumption of 3.916 gph. To conform with A.S.A.E. and S.A.E. rating codes, test notes indicated this tractor should not have been rated higher than 32 belt hp.

COLLECTOR VALUES	1	2	3	4
MODEL F 18-35	$6,500	$4,500	$2,500	–

Rock Island G-2, 15-25 tractor

In 1929 the Rock Island G-2, 15-25 tractor appeared. This tractor was of a design similar to the Model F. Weighing 4,200 lbs., the G-2 was furnished with a Waukesha four-cylinder engine with a 4-1/4 x 5-3/4-inch bore and stroke. Starting and lighting equipment were available for the Model F and Model G-2 tractors as extra-cost options. When J. I. Case bought out Rock Island Plow Co. in 1937, all production of Rock Island tractors ceased.

Nebraska Test Data

Model: Rock Island G-2, 15-25
Test No. 157
Date Tested: April 24 to May 3, 1929

Waukesha supplied the engine for this tractor. Of four-cylinder vertical, L-head design, it was rated at 1,100 rpm and featured a 4-1/4 x 5-3/4-inch bore and stroke. Also included was a Splitdorf 46T magneto, Stromberg M-2 carburetor, Pomona air cleaner and full-pressure lubrication. Distillate fuel was used in this test, with the G-2 yielding 8.41 hp-hours per gallon at rated brake hp. Under maximum load, 29 hp appeared, along with 8.01 hp-hours per gallon. Rated drawbar testing was done in low gear. In this test, the G-2 produced 5.22 hp-hours per gallon. Maximum drawbar tests were conducted in both forward gears, but in low, the G-2 pulled 2,880 lbs. at 2.84 mph for a maximum of 22.08 drawbar hp. No repairs or adjustments were required during the 30 hours of running time. Test weight, with operator, was 5,070 lbs.

Nebraska Test Data

Model: Rock Island G-2, 18-30
Test No. 158
Date Tested: May 4 to May 8, 1929

The only difference between this test and No. 157 was that gasoline was used in Test No. 158, compared to distillate in No. 157. Results were quite different between the two tests. When operating at rated load, the 18-30 delivered 30.16 brake hp with an economy of 9.24 hp-hours per gallon. This figure dropped to 9.14 on the operating maximum load test, but total hp rose to 35.69. Drawbar tests revealed that on rated load the 18-30 delivered 5.22 hp-hours per gallon, with total consumption of 2.934 gph. The highest drawbar pull came in low gear, where the 18-30 attained 22.08 drawbar hp, and pulled a 2,880-lb. load at 2.88 mph. Only 25 hours were required to complete this test, and during that time, no repairs or adjustments were necessary. Coolant temperatures never rose above 175 degrees F. during the entire test.

COLLECTOR VALUES	1	2	3	4
MODEL G-2	$5,500	$4,000	$2,500	–

Rockford Engine Works

ROCKFORD, ILLINOIS

This firm was listed as a tractor manufacturer between 1906 and 1908. Rockford certainly was an active engine builder at the time and most likely produced a few "gasoline traction engines" using its stationary designs. No illustrations of the Rockford tractors have been found.

Rogers Tractor & Trailer Company

ALBION, PENNSYLVANIA

Rogers four-wheel-drive tractor

Rogers offered this four-wheel-drive tractor in 1923. Little information can be found on the company, so it may have been on the market for a few years during the early 1920s. The Rogers had two speeds: forward and reverse. It was powered by a Buffalo four-cylinder engine.

Nebraska Test Data

Model: Rogers

Test No. 84

Date Tested: April 1 to May 10, 1922

Starting off the 1922 testing season was a unique four-wheel-drive tractor produced by Rogers Tractor & Trailer Company. This was the first tractor to be tested using a hydraulic steering gear. Using low gear, a maximum pull of 10,000 lbs. was achieved at 1.31 mph for 34.85 drawbar hp. High gear was rated at 3.6 mph. On rated drawbar load, 35.47 hp was developed pulling a 3,979-lb. load at 3.34 mph. Gasoline was the chosen fuel throughout Test No. 84, with 6.33 hp-hours per gallon resulting on the rated brake hp test. Total consumption was 9.687 gph with a 61.3 hp load. A total of 78 hours running time was required to complete the tests, with the engine using 9 gallons of oil to fill the crankcase initially and then requiring the addition of another 14-1/2 gallons during the tests. A number of minor adjustments were made, including frequent attention to the magneto and spark plugs. Standard equipment included a Berling magneto and a Zenith carburetor. A Buffalo four-cylinder vertical, L-head engine was used. It carried a 6-3/4 x 9-inch bore and stroke with a rated speed of 800 rpm. The Rogers tractor weighed 19,500 lbs.

Ross Motors Ltd.

CHICAGO, ILLINOIS

This firm is listed as a tractor manufacturer but no other information has been found.

Roths Industries

ALMA, MICHIGAN

Model R Bes-Ro tractor

By 1947, Roths was offering several styles of garden tractors. The Model R Bes-Ro tractor was on the market by 1950. It was equipped with a 7-1/2-hp engine and an automotive-type differential. Also included was the Model W Garden King, a two-wheeler with a 5-hp engine, and the Model G, a two-wheeler with the choice of a 2- or 3-hp engine. The company was active in the tractor business at least into the late 1950s.

Roto-Hoe & Sprayer Company

NEWBURY, OHIO

Roto-Hoe 148H rotary tiller

In the early 1950s, the Roto-Hoe 148H rotary tiller was available. It was equipped with a Lauson Model RSH engine that used a 2 x 1-7/8-inch bore and stroke. It was capable of 2 hp.

COLLECTOR VALUES	1	2	3	4
148H	$150	$100	$75	$35

Rototiller Incorporated

TROY, NEW YORK

Rototiller

Rototiller first used its trade name for soil cultivators on February 9, 1929. The company built various models of Rototillers during the years. The firm initially operated at Wilmington, Delaware, but by the late 1940s was located at Troy, New York. Shown here is the Model T Rotoette.

This 1950 model was equipped with a Briggs & Stratton Model N engine with a 2-inch bore and stroke.

COLLECTOR VALUES	1	2	3	4
ALL MODELS	$750	$600	$450	$175

Royal Motors Company

NAPOLEON, OHIO

Royal Line-Drive tractor

In 1917 Royal Motors announced its new line-drive tractor. Rated at 35 belt hp, it also featured electric starting and lights. The Royal Line-Drive remained on the market for only a short time. Virtually nothing is known about the machine aside from introductory announcements.

Royer Tractor Company

WICHITA, KANSAS

Royer Ensilage Harvester Co. was organized and incorporated at Wichita in 1914. By 1919, the company was building its 12-25 Royer tractor. It was equipped with a four-cylinder Erd engine with a 4 x 6-inch bore and stroke. The company was incorporated in 1920, but little is known of the Royer enterprise after that time.

Ruby Tractor Company

MINNEAPOLIS, MINNESOTA

This firm is listed as a tractor manufacturer in 1916 and remained listed as late as 1920. The company exhibited its tractor at various shows during this period but operated from the same address as the Pullet Tractor Company, so they were actually one and the same. No specific information has been found on the Ruby tractor.

12-25 Royer tractor

Hoosier tractor

Leo Rumely Tractor Company

LAPORTE, INDIANA

The Hoosier tractor was announced in January 1916. It was a revised version of the Wolf tractor, previously built in LaPorte by Wolf Tractor Company. The Hoosier had a rating of 8 drawbar and 18 belt hp. Power came from a Waukesha four-cylinder engine with a 3-3/4 x 5-1/4-inch bore and stroke. The Hoosier remained on the market for only a short time.

Rumely Products Company

LAPORTE, INDIANA

Russell & Company

MARION, OHIO

Russell & Company had its roots all the way back to 1842 when the Russell brothers formed a company to build threshing machines. In 1878 the company was incorporated, and a couple of years later, they began building steam traction engines.

Russell & Co. entered the gasoline traction engine business in 1909 and subsequently offered several sizes of tractors. The company was sold at auction in March 1927 and Russell Service Co. provided repair parts until 1942.

The three-cylinder American Gas Traction Engine made its debut in 1909. It used a three-cylinder engine with an 8 x 10-inch bore and stroke for 22 drawbar hp. The American weighed 17,000 lbs. and sold for $2,400. This tractor was available as late as 1914.

American Gas Traction Engine

Russell 30-60 tractor

Between 1911 and 1913, Russell offered this 30-60 tractor with a single front wheel. A four-cylinder engine powered this model, but no specifications or detailed information has been found.

Russell Giant 40-80 tractor

Russell 30-60 tractor

During 1913, the Russell 30-60 tractor was redesigned to include a conventional front axle instead of the single front wheel as before. Another change was the use of a large tubular radiator. From this design came the Russell Giant of 1914.

From 1914 until 1921, the Russell Giant was rated as a 40-80 tractor. The big four-cylinder engine used an 8 x 10-inch bore and stroke, but in Nebraska Test No. 78, it only developed 66 belt hp. From that time on, until production ended in 1927, it was sold as a 30-60 tractor. The Russell Giant weighed 24,000 lbs.

Nebraska Test Data

Model: Russell 30-60 Giant

Test No. 78

Date Tested: June 6 to June 25, 1921

Originally rated by the company as a 40-80 tractor, the 30-60 Russell Giant came through Test No. 78 without serious problems. Test engineers noted that during preliminary tests the engine overheated. By substituting a larger radiator and making it standard equipment, the problem was rectified. All valves were ground prior to taking any official test data. One exhaust valve spring broke during the maximum drawbar test and was repaired. Specifications included Russell's own four-cylinder vertical, L-head engine with an 8-inch bore and 10-inch stroke, and rated at 525 rpm. The two forward speeds gave selections of either 2 or 3.2 mph. Total weight of the 30-60 was 23,380 lbs. Using low gear, the Russell 30-60 yielded a maximum drawbar pull of 8,800 lbs. at 1.85 mph, for a corresponding maximum of 43.53 drawbar hp. On the rated brake hp test, fuel consumption totaled 11.98 gph for an economy of only 5.04 hp-hours per gallon of kerosene. This dropped to 4.09 hp-hours per gallon when on the maximum brake test, although 66.13 maximum brake hp was developed. Kerosene fuel was used throughout Test No. 78.

Collector Value: The last reported sale of a Russell 30-60 was $262,500.

Russell Jr. 12-24 tractor

Production of the Russell Jr. 12-24 tractor began in late 1915. This model used a Waukesha engine with a 4-1/2 x 5-3/4-inch bore and stroke. This tractor was available into the mid-1920s.

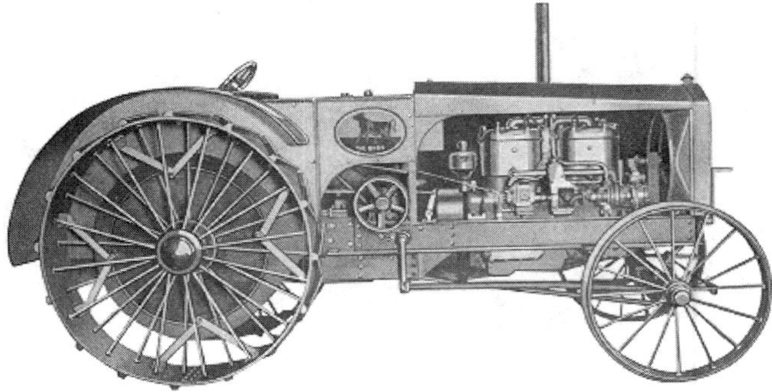

Russell Little Boss 15-30

The Russell Little Boss 15-30 tractor first appeared in 1917. It used a four-cylinder Climax engine with a 5 x 6-1/4-inch bore and stroke. Test No. 93 was run at Nebraska in 1923, and the 15-30 delivered over 24 drawbar hp.

Nebraska Test Data

Model: Russell "Little Boss," 15-30 Model C

Test No. 93

Date Tested: May 16 to May 23, 1923

Weighing 6,035 lbs., Russell's Little Boss carried a Climax four-cylinder vertical, L-head engine. Rated at 950 rpm, it used a 5 x 6-1/2-inch bore and stroke. Low gear gave a speed of 2.4 mph, compared to 3.7 mph in high gear. Also included was a Kingston Model L carburetor, a Splitdorf Aero "448" magneto and a Bennett dry centrifugal air cleaner. All tests were made with kerosene. At rated load of 30.10 brake hp, the 15-30 gave an economy of 7.61 hp-hours per gallon, or a total consumption of 3.956 gph. Under maximum load, 33.57 hp was achieved. Using low gear, the 15-30 pulled a 3,870-lb. load at 2.33 mph for 24.05 maximum drawbar hp. No apparent problems developed under the 10-hour rated drawbar test with the 15-30 pulling a 2,499-lb. load at 2.51 mph. Test notes indicated that repairs and adjustments were confined to tightening the fan belt once and adjusting the clutch on another occasion.

Nebraska Test No. 94 was run on the Russell 20-40 Big Boss tractor in 1923, although production of this model had already begun in 1917. This model used a Climax four-cylinder engine with a 5-1/2 x 7-inch bore and stroke. In Test No. 94, the Big Boss was capable of almost 31 drawbar hp, considerably more than its manufacturer's rating. Production of the Russell tractors ended in 1927 when the company was sold at auction.

Nebraska Test Data

Model: Russell "Big Boss," 20-40 Model C

Test No. 94

Date Tested: May 16 to May 25, 1923

Using a Climax four-cylinder, 5-1/2 x 7-inch engine, the Russell 20-40 was, for all practical purposes, an overgrown version of the 15-30 model noted in Test No. 93. Again, an L-head design was used, but the 20-40 carried a rated speed of 900 rpm. Weighing 8,000 lbs., the 20-40 was a full ton heavier than its counterpart and came up with substantially greater power ratings during Test No. 94. On the two-hour rated brake hp test, 40.21 hp was developed, with kerosene consumption totaling 5.453 gph for an economy of 7.37 hp-hours per gallon. Under maximum load, the 20-40 came out with a recorded 43 hp. A maximum drawbar load test run in high gear revealed 30.9 hp, with a pull of 3,590 lbs. at 3.23 mph. Maximum pull was achieved in low gear, with the dynamometer recording 5,070 lbs. of drawbar pull at 2.37 mph for 32.05 maximum hp. Few adjustments were necessary during the 32-hour test. Regular equipment included a Kingston Model L carburetor, Splitdorf Aero "448" magneto and a Bennett dry centrifugal air cleaner. The 20-40 was equipped with a governor designed and built by Climax. It operated on an elliptical butterfly valve.

COLLECTOR VALUES	1	2	3	4
20-40 BIG BOSS	$25,000	$15,000	$10,000	$5,000

Russell Tractor Company

CHICAGO, ILLINOIS

This firm was organized in 1914 to manufacture tractors, but no other information has been located.

Russell 20-40 Big Boss tractor

[Throughout this section, assume that gasoline was used for fuel unless another fuel source is indicated.]

Sageng Threshing Machine Company

ST. PAUL, MINNESOTA

Halvor O. and Ole O. Sageng organized the Sageng Threshing Machine Company in 1908. The company went broke and closed down in April 1912.

The Sageng Combination Gasoline Thresher was its primary interest, and was one of the first such machines to be built. A large four-cylinder engine was situated beneath the driver's platform. The machines were built by Minneapolis Steel & Machinery Company.

During 1911, the Sageng Farmer's Tractor appeared. Rated at 16 drawbar and 30 belt hp, it used a two-cylinder opposed engine with a 7 x 8-inch bore and stroke. Unfortunately, the Farmer's Tractor lasted only a short time because of the company's financial problems.

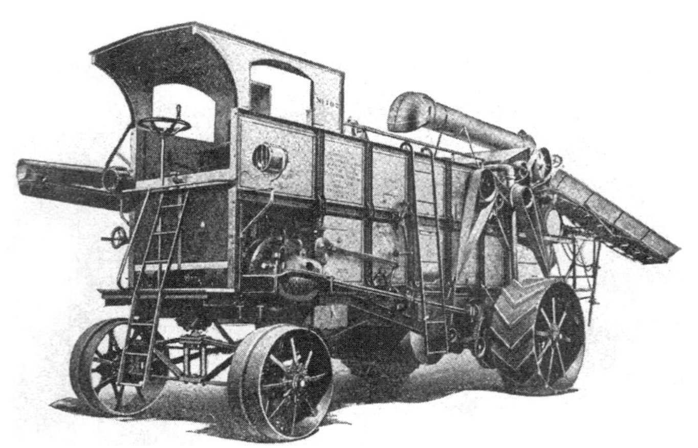

Sageng Combination Gasoline Thresher

Samson Iron Works

STOCKTON, CALIFORNIA

Samson Iron Works had its start in the gasoline engine business as early as 1904, and started making tractors around 1914. General Motors Corporation bought out the Samson tractor line in 1918 and moved the manufacturing operation to Janesville, Wisconsin.

See: General Motors

Sageng Farmer's Tractor

Samson tractor

As early as 1914 the Samson tractor was on the market. The smallest model used a single-cylinder engine with a 7 x 9-inch bore and stroke. It was rated at 10 belt hp. Weighing 4,200 lbs., it was priced at $675. This model was built until about 1917. Only three specimens are known to exist.

Samson Sieve Grip tractor

By 1916, the Samson Sieve Grip tractor line included a four-cylinder model with a rating of 20 belt hp. It was furnished with an engine with a 4-1/4 x 6-3/4-inch bore and stroke. Weighing 5,500 lbs., it sold for $1,150.

COLLECTOR VALUES	1	2	3	4
SIEVE GRIP	$30,000	$26,000	–	–

Savage Harvester Company

DENVER, COLORADO

Savage 20-35 tractor

A full cab came as standard equipment on the Savage 20-35 tractor. Listed only in 1921, this model weighed 7,500 lbs. and was priced at $3,500. Power came from a Climax four-cylinder engine with a 5-1/2 x 7-inch bore and stroke. Little else is known about the Savage 20-35.

Savidge Tractor Mfg. Company

ALTON, ILLINOIS

Although this firm was organized and incorporated in 1917, no other information has been located.

Savoie-Guay Company Ltd.

PLESSISVILLE, QUEBEC

Savoie-Guay one-man motor plow

In 1914 Savoie-Guay developed a one-man motor plow and advertised it the following year. This machine used a three-cylinder engine capable of 35 belt hp. Very little information was found on this unit, and it seems unlikely that a large number were built.

Sawyer-Massey Company

HAMILTON, ONTARIO

During 1910, Sawyer-Massey introduced its new tractor, demonstrating it at various fairs and expositions. Its performance was sufficiently good to warrant continued tractor development, and from this prototype came the Sawyer-Massey 22-45 of the following year. Production of the Sawyer-Massey tractors ended in the early 1920s when the company moved into the construction of road-building machinery.

Sawyer-Massey 22-45 tractor

The 22-45 was typical of the Sawyer-Massey line until production ended in the early 1920s. In the 1912 through 1917 period, Sawyer-Massey offered the 10-20, 16-32 and 25-50 models. The latter was nothing more than the original 22-45 production model of 1911.

Sawyer-Massey 11-22 tractor

By 1918, the Sawyer-Massey line included the 11-22 tractor. This model was designed with a four-cylinder Erd motor with a 4 x 6-inch bore and stroke. Weighing 5,400 lbs., it was priced at $1,750.

Sawyer-Massey 17-34 tractor

A Twin City four-cylinder engine was used in the Sawyer-Massey 17-34 tractor. It used a 5-1/2 x 7-1/2-inch bore and stroke. The 17-34 weighed 11,500 lbs. and was priced at $2,900. Production continued into the early 1920s.

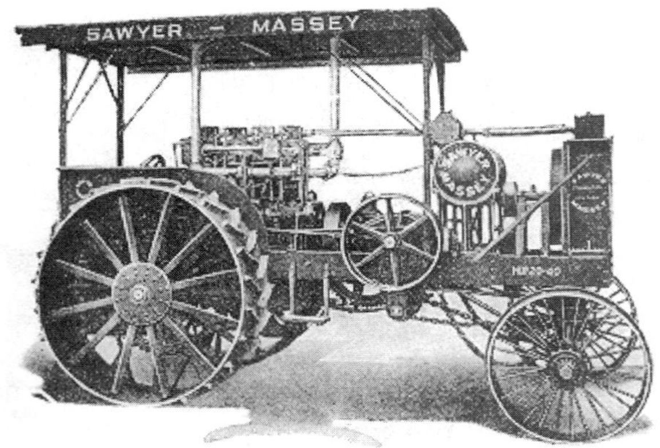

Sawyer-Massey 20-40 tractor

Sawyer-Massey used its own four-cylinder engine in the 20-40 tractor. It was designed with a 5-5/8 x 7-inch bore and stroke. Apparently this tractor was built over the same chassis as the 17-34 tractor. The 20-40 was priced at $3,750.

Sawyer-Massey 27-50 tractor

Priced at $4,000, the Sawyer-Massey 27-50 weighed 17,500 lbs. This model was equipped with the company's own four-cylinder engine with a 6-1/4 x 8-inch bore and stroke.

COLLECTOR VALUES	1	2	3	4
10-20	$20,000	$18,000	$10,000	$6,500
11-22	$20,000	$18,000	$10,000	$6,500
16-32	$25,000	$20,000	$18,000	$15,000
17-36	$25,000	$20,000	$18,000	$15,000
20-40	$35,000	$30,000	$20,000	$15,000
25-50, 25-45 OR 30-60	$50,000	$40,000	$20,000	$15,000

Schofield Auto Tractor Company

KANSAS CITY, MISSOURI

The Schofield Auto Tractor Attachment was offered in 1919, and perhaps for a few seasons on either side of that year. Nearly 50 different companies built automobile-tractor conversion kits at the time. One simply drove the entire automobile onto a chassis, connected the drive chains and the steering linkage for an instant tractor.

Schofield Auto Tractor Attachment

Scientific Farming Machinery Company

MINNEAPOLIS, MINNESOTA

Incorporated in 1916, this firm offered its machines to the U. S. Government the following year in a "Win the War" effort. During 1920, the company gave a manufacturing franchise to Once-Over Tiller Corporation to build a similar machine. The latter was also known as U. S. Farming Machinery Co.

Princess Pat VI 10-20 model

The Princess Pat VI 10-20 model is shown here. Its two plow bottoms were equipped with powered revolving blades that pulverized the soil as it left the moldboards.

Mark 4 tractor

By 1922, the "Once-Over" design was available as the Mark 4, a one-plow horsedrawn unit, the Mark 5 one-plow "Baby" tractor, the Mark 6 two-plow tractor shown here, and the Mark 10 four-plow crawler unit. The plowing units could be removed so other implements could be used, and a belt pulley was also provided.

Mark 10 tractor also known as the Tank-Tread X tractor

For 1922 the equipment line included the Mark 10 shown here. It was also known as the Tank-Tread X tractor. This unit had a 25-50 hp rating and the higher hp was required to operate the whirling tines that pulverized the soil as it left the plows. This machine sold for $3,750, compared to $1,750 for the Princess Pat model of 1919. The company does not appear in the trade directories after 1924.

Seager Engine Works

LANSING, MICHIGAN

Seager tractor

In 1910, Seager Engine Works, manufacturers of the Olds gasoline engines, came out with the Seager tractor. It was rated at 20 drawbar hp and used a four-cylinder engine. The tractor weighed 6,000 lbs. and had two forward and two reverse speeds. Few specific details of this tractor have been found.

Sears, Roebuck & Company

CHICAGO, ILLINOIS

Starting in 1930, Sears Roebuck offered a variety of small tractors and garden tractors. In the 1950s, several models from Sears' line of David Bradley garden tractors were tested at Nebraska.

Handiman garden tractor

About 1930, Sears Roebuck introduced its Handiman garden tractor. It was equipped with a 2-1/2 hp gasoline engine with a 2-1/2-inch bore and stroke. Ordinarily, it was furnished with battery ignition and priced at $149.50, but in 1932, it was also available with magneto ignition at a price of $165. This unit weighed 400 lbs.

COLLECTOR VALUES	1	2	3	4
HANDIMAN GARDEN TRACTOR	$1,250	$650	$450	$250

Sears Bradley General Purpose tractor

Few details have been found on the Sears Bradley General Purpose tractor. It was listed briefly in the 1932 catalog, but reference was given to a special tractor catalog detailing this machine. It was available with a single-row or a two-row cultivator. The rear wheel tread width was adjustable to accommodate various row spacings.

Nebraska Test Data

Model: Bradley General Purpose
Test No. 192
Date Tested: June 10 to June 18, 1931

Under recommendations of the A.S.A.E. and S.A.E. tractor rating codes, this tractor carried a maximum of 15.89 drawbar and 22.93 belt hp, although it was not rated by the manufacturer. Advertised speeds of 1-3/4, 2-1/2, 3 and 4-1/2 mph were built into the Bradley. Using third gear, it delivered 14.83 hp in the rated drawbar test. Also resulting from this test was a pull of 1,626 lbs. at 3.42 mph and an economy of 5.81 hp hours per gallon. Maximum 20.05 drawbar hp came in second gear, with the Bradley pulling 2,728 lbs. at 2.76 mph. Fuel economy at maximum brake hp came in at a respectable 9.22 lbs. per hp hour while cranking out 24.96 hp. The economy figure dropped to 8.23 at rated load of 22.01 hp. Bradley featured a Waukesha four-cylinder vertical engine of L-head design. Rated at 1,250 rpm, it used a 3-3/4 x 4-3/4-inch bore and stroke. An American Bosch U4 magneto, Kingston Model Z carburetor, and Pomona Vortox air cleaner all came as standard equipment, along with a Borg & Beck clutch. Total weight was 4,150 lbs. No repairs or adjustments were required during the 43-hour test.

Sears & Roebuck conversion attachment

During the 1930s Sears & Roebuck offered a conversion attachment whereby any Ford Model T or Model A could be converted into a small utility tractor. Priced at $100, this conversion was capable of ground speeds up to 2-1/2 mph. Various tillage equipment was also available for this unit.

Sears New Economy tractor

For 1938, Sears & Roebuck offered the Sears New Economy tractor. Priced at $495, it was powered by a rebuilt Ford Model A engine. This tractor could be furnished on steel wheels, with rubber tires being an extra-cost option. Various cultivators and implements were available for use with this tractor.

Sears Handiman garden tractor

By 1942, the Sears Handiman garden tractor was available in an entirely new design that featured rubber tires and weighed only 220 lbs. It was powered by a 1-hp Briggs & Stratton engine and was available with numerous implements and attachments.

COLLECTOR VALUES	1	2	3	4
HANDIMAN GARDEN TRACTOR	$650	$500	$300	$200

Nebraska Test Data

Model: Bradley Handiman

Test NNo. 732

Date Tested: November 30 to December 9, 1959

Complete with 23 lbs. of added ballast, the Bradley Handiman weighed 175 lbs. It featured a Briggs & Stratton single-cylinder air-cooled engine rated at 3,600 rpm. Using a 2-3/8 x 1-3/4-inch bore and stroke, it had a 7.75-cubic inch displacement. A fixed-sheave V-belt drive and a planetary gear set gave forward speeds ranging from 0.60 to 2.5 mph. Fuel economy was registered at 2.88 hp-hours per gallon at a maximum available output of 0.69 drawbar hp. This two-hour run indicated a pull of 115 lbs. at 2.24 mph, slippage of 14.18 percent and a fuel economy of 2.88 hp-hours per gallon. A 10-hour run made at 75 percent pull noted 0.55 drawbar hp, a pull of 88 lbs. at 2.35 mph and slippage of 10.36 percent for a fuel economy figure of 2.53 hp-hours per gallon. Belt testing indicated 2.19 maximum hp with a fuel economy of 6.76 hp-hours per gallon. No repairs or adjustments were noted during 37 hours of running time.

The David Bradley Super Power garden tractor was tested at Nebraska in 1953. Test No. 515 indicated a maximum of 6.7 belt hp for this unit. It was powered by a Continental Red Seal engine with a single cylinder with a 2-1/4 x 2-inch bore and stroke.

David Bradley Super Power garden tractor

Nebraska Test Data

Model: David Bradley Super Power

Test No. 515

Date Tested: November 16 to November 20, 1953

Closing out the 1953 testing season, the David Bradley Super Power garden tractor carried a single forward speed of 2.4 mph. Standard equipment included a Continental Red Seal engine of single cylinder, L-head design. Using a 2-1/4 x 2-inch bore and stroke, this engine had a 7.95-cubic inch displacement. Rated at 3,200 rpm, it developed a maximum torque of 7.33 lbs.-ft. at 2,790 rpm. Bare tractor weight was 329 lbs. During Tests F, G and H, an additional 82 lbs. of cast iron was added to each rear wheel. Test G indicated a maximum drawbar pull of 268 lbs. at 2.29 mph with a slippage of 4.89 percent. Test H, run for 10 hours with a rated load of 1.31 drawbar hp, elicited a pull of 209 lbs. at 2.35 mph and a recorded slippage of 3.3 percent. Fuel economy came to 5.04 hp-hours per gallon. Belt testing indicated a fuel economy of 6.19 hp hours per gallon under a Test D-rated load of 1.79 hp, increasing to 6.70 at a Test C maximum belt load of 2.01 hp. No repairs or adjustments were noted during 33 hours of engine operating time.

David Bradley Tri-Trac tractor

In 1954, Sears Roebuck offered its David Bradley Tri-Trac tractor. It used a 6-hp Wisconsin engine with a 2-7/8 x 2-3/4-inch bore and stroke. The Tri-Trac weighed 894 lbs. and had a cultivating clearance of nearly 20 inches.

COLLECTOR VALUES	1	2	3	4
DAVID BRADLEY TRI-TRAC	$650	$500	$300	$200

Nebraska Test Data

Model: David Bradley Suburban
Test No. 729
Date Tested: November 17 to December 7, 1959

The David Bradley Suburban featured a Briggs & Stratton single-cylinder air-cooled engine rated at 3,600 rpm. Using a 2-3/4 x 2-3/8-inch bore and stroke, it had a 14.1-cubic inch displacement. Also included was a 12-volt electrical system. Belt testing indicated a maximum of 3.90 hp at rated speed. Fuel economy was recorded at 6.26 hp-hours per gallon. Using a manually controlled variable speed V-belt drive, the Suburban had a speed range of 2.1 to 4.6 mph. At a maximum drawbar output of 2.80 hp, a pull of 431 lbs. was recorded at 2.43 mph against an 8.4 percent slippage. Fuel economy totaled 4.31 hp- hours per gallon. In contrast, a 10-hour run made at 75 percent pull yielded a figure of 3.77. The latter test also noted an output of 2.35 drawbar hp, a pull of 322 lbs. at 2.74 mph and slippage of 5.65 percent. During preliminary belt runs, a new spark plug was installed and a new carburetor substituted for the original unit. With these exceptions, no repairs or adjustments were required during 52-1/2 hours of operating time.

Nebraska Test Data

Model: David Bradley Super 575
Test No. 730
Date Tested: November 19 to November 28, 1959

Weighing 375 lbs., the Super 575 was burdened with 75 lbs. of ballast on each rear wheel during most of the drawbar tests. At maximum available power, a drawbar output of 3.13 hp was observed, together with a pull of 292 lbs. at 4.02 mph and slippage of 4.34 percent. Fuel economy in this two-hour run totaled 5.7 hp-hours per gallon. A 10-hour run, made at 75 percent pull, produced an economy figure of 5.10. This was balanced against an output of 2.64 hp, a pull of 231 lbs. at 4.28 mph, and slippage of 3.18 percent. Like the tractor noted in Test No. 729, a manually controlled variable-speed V-belt drive was used. Also featured was a single-cylinder Briggs & Stratton engine with a 14.1-cubic inch displacement and using a 2-3/4 x 2-3/8-inch bore and stroke. Belt testing produced a maximum of 3.88 hp at rated engine speed of 3,600 rpm. Fuel economy in this 2-hour test came to 6.54 hp-hours per gallon. No repairs or adjustments were noted during 40-1/2 hours of operating time.

Nebraska Test Data

Model: David Bradley Super 300
Test No. 731
Date Tested: November 19 to December 7, 1959

Weighing only 486 lbs., even with the addition of 152 lbs. of ballast, the Super 300 delivered 1.65 maximum available drawbar hp, pulling 241 lbs. at 2.57 mph with 3.23 percent slippage. Under this load, fuel economy was pegged at 4.84 hp-hours per gallon. A 10-hour drawbar run, made at 75 percent pull, yielded an output of 1.38 hp, together with a pull of 190 lbs. at 2.72 mph and 2.58 percent slippage. The fuel economy test came to 4.33 hp-hours per gallon. The Super 300 was equipped with a fixed-sheave V-belt drive giving an advertised forward speed of 2.7 mph at the rated engine speed of 3,600 rpm. Standard equipment included a Briggs & Stratton single-cylinder engine with a 2-3/8 x 1-3/4- inch bore and stroke for a displacement of 7.75-cubic inches. Belt testing at rated engine speed recorded a maximum output of 1.77 hp and a fuel economy of 4.69 hp-hours per gallon. No repairs or adjustments were noted during 37 hours of operating time.

Self-Contained Power Plow Company

CHAPMAN, KANSAS

Trade reports indicated this firm was in operation in 1913, but no details or illustrations of this machine have been found.

Sexton Tractor Company

ALBERT LEA, MINNESOTA

No information was found regarding this company, but it appears a company of similar name at Asbury Park, New Jersey, was led by the same George L. Sexton who also was the moving force behind this company.

Sexton 12-25 tractor

In 1918, the Sexton 12-25 tractor appeared. This tractor was designed around an Erd four-cylinder engine with a 4 x 6-inch bore and stroke. Westinghouse electric starting and lighting equipment came as an extra-cost option. After a very short time, the Sexton tractor disappeared from the scene.

S.G. Stevens Company

DULUTH, MINNESOTA

Stevens Auto Cultivator

Early in 1913, the Stevens Auto Cultivator was announced, the invention of S.G. Stevens. The cultivating units revolved about an axis and were powered by a 5-hp motorcycle engine. Little else is known of this machine; it is assumed that production lasted for only a short time.

Collector Values: The Stevens Auto Cultivator is valued at $1,000 to $2,500 depending on condition.

Sharpe Mfg. Company

JOLIET, ILLINOIS

Sharpe tractor

In 1917, Sharpe offered this design, noting its heavy use of ball and roller bearings in the tractor. Few details can be found regarding the Sharpe tractor and apparently it was in production for only a short time.

Shaw-Enochs Tractor Company

MINNEAPOLIS, MINNESOTA

In 1918, the Midget Tractor Co. was organized at Minneapolis. By November of the following year, the company was renamed as Shaw-Enochs Tractor Co.

The Shawnee 6-12 shown here was a 2,600-lb. machine that was powered by a four-cylinder LeRoi engine with a 3-1/8 x 4-1/2-inch bore and stroke. In this instance, it is connected to a cultivator, but the Shawnee could be used with a variety of implements.

Shawnee 9-18 model tractor

During 1919, the Shaw-Enochs tractor line included the Shawnee 9-18 model. This one was powered by a four-cylinder Gray engine with a 3-1/2 x 5-inch bore and stroke. This 9-18 is shown with a road grader, and from this design came the Shawnee Township Road Boss road grader. Its success prompted the firm to discontinue farm tractors in 1921 and concentrate solely on road building machinery.

Nebraska Test Data

Model: Shawnee Thirty

Test No. 115

Date Tested: May 16 to May 28, 1925

Primarily intended as a road maintainer rather than a farm tractor, the Shawnee Thirty was not equipped with a belt pulley and no brake hp tests were made. The drive wheels were to the front of the machine, and the two non-drivers in the rear carried the road working equipment and the operator. Two forward speeds of 1.5 and 3 mph were available. Total weight of this unit was 9,840 lbs. Since the Shawnee Thirty was not equipped with an ordinary drawbar, the dynamometer car was pulled behind the complete machine through a chain attached to the front end of the grader frame. The rated drawbar load test revealed an average pull of 1,732 lbs. at 2.59 mph for 11.95 drawbar hp. A maximum load test in low gear gave a pull of 3,533 lbs. at 1.23 mph for 11.57 drawbar hp. Slippage in this test exceeded 22 percent. Standard equipment included a Waukesha four-cylinder vertical engine using the Ricardo L-head design. With a 3-3/4x 5-3/4-inch bore and stroke, it was rated at 1,200 rpm. Accessory items included a United air cleamer, Eisemann GS4 magneto and a Zenith carburetor.

Shawnee 6-12 tractor

Shaw Mfg. Company

GALESBURG, KANSAS

Shaw Du-All garden tractor

By 1930, the Shaw Du-All garden tractor was being actively promoted and sold. This early model used a Briggs & Stratton one-cylinder engine, but few specifics have been found on this early model. Shaw Mfg. Company apparently started in the manufacturing business already in 1903.

Shaw tractor conversion unit

During the 1930s, Shaw promoted its tractor conversion units, using the Ford Model A or Model T engine and parts of the chassis. These units were offered for a number of years, and were fairly successful. Of course, much of the success laid with the condition of the engine that was used and the skill of the mechanic assembling this unit.

COLLECTOR VALUES	1	2	3	4
SHAW DU-ALL GARDEN TRACTOR	$850	$650	$450	$250

In 1934 the Shaw Du-All T45D tractor appeared. It was built in 2-, 3- and 4-hp sizes. All models were equipped with Briggs & Stratton engines. These tractors were available with steel wheels or rubber tires. In 1934, the 4-hp unit on steel wheels was priced at $221.50. By 1936, these tractors became known as the Du-All Model D tractors and they remained on the market until about 1940.

Shaw Du-All T45D Tractor

COLLECTOR VALUES	1	2	3	4
SHAW DU-ALL T45D	$850	$600	$450	$200

Shaw HY-8 tractor

The Shaw HY-8 tractor first appeared about 1940. This small tractor used a Wisconsin single-cylinder engine with a 3-5/8 x 4-inch bore and stroke. A belt pulley was standard equipment. The plow shown here was one of many optional implements.

COLLECTOR VALUES	1	2	3	4
SHAW HY-8 TRACTOR	$2,800	$2,000	$1,500	$550

Model H2 Peppy Pal garden tractor

Shaw T-24 riding tractor

Several models of Peppy Pal garden tractors appeared about 1945. One was the 1-1/2 hp model available with several different attachments. The Model H2 Peppy Pal offered many features, including an adjustable tread width ranging from 18 to 28 inches.

About 1954, the Shaw T24 riding tractor appeared. It was offered with the choice of 2-1/2, 2-3/4, 3 and 3-1/2 hp engines. A mower attachment was a $45 extra, and various other implements were available, such as a cultivator, a plow and a snowplow. At this time, Shaw also offered a Model D24 riding mower and a Model D32 riding mower. It was equipped with a 6-hp engine.

COLLECTOR VALUES	1	2	3	4
SHAW T-24 RIDING TRACTOR	$350	$250	$100	$50

Nebraska Test Data

Model: Shaw Du-All Model T-25

Test No. 136

Date Tested: June 7 to June 22, 1927

The Shaw Du-All T-25 carried a Briggs & Stratton single-cylinder air-cooled engine with a rated speed of 2,200 rpm. Featuring an F-head design, this engine carried a 2-1/2-inch bore and stroke. Briggs & Stratton supplied its own magneto, plus a Tillotson MS6A carburetor. No air cleaner or governor were used. Weighing 400 lbs., the Du-All had two forward speeds ranging from 1/2 to 2-1/2 mph. Designed for use only with gasoline, the Du-All came up with only 3.3 hp-hours per gallon in the rated brake hp test, and developed 1.08 hp at maximum load. Drawbar tests indicated a maximum of 0.73 hp. At a speed of 1.94 mph, the Du-All pulled 140-1/2 lbs. Numerous engine problems developed during the test. The exhaust valve stem stuck and it was removed and polished, along with reaming the valve guide. The piston rings stuck in the grooves, requiring replacement. Although these and other minor problems plagued the Du-All during the test; the unit was in good running order after revisions were made.

Nebraska Test Data

Model: Shaw Du-All Model T-45

Test No. 137

Date Tested: June 7 to June 23, 1927

Following the same basic design as the Shaw Du-All noted in Test No. 136, the T-45 featured a somewhat larger Briggs & Stratton engine. Of air-cooled, L-head design, this model carried a 2-3/4 x 3-inch bore and stroke with a rating of 1,600 rpm. A Tillotson MS7A carburetor was used, along with a magneto designed and built by Briggs & Stratton. Also featured was a pneumatic governor by the same manufacturer. Weighing 437 lbs., the T-45 managed a maximum pull of 222.5 lbs. at a speed of 0.93 mph for a total of 0.55 drawbar hp. Slippage totalled 37.75 percent during this test. At rated drawbar load, fuel economy was 1.77 hp-hours per gallon. Slippage of 28.64 percent shared part of the blame. At its rated 1-1/2 brake hp, the T-45 burned 0.319 gallons of gasoline per hour for 4.73 hp-hours per gallon. The maximum load test yielded 1.68 brake hp at a speed of 1,610 rpm.

John Shelburne

NEW LONDON, MISSOURI

A trade note of 1912 indicated this individual or firm was beginning to build a new tractor design. No other information has been found.

Shelby Truck & Tractor Company

SHELBY, OHIO

Little is known of the company, despite the fact that it operated for at least three years, and it produced two different models of tractors starting in 1919.

Shelby 9-18 tractor

In 1919 the Shelby 9-18 tractor appeared. It was powered by a four-cylinder Waukesha engine with a 3-3/4 x 5-1/4-inch bore and stroke. In 1921 this model was given a 10-20 hp rating, but production ended shortly thereafter.

Shelby 15-30 tractor

Between 1919 and 1921, Shelby produced its 15-30 tractor. Weighing 5,000 lbs., it was equipped with a four-cylinder Erd engine with a 4-3/4 x 6-inch bore and stroke.

Sheldon Engine & Sales Company

WATERLOO, IOWA

During World War One, the Sheldon Three Purpose Tractor Attachment appeared. This device was intended primarily for use with the Ford Model T, but could also be adapted to other automobiles. The complete conversion kit was priced at $175. The company rated this machine to have a drawbar pull of 900 lbs., assuming that the Model T engine was in good condition.

Sheldon Three Purpose Tractor Attachment

R. H. Sheppard Company

HANOVER, PENNSYLVANIA

Sheppard began building its own diesel engines in 1940. During World War II the firm developed several sizes and styles of diesel engines using the unique Sheppard design. Production of the Sheppard tractors continued into the late 1950s.

Sheppard SD-1 tractor

The Sheppard SD-1 tractor first appeared about 1948. Weighing 1,100 lbs., it was equipped with a Sheppard single-cylinder diesel engine with a 3 x 4-inch bore and stroke. This tractor was apparently out of production by 1950.

Sheppard SD-2 Diesel tractor

The Sheppard SD-2 Diesel tractor first emerged about 1948, with production continuing for about 10 years. This model used a two-cylinder diesel engine of Sheppard's own design. Rated at 1,650 rpm, it used a 4-1/4 x 5-inch bore and stroke for a displacement of 141.9 cubic inches.

COLLECTOR VALUES	1	2	3	4
SHEPPARD SD-2 DIESEL TRACTOR	--	$9,500	--	--

Sheppard SD-3 Diesel tractor

A three-cylinder Model 6B Sheppard engine was used in the SD-3 Diesel tractor. The design was built around a 4 x 5-inch bore and stroke for a displacement of 188.5 cubic inches.

Sheppard SDO-3 model

In addition to standard row-crop farm tractors, Sheppard also provided various Industrial and Orchard models, including this SDO-3 model. It was essentially built over the SD-3 chassis but included the necessary fenders, hood and other accessories for orchard and vineyard work.

Sheppard SD-4 Diesel tractor

Production of the SD-4 Sheppard Diesel began about 1948 and continued into the late 1950s. This model used the company's own Model 16, four-cylinder diesel engine. It had a 319-cubic inch displacement. Rated speed was 1,650 rpm. A Sheppard-built transmission was used in the Sheppard tractors. The SD-4 had 10 forward speeds. Another important feature was the independent hydraulic system, introduced at a time when few farm tractors were equipped this way. The engine in this tractor used a 4-1/2 x 5-inch bore and stroke. Sheppard also built a conversion unit so the Farmall M and selected other models could be converted to Sheppard Diesel power.

P. E. Shirk

BLUE BALL, PENNSYLVANIA

Shirk announced its first products in 1911, but little was heard from the company after that time.

Shirk tractor

By 1911, the Shirk tractor was on the market and it consisted of a traction chassis that P. E. Shirk had designed. In this instance, a Woodpecker engine from Middletown Machine Co., Middletown, Ohio, served as the power plant. It was capable of 8 belt hp. Probably the chassis could be fitted with other engines as well.

Shirk gasoline tractor

The Shirk gasoline tractor was capable of plowing and various other farm duties. Although the 8-hp model is shown here, the company was prepared to furnish this machine in 4-, 6-, 10-, 12- and 15-hp sizes.

Short Turn Tractor Company

BEMIDJI, MINNESOTA

Short Turn 20-30 tractor

Short Turn Tractor Co. was organized in 1916, and by 1918, a factory was established at Bemidji. The Short Turn 20-30 of that year was built with a four-cylinder engine and a 4 x 6 -inch bore and stroke. Production continued into 1920, and during the last year of production, the Short Turn got a larger engine with a 4-3/4-inch bore. At that time it sold for $1,500.

Siemon Tractor Corporation

BUFFALO, NEW YORK

Siemon's Iron Horse Tractor

During 1919, Siemon's Iron Horse Tractor was demonstrated at various points, and company advertising noted: "The Siemon-McCloskey Tractor has already created a sensation in many parts of the world." Aside from some advertisements, little is known of this tractor; it is not believed that production lasted more than a short time.

Silver King

PLYMOUTH, OHIO

See: Fate-Root-Heath; Mountain State Engineering

Simplex Tractor Company

MINNEAPOLIS, MINNESOTA

Simplex Tractor Company

WICHITA, KANSAS

Simplex 15-30 tractor

The Simplex tractor first appeared in 1914. Rated as a 15-30, it weighed 5,500 lbs. and sold for $950. The Simplex was displayed at various fairs and expositions into 1917. Late that year, the company folded at Minneapolis and reorganized itself in Wichita, Kansas. Little came of the Wichita venture.

Simplicity Mfg. Company

PORT WASHINGTON, WISCONSIN

Simplicity Mfg. Co. began as Turner Mfg. Company in 1911. This firm built Simplicity gasoline engines in many sizes, and began building the Turner Simplicity tractor in 1915. The company was liquidated in 1920 and the following year Simplicity Mfg. Co. was organized. Simplicity began in the garden tractor business by building a version for Montgomery, Ward & Co. in 1937. In 1961, Simplicity began building garden tractors for Allis-Chalmers, and in 1965 Allis-Chalmers bought out the Simplicity factories.

Simplicity L 2 garden tractor

Simplicity had an extensive garden tractor line. The model shown here is the Model L 2 hp tractor of about 1950.

Model M 3 hp garden tractor

During the 1950s, the Simplicity garden tractor line expanded considerably to include the Model M 3 hp size shown here.

COLLECTOR VALUES	1	2	3	4
MODEL M	$600	$500	$250	$125

Sioux City Foundry & Mfg. Company

SIOUX CITY, IOWA

Sioux City Foundry & Mfg. Company tractor

This lightweight tractor appeared in 1911. The company noted it was an experimental model, and full production had not yet begun. Apparently it never got into production, since nothing further was heard of the machine. The engine was a two-cycle model built by Ottumwa-Moline Pump Co. at Ottumwa, Iowa.

S. K. & S. Company

EL PASO, ILLINOIS

This firm developed the Jim Dandy Motor Cultivator about 1916 and subsequently General Motors bought it out. The latter redesigned the Jim Dandy and produced the Samson Iron Horse cultivator.

Smathers Mfg. Company

BREVARD, NORTH CAROLINA

Inexco garden tractor

In 1948 Smathers was building the Inexco garden tractor, also known as the Acme. Inexco Tractor Co. was the exclusive foreign distributor, and it appeared the majority of production was for export. The Inexco used a Clinton Model 1100 engine, capable of about 3 hp. Total weight of this machine was 500 lbs.

Smith Form-A-Truck Company

CHICAGO, ILLINOIS

Smith Form-A-Tractor

About 1920, the Smith Form-A-Tractor appeared. It was a sister device to the Smith Form-A-Truck, which was intended to convert an automobile into a light truck. Numerous tractor attachments were available in the 1915 through 1930 period, but only a few continued into the 1930s.

Smith Tractor Mfg. Company

HARVEY, ILLINOIS

This company was bought out by Ohio Steel Wagon Company at Wapokoneta, Ohio, in 1911. Little else is known of either firm.

H. J. Smith Tractor Company

MINNEAPOLIS, MINNESOTA

It was announced in 1915 that this firm would begin building tractors at Minneapolis. No other information has been located.

Sollberger Engineering Company

MARSHALL, TEXAS

Sollberger C-24 tractor

Sollberger listed its C-24 tractor in 1948. It was also known as the Laughlin C-24 tractor and was sold by Laughlin Engineering under that title until the early 1950s. The C-24 used a Continental F162, four-cylinder engine. It was designed with a 3-7/16 x 4-3/8-inch bore and stroke.

South Texas Tractor Company

HOUSTON, TEXAS

This firm was incorporated in 1917, but no other information is available.

Southern Corn Belt Tractor Company

SIOUX FALLS, SOUTH DAKOTA

Organized in 1916, this company displayed its tractor at the 1917 Tractor Demonstration at Atchison, Kansas. The company was building the Corn Belt 7-18 tractor. Priced at $750, it weighed 3,700 lbs. It was powered by a Gile two-cylinder engine with a 5 x 6-1/2-inch bore and stroke. No illustrations of the Corn Belt 7-18 have been found.

Southern Motor Mfg. Company Ltd.

HOUSTON, TEXAS

Ranger Motor Cultivator

The Ranger Motor Cultivator was developed in 1918. Initially given a 6-12 hp rating, this was soon raised to an 8-16 rating. Southern apparently remained in business until 1923 or 1924, and then disappeared from the scene. The Ranger 8-16 sold for $1,100.

Southern Tractor Mfg. Corporation

CAMDEN, SOUTH CAROLINA

This firm was listed as the manufacturer of the Southern garden tractor in 1953, but no other information has been found.

Speedex Tractor Company

RAVENNA, OHIO

See: Pond Garden Tractor Company.

Springfield Boiler Mfg. Company

SPRINGFIELD, ILLINOIS

No information was available about the tractors manufactured by this company.

Springfield Gas Engine Company

SPRINGFIELD, OHIO

This company was listed as a tractor manufacturer in the 1906 through 1910 period, but no illustrations of the Springfield tractors were found. The company was a well-known manufacturer of gasoline engines.

Square Deal Mfg. Company

DELAWARE, OHIO

This firm is listed as a tractor manufacturer in 1909, but no other information has been located.

Square Turn Tractor Company

NORFOLK, NEBRASKA

In December 1917, Square Turn Tractor Co. was organized from the Kenney-Colwell Co., also of Norfolk. The company was sold at a sheriff's sale in 1925.

Square Turn 18-35 tractor

The Square Turn 18-35 was powered by a four-cylinder Climax engine with a 5 x 6-1/2-inch bore and stroke. A three-bottom Oliver plow came as standard equipment, and the friction drive transmission eliminated clutch, transmission gears and differential. Total weight of the tractor was 7,800 lbs., and in 1920 it sold for $1,875.

Nebraska Test Data

Model: Square Turn, 18-35

Test No. 66

Date Tested: September 27 to October 7, 1920

As submitted for Test No. 66, the Square Turn 18-35 was the first tractor tested at Nebraska that was equipped with a Climax engine. In this case, a four-cylinder L-head style was used, with a 5-inch bore and 6-1/2-inch stroke. Rated speed was 850 rpm. Of three-wheel design, the Square Turn also featured a friction drive transmission, with rated speeds varying from 2 to 3 mph. Total weight was 7,800 lbs. The first tractor submitted for testing had a defective engine, so another unit was substituted prior to the recording of any official test data. Regular equipment on the 18-35 included a Dixie Model 46 magneto and Stromberg Model M carburetor. Kerosene was used throughout the test except for a maximum brake hp test made on gasoline. It indicated 36.66 maximum brake hp with a fuel economy of 7.35 hp-hours per gallon. The same test on kerosene yielded 30.69 hp and 6.02 hp-hours per gallon. Travelling at 2.85 mph, the 18-35 mustered a maximum pull of 3,090 lbs. for 23.45 drawbar hp.

COLLECTOR VALUES	1	2	3	4
SQUARE TURN	–	–	–	$10,000

Standard-Detroit Tractor Company

DETROIT, MICHIGAN

Standard-Detroit tractor

The Standard-Detroit tractor appeared in 1916. Rated at 10 drawbar and 20 belt hp, the Standard-Detroit was equipped with a four-cylinder engine with a 3-1/4 x 5-inch bore and stroke. Tractor production continued for a couple of years.

Tracford Tractor conversion attachment

The Tracford tractor conversion attachment appeared about 1916 and remained on the market for several years. It was one of many tractor conversion kits available at the time, and was built especially for the Ford Model T automobile chassis.

Standard Engine Company

MINNEAPOLIS, MINNESOTA

Standard began building garden tractors in the early 1930s. A confusing picture of makes and models emerged from Standard into the 1950s. These also included the Standard Twin and the Viking garden tractors.

Standard 3-1/2 model garden tractor

For 1933, the Standard 3-1/2 model used the company's own engine with a 3-inch bore and stroke. This unit weighed 300 lbs. and retailed at $219. Ignition was by battery and timer, but a magneto could be supplied at extra cost.

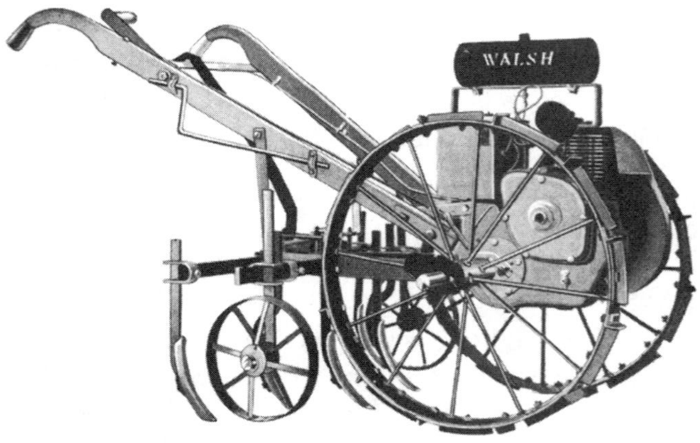

Walsh tractor

At an undetermined point, Standard took over the Walsh Garden Tractor Co. and continued building and selling the Walsh tractor. It was quite similar in design to the Standard 3-1/2 model.

COLLECTOR VALUES	1	2	3	4
WALSH	$750	$500	$350	$250
VIKING TWIN	$1,200	$950	$600	$350
STANDARD TWIN	$1,200	$950	$600	$350
VIKING SINGLE	$1,500	$1,000	$800	$450

Standard Mfg. & Sales Company

LEBANON, INDIANA

This firm is listed in 1953 as the builder of the Standard-Bantam tractor, but no photographs or specifications have been located.

Standard Tractor Company

ST. PAUL, MINNESOTA

Standard 22-45 tractor

Originally, this firm was organized in 1913 as Humber-Anderson Co. In 1915 the company moved to Willmar, Minnesota, and operated as Willmar Tractor Co. Standard Tractor Co. emerged in 1917, and continued building the Standard 22-45 into 1920. This model was originally built as the 20-40. It weighed 8,000 lbs. and was designed around a Waukesha four-cylinder engine with a 4-3/4 x 6-3/4- inch bore and stroke.

Standard Tractor Company

NEW YORK, NEW YORK

This firm was organized in 1914 to manufacture tractors, but no other information has been found.

Star Tractor Company

FINDLAY, OHIO

Developed in 1917, the Star 5-10 tractor made its appearance in 1918. This small tractor used a LeRoi four-cylinder engine with a 3-1/8 x 4-1/2-inch bore and stroke. Indiana Tractor Company took over Star Tractor Company in 1919.

E. G. Staude Mfg. Company

ST. PAUL, MINNESOTA

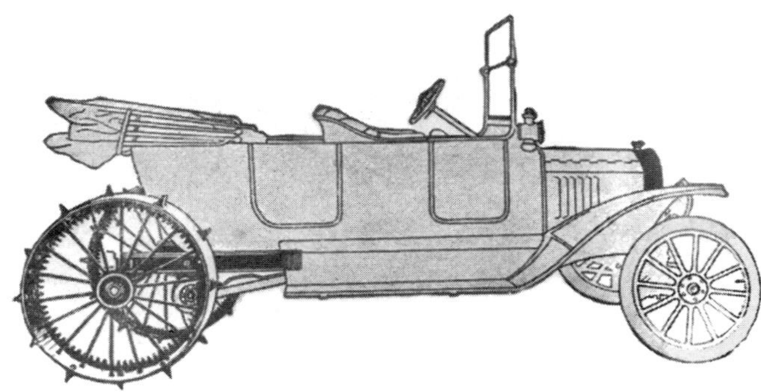

Staude Mak-a-Tractor

The Staude Mak-a-Tractor first appeared in 1918 and remained on the market for several years. Priced at $225, this conversion unit was designed especially for the Ford Model T automobile.

Steam Tractor & Auto Mfg. Company

SIOUX CITY, IOWA

In about 1912, this firm attempted to get into the tractor business with a special steam tractor design, but apparently it never got past the experimental stage. No other information has been found.

Star 5-10 tractor

Stearns Model Q 15-35 tractor

Stearns Motor Mfg. Company

LUDINGTON, MICHIGAN

Stearns bought out Gile Engine & Tractor Co. in 1919 and began producing the Stearns Model Q 15-35 tractor. It was essentially the same as the Gile Model Q 15-35 of the previous year. The four-cylinder Stearns engine used a 4-3/4 x 6-1/2-inch bore and stroke. The 15-35 weighed 6,800 lbs. Production continued for only a short time.

Steel King Motor Plow Company

DETROIT, MICHIGAN

Steel King Motor Plow

During 1914 the Steel King Motor Plow appeared. The rear-mounted plows were detachable so the tractor could be used for other drawbar work. Rated as a 9-18 tractor, the Steel King was priced at $950. Production continued for only a short time.

Chas. H. Stehling Company

MILWAUKEE, WISCONSIN

In 1948, this company was listed as supplying "repairs only" for the Dependable garden tractors. No other information has been located.

Steiger Tractor Company

FARGO, NORTH DAKOTA

Steiger Tractor Company began operations in 1957 and 1958 when Douglass and Maurice Steiger built their first prototype model. The original four-wheel-drive design was powered with a 238-hp Detroit Diesel engine. This machine logged over 10,000 hours of farm duty. From this model came an extensive line of Steiger tractor models, beginning in the mid-1960s.

Steiger Bearcat Series

Nebraska Test Data

Model: Steiger Bearcat Diesel
Test No. 1079
Date Tested: September 27 to October 6, 1971

Steiger's first entry in the Nebraska Tractor Tests featured a Caterpillar V-8 diesel engine. Rated at 2,800 rpm, it used a 4.5 x 5.0-inch bore and stroke for a 636-cubic inch displacment. No PTO shaft was provided, so no brake hp output or economy tests were run. Weighing 19,564 lbs., this tractor featured 23.1-26 inch tires on all four corners. An additional 212 lbs. of liquid ballast was added to each rear wheel, plus an additional 560 lbs. of liquid to each front wheel, for a total test weight of 22,650 lbs. A selective-gear fixed-ratio transmission was used with 10 forward speeds that ranged from 2.4 to 19.3 mph. Operating in fourth gear, the Bearcat achieved 158.91 maximum available drawbar hp in the two-hour economy run. This test also indicated a pull of 12,961 lbs. at 4.6 mph, a slippage of 5.4 percent, and an economy of 12.91 hp-hours per gallon. The 10-hour run at 75 percent pull noted an economy of 12.46 hp-hours per gallon with a load of 129.91 hp. Other statistics included a pull of 9,827 lbs. at 4.96 mph and 3.93 percent slippage. Also, a maximum pull of 21,287 lbs. was recorded in second gear, with an equivalent output of 147.4 hp. Except for replacement of an inner tube, no repairs or adjustments were reported during 44 hours of running time.

Nebraska Test Data

Model: Steiger Bearcat II
Test No. 1162
Date Tested: September 13 to September 20, 1974

Weighing 21,435 lbs., this tractor was equipped with four 23.1-30-inch tires. Additional front-wheel ballast raised the total test weight to 23,020 lbs. The selective-gear fixed-ratio transmission offered 10 forward speeds ranging from 2.0 to 16.0 mph. Using sixth gear, the two-hour economy run at 178.24 maximum available drawbar hp indicated a pull of 10,179 lbs. at 6.57 mph. Slippage totaled 2.96 percent, and fuel economy was 12.79 hp-hours per gallon. The 10-hour run at 75 percent pull noted an economy of 12.37 hp-hours per gallon under a load of 149.01 drawbar hp. Other test statistics included a pull of 7,791 lbs. at 7.17 mph with 2.23 percent slippage. Except for a broken fuel line fitting, no repairs or adjustments were required during 39 hours of engine operating time. The Bearcat II was equipped with a Caterpillar 3208, eight-cylinder diesel engine. Rated at 2,800 rpm, it used a 4.5 x 5.0-inch bore and stroke for a 636-cubic inch displacement. No PTO hp tests were made on this tractor.

Nebraska Test Data

Model: Steiger Bearcat IV, KM-225 Diesel
Test No. 1542
Date Tested: October 10 to October 23, 1984

This Steiger model featured a Cummins six-cylinder turbocharged diesel engine. Rated at 1,700 to 2,100 rpm, it carried a 4.921 x 5.354-inch bore and stroke for a displacement of 611-cubic inches. No PTO shaft was provided, and no brake hp tests were made. No repairs or adjustments were necessary during 48-1/2 hours of operating time. The selective-gear fixed-ratio transmission offered 20 forward speeds ranging from 1.8 to 18.0 mph. Weighing 28,400 lbs., a total test weight of 33,830 lbs. was noted after additional front and rear ballast was added. Drawbar performance tests were run at the maximum rated speed of 2,100 rpm, and supplementary tests were made both at 1,700 rpm and 1,900 rpm. With an engine speed of 2,100 rpm, and operating in 10th gear, a two-hour run at 188.03 maximum available drawbar hp saw a pull of 13,209 lbs. at 5.34 mph and slippage of 3.41 percent. Fuel economy was 16.43 hp-hours per gallon. A two-hour drawbar run at an engine speed of 1,700 rpm yielded a maximum drawbar output of 198.75 hp, together with 17.47 hp-hours per gallon. Also recorded in this test was a pull of 17,396 lbs. at 4.28 mph and slippage totaling 4.18 percent. Standard equipment for this tractor included dual 23.1-34-inch tires.

Steiger Cougar Series

Nebraska Test Data

Model: Steiger Cougar II Diesel
Test No. 1170
Date Tested: November 20 to November 27, 1974

Weighing 26,690 lbs., the Cougar 11 took on additional front and rear ballast for a total test weight of 27,995 lbs. Dual 23.1-34-inch tires were used. Using sixth gear, the two-hour economy run at 222.16 maximum available drawbar hp saw a pull of 14,508 lbs. at 5.74 mph with slippage totaling 3.96 percent. Fuel economy was 13.15 hp-hours per gallon. For comparison, the 10-hour run at 75 percent pull achieved 12.77 hp-hours per gallon against a load of 182.43 drawbar hp. This test also indicated a pull of 11,160 lbs. at 6.13 mph with slippage totaling 2.84 percent. No repairs or adjustments were recorded during 39-1/2 hours of operation, and no PTO tests were run. The Cougar II was equipped with a Caterpillar 3306 Diesel engine. Of six-cylinder, turbocharged design, it was rated at 2,200 rpm, and used a 4-3/4 x 6-inch bore and stroke for a 638-cubic inch displacement. The selective-gear fixed-ratio transmission offered 10 forward speeds ranging from 1.7 to 15.0 mph.

Nebraska Test Data

Model: Steiger Cougar III ST-251 Diesel
Test No. 1233
Date Tested: March 26 to April 30, 1977

The Cougar III featured a Cummins six-cylinder turbocharged diesel engine. Rated at 2,100 rpm, it used a 5.5 x 6.0-inch bore and stroke for an 855-cubic inch displacement. This tractor was not equipped with a PTO shaft, so no brake hp tests were run. The selective-gear fixed-ratio transmission offered 10 forward speeds ranging from 1.8 to 16.0 mph. Operating in sixth gear, the two-hour economy test at 199.04 maximum available drawbar hp yielded a pull of 12,252 lbs. at 6.09 mph with slippage of 2.59 percent. Fuel economy was recorded at 14.74 hp-hours per gallon. The 10-hour run at 75 percent pull noted 13.69 hp-hours per gallon under a load of 161.89 drawbar hp. Other test data included a pull of 9,371 lbs. at 6.48 mph with 1.76 percent slippage. Also, this tractor made a maximum pull of 26,880 lbs. at 2.13 mph using second gear. Slippage in this test totaled 14.64 percent. Weighing 30,840 lbs., the Cougar III was tested without the use of additional ballast. Standard equipment included dual 23.1-34-inch tires on all four corners.

Nebraska Test Data

Model: Steiger Cougar III ST-280 Diesel (Also Cougar IV CM-280 Diesel)
Test No. 1412
Date Tested: October 19 to October 30, 1981

This tractor was not furnished with a PTO shaft and no brake hp tests were run. The Caterpillar six-cylinder turbocharged engine was rated at 1,700 to 2,100 rpm. Its 5.4 x 6.5-inch bore and stroke gave an 893-cubic inch displacement. The selective-gear fixed-ratio transmission offered 20 forward speeds ranging from 2.3 to 23.1 mph. Using 10th gear, the two-hour drawbar run at 238.27 maximum available hp indicated a pull of 12,586 lbs. at 7.1 mph. Slippage totaled 2.67 percent, and fuel economy came in at 14.85 hp-hours per gallon. The 10-hour run at 75 percent pull noted 13.76 hp-hours per gallon under a load of 192.43 maximum available hp. Also recorded was a pull of 9,715 lbs. at 7.43 mph and 2.11 percent slippage. This tractor made a second-gear maximum pull of 32,099 lbs. at 2.41 mph with 14.48 percent slippage. Weighing 30,640 lbs., it was equipped with dual 23.1-34-inch tires. Additional front and rear ballast gave a total test weight of 33,345 lbs. Repairs and adjustments during 45 hours of operation included a malfunction of the fuel shut-off system during the preliminary drawbar tests.

Steiger Panther Series

Nebraska Test Data

Model: Steiger Panther III ST-325 Diesel 10-Speed (Also Steiger Panther IV CM-325 Diesel 20-Speed)
Test No. 1236
Date Tested: April 11 to May 2, 1977

This four-wheel-drive model offered a selective-gear fixed-ratio transmission with 10 forward speeds ranging from 2.3 to 19.9 mph. Operating in fifth gear, the two-hour economy run at 269.86 maximum available hp yielded a pull of 16,535 lbs. at 6.12 mph with slippage totaling 4.03 percent. Fuel economy came in at 14.82 hp-hours per gallon. The 10-hour run at 75 percent pull noted 14.19 hp-hours per gallon under a load of 225.6 drawbar hp. Also recorded was a pull of 12,862 lbs. at 6.58 mph and slippage totaling 2.93 percent. Weighing 31,080 lbs., this tractor was tested without the use of additional ballast. Standard equipment included dual 23.1-34-inch tires. During 47 hours of operating time it was reported that the transfer case control shift lever linkage was broken. This was repaired and the test continued. No PTO shaft was provided, and no brake hp tests were run. The Panther III was equipped with a Caterpillar six-cylinder turbocharged engine. Rated at 2,100 rpm, it used a 5.4 x 6.5-inch bore and stroke for an 893-cubic inch displacement.

Nebraska Test Data

Model: Steiger Panther CP-1325 Diesel
Test No. 1453
Date Tested: September 27 to October 13, 1982

At its rated engine speed of 2,100 rpm, the CP-1325 delivered 299.10 maximum PTO hp while achieving 16.55 hp-hours per gallon. This tractor was equipped with a Caterpillar six-cylinder turbocharged engine. The 5.4 x 6.5-inch bore and stroke gave an 893-cubic inch displacement. Also featured was a selective-gear fixed-ratio transmission with full range power shifting. The 12 forward speeds ranged from 2.4 to 16.5 mph. Using seventh gear, a two-hour drawbar run at 261.75 maximum available drawbar hp saw a pull of 14,136 lbs. at 6.94 mph. Slippage totaled 2.94 percent and fuel economy was 14.71 hp-hours per gallon. The 10-hour run at 75 percent pull saw an economy of 13.86 under a load of 209.22 drawbar hp. Other test data included a pull of 10,811 lbs. at 7.26 mph and slippage of 2.26 percent. No repairs or adjustments were necessary during 48 hours of operating time. Standard equipment included dual 23.1-34-inch tires. Weighing 35,460 lbs., this Steiger assumed a total test weight of 35,870 lbs. by the addition of front ballast. Supplementary tests covering drawbar and PTO performance were also made at engine speeds of 1,700 rpm and 1,900 rpm. These are fully detailed in the Official Test Report.

Nebraska Test Data

Model: Steiger Panther IV SM-325 Diesel
Test No. 1550
Date Tested: November 16 to November 26, 1984

Weighing 28,900 lbs., this Steiger model featured dual 23.1-34-inch tires. Additional front and rear ballast gave a total test weight of 33,930 lbs. This tractor was not provided with a PTO shaft so no brake hp tests were run. Twenty forward speeds, ranging from 2.3 to 23.1 mph, were provided by the selective-gear fixed-ratio transmission. The six-cylinder turbocharged and inter-cooled Komatsu engine was rated at 1,700 to 2,100 rpm. Its 4.921 x 5.906-inch bore and stroke gave a displacement of 674-cubic inches. Using 10th gear and operating at 2,100 rpm, a two-hour drawbar run at 270.89 maximum available hp saw a pull of 14,996 lbs. at 6.77 mph. Slippage totaled 3.52 percent and 17.12 hp-hours per gallon. The same two-hour run using an engine speed of 1,700 rpm established 18.08 hp-hours per gallon against a load of 265.92 drawbar hp. Also witnessed was a pull of 18,334 lbs. at 5.44 mph and slippage of 4.19 percent. Repairs and adjustments over 39-1/2 hours of operating time included replacing the injector gaskets.

Steiger Tiger Series

Nebraska Test Data

Model: Steiger Tiger II Diesel

Test No. 1169

Date Tested: November 15 to November 26, 1974

A Cummins VT-903 V-8 diesel engine was featured in the Tiger II. Rated at 2,600 rpm, this turbocharged unit carried a 5.50 x 4.75-inch bore and stroke for a 903-cubic inch displacement. No PTO tests were run on this tractor, and no repairs or adjustments were reported during 45 hours of engine operating time. Dual 23.1-34-inch tires were used on all four corners of this 27,600-lb. unit. Additional front and rear ballast raised the total test weight to 29,930 lbs. The selective-gear fixed-ratio transmission included 10 forward speeds ranging from 2.0 to 17.6 mph. Operating in sixth gear, the two-hour economy run at 262.13 maximum available drawbar hp recorded a pull of 14,606 lbs. at 6.73 mph with slippage totaling 3.53 percent. Fuel economy was posted at 13.88 hp-hours per gallon. The 10-hour run at 75 percent pull indicated 12.7 hp-hours per gallon against a load of 211.66 drawbar hp. Also recorded was a pull of 11,286 lbs. at 7.03 mph with slippage totaling 2.49 percent. The Official Test Report noted the engine manufacturer's warranty was voided if the fuel flow rate exceeded 18.9 gph for this model and application. In the two-hour maximum available power test noted above, fuel consumption totaled 18.886 gph.

Nebraska Test Data

Model: Steiger Tiger III ST-450

Test No. 1282

Date Tested: July 6 to July 13, 1978

Without ballast, this tractor weighed 42,725 lbs. Additional front ballast gave a total test weight of 47,370 lbs. The ST-450 was equipped with dual 30.5L-32-inch tires. Among the features were a selective-gear fixed-ratio torque converter transmission with automatic lockup and full range power shifting. The six forward speeds ranged from 3.3 to 19.5 mph. Using third gear, the 2-hour drawbar run at 356.58 maximum available drawbar hp witnessed a pull of 20,385 lbs. at 6.56 mph with slippage totaling 4.07 percent. Fuel economy came to 14.18 hp-hours per gallon, or expressed differently, fuel consumption totaled 25.143 gph. The 10-hour run at 75 percent pull noted a figure of 12.70 under an output of 309.97 drawbar hp. Also recorded was a pull of 16,024 lbs. at 7.25 mph and slippage totaling 3.14 percent. Operating in first gear, this tractor made a maximum pull of 42,610 lbs. at 2.94 mph with total slippage of 14.71 percent. No brake hp tests were run on this tractor, nor were any repairs or adjustments required during 39 hours of operating time. Steiger equipped this model with a Cummins six-cylinder turbocharged and intercooled engine. Rated at both 2,100 and 1,700 rpm, this engine carried a 6.25-inch bore and stroke for a displacement of 1,150 cubic inches.

Nebraska Test Data

Model: Steiger Wildcat III ST-210 & RC-210 Diesel

Test No. 1237

Date Tested: April 23 to April 25, 1977

The ST-210 Wildcat featured a Caterpillar V-8 diesel engine. Rated at 2,800 rpm, it used a 4.5 x 5.0-inch bore and stroke for a displacement of 636-cubic inches. No PTO shaft was provided, and no brake hp tests were run on this tractor. No repairs or adjustments were reported on this four-wheel-drive unit during 43-1/2 hours of operation. Standard features included a selective-gear fixed-ratio transmission with 10 forward speeds and a range of 2.2 to 19.6 mph. Weighing 22,260 lbs., the ST-210 was tested without additional ballast. The test model was equipped with dual 23.1-30-inch tires. Operating in fifth gear, the 2-hour drawbar run at 163.78 maximum available hp saw a pull of 10,505 lbs. at 5.85 mph with slippage totaling 4.01 percent. Fuel economy for this test came to 12.71 hp-hours per gallon. The 10-hour run at 75 percent pull noted 12.58 hp-hours per gallon against a load of 135.23 drawbar hp. Also established was a pull of 8,256 lbs. at 6.14 mph. Slippage totaled 2.95 percent. The maximum power runs noted a pull of 21,052 lbs. at 2.57 mph using second gear. Slippage totaled 14.91 percent.

Steiger Wildcat Series

Sterling Engine Works Ltd.

WINNIPEG, MANITOBA

Sterling 12-24 tractor

During 1916, the Sterling 12-24 tractor was offered to the market. This $1,170 tractor weighed 5,400 lbs. and was sold direct to the farmer. Sterling offered to pay the travel expenses for anyone wishing to come to Winnipeg and inspect the new tractor. This was a novel approach to selling tractors. Aside from its 1916 advertising, little else has been found on this tractor.

Sterling Machine & Stamping Company

WELLINGTON, OHIO

Wellington tractor

In 1920, Sterling offered its Wellington tractor in two sizes. The Wellington F 12-22 tractor shown here sold for $1,600. It was equipped with an Erd four-cylinder engine with a 4 x 6-inch bore and stroke. The Wellington B 16-30 tractor used a Chief four-cylinder engine with a 4-3/4 x 6-inch bore and stroke. It weighed 5,000 lbs.

Stewart Tractor Company

WAUPACA, WISCONSIN

See: Topp-Stewart

Stinson Tractor Company

MINNEAPOLIS, MINNESOTA

This company started a five-year foray into the tractor business around 1917. Numerous changes were ultimately made in the company organization, including a move to Superior, Wisconsin, about 1922—just at the end of production.

Stinson 15-30 tractor

The Stinson 15-30 tractor made its first appearance in 1917. This model used an Erd four-cylinder engine with a 4-1/2 x 5-inch bore and stroke, but it could also be equipped with a Herschell-Spillman V-8 engine.

Stinson 18-36 tractor

For 1918, the Stinson tractor gained an 18-36 hp rating. In 1917, the Stinson was manufactured by Gile Engine Co. at Ludington, Michigan. The 1918 model was built by Imperial Machinery Company at Minneapolis. This model used a four-cylinder Beaver engine with a 4-3/4 x 6-inch bore and stroke.

Stinson Heavy Duty 18-36 tractor

In 1920, the Stinson Heavy Duty 18-36 tractor appeared. From then until production ended in 1922, this was the only model in the Stinson tractor line.

St. Marys Machinery Company

ST. MARYS, OHIO

This company is listed as a tractor manufacturer about 1910 and actually may have mounted some of its stationary engines to a tractor chassis, but no illustrations have been found.

Stockton Tractor Company

STOCKTON, CALIFORNIA

This company made a very brief entrance into the tractor business. Its models were announced in 1920, but by 1921 the company had disappeared from tractor directories.

Stockton Model A 8-16 tractor

In 1920, the Stockton Model A 8-16 tractor appeared. Very little is known of this model, probably because it was on the market for only a short time.

Stockton Model B Sure-Grip tractor

The Stockton Model B Sure-Grip tractor made its debut in 1920. Apparently, the Model A and Model B tractors both used a four-cylinder Herschell-Spillman engine with a 3-1/2 x 5-inch bore and stroke.

Stone Tractor Company

TEXARKANA, TEXAS

Stone 20-40 tractor

In 1917, Stone Tractor Co. was organized and began building the Stone 20-40 tractor. Weighing 5,450 lbs., it was built with a Beaver four-cylinder engine with a 4-1/2 x 6-inch bore and stroke. The 20-40 sold for $1,850. Production continued until about 1920.

Stone Tractor Mfg. Company

QUINCY, ILLINOIS

This firm was incorporated in 1917, presumably to manufacture a new tractor design, but no other information has been found.

Stover Engine Works

FREEPORT, ILLINOIS

Stover tractor

In 1906, Stover shipped three of these 40-hp tractors to Argentina. This model used a single-cylinder Stover engine with a 12-1/2 x 18-inch bore and stroke. Between 1906 and 1911, Stover built a handful of these tractors. The last one was a 30-hp model built in 1911.

Stover prototype

Stover built this prototype in 1915. Aside from the photograph, nothing is known about the tractor, even though extensive Stover company records are available. Compared to other tractors of the day, this one was fairly attractive. Given the size of the company, it could have sold in quantity. However, an internal company photograph is the only evidence that this tractor ever existed.

St. Paul Machinery & Mfg. Company

ST. PAUL, MINNESOTA

Organized in 1910, St. Paul Machinery & Mfg. began building tractors shortly after that time. By 1912, the St. Paul had taken the form shown here and was equipped with a four-cylinder engine capable of about 35 belt hp. The mounted plows came as standard equipment and were detachable for other drawbar work. Production of this tractor continued as late as 1917. By that time, the tractor had a 24-40 hp rating.

Strite Tractor Company

MINNEAPOLIS, MINNESOTA

Strite 3-Point tractor

St. Paul 24-40 tractor

Already in 1913, the Strite 3-Point tractor was on the market. It was thus named because of its three-wheel chassis configuration. By 1917, this model had an 18-36 hp rating and used a Waukesha four-cylinder engine with a 4-1/2 x 6-3/4-inch bore and stroke. It was priced at $1,485.

Strite 12-25 tractor

In 1919, the Strite 12-25 tractor appeared. At this point, Strite Tractor Co. had its offices in New York City, but the connection between the Minneapolis and the New York offices has not been established. The 12-25 used a four-cylinder engine with a 3-1/2 x 5-1/4-inch bore and stroke. Production of this model apparently ended by 1921.

Stroud Motor Mfg. Association

SAN ANTONIO, TEXAS

Stroud 16-30 tractor

In 1919, Stroud developed its 16-30 tractor. It was powered by a Climax four-cylinder engine with a 5 x 6-1/2-inch bore and stroke. Curiously, the Stroud 16-30 embodied most of the features that would be essential for the Farmall row-crop tractor that would soon appear. For reasons unknown, Stroud did not put the features into practice, or did not remain in business long enough to implement them.

Stuts-Mar Tractor Company

SAN JOSE, CALIFORNIA

This firm is listed as a tractor manufacturer in 1918 and 1919, but no other information has been found.

Sullivan Tractor Company

OAKLAND, CALIFORNIA

Sullivan 8-28 tractor

A 1915 industry listing showed the Sullivan 8-28 tractor. It used a four-cylinder Beaver engine and weighed 4,000 lbs. The engine carried a 4-3/4 x 5-1/2-inch bore and stroke. In 1916, this tractor listed at $1,250. Production apparently ended after 1916.

Sumner Iron Works

EVERETT, WASHINGTON

This company was listed as a tractor manufacturer in 1921 but no other information has been found.

Sun Tractor Company

COLUMBUS, OHIO

Sun 8-16 tractor

About 1916 the Sun 8-16 tractor appeared. It was of the universal design, meaning it hinged in the middle and the driver was seated on the towed implement. This model remained on the market for only a short time.

Super-Diesel Tractor Company

MANHATTAN, NEW YORK

In 1917, Edward A. Rumely and others incorporated the Super-Diesel Tractor Co. Rumely had formerly been the moving force at M. Rumely Company, builders of the Rumely OilPull tractors. Rumely had been a close friend of Rudolph Diesel and others. Rumely was convinced diesel power was ultimately the way to go in the tractor business. Unfortunately, Rumely's ideas were ahead of his time and technology, so the Super-Diesel never made it into production.

Super-Trac Incorporated

CHICAGO, ILLINOIS

This company was listed as the manufacturer of the Super-Trac tractor in 1948, but no other information has been found.

Superior Traction Company

DULUTH, MINNESOTA

This firm announced in 1910 they would be build a new tractor, but no other information was found.

Superior Tractor Company

CLEVELAND, OHIO

Superior 15-30 tractor

The Superior 15-30 was developed in 1919 and remained on the market until about 1922. This model was powered by a four-cylinder Beaver engine with a 4-3/4 x 6-inch bore and stroke. Weighing 4,500 lbs., it had two forward speeds.

Sweeney Tractor Company

KANSAS CITY, MISSOURI

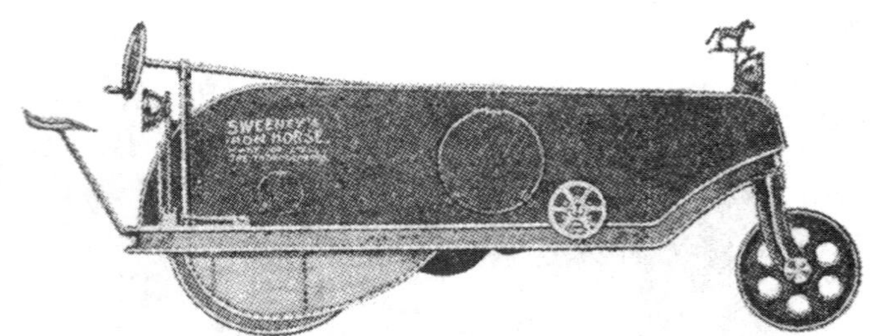

Sweeney 15-25 tractor

During 1916, the Sweeney tractor appeared. Sweeney also operated a tractor school so interested parties could learn how to operate and repair tractors. Rated as a 15-25, the Sweeney was built for only a short time.

SWH Engineering Company

CLEVELAND, OHIO

SWH 15-30 tractor

Little information is available on the SWH 15-30 tractor. Introduced in 1919, it left the market the same year. The 15-30 was equipped with a four-cylinder engine with a 4-3/4 x 6-inch bore and stroke. It weighed 4,800 lbs. and had two forward speeds.

Sylvester Mfg. Company Ltd.

LINDSAY, ONTARIO

Sylvester began building farm implements at Lindsay, Ontario, in 1876 and began building gasoline engines in 1902. In 1907 the firm had worked its way into the tractor business. In 1920, the firm quit the farm equipment business to concentrate on railway equipment and track cars and remained in operation until 1956.

Sylvester auto thresher

In 1907 Sylvester Mfg. Co. developed its first auto thresher, or in other words, a self-propelled threshing machine. This machine differed from most other auto threshers because it was capable of heavy drawbar work, while the rest were content to just move themselves from place to place.

Sylvester gasoline traction engine

With the 1907 introduction of the auto thresher came the announcement of the Sylvester gasoline traction engines. These were powered by a two-cylinder opposed engine, but few details have been found.

Sylvester tractor

By 1910, the Sylvester tractors were modified somewhat, although the basic design remained the same. These tractors were offered until 1914 when the company reverted back to its farm equipment line.

[Throughout this section, assume that gasoline was used for fuel unless another fuel source is mentioned.]

Taylor-Jenkins Tractor Company

JONESBORO, ARKANSAS

In 1918 this company was listed as the manufacturer of the T-J 30-40 tractor. No other information has been found.

Temple Pump Company

CHICAGO, ILLINOIS

This firm dated back to the 1850s in the pump business, and began building gasoline engines by 1903. In 1908 the company offered a tractor, noting in its advertising that its had been building its "traction engine" for some time. It was built in 5, 7, 10, 15, 20, 30, and 45 horsepower sizes; the largest two were of four-cylinder design, and the others featured two-cylinder engines.

Termaat & Monahan Company

OSHKOSH, WISCONSIN

Termaat & Monahan tractor

In 1913 Termaat & Monahan offered small tractor with a 7 hp engine of its own manufacture. Weighing 4,200 lbs., it had two forward speeds. The company also indicated that larger engines could be mounted on the same chassis if

Temple Pump Co. tractor

desired. Termaat & Monahan was a sizable gasoline engine builder. The company went into receivership in 1917, then recovered and built the Wiscona Pep engines.

Texas Motor Car Association

FORT WORTH, TEXAS

A trade note of 1918 indicates that this firm was organized to "build a tractor." The company was formed in December 1917 to build the Texan automobile, but the latter didn't make it to the market until 1920, and was gone by 1922. It is assumed that if, in fact, the tractor was ever built, it met the same fate.

Texas Tractor & Farm Machinery Company

AMARILLO, TEXAS

In 1917 this firm was organized to build a farm tractor, but no further information has been found.

Texas Truck & Tractor Company

DALLAS, TEXAS

This firm is said to have built an assembled automobile in 1920. The Wharton Pull 12-22 tractor was listed from this company in 1920. It used a four-cylinder engine with a 4 x 6-inch bore and stroke. The Wharton Pull weighed 3,700 pounds.

Thieman Harvester Company

ALBERT CITY, IOWA

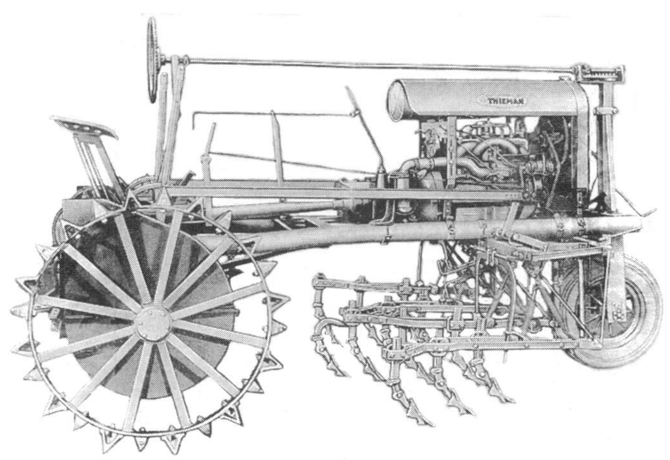

Thieman tractor

In 1936 the first Thieman tractor appeared. This was actually a $185 tractor chassis to which the customer fitted a Ford Model A engine, driveshaft, and rear axle. The Thieman chassis could also be supplied for the 1928 Chevrolet or the Dodge Four. The Thieman chassis was sold until World War II, when production was halted because of the war effort.

COLLECTOR VALUES	1	2	3	4
THIEMAN	–	$2,100	–	–

Thompson-Breese tractor

Thompson-Breese Company

WAPOKONETA, OHIO

During 1911 Thompson-Breese was formed from the Ohio Steel Wagon Company. Its tractor was also announced that year, but few details have been found. It was powered by a two-cylinder opposed engine and was equipped with a rear-mounted plow.

Thomson Machinery Company

THIBODAUX, LOUISIANA

Thomson UCD tractor

The Thomson UCD tractor was originally built as the Allis-Chalmers Model U Cane Tractor. When production of this tractor ended in 1941, Allis-Chalmers apparently continued building the UC rear end for Thomson, and they in turn modified it suitably for a cane tractor. By the mid-1950s the UCD appeared with a GM 2-71 diesel engine.

Thomson XTD four-wheel-drive tractor

By the late 1950s Thomson Machinery Co. was offering its XTD four-wheel-drive tractor. Like the UCD, it was equipped with a General Motors 2-71 diesel engine. This 12,600 lb. tractor included features such as four hydraulic brakes and an optional hydraulic system.

Thorobred Tractor & Mfg. Company

MOBRIDGE, OHIO

This company is listed as a tractor manufacturer in 1918, but no further information has been found.

Three-P Auto Tractor Company

DAVENPORT, IOWA

Three-P was incorporated in 1917 to manufacture tractors, but no other information has been found.

Three Wheel Drive Tractor Company

INDIANAPOLIS, INDIANA

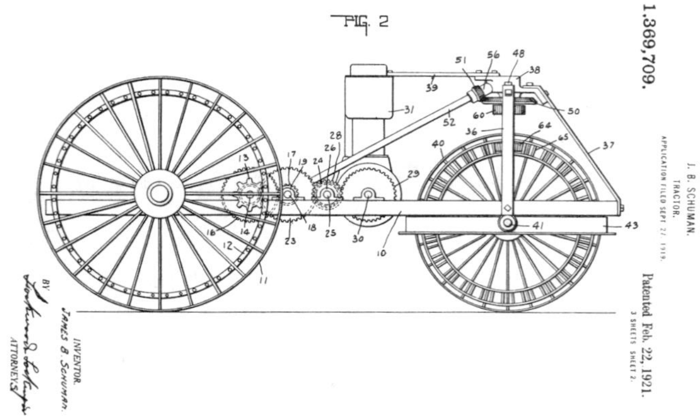

Patent 1,369,709 copy

In 1919 J. B. Schuman applied for a patent covering a three-wheel-drive tractor design. It was issued in February 1921, and assigned to the above company. Aside from the patent, nothing more has been found regarding this tractor or the company organized for its manufacture.

Tiger Tractor Corporation

KEYSER, WEST VIRGINIA

Tiger tractor

In the late 1940s the Tiger tractor was being built by Inexco Tractor Company. By 1953 the Tiger was being produced by Tiger Tractor Corporation. The Tiger PTD6 shown here was built with a Briggs & Stratton Model 14 engine, capable of over 5 hp. Priced at $520, it was available with numerous attachments.

See: Inexco Tractor Corporation

COLLECTOR VALUES	1	2	3	4
PTD 6	$750	$650	$350	$150

Tillavator Company

NEW YORK, NEW YORK

By the late 1930s the Tillavator DP55 rotary tiller was on the market. It was designed with single-cylinder, two-cycle engine capable of 5 hp. The company was listed as a garden tractor manufacturer at least into the early 1950s.

COLLECTOR VALUES	1	2	3	4
TILLAVOTOR LATE MODELS	–	–	$100	–

Tillavator DP55 rotary tiller

Tillermobile Company

MINNEAPOLIS, MINNESOTA

Tillermobile Company was organized in 1920, and offered the Tillermobile 2-6 garden tractor that same year. It used the company's own single-cylinder horizontal engine with a 4-inch bore and stroke. Weighing 625 lbs., it sold for $350. Production apparently ended soon after it began.

Tioga 15-27 tractor

Tillermobile 2-6 garden tractor

Tioga Mfg. Company

PHILADELPHIA, PENNSYLVANIA

Tioga Tractor Company apparently began operations at Philadelphia, Pennsylvania, about 1920. Initially the Tioga 15-27 was equipped with a Wisconsin four-cylinder engine with a 4-1/2 x 6-inch bore and stroke. By 1923 the company had moved to Baltimore, Maryland, and by 1925 had begun building the Tioga 3 18-32 tractor. It was of the same essential design, and even continued to use the same Wisconsin engine as the 15-27 model. Production ended in the late 1920s.

Titan Truck & Tractor Company

MILWAUKEE, WISCONSIN

This firm was organized in 1917 to build trucks and tractors. Before the year ended, the firm had dropped "Tractor" from the corporate name, probably indicating a hasty end to the tractor business. The company continued building trucks into the late 1920s.

Tom Thumb Tractor Company

MINNEAPOLIS, MINNESOTA

Tom Thumb 12-20 tractor

Developed during 1915, the Tom Thumb 12-20 tractor featured a Waukesha four-cylinder engine with a 4-1/4 x 5-3/4-inch bore and stroke. This 4,500 lb. tractor was propelled by a single rear- mounted track, and the two large front wheels gave a three-point chassis design. The firm was taken over by Federal Tractor Company in 1917.

Topeka Farming and Machinery Company

TOPEKA, KANSAS

No information has been found about this company.

Topp-Stewart Tractor Company

CLINTONVILLE, WISCONSIN

G.F. Stewart, a native of Antigo, Wisconsin, developed the principle of a four-wheel-drive tractor using conventional straight drive axles mounted on wagon-type (bolster) drive axles and driven by conventional universal joint drive shafts front and rear. The bolster-type axles were used because this tractor featured four-wheel steer. The front and rear axles were connected with cross chains that caused both axles to turn in opposite directions for a shorter turning radius.

Lacking the financial resources to proceed with production in Antigo, Stewart moved to Waupaca, Wisconsin. Still in need of funding, the company received the investment it needed from Dr. Charles Topp of Clintonville, Wisconsin. At that point the company moved to Clintonville and was renamed the Topp-Stewart Tractor Company, and there it thrived until it was sold to the Atlas Tractor Company. Later the company ceased making tractors and became known as the Atlas Conveyor Company. It was later sold to the Rex-Nord Company of Milwaukee, Wisconsin.

At no time was the Topp-Stewart Tractor Company associated with the FWD Auto Company of Clintonville.

Topp-Stewart tractor

The Topp-Stewart tractor featured a Waukesha engine of 4-3/4-inch bore by 6-3/4-inch stroke, mounted conventionally. Because of the axle arrangement the engine could not be cranked from the front and a disengageable bevel-gear system was devised to crank the engine from the left side in a counter-clockwise manner.

Topp-Stewart 30-45

By 1918 the Topp-Stewart tractor was furnished with an upholstered seat and a styled hood. This tractor continued to use the same engine as before, giving it 30 drawbar and 45 belt hp. The 30-45 weighed 7,500 lbs. and sold for $3,250.

Toro Motor Company

MINNEAPOLIS, MINNESOTA

The "Toro" name reflected an earlier connection with the Bull Tractor Company. "Toro" is the Spanish word for "bull." In addition to tractors, the company also built engines for power lawn mowers, beginning in 1914. Self-propelled tractors for pulling mowers were added in 1919, and self-contained lawn mowers were added in 1925. The company sold its farm tractor line to Advance-Rumely in 1927, but the company continued manufacturing an extensive line of garden tractors and mowers for several years.

See: Bull Tractor Company; Advance-Rumely Thresher Company

Toro two-row power cultivator

Toro Motor Co. announced its two-row power cultivator in 1918. It was powered by a LeRoi four-cylinder engine with a 3-1/8 x 4-1/2-inch bore and stroke.

Toro cultivator, 1920s

An interesting play on words is noted on the radiator shell of this Toro cultivator of the 1920s. Splitting the word To-Ro also could be pronounced as "two-row" and that described the Toro cultivator exactly. During the 1920s this outfit sold for about $500. In September 1927 the Toro Motor Cultivator was sold to Advance-Rumely Thresher Company. This model was later revamped into the Rumely DoAll Tractor.

Toro 6-10 tractor

During the 1920s Toro offered its small Toro 6-10 tractor. This model was evaluated at Nebraska during the first year of tractor testing.

Nebraska Test Data

Model: Toro 6-10

Test No. 65

Date Tested: September 23 to September 29, 1920

Once again the LeRoi 3 1/8 x 4 ½-inch engine appeared and this time it was in the Toro 6-10 tractor. This company rated the engine at 1,200 rpm, somewhat faster than the ratings shown by competitive tractor builders. Although this tractor was readily convertible to a cultivator, it appears the standard tread style was evaluated in this test. Total weight was only 2,600 lbs. A Kingston Model L carburetor and Eisemann GS4 magneto came as standard equipment, with gasoline being the chosen fuel. At rated brake horsepower (10.56) a fuel economy of 8.48 hp-hours per gallon resulted, with consumption totaling only 1.25 gph. At maximum load, 13.31 brake hp was recorded. The rated drawbar test averaged 6.32 hp, yielding a pull of 893 lbs. at a speed of 2.66 mph. Slightly over 1,300 lbs. was noted on the maximum drawbar test with a yield of 9.92 drawbar hp. Provided were two forward speeds of 2.6 and 3.7 mph.

E. F. Townsend Tractor Company

LOS ANGELES, CALIFORNIA

EFT 6-12 crawler

The EFT 6-12 crawler appeared in 1921 and remained on the market at least into 1922. This small tractor was powered by a Light four-cylinder engine with a 3-1/4 x 4-1/2-inch bore and stroke. Towed implements were attached to the trailing trucks.

Townsend Mfg. Company

JANESVILLE, WISCONSIN

Townsend began the tractor business by offering a 10-20 two-cylinder model in 1915. Known as the Bower City 10-20, it was sold until 1918. The 10-20 used a 6 x 8-inch bore and stroke.

In 1931 LaCrosse Boiler Co. at LaCrosse, Wisconsin, bought out the company and continued building several models of Townsend tractors until the onset of World War II.

See: Fairbanks-Morse; La Crosse Boiler Co.

Townsend 12-25 tractor

Townsend 25-50 and 30-60 tractors

The Townsend 12-25 replaced the 10-20 in 1918. The two-cylinder engine on the 12-25 carried a 7 x 8- inch bore and stroke.

Townsend 15-30 tractor

In 1919 the 12-25 was rerated as the 15-30 tractor. In testing at Nebraska the 15-30 delivered nearly 18 drawbar hp. Even though the Townsend was a gasoline and kerosene-powered tractor, its outward appearance would make one believe it was really a steam traction engine. R. B. Townsend, who was almost totally responsible for the design, referred to it as a "boiler frame" concept. The locomotive-style cab was standard equipment.

Nebraska Test Data

Model: Townsend 15-30

Test No. 63

Date Tested: September 9 to September 23, 1920

Initially presented as Test No. 34, the locomotive-like Townsend 15-30 was withdrawn on order of R. B. Townsend on July 21, 1920. Test No. 63 on the 15-30 was completed and certified, but not without some difficulty. Notes in the test report indicate that several adjustments and repairs were made, along with a new magneto about halfway through the test, plus a new carburetor. Because of the small clearance between the drive wheel and the flywheel, accumulated dirt acted as a brake on the engine flywheel, stalling the motor, and necessitating a readjustment of the clutch. Townsend used its own two-cylinder horizontal engine. Rated at 500 rpm, it carried a 7 x 8-inch bore and stroke. The carburetor was also of Townsend's design, but ignition was furnished by a Dixie Model 462 "C" magneto. Kerosene was used for fuel throughout the test. At maximum brake horsepower, 29.51 was recorded, with a fuel economy of 8.66 hp-hours per gallon and total consumption of 1.75 gph. At rated load of 28.35 hp, fuel economy rose to 9.38 hp hours per gallon and 3.02 gph. A maximum pull of 2,681 lbs. was recorded at the drawbar for an equivalent of 17.85 hp.

COLLECTOR VALUES	1	2	3	4
12-25, 15-30	–	$35,000	–	–

By 1924 the Townsend line included the 25-50 and 30-60 tractors. Both were of two-cylinder design, and like previous Townsend models, used a boiler shell that served as the tractor frame as well as the engine radiator. The 25-50 carried an 8-1/2 x 10-inch bore and stroke, while the 30-60 was designed with a 9-1/2 x 12-inch bore and stroke.

COLLECTOR VALUES	1	2	3	4
25-50	–	$63,500	–	–

Production of the Townsend 20-40 began about 1923 and continued for several years after the company sold out in 1931 to La Crosse Boiler Co.

Townsend 20-40

Townsend 12-20

During 1924 the Townsend 12-20 tractor appeared. This model used a two-cylinder engine with a 6 x 8-inch bore and stroke, as did the original 10-20 tractor of 1915. The 12-20 weighed 4,000 lbs. After the 1931 takeover by La Crosse Boiler Co., the 12-20 was rerated upwards to a 12-25 tractor.

Traction Engine Company

BOYNE CITY, MICHIGAN

Heinze four-wheel-drive tractor

In 1918 this company was incorporated to build the Heinze four-wheel-drive tractor. This design remained on the market into 1919. The company used its own four-cylinder engine with a 4-1/4 x 6- inch bore and stroke. Weighing 4,000 lbs., this tractor retailed at $2,000.

Traction Motor Corporation

KALAMAZOO, MICHIGAN

Traction Motor tractor

In 1920 the Traction Motor tractor appeared. It was quite a modern tractor for the time, with electric starting and lights, a three-speed transmission, and full pressure lubrication to all engine bearings. The engine was a 65 horsepower V-8 from Herschell-Spillman. Nothing is known about this tractor after its 1920 appearance.

Tractor Mfg. Company

SOUTH GATE, CALIFORNIA

In 1947 and 1948 the Garden Master Model B garden tractor was listed in the trade directories. It was powered by a Briggs & Stratton Model B engine. Ratchet hubs were used for steering. This tractor weighed 525 pounds. No illustrations of the Garden Master have been found.

Tractor Motor Corporation

KALAMAZOO, MICHIGAN

This company was incorporated in 1918 to build the "Hans" tractor, but no other information has been found.

Tractor Producing Corporation

NEW YORK, NEW YORK

A 1918 trademark application from this firm indicates that it was building the Liberty tractor and first used this tradename on February 1, 1917. No other information has been found.

Traylor 6-12 tractor

Transit Thresher Company

MINNEAPOLIS, MINNESOTA

Transit Thresher Co. was organized in 1907 to build the Transit 35 (drawbar) hp tractor. The four-cylinder engine had a 6 x 8-inch bore and stroke. This was one of the first four-cylinder tractors built. In 1908 the firm was reorganized as Gas Traction Company. In 1912 the latter was bought out by Emerson-Brantingham Co., Rockford, Illinois.

See: Gas Traction Company; Emerson-Brantingham Company

Transit 35 tractor

Traylor Engineering Company

CORNWELLS, PENNSYLVANIA

About 1920 the Traylor 6-12 tractor appeared. It remained on the market, virtually unchanged, until the late 1920s. A four-cylinder engine was used, a LeRoi with a 3-1/8 x 4-1/2-inch bore and stroke. A cultivator could be attached and removed at will.

Trenam Tractor Company

STEVENS POINT, WISCONSIN

Built in the 1917 through 1920 period, the Trenam 12-24 was fairly popular. This 4,500-lb. tractor used various engines, including the Erd four-cylinder style with a 4 x 6-inch bore and stroke.

Triple Tractor Truck Company

MINNEAPOLIS, MINNESOTA

During 1915 the Triple Tractor Truck appeared. It was an all-wheel-drive affair powered by a four-cylinder engine. The latter used a 4-1/4 x 5-1/4-inch bore and stroke. It was also designed with a pulley for belt work. Nothing is heard of this design after its 1915 announcement.

Triple Tractor Truck

Triumph Truck & Tractor Company

KANSAS CITY, MISSOURI

Triumph 18-36 tractor

During 1920 the Triumph 18-36 tractor was offered to the market. This model was built with a Climax four-cylinder engine with a 5 x 6-1/2-inch bore and stroke. Weighing 5,200 lbs., it sold for $2,250. Nothing is known of the Triumph after the 1920 listings.

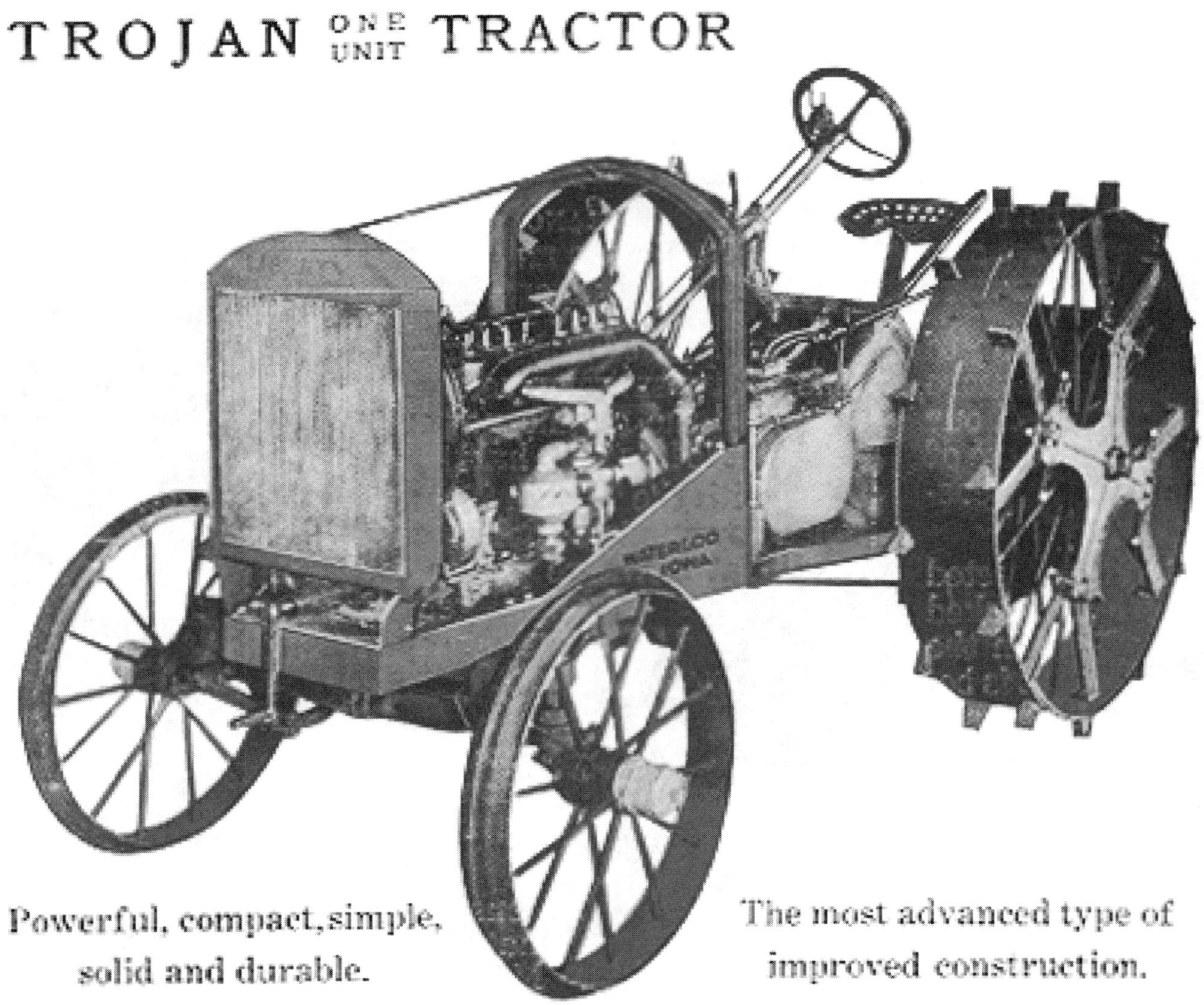

TROJAN ONE UNIT TRACTOR

Powerful, compact, simple, solid and durable.

The most advanced type of improved construction.

Trojan Unit tractor

Trojan Unit Tractor Company

WATERLOO, IOWA

In 1917 the Trojan Unit Tractor appeared. This design had a manufacturer's rating of 32 drawbar and 40 belt hp. Power came from a Waukesha Type L, four-cylinder engine with a 4-3/4 x 6-3/4-inch bore and stroke. The combination planetary transmission provided three forward speeds. Production of this tractor continued for only a short time.

Turner Mfg. Company

PORT WASHINGTON, WISCONSIN

Turner Mfg. Co. had a career as a gas engine builder going back to 1902. The company entered the tractor business in 1915. Turner went into receivership in 1920, and the following year it was reorganized as Simplicity Mfg. Company.

See: Simplicity Mfg. Company

Turner Simplicity 12-20 tractor

In 1915 the Turner Simplicity 12-20 tractor appeared. Weighing 4,200 lbs., it sold for $1,350. Power came from a Waukesha four-cylinder engine with a 3-3/4 x 5-1/4-inch bore and stroke. Production of this model continued until about 1919.

Turner Simplicity 14-25 tractor

The Turner Simplicity 14-25 tractor first appeared about 1918. This model was of the same general design as the 12-20 but used a larger Buda four-cylinder engine; it was designed with a 4-1/4 x 5-1/2-inch bore and stroke.

COLLECTOR VALUES	1	2	3	4
12-20 OR 14-25	$26,000	--	--	--

Twin Ports Steel and Machinery Company

SUPERIOR, WISCONSIN

No information is available about this company or its tractors.

Two-Way Tractor Plow Company

DENVER, COLORADO

In 1921 this company was listed as a tractor manufacturer, but no other information is available.

[Throughout this section, assume that gasoline was used for fuel unless another fuel source is indicated.]

Uncle Sam Tractor & Machinery Company

MENASHA, WISCONSIN

See: U. S. Tractor & Machinery Company

Union Iron Works

MINNEAPOLIS, MINNESOTA

New Gearless tractor

In 1913 the New Gearless tractor appeared from Union Iron Works. This unique design transmitted power to the rear wheels without the use of gears, chains, and sprockets. It soon proved itself impractical, although it stayed on the market until about 1915. The New Gearless was rated at 12 belt hp.

Union Tool Corporation

TORRANCE, CALIFORNIA

The Union 12-25 crawler was listed in the tractor directories for 1921 and 1922, though may have been built before and after those years. Power came from the company's own four-cylinder engine and was designed with a 4-3/4 x 6-inch bore and stroke. The company had introduced its Velvettread crawler by about 1914, but no information has been found on this unit.

Union Tractor Company

SAN FRANCISCO, CALIFORNIA

The Union Bulldog 18-30 crawler appeared for a short time in 1917 and then disappeared from the scene. Little is known of this tractor. In many instances, new tractors like this one barely advanced past a few prototypes. Sometimes they never got past the drawing board.

Unit Power Wheel Company

CLEVELAND, OHIO

No information is available on this company or any tractors it manufactured.

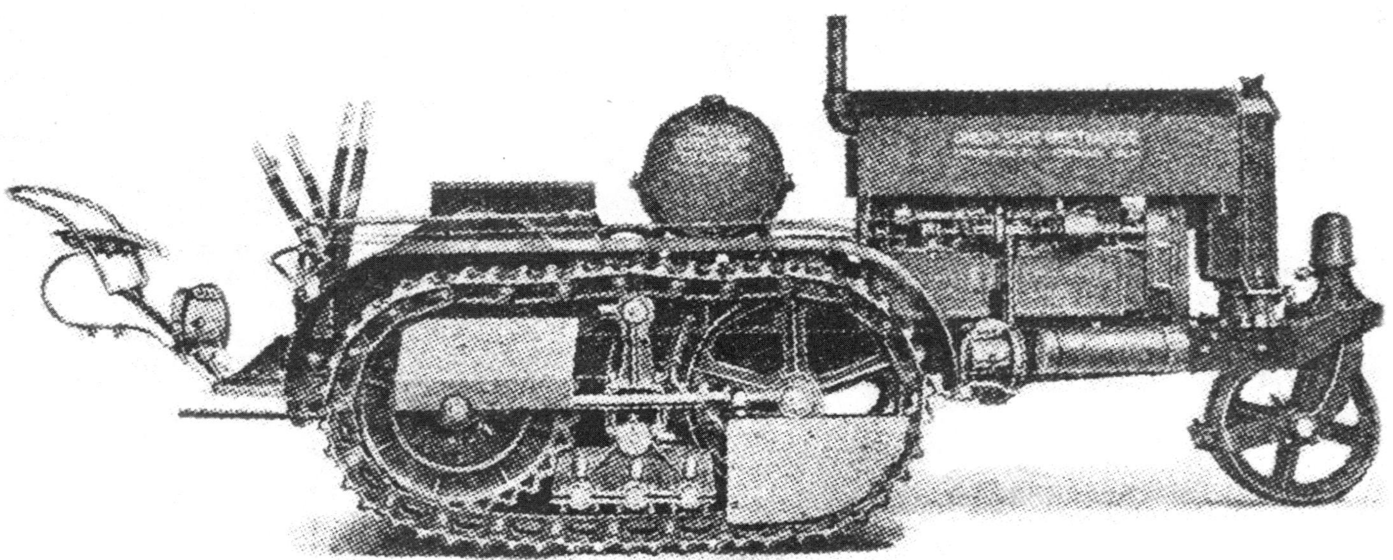

Union 12-25 crawler

United tractor

United States Tractor Corporation

DOVER, DELAWARE

No information has been found on this company or its tractors except that it was organized and incorporated in 1917.

United Tractor & Equipment Company

CHICAGO, ILLINOIS

First appearing in 1929, the United was actually a Model U Allis-Chalmers—identical except for the "United" logo appearing on the radiator. Over 30 independent implement makers and distributors banded together to form this company, but it marketed the United only into 1930.
See: Allis-Chalmers

United Tractor Company

DES MOINES, IOWA

This firm was incorporated in 1917 to build tractors, but no other information has been found.

United Tractors Corporation

NEW YORK, NEW YORK

About 1918 the 7-12 Cultitractor appeared. This small tractor used a Light Model H, four-cylinder engine with a 3-1/4 x 4-1/2-inch bore and stroke. Weighing 2,350 lbs., the Cultitractor retailed at $785. By 1920, essentially the same tractor was known as the Mohawk 8-16.

7-12 Cultitractor

For 1921 the Mohawk 8-16 was slightly redesigned, but continued to use the same engine, chassis, and drivetrain as before. The company guaranteed this tractor would pull at least 1,000 lbs. on the drawbar, and deliver at least 16 hp in the belt. Production ended in the early 1920s.

Mohawk 8-16 tractor

Unitractor Company

INDIANAPOLIS, INDIANA

Unitractor Model 47

The Unitractor first appeared in June 1939. By 1947 it had taken the form shown here, with this being the Model 47. It was equipped with a Briggs & Stratton Model N engine with a 2-inch bore and stroke. Various accessory equipment was available for the Unitractor.

Unity Steel Tractor Company

ANTIGO, WISCONSIN

This company was organized in 1914 by D. S. Stewart and others. Stewart was involved with the Topp-Stewart Tractor Company, as well as the Antigo Tractor Company of 1919.

See: Topp-Stewart Tractor Company

Universal Machinery Company

PORTLAND, OREGON

By 1948 the Universal garden tractor line was on the market. A typical model of 1950 was the Universal pattern shown here, a tractor powered by a Lauson single-cylinder engine with a 2-1/4 inch bore and stroke. The Universal was available at least into the mid-1950s.

Universal garden tractor

Universal Mfg. Company

INDIANAPOLIS, INDIANA

In 1953 this company is listed as the manufacturer of the McLean garden tractor. No other information is available.

COLLECTOR VALUES	1	2	3	4
MCLEAN GARDEN TRACTOR	$1,500	$1,200	$850	$500

Universal Motor Company

NEWCASTLE, INDIANA

Universal Model G combination truck and tractor

Universal tractor

In 1910 the concept of a combination truck and tractor was common. The Universal Model G was a unique combination outfit in several ways. First, a large six-cylinder engine was direct-coupled to a generator. Electric motors were connected to each wheel, and operated from the generator. Production of this unit continued for only a short time.

Universal Motor Truck & Traction Engine Company

ST. LOUIS, MISSOURI

Although it was organized and incorporated in 1912, no other information has been found on this company.

Universal Motor Company

OSHKOSH, WISCONSIN

Aside from a single illustration, almost nothing is known of the Universal motor cultivator of 1920. It used a single rear drive wheel, and the operator was seated to the very front of the machine.

Universal motor cultivator

Universal Products Company

MADISON, WISCONSIN

Although organized and incorporated in 1919, no other information has been found for this company.

Universal Tractor Company

INDIANAPOLIS, INDIANA

Universal was organized and incorporated in 1913, but no other information has been found.

Universal Tractor Company

STILLWATER, MINNESOTA

Production of the Universal tractor began at Crookston, Minnesota, in July 1909. The following year the company was taken over by Northwest Thresher Company at Stillwater, and in 1912 the latter was bought out by M. Rumely Company, LaPorte, Indiana. At that point the Universal became the Rumely GasPull tractor. The Universal used a two-cylinder opposed engine with a 7-1/2 x 8-inch bore and stroke, and capable of 18 hp.

See: Advance-Rumely Thresher Company

Universal Tractor Mfg. Company

COLUMBUS, OHIO

Universal 10 hp motor cultivator

Beginning in 1914, Universal came out with a 10 hp motor cultivator outfit. It used a two-cylinder engine and was priced at $385. Moline Plow Company bought out the company in November 1915 for $150,000. Initially, Moline continued to build the two-cylinder design pioneered by Universal, but eventually converted to a larger four-cylinder model.

COLLECTOR VALUES	1	2	3	4
10HP CULTIVATOR	$8,000	$7,000	$5,000	$2,000

Universal Tractor Mfg. Company

NEWCASTLE, INDIANA

The beginnings of this company are unknown, but in 1913 Universal went into receivership, and late that year, merged with Lawter Tractor Company, also of Newcastle.

See: Lawter Tractor Company

Universal Tractors Ltd.

BARTONVILLE, ONTARIO

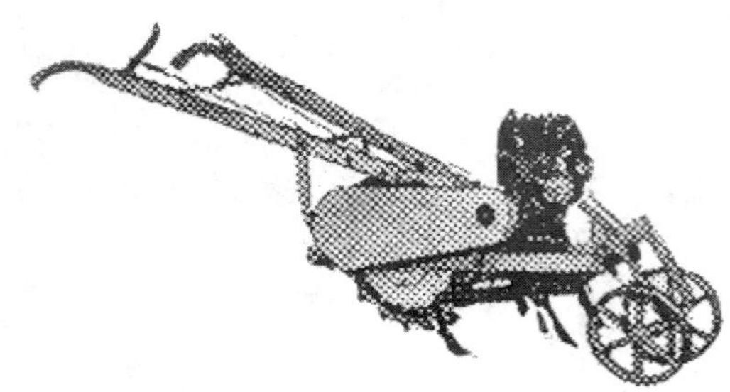

Universal garden tractor

In 1947 the Universal garden tractor was listed and it is unknown if the company built other models. The Universal was equipped with a Briggs & Stratton NPR-6 engine with a 2-inch bore and stroke. Total weight was 200 lbs.

Uncle Sam 20-30 tractor

U.S. Tractor & Machinery Company

MENASHA, WISCONSIN

Organized at Chicago, Illinois in 1918, this company moved to Menasha, Wisconsin, by 1919. U.S. Tractor & Machinery built two sizes of the Uncle Sam tractor —initially a 12-20 model, followed by the 20-30.

The Uncle Sam 20-30 was equipped with a Beaver four-cylinder engine with a 4-3/4 x 6-inch bore and stroke. Production of this tractor continued into the early 1920s.

Nebraska Test Data

Model: Uncle Sam 20-30

Test No. 64

Date Tested: September 21 to September 28, 1920

Although the Uncle Sam tractor was marketed for only a short time, it managed to last long enough to go through the Nebraska Tractor Test. Weighing 4,500 lbs., the 20-30 negotiated a maximum drawbar pull of 3,264 lbs. at 2.79 mph, for 21.98 maximum drawbar hp. For those who enjoy statistics, this represented over 72 percent of the total weight available at the drawbar! Negating this effort was a recorded figure of 18 percent for drivewheel slippage. During the 34-hour test, kerosene was the chosen fuel. Specifications included a Beaver four-cylinder vertical, valve-in-head engine with a 4-3/4 x 6-inch bore and stroke and a rated speed of 1,000 rpm. Two forward speeds of 2-1/2 and 3-3/4 mph were provided. A Bennett carburetor and Dixie Model 46C magneto came as standard equipment. Brake hp tests did not prove the Uncle Sam to be exceptionally stingy on fuel. At 30.75 hp, fuel consumption totaled 6.34 gph for an economy of only 4.85 hp-hours per gallon.

U.S. Tractor Company

MINNEAPOLIS, MINNESOTA

U.S. 12-24 tractor

In 1917 the Challenge Tractor Co. was organized at Minneapolis. Challenge Co. of Batavia, Illinois, also had a major division at Minneapolis, and the latter also was building a tractor—lots of confusion ensued. Finally, Challenge Tractor Co. changed its name to U.S. Tractor Co. in 1918. The U.S. 12-24 tractor only remained on the market a short time.

U. S. Tractor Corporation

WARREN, OHIO

U. S. Tractor Sales Inc.

PEORIA, ILLINOIS

In 1948 U.S. Tractor Sales Division and U.S. Tractor Corp. were both listed as manufacturers of the USTRAC Model 10 crawler. Within a year or so, production was taken over by Federal Machine & Welder Company.

See: Federal Machine & Welder Company

USTRAC Model 10 crawler

The USTRAC Model 10 was capable of about 27 belt hp. It used a Continental F-124 engine and had four forward and four reverse speeds.

Nebraska Test Data

Model: USTRAC Model 10

Test No. 414

Date Tested: June 22 to June 30, 1949

Weighing 3,695 lbs., the little USTRAC crawler featured a Continental four-cylinder L-head engine with a 3 x 4 3/8-inch bore and stroke with a rated speed of 1,900 rpm. Also featured were an Auto-Lite electrical system and a Zenith 161-7 carburetor. After all tests, that required 45 hours of engine running time, it was noted that oil leaked from the PTO shaft during belt testing. The ignition coil failed during the drawbar tests, and at the end of the tests it was discovered the hood bracket had come loose, leaving a hole in the fuel tank. Test C at 100 percent maximum load indicated 8.57 hp-hours per gallon under a load of 21.33 belt hp. By comparison, fuel economy settled in at 8.03 under a Test D rated load of 19.35 belt hp. Advertised speeds of 1.06, 2.17, 3.97, and 6.75 were built into this tractor, with third gear used for Test H. When this 10-hour run concluded, fuel economy rested at 5.56 hp-hours per gallon under a rated load of 12.48 drawbar hp. Other Test H data included a pull of 1,416 lbs. at 3.31 mph and slippage of 1.45 percent. A low-gear maximum pull of 3,256 lbs. was noted in Test G.

Utilitor Company

DAYTON, OHIO

The exact origins of Utilitor are unknown, but about 1925 the Utilitor Model 502 garden tractor appeared. It used the company's own single-cylinder engine with a 3-1/2 x 4-1/2-inch bore and stroke.

Model 7 garden tractor

Around 1927 the Model 502 was replaced with the Utilitor Model 7. This model was nearly identical except that the engine size was increased to 3-5/8 x 5 inches.

Model 8 Utilitor

In the early 1930s the Model 8 Utilitor appeared. It remained in production until about 1940. During later years it could be purchased with steel wheels or rubber tires. The Model 8 used a Novo engine with a 3-3/8 x 4-inch bore and stroke. Total weight of this tractor was 840 lbs.

Late in the 1930s the Utilitor Model 25 appeared, and it remained in production until the company faded from view in the early 1950s. The Model 25 weighed 640 lbs., and was equipped with a Wisconsin engine with a 3 x 3-1/4-inch bore and stroke. The Model 25 had three forward speeds ranging from 1/2 to 5 mph.

In addition to above models, Utilitor Company also manufactured a riding tractor called the "Red Label." Produced in the 1930s it had rubber tires all around, a PTO, and was powered by a two-cylinder water-cooled Wisconsin engine. Apparently only one exists and is owned by a collector in Wisconsin.

Utilitor Model 25

COLLECTOR VALUES	1	2	3	4
EARLY UTILITORS	$2,500	$2,000	$1,500	$850
MODEL 7/MODEL 8	$1,200	$1,000	$850	$600
MODEL 25	$800	$500	$300	$150
RED LABEL	$5,000	$4,000	$3,000	$2,500

Utility Products Company

AUBURN, INDIANA

In 1948, Utility Products Co. was listed as the manufacturer of the Tractorette garden tractor.

Utility Steel Tractor Company

ANTIGO, WISCONSIN

Utility Steel Tractor

Announced in 1915, the Utility Steel Tractor was one of the first successful four-wheel-drive designs, and ultimately led to the FWD designs of Atlas Engineering Company, Clintonville, Wisconsin. The model shown here weighed about 5,000 lbs. and was equipped with a four-cylinder engine capable of about 40 belt hp. All parts of the tractor were cast steel wherever it was possible to use it.

Vail-Rentschler Tractor Company

HAMILTON, OHIO

Vail Oil Tractor

Incorporated in 1916, Vail-Rentschler began producing its Vail Oil Tractor that same year. Initially it was rated as a 9-18, but by 1918 it was rated as a 10-20 model. The Vail used a two-cylinder engine with a 6 x 7-inch bore and stroke and the tractor weighed 3,700 lbs. Production ended about 1920.

Valentine Bros. Mfg. Company

MINNEAPOLIS, MINNESOTA

During 1908 Valentine Bros. announced its Imperial tractor. Priced at $3,400 it was equipped with a horizontal opposed four-cylinder engine with a 7-1/2 x 9-inch bore and stroke. In 1910 Valentine Bros. and the Shock & Hay Loader Company merged to form Imperial Mfg. Company.
See: Imperial Mfg. Company

Van Duzen Gas & Gasolene Engine Company

CINCINNATI, OHIO

Benjamin C. Van Duzen was a prolific inventor of gasoline engines and their accessory parts. Shown here is the 1898 Van Duzen gasoline traction engine, for which he received Patent No. 609,253. Huber Mfg. Company of Marion, Ohio, bought out Van Duzen in 1898, and built a prototype or two, then left the gasoline traction engine business for a decade. Later they returned with a different design.

Van Duzen gasoline traction engine

Van Nostrand Plow Company

OMAHA, NEBRASKA

This company announced a rotary motor plow design about 1912, but no more is known after this time.

Vaughan Motor Company

PORTLAND, OREGON

In the late 1930s Vaughan developed its Flextread garden tractors. The Model W shown here is of 1939 vintage, and was powered by the company's own single-cylinder engine. It used a 3-3/4 x 4-inch bore and stroke. Vaughan manufactured its Flextread tractors into the 1950s.

COLLECTOR VALUES	1	2	3	4
FLEXTREAD MODEL W	$2,000	$1,500	$850	$450

Flex-tread Model W garden tractor

Velie Motors Corporation

MOLINE, ILLINOIS

This company was organized around 1901 as the Velie Carriage Company and in 1908 the Velie Motor Vehicle Company was organized to build automobiles. Another firm, Velie Engineering Co. was organized in 1911 to build trucks. Tractor manufacturing followed a few years later.

Velie began building tractors in 1916. The Velie Biltwell had a rating of 12 drawbar and 24 belt hp.

Velie 12-24 tractor

About 1917 Velie modified the 12-24 tractor by giving it a different hood and removing the canopy. Velie built its own engine for the 12-24. It was a four-cylinder design and used a 4-1/8 x 5-1/2-inch bore and stroke. Production of the 12-24 continued until 1920.

Versatile Mfg. Company

WINNIPEG, MANITOBA

Versatile Mfg. Co. began building farm equipment in 1945, and began making self-propelled swathers in 1954. The company did not begin building tractors until 1966. The D-100 and G-100 were the first models, followed by the Versatile 145. Built in various styles, the Versatile remained in production until about 1976. During the late 1960s the Versatile line grew to include the 700, 800, 850, and 900 models. The Model 750 was added in 1976. The big 210 hp Model 700 was introduced in 1971. Its companion, the Versatile 900, used a 295 hp Cummins engine.

Imperial tractor

Velie Biltwell tractor

Versatile 256 tractor

Nebraska Test Data

Model: Versatile 256 Diesel, Hydrostatic

Test No. 1518

Date Tested: May 10 to May 21, 1984

The Versatile 256 featured an infinitely variable hydrostatic drive plus a three-speed manual transmission. Using the second range and a speed setting of 5.5 mph, the two-hour drawbar run at 60.62 maximum available hp indicated a pull of 4,122 lbs. at 5.51 mph. Slippage totaled 3.54 percent, and fuel economy was 11.82 hp-hours per gallon. The 10-hour run at 75 percent pull, noted an economy of 11.07 against a load of 51.69 drawbar hp. Also recorded was a pull of 3,219 lbs. at 6.02 mph and slippage totaling 2.53 percent. No repairs or adjustments were required during 48-1/2 hours of operating time. Standard equipment for this 9,150-lb. tractor included 16.9-28-inch tires. Additional front and rear ballast gave a total test weight of 10,460 lbs. The hydrostatic transmission offered a total speed range of 0 to 19.9 mph. A four-cylinder turbocharged engine by Consolidated Diesel Corporation was rated at 2,500 rpm, and it carried a 4.02 x 4.72-inch bore and stroke for a 239-cubic inch displacement. At rated engine speed, 84.36 maximum PTO hp was observed, with 16.19 hp-hours per gallon. Operating at 540 PTO rpm and an engine speed of 2,447 rpm, the economy figure rested at 16.45 under a load of 85.08 PTO hp.

Versatile 555 tractor

Nebraska Test Data

Model: Versatile 555 Diesel, 15-Speed
Test No. 1331
Date Tested: October 29 to November 15, 1979

At a rated engine speed of 2,850 rpm, a two-hour drawbar run was made in eighth gear and under a load of 150.39 maximum available hp. This test saw a pull of 10,331 lbs. at 5.46 mph with slippage totaling 3.37 percent. Fuel economy totaled 12.96 hp-hours per gallon. Another two-hour test at 2,550 engine rpm and under a maximum output of 157.09 drawbar hp gave 14.61 hp-hours per gallon. Also witnessed in this test was a pull of 12,124 lbs. at 4.86 mph and slippage of 3.84 percent. Weighing 19,650 lbs., the 555 Diesel was equipped with dual 18.4-38-inch tires. Additional front and rear ballast gave a total test weight of 25,980 lbs. No repairs or adjustments were required during 53 hours of operation. Features included a selective gear fixed-ratio transmission with 15 forward speeds in a range of 2.0 to 17.4 mph. A Cummins V-8 turbocharged diesel engine had a 4.625 x 4.125-inch bore and stroke gave 555-cubic inches. At a rated engine speed of 2,850 rpm, 182.52 maximum PTO hp was observed, with an economy of 15.52 hp-hours per gallon. With a PTO speed of 1,000 rpm, and a corresponding engine speed of 2,667 rpm, an economy of 16.33 hp-hours per gallon resulted from a load of 184.35 PTO hp.

Nebraska Test Data

Model: Versatile 835 Diesel, 12-Speed
Test No. 1356
Date Tested: June 13 to July 3, 1980

At its rated engine speed of 2,100 rpm, the 835 Diesel delivered 198.23 maximum PTO hp, with an economy of 15.13 hp-hours per gallon. A Cummins six-cylinder, 855-cid turbocharged engine was featured with a 5.5 x 6.0-inch bore and stroke. While the engine was rated at 2,100 rpm, it had a constant power range of 1,750 to 2,100 rpm. Drawbar performance at the higher speed indicated an output of 171.41 drawbar hp using seventh gear. This test also saw a pull of 10,488 lbs. at 6.13 mph and slippage totaling 3.32 percent. Fuel economy was 13.16 hp-hours per gallon. The same test run at 1,900 rpm, and using seventh gear again indicated a maximum drawbar output of 191.23 hp, a pull of 12,714 lbs. at 5.02 mph, and slippage totaling 4.27 percent. Fuel economy totaled 14.25 hp-hours per gallon. Weighing 24,280 lbs., the 835 assumed a total test weight of 28,000 lbs. through additional front and rear ballast. Standard equipment included dual 18.4-38-inch tires. No repairs or adjustments were necessary during 70-1/2 hours of operating time.

Versatile 835 tractor

Nebraska Test Data

Model: Versatile 835 Series 3 Diesel
Test No. 1482
Date Tested: May 31 to June 9, 1983

This version of the 835 also featured a Cummins six-cylinder turbocharged engine. Rated at 1,750 to 2,100 rpm, it carried a 5.5 x 6.0-inch bore and stroke for an 855-cubic inch displacement. With an engine speed of 2,100 rpm, 200.30 maximum PTO hp was observed, with an economy of 15.82 hp-hours per gallon. The selective-gear fixed-ratio transmission offered 12 forward speeds ranging from 2.6 to 14.3 mph. Operating in seventh gear, with an engine speed of 2,100 rpm, 178.82 maximum available drawbar hp was demonstrated with 14.45 hp-hours per gallon. Also indicated was a pull of 10,829 lbs. at 6.19 mph and slippage totaling 2.97 percent. A supplementary test at 1,750 rpm, still using seventh gear, saw 16.11 hp-hours per gallon under an output of 188.51 drawbar hp. Other test data included a pull of 13,844 lbs. at 5.11 mph and slippage of 3.94 percent. No repairs or adjustments were necessary during 47 hours of operating time. Standard equipment included dual 18.4-38-inch tires. Weighing in at 24,385 lbs., the 835 took on a total test weight of 27,980 lbs. by the addition of front and rear ballast.

Versatile 875 tractor

Nebraska Test Data

Model: Versatile 875 Diesel
Test No. 1279
Date Tested: June 3 to June 8, 1978

Weighing 24,520 lbs., the 875 was equipped with dual 18.4-38-inch tires. Additional rear wheel ballast gave a total test weight of 29,500 lbs. A selective gear fixed-ratio transmission was used—its 12 forward speeds ranged from 2.6 to 14.3 mph. Seventh gear was used for the two-hour economy run made at 220.20 maximum available drawbar hp. This test indicated 13.6 hp hours per gallon. Also revealed was a pull of 13,410 lbs. at 6.16 mph and slippage of 4.46 percent. The 10-hour run at 75 percent pull noted 12.28 hp-hours per gallon under a load of 186.11 drawbar hp. Also recorded was a pull of 10,398 lbs. at 6.71 mph and slippage totaling 3.39 percent. Replacement of fuel filters and repair of an oil filter were noted during 38-1/2 hours of operating time. A Cummins six-cylinder turbocharged diesel engine was featured—rated at 2,100 rpm, it carried a 5.5 x 6.0-inch bore and stroke for an 855-cubic inch displacement. At rated engine speed, the 875 developed 248.07 maximum PTO hp and achieved 15.45 hp-hours per gallon.

Nebraska Test Data

Model: Versatile 875 Diesel, 12-Speed

Test No. 1332

Date Tested: October 30 to November 13, 1979

At its rated engine speed of 2,100 rpm, the Versatile developed 247.16 maximum PTO hp while achieving 16.06 hp-hours per gallon. Standard equipment included a Cummins six-cylinder turbocharged engine. Rated at from 1,750 to 2,100 rpm, it used a 5.5 x 6.0-inch bore and stroke for an 855-cubic inch displacement. The selective-gear fixed-ratio transmission included 12 forward speeds ranging from 2.7 to 14.6 mph. No repairs or adjustments were required during 53-1/2 hours of operation. Using seventh gear, and under a maximum load of 217.55 drawbar hp, the two-hour economy run saw a pull of 12,386 lbs. at 6.59 mph, slippage of 2.97 percent and fuel economy of 14.35 hp-hours per gallon. The 10-hour run at 75 percent witnessed a pull of 9,425 lbs. at 7.32 mph and slippage totaling 2.25 percent. This test also saw an output of 184.02 drawbar hp and 12.53 hp-hours per gallon. The 875 weighed in at 25,320 lbs., but additional front and rear ballast gave a total test weight of 29,480 lbs. Standard equipment included dual 20.8-38-inch tires.

Nebraska Test Data

Model: Versatile 875 Series 3 Diesel

Test No. 1483

Date Tested: May 31 to June 10, 1983

Operating at 2,100 rpm and using seventh gear, the 875 delivered 224.08 maximum available drawbar hp in a two-hour test. Also recorded was a pull of 12,851 lbs. at 6.54 mph, slippage of 3.18 percent, and 15.25 hp-hours per gallon. A supplementary two-hour run at an engine speed of 1,750 rpm, again using seventh gear, saw 16.62 hp-hours per gallon under a load of 229.39 maximum available hp. Other data included a pull of 15,957 lbs. at 5.39 mph and slippage of 4.27 percent. No repairs or adjustments were required during 41 hours of operating time. Weighing in at 25,360 lbs., the 875 assumed a total test weight of 29,500 lbs. by the addition of front and rear ballast. Standard equipment included dual 20.8-38-inch tires. The six-cylinder Cummins turbocharged diesel engine was rated at 1,750 to 2,100 rpm. Its 5.5 x 6.0 inch bore and stroke gave an 855-cubic inch displacement. At a rated speed of 2,100 rpm, 252.67 maximum PTO hp was observed, 16.82 hp-hours per gallon. Standard equipment included a selective-gear fixed-ratio transmission with 12 forward speeds ranging from 2.7 to 14.6 mph.

Versatile 895 tractor

Nebraska Test Data

Model: Versatile 895 Diesel, 12-Speed

Test No. 1335

Date Tested: March 25 to April 3, 1980

Dual 24.5-32-inch tires were used on this tractor. Weighing 24,620 lbs., it assumed a total test weight of 32,500 lbs. through added front and rear ballast. The selective-gear fixed-ratio transmission offered 12 forward speeds ranging from 2.6 to 14.3 mph. Using seventh gear, and operating at 2,100 engine rpm, a maximum available output of 251.51 drawbar hp was delivered, with a pull of 14,609 lbs. at 6.46 mph and slippage totaling 3.35 percent. Fuel economy came in at 15.15 hp-hours per gallon. At an engine speed of 1,900 rpm, the test gave an output of 255.07 maximum available hp and achieved 16.05 hp hours per gallon. Also recorded was a pull of 16,462 lbs. at 5.82 mph with slippage totaling 3.72 percent. No repairs or adjustments were reported during 54 hours of operating time. The 895 Diesel was equipped with a Cummins six-cylinder turbocharged and intercooled engine. Rated at 1,750 to 2,100 rpm, it carried a 5.5 x 6.0-inch bore and stroke for a displacement of 855-cubic inches. No PTO shaft was furnished and no brake hp tests were run on this tractor.

Versatile 1150 tractor

Nebraska Test Data

Model: Versatile 1150 Diesel

Test No. 1462

Date Tested: November 11 to November 19, 1982

This tractor was not equipped with a PTO shaft so no brake hp tests were run. Weighing 35,140 lbs., the 1150 featured dual 30.5L-32-inch tires. Additional front and rear ballast gave a total test weight of 46,500 lbs. The Cummins six-cylinder turbocharged and inter-cooled engine was rated at 1,750 to 2,100 rpm. Its 6.25-inch bore and stroke displaced 1,150 cubic inches. The eight-speed selective-gear fixed-ratio transmission offered a total speed range of 3.0 to 16.0 mph. Using fourth gear and operating at 2,100 rpm, the 1150 delivered 390.69 maximum available drawbar hp while achieving 15.84 hp-hours per gallon. Also indicated by this test was a pull of 24,626 lbs. at 5.95 mph, with slippage totaling 3.52 percent. The same two-hour test run at an engine speed of 1,750 rpm indicated 17.10 hp-hours per gallon under a load of 411.32 drawbar hp. Also revealed was a pull of 31,691 lbs. at 4.87 mph with 5.09 percent total slippage. This tractor made a second gear maximum drawbar pull of 43,219 lbs. at 3.07 mph. Slippage totaled 14.59 percent. No repairs or adjustments were required during 35-1/2 hours of operating time.

Victor tractor

Victor Tractor Company

MINNEAPOLIS, MINNESOTA

The Victor tractor was first built in 1918 and remained on the market for only a short time. It was powered by a Climax four-cylinder engine with a 5 x 6-1/2-inch bore and stroke. Weighing 4,500 lbs., the Victor sold for $1,685.

Victor Traction Gear Company

LOUDONVILLE, OHIO

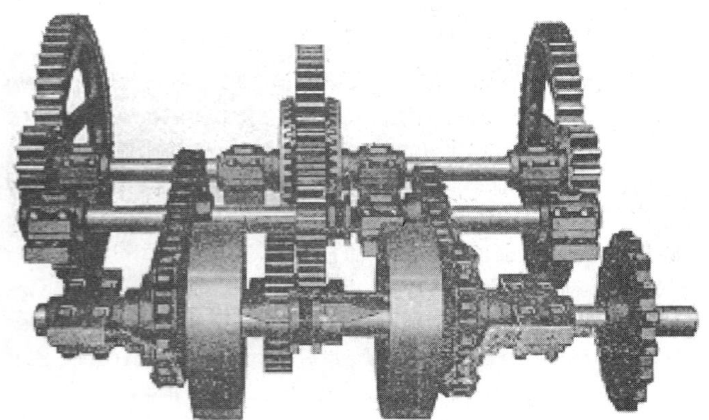

Victor conversion attachment

At least into the early 1920s, Victor offered a variety of "Traction Equipment for Converting Portable Engines into Tractors." Shown here are the components of a two-speed system, complete with all gears, clutches, and other items. The concept was popular enough at the time to provide room for several manufacturers of these conversions.

Victory Tractor Company

GREENSBURG, INDIANA

Victory 9-18 tractor

Vim 15-30 tractor

This company was organized in 1918 and built Victory tractors until 1921. The best-known model was the 9-18, which was built during the entire existence of the company. It was equipped with a Gray four-cylinder engine with a 3-1/2 x 5-inch bore and stroke. In the 1919 to 1921 period the company also built a 15-30 model. It was of the same design as the 9-18 but used a Waukesha four-cylinder engine with a 4-1/4 x 5-3/4-inch bore and stroke.

Vim Tractor Company

SCHLEISINGERVILLE, (NOW SLINGER), WISCONSIN

Vim took over the factories of Standard Machinery Company in 1919 and built the 10-20 Vim tractor. Shortly after this, the firm added the Vim 15-30, shown here. The 10-20 was of similar appearance. It used a Waukesha four-cylinder engine with a 3-3/4 x 5-1/2-inch bore and stroke. No specifications have been found for the 15-30 model. Production ended by 1920 or shortly thereafter.

Vincennes Tractor Company

VINCENNES, INDIANA

During 1911 this company was organized to manufacture tractors, and in 1913 the first Vincennes tractor appeared. It was powered by a four-cylinder engine with a 6 x 7-1/2-inch bore and stroke, producing around 50 belt hp. Little is known of the company, and it is entirely possible that the prototype shown here was the only copy built.

Vincennes tractor

James Vis

GRAND RAPIDS, MICHIGAN

Peters garden tractor

In the early 1930s the Peters garden tractor was built by Progressive Mfg. Company of Minneapolis, Minnesota. Later in the decade, the Peters was offered by James Vis, at least until the beginning of World War II. The 1939 model used a Briggs & Stratton Model PB engine with a 2-1/2-inch bore and stroke. The Peters also could be supplied with a Briggs & Stratton Type T engine with a 2-5/8 x 3-1/4-inch bore and stroke.

Motox 18-20 tractor

Wabash Tractor Company

WABASH, INDIANA

The Motox 18-30 was advertised by Wabash in 1919, and at the same time, the Motox was promoted by Plano Tractor Company at Plano, Illinois. The connection between the two firms has not been established. A Buda four-cylinder engine with a 4-1/4 x 6-inch bore and stroke was used in the Motox. This 5,000 lb. tractor retailed for $2,000.

R. M. Wade & Company

PORTLAND, OREGON

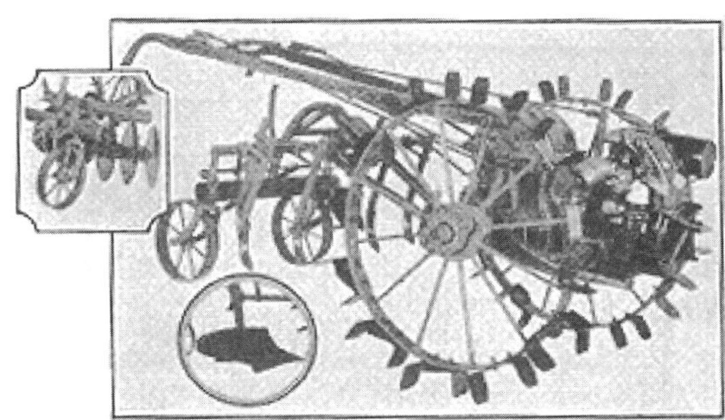

Wade garden tractor

In the late 1930s the Wade garden tractor was on the market; this one is of 1937 vintage. It was powered by a 4 hp Briggs & Stratton engine and permitted power turns through ratchet hubs. The Wade garden tractor remained in production as late as 1953.

Wagner TR-14 tractor

Wagner Tractor Inc.

PORTLAND, OREGON

In the early 1950s the Wagner four-wheel-drive tractors were introduced. For 1955 three models were available. The TR-6 was equipped with a 302 cubic inch diesel engine. The TR-9 was built with a 495-cid diesel. The TR-14 weighed about 16,000 lbs. and was designed around a 672 cubic inch diesel. The company was later renamed FWD Wagner. Wagner tractors were built through the 1960s. In the late 1960s FWD Wagner built the WA-14 and WA-17 tractors for John Deere.

Nebraska Test Data

Model: Wagner TR-9 Diesel
Test No. 631
Date Tested: September 24 to October 3, 1957

No belt pulley was available for this tractor, consequently no belt or torque tests were made. The test report also indicated that agricultural type R-1 tires were not available in the recommended ply rating, so an industrial tread was used. The TR-9 featured a four-cylinder Cummins diesel engine. Rated at 1,800 rpm, it carried a 5-1/8 x 6-inch bore and stroke for a 495-cubic inch displacement. The test tractor weighed 15,445 lbs. and used 15-26 10-ply tires on all four wheels. During the tests an additional 860 lbs. of liquid ballast was added to each rear wheel, with an additional 465 lbs. of liquid ballast on each front wheel. Featuring forward speeds of 1.22, 1.61, 2.28, 3.08, 4.24, 5.64, 6,68, 8.84, 11.46, and 14.99 mph, the TR-9 made a low-gear maximum pull of 15,975 lbs. at 1.22 mph with 14.58 percent slippage. Test H was run in fifth gear. At a rated output of 68.93 hp, it achieved 12.56 hp-hours per gallon of fuel. This test also noted a pull of 6,013 lbs. at 4.3 mph against a slippage of 2.68 percent. No repairs or adjustments were noted during 44 hours of operating time.

Nebraska Test Data

Model: Wagner TR-14 Diesel
Test No. 700
Date Tested: June 4 to June 10, 1959

This four-wheel-drive tractor weighed in at 21,255 lbs. and went through the entire series of drawbar tests without the use of additional ballast. No belt or PTO tests were run, since this tractor was not equipped with a belt pulley or a PTO shaft. Tire equipment included 18-26-inch tires on all four wheels. Also featured were 10 forward speeds ranging from 2.1 to 20.9 mph. The water pump leaked during the test runs and continued to do so through the remainder of the testing. Otherwise, no repairs or adjustments were noted during 41 hours of operating time. In second gear, a maximum pull of 19,357 lbs. was made at a speed of 2.27 mph with 14.46 percent slippage. Fifth gear was used for the varying drawbar power runs, with 148.56 maximum hp noted, with a pull of 10,749 lbs. at 5.18 mph and a 4.47 percent slippage. Fuel economy was registered at 13.52 hp-hours per gallon of diesel fuel. The same test, run at 75 percent of maximum pull, indicated an output of 122.29 hp, a pull of 8,469 lbs. at 5.41 mph and 3.39 percent slippage. This 10-hour run produced 12.89 hp-hours per gallon. The TR-14A was equipped with a Cummins six-cylinder diesel engine rated at 2,100 rpm that carried a 5 1/8 x 6-inch bore and stroke for a 743-cubic inch displacement.

Nebraska Test Data

Model: FWD Wagner WA-4 Diesel
Test No. 864
Date Tested: June 6 to June 12, 1964

No belt pulley or PTO shaft were available for this tractor, so no PTO output or economy tests were run. Standard equipment included a General Motors four-cylinder, two-cycle, blower-equipped engine rated at 2,500 rpm. Its 212.3-cubic inches resulted from a 3-7/8 x 4-1/2-inch bore and stroke. The selective-gear fixed-ratio transmission included a partial syncro-mesh design. Eight forward speeds were available in a range from 1.61 to 18.29 mph. The WA-4 featured 18.4-26-inch tires on all four wheels. They supported a bare weight of 11,035 lbs., compared to a test figure of 18,795 lbs. The latter figure was attained through the use of front and rear ballast. Using fourth gear, and operating at 93.87 maximum available drawbar hp, fuel economy came to 12.5 hp-hours per gallon. This test further indicated a pull of

Waite tractor

Ward tractor

6,598 lbs. at 5.34 mph with 4.4 percent slippage. A 10-hour run at 75 percent pull noted 12 hp-hours per gallon against an output of 76.98 drawbar hp. In this test a pull of 5,109 lbs. was recorded at 5.65 mph and 3.49 percent slippage. Also, this tractor made a low-gear maximum pull of 14,968 lbs. at 1.86 mph with 14.87 percent slippage. No repairs or adjustments were noted during 33-1/2 hours of running time.

Waite Tractor Sales Corporation

CHICAGO, ILLINOIS

H. C. Waite designed this tractor, going back to 1913 and a factory at Elgin, Illinois. The company continued building this model, and attempted to raise the capital for the firm in 1916. In July 1916, the company was forced into reorganization. Waite tractors used a friction-drive system.

Wallis Tractor Company

RACINE, WISCONSIN

See: J. I. Case Plow Works

Walsh Tractor Company

MINNEAPOLIS, MINNESOTA

The 1931 Walsh garden tractor used the comany's own single-cylinder engine with a 2-1/2-inch bore and stroke and a 2-1/2 hp rating. With an engine speed of 800 to 2,000 rpm, it could travel from 1/2 to 2 mph. This machine weighed 231 lbs. and could be furnished with a variety of implements. The tractor shown here was equipped with a double engine, an option that effectively doubled the hp.

See: Standard Engine Co.

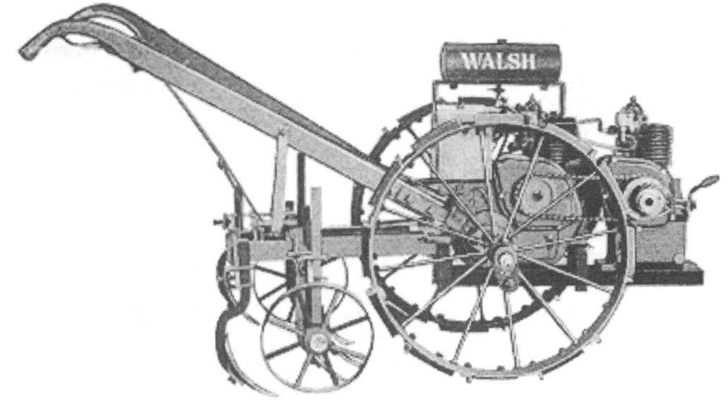

Walsh garden tractor

COLLECTOR VALUES	1	2	3	4
WALSH	$750	$500	$350	$250
VIKING SINGLE	$1,500	$1,000	$850	$450
VIKING TWIN	$1,200	$950	$600	$350
STANDARD TWIN	$1,200	$950	$600	$350

Ward Tractor Company

LINCOLN, NEBRASKA

During 1912 the Ward tractor was announced. This unique design was powered by a Cushman 20 hp, two-cylinder engine. (The Cushman was also built at Lincoln, Nebraska.) Despite many favorable comments on this tractor, it was not built beyond 1914.

Warehouse Point Company

WAREHOUSE POINT, CONNECTICUT

Terra Farma garden tractor

In 1946 this firm offered its Terra Farma garden tractor. It was powered by a 1-1/2 hp engine. This machine retailed for $350. According to advertising, it was offered to "distributors and exporters." Nothing further is known about this machine.

Warren Motor & Mfg. Company

MINNEAPOLIS, MINNESOTA

In 1919 this company was listed as the manufacturer of the Dakota King tractor. No other information has been found.

Waterbury Tool Division

WATERBURY, CONNECTICUT

Waterbury Model R riding tractor

In the early 1950s Waterbury offered several different models of garden tractors. Shown here is the Waterbury

Waterloo Boy One-Man tractor

Model R riding tractor. Weighing 545 lbs., it sold for $395. Power came from a Briggs & Stratton engine capable of over 5 hp. This firm was a subsidiary of Vickers Incorporated.

COLLECTOR VALUES	1	2	3	4
WATERBURY MODEL R RIDING TRACTOR	$850	$450	$225	$100

Waterloo Boy Kerosene Tractor Company

CHICAGO, ILLINOIS

Little is known about this company except that it was organized and incorporated in 1916. It had no connection with Waterloo Gasoline Engine Company, the builders of the Waterloo Boy tractors.

Waterloo Foundry Company

WATERLOO, IOWA

Big Chief 8-15 tractor

In 1911 the Big Chief 8-15 tractor was announced. Little is known about this tractor, although it bears unmistakable signs of being a forerunner to the Waterloo Boy tractor. The latter was built by Waterloo Gasoline Engine Company.

Waterloo Gasoline Engine Company

WATERLOO, IOWA

As early as 1886 John Froehlich conceived the idea of building a replacement for the steam traction engine and was soon building gas engines. Froehlich was an organizer of the Waterloo Gasoline Traction Engine Company, but due to the limited market at the time, the company preferred to build gasoline engines. The resulting Waterloo Gasoline Engine Co. became a major gas engine builder until the company entered the tractor business in 1912. The company was bought out by Deere & Company in 1918, launching that venerable manufacturer into the tractor business.

See: Deere & Company

In 1892 John Froehlich built his first engine in Clayton County, Iowa. That year his gasoline traction engine was shipped to South Dakota where it threshed over 62,000 bushels of grain without a single breakdown.

Waterloo Boy Sure-Grip (Waterloo Catapillar)

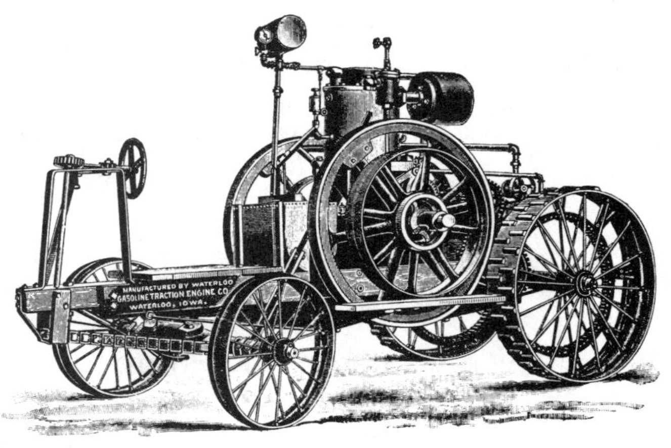

Froehlich gasoline traction engine

After the Froehlich tractor of the 1890s, Waterloo Gasoline Engine Co. stayed out of the tractor business until announcing the Waterloo Boy One-Man tractor in 1912. It used a four-cylinder engine with a 5-1/2 x 6-inch bore and stroke. The Waterloo Boy was available with rear-mounted plows. Production of this model ended in 1913.

The Waterloo Boy Sure-Grip, also known as the Waterloo Catapillar, used the same engine as the One-Man tractor of 1912. This tractor, like the One-Man, owed its existence to the design work of Harry Leavitt.

By 1913 the Waterloo One-Man tractor was discontinued, and in its place came a new Waterloo One-Man tractor of an entirely different design. This 15 hp model used a two-cylinder opposed engine with a 5-1/2 x 7-inch bore and stroke. Production continued into 1914.

Waterloo One-Man tractor

Waterloo Boy Small Farm tractor

Sometime in 1914 the Waterloo Boy Small Farm tractor appeared. This model continued to use the same engine as the 15 hp One-Man, but used a cellular radiator, along with other changes.

During 1914 the first Waterloo Boy Style R tractor appeared. It used a two-cylinder engine with a 5-1/2 x 7-inch bore and stroke. First known as the Type A, this tractor underwent numerous changes in the coming months. By 1915 it was the Model R, Style D, but all used the same 5-1/2 x 7 engine. In 1916 the engine of the Style R

Waterloo Boy Style N tractor

Waterloo Boy was changed to a 6 x 7-inch bore and stroke. It remained thus until 1917 when it was again changed to include a 6-1/2 x 7-inch bore and stroke. Production of the Style R ended in 1918.

Waterloo Boy Style R tractor

Production of the famous Waterloo Boy Style N tractor began in 1917 and continued until 1924. When the Nebraska Tractor Tests began in 1920, the Model N, 12-25 was the first tractor tested. It yielded almost 16 maximum drawbar hp during Test No. 1. This tractor carried a two-cylinder engine with a 6-1/2 x 7-inch bore and stroke.

Waterloo Mfg. Company Ltd.

WATERLOO, ONTARIO

In 1953 the Waterloo Bronco Model 100 was listed in a few of the tractor directories. This small tractor was equipped with a Wisconsin two-cylinder Model TE engine with a 3 x 3-1/4-inch bore and stroke. It was rated at slightly over 11 hp. Options included a pto shaft and a belt pulley. Also available was a hydraulic lift system. Exact production dates of the Bronco 100 are not known.

Waterloo Bronco Model 100 tractor

COLLECTOR VALUES	1	2	3	4
BRONCO MODEL 100	$3,500	$3,000	$2,500	$1,000

Waterloo Motor Works

WATERLOO, IOWA

This firm was organized in 1902 after a buyout of the Davis Gasoline Engine Works of Waterloo, Iowa. The latter had also organized the Davis Gasoline Traction Engine Works, and possibly built a few tractors. In any event, the activities of Waterloo Motor Works in the tractor business probably followed the pioneering work of Davis.

Waterous Engine Company

ST. PAUL, MINNESOTA

Waterous tractor

By 1904 the Waterous tractor was on the market, and remained so until 1911. Few details of this tractor have been found, although it appears to be of 30 or more hp. Waterous began building steam fire engines in the 1880s, and began building gasoline engines in the late 1890s. After leaving the tractor business, Waterous Fire Engine Co. specialized in building firefighting equipment.

Wayne Tractor Company

DETROIT, MICHIGAN

Although it was organized and incorporated in 1916, nothing further is known about this company or its tractors.

Welborn Corporation

KANSAS CITY, KANSAS

This firm succeeded Coleman Tractor Company in 1920. A few tractors may have been built by Coleman-Welborn Corporation, and even a few by Welborn Corporation, but the Coleman was essentially gone after 1920.

Wellman-Seaver-Morgan Company

AKRON, OHIO

During the 1920 through 1922 period Wellman-Seaver-Morgan offered its Akron 15-30 tractor. The company used its own four-cylinder engine, designed with a 4-3/4 x 6-inch bore and stroke. Four forward speeds were provided, ranging from 1-1/2 to 6 mph.

Akron 15-30 tractor

Western American Industries

LONGMONT, COLORADO

In the late 1950s Western American appeared as the manufacturer of the Gibson tractors, apparently succeeding Gibson Mfg. Corporation of Longmont, Colorado. Shown here is the Gibson Super D tractor. This model was equipped with a Wisconsin single-cylinder engine with a 3 x 3-1/4-inch bore and stroke. It was rated at nearly 8-1/2 hp.

Gibson Super D tractor

Western Implement & Motor Company

DAVENPORT, IOWA

In 1912 Western Implement & Motor Company was organized. This was a new name for the former National Co-operative Farm Machinery Company. To launch itself into the tractor business, Western bought out the Colby Motor Works at Mason City, Iowa. Western went out of business late in 1913.

Western 16-32 tractor

Creeping Grip 40-30 tractor

Western Implement built tractors under the Creeping Grip brand name. This was the 40-30 model, rated to have 40 drawbar hp.

Creeping Grip 75-55 tractor

The 75-55 model shown here was built with a four-cylinder engine. Aside from an occasional illustration, few specifications were found on the Creeping Grip tractors.

Western Mfg. Company

WATERTOWN, SOUTH DAKOTA

In 1914 this company offered a 20-35 tractor weighing 8,200 lbs. and using a two-cylinder opposed engine. No other information has been found, nor have any photographs been located.

Western Tractor Company

EL MONTE, CALIFORNIA

In 1947 this company offered the Western "400" garden tractor. It was powered by a Briggs & Stratton engine with a 2-1/4-inch bore and stroke. Shipping weight was 400 lbs. Little else is known about this garden tractor.

Western Tractor Company

MINNEAPOLIS, MINNESOTA

This company announced in early 1917 that it would soon build tractors, but no other information has been found.

Western Tractor Company

REGINA, SASKATCHEWAN

No information has been located on this company except that it went out of business in 1919.

Wharton 3WD, 12-22 tractor

Wharton 20-40 tractor

Western Tractor Company

TULSA, OKLAHOMA

Organized in 1916, this firm offered the Western 8-15 tractor at least into 1917. It used a Toro two- cylinder vertical engine with a 5-1/4 x 6-1/2-inch bore and stroke. Weighing 4,200 lbs., it sold for $735.

Western Tool and Manufacturing Company

KANSAS CITY, MISSOURI

No information has been located for this company or its tractors.

Western Tractor Company

WICHITA, KANSAS

Developed about 1919, the Western 16-32 tractor remained on the market for only a short time. This 5,900-lb. tractor had a 1920 retail price of $2,100. It featured a Climax four-cylinder engine with a 5 x 6-1/2-inch bore and stroke.

Wetmore Tractor Company

SIOUX CITY, IOWA

Wetmore 12-25 tractor

During 1919 the Wetmore 12-25 tractor appeared. This lightweight design weighed only 3,000 lbs. and had a list price of $1,385. Power came from a Rutenbur four-cylinder engine with a 4-1/8 x 5-1/2- inch bore and stroke. Originally the tractor was built by H. A. Wetmore, but the company name was changed to Wetmore Tractor Co. in the early 1920s. Production of the 12-25 continued into the early 1930s.

Nebraska Test Data

Model: Wetmore 12-25
Test No. 73
Date Tested: April 6 to April 12, 1921

Kerosene was used throughout the test procedures of the Wetmore 12-25. Specifications indicate many of the Wetmore's components were OEM items. Included were a Weidely four-cylinder vertical, valve-in-head engine with a 4 x 5-1/2-inch bore and stroke. It was rated at 1,265 rpm. Also featured was a Torbenson axle, Fuller transmission, Splitdorf magneto and a Schebler Model ATX 47 carburetor. Three forward speeds of 2, 3.5 and 5.9 mph were standard equipment. No adjustments or repairs were made throughout the 32 hours of running time. At rated brake hp, 6.95 hp-hours per gallon of kerosene was demonstrated for a total consumption of 3.65 gph at 25.27 hp. Using second gear, a maximum drawbar load test revealed 16.1 hp and a pull of 1,162 lbs. at 2.67 mph. Total weight of this unit was 3,000 lbs.

Wharton Motors Company

DALLAS, TEXAS

Wharton Motors Company was building tractors by 1920. In 1921, the Wharton tractors were built by Texas Truck & Tractor Company, but it is likely that very few tractors were produced by the new builder before the Wharton models disappeared from the market.

By 1920 the Wharton 3WD, 12-22 tractor was on the market. It was a unique three-wheel-drive design, and was powered by an Erd four-cylinder engine with a 4 x 6-inch bore and stroke.

The Wharton 20-40 was a four-wheel-drive design, but few details have been found for this tractor. Probably, as with the 12-22, production was rather limited.

Wheat Tiller & Tractor Company

BUFFALO, NEW YORK

The Wheat 12-24 tractor appeared in 1921, formerly built by Hession Tiller & Tractor Corporation. This unique design was a combination farm and road tractor. As shown in the top illustration, the tractor was ready for the road, but in the bottom illustration it was field-ready. In the 1922-1924 period the Wheat tractor was built by Matthews Tractor Company at Brockport, New York.

See: Hession Tiller & Tractor Corporation

Wheat 12-24 tractor

White Farm Equipment Company,

OAK BROOK, ILLINOIS

After buying out and merging Oliver Farm Equipment, Minneapolis-Moline, and other companies, White consolidated its interests, closed its other plants, and concentrated its tractor building efforts at its Illinois plant by the mid-1970s.

White Field Boss 2-105 tractor

Nebraska Test Data

Model: White Field Boss 2-105 Diesel

Test No. 1181

Date Tested: June 16 to June 23, 1975

This tractor featured a Perkins six-cylinder, 354-cubic inch turbocharged engine. Rated at 2,200 rpm, it used a 3.875 x 5-inch bore and stroke. Operating at rated engine speed, 105.61 maximum PTO hp was observed, as was 15.76 hp-hours per gallon. The selective-gear fixed-ratio transmission offered partial-range power shifting. Its 18 forward speeds ranged from 1.6 to 18.9 mph. Using ninth gear, the two-hour economy run was made at 84.96 maximum available drawbar hp. This test saw a pull of 6,147 lbs. at 5.18 mph with slippage of 7.4 percent. Fuel economy was 12.89 hp-hours per gallon. The 10-hour run at 75 percent pull noted 11.95 hp-hours per gallon against a load of 70.71 drawbar hp. Other test data included a pull of 4,738 lbs. at 5.6 mph with slippage totaling 5.16 percent. Weighing 11,810 lbs., the 2-105 was tested without additional ballast. Standard equipment included 20.8-38-inch rear and 11L-15-inch front tires. In the "Repairs and Adjustments" section it was reported that a fuel tank leak was repaired, as was an oil supply line to the turbocharger, during 41 hours of engine operating time.

Nebraska Test Data

Model: White Field Boss 2-150 Diesel

Test No. 1182

Date Tested: June 16 to June 30, 1975

Weighing 16,940 lbs., the 2-150 was equipped with dual 18.4-38-inch rear tires and 11.00-16-inch front rubber. No additional ballast was used during drawbar testing. The 2-150 was equipped with an 18-speed transmission, which also featured partial-range power shifting. Speed varied from 1.5 to 17.7 mph. Using ninth gear, the two-hour economy run saw 121.35 maximum available drawbar hp and 12.07 hp-hours per gallon. Also recorded was a pull of 9,865 lbs. at 4.61 mph with slippage totaling 6.34 percent. The 10-hour run at 75 percent pull noted 12.14 hp-hours per gallon under a load of 99.49 drawbar hp. Other statistics included a pull of 7,643 lbs. at 4.88 mph with 4.45 percent slippage. After a total of 50-1/2 hours operating time it was reported that an oil seal on the left rear axle was replaced. Also, No. 6 piston seized and scored the cylinder wall. After replacement of the piston and the rear cylinder block, the 10-hour drawbar test was run again. White featured its own six-cylinder, 585-cid engine. Rated at 2,200 rpm, it carried a 4.75 x 5.50-inch bore and stroke. At rated engine speed a maximum output of 147.49 PTO hp appeared, and an economy of 14.46 hp-hours per gallon was observed.

White Field Boss 2-150 tractor

White Field Boss 2-155 and 2-180 tractors

White Field Boss 2-50 and 2-60 tractors

Nebraska Test Data

Model: White Field Boss 2-155 Diesel

Test No. 1276

Date Tested: May 12 to May 19, 1978

Weighing 16,650 lbs., this White tractor was tested without the use of additional ballast. Standard equipment included dual 20.8-38-inch rear and 14L-16-inch front tires. The selective-gear fixed-ratio-transmission offered partial-range power shifting. Its 18 forward speeds ranged from 2.2 to 17.8 mph. Tenth gear was used for the two-hour economy run made at 131.33 maximum available drawbar hp. This test saw a pull of 9,145 lbs. at 5.39 mph, slippage of 5.56 percent, and an economy of 12.69 hp hours per gallon. The 10-hour run at 75 percent pull indicated 11.53 hp-hours per gallon under a load of 106.18 drawbar hp. Also revealed was a pull of 6,969 lbs. at 5.71 mph and slippage totaling 3.95 percent. A White six-cylinder turbocharged engine was featured in the 2-155 tractor. Rated at 2,200 rpm, it carried a 4.56 x 4.87-inch bore and stroke for a 478-cubic inch displacement. At rated engine speed, 157.73 maximum PTO hp was observed, with 15.12 hp-hours per gallon. Operating at 1,000 PTO rpm and a corresponding engine speed of 2,167 rpm, an economy of 15.38 hp-hours per gallon was indicated against a load of 162.37 PTO hp. No repairs or adjustments were indicated during 35 hours of operating time.

Nebraska Test Data

Model: White Field Boss 2-180 Diesel

Test No. 1287

Date Tested: September 15 to September 23, 1978

Weighing 18,280 lbs., this tractor was tested without additional ballast. Standard equipment included dual 20.8-42-inch rear and 16.5L-16-inch front tires. Also featured was a selective-gear fixed-ratio transmission with partial-range power shifting. Its 18 forward speeds ranged from 2.4 to 20.1 mph. Using eleventh gear, the two-hour drawbar run at 158.97 maximum available hp indicated a pull of 9,157 lbs. at 6.51 mph, slippage of 5.39 percent, and 12.85 hp-hours per gallon. The 10-hour run at 75 percent pull noted 12.48 hp-hours per gallon under a load of 129.81 drawbar hp. Also recorded was a pull of 7,083 lbs. at 6.87 mph and slippage totaling 3.89 percent. No repairs or adjustments were required during 35-½ hours of operating time. At its rated engine speed of 2,800 rpm, the 2-180 developed 181.89 maximum PTO hp while delivering 14.38 hp-hours per gallon. Standard equipment for this model included a Caterpillar V-8 diesel engine. Its 4.5 x 5.0-inch bore and stroke gave a displacement of 636-cubic inches.

Nebraska Test Data

Model: White Field Boss 2-50 Diesel

Test No. 1231

Date Tested: March 15 to March 25, 1977

Weighing 4,555 lbs., the 2-50 was equipped with 14.9-28-inch rear and 6.50-16-inch front tires. Additional front and rear ballast brought the total test weight to 6,880 lbs. The selective-gear fixed-ratio transmission offered eight forward speeds ranging from 1.5 to 15.1 mph. Fifth gear was used for the two-hour drawbar economy run. At 40.38 maximum available hp, a pull of 3,159 lbs. was recorded at 4.79 mph with slippage totaling 6.75 percent. Fuel economy was 13.26 hp-hours per gallon. The 10-hour run at 75 percent pull noted 13.49 hp hours per gallon under a load of 33.74 drawbar hp. Also recorded was a pull of 2,457 lbs. at 5.15 mph and 4.9 percent slippage. No repairs or adjustments were reported during 45-1/2 hours of operating time. The 2-50 was equipped with a Fiat three-cylinder diesel engine. Rated at 2,500 rpm, it used a 3.94 x 4.33-inch bore and stroke for a 158-cubic inch displacement. At rated engine speed, fuel economy stood at 15.22 hp-hours per gallon under a maximum load of 47.02 PTO hp. Operating at 540 PTO rpm and a corresponding engine speed of 2,159 rpm, 15.8 hp-hours per gallon was established under an observed output of 43.94 PTO hp.

Nebraska Test Data

Model: White Field Boss 2-60 Diesel

Test No. 1232

Date Tested: March 15 to March 28, 1977

Weighing in at 5,160 lbs., the 2-60 was equipped with 16.9-30-inch rear and 7.50-16-inch front tires. Additional front and rear ballast gave a total test weight of 8,990 lbs. Also featured was a selective-gear fixed-ratio transmission with eight forward speeds ranging from 1.5 to 15.5 mph. Operating in fifth gear, the two-hour economy run at 53.16 maximum available drawbar hp indicated a pull of 3,928 lbs. at 5.07 mph with slippage of 6.14 percent. Fuel economy was 14.4 hp-hours per gallon. The 10-hour run at 75 percent pull noted 13.87 hp-hours per gallon under a load of 44.18 drawbar hp. Also recorded was a pull of 3,041 lbs. at 5.45 mph and 4.66 percent slippage. No repairs or adjustments were reported during 44 hours of operation. This tractor was equipped with a Fiat four-cylinder diesel engine. Rated at 2,4000 rpm, it used a 3.94 x 4.33-inch bore and stroke for a 211-cubic inch displacement. At rated engine speed, 63.22 maximum PTO hp was observed, with an economy of 17.06 hp-hours per gallon. Operating at 540 PTO rpm and a corresponding engine speed of 1,966 rpm, 17.63 hp hours per gallon was established under a load of 54.35 PTO hp.

White Field Boss 2-70 and 2-85 tractors

Nebraska Test Data

Model: White Field Boss 2-70 Diesel
Test No. 1212
Date Tested: May 18 to May 28, 1976

At its rated engine speed of 2,200 rpm, the 2-70 Diesel developed 70.71 maximum PTO hp while achieving an economy of 14.56 hp-hours per gallon. Standard features included a White Farm Equipment six-cylinder engine. Its 283-cubic inches resulted from a 3.875 x 4.0-inch bore and stroke. This tractor experienced no repairs or adjustments during 41-1/2 hours of operation. The selective-gear fixed-ratio transmission included partial-range power shifting. Its 18 forward speeds ranged from 2.1 to 16.6 mph. Using 10th gear, the two-hour economy run at 57.29 maximum available drawbar hp saw a pull of 4,097 lbs. at 5.24 mph with a 6.21 slippage. Fuel economy was 11.92 hp-hours per gallon. The 10-hour run at 75 percent pull noted 12.13 hp-hours per gallon under a load of 48.06 drawbar hp. Also recorded was a pull of 3,171 lbs. at 5.68 mph with slippage totaling 4.52 percent. Weighing 8,630 lbs., the 2-70 was equipped with 18.4-34-inch rear and 11L-15-inch front tires. Additional front and rear ballast gave a total test weight of 9,630 lbs.

Nebraska Test Data

Model: White Field Boss 2-85 Diesel
Test No. 1213
Date Tested: May 18 to June 1, 1976

Weighing 11,700 lbs., this White had 18.4-34-inch rear and 11L-15-inch front tires. Additional front and rear ballast raised the total test weight to 12,280 lbs. The selective-gear fixed-ratio transmission offered partial-range power shifting. Its 18 forward speeds ranged from 1.5 to 17.0 mph. Using 11th gear, the two-hour economy test at 71.33 maximum available drawbar hp noted a pull of 4,688 lbs. at 5.71 mph with slippage totaling 5.51 percent. Fuel economy was pegged at 12.24 hp-hours per gallon. The 10-hour run at 75 percent pull noted an economy of 11.64 under a load of 56.26 drawbar hp. Also recorded was a pull of 3,513 lbs. at 6.01 mph and a 3.72 percent slippage. The 2-85 was equipped with a six-cylinder Perkins diesel engine. Rated at 2,200 rpm, it carried a 3,875 x 5.0-inch bore and stroke for a 354-cubic inch displacement. At rated engine speed, 85.54 maximum PTO hp was observed, with an economy of 14.62 hp-hours per gallon. No repairs or adjustments were indicated during 41 hours of operating time.

White Field Boss 4-150, 4-175, 4-180, and 4-210 tractors

Nebraska Test Data

Model: White Field Boss 4-150 Diesel
Test No. 1159
Date Tested: May 21 to May 29, 1974

Weighing 16,960 lbs., the 4-150 was tested without additional ballast. Standard equipment for this four-wheel-drive unit included 18.4-38 inch tires. No repairs or adjustments were reported during 54 hours of operating time. The selective-gear fixed-ratio transmission included partial-range power shifting. Its 18 forward speeds ranged from 1.6 to 19.2 mph. Operating in eighth gear, the two-hour economy run at 125.79 maximum available hp saw a pull of 10,141 lbs. at 4.65 mph with 4.43 percent total slippage.. Fuel economy was 12.46 hp-hours per gallon. By comparison, the 10-hour run at 75 percent pull noted an economy of 11.34 under a load of 100.60 drawbar hp. Also recorded was a pull of 7,849 lbs. at 4.81 mph with slippage totaling 3.13 percent. At its rated speed of 2,800 rpm, the 4-150 delivered 151.87 maximum PTO hp while achieving 14.82 hp-hours per gallon. With a PTO speed of 1,000 rpm and a corresponding engine speed of 2,739 rpm, an economy figure of 15.09 was presented under a load of 152.45 PTO hp. This unit was equipped with a Caterpillar V-8 diesel engine. Its 636-cubic inches resulted from a 4.5 x 5.0-inch bore and stroke.

Nebraska Test Data

Model: White Field Boss 4-175 Diesel
Test No. 1375
Date Tested: October 24 to November 6, 1980

This 20,420-lb. tractor was tested without additional ballast. Standard equipment included dual 18.4-38-inch tires. The four-wheel-drive design featured partial-range power shifting within the selective-gear fixed-ratio transmission. Its 18 forward speeds ranged from 1.6 to 19.0 mph. Operating in eighth gear the two-hour drawbar run at 127.15 maximum available hp saw a pull of 10,107 lbs. at 4.72 mph with slippage totaling 3.25 percent. Fuel economy was 12.96 hp-hours per gallon. In contrast, an economy of 11.98 hp- hours per gallon was witnessed in the 10-hour run at 75 percent pull. This test, run at 103.70 drawbar hp, indicated a pull of 7,789 lbs. at 4.99 mph with slippage totaling 2.33 percent. No repairs or adjustments were noted during 40 hours of operating time. The 4-175 featured a Caterpillar V-8 diesel engine. Rated at 2,600 rpm, the 636-cid engine carried a 4.5 x 5.0-inch bore and stroke. At rated engine speed, 151.69 maximum PTO hp appeared, and 15.29 hp-hours per gallon was observed. Operating at 1,000 PTO rpm and a corresponding engine speed of 2,542 rpm, 15.50 hp-hours per gallon was achieved under a load of 151.29 PTO hp.

Nebraska Test Data

Model: White Field Boss 4-180 Diesel
Test No. 1184
Date Tested: August 20 to August 29, 1975

This four-wheel-drive articulated design was equipped with dual 18.4-38-inch wheels. Weighing 20,600 lbs., it was tested without the use of additional ballast. The selective-gear fixed-ratio transmission offered 12 forward speeds ranging from 1.9 to 18.9 mph. Operating in sixth gear, the two-hour run at 150.52 maximum available drawbar hp saw a pull of 10,131 lbs. at 5.57 mph and slippage of 3.52 percent. Fuel economy came in at 11.79 hp-hours per gallon. The 10-hour run at 75 percent pull noted 11.56 hp-hours per gallon under a load of 122.98 drawbar hp. Other test statistics included a pull of 7,853 lbs. at 5.87 mph with slippage totaling 2.75 percent. White equipped this model with a Caterpillar 3208 V-8 diesel engine. Rated at 2,800 rpm, it used a 4.5 x 5.0-inch bore and stroke for a 636-cubic inch displacement. At rated engine speed, 181.07 maximum PTO hp was observed, and 13.95 hp-hours per gallon. Operating at 1,000 PTO rpm and a corresponding engine speed of 2,739 rpm, 14.19 hp-hours per gallon was established with a load of 182.30 PTO hp. During 49-1/2 hours of operating time, it was reported that replacement of the alternator fan guard was necessary, and that during the two-hour maximum PTO run an air conditioner line was melted off with a subsequent loss of freon.

Nebraska Test Data

Model: White Field Boss 4-210 Diesel, 18-Speed
Test No. 1318
Date Tested: June 12 to June 20, 1979

Weighing 23,735 lbs., this tractor was tested without additional ballast. Standard equipment included dual 18.4-38-inch tires. Partial-range power shifting was featured in the selective-gear fixed-ratio transmission. Its 18 forward speeds ranged from 2.2 to 18.3 mph. Operating in 11th gear, the two-hour drawbar test at 158.77 maximum available hp saw a pull of 10,120 lbs. at 5.88 mph with slippage totaling 3.06 percent. Fuel economy was 12.34 hp-hours per gallon. The 10-hour run at 75 percent pull indicated 12.10 hp- hours per gallon with a load of 126.70 drawbar hp. Other test data included a pull of 7,744 lbs. at 6.14 mph and 2.31 percent slippage. The 4-210 featured a Caterpillar V-8 diesel engine. Rated at 2,800 rpm, it carried a 4.5 x 5.0-inch bore and stroke for a 636-cubic inch displacement. At rated engine speed, 182.44 maximum PTO hp was observed and 14.26 hp-hours per gallon was achieved. During 36 hours of engine operating time, no repairs or adjustments were required.

Whitney Tractor Company

CLEVELAND, OHIO

Whitney 9-18 tractor

About 1918 the Whitney 9-18 tractor appeared, but remained on the market for only a short time. Whitney succeeded the Ohio Mfg. Company, and the latter had roots going back to the late 1890s. The 9-18 was powered by a Gile two-cylinder engine. It sold for $1,175. The Whitney 9-18 weighed 3,000 lbs.

Wichita Falls Motor Company

WICHITA FALLS, TEXAS

Wichita 20-30 tractor

By 1920 the Wichita 20-30 was on the market. Weighing 5,500 lbs., this tractor listed at $2,500. Power came from a Beaver four-cylinder engine with a 4-1/2 x 6-inch bore and stroke. The Wichita did not appear in the 1921 listings.

Wichita Tractor Company

WICHITA, KANSAS

Wichita 8-16 tractor

The Wichita 8-16 tractor was announced in 1917 and was built until 1920. At that time it was taken over by Agrimotor Mfg. Company, also of Wichita. This tractor was also known as the Midwest 8-16. Power came from a Gile two-cylinder opposed engine with a 5 x 6-1/2-inch bore and stroke. For 1920, this 3,300 lb. tractor sold for $1,085.

Will-Burt Company

ORRVILLE, OHIO

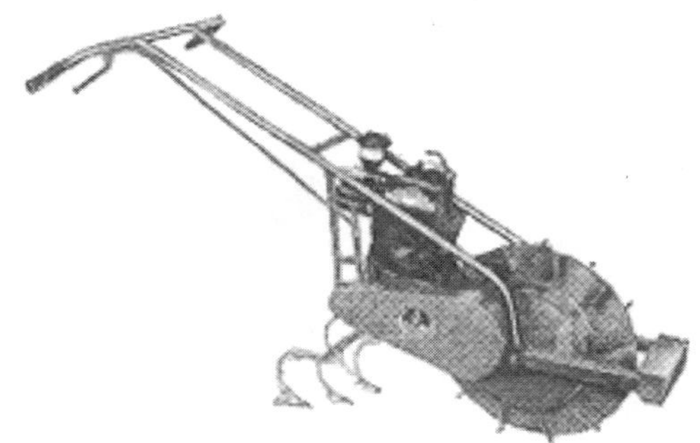

Little Farmer garden tractor

In the early 1950s the Little Farmer garden tractor appeared from Will-Burt. Weighing only 180 lbs., it sold for $100. Power came from a Briggs & Stratton Model 5S engine capable of 1 hp. Very little information was available about this company.

COLLECTOR VALUES	1	2	3	4
LITTLE FARMER	$700	$500	$250	$100

H. C. Williams Mfg. Company

ROOTSTOWN, OHIO

In 1950 Williams offered its Norm Garden Tractor in two different sizes. The 14R6 weighed 435 lbs. and was powered by a 4 hp Briggs & Stratton engine. Shown here is the Norm U-2R6 garden tractor. This model was equipped with a 3-1/2 hp Ultimotor engine. Little more is known about the Norm garden tractors aside from a 1950 listing.

COLLECTOR VALUES	1	2	3	4
NORM U-2R6 GARDEN TRACTOR	$475	$275	$150	$75

Norm U-2R6 garden tractor

Willmar Tractor Company

WILLMAR, MINNESOTA

Humber-Anderson Mfg. Co. was organized at St. Paul, Minnesota in 1913 to build the Little Oak tractor. Shortly afterward, Willmar Tractor Mfg. Company took over the Little Oak, and the latter continued until December 1916. At that time the company was reorganized as Standard Tractor Co. As built by Willmar, the Little Oak carried a 22-44 hp rating. It was equipped with a four- cylinder engine with each cylinder cast separately. It used a 5-5/8 x 7-1/2-inch bore and stroke.

See: Humber-Anderson Mfg. Co.

Little Oak tractor

Willys CJ-2A

Willys-Overland Motors

TOLEDO, OHIO

In the late 1940s and early 1950s, Willys offered its famous Jeep CJ-3A for farm use. A wide number of options were available, including a three-point hitch system, PTO shaft, and belt pulley. The CJ-3A was equipped with the Jeep four-cylinder engine that used a 3-1/8 x 4-3/8-inch bore and stroke. In 1951, Willys created a CJ-3A "Farm Jeep" as well as a stripped-down version with no windshield or headlights called the "Jeep Tractor." The Farm Jeep was not produced until 1953 (when it was tested at Nebraska) and 1954 and it appeared that only about 77 were built before being discontinued.

Nebraska Test Data

Model: Jeep CJ-3A

Test No. 432

Date Tested: October 25 to November 2, 1949

The official test report for the Universal Jeep stated: "A small amount of oil leaked from the transmission drive during test." Otherwise, no repairs or adjustments were noted during 37 hours of operation. This unit featured the company's own four-cylinder L-head engine rated at 2,000 rpm and using a 3-1/8 x 4-3/8-inch bore and stroke. Advertised speeds of 4.6, 8.2, 11.2, 12.9, 20.2, and 31.3 mph were provided, with the 10-hour run of Test H made in first gear. At a rated drawbar load of 19.15 hp, a pull of 1,676 lbs. was achieved at 4.28 mph with a 4.5 percent slippage. Fuel economy was recorded at 8.67 hp-hours per gallon. This four-wheel-drive unit was equipped with 7.00-15-inch tires and weighed 2,819 lbs. Additional ballast was added to the frame during Tests F, G, and H. Test G indicated a low-gear maximum pull of 2,148 lbs. at 4.25 mph under a slippage of 5.46 percent. Belt testing showed a Test C operating maximum load of 28.43 hp with an economy of 7.73 hp-hours per gallon. This figure rose to 9.86 under a Test D rated load of 25.46 belt hp.

Nebraska Test Data

Model: Willys Farm Jeep

Test No. 502

Date Tested: August 28 to September 4, 1953

Six forward speeds of 4.6, 8.2, 11.2, 12.9, 20.2, and 31.3 mph were in the Willys Farm Jeep. Weighing 2,714 lbs., this four-wheel-drive unit was equipped with 7.00-15-inch tires. During the drawbar testing, 755 lbs. were added to each front wheel, with no additional ballast on the rear. Test H, with a rated drawbar output of 20.69 hp, was run in first gear. At 4.21 mph, the Jeep pulled 1,843 lbs. with a slippage of 5.97 percent and yielded 8.55 hp-hours per gallon. Test G produced a low gear maximum pull of 2,317 lbs. at 4.11 mph with an 8.32 percent slippage. A Willys-built four-cylinder F-head engine was featured. Rated at 2,400 rpm on the belt and 2,000 rpm at the drawbar, it used a 3 7/8 x 4 3/8-inch bore and stroke for a 134.2-cubic inch displacement. Except for a minor adjustment, no repairs were required during 42-1/2 hours of operation. Tests B & C at a 100 percent maximum belt load of 35.23 hp produced an economy of 10.39 hp-hours per gallon, sagging to 9.94 under a Test D rated load of 31.61 belt hp.

Wilson Tractor Company

PEORIA, ILLINOIS

Developed by 1918, this two-row cultivator appeared in 1919. It was powered by a four- cylinder LeRoi engine with a 3-1/8 x 4-1/2-inch bore and stroke. Parrett Motors Corporation of Chicago, Illinois, took over Wilson cultivator in 1919, and marketed its own machine in 1920 and 1921.

Two-row cultivator

Wilson Tractor Mfg. Company

OTTUMWA, IOWA

Rated as a 12-20, the Wilson four-wheel-drive tractor appeared in 1920. Weighing only 3,700 lbs., it was powered by a Weidely four-cylinder engine with a 4 x 5-1/2-inch bore and stroke. This company was bought out by Austin Mfg. Company, Chicago, Illinois, in 1922, and from this design the latter built its own four-wheel-drive tractor for a time.

Winchell Mfg. Company

FORT SCOTT, KANSAS

The Clean Row Garden Tractor was offered by this firm in the late 1940s and at least into the early 1950s. No specifications for the Clean Row have been found.

COLLECTOR VALUES	1	2	3	4
CLEAN ROW	$300	$200	$150	$75

Windolph Tractor Company

PORTLAND, OREGON

Starting in the early 1950s and extending through the decade, Windolph offered several models of garden tractors.

Windolph Garden Maker "M" tractor

Wilson 12-20 four-wheel-drive tractor

Shown here is the Windolph Garden Maker "M" which was essentially a rotary tiller. This small machine was powered by a Clinton Model 700 engine of 1-1/2 hp.

COLLECTOR VALUES	1	2	3	4
GARDEN MAKER M	$200	$150	$75	$50

Windolph Chain-Tred Deluxe garden tractor

Weighing 480 lbs., the Windolph Chain-Tred Deluxe garden tractor was a crawler machine that sold for $549. Power came from a 6 hp Wisconsin Model AK engine.

Topping the Windolph line was the Riding "C" tractor, a crawler design that weighed 1,500 lbs. This model was powered by a 13 hp Wisconsin Model TF engine. Numerous attachments were available for this tractor, including a moldboard plow, various harrows, cultivators, and mowers.

COLLECTOR VALUES	1	2	3	4
ALL MODELS	$4,000	$3,000	$1,200	$800

Windolph Riding "C" tractor

Winkley Company

MINNEAPOLIS, MINNESOTA

This firm is listed as the manufacturer of the Winkley garden tractor in 1953, but no other information has been found.

Winnebago Tractor Company

ROCKFORD, ILLINOIS

About 1920 the Winnebago Chief tractor made a very brief appearance. Little is known about this model except that it used the company's own four-cylinder engine.

Winnebago Chief tractor

Winona Mfg. Company

WINONA, MINNESOTA

In 1896 this company gained manufacturing rights for the Otto Gasoline Traction Engines with a territory covering much of the northwest. The manufacturing arrangement lasted for only a year or two. No illustrations of the Winona-built Otto gasoline traction engines have been found.

Winslow Mfg. Company

KANSAS CITY, MISSOURI

This company appeared in 1917 as the manufacturer of the Coleman 10-20 tractor. The Coleman operation went through numerous title changes and reorganizations. The role of Winslow is unknown.

Winter Mfg. Company

TACOMA, WASHINGTON

The Mighty Man garden tractors first appeared in April 1946. Beyond this, little information is available.

COLLECTOR VALUES	1	2	3	4
MIGHTY MAN	$750	$500	$250	$100

Wisconsin Farm Tractor Company

SAUK CITY, WISCONSIN

In 1917 McFarland & Westmont Tractor Co. began building tractors. Within a short time the name was changed to Wisconsin Farm Tractor Company. Production of the Wisconsin tractors ceased in 1923.

Wisconsin "Thirty" (16-30) tractor

Initially this tractor was known as the Wisconsin "Thirty" and had a 15-30 hp rating. The rating was soon changed to 16-32, though after testing at Nebraska this model was officially given a 16-30 hp rating. Power came from a Climax four-cylinder engine with a 5 x 6-1/2-inch bore and stroke. Toward the end of production in 1923 this model took on a 20-35 hp rating.

Wisconsin 22-40 tractor

Nebraska Test Data

Model: Wisconsin 16-30

Test No. 21

Date Tested: 1920

Except for a broken fan belt, the 16-30 Wisconsin went through its paces without major difficulties. Some 31-1/2 hp was derived in the maximum brake hp test, although fuel consumption came to 5.64 gph or an equivalent of 5.58 hp-hours per gallon of kerosene. Nearly 22-1/4 hp was achieved on the drawbar, with a maximum pull of 3,426 lbs. at 2.43 mph. Drivewheel slippage under this load was 15.3 percent. A four-cylinder vertical engine of 5 x 6-1/2-inch bore and stroke was featured—rated at 900 rpm. Standard equipment included two forward speeds of 2.53 and 3.66 mph, but the gears could be changed to give 1.83 and 2.57 mph speeds instead. Total weight was 6,060 lbs. Regular equipment included an Eisemann G4 magneto and a Schebler Model A carburetor. Total running time was 34 hours.

By 1918 the Wisconsin 22-40 tractor was on the market. It was built over the same chassis as the 16-30. This model used a Climax four-cylinder engine with a 5-1/2 x 7-inch bore and stroke. At its rated speed of 800 rpm, this engine was capable of 50 belt hp.

Wisconsin 25-45 tractor

The 22-40 and the 25-45 Wisconsin tractors used the same Climax engine. The 25-45 was claimed to have a maximum of 60 belt hp, even though the rated engine speed was the same 800 rpm for both models.

COLLECTOR VALUES	1	2	3	4
WISCONSIN 25-45	--	$14,000	--	--

Wisconsin Truck & Tractor Company

MADISON, WISCONSIN

Although it was organized and incorporated in 1917 to manufacture tractors, nothing further is known about this company or its activities.

Wizard Tractor Corporation

LOS ANGELES, CALIFORNIA

During the 1920s the Wizard 4-Pull tractor was marketed. Rated as a 20-35 tractor, this machine was of the four-wheel-drive design. Power came from a four-cylinder engine with a 5-1/4 x 6-1/2-inch bore and stroke.

Wolf Tractor Company

LAPORTE, INDIANA

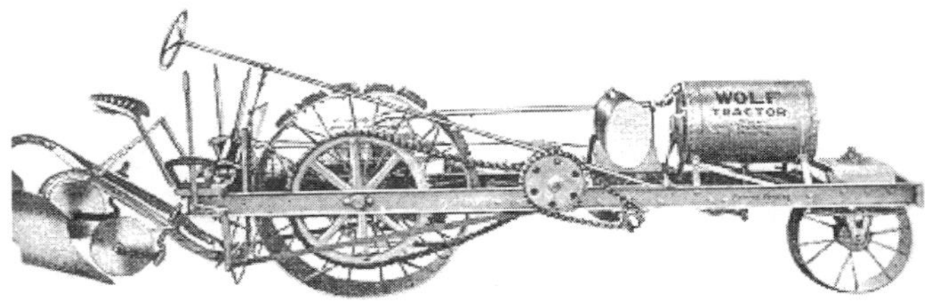

Wolf tractor

Wizard 4-Pull tractor

In 1913 or 1914 the Wolf Tractor Company was organized. John Wolf was the inventor, and formerly had managed the Rumely Hotel in LaPorte. During 1915 the Leo Rumely Tractor Co. was organized to take over the Wolf operation. No details about the Wolf tractor have been found.

Wolverine Tractor Company

DETROIT, MICHIGAN

Wolverine Tractor Company

SAGINAW, MICHIGAN

Wolverine 15-30 tractor

In 1917 Wolverine purchased a factory at Dearborn, Michigan, to build the Wolverine 15-30 tractor. This model was designed with an Erd four-cylinder engine with a 4 x 6-inch bore and stroke. The tractor weighed 5,500 lbs. In 1918 the company moved to a different factory at Saginaw, Michigan. Little is known about the Wolverine activities after that time.

Wood, Knight, Hawk Plow Company

OKLAHOMA CITY, OKLAHOMA

This company was incorporated in 1911 to build a motor plow. The prototype machine shown here was equipped with a three-cylinder engine. A descriptive article noted this was merely an experimental engine and that the production model would use an engine ranging from 60 to 75 belt hp. No further information has been found on this machine, built under the tradename of Alivator.

S. A. Woods Machine Company

BOSTON, MASSACHUSETTS

During 1953 this firm was listed as the manufacturer of the GHN and Sprywheel garden tractors. No other information has been located.

Wood, Knight, Hawk motor plow

COLLECTOR VALUES	1	2	3	4
ALL MODELS	$3,500	$3,000	$2,000	$800

World Harvester Corporation

NEW YORK, NEW YORK

World Harvester Auto-Tiller

In 1919 the Auto-Tiller was available from World Harvester Corp. This machine was large, and used a single-cylinder engine with a 5 x 7-inch bore and stroke. It weighed 800 lbs. Few other details have been found on this machine; none are known to exist.

Worthington Pump & Machinery Corporation

CUDAHY, WISCONSIN

Worthington bought out International Gas Engine Company of Cudahy in 1916. The latter had brought out its Ingeco 10-20 tractor. Worthington revamped the Ingeco 10-20 and sold it as late as 1919. At that time it was priced at $1,175. Power came from the company's own two-cylinder engine; it used a 6 x 7-inch bore and stroke.
See: International Gas Engine Company

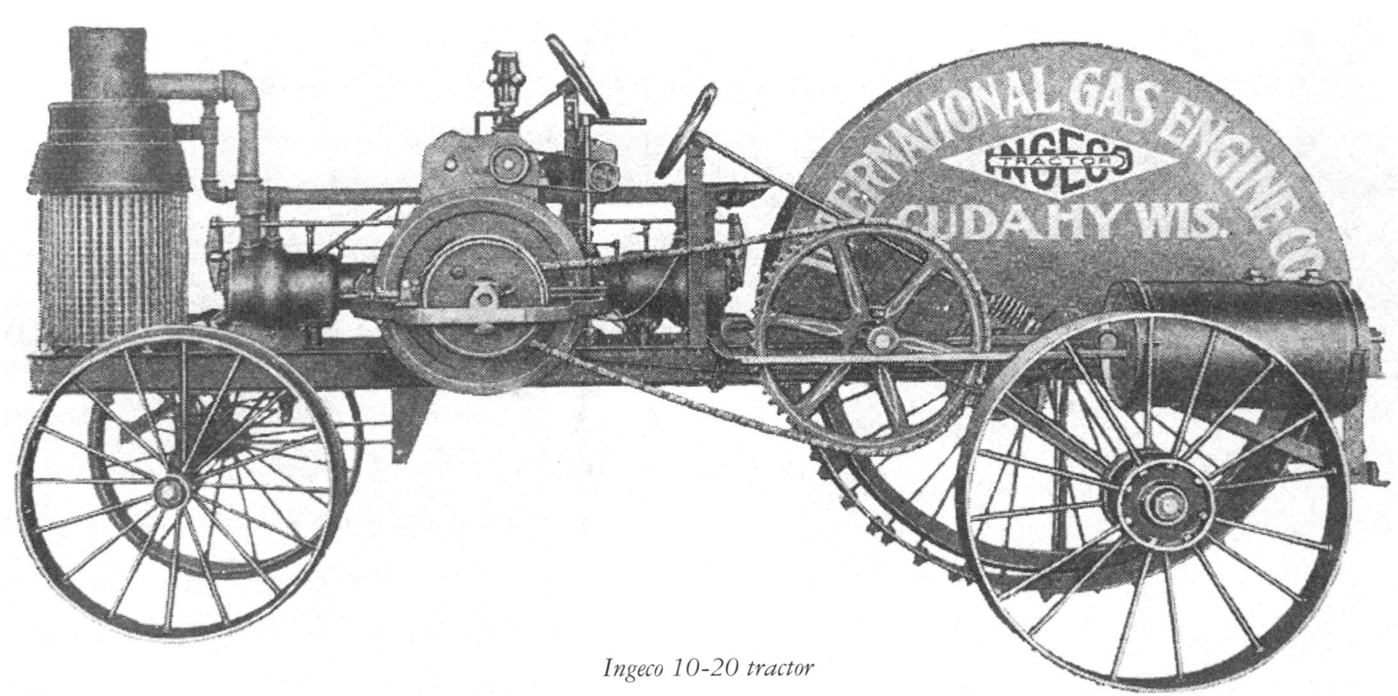

Ingeco 10-20 tractor

Yankee Boy Tractor Corporation

CHICAGO, ILLINOIS

Yankee Boy 16-32 tractor

Developed in 1918, the Yankee Boy 16-32 remained on the market for a couple of years. Power came from a Buda engine, but other specifications are unknown. In 1919 the Yankee Boy sold for $2,295.

Ypsilanti Hay Press Company

YPSILANTI, MICHIGAN

Wolverine tractor

In 1912 the Wolverine tractor was offered in 18, 25, and 35 hp sizes. Little is known about these tractors, and it is believed they weren't marketed for any length of time. About the only evidence they existed came from a few magazine advertisements.

Yuba Mfg. Company

MARYVILLE, CALIFORNIA

The Yuba Ball Tread tractor began with the Ball Tread Tractor Co., Detroit, Michigan. In 1912 the company built its first 12-25 tractor. Yuba Construction bought the company in 1914, and continued building tractors in California until 1931, when it disappeared from the trade directories.

Yuba Model 12 and Model 18 tractors

Yuba Mfg. continued buiding its own version of 12-25 and 18-35 models developed by Ball Tread Co. Shown here is the early design of the Yuba Model 12 and Model 18 tractors.

Yuba Ball Tread 12-20 tractor

Production of the Yuba Ball Tread 12-20 tractor ran from 1916 to 1921. This model became the 15-25 tractor and was built from 1921 to 1925. Initially a Continental four-cylinder engine powered the 12-20, but the 15-25 used a Waukesha engine.

The Yuba Ball Tread 20-35 was a takeoff from the Yuba Model 18 that originally had been developed by Ball Tread Company. Production of this model ran from 1916 to 1921. Various engines were used during the production run. Toward the latter part of production a Wisconsin four-cylinder engine was used. It had a 5-3/4 x 7-inch bore and stroke.

Yuba Ball Tread 20-35 tractor

Yuba Ball Tread 40-70 tractor

The Yuba Ball Tread 40-70 tractor was probably developed in 1918 and remained on the market into 1920. This big crawler weighed 21,000 lbs. and used a four-cylinder engine with a 6-1/2 x 8-1/2-inch bore and stroke. It had three forward speeds.

In the early 1920s the Yuba Rodebilder appeared. The 25-40 model was a takeoff from the earlier 20-35 model. This tractor used a four-cylinder Yuba-built engine with a 5-1-4 x 7-inch bore and stroke. Production of this model continued until the company ceased building tractors about 1931.

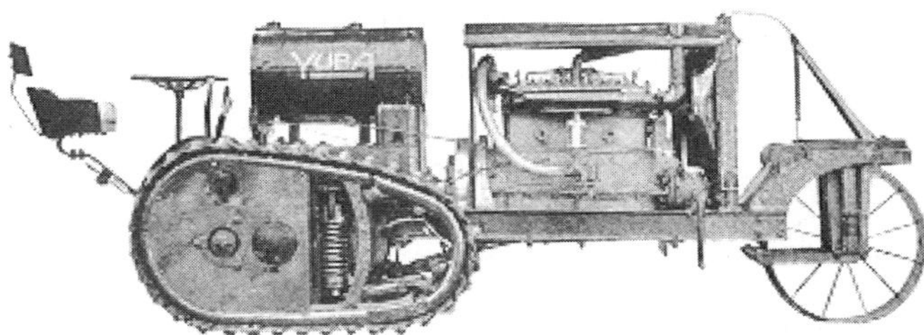

Model 15-25 Yuba tractor

The Model 15-25 Yuba tractor was equipped with a Wisconsin four-cylinder engine with a 4-1/4 x 6-inch bore and stroke. This model appeared to have been an improved version of the earlier 12-20 tractor.

Yuba Rodebilder 25-40 tractor

Geo. Zalesky & Company

CEDAR RAPIDS, IOWA

This firm was organized to build the G-O tractors after General Ordnance Company closed its doors in the early 1920s. The venture lasted only a short time.

Zelle Tractor Company

ST. LOUIS, MISSOURI

Zelle Tractor Company was organized and incorporated in 1916, with the takeover of Plantation Equipment Co. Zelle offered its 12-25 tractor in the 1916 through 1921 period. It was rated at 12 drawbar and 25 belt hp, using a four-cylinder engine with a 4-1/4 x 5-1/2-inch bore and stroke. Weighing 4,000 lbs., it sold for $1,500.

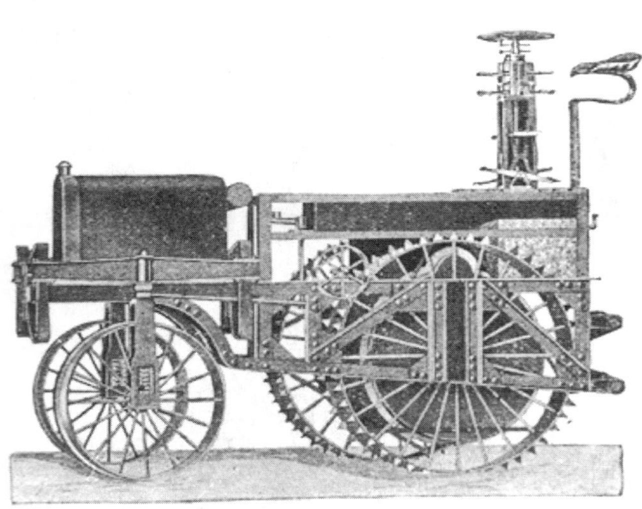

Zelle 12-25 tractor

Zimmerman Auto Tractor Company

CHICAGO, ILLINOIS

This company built a tractor conversion unit and may also have built farm tractors, but no other information has been found.

The Nebraska Tractor Tests

In 1985 we completed the first book presenting all of the Nebraska Tractor Tests in a single volume. Although this title, *Nebraska Tractor Tests Since 1920* has been out of print for several years, there is a continuing need for the data from these tests. We have included them where appropriate throughout this second edition.

Those desiring specific test data should contact: Tractor Testing Laboratory, University of Nebraska-Lincoln, Lincoln, NE 68583-0832 or via the Internet at http://tractortestlab.unl.edu.

Tractor testing at Nebraska officially began in 1920. The idea, however, went back to the Winnipeg Industrial Exhibition of 1908 in Manitoba. The Winnipeg Test Scores were the first formal attempt to classify steam and gas tractors on their abilities and quickly pointed out their shortcomings. After a few years the Winnipeg Trials were discontinued. There were several attempted organized tests, and with the great demand for tractors, more than a few companies built poor quality machines. In many instances, these companies left the market, often in a couple of years, and rendered the need for replacement parts an impossibility.

In 1919 Wilmot F. Crozier, with the help of L. W. Chase and others, wrote the Nebraska Tractor Test Law and presented it to the Nebraska House of Representatives. Essentially, this statute required that all tractors sold in Nebraska had to be tested at the Tractor Test Laboratory, and that companies selling tractors in Nebraska had to maintain service stations in the state.

Within a short time, most manufacturers sent their tractors to Nebraska, seeing in these tests the opportunity to offer customers all over the country a check of the performance and economy of their models.

An interesting sidebar is the Nebraska Tractor Tests have provided a detailed historical record that demonstrates not only the mechanical evolution of the tractor, but the use of various fuels, various chassis designs, and quite noticeably, the change from belt power to PTO power.

As previously noted, those requiring precise test data should contact the Tractor Test Laboratory for official test transcripts or further information.

Unless another fuel is mentioned for a particular test, the reader can assume that gasoline was the propellent that fueled the engine of the particular tractor tested.

NEBRASKA TRACTOR TEST 839 - OLIVER 1800 SERIES B GASOLINE

The University of Nebraska Agricultural Experiment Station
E. F. Frolik, Dean; H. H. Kramer, Director, Lincoln, Nebraska

POWER TAKE-OFF PERFORMANCE

Hp	Crank-shaft speed rpm	Fuel Consumption Gal per hr	Lb per hp-hr	Hp-hr per gal	Temperature Degrees F Cooling medium	Air wet bulb	Air dry bulb	Barometer inches of Mercury
MAXIMUM POWER AND FUEL CONSUMPTION								
Rated Engine Speed—Two Hours								
80.16	2200	6.601	0.505	12.14	173	58	75	29.058
VARYING POWER AND FUEL CONSUMPTION—TWO HOURS								
70.31	2269	6.205	0.541	11.33	174	58	76	....
0.00	2400	2.378	....	....	166	57	73	....
36.14	2334	4.311	0.731	8.38	173	58	75	....
80.15	2200	6.581	0.503	12.18	174	58	75	....
18.31	2365	3.347	1.121	5.47	168	58	74	....
53.63	2309	5.314	0.607	10.09	174	57	73	....
Av 43.09	2313	4.689	0.667	9.19	172	57	74	29.043

DRAWBAR PERFORMANCE

Hp	Draw-bar pull lbs	Speed miles per hr	Crank-shaft speed rpm	Slip of drivers %	Fuel Consumption Gal per hr	Lb per hp-hr	Hp-hr per gal	Temp Degrees F Cool-ing med	Air wet bulb	Air dry bulb	Barometer inches of Mercury
VARYING DRAWBAR POWER AND FUEL CONSUMPTION WITH BALLAST											
Maximum Available Power—Two Hours—4th Gear Hydra-Power											
67.81	6839	3.72	2204	7.16	6.875	0.622	9.86	182	67	79	28.900
75% of Pull at Maximum Power—Ten Hours—4th Gear Hydra-Power											
55.47	5275	3.94	2289	5.27	6.033	0.667	9.19	180	64	77	29.037
50% of Pull at Maximum Power—Two Hours—4th Gear Hydra-Power											
37.96	3493	4.08	2325	3.69	4.934	0.797	7.69	179	72	85	28.813
MAXIMUM POWER WITH BALLAST											
58.33	10827	2.02	2258	14.94	2nd Gear Hydra-Power			172	55	62	29.010
67.72	8946	2.84	2201	10.09	2nd Gear			178	56	63	29.000
68.49	8805	2.92	2201	9.77	3rd Gear Hydra-Power			177	56	63	29.000
69.52	7042	3.70	2201	7.53	4th Gear Hydra-Power			178	56	58	28.890
69.04	6282	4.12	2204	6.57	3rd Gear			178	61	68	28.920
69.01	5013	5.16	2199	5.17	4th Gear			178	61	68	28.920
70.13	4429	5.94	2199	4.67	5th Gear Hydra-Power			180	61	68	28.920
68.81	3145	8.20	2199	3.28	5th Gear			182	61	68	28.920
67.25	2410	10.46	2197	2.69	6th Gear Hydra-Power			180	65	75	28.920
62.41	1623	14.42	2201	1.63	6th Gear			180	65	75	28.920
MAXIMUM POWER WITHOUT BALLAST											
64.99	6815	3.58	2203	11.30	4th Gear Hydra-Power			182	75	85	28.830

VARYING DRAWBAR PULL AND TRAVEL SPEED WITH BALLAST

4th Gear Hydra-Power

Pounds pull	7042	7378	7541	7580	7628	7658	7415
Horsepower	69.52	65.22	58.80	51.75	44.61	37.03	29.03
Crankshaft speed rpm	2201	1982	1750	1534	1316	1089	879
Miles per hour	3.70	3.31	2.92	2.56	2.19	1.81	1.47
Slip of drivers %	7.53	8.14	8.27	8.27	8.40	8.40	8.27

TIRES, BALLAST and WEIGHT		With Ballast	Without Ballast
Rear tires	—No, size, ply & psi	Two 18.4-34; 8; 20	Two 18.4-34; 8; 16
Ballast	—Liquid	1170 lb each	None
	Cast iron	1350 lb each	None
Front tires	—No, size, ply & psi	Two 7.50-15; 8; 40	Two 7.50-15; 8; 32
Ballast	—Liquid	None	None
	Cast iron	208 lb each	None
Height of drawbar		20½ inches	21 inches
Static weight	—Rear	11300 lb	6260 lb
	—Front	2960 lb	2545 lb
Total weight with operator		14435 lb	8980 lb

Department of Agricultural Engineering
Dates of Test: May 22 to June 4, 1963
Manufacturer: OLIVER CORPORATION, CHARLES CITY, IOWA
Manufacturer's Power Rating: Not rated

FUEL, OIL and TIME Fuel regular gasoline **Octane No Motor** 84.4 **Research** 92.2 (rating taken from oil company's typical inspection data) **Specific gravity converted to 60°/60°** 0.7365 **Weight per gallon** 6.131 lb **Oil SAE** 10W **API service classification** MS DM **To motor** 1.977 gal **Drained from motor** 1.596 gal **Transmission and final-drive lubricant** SAE 80 **Total time engine was operated** 43 hours.

ENGINE Make Oliver gasoline **Type** 6 cylinder vertical **Serial No** 221120 **Crankshaft mounted** lengthwise **Rated rpm** 2200 **Bore and stroke** 3⅞" x 4" **Compression ratio** 8.5 to 1 **Displacement** 283 cu in **Carburetor size** 1½" **Ignition system** battery **Cranking system** 12 volt electric **Lubrication** pressure **Air cleaner** oil washed wire screen **Oil filter** full flow replaceable paper element **Oil cooler** engine coolant heat exchanger for Hydra-Power oil **Fuel filter** screen in sediment bowl **Muffler** was used **Cooling medium temperature control** thermostat.

CHASSIS Type standard **Serial No** 124925844 **Tread width** rear 68" to 89½" front 60" to 84" **Wheel base** 109¼" **Center of gravity** (without operator or ballast, with minimum tread, with fuel tank filled and tractor serviced for operation) Horizontal distance forward from center-line of rear wheels 30.9" Vertical distance above roadway 35.5" Horizontal distance from center of rear wheel tread 0" to the right/left **Hydraulic control system** direct engine drive **Transmission** selective gear fixed ratio with partial range operator controlled power shifting **Advertised speeds mph** first 1.60 second 3.09 third 4.31 fourth 5.34 fifth 8.32 sixth 14.37 reverse 1.81 and 4.87 (using Hydra-Power drive) first 1.17 second 2.27 third 3.16 fourth 3.92 fifth 6.11 sixth 10.55 reverse 1.33 and 3.57 **Clutch** single plate dry disc operated by foot pedal **Brakes** double disc operated by two foot pedals which can be locked **Steering** mechanical with power assist **Turning radius** (on concrete surface with brake applied) right 152" left 152" (on concrete surface without brake) right 172" left 172" **Turning space diameter** (on concrete surface with brake applied) right 312" left 312" (on concrete surface without brake) right 352" left 352" **Belt pulley** 1056 rpm at 2200 engine rpm diam 11⁵⁄₁₆" face 8¾" **Belt speed** 3111 fpm **Power take-off** 1004 rpm at 2200 engine rpm.

REPAIRS and ADJUSTMENTS No repairs or adjustments.

REMARKS All test results were determined from observed data obtained in accordance with the SAE and ASAE test code.

First gear and first gear Hydra-Power drive were not run as it was necessary to limit the pull in second gear Hydra-Power drive to avoid excessive wheel slippage.

We, the undersigned, certify that this is a true and correct report of official Tractor Test 839.

L. F. LARSEN
Engineer-in-Charge

L. W. HURLBUT, Chairman
G. W. STEINBRUEGGE
J. J. SULEK
Board of Tractor Test Engineers

1957 TRACTOR FIELD BOOK

Nebraska Test No. 517–Oliver OC-6 Diesel

University of Nebraska Agricultural Engineering Department, Agricultural College, Lincoln

Copy of Report of Official Tractor Test No. 517

Dates of test: April 17, to May 7, 1954
Name and model of tractor: Oliver OC-6 Diesel
Manufacturer: The Oliver Corporation, Cleveland, Ohio
Manufacturer's rating: Not Rated

DRAWBAR HORSE POWER TESTS

H.P.	Draw bar pull Lbs.	Speed miles per hr.	Crank shaft speed R.P.M.	Slip of drive wheels %	Fuel Consumption			Water used Gal. per hr.	Temp. Deg. F.		Barometer Inches of Mercury
					Gal. per hour	Hp.-hr. per Gal.	Lb. per Hp.-hr.		Cool-ing med.	Air	
TESTS F AND G - 100% MAXIMUM LOAD											
33.01	6779	1.83	1599	3.41	Not Recorded				174	66	28.830
33.46	5204	2.41	1601	1.67	"	"			174	63	28.900
31.80	3708	3.22	1597	0.93	"	"			178	67	28.875
30.48	2729	4.19	1604	0.80	"	"			175	67	28.800
28.90	2104	5.15	1601	0.58	"	"			177	66	28.800
21.98	922	8.94	1609	0.17	"	"			178	66	28.800
TEST H—RATED LOAD - TEN HOURS -2nd GEAR											
26.21	4066	2.42	1602	1.42	2.159	12.14	0.575	0.00	175	61	28.710
TEST J—OPERATING MAXIMUM LOAD -2nd GEAR											
33.19	5193	2.40	1601	2.34	Not Recorded				176	64	28.700

FUEL, OIL and TIME—Fuel: Diesel fuel, Cetane No. 50 (rating taken from oil company's typical inspection data); weight per gal 6.979 lb. Oil: SAE 10; to motor 1.966 gal.; drained from motor 1.037 gal. Total time motor was operated: 37½ hours.

CHASSIS—Type: Tracklayer. Serial No. 4501134. Tread width: 68 in. Wheel base: 54 3/16 in. Measured length of track: 196 in. Cleats per track: 33. Size of cleats: 12 x 1¼ in. Cleats integral with shoes. Hydraulic control system: Direct engine drive. Advertised speeds, mph: First 1.88, second 2.44, third 3.23, fourth 4.19, fifth 5.15, sixth 8.86, reverse 1.92 and 3.31. Belt pulley: Not available. Clutch: Single plate dry disc operated by foot pedal. Seat: Pressed steel cushioned by rubber in torsion. Brakes: Contracting bands operated by steering levers that can be locked by latches. Power take-off: Direct engine drive with independent hand clutch.

ENGINE—Make: Oliver Diesel. Type: 6-cylinder vertical. Serial No. D1-922054. Crankshaft mounted lengthwise. Head: I. Lubrication: Pressure. Bore and stroke: 3 5/16 x 3¾ in. Rated rpm: 1600. Compression ratio: 15.75 to 1. Displacement: 193.9 cu. in. Port diameter valves: Inlet 1 5/64 in., exhaust 15/16 in. Governor: Variable speed centrifugal. Starting system: 12-volt electric. Air cleaner: Oil-washed wire mesh. Muffler was used. Oil filter: Two replaceable waste packed elements. Fuel filters: One brass screen, one replaceable waste type element and one replaceable paper cartridge element. Cooling medium temperature control: Thermostat.

TOTAL WEIGHT AS TESTED (WITH OPERATOR)—(F, G & H)—7560 lbs.

TOTAL WEIGHT AS TESTED (WITH OPERATOR)—(J)—6742 lbs.

REPAIRS and ADJUSTMENTS—The 14-in. tracks were replaced with 12-in. tracks before starting test F because of soil conditions.

REMARKS—All test results were determined from observed data and without allowances, additions or deductions. Test F was made with fuel pumps set to develop approximately 34.5 maximum drawbar horsepower and data from this test was used in determining the horsepower to be developed in test H. Tests F, G, H, and J were made with the same setting.

HORSEPOWER SUMMARY

	Drawbar
1. Sea level (calculated) maximum horsepower (based on 60° F and 29.92" Hg.)	34.74
2. Observed maximum horsepower (test F)	33.46
3. Seventy-five percent of calculated maximum drawbar horsepower (formerly ASAE and SAE ratings)	26.06

We, the undersigned, certify that this is a true and correct report of official tractor test No. 517.

L. F. Larsen
Engineer in Charge

C. W. Smith (Chairman)
L. W. Hurlbut
F. D. Yung
Board of Tractor
Test Engineers

See page 142 for Nebraska Test Index.

NEBRASKA TRACTOR TEST 839 - OLIVER 1800 SERIES B GASOLINE

The University of Nebraska Agricultural Experiment Station

E. F. Frolik, Dean; H. H. Kramer, Director, Lincoln, Nebraska

POWER TAKE-OFF PERFORMANCE

Hp	Crank-shaft speed rpm	Fuel Consumption Gal per hr	Lb per hp-hr	Hp-hr per gal	Temperature Degrees F Cooling medium	Air wet bulb	Air dry bulb	Barometer inches of Mercury
MAXIMUM POWER AND FUEL CONSUMPTION								
Rated Engine Speed—Two Hours								
80.16	2200	6.601	0.505	12.14	173	58	75	29.058
VARYING POWER AND FUEL CONSUMPTION—TWO HOURS								
70.31	2269	6.205	0.541	11.33	174	58	76	....
0.00	2400	2.378	....	....	166	57	73	....
36.14	2334	4.311	0.731	8.38	173	58	75	....
80.15	2200	6.581	0.503	12.18	174	58	75	....
18.31	2365	3.347	1.121	5.47	168	58	74	....
53.63	2309	5.314	0.607	10.09	174	57	73	....
Av **43.09**	**2313**	**4.689**	**0.667**	**9.19**	**172**	**57**	**74**	**29.043**

DRAWBAR PERFORMANCE

Hp	Draw-bar pull lbs	Speed miles per hr	Crank-shaft speed rpm	Slip of drivers %	Fuel Consumption Gal per hr	Lb per hp-hr	Hp-hr per gal	Temp Degrees F Cool-ing med	Air wet bulb	Air dry bulb	Barometer inches of Mercury
VARYING DRAWBAR POWER AND FUEL CONSUMPTION WITH BALLAST											
Maximum Available Power—Two Hours—4th Gear Hydra-Power											
67.81	6839	3.72	2204	7.16	6.875	0.622	9.86	182	67	79	28.900
75% of Pull at Maximum Power—Ten Hours—4th Gear Hydra-Power											
55.47	5275	3.94	2289	5.27	6.033	0.667	9.19	180	64	77	29.037
50% of Pull at Maximum Power—Two Hours—4th Gear Hydra-Power											
37.96	3493	4.08	2325	3.69	4.934	0.797	7.69	179	72	85	28.813
MAXIMUM POWER WITH BALLAST											
58.33	10827	2.02	2258	14.94	2nd Gear Hydra-Power			172	55	62	29.010
67.72	8946	2.84	2201	10.09	2nd Gear			178	56	63	29.000
68.49	8805	2.92	2201	9.77	3rd Gear Hydra-Power			177	56	63	29.000
69.52	7042	3.70	2201	7.53	4th Gear Hydra-Power			178	56	58	28.890
69.04	6282	4.12	2204	6.57	3rd Gear			178	61	68	28.920
69.01	5013	5.16	2199	5.17	4th Gear			178	61	68	28.920
70.13	4429	5.94	2199	4.67	5th Gear Hydra-Power			180	61	68	28.920
68.81	3145	8.20	2199	3.28	5th Gear			182	61	68	28.920
67.25	2410	10.46	2197	2.69	6th Gear Hydra-Power			180	65	75	28.920
62.41	1623	14.42	2201	1.63	6th Gear			180	65	75	28.920
MAXIMUM POWER WITHOUT BALLAST											
64.99	6815	3.58	2203	11.30	4th Gear Hydra-Power			182	75	85	28.830

VARYING DRAWBAR PULL AND TRAVEL SPEED WITH BALLAST
4th Gear Hydra-Power

Pounds pull	7042	7378	7541	7580	7628	7658	7415
Horsepower	69.52	65.22	58.80	51.75	44.61	37.03	29.03
Crankshaft speed rpm	2201	1982	1750	1534	1316	1089	879
Miles per hour	3.70	3.31	2.92	2.56	2.19	1.81	1.47
Slip of drivers %	7.53	8.14	8.27	8.27	8.40	8.40	8.27

TIRES, BALLAST and WEIGHT		With Ballast	Without Ballast
Rear tires	—No, size, ply & psi	Two 18.4-34; 8; 20	Two 18.4-34; 8; 16
Ballast	—Liquid	1170 lb each	None
	Cast iron	1350 lb each	None
Front tires	—No, size, ply & psi	Two 7.50-15; 8; 40	Two 7.50-15; 8; 32
Ballast	—Liquid	None	None
	Cast iron	208 lb each	None
Height of drawbar		20½ inches	21 inches
Static weight	—Rear	11300 lb	6260 lb
	—Front	2960 lb	2545 lb
Total weight with operator		14435 lb	8980 lb

Department of Agricultural Engineering
Dates of Test: May 22 to June 4, 1963
Manufacturer: OLIVER CORPORATION, CHARLES CITY, IOWA
Manufacturer's Power Rating: Not rated

FUEL, OIL and TIME Fuel regular gasoline **Octane No** Motor 84.4 Research 92.2 (rating taken from oil company's typical inspection data) **Specific gravity converted to 60°/60°** 0.7365 **Weight per gallon** 6.131 lb **Oil** SAE 10W **API service classification** MS DM **To motor** 1.977 gal **Drained from motor** 1.596 gal **Transmission and final-drive lubricant** SAE 80 **Total time engine was operated** 43 hours.

ENGINE Make Oliver gasoline **Type** 6 cylinder vertical **Serial No** 221120 **Crankshaft mounted** lengthwise **Rated rpm** 2200 **Bore and stroke** 3⅞″ x 4″ **Compression ratio** 8.5 to 1 **Displacement** 283 cu in **Carburetor size** 1½″ **Ignition system** battery **Cranking system** 12 volt electric **Lubrication** pressure **Air cleaner** oil washed wire screen **Oil filter** full flow replaceable paper element **Oil cooler** engine coolant heat exchanger for Hydra-Power oil **Fuel filter** screen in sediment bowl **Muffler** was used **Cooling medium temperature control** thermostat.

CHASSIS Type standard **Serial No** 124925844 **Tread width** rear 68″ to 89½″ front 60″ to 84″ **Wheel base** 109¼″ **Center of gravity** (without operator or ballast, with minimum tread, with fuel tank filled and tractor serviced for operation) Horizontal distance forward from center-line of rear wheels 30.9″ Vertical distance above roadway 35.5″ Horizontal distance from center of rear wheel tread 0″ to the right/left **Hydraulic control system** direct engine drive **Transmission** selective gear fixed ratio with partial range operator controlled power shifting **Advertised speeds mph** first 1.60 second 3.09 third 4.31 fourth 5.34 fifth 8.32 sixth 14.37 reverse 1.81 and 4.87 (using Hydra-Power drive) first 1.17 second 2.27 third 3.16 fourth 3.92 fifth 6.11 sixth 10.55 reverse 1.33 and 3.57 **Clutch** single plate dry disc operated by foot pedal **Brakes** double disc operated by two foot pedals which can be locked **Steering** mechanical with power assist **Turning radius** (on concrete surface with brake applied) right 152″ left 152″ (on concrete surface without brake) right 172″ left 172″ **Turning space diameter** (on concrete surface with brake applied) right 312″ left 312″ (on concrete surface without brake) right 352″ left 352″ **Belt pulley** 1056 rpm at 2200 engine rpm diam 11⁵⁄₁₆″ face 8¾″ Belt speed 3111 fpm Power take-off 1004 rpm at 2200 engine rpm.

REPAIRS and ADJUSTMENTS No repairs or adjustments.

REMARKS All test results were determined from observed data obtained in accordance with the SAE and ASAE test code.

First gear and first gear Hydra-Power drive were not run as it was necessary to limit the pull in second gear Hydra-Power drive to avoid excessive wheel slippage.

We, the undersigned, certify that this is a true and correct report of official Tractor Test 839.

L. F. LARSEN
Engineer-in-Charge

L. W. HURLBUT, Chairman
G. W. STEINBRUEGGE
J. J. SULEK
Board of Tractor Test Engineers

NEBRASKA TRACTOR TEST 842 - FORD 6000 GASOLINE

The University of Nebraska Agricultural Experiment Station

E. F. Frolik, Dean; H. H. Kramer, Director, Lincoln, Nebraska

POWER TAKE-OFF PERFORMANCE

Hp	Crank-shaft speed rpm	Fuel Consumption Gal per hr	Lb per hp-hr	Hp-hr per gal	Temperature Degrees F Cooling medium	Air wet bulb	Air dry bulb	Barometer inches of Mercury
MAXIMUM POWER AND FUEL CONSUMPTION								
Rated Engine Speed—Two Hours								
62.25	2300	5.942	0.585	10.48	189	71	79	28.945
Standard Power Take-off Speed (1000 rpm)—One hour								
60.98	2227	5.780	0.581	10.55	192	72	81	28.955
Standard Power Take-off Speed (1000 rpm)—One hour								
49.35	1731	4.614	0.573	10.70	199	77	92	29.000
VARYING POWER AND FUEL CONSUMPTION—TWO HOURS								
57.23	2487	6.229	0.667	9.19	185	73	84	....
0.00	2646	2.388	....	....	170	74	85	....
29.57	2569	3.983	0.826	7.42	182	75	86	....
61.64	2300	5.945	0.591	10.37	196	75	88	....
14.99	2608	3.112	1.273	4.82	180	76	90	....
43.79	2537	5.015	0.702	8.73	191	76	89	....
Av 34.54	2524	4.445	0.789	7.77	184	75	87	28.983

DRAWBAR PERFORMANCE

Hp	Draw-bar pull lbs	Speed miles per hr	Crank-shaft speed rpm	Slip of drivers %	Fuel Consumption Gal per hr	Lb per hp-hr	Hp-hr per gal	Temp Degrees F Cool-ing med	Air wet bulb	Air dry bulb	Barometer inches of Mercury
VARYING DRAWBAR POWER AND FUEL CONSUMPTION WITH BALLAST											
Maximum Available Power—Two Hours—6th Gear											
53.56	4307	4.66	2300	7.33	5.915	0.677	9.05	189	68	73	29.078
75% of Pull at Maximum Power—Ten Hours—6th Gear											
45.22	3259	5.20	2512	5.29	5.683	0.771	7.96	197	74	88	29.012
50% of Pull at Maximum Power—Two Hours—6th Gear											
30.86	2145	5.40	2565	3.82	4.405	0.875	7.01	184	70	74	29.030
MAXIMUM POWER WITH BALLAST											
43.76	7326	2.24	2467	14.89	4th Gear			178	66	73	28.930
52.62	5555	3.55	2304	9.40	5th Gear			183	67	74	28.940
53.90	4347	4.65	2292	7.30	6th Gear			189	68	73	29.080
51.86	3567	5.45	2298	5.71	7th Gear			183	67	74	28.940
52.27	2758	7.11	2299	4.41	8th Gear			182	67	74	28.940
50.65	1618	11.74	2301	2.79	9th Gear			183	67	74	28.940
MAXIMUM POWER WITHOUT BALLAST											
52.15	4263	4.59	2300	8.86	6th Gear			193	72	84	28.960

VARYING DRAWBAR PULL AND TRAVEL SPEED WITH BALLAST—6th Gear

Pounds pull	4347	4417	4552	4617	4611	4652	4525
Horsepower	53.90	49.32	45.02	39.96	34.15	28.73	22.16
Crankshaft speed rpm	2292	2062	1829	1604	1373	1146	907
Miles per hour	4.65	4.19	3.71	3.25	2.78	2.32	1.84
Slip of drivers %	7.30	7.10	7.49	7.62	7.62	7.75	7.62

TIRES, BALLAST and WEIGHT		With Ballast	Without Ballast
Rear tires	—No, size, ply & psi	Two 15.5-38; 6; 18	Two 15.5-38; 6; 14
Ballast	—Liquid	880 lb each	None
	Cast iron	390 lb each	None
Front tires	—No, size, ply & psi	Two 6.50-16; 6; 32	Two 6.50-16; 6; 28
Ballast	—Liquid	None	None
	Cast iron	47 lb each	None
Height of drawbar		21½ inches	22½ inches
Static weight	—Rear	7290 lb	4750 lb
	Front	2155 lb	2060 lb
Total weight with operator		9620 lb	6985 lb

Department of Agricultural Engineering

Dates of Test: June 17 to July 3 ,1963

Manufacturer: FORD MOTOR COMPANY, BIRMINGHAM, MICHIGAN

Manufacturer's Power Rating: 64.5 PTO Horsepower (corrected to standard conditions)

FUEL OIL and TIME Fuel regular gasoline **Octane No Motor** 84.4 **Research** 92.2 (rating taken from oil company's typical inspection data) **Specific gravity converted to 60°/60°** 0.7365 **Weight per gallon** 6.131 lb **Oil** SAE 20-20W **API service classification** MS, DG **To motor** 1.474 gal **Drained from motor** 0.817 gal **Transmission and final-drive lubricant** Ford hydraulic oil M-2C-41 **Total time engine was operated** 47½ hours.

ENGINE Make Ford gasoline **Type** 6 cylinder vertical **Serial No** 18524 **Crankshaft mounted** lengthwise **Rated rpm** 2300 **Bore and stroke** 3.62" x 3.60" **Compression ratio** 8.4 to 1 **Displacement** 223 cu in **Carburetor size** 1¼" **Ignition system** battery **Cranking system** 12 volt electric **Lubrication** pressure **Air cleaner** oil washed wire mesh with centrifugal precleaner **Oil filter** treated paper element in replaceable cartridge **Oil cooler** heat exchanger in lower radiator tank for transmission oil **Fuel filter** screen in sediment bowl **Muffler** was used **Cooling medium temperature control** thermostat.

CHASSIS Type tricycle **Serial No** 18524 **Tread width** rear 56" to 84" front 8.3" to 16.3" **Wheel base** 95.5" **Center of gravity** (without operator or ballast, with minimum tread, with fuel tank filled and tractor serviced for operation) Horizontal distance forward from center-line of rear wheels 28.0" Vertical distance above roadway 35.5" Horizontal distance from center of rear wheel tread 0" to the right/left **Hydraulic control system** direct engine drive with accumulator **Transmission** fixed ratio operator controlled full range power shifting **Advertised speeds mph** first 1.2 second 1.6 third 1.7 fourth 2.4 fifth 3.8 sixth 5.0 seventh 5.7 eighth 7.3 ninth 11.9 tenth 17.5 reverse 3.4 and 5.0 **Clutch** four multiple disc wet clutches within transmission hydraulically operated **Brakes** wet disc hydraulically power actuated **Steering** mechanical with power assist **Turning radius** (on concrete surface with brake applied) right 109" left 109" (on concrete surface without brake) right 131" left 131" **Turning space diameter** (on concrete surface with brake applied) right 238" left 238" (on concrete surface without brake) right 281" left 281" **Power take-off** 540 or 1000 rpm at 1730 or 2225 engine rpm.

REPAIRS and ADJUSTMENTS Preliminary PTO runs indicated a loss of power. The cylinder head was removed and combustion chamber cleaned. Head was replaced and test continued with improved performance.

A crack in exhaust manifold made it necessary to install a new exhaust manifold.

REMARKS All test results were determined from observed data obtained in accordance with the SAE and ASAE test code.

First, second, and third gears were not run as it was necessary to limit the pull in fourth gear to avoid excessive wheel slippage. Tenth gear was not run as it exceeded 15 mph.

We, the undersigned, certify that this is a true and correct report of official Tractor Test 842.

L. F. LARSEN
Engineer-in-Charge

L. W. HURLBUT, Chairman
G. W. STEINBRUEGGE
J. J. SULEK
Board of Tractor Test Engineers

Tractor Collectors' Resources

List Compiled by Brian Rukes

Magazines:

General Interest:

Ageless Iron (by *Successful Farming*), http://www.agriculture.com/ag/files/agelessiron/

Antique Power, http://www.antiquepower.com/

Belt Pulley, http://www.beltpulley.com/

Farm Collector Magazine, www.farmcollector.com

Gas Engine Magazine, http://www.gasenginemagazine.com/

Old Tractor Magazine (in the UK), http://www.oldtractor.co.uk/

Steam Traction Magazine, http://www.steamtraction.com/

Brand Specific, Case:

Old Abe's News, http://www.jicca.org/Oldabesnews.htm

The Heritage Eagle, http://www.caseheritage.org

Brand Specific, Ferguson:

Ferguson Heritage, http://www.fofh.co.uk/magazine/magazine.htm

Brand Specific, Ford:

9N-2N-8N-NAA Newsletter, http://www.n-news.com/

Brand Specific, International Harvester:

Harvester Highlights, http://members.aol.com/ihcollectors/harvesterhighlights.htm

Brand Specific, John Deere:

Green Magazine, http://www.greenmagazine.com/

Two-Cylinder Magazine, http://www.twocylinder.com/

Brand Specific, Minneapolis-Moline:

MM Corresponder, http://www.minneapolismolinecollectors.org/magazine/corresponder.asp

Prairie Gold Rush, http://www.prairiegoldrush.com/

Brand Specific, Oliver:

Hart-Parr Oliver Collectors Magazine, http://www.hartparroliver.org/magazine.html

Oliver Heritage Magazine, http://www.oliverinformation.com/

Brand Specific, Rumely (and related):

Rumely Collectors News, http://www.rumely.com/

- Magazine For Fans of Rumely, Advance, Gaar-Scott, Aultman-Taylor & More!

Clubs and Organizations:

General Interest / All Brand:

Early Day Gas Engine and Tractor Association (E.D.G.E. & T.A.) http://www.edgeta.org/oldsite/index.php

Historical Construction Equipment Association, http://www.hcea.net/

Rough and Tumble Engineers Historical Association, http://www.roughandtumble.org/

Brand Specific, Allis-Chalmers:

Allis Chalmers Club of Ontario, http://www3.sympatico.ca/michael.greer/

Brand Specific, Case:

J.I. Case Collectors Association, http://www.jicca.org/

The J.I. Case Heritage Foundation, Inc., http://www.caseheritage.org/

Brand Specific, Caterpillar:

Antique Caterpillar Machinery Owners Club, http://www.acmoc.org/

Brand Specific, Cockshutt:

The International Cockshutt Club, Inc., http://www.cockshutt.com/

Brand Specific, David Brown:

David Brown Tractor Club, Ltd., http://www.davidbrowntractorclub.com/

Brand Specific, Ferguson:

The Friends of Ferguson Heritage, Ltd., http://www.fofh.co.uk/

Brand Specific, Ford:

Ford/Fordson Collectors Association, Inc., http://www.ford-fordson.org/

N Tractor Club, http://www.ntractorclub.com/

Brand Specific, International Harvester:

International Harvester Collectors Club, Inc. Home Page, http://members.aol.com/ihcollectors/

Brand Specific, John Deere:

Two-Cylinder Club, http://www.twocylinder.com/

Brand Specific, Minneapolis-Moline:

The MM Collectors Club, The M-M Registry, http://www.angelfire.com/ok/mmreg/

Brand Specific, Oliver:

Hart-Parr Oliver Collectors Association, http://www.hartparroliver.org/

Brand Specific, Rumely:

Rumely Product Collectors, Inc., http://www.rumelycollectors.com/

Parts Sources / Restoration Resources:

Manuals:

Antique Tractor Source, http://www.antiquetractorsource.com

Binder Books (specializes in IH items), http://www.binderbooks.com/

Historic Tractor Manuals (specializing in Oliver items), http://www.olivertractormanuals.org/

Jensales, http://www.jensales.com/

Restoration Services:

Old South Tractor - Restorations Unlimited (specializing in IH products), http://www.oldsouthtractor.com/

Spiegelberg Restoration & Service, Birmingham, OH (specializing in JD), http://www.kellnet.com/tractor/

Tires:

M.E. Miller Tire, http://www.millertire.com/ Goodyear Tires,

Carburetors:

Denny's Carb Shop, Fletcher, OH, http://www.dennyscarbshop.com/

Tractor Parts, Various Brands:

Rural King (various locations), http://ruralking.com/

Tractor Supply Co. (TSC - various locations), http://www.mytscstore.com/

Valu-Bilt Tractor Parts (formerly Central Tractor), http://www.valu-bilt.com/

Antique Tractor Parts, Martin's Farm Supply, Vevay, IN, http://www.antiquetractorparts.com/

Antique Tractor Store (online store), http://www.antiquetractorstore.com/

Dennis Polk Equipment, New Paris, IN, http://www.dennispolk.com/

Steiner Tractor Parts, Inc., Lennon, MI, http://www.steinertractor.com/

British Tractor Wreckers; Unity, Sask., Canada; http://www.britishtractor.com/

Brand Specific, Allis-Chalmers:

OK Tractor, Mounds, OK, http://www.oktractor.com/

Brand Specific, Ford:

N-Complete, http://www.n-complete.com/, specializing in N-series Fords

Just 8Ns, http://www.just8ns.com/

Brookfield Vintage Tractors (in UK), http://www.vintagetractors.freeserve.co.uk/

Brand Specific, Oliver:

Larry Harsin's Oliver Tractors, http://olivertractor.com/

Korves Oliver, http://www.korvesoliver.com/

Oliver Decals, http://www.oliverdecals.com/

OllieOliver.com, http://www.ollieoliver.com/

Websites (not listed above):

General Interest / All Brand:

Antique Tractor Internet Service (ATIS), http://www.atis.net/

Classic Tractor Fever, http://www.classictractors.com/

Yesterday's Tractors, http://www.ytmag.com

Brand Specific, Allis-Chalmers:

Unofficial Allis Home Page, http://www.allischalmers.com

Jim's Allis-Chalmers Web Page, http://www.geocities.com/jpessek/index.html

Brand Specific, Cockshutt:

The Cockshutt Shed, http://www.ciaccess.com/~jackson1/shed/homepage.html

Cockshutt West, http://www.cockshuttwest.com/

Brand Specific, Ferguson:

The Unofficial Harry Ferguson Web Page, http://www.geocities.com/motorcity/downs/9828/

CTV Motors Ferguson Tractor website, http://home.ntelos.net/~ctvert/ft.htm

The Un-official Massey Harris Pony Website, http://www.bealenet.com/~ron/mainpony.htm

Brand Specific, Ford:

The Smith's 8N Ford Tractor Page, http://www.8nford.com

Tyler's Ford-Ferguson 9N Web Site, http://www.my9n.com/

Brand Specific, International Harvester:

McCormick-International Harvester Company Collection of the Wisconsin

Historical Society, http://www.wisconsinhistory.org/libraryarchives/ihc/

Brian's Farmall Tractor Page, http://www.geocities.com/mck357/

The Farmall Page, http://redpower.higginsonequip.com/

International Harvester, McCormick-Deering and Farmall Tractors, http://www.international-farmall-tractors.com/

International Harvester Tractors, http://falcon.fsc.edu/~craymond/farm/main.html

International Harvester Farmall Tractors, http://members.iquest.net/~jgrodey/tractori.htm

Joels Antique International Farmall Tractor Page, http://www.fmtc.com/~fm_jands/

JW's Page: The Unofficial Farmall tractors, McCormick-Deering tractors, and

Chevrolet page, http://www.geocities.com/MotorCity/Garage/9399/

Tom's IH Antique Tractors (specializing in the Super Series tractors), http://www.tomsihantiquetractors.com/

Bowen's Antique Tractor and International Harvester Site, http://www.angelfire.com/ky2/ihbowen/

Pauls Antique Tractors, http://home.att.net/~loraed/wsb/html/view.cgi-home.html-.html

Strait's Antique Tractors, http://www.angelfire.com/mi/straitsoldtractors/

Farmall Promenade Square Dancing Tractors, http://www.farmallpromenade.com/

Old Oak Farmalls, http://www.oldoakfarmalls.com/

Farmall H Page, http://www.farmall-h.com/

Kelly's Farmall H Page, http://ns2.genesis-technology.com/~kvp/

Mike's Farmall F12 Site, http://home.austin.rr.com/hadleyhouse/F12/F12-F14.html

Rebuilding an IHC F-14, http://www.angelfire.com/me4/pfoxy/38farmall.html

Restoration of an International Harvester Super BWD-6 (in Belgium), http://users.pandora.be/IH-SBWD6/IndexEng.html

Cub Cadet Garden Tractor by International Harvester Unofficial Home Page, http://www.ihcubcadet.com/

Brand Specific, John Deere:

The First Numbered Series, http://hometown.aol.com/jdmodel80/index.html?f=fs

Brand Specific, Massey-Harris:

The Unofficial Massey-Harris Home Page, http://m-h.cs.uoguelph.ca/

Brand Specific, Minneapolis-Moline:

The Unofficial Minneapolis-Moline Homepage, http://www.minneapolis-moline.com

Brand Specific, Oliver and Hart-Parr:

Oliver Information, http://www.oliverinformation.com/

Greenleigh Farm Oliver Tractor Web Site, http://www.olivertractors.ca/

Hart-Parr Tractors, http://www.geocities.com/hartparrtractors/

Geoff's Oliver Site, http://www.geocities.com/olivercollector/

Oliver Haven, http://www.geocities.com/Heartland/Meadows/3420/

Brand Specific, Rumely:

Epping's Rumely and Other OLD Tractor and Gas Engine Homepage, http://www.oilpull.com

Rumely Tractor Page, http://www.chem.utoronto.ca/~jford/

Brand Specific, Zetor:

Zetor World, http://www.zetorworld.com

Garden Tractors, Brand Specific, Planet Jr.:

Yahoo! Groups, Planet Jr., http://groups.yahoo.com/group/planetjr/

Museums and Living History Farms:

General Interest / All Brand:

The Association for Living History, Farm and Agricultural Museums, http://www.alhfam.org/

Located in Arkansas, USA:

The Museum of the Arkansas Grand Prairie (formerly Stuttgart Agricultural Museum)

P.O.Box 65
Stuttgart, AR 72160

Website: http://www.shareyourstate.com/Ark/grandprairiemuseum.htm

Located in California, USA:

Antique Gas & Steam Engine Museum, Inc.

2040 North Santa Fe Ave.

Vista, CA 92083

Phone: 760-941-1791 or 1-800-587-2286

Fax: 760-941-0690

Website:http://www.agsem.com/

Heritage Complex Farm Equipment Museum & Learning Center

(at the International Agri-Center)

4450 S. Laspina St.

Tulare, CA 93274

Phone: (559) 688-1030
Fax: (559) 686-5527

Website: http://www.heritagecomplex.org/contact/default.asp

Located in Delaware, USA:

Delaware Agricultural Museum and Village

866 North DuPont Highway
Dover, DE 19901

Phone: 302-734-1618

Fax: 302-734-0457

Website: http://www.agriculturalmuseum.org/

Located in Florida, USA:

Florida Agricultural Museum

1850 Princess Place Road
Palm Coast, Florida 32137
Phone: 386-446-7630
Fax: 386-446-7631
E-mail: famuseum@pcfl.net

Website: http://www.flaglerlibrary.org/history/agrimuseum/agri1.htm

Located in Illinois, USA:

Garfield Farm and Inn Museum

PO Box 403

LaFox, IL 60147

Phone: 630-584-8485

E-mail: info@garfieldfarm.org

Website: http://www.garfieldfarm.org/

Located in Indiana, USA:

Skinner Farm Museum Steam & Gas Show;

Vermillion County Indiana Historical Society, Inc.

220 East Market Street

P.O. Box 273

Newport, IN 47966

Website: http://vcihs.homestead.com/Skinner.html

Wabash Valley Living History Farm / Historic Prophetstown

3549 Prophetstown Trail

P.O. Box 331

Battle Ground, IN 47920
Phone: 765-567-4700

Email: prophet@prophetstown.org

Website: http://www.prophetstown.org/1920sfarmhouse.html

Located in Iowa, USA:

Heartland Museum

119 9th Street S.W.; Hwy. 3 W.

P.O. Box 652

Clarion, IA 50525

Phone: 515-602-6000

Website: http://www.heartlandmuseum.org/

Heritage Museum
(by the Midwest Old Threshers)

405 E Threshers Road

Mt. Pleasant, IA 52641

Phone: 319-385-8937

Fax: 319-385-0563

Website: http://www.oldthreshers.com/

Living History Farms (in Iowa, various sites)

Website: http://www.lhf.org/farmsites.html

Located in Kansas, USA:

The National Agricultural Center
& Hall of Fame

630 Hall of Fame Drive
Bonner Springs, Kansas 66012
Phone: 913-721-1075

Website: http://aghalloffame.com/

Yesteryear Museum:
Central Kansas Flywheels Museum

1100 W Diamond Dr.

Salina, KS 67401

Phone: 785-825-8473

Website: http://www.yesteryearmuseum.com/

Located in Maryland, USA:

Carroll County Farm Museum

500 South Center Street

Westminster, MD 21157

Phone: 410-386-3880 or 1-800-654-4645

Related website: http://tourism.carr.org/todo/farm-mus.htm

Cecil County Farm Museum, Inc.

954 England Creamery Road

Rising Sun, MD 21911

E-mail: info@ccfarmmuseum.org

Website: http://www.ccfarmmuseum.org/

Located in Michigan, USA:

Henry Ford Museum

Dearborn, MI

Website: http://www.hfmgv.org/

Located in Minnesota, USA:

Farmamerica: The Minnesota Agricultural Interpretive Center

Phone: 507-835-2052

E-mail: farmamer@mnic.net

Website: http://www.farmamerica.org/

Minnesota History Center Museum of the Minnesota Historical Society

345 Kellogg Blvd. W.

St. Paul, MN 55102-1903

Phone: 651-296-6126 or 1-800-657-3773

Website: http://www.mnhs.org/historycenter/index.htm

Located in Montana, USA:

Louis Toavs' John Deere Tractor Museum

Box 2045

Wolf Point, MT 59201

Phone: 406-392-5294

Related Website:

http://virtualmontana.com/montanadirectory/montanalistings/MR/montana10099.htm

Located in Nebraska, USA:

Lester F. Larsen Tractor Test & Power Museum

University of Nebraska-Lincoln

PO Box 830833

Lincoln, Nebraska 68583-0833

Phone: 402-472-8389

FAX: 402-472-8367

E-mail: tractormuseum2@unl.edu

Website: http://tractormuseum.unl.edu/

Located in New Jersey, USA:

New Jersey Museum of Agriculture

103 College Farm Rd

P.O. Box 7788

North Brunswick, NJ 08902

Phone: 732-249-2077

Fax: 732-247-1035

Email: info@agriculturemuseum.org

Website: http://www.agriculturemuseum.org/

Located in New York, USA:

Tired Iron Tractor Museum

Route 20A

Leicester, NY 14481

Related website: http://www.rochester.lib.ny.us/clubs/920jo3d2.htm

Located in North Carolina, USA:

Wilbur A. Tyndall Tractor Museum

406 North Front Street

Pink Hill, NC 28501

Related Website:

http://blue.dcr.state.nc.us/servlet/ascwg/search?ss=no&qry=county&tm1=Lenoir

Located in Ohio, USA:

Huber Museum, Marion, OH

Phone: 740-389-1098

E-mail: hubermuseum@aol.com

Website: http://www.mariononline.com/hubermuseum/

Located in Pennsylvania, USA:

Rough and Tumble Museum, http://www.roughandtumble.org/rt_visit.asp

P.O. Box 9

Kinzers, PA 17535

Phone: 717-442-4249

Website: http://www.roughandtumble.org/rt_visit.asp

Located in South Dakota, USA:

South Dakota State Agricultural Heritage Museum

South Dakota State University

Box 2207C

Brookings, SD 57007-0999

Phone: 605-688-6226

Fax: 605-688-6303

E-mail : sdsu.agmuseum@sdstate.edu

Website: http://www.agmuseum.com/

South Dakota Tractor Museum

P.O. Box 418

Kimball, SD 57355

Phone: 605-778-6513

E-mail: rbickner@midstatesd.net

Website: http://sdtractormuseum.home.comcast.net/

Located in Tennessee, USA:

Tennessee Agricultural Museum / Ellington Agricultural Center

P.O. Box 40627,

Nashville, TN 37204

Phone: 615-837-5197

Website: http://picktnproducts.org/agmuseum/

Located in Texas, USA:

Agricultural Heritage Center & Museum, and Tractor Show

P.O. Box 1076

Boerne, TX 78006

Phone: 830-249-6007

Website: http://www.agmuseum.org/intro.html

Located in West Virginia, USA:

West Virginia State Farm Museum

Route 1, Box 479

Pleasant Point, WV 25550

Phone: 304-675-5737

http://www.pointpleasantwv.org/Museums/FarmMuseum/farm_museum_hello.htm

Located in Wisconsin, USA:

State Agricultural Museum of the Wisconsin Historical Society

P.O. Box 125

Cassville, WI 53806

Website: http://www.wisconsinhistory.org/stonefield/agmuseum.asp

Located in Washington, D.C., USA

Smithsonian Institution, http://www.si.edu/

Located in Canada:

Agricultural Museum of New Brunswick, and Antique Power Show

28 Perry St.

Sussex, New Brunswick, Canada E4E-2N7

Website: http://www.agriculturalmuseumofnb.com/

British Columbia Farm Equipment & Agriculture Museum

9131 King St

Fort Langley

British Columbia, Canada V0X-1J0

Phone: 604-888-2273

Email: bcfarm@vcn.bc.ca

Website: http://www.bcfma.com/

Canada Agriculture Museum

Prince of Wales Drive Ottawa, Canada

Phone: 613-991-3044 or 1-866-442-4416

Fax: 613-993-7923

Website: http://www.agriculture.technomuses.ca/

Manitoba Agricultural Museum

Box 10

Austin, Manitoba, Canada R0H-0C0

Phone: 204-637-2354

Fax: 204-637-2395

Website: http://www.ag-museum.mb.ca/index.htm

Located in Australia:

The Aussie Tractor Page (list of Australian Tractor Museums and Rallies)

http://members.ozemail.com.au/~bobkav/aussietractorpage/

National Steam Center / Melbourne Steam Traction Engine Club, Inc.

1200 Ferntree Gully Rd.

Scoresby, Melway, Australia

Website: http://home.vicnet.net.au/~mstec/

Serpentine Vintage Tractors & Machinery

Wellard St.

P.O. Box 64

Serpentine, Western Australia 6125

Phone: +61 (8) 9525 2129

Fax: +61 (8) 9525 2549

Website: http://www.serpentinetractors.asn.au/

Located in Denmark:

Zealand Tractor Museum

Overdrevsgården - Lidemarksvej 45, Svansbjerg - 4681 Herfølge

Phone: 56 27 52 12

Website: http://www.svtk.dk/eng/

Located in England:

Stonehurst Family Farm and Museum

Loughborough Road

Mountsorrel, Leicestershire, England

E-mail: Stonehurst@farm18.fsnet.co.uk

Website: http://www.farm18.fsnet.co.uk/

David Brown Tractor Club Museum

Spinks Mill

Huddersfield Road

Meltham, West Yorkshire, England

Website: http://www.davidbrowntractorclub.com/

Located in Finland:

Kovela Tractor Museum

Kovelantie 130,

Nummi-Pusula, Finland
Phone: +358-19-373311

Related Website: http://www.nummi-pusula.fi/TourismENG.asp

Located in France:

Agropolis-Museum

951 Av. Agropolis 34394

Montpellier Cedex 5 FRANCE
Phone: (33) 4 67 04 75 00

Fax: (33) 4 67 04 13 69
E-mail: museum@agropolis.fr

Website: http://museum.agropolis.fr/english/default.htm

Located in Italy:

The Farm Tractor Museum

Senago (Milano)
Azienda Tosi, via Brodolini, 2
Phone: 02/9988435

Related Website: http://www.museionline.it/eng/cerca/museo.asp?id=2833

Brand Specific, Oliver (and related):

Floyd County Historical Society and Museum

500 Gilbert St.

Charles City, IA 50616

Phone: 641-228-1099

Fax: 641-228-1157

E-mail:fchs@fiai.net

Website: http://www.floydcountymuseum.org/

The new BIG D . . . newly designed from the tire tracks up for the man who farms big, thinks big. Top of the long leadership line.

We rewrote the "big tractor book" with the new D21...

AND OUR DEALERS ARE REWRITING THE SALES BOOK THANKS TO WHAT OUR ENGINEERS AND DESIGNERS HAVE DONE

We feel fortunate to be teamed with the greatest group of farm equipment dealers you can find.

They're all tractor folks, like us.

We're proud that our factory people work so hard to design and manufacture high quality products. And that our retail tractor folks believe in high quality service.

What does it all mean?

Careers in farm machinery.

Dealers with get up and go. Men who think like we do . . . who are proud to handle the leadership line.

Community leaders.

ALLIS-CHALMERS

MILWAUKEE, WISCONSIN

THE COMPANY WITH GET UP AND GO

1957 TRACTOR FIELD BOOK

It PAYS to Sell the CASE System of Overlapping Gears

A speed for every need balances engine power and torque with ground speed and traction for any job. This combination gives Case dealers a big competitive lead in each power class.

In the 3-plow range, the Case 300 offers 12 speeds from a smooth, steady creep to a brisk highway clip—versatility that permits disking up to 18% extra acres every day. The 4-plow Case 400 matches every load with 8 gears for plowing up to 4½ more acres daily. The new 6-cylinder, 6-speed Case 600 puts Case dealers at the top of the 6-plow class.

The beautiful 2-tone color harmony of all Case tractors, their easy handling and comfortable riding, their ability to cover extra acres daily at rock-bottom economy with the Case system of overlapping gears—all enable Case dealers to out-demonstrate all contenders. The wonderfully flexible Case Crop-Way Purchase Plan clinches many an extra sale, too.

Both the 3-plow Case 300 (above) and 4-plow Case 400 (below) have speedy 3-point Case Eagle-Hitch; models for diesel, gasoline, LPG and distillate. Case Drive-In cultivators take but minutes to mount.

CASE®

J. I. CASE CO.
Racine, Wisconsin
Serving Agriculture Since 1842

New Case implements open doors to additional tractor sales. The new Super-Strength Case A plow (above) is built ruggedly for the toughest soils. It has extra clearance and extra rank for covering heavy trash. The 115-year Case tradition of quality simplifies your service problems, too. It pays to deal—as it pays to farm—with Case.

1957 TRACTOR FIELD BOOK

IT'S *The Newest Family in Town*

The

JOHN DEERE

TRACTOR LINE for 1957

•

6 Power Sizes...

30 Basic Models...

Every One Is *New* in LOOKS . . . PERFORMANCE . . . VALUE

Quality Farm Equipment Since 1837

1957 TRACTOR FIELD BOOK

Ferguson "40"

Ferguson "35"

4-wheel "Hi-40"

Double-wheel tricycle "Hi-40"

Single-wheel tricycle "Hi-40"

SALES ASSET...The Ferguson System

Herein lies the greatest single sales story that a farm equipment dealer could ever hope to have. It begins with the creation of the advanced Ferguson System for five great Ferguson Tractors. And it ends with satisfied customers for every Ferguson dealer.

Among other things, the Ferguson System means power control for more accurate, easy handling of all implements, right from the tractor seat. It means *full* use of power without tedious, time-wasting adjustments. It means better seedbed preparation, more accurate planting and faster harvesting—at amazingly lower costs.

Simply: It means your customers have all the benefits of the famous Ferguson System, the one system with complete power control.

If you'd like to handle this advanced tractor line and increase your farm equipment profits, be sure to investigate a Ferguson Franchise without delay. Wire or write: *Ferguson, Racine, Wisconsin.*

Ferguson

1957 TRACTOR FIELD BOOK

Power is up 138%

FORD TRACTORS

The chart at right shows the big bonus of pull-power delivered by new Ford Tractors—especially the super-powered 800 and 900 Series. This is a big selling advantage. Farmers can turn furrows faster—pull through tough spots where other tractors often "give up the ghost"—pull more tools in tandem—avoid needless stalls and down-shifting.

New Ford Tractors are priced low. They're easier to operate; built to last longer. And more quick-attached tools are designed for use with Ford Tractors than with any other.

These are all good reasons why it's better to be *with* Ford than to *watch* Ford. So talk over a dealership opportunity with your nearby Ford Tractor and Implement distributor. Or write to Tractor and Implement Division, Ford Motor Company, Birmingham, Mich.

Ford Farming

IS NEW DAY FARMING

LOOK AT THE INCREASE IN *HORSEPOWER!**

NOW 40.2 H.P.

1953 26.8 H.P.

1948 23.1 H.P.

1942 16.9 H.P.

*Drawbar Horsepower

Ford

Ford

Ford

Ford

Watch the work fly!

FARM IMPLEMENT NEWS'

Now, America's top ten—5 new Farmall® and 5 new International® tractors! *Models unlimited!* The new 1957 Power Line gives IH dealers the greatest line-up of sales power in history.

All that's new is skillfully engineered with the best of the past to put engine horsepower to better use . . . to give farmers greater value for every power dollar. Better than ever before, IH dealers can match the exact needs of more prospects and expand sales, with new power in most models . . . two new 3-plow diesels . . . new Fast-Hitch with Traction-Control . . . new power adjusted rear wheels . . . new conveniences, plus incomparable TA,

1957 TRACTOR FIELD BOOK

LINE FOR '57...

UNLIMITED!

Hydra-Touch, independent pto, power steering . . . unmatched IH stamina . . . and countless more work-easing, cost-cutting features.

And now in 1957, an IH dealer franchise—with the most complete line of power sizes, models, and options ever offered—has greater appeal and is more valuable than ever.

INTERNATIONAL HARVESTER

International Harvester products pay for themselves in use—McCormick Farm Equipment and Farmall Tractors . . . Motor Trucks . . . Construction Equipment—General Office, Chicago 1, Illinois.

FARMALL
FIRST WITH
FOUR MILLION TRACTORS

MF
DIESEL
1100
MASSEY-FERGUSON

1957 TRACTOR FIELD BOOK

Now the tractor triumph of our time... The *Miracle* from MASSEY-HARRIS

MH50 with Hydramic Power

built to trigger a new tractor age!

HYDRAMIC Power! Miracle Design! Dramatic new reasons why a Massey-Harris dealership is the franchise of the future.

A bold new concept of farm power . . . the one sytem that puts power where it is needed — to push, pull, lift, lower, adjust, operate. Miracle Design that breaks through the engineering barrier to command traction automatically and broaden the scope of jobs a tractor can do.

New sales features! New profit potential! Yours in the most progressive franchise in the farm field. Get complete details. Write or wire the Massey-Harris Branch nearest you. MASSEY-HARRIS, QUALITY AVE., RACINE, WISCONSIN. Dept. M-200.

3 more to see . . . paving the way to new sales heights on the big-equipment farms

333 . . . New 208 cu. in. Engine. Power Steering. Power Adjusted Wheels. Level-Drive PTO. 10 Speeds Forward. 12-Volt battery.

444 ... inspired by miracle design. Power Steering. Power Adjusted Wheels. Level-Drive PTO. 10 Speeds Forward. 12-Volt battery.

555 . . . inspired by miracle design. Power Steering. 12-Volt Electrical System. Stronger, tougher design throughout. 4-5-plow power.

BRANCHES AT:

Atlanta, Ga.; Baltimore, Md.; Batavia, N. Y.; Columbus, Ohio; Dallas, Texas; Denver, Colo.; Des Moines, Iowa; Fargo, N. D.; Indianapolis, Ind.; Kansas City, Kan.; Memphis, Tenn.; Minneapolis, Minn.; Oklahoma City, Okla.; Omaha, Nebr.; Pocatello, Idaho; Portland, Ore.; Racine, Wis.; Springfield, Ill.; Stockton, Cal. Sub-branches: Amarillo, Texas; Billings, Mont.; Los Angeles, Cal.; Spokane, Wash.

Always **Keep your eye on**

Massey-Harris

1957 TRACTOR FIELD BOOK

THE EXCLUSIVE UNI-FARMOR

America's newest way to farm!
Six self-propelled machines built around one money-saving power source.
Uni-Windrower, Uni-Foragor, Uni-Balor, Uni-Harvestor, Uni-Huskor and Uni-Picker-Sheller!

THE MIGHTY GB

Five-plow power at its money-making best!

...on the march with tomorrow's machines...today!

New advances in farm machinery don't *just happen*. They have to be *planned* . . . years ahead of the market. Ideas have to be developed; money and materials and time have to be invested; long years have to be spent in research and testing. It takes vision and faith to build the machines of the future.

That's how the present-day line of Minneapolis-Moline machinery was developed—years ahead of its time, to meet the farming needs of today. Tractors like the mighty GB and the all-new POWERlined series; the complete new line of big-capacity tillage implements and high-speed planters; fully self-propelled machinery systems like the exclusive Uni-Farmor—these machines have established MM Idea Leadership more surely than ever before.

These are the machines of tomorrow . . . opening an expanding future to the farmer who buys them and the businessman who sells them. They are MM's answer to the New Agriculture . . . here and working today!

Some choice territories are now open in MM's growing dealer organization. Your inquiry will bring full details.

MINNEAPOLIS-MOLINE MINNEAPOLIS 1, MINNESOTA

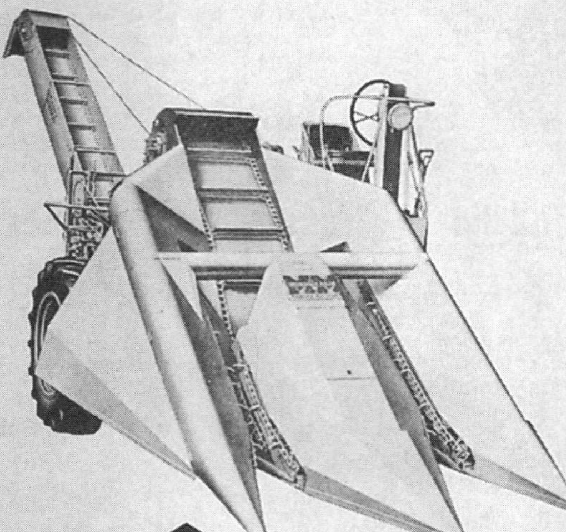

THE CHAMPION UNI-HUSKOR

One of the Uni-Farmor family—United States and Canadian Corn Picking Champion two years in a row!

THE POWERLINED TRACTORS!

The completely new farm tractors—built to make *today's* farming pay better than ever!

Big MM tractors lead the parade—Standard and Universal types—4-wheel and 2-wheel drive, 40 to 100 horsepower

Minneapolis-Moline dealers are growing with a full line of tractors and implements

You just can't beat this new combination—the World's Finest Tractors, plus a full line of the finest farm machines and implements—many of them added to the line this year—all of them tested and proved for perfect performance.

But that is not all! MM parts service is the best—with a full line of parts for all makes and models of tractors and equipment. Company help is strong and dependable—with merchandising and advertising support designed to help build each dealer's business to the full. And Big MM salesmen are experienced and trained to work for the dealers' greatest growth and prosperity. No wonder business is booming at the sign of the Big MM.

We'll be glad to give you more information. Write to B. F. Shipman, General Sales Manager, Minneapolis-Moline, Inc., 130 Ninth Avenue South, Hopkins, Minnesota.

MINNEAPOLIS-MOLINE, INC. HOPKINS, MINNESOTA

TRACTORS • TILLAGE TOOLS • PLANTERS AND DRILLS • HAY MACHINES • HARVESTING MACHINES • A FULL AND COMPLETE LINE

Full 4-plow, diesel-powered Super 88.

Standard front axle Super 77.

Profit-Producing POWER!

There's more in the Oliver tractor line—in power range, features, modern design! Look at the broad choice Oliver dealers can offer: wheel or crawler... 2-plow to 6-plow...diesel, gasoline or LP-gas engines.

In features, too, the Oliver dealer can give the farmer exactly what he wants: power steering...power-shift wheels...key starting...12-volt electrical system ...oil-saving lubrication...pressurized, by-pass cooling...double-disc brakes...rubber spring seat.

Add to them such conveniences as the completely independent PTO, hydraulic depth adjustment on the "go," 3-point hitching and full ground-speed coverage.

Here are the real profit-producers! They save days and dollars for the farmers who buy them. They can increase the profit possibilities for the dealers who sell them.

The Oliver Corporation, 400 West Madison Street, Chicago 6, Illinois.

"FINEST IN FARM MACHINERY"

Mighty 5-6 plow Super 99 GM.

Versatile 3-plow OC-6 crawler.

1957 TRACTOR FIELD BOOK

JOHN DEERE 70 ROW-CROP DIESEL
Deere & Co., Moline, Ill.

FERGUSON MODEL 35
Ferguson Division, Massey-Harris-Ferguson, Inc., Racine, Wis.

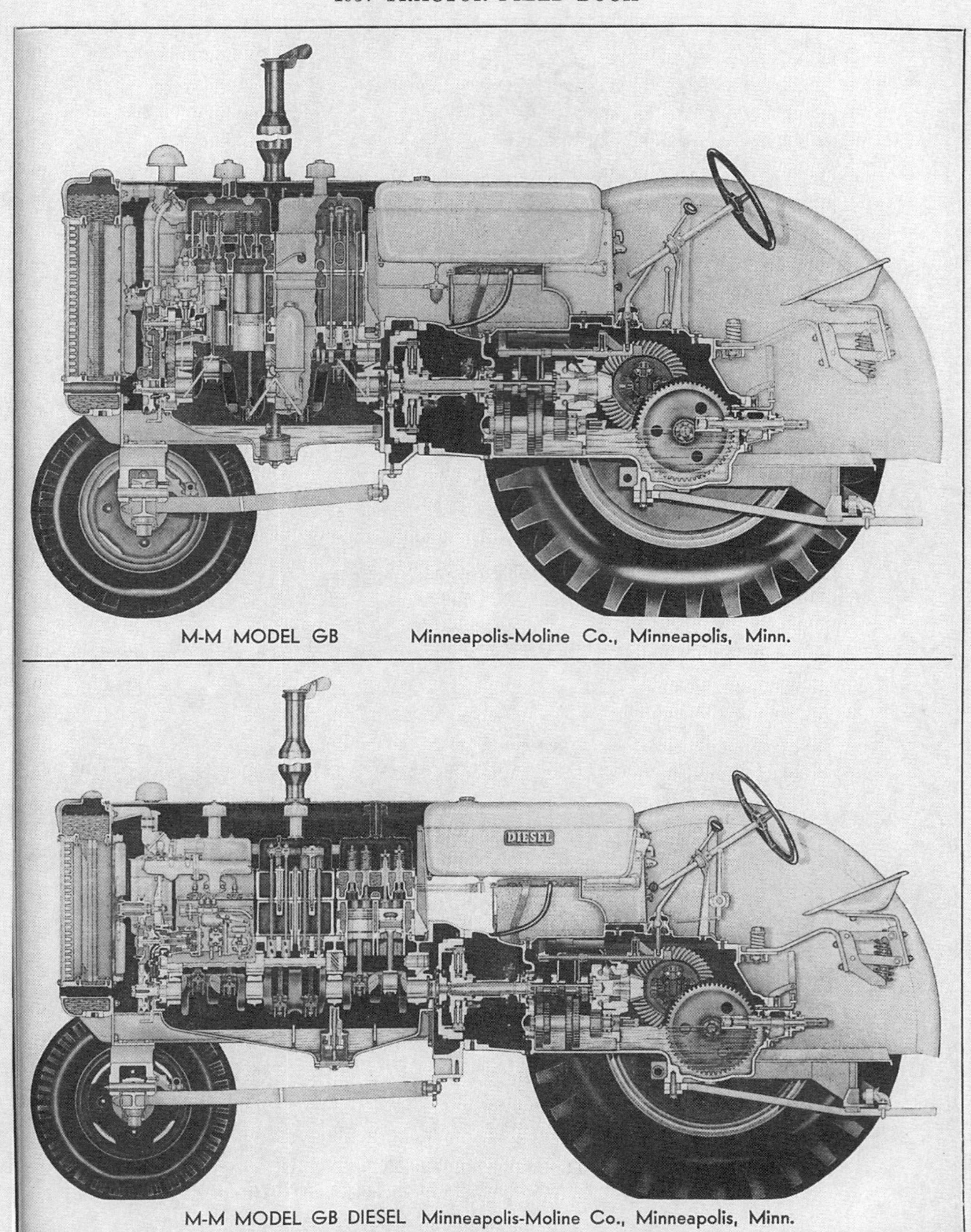

M-M MODEL GB Minneapolis-Moline Co., Minneapolis, Minn.

M-M MODEL GB DIESEL Minneapolis-Moline Co., Minneapolis, Minn.

TRACTOR CROSS-SECTION VIEWS

Massey-Ferguson "50" Diesel

Massey-Ferguson "65" Gas

TRACTOR CROSS-SECTION VIEWS

Oliver "550"

Oliver "1600"

Tractors at Work

7045
ALLIS-CHALMERS

8550

AC 7050

7080
ALLIS-CHALMERS

Special Contributions:

Andrew Morland: Massey-Ferguson 2745 p. 513

Brian Rukes:

Collector resource information: pp. 718-728

Original images: Minneapolis-Moline GB p. 531, 5-Star p. 532. 455 series p. 535,
G-704 p. 535, G-900 series (top, middle) p. 537,
G-1000 and G-1355, p 539
Oliver 1650, p. 592

Tractor ads and miscellaneous images:
Massey-Ferguson 135, 150 and 165 p. 506
Massey-Ferguson 180 p. 507
Minneapolis-Moline U302 p. 534
Nebraska Test page images: pp. 714-717
Tractor ads: pp. 729-742
Tractor cutaways: pp. 734-744

Tractor catalog images: Baird p. 98, John Deere 1010 p. 248, Ford 6000 p. 321, I-H 130 p. 417, I-H 350 p. 418, Massey-Ferguson 35 p. 504, Minneapolis-Moline, 4-Star p. 532, Oliver DG p. 599, Oliver OC-12 p. 601, Oliver 550 p. 586, Oliver 880 p. 587, Oliver 1800 p. 590 and Oliver 1900 p. 591

Don Voelker, Voelker Enterprises Inc.:

Original images: John Deere 1020 p. 252 and 3020 p. 255
Ford 5000 p. 322
International-Harvester (I-H) 460 p. 421,
966 p. 431 and 1066 p. 432
Massey-Ferguson 90 p. 505
Minneapolis-Moline G p. 530, Gvi and M-5 p. 533,
G-900 (bottom) p. 537and G-1000 Vista Diesel p. 538
Oliver 1600 p. 588, 1800 p. 590, 1850 p. 594 and 1950 p. 596
White 2-105 (top) p. 698